S0-BEZ-415

Annotated Teacher's Edition

Author

Jacqueline King Donnelly

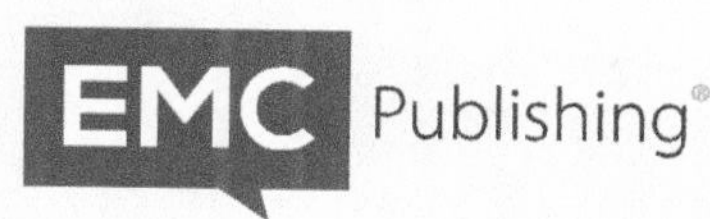

ST. PAUL

Editorial Director: Alejandro Vargas
Developmental Editor: Diana Moen
Associate Editor: Nathalie Gaillot
Assistant Editor: Kristina Merrick
Copy Editor: Kristin Hoffman

Director of Production: Deanna Quinn
Production Editor: Bob Dreas
Cover Designer: Leslie Anderson
Text Designers: Diane Beasley Design, Leslie Anderson
Production Specialist: Julie Johnston
Reviewer: Linda Christen

ISBN 978-0-82196-000-4

875 Montreal Way
St. Paul, MN 55102
Email: educate@emcp.com
Website: www.emcp.com

Printed in the United States of America
22 21 20 19 18 17 16 15   3 4 5 6 7 8 9 10

Meet the Textbook Authors

Toni Theisen, the 2009 ACTFL Teacher of the Year and ACTFL President in 2013, is a National Board Certified Teacher of French at Loveland High School in Loveland, Colorado and the Thompson School District World Language Curriculum Representative. She holds an M.A. in Foreign Language Teaching and an M. A. in Education of Diverse Learners. She is also a Google Certified teacher.

A passionate and active world language advocate, Theisen has presented numerous workshops, keynotes, and webinars for national, regional, and state conferences and institutes. Also an author, she has written several middle and high school French language series and many articles on Multiple Intelligences, Differentiated Instruction, and Technology for the 21st-century learner. Theisen presented "Activating Communication" as part of the first ACTFL Webinar series and also presented at the 2011 LARC (National Language Acquisition Resource Center) STARTALK Institute at San Diego State University.

Theisen led the effort in 2009 to revise the Colorado World Languages Academic Standards and co-chaired the revision committee of the National Board for Professional Teacher Standards for WLOE (World Languages Other than English) in 2009. Most recently she chaired the ACTFL 21st Century Skills Map committee in collaboration with the Partnership for 21st Century Learning.

Thiesen's many additional honors include the ACTFL Nelson Brooks Award for the Teaching of Culture, the Colorado Governor's Award for Excellence in Teaching, the SWCOLT Excellence in Teaching Award, and the Genevieve Overman Memorial Service Award from the Colorado Congress of Foreign Language Teachers.

Jacques Pécheur is the Chief Editor of the French review *Le français dans le monde*. He has worked as Director of the Cultural Center of Palermo and Sicily, and as Cultural Ambassador to the French Embassy in Switzerland. As head of the Mission to the General Delegation for the Languages of France (DGLF), Pécheur has conducted numerous missions to promote multilingualism, the French language, and la Francophonie in the world. He also worked for the French Ministry of Foreign Affairs, the European Council, the European Union, and the Intergovernmental Agency of la Francophonie (AIF). As such he was entrusted with conducting and managing conferences and training workshops in more than 50 countries.

Pécheur's numerous involvements in political, cultural, and language-related occupations have led him to gain expertise in language policies and the language marketplace. As someone who has developed many strategies to promote the learning of French, Pécheur has been a spokesman in numerous conferences related to language learning, and has published many articles. His 20 years of experience in *Le francais dans le monde*, as well as his many publications on French civilization, cinema, and contemporary literature, have shaped his proactive approach to the editorial world.

Honorary member of the AATF, Pécheur is recognized in the United States by the Cultural Services of the French Consulate in the United States (SCAC), the Alliance Française, and many American universities.

Table of Contents

Scope and Sequences

T'es branché? Level 1

Vocabulaire	Fonctions	Culture	Structure	Stratégies
Unité 1 Bonjour, tout le monde!				
Essential question: In what ways is learning another language beneficial?				
• Greetings • Nationalities (in **Vocabulaire actif**)	• Introduce oneself • Introduce someone else • Respond to an introduction • Ask someone's name (in **Pour la conversation**)	• Greetings • Popular first names • **La Francophonie:** Francophones in France and North America (in **Points de départ**)		
• Respond to **Ça va?** • Say good-bye	• Ask how someone is • Say how I am doing	• Back to school • Ways to say good-bye • **La Francophonie:** Europe and North Africa		**Communication:** Register in speaking and writing (in **Stratégies communicatives**)
• Locations • Parents	• Extend an invitation • Accept an invitation • Refuse an invitation	• French teens • **La Francophonie:** Sub-Saharan Africa, Caribbean, and South America **Produits:** **La Négritude**		**Culture:** Assess comfort level with Francophone cultures (in **La culture sur place**) **Fine art:** Impressionistic techniques (Jean Béraud) (in **Le monde visuel**) **Reading:** Answer the five "W" questions and decipher words (in **Lecture thématique**)
Unité 2 Les passe-temps				
Essential question: What do activities and pastimes reveal about a culture?				
• Pastimes • Olympic sports • Weather • Food	• Ask what someone likes to do • Say what I like to do • Say what I don't like to do	• **Pari Roller** • Olympics • Paris **La Francophonie (Sports):** • **Tour de France** • Hockey in Canada **Produits:** Cubism in Paris	• Subject pronouns • **tu** vs. **vous** • Present tense of regular **-er** verbs	
• More pastimes • Adverbs	• Ask how much someone likes to do something • Say how much I enjoy doing things	• Lyon **La Francophonie (Les passe-temps):** • Mancala in Africa **Produits:** Guignol	• Position of adverbs	**Communication:** Cognates

Vocabulaire	Fonctions	Culture	Structure	Stratégies
• Nouns: Sports Music Pastimes • Numbers 0–20	• State my preferences • Ask what someone prefers • Agree and disagree	• Count on fingers • Rachid Taha and World music • Singer Corneille • **Fête de la musique** **La Francophonie (Instruments):** • Kora in Africa	• Gender of nouns and definite articles • The verb **préférer** • Negation with **ne... pas**	**Culture:** Sports viewing habits **Fine art:** Coloration (Béatrice Boisségur) **Reading:** Paraphrasing and finding meaning in repetition
Bilan cumulatif: Unités 1 – 2				
Unité 3 À l'école				
Essential question: How does education shape individuals and societies?				
• Classroom objects • Numbers 20–100	• Say what I need • Ask what someone else needs • Ask what something costs • State what something costs	• Carrefour • School supplies • The euro and the Eurozone • Online instruction	• Indefinite articles • Plurals of articles and nouns • Present tense of the irregular verb **avoir** • **Avoir besoin de**	
• Classroom subjects • Adjectives • Time expressions	• Describe a class • Ask for a description of someone • Describe someone	• 24-hour clock • Wednesday afternoon • Classes and exams • The **lycée** and the **bac** • Naming schools **La Francophonie:** • French Polynesia **Produits:** **Le paréo** in French Polynesia	• Telling time • Present tense of the irregular verb **être** • Agreement and position of regular adjectives	**Communication:** Combine sentences
• Places in school • Places in the city	• Ask where someone is going • Ask when someone is going somewhere • Ask why someone cannot do something • Establish a place and time to meet	• **La cantine** and school meals • **Lycées hôteliers** • **Fête de la musique** • English words of French origin **La Francophonie (Éducation):** • Education in Mali	• Present tense of the irregular verb **aller** • **À** + definite articles • Forming questions with **est-ce que**	**Culture:** Reflect on learning about French schools and compare them to schools in the United States **Fine art:** Focal point (Robert Doisneau) **Reading:** Point of view and Context clues

Vocabulaire	Fonctions	Culture	Structure	Stratégies
Unité 4 Le weekend ensemble				
Essential question: What activities do friends in other countries do together?				
• Soccer • Soccer clothes • The **métro**	• Give a reason • Set a time and place to meet • Suggest a different time	• Soccer in France • Soccer clubs • Famous soccer players **Produits:** The media and soccer in France	• **Aller** + infinitive • Forming questions	
• Food and drink • Numbers 100–1.000	• Understand what the server will ask • Order food • Ask for the bill	• Cafés and **bistrots** • Paris cafés and famous writers • Fast food chains in France **Produits:** **Le croissant**	• Present tense of the irregular verb **prendre** • Avoir expressions: **avoir faim/soif**	**Communication:** Use adjectives and adverbs
• Movie genres • Early, on time, and late	• Make a prediction • Respond to a prediction	• French cinema • French comedies • ***Bienvenue chez les Ch'tis***, French comedy **Produits:** French film starring Johnny Depp	• The interrogative adjective **quel** • Present tense of the irregular verb **voir**	**Culture:** Remakes of French films **Fine art:** Poster art **Reading:** Identify the conflict in a story and recognize false cognates
Bilan cumulatif: Unités 3 – 4				
Unité 5 Les gens que je connais				
Essential question: What is the nature of relationships in other cultures?				
• Family members • Physical descriptions • Numbers 1.000–1.000.000	• Ask for a description • Point out resemblances	• The metric system **La Francophonie:** • Martinique **Produits:** Zouk music	• Possessive adjectives • Indefinite articles in negative sentences	
• Months of the year • Birthdays • Descriptions of character	• Ask someone's age • Tell my age • Tell what gift I am giving • Plan a party with others	• Birthdays and saints' days • **La FNAC** **La Francophonie (Fêtes d'anniversaire):** • Birthday celebrations in Guadeloupe, North Africa, and Sub-saharan Africa	• Present tense of regular verbs ending in **-ir** • Dates • Expressions with **avoir: J'ai... ans** • Present tense of the irregular verb **offrir**	**Communication:** Ask questions to extend a conversation
• French-speaking African countries and nationalities • Professions	• Find out someone's profession • Ask where someone comes from • Tell where I come from	• Singers Amadou and Mariam **La Francophonie:** Sub-saharan Francophone Africa **Produits:** African masks	• **C'est** vs. **il/elle est** • Present tense of the irregular verb **venir** • **De** + definite articles	**Culture:** Collect anecdotal evidence about a Francophone family **Fine art:** Composition (Alfred Wolf) **Reading:** Theme and Monitoring comprehension

Vocabulaire	Fonctions	Culture	Structure	Stratégies
Unité 6 La rue commerçante				
Essential question: How is shopping different in other countries?				
• Articles of clothing • Colors	• What to ask the salesperson • What the salesperson says	• Shopping online • French flea markets • High fashion houses in Paris **La Francophonie (Vêtements):** Clothing in West Africa	• Present tense of the verb **acheter** • Present tense of the irregular verb **vouloir** • Demonstrative adjectives	
• Stores and grocery items • Quantities	• Sequence my activities	• Superstores vs. small shops • French cheeses • Metric measurements **Produits:** **Le pâté**	• Present tense of regular verbs ending in **-re** • Expressions of quantity	**Communication:** Tell a story through pictures
• Fruits and vegetables	• Make a purchase at the market • Respond to questions from the vendor	• Outdoor markets • Slow food movement **La francophonie (Le marché):** **Les souks** in North Africa **Produits:** North African arts and crafts	• The partitive article • The partitive in negative sentences	**Culture:** Go shopping online **Fine art:** Black and white photography **d'après-guerre** (Sabine Weiss) **Reading:** Setting and Word families
Bilan cumulatif: Unités 5 – 6				
Unité 7 À la maison				
Essential question: What makes a house a "home"?				
• Stories in a building • Rooms in a house • Furniture in the kitchen and living room	• Give a tour of a house or an apartment • Ask where someone lives • Agree and disagree	• Housing in France • Bathrooms in France **La Francophonie (Habitations):** North African dwellings, focus on Algeria **Produits:** **Le raï**	• Ordinal numbers	
• Meals • Table setting	• Give directions in the kitchen	• Marseille • Provence • Regional culinary specialties **Produits:** *The Starry Night* by Van Gogh And "**La Marseillaise**"	• Comparative of adjectives • Present tense of the irregular verb **devoir** • Present tense of the irregular verb **mettre**	**Communication:** Write descriptions

Vocabulaire	Fonctions	Culture	Structure	Stratégies
• The bedroom and bathroom • Computer and other technology	• Say that I don't understand • Talk about computers	• Technology and French youth **La Francophonie:** • New Brunswick • The **Grand Dérangement** of the Acadians • Singer Natasha St-Pier **Produits:** Zydeco music	• Present tense of the irregular verb **pouvoir**	**Culture:** Evaluate whether student's home is like or unlike Francophone homes **Fine art:** Impressionism and Cubism (Paul Cézanne) **Reading:** Rhyme Scheme and Deciphering new grammatical structures
Unité 8 À Paris				
Essential question: How do major world cities tell their stories?				
• Weather • Seasons • Pets	• Extend an invitation • Accept or refuse an invitation	• Paris • Parisian pastries **La Francophonie (Une autre capitale):** Port-au-Prince **Produits:** **La galette des rois**	• Present tense of the irregular verb **faire** • Expressions with **avoir: avoir froid**, **avoir chaud**, **avoir envie de**	
• Places in the city • Monuments in Paris	• Excuse oneself • Describe actions that took place in the past • Sequence past events	• **Notre-Dame** • **L'arc de triomphe** • **La tour Eiffel**	• **Passé composé** with **avoir** • Irregular past participles • Position of irregular adjectives	**Communication:** Personal narrative
• Time expressions	• Express actions that took place in the past • Sequence past events	• **Le jardin des Tuileries** • **Le métro**	• **Passé composé** with **être** • Position of adverbs in the **passé composé**	**Culture:** Identify customs and React to French culture **Fine art:** Pointillism (Paul Signac) **Reading:** Personification and Making inferences
Bilan cumulatif: Unités 7 – 8				
Unité 9 En forme				
Essential question: How do people stay healthy and maintain a healthy environment?				
• Parts of the body • Parts of the face	• Say it is necessary to do, or not do, something	• **La sécu** in France • **"Manger-bouger"** ad campaign • **Le thermalisme** **Produits:** Homeopathic medications	• Present tense of the irregular verb **falloir**	

Vocabulaire	Fonctions	Culture	Structure	Stratégies
• Illnesses and other health expressions	• Ask for advice • Give advice	**La Francophonie:** Rwanda • Fighting AIDS in Rwanda • Home health care workers in Rwanda **Produits:** Languages and language education in Rwanda	• The imperative	**Communication:** "How-to" writing
• Environmental problems • Environmental solutions • Endangered species	• Persuade someone • Respond to persuasion	• **Les Verts** in France • **Vélib' Paris** **Produits:** ***La souris verte***, online magazine for young people	• Verbs + infinitives • **De** + plural adjectives	**Culture:** Hunting for diabetes education aids in Francophone countries **Fine art:** Cubism (Roger de La Fresnaye) **Reading:** Characterization, Text organization, and Making a prediction
Unité 10 Les grandes vacances				
Essential question: How do travel experiences shape our worldview?				
• Places in North America • Quebec essentials • Compass directions	• Tell someone where a place is located	**La Francophonie:** • Quebec • Montreal • **FrancoFolies** festival in Montreal **Produits:** Maple syrup	• Prepositions before cities, countries, and continents	
• At the train station • Features of the countryside	• Remind someone to do something • Wish someone a good trip	• Departments and regions of France • Loire castles • Tours	• Other negative expressions	**Communication:** Writing a postcard
• European countries • European nationalities • Expressions for giving directions	• Ask for directions • Give directions	**La Francophonie:** • Switzerland • Geneva • International museum of the **Croix-Rouge** **Produits:** Swiss watches	• Superlative of adjectives	**Culture:** Interviewing a traveler who has visited a Francophone location **Fine art:** Perspective (Achille Varin) **Reading:** Imagery and the Progression of stanzas
Bilan cumulatif: Unités 9 – 10				

T'es branché? Level 2

Vocabulaire	Fonctions	Culture	Structure	Stratégies
Unité 1 Comment je passe l'été				
Essential question: What do young people do in the summer in other cultures?				
• Holidays in France, Quebec, and the United States	• Ask someone if they celebrate a particular holiday • Ask when something takes place and respond	• Quebec City • 400th anniversary of the founding of Québec **La Francophonie (Les fêtes):** • Celebrations in Quebec and France • Native Singer Samian **Produits:** **Le cirque du soleil**	• Present tense of regular verbs ending in **-er**, **-ir**, and **-re** • Negation • Possessive adjectives • Forming questions • Dates	
• Television programs • Television professions	• Ask for an opinion • Give an opinion • Find out what someone is thinking • Agree or disagree	**La Francophonie:** • Luxemburg • French and Luxemburg TV channels • Reality shows in France **Produits:** • Canal + • **"La Nouvelle Star"**	• Present tense of the irregular verbs **avoir** and **être** • Indefinite articles in negative sentences • Demonstrative adjectives • Agreement and position of adjectives • Comparative of adjectives	**Communication:** Create a TV commercial
• Rides and attractions at amusement parks	• Inquire about future plans • Respond	• French fair **la Fête des Loges** • Amusement parks and other attractions in France **La Francophonie (Parcs d'attractions): La Ronde** **Produits:** **Le Parc d'Astérix**	• Present tense of the irregular verbs **aller** and **faire** • **De** and **à** + definite articles • The irregular verb **venir** and **venir de** + infinitive • Telling time	**Culture:** Investigate bilinguism in Canada **Fine art:** Realism (Jean-Louis Ernest Meissonier) **Reading:** Paraphrasing and Learning from the title
Unité 2 Dans la capitale				
Essential question: What stories does Paris tell about art and architecture?				
• Art terms • Types of paintings	• Describe a painting	• The **Louvre** • The **musée d'Orsay** • The **Centre Pompidou** **Produits:** **La *Joconde***	• Present tense of the irregular verb **suivre** • **Passé composé** with **avoir** • Present tense of the irregular verbs **mettre**, **prendre**, and **voir**	
• Places in the neighborhood	• Say I'm lost • Tell someone not to worry • Ask for directions • Give directions	• Paris **arrondissements** • **Le Quartier latin** • **Saint-Germain des Prés** **Produits:** **La Sainte-Chapelle**	• Present tense of the irregular verbs **vouloir**, **pouvoir**, **devoir**, and **falloir** • Irregular past participles • Imperative	**Communication:** Describe art

Vocabulaire	Fonctions	Culture	Structure	Stratégies
• Modes of transportation • Versailles	• Ask about transportation • Respond	• Tourist offices • The R.E.R. • **Versailles**	• Present tense of the irregular verbs **partir** and **sortir** • **Passé composé** with **être** • Superlative of adjectives	**Culture:** Explore **le musée d'Orsay** **Fine art:** Modern Art (Marc Laberge) **Reading:** Drama basics and Finding evidence in the text
Bilan cumulatif: Unités 1 – 2				
Unité 3 La vie quotidienne				
Essential question: How do the routines of people in other cultures differ from mine?				
• Toiletries • Daily routine	• Complain • Respond to a complaint • Express frustration • Respond	**La Francophonie:** • Cameroon • Goals of the community of **la Francophonie** **Produits:** **Le Ngondo**	• Present tense of reflexive verbs • Irregular plural forms of nouns and adjectives	
• Household items • Household chores	• Make comparisons • Respond to comparisons • Express injustice	**La Francophonie:** • Ivory Coast • Artists from the Ivory Coast • Africa today • African immigrants in France today **Produits:** **Zouglou** music	• Present tense of the irregular verb **s'asseoir** • The imperative of reflexive verbs	**Communication:** Tell a story through pictures
• More reflexive verbs	• Find out if someone remembers something • Recount past events	**La Francophonie:** • Senegal • Senagalese artists • **Griots** • Singer Youssou N'Dour **Produits:** **L'hymne national sénégalais**	• **Passé composé** of reflexive verbs	**Culture:** Examine the controversy of Halal meat in fast-food restaurants **Fine art:** Batik (Anonyme) **Reading:** Sensory details and Making inferences
Unité 4 Autrefois				
Essential question: How does the past shape us?				
• Farm • Farm animals	• Reminisce • Describe past events	• Agriculture in France • World ranking of France's agricultural products • French rural life today **Produits:** **Emmental**	• Imperfect tense • Present tense of the irregular verb **croire**	

Vocabulaire	Fonctions	Culture	Structure	Stratégies
• Professions of the past	• Describe past events	• Montmartre • Toulouse-Lautrec **Produits:** Poster art	• **Il y a** + time • Imperfect and **passé composé**	**Communication:** Write an oral history
• University life	• Make a suggestion	• Demonstrations • May 1968 • University of Vincennes vs. Sorbonne	**Si on** + imperfect	**Culture:** Discover the reasons why people demonstrate **Fine art:** Impressionism's use of light (Camille Pissarro) **Reading:** Text organization and Fact vs. opinion
Bilan cumulatif: Unités 3 – 4				
Unité 5 Bon voyage et bonne route!				
Essential question: What do you need to know to travel successfully?				
• At the airport	• Describe a health problem • Give instructions	• **Air France** • Airports in Paris • Bordeaux **Produits:** **Les Nubians**, hip-hop group from Bordeaux	• Direct object pronouns: **me**, **te**, **nous**, **vous**	
• Types of cars • Exterior of cars • Interior of cars	• Express that I'm looking forward to something	• **Peugeot-Citroën** and **Renault** car companies • Learning to drive in France **Produits:** **Renault** and General Motors	• Direct object pronouns: **le**, **la**, **l'**, **les** • Direct object pronouns in the **passé composé** • Present tense of the irregular verb **conduire**	**Communication:** Write a dialogue
• Hotel room • French breakfast • North American breakfast	• Ask for a hotel room • Ask if something's included in the price • Understand what the receptionist asks	• Hotels, inns, and bed & breakfasts in France • Luxury hotels and the movies **Produits:** Sofitel, hotel chain	• Indirect object pronouns: **lui**, **leur** • Indirect object pronouns: **me**, **te**, **nous**, **vous** • Present tense of the irregular verb **boire** • The adjective **tout**	**Culture:** Find a hotel that meets your needs **Fine art:** Pop art (François Le Diascorn) **Reading:** Motif and Cause and effect
Unité 6 Les arts maghrébins				
Essential question: How do other cultures enrich our lives?				
• Things we read • Things we write	• Say what a book is about • Introduce an author or a novel • Borrow something	**La Francophonie:** • Morocco • French language comic books **Produits:** • Henna decoration in North Africa • ***Le racisme expliqué à ma fille*** by Tahar Ben Jelloun	• Present tense of the irregular verb **lire** • Present tense of the irregular verb **écrire**	

Vocabulaire	Fonctions	Culture	Structure	Stratégies
• Music genres • Musical instruments	• Ask if someone plays a particular instrument • Say what instrument I play	**La Francophonie:** • Algeria • **Raï** music • Singer Faudel • North African music instruments **Produits:** ***Indigènes***, French film about North African soldiers	• Present tense of the irregular verb **savoir** • Present tense of the irregular verb **connaître**	**Communication:** Write a character sketch
• Accessories and fabrics • Jewelry	• Begin and end a letter • Thank someone formally	**La Francophonie:** • Tunisia • **Souks** • How to write a formal letter **Produits:** Carthage	• Present tense of the irregular verb **recevoir** • Present tense of the irregular verb **ouvrir**	**Culture:** Reflect on negotiating a price in North African souks and in North America **Fine art:** Perspective in modern photography (Peet Simard) **Reading:** Images and Refrain
Bilan cumulatif: Unités 5 – 6				
Unité 7 En province				
Essential question: How do smaller communities enrich a country's culture?				
• Foods and courses	• Compliment the host or hostess • Politely refuse more food • Offer help	• Alsace • Strasbourg **La Francophonie (Une autre province):** **Kabylie** in Algeria **Produits:** **La choucroute garnie**	• The relative pronouns **qui** and **que** • The partitive • The pronoun **en**	
• French regions and their adjectives	• Ask a friend what's new • Find out someone's associations with a place • Say I like a suggestion	• Normandy • Rouen **Produits:** • French influence on the English language • Bayeux tapestry • Cider • Claude Monet museum in Giverny	• Interrogative pronouns	**Communication:** Combine sentences
• Things to eat and drink in a **crêperie** • Youth hostels	• Understand what the server asks • Order food	• Brittany • Saint-Malo • Youth hostels **Produits:** Food specialties of Brittany	• Stress pronouns	**Culture:** Explore regional identity **Fine art:** Still lifes (Paul Cézanne) **Reading:** Refrain and tone, and Anticipating vocabulary

Vocabulaire	Fonctions	Culture	Structure	Stratégies
Unité 8 Les Antilles				
Essential question: What are the benefits of encountering other cultures?				
• Flora in Guadeloupe • Fauna in Guadeloupe	• Ask what someone prefers • State ambivalence	**La Francophonie:** • Guadeloupe • **Parc national de la Guadeloupe** • Green tourism **Produits:** **"Prière d'un Petit enfant nègre"** by Guy Tirolien	• Present tense of the irregular verb **vivre** • Pronoun **y**	
• Carnival in Martinique • Weddings	• Make an observation	**La Francophonie:** • Martinique • Carnival in Martinique **Produits:** ***La Rue Cases-Nègres***	• Double object pronouns	**Communication:** Circumlocution
• Water management • Seafood	• Say what I'm in charge of • Express appreciation	**La Francophonie:** • Haiti • Toussaint Louverture • Haitian cuisine **Produits:** Haitian music	• **Depuis** + present tense	**Culture:** Find a good humanitarian organization **Fine art:** Seascapes (Claude Salez) **Reading:** Theme and Citing others' works
Bilan cumulatif: Unités 7 – 8				
Unité 9 La vie contemporaine				
Essential question: What influences and changes contemporary society?				
• Features of smartphones • Steps for taking a digital photo	• Ask someone to lend me something • Say that I know or do not know how to use something • Express what someone was happy about	• French transportation technologies: aviation, space program, rail **Produits:** Rubber from Indochina and Michelin	• Conditional tense	
• Problems in contemporary society • Possible solutions	• Hypothesize • Propose solutions	• Nuclear energy • Objectives and problems in French education • Unemployed young people **Produits:** French **Grandes Écoles**	• Conditional tense in sentences with **si**	**Communication:** Write a proposal

Vocabulaire	Fonctions	Culture	Structure	Stratégies
• Job sectors • Today's professions	• Express my future goals • Give a reason	**La Francophonie:** • Belgium • Famous Belgians • Brussels • European Union **Produits:** Flemish/French song by Jacques Brel	• Future tense	**Culture:** Investigate what new words in ***Le Petit Larousse*** reveal about contemporary French culture **Fine art:** Textures of acrylic paints (Daniel Cacouault) **Reading:** Dystopias in fiction and Social commentary
Unité 10 En vacances				
Essential question: What opportunities does travel afford us?				
• At the beach	• Say I've been wanting to do something for a long time	• French Riviera • Nice • Chagall museum • Matisse museum **Produits:** The **promenade des Anglais** in Nice	• Adverbs • Verbs + infinitives	
• Camping	• Say I need something • Ask someone to return something as soon as possible	• Alps • Grenoble • Camping in France **Produits:** **Téléphérique** in Grenoble	• Present tense of the irregular verb **dormir** • Comparative of adverbs	**Communication:** Travel writing
• Continents and bodies of water • Adventure tourism	• Ask what to bring	**La Francophonie:** • French Guiana • Kourou • Prisons **La Francophonie (Tourisme d'aventure):** Adventure tourism in France and French Guiana **Produits:** • Poems of Léon Gontran-Damas • *Papillon*	• Superlative of adverbs	**Culture:** Compare French and American vacation destinations **Fine art:** Point of view (Delphine D. Garcia) **Reading:** Point of view and Characterization
Bilan cumulatif: Unités 9 – 10				

T'es branché? Level 3

Vocabulaire	Fonctions	Culture	Structure	Stratégies
Unité 1 Les moments de la vie				
Essential question: Comment les objectifs et les intérêts des Francophones évoluent-ils avec le temps?				
• Human emotions • Teen destinations	• Say where I met someone • Advise someone • Tell someone not to worry • Describe how someone seems	• Teen socialization • **Maisons des Jeunes et de la Culture (MJC)** **Produits:** French blogs	• Present tense of regular **-er**,**-ir**, and **-re** verbs • Present tense of irregular verbs • **Depuis** + present tense	
• Different types of families • Childhood games and activities	• Explain how something happened • Say what I discovered • Ask for a suggestion	• Different types of families in France **La Francophonie (Les familles):** • Families and family values in Africa • **Provence-Alpes-Côte d'Azur** **Produits:** Perfumes and Grasse	• The irregular verb **courir** • **Passé composé** with **avoir** • **Passé composé** with **être** • Imperfect tense • Imperfect and **passé composé**	**Communication:** Write a personal narrative
• Weddings • Workplaces	• Say I don't care • Say where I'd like to work	• Preparatory and Ivy league schools • Civil and religious marriage ceremonies **La Francophonie (Le mariage):** • Marriage ceremony in Maghreb **Produits:** French wedding cake	• Conditional tense • Conditional tense with **si** • Future tense	**Culture:** Describing adolescent cultures **Fine art:** Line drawing (Édouard Albert) **Reading:** Setting and Using context clues (***Les petits enfants du siècle***, Christiane Rochefort)
Unité 2 Les rapports personnels				
Essential question: Qu'y a-t-il d'universel dans les rapports entre les gens?				
• Christmas eve dinner	• Talk on the phone • Invite someone • Respond affirmatively to an invitation • Say that a proposal works for me	• Christmas Eve holiday **Produits: Bûche de Noël** **La Francophonie (Les fêtes):** • Ramadan • **Aïd-el-Fitre**	• Interrogative pronouns • Direct object pronouns	
• Descriptions: shapes, sizes, material, and usage • Kitchen utensils	• Ask for help • Respond to a request for help	• Classic French cooking • **La nouvelle cuisine** **Produits: Le Cordon Bleu**	• Indirect object pronouns • **C'est** vs. **il/elle est**	**Communication:** Using circumlocution

Vocabulaire	Fonctions	Culture	Structure	Stratégies
• Dinner table topics of conversation	• Express that I can't stop myself • Say someone is right • Ask about dinner table topics	• Traditional meal for Christmas Eve • Rules of table etiquette **Produits:** French wine	• Relative pronouns **qui**, **que** • Relative pronouns **ce qui**, **ce que**	**Culture:** Identify food preferences **Fine art:** Landscapes behind portraits (Jules Ernest Renoux) **Reading:** Dialogue and Conflict (***Deux couverts***, Sacha Guitry)
Bilan cumulatif: Unités 1 – 2				
Unité 3 La Francophonie				
Essential question: Comment les Francophones restent-ils fidèles à leurs traditions?				
• Extended family members • States in the United States	• Say where my ancestors came from • Say where my ancestors settled	• **Alliance Française** and its outreach programs • French immigration to Quebec and **île d'Orléans** • French-Canadian immigration to New England	• Pronouns **y**, **en** • Double object pronouns	
• Types of stories • Words from a North African children's story	• Start a fairy-tale	**La Francophonie:** • Tunisia • Immigration of **Maghrébins** in France **La Francophonie (Les contes):** • Overview of **contes maghrébins** **Produits:** North African cuisine	• Reflexive verbs	**Communication:** Describe in detail
• Types of housing • Home repair terms	• Respond to an introduction • Say where I grew up • Give a compliment	• HLMs and **allocations familiales** **La Francophonie:** • Senegal **(Logement):** • African housing **Produits:** Oral tradition in Africa	• Comparative of adverbs • Superlative of adverbs	**Culture:** Needs of new immigrants **Fine art:** Primitive Art (Cécile Delorme) **Reading:** Make cultural inferences, Gender criticism (***Une si longue lettre***, Mariama Bâ)

Vocabulaire	Fonctions	Culture	Structure	Stratégies
Unité 4 Préparatifs de départ				
Essential question: Qu'est-ce qu'on doit connaître de sa destination pour réussir son voyage?				
• Sports and activities to do on vacation	• Ask someone's opinion • React positively to someone's opinion • React negatively to someone's opinion	**La Francophonie: La Réunion** • Chamonix and other **stations de ski** in France **La Francophonie (Stations de ski):** • Switzerland **Produits:** Training Saint Bernard dogs	• Present participle • Negation • Other negative expressions	
• At the ski resort • Ski clothing and equipment	• Say what I must do • Tell someone they'll have an opportunity • Say I was expecting something	• Haute Savoie traditions and specialties • **Classes de neige** **Produits: La raclette savoyarde** **La Francophonie (La récréation):** Aquatic or "bleu" activities in Saint-Martin	• **Savoir** vs. **connaître** • Subjunctive of regular verbs after **il faut que** • Subjunctive of irregular verbs	**Communication:** Write a "how-to" piece using subjunctive
• Other winter sports • Travel planning expressions	• Say I'm doing something different • Tell someone to not hurt himself or herself	• Volunteer travel experiences in Francophone countries **Produits:** Sports in the Winter Olympics	• Subjunctive after impersonal expressions	**Culture:** Volunteer travel experiences **Fine art:** Classicism (Sébastien Bourdon) **Reading:** Structure and Meaning, Allusions ("**Heureux qui, comme Ulysse, a fait un beau voyage,**" Joachim du Bellay)
Bilan cumulatif: Unités 3 – 4				
Unité 5 Comment se renseigner en voyage				
Essential question: De quelles compétences ai-je besoin pour réussir un séjour?				
• At the hotel • Hotel amenities	• Ask for information	**La Francophonie:** • Monaco • Monte Carlo • Rainier family **Produits: Le Bal de la Rose**	• Subjunctive after expressions of wish, will, desire	
• Food in Bourgogne: meats, dishes, sauces	• Ask about restaurant specialties • Ask what a dish is served with	• Dijon and its region • Food specialties in Bourgogne **Produits:** Dijon museum and mustard **La Francophonie (La cuisine):** • North African dishes	• Subjunctive after expressions of emotion • Subjunctive after expressions of doubt or uncertainty	**Communication:** Write a movie review

Vocabulaire	Fonctions	Culture	Structure	Stratégies
• Movie expressions	• Say what I'm not in the mood for • Report a review of a film • Ask someone's reaction (to a piece of art) • Express disagreement	• **Le septième art** • **Les Césars** **Produits:** Lumière brothers and birth of cinematography	• Interrogative adjective **quel** • Interrogative pronoun **lequel** (**duquel**, **auquel**)	**Culture:** Planning a trip online **Fine art:** Bright colors (Georges Rouault) **Reading:** Epistolary novel ("**La quarantaine**", Jean-Marie Le Clézio)
Unité 6 **On se débrouille en France.**				
Essential question: Comment s'intégrer à une autre culture?				
• Banking terms • University departments	• Open a bank account • Get a credit card • Make a promise	• French banks • French universities and free education **Produits:** **La Carte bleue**	• Future tense in sentences with **si** • Future tense after **quand**	
• Things to read	• Ask what a book is about • Say I can't decide	• French reading habits • Le Clézio **Produits:** French TV shows about books **La Francophonie (Les écrivains):** Maryse Condé	• Verbs + **de** + nouns • Relative pronoun **dont**	**Communication:** Persuade someone to read a book or see a movie
• At the post office	• Say what I need • Specify items	• French post office and its services **Produits:** Films that feature mail carriers	• Demonstrative adjectives • Demonstrative pronouns	**Culture:** Problem solving **sur place** **Fine art:** Cartoon art (Marjane Satrapi) **Reading:** Narrator and Narration, Direct and Indirect Reporting (***Petropolis***, Marjane Satrapi)
Bilan cumulatif: Unités 5 – 6				
Unité 7 **Les Arts**				
Essential question: Comment l'art est-il un reflet de la culture?				
• Art descriptions • Art movements	• Say when a painting was painted • Describe an artist's approach • Describe colors in a painting	• **Académie, salons** • **Atelier** vs. **en plein air** • **Salon des refusés** **Produits:** Monet painting that gave name to Impressionnists, *Sunday in the Park with George*	• Agreement and position of adjectives • Comparative of adjectives • Superlative of adjectives	

Vocabulaire	Fonctions	Culture	Structure	Stratégies
• Music	• Describe an artist's development • Say that an artist was successful • Describe an artist's ability to connect with his or her audience	• The modern French song and its themes **Produits:** "La vie en rose" **La Francophonie (Les chansons):** Quebec group **Produits:** "Mon pays," Gilles Vigneault	• The irregular verb **plaire**	**Communication:** Compare and Contrast
• Poetry	• Describe how an artist raises themes • Describe how a work of art takes a position • Describe what an artist worked on • Attribute new inventions • Describe how an artist fits into a culture	• French poets **Produits:** Apollinaire's **calligrammes**	• **Pour** + infinitive • Subjunctive after **pour que**	**Culture:** Compare French and American music **Fine art:** Multiple exposure (Walter Limot) **Reading:** Free Verse and Oxymorons ("**Familiale**," Jacques Prévert)
Unité 8 La France hier et aujourd'hui				
Essential question: Comment le passé influence-t-il le présent?				
• French Revolution	• Express what someone was obligated to do • Find that someone is forced to do something	• Louis XVI and Marie-Antoinette • **Les États généraux** • La ***Déclaration des Droits de l'homme et du citoyen*** **Produits:** **La Conciergerie**, guillotine, **La *Déclaration des Droits de la femme et de la citoyenne*** **La Francophonie (La révolution):** Arab Spring in Tunisia	• Expressions with **faire** • **Faire** + infinitive	
• Applying and interviewing for a job	• Indicate quantity • Say I did something in vain	• European Union Institutions **Produits:** Flag of E.U.	• Expressions with **avoir** • Past infinitive	**Communication:** Write a CV
• Health care terms • Debate terms	• Express that someone has a right • Express that someone can afford something • Say I want to discuss something more later	• Rights of the French citizen under **la sécu:** unemployment, health care, family, disabled protection, retirement **Produits:** **La crèche**	• Expressions with **être** • Pluperfect tense	**Culture:** Rights issues and challenges the press faces abroad **Fine art:** Theatrical photography (Joseph Nicéphore Niépce) **Reading:** Word families and setting (***Le bourgeois gentilhomme***, Molière)
Bilan cumulatif: Unités 7 – 8				

Vocabulaire	Fonctions	Culture	Structure	Stratégies
Unité 9 Récits de la vie contemporaine				
Essential question: Quels sont les défis de la vie contemporaire?				
• Emotions	• Express how someone looked	• Recent changes to French school system • **Le bac** and student stress **Produits: Les annales du bac**	• Past conditional tense • Past conditional tense with **si**	
• Physical description: hair, age, ethnicity, clothing	• Say I realized something	• Different types of French police • Crime in France **Produits: Une déclaration de vol Le château d'If**	• Possessive adjectives • Possessive pronouns	**Communication:** Tell a story through pictures
• Reactions	• Say I did not expect something	• Internet resources for teens **Produits: Loisirs ados**	• Indefinite adjectives • Indefinite pronouns	**Culture:** Interview a French speaker about challenges of life today **Fine art:** Book illustrations (Anonymous) **Reading:** Characterization and **Le passé simple** (**Les Misérables**, Victor Hugo)
Unité 10 La culture des affaires				
Essential question: Qu'est-ce qu'on apprend de la culture d'un pays en étudiant son économie?				
• Export products	• Say where an item was made	• French attitude toward globalization • **Luxury products** and LVMH **Produits:** Louis Vuitton brand		
• Types of companies • French and U.S. trade	• Ask if someone's been here a long time • Say I wanted to get away	• France's position in world trade • Multinational companies • French business etiquette and taboos **Produits:** Ariane rockets		**Communication:** Make a storyboard to sell a North American product in France
• Professional qualifications • Job positions within a company	• Describe adaptability • Say what I'm interested in	• Evolution of French marketing strategies **Produits:** Advertisements for **La vache qui rit**		**Culture:** How globalization affects our lives **Fine art:** Advertising photography **Reading:** (***14.99 €***, Frédéric Beigbeder)
Bilan cumulatif: Unités 9 – 10				

Introduction

T'es branché? was designed to give French teachers a program that focuses on the three modes of communication—interpersonal, presentational, and interpretive—while ensuring their students become proficient in the five skill areas. Based on detailed surveys involving hundreds of experienced French educators, the textbook program responds to teachers' expressed interests and priorities. The filmed dialogues in the *Rencontres culturelles* section were written in France by native speakers, so that students learn idiomatic and natural expression. Grammar exercises are designed to build proficency. Students develop reading skills with comprehensible input paragraphs in the vocabulary practice section. They also learn to appreciate literary writing in *Lecture thématique*. Activities move from mechanical exercises to more creative and open-ended projects. An essential question molds all the learning in any given unit.

Because paired, small group, and cooperative group activities are at the heart of today's student-centered classroom, *T'es branché?* offers many opportunities for students to work with their classmates on activities and projects that have clear guidelines and expectations. Students assume a more active role in their learning as they focus on how to learn as well as how to communicate in French. Opportunities for critical thinking can be found throughout the program, for example, in comparing francophone cultures to American culture and French grammar to English grammar.

Finally, the *T'es branché?* program was written to incorporate the National Standards. Let's look at how the textbook covers 2.1 and 2.2 from the standards below, for example. Students read culture notes about practices in the francophone world, as well as the content in *Produits* boxes that describe products from these locations. *Perspectives* are presented that may be in the form of a poem or song or quote from a French-speaker about their beliefs, experience, or observations. A new approach to teaching culture is presented in *La culture sur place*, allowing students to engage with francophone culture as they investigate topics of interest to teens and reflect on their "experience." Whatever element you are teaching, *T'es branché?* provides the tools you need to address standards in the following areas:

Communication

Communicate Effectively in More than one Language in Order to Function in a Variety of Situations and for Multiple Purposes

Interpersonal Communication (formerly Standard 1.1): Learners interact and negotiate meaning in spoken, signed, or written conversations to share information, reactions, feelings, and opinions.

Interpretive Communication (formerly Standard 1.2): Learners understand, interpret, and analyze what is heard, read, or viewed on a variety of topics.

Presentational Communication (formerly Standard 1.3): Learners present information, concepts, and ideas to inform, explain, persuade, and narrate on a variety of topics using appropriate media and adapting to various audiences of listeners, readers, or viewers.

Cultures

Interact with Cultural Competence and Understanding

Relating Cultural Practices to Perspectives (formerly Standard 2.1): Learners use the language to investigate, explain, and reflect on the relationship between the practices and perspectives of the cultures studied.

Relating Cultural Products to Perspectives (formerly Standard 2.2): Learners use the language to investigate, explain, and reflect on the relationship between the products and perspectives of the cultures studied.

Connections

Connect with Other Disciplines and Acquire Information and Diverse Perspectives in order to Use the Language to Function in Academic and Career-Related Situations

Making Connections (formerly Standard 3.1): Learners build, reinforce, and expand their knowledge of other disciplines while using the language to develop critical thinking and to solve problems creatively.

Acquiring Information and Diverse Perspectives (formerly Standard 3.2): Learners access and evaluate information and diverse perspectives that are available through the language and its cultures.

Comparisons

Develop Insight into the Nature of Language and Culture in order to Interact with Cultural Competence

Language Comparisons (formerly Standard 4.1): Learners use the language to investigate, explain, and reflect on the nature of language through comparisons of the language studied and their own.

Cultural Comparisons (formerly Standard 4.2): Learners use the language to investigate, explain, and reflect on the concept of culture through comparisons of the cultures studied and their own.

Communities

Communicate and Interact with Cultural Competence in order to Participate in Multilingual Communities at Home and Around the World

School and Global Communities (formerly Standard 5.1): Learners use the language both within and beyond the classroom to interact and collaborate in their community and the globalized world.

Lifelong Learning (formerly Standard 5.2): Learners set goals and reflect on their progress in using languages for enjoyment, enrichment, and advancement.

Since a modern challenge in world language instruction is reaching all students—those with varying abilities, backgrounds, interests, and learning styles—the *T'es branché?* program has many opportunities beyond the textbook to help meet those needs. The Annotated Teacher's Edition provides suggested activities for different types of learners, from those with special needs to those who would benefit from enrichment. The online Drill and Practice games provide immediate feedback, allowing students to find out what they need more practice on well in advance of the test. Online Pre-tests also have immediate feedback, so that students can find out what they need to study more before their assessment experiences. Tailor-made products such as these ensure that each student makes progress and meets their potential as they embrace the French language and francophone culture.

Common Core State Standards

The Common Core State Standards (CCSS) initiative seeks to raise academic standards for students and provide articulation of academic standards between states. The CCSS is designed for courses in English Language Arts, History/Social Studies, Science, and Technical Subjects, each containing four strands: Reading, Writing, Speaking and Listening, and Language. Having CCSS drive curricula will result in new assessment benchmarks for students.

T'es branché? was designed with the CCSS in mind. It emphasizes the purpose behind the communication by labeling activities that provide interpersonal (speaking-listening or writing-reading), interpretive (reading, listening, viewing), and presentational (writing, speaking, representing visually) communication. The goal of the textbooks is to move students from novice, to intermediate, to the advanced mid-level by the time they complete the *T'es branché?* four-level program. Connections activities in *T'es branché?* that are specific to history and science allow students to learn about francophone history and scientific contributions made by Francophones. Technology skills are developed, as in the readings of *Points de départ*, where students research online using search words provided, and the *Projets finaux*, which allows for individual, pair, and group work using technology such as the Internet, video, smartphone, and online programs. *T'es branché?* uses the CCSS to make sure all students are ready for post-secondary learning, working, and becoming global citizens. A correlation of *T'es branché?* to the CCSS is at the end of the Annotated Teacher's Edition front pages.

Welcome to *T'es branché?*!

Key Features: Student Textbook

Students are excited to speak in French with abundant, targeted communicative practice…

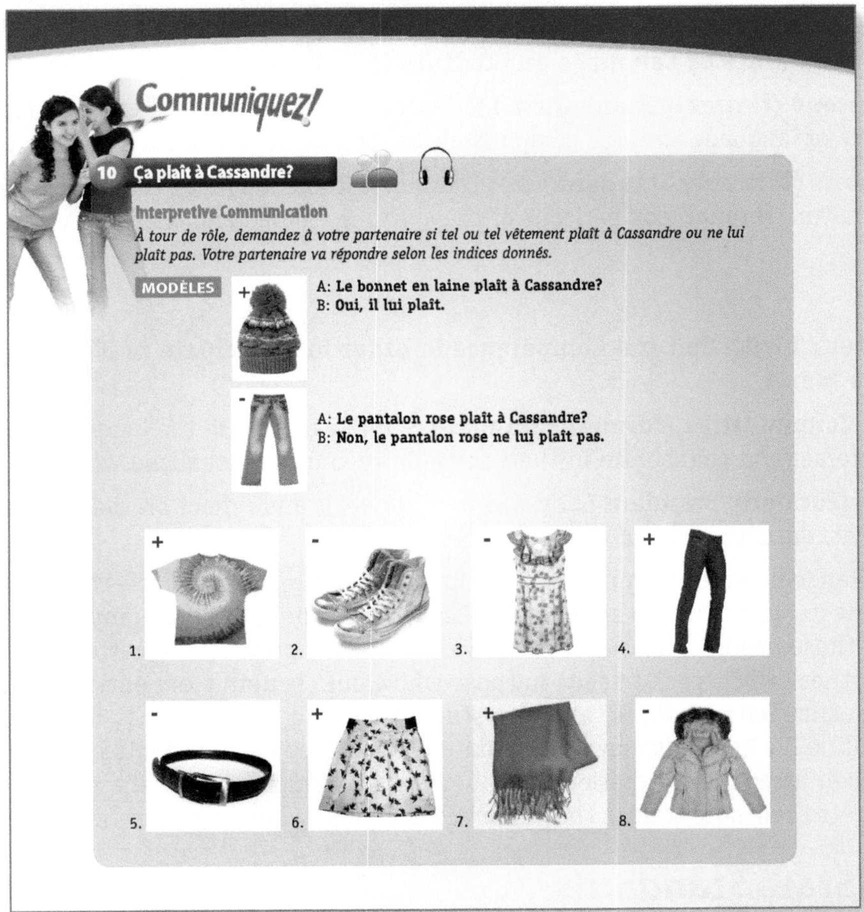

and opportunities for creative self-expression.

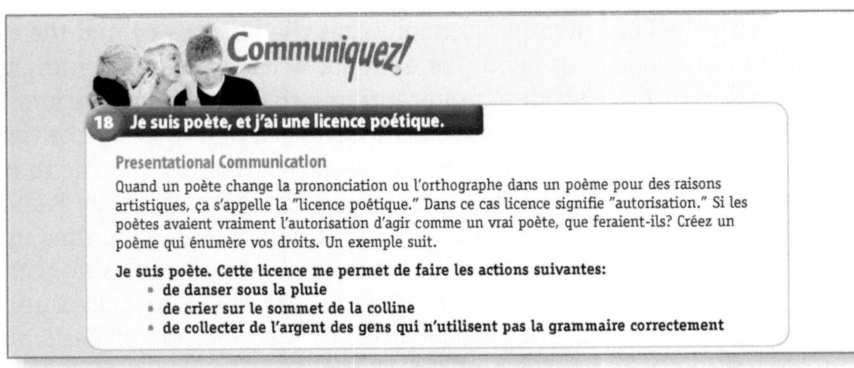

Unit content is centered on an essential question to anchor learning:

Students analyze the essential question in the *Projets finaux* section.

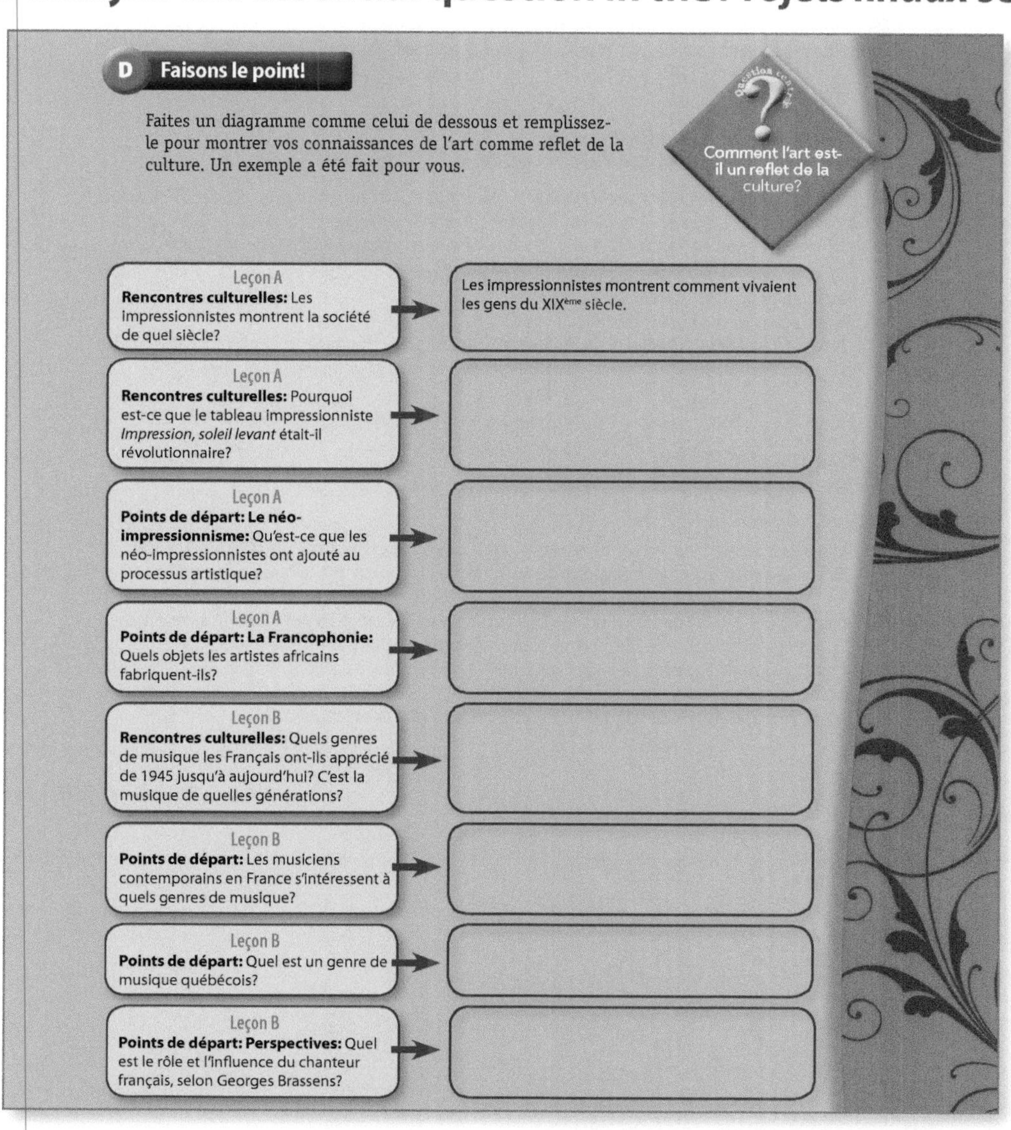

D Faisons le point!

Faites un diagramme comme celui de dessous et remplissez-le pour montrer vos connaissances de l'art comme reflet de la culture. Un exemple a été fait pour vous.

Leçon A **Rencontres culturelles:** Les impressionnistes montrent la société de quel siècle?	Les impressionnistes montrent comment vivaient les gens du XIXème siècle.
Leçon A **Rencontres culturelles:** Pourquoi est-ce que le tableau impressionniste *Impression, soleil levant* était-il révolutionnaire?	
Leçon A **Points de départ: Le néo-impressionnisme:** Qu'est-ce que les néo-impressionnistes ont ajouté au processus artistique?	
Leçon A **Points de départ: La Francophonie:** Quels objets les artistes africains fabriquent-ils?	
Leçon B **Rencontres culturelles:** Quels genres de musique les Français ont-ils apprécié de 1945 jusqu'à aujourd'hui? C'est la musique de quelles générations?	
Leçon B **Points de départ:** Les musiciens contemporains en France s'intéressent à quels genres de musique?	
Leçon B **Points de départ:** Quel est un genre de musique québécois?	
Leçon B **Points de départ: Perspectives:** Quel est le rôle et l'influence du chanteur français, selon Georges Brassens?	

Students investigate francophone cultures "on location."

La culture sur place

Mes expériences avec la mondialisation

Dans cette *Culture sur place*, vous allez rechercher les marques internationales dans votre vie. D'où viennent les produits que vous utilisez chaque jour? Quel est le lien entre ces produits et la culture?

11 Première Étape: Chercher et rechercher

Choisissez une catégorie de la liste suivante. Vous allez rechercher d'où viennent ces produits dont vous vous servez régulièrement.

- les vêtements
- l'équipement sportif
- la nourriture
- les boissons
- les produits électroniques
- les produits cosmétiques, produits d'entretien et d'hygiène

Faites une liste des produits, donnez le pays de fabrication et des marques pour chacun. Préparez des pourcentages où c'est possible, par exemple, "Soixante pourcent de mes vêtements viennent d'Asie."

12 Deuxième Étape: Comparer

Partagez les informations de votre liste avec celles de quelques camarades de classe. Si plusieurs élèves ont choisi la même catégorie, combinez vos listes de marques et de pays de fabrication. Ensuite, discutez de vos découvertes avec les autres élèves en répondant à ces questions:

1. Est-ce que la plupart de ces produits (dans la catégorie que vous avez choisie) viennent de la même région ou du même pays?
2. Remarquez-vous d'autres motifs?
3. Quelle est votre hypothèse économique pour expliquer ces motifs et pourquoi un tel pays fabrique ceci ou cela?

13 Faire l'inventaire!

Discutez ces questions en classe.

1. Après vos recherches, est-ce que vous pensez que vous vivez dans un marché mondial? Est-ce que votre point de vue a changé au cours de cette activité? Si oui, comment?
2. Est-ce que vous pensez qu'il y a un lien entre les produits et les cultures? Avez-vous trouvé, par exemple, un produit que vous pensez typiquement américain qui a été fabriqué à l'étranger?
3. Quelle est la fonction des frontières (*borders*) entre nations dans une époque de mondialisation? Trouvez-vous que les frontières entre les pays sont plus importantes, ou moins importantes, maintenant?
4. Selon vous, la mondialisation est-elle une menace ou un avantage?

Leçon C | six cent trois 603

The francophone world is seen through its

- **Practices**

Bonnes manières

Réunion*, repas d'affaires, invitations—à chaque moment ses codes pour réussir un rapport avec une entreprise française.

Rendez-vous et réunions: Depuis le Moyen-Âge*, les Français ont la réputation de n'être jamais à l'heure à un rendez-vous. Pourtant les rendez-vous et réunions commencent en général à l'heure dite. L'internationalisation a mis de la rigueur* dans la gestion du temps. Un écart* de cinq minutes reste toutefois toléré. Les Français ne fixent que rarement l'heure de fin d'une réunion. Dans les premiers rendez-vous, le "vous" est de rigueur au premier contact; si le "tu" doit s'imposer, il le fera naturellement, par consensus. Généralement, c'est dans les moments de convivialité, hors* l'officialité qu'il s'imposera. Attention, les Français respectent peu les tours de parole et ont tendance à couper la parole: c'est le produit d'une culture du débat et de la polémique*.

- **Products**

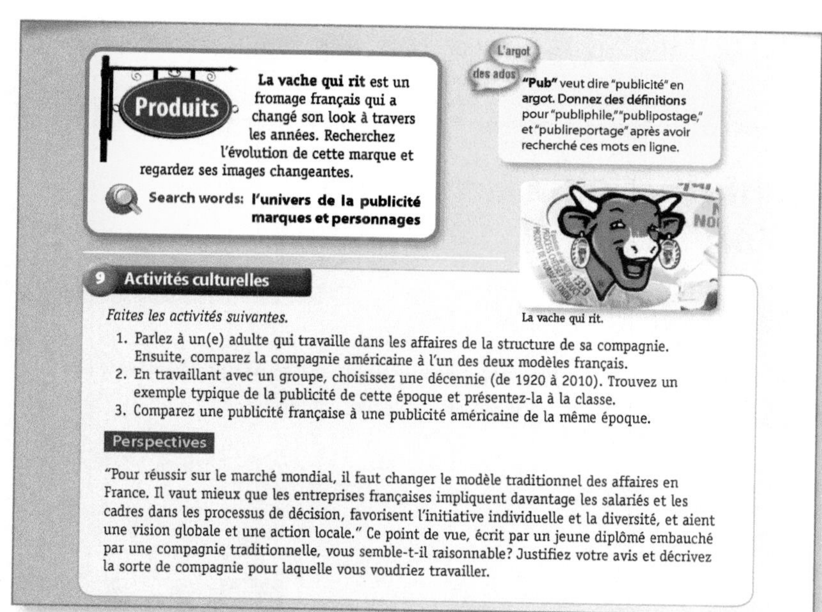

Produits

La vache qui rit est un fromage français qui a changé son look à travers les années. Recherchez l'évolution de cette marque et regardez ses images changeantes.

Search words: **l'univers de la publicité marques et personnages**

L'argot des ados

"Pub" veut dire "publicité" en argot. Donnez des définitions pour "publiphile," "publipostage," et "publireportage" après avoir recherché ces mots en ligne.

La vache qui rit.

9 Activités culturelles

Faites les activités suivantes.

1. Parlez à un(e) adulte qui travaille dans les affaires de la structure de sa compagnie. Ensuite, comparez la compagnie américaine à l'un des deux modèles français.
2. En travaillant avec un groupe, choisissez une décennie (de 1920 à 2010). Trouvez un exemple typique de la publicité de cette époque et présentez-la à la classe.
3. Comparez une publicité française à une publicité américaine de la même époque.

Perspectives

"Pour réussir sur le marché mondial, il faut changer le modèle traditionnel des affaires en France. Il vaut mieux que les entreprises françaises impliquent davantage les salariés et les cadres dans les processus de décision, favorisent l'initiative individuelle et la diversité, et aient une vision globale et une action locale." Ce point de vue, écrit par un jeune diplômé embauché par une compagnie traditionnelle, vous semble-t-il raisonnable? Justifiez votre avis et décrivez la sorte de compagnie pour laquelle vous voudriez travailler.

- **and Perspectives.**

Perspectives

"Avant d'aller faire la prière rituelle à la mosquée, nous distribuons la *Zakat el-Fitr*, l'aumône donnée aux pauvres par acte de générosité et de compassion. Ce don purificateur permet aux personnes pauvres de ne pas avoir faim et représente une libération de la mendicité (*begging*) en ce jour sacré." Selon ce Musulman, quel est le but de la *Zakat el-Fitr*?

Students master core vocabulary by reading comprehensible-input texts…

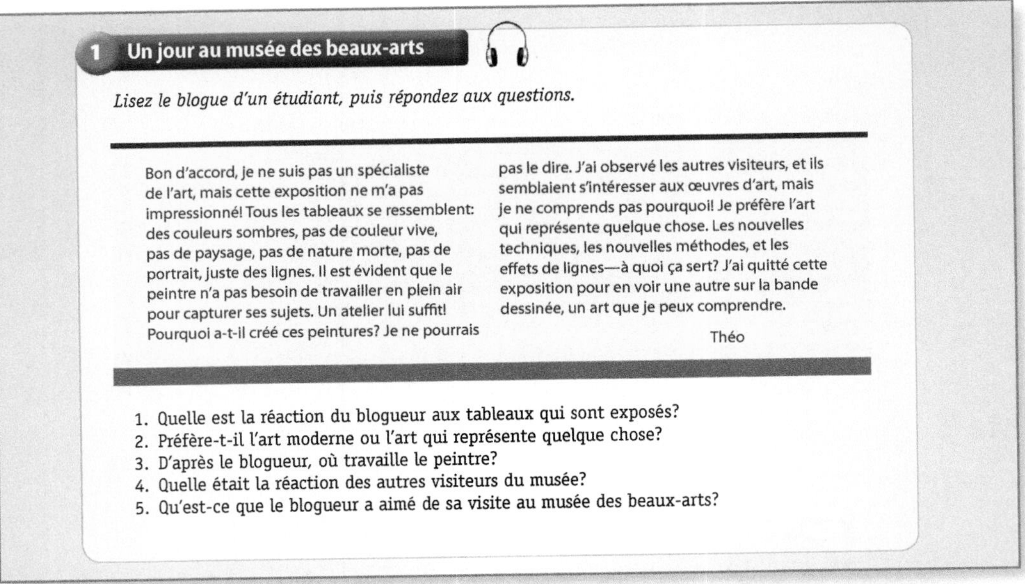

1 Un jour au musée des beaux-arts

Lisez le blogue d'un étudiant, puis répondez aux questions.

Bon d'accord, je ne suis pas un spécialiste de l'art, mais cette exposition ne m'a pas impressionné! Tous les tableaux se ressemblent: des couleurs sombres, pas de couleur vive, pas de paysage, pas de nature morte, pas de portrait, juste des lignes. Il est évident que le peintre n'a pas besoin de travailler en plein air pour capturer ses sujets. Un atelier lui suffit! Pourquoi a-t-il créé ces peintures? Je ne pourrais pas le dire. J'ai observé les autres visiteurs, et ils semblaient s'intéresser aux œuvres d'art, mais je ne comprends pas pourquoi! Je préfère l'art qui représente quelque chose. Les nouvelles techniques, les nouvelles méthodes, et les effets de lignes—à quoi ça sert? J'ai quitté cette exposition pour en voir une autre sur la bande dessinée, un art que je peux comprendre.

Théo

1. Quelle est la réaction du blogueur aux tableaux qui sont exposés?
2. Préfère-t-il l'art moderne ou l'art qui représente quelque chose?
3. D'après le blogueur, où travaille le peintre?
4. Quelle était la réaction des autres visiteurs du musée?
5. Qu'est-ce que le blogueur a aimé de sa visite au musée des beaux-arts?

and doing meaningful activities with high frequency vocabulary.

3 Les réactions

Regardez les illustrations pour identifier les réactions des personnes. Choisissez un adjectif de la liste.

MODÈLE **M. Dugas est complètement accablé.**

accablé seul surpris surexcité choqué frustré

M. Dugas

1. M. et Mme Laroche
2. Mme Dufour
3. Matthieu
4. M. Carré
5. Isabelle

Students connect to each structure topic...

- **visually**

- **contextually**

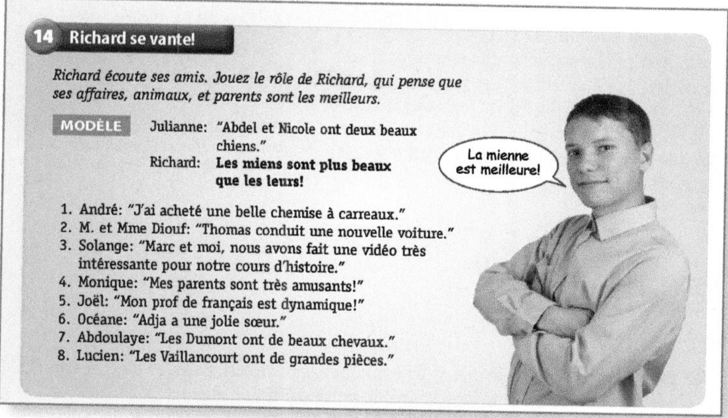

14 Richard se vante!

Richard écoute ses amis. Jouez le rôle de Richard, qui pense que ses affaires, animaux, et parents sont les meilleurs.

MODÈLE Julianne: "Abdel et Nicole ont deux beaux chiens."
Richard: **Les miens sont plus beaux que les leurs!**

1. André: "J'ai acheté une belle chemise à carreaux."
2. M. et Mme Diouf: "Thomas conduit une nouvelle voiture."
3. Solange: "Marc et moi, nous avons fait une vidéo très intéressante pour notre cours d'histoire."
4. Monique: "Mes parents sont très amusants!"
5. Joël: "Mon prof de français est dynamique!"
6. Océane: "Adja a une jolie sœur."
7. Abdoulaye: "Les Dumont ont de beaux chevaux."
8. Lucien: "Les Vaillancourt ont de grandes pièces."

- **meaningfully**

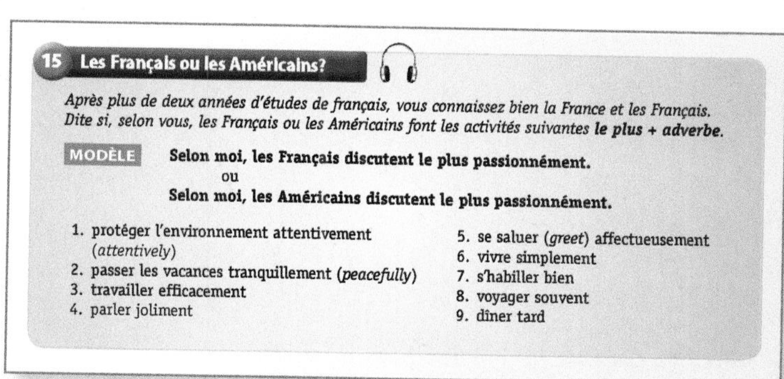

15 Les Français ou les Américains?

Après plus de deux années d'études de français, vous connaissez bien la France et les Français. Dite si, selon vous, les Français ou les Américains font les activités suivantes **le plus + adverbe**.

MODÈLE **Selon moi, les Français discutent le plus passionnément.**
ou
Selon moi, les Américains discutent le plus passionnément.

1. protéger l'environnement attentivement (*attentively*)
2. passer les vacances tranquillement (*peacefully*)
3. travailler efficacement
4. parler joliment
5. se saluer (*greet*) affectueusement
6. vivre simplement
7. s'habiller bien
8. voyager souvent
9. dîner tard

Students make meaningful reading/writing connections.

Deux couverts

Post-lecture

Pelletier est-il un bon ou mauvais père? Pourquoi?

Le monde visuel

Dans ce tableau, Jules Ernest Renoux (1863–1932) a peint un petit garçon de manière réaliste, sur un arrière-plan de style différent. L'interprétation artistique des paysages d'arrière-plan en peinture a changé à travers l'histoire de l'art. Au XVIème siècle, on peut voir derrière la *Joconde*, de Léonard de Vinci, un arrière-plan qui annonce la peinture de paysage. Au XVIIIème siècle, Claude Lorrain a essayé de peindre ses paysages d'arrière-plan de manière plus réaliste que les peintres de son époque. Mais au XIXème siècle, les peintres voulaient plutôt montrer des impressions de paysage. Quel est le style dans lequel est peint le paysage d'arrière-plan dans ce portrait du fils de Renoux? Qu'est-ce qui frappe l'œil en premier, le sujet ou le paysage? Selon vous, pourquoi une telle juxtaposition du portrait réaliste et d'un paysage de style différent?

Portrait de Marcel Renoux vers 13 ou 14 ans, c. 1912. Jules Ernest Renoux. Collection privée.

19 Activités d'expansion

Complétez les activités suivantes.

1. Écrivez un paragraphe dans lequel vous expliquez les conflits entre le père et son fils dans cette pièce. Servez-vous des informations de votre grille.
2. Jouez le rôle du père et écrivez une lettre que vous allez glisser (*slip*) sous la porte de la chambre de votre fils qui explique ce que vous voulez pour lui et pourquoi.
3. Imaginez que le père et le fils dînent ensemble et discutent de l'avenir du fils. Écrivez le dialogue pour cette scène entre le père et le fils.

T'es branché? provides two opportunities for reviewing:

Évaluation

E Évaluation visuelle

Imaginez que vous devez écrire un paragraphe sur ce tableau. Expliquez:

- le mouvement auquel cette œuvre appartient (*belongs*).
- quand ce mouvement a eu lieu.
- qui est l'artiste.
- ce que le peintre recherche dans cette œuvre ou son œuvre en général.
- comment l'artiste s'éloigne des peintres qui l'ont précédé.
- ce qu'il a peint dans ce tableau.
- pourquoi vous aimez cette peinture ou pourquoi vous ne l'aimez pas.

Servez-vous des expressions de Pour la conversation.

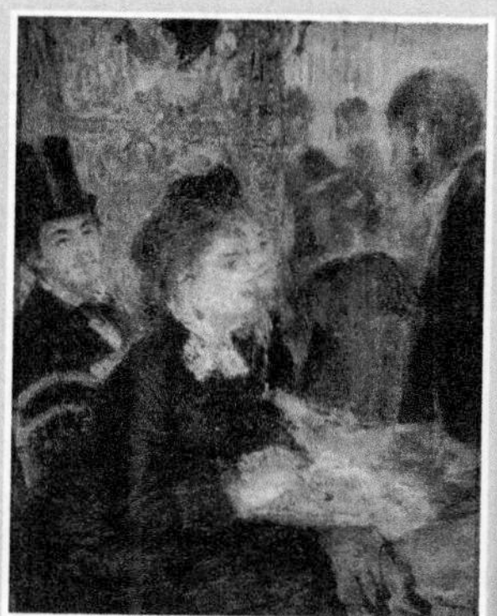

Unité 10 Bilan cumulatif

IV. Interpersonal Speaking: Conversation

Vous allez avoir une conversation avec un agent de police au commissariat. Vous êtes touriste en France, et on vous a volé quelque chose d'important. Suivez les indications ci-dessous.

L'agent: Je peux vous aider, Monsieur?
Vous: **Dites ce qu'on vous a volé.**
L'agent: Et où ce vol a-t-il eu lieu?
Vous: **Dites qu'on vous a volé dans le métro en route vers la station Châtelet.**
L'agent: Et vous avez vu le voleur?
Vous: **Dites que oui, et décrivez le voleur: sa taille, son âge, la couleur de ses cheveux, son origine ethnique, ses vêtements.**
L'agent: (Il vous montre une photo.) C'est lui?
Vous: **Dites que vous êtes sûr que c'est lui, mais qu'il a les cheveux plus courts maintenant.**
L'agent: On l'a presque arrêté la semaine dernière. Ses vols sont toujours dans le métro. Comment est-ce qu'on peut vous contacter?
Vous: **Donnez-lui votre numéro de portable.**
L'agent: Auriez-vous le temps de remplir cette déclaration de vol?
Vous: **Dites que vous le remplirez à l'hôtel et que vous reviendrez demain matin.**
L'agent: Merci d'être venu. Je vous reverrai demain, alors.
Vous: **Remerciez l'agent et dites que vous le reverrez demain.**

Key Features: Technology for Students

Students have the technological tools they need to excel and learn at their own pace:

- **EMCL (emcl.com)**
  EMCL is the ideal blended-learning environment for world language students, and the ultimate, time-saving companion for teachers. This innovative online Learning Management System integrates proven methodologies with EMC's rich content to deliver authentic, interactive, and engaging learning experiences.
- **EPUB multimedia eBook offers delivery on multiple devices.**

- **Electronic flash cards help students master core vocabulary.**

le service après-vente

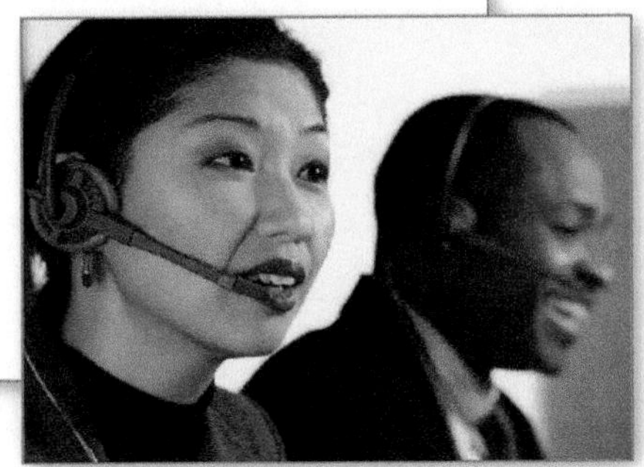

- **e-visuals allow for motivating vocabulary practice.**

- **Online Pre-tests offer immediate feedback.**

Unité 5

Leçon B

Complete the mini-dialogues by filling in the blanks.

1. -Tu as mis ta veste préférée?
   -Oui, ______.
2. -Georges a pris le metro?
   -Non, ______.
3. -Vous avez ouvert le cadeau?
   - Non, ______.
4. -Nous avons envoyé la lettre?
   -Oui, ______.
5. -Tu as acheté les provisions?
   -Oui, ______.

- **Documentaires, DVD... location in Nice.**

- **QR codes provide access to videos.**

Key Features: Teacher's Edition

Online, print, and electronic resources for the page in question are listed here.

The Reference Desk offers additional background information, linguistic and pronunciation notes, and other relevant information about items on the page.

The Communication box includes Interpersonal, Presentational, and Interpretive activities for additional practice.

The culture box contains information and/or activities about the practices, products, and perspectives of francophone cultures.

RESOURCES

 e-visual 6

 Workbook 1–4

 Flash Cards

 Listening Activities 1–2

 Drill & Practice Games

Reference Desk

1. Put the following terms on the board: **le socialisme, l'entraîneur, réaliser, champion, la candidature.** Ask students what expressions these new words are related to, whether they're nouns or verbs, and to guess what they might mean. For students interested in increasing their vocabulary, one strategy is to learn other words related to a new vocabulary word.
2. A lot of American citizens might bristle at the word **socialiste**, but in France and Europe socialism is an important political option.
3. Explain why **réaliser** is a **faux ami**.

Communication

Interpersonal: Paired Practice

To practice the expressions in **L'art de la conversation** and **Pour la conversation**, have students work in pairs to prepare a dialogue about topics discussed at their dinner table. Ask students to expand and include many points of view from the various family members.

Culture

Perspectives: Information

High fashion in France has a worldwide reputation, and the French created the term **haute couture**. The fashion houses where this luxurious apparel is created must adhere to strict rules, such as their work must be done by hand, and they must not exceed a certain number of employees.

108

Leçon C — Vocabulaire actif

L'art de la conversation

la politique

C'est bientôt **les élections présidentielles.** Les Français vont-ils **voter** pour **le candidat** du **parti politique socialiste** cette année?

les médias

On **passe** le nouveau **hit** de Faudel à la radio. Ce **blogueur** suit les manifestations à Paris.

la mode

Pour le **prêt-à-porter** femmes, on remarquera la **longueur des jupes** cette saison. Le **look tradi** sera à la page.

le sport

Sylvain **s'est entraîné** au **club** pour le **championnat d'athlétisme.** Il a gagné **une médaille.**

le cinéma

On passe une comédie **dramatique** au Gaumont. **Réalisé** par Noémie Lvovsky, le film *Camille redouble* a été **tourné** en France et a reçu deux **récompenses.**

l'économie

À cause de l'**endettement** des pays, le **PNB** de l'Europe a **baissé.** **La hausse** du **taux d'inflation réduit la valeur** des **revenus.**

108 cent huit | Unité 2

Essential Instruction

1. Introduce the new vocabulary with the e-visuals for this lesson.
2. Tell students they will listen to news on the radio. Play the recording twice with textbooks closed. The third time, play the recording, stopping at specific points to ask students to identify what is being discussed.
3. Have students listen again, this time with their books open. Make sure students understand each bolded word.
4. Have students listen to the three expressions in **Pour la conversation** with their books open. Ask them to respond to the last question.
5. You might have pairs of students read each mini-dialogue in **Activité 1**, then turn to the class to identify the **thème.**

Here you can find the essential parts of the day's lesson; these tips will help teachers organize the lesson and suggest a logical order of approach.

Pour la conversation

1.1, 5.2

How do I express I can't stop myself from doing something?

> **Je ne peux pas m'empêcher de** penser aux gens qui souffrent dans le monde.
> *I can't help but think about the people who are suffering in the world.*

How do I say that someone is right?

> Élodie **a raison**.
> *Elodie is right.*

How do I ask about dinner table topics?

> Et à votre table, **vous parlez de quoi**?
> *And at your dinner table, what do you talk about?*

Et si je voulais dire...?

le scrutin, le bulletin	*ballot*
un électeur, une électrice	*voter*
le dirigeant	*leader*
un programme électoral	*political platform*
une crise économique	*economic crisis*
un défilé de mode	*fashion show*
une station de radio	*radio station*

1 Thèmes de conversation

1.1,1.2

Indiquez le thème des conversations suivantes.

la politique l'économie la mode le sport le cinéma les médias

1. -C'est une co-production franco-canadienne.
   -De vrais serveurs jouent les rôles principaux, pas des vedettes.
2. -Tu as remarqué la longueur des manteaux cette saison?
   -Oui, ça me fait penser aux années 1950.
3. -Tu suis les manifestations à Paris?
   -Oui, je lis le blogue d'un blogueur qui y participe.
4. -Tes parents soutien le parti socialiste?
   -Oui, ils tendent à le soutienir cette fois-ci.
5. -L'endettement change notre mode de vivre.
   -Le gouvernement va augmenter les impôts (*taxes*), c'est sûr!
6. -Il a gagné ses deux courses (*races*) au championnat de France indoor.
   -Il se prépare pour ça depuis des mois.

En politique européenne, on se rénit au Parlement pour prendre de nouvelles mesures écologiques.

Answers

1. le cinéma
2. la mode
3. les médias
4. la politique
5. l'économie
6. le sport

Reference Desk

Here is some useful supplemental vocabulary about politics: **une campagne électorale** (*political campaign*); **un challenger** (*challenger*); **un movement populaire** (*grassroots movement*); **le/la perdant(e)** (*the loser*); **une urne** (*voting box*).

Critical Thinking

Comparisons

The French are known for their skills in **la polémique**, or argument, practicing it even at the dinner table. Ask students if their families get into heated discussions at the dinner table. What topics are the most controversial?

Games

Dinner Topics

Divide the class into two teams. The first player of the first team picks a card; the cards have the six topics, or themes, from page 108 on them. The player has 20 seconds to state a sentence that pertains to the topic. If it is accepted by the teacher, the player earns a point for his or her team.

Critical Thinking activities ask students to apply, choose, interpret, solve, categorize, compare, contrast, criticize, distinguish, compose, construct, create, propose, etc.

Games may practice vocabulary, grammar, or culture knowledge.

Differentiated Learning

Accelerate

Have students learn the **Et si je voulais dire...?** and **supplemental vocabulary** from **Reference Desk** to create a radio or television broadcast.

Learning Styles

Visual Learners

Have these students create a campaign poster for a real or imaginary political candidate.

Multiple Intelligences

Visual-Spatial

Ask these students to find clips on You Tube about the six topics, or themes: politics, the media, fashion, sport, cinema, and the economy in France. Have them play the clips for the class. While they watch, students write down a theme for each one. You may want to award points for those students who can even grasp some of the details in the clips.

Differentiated Learning tips help the teacher make sure advanced and slower-paced students have successful learning experiences.

Here teachers find tips for how to reach students with different learning styles, including multiple intelligences, or special needs.

Components

T'es branché? is a comprehensive four-level French language program written to meet the needs of French students of all abilities in the twenty-first century. The third-level program includes the following components:

- Student Textbook
- Annotated Teacher's Edition
- Workbook
- Workbook Teacher's Edition
- At-Standard Assessment Manual
- Communicative Activities
- Listening Activities
- Audio Program
- DVD Manual
- EMCL

Student Textbook

T'es branché? contains ten units. Each unit is composed of three lessons, labeled A, B, and C. All the units are designed similarly so that both teachers and students will know what to expect. Each lesson gives students the vocabulary, functions, structures, and cultural information necessary to communicate in authentic French about a variety of everyday situations designed to appeal to teenagers. Vocabulary and structures are recycled in the third-level textbook so that students can attain mastery of the concepts that are introduced by the time they complete the program. The headphones icon 🎧 indicates activities that are recorded in the audio program.

Unit Opener – The unit begins with a photo spread, quotation (**Citation**) by a Francophone person of note, and fact (**À savoir**) that connect to the unit theme. The **Question centrale** is an essential question that frames the unit's contents, and that reappears throughout the unit. There are also two culture questions accompanied by a photo for which students will find the answer somewhere in the culture readings of the unit.

Vocabulaire actif – Each lesson begins with colorful photos or illustrations that introduce coherent vocabulary groupings in a meaningful context. Students need to know that they are expected to learn these words and expressions. Also in this section are one or more functions under the *Pour la conversation* heading, and more advanced vocabulary for the students who want to move at a faster pace (*Et si je voulais dire...?*) and assimilate even more vocabulary in order to express themselves. Vocabulary practice activities follow the presentation, culminating in questions that are designed to elicit responses from students about their lives (*Questions personnelles*). One of the vocabulary practice options includes a listening activity. Another is a paragraph or other text that puts comprehensible input into practice, allowing students to "read" and understand the vocabulary words before using them.

Rencontres culturelles – Next comes a short dialogue that dramatizes a situation typical of everyday life in francophone regions. Written in France, these dialogues use authentic French speech and current expressions. Speakers may include one or more of the four main characters, their friends, parents, other relatives, or teachers. These teens all live in Nice.

> **Élodie** is a 17-year-old French girl who lives in Nice with her parents and older brother, Léo. She is in her last year of high school, preparing for the *baccalauréat*. She loves movies, and likes Karim a lot.
>
> **Léo** is Élodie's older brother. He is in his first year of college. His best friend is Justin, an American. He is also good friends with Karim.
>
> **Karim** is an 18-year old boy from a Tunisian background. He lives with his mother and little sister. His family moved to Nice from the countryside. Karim is good friends with Léo. He is dating Élodie.
>
> **Justin** is an American student who has come to France to study and immerse himself in French culture. He goes to college with Léo, and spends a lot of time with him.

These dialogues include the functions from the *Pour la conversation* box in the vocabulary spread. Also in the dialogue you will find an example of each structure topic that models for students how it can be used. All words in the dialogue are active vocabulary, though not all of them appear in the vocabulary presentation that precedes it. All dialogues were filmed in France, and the accompanying photo is a still shot from the film. A comprehension activity follows the dialogue to make sure students understand what transpired.

Extension – This is another dialogue but of a more advanced nature that requires students to read in context and perhaps even look up some words in their French-English dictionary. A critical thinking question follows each of these dialogues. The vocabulary in this dialogue will not be tested.

Points de départ – Directly after the dialogues, information about the francophone world is presented. These notes reflect the themes introduced in the first dialogue in the *Rencontres culturelles* section. Accompanying photos open a window on cultural practices, perspectives, and products. Certain products are defined and described in the *Produits* boxes. In this section, students are also asked to draw comparisons between francophone cultures and their own (see *Comparaisons* graphic). After answering the *Questions culturelles*, students engage with culture further by participating in a discussion (*À discuter*) or reading a *Perspectives* note and answering a critical thinking question.

Du côté des medias – In this section, students read or skim or scan francophone realia and answer questions or complete an activity based on it. The realia ties into one of the notes in the *Points de départ*. Students might see a grocery store advertisement, a restaurant menu, or film ratings.

La culture sur place – In Lesson C, this section follows the culture notes and gets students to investigate and engage in an aspect of French culture. For example, students learn how to examine culinary preferences of French speakers, apply Maslow's hierarchy of needs to the needs of immigrants, or plan a trip around volunteer tourism. The philosophy behind this section is explained in the Philosophy and Approach section of the Annotated Teacher's Edition front pages.

Structure de la langue – One or more grammar topics is presented and practiced in this section. You can find all the grammar topics covered in *T'es branché?* in the Scope and Sequence at the beginning of this Annotated Teacher's Edition. The contextualized practice activities that follow move from more mechanical activities to those that are more creative and open-ended. The activities allow for oral and written practice of the language structures, and students may be asked to work with a partner or group. Practice for one of the grammar topics includes a listening activity. (Unit 10 contains no grammar.) Where there is a model, the model sentence is highlighted so students know which parts of the sentence to replace.

À vous la parole – A series of proficiency-based activities follows the grammar section. Students have an opportunity to practice interpersonal, presentational, and interpretive communication here as well as in the vocabulary and grammar sections. In this section, the vocabulary, structures, and culture all come together and are integrated into activities that may be cooperative, task-based, oral, or written. For example, students may be asked to conduct a survey, create a graphic or smartphone application to entice skiers to **les Alpes**, or plan **un voyage en péniche** in la Bourgogne.

Prononciation – This section is presented at the end of Lesson A in each unit. Written by a pronunciation expert in France who works with English speakers, it centers on pronunciation problems English speakers have with French sounds and pronunciation patterns.

Stratégie communicative – This section is presented at the end of Lesson B in each unit. Students learn various strategies for successful function-based oral and written communication activities. For example, students learn how to extend conversations, create an advertisement to sell an American product on the French market, or compare and contrast two paintings.

Lecture thématique – This section is presented at the end of Lesson C in each unit. Authentic texts in French are studied with scaffolding that allows students to learn about literature, francophone authors, and francophone art. First, students read a paragraph about the author, which concludes with a question designed to get students to focus on one of the main ideas of the text. Next, students learn a strategy with which to approach the text, always accompanied by a graphic organizer. A secondary tool for understanding another aspect of the text is highlighted with the *Outil de lecture*. With the pre-reading question, students connect to the theme of the text by comparing it to their own experience or observations. During reading questions, alongside the text, check to make sure students comprehend what is happening in the text. A post-reading question asks students to draw a main conclusion about the text. A painting or other art form accompanies the text. Students learn to appreciate art and art periods and techniques in *Le monde visuel*, which is designed to promote literacy in the visual arts. In the *Activités d'expansion*, students use the information from their graphic organizer to write about the meaning of the text in the first activity. The *Lecture thématique* section provides students opportunities to improve their reading skills and helps to prepare them for the AP language exam.

Projets finaux – This section was designed for teachers who prefer performance-based assessment to traditional testing, or who like unit work to culminate in a meaningful project. The first activity, *Connexions par Internet*, provides a cross-curricular project that may be connected to art, architecture, math, science, or any number of academic disciplines. The focus of *Communautés en ligne* is to have students build online communities in the French-speaking world in projects that relate to the unit's theme. *Passez à l'action!* provides an engaging activity for students to work with their classmates to complete a project. Finally, *Faisons le point!* asks students to pull together all their learning from the unit and analyze it; one format occurs in odd-numbered units, another in even-numbered units.

Évaluation – There are six opportunities for reviewing unit content in this section: (A) listening comprehension; (B) oral communication; (C) culture comparisons; (D) written expression; (E) oral or written response to a visual; and (F) telling a story that uses unit content.

Vocabulaire – All words and expressions introduced as active vocabulary in *T'es branché?* appear in the end-of-unit vocabulary list.

Bilan cumulatif – Based on the AP exam, this section appears after every even-numbered unit and provides students practice interpreting print texts, listening listening practice followed by multiple choice questions, and opportunites to practice four types of free response.

Annotated Teacher's Edition

This Annotated Teacher's Edition contains a front section and an annotated version of the student textbook.

Front Section:

- Scope and Sequence charts for Levels 1 – 3
- Introduction
- Key program features
- Description of all the components in the program
- Author biographies
- Philosophy and approach
- Transcript of Textbook Listening Activities
- Correlation to Common Core State Standards

Annotated Version of the Student Textbook:

- Correlations of ancillary materials to the textbook (*Resources*)
- Answers to both oral and written activities
- Informational notes for teachers in the *Reference Desk*
- Culture notes or activities about products, practices, or perspectives (*Culture*)
- Interpersonal, presentational, or interpretive communicative activities (*Communication*)
- Total Physical Response (TPR) activities
- Activities that use critical thinking skills (*Critical Thinking*)

- Additional cross-curricular activities (*Connections*)
- Games
- Additional activities or adaptations of textbook activities (*Expansion*)

The annotated version of the expanded student textbook contains icons in the Resource boxes at the top of the wraparound pages. These icons are:

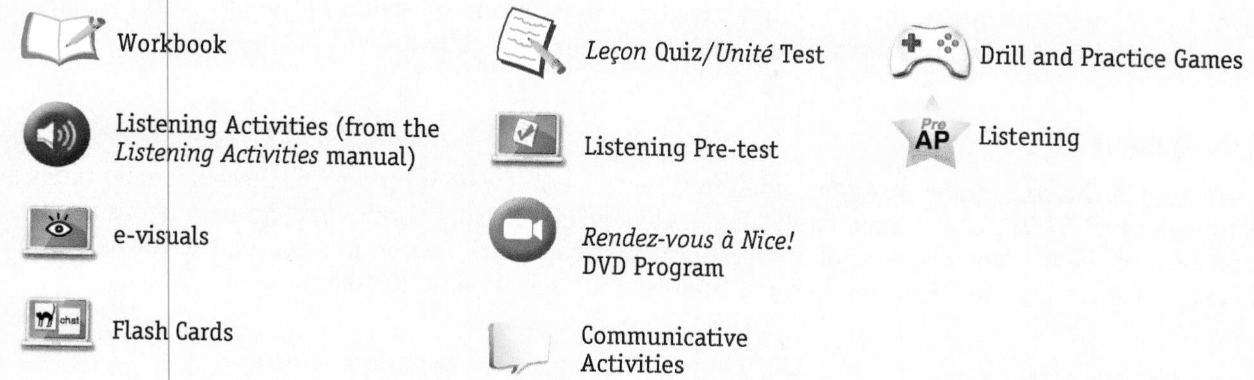

Workbook

The workbook reviews and expands on the material covered in the textbook with additional written exercises that reinforce students' language skills and cultural awareness.

Workbook Teacher's Edition

This is the student workbook, but with answers in boldface.

Communicative Activities

Since effective communicative activities are integral to the success of a proficiency-oriented French-language program, this online manual provides additional oral and written communicative practice for students. Information gap activities and situation cards allow for interpersonal communication and student-to-student interaction. Also in this manual are conversation grids, activities based on an illustration, and surveys; an e-mail writing activity; and a writing activity based on the conversation grids, activities based on an illustration, or surveys.

Listening Activities

This online manual provides seven additional listening comprehension activities for each unit, two for each lesson and a cumulative dialogue that synthesizes the vocabulary and grammar from the whole unit. Students are provided with an answer sheet they fill in while they listen. These activities help prepare students for the listening comprehension sections of the Unit Tests in the Assessment Program. An answer key is provided at the end of the manual that also includes complete scripts.

Textbook Audio Program

The online audio program contains language-production activities, and all the listening comprehension activities in the textbook: one vocabulary and grammar activity for every lesson, the listening activity in the *Évaluation* section, and the listening activity in the *Bilan cumulatif*. The *Vocabulaire actif*, dialogues, *Points de départ*, and reading selection have also been recorded.

Assessment Manual

The *T'es branché? Assessment Manual* is a print version of the At-Standard test that is also found as a prescribed test on the *Teacher Resources DVD* (see Multimedia Technology and Teacher Resources DVD). It contains Lesson Quizzes, Unit Tests, and Proficiency Tests. Each quiz tests student achievement in vocabulary, culture, structure, and speaking. There are three quizzes for each unit, or one per lesson. The Unit Tests contain these sections: vocabulary, structure, proficiency writing, speaking, listening comprehension, reading, and culture. Teachers are encouraged to test their students in the areas that have been practiced in class during the unit. For teachers who want to adapt or modify the test, the tests are available on ExamView® software.

DVD Program

Five of the actors in the continuous storyline video for Levels 1 and 2 were interviewed; these documentaries are the basis for the Level 3 DVD. These actors are Laurent, Clémentine, Nelson, Sarah, and Tigran; there is a video segment on each of them. They discuss their interests, such as painting, theater, and sports; the towns in the south of France where they live; their families and friends; and their hopes and dreams for the future.

Lectures thématiques

Additional readings, including some realia pieces, are available in this manual. The format is similar to the *Lecture thématique* section of the student book.

Copy Masters

To save time in the class, there is a manual with blackline masters for all the graphs, charts, maps and other graphics that are in the student edition.

Multimedia Technology

EMCL

EMCL is EMC Publishing's online environment for many of the *T'es branché?* ancillary materials. Online delivery of classroom materials allows students to access them in an electronic, interactive format and connect to the classroom in new ways using blended instruction. Visit EMCL at emcl.com to see all that is available for your students.

- **Lesson Planner**
  Each day's lesson plan, whether for a traditional class or block scheduling, presents the core materials from the textbook and key ancillaries to include in instruction. Teachers can access the ancillary manuals within the lesson planner.
- **e-visuals**
  These digital "transparencies" reinforce the vocabulary presented in the textbook.
- **Electronic Flash Cards**
  These flash cards are an essential component of the differentiated-learning classroom because students can practice over and over again until they master the vocabulary. Each vocabulary word is illustrated and the vocabulary word or expression is also visible spelled out.
- **Drill and Practice Games**
  Students master the vocabulary and structures in *T'es branché?* with activities that provide immediate feedback, telling students if their answer is right or wrong.
- **WebQuests**

A WebQuest is an inquiry-oriented activity for which students use online resources. There is a WebQuest for each lesson of *T'es branché?*

- **Pre-AP Listening**

  Students hear a short listening segment and answer multiple-choice questions as on the AP test. If they get any of the questions wrong, they can then see and hear the video in order to have a more successful listening experience.

- **Pre-tests**

  There is a pre-test for each lesson of *T'es branché?* Students receive immediate feedback by completing sentences about vocabulary, grammar, culture, and listening so that they know what they need to review before they take each Lesson Quiz or Unit Test.

- **ExamView® Assessment Program**

  Teachers choose between a prescribed test for At-Standard, Slower-Paced, or Advanced students, or they can make their own test that responds to the needs of their students. There is a quiz for every lesson. Each quiz consists of vocabulary, culture, structure, and speaking. Each prescribed Unit Test covers vocabulary, structure, proficiency writing, speaking prep, speaking, listening comprehension, reading, and culture.

Teacher Resources DVD

The Teacher Resources DVD is a one-stop resource where teachers can find all the resources for the program:

- Annotated Teacher's Edition
- Textbook Audio Program
- Lesson Plans
- Workbook
- Drill and Practice Games
- e-visuals
- Textbook Dialogue Videos
- DVD Program
- Listening Activities
- Communicative Activities
- Copy Masters
- *Lectures thématiques* Manual
- Pre-AP Listening
- Electronic Flash Cards
- Assessment (ExamView® and Print)

World Language Learning in the 21st Century

By Toni Theisen

Our world is an ever increasingly diverse, globalized, and complex, media-saturated society. Our 21st-century learners need a multi-sensory and multi-layered learning environment that is designed to inspire creativity, synthesis, and collaboration, as well as provide opportunities to analyze, reflect, and evaluate. So what are the critical skills and multiple literacies that our students will need in order to successfully participate in the global community of today's world? How do we engage them in meaningful contexts that are relevant and challenging? How do we provide project-based learning opportunities that help students reach higher levels of proficiency? How do we help students set personal learning goals and become self-directed learners? How do we personalize learning?

Quite often 21st-century skills are equated with technology. True, technology is a part of the skills learners will need to master, but this concept is much broader. In 2010 ACTFL, in collaboration with the Partnership for 21st Century Skills organization, created the ACTFL World Languages 21st Century Skills Map for Pre-K-16. The Partnership for 21st Century Skills P21 is a national organization that advocates for 21st-century readiness for every student framed within 12 skill areas and four interdisciplinary themes.

Here are the twelve skills statements from the ACTFL World Languages 21st Century Skills Map and their topics:

1. **Communication**
   Students as effective communicators use languages to engage in meaningful conversation; to understand and interpret spoken language and written text; and to present information, concepts, and ideas.
2. **Collaboration**
   Students as collaborators use their native and acquired languages to learn from and work cooperatively across cultures with global team members, sharing responsibility and making necessary compromises while working toward a common goal.
3. **Critical Thinking and Problem Solving**
   Students as inquirers frame, analyze, and synthesize information as well as negotiate meaning across language and culture in order to explore problems and issues from their own and different perspectives.
4. **Creativity and Innovation**
   Students as creators and innovators respond to new and diverse perspectives as they use language in imaginative and original ways to make useful contributions.
5. **Information Literacy**
   Students as informed global citizens access, manage, and effectively use culturally authentic sources in ethical and legal ways.
6. **Media Literacy**
   Students as active global citizens evaluate authentic sources to understand how media reflect and influence language and culture.
7. **Technology Literacy**
   Students as productive global citizens use appropriate technologies when interpreting messages; interacting with others; and producing written, oral, and visual messages.
8. **Flexibility and Adaptability**
   Students as flexible and adaptable language learners are open-minded, willing to take risks, and accept the ambiguity of language while balancing diverse global perspectives.
9. **Initiative and Self-Direction**
   Students as life-long learners are motivated to set their own goals and reflect on their progress as they grow and improve their linguistic and cultural competence.

10. **Social and Cross-Cultural Skills**
Students as adept language learners understand diverse cultural perspectives and use appropriate sociolinguistic skills in order to function in diverse cultural and linguistic contexts.
11. **Productivity and Accountability**
Students as productive and accountable learners take responsibility for their own learning by actively working to increase their language proficiency and cultural knowledge.
12. **Leadership and Responsibility**
Students as responsible leaders leverage their linguistic and cross-cultural skills to inspire others to be fair, accepting, open, and understanding within and beyond the local community.

Interdisciplinary Themes

Global Awareness

Language education and cultural understanding are at the heart of developing global awareness for students. In order to understand and address global issues, it is important to understand the perspectives on the world that speakers of other languages bring to the table. By learning other languages, students develop respect and openness to those whose culture, religion, and views on the world may be different. Language students are able to interact with students from the target language in order to discuss and reach solutions regarding global issues.

Financial, Economic, Business, and Entrepreneurial Literacy

Students in language classes learn about the financial and economic issues from the target language culture and are able to compare and contrast with those of the United States. According to the Committee for Economic Development (CED), "...cultural competence and foreign language skills can prove invaluable when working on global business teams or negotiating with overseas clients." Those who are able to communicate with others in their native language will naturally feel more empowered to negotiate with those around the world as they engage in entrepreneurial activities.

Civic Literacy

Language learners become aware of the judicial, legislative, and government functions of the target language country/countries and are able to compare and contrast those with the civil liberties and responsibilities in the United States. Because they can communicate in the target language, they are able to engage in discussions with other students to participate in activities in which they discuss civic life in their respective countries.

Health Literacy

Language learners are engaged in a value-added activity as they can address global health and environmental issues in the target language and understand materials that were written for native speakers of that language. They have access to information because they can understand the language and can thus engage in global discussions on health, environmental, and public safety issues as they prepare for careers in these fields.

So by focusing on these essential skills, the interdisciplinary themes and the integration of technology in a meaningful, relevant standards-based curriculum, teachers can empower students to actively participate in the global community.

Sources:

ACTFL World Languages 21st Century Skills Map

Partnership for 21st Century Skills

Oral Proficiency in the 21st Century

By Toni Theisen

"I want to learn how to speak the language" is the most common goal of most world language learners. But what is oral proficiency and how do learners demonstrate their progress toward this goal?

At the center of the national standards are the three modes of communication. The interpersonal and the presentational modes are focused on both oral and written communication. In the interpersonal mode learners engage in conversation, provide and obtain information, express feeling and emotion, and exchange opinions. This mode occurs in two-way, spontaneous exchanges that involve negotiation of meaning and is unrehearsed. Activities and strategies include debates, discussions, phone calls, Skyping, asking for and giving directions, and conversations with friends about making plans.

In the presentational mode, learners present information, concepts and ideas to an audience of listeners or readers on a variety of topics. It is one-way, planned and can be rehearsed. There is no feedback from another person. Some activities and strategies include creating videos, telling a story, delivering a speech, creating a public service announcement or other podcasts, or presenting a skit or play.

Teachers can assess language performance in terms of ability to use the language effectively and appropriately in real-life situations using a rubric that can measure proficiency. Students need to demonstrate what they "can do." The Linguafolio is an excellent source for "can do" statements at different proficiency levels. The "can do" statements are a perfect resource to use to create learner targets for each thematic unit, help students set personal goals and provide a clearer explanation to parents about what their children are learning in their language classes.

Open-ended performance assessments are the best ways to determine growth in oral proficiency. Rubrics and feedback should be put in kid-friendly terms, so students know what they can do to improve. Each assessment needs to be designed to show what a student is able to do with the language in order to elicit meaningful feedback.

With *T'es branché?*, students gain practice in the three modes of communication in vocabulary and structure activities, as well as the *À vous la parole* and *Projets finaux* sections. Rubrics for spoken and written communication can be found at EMCL. A student contract on the Unit Opener page makes it clear to students what material they will be responsible for learning and helps them take ownership of this content from the beginning. Students reflect on what they can do and what they can learn to do better in *Faisons le point!* at the end of each unit. The final projects are designed to showcase student learning and make students feel successful, engaged, and purpose-driven in their French language learning experiences with *T'es branché?*

A New Emphasis in Teaching Culture: Explore and Investigate *sur place*

By Pamela M. Wesely

Foreign language teachers have examined and debated the issue of teaching culture in the foreign language classroom for many years. One of the ways that *T'es branché?* attempts to respond to this debate is through the presentation of *La culture sur place* sections in every unit. They are designed to engage students differently with francophone culture(s) by promoting a spirit of inquiry and treating the students as social actors, not as passive recipients of culture. The idea of developing intercultural competence in the language classroom rather than relying solely on teaching *about* the target culture(s) is not a new one, but it is one that has rarely been incorporated into a textbook.

The format of these sections varies throughout the text, but generally one of six different styles of activity is used for each one.

- **Submersion:** Students are encouraged to feel that they are "on location" in a francophone culture observing, asking questions, finding answers, drawing conclusions, and finding different perspectives and viewpoints. They report on their findings to the class.
- **Poll:** Students conduct a survey of their fellow students that parallels a survey of French or Francophone people. The students can then draw conclusions from a comparison of the results, focusing on current characteristics and realities in francophone cultures, as well as the diversity of their own lives.

- **Advocacy:** Students write a plan for taking action, getting their voices heard, and/or advocating for a specific population in the face of human rights abuses, current events issues, or other potential areas for discussion.
- **Reaction:** Via self-assessment, students examine potential areas of discomfort with French or Francophone cultures, and perhaps identify what they might need to do to gain more comfort in or become more habituated to the practices of these cultures.
- **Comparison:** Students take two explicitly different but related phenomena (encompassing products, practices, and perspectives) in their own culture and the target culture(s) and examine why those two phenomena might be different.
- **Contact:** Students investigate the reality of one individual from a French-speaking culture through an interview conducted in written form or face-to-face.

  "Culture" in *La culture sur place* is thus not intended to be something to be learned, but rather something to be explored, questioned, and examined. Students will be able to use their 21st-century skills in applying themselves to get through the steps of these activities that are meaningful, structured, and that allow for student self-expression.
- **Note**: Some of the activities in *La Culture sur place* might take some preparation several weeks before the actual activity takes place. One notable example of this is the *Unité 5* activity involving identifying individuals from French-speaking countries for the students to interview.

Teaching Grammar to Enhance Communication

"I took French for three years and I can't say anything." Perhaps you know someone with such an experience with language instruction. The drill-and-practice instruction of yesteryear relied on mechanical, repetitive exercises that were not linked to meaningful expression. Today's teachers still want their students to learn grammatical concepts incrementally so that their language production doesn't fossilize. They also want their students' oral and written expression to be comprehensible to native speakers, acceptable in different social contexts, and accurate. To reach these goals, today's teachers often provide activities that allow for structured input (learning the grammar rules and examining models), structured output (practicing the grammar point in communicative exercises), and communicative output (doing a communicative task that uses the grammar point).

Structured Input

In *T'es branché?*, grammar points are presented concisely with the use of charts and examples. Students can use these pages as reference when they want to try to expand on their expression; they don't have to learn everything at once. For example, they may learn quickly how to use the **plus-que-parfait** in declarative sentences, but can refer back to the grammar presentation later in order to see how to **être** with a reflexive verb. Some of the examples used in the grammar presentation come from the first *Rencontres culturelles* dialogue that students can hear and see as many times as they'd like on their mobile devices.

Structured Output

T'es branché? begins with more mechanical activities, then builds to activities that are more creative, meaningful, and open-ended. A mechanical activity might ask students to insert the right preposition before the names of cities, countries, and continents they learned about in the culture readings. A creative activity might have students interpret a survey about what music teens like using **plaire**. A meaningful and more open-ended activity might have students writing a dialogue using the forms of **lequel** to identify their classmates' cultural preferences.

Communicative Output

In the *À vous la parole* section, students put their knowledge of grammar to use in interpretive, presentational, and interpersonal communication activities. For example, they might use **il faut que** to write a to-do list for an overseas trip or write a biography of the **slameur**, **Grand Corps Malade**, in the **imparfait** and the **passé composé**.

Communicative Competence

Students build communicative competence by using *T'es branché?* in part because they learn grammar from a logical grammatical syllabus that builds on and recycles grammar points. Some teachers like to provide an immersion experience, having their students build structural knowledge naturally. For these teachers we have the TPR Storytelling manual, which is correlated to the textbook. Students will pick up on the grammar topics in the original story and soon be able to tell their own variation, using accurate and comprehensible grammar.

Meeting the Needs of the 21st-Century Reader

"Qui que vous soyez qui voulez cultiver, vivifier, edifier, attendrir, apaiser, mettez des livres partout."

—Victor Hugo

Whoever wishes to cultivate, enliven, edify, soften, pacify, put books everywhere.

Reading research shows that successful readers read extensively, integrate information in the text with pre-existing knowledge, have a reading style that adapts to the text, are motivated, read for a purpose, and rely on different skills to comprehend a text. The readings in *T'es branché?* were designed to provide contextual reading activities that hone all of these skills and guide the reader to greater comprehension. These readings are always accompanied with supports to make every French student a successful reader.

Successful Readers Read Extensively

In *T'es branché?* students read the dialogues (the second one in *Rencontres culturelles* is for students who want to go farther and faster), which incorporate the vocabulary, functions, structure, and culture of the lesson. In each lesson there is a comprehensible-input paragraph so that students can build understanding of the new vocabulary before using it. A piece of realia, such as a quiz about the European Union, a play review, movie schedule, an advertisement for an **école matermelle**, or tourism website, appears in the section *Du côté des médias*. Student's unit learning culminates in a literary selection, linked to the theme of the unit; pre-reading questions, strategies, guided reading questions, and post-reading questions help students feel that they can tackle literary selections with ideas and themes.

Successful Readers Integrate Information in the Text With Pre-Existing Knowledge and Adapt to the Text

In the culture section, students are asked to connect to what they know about culture in the United States and Canada with *Comparaisons* questions, which become their starting point for comparisons with francophone cultures. The *Perspectives* questions ask students to consider a certain point of view of a French speaker in excerpts from songs, poems, blogs, etc. In the literary selection, students are asked a pre-reading question to connect the theme of the selection to their own experience. The repeated supports in these sections help students to adapt to the text, whether it is experiential (*Rencontres culturelles*), factual (*Points de départ*), opinion (*Perspectives*), informational (*Du côté des médias*), or literary (*Lecture thématique*).

Successful Readers Are Motivated and Read for a Purpose

For whatever reason students are learning French (a love of languages, to test out of college French, to travel to French-speaking countries, to have an interesting career, etc.), the texts in *T'es branché?* underline their reasons for study, thus motivating them toward their goal. Students also read with a purpose: for enjoyment (the cartoons in the section Structure de la langue, for information (the culture section), to confirm prior knowledge (dialogues and the culture section), or to evaluate ideas (the literary selections), and to grapple with other points of view (*Perspectives*). Students who want to learn more about a certain culture topic will benefit from the "Search words" underneath each culture paragraph that connect them to texts online.

Successful Students Rely on Different Skills to Comprehend a Text

Although woven throughout the various reading activities of each unit, specific strategies that can help students read more quickly and effectively receive greater focus in *Lecture thématique* and the manual with the same name, and include previewing, predicting, skimming and scanning, monitoring their comprehension, using text organization, tacking difficult vocabulary, visualizing, writing things down (with the help of graphic organizers), guessing from context, and paraphrasing.

Since research has shown that reading is the skill that endures the longest, French students who study with *T'es branché?* will be on their way to becoming life-long readers of French: successfully reading literary selections; reading nonfiction; and reading Internet, reference, and visual materials.

Immersion Lessons in the Non-immersion Classroom

Connecting to Literature and Art

"The subject matter class is a language class if it is made comprehensible to the language student."

—Krashen

Research has shown that immersion experiences provide the best experience for language acquisition outside of interaction with a native community. The sections of *T'es branché?* that easily lend themselves to immersion experiences are the *Lecture thématique* and *Le monde visuel*, both in Lesson C. Students can build a literary and artistic vocabulary, which will result in an appreciation and understanding of literature and art.

La littérature

Begin the reading lesson by asking students to read the **Rencontre avec l'auteur**. Identify the time period of the writer by making a timeline on the wall and placing the names of the authors, as you encounter them, where they belong, along with a flag identifying their nationality. Have students identify the question at the end of the paragraph that they should be able to answer after having read the selection; you may want them to write it in their notebook and jot down ideas as they come to them when they read. Have students share responses to the **Pré-lecture** question as a class, unless you consider the question personal and want students to write a response in their notebook. Since interaction is the key to a good immersion experience, have students compare their graphic organizers in pairs or small groups. Put useful expressions on the board to help students share information, such as, **J'ai mis....**, **Pourquoi n'as-tu pas considéré**...?, **J'ai une autre idée**, etc.

You may want to begin the selection by playing the audio recording. Point out that there will be words students won't know, but these words are glossed below the selection. Wherever possible, a French synonym is given. Ask students to answer the **Pendant la lecture** questions after listening to the recording, or pause the recording where there is a question in order to monitor their comprehension. Then have students share their responses to the **Post-lecture** question in pairs or small groups, and ask for volunteers to share once you reassemble as a class. Finally, students do the **Activités d'expansion.** Encourage students to publish their writings on the Internet and put some in their portfolio so they can see how they improve at analyzing literature over time.

L'art

To familiarize your students with keys to understanding art as presented in **Le monde visuel**, you may want to have students keep a notebook in which they define the art terms they encounter with each new painting. Provide them with some words and expressions to answer the question(s) at the end of each paragraph. Have students work in pairs to answer the question(s).

In Level 2, you might begin with an overview of the basic art movements, since not all the art movements are covered in *T'es branché?*, so that students understand the basic characteristics of each movement. The chart that follows provides simple phrases you can use to distinguish these movements. Bring in art books and pass around paintings by the artists mentioned so students understand which artists are associated with each movement and the evolution of French art. Students should learn these types of paintings: **la nature morte**, **le portrait**, **l'autoportrait**, **le paysage**, **la scène.** Post some examples in class and do a station activity in which they identify the type of painting and the movement.

Overview of Art Movements

Mouvement	Dates approximatives	Charactéristiques	Peintres
Renaissance	1492 – 1600	Inspirée par la Renaissance italienne Conception nouvelle du portait Débuts du paysage, par exemple, dans la *joconde*	Léonard de Vinci Fouquet Clouet Dubreuil (Ambroise) Dubois
Classicisme	1575 – 1700	Sujets nobles de l'antiquité, de la mythologie, de la Bible La symétrie dans la composition	Poussin Charles Le Brun
Baroque	1625 – 1700	Histoires viennent des légendes, de la mythologie, de la Bible Couleurs chaudes et vives Sentiments visibles sur les visages L'asymétrie dans la composition Impression du mouvement	Chardin Fragonard Lebrun Lorrain Poussin
Rococo	1730 – 1789	Compositions frivoles et légères Scènes pastorales et aristocrates	Boucher Watteau
Néo-classicisme	1760 – 1830	Inspiré par Rome antique Style plus simple que rococo Allégories, mythologie comme sujets	David Gérard Gros
Romantisme	1775 – 1850	Rejet du classicisme (trop rigide) Désir de montrer l'idéal, les sentiments, l'exotique, les fantaisies du peintre	Delacroix Gros Géricault
Réalisme	1830 – 1890	Sujets les scènes de la vie courante Observation Stylisation Coloration sombre	Corot Courbet Daumier Millet Fantin-Latour
Impressionnisme	1850 – 1900	Rejet de l'art académique Note les impressions fugitives avec une touche rapide Taches de couleurs juxtaposées se recomposent à une distance	Monet Renoir Pissarro Sisley Morisot Bazille Manet
Cubisme	1907 – 1914	Sujets décomposés Formes géométriques	Picasso, Gris Braque

Differentiated Instruction and *T'es branché?*

Differentiated instruction occurs when teachers design learning to meet individual student needs. It differentiates between **content** (the materials the student needs to learn); **process** (practice that allows the student to learn the material; **products** (projects that get the student to rehearse, apply, and extend his or her learning); and, according to Carol Ann Tomlinson, fosters a positive **learning environment** (the way the classroom functions and feels).

Tailoring activities to different ability levels in your classroom can be time-consuming, so having a program like *T'es branché?* that is designed to meet differing ability levels and learning styles means you won't have to develop many materials on your own. Below are a few examples from *T'es branché?* for each aspect of differentiated instruction.

Content

1. **Use reading materials for different ability levels.**
   T'es branché? has a basic dialogue and a more advanced dialogue in each lesson; the advanced dialogue is called *Extension*. If a literary selection in *Lecture thématique* is too easy or hard for a student, pick an alternative for him or her in the *Lectures thématiques* manual. Ideas for differentiated learning appear in the Annotated Teacher's Edition wraparound notes.
2. **Present materials visually and auditorily.**
   For the visual learner, *T'es branché?* includes many activities based on a visual illustration, piece of realia, or graphic. Take advantage of the e-visuals and electronic flash cards for learning vocabulary, for example. Students are encouraged to fill out graphic organizers throughout *T'es branché?* to help them conceptualize and form ideas. *T'es branché?* has seven listening activities in every odd-numbered unit, eight for even-numbered units; also, the first dialogue in the *Rencontres culturelles* section is available as a video and an audio mp3 file; these listening activities will help students who learn best aurally.
3. **Use materials that result in analysis and evaluation.**
   While some students may find their comfort area in knowledge, comprehension, and application, *T'es branché?* allows for analysis and evaluation as students progress and move forward to reach their potential.

Process

1. **Provide opportunities for students to work in pairs and groups.**
   Students learning with *T'es branché?* receive many opportunities to work cooperatively in pairs and groups.
2. **Adapt instruction to meet Multiple Intelligences and other learning styles.**
   Different learning styles are built into the activities of *T'es branché?*; suggestions for implementation appear in the Annotated Teacher's Edition wraparound notes.
3. **Provide differentiated testing.**
   With *T'es branché?*, students can be tested with a slower-paced test, an at-standard test, or an advanced test.

Products

1. **Provide opportunities for communication.**
   With the *T'es branché?* program, students learn to enact dialogues (interpersonal communication); write memos, e-mails, postcards, etc. (presentational communication); and make presentations based on online research (interpretive/presentational communication).
2. **Provide challenging and engaging tasks.**
   The activities in *T'es branché?* move from those that are more mechanical to those that are meaningful, open-ended, and creative. Students practice recalling, check their comprehension, apply what they have learned, analyze, synthesize, and evaluate using *T'es branché?*
3. **Provide a variety of final projects based on learning styles.**
   Students have the opportunity to develop three types of final projects in *T'es branché?*: *Connexions par Internet*, *Communautés en ligne*, and *Passez à l'action!* In the first students do cross-disciplinary research in

French using presentational communication. In the second they reach out to or learn about a francophone community online that results in interpersonal or presentational communication. The third activity may have them designing the house of the future, researching French links to the Olympics, or donating books to Africa, often as a group activity.

Learning Environment

People passing by your classroom will see a lot of activity when you teach with *T'es branché?*, but it is a good idea to have days for working quietly without distraction too to keep all your students comfortable. Qualitative assignments in *T'es branché?* mean that students dig deeper and go beyond comprehension questions; learning revolves around an essential question that ties each unit together and that allows for reflection on learning in *Faisons le point!* The technology that accompanies *T'es branché?* means that your students can be engaged every day with video, audio, interactive e-visuals, electronic flash cards—using a variety of electronic devices—having fun while they learn at their own pace because you have planned and organized instruction that accommodates their learning styles.

Blended Learning in the Second Language Environment

A Blended Learning Success Story

The overwhelming success of the Khan Academy, which provides free lessons on the Internet, is a wake-up call for teachers who are not using much online instruction in the classroom. Khan Academy currently has 3.5 million users per month, and its free lessons have been viewed more than 82 million times. The increased success rate of students using this free tool is a testament to the potential of blended learning.

What Is Blended Learning?

Blended learning occurs when teachers combine face-to-face learning with online learning. With self-paced e-learning, students experience differentiated learning. In a blended learning environment activities that may have previously taken place during classroom time are moved online. In one model, student might meet in the traditional classroom only a couple times per week and do the rest of their learning online.

What Kind of Blended Learning Experience Can I Create for My Students with *T'es branché?*

Today's students are digitally literate, interactive, experiential, social, and possess strong visual-spatial skills. They look for fast response times and are adept at multi-tasking. *T'es branché?* is motivated by the belief that to be successful teachers need to communicate in the language and style of today's students. To achieve this goal, we have created materials that coordinate with a blended learning approach that allows for three types of learning:

Face-to-Face Learning	Self-Paced Learning	Online Collaborative Learning

Face-to-Face Learning

Classroom learning with *T'es branché?* centers on the three modes of communication: interpersonal, presentational, and interpretive, or a combination of these. Activities move from mechanical to meaningful to more creative and open-ended as students progress with concepts and information. Assessment is geared to the level of the student with three possibilities for testing: tests for the advanced learner, tests for the at-standard learner, and tests for the slower-paced learner.

Self-Paced Learning

In today's student-centered classroom, students need to be able to learn at their own pace. To learn vocabulary, *T'es branché?* allows for students to learn words and expressions at their own pace with electronic flash cards and e-visuals, some of which are interactive. In the culture section, called *Points de départ*, students can find out more online about any covered topic by using Search words that are provided under each informational (cultural practices) paragraph. Students can learn each unit's content at their own pace with the interactive textbook; for example, they can listen to and watch the dialogues as many times as they need to. Students can see if they have learned the vocabulary and structure content by playing the *Drill and Practice Games*, which allow for immediate feedback. Immediate feedback is also provided in the online *Pre-tests* so that students can see what they need to go back and review before the Unit Tests. These are a few of the features of *T'es branché?* available on EMC's platform for online learning, EMCL.

Online Collaborative Learning

Students work collaboratively using *T'es branché?* in the *À vous la parole*, *La culture sur place*, and *Projets finaux* sections. Fun and worthwhile activities that they can participate in online include interviewing or surveying francophone teens, communicating with francophone communities, exchanging videos with other French or francophone classes, participating in a service project with other French speakers, posting and commenting on movie reviews, sharing and describing personal photos, and planning a class trip to a French-speaking location.

The blended learning approach of *T'es branché?* provides a technology-rich learning environment that responds to the needs and expectations of students and teachers of the 21st century and extends the second-language environment beyond the classroom. *T'es branché?* in conjunction with EMCL speak the multi-media language of students today. *On est branché!*

Pre-AP French Language and Culture

The new AP French Language and Culture exam is centered around themes, incorporates overarching essential questions, and focuses on the three modes of communication (interpersonal, presentational, interpretive). It also relies on authentic print, audio, and video materials, and requires students to comprehend cultural perspectives and make comparisons among cultures. These are some ways in which *T'es branché?* prepares students for the eventual AP French language exam:

- Units are organized thematically, for example, **Les arts**, **La France hier et aujourd'hui**, and **La culture des affaires.**
- All units have an overarching question, a *Question centrale*, or essential question around which students frame their learning, for example: **Qu'y a-t-il d'universel dans les rapports entre les gens? Comment les Francophones restent-ils fidèles à leurs traditions? Comment s'intégrer à une autre culture?**
- The culture readings (*Points de départ*) take students to French-speaking locations. The *Produits* boxes introduce key cultural products in French-speaking countries. The *Perspectives* questions get students to read excerpts from songs, poems, blogs, etc. and think about cultural perspectives in **la Francophonie**. Students also make comparisons to the cultures they know in this culture section. In *La culture sur place*, students experience French culture by investigating it and reflecting on it.
- Filmed dialogues (*Rencontres culturelles*) and a documentary video filmed in France allow for student engagement with authentic listening experiences. There are also seven listening opportunities in each unit, eight in the even units.
- *The Stratégies communicatives* provide clear and effective strategies to help students use the three modes of communication in activities that are meaningful, creative, and use criticial thinking skills.
- The *Lectures thématiques* present authentic texts from the French-speaking world (novels, poetry, dialogues, blogs, etc.) that students engage with using critical thinking skills. There are also readings in French in the culture section and authentic texts in *Du côté des médias*.
- The *Projets finaux* allow students to build communities (*Communautés en ligne*), make connections (*Connexions par Internet*), and communicate in French to complete a French-based project (*Passez à l'action!*).

- Finally, the *Bilan cumulatif*, at the end of every other unit, provides a practice test experience in listening, reading, writing, composition, and speaking. It is modeled after the new AP language exam from the College Board.
- The online resource Pre-AP Listening allows students to listen to audio that is followed by multiple-choice questions as on the AP French exam. However, since this is Pre-AP, students who can't answer the questions with audio alone are prompted to "watch" the video to help them understand before trying the questions again.

Students who use *T'es branché?* will learn to use French in real-life settings (Communities), demonstrate an understanding of francophone cultures (Culture), incorporate interdisciplinary learning (Connections), make comparisons between their cultures and languages and French-speaking cultures and French language (Comparisons), all the while communicating in French (Communication).

T'es branché? and the International Baccalaureat

The International Baccalaureat (IB) program is recognized in many schools in 141 countries, with more than 1,300 schools participating in the United States. It seeks to develop global citizens with a strong sense of cultural awareness who recognize and develop universal human values. The program stimulates curiosity and inquiry as students learn and acquire knowledge across different disciplines in a quest toward lifelong learning.

With *T'es branché?,* students are exposed to **la Francophonie** in culture readings, activities, projects, and literature selections, so they move towards becoming global citizens who can embrace the big "C" and small "c" of places where French is spoken. They interact with Francophone students in *À vous la parole* and *Projets finaux* activities and projects. The section *La culture sur place* asks students to interact directly with Francophone culture as participants. Students see universal human values at work in the *Lecture thématique* selections and *Points de départ* sections, and build relationships working collaboratively with others in pair and group work. Pushing the boundaries of their knowledge in cross-disciplinary activities, they connect to math, literature, meteorology, art, science, technology, and many other subject areas.

Each unit of *T'es branché?* is organized around a *question centrale*, in a sense an umbrella under which all the content of the unit falls. At the end of the unit, students are asked to recapture and reflect on what they have learned and self-assess in the *Faisons le point!* section.

As students learn with *T'es branché?*, they begin to acquire important IB characteristics, becoming....

- **knowledgeable** about French language and culture
- **inquiring** about many subject areas
- **reflective** about human values, social issues, and their own learning process
- **open-minded** about other cultures, their values, and points of view
- **caring** about their classmates and Francophone students with whom they collaborate
- **communicative** as they interact orally and write memos, web pages, formal and informal letters, journal articles, reports on surveys they have taken, brochures, and critiques of books and films

With ***T'es branché?*** as a tool, IB students become great communicators who practice interpersonal, presentational, and interpretive language skills in activities and projects that are engaging, challenging, penetrating, and open-ended.

Transcript of Textbook Listening Activities

The following is the transcript of the listening comprehension activities included in the *T'es branché?* Student Textbook, Level 3. These activities are recorded in the Audio Program. The following section contains a transcript of these recorded activities for teachers who prefer to read the activities aloud instead of using the recorded version. There is one vocabulary and one structure listening activity in each section, plus one in the *Évaluation* section. In every even unit there is also one recorded activity for the *Bilan cumulatif*.

Unité 1

Leçon A

Vocabulaire

4 Où sont-ils allés?

Écrivez les numéros 1–8 sur votre papier. Dites pour chaque conversation où les personnes sont allées ou où ils vont en écrivant la bonne lettre.

1. Jean: Quels chanteurs étaient là?
   Mme Martin: Rachid Taha et Faudel.
2. Karine: Tu as l'air fâché. Qu'est-ce qu'il y a?
   Juliette: Je devais voir Karim. On allait danser, mais il n'est pas venu.
3. David: Tu as l'air de détester ta classe d'allemand!
   Karim: Oui, je suis nul! Mais M. Morel va m'aider samedi après-midi.
4. Aude: Tu as l'air content. Qu'est-ce que tu as fait ce weekend?
   Rachida: J'ai suivi un cours d'art avec d'autres ados. C'était super!
5. Kevin: Tu veux faire du footing?
   Xavier: Oui, je veux bien.
6. Anissa: Si on faisait du skate?
   Koffi: D'accord. Je suis libre à 14h00.
7. Marie: Qui était chez Chloé?
   Éric: J'ai rencontré une fille super belle et sympa. Tu vas l'aimer.
8. Virginie: Tu veux voir le drame de Scorsese?
   François: Oui, si tu veux. Ça a l'air intéressant!

Grammaire

14 On étudie ou pas?

Écrivez les numéros 1–8 sur votre papier. Écoutez les dialogues et décidez si la personne étudie. Si oui, écrivez ***oui****. Si non, écrivez* ***non****.*

1. -Tu as envie d'aller à la discothèque ce soir?
   -Désolée, mais je ne peux pas. Il y a un contrôle de maths demain.
2. -Vous suivez un cours d'anglais?
   -Oui, nous sommes en train de lire *Huckleberry Finn*.
3. -Tu veux aller en ville avec moi?
   -Si on peut jouer au basket au complexe sportif.
4. -Je conduis ou tu conduis au festival?
   -Je ne peux pas conduire. Je n'ai pas de permis de conduire.
5. -Vous écrivez une rédaction sur la pièce de Molière?
   -Oui, il faut la rendre lundi, et je viens d'écrire le premier paragraphe.
6. -Chéri, tu mets le couvert pour moi?
   -Non, maman, je ne peux pas. Je lis ma leçon d'histoire.
7. -Vous venez à la soirée de Guillaume vendredi soir?
   -Non, nous ne connaissons pas ses amis.
8. -Vous faites vos devoirs de français?
   -Non, nous recevons nos amis.

Leçon B

Vocabulaire

5 Ce que j'aime faire.

*Écrivez les numéros 1–8 sur votre papier. Écoutez la petite Marie parler de sa vie. Écrivez **V** si les phrases sont vraies ou **F** si elles sont fausses.*

Moi, c'est Marie. Tous les lundis, je vais à l'école. C'est ma maman qui m'emmène. Nous habitons dans un bel appartement, elle et moi. À l'école, j'ai une copine qui s'appelle Julie et un copain Karim. Pendant la récréation, on joue à cache-cache ou on fait semblant d'être des superhéros. Moi, j'aime jouer à la poupée à la maison, mais pas à l'école. Julie adore jouer à la marelle et sauter à la corde. Moi aussi, mais je préfère jouer aux billes parce que je gagne toujours. Karim lui, il préfère faire des courses de petites voitures chez lui. Moi, je n'aime pas ça.

Grammaire

21 La journée de Mme Aknouch

*Écrivez les numéros 1–6 sur votre papier. Écoutez l'histoire. Ensuite, dites si chaque phrase est vraie (**V**) ou fausse (**F**).*

Hier Mme Aknouch a quitté la maison à une heure. D'abord, elle est allée au complexe sportif pour courir. Puis elle est allée à la station de métro. Là, elle a pris le métro et elle est descendue au supermarché. Elle a fait les courses avant d'aller chercher sa fille à l'école. Sa fille Amina jouait à la marelle avec une amie. Elle était contente de voir sa maman. Mme Aknouch et sa fille sont rentrées à l'appartement à pied.

Leçon C

Vocabulaire

3 Le mariage de Claudia et Philippe

*Écrivez les numéros 1–7 sur votre papier. Écrivez **E** si la phrase décrit la cérémonie à l'église ou **R** si la phrase décrit la réception.*

1. Le marié met un morceau de gâteau dans la bouche de la mariée.
2. Chloé met une longue robe blanche.
3. Beaucoup des invités dansent et chantent.
4. Chloé met une alliance sur le doigt de Thomas.
5. On prend une photo de la demoiselle d'honneur avant la cérémonie.
6. Thomas, dans un smoking noir, attend que le père de Chloé l'accompagne.
7. Le garçon d'honneur donne l'alliance à Thomas.

Grammaire

18 Le conditionnel ou le futur?

*Écrivez les numéros 1–8 sur votre papier. Écoutez les phrases suivantes. Écrivez **C** si la phrase est au conditionnel et **F** si la phrase est au futur.*

1. J'aimerais bien travailler dans un laboratoire de recherches.
2. Si tu étais un garçon, tu serais le garçon d'honneur à mon mariage.
3. Nous irons en Italie après la cérémonie.
4. Amélie aura beaucoup d'invités à sa réception.
5. Nous préférerions aller à Nice qu'à Cannes.
6. Tu achèteras un cadeau pour le couple?
7. Si son fiancé avait de l'argent, il lui achèterait une bague avec un gros diamant.
8. Ils prendront le train quand ils iront en voyage de noces.

Évaluation

A Évaluation de compréhension auditive

Les vacances

Écrivez les numéros 1–7 sur votre papier. Ensuite, écoutez l'histoire et écrivez la lettre qui correspond à l'endroit où les personnes feront les activités suivantes pendant les vacances.

Les ados du lycée Lafontaine ont beaucoup de projets pour les vacances. Caroline s'intéresse à la peinture; donc, elle compte suivre un cours de peinture avec d'autres ados. Serge passera beaucoup de temps à faire du skate. Amélie et Amadou verront tous les drames de Truffaut parce qu'ils adorent le cinéma français. Jacques aimerait assister aux FrancoFolies à LaRochelle. Martine n'a pas réussi en anglais; donc, elle étudiera avec le prof anglais. Yasmine courra et Julien jouera au foot. Chloé dansera tous les vendredis et samedis soirs.

Unité 2

Leçon A

Vocabulaire

5 Un réveillon traditionnel!

Écrivez les numéros 1–6 sur votre papier. Écoutez la description du réveillon de Noël chez les Dupont. Ensuite, écrivez un mot ou une expression pour répondre aux questions que vous entendez.

Le soir du réveillon de Noël, M. et Mme Dupont accueillent leurs invités à 19h20. M. Dupont range leurs manteaux. Les enfants, Martine et Guy, emmènent les invités au salon. Mme Dupont leur sert des toasts avec des œufs de lump. Avant le dîner, les invités offrent des cadeaux aux enfants. Mme Dupont sert la dinde aux marrons dans la salle à manger. À table, Guy embête sa sœur. Dans le salon on mange la bûche de Noël et des mandarines. Avant de se coucher, les enfants mettent leurs chaussures devant le sapin de Noël. Le lendemain Guy et Martine ont beaucoup de cadeaux à ouvrir.

1. Quelle est la date?
2. Qui arrive chez les Dupont?
3. Qui range leurs manteaux?
4. Où est-ce que Mme Dupont sert des toasts avec des œufs de lump?
5. Qu'est-ce qu'on mange avec la bûche de Noël?
6. Qui a des beaucoup de cadeaux le lendemain?

Grammaire

12 Qui et quoi à Noël?

Écoutez les réponses suivantes. Ensuite, choisissez la question correspondante.

1. Cette année je vais manger des huîtres en hors-d'œuvre.
2. Mon frère va mettre les huîtres dans des assiettes.
3. Mes parents vont offrir des cadeaux à leurs enfants.
4. Je vais préparer les toasts avec les œufs de lump.
5. Ma mère va avoir besoin de marrons pour la dinde.
6. Nous allons inviter mes grands-parents.
7. Je vais préparer la bûche pour toute la famille.
8. Nous allons accueillir notre famille.

Leçon B

Vocabulaire

5 À quoi ça sert?

Écrivez les numéros 1–6 sur votre papier. Écoutez les descriptions suivantes. Ensuite, choisissez l'objet qui correspond à la définition.

1. C'est un machin en métal ou plastique. Ça sert à passer l'eau des spaghettis.
2. C'est un ustensile souvent en métal. Ça sert à filtrer les herbes.
3. C'est un machin souvent en verre. Ça sert à mesurer le sucre.
4. C'est un ustensile en bois et plastique. Ça sert à racler toute la sauce.
5. C'est une petite machine en métal et verre. Ça sert à mélanger les ingrédients.
6. C'est un machin en métal. Ça sert à faire chauffer la soupe.

Grammaire

13 C'est qui?

Écrivez les numéros 1–6 sur votre papier. Écoutez les descriptions. Puis, choisissez la personne décrite.

1. C'est un homme d'affaires. Il est américain. Il a une émission de télé-réalité. C'est un homme riche.
2. C'est un Français. Il est drôle. Il a joué un rôle important dans le film *Bienvenue chez les Ch'tis*.
3. C'est une bonne actrice. C'est une Américaine. Elle a fait des films avec Robert Pattinson.
4. C'est un bon artiste. Il est français. Il aime peindre en plein air.
5. Elle est canadienne. C'est une chanteuse. Elle vient du Nouveau-Brunswick.
6. C'est une femme intelligente. C'est elle qui travaille à Washington. C'est une femme politique.

Leçon C

Vocabulaire

5 De quoi parle-t-on?

Écrivez les numéros 1–6 sur votre papier. Écoutez les histoires et descriptions. Ensuite, choisissez la catégorie à laquelle chacun correspond.

1. C'est bientôt les élections pour la ville! Allez voter pour cette femme politique. Vous la connaissez depuis longtemps. Elle est intelligente et prête à vous servir. C'est le candidat du parti socialiste.
2. Un nouvel athlète africain a couru aux Jeux olympiques et a gagné une médaille. Est-ce l'homme le plus vite du monde? On verra demain.
3. Cette semaine, sortie d'un bon film réalisé par un jeune metteur en scène. On va le passer dans un cinéma près de chez vous.
4. À cause de l'endettement, le PNB d'Italie a baissé. Ce n'est pas une question d'inflation. Les revenus du pays déclinent face à l'endettement public.
5. On va parler des blogueurs célèbres. Qui est-ce que vous suivez? Téléphonez-nous!
6. La collection prêt-à-porter automne/hiver vient de sortir. À cause de la longueur des jupes, on dirait un look années 1960.

Grammaire

13 Qui ou que? Là est la question!

Écrivez les numéros 1–8 sur votre papier. Écoutez les deux phrases. Puis, écrivez le pronom relatif ***qui*** *ou* ***que*** *que vous utiliseriez pour faire une seule phrase.*

1. Je préfère le réveillon de Noël. Le réveillon de Noël a lieu le 24 décembre.
2. Le candidat fait partie de la droite. J'aime ce candidat.
3. L'équipe de foot a gagné. Elle vient de Nantes.
4. J'ai l'ustensile. Il filtre les herbes.
5. L'athlète s'appelle Zinédine Zidane. Les Français le préfèrent.
6. Elle porte un look à la mode. C'est des années 1960.
7. Ils choisissent le candidat socialiste. Il est le meilleur homme politique.
8. J'ai vu le film *Bienvenu chez les Ch'tis*. C'est un bon film.

Évaluation

A Évaluation de compréhension auditive

Une fête

*Écrivez les numéros 1–6 sur votre papier. Écoutez Laure parler d'une fête dans sa famille. Puis, écrivez **V** si la phrase que vous entendez est **vraie** et **F** si la phrase que vous entendez est **fausse**.*

Chez moi, on fête le Nouvel An avec les amis et la famille. En général, on loue une salle des fêtes que l'on décore. On achète des vêtements et des jouets de fêtes. Ma cousine est toujours à la dernière mode et papa porte le même smoking tous les ans. Maman et ma tante font les courses et c'est Jean-François, mon cousin qui est chef, qui prépare la cuisine. Bien sûr, on l'aide tous un peu! Au menu, il y a toujours des huîtres, du foie gras, une dinde, et des pâtisseries. C'est moi qui accueille tout le monde et je range les manteaux. C'est une grande soirée avec un DJ et on écoute tous les hits de l'année. On mange bien, on discute politique et cinéma, on danse jusqu'à minuit quand on boit un verre de champagne.

1. Laure parle du réveillon de Noël.
2. On porte des vêtements spéciaux pour cette fête.
3. La mère et la tante de Laure font la cuisine.
4. Laure accueille tout le monde.
5. On écoute tous les hits de l'année et on danse jusqu'à minuit.
6. On invite juste des amis.

Bilan cumulatif

II. Interpretive communication: Audio texts

Écoutez le dialogue suivant deux fois, puis complétez les phrases.

-Bonjour, Victoria et félicitations tout d'abord pour vos fiançailles avec Alexandre. Merci bien de nous avoir contactés pour parler du mariage en France.

-Oui, c'est bien ça. Comme vous le savez déjà peut-être, aux États-Unis, on a toutes sortes de traditions pour le mariage. Mes parents se sont mariés en plein air, mais moi et Alexandre, mon futur mari, nous souhaitons avoir un mariage traditionnel français à la cathédrale de Chartres. Je ne connais que très peu de choses sur les traditions françaises et encore moins sur comment on se marie en France. Vous avez l'air de tout savoir sur le mariage, alors je vous écoute.

-Ce n'est pas la peine de vous inquiéter. Nous sommes là pour vous aider et vous guider. Des invitations à la réception, nous pouvons tout organiser pour vous. Commençons par le domaine de la culture. Tout d'abord en France, il a la cérémonie civile qui est obligatoire et, si vous le désirez, vous pouvez avoir une cérémonie religieuse. La demoiselle et le garçon d'honneur sont en général les parents ou amis du couple. Le garçon d'honneur, lui, porte l'anneau des futurs mariés. Le gâteau traditionnel est ce que l'on appelle une pièce montée, donc il est grand, beau, et délicieux! Maintenant, que vous en savez un peu plus sur le mariage en France, avez-vous des questions, Victoria?

-Oh, merci. Je me sens vraiment en sécurité chez vous! Oui, j'ai une question sur ce qui va se passer après le mariage et la réception.

Unité 3

Leçon A

Vocabulaire

5 Qui sont vos aïeux?

*Écrivez les numéros 1–6 sur votre papier. Écoutez la discussion entre le prof d'histoire et ses élèves. Ensuite, indiquez si les phrases sont vraies (**V**) ou fausses (**F**).*

Professeur:	Alors, vous avez trouvé des informations en ligne sur vos aïeux? Annie?
Annie:	Oui, moi, j'ai découvert que mon arrière-grand-mère était québécoise. Elle s'est installée dans le Maine et c'est là qu'elle a rencontré mon arrière-grand-père.
Professeur:	Et lui, il était de quelle origine?
Annie:	Il était anglais.

Professeur:	Et vous, Roger, qu'as-tu découvert?
Roger:	Et bien, ma famille vient d'Allemagne. Ils se sont installés dans le Minnesota où ils étaient fermiers.
Professeur:	Chase, tu veux nous dire ce que vous avez trouvé?
Chase:	Ma grand-tante Mathilde, ses ancêtres viennent d'Acadie et ils ont quitté le Canada et se sont installés en Louisiane.
Professeur:	C'est passionnant! Quelqu'un d'autre? Oui, Melissa.
Melissa:	Moi, mon arrière-grand-père de Moscou habitait en Alaska. C'est là où une partie de ma famille habite.

Grammaire

12 De petites conversations

Écrivez les numéros 1–8 sur votre papier. Écoutez les questions et indiquez si vous répondriez avec **y** *ou* **en**.

1. Tu es allé dans le Delaware l'été dernier?
2. Est-ce que tu prends souvent de la soupe à l'oignon?
3. Est-ce que vous avez vu tes cousins au Texas?
4. Où ont-ils acheté des fraises?
5. Quand vas-tu en Louisiane?
6. Tes grands-parents ont vécu au Québec?
7. Combien de fois par semaine l'enfant mange-t-il des légumes?
8. Combien de CDs Michèle a-t-elle acheté?

Leçon B

Vocabulaire

4 Une princesse rusée

Écoutez le conte de fées, puis choisissez la lettre de la partie qui complète la phrase.

Il était une fois une très belle princesse. Elle habitait dans un grand château. Tous les matins, la princesse se levait, se lavait, se maquillait, et se brossait les cheveux pour se préparer pour la journée avant de sortir pour faire une longue promenade dans la forêt. Un jour, un magicien a décidé de lui jouer un mauvais tour. Il a changé le chemin de la promenade de la princesse. Mais la princesse était aussi rusée que belle. Elle se méfiait des magiciens et savait qu'un magicien méchant habitait dans la forêt. Donc, elle a mis des cordes jaunes aux arbres pour lui indiquer le chemin. Comme ça, elle a pu déjouer le tour du magicien et rentrer au château.

Grammaire

11 Le bal

Écrivez les numéros 1–5 sur votre papier. Écoutez l'histoire et écrivez une réponse courte à la question que vous entendez.

Jacqueline rêvait de devenir princesse. Un jour, elle a reçu une invitation à un bal au château du prince Jean. Elle s'est habillée d'une très jolie robe rose et je jour du bal, elle s'est levée très tôt. Elle s'est lavée et s'est maquillée. Elle s'est regardée dans la glace. Elle était très belle. Enfin, elle a mis ses petites chaussures en soie. Elle s'est rendue au château du roi et de la reine. Au bal, le prince a tout de suite voulu danser avec Jacqueline et les deux jeunes gens sont tombés amoureux. Jacqueline est rentrée chez elle à minuit et s'est couchée tout de suite. Elle ne s'est même pas brossé les dents. Elle rêvait d'une grande bague de fiançailles.

1. De quoi Jacqueline s'est-elle habillée?
2. Comment s'est-elle préparée pour le bal?
3. Où s'est-elle rendue ce soir-là?
4. Comment s'est-elle amusée?
5. Avec qui veut-elle se marier?

Leçon C

Vocabulaire

5 Comment réparer?

Écrivez les numéros 1–6 sur votre papier. Écoutez les descriptions suivantes. Choisissez la solution pour chaque problème de logement.

1. J'habite dans un HLM en banlieue. J'aime mon logement, mais le HLM n'est pas très propre. Je déteste les graffitis sur les murs de ma cité!
2. Henri vient d'acheter un appartement dans un grand immeuble. Il adore bricoler, peindre les murs, réparer les meubles. Son projet aujourd'hui est le parquet qui est sale.
3. Les Dumas habitent une nouvelle maison individuelle. Mr. Dumas n'aime pas bricoler. C'est sa femme, Mme Dumas qui veut décorer les salles, mais pas avec des affiches!
4. Mes grands-parents habitent une ancienne ferme. Ma grand-mère veut que mon grand-père répare un placard dans la cuisine.
5. Aïcha habite une maison mitoyenne très jolie. Mais elle n'aime pas peindre; elle préfère plus de décoration aux murs.
6. Les Fleury ont une maison individuelle à Tours. Mais ils veulent passer toutes les vacances à la campagne.

Grammaire

14 Qui est le meilleur élève?

Écoutez le paragraphe qui compare Abdoulaye et Étienne. Dites quel élève travaille le plus sérieusement, Abdoulaye ou Étienne.

Abdoulaye se couche à 10h00, mais Étienne se couche à minuit. Abdoulaye se couche plus tôt qu'Étienne. Abdoulaye se lève à 7h30, mais Étienne se lève à 8h15. Étienne se lève plus tard qu'Abdoulaye et arrive souvent en retard au lycée. Pendant la semaine, après les cours, Étienne fait du sport. Il va à la bibliothèque une fois par semaine, mais Abdoulaye y va quatre fois par semaine pour étudier et faire ses devoirs. Abdoulaye va plus souvent à la bibliothèque qu'Étienne. Abdoulaye réussit plus aux contrôles qu'Étienne.

Évaluation

A Évaluation de compréhension auditive

*Écoutez la conversation entre Amina et Ahmed, qui décrit un conte de fées. Ensuite, indiquez si les phrases sont vraies (**V**) ou fausses (**F**).*

Amina:	Qu'est-ce que tu fais?
Ahmed:	Bon, j'écris un conte de fées moderne pour mon cours de français.
Amina:	Moderne comment?
Ahmed:	Et bien, il y a un garçon. Il s'appelle David. Il habite dans une cité HLM. La cité est sale est il y a plein de graffitis sur les murs.
Amina:	Et qu'est-ce qui se passe ensuite?
Ahmed:	Et bien, David a un arrière-grand-père africain qui est magicien. Cet ancêtre a donné un marteau magique au père de David. Tu devines ce que David va faire avec le marteau?
Amina:	Il va enfoncer un clou, bricoler dans sa chambre....
Ahmed:	Mais non, utilise ton imagination! Avec le marteau, David va réparer la cité. Les HLM vont devenir de belles maisons mitoyennes. Chaque locataire aura un beau petit jardin. Tout va être propre! Plus de graffitis sur les murs, plus de passants méchants. Ce sera le quartier le plus beau de la ville.
Amina:	Et comment va-t-il réussir?
Ahmed:	Et bien, il va frapper trois fois le marteau sur sa porte etdire ce qu'il veut avant d'aller se coucher. Le lendemain, quand il va se réveiller, la cité sera transformée.
Amina:	C'est un conte moderne formidable. Bravo, Ahmed!

Unité 4

Leçon A

Vocabulaire

4 La Réunion, je kiffe!

*Écrivez les numéros 1–5 sur votre papier. Écoutez Stéphane décrire sa vie à la Réunion. Écrivez **V** si la phrase que vous lisez est vraie et **F** si la phrase est fausse.*

Mes parents et moi habitons à la Réunion depuis trois mois. Il y a beaucoup de choses à faire ici. Je parle des activités en plein air. Le lundi après les cours, je fais de la planche à voile avec des copains. Le mardi matin, je fais de la randonnée équestre avec mon école. C'est génial, on découvre beaucoup de paysages superbes. Le mercredi après-midi, je fais de l'escalade et du parapente en descente. Le weekend, j'aime sauter à l'élastique. Quelles activités en plein air est-ce que vous aimez faire?

Grammaire

13 Questions simples

*Écrivez les numéros 1–8 sur votre papier. Écoutez les mini-dialogues. Puis, écrivez **oui** si la personne mentionnée fait le sport dont on parle ou **non** si elle n'en fait pas.*

1. -Les Alpes cet été, ça te dit?
   -Bien sûr. On peut faire de la randonnée.
2. -Tu aimes faire des sauts à ski?
   -Non, je n'aime ni skier, ni le saut à ski.
3. -En sortant du lycée, tu veux faire de la planche à voile?
   -Oui, bonne idée. Invitons André! Il me l'a proposé aussi.
4. -Personne ne veut faire de saut à l'élastique avec nous samedi?
   -Si, Aurélie veut venir.
5. -Ils n'offrent aucune randonnée équestre? J'ai envie de le faire ce weekend.
   -Si, ils offrent des randonnées équestres le samedi matin.
6. -Tu aimes faire du parapente?
   -Non, je n'aime ni le parapente ni le saut à l'élastique. J'ai horreur de ces sports!

7 -Tu fais souvent de l'escalade?
   -Non, je ne fais jamais d'escalade.

8. -Martin ne fait pas de ski?
   -Si, et il fait aussi du saut à ski!

Leçon B

Vocabulaire

5 La classe de neige

Écrivez les numéros 1–6 sur votre papier. Écoutez ce que chacun des enfants emporte en classe de neige. Puis, choisissez le mot qui qui n'est pas mentionné.

1. un bonnet, un blouson, des bottes de ski
2. des lunettes de ski, des gants, de la crème solaire, un bonnet
3. des chaussures de ski, des bâtons de ski
4. un fuseau de ski, une écharpe, un bonnet, des skis
5. un fuseau de ski, une écharpe, des chaussures de ski
6. des skis, un forfait, des chaussures

Grammaire

13 Une leçon de ski

*Écrivez les numéros 1–7 sur votre papier. Écoutez les conseils de la monitrice. S'il faut que les enfants fassent quelque chose, écrivez **oui**; s'il ne faut pas qu'ils fassent quelque chose, écrivez **non**.*

1. Il ne faut pas que vous téléphoniez sur la piste.
2. Il ne faut pas que vous achetiez de nouveaux skis.
3. Il ne faut pas que vous quittiez la piste.
4. Il faut que vous écoutiez les conseils des moniteurs.
5. Il faut que vous skiiez vite.
6. Il faut que vous choisissiez le télésiège.
7. Il faut que vous jouiez dans la neige.
8. Il ne faut pas que vous vendiez votre forfait de ski.
9. Il faut que vous finissiez votre chocolat chaud avant de skier.

Leçon C

Vocabulaire

3 On part où?

*Écrivez les numéros 1–8 sur votre papier. Puis, écrivez **oui** si la phrase décrit des préparatifs de voyage ou **non** s'il ne s'agit pas d'un voyage.*

1. M. et Mme Morin remplissent des papiers pour obtenir un passeport.
2. Suzanne prend le télésiège à la station de ski.
3. Marc et moi, nous faisons de saut à l'élastique en été.
4. Julie et Martine font leurs valises.
5. Les Delpy planifient un séjour au Maroc.
6. Aujourd'hui les Dumont se font vacciner au cabinet du médecin.
7. Jacques se renseigne sur l'Espagne en surfant sur Internet.
8. Nous achetons un guide sur le Sénégal.

Grammaire

13 Notre séjour au Sénégal

Écrivez les numéros 1–7 sur votre papier. Écoutez les phrases, puis choisissez l'image qui correspond.

1. Il est nécessaire que vous obteniez un passeport.
2. Il est important que vous réserviez une chambre d'hôtel.
3. Il est indispensable que vous planifiiez en surfant sur Internet.
4. Il est essentiel que vous vous fassiez faire vacciner.
5. Il vaut mieux que vous alliez au consulat.
6. Il est bon que vous écoutiez la météo avant de faire votre valise.
7. Il est utile que vous ayez toujours une pièce d'identité sur vous.

Évaluation

A Évaluation de compréhension auditive

On part à la montagne.

*Écrivez les numéros 1–7 sur votre papier. Écoutez Armelle et Amadou discuter de leur projet de vacances à la montagne. Ensuite, indiquez si les phrases que vous entendez sont vraies (**V**) ou fausses (**F**).*

Armelle: Tu fais ta valise?
Amadou: Oui, j'essaie de penser à ce que je dois prendre.
Armelle: Il est indispensable que tu prennes la crème solaire, une écharpe, un bonnet, et des gants.
Amadou: Et toi, tu as confirmé notre réservation à l'hôtel?
Armelle: Oui, et j'ai réservé un taxi pour aller à l'aéroport.
Amadou: Super. Tu as bien pris nos pièces d'identité?
Armelle: Oui, j'ai les billets d'avions, notre réservation à l'hôtel, ma carte de crédit, et nos pièces d'identité dans mon sac à main.
Amadou: Alors, on est prêt pour le ski alpin, le snowboard, et les randonnées.
Armelle: Moi, je vois les choses un peu différemment. Si on faisait du ski de fond et qu'on allait à la piscine?
Amadou: Pourquoi pas! Tu as vérifié qu'on n'a rien oublié?
Armelle: Oui, allons-y!

1. Il est indispensable qu'Amadou prenne des gants, selon Armelle.
2. Armelle a oublié de confirmer la réservation de l'hôtel.
3. On a réservé un taxi pour aller à l'aéroport.
4. Armelle a les passeports, les visas, et les permis de conduire dans son sac à main.
5. Amadou veut faire du ski et du snowboard.
6. On change d'avis et on va faire des randonnées équestres.
7. Amadou et Armelle vont profiter de la piscine.

Bilan cumulatif

II. Interpretive communication: Audio texts

Écoutez le dialogue suivant deux fois, puis répondez aux questions en choisissant la lettre correcte.

Nora: Il faut que vous voyiez la Savoie, surtout en hiver.
Bruno: Qu'est-ce que tu me conseilles de faire?
Nora: Il est possible que tu aimes le ski alpin. Il y a de belles pistes dans les stations de ski.
Bruno: Il se pourrait que je t'accompagne.... J'ai hâte d'essayer le ski alpin dans les Alpes. Mais je n'ai ni skis ni bâtons!
Nora: Tu peux tout louer sur place. Si on planifie un weekend?
Bruno: Il faut que nous obtenions des forfaits de ski.
Nora: Je les trouverai en surfant sur Internet.
Bruno: J'aurai besoin d'une leçon avant de descendre la piste.
Nora: On peut parler à un moniteur quand on arrive.
Bruno: J'aimerais bien regarder le taxi-ski et la luge.
Nora: Bien sûr. On aura un séjour formidable. Et n'oubliez pas la cuisine! On va goûter la raclette savoyarde.
Bruno: J'adore essayer de nouveaux plats! On a fini de planifier?
Nora: Mais non, il faut réserver un condo et des billets de train. Il est bon qu'on n'ait pas besoin d'un passeport parce que je voudrais y aller le weekend prochain.

Unité 5

Leçon A

Vocabulaire

2 Un bon ou un mauvais hôtel?

Écrivez les numéros 1–6 sur votre papier. Écoutez Élise décrire son expérience dans un hôtel de Monaco. Écrivez une courte réponse pour répondre à chaque question, par exemple, "à la réception."

J'avais hâte de passer mes vacances à Monaco. J'avais réservé un hôtel qui semblait très bien en ligne mais les prestations étaient fausses. D'abord, la réception n'était ouverte que jusqu'à 23 heures et le réceptionniste n'était pas sympa. Ensuite, il n'y avait pas de concierge comme c'était indiqué en ligne. Bien sûr, c'était une vieille clé et pas une clé électronique. Ensuite, il n'y avait pas de chaines câblées à la télé. Heureusement, la climatisation marchait parce qu'il faisait très chaud. J'ai mis mon passeport et mon argent dans un coffre-fort dans le hall derrière la réception. Je me servais du sèche-cheveux chaque jour après la piscine chaque matin. Le service de chambre offrait de bonnes spécialités de la région. Mais tout n'était pas comme il faut, donc j'ai changé d'hôtel et après, j'ai passé des vacances super géniales.

Grammaire

10 Souhaits de vacanciers

Écrivez les numéros 1–8 sur votre papier. Écoutez les souhaits des vacanciers. Puis, choisissez l'image qui y correspond.

1. Je veux que l'hôtel ait un concierge.
2. Je souhaite que la réception soit ouverte jour et nuit.
3. Je désire qu'il y ait un accès Wifi dans ma chambre.

4. J'aimerais que ma chambre soit équipée d'une clé électronique.
5. Je préfère qu'il y ait un jacuzzi dans ma chambre.
6. Je souhaite qu'on offre le service de chambre.
7. J'exige qu'on change mes serviettes de bain tous les jours.
8. Je veux que la chambre ait la climatisation.

Leçon B

Vocabulaire

4 Les plats cuisinés, délicieux!

Écrivez les numéros 1–7 sur votre papier. Puis, écoutez Stéphane décrire ses goûts culinaires. Enfin, écrivez ***oui*** *ou* ***non*** *pour répondre à la question que vous entendez.*

Moi, j'adore la cuisine française. Je suis bourguignon, alors j'adore le bœuf bourguignon. Par contre, je n'aime pas le chevreuil ou le jambon persillé. J'adore les plats en sauces. Mes préférés sont le jambon sauce béchamel, les moules marinières, et le saumon sauce hollandaise. Je déteste la sauce béarnaise. À la maison, maman fait souvent du lapin à la moutarde. C'est délicieux! Mon frère adore le faisan. Moi je n'aime pas trop. Je préfère le veau Orloff. Miam!

1. Est-ce que Stéphane aime le bœuf bourguignon parce qu'il est provençal?
2. Est-ce que Stéphane préfère le chevreuil et le jambon persillé?
3. Est-ce qu'il aime les plats servis avec une sauce?
4. Est-ce qu'il adore la sauce béarnaise?
5. Est-ce que sa mère lui sert souvent du lapin à la moutarde?
6. Est-ce qu'il aime le faisan plus que son frère?
7. Il prend souvent du veau Orloff?

Grammaire

15 La cuisine, c'est bon!

Écrivez les numéros 1–8 sur votre papier. Écoutez les phrases. Écrivez ***D*** *si vous pensez que la phrase exprime (expresses) un doute, ou* ***C*** *si vous pensez qu'elle exprime une certitude.*

1. Je doute que tu goûtes les trompettes de la mort.
2. Tu ne doutes pas que Clara aime la gastronomie de la Bourgogne.
3. Le chef est sûr que ses clients aiment sa sauce marinière.
4. Marie-Alix est certaine que la viande est servie avec de la moutarde.
5. Nous ne sommes pas certains que les enfants prennent des escargots.
6. Il n'est pas évident que l'entrée ait bon goût.
7. Crois-tu que les spécialités soient bonnes?
8. Félix ne croit pas que le faisan soit frais.

Leçon C

Vocabulaire

4 Quel film on va voir?

Écoutez la conversation, puis écrivez un mot ou une expression pour répondre aux questions.

Ahmed: Quelles sont les nouveautés cette semaine?

Yasmina: Il y a un film en version originale avec Adam Sandler.

Ahmed: Je ne suis pas d'humeur pour un film en version originale. Il faut lire les sous-titres. C'est nul!

Yasmina: Le film avec Adam Sandler semble intéressant. Le casting est sympa et il paraît que c'est drôle.

Ahmed:	Qui est le réalisateur et tu as regardé la critique?
Yasmina:	Je ne connais ni l'un ni l'autre, mais la bande-annonce est très bonne.
Ahmed:	C'est quel genre ?
Yasmina:	C'est une comédie. Tu as envie de rire, non?
Ahmed:	Oui, d'accord, allons-y pour une comédie!

1. Quel est le genre du film qu'Ahmed et Yasmina vont voir?
2. Qui joue le rôle principal?
3. Ahmed et Yasmina veulent-ils pleurer au cinéma?
4. Yasmina a-t-elle lu la critique?
5. Qu'est-ce qu'elle a vu du film?
6. C'est un film français?

Grammaire

15 Quel cinéma?

Écrivez les numéros 1–7 sur votre papier. Écoutez les questions suivantes. Choisissez la réponse logique.

1. Il y a beaucoup de bons films au cinéma. Lequel veux-tu voir ce weekend?
2. Quel est le meilleur film de l'année en France?
3. Tu as vu ces deux comédies. Laquelle préfères-tu?
4. Quelle bande-annonce te semble la meilleure?
5. Entre tous ces artistes, lesquels préfères-tu?
6. Pour toi, lequel de ces réalisateurs est le meilleur?
7. Quelle dernière sortie as-tu choisi de voir?

Évaluation

A Évaluation de compréhension auditive

Un hôtel à Dijon

*Écoutez Aude et Rachid discuter de leur réservation dans un hôtel en Bourgogne. Ensuite, écrivez **V** si les phrases sont vraies ou **F** si elles sont fausses.*

Aude:	Tu as choisi un hôtel en Bourgogne?
Rachid:	Oui, à Dijon. Il y a beaucoup de sites à visiter et les spécialités sont formidables.
Aude:	L'hôtel, il est moderne au moins! Rappelle-toi notre hôtel à Monaco l'année dernière. Il n'y avait même pas la climatisation.
Rachid:	Je ne suis pas sûr que la réception soit ouverte 24h sur 24, mais il semble qu'ils aient des sèche-cheveux dans la chambre et les critiques sont bonnes.
Aude:	Penses-tu qu'il y a un bon restaurant dans l'hôtel ou, au moins, proche de l'hôtel?
Rachid:	Oui, j'ai appelé et j'ai demandé à la réception. La réceptionniste m'a dit que le concierge connaît les meilleurs restaurants de la ville et que le restaurant de l'hôtel sert toutes les spécialités bourguignonnes.
Aude:	Quelles sont leurs spécialités?
Rachid:	Le bœuf bourguignon et les escargots.
Aude:	Tu crois qu'ils ont du lapin à la moutarde? J'adore ça!
Rachid:	Je ne suis pas sûr qu'ils aient du lapin au restaurant de l'hôtel, mais en ville certainement.
Aude:	Et quelles sont les autres prestations de l'hôtel?
Rachid:	Ils offrent les chaines câblées et une connexion Wifi, en plus un centre de remise en forme et le service de chambre.
Aude:	Il n'y a pas de piscine?
Rachid:	Non, juste un bain à remous.
Aude:	C'est dommage qu'il n'y ait pas de piscine mais le centre de remise en forme, ça c'est très bien!

Unité 6

Leçon A

Vocabulaire

2 Nouveau compte en banque!

Écrivez les numéros 1–7 sur votre papier. Écoutez Jonathan décrire son expérience dans une banque en France. Faites correspondre la phrase que vous entendez avec la bonne image.

1. Hier, je suis allé à la banque pour ouvrir un compte. D'abord, j'ai attendu au guichet.
2. J'ai dit à la caissière que je voulais ouvrir un compte et faire une demande de carte bancaire.
3. Elle m'a demandé ma carte d'identité et mon adresse en France.
4. Puis, elle m'a donné une carte bancaire et un chéquier.
5. Comme je voulais échanger mes dollars pour des euros, elle m'a indiqué le bureau de change.
6. Là, l'employé m'a donné de l'argent liquide, des pièces et des billets.
7. Alors, je suis sorti de la banque et j'ai retiré de l'argent au distributeur avec ma nouvelle carte. Ouvrir un compte bancaire, c'est facile!

Grammaire

11 Quand je serai en France

Écrivez les numéros 1–8 sur votre papier. Écoutez les questions suivantes. Choisissez la lettre qui correspond à la meilleure réponse.

1. Qu'est-ce que tu feras après le bac?
2. Qu'est-ce que tu étudieras lorsque tu seras à la fac en France?
3. Quand tu seras médecin, tu rentreras au Canada?
4. Qu'est-ce que tu feras si tu ne peux pas devenir médecin en France?
5. Comment vas-tu retirer de l'argent en France?
6. Qu'est-ce que tu feras si tu ne peux pas ouvrir de compte en banque en France?
7. Et si ta carte ne marche pas, que feras-tu alors?
8. Et si on te vole ton portefeuille?

Leçon B

Vocabulaire

4 Ce que je lis

*Écrivez les numéros 1–8 sur votre papier. Écoutez Stéphanie interviewer des passagers à la gare du Nord sur ce qu'ils lisent dans le train. Écrivez **F** si on lit de la fiction, ou **NF** si on ne lit pas de fiction.*

1. -Bonjour, mademoiselle. Qu'est-ce que vous lisez en ce moment dans le train?
   -Un roman de science-fiction de Jules Verne. Il est passionnant!
2. -Madame, excusez-moi. Quel type de livre lisez-vous?
   -Je lis une biographie de Charles de Gaulle. Un vrai homme politique.
3. -Monsieur. Est-ce que vous pouvez me dire ce que vous lisez?
   -Oui, bien sûr. C'est le dernier thriller de Stieg Larsson.
4. -Madame, quelle est votre type de lecture favorite?
   -J'adore les nouvelles. C'est facile et rapide comme lecture dans les transports. Je lis un recueil de nouvelles de Maupassant en ce moment.
5. -Excuse-moi. Tu peux me dire ce que tu lis?
   -Moi, je lis des mangas. J'adore ça!
6. -Madame, vous préférez quel genre de livres?
   -Je préfère un livre de poche… normalement un roman policier de Georges Simenon.
7. -Bonjour, mademoiselle. Est-ce que c'est un livre de poésie que vous lisez?
   -Non, c'est les mémoires de Simone de Beauvoir, une femme pour notre temps aussi.
8. -Bonjour, monsieur. Est-ce que vous lisez quelque chose dans le train?
   -Oui, une série d'articles sur l'économie. C'est une crise! Il faut se renseigner.

Grammaire

12 Dans le cours de littérature

Écrivez les numéros 1–7 sur votre papier. Écoutez les phrases. Puis, écrivez le genre de livres dont tout le monde se sert pour son cours de littérature.

1. L'histoire dont Sébastien se sert est dans un recueil de Maupassant.
2. L'anthologie poétique dont Martine et Chloé se servent est anglaise.
3. Les mangas dont Julie se sert sont japonais.
4. Le roman dont nous nous servons est un best-seller. Ça parle d'un crime à Paris. L'inspecteur est très intelligent.
5. Le dico dont Jérémy se sert est anglais-français.
6. Le roman policier dont Théo et Karim se servent est américain.
7. Le livre de Jules Verne dont Clarisse se sert est aussi un film.

Leçon C

Vocabulaire

4 Le courrier

Écrivez les numéros 1–6 sur votre papier. Écoutez chaque phrase, puis choisissez la lettre qui correspond à la chose ou la personne indiquée.

1. Tu peux la mettre dans la boîte aux lettres quand tu sors?
2. J'ai fini ma lettre à tante Adja en Côte-d'Ivoire. J'y vais maintenant.
3. Tiens, mon chéri. Il faut le mettre sur ton enveloppe. Non, en haut à droite.
4. Oui, bien sûr, monsieur. Ça coûte 2, 89€.
5. Elle est déjà passée; le courrier est sur la table.
6. Tu mets où tu habites ici, chéri. Non, à gauche.

Grammaire

12 À la poste

Écrivez les numéros 1–6 sur votre papier. Écoutez les phrases. Choisissez la réponse logique.

1. Tu préfères cette boite-ci ou celle-là pour envoyer tes cadeaux?
2. De quelle enveloppe avez-vous besoin?
3. Quelles lettres pèsent le plus?
4. Quelle adresse est la bonne?
5. Tu veux ces timbres-ci ou ceux-là?
6. Quel paquet est le plus gros?

Évaluation

A Évaluation de compréhension auditive

*Écrivez les numéros 1–8 sur votre papier. Écoutez David et Paulette discuter de la poste en France. Ensuite, écrivez **(V)** si les phrases que vous entendez sont vraies, ou **(F)** si elles sont fausses.*

David: Tu vas à la poste?
Paulette: Oui, j'ai besoin de retirer de l'argent et d'acheter des timbres.
David: Tu peux retirer de l'argent à la poste?
Paulette: Bien sûr, la poste a aussi un service bancaire. C'est très pratique!
David: De quoi penses-tu que j'aurai besoin pour ouvrir un compte chez eux?
Paulette: En général, ils demandent une carte d'identité et une adresse. Mais toi, comme tu es étudiant étranger, il faut que tu prennes ton passeport, je pense, et que tu aies une lettre de l'école.
David: Je peux venir avec toi? J'en profiterais pour changer mes dollars en euros au bureau de change et je demanderai au banquier si je peux ouvrir un compte.
Paulette: Oui, on y va?

David: Tu crois que je pourrai envoyer un colis à ma famille?
Paulette: Bien entendu. Ton colis est prêt?
David: Oui, le voici.
Paulette: Il faut mettre ton adresse.
David: Et les timbres?
Paulette: Et bien, tu demanderas à la postière. Elle te dira le prix de l'affranchissement.
David: D'accord. La poste en France, c'est super!

1. Paulette veut retirer de l'argent à la poste.
2. En France, la poste propose à la fois un service bancaire et un service postal.
3. David ne pourra pas ouvrir un compte à la poste parce qu'il n'est pas français.
4. Il faut une adresse et une carte d'identité pour acheter des timbres.
5. David peut changer son argent à la poste.
6. David peut changer de l'argent, envoyer un colis, et ouvrir un compte au même endroit.
7. David doit affranchir son colis à la poste.
8. L'employé de banque va aider David avec son colis.

Bilan cumulatif

II. Interpretive Communication: Audio Texts

Madison va en France pour les vacances. Avec son amie Sidney, elle regarde les guides touristiques. Écoutez le dialogue suivant deux fois, puis complétez les phrases.

Sidney: Tiens Madison, voilà un guide sur les régions de France. Il décrit les hôtels, les prestations et les descriptions des spécialités de chaque région. Le seul problème, ce n'est pas une édition de poche.

Madison: Oh, ça a l'air super pour planifier mon séjour. J'aime bien la liste des préparatifs de voyage qu'il y a. Oh, je n'arrive pas à me décider! Il y a aussi ces deux éditions de poche sur la Bourgogne et la côte d'Azur, et ce gros guide qui comprend tout et qui a aussi un bon dico à la fin.

Sidney: Je ne sais pas. À mon avis, il faut que tu fasses surtout attention aux bagages. On exigera que tu paies pour chaque kilo en plus de 32 kilos! Pourquoi pas acheter un bouquin sur place?

Madison: Tu as tout à fait raison. Je veux que mon séjour soit un peu planifié, au moins.... Je pourrais trouver ce que je veux là-bas et improviser. Finalement, je ne vais prendre que ce magazine sur la cuisine provençale.

Sidney: Bon, on va au ciné après? La dernière comédie de Dany Boon vient de sortir. J'ai vu la bande-annonce et ça a l'air vraiment drôle.

Madison: Excellente idée.

Unité 7

Leçon A

Vocabulaire

4 Quel beau tableau!

*Écrivez les numéros 1–7 sur votre papier. Écoutez Pablo et Chloé parler peinture. Ensuite, indiquez si les phrases que vous entendez sont vraies (**V**) ou fausses (**F**).*

Pablo: Salut, Chloé! Je ne savais pas que tu aimais peindre.
Chloé: Bien sûr! J'adore peindre en plein air. Mon atelier, c'est la nature!
Pablo: Qu'est-ce que tu peins?
Chloé: C'est un paysage. Regarde, au premier plan tu vois les gens sur la plage et à l'arrière-plan, la mer et les bateaux.
Pablo: C'est très beau. Est-ce que tu aimes les natures mortes?
Chloé: Pas vraiment. Je préfère peindre la vie, les saisons, les gens. J'adore les toiles de Monet. C'est mon inspiration. Tu peux me passer le pinceau là?

Pablo:	Celui-ci? Tu aimes les impressionnistes, alors?
Chloé:	Oui, mais j'aime aussi le fauvisme et le cubisme d'une manière différente.
Pablo:	Alors, tu peins des toiles modernes?
Chloé:	Non, j'aime avoir des modèles à regarder et je préfère peindre les choses de la vie réelle.
Pablo:	Et bien tu devrais continuer. J'adore ton style! À plus!

1. Pablo est surpris de découvrir que Chloé peint.
2. Chloé adore peindre dans son atelier.
3. Cette conversation a lieu dans un musée de beaux-arts.
4. Au premier plan du tableau de Chloé, il y a les bateaux et la mer.
5. Chloé n'aime pas beaucoup peindre des natures mortes.
6. Chloé adore les impressionnistes et Monet est son inspiration.
7. Chloé préfère peindre la vie imaginaire.

Grammaire

13 Les plus grands peintres!

*Écrivez les numéros 1–7 sur votre papier. Écoutez les phrases. Ensuite, indiquez si chaque phrase que vous entendez représent un fait (**F**) ou une opinion (**O**).*

1. *Impression, soleil levan*t est la peinture la plus sombre de Monet.
2. Renoir et Monet sont les peintres les plus connus des impressionnistes.
3. C'est la plus grande fête champêtre dans les jardins de Versailles.
4. La peinture de Van Gogh montre le café le plus charmant de Provence.
5. Les impressionnistes sont les peintres les plus importants.
6. Seurat est le plus grand peintre du XXème siècle.
7. Van Gogh est considéré un artiste expressionniste.

Leçon B

Vocabulaire

5 Ce que j'écoute.

Écrivez les numéros 1–6 sur votre papier. Écoutez Amina et Antoine discuter de leurs interprètes préférés. Puis choisissez la réponse qui correspond aux questions posées.

Antoine:	Qu'est-ce que tu écoutes?
Amina:	J'écoute "Ne me quitte pas" de Jacques Brel.
Antoine:	Tu n'es pas contente aujourd'hui?
Amina:	Pas du tout! J'adore Brel comme auteur et pour son interprétation si dramatique. Tu n'aimes pas les chansons à texte?
Antoine:	Si, mais moi, je préfère Serge Gainsbourg.
Amina:	Et Charles Aznavour, tu l'aimes?
Antoine:	Oui, j'aime ses chansons, et c'est un très bon interprète, je trouve.
Amina:	Oui, je pense aussi. Tu sais qu'on l'a nommé "Artiste de variétés du siècle"?
Antoine:	Vraiment? Quelle autre musique te plaît?
Amina:	Et bien, j'aime la pop, le rap, le jazz, et le swing. J'adore danser le swing aussi.
Antoine:	Ah bon, tu me montres.
Amina:	Maintenant?

Grammaire

13 La musique qui leur plaît

Écrivez les numéros 1–6 sur votre papier. Écoutez les conversations. Puis, mettez un + si la personne aime la chose mentionnée dans la question, ou un – si elle ne l'aime pas.

1. -Est-ce que la peinture française te plaît?
   -Oui, surtout les impressionnistes avec leurs tableaux peints en plein air.
2. -Est-ce que les chansons de Gainsbourg vous plaisent?
   -Oui, ses chansons nous plaisent plus que sa personne.

3. -Les chansons pop vous plaisent-elles?
   -Oui, elles nous plaisent mieux que le rock et le hip-hop.
4. -Est-ce que cette mélodie te plaît?
   -Non, elle ne me plaît pas du tout; j'ai mal à la tête.
5. -C'est de la musique classique?
   -Non, c'est la world. Ce qui me plaît, c'est la musique qui vient de l'Afrique.
6. -Les tableaux de Van Gogh te plaisent?
   -Non, je préfère ceux de Monet… les beaux paysages, la mer, le soleil.

Leçon C

Vocabulaire

4 Ah, la poésie!

*Écrivez les numéros 1–5 sur votre papier. Écoutez la conversation entre Manon et son père, puis indiquez si la phrase que vous entendez est vraie (**V**) ou fausse (**F**).*

Papa: Tu lis les fables de La Fontaine? C'est une figure de la littérature française!
Manon: Oui, c'est pour mon cours de français. On étudie la poésie du XVIIème siècle. Je dois choisir une fable du recueil et la présenter en classe.
Papa: Quand j'avais ton âge, j'adorais la satire dans "Les animaux malades de la peste."
Manon: Moi, "Le corbeau et le renard" me plait beaucoup. J'aime la morale et surtout comment le renard ment au corbeau pour obtenir le fromage. C'est assez amusant. Je connais des gens comme ça.
Papa: À mon avis, les poèmes de Victor Hugo sont meilleurs. Quand tu lis c'est comme si tu voyais vraiment le brouillard ou l'aube.
Manon: Chacun ses goûts!

1. Manon lit un poème de Victor Hugo.
2. Elle lit un recueil parce qu'elle doit faire une présentation en classe.
3. "Les animaux malades de la peste" et "Le corbeau et le renard" sont des fables de La Fontaine.
4. Manon connaît des gens qui ressemblent aux animaux dans la fable.
5. Le père de Manon préfère les poèmes de Jacques Prévert.

Grammaire

15 Pour vs. Pour que

Écrivez les numéros 1–5 sur votre papier. Écoutez les phrases. Choisissez la réponse logique.

1. Pourquoi veux-tu que je lise les poèmes de Jacques Prévert?
2. Pourquoi Mamy regarde-t-elle son album de photos si souvent?
3. Pourquoi les poètes et les romanciers du XIXème siècle mettent-ils toujours le brouillard dans leurs œuvres?
4. Pourquoi regardes-tu ma collection de livres?
5. Pourquoi lis-tu le dictionnaire?

Évaluation

A Evaluation de compréhension auditive

Deux artistes

*Écoutez Kevin et Annie discuter de leurs intérêts artistiques. Ensuite, indiquez si chaque phrase que vous entendez et vraie (**V**) ou fausse (**F**).*

Annie: Tu aimes les arts?
Kevin: Bien sûr, toutes les formes artistiques me plaisent, mais je préfère la peinture et la musique.

Annie:	Moi aussi, j'aime la peinture. Quel mouvement tu préfères? Pour moi, c'est l'impressionnisme, le fauvisme, le néo-impressionnisme.
Kevin:	J'adore le fauvisme et les tableaux de Vlaminck pour les couleurs vives et l'intensité de l'expression plus que les peintres néo-impressionnistes. Et toi?
Annie:	Moi, je suis fan de Monet. Quelle autre forme d'art tu aimes?
Kevin:	Moi, j'adore la musique. Je joue de la guitare dans un groupe et je suis auteur-compositeur et interprète.
Annie:	Super! Quel genre de musique vous jouez?
Kevin:	On joue de la musique folklorique et du rock. On a même sorti un album avec des chansons poétiques et réalistes.
Annie:	J'aimerais beaucoup l'écouter. Moi, tu sais, j'aime la littérature et j'écris beaucoup de poèmes et de fables que je publie sur Internet. On pourrait peut-être travailler ensemble sur de nouvelles chansons.
Kevin:	Ça, c'est une idée géniale. Avec nos intérêts artistiques, on est sûr de réussir et de devenir célèbre!

1. Annie et Kevin parlent de cinéma.
2. Kevin préfère la peinture et la littérature.
3. Annie aime le néo-impressionnisme.
4. Kevin admire le peintre Vlaminck.
5. Annie est fan de Seurat.
6. Les deux ados aiment la musique.
7. Kevin joue de la musique classique.
8. Les deux ados vont écrire des nouvelles ensemble.

Unité 8

Leçon A

Vocabulaire

3 L'histoire de France

*Écrivez les numéros 1–6 sur votre papier. Écoutez Camille et sa mère parler de la Révolution française. Ensuite, indiquez si les phrases sont vraies (**V**) ou fausses (**F**).*

Maman:	Regarde, Camille, le beau livre que je t'ai acheté sur la Révolution française!
Camille:	On peut le lire maintenant maman? Ça m'intéresse beaucoup!
Maman:	Si tu veux. Tu te rappelles, l'année dernière quand la maîtresse vous a raconté l'histoire du roi Louis XVI et de sa famille?
Camille:	Oui, un peu. Quand on a visité Versailles avec l'école?
Maman:	Oui. Qu'est-ce que tu as aimé?
Camille:	La grande salle avec les miroirs et la belle chambre de la reine. Aussi sur les portraits, la reine avait de belles robes et des perruques ridicules.
Maman:	Qu'est-ce qui est arrivé au dernier roi qui a vécu à Versailles?
Camille:	Il a fait ses adieux à sa famille et on l'a «guillomé.»
Maman:	Oui, il est mort guillotiné.
Camille:	Il avait fait un discours devant les États généraux mais on l'a fait prisonnier quant même! Et sa femme, elle est morte aussi.
Maman:	Très bien. Et bien, tu te souviens de beaucoup de choses. C'est bien! Lisons ton nouveau livre alors!

Grammaire

13 Louis XVI et Marie-Antoinette

Écrivez les numéros 1–6 sur votre papier. Écoutez les phrases suivantes et associez-les à la bonne illustration.

1. Louis XVI a fait venir Marie-Antoinette en France.
2. Louis XVI et Marie-Antoinette ont fait préparer de bons repas pour leurs invités à Versailles.

3. Marie-Antoinette a fait construire un petit village à Versailles.
4. Louis XVI a fait venir les États généraux en 1789.
5. Le gouvernement français l'a fait prisonnier.
6. Le nouveau gouvernement l'a fait guillotiner.

Leçon B

Vocabulaire

3 Jeanne dans le marché du travail

Écrivez les numéros 1–6. Écoutez le parcours de Jeanne pour trouver un emploi. Si l'ordre des deux phrases est logique, écrivez ***oui****; sinon, écrivez* ***non****.*

1. Jeanne finit ses études universitaires.
   Elle regarde les petites annonces en ligne.
2. Jeanne envoie son CV et sa lettre à Bruxelles.
   Elle écrit son CV où elle parle de ses connaissances acquises.
3. Jeanne envoie son CV et sa lettre.
   Le Chef du Personnel à la Commission lui téléphone et lui demande de se présenter pour une interview.
4. Le Chef du Personnel de la Commission Européenne l'embauche.
   Elle va à Bruxelles par le train pour un entretien.
5. Jeanne signe un contrat d'une année avec le Chef du Personnel.
   Elle entre dans son bureau pour la première fois.
6. Jeanne reçoit son premier chèque.
   Elle commence à travailler à plein-temps à la Commission.

Grammaire

12 Qu'est-ce qui s'est passé après?

Écrivez les numéros 1–6. Ensuite, écoutez les phrases. Si la phrase est logique, écrivez L. Sinon, écrivez I pour illogique.

1. Après été embauchée par une entreprise, Coralie s'est inscrite à l'université.
2. Après s'être spécialisée en chimie, Coralie est devenue pilote.
3. Après avoir trouvé une bonne petite annonce en ligne, Coralie a écrit une lettre de motivation.
4. Après avoir envoyé son CV à l'entreprise, Coralie a été convoquée pour un entretien.
5. Après avoir parlé à Coralie, le Chef du Personnel l'a embauché.
6. Après avoir travaillé pour deux semaines, Coralie a reçu son premier chèque.

Leçon C

Vocabulaire

2 Quel débat!

Écoutez le débat entre Juliette et Luc sur l'assurance maladie. Puis, identifiez la personne décrite.

Juliette: Toi, tu es pour ou contre une assurance médicale privée?

Khaled: Personnellement, je suis contre. Premièrement, parce que les gens qui n'ont pas les moyens n'auront pas accès aux soins et deuxièmement parce que je pense que les assurances vont devenir plus chères, mais pas la qualité.

Juliette: Je suis de ton avis dans un sens mais si les gens payaient leur propre assurance, ils feraient plus attention à leurs visites médicales et ils n'iraient pas assez souvent à l'hôpital.

Khaled: J'ai un autre point de vue. Pour moi, se faire soigner est un droit. Une personne âgée doit avoir le droit d'aller chez le kiné si elle tombe. Par contre, je suis d'avis qu'il doit y avoir plus de contrôles par la Sécurité Sociale pour éviter les abus.

Juliette: Je dois partir. On peut discuter du sujet davantage chez moi après les cours si tu veux. Dix-sept heures, ça te convient?

Khaled: Oui, bonne idée!

Grammaire

13 Papy à l'hôpital

Écrivez les numéros 1–6 sur votre papier. Écoutez le dialogue entre Chantal et son frère Théo. Ensuite, choisissez la bonne réponse à la question que vous entendez.

Chantal:	Écoute, Papy est à l'hôpital.
Théo:	Qu'est-ce qui s'est passé?
Chantal:	Il avait acheté un billet de concert, mais il est tombé devant le théâtre en sortant.
Théo:	Mamy était avec lui ?
Chantal:	Non, elle avait pris rendez-vous chez le kiné.
Théo:	Il avait sa carte d'assurance sur lui?
Chantal:	Oui, dans son portefeuille.
Théo:	On lui a servi un dîner?
Chantal:	Non, il avait déjà mangé à la maison.
Théo:	Mamy est avec lui maintenant?
Chantal:	Oui, j'y suis allée avec elle, mais j'ai dû partir pour travailler.
Théo:	Je vais à l'hôpital tout de suite!

1. Pourquoi le grand-père de Chantal et Théo était-il en ville?
2. Pourquoi sa femme n'était-elle pas avec lui?
3. Le grand-père avait-il sa carte d'assurance sur lui?
4. À l'hôpital a-t-on servi un repas au grand-père?
5. Où Chantal était-elle allée avant de travailler?
6. Qu'est-ce que Théo va faire?

Évaluation

A Évaluation de compréhension auditive

Voyage scolaire

Écoutez Benoît et Margot discuter de leurs projets et voyages d'études. Ensuite, complétez la phrase avec un mot ou une expression convenable.

Benoît:	Qu'est-ce que vous allez faire comme voyage cette année avec ta classe d'histoire? Vous allez aller au château de Versailles?
Margot:	Non, on a étudié la Révolution française l'année dernière. Cette année, on étudie l'Europe et la France de l'après-guerre.
Benoît:	Pas de roi et de reine, alors vous allez visiter l'Assemblée?
Margot:	Bien mieux, cette année on va à Bruxelles pendant deux jours. On va visiter la Commission européenne.
Benoît:	Super! Moi, je voudrais travailler là plus tard.
Margot:	Si tu me donnes une lettre de candidature et un C.V., je peux les donner pour toi....
Benoît:	C'est une bonne idée. Je dois faire un stage cet été et la Commission Européenne, ce serait génial! J'ai déjà regardé leur site et je sais qu'ils embauchent des stagiaires pendant l'été, et qu'en plus ils leur donnent un petit salaire.
Margot:	D'accord, alors rédige ta lettre et donne-la moi. Toi, tu peux m'aider avec mon projet sur la santé en France?
Benoît:	Bien-sûr, qu'est-ce que tu dois faire ?
Margot:	Je dois présenter le pour et le contre de l'assurance privée comparée à notre assurance sociale.
Benoît:	Tu peux commencer par une question: Est-ce un droit ou un privilège de se faire soigner? Et puis tu introduis ta position.
Margot:	Super. Tu peux venir chez moi ce soir?
Benoît:	Oui, dix-huit heures, ça te va?

1. Margot a déjà étudié... dans son cours d'histoire l'année dernière.
2. Margot fait une excursion à... en....

3. Benoît voudrait faire un stage à la....
4. Si on l'embauche, il recevra un....
5. Margot doit faire une présentation sur l'....

Bilan cumulatif

II. Interpretive Coummunication: Audio texts

Écoutez le dialogue suivant deux fois, puis répondez aux questions.

-Il paraît que ton mari est tombé d'un arbre ce week-end en essayant de couper les branches?

-Il s'est cassé le bras droit et il a mal. Il ne va pas pouvoir travailler pendant un moment, vu qu'il dessine avec la main droite.

-Par contre on peut dire qu'il a eu beaucoup de chance que cela lui soit arrivé en France et pas aux États-Unis où tout le monde n'a pas d'assurance médicale.

-Ah, ne m'en parle pas. Ma sœur m'a dit que là-bas se faire soigner est un privilège, alors qu'en France c'est un droit. Qu'on ait les moyens ou pas, on peut tous aller chez le médecin, consulter un psychiatre ou voir un kiné; c'est quand même formidable; tu crois pas?

-Complètement! Je suis entièrement de ton avis. C'est fou cette histoire d'assurance médicale privée en Amérique. Je ne comprends pas qu'au vingt-et-unième siècle on n'a pas tous droit à se faire soigner.

-Évidemment je ne suis pas économiste et je ne comprends rien à la politique, mais je suis pour le système social français et entièrement contre le système capitaliste américain.

Unité 9

Leçon A

Vocabulaire

4 Une mauvaise journée

*Écrivez les numéros 1–5 sur votre papier. Écoutez Sandrine et Ahmed discuter de la matinée de Sandrine. Ensuite, dites si les phrases que vous entendez sont vraies (**V**) ou fausses (**F**).*

Ahmed: Pourquoi tu étais en retard ce matin? Tu ne semblais pas très bien en cours de maths.

Sandrine: Oh, tu ne sais pas ce qui s'est passé! D'abord, je me suis réveillée en retard et quand je me suis levée j'ai tout juste évité de trébucher sur mon livre de révision pour le bac.

Ahmed: Tu as aussi évité l'interro-surprise pendant le cours de français.

Sandrine: Oui, je sais. Je me sens honteuse. J'étais incapable de me rappeler quels cours on avait, alors j'ai pris les mauvais cahiers. Mon père m'a emmenée. Quand on a quitté la maison, la grêle a commencé à tomber, et on a évité de se faire arrêter devant le lycée.

Ahmed: Et bien, ce n'est vraiment pas de chance.

Sandrine: Et en plus, je me suis fait bousculé dans les couloirs et je n'ai pas pu éviter les commérages de Marie-Hélène pendant le cours de maths.

Ahmed: Peut-être que tu aurais dû rester chez toi!

1. Sandrine a évité l'interro-surprise de français.
2. Sandrine a pris un taxi au lycée.
3. Le père de Sandrine s'est faire arrêter devant le lycée.
4. Sandrine s'est réveillée en retard.
5. La grêle a commencé à tomber ce matin.

Grammaire

12 Et si et si!

Écrivez les numéros 1–6 sur votre papier. Écoutez les descriptions des situations. Ensuite, faites correspondre l'illustration avec la phrase que vous entendez.

1. S'il s'était levé à l'heure, il n'aurait pas raté le bus.
2. Si nous avions bossé plus auparavant, nous aurions réussi au bac.
3. Si vous aviez évité de trébucher, vous ne seriez pas cassé la jambe.
4. Si Amanda n'avait pas séché les cours, elle aurait dû faire un exposé.

5. Si j'étais venu en bus, j'aurais évité la grêle.
6. Si Julien ne s'était pas senti heureux, il n'aurait pas fait la connaissance de Julie.

Leçon B

Vocabulaire

5 Comment sont-ils?

Écrivez les numéros 1–6 sur votre papier. Ensuite, écoutez les descriptions des personnes. Finalement, choisissez la bonne photo.

1. Aminata est grande. Elle a les cheveux courts et bouclés. Elle est mince et a une trentaine d'années. Elle est d'origine africaine.
2. La maman d'Anne est d'origine méditerranéenne. . Elle a une quarantaine d'années. Elle a les cheveux noirs longs et raides. Elle est musclée et mince. Elle est vêtue d'une robe à pois sur cette photo.
3. Mon grand-père, c'est un type costaud. Il est d'origine scandinave. Il a les cheveux blonds et bouclés, et il est fort. Il porte une chemise à carreaux sur la photo. Il a une soixantaine d'années.
4. Alima est d'origine arabe. Elle a une trentaine d'années et elle est vêtue d'un jean et d'un chemisier à carreaux. Elle a les cheveux mi-longs et frisés.
5. Julien, c'est un type africain. Il est chauve et costaud. Il a une quarantaine d'années.
6. Ma tante est grande et mince avec les cheveux marron courts et raides. Elle porte une jupe et un chemisier à rayures, un ensemble qui n'est pas très chic. Elle a une cinquantaine d'années et est vraiment sympa.

Grammaire

15 C'est à qui?

Écrivez les numéros 1–5 sur votre papier. Écoutez les mini-dialogues. Dites à qui appartient chaque chose; écrivez son prénom.

1. -C'est ton maillot, Christian?
   -Non, ce n'est pas le mien. Le mien est plus grand.
   -C'est celui de Julien?
   -Oui, c'est probablement le sien. Il est plus petit que moi.
2. -C'est à qui cette trousse, Chantal?
   -Ce n'est pas la mienne. J'ai un taille-crayon dans le mien.
   -C'est à ta camarade Anne-Marie?
   -Oui, c'est probablement la sienne. Elle aime le bleu.
3. -Ce sont à qui, ces magazines, Cédric?
   -Ce sont à mes amis Jean et Luc.
   -Tu es sûr, ce sont les leurs?
   -Oui, maman; ils aiment les bandes dessinées dans ces magazines.
4. -C'est votre chien, Benoît?
   -Non, ce n'est pas le nôtre. Le nôtre est la même taille, mais il est noir. Je crois que c'est le chien de M. et Mme Blanchard.
   -Je vais vérifier si c'est le leur.
5. -À qui vas-tu rendre cette casserole?
   -Je ne sais pas.
   -Réfléchis bien. C'était dans le caravane. Quand tu as fait du camping, qui a sorti la casserole?
   -Juliette et Sylvie, les sœurs LeBlanc. Je sais que c'est la leur.

Leçon C

Vocabulaire

4 Quelle surprise!

*Écrivez les numéros 1–5 sur votre papier. Ensuite, écoutez la discussion entre Aminata et l'animateur M. Aknouch sur un concours vidéo. Finalement, indiquez si les phrases que vous entendez sont vraies **(V)** ou fausses **(F)**.*

M. Aknouch:	Alors Aminata, tu as gagné le concours de plus belle vidéo musicale sur YouTube.
Aminata:	Oui, je ne m'y attendais pas. Quelle surprise!
M. Aknouch:	Tu as eu l'idée de mettre ta vidéo comment?
Aminata:	C'est mon frère qui m'a parlé du concours. Il m'a dit que je devrais essayer et comme on avait cette vidéo de la fête d'une copine, alors....
M. Aknouch:	Tu es charmante dans le clip avec ta robe à rayures.
Aminata:	Merci beaucoup. J'étais complètement choquée de gagner, mais maintenant je me sens surexcitée et je veux continuer et faire d'autres vidéos et peut-être devenir célèbre!

1. Aminata a gagné le concours de plus belle vidéo musicale sur YouTube.
2. Aminata savait qu'elle allait gagner.
3. Son père a eu l'idée de mettre la vidéo sur YouTube.
4. Aminata a filmé la vidéo à un mariage.
5. Aminata se sent attristée.

Grammaire

19 On est branché!

Écrivez les numéros 1–5 sur votre papier. Écoutez les phrases suivantes. Faites correspondre la phrase à une image.

1. Vincent a posté toutes les vidéos de ses vacances sur YouTube.
2. J'ai vu quelques messages de mes copains sur mon réseau social.
3. La plupart des parents dans cet immeuble achètent des tablettes pour leurs enfants.
4. Sandrine regarde ses mails chaque jour et ses textos toutes les dix minutes.
5. Rachid et Jean-Pierre parlent de tout et n'importe quoi en ligne.

Évaluation

A Évaluation de compréhension auditive

Récit d'un vol

Écoutez Marion décrire à un policier le vol auquel elle vient d'assister. Ensuite, dites oui ou non si elle a aidé avec les catégories ci-dessous.

Le policier:	Bonjour, mademoiselle. Vous avez vu ce qui s'est passé? Vous pouvez me décrire la scène?
Marion:	Oui, je retournais chez moi quand j'ai vu un homme sortir de la banque avec une arme dans une main et un sac à dos dans l'autre.
Le policier:	Pouvez-vous me décrire cet homme?
Marion:	Bien entendu. Il était grand et costaud avec des cheveux raides et courts. Je pense qu'il avait une trentaine d'années. Il semblait être excité par ce qu'il venait de faire.
Le policier:	Vous avez fait attention à comment il était vêtu?
Marion:	Il portait un jean délavé et une liquette rouge.
Le policier:	Il avait un masque?
Marion:	Non, pas de masque, juste une casquette de baseball bleue. Le sac à dos était rouge.
Le policier:	Qu'est-ce qu'il a fait après être sorti de la banque?
Marion:	Il a couru jusqu'à la rue et a arrêté la voiture d'un vieux monsieur. Il lui a volé sa voiture.
Le policier:	Merci pour toutes ces informations, mademoiselle. Où puis-je vous contacter si j'ai plus de questions?
Marion:	Vous pouvez m'envoyer un texto au 06.25.35.12 ou vous pouvez m'envoyer un mail.
Le policier:	Merci de votre aide et bonne journée.

1. Description physique
2. Description des cheveux
3. Description d'âge
4. Description psychologique
5. Description de vêtments
6. Description de caractère
7. Description d'actions
8. Description de bijoux

Unité 10
Leçon A

Vocabulaire
4 Fabriqué au Maroc

Écrivez les numéros 1–8. Écoutez David et sa maman discuter des produits qu'ils achètent au Maroc. Ensuite, dites si les phrases que vous entendez sont vraies (V) ou fausses (F).

David: Alors, qu'est-ce que tu as trouvé chez ce marchand marocain?
Maman: J'ai trouvé des lunettes Dior pour ta tante et une montre Cartier pour ta grand-mère.
David: Maman, tu sais que ce sont des faux. Regarde, tes lunettes ont été fabriquées au Vietnam et ta montre en Chine, bien sûr.
Maman: C'est bien ce que je craignais mais ta grand-mère, elle va pouvoir impressioner ses copines quand même.
David: Tu sais, au Maroc, il faut acheter des produits locaux. Les parfums, la maroquinerie de luxe et les bijoux sont tous des faux et on risque d'avoir des problèmes avec les douanes françaises.
Maman: Alors, le tee-shirt Nike que j'ai acheté à ton père, c'est un faux aussi?
David: Je ne sais pas. Beaucoup de produits américains sont fabriqués en Chine ou au Mexique alors.... Regarde, tu peux acheter de beaux sacs à mains en cuir ici ou une ceinture pour oncle Edouard.
Maman: Oui, et bien, mais un sac à main Vuitton, ce serait plus chic!
David: Maman!!! Quelle snob tu es!!!

1. David pense que sa mère est snob.
2. Beaucoup de produits américains sont fabriqués en Chine et au Mexique.
3. Les lunettes Dior que la maman de David a achetés ont été fabriquées en Asie.
4. David recommande à sa mère d'acheter les produits locaux au Maroc.
5. La maman de David a acheté une vraie montre Cartier pour la grand-mère.
6. Les produits de luxe pas chers au Maroc sont en général des faux.
7. La mère de David craint que le tee-shirt Nike du Père de David soit un faux.
8. David recommande que sa mère achète une ceinture en cuir pour l'oncle Edouard.

5 Les produits de luxe

Écrivez les numéros 1–5 sur votre papier. Écoutez Rachida et Caroline discuter de l'industrie de luxe française. Ensuite, écrivez une réponse brève pour chaque question que vous entendez.

Rachida: Alors, ton exposé pour la classe d'économie, comment ça se passe?
Caroline: Super, j'ai trouvé plein d'info sur l'industrie de luxe et j'ai pu parler à quelques personnes qui travaillent dans le secteur et qui m'ont donnée plein d'idées. J'ai même trouvé un stage pour l'été chez Guerlain.
Rachida: Le parfumeur? Tu as de la chance.
Caroline: Guerlain ne fait pas que du parfum. Ils ont toute une ligne de produits de beauté également et c'est un des seuls parfumeurs qui fabrique toujours son parfum avec de vraies essences de fleurs.
Rachida: Oui, c'est vrai que la plupart des produits de luxe sont fabriqués à l'étranger maintenant. Moi je trouve des montres Cartier et des tee-shirts Chanel bon marché quand je vais en Tunisie l'été.
Caroline: Oui, mais ce sont des faux et tu risques d'être arrêté par les douanes françaises pour avoir des faux. Les produits de luxe français comme la joaillerie, la faïence, la maroquinerie et les vêtements de marques sont fabriqués en France. Et c'est un secteur en pleine expansion. Par exemple, la maison Hermès...
Rachida: Celle qui fait les foulards en soie?
Caroline: Oui, et bien, ils vont ouvrir deux nouvelles usines cette année.
Rachida: Pourtant, Hermès c'est très cher. Qui achète leurs produits?
Caroline: Les États-Unis, la Chine, les pays arabes...La France a 40 % du marché mondial des produits de luxe.

Rachida: Et bien, c'est peut-être dans ce secteur que je devrais chercher du travail alors. Tu as eu des réductions sur certains produits au moins.

Caroline: Non, mais la maison LVMH m'a offert une carte cadeau pour l'une de leurs boutiques!

1. Caroline fait un exposé sur quoi?
2. Où est-ce que Caroline a pu trouver des informations?
3. Que va faire Rachida pendant l'été?
4. Dans quoi se spécialise la maison Guerlain?
5. Que trouve Rachida de pas cher en Tunisie?
6. Où sont fabriqués les produits de luxe français?
7. Quelle société est connue pour ses foulards en soie?
8. Quel pourcentage du marché mondial du luxe représente la France?

Leçon B

Vocabulaire

4 Tu travailles pour qui?

Écrivez les numéros 1–6 sur votre papier. Écoutez les personnes décrire où elles travaillent. Ensuite, choisissez la lettre qui correspond au lieu de travail.

1. Je m'appelle Amina. Moi, je travaille pour une grande compagnie française dans le secteur de la cosmétologie. On vend nos produits dans l'eurozone, en Amérique du Nord, et en Asie.
2. Bonjour. Mon nom est Rachid. Je travaille dans l'épicerie du coin. Mes clients habitent dans mon quartier.
3. Salut, moi c'est Arnaud. Je travaille pour Apple à Paris. Vous connaissez les produits d'Apple, n'est-ce pas?
4. Moi, c'est Isabelle. Je suis américaine, mais ça fait longtemps que je travaille ici en France dans ce bureau qui gère les opérations de Danone dans le monde.
5. Bonjour. Je m'appelle Julien et j'ai ma propre boulangerie aux environs de Paris.
6. Je suis Brigitte. Je travaille dans le secteur agroalimentaire; on a des filiales partout dans le monde

5 Je travaille chez GM.

Écrivez les numéros 1–6 sur votre papier. Écoutez l'histoire et, ensuite, répondez aux questions que vous entendez.

Julie voulait s'éloigner de Paris et de sa famille après ses études. Elle a eu de la chance de trouver un stage au siège social de GM à Detroit. D'abord, elle a commencé par servir le café et faire de petits travaux au service comptabilité. Puis, elle a travaillé au service ressources humaines et au service vente. Aujourd'hui, elle est directrice des ventes dans une filiale de GM à Paris où elle supervise la vente de voiture fabriquées aux USA.

1. Qu'est-ce que Julie voulait faire après ses études?
   A. Elle voulait faire le tour du monde.
   B. Elle voulait s'éloigner de Paris et de sa famille.
   C. Elle voulait trouver un travail à Paris.
2. Où Julie a-t-elle trouvé un stage?
   A. Elle a fait un stage chez GM à Paris.
   B. Elle a fait un stage chez Renault.
   C. Elle a fait un stage chez GM à Détroit.
3. Qu'est-ce qu'elle a dû faire d'abord dans cette compagnie?
   A. D'abord, elle a servi le café et fait de petits travaux.
   B. D'abord elle a travaillé comme comptable.
   C. D'abord, elle est devenue directrice du service des ventes.
4. Dans quels services a-t-elle travaillé?
   A. Au service comptabilité, ressources humaines, et vente.
   B. Au service comptabilité, gestion, et secrétariat.
   C. Au service comptabilité, ressources humaines, et marketing.
5. Quelle est son poste aujourd'hui?
   A. Julie est directrice du marketing chez GM à Paris.
   B. Julie est directrice des ventes chez GM à Détroit.
   C. Julie est directrice des ventes chez GM à Paris.

6. Où est fabriqué le produit qu'elle vend?
   A. Il est fabriqué aux États-Unis.
   B. Il est fabriqué en France.
   C. Il est fabriqué au Mexique.

Leçon C

Vocabulaire

4 Tu fais quoi?

Écrivez les numéros 1–6 sur votre papier. Écoutez les descriptions. Puis, faites correspondre la description avec la bonne illustration.

1. Voici madame Roger. Elle travaille comme vendeuse chez Carrefour.
2. Ça, c'est Monsieur Dupont. Il est PDG chez Dior.
3. Voici la DRH de la SNCF, Madame Radjad.
4. C'est Julien, le nouveau comptable au département comptabilité de chez Renault.
5. Je te présente Madame Longchamp, la secrétaire du PDG de Danone.
6. Ça c'est le responsable marketing de chez BMW. Il s'appelle Monsieur Garcia.

5 Le travail en France

Écrivez les numéros 1–6 sur votre papier. Écoutez la conversation entre Marc et Henrike, une stagiaire allemande. Ensuite, indiquez si les phrases que vous entendez sont vraies (V) ou fausses (F).

Marc: Alors, comment s'est passé ta première semaine de stage dans la société?

Henrike: C'était très intéressant, mais difficile aussi. En Allemagne, tout est beaucoup plus structuré, je pense, et on travaille plus.

Marc: Comment ça?

Henrike: Ici, c'est assez rigide. Tu as un chef qui a fait des études et tu dois suivre la hiérarchie. En Allemagne, chacun propose des idées et on obtient un poste en travaillant dur pas juste parce qu'on est allée à une grande école.

Marc: C'est vrai qu'ici on a peur du PDG, même si parfois il ne fait pas grand-chose.

Henrike: Oui, et puis, vous êtes toujours en pause. Pause-café, pause-conversation, pause-portable. Nous, on travaille non-stop jusqu'au déjeuner et on ne se plaint pas.

Marc: Tu as fait un stage dans quel département en Allemagne?

Henrike: J'étais au service marketing chez Mercedes. Il y avait beaucoup de jeunes qui donnaient leurs idées et le responsable marketing avait juste 35 ans.

Marc: Vraiment? Ici, notre PDG a plus de 60 ans et le responsable marketing doit prendre sa retraite à la fin de l'année. Avec la mondialisation, il va falloir que l'on s'adapte comme en Allemagne et aux États-Unis.

Henrike: Oui, mais je pense que votre marketing ici est bien alors.

1. Henrike vient d'être embauché à plein temps.
2. Henrike trouve les compagnies françaises hiérarchiques.
3. Marc n'a pas peur du PDG.
4. On travaille plus en Allemagne.
5. Le PDG d'Henrike en Allemagne était plus âgé que le PDG de Marc en France.
6. Henrike n'aime pas le marketing en France.

Évaluation

A Évaluation de compréhension auditive

Le travail et l'économie

Écrivez les numéros 1–8 sur votre papier. Écoutez une femme et un homme discuter des métiers des membres de leur famille. Ensuite, écrivez une réponse brève à la question que vous entendez.

Madame Picard: Alors, ta nièce a eu le travail chez LVMH?

Monsieur Boucher: Oui, elle a commencé lundi aux ressources humaines.

Madame Picard:	Elle est DRH?
Monsieur Boucher:	Non, elle est assistante de la DRH. Elle est super contente.
Madame Picard:	En tout cas, c'est un bon travail ! C'est une multinationale et elle travaille dans le secteur des produits de luxe qui est en pleine expansion. Elle aura peut-être des avantages pour acheter du bon champagne ou des vêtements et des parfums de marques pour moins cher.
Monsieur Boucher:	Et toi, ton petit-fils, il travaille toujours chez Apple aux États-Unis?
Madame Picard:	Oui, ça fait longtemps qu'il est là-bas. Il voulait s'éloigner de la France. Mais maintenant qu'il est marié, il voudrait rentrer en France et travailler pour une filiale d'Apple à Paris.
Monsieur Boucher:	Qu'est-ce qu'il fait déjà ?
Madame Picard:	Il travaille au service marketing. Il est responsable.
Monsieur Boucher:	Et bien, lui aussi, a bien réussi!
Madame Picard:	Oui, ma fille est très fière, et mon beau-fils adore tous les gadgets électroniques que son fils lui achète.
Monsieur Boucher:	Et ta petite-fille, qu'est-ce qu'elle fait maintenant qu'elle a fini ses études?
Madame Picard:	Elle a aussi trouvé du travail, dans une PME. Elle est au service des ventes et choisit et commande de nouveaux vêtements pour 1, 2, 3. Elle adore son poste et surtout elle voulait s'éloigner de Paris.
Monsieur Boucher:	1, 2, 3, leurs vêtements sont fabriqués en France?
Madame Picard:	Non, surtout en Chine et en Tunisie.
Monsieur Boucher:	C'est dommage! Maintenant tout est fabriqué dans d'autres pays.
Madame Picard:	À moins que tu t'habilles chez Dior, Chanel ou Saint Laurent…

1. Où travaille la nièce de Monsieur Boucher?
2. Qu'est-ce qu'elle fait dans la multinationale?
3. Est-ce que c'est un bon travail? Pourquoi?
4. Pourquoi le petit-fils de Madame Picard habite aux États-Unis?
5. Pour quelle compagnie travaille-t-il?
6. Pourquoi veut-il renter en France?
7. Dans quel type d'entreprise est-ce que la petite-fille de Madame Picard travaille?
8. Est-ce que les vêtements de chez 1,2,3 sont fabriqués en France?

Bilan cumulatif

II. Interpretive Communication: Audio texts

Écoutez le dialogue entre Taylor et son meilleur ami, puis répondez aux questions.

-Ah non, tu ne vas pas nous quitter!

-Si, j'ai besoin de perfectionner mon français, et pour ça je dois aller en France pour au moins un an.

-Mais qu'est-ce que tu vas y apprendre que tu ne peux pas apprendre ici? Ta prof est française.

-Oui, elle est française et formidable mais elle ne peut pas remplacer l'expérience sur place. Je voudrais m'éloigner de la culture américaine et m'immerger le plus possible dans la culture et la langue française. Ça fait longtemps que j'en rêve; je vais observer les Français et m'adapter à leur mode de vie. Je pourrai parler français jour et nuit, mon désir le plus cher!

-Comment vas-tu faire pour vivre?

-J'y ai pensé. Je vais chercher un stage dans le service marketing d'une multinationale américaine dont le siège social est dans la capitale. Comme tu sais, j'ai suivi des cours de marketing à l'université.

-Quelle bonne idée, même si je suis triste de te voir partir.

Correlation of Common Core State Standards

Common Core State Standards—ELA	Standards for Learning Languages	*T´es branché?* Level 3
Key Ideas and Details		
Reading 1–3	**Interpretive (Reading, Listening, Viewing)**	**Page Number**
1. Read closely to determine what the text says explicitly and to make logical inferences from it; cite specific textual evidence when writing or speaking to support conclusions drawn from the text 2. Determine central ideas or themes of a text and analyze their development; summarize key supporting details and ideas 3. Analyze how and why individuals, events, or ideas develop and interact over the course of a text	**Interpretive Communication (Standard 1.2)**	2, 3, 4, 5, 8, 9, 10, 11, 12, 19, 20, 23, 24, 27, 28, 29, 30, 31, 32, 48, 49, 50, 51, 52, 53, 54, 55, 65, 66, 67, 73, 74, 75, 76, 77, 78, 79, 80, 81, 82, 83, 84, 85, 90, 91, 93, 94, 95, 96, 97, 98, 99, 100, 101, 103, 106, 107, 108, 109, 110, 111, 112, 113, 114, 115, 116, 117, 118, 119, 120, 121, 122, 123, 124, 125, 126, 127, 128, 129, 130, 131, 134, 135, 137, 138, 139, 140, 141, 144, 145, 146, 147, 148, 149, 150, 151, 152, 154, 156, 157, 158, 159, 160, 161, 162, 163, 164, 165, 166, 167, 168, 169, 170, 171, 172, 173, 174, 175, 176, 177, 178, 179, 180, 181, 182, 183, 184, 185, 186, 187, 189, 192, 193, 194, 195, 196, 197, 198, 201, 202, 203, 204, 205, 206, 207, 208, 209, 210, 211, 212, 213, 214, 215, 216, 218, 220, 221, 222, 223, 224, 225, 226, 227, 228, 229, 230, 231, 232, 233, 234, 235, 236, 237, 238, 240, 241, 242, 243, 244, 245, 246, 247, 248, 249, 250, 251, 255, 256, 257, 258, 259, 262, 263, 265, 266, 267, 268, 269, 270, 271, 272, 273, 274, 275, 276, 278, 279, 280, 281, 282, 285, 286, 287, 288, 289, 290, 292, 293, 295, 298, 299, 300, 301, 302, 303, 304, 305, 306, 307, 309, 310, 311, 312, 313, 314, 315, 316, 317, 318, 319, 322, 323, 324, 325, 326, 327, 328, 329, 330, 331, 332, 336, 340, 342, 351, 355, 359, 364, 370, 372, 375, 382, 390, 391, 404, 405, 406, 407, 408, 417, 491, 420, 421, 422, 424, 426, 427, 433, 434, 444, 448, 453, 462, 465, 485, 493, 494, 495, 496, 497, 498, 503, 504, 509, 512, 513, 514, 520, 521, 522, 526, 530, 531, 539, 544, 548, 554, 560, 561, 562, 563, 573, 584, 576, 577, 578, 584, 586, 588, 589, 595, 599, 600, 601, 602, 615, 616
	Cultures: Practices and Products (Standard 2.1 and 2.2)	2, 4, 5, 8, 9, 10, 11, 12, 19, 23, 24, 28, 29, 30, 31, 32, 48, 49, 50, 51, 52, 53, 54, 55, 65, 73, 74, 75, 76, 77, 78, 81, 82, 83, 84, 85, 91, 94, 95, 96, 97, 98, 99, 100, 101, 103, 106, 108, 109, 111, 112, 114, 115, 116, 117, 121, 122, 123, 124, 125, 126, 127, 128, 129, 130, 131, 134, 135, 137, 138, 139, 140, 141, 144, 145, 146, 147, 148, 149, 150, 151, 156, 157, 158, 160, 161, 162, 164, 165, 166, 167, 168, 169, 170, 174, 175, 176, 177, 178, 181, 182, 183, 184, 185, 186, 190, 191, 192, 193, 194, 195, 196, 197, 198, 199, 202, 203, 204, 205, 206, 207, 208, 209, 210, 211, 212, 213, 220, 221, 222, 223, 224, 225, 226, 227, 228, 229, 230, 231, 232, 240, 242, 243, 244, 245, 246, 247, 248, 249, 250, 254, 256, 257, 258, 259, 262, 263, 266, 267, 268, 269, 271, 272, 273, 274, 275, 278, 279, 281, 282, 283, 285, 286, 287, 288, 289, 292, 298, 299, 300, 301, 302, 303, 304, 305, 306, 307, 312, 313, 314, 315, 316, 317, 318, 319, 328, 329, 330, 331, 340, 343, 344, 345, 357, 361, 390, 391, 404, 405, 406, 407, 408, 444, 448, 453, 468, 482, 485, 493, 494, 495, 496, 497, 503, 504, 514, 526, 531, 560, 575, 576, 577, 578, 587, 589, 599, 600, 601
	Connections: Acquiring New Information (Standard 3.2)	4, 5, 8, 20, 28, 32, 33, 49, 51, 52, 53, 65, 72, 75, 76, 77, 78, 83, 84, 85, 91, 94, 95, 96, 97, 98, 99, 100, 101, 102, 104, 105, 106, 107, 108, 109, 110, 111, 113, 114, 115, 116, 121, 129, 131, 137, 138, 139, 141, 145, 146, 147, 148, 149, 150, 151, 152, 154, 159, 161, 165, 166, 167, 168, 169, 170, 171, 176, 177, 178, 181, 182, 183, 184, 185, 186, 187, 189, 202, 203, 204, 205, 206, 207, 210, 211, 212, 213, 214, 223, 224, 225, 228, 229, 230, 231, 233, 234, 235, 237, 238, 241, 242, 243, 246, 247, 248, 249, 250, 254, 256, 257, 266, 267, 268, 269, 271, 272, 273, 274, 275, 276, 278, 279, 282, 285, 286, 287, 288, 289, 290, 292, 293, 298, 299, 302, 303, 304, 305, 306, 307, 309, 310, 312, 313, 314, 315, 322, 324, 325, 326, 339, 343, 345, 346, 347, 352, 354, 357, 358, 360, 367, 368, 369, 575, 588, 589, 590, 600

Common Core State Standards—ELA	Standards for Learning Languages	*T´es branché?* Level 3
Craft and Structure		
Reading 4–6	**Interpretive (Reading, Listening, Viewing)**	**Page Number**
4. Interpret words and phrases as they are used in a text, including determining technical, connotative, and figurative meanings, and analyze how specific word choices shape meaning or tone 5. Analyze the structure of texts, including how specific sentences, paragraphs, and larger portions of the text relate to each other and the whole 6. Assess how point of view or purpose shapes the content and style of a text	**Interpretive Communication (Standard 1.2)**	4, 8, 9, 10, 11, 12, 17, 19, 28, 29, 30, 31, 32, 33, 44, 47, 49, 50, 51, 52, 53, 55, 65, 66, 67, 76, 77, 78, 79, 81, 82, 83, 84, 91, 94, 95, 96, 97, 98, 99, 100, 101, 106, 107, 108, 109, 110, 111, 112, 113, 114, 115, 116, 117, 118, 119, 120, 121, 122, 123, 124, 125, 126, 127, 128, 129, 131, 134, 135, 140, 141, 144, 145, 146, 147, 148, 149, 150, 151, 152, 154, 156, 157, 158, 159, 160, 161, 162, 163, 164, 165, 166, 167, 168, 169, 170, 171, 172, 173, 174, 175, 176, 177, 178, 179, 181, 182, 183, 184, 185, 186, 187, 189, 190, 191, 192, 193, 194, 195, 196, 198, 202, 203, 204, 205, 206, 207, 208, 209, 210, 211, 212, 213, 214, 215, 216, 218, 220, 221, 222, 224, 225, 226, 227, 228, 229, 230, 231, 232, 233, 234, 235, 236, 237, 238, 240, 241, 242, 243, 244, 245, 246, 247, 248, 249, 250, 251, 255, 256, 257, 258, 259, 262, 263, 266, 267, 268, 269, 271, 272, 273, 274, 275, 276, 278, 279, 278, 279, 282, 283, 285, 286, 287, 288, 289, 290, 292, 293, 298, 299, 300, 301, 302, 303, 304, 305, 306, 307, 309, 310, 312, 313, 314, 315, 316, 317, 318, 319, 322, 325, 327, 328, 329, 330, 331, 334, 336, 341, 343, 344, 345, 346, 349, 350, 351, 355, 356, 361, 362, 363, 364, 367, 368, 369, 370, 372, 375, 380, 381, 382, 383, 384, 385, 387, 388, 389, 400, 404, 405, 406, 407, 415, 424, 444, 449, 450, 451, 453, 465, 466, 467, 468, 469, 492, 493, 494, 495, 496, 497, 509, 512, 513, 514, 520, 521, 549, 550, 561, 562, 574, 577, 590, 592, 593, 600, 601, 602, 605, 615
	Cultures: Practices and Products (Standards 2.1 and 2.2)	4, 5, 8, 9, 10, 11, 12, 31, 32, 47, 48, 49, 50, 51, 53, 54, 55, 65, 76, 77, 78, 79, 81, 82, 83, 84, 91, 94, 95, 96, 98, 99, 100, 101, 106, 108, 109, 112, 114, 115, 116, 117, 121, 122, 123, 124, 125, 126, 127, 128, 129, 131, 134, 135, 141, 144, 145, 146, 147, 148, 149, 150, 151, 156, 157, 158, 160, 161, 162, 165, 166, 167, 168, 169, 170, 174, 175, 176, 177, 178, 181, 182, 183, 184, 185, 186, 190, 191, 192, 193, 194, 195, 196, 197, 198, 199, 202, 203, 204, 205, 206, 207, 208, 209, 210, 211, 212, 213, 220, 221, 222, 224, 225, 226, 227, 228, 229, 230, 231, 232, 240, 242, 243, 244, 245, 246, 247, 248, 249, 250, 251, 254, 256, 257, 258, 259, 262, 263, 266, 267, 268, 269, 271, 272, 273, 274, 275, 278, 279, 278, 279, 282, 283, 285, 286, 287, 288, 289, 298, 299, 300, 301, 302, 303, 304, 305, 306, 307, 312, 313, 314, 315, 318, 319, 347, 357, 367, 387, 389, 415, 444, 449, 450, 451, 466, 467, 468, 493, 494, 495, 496, 497, 513, 549, 587, 590, 592, 593, 600, 601
	Connections: Reinforce Other Disciplines (Standard 3.1)	13, 14, 15, 28, 34, 42, 44, 57, 58, 60, 61, 62, 72, 84, 86, 88, 89, 91, 93, 99, 100, 102, 104, 106, 114, 115, 116, 118, 119, 121, 129, 131, 145, 146, 147, 148, 149, 150, 151, 152, 154, 155, 167, 168, 169, 170, 171, 172, 174, 175, 182, 183, 184, 185, 187, 189, 190, 191, 194, 195, 198, 199, 200, 208, 209, 210, 211, 214, 215, 216, 218, 228, 229, 233, 237, 240, 241, 246, 251, 255, 261, 262, 263, 272, 273, 274, 275, 276, 281, 287, 288, 289, 290, 293, 298, 304, 306, 307, 309, 310, 315, 325, 331, 333, 335, 339, 341, 345, 347, 348, 349, 350, 354, 358, 362, 363, 364, 371, 374, 380, 381, 383, 383, 384, 385, 387, 388, 389, 404, 405, 406, 407, 415, 424, 444, 449, 450, 451, 453, 466, 467, 468, 469, 492, 493, 494, 495, 496, 497, 512, 513, 514, 587, 600, 601, 602
	Comparisons: Language (Standard 4.1)	28, 30, 51, 52, 57, 58, 60, 61, 62, 72, 76, 80, 81, 83, 84, 85, 86, 87, 88, 89, 91, 93, 94, 95, 99, 100, 102, 104, 105, 106, 107, 108, 109, 110, 116, 118, 119, 121, 152, 153, 154, 155, 159, 171, 172, 173, 174, 175, 178, 180, 187, 195, 214, 215, 216, 218, 225, 228, 229, 233, 234, 235, 236, 237, 238, 240, 241, 242, 243, 244, 245, 246, 247, 251, 258, 259, 261, 262, 263, 268, 269, 271, 274, 276, 277, 278, 279, 278, 280, 282, 284, 290, 293, 298, 299, 300, 302, 303, 306, 307, 309, 310, 312, 313, 314, 315, 316, 317, 318, 319, 334, 335, 350, 354, 409, 449, 450, 456

Common Core State Standards—ELA	Standards for Learning Languages	*T'es branché?* Level 3
	Comparisons: Cultures (Standard 4.2)	4, 5, 23, 28, 30, 31, 32, 33, 49, 51, 52, 53, 54, 73, 74, 80, 81, 82, 83, 84, 85, 91, 94, 95, 97, 98, 99, 100, 101, 106, 108, 109, 110, 114, 115, 116, 117, 129, 131, 138, 139, 146, 147, 148, 149, 150, 151, 156, 157, 158, 160, 161, 162, 165, 166, 167, 168, 169, 170, 174, 175, 176, 177, 178, 181, 182, 183, 184, 185, 186, 190, 191, 192, 193, 194, 195, 196, 197, 198, 199, 202, 203, 204, 205, 206, 207, 210, 211, 212, 213, 220, 221, 222, 224, 225, 228, 229, 230, 231, 232, 240, 241, 242, 243, 246, 247, 248, 250, 254, 256, 257, 258, 259, 262, 263, 266, 267, 268, 269, 270, 271, 272, 273, 274, 275, 278, 279, 281, 282, 283, 285, 286, 287, 288, 289, 298, 299, 300, 302, 303, 304, 305, 306, 307, 312, 313, 314, 315, 316, 317, 318, 319, 345, 358, 367, 373, 387, 450, 492, 588, 589, 600, 601, 602

Integration of Knowledge and Ideas

Reading 7–9	Interpretive (Reading, Listening, Viewing)	Page Number
7. Integrate and evaluate content presented in diverse formats and media, including visually and quantitatively, as well as in words 8. Delineate and evaluate the argument and specific claims in a text, including the validity of the reasoning as well as the relevance and sufficiency of the evidence 9. Analyze how two or more texts address similar themes or topics in order to build knowledge or to compare the approaches the authors take 10. Read and comprehend complex literary and informational texts independently and proficiently	**Interpretive Communication (Standard 1.2)**	10, 12, 28, 29, 30, 31, 32, 33, 47, 52, 53, 55, 57, 58, 60, 62, 65, 76, 77, 78, 80, 81, 82, 83, 84, 85, 86, 87, 88, 89, 90, 91, 93, 94, 95, 96, 97, 98, 99, 100, 101, 102, 103, 104, 105, 106, 107, 108, 110, 111, 112, 113, 114, 116, 118, 119, 120, 121, 122, 123, 124, 125, 126, 127, 128, 129, 130, 134, 135, 137, 138, 139, 140, 141, 145, 147, 148, 149, 150, 151, 152, 156, 157, 160, 161, 162, 163, 164, 165, 166, 167, 168, 169, 170, 171, 172, 173, 174, 175, 176, 177, 178, 181, 182, 183, 184, 185, 186, 187, 189, 190, 191, 192, 193, 194, 195, 196, 197, 198, 199, 202, 203, 204, 205, 206, 207, 208, 209, 210, 211, 212, 213, 214, 215, 216, 218, 220, 221, 222, 224, 225, 226, 227, 228, 229, 230, 231, 232, 233, 234, 235, 236, 237, 238, 240, 241, 242, 243, 246, 247, 248, 249, 250, 251, 254, 255, 256, 257, 258, 259, 262, 263, 266, 267, 268, 269, 271, 272, 273, 274, 275, 276, 279, 281, 282, 283, 285, 286, 287, 288, 289, 290, 293, 298, 299, 300, 302, 303, 304, 305, 306, 307, 309, 310, 312, 313, 314, 315, 316, 317, 318, 319, 347, 355, 360, 370, 381, 382, 383, 384, 385, 388, 389, 391, 392, 404, 405, 406, 407, 408, 415, 419, 420, 421, 422, 423, 426, 435, 444, 448, 449, 452, 453, 462, 465, 467, 468, 469, 473, 477, 482, 492, 493, 494, 495, 496, 497, 498, 503, 504, 509, 512, 514, 517, 520, 524, 525, 526, 530, 531, 534, 539, 543, 544, 548, 573, 574, 575, 577, 578, 579, 584, 586, 587, 589, 591, 593, 596, 615
	Cultures: Practices and Products (Standards 2.1 and 2.2)	8, 9, 10, 12, 23, 24, 28, 29, 30, 31, 32, 50, 51, 52, 53, 54, 55, 64, 65, 66, 67, 76, 77, 80, 81, 82, 83, 84, 85, 91, 94, 95, 97, 98, 99, 100, 101, 106, 108, 110, 111, 114, 115, 116, 117, 122, 123, 124, 125, 126, 127, 128, 129, 130, 131, 134, 137, 138, 139, 140, 141, 145, 147, 148, 149, 150, 151, 156, 157, 160, 161, 162, 165, 166, 167, 168, 169, 170, 174, 175, 176, 177, 178, 181, 182, 183, 184, 185, 186, 190, 191, 192, 193, 194, 195, 196, 197, 198, 199, 202, 203, 204, 205, 206, 207, 208, 209, 210, 211, 212, 213, 220, 221, 222, 224, 225, 226, 227, 228, 229, 230, 231, 232, 240, 241, 242, 243, 246, 247, 248, 249, 250, 254, 256, 257, 258, 259, 262, 263, 266, 267, 268, 269, 271, 272, 273, 274, 275, 278, 279, 280, 281, 282, 283, 285, 286, 287, 288, 289, 298, 299, 300, 302, 303, 304, 305, 306, 307, 312, 313, 314, 315, 316, 317, 318, 319, 358, 368, 369, 391, 404, 405, 406, 407, 408, 415, 444, 448, 462, 468, 482, 492, 493, 494, 495, 496, 497, 503, 504, 509, 512, 532, 548, 549, 565, 579, 592, 593
	Connections: Reinforce Other Disciplines (Standard 3.1)	28, 57, 60, 61, 62, 84, 86, 88, 91, 93, 99, 102, 104, 106, 108, 109, 114, 115, 118, 119, 121, 129, 133, 137, 138, 139, 140, 141, 145, 147, 148, 149, 150, 151, 152, 154, 155, 167, 168, 169, 170, 171, 172, 174, 175, 182, 183, 184, 185, 186, 187, 189, 190, 191, 195, 202, 203, 206, 210, 211, 214, 216, 218, 228, 229, 233, 237, 246, 247, 251, 257, 262, 263, 272, 273, 274, 275, 276, 281, 282, 287, 288, 289, 290, 293, 298, 304, 306, 307, 309, 320, 339, 354, 374, 381, 384, 385, 391, 404, 405, 406, 407, 408, 415, 419, 420, 421, 422, 423, 426, 435, 448, 449, 452, 453, 462, 465, 468, 469, 473, 477, 482, 492, 493, 494, 495, 496, 497, 498, 503, 504, 513, 514, 531, 532, 539, 550, 578, 589, 591, 601, 615

Common Core State Standards—ELA	Standards for Learning Languages	*T´es branché?* Level 3
	Comparisons: Cultures (Standard 4.2)	9, 10, 12, 27, 29, 32, 49, 51, 52, 53, 54, 55, 56, 64, 65, 66, 67, 75, 77, 78, 80, 81, 82, 83, 84, 85, 91, 94, 95, 97, 99, 100, 101, 106, 108, 109, 110, 114, 115, 116, 117, 129, 131, 134, 137, 138, 139, 145, 147, 148, 149, 150, 151, 156, 157, 158, 159, 161, 162, 165, 166, 167, 168, 169, 170, 174, 175, 176, 177, 178, 181, 182, 183, 184, 185, 186, 190, 191, 192, 193, 194, 195, 196, 197, 198, 199, 202, 203, 204, 205, 206, 207, 208, 209, 210, 211, 212, 213, 214, 215, 222, 224, 225, 226, 227, 228, 229, 232, 240, 241, 242, 243, 246, 247, 248, 250, 254, 256, 257, 258, 259, 262, 263, 266, 267, 268, 269, 271, 272, 273, 274, 275, 278, 279, 281, 282, 283, 285, 286, 287, 288, 289, 298, 299, 300, 302, 303, 304, 305, 306, 307, 312, 313, 314, 315, 316, 317, 324, 325, 345, 346, 358, 388, 392, 404, 423, 452, 466, 484, 492, 591, 592, 593, 601
	Communities: Beyond the School Setting (Standard 5.1)	21, 68, 71, 83, 84, 91, 99, 100, 106, 114, 129, 147, 148, 149, 151, 157, 158, 167, 168, 169, 174, 182, 183, 190, 195, 198, 199, 210, 211, 212, 222, 229, 230, 240, 241, 247, 248, 250, 254, 257, 258, 262, 263, 272, 273, 274, 279, 288, 289, 304, 305, 306, 307, 308, 312, 316, 345, 346, 358, 367, 373, 375, 381, 382, 383, 384, 385, 391, 392, 404, 405, 406, 407, 408, 415, 419, 420, 421, 422, 423, 426, 435, 444, 448, 449, 452, 453, 462, 465, 466, 467, 468, 469, 473, 477, 482, 492, 493, 494, 495, 496, 497, 498, 503, 504, 509, 512, 517, 520, 524, 525, 526, 530, 532, 534, 539, 543, 544, 548, 574, 575, 576, 577, 578, 579, 584, 585, 586, 588, 589, 590, 592, 593, 597, 600, 601, 615
Range of Reading and Level of Text Complexity		
Reading 10	**Interpretive (Reading, Listening, Viewing)**	**Page Number**
10. Read and comprehend complex literary and informational texts independently and proficiently	**Interpretive Communication (Standard 1.2)**	65, 66, 67, 78, 95, 101, 110, 112, 113, 114, 116, 122, 123, 124, 125, 126, 127, 128, 134, 138, 145, 147, 148, 149, 150, 151, 160, 161, 162, 163, 165, 166, 167, 168, 169, 170, 181, 182, 183, 184, 185, 186, 192, 193, 194, 196, 197, 198, 205, 208, 209, 210, 211, 212, 213, 214, 215, 218, 225, 228, 229, 230, 231, 246, 247, 248, 249, 255, 256, 257, 262, 263, 271, 272, 273, 275, 285, 286, 287, 288, 289, 293, 298, 299, 300, 304, 305, 306, 307, 312, 313, 314, 315, 330, 331, 345, 346, 358, 367, 368–370, 371, 375, 384, 385, 387, 388, 389, 390, 392, 404, 405, 406, 407, 408, 419, 420, 421, 422, 423, 424, 426, 427, 433, 434, 435, 449, 450, 451, 452, 466, 467, 468, 483, 492, 493, 494, 495, 496, 497, 498, 504, 513, 514, 531, 532, 549, 560, 561, 562, 563, 564, 565, 578, 579, 588, 590, 592, 593, 602, 605, 616
	Comparisons: Cultures (Standard 4.2)	65, 66, 67, 95, 108, 109, 110, 111, 112, 113, 114, 115, 116, 117, 121, 122, 134, 145, 147, 148, 149, 150, 151, 156, 157, 159, 161, 162, 165, 166, 167, 168, 169, 170, 173, 174, 175, 176, 177, 178, 181, 182, 183, 184, 185, 186, 190, 191, 192, 193, 194, 195, 196, 197, 198, 199, 202, 203, 208, 209, 210, 211, 212, 213, 222, 224, 225, 228, 229, 230, 231, 240, 241, 246, 247, 248, 249, 254, 256, 257, 262, 263, 271, 272, 273, 274, 275, 286, 287, 288, 289, 298, 299, 300, 304, 305, 306, 307, 312, 313, 314, 315, 330, 345, 346, 358, 361, 371, 373, 376, 388, 390, 392, 423, 466, 484, 500, 513, 514, 531, 532, 592, 593, 601, 602
	Communities: Beyond the School Setting (Standard 5.1)	21, 99, 100, 106, 114, 129, 147, 148, 149, 151, 157, 158, 167, 168, 169, 174, 182, 183, 186, 190, 195, 198, 199, 210, 211, 212, 222, 229, 230, 240, 241, 247, 248, 250, 254, 257, 262, 263, 272, 273, 274, 275, 279, 282, 287, 288, 289, 296, 304, 305, 306, 307, 312, 315, 367, 368–370, 384, 385, 387, 388, 389, 390, 392, 404, 405, 406, 407, 408, 419, 420, 421, 423, 424, 426, 427, 449, 450, 451, 453, 466, 467, 468, 483, 492, 493, 494, 495, 496, 497, 498, 504, 513, 514, 531, 532, 549, 560, 561, 562, 563, 564, 578, 579, 584, 585, 590, 592, 593, 601, 602, 605, 616, 656

Common Core State Standards—ELA	Standards for Learning Languages	*T´es branché?* Level 3
Text Types and Purposes		
Writing 1–3	**Interpretive (Reading, Listening, Viewing)**	**Page Number**
1. Write arguments to support claims in an analysis of substantive topics or texts using valid reasoning and relevant and sufficient evidence 2. Write informative/ explanatory texts to examine and convey complex ideas and information clearly and accurately through the effective selection, organization, and analysis of content 3. Write narratives to develop real or imagined experiences or events using effective technique, well-chosen details, and well-structured event sequences	**Presentational Communication (Standard 1.3)** Present information, concepts, and ideas to an audience of listeners or readers on a variety of topics. • Produce a variety of creative oral and written presentations (e.g. original story, personal narrative, script). • Retell or summarize information in narrative form, demonstrating a consideration of audience. • Create and give persuasive speeches and write persuasive essays. • Produce expository writing.	6, 9, 12, 14, 15, 21, 27, 33, 44, 46, 47, 49, 50, 51, 54, 55, 56, 58, 59, 61, 62, 63, 64, 65, 67, 68, 69, 71, 77, 78, 79, 80, 81, 82, 83, 84, 85, 87, 89, 90, 91, 94, 95, 96, 97, 99, 100, 101, 102, 103, 106, 107, 109, 110, 111, 112, 113, 114, 115, 116, 117, 118, 120, 121, 122, 128, 129, 130, 131, 132, 134, 135, 140, 141, 142, 143, 144, 146, 147, 149, 151, 153, 155, 156, 157, 158, 162, 163, 164, 166, 168, 169, 170, 173, 174, 175, 178, 179, 180, 181, 182, 184, 185, 186, 188, 189, 190, 191, 192, 194, 195, 196, 197, 198, 199, 205, 206, 207, 209, 212, 213, 215, 217, 219, 220, 221, 222, 225, 226, 227, 229, 230, 231, 232, 234, 236, 237, 238, 239, 240, 241, 243, 244, 245, 246, 247, 248, 249, 250, 252, 253, 254, 256, 257, 258, 259, 260, 262, 263, 266, 267, 270, 271, 272, 274, 275, 277, 278, 279, 282, 283, 284, 285, 286, 288, 289, 291, 292, 294, 295, 296, 297, 299, 300, 301, 302, 303, 305, 306, 307, 308, 309, 311, 312, 315, 316, 317, 318, 319, 351, 370, 373, 376, 390, 391, 397, 402, 407, 414, 418, 422, 426, 428, 436, 446, 452, 462, 473, 475, 480, 491, 499, 500, 501, 504, 515, 522, 530, 540, 552, 563, 567, 578, 579, 584, 585, 590, 592, 593, 601, 602, 605, 616
	Comparisons: Language (Standard 4.1) Demonstrate understanding of the nature of language through comparisons of the language studied and one's own.	6, 9, 10, 11, 12, 21, 27, 34, 42, 44, 45, 46, 47, 49, 52, 54, 60, 62, 71, 77, 78, 80, 81, 82, 83, 87, 89, 90, 91, 92, 100, 102, 106, 109, 110, 114, 118, 128, 129, 134, 135, 140, 141, 144, 152, 153, 155, 156, 157, 159, 171, 173, 174, 175, 178, 179, 180, 182, 186, 188, 189, 190, 191, 197, 198, 199, 214, 215, 216, 217, 218, 219, 225, 229, 230, 231, 234, 235, 237, 238, 239, 240, 241, 243, 244, 245, 246, 247, 250, 251, 254, 256, 257, 258, 259, 260, 262, 263, 270, 274, 275, 277, 278, 279, 282, 283, 284, 286, 288, 289, 291, 292, 294, 295, 296, 297, 299, 300, 301, 302, 303, 305, 306, 307, 308, 309, 311, 312, 315, 316, 317, 318, 319, 326, 332, 336, 342, 347, 350, 364, 516, 592
Production and Distribution of Writing		
Writing 4–6	**Interpretive (Reading, Listening, Viewing)**	**Page Number**
4. Produce clear and coherent writing in which the development, organization, and style are appropriate to task, purpose, and audience	**Presentational Communication (Standard 1.3)** Present information, concepts, and ideas to an audience of listeners or readers on a variety of topics, knowing how, when, and why to say what to whom. • Retell or summarize information in narrative form, demonstrating a consideration of audience. • Self-edit written work for content, organization, and grammar.	9, 12, 21, 24, 33, 44, 46, 47, 49, 50, 54, 55, 56, 59, 61, 62, 63, 64, 67, 68, 69, 71, 78, 79, 81, 82, 83, 84, 85, 87, 89, 90, 91, 94, 96, 97, 99, 100, 106, 107, 109, 110, 111, 112, 113, 114, 115, 117, 118, 120, 121, 128, 129, 130, 131, 132, 134, 135, 141, 142, 143, 144, 146, 147, 149, 151, 153, 155, 156, 157, 158, 162, 163, 164, 166, 168, 169, 170, 173, 174, 175, 178, 179, 180, 181, 182, 184, 185, 186, 188, 189, 190, 191, 192, 194, 195, 196, 197, 198, 199, 205, 206, 207, 209, 212, 213, 215, 217, 219, 220, 221, 222, 225, 226, 227, 229, 230, 231, 234, 235, 236, 237, 238, 239, 240, 241, 244, 245, 248, 249, 250, 252, 253, 254, 256, 257, 258, 259, 260, 262, 263, 270, 271, 274, 275, 277, 278, 279, 282, 283, 284, 288, 289, 291, 292, 294, 295, 296, 297, 299, 300, 301, 305, 306, 307, 308, 311, 312, 315, 316, 317, 318, 319, 328, 329, 331, 340, 343, 344, 347, 352, 353, 355, 357, 359, 360, 366, 370, 371, 373, 376, 386, 391, 405, 408, 414, 422, 425, 426, 428, 432, 437, 446, 452, 453, 473, 475, 480, 484, 500, 501, 515, 522, 528, 534, 538, 540, 550, 551, 559, 564, 565, 578, 585, 591, 592, 598, 602, 603, 604, 608, 609, 612, 615

Common Core State Standards—ELA	Standards for Learning Languages	*T´es branché?* Level 3
5. Develop and strengthen writing as needed by planning, revising, editing, rewriting, or trying a new approach	**Cultures: Practices and Perspectives (Standard 2.1):** Demonstrate an understanding of the relationship between the practices and perspectives of the cultures studied.	10, 11, 12, 22, 29, 49, 50, 51, 54, 55, 56, 59, 64, 65, 68, 69, 71, 78, 80, 81, 82, 83, 84, 85, 87, 89, 91, 92, 94, 95, 99, 100, 106, 109, 110, 111, 112, 114, 115, 116, 117, 121, 128, 129, 131, 132, 134, 135, 140, 141, 142, 143, 146, 147, 149, 151, 156, 157, 158, 162, 164, 166, 168, 169, 170, 174, 175, 178, 179, 180, 182, 184, 185, 186, 190, 191, 194, 195, 196, 197, 198, 199, 205, 206, 207, 209, 212, 213, 220, 221, 222, 225, 226, 227, 229, 230, 231, 232, 240, 241, 244, 245, 248, 249, 250, 254, 256, 257, 258, 259, 260, 262, 263, 271, 274, 275, 278, 279, 282, 284, 288, 289, 296, 297, 299, 300, 301, 305, 306, 307, 308, 312, 314, 315, 316, 317, 318, 319, 347, 370, 390, 391, 422, 425, 428, 452, 453, 484, 491, 500, 501, 515, 522, 550, 559, 564, 565, 592, 600
6. Use technology, including the Internet, to produce and publish writing and to interact and collaborate with others	**Cultures: Products and Perspectives (Standard 2.2)** Demonstrate an understanding of the relationship between the products and perspectives of the cultures studied.	10, 11, 24, 25, 33, 52, 53, 54, 55, 56, 64, 65, 69, 71, 78, 80, 81, 83, 84, 85, 91, 95, 99, 109, 111, 114, 115, 116, 117, 121, 128, 129, 131, 132, 134, 135, 141, 146, 147, 151, 156, 157, 158, 168, 169, 170, 174, 175, 178, 179, 182, 184, 185, 186, 190, 191, 194, 195, 196, 197, 198, 199, 205, 212, 213, 222, 230, 231, 240, 241, 248, 249, 250, 254, 256, 257, 258, 259, 260, 262, 263, 271, 274, 275, 278, 279, 288, 289, 296, 297, 300, 301, 306, 307, 308, 312, 315, 316, 317, 318, 319, 331, 602, 603, 604, 612
	Comparisons: Language (Standard 4.1) Demonstrate understanding of the nature of language through comparisons of the language studied and one's own.	12, 14, 15, 22, 27, 33, 34, 35, 36, 37, 38, 39, 40, 41, 42, 43, 44, 47, 49, 55, 56, 68, 69, 78, 83, 84, 85, 89, 91, 94, 102, 103, 104, 105, 106, 109, 114, 118, 120, 121, 131, 132, 134, 135, 140, 141, 155, 156, 157, 171, 173, 188, 189, 195, 197, 198, 199, 214, 215, 217, 218, 219, 225, 229, 233, 234, 235, 236, 237, 238, 240, 241, 248, 251, 254, 255, 258, 259, 260, 262, 263, 270, 274, 275, 277, 278, 279, 312,284, 288, 289, 291, 292, 294, 295, 296, 297, 299, 300, 301, 305, 306, 307, 308, 311, 315, 316, 317, 318, 319, 360, 409, 410, 472, 489, 516, 593, 594
	Communities: Beyond the School Setting (Standard 5.1) Use the language both within and beyond the school setting.	10, 12, 21, 31, 32, 33, 46, 56, 68, 84, 85, 91, 99, 100, 106, 114, 129, 147, 151, 157, 158, 167, 168, 169, 174, 182, 183, 184, 186, 190, 210, 211, 212, 222, 229, 230, 240, 241, 247, 248, 250, 254, 257, 258, 260, 262, 263, 274, 275, 279, 287, 288, 289, 296, 304, 305, 306, 307, 308, 316, 386, 390, 391, 405, 408, 414, 425, 426, 428, 432, 446, 452, 453, 462, 475, 480, 484, 491, 500, 501, 515, 522, 528, 534, 538, 540, 550, 551, 559, 565, 565, 592, 593, 594, 600, 601, 602, 603, 604, 608, 615
Research to Build and Present Knowledge		
Writing 7–9	**Interpretive (Reading, Listening, Viewing)**	**Page Number**
7. Conduct short as well as more sustained research projects based on focused questions, demonstrating understanding of the subject under investigation	**Presentational Communication (Standard 1.3)** • Present information, concepts, and ideas to an audience of listeners or readers on a variety of topics. • Expound on familiar topics and those requiring research. • Produce expository writing including researched reports. • Use reference tools, acknowledge sources and cite them appropriately. • Demonstrate an understanding of features of target culture communities (e.g. geographic, historical, artistic, social and/or political). • Demonstrate knowledge and understanding of content across disciplines.	10, 11, 12, 18, 19, 21, 33, 46, 49, 50, 52, 54, 55, 56, 59, 61, 63, 64, 65, 67, 68, 69, 71, 83, 84, 85, 91, 97, 99, 100, 101, 109, 110, 111, 112, 113, 114, 115, 116, 117, 118, 120, 121, 122, 128, 129, 130, 131, 132, 134, 140, 141, 142, 146, 147, 149, 151, 153, 155, 156, 157, 158, 162, 163, 164, 166, 168, 169, 170, 173, 174, 175, 178, 179, 180, 181, 182, 184, 185, 186, 188, 189, 190, 191, 192, 194, 195, 196, 197, 198, 199, 205, 206, 207, 209, 212, 213, 215, 217, 219, 221, 222, 225, 226, 229, 231, 240, 241, 244, 245, 248, 250, 252, 253, 254, 256, 257, 258, 259, 260, 262, 263, 274, 275, 279, 282, 288, 289, 296, 297, 305, 306, 307, 308, 312, 316, 317, 318, 319, 331, 337, 340, 347, 351, 359, 360, 370, 371, 373, 390, 397, 407, 408, 414, 425, 428, 436, 438, 439, 452, 453, 459, 462, 463, 469, 470, 475, 484, 486, 491, 498, 499, 500, 501, 504, 515, 522, 533, 534, 550, 551, 552, 559, 563, 564, 565, 567, 579, 581, 591, 592, 593, 594, 601, 602, 603, 604, 609, 613

Common Core State Standards—ELA	Standards for Learning Languages	*T'es branché?* Level 3
8. Gather relevant information from multiple print and digital sources, assess the credibility and accuracy of each source, and integrate the information while avoiding plagiarism	**Interpretive Communication (Standard 1.2)** Understand and interpret written and spoken language on a variety of topics.	10, 11, 12, 21, 30, 31, 33, 34, 35, 36, 37, 38, 39, 40, 41, 42, 43, 45, 46, 49, 51, 54, 55, 56, 58, 59, 60, 61, 62, 64, 65, 67, 68, 69, 71, 78, 80, 81, 82, 83, 84, 85, 86, 87, 88, 89, 90, 91, 94, 95, 97, 98, 99, 100, 101, 103, 104, 106, 107, 109, 110, 111, 112, 113, 114, 116, 117, 118, 120, 128, 129, 131, 132, 134, 140, 141, 142, 143, 146, 147, 149, 151, 153, 155, 156, 157, 158, 162, 163, 164, 166, 168, 169, 170, 173, 174, 175, 178, 179, 180, 182, 184, 185, 186, 188, 189, 190, 191, 192, 194, 195, 196, 197, 198, 199, 205, 206, 207, 209, 212, 213, 215, 217, 218, 219, 220, 221, 222, 225, 226, 229, 230, 231, 240, 241, 248, 250, 254, 256, 257, 258, 259, 260, 262, 263, 274, 275, 279, 282, 286, 288, 289, 296, 297, 305, 306, 307, 308, 312, 316, 317, 318, 319, 331, 337, 340, 347, 351, 359, 360, 370, 371, 373, 390, 397, 407, 408, 414, 425, 428, 436, 438, 439, 452, 453, 459, 462, 463, 465, 470, 475, 484, 486, 491, 498, 499, 500, 501, 504, 515, 522, 533, 534, 550, 551, 552, 559, 563, 564, 565, 567, 584, 591, 596, 597, 600, 601, 602
9. Draw evidence from literary or informational texts to support analysis, reflection, and research	**Cultures: Practices and Perspectives (Standard 2.1)** Demonstrate an understanding of the relationship between the practices and perspectives of cultures studied.	10, 11, 12, 21, 29, 30, 31, 32, 36, 49, 50, 54, 55, 56, 64, 67, 68, 69, 71, 78, 79, 80, 81, 82, 83, 84, 85, 87, 91, 94, 95, 97, 98, 99, 100, 101, 106, 109, 110, 111, 112, 113, 116, 117, 128, 129, 131, 132, 134, 140, 141, 142, 143, 146, 147, 149, 151, 156, 157, 158, 162, 164, 166, 168, 169, 170, 174, 175, 178, 179, 180, 182, 184, 185, 186, 190, 191, 194, 195, 197, 198, 199, 205, 206, 207, 209, 212, 213, 220, 221, 222, 225, 226, 227, 228, 229, 240, 241, 244, 245, 248, 249, 254, 256, 257, 258, 259, 260, 262, 263, 274, 275, 278, 279, 282, 288, 289, 296, 297, 305, 306, 307, 308, 312, 316, 317, 318, 319, 331, 340, 345, 347, 359, 370, 390, 408, 425, 428, 436, 438, 439, 452, 459, 484, 486, 498, 499, 500, 501, 504, 522, 533, 550, 552, 559, 563, 564, 565, 567, 597, 600, 601
	Cultures: Products and Perspectives (Standard 2.2) Demonstrate an understanding of the relationship between the products and perspectives of cultures studied.	10, 11, 12, 21, 33, 54, 55, 56, 64, 67, 68, 69, 71, 78, 79, 83, 84, 85, 91, 95, 99, 100, 106, 109, 110, 114, 116, 129, 131, 132, 134, 141, 142, 146, 147, 149, 151, 156, 157, 158, 162, 164, 166, 168, 169, 170, 174, 175, 178, 179, 182, 184, 185, 186, 190, 191, 194, 195, 197, 198, 199, 205, 206, 207, 212, 213, 222, 230, 231, 240, 241, 248, 250, 254, 256, 257, 258, 259, 262, 263, 274, 275, 282, 288, 289, 296, 297, 306, 307, 308, 316, 317, 318, 319, 331, 345, 347, 359, 361, 534, 550, 597, 602
	Connections: Reinforce Other Disciplines (Standard 3.1) Reinforce and further knowledge of other disciplines through the target language.	21, 32, 33, 44, 68, 71, 84, 85, 86, 87, 88, 89, 91, 95, 99, 100, 102, 106, 114, 116, 118, 129, 141, 147, 149, 151, 153, 157, 158, 168, 169, 170, 171, 182, 186, 195, 198, 206, 212, 213, 214, 217, 218, 229, 251, 254, 256, 257, 262, 263, 274, 275, 279, 288, 289, 306, 307, 312, 390, 391, 407, 408, 425, 428, 436, 438, 439, 459, 452, 453, 462, 463, 465, 469, 470, 475, 484, 486, 491, 498, 499, 500, 501, 504, 522, 533, 534, 550, 551, 552, 559, 563, 565, 567, 579, 591, 597, 600, 601
	Connections: Acquiring New Information (Standard 3.2) Acquire information and recognize the distinctive viewpoints that are only available through the target language and its cultures.	10, 11, 21, 30, 31, 54, 56, 64, 68, 71, 78, 80, 82, 83, 84, 85, 91, 100, 102, 106, 109, 114, 116, 118, 121, 129, 131, 132, 141, 146, 147, 149, 151, 156, 157, 158, 166, 168, 169, 170, 174, 175, 178, 179, 182, 184, 185, 186, 190, 191, 195, 198, 205, 206, 207, 212, 213, 225, 228, 229, 230, 231, 238, 239, 248, 249, 251, 256, 257, 258, 259, 274, 275, 279, 282, 288, 289, 306, 307, 309, 312, 316, 317, 345, 347, 361, 370, 459, 486, 491, 498, 499, 500, 501, 504, 533, 552, 559, 563, 564, 565, 567, 593, 600
	Comparisons: Culture (Standard 4.2) Demonstrate understanding of the concept of culture through comparisons.	12, 21, 54, 55, 56, 67, 68, 71, 78, 80, 81, 82, 83, 84, 85, 91, 95, 97, 99, 100, 101, 106, 109, 110, 114, 117, 121, 128, 129, 131, 132, 140, 142, 143, 146, 147, 149, 151, 157, 158, 162, 164, 168, 169, 170, 174, 175, 178, 179, 180, 182, 184, 185, 186, 190, 191, 195, 196, 197, 198, 199, 205, 206, 207, 209, 212, 213, 221, 222, 225, 228, 229, 230, 231, 240, 241, 248, 249, 250, 254, 256, 257, 258, 259, 260, 262, 263, 274, 275, 278, 279, 282, 288, 289, 306, 307, 308, 312, 316, 317, 318, 319, 347, 428, 438, 439, 459, 484, 486, 500, 515, 533, 551, 559, 564, 567, 591, 593, 601

Common Core State Standards—ELA	Standards for Learning Languages	*T'es branché?* Level 3
Range of Writing		
Writing 10	**Interpretive (Reading, Listening, Viewing)**	**Page Number**
10. Write routinely over extended time frames (time for research, reflection, and revision) and shorter time frames (a single sitting or a day or two) for a range of tasks, purposes, and audiences	**Presentational Communication (Standard 1.3)** Present information, concepts, and ideas to an audience of listeners or readers on a variety of topics. • Self-monitor and adjust language production. • Self-edit written work for content, organization, and grammar.	6, 7, 21, 25, 26, 27, 29, 33, 34, 36, 37, 39, 40, 42, 43, 45, 46, 54, 56, 58, 59, 60, 61, 62, 63, 64, 67, 68, 69, 71, 78, 79, 80, 81, 82, 83, 84, 85, 87, 89, 90, 91, 94, 97, 99, 100, 106, 107, 110, 111, 114, 115, 117, 121, 122, 128, 129, 131, 132, 134, 135, 142, 146, 147, 149, 151, 153, 155, 156, 157, 158, 162, 164, 166, 168, 169, 170, 173, 174, 175, 178, 179, 180, 181, 182, 184, 185, 186, 188, 189, 190, 191, 192, 194, 195, 196, 197, 198, 199, 205, 207, 209, 212, 213, 215, 217, 219, 221, 222, 226, 227, 229, 231, 240, 241, 248, 250, 254, 256, 257, 258, 259, 260, 262, 263, 274, 275, 279, 288, 289, 296, 306, 307, 308, 312, 316, 317, 318, 319, 331, 337, 347, 352, 353, 359, 370, 371, 390, 414, 428, 439, 459, 484, 486, 499, 500, 504, 540, 541, 542, 550, 552, 559, 563, 564, 567, 593, 594, 608, 609, 612, 615
	Cultures: Practices and Perspectives (Standard 2.1) Demonstrate an understanding of the relationship between practices and perspectives of the cultures studied.	6, 9, 12, 21, 29, 33, 49, 54, 55, 56, 69, 71, 78, 79, 80, 81, 82, 83, 84, 85, 89, 95, 99, 100, 114, 115, 121, 129, 131, 134, 142, 143, 146, 147, 149, 151, 156, 157, 158, 162, 164, 166, 168, 169, 170, 174, 175, 178, 179, 180, 182, 184, 185, 186, 190, 191, 194, 195, 197, 198, 199, 205, 207, 209, 212, 213, 220, 221, 222, 226, 227, 229, 230, 231, 240, 241, 248, 249, 250, 254, 256, 257, 258, 259, 260, 262, 263, 274, 275, 279, 288, 289, 296, 297, 306, 307, 308, 312, 316, 317, 318, 319, 331, 344, 347, 352, 371, 373, 376, 428, 439, 459, 484, 486, 499, 500, 504, 550, 552, 559, 563, 564, 567, 591, 593, 594
	Cultures: Products and Perspectives (Standard 2.2) Demonstrate an understanding of the relationship between the products and perspectives of the cultures studied.	10, 12, 21, 32, 54, 55, 56, 68, 69, 71, 78, 83, 85, 99, 100, 114, 115, 129, 131, 142, 147, 149, 151, 156, 157, 158, 164, 168, 169, 170, 174, 175, 178, 179, 180, 182, 184, 185, 186, 190, 191, 194, 195, 197, 198, 199, 205, 212, 213, 222, 229, 230, 231, 240, 241, 250, 254, 256, 257, 258, 259, 260, 262, 263, 274, 275, 279, 288, 289, 306, 307, 308, 312, 316, 317, 318, 319, 359, 550, 593
Comprehension and Collaboration		
Speaking and Listening 1–3	**Interpretive (Reading, Listening, Viewing)**	**Page Number**
1. Prepare for and participate effectively in a range of conversations and collaborations with diverse partners, building on others' ideas and expressing their own clearly and persuasively	**Interpersonal Communication (Standard 1.1)** • Engage in conversations, provide and obtain information, express feelings and emotions, and exchange opinions. • Engage in the oral exchange of ideas in formal and informal situations. • Elicit information and clarify meaning by using a variety of strategies. • State and support opinions in oral interactions. • Self-monitor and adjust language production. • Converse in ways that reflect knowledge of target culture communities (e.g., geographic, historical, artistic, social and/or political.	4, 5, 6, 7, 8, 9, 11, 12, 13, 14, 15, 16, 17, 18, 20, 22, 23, 24, 25, 26, 27, 28, 29, 34, 35, 36, 37, 38, 39, 40, 41, 42, 43, 44, 45, 46, 48, 49, 50, 51, 54, 55, 56, 58, 59, 60, 61, 62, 63, 64, 65, 66, 67, 68, 69, 70, 72, 76, 77, 78, 79, 80, 81, 82, 84, 85, 90, 91, 92, 94, 95, 96, 97, 98, 99, 100, 101, 102, 103, 104, 105, 106, 107, 108, 109, 110, 111, 112, 113, 114, 115, 116, 117, 118, 119, 120, 121, 129, 131, 133, 134, 136, 138, 139, 140, 141, 142, 143, 144, 145, 146, 147, 149, 151, 153, 154, 155, 156, 157, 158, 159, 161, 162, 163, 164, 166, 168, 169, 170, 172, 173, 174, 178, 179, 180, 181, 182, 184, 186, 188, 189, 190, 191, 194, 195, 199, 200, 203, 204, 205, 206, 207, 208, 209, 212, 215, 217, 219, 220, 221, 222, 223, 224, 225, 226, 227, 228, 229, 230, 231, 232, 234, 236, 237, 238, 240, 241, 242, 243, 244, 245, 246, 247, 248, 249, 250, 252, 253, 254, 256, 257, 258, 259, 260, 261, 264, 266, 267, 268, 269, 270, 271, 272, 274, 277, 278, 279, 280, 281, 282, 283, 284, 285, 286, 287, 288, 289, 291, 292, 294, 295, 296, 297, 298, 299, 300, 301, 302, 303, 304, 305, 306, 307, 308, 309, 311, 312, 315, 316, 317, 318, 319, 320, 325, 334, 336, 337, 342, 354, 359, 361, 362, 365, 366, 371, 372, 376, 380, 383, 393, 396, 397, 398, 399, 401, 403, 411, 412, 413, 414, 415, 416, 418, 425, 431, 433, 438, 444, 445, 446, 455, 456, 459, 460, 461, 462, 463, 464, 465, 471, 474, 479, 480, 481, 486, 490, 491, 492, 493, 494, 495, 496, 497, 498, 499, 500, 501, 509, 511, 517, 518, 519, 520, 524, 525, 529, 530, 538, 540, 543, 546, 547, 555, 557, 558, 560, 561, 562, 566, 573, 575, 577, 581, 585, 586, 595, 597, 598, 599, 603, 604, 605, 606, 609, 611, 615, 616

Common Core State Standards—ELA	Standards for Learning Languages	*T´es branché?* Level 3
2. Integrate and evaluate information presented in diverse media and formats, including visually, quantitatively, and orally	**Cultures: Practices and Perspectives (Standard 2.1)** • Use appropriate verbal and non-verbal behavior in interpersonal communication.	6, 7, 9, 10, 11, 18, 20, 24, 25, 27, 28, 30, 31, 46, 49, 50, 51, 64, 67, 68, 70, 71, 77, 78, 79, 80, 81, 82, 84, 85, 91, 94, 95, 97, 98, 99, 100, 107, 109, 110, 111, 112, 113, 114, 116, 117, 121, 129, 131, 134, 136, 138, 139, 140, 141, 142, 143, 144, 145, 146, 147, 149, 151, 156, 157, 158, 161, 162, 168, 169, 170, 174, 178, 179, 180, 182, 184, 186, 190, 191, 195, 198, 199, 203, 205, 206, 207, 208, 209, 212, 220, 221, 222, 223, 224, 225, 226, 227, 228, 229, 232, 240, 241, 242, 243, 244, 245, 246, 247, 248, 249, 250, 254, 256, 257, 258, 259, 260, 264, 266, 267, 268, 269, 271, 272, 274, 278, 279, 280, 281, 282, 283, 284, 285, 286, 287, 288, 289, 296, 297, 298, 299, 300, 301, 302, 303, 304, 305, 306, 307, 308, 312, 314, 315, 316, 317, 318, 319, 334, 336, 337, 342, 361, 362, 365, 366, 372, 509, 511
3. Evaluate a speaker's point of view, reasoning, and use of evidence and rhetoric	**Cultures: Products and Perspectives (Standard 2.2)** • Compare and contrast artifacts, themes, ideas, and perspectives across cultures	10, 32, 46, 49, 64, 68, 76, 77, 78, 84, 91, 100, 107, 110, 114, 115, 117, 121, 129, 131, 136, 138, 139, 142, 143, 147, 149, 151, 168, 169, 170, 174, 182, 184, 186, 190, 191, 195, 198, 199, 205, 206, 207, 220, 221, 222, 228, 229, 231, 240, 241, 247, 248, 249, 250, 254, 257, 260, 264, 266, 267, 268, 269, 271, 272, 274, 278, 279, 281, 282, 283, 286, 287, 288, 289, 296, 297, 298, 299, 300, 301, 304, 305, 306, 307, 308, 312, 315, 316, 317, 318, 319, 334, 361, 365, 366, 372, 397, 399, 403, 407, 411, 412, 413, 428, 438, 444, 445, 446, 492, 493, 494, 495, 496, 497, 500, 533, 546, 547, 565, 581, 585, 595, 597, 599, 603
	Connections: Acquiring New Information (Standard 3.2) • Use age-appropriate authentic sources to prepare for discussions.	10, 11, 12, 21, 29, 33, 46, 49, 55, 56, 64, 68, 78, 81, 82, 83, 84, 91, 94, 95, 99, 100, 107, 109, 114, 115, 117, 129, 131, 136, 138, 139, 140, 144, 145, 148, 149, 151, 156, 157, 158, 161, 162, 174, 178, 179, 182, 184, 186, 195, 198, 199, 205, 206, 207, 209, 225, 226, 227, 229, 230, 231, 238, 240, 241, 246, 247, 248, 249, 250, 252, 253, 254, 257, 258, 259, 264, 272, 274, 277, 279, 281, 282, 283, 284, 287, 288, 289, 291, 296, 297, 300, 301, 306, 307, 308, 312, 314, 315, 334, 342, 336, 337, 361, 372
	Comparisons: Language (Standard 4.1) • Demonstrate an awareness of formal and informal language expressions in other languages and one's own.	8, 9, 21, 27, 46, 49, 51, 56, 59, 61, 64, 68, 70, 77, 78, 84, 86, 87, 88, 89, 91, 94, 99, 100, 102, 104, 105, 107, 111, 118, 119, 120, 129, 133, 153, 154, 155, 172, 173, 188, 189, 200, 214, 215, 217, 219, 225, 229, 234, 235, 236, 237, 238, 239, 240, 241, 242, 243, 246, 247, 251, 252, 253, 254, 257, 258, 259, 260, 261, 264, 270, 274, 277, 278, 279, 284, 286, 288, 289, 291, 292, 294, 295, 296, 297, 298, 299, 300, 301, 304, 305, 306, 307, 308, 311, 312, 314, 315, 316, 317, 318, 319, 320, 529, 530, 540, 555, 577, 581, 586, 599, 606, 607, 611, 615, 616
	Communities: Lifelong Learning (Standard 5.2) • Establish and/or maintain interpersonal relations with speakers of the target language.	16, 17, 21, 46, 56, 68, 91, 129, 151, 174, 231, 240, 250, 254, 274, 275, 308, 361, 397, 403, 411, 412, 425, 431, 438, 446, 447, 448, 455, 459, 462, 463, 464, 465, 471, 474, 479, 480, 481, 500, 501, 511, 517, 518, 519, 520, 524, 525, 529, 530, 540, 546, 547, 581, 586, 611, 615, 616

Common Core State Standards—ELA	Standards for Learning Languages	*T´es branché?* Level 3
Presentation of Knowledge and Ideas		
Speaking and Listening 4–6	**Interpretive (Reading, Listening, Viewing)**	**Page Number**
4. Present information, findings, and supporting evidence such that listeners can follow the line of reasoning and the organization, development, and style are appropriate to task, purpose, and audience	**Presentational Communication: (Standard 1.3)** Present information, concepts, and ideas to an audience of listeners or readers on a variety of topics. • Produce a variety of creative oral presentations (e.g. original story, personal narrative, speech, performance). • Retell or summarize information in narrative form, demonstrating a consideration of audience. • Create and give persuasive speeches. • Expound on familiar topics and those requiring research. • Self-monitor and adjust language production. • Use information about features of target culture communities (e.g. geographic, historical, artistic, social and/or political) in presentations. • Incorporate content across disciplines in presentations.	7, 9, 11, 12, 14, 18, 21, 24, 25, 26, 27, 29, 33, 34, 36, 37, 39, 40, 42, 43, 45, 46, 49, 50, 51, 54, 56, 59, 60, 61, 63, 64, 67, 68, 70, 71, 77, 78, 79, 80, 81, 82, 83, 84, 85, 87, 89, 91, 92, 95, 96, 97, 99, 100, 102, 103, 104, 105, 106, 107, 109, 110, 111, 112, 113, 114, 115, 116, 117, 128, 131, 132, 133, 134, 136, 138, 139, 140, 141, 142, 143, 144, 145, 146, 147, 149, 151, 153, 154, 155, 156, 157, 158, 159, 161, 162, 163, 164, 166, 168, 169, 170, 172, 173, 174, 178, 179, 180, 181, 182, 184, 186, 188, 189, 190, 191, 194, 195, 199, 200, 205, 206, 207, 209, 212, 215, 217, 219, 220, 221, 222, 224, 225, 226, 227, 228, 229, 230, 231, 232, 234, 235, 236, 237, 238, 239, 240, 241, 242, 243, 244, 245, 246, 247, 248, 249, 250, 252, 253, 254, 256, 257, 258, 259, 260, 261, 264, 266, 267, 268, 269, 270, 271, 272, 274, 275, 277, 278, 279, 281, 282, 283, 284, 285, 286, 287, 288, 289, 291, 292, 294, 295, 296, 297, 298, 299, 300, 301, 302, 303, 304, 305, 306, 307, 308, 311, 312, 318, 319, 320, 366, 376, 397, 407, 414, 425, 432, 436, 438, 439, 453, 459, 475, 491, 498, 499, 500, 522, 540, 541, 542, 550, 552, 564, 565, 581, 591, 602, 603, 604, 609
5. Make strategic use of digital media and visual displays of data to express information and enhance understanding of presentations 6. Adapt speech to a variety of contexts and communicative tasks, demonstrating command of formal English when indicated or appropriate	**Connections: Acquiring Information (Standard 3.2)** • Use age-appropriate authentic sources to prepare for discussions.	10, 11, 12, 21, 24, 33, 46, 49, 52, 55, 56, 64, 68, 71, 76, 77, 78, 79, 83, 84, 91, 97, 100, 106, 110, 111, 112, 113, 114, 115, 117, 134, 136, 138, 139, 142, 143,144, 145, 146, 147, 148, 149, 151, 156, 157, 158, 161, 162, 174, 178, 179, 182, 184, 186, 198, 199, 205, 206, 207, 209, 212, 225, 226, 227, 229, 230, 231, 238, 239, 240, 241, 247, 248, 249, 250, 252, 253, 254, 257, 258, 259, 260, 264, 270, 271, 272, 274, 275, 277, 279, 281, 282, 283, 284, 287, 288, 289, 291, 292, 296, 297, 300, 301, 304, 305, 306, 307, 308, 311, 312, 314, 315, 316, 317, 318, 319, 371

Author

Toni Theisen

With the collaboration of

Jacques Pécheur

Contributing Writers

Stephen R. Adamson
Rogers, AR

Caroline Busse
Pasadena, CA

Nathalie E. Gaillot
Lyon, France

Lynne I. Lipkind
West Hartford, CT

Diana I. Moen
St. Paul, MN

Annie-Claude Motron
Paris, France

Virginie Pied
Salt Lake City, UT

Emily Wentworth
Branford, CT

Pamela M. Wesely
Iowa City, IA

ST. PAUL

Developmental Editor: Diana Moen
Associate Editor: Nathalie Gaillot
Assistant Editor: Kristina Merrick
Production Editor: Bob Dreas
Cover Designer: Leslie Anderson
Text Designers: Diane Beasley Design, Leslie Anderson
Illustrators: TSI Graphics
Production Specialists: Leslie Anderson, Julie Johnston
Copy Editor/Proofreader: Jamie Bryant, B-books Ltd.
Reviewers: Sébastien De Clerck, Mary Lindquist, Gretchen Petrie, Anne Marie Plante

Credits: Photo Credits, Reading Credits, Art Credits, and Realia Credits follow the Index.

ISBN 978-0-82195-999-2

875 Montreal Way
St. Paul, MN 55102
Email: educate@emcp.com
Website: www.emcp.com

Printed in the United States of America

22 21 20 19 18 17 16 15 14 4 5 6 7 8 9 10

To the Student

Pensez-vous à votre avenir?

Ms. Brown used her knowledge of French to become a conference interpreter for the UN Development Program.

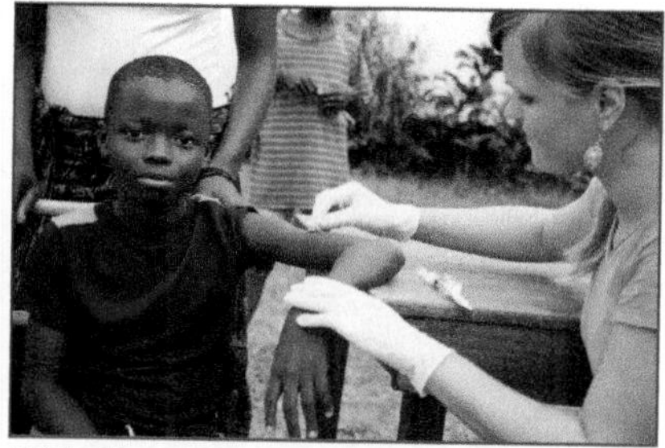

Médecins sans Frontières recruits medical professionals who speak French to help African countries such as the Ivory Coast.

A career using French may be in your future. Combining your French skills with training in a profession of your choice may open doors when entering the workforce. With a degree in law, medicine, or political science you could work as a lawyer in international law or as a paralegal, be a doctor or nurse working for **Médecins Sans Frontières**, or work for a Non-Governmental Organization (NGO) in a francophone country. You might choose to teach English in a francophone country, or apply for a Fulbright Teacher Exchange in a francophone location. French speakers are in high demand for all Peace Corps assignment sectors right now including: environment, agriculture, health, business, education, and community/youth development. There are also jobs in the foreign service, a branch of the government that offers diplomatic services overseas in embassies and consulates.

Universities such as Thunderbird in Arizona prepare students for jobs in business and French. You could work for an American company with a presence in France like 3M, Bank of America, or Hewlett-Packard, or for a French company with a presence in the United States such as Air France (air travel), Accor (hotels), or L'Oréal (cosmetics). According to Bloomberg Rankings, French is the second most useful language in the world for business, after English. You might want to apply for **un stage**, or apprenticeship, at a company while in college or right after you've earned your degree. You might consider working as an insurance agent, banker, financial services provider, public relations specialist, or marketing director using your French.

If you're interested in communications, there are jobs as reporters, production assistants, news anchors, book editors, translators, or editors and proofreaders. The areas of hospitality and recreation offer jobs such as tour guides, sales coordinators, and museum tour guides. Whatever job you're interested in pursuing, think about positioning yourself in a company, agency, or NGO with your bilingual skills.

This year you will learn about French history, more francophone travel destinations, French companies and luxury products, famous French singer-songwriters, and much more! **Bonne continuation** as you continue your learning about French language and francophone cultures!

Search words: **careers in french, thunderbird, state department, careerinsider/vault, concordia language villages, gale's public relations career directory**

Table of Contents

Unité 1

Les moments de la vie 1

Unité 2

Les rapports personnels 73

Unité 3

La Francophonie 137

Unité 4

Préparatifs de départ 201

Unité 5

Comment se renseigner en voyage 265

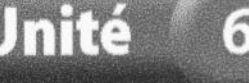

Unité 6

On se débrouille en France. 321

Unité 7

Les arts francophones 377

La France d'hier et d'aujourd'hui 441

Unité 9

Récits de la vie contemporaine 505

Unité 10

La culture des affaires 569

Le monde francophone

Vieille maison de Québec.

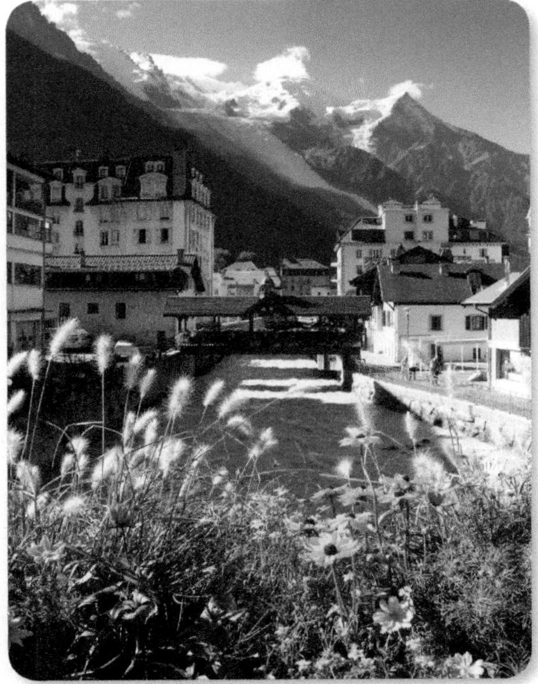

La ville de Chamonix dans les Alpes françaises.

Ville de Basta, Corse.

Des Sénégalaises attendant le retour des pêcheurs.

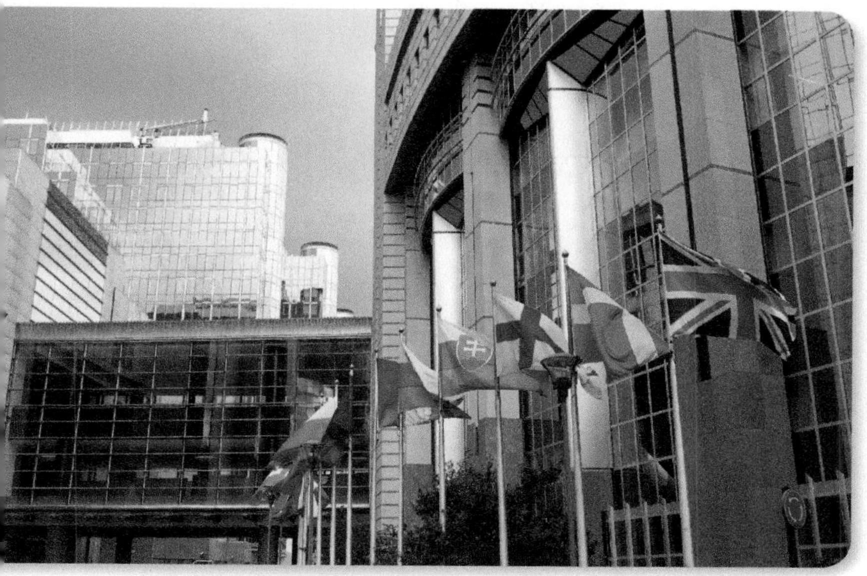

Le Parlement Européen à Bruxelles, en Belgique.

Plage à Saint-Martin, Antilles françaises.

Dans les rues d'Alger, en Afrique du Nord.

Le port de Monaco, de nuit.

Map of France

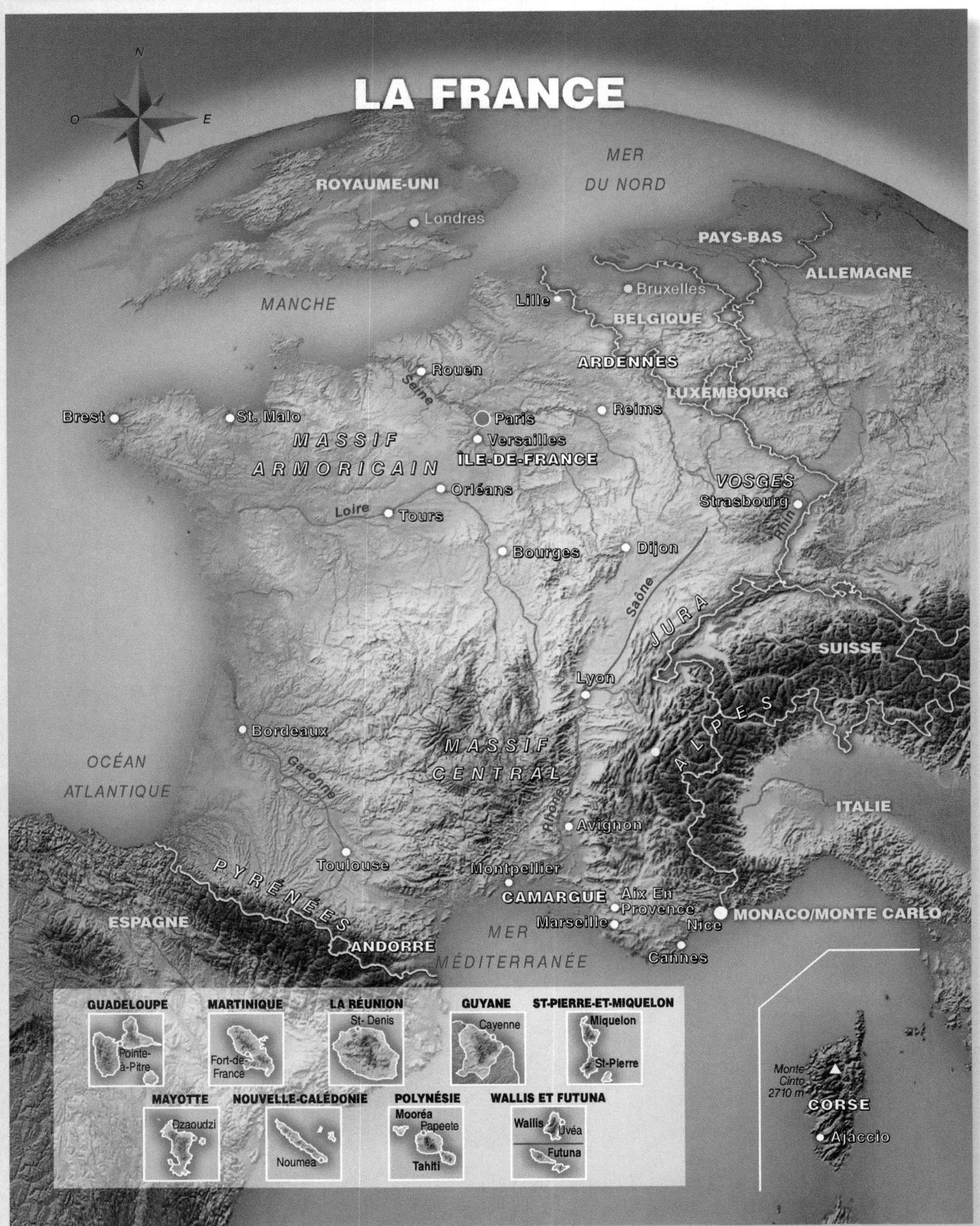

Francophone World Map

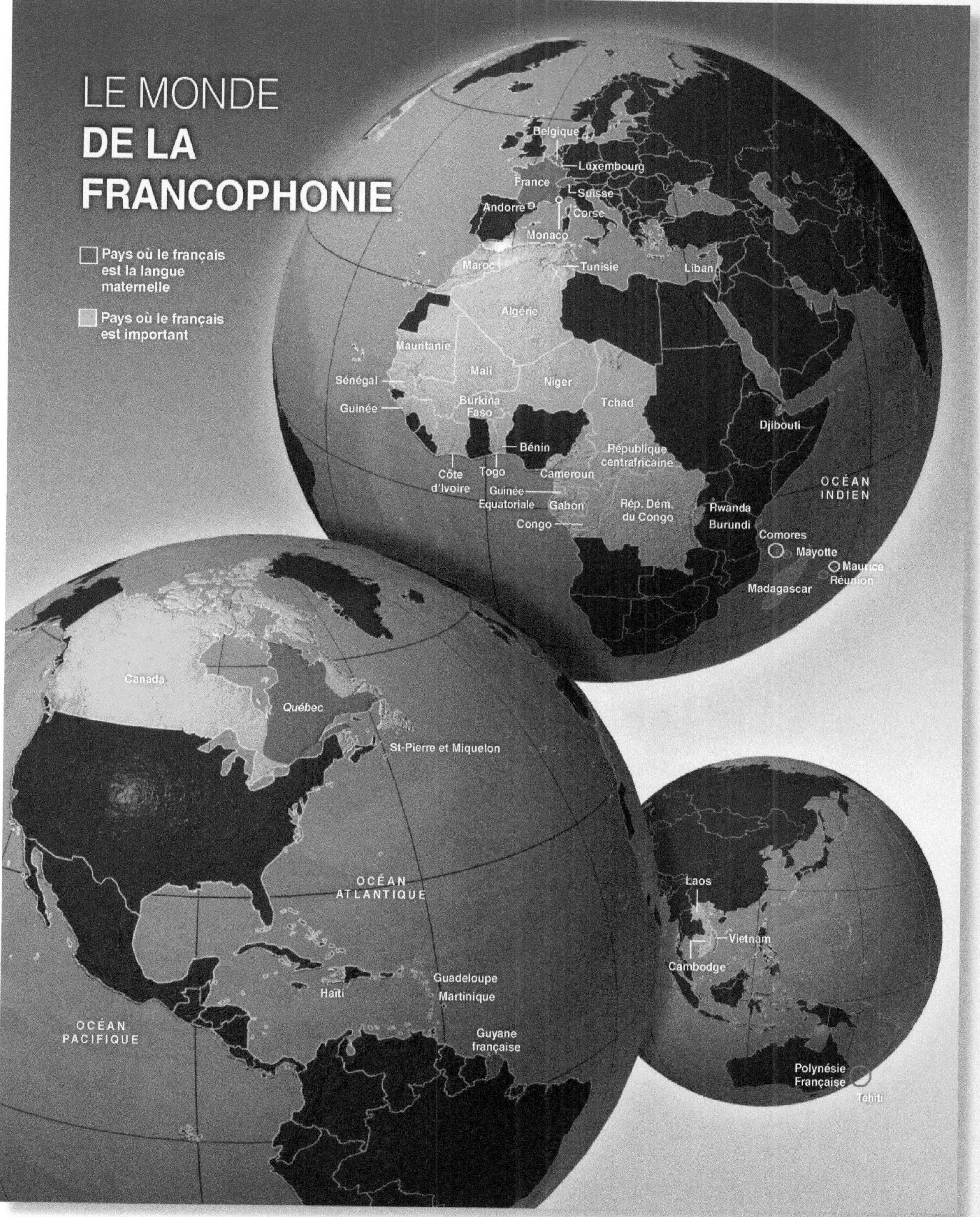

Map of Paris

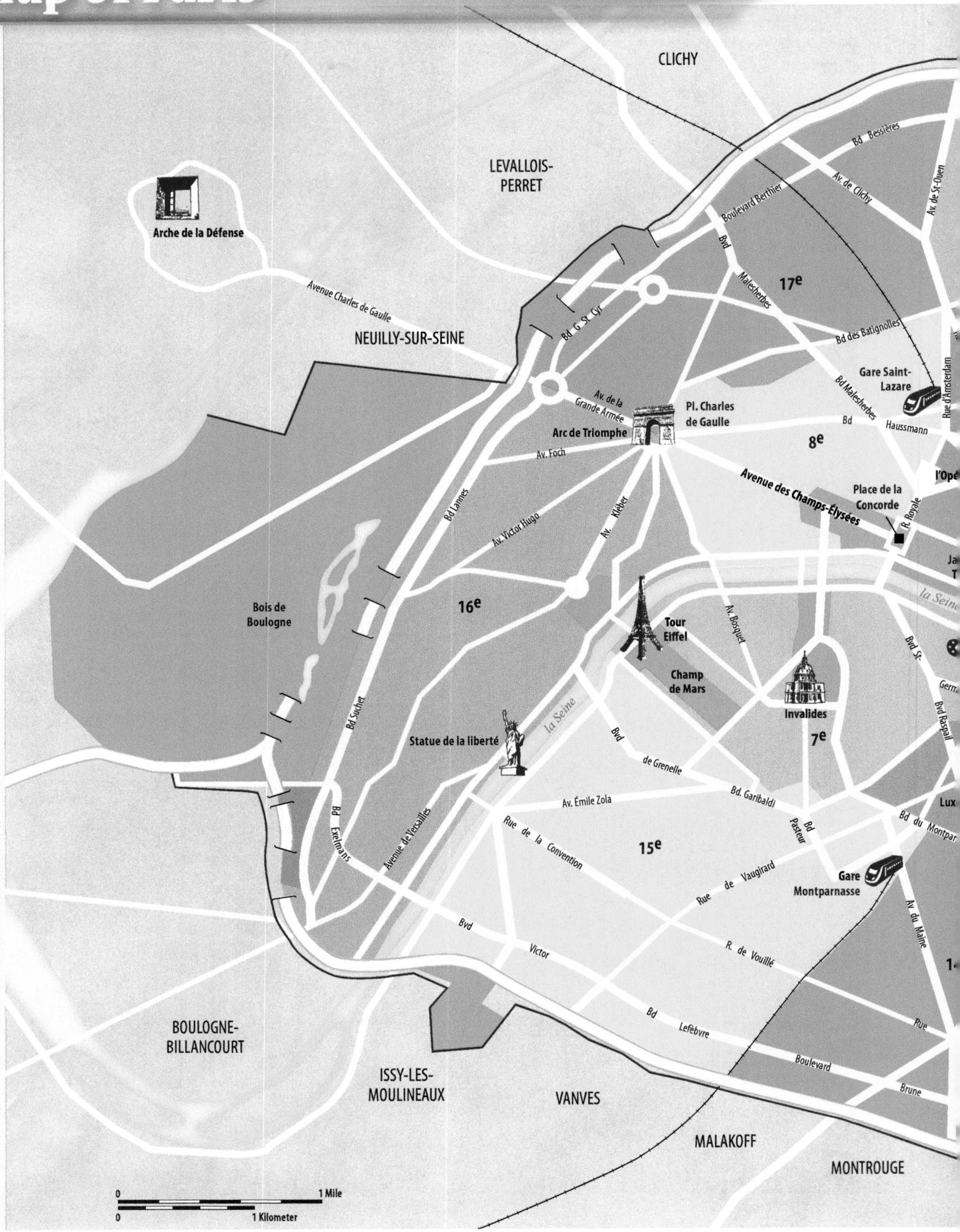

CLICHY
LEVALLOIS-PERRET
Arche de la Défense
Avenue Charles de Gaulle
NEUILLY-SUR-SEINE
Bd Bessières
Av. de St-Ouen
Boulevard Berthier
Av. de Clichy
Bvd Malesherbes
17e
Bd G. St. Cyr
Bd des Batignolles
Gare Saint-Lazare
Bd Malesherbes
Rue d'Amsterdam
Av. de la Grande Armée
Pl. Charles de Gaulle
Arc de Triomphe
Bd Haussmann
8e
Av. Foch
l'Opé
Avenue des Champs-Élysées
Place de la Concorde
R. Royale
Bd Lannes
Av. Victor Hugo
Av. Kléber
la Seine
Bois de Boulogne
16e
Tour Eiffel
Av. Bosquet
Bd St-Germ
Champ de Mars
Invalides
Bd Raspail
Bd Suchet
Statue de la liberté
la Seine
Bvd de Grenelle
7e
Bd. Garibaldi
Av. Émile Zola
Lux
Bd Pasteur
Bd du Montpar
Bd Exelmans
Avenue de Versailles
Rue de la Convention
15e
Rue de Vaugirard
Gare Montparnasse
Av. du Maine
Bvd Victor
R. de Vouillé
Bd Lefèbvre
Rue
Boulevard Brune
BOULOGNE-BILLANCOURT
ISSY-LES-MOULINEAUX
VANVES
MALAKOFF
MONTROUGE
0 1 Mile
0 1 Kilometer

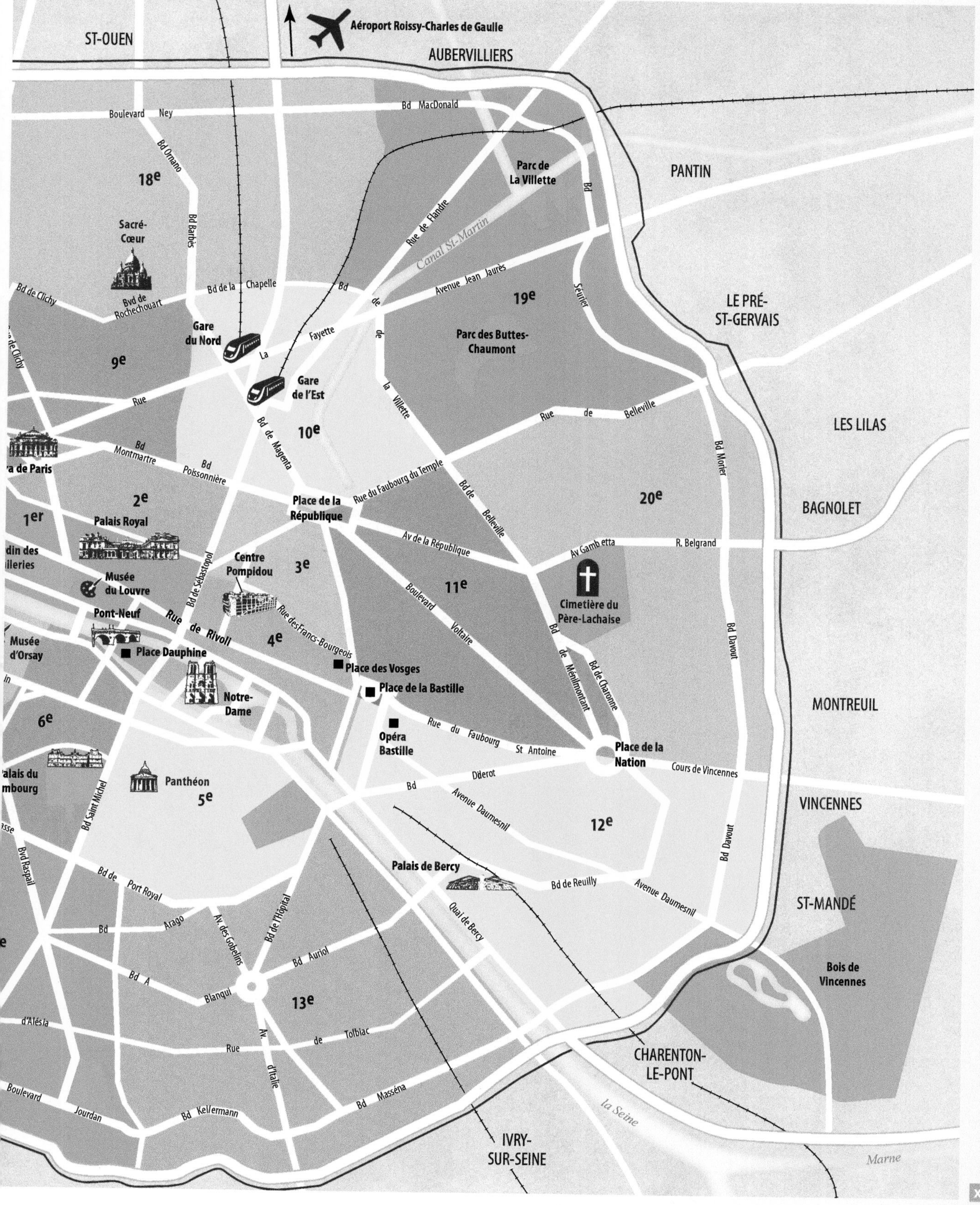

ST-OUEN
Aéroport Roissy-Charles de Gaulle
AUBERVILLIERS
Boulevard Ney
Bd MacDonald
Bd Ornano
18e
Parc de La Villette
PANTIN
Sacré-Cœur
Bd Barbès
Rue de Flandre
Canal St-Martin
Bd de la Chapelle
Bvd de Rochechouart
Avenue Jean Jaurès
19e
Sérurier
LE PRÉ-ST-GERVAIS
Bd de Clichy
Gare du Nord
Parc des Buttes-Chaumont
9e
Rue La Fayette
Bd de la Villette
Gare de l'Est
Rue de Belleville
LES LILAS
10e
Bd Montmartre
Bd Poissonnière
Bd de Magenta
Bd Mortier
Opéra de Paris
2e
Place de la République
Rue du Faubourg du Temple
Bd de Belleville
20e
BAGNOLET
1er
Palais Royal
Av de la République
Av Gambetta
R. Belgrand
Jardin des Tuileries
Centre Pompidou
3e
11e
Musée du Louvre
Bd de Sébastopol
Boulevard Voltaire
Cimetière du Père-Lachaise
Pont-Neuf
Rue de Rivoli
Rue des Francs-Bourgeois
Musée d'Orsay
4e
Place Dauphine
Place des Vosges
Bd de Ménilmontant
Bd de Charonne
Bd Davout
Place de la Bastille
Notre-Dame
MONTREUIL
6e
Opéra Bastille
Rue du Faubourg St Antoine
Place de la Nation
Cours de Vincennes
Palais du Luxembourg
Panthéon
5e
Bd Diderot
Avenue Daumesnil
VINCENNES
Bd Saint Michel
12e
Bd Raspail
Palais de Bercy
ST-MANDÉ
Bd de Port Royal
Bd de Reuilly
Avenue Daumesnil
Bd Arago
Av. des Gobelins
Bd de l'Hôpital
Quai de Bercy
Bois de Vincennes
Bd Auriol
Bd A Blanqui
13e
d'Alésia
Rue de Tolbiac
Av. d'Italie
CHARENTON-LE-PONT
Boulevard Jourdan
Bd Kellermann
Bd Masséna
la Seine
IVRY-SUR-SEINE
Marne

Administrative Map of France

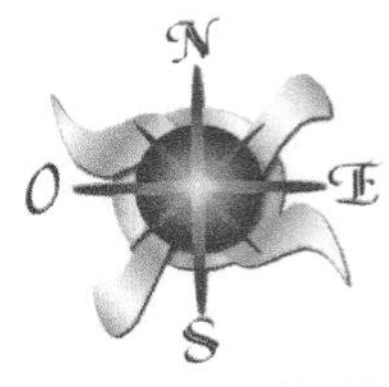

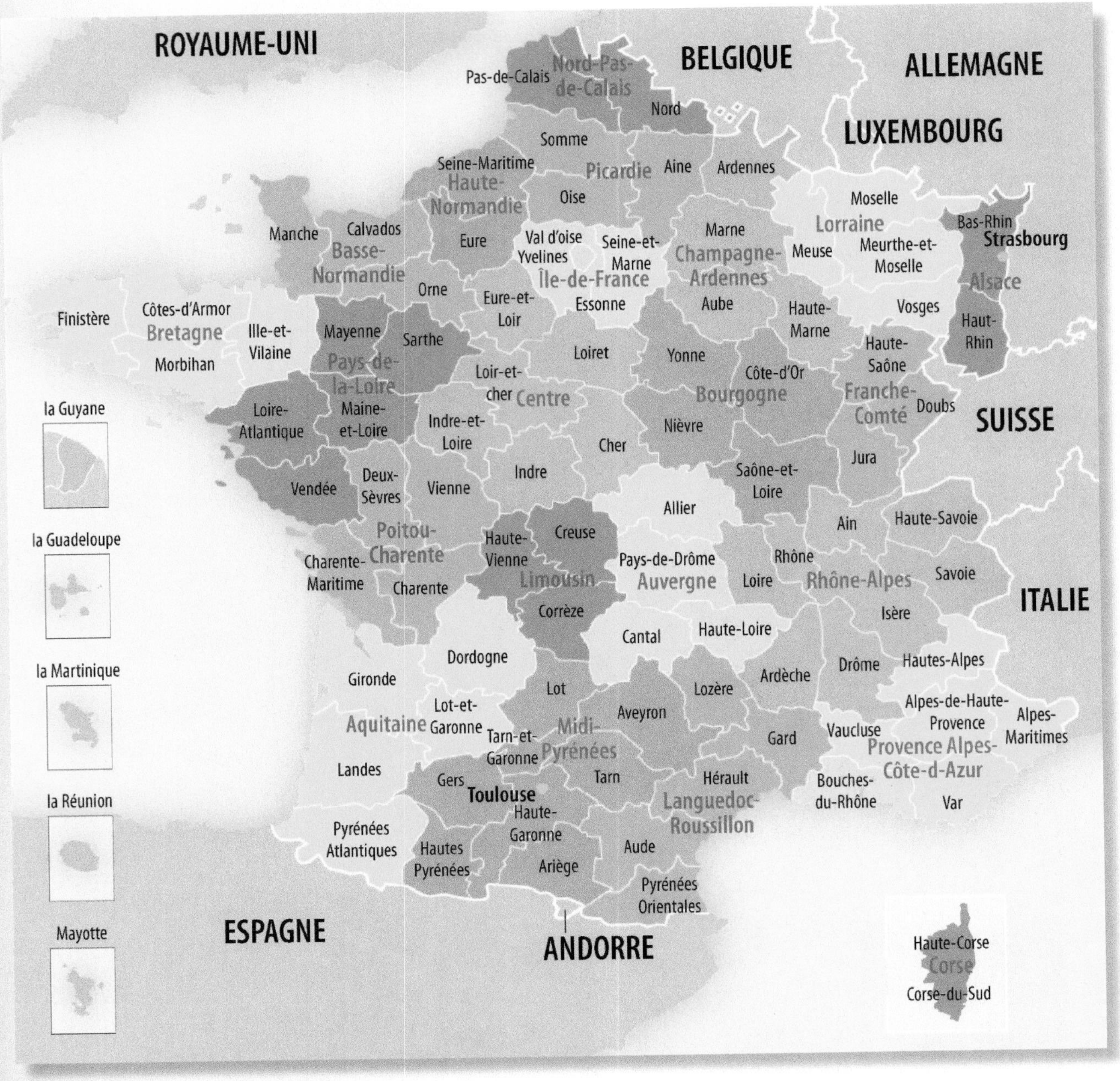

ROYAUME-UNI
BELGIQUE
ALLEMAGNE
LUXEMBOURG
SUISSE
ITALIE
ESPAGNE
ANDORRE

Pas-de-Calais
Nord-Pas-de-Calais
Nord
Somme
Seine-Maritime
Haute-Normandie
Picardie
Aine
Ardennes
Moselle
Lorraine
Bas-Rhin
Strasbourg
Oise
Manche
Calvados
Basse-Normandie
Eure
Val d'oise
Yvelines
Seine-et-Marne
Île-de-France
Marne
Champagne-Ardennes
Meuse
Meurthe-et-Moselle
Alsace
Orne
Eure-et-Loir
Essonne
Aube
Haute-Marne
Vosges
Haut-Rhin
Finistère
Côtes-d'Armor
Bretagne
Ille-et-Vilaine
Morbihan
Mayenne
Sarthe
Pays-de-la-Loire
Loiret
Yonne
Haute-Saône
Loir-et-cher
Centre
Côte-d'Or
Bourgogne
Franche-Comté
Doubs
Loire-Atlantique
Maine-et-Loire
Indre-et-Loire
Cher
Nièvre
Jura
Vendée
Deux-Sèvres
Vienne
Indre
Saône-et-Loire
Allier
Ain
Haute-Savoie
Poitou-Charente
Haute-Vienne
Creuse
Pays-de-Drôme
Rhône
Charente-Maritime
Charente
Limousin
Auvergne
Loire
Rhône-Alpes
Savoie
Corrèze
Isère
Cantal
Haute-Loire
Dordogne
Gironde
Ardèche
Drôme
Hautes-Alpes
Lot
Lozère
Lot-et-Garonne
Aveyron
Alpes-de-Haute-Provence
Alpes-Maritimes
Aquitaine
Tarn-et-Garonne
Midi-Pyrénées
Gard
Vaucluse
Provence Alpes-Côte-d'Azur
Landes
Gers
Tarn
Hérault
Bouches-du-Rhône
Var
Toulouse
Haute-Garonne
Languedoc-Roussillon
Pyrénées Atlantiques
Hautes Pyrénées
Ariège
Aude
Pyrénées Orientales
Haute-Corse
Corse
Corse-du-Sud

la Guyane
la Guadeloupe
la Martinique
la Réunion
Mayotte

Unité

1 Les moments de la vie

Reference Desk

Each unit begins with a photo montage that previews the content of each lesson. In this unit, students will learn about stages in the lives of young people: their personal lives and loves, education, marriage, and future careers. American students may find that their own values, lives, and dreams are closely aligned to their French counterparts'.

Essential Instruction

Ask students to describe in French what they see in the photos. Divide the class into three groups and ask each group to create a story about one of the photos. They can include what happened before the photo was taken, what is happening now, and what will happen later.

Reference Desk

1. Each unit opener spread will have a **Citation**, or quote, designed to connect students to the theme of the unit. The quotation on p. 2, how time reveals secrets, brings opportunities to life, and confirms good counsel, is closely linked to the overriding question of the unit: How do the lives of French-speaking people evolve?
2. The photo on the opening-page spread is intended to highlight a topic from the unit, here teens who may be on their way to the local **Maison des Jeunes et de la Culture**. The teen years are the focus of **Leçon A**, childhood is the focus of **Leçon B**, and early adulthood is the focus of **Leçon C**.
3. **À savoir** provides a fact or statistic about unit content.

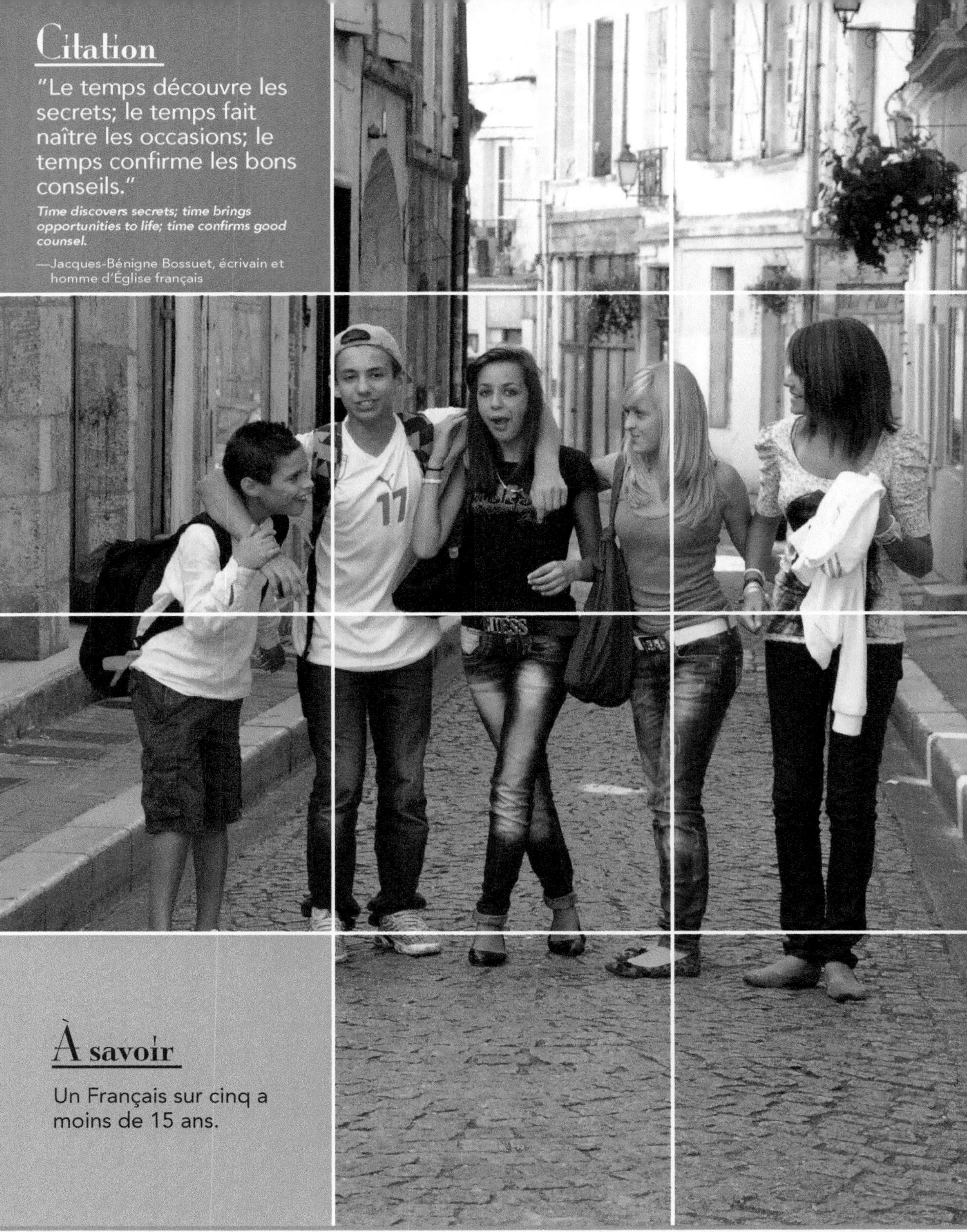

Citation

"Le temps découvre les secrets; le temps fait naître les occasions; le temps confirme les bons conseils."

Time discovers secrets; time brings opportunities to life; time confirms good counsel.

—Jacques-Bénigne Bossuet, écrivain et homme d'Église français

À savoir

Un Français sur cinq a moins de 15 ans.

Essential Instruction

1. Ask your students to make a list of ideas that they have about French young people, childhood in France, preparing for college in France, and French weddings.
2. Use their perceptions as the basis of a class discussion, including questions they have.
3. Ask students if they remember which grammar topics are review (all but **courir**).
4. Go over the student contract with the class.

Unité 1

Les moments de la vie

Comment la vie des Francophones évolue-t-elle avec le temps?

Cette femme se prépare pour quelle cérémonie?

Comment s'appelle ce village?

Contrat de l'élève

Leçon A **I will be able to:**

- say where I met someone and how someone looks; advise someone; and tell someone not to worry.
- talk about French young people and the **Maisons des Jeunes et de la Culture** that they frequent.
- review the present tense of regular and irregular verbs and **depuis** + present tense.

Leçon B **I will be able to:**

- explain how something happened, say what I discovered, and ask for a suggestion.
- talk about childhood and the composition of French families and the **département Provence-Alpes-Côte d'Azur**.
- use the verb **courir** and use the **passé composé** and imperfect.

Leçon C **I will be able to:**

- say I don't care and where I'd like to work.
- talk about college preparatory classes, elite universities, and weddings.
- use the conditional, including sentences with **si**; and the future.

Reference Desk

1. The **Question centrale** is designed to help frame students' learning around an essential question for the entire unit. Students will wrap up their ideas about the question in the **Faisons le point!** section in **Leçon C**.
2. The **Contrat de l'élève** shows students the core content of the unit that they must master: the functions, culture topics, and structure topics.
3. In each unit opener there will be two culture questions, like this unit's question about identifying the village in the photo. This question will be answered in one of the cultural readings, and the students should be encouraged to search for the correct response.

Differentiated Learning

Accelerate

Ask students to write a paragraph about their summer using the **passé compose** and **imparfait**, review topics in **Leçon B**.

Decelerate

Ask students questions about their summer using the **passé composé** and **imparfait**, review topics in **Leçon B**. You may need to give them cues to initiate proper responses, or as a hint tell them they should listen to the verb form and tense in each question.

RESOURCES

 **e-visual 1**

 **Workbook 1–4**

 **Flash Cards**

 **Listening Activity 1**

 **Drill & Practice Games**

Reference Desk

1. Lesson vocabulary is presented with photos or illustrations. Vocabulary practice activities follow the vocabulary presentation.
2. Young Americans enjoy many extracurricular activities organized by their schools. French students, by contrast, enjoy activities at **la Maison des Jeunes et de la Culture** where they can take art and photography classes, or participate in music, theater, and dance. For student athletes, parents in France depend on local clubs to which they pay fees; the sports complex may offer basketball and tennis courts, a pool, and/or soccer fields, depending on the community assets (see p.11).
3. **La soirée** is a more formal word for "party."

Critical Thinking

Comparisons

Two of the lexical items on this page make this a good time to review with students that idiomatic expressions cannot be translated word for word. To express how someone looks, French speakers use **avoir l'air de**, meaning "to seem to be" as in **Il a l'air d'être fâché.** (*He seems to be angry* is more natural in English than *He has an air of being angry.*) The same would be true of the key phrase **Je fréquente**, which could be translated into English as "I often go" rather than "I frequent."

Vocabulaire actif

emcl.com
WB 1–3
LA 1
Games

Quand je sors....   1.2, 5.1

avoir l'air de (d')....

détester quelque chose | être fâché(e) | être affolé(e)

réfléchir

Je fréquente....

le ciné-club | la discothèque | le festival | le skatepark | la MJC | l'aquaparc (m.) | le cours particulier | la soirée | le complexe sportif

Essential Instruction

1. Ask students which sentence is definitive and which is conjecture: **Il est fâché** and **Il a l'air d'être fâché.**
2. Ask students to suggest other examples using adjectives that they have learned such as **content**, **triste**, **pauvre**. Vary the subject forms of **avoir** for more practice.
3. Ask students where they met their **meilleur(e) ami(e)** to elicit the response **Je l'ai rencontré(e)....** For the remaining expressions in **Pour la conversation**, model the expressions or ask students to help you create scenarios such as: **Tu vas sortir avec Jean? Tu ferais bien de l'inviter à la maison./Tu ne le connais pas bien? Oui, mais ce n'est pas la peine de t'inquiéter./Tu as l'air de bien l'aimer. Oui, il est super sympa!**
4. You may want to put students in pairs to do **Activité 1.**

emcl.com
WB 4

Pour la conversation 

1.2, 5.1, 5.2

How do I say where I met someone?

> **Je l'ai rencontré** au ciné-club.
> *I met him/her at the film club.*

How do I advise someone?

> **Tu ferais bien de** l'inviter à la maison.
> *You would do well to invite him to the house.*

How do I tell someone not to worry?

> **Ce n'est pas la peine de t'inquiéter.**
> *It's not worth worrying about.*

How do I describe how someone looks?

> **Tu as l'air de** bien l'aimer.
> *It looks like you really like him.*

Et si je voulais dire...? 

l'auto-école (f.)	*driving school*
l'école (f.) de conduite	*driving school*
la bibliothèque	*library*
la fête foraine	*funfair*
la salle de jeux vidéo	*video arcade*
la patinoire	*ice rink*
Tu as l'air crevé(e).	*You look exhausted.*
Ça n'a pas l'air d'aller.	*You don't seem so well.*
Ils ont l'air de bien s'entendre.	*They look like they get along well.*
Tu as l'air d'être déprimé(e).	*You look depressed.*

1 Vendredi soir   1.2

Certains élèves du lycée Victor Hugo ne sont pas restés à la maison ce soir. Lisez le paragraphe ci-dessous. Puis, répondez à la question qui suit.

Pierre a bien réfléchi, puis il a choisi d'aller au ciné-club à la MJC. Marie-Alix a décidé de jouer au foot au complexe sportif. Maxime s'est rendu à la soirée de Chantal. Julien est allé au skatepark. Julianne voulait voir un film gratuit. Monique voulait fêter l'anniversaire de sa copine Chantal. Marc et Annie se sont rencontrés à la discothèque. Chloé voulait voir ses copains à la MJC.

Qui a vu un(e) autre camarade de classe ce soir?

Answers

Maxime, Monique, Marc, Annie, et Chloé

Reference Desk

1. **Pour la conversation** showcases the functions for the lesson. Encourage students to learn and practice these functions.
2. **Activité 1** is an example of a comprehensible input paragraph. It is designed so students read the new vocabulary words in context before using them in oral and written activities.
3. The vocabulary in **Et si je voulais dire...?** is not included in the end-of-textbook glossary and is included for students who want to learn more or move at a faster pace in learning French.

Differentiated Learning

Adapt

You may want to ask some comprehension questions before assigning the critical thinking question below the paragraph.

Learning Styles

Visual Learners

These students would benefit from creating vocabulary lists by illustrating the terms that they are learning. Artistic students are great assets for making charts, posters, and flash cards for your classroom if you yourself are not a Picasso.

Answers

2

1. Les ados ont l'air d'être contents.
2. Simon a l'air de détester les haricots verts.
3. Alex et Claire ont l'air d'être tristes.
4. Éric et Sébastien ont l'air d'être affolés.
5. Les garçons ont l'air de s'amuser.

Expansion

After completing **Activité 2**, put students in pairs. Challenge each pair to expand on the activity by adding **parce que** or **quand** to provide additional examples of how to use **avoir l'air de**. Example: **Martine a l'air triste parce qu'elle a eu 10/20 sur son contrôle de maths**.

2 Avoir l'air de....

1.2, 5.1

*Regardez les illustrations, puis utilisez **avoir l'air de (d')** et choisissez les expressions de la liste ci-dessous.*

être triste | détester (quelque chose) | s'amuser
être affolé(e) | réfléchir | être content(e)

MODÈLE

Martine
Martine a l'air de réfléchir.

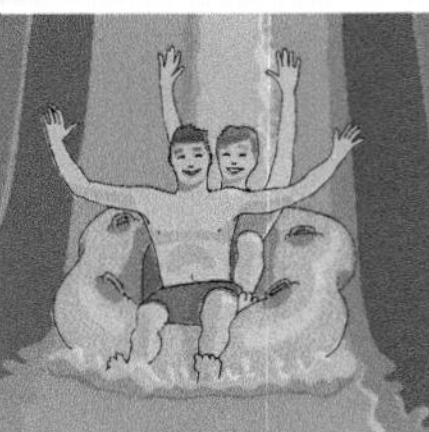

1. les ados

2. Simon

3. Alex et Claire

4. Éric et Sébastien

5. Les garçons

Essential Instruction

1. Remind students that adjectives usually agree with the noun in gender and number. Here, however, the adjective agrees with **l'air**, which is masculine: **Elle a l'air content.**
2. Have students write the answers to **Activité 2** on the board.
3. Check answers to **Activité 4** as a class.
4. You may choose to do the **Questions personnelles** as a teacher/student exchange or put students in pairs.

3 Je l'ai rencontré(e)....

 1.2, 5.1

Dites où chaque ado a rencontré son/sa meilleur(e) ami(e). Choisissez un endroit de la liste.

le ciné-club | la discothèque | la MJC | le complexe sportif
l'aquaparc | le festival de musique | le skatepark | la soirée de Yasmine

MODÈLE Jérémy aime les activités avec d'autres ados. Où a-t-il rencontré Amadou?
Il l'a rencontré à la MJC.

Maylis aime les concerts en plein air. Où a-t-elle rencontré Camille?
Elle l'a rencontrée au festival de musique.

1. Géraldine aime les films chinois. Où a-t-elle rencontré Florence?
2. Sophie aime danser. Où a-t-elle rencontré Julie?
3. Karim aime s'amuser dans l'eau. Où a-t-il rencontré Théo?
4. Sarah aime faire du sport et regarder les matchs de basket. Où a-t-elle rencontré Marianne?
5. Marco aime faire du skate. Où a-t-il rencontré Antoine?
6. Béatrice aime faire la fête. Où a-t-elle rencontré Fatima?

4 Où sont-ils allés?

  1.2

Écrivez les numéros 1–8 sur votre papier. Dites pour chaque conversation où les personnes sont allées en écrivant la bonne lettre.

A. la discothèque
B. le complexe sportif
C. la soirée
D. le festival de musique
E. le cours particulier
F. le skatepark
G. la MJC
H. le ciné-club

5 Questions personnelles

   1.2, 5.1

Répondez aux questions suivantes.

1. Qu'est-ce que tu fais quand un(e) ami(e) a l'air triste?
2. Quels genres de films est-ce que tu détestes?
3. Est-ce que tu réfléchis bien avant de prendre une décision?
4. Où as-tu rencontré tes meilleur(e)s ami(e)s?
5. Y a-t-il un complexe sportif sympa dans ta ville ou ta région? Quels sports peut-on y pratiquer?

Answers

1. Elle l'a rencontrée au ciné-club.
2. Elle l'a rencontrée à la discothèque.
3. Il l'a rencontré à l'aquaparc.
4. Elle l'a rencontrée au complexe sportif.
5. Il l'a rencontré au skatepark.
6. Elle l'a rencontrée à la soirée de Yasmine.

1. D
2. A
3. E
4. G
5. B
6. F
7. C
8. H

5 *Answers will vary.*

Reference Desk

Activité 4 is a listening activity that has been recorded; scripts of textbook listening activities can be found in the front pages of this Annotated Teacher's Edition. There is one vocabulary listening activity in every lesson. Other listening activities have been adapted to provide more listening/speaking practice. These activities can be found in the **Audio Program Manual**.

Communication

Interpersonal: Paired Practice

Have each student write a problem on a slip of paper. Put the slips in a bowl or hat and ask half the students to take one. Move the desks so that the class is in two circles facing each other. Students in the inner circle will read their "problem" to the opposing partner, for example: **Je voudrais organiser une soirée, mais je n'ai pas d'argent.** The student opposite presents a solution using **Tu ferais bien de (demander à tes amis d'apporter de la nourriture).**

Differentiated Learning

Adapt

There are many different ways to organize your classroom to maximize productive interaction among students. Some activities work well in pairs, others in groups of three and four. You can randomly group students by organizing a deck of playing cards according to the number of students in your class. The four students who draw the same number will be working together. Or you might want to organize groups intentionally by pairing two students who perform well with two students who might need more help.

Special Needs Students

Auditory Impairment

To help students who have trouble listening to recorded French audio, make sure they understand the direction line for **Activité 4**. You may also want to allow them to have their books open to the vocabulary presentation.

RESOURCES

Dialogue Video

Workbook 5–6

Answers

1. Élodie
2. Léo
3. Léo
4. Élodie
5. Élodie
6. Élodie et Léo

Reference Desk

1. In **Rencontres culturelles**, students can watch the dialogue, which has been filmed, or just listen to the audio.
2. **Mots-clé** is a new feature in Level 3 that highlights the etymology of key words so that students see the link between Latin and French and learn that languages are constantly evolving.
3. Point out some lexical items in the dialogue. The past participle **connu** comes from **connaître.** Ask students to find direct objects that precede verbs: **l'aimer**, **te regarde**, **te sourit**, **tu le trouves**, etc. The infinitive for **vous ne vous quittez plus** is **se quitter**.
4. The expression **au courant** is also in the English dictionary.
5. Have students make a list of reasons why Leo thinks that Karim likes Elodie. Example: **"Il la regarde."**

Critical Thinking

Comparisons

Point out to students the verb **trouver** has two meanings, just as in English. **Trouver** means "to find something that is missing or lost." It also means "to find," as in to have an opinion: **Je trouve que le chocolat est délicieux.**

Rencontres culturelles

emcl.com
WB 5

1.1, 1.2, 5.1

Comment tu le trouves?

Élodie montre à Léo des photos de ses amis sur son portable.

Élodie: On fait une super bande… je n'avais jamais connu ça avant.
Léo: Et lui? Tu as l'air de bien l'aimer.
Élodie: Pourquoi tu dis ça?
Léo: Comme ça… il te regarde, il te sourit… ça s'appelle de la complicité….
Élodie: Comment tu le trouves?
Léo: Karim? C'est le frère d'un copain, je l'aime bien: il réussit à ses examens; il adore le cinéma…. Tu le connais depuis quand?
Élodie: Je l'ai rencontré au ciné-club: ce soir-là, on n'était absolument pas d'accord sur le film….
Léo: Et maintenant il te fait de beaux sourires; il t'attend après les cours; et vous ne vous quittez plus… tu ferais bien de l'inviter à la maison….
Élodie: Mais que va dire maman?
Léo: Ce n'est pas la peine de t'inquiéter, elle est déjà au courant!

Bande. (provençal XVème siècle, *banda*: "la troupe," la "compagnie des gens"). Une bande se définit comme un groupe de personnes ayant des activités et des intérêts en commun. Par exemple: Je vais toujours au ciné avec la même *bande de* copains. L'expression "bande de…" est une insulte qui s'adresse à un groupe.

6 Comment tu le trouves?

1.2, 5.1

Identifiez la personne décrite.

1. Cette personne aime bien Karim.
2. Cette personne connaît le frère de Karim.
3. Cette personne sait qu'Élodie aime bien Karim.
4. Cette personne a rencontré Karim au ciné-club.
5. Cette personne passe beaucoup de temps avec Karim.
6. Cette personne a une super bande.

Essential Instruction

1. Before watching the video, ask students to look at the photos. What might Élodie and Léo be looking at? Have the students scan the dialogue for cognates like **complicité** and to use context clues to guess other words they may not know. Ask them to predict what they think the video is about. Watch the video together so students can confirm if their predictions were correct.
2. To make sure students understood the dialogue, do **Activité 6** as a class.
3. The **Extension** is a dialogue for advanced students who want to go faster or like being challenged; a critical-thinking question always follows this dialogue. The words in **Extension** dialogues are not in the end-of-unit or end-of-book vocabulary list.

Extension **Le profil d'une lycéenne**   **1.1, 1.2, 5.1**

emcl.com WB 6

Un journaliste interviewe une lycéenne pour faire un profil de l'ado typique.

Journaliste: Tu as beaucoup de copains et copines au lycée?

Julie: On est toute une bande: on se retrouve tout le temps à la fin des cours, pour sortir, pour aller prendre un verre au café, on organise des soirées....

Journaliste: Ton petit ami fait partie du groupe?

Julie: Ben, oui.

Journaliste: Mais ce n'est pas gênant de ne pas avoir de temps à toi?

Julie: Au contraire! On a tous notre profil sur Facebook; comme ça on sait toujours ce que tout le monde fait. Même les copains des copains!

Journaliste: Alors, tu es toujours connectée avec tes amis?

Julie: Notre génération est toujours connectée!

Extension Qu'est-ce que le reporter apprend sur la vie des lycéens?

Answers

Extension

Il apprend que les lycéens aujourd'hui sont très connectés par les réseaux sociaux comme Facebook.

Reference Desk

1. The **Extension** dialogue is for advanced students who want to go further. The dialogue is followed by one critical-thinking question.
2. **Ben** is the shortened form of **bien** used as a filler in the conversation the way we might say "well."
3. This would be a good time to review the forms of **tout**. Ask students to find examples of these forms in the dialogue.

Culture

Practices: Information

Level 3 is a good time to start discussing language patterns. The French love to truncate words. For example, **un ado** is short for **un adolescent; un dico**, **un dictionnaire; un appart**, **an appartement**; and **un ordi**, **un ordinateur**. Ask the students reading the **Extension** dialogue to make a list to share with the class. Encourage students to add to this list throughout the year.

Differentiated Learning

Accelerate

Have these advanced students interview a peer in the class, asking the same questions as **le journaliste** in the **Extension** dialogue. Have the pairs present their dialogues to the rest of the class.

Decelerate

As you read the dialogue in **Rencontres culturelles** aloud, ask your students to sub-vocalize the words as you speak. (They will mouth the words without speaking.) In doing so, they will register the correct pronunciation without the stress of reading aloud. Ask them after each line of the interview what words or expressions they do not understand. Encourage even the most basic questions.

Learning Styles

Auditory Learners

After listening to the main dialogue, ask these students to share what they understand. Only then ask students to look at the text in their books.

Workbook 7

Reference Desk

1. **Points de départ** is the name of the culture section. Note that the **Question centrale** reappears here. Besides the paragraphs about francophone practices, there are **Produits** boxes and **Comparaisons** questions that allow students to connect French and American cultures.
2. Students are not expected to remember, and they will not be tested on, the glossed vocabulary.

Culture

Products: Information

For your students who are **branché**, here are the terms they would find on a French social media page. Ask students if they can figure out the equivalents in English for these: **mentions j'aime** (*like*), **actualiser une photo de profil** (*post a photo*), **historique personnel** (*personal information*), **Exprimez-vous?** (*What's on your mind?*), **mot de passe** (*password*), **mises à jour** (*updates*), **signaler comme indésirable** (*unfriend*).

Points de départ

Pre AP

emcl.com WB 7

Question centrale

Comment la vie des Francophones évolue-t-elle avec le temps?

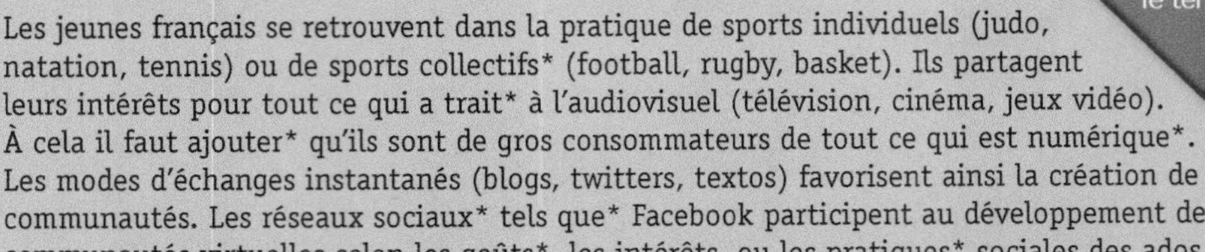

Modes de vie des adolescents 1.2, 2.1, 2.2, 5.1

Les jeunes français se retrouvent dans la pratique de sports individuels (judo, natation, tennis) ou de sports collectifs* (football, rugby, basket). Ils partagent leurs intérêts pour tout ce qui a trait* à l'audiovisuel (télévision, cinéma, jeux vidéo). À cela il faut ajouter* qu'ils sont de gros consommateurs de tout ce qui est numérique*. Les modes d'échanges instantanés (blogs, twitters, textos) favorisent ainsi la création de communautés. Les réseaux sociaux* tels que* Facebook participent au développement de communautés virtuelles selon les goûts*, les intérêts, ou les pratiques* sociales des ados.

Autour* de la mode, de la musique, du sport, ou de la vidéo se rassemblent* des groupes qui partagent les mêmes styles de vêtements, se reconnaissent* dans les mêmes héros de séries télé, écoutent le même style de musique, ou encore sont fans des mêmes sportifs. Ils s'inventent aussi un vocabulaire, des gestes (souvent empruntés à leurs "idoles"), et parfois une façon* de parler. Les jeunes ont surtout un goût commun pour faire la fête, et la musique y occupe une place importante: c'est un moment pour "s'éclater*."

Pascal passe deux heures par jour sur Internet.

Search words: club de sport (+ nom de la ville), allociné, télé 7 jours

sport collectif *team sport;* **a trait** *is linked;* **ajouter** *to add;* **numérique** *digital;* **réseaux sociaux** *social networks;* **tels que** *such as;* **goûts** *tastes;* **pratiques** *practices;* **Autour** *Around;* **se rassemblent** *gather;* **se reconnaissent** *identify with;* **façon** *manner;* **s'éclater** *to have a ball*

Les jeunes français aiment se servir des **blogues** pour parler de leurs vies et leurs intérêts, comme Skyrock France et MSN. Il y a plus de blogueurs en France que dans n'importe quel autre pays européen.

COMPARAISONS

Comparez les modes de vie des jeunes français avec les vôtres.

Essential Instruction

1. To compare the interests of the French students with their own, students should make two columns on a piece of paper. The first column will be a numbered list of interests of French teens mentioned in the **Points de départ.** Across from each item is the corresponding interest of American youth, according to what American students have observed. To add to the list, encourage students to find a teen blog online and follow it for a few days. At the end of the week ask students to share what they have learned.
2. Have each student look at the website of an **MJC** online, then divide the class into groups to share what they learned.

Les MJC  1.2, 2.1, 2.2, 4.1, 4.2, 5.1

La MJC organise toujours des sorties pour les jeunes.

Les Maisons des Jeunes et de la Culture (MJC) sont des lieux de rencontre pour les jeunes; elles existent dans pratiquement toutes les villes de France. Ce sont des centres sportifs, éducatifs, culturels, et artistiques fréquentés premièrement par les enfants, les ados, et les jeunes de moins de 25 ans, mais aussi par les adultes. Les MJC offrent des activités éducatives et récréatives, telles que le sport, la peinture, la musique, des séances de cinéma. Les MJC sont de vrais centres d'information et d'échange*, où l'on peut voir ou participer à des expositions, et prendre part* à des projets de bénévolat*.

Ce sont aussi des centres d'accueil où l'on peut se renseigner pour obtenir des aides. Elles représentent donc un espace de relations sociales, d'informations, et d'aide sociale pour les habitants d'une commune. On peut s'inscrire à la MJC de sa ville et participer aux événements régulièrement, ou y aller de temps en temps pour participer à des activités, des forums d'échange, etc. Les tarifs d'adhésion* ou de participation sont toujours raisonnables, car les MJC sont partenaires de fédérations régionales et reçoivent des aides de l'état.

 **Search words: mjc (+ nom de la ville)**

échange *exchange;* **prendre part** *participate;* **bénévolat** *volunteer;* **adhésion** *subscription*

L'argot des ados

Les expressions argotiques utilisées par les ados évoluent. Voici quelques-unes de cette génération:

Ça kiffe. / Ça déchire.	C'est génial.
faire la teuf	faire la fête
un reuf	un frère
un mec	un garçon
Il est grave.	Il est bizarre.
J'hallucine.	Je n'y crois pas.

COMPARAISONS

Y a-t-il un endroit où vous passez du temps avec d'autres ados? Si non, où allez-vous quand vous avez du temps libre? Qu'est-ce que vous y faites?

Reference Desk

L'argot des ados is a new feature in Level 3 that highlights slang words.

Culture

Practices: Information

For generations, young French people have spoken a unique sub-language called **le verlan.** It is basically inverted French. The very name is a good illustration. **L'envers** means "the reverse." Take the two syllables and reverse them with a slight spelling change and you have **verlan.** Ask your students if they can guess what the following words mean: **ripa** (**Paris**), **rempes** (**parents**), **meuf** (**femme**), **blèmpro** (**problème**). For more information, use the search words **verlan** and **dictionnaire de la zone.**

Differentiated Learning

Decelerate

1. Pair students needing more assistance with above-level students to collaborate reading **Les MJC.** Have the stronger students ask comprehension questions.
2. Have students participate in a lexical scavenger hunt in which pairs have to search for clues that you have prepared in English. For example, "Find the sentence that states that one can find volunteer opportunities at the youth center." (**On peut prendre part à des projets de bénévolat.**)

Special Needs Students

Reading Difficulties

For those students who have trouble reading longer texts in French and finding the main ideas, make an outline for them to complete.

Answers

7 *Answers will vary.*

À discuter
Answers will vary.

8
une salutation: 3 (*Sympa ce petit bonjour furtif...*) ; 7 (*nous nous sommes croisés, timidement souris...*)
une conversation: 6 (*je t'ai demandé...*); 9 (*Nous avons dicuté...*)
une interaction: 1 (*On s'est rencontré...*); 4 (*Tu m'as souri dans les escaliers...*)
une remarque politique: 9 (*Nous avons discuté (de ce fournisseur d'énergie écologique...*)
une trahison: 5 (*amour trahi...*)
un remerciement: 2 (*un grand merci à...*)
un regret: 7 (*Pourquoi ne nous sommes-nous pas arrêtés?...*); 8 (*Je n'ai jamais eu de regret plus grand...*)

Reference Desk

1. Review with students what they learned about **le Métro** in previous levels. It is composed of 16 routes, mostly underground, transporting over 4.5 million people per day. It is 133 miles long, composed of 301 stations with 62 transfer stations. The lines are indicated by color and number. The directions are listed by the last station on the line called **a terminus.** The Paris metro operates from 5:30 A.M. to 1:15 A.M. daily.
2. The **RER** is a commuter train system that runs through Paris, servicing a limited number of stations. There are five lines indicated by colors: A (red), B (blue), C (yellow), D (green), and E (pink). Travelers can take the **RER** to Charles de Gaulle airport as well as to Eurodisney, among other destinations. For more information, search the words **RATP**, **RER**. Naturally, people using public transportation notice others, which leads to many attempts by people to find those who caught their attention.

7 Activités culturelles

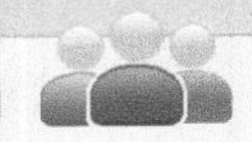

1.2, 1.3, 2.1, 3.2, 5.1

Complétez les activités suivantes.

1. Recherchez des clubs où les ados français peuvent pratiquer les sports mentionnés à la page 10.
2. Allez sur le site Web d'une MJC d'une ville française. Évaluez cette MJC en termes et de la variété des activités, du tarif de participation, des heures et jours d'ouverture, etc. Dites à quelles activités vous participeriez. Vous pouvez travailler en groupes.
3. Trouvez deux projets de bénévolat dans les MJC. Citez les villes.
4. Écrivez un dialogue avec un partenaire dans lequel vous utilisez deux ou trois expressions argotiques. Présentez-le à la classe.

Search words: judo, natation, tennis, football, rugby, basket (+ club ou association)

À discuter

Comment est-ce que l'Internet change les rapports entre ados?

Du côté des médias

Interpretive Communication

Lisez le courrier du cœur de Métrofrance.

Métrofrance - Courrier du cœur

1. RER A ingénieur travaillant à la banque Je te cherche depuis un bon moment mais impossible de trouver… toi que j'ai rencontré un mercredi ensoleillé. On s'est rencontré à Nanterre préfecture, à auber tu voulais me...
2. un grand merci à la jeune femme, qui, Mardi 26 Mai m'a rattrapé dans l'escalator du RER E à Magenta vers Haussmann.à 7h 15. Plus de peur que de mal...
3. le 25 mai RER A direction poissy 16h15 Sympa ce petit bonjour furtif dans le RER A direction poissy je suis decendu a houilles et toi tu as continué .... moi bermuda et pull à bientôt peut être...
4. Belle brune à la Pena Festayre Tu m'as souri dans les escaliers, je tai embrassé. On a dansé. Cétait bien! Je voudrais te revoir. A bientôt jespère. Erwan...
5. amour trahi je croyais t'aimé heureusement que non, tu m'as trahi, abandonné comme un chien, tu es ignoble, horrible, et j'ai vu ton vrai visage croyant que tu étais bien sur...
6. A toi la belle brune de la ligne 8 lundi 02 mai vers 19h00, je tai demandé si tu descends à la station république, hélas tu mas répondus que tu...
7. Place d'Italie, hier. Pourquoi ne nous sommes nous pas arrêtés? Sur ce quai où nous nous sommes croisés, timidement souris, puis franchement souris, avant que je ne tourne et ne prenne ce fichu...
8. La Demoiselle au vélo pliant et le RER. Chère Demoiselle au vélo pliant, Je nai jamais eu de regret plus grand que cet acte manqué le jour où nous nous sommes croisés. Vous en souvenez-vous ? Cétait un...
9. A vous qui portiez un Tee-shirt "Enercoop", jeudi 7 avril en direction de Montreuil. Bonjour, Je madresse à vous que jai rencontré il y a une semaine, sur la ligne 9 en direction de Montreuil. Nous avons discuté (de ce fournisseur dénergie écologique et...

8 Le courrier du cœur de Métrofrance

1.2, 2.1, 4.1, 5.1

Retrouvez dans le courrier du cœur….

- une salutation
- une conversation
- une interaction
- une remarque politique
- une trahison (*betrayal*)
- un remerciement
- un regret

Essential Instruction

1. You may want to allow students to work in pairs to complete the **Activités culturelles**.
2. Here is a list of supplemental vocabulary to aid in understand the **Metrofrance—Courrier du cœur: la prefecture** (*police station*), **auber** (*metro stop*), **vélo pliant** (*foldable bike*). This is a challenging reading because it is written in a sort of condensed language with much implied. Begin by asking students to determine if each chance meeting was a positive, negative, uplifting, or frustrating experience. Ask them to find the word clues that indicate the emotion of the writer.
3. Before reviewing the formation of regular verbs, have students see if they can do the activity in yellow. Students who are ready can proceed to **Activités 9–11** while you review with the rest of the class.

Structure de la langue

emcl.com
WB 8–11
LA 2
Games

Révision: Present Tense of Regular Verbs Ending in *–er, –ir,* and *–re* 1.2

Do you remember the endings to regular verbs in the present tense? See if you can match the endings below to the correct pattern for regular verbs.

1. **–s, –s, –, –ons, –ez, –ent**
2. **–e, –es, –e, –ons, –ez, –ent**
3. **–is, –is, –it, –issons, –issez, –issent**

A. regular **–er** verbs
B. regular **–ir** verbs
C. regular **–re** verbs

If you got one or more wrong, then read the summary below.

To form the present tense of a regular **–er** verb, add the endings **–e**, **–es**, **–e**, **–ons**, **–ez**, and **–ent** to the stem of the verb depending on the corresponding subject pronouns.

trouver			
je	**trouve**	nous	**trouvons**
tu	**trouves**	vous	**trouvez**
il/elle/on	**trouve**	ils/elles	**trouvent**

Comment tu **trouves** le garçon? — *What do you think of the boy?*
Je le **trouve** génial! — *I think he is fantastic!*

To form the present tense of a regular **–ir** verb, add the endings **–is**, **–is**, **–it**, **–issons**, **–issez**, and **–issent** to the stem of the verb depending on the corresponding subject pronouns.

réussir			
je	**réussis**	nous	**réussissons**
tu	**réussis**	vous	**réussissez**
il/elle/on	**réussit**	ils/elles	**réussissent**

Réussissez-vous à vos contrôles? — *Are you passing your tests?*
Oui, nous y **réussissons.** — Yes, we are passing.

PRESENT TENSE OF REGULAR VERBS:
The answers are: 1. C; 2. A; 3. B

RESOURCES

 Workbook 8–11

 Listening Activity 2

 Drill & Practice Games

Reference Desk

1. **Structure de la langue** is the grammar section of the textbook. Here students review grammar topics from Levels 1–2, learn new grammar, and practice each grammar concept, whether new or reviewed. There is more practice for new grammar topics than for review topics.
2. Students originally learned regular verbs in Level 1: –**er** verbs, **Unité 2**; –**ir** verbs, **Unité 5**; –**re** verbs, **Unité 6.** All three types of regular verbs were reviewed in Level 2, **Unité 1.**

Game

Dice Conjugation

Distribute a die to groups of three or four students. Explain that each number corresponds to a subject pronoun you write on the board: 1 is for **je**, 2 for **tu**, etc. Call out a verb. Students take turns rolling the die and conjugating the regular verbs according to the subject pronoun. Have a sample verb from each conjugation on the board so that students can correct their work. Circulate to see what pronunciation errors you are hearing and point out a few tips to remember when the class reconvenes.

Differentiated Learning

Decelerate

Prepare an alternate version of the realia in which these students only see the entries that link to what they are asked to do in **Activité 8**, and tell them the type of message it is. Ask them to explain why that description is appropriate.

Multiple Intelligences

Musical-Rythmic/Bodily-Kinesthetic

Have students tap out the verbs as they conjugate them. They will "feel" the syllables change in the **nous** and **vous** forms as they tap the beat.

Answers

Leïla et Karim arrivent au parc.
Amadou joue de la guitare.
Mathis et moi mangeons des sandwichs.
Philippe aide Océanne.
Léa apporte des boissons.
Julie et Claire jouent au foot.
Salim et toi préparez des hamburgers.

Reference Desk

Activité 9 reviews regular –**er** verbs, **Activités 10–11** all three regular types of verbs.

To form the present tense of a regular **–re** verb, add the endings **–s**, **–s**, **–**, **–ons**, **–ez**, and **–ent** to the stem of the verb depending on the corresponding subject pronouns.

attendre			
je	**attends**	nous	**attendons**
tu	**attends**	vous	**attendez**
il/elle/on	**attend**	ils/elles	**attendent**

Qui attends-tu? *Who are you waiting for?*
J'attends mon copain. *I'm waiting for my friend.*

COMPARAISONS

Are "to find," "to succeed," and "to wait for" regular verbs in the present tense in English?

4.1

9 Un après-midi au parc

1.1, 1.2, 5.1

Dites ce que ces jeunes font au parc. Utilisez un verbe de la liste.

apporter des boissons | jouer de la guitare | arriver au parc
manger des sandwichs | aider | jouer au foot | préparer des hamburgers

COMPARAISONS: Yes, all three verbs are also regular in the present tense in English:
I find, You find, He finds, We find, They find
I succeed, You succeed, She succeeds, We succeed, They succeed
I wait, You wait, He waits, We wait, They wait

Essential Instruction

1. Reintroduce regular –**er**, –**ir**, and –**re** verbs as bargain verbs by telling students that with these patterns they can conjugate hundreds of verbs! Brainstorm with them the verbs from these conjugations that they learned in Levels 1 and 2.
2. Have the students conjugate a sample verb of each type side by side in their notebook. What forms do these verbs have in common?
3. Do **Activité 9** as a class, **10** in small groups, and **11** individually or in pairs.

10 La rentrée

 1.2, 2.1, 5.1

Complétez chaque phrase pour indiquer ce que Marine et sa sœur font pour se préparer pour la rentrée.

1. Marine… une nouvelle jupe dans son magasin préféré. (*chercher*)
2. Elle… une belle jupe grise qui… 25 €. (*choisir, coûter*)
3. Elle… un pull à sa meilleure amie Amélie pour le premier jour de classe. (*emprunter*)
4. Le jour de la rentrée, Marine et sa sœur… des sandwiches parce qu'elles n'aiment pas ce qu'il y a à la cantine. (*préparer*)
5. Il est 7h45 quand elles… de nettoyer la cuisine. (*finir*)
6. Marine… son sac à dos avec ses cahiers, son dictionnaire anglais-français, et sa trousse. (*remplir*)
7. Marine… sa sœur au collège. (*accompagner*)
8. Elle… que sa sœur…. (*remarquer, grandir*)
9. Marine… à sa sœur de bien étudier. (*conseiller*)
10. Ensuite, Marine… Amélie devant le lycée. (*attendre*)

11 Qu'est-ce qu'on fait pendant les vacances?

 1.2, 1.3, 5.1

Choisissez un élément de chaque colonne (A, B, et C), puis formez des phrases logiques. Attention à la conjugaison des verbes en **–er**, **–ir**, *et* **–re**.

A	B	C
mes copains et moi	écouter un concert de jazz	au parc
tu	finir ses devoirs	à la discothèque
je	dessiner nos familles	au festival de musique
Marco	attendre tes amis	à la soirée
ton cousin et toi	danser la salsa	au cours particulier
les ados	regarder un documentaire	au ciné-club de la MJC
Sophie et Ahmed	nourrir les chevaux	à la ferme

Multiple Intelligences

Intrapersonal

Students who like to work on their own can find extra practice with wonderful interactive verb web sites that provide activities online.

Search words: **conjuguemos**, **verbs-online**, **funtrivia**

Answers

1. cherche
2. choisit…coûte
3. emprunte
4. préparent
5. finissent
6. remplit
7. accompagne
8. remarque…grandit
9. conseille
10. attend

11 *Possible Answers:*

Mes copains et moi dessinons nos familles au cours particulier.
Tu attends tes amis à la soirée.
J'écoute un concert de jazz au festival de musique.
Marco finit ses devoirs au parc.
Ton cousin et toi dansez la salsa à la discothèque.
Les ados regardent un documentaire au ciné-club de la MJC.
Sophie et Amed nourrissent les chevaux à la ferme.

TPR

To anchor the pronunciation of regular present-tense verbs in the three conjugations, ask the students to put their index finger to their mouth as if to say "shhh" each time you say a conjugation that has a silent ending. Through this physical action, they will internalize that the **nous** and the **vous** forms are the only ones that have pronounced endings.

Expansion

Select students to put the sentences on the board for correction after they have completed **Activité 11**. Then have the students do the exercise orally, ideally without consulting their written work.

RESOURCES

 Workbook 12–13

 Drill & Practice Games

Révision: Present Tense of Irregular Verbs  1.2

emcl.com
WB 12–13
Games

See if you can figure out the meanings of the verbs below. You will find the answers at the bottom of the page. If you have any trouble, then read the grammar summary that follows.

1. **ils ont**	A. you do, you make
2. **vous faites**	B. you are
3. **ils vont**	C. they have
4. **tu es**	D. they are going

Many French verbs are considered irregular because they do not follow a regular pattern like **–er**, **–ir**, and **–re** verbs. Here are the present tense forms of the "building block" irregular verbs **aller**, **être**, **avoir**, and **faire**.

	aller	avoir	être	faire
je	**vais**	**ai**	**suis**	**fais**
tu	**vas**	**as**	**es**	**fais**
il/elle/on	**va**	**a**	**est**	**fait**
nous	**allons**	**avons**	**sommes**	**faisons**
vous	**allez**	**avez**	**êtes**	**faites**
ils/elles	**vont**	**ont**	**sont**	**font**

Vous **allez** au ciné-club? — *Are you going to the film club?*
Non, nous n'**avons** pas envie d'y aller. — *No, we don't feel like going there.*

Qu'est-ce que vous **faites**? — *What are you doing?*
Je **suis** au skatepark et Djamel **est** au cinéma. — *I am at the skate park and Djamel is at the movies.*

On the next page you will find the **je** form of the other irregular verbs that you have already learned. An example sentence is included containing one of the other forms of the verb. Do you remember what these verbs mean? To review them, turn to the Grammar Summary at the back of the book.

PRESENT TENSE OF REGULAR VERBS:
The answers are: 1. C; 2. A; 3. D; 4. B

Essential Instruction

1. Explain to the students that **aller**, **avoir**, **être**, and **faire** are four high-frequency verbs that are the basis for many idiomatic expressions, so they need to be mastered.
2. Allow students who already know these verbs to write a group story using them.
3. Give students who need additional practice with these verbs the assignment of writing an original sentence for each one in the list on p. 17, using a pronoun other than **je**.

Verb	Present	Example
s'asseoir	je **m'assieds**	Élodie **s'assied** devant moi.
boire	je **bois**	Que **buvez**-vous au café?
conduire	je **conduis**	Ils **conduisent** mal!
connaître	je **connais**	Nous ne **connaissons** pas cette fille.
croire	je **crois**	Elle ne le **croit** pas.
devenir	je **deviens**	Vous **devenez** un pro des blogues?
devoir	je **dois**	Elles **doivent** travailler.
dire	je **dis**	Le prof me **dit** de faire mes devoirs.
dormir	je **dors**	Tu **dors** beaucoup pendant le weekend!
écrire	j'**écris**	Elle **écrit** une composition.
falloir	il **faut**	Il **faut** étudier pour le contrôle.
lire	je **lis**	Qu'est-ce que tu **lis**?
mettre	je **mets**	Elle **met** toujours la table.
offrir	j'**offre**	Qu'**offrez**-vous à vos parents?
ouvrir	j'**ouvre**	N'**ouvrez** pas le cadeau avant Noël!
partir	je **pars**	L'autobus **part** à huit heures.
pouvoir	je **peux**	Nous **pouvons** aller à l'aquaparc.
prendre	je **prends**	Tu **prends** des notes?
recevoir	je **reçois**	Qu'est-ce qu'il **reçoit** pour son anniversaire?
revenir	je **reviens**	Quand **revenez**-vous?
savoir	je **sais**	Elle **sait** faire du roller?
sortir	je **sors**	Nous **sortons** avec notre bande de copains.
suivre	je **suis**	Quel cours **suivent**-elles à 10h00?
venir	je **viens**	D'où **viens**-tu?
vivre	je **vis**	Nous ne **vivons** pas à Nice.
voir	je **vois**	Elle ne **voit** personne à la plage.
vouloir	je **veux**	Raoul **veut** devenir infirmier.

12 Un weekend chargé

1.1, 1.2, 2.1, 5.1

Dites où on est et ce qu'on fait ce weekend.

MODÈLE

les ados/faire une randonnée à pied
Les ados sont dans la forêt. Ils font une randonnée à pied.

1. tu/faire du sport

2. Luc et moi/faire du camping

3. je/faire des hamburgers

4. Alima/faire la vaisselle

5. Les Castinot/faire une excursion

6. vous/faire du shopping

Answers

1. Tu es au complexe sportif. Tu fais du sport.
2. Luc et moi sommes au terrain de camping. Nous faisons du camping.
3. Je suis à la maison. Je fais des hamburgers.
4. Alima est à la maison. Elle fait la vaisselle.
5. Les Castinot sont à la montagne. Ils font une excursion.
6. Vous êtes en ville. Vous faites du shopping.

Reference Desk

Of the irregular verbs in the chart, these verbs were introduced in Level 1: **aller**, **avoir**, **devenir**, **devoir**, **être**, **faire**, **falloir**, **mettre**, **offrir**, **pouvoir**, **prendre**, **revenir**, **venir**, **voir**, **vouloir**. The remaining verbs were introduced in Level 2.

TPR

Because this is a daunting list of infinitives for the average student to learn, break down the list into groups of six and work on only those verbs. Ask the students to invent with you a gesture which illustrates the meaning of each verb for the first six. Here are a few suggestions:

Je m'assieds (Pretend you are sitting down.); **Je bois** (Put your thumb to your mouth.); **Je conduis** (Turn the wheel of a car.); **Je connais** (Shake hands.); **Je crois** (Put your hands in a prayer position.); **Je deviens** (Pretend you are a dancer.) Write a pronoun on the board, for example, **nous**. Then say **nous nous asseyons** and have students do the corresponding gesture.

Differentiated Learning

Accelerate

Ask these students to write cloze activities that you will distribute to those who need more practice. Make sure students provide an answer key on a separate piece of paper.

Decelerate

Prepare bell-ringers for these students to do at the beginning of class for a few days. Tell them each day they will need to learn all the forms of 5–6 verbs, and tell them which ones you are testing them on each day.

Learning Styles

Kinesthetic/Visual Learners

For **Activité 12**, ask these students to draw other locations on the board to use for additional practice. Ask the class for expressions to use to continue the textbook activity.

Answers

13

1. Ma famille et moi avons envie de manger des pâtes. Nous allons au restaurant.
2. Mon meilleur ami a envie d'acheter des billets de concert. Il va à la FNAC.
3. Tu as envie de faire du cheval. Tu vas à la ferme.
4. Mon oncle a envie d'acheter une voiture. Il va à la banque.
5. J'ai envie de faire la cuisine. Je vais au supermarché.
6. Nathan et toi avez envie de faire un tour de grande roue. Vous allez au parc d'attractions.
7. Jean et Clara ont envie de voir un film. Ils vont au ciné-club.
8. Awa a envie de danser. Elle va à la discothèque.

14

1. oui
2. oui
3. non
4. non
5. oui
6. oui
7. non
8. non

15

Questions will have the following forms:

3. Tu vas souvent...?
4. Tu fais du jogging...?
5. Tu conduis...?
6. Tu veux devenir...?
7. Tu peux sortir...?
8. Tu connais...?
9. Tu écris...?
10. Tu lis...?
11. Tu suis...?
12. Tu dors...?
13. Tu offres...?
14. Tu sais...?
15. Tu vis...?

Reference Desk

1. **Pariscope** and **L'Officiel des spectacles** are booklets Parisians buy at **les kiosques de journaux**, or subscribe to, that provide detailed information about movies, museum exhibits, plays, etc.
2. The **Communiquez!** heading indicates that the activity allows for practice with the three modes of communication.

13 On a envie de.... 1.1, 1.2, 2.1, 5.1

Selon ce qu'on a envie de faire, dites où on va.

MODÈLE Julien/lire *Pariscope*
Julien a envie de lire *Pariscope*. Il va au kiosque à journaux.

à la FNAC · au parc d'attractions · au restaurant · au supermarché · à la ferme · à la banque · au kiosque à journaux · à la discothèque · au ciné-club

1. ma famille et moi/manger des pâtes
2. mon meilleur ami/acheter des billets de concert
3. tu/faire du cheval
4. mon oncle/acheter une voiture
5. je/faire la cuisine
6. Nathan et toi/faire un tour de grande roue
7. Jean et Clara/voir un film
8. Awa/danser

14 On étudie ou pas?

1.1, 1.2

*Écrivez les numéros 1–8 sur votre papier. Écoutez les dialogues et décidez si la personne étudie. Si oui, écrivez **oui**. Si non, écrivez **non**.*

Communiquez!

15 Trouvez quelqu'un qui....

1.1, 1.2, 5.1

Interpersonal Communication

Préparez des questions pour vos camarades de classe. Trouvez quelqu'un dans la classe qui répond oui à votre question. Chaque personne qui répond affirmativement doit signer votre grille.

Questions	Prénom	Signature
1. Tu as un chat ou un chien?		
2. Tu dois faire la vaisselle après le dîner?		

1. avoir un chat ou un chien
2. devoir faire la vaisselle après le dîner
3. aller souvent au skatepark
4. faire du jogging tous les jours
5. conduire une décapotable
6. vouloir devenir homme ou femme d'affaires
7. pouvoir sortir avec tes amis pendant la semaine
8. connaître un homme ou une femme politique
9. écrire des poèmes ou des chansons
10. lire des blogues chaque jour
11. suivre un cours d'art
12. dormir jusqu'à midi samedi matin
13. offrir des cartes pour la Saint-Valentin
14. savoir faire de la plongée sous-marine
15. vivre à la campagne

Essential Instruction

1. Do **Activité 13** as a class or in small groups. Ask for synonyms for **avoir envie de** (**voudrait, aimerait**).
2. Read the listening script before having students do **Activité 14** in case you need to review some words.
3. Allow 20 minutes for students to do **Activité 15**.
4. You may want students to create a French social media page similar to Zach's using the review verbs and new lesson vocabulary.

16 Le réseau social de Zach

Zach passe l'année en France avec une famille française. Aidez-le à finir sa lettre pour son réseau social.

Mon réseau social Accueil Profil Compte

Zach

Mur	Infos	Photos
Exprimez-vous...		

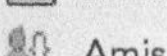

Nouvelle
Messages
Événements
Amis

Partager

Me voici à Marseille chez les Simenon. Je (être) un vrai membre de la famille. Je (mettre) le couvert et (faire) la vaisselle tous les soirs. Les Simenon (recevoir) beaucoup d'amis qui viennent le weekend. M. Simenon (travailler) pour la ville et il (connaître) le maire. À leurs soirées, il (falloir) parler français.

Au lycée je (suivre) un cours d'informatique super! Ça va m'aider quand je vais (devenir) graphiste.

Avec mes copains, on (aller) au café après les cours où on (boire) un coca et (prendre) un goûter. Mon meilleur ami, David, (savoir) parler trois langues—le français, l'anglais, et l'italien. Nous (aller) souvent à la MJC pour le ciné-club et au cours de musique. Nous (vouloir) commencer un groupe de rock, mais nous (avoir) besoin d'un guitariste. Moi, je (jouer) de la batterie et David (chanter).

Les Simenon et moi, nous (partir) vendredi soir pour Nice. Nous (pouvoir) nager dans la mer parce qu'ils (avoir) une villa près de la plage. Nous (revenir) dimanche soir. Je (aller) prendre beaucoup de photos, c'est sûr!

Qu'est-ce que vous (voir) au cinéma? Qu'est-ce que vous (lire)? Vous (venir) me voir en France?

Zach

samedi le 10 septembre

Answers

16 suis...mets...fais...reçoivent... travaille...connaît...faut...suis... devenir...va...boit...prend...sait... allons...voulons...avons...joue... chante...partons...pouvons...ont... revenons...vais...voyez...lisez... venez...

Reference Desk

Some highlights to help your students understand the passage **Mon réseau social:**

1. **Le réseau social** means social media.
2. In French one does not add an **s** to the family name: *I am going to the Simenons'*; the definite article indicates more than one person: **Je vais chez les Simenon.**
3. A synonym for **mettre le couvert** is **mettre la table. Un couvert** is a place setting.
4. **Le weekend** in this reading means "on weekends."

Game

Debate

Students can take sides or write in their journal arguing that social media is valuable for connecting people to each other, or a threat to the privacy of individuals and perhaps even a danger to their security.

Differentiated Learning

Accelerate

Ask these students to prepare a written or oral summary of what they learned about their classmates after doing **Activité 15**.

Decelerate

To prepare for **Activité 15**, which requires the mastery of many irregular verbs, have these students prepare by writing down the **Tu** form and the **Je** form of each infinitive so that they can be successful in interviewing their classmates and responding.

RESOURCES

Workbook 14

Drill & Practice Games

Answers

1. Depuis quand
2. Depuis combien de temps
3. depuis quand
4. Depuis quand
5. depuis quand
6. depuis combien de temps
7. depuis quand
8. Depuis combien de temps

Reference Desk

1. Students learned **Depuis** + Present Tense in **Leçon C** of **Unité 8** in the Level 2 textbook.
2. To illustrate that **depuis** expresses an action that started in the past and is still continuing, you might want to dramatize the concept. Write a series of commands on pieces of paper and put them in a hat (**danse**, **conduis**, **dors**, **bois**). Ask for student volunteers to do the activity until you say **Arrête!** Then ask the class to answer your questions in writing: **Depuis combien de temps Annie danse-t-elle?** (**Quinze secondes**, for example).
3. All review activities are labeled with **Révision**.

Révision: *Depuis* + Present Tense

1.1, 1.2

emcl.com
WB 14
Games

See if you can select the correct question for each answer below.

A. **Depuis quand...?** B. **Depuis combien de temps...?**

1. J'étudie le français depuis trois ans.
2. Nous sommes en cours depuis hier.

If you couldn't match the questions and answers correctly, then read the grammar review below to review how to use **depuis**.

Depuis quand followed by a verb in the present tense is used to ask when an action began in the past that is still going on in the present. To answer this question in a complete sentence, use a present tense verb form, **depuis**, and an expression of time.

Depuis quand est-ce que Léo travaille à la MJC?	*Since when has Leo been working at the youth center?*
Il y **travaille depuis mars.**	*He has been working there since March.*

Depuis combien de temps (*how long*) followed by a verb in the present tense is used to ask how long an action has been going on. To answer this question in a complete sentence, use a present tense verb form, **depuis** (*for*), and an expression of time.

Depuis combien de temps êtes-vous au complexe sportif?	*How long have you been at the sports complex?*
Nous y sommes **depuis deux heures.**	*We have been here for two hours.*

17 Complétez!

1.1, 1.2

Complétez chaque dialogue avec **depuis quand** *ou* **depuis combien de temps**, *selon les réponses.*

MODÈLES

... regardes-tu le match?
Je le regarde depuis 14h00.
Depuis quand

... vit-il en France?
Il y vit depuis cinq ans.
Depuis combien de temps

1. ... est-ce qu'elle travaille à la ferme?
   Elle y travaille depuis le 10 juin.
2. Désolé! ... m'attends-tu?
   Je t'attends depuis dix minutes.
3. Vous vivez à Lyon...?
   Nous y vivons depuis l'année 2010.
4. ... est-ce que tu écris cette composition?
   Je l'écris depuis ce matin.
5. Tu lis les bandes dessinées d'*Astérix*...?
   Je lis *Astérix* depuis l'âge de sept ans.
6. Vous cherchez une nouvelle voiture...?
   J'en cherche une depuis un mois.
7. Tu es fâché...?
   Depuis ce matin.
8. ... suis-tu ce cours particulier?
   Depuis six mois.

DEPUIS: The answers are: 1. B; 2. A

Essential Instruction

1. Now that the students have reviewed regular and irregular verbs in the present tense, they are asked to use them with **depuis** + present tense.
2. For students who successfully completed the top section, have them write questions they can address to you once you have reviewed the material with those students who need the help and who have completed **Activité 17.**
3. You may want to divide the class into three groups and have each group complete one of the activities in **À vous la parole.**

À vous la parole

18 On a hâte de passer de bonnes vacances.

1.1, 1.2, 1.3, 5.1, 5.2

Interpersonal Communication

C'est presque la fin de l'année scolaire. Avec votre partenaire, vous planifiez vos vacances et parlez d'où vous voulez aller cet été. Vous devez choisir des endroits (à la campagne, au bord de la mer, etc.) et conseiller votre partenaire sur ce qu'on peut y faire, par exemple:

A: **Je voudrais passer les vacances en ville.**
B: **Tu peux suivre un cours à la MJC et aller à la discothèque tous les weekends.**

19 Ma vie d'ado

1.2, 1.3, 2.1, 3.2, 4.2, 5.1, 5.2

Presentational Communication

Vous avez décidé de créer un blogue pour un site d'ados en France. Vous voulez partager votre vie d'ado américain… ce que vous aimez, où vous allez, ce que vous y faites, ce que vous pensez. Parce que vous avez lu des blogues français, comparez votre vie avec celles des ados français que vous avez rencontrés en ligne, et faites une présentation.

Communiquez!

20 Un sondage

1.1, 1.2, 1.3, 2.1, 3.2, 4.2, 5.1, 5.2

Interpersonal/Presentational Communication

Pour le site Web de votre classe, vous devez préparer un sondage pour la classe d'ados français avec qui vous communiquez. Vous voulez connaître leurs préférences et leurs habitudes. Préparez dix questions au minimum. Cherchez un thème avant de commencer, comme les passe-temps, le sport, les communautés, les expressions argotiques, les soirées. Ensuite, envoyez votre sondage à dix ados français que vous connaissez en ligne. Finalement, faites un résumé des résultats pour vos camarades de classe, et postez votre sondage sur le site de votre classe.

RESOURCES

Communicative Activities

Answers

Activities will vary.

Reference Desk

1. In **À vous la parole**, students will engage in interpersonal, presentational, or interpretive communication to build their proficiency.
2. **Activité 18** is ideal for your students who like to work with a partner whereas **Activités 19** and **20** would appeal to students who like to work on their own. Their choice of project will give you an insight into your students' working style.

Blended Instruction

Consider using blended instruction, a combination of in-class learning and computer-mediated instruction or learning opportunities. Ask students to complete activities on the computer, using their cell or smartphone, or other emerging electronic technology. This will allow students to hone their tech skills and become more independent learners. Schedule routine Internet and e-book learning in class and in the lab.

Differentiated Learning

Adapt

In your class there are students who are very advanced users of technology. Not all will be your high-ability students; often they will be your low-ability language students who are gifted computer users. Enlist their aid in structuring and executing tech projects. This will give them a sense of satisfaction and pride that even though their language skills aren't as keen as other students, they can still make a valuable contribution to the classroom.

Multiple Intelligences

Intrapersonal

Your tech-savvy students may want to do **Activité 19** or **20.** They can report on blog postings, thus encouraging the other students to take a look; the blog could be an ongoing class project spearheaded by these students.

RESOURCES

 Pre-test

 *Leçon* Quiz

Answers

1. u
2. u
3. ø
4. u
5. u
6. ø

Prononciation 1.1, 1.2

Accentuation in Phrases

- Only the last word or syllable in a phrase is accentuated. The rest of the words in the group are not accentuated.

Le mariage

Répétez les phrases suivantes sur le mariage. Accentuez uniquement la syllabe en caractère gras (bold).

1. la bague de fian**çaill**es
2. une demoiselle d'ho**nneur**
3. un garçon d'ho**nneur**
4. le gâteau de ma**riag**e
5. la lune de **miel**
6. le voyage de **noc**es

Les objets technologiques

Répétez les noms à gauche; faites attention à les accentuer correctement. Les caractères gras indiquent les syllabes qu'il faut accentuer. Ensuite, répétez en ajoutant (adding) le deuxième mot. N'accentuez que les syllabes en caractères gras!

1. un mi**cro** ... ordinateur (un micro-ordina**teur**)
2. un télé**phon**e ... portable (un téléphone por**tabl**e)
3. une impri**mant**e ... laser (une imprimante la**ser**)

The Vowels /y/ - /u/ - /ø/ - /o/

- These four vowels are pronounced with the mouth closed and the lips pursed. Place your tongue as far forward as possible for **/y/**, far back for **/u/**, and in the middle for **/ø/** and **/o/**.

Quelle vue!

Répétez les phrases suivantes, en faisant attention aux sons ***/y/*** *et* ***/o/***.

1. Quelle vue des roses!
2. Quelle vue des eaux!
3. Quelle vue des autos!
4. Quelle vue des beaux bureaux!

Deux euros ou douze euros?

Répétez les phrases suivantes, en faisant attention au son ***/ø/*** *comme dans* ***deux***, *et au son* ***/u/*** *comme dans* ***douze***.

1. Tu as dit deux ‿ euros ⁀ ou dou|ze euros?
2. Qu'est-ce que tu veux, deux ‿ euros ⁀ ou dou|ze euros?
3. Excusez-moi, ça coûte deux ‿ euros ⁀ ou dou|ze euros?

Distinguez!

Écrivez ***/ø/*** *si vous entendez le son* ***/ø/*** *de* ***deux***, *ou* ***/u/*** *si vous entendez le son* ***/u/*** *de* ***douze***.

Essential Instruction

1. Introduce the concept of Accentuation in Phrases, then have students listen and repeat **Activités A** and **B.** Repeat the recordings as necessary.
2. Make a list of words students know that incorporate the sounds of the four vowels. Ask for volunteers to read the words. (Some students would be stressed to do that in front of others so be selective.) Put the students in paired groups to read each section to each other. Circulate to correct pronunciation errors. Have the whole class listen to **Activité E.**
3. Have students write the three types of families in their notebooks, listing names of families they know that belong to each type.
4. Provide supplemental vocabulary expressions for **Les activités enfantines** that reflect the experiences of your students.

Vocabulaire actif

emcl.com
WB 1–3
LA 1
Games

La famille et les activités enfantines

1.2

Les types (m.) de familles

une famille nucléaire

une famille monoparentale

une famille recomposée

Les activités enfantines

jouer à cache-cache

collectionner des coquillages/timbres...

faire semblant d'être une princesse/

un super-héros

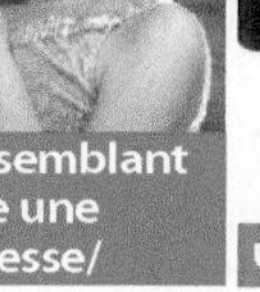
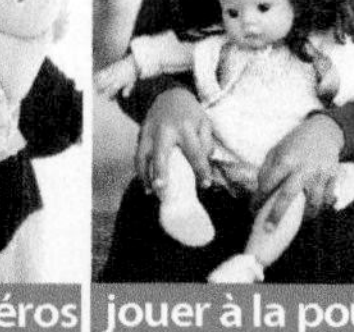
jouer à la poupée

jouer à la marelle

sauter à la corde

jouer aux petites voitures/billes

faire des châteaux de sable

courir

RESOURCES

e-visual 2

Workbook 1–3

Flash Cards

Listening Activity 1

Drill & Practice Games

Reference Desk

1. The three types of families are: a nuclear family, a single-parent family, and a blended family.
2. Have students offer other **activités enfantines** in which they participated as a child; write all these terms on the board and use them in subsequent in-class activities.

Differentiated Learning

Adapt

Make a list of TV shows and ask students to identify the types of families in them. This is often preferable to asking students personal questions about their own families.

Decelerate

Make three columns on the board: **les filles**, **les garcons**, **les filles et garçons** and ask students to put the illustrated activities in the category that is, in their experience, correct.

Answers

1. Martin fait un château de sable, il collectionne des timbres, il fait semblant d'être un super-héros, il joue aux petites voitures, il saute à la corde, puis il joue aux billes.

Reference Desk

In **Activité 3**, **découvrir** is a new verb from the **Rencontres culturelles** dialogue. Tell students it works like **ouvrir**.

Expansion

After students read **Martin s'ennuie?**, ask them some questions. How old do they think he is? Why is he bored? What does he do to keep himself busy? Why does he not play with the babysitter? How does he treat the dog? Is he a typical child? If so, why?

Pour la conversation 

How do I explain how something happened?

› **J'ai découvert** la vie des supermarchés ici.

I discovered (the experience of) shopping in supermarkets here.

How do I say what I discovered?

› **C'est comme ça que** l'on est arrivé à Nice.

That's how we arrived in Nice.

How do I ask for a suggestion?

› **Tu proposes** quoi?

What are you suggesting?

Et si je voulais dire...? 

la famille éloignée	*extended family*
un enfant mixte	*biracial child*
un enfant adopté	*adopted child*
une mère/un père célibataire	*single parent*
un animal en peluche	*stuffed animal*
un jouet à piles	*battery-operated toy*
un jouet mécanique	*wind-up toy*

1 Martin s'ennuie? 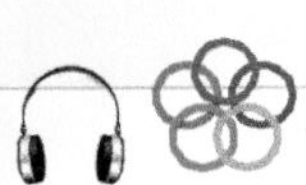 1.2, 1.3

Lisez le paragraphe sur Martin. Ensuite, répondez à la question qui suit.

Martin habite sur la côte Atlantique en France. Il n'a pas de frère ou sœur. Ses parents sont en ville cet après-midi. Martin n'aime pas sa baby-sitter. Elle ne joue pas avec lui. Elle lui propose d'aller à sa chambre, mais lui, il n'est pas d'accord. D'abord, il est fâché, mais il a des idées pour passer le temps. Il s'amuse à faire un château de sable avec quatre tours. Il met des timbres dans son album; il aime collectionner les timbres des pays différents. Il fait semblant d'être un super-héros dans le jardin, mais il fait peur au chien. Ensuite, il joue aux petites voitures. Enfin, il saute à la corde et joue aux billes.

Comment est-ce que Martin passe l'après-midi?

Essential Instruction

1. To review family vocabulary from Level 1, have the students make a family tree of their own, of an imaginary family, of a family from the media, or of a family from a work of fiction. There are free family tree templates online to make the task simpler.
2. For **Activité 2**, have students pick a family about which to write a description or story.

2 Les familles

1.2, 1.3, 5.1

Décrivez chaque famille.

MODÈLE

C'est une famille monoparentale.

1. 

2. 

3. 

4. 

3 Les découvertes

1.2, 1.3

Dites ce que vous avez découvert quand vous étiez petit(e).

MODÈLE

J'ai découvert les châteaux de sable.

1. 

2. 

3. 

4. 

5. 

Answers

1. C'est une famille nucléaire.
2. C'est une famille recomposée.
3. C'est une famille nucléaire.
4. C'est une famille monoparentale.

1. J'ai découvert les coquillages.
2. J'ai découvert le saut à la corde.
3. J'ai découvert les billes.
4. J'ai découvert les poupées.
5. J'ai découvert les timbres.

Expansion

Have the students imagine that they are seven years old and it is time to make up a Christmas list. Have them visit a French toy store's web site for ideas. They have a 100€ budget. They must write the name of the toy, a brief description, and the price. They will then write a letter to **le Père Noël**.

Answers

4

1. Ils jouaient à cache-cache.
2. Ils faisaient des châteaux de sable.
3. Ils jouaient aux petites voitures.
4. Ils jouaient à la marelle.
5. Ils sautaient à la corde.

5

1. V
2. F
3. V
4. V
5. F
6. V
7. F
8. F

Communication

Interpersonal: Paired Practice

Have students, working in pairs, ask each other what they "used to do" when they were children, using the new vocabulary and the imperfect tense.

4 Quand Louis et Lola étaient petits

 1.1

Dites ce que Louis et Lola faisaient quand ils étaient petits.

MODÈLE  **Louis et Lola faisaient semblant d'être des super-héros.**

1. 
2. 
3. 
4. 
5. 

5 Ce que j'aime faire.

  1.1, 1.2, 5.1

*Écrivez les numéros 1–8 sur votre papier. Écoutez la petite Marie parler de sa vie. Écrivez **V** si les phrases sont vraies ou **F** si elles sont fausses.*

1. Marie vient d'une famille monoparentale.
2. Marie n'a pas d'amis.
3. Marie, Karim, et Julie jouent à cache-cache.
4. Marie joue à la poupée chez elle.
5. Marie aime courir avec Karim.
6. Julie adore jouer à la marelle et à la corde à sauter.
7. Karim gagne toujours aux billes.
8. Julie et Marie aiment jouer aux petites voitures.

Essential Instruction

1. Since the imperfect tense will be reviewed in Lesson B on p. 41, only a brief explanation will be necessary to complete **Activité 4**.
2. Have the students suggest other activities that they might have done when they were young.
3. Before playing the recording that goes with **Activité 5**, ask students to read sentences 1–8 so they can prepare for what they are going to hear.
4. Play the recording as many times as it takes so that all students are successful.

6 Chère Mamy

1.2, 1.3, 5.1

Lisez le mail que Cédric, qui a neuf ans, a écrit à sa grand-mère. Puis, répondez aux questions.

À: Mamy
Cc:
Sujet: Halloween

Chère Mamy,

C'est bientôt Halloween. Je vais mettre un costume de Superman. Cécile fait toujours semblant d'être une princesse. Donc, elle va mettre son costume de Cendrillon. Samedi, j'ai joué avec mes copains aux petites voitures. J'ai gagné. Papa a dit que j'avais l'air d'être très content! Je continue de collectionner les timbres. Tu peux m'apporter des timbres de ton voyage? Cécile collectionne les coquillages maintenant. Quand est-ce que tu viens nous voir à Nice?

Bisous,

Cédric

1. C'est bientôt quelle fête?
2. Cédric et sa sœur vont faire semblant d'être qui?
3. À quoi est-ce que Cédric a gagné?
4. Il avait l'air d'être triste?
5. Qu'est-ce que Cédric voudrait savoir?
6. Qu'est-ce que sa sœur collectionne?

7 Questions personnelles

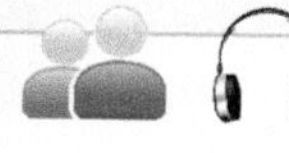

Je faisais semblant d'être une princesse quand j'avais sept ans.

Répondez aux questions suivantes.

1. Est-ce que tu fais partie d'une famille nucléaire, monoparentale, ou recomposée?
2. Est-ce que tu collectionnes quelque chose? Si oui, quoi?
3. Que faisais-tu quand tu étais petit(e)?
4. Quand tu étais petit(e), est-ce que tu faisais semblant d'être une princesse ou un super-héros?
5. Aimes-tu courir en plein air?
6. Qu'est-ce que tu as découvert pendant tes dernières vacances?
7. Tu proposes quoi à tes amis pour le weekend?

1.2, 1.3, 5.1

Answers

1. Halloween
2. Superman, une princesse
3. une course de petites voitures
4. Non, il avait l'air très content.
5. Quand sa grand-mère vient les voir, et si elle peut lui apporter des timbres de son voyage.
6. les coquillages

7 *Answers will vary.*

Reference Desk

You may want to vary how you approach the **Questions personnelles**. They are intended to get students to ask each other questions, but you may want to ask students the questions individually using **vous**.

Differentiated Learning

Expand

You may want students to create a digital or traditional storybook using clipart, photos from magazines, or personal photos illustrating what they did **quand j'étais petit(e)**. Tell them how many pages with commentary in French you expect. Have the students submit their sentences for correction before putting them in the storybook. They can use online storybook programs or storybook apps.

RESOURCES

Dialogue Video

Workbook 4

Answers

2, 6, 4, 5, 1, 3

Reference Desk

1. Explain that this dialogue is written in the imperfect tense because Karim is talking about what life was like when he was younger. Ask students what they remember about the **imparfait**.
2. Point out that **se connaissait** is an example of a reflexive thought: Everyone knew "each other." Ask students where they see another such example.
3. The past participle **vécu** comes from **vivre**.
4. Point out the difference between **en fait** (*in fact*) and **au fait** (*by the way*).

Rencontres culturelles

emcl.com
WB 4

L'enfance de Karim

1.1, 1.2, 5.1, 5.2

Karim et Léo se promènent à Nice.

Karim: C'était plus possible… un jour ma mère est partie… nous, on a suivi… c'est comme ça que l'on est arrivé à Nice.

Léo: Et tu n'as pas eu de regrets?

Karim: Si, le village où on habitait… tout le monde se connaissait. Il n'y avait qu'une école dans le village; les commerçants nous appelaient par notre prénom; on se retrouvait tous au foot, on y jouait le mercredi après-midi…. Et puis on avait une grande maison avec une piscine….

Léo: En fait, tu n'avais jamais vécu en ville?

Karim: Non, jamais! J'ai découvert la vie des supermarchés ici. Dans l'immeuble, à l'étage où on habitait, personne ne nous parlait au début… et puis le foot aussi ça a été fini… je n'y ai jamais plus joué. Heureusement, il y a eu le cinéma….

Léo: Et c'est comme ça qu'on s'est connu….

Karim: Au fait, on va voir quoi ce soir?

Léo: Élodie, elle propose quoi?

Connaître. Le verbe *connaître* vient de l'infinitif latin *cognoscere*. Le latin est la base de plusieurs langues européennes, dites *langues romanes*. *Connaître* est la racine des verbes *reconnaître* ("to recognize") et *méconnaître* ("to misread / to be un aware of").

8 L'enfance de Karim

1.2, 1.3

Remettez les phrases en ordre chronologique.

1. Karim a arrêté de jouer au foot.
2. La mère de Karim est arrivée à Nice.
3. Léo a fait la connaissance de Karim au ciné-club.
4. Karim a découvert les supermarchés.
5. Les gens de l'immeuble à Nice n'ont pas parlé à Karim et à sa famille.
6. Karim a déménagé (*moved*) à Nice.

Essential Instruction

1. Discuss the title of the video dialogue, **L'enfance de Karim**, asking what past tenses Karim will be using.
2. Watch the video and ask students to summarize what they understood.
3. Ask the students to read the dialogue and the sentences in **Activité 8** and watch the video a second time.
4. Do **Activité 8** in pairs and write the sentences in the correct order on the board.

Extension **Les enfants vont bien?**   **1.1, 1.2**

Au café, deux femmes parlent de leurs nouvelles vies.

Mme Duhamel: Avec Pierre, nous nous sommes arrangés. J'ai les enfants une semaine, et il les prend la semaine suivante, et ainsi de suite. C'est plus simple.

Mme Laforge: Mon ex-mari ne prend les enfants qu'un weekend sur deux. Je lui ai dit que ce n'était pas bon pour les enfants. Ils veulent le voir plus. Mais, non!

Mme Duhamel: Je vois: la règle, c'est la règle. Et les enfants, ils le vivent comment?

Mme Laforge: Pas très bien. Ils ont été très déstabilisés au début. Avec Sandrine, la compagne de Julien, ça se passe moyennement bien. Ils sont très nostalgiques de notre vie d'avant. Toi, tu as de la chance.

Mme Duhamel: Pierre n'a pas de compagne fixe pour le moment, il est très attentif aux enfants et puis il s'entend bien avec Marc. Il passe souvent à la maison.

Extension Qu'est-ce qui a changé dans les vies de Mme Duhamel, de Mme Laforge, et de leurs enfants?

1.1, 1.2

Answers

Extension

Mme Duhamel et Mme Laforge ont divorcé.

Reference Desk

Here are some expressions students may need help understanding: **Nous nous sommes arranges.** (*We have worked things out.*) **Ainsi de suite.** (*And so on.*) **Ils le vivent comment?** (*How are they taking it?*)

Differentiated Learning

Adapt

Ask students to determine which lines of the main dialogue fit this outline: 1. Change in Karim's life as a child. 2. His old life. 3. His new life. 4. His friendship with Léo and Élodie.

Special Needs Students

At-Risk Students

The **Extension** dialogue relates the difficulty children have adapting to divorce. Look for signs that certain students are struggling with the topic, and talk to them after class, or discuss their reactions with a school counselor to find out what you can do to help.

RESOURCES

Workbook 5

Reference Desk

Other common family words include **Mamy** (*Grandma*) and **Papy** (*Grandpa*). Children may be called **les gamins** or **les gosses.**

Culture

Practices: Activity

To make a comparison to American culture, write the facts from the paragraph **L'enfance en France** on the board in the left column. Then discuss with students what they think is true about childhood in America, and write those observations down on the right. Point out that anecdotal evidence is not scientific evidence. See if any students would like to uncover the facts, statistics, and percentages to verify the observations about American culture.

Points de départ

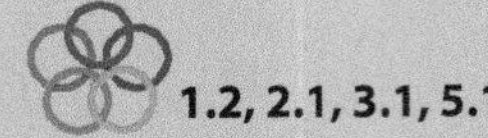

emcl.com
WB 5

Question centrale: Comment la vie des Francophones évolue-t-elle avec le temps?

L'enfance en France 1.2, 2.1, 3.1, 5.1

En France, le nombre de naissances* augmente de 2,02 enfants par mère, mais plus de 50% des naissances ont lieu hors* du mariage. En plus, cinquante pourcent de parents sont divorcés. Pour répondre à ces changements sociaux, l'État subventionne* fortement* les "assistantes maternelles" et les "nounous*" à domicile* pour les enfants de 0 à 2 ans, et les villes multiplient les crèches, des lieux d'accueil pour garder les enfants pendant que les mères travaillent. À partir de trois ans, tous les enfants vont à l'école. Depuis 1980, six fois plus d'enfants de plus de cinq ans sont obèses* aujourd'hui. Pour les enfants de huit à dix ans, plus de 70 % font du sport, mais souvent individuel. Ils passent plus de temps devant la télé qu'en classe et entrent plus tôt dans l'adolescence.

Voici quelques expressions françaises qui sont liées* à l'enfance:

C'est le berceau de son enfance. *C'est là qu'il a grandi.*

C'est l'enfance de l'art. *C'est très simple.*

C'est un jeu d'enfant. *C'est facile à faire.*

Il a replongé dans l'enfance. *Il régresse.*

naissances *births;* **hors** *outside of;* **subventionne fortement** *strongly subsidizes;* **nounous** *nannies;* **à domicile** *at home;* **obèses** gros; **liés** tied

La famille 1.2, 2.1, 3.1, 4.1, 5.1

Si les Français restent très attachés à la famille, les modèles familiaux ont considérablement évolué. Environ 80% des adultes qui vivent en couples sont mariés: on enregistre environ 270.000 mariages par an.

Face au mariage on trouve l'union libre qui concerne plus de trois millions de couples. Aujourd'hui, un couple sur cinq n'est pas marié, et l'arrivée d'un premier enfant se fait dans la moitié des cas hors mariage. Institué en 1999, le PACS* (Pacte civil de solidarité) est une forme d'union civile contractuelle* entre deux personnes, du même sexe ou de sexe différent. Aujourd'hui, on compte un PACS pour deux mariages.

Le nombre de familles monoparentales avec un ou plusieurs enfants (20% des enfants vivent dans une famille monoparentale) ne cesse* d'augmenter*: on compte 1,8 million de familles monoparentales apparues le plus souvent à la suite d'une séparation ou d'un divorce.

En effet un mariage sur deux se termine par un divorce. Les remariages donnent naissance aux familles recomposées où cohabitent souvent demi-frères et demi-sœurs.

L'argot des ados

La famille

le vieux:	le père
la vieille:	la mère
les vieux:	les parents
le frangin:	le frère
la frangine:	la sœur
la reusse:	la sœur
tonton:	l'oncle
tatie/tata:	la tante
mon zinc:	mon cousin

PACS *civil pact of union between two adults;* **contractuelle** *contractual;* **ne cesse d'** *does not cease;* **augmenter** *to increase*

Essential Instruction

1. Here are questions that you could ask to ascertain how much the students understood of **L'enfance en France**: What is the percentage of children born to unmarried couples? How has the French government made adjustments to help single parents? At what age do children start school in France? What has contributed to the increasing rate of overweight children?
2. Here are questions to check reading comprehension for the paragraph on **La famille:** How many couples are not married in France? What is a PACS and why was it established? Approximately how many one-parent families are there in France? How many people in France choose to live alone? Is the number growing?
3. After students have read the paragraph on **Les familles en Afrique**, help them compare African families with French families or families in your country.

Reste les personnes qui vivent seules. On compte aujourd'hui plus de huit millions de célibataires*. Une vie en solitaire par choix tend à devenir un véritable phénomène de société.

Search words: statistiques sur les familles françaises, enquête familles françaises, familles de france, repas de famille

un(e) célibataire *single person*

COMPARAISONS

Quel est le taux de mariage aux États-Unis? De divorce?

1.2, 2.1, 4.2, 5.1

La Francophonie

Les familles en Afrique

Dans la plupart des pays d'Afrique, la structure familiale est déterminée par des valeurs traditionnelles. Le père a le statut de chef de famille: il lui incombe* de travailler pour faire vivre sa famille. La mère est responsable des tâches* domestiques, et surtout d'élever les enfants et de leur inculquer* les valeurs de leur culture. Toutefois, contrairement à la notion de famille nucléaire occidentale, les familles africaines sont souvent des familles élargies*; souvent, les grands-parents, et quelques fois, les oncles, les tantes, et les cousins, etc. vivent sous un même toit. Aussi, la notion de la famille a un sens communautaire où des groupes ethniques, ou même les habitants d'un village, constituent un macrocosme familial solidaire. La polygamie est aussi pratiquée par certaines ethnies et communautés religieuses, plus ou moins acceptée par les jeunes générations.

Mais il faut aussi reconnaître que les valeurs familiales sont différentes selon la situation économique, religieuse, et culturelle des pays et des peuples d'Afrique. Aussi, les plus jeunes générations, hommes ou femmes, ont tendance à privilégier* l'éducation et la réussite économique. Ces générations transforment les valeurs traditionnelles. On peut dire que les familles africaines connaissent aussi le divorce, les familles monoparentales, et les familles recomposées.

il lui incombe *it's up to him;* **tâches** corvées; **inculquer** *to implant;* **élargies** *extended;* **privilégier** *to favor*

Un jeune couple africain.

Critical Thinking

Analysis

The article **La Francophonie** states "Mais il faut aussi reconnaître que les valeurs familiales sont différentes selon la situation économique, religieuse, et culturelle des pays...." Est-ce valable pour la France aussi? Pour votre pays? Pourquoi?

Differentiated Learning

Accelerate

Have these students write a dialogue in which they use one of the expressions linked to childhood.

Adapt

Divide the class into three groups and have each group present the content of their culture paragraph.

Special Needs Students

Linguistically Challenged

The culture paragraphs may be difficult for these students. Provide a cloze activity for them that focuses only on the main ideas.

Dyslexia

Give these students a paper that they can refer to when they read, with the key words to understand the main ideas in each paragraph.

Connections

Cinema

Since Cannes is the site of the international film festival, assign pairs of students to find interesting film footage to share with the class, going back as far as they can. Some interesting things to look for include: What American films have premiered at Cannes? What films won the **Palme d'Or**? What are some themes of the winning films? How many of the French films were subsidized by the French government?

Culture

Products: Information

1. Marcel Pagnol (1895–1974) was born in Aubagne, near Marseille. Originally a teacher, he resigned to become a playwright and filmmaker. His notable films reflect the life of lower-class French living in the Marseille area, capturing their unique accent and traditions. Films that the students would enjoy are: ***Marius, Jean de Florette; Manon des Sources; La Gloire de mon père***; and ***Le Château de ma mère***.
2. The **Festival de Film de Cannes**, which takes place every year in May, draws worldwide attention to the work of international film directors and actors. The coveted **Palme d'Or** is awarded to the director. Brad Pitt, Sean Penn, Alec Baldwin, and Bruce Willis are among the American stars who have climbed the famous red stairs to the **Palais des Festivals**.

2.1, 5.1

Provence-Alpes-Côte d'Azur (la région PACA)

St-Paul de Vence.

Comme le dit si bien la chanson, "Il y a le ciel, le soleil, et la mer." Il y a aussi des paysages immortalisés par Van Gogh et Cézanne, et des villes mythiques telles que Cannes, Nice, et Saint-Tropez. Marseille, deuxième plus grande ville de France, est l'un des plus vieux ports d'Europe (fondée en 600 av. J-C). C'est une ville cosmopolite et le symbole du lien de la France avec le monde méditerranéen, maghrébin, africain, ou proche oriental*. La région PACA, c'est aussi un accent inimitable popularisé par le cinéma et des acteurs de légende (Raimu, Fernandel, ou Daniel Auteuil). La région a été popularisée par des écrivains comme Marcel Pagnol qui en ont fait une légende, par des artistes français et étrangers qui ont associé leur nom à ces lieux (Picasso, Matisse, Colette, F. Scott Fitzgerald, Françoise Sagan, Brigitte Bardot, Alfred Hitchcock, Winston Churchill). Et bien entendu, la côte d'Azur est aussi l'un des lieux de rendez-vous favoris des vedettes* internationales du cinéma et des célébrités d'aujourd'hui.

Au-delà* de la légende, la région Provence-Alpes-Côte d'Azur est la troisième région la plus dynamique de France: pôle scientifique (Nice) et universitaire (Aix-Marseille); industries chimiques et pétrochimiques (Marseille); industries du numérique* (Nice); industries aéronautiques dans la Vallée du Rhône; industries du luxe (parfums de Grasse); et, agriculture (vignoble, fruits). Et sans oublier le tourisme avec la mer et les paysages (Alpes de haute Provence, Montagne de la Sainte Victoire, du Lubéron), la beauté des villages (Saint-Paul de Vence, Saint-Tropez), et aussi le tourisme de luxe (Cannes, Nice, Antibes).

Search words: région provence-alpes-côte d'azur, tourisme provence-alpes-côte d'azur

proche oriental *Near East*; **vedettes** stars; **Au-delà** *Beyond*; **numérique** *digital*

Grasse est une ville située dans l'arrière-pays niçois connue pour sa production de fleurs. Elle est célébrée comme **la capitale des parfums**. Grasse envoie ses parfums partout dans le monde. Au Musée International de la Parfumerie de Grasse, on apprend comment un parfum se fait et on peut aussi y découvrir l'histoire de l'industrie. 2.1

Des paniers pleins de jasmin dont on fera du parfum.

Essential Instruction

1. Play a trivia game such as Jeopardy with your class, asking questions about PACA and other regions students have studied such as **la Bretagne** and **la Normandie: Quelle ville est connue pour ses fleurs? PACA est connue pour quels produits agricoles?**
2. Consider having students work in pairs to do **Activités culturelles 4–5.**
3. Have students look at the photos and subheadings in **Du côté des médias** to prepare for the reading.
4. Organize a game of **pétanque**, also known as **boules**, for your class.

9 Activités culturelles

 1.2, 1.3, 2.1, 3.1, 3.2, 5.1

Faites les activités suivantes.

1. Retrouvez à quoi correspondent ces chiffres qui concernent la famille française:
   - 270.000
   - 3 millions
   - 1,8 millions
2. Faites une liste des genres de couples éventuels (*potential*) qui peuvent former un PACS.
3. Faites un graphique en barres (*bar graph*) qui montre le nombre de divorces en France en 1980, 1990, et 2000.
4. Choisissez une personne célèbre liée à la région Provence-Alpes-Côte d'Azur et faites une recherche sur Internet de ce qui la lie à la région. Présentez ce que vous avez découvert à la classe.
5. Choisissez une de ces villes: Saint-Tropez, Cannes, ou Saint-Paul de Vence, et recherchez ce qui les rend célèbres. Préparez un album de photos avec une carte et un texte.

Perspectives

Selon le romancier Honoré de Balzac, "La famille sera toujours la base des sociétés." Êtes-vous d'accord? Pourquoi, ou pourquoi pas?

Du côté des médias

Pre AP

 1.2, 1.3, 3.1, 5.1

Interpretive Communication

Saint-Paul de Vence

Lisez les informations suivantes sur les visites à faire à Saint-Paul de Vence. Préparez huit questions. Puis, échangez votre liste de questions avec celle de votre partenaire.

Histoire et Patrimoine

A Saint-Paul, chaque pierre raconte quelque chose : la venue de François 1er, les inspections de Vauban, le destin des grandes familles telles les Alziary et les Bernardi qui ont chacune laissé leur empreinte au village. Les façades, les remparts, les maisons et les tours racontent à qui sait les regarder le riche passé du village.

Durée de la visite : 1 heure + entrée au Musée d'Histoire Locale et à la chapelle Folon
Visite en français, anglais, italien, allemand et espagnol

Sur les pas de Marc Chagall

Marc Chagall vécut à Saint-Paul pendant près de 20 ans. Admirez les mêmes paysages que l'artiste contempla avant de les reproduire sur la toile. Découvrez les liens étroits qui l'ont uni à Saint-Paul de 1966 à 1985 à travers 3 œuvres reproduites sur lutrins, la mosaïque de l'école et la sépulture de l'artiste.

Durée de la visite : 1 h 30
Visite en français et anglais

La Pétanque

Sous les platanes de la plus célèbre place en sable dur du monde, l'Office de Tourisme vous propose une initiation au célèbre jeu de boules provençal. Se tenir "pieds tanqués" ? Faire Fanny ? La pétanque n'aura plus de secret pour vous. Yves Montand pointait, Lino Ventura tirait...et vous ?

Durée du jeu : 1 heure
Animation en français, anglais, allemand et espagnol

A Saint-Paul de Vence avec Jacques Prévert

Pour Jacques Prévert, Saint-Paul était un refuge loin de l'agitation de la capitale. C'est au village qu'il a cultivé son amitié avec Picasso et Verdet, qu'il a exercé ses talents de scénariste, qu'il a écrit ses plus belles pages...

Durée de la visite : 1 heure
Visite en français - sur réservation

Answers

1. 270.00: le nombre de mariages en France par an; 3 millions: le nombre de couples qui vivent en union libre; 1,8 millions: le nombre de familles monoparentales en France
2. un couple hétérosexuel non marié; un couple homosexuel

3–5. *Answers will vary.*

Perspectives
Answers will vary.

Differentiated Learning

Accelerate
Have students create a travel brochure in French for a city in the PACA region. It will contain photos, statistics, hotel and restaurant suggestions, and a list of things to do.

Decelerate
Prepare a matching activity for the second paragraph of the reading about the PACA region.

Multiple Intelligences

Naturalist
Have these students look for paintings by artists such as Van Gogh and Cézanne who lived in the PACA region. Ask them to label six paintings with what they learned about the natural world in this area: olive trees, vineyards, red soil, bright sunlight, azure seawater, etc.

RESOURCES

Workbook 6

Drill & Practice Games

Answers

1. Aimée court depuis quatre heures et demie.
2. Tu cours depuis quinze minutes.
3. Ils courent depuis trois heures.
4. Il court depuis une demi-heure.
5. Nous courons depuis deux heures quinze.
6. Vous courez depuis une heure et demie.
7. Il court depuis une heure quarante.
8. Je cours depuis deux heures quinze.

Reference Desk

1. **Parcourir** is conjugated like **courir.** It means "to cover a distance." **Je peux parcourir le village en une heure.** (*I can get through the village in one hour.*)
2. **Parcourir** also means "to skim." **J'ai parcouru le livre.** (*I skimmed the book.*)

Structure de la langue

emcl.com
WB 6
Games

Present Tense of the Irregular Verb *courir*

1.2

The verb **courir** (*to run*) is irregular.

courir			
j'	**cours**	nous	**courons**
tu	**cours**	vous	**courez**
il/elle/on	**court**	ils/elles	**courent**

Alain court le plus vite dans le marathon.

Est-ce que tu **cours** quand tu es au complexe sportif? — *Do you run when you are at the sports complex?*

Non, je ne **cours** jamais là-bas. — *No, I never run there.*

The irregular past participle of **courir** is **couru.**

J'ai **couru** jusqu'à la maison. — *I ran home.*

10 Le marathon

1.2, 1.3

Les personnes ci-dessous s'entraînent (are training) *pour le marathon. Il est 13h30. Dites depuis combien de temps elles courent aujourd'hui.*

MODÈLE Julien/9h30
Julien court depuis quatre heures.

1. Aimée/9h00
2. toi/13h15
3. Marion et Théo/10h30
4. M. Dupont/13h00
5. Chloé et moi/11h15
6. M. Roger et toi/12h00
7. Thomas/11h50
8. moi/11h15

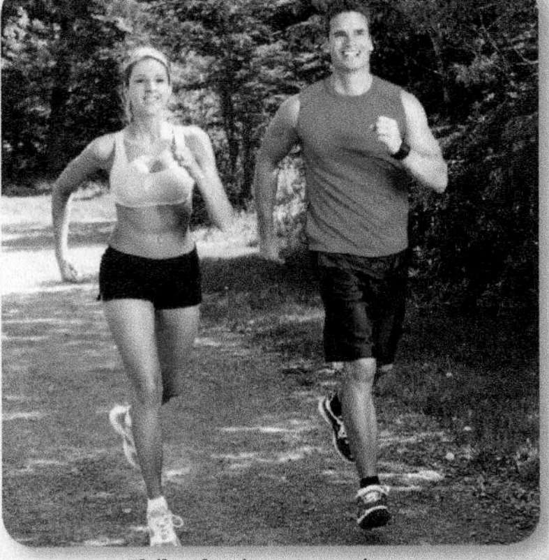
Jeanne et Thibault aiment courir.

COMPARAISONS

What are the three ways to express **Je cours** in English?

4.1

COMPARAISONS: Je cours is the equivalent of "I run," "I am running," and "I do run" in English.

Essential Instruction

1. Ask students why **courir** is an irregular verb. Compare its endings to those of **finir.**
2. The past participle ends in **u.** Is that typical of an **–ir** verb? Point out that **venir** and other verbs with that stem (**revenir, devenir**) also have a past participle ending in **u: venu.**
3. Ask the class the questions about the **passé composé** with **avoir** in the first yellow box. Depending on what students remember, move to practice activities or do a thorough review.
4. Ask students to place a piece of paper over the left two columns of the irregular past participles chart. They then take turns reading the sentences aloud and giving the infinitive; a volunteer writes the infinitives and past participles in two columns on the board.

Révision: *Passé composé* with *avoir*

1.2

emcl.com
WB 7–11
Games

Do you remember how to form the **passé composé** with **avoir**? What follows the conjugated form of **avoir**? Are most verbs in the **passé composé** conjugated with **avoir** or **être**? If you can't answer these questions, then read the summary below.

The **passé composé** tells what happened in the past. For most verbs the **passé composé** consists of the appropriate present tense form of **avoir** and the past participle of the main verb.

subject	+	present tense of **avoir**	+	past participle
(**–er** verbs) Lise *Lise played hide and seek.*		**a**		**joué** à cache-cache.
(**–ir** verbs) Nous *We chose soccer trading cards.*		**avons**		**choisi** des cartes de foot.
(**–re** verbs) Elles *They lost their dolls.*		**ont**		**perdu** leurs poupées.

Here are the verbs you've already studied that have irregular past participles in the **passé composé** formed with **avoir.** Note the position of negative expressions in the **passé composé** and how to form questions using inversion. Remember that the past participle agrees in number and in gender with a preceding direct object pronoun. Note how to use negation and form questions.

Verb	Past Participle	*Passé Composé*
avoir	**eu**	Elle n'**a** pas **eu** la grippe.
boire	**bu**	**As**-tu **bu** toute la limonade?
conduire	**conduit**	J'**ai conduit** une voiture de sport.
connaître	**connu**	Où les **avez**-vous **connus**?
courir	**couru**	Après l'accident, il n'**a** plus **couru**.
croire	**cru**	La voyante? Nous ne l'**avons** pas **crue**.
devoir	**dû**	Tu **as dû** faire la vaisselle après le dîner.
dire	**dit**	Ils **ont dit** oui.
écrire	**écrit**	Ces lettres? Thomas me les **a écrites**.
être	**été**	Nous **avons été** contents.
faire	**fait**	Tu n'**as** jamais **fait** des châteaux-forts?
falloir	**fallu**	Il n'**a** pas **fallu** partir!
lire	**lu**	**Avez**-vous **lu** le blogue d'Alima?
mettre	**mis**	Tes chemises? Mamy les **a mises** dans ta chambre.
offrir	**offert**	Il n'**a** rien **offert** comme cadeau.
ouvrir	**ouvert**	La porte? Richard l'**a ouverte**.
pleuvoir	**plu**	Il n'a pas **plu** hier, mais il a neigé.
pouvoir	**pu**	On **a pu** profiter de la neige.
prendre	**pris**	J'**ai pris** le petit déjeuner chez moi.
recevoir	**reçu**	Djamel n'**a** pas **reçu** mes textos.
savoir	**su**	L'**ont**-elles **su**?
suivre	**suivi**	J'**ai suivi** un cours de chimie.
vivre	**vécu**	Nous n'**avons** jamais **vécu** au Canada.
voir	**vu**	Non, je n'**ai vu** personne.
vouloir	**voulu**	Notre bande **a voulu** partir après le film.

PASSÉ COMPOSÉ WITH AVOIR: After the conjugated form of **avoir**, which agrees with the subject, there is a past participle, which may be regular or irregular. Most verbs in the passé composé are conjugated with **avoir**.

RESOURCES

Workbook 7–11

Drill & Practice Games

Reference Desk

The **passé compose** with **avoir** was introduced in Level 1 in **Unité 8** and reviewed in Level 2 in **Unité 2.**

Critical Thinking

Analysis

Have students look at the sentences to deduce language patterns and answer these questions: How are negative sentences formed in the **passé composé**? What are some of the negative expressions? How do you form a question using inversion? Where are direct object pronouns placed? How do you make direct object pronouns agree?

Game

Line-up

Arrange the class into two teams, A and B, facing each other in two lines. Throw a ball to the first student in line A as you conjugate a verb in the present tense: **Il écrit.** The student has to catch the ball and conjugate the verb in the **passé compose: Il a écrit.** If the student is successful, he/she may stay in line. If the student misses the verb or the ball, the student must sit down. Do the same thing for the first student in line B. The object of the game is to see which team is left standing the longest. Seated students can get back in the game if a team member doesn't know the answer and gets him/her the ball within five seconds.

Differentiated Learning

Accelerate

Have these students tell a group story in front of the class that uses some of the irregular past participles in the chart.

Decelerate

Practice the verbs in the chart by introducing gestures to anchor the meaning for these students. For example, for the verb **prendre**, take a student's textbook and bring it to your desk, saying, **"J'ai pris le livre de Martine."**

Answers

11

1. Djamel et toi avez étudié la biologie. Vous avez eu 19 et 18 sur 20 au contrôle. Vous avez réussi.
2. Nadia a étudié la physique. Elle a eu 17 sur 20 au contrôle. Elle a réussi.
3. Karim et Rania ont étudié la physique. Ils ont eu 15 et 16 sur 20 au contrôle. Ils ont réussi.
4. Léo et Djamel ont étudié la biologie. Ils ont eu 17 et 19 sur 20 au contrôle. Ils ont réussi.
5. Sandrine et moi avons étudié la chimie. Nous avons eu 11 et 10 sur 20 au contrôle. Nous n'avons pas réussi.
6. Tu as étudié la biologie. Tu as eu 18 sur 20 au contrôle. Tu as réussi.
7. Yasmine a étudié la chimie. Elle a eu 16 sur 20 au contrôle. Elle a réussi.

Expansion

Use the context of **Activité 11** as an opportunity to talk about careers in math and science. Have students help you make a list of careers that require courses in those subjects: aeronautics, computer programming, laboratory research, space technology, oceanography, etc.

Culture

Practices: Information

French students are graded on a 20-point scale; they do not receive letter grades. A grade of 16–20 is considered excellent, 14–15 good, 12–13 satisfactory, 10–11 passing, 0–9 failing.

COMPARAISONS

What is the past participle in these English sentences?

Djamel **has** not **received** my texts.

They **have said** yes.

Have you **drunk** all the lemon-lime soda?

4.1

11 Les sciences

1.1, 1.2, 1.3, 5.1

Les élèves suivants ont suivi un cours de sciences. Pour réussir au premier contrôle, il fallait avoir 12 ou plus. Dites quelle matière chaque ado a étudié, combien de points il/elle a reçu, et s'il/elle a réussi.

Élève	Cours	Contrôle
Sandrine	chimie	11
Djamel	biologie	19
Léo	biologie	17
Karim	physique	15
moi	chimie	10
Rania	physique	16
toi	biologie	18
Nadia	physique	17
Yasmine	chimie	16

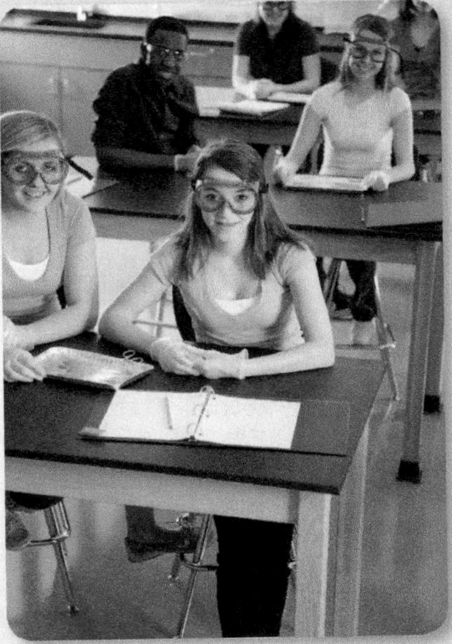

MODÈLE Sandrine
Sandrine a étudié la chimie. Elle a eu 11 sur 20 au contrôle. Elle n'a pas réussi.

1. Djamel et toi
2. Nadia
3. Karim et Rania
4. Léo et Djamel
5. Sandrine et moi
6. toi
7. Yasmine

COMPARAISONS: The past participles are "received," "said," and "drunk."

Essential Instruction

1. Ask students for the past participles of **étudier**, **avoir**, and **réussir** before doing **Activité 11** as a class.
2. If your students are struggling with the **passé composé**, have them write out the answers to **Activité 12**; otherwise have students work with a partner.
3. Remind students that questions using inversion do not take **est-ce que**. After students write out the questions, have them close their notebooks and do **Activité 13** orally.

12 Dans quel ordre?

1.2, 1.3, 5.1

Composez deux phrases grâce aux indices qui vous sont donnés, et mettez-les dans l'ordre. Suivez le modèle.

MODÈLE Jacques/vivre à Lyon/grandir à Marseille
Jacques a grandi à Marseille.
Puis, il a vécu à Lyon.

Romain est venu chez Alex. Puis, il l'a aidé à faire ses devoirs.

1. ma famille et moi/choisir un terrain de camping/pêcher
2. toi/atterrir en Côte-d'Ivoire/décoller de Paris
3. les Lambert/faire les magasins/finir leurs corvées
4. je/emprunter une tondeuse/tondre la pelouse
5. Alex/composter son billet/acheter son billet de train
6. Luc et toi/mettre le couvert/dîner en famille avec vos grands-parents

13 Au parc d'attractions

1.2, 1.3, 5.1, 5.2

Pendant l'été, tes copains sont allés dans un parc d'attractions. Écrivez les questions que vous voulez leur poser. Utilisez le passé composé.

MODÈLE avec qui/tu/faire un tour de montagnes russes
Avec qui as-tu fait un tour de montagnes russes?

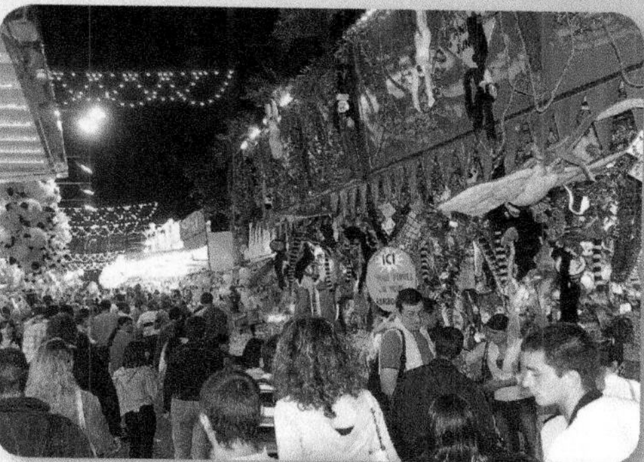

1. pourquoi/Alexandre/faire un tour de grande roue
2. avec qui/Julie/essayer des jeux d'adresse
3. pourquoi/Cécile et Eva/avoir une consultation avec la voyante
4. comment/vous/conduire les autos tamponneuses
5. que/on/boire au parc d'attractions
6. quand/vous/devoir partir

Answers

1. Ma famille et moi avons choisi un terrain de camping. Puis, nous avons pêché.
2. Tu as décollé de Paris. Puis, tu as atterri en Côte-d'Ivoire.
3. Les Lambert ont fini leurs corvées. Puis, ils ont fait les magasins.
4. J'ai emprunté une tondeuse, puis j'ai tondu la pelouse.
5. Alex a acheté son billet de train. Puis, il la composté.
6. Luc et toi avez mis le couvert. Puis, vous avez dîné en famille avec vos grands-parents.

1. Pourquoi Alexandre a-t-il fait un tour de grande roue?
2. Avec qui Julie a-t-elle essayé les jeux d'adresse?
3. Pourquoi Cécile et Eva ont-elles eu une consultation avec la voyante?
4. Comment avez-vous conduit les autos tamponneuses?
5. Qu'a-t-on bu au parc d'attractions?
6. Quand avez-vous dû partir?

Reference Desk

Most short, common adverbs come before the past participles, for example, **Julien est vite descendu de l'auto tamponneuse.**

Expansion

For additional practice, have students complete this activity in the **passé composé.**

Le matin de la rentrée, Aïcha (mettre) un nouvel ensemble. Elle (prendre) une tartine et un jus d'orange. Puis, elle (chercher) ses cahiers et ses livres. Elle (attendre) Chloé devant leur immeuble. Mais elle (être) en retard. Donc, les filles ont (courir vite) au lycée. En cours, Aïcha (ne pas pouvoir) prendre des notes. Elle (oublier) d'apporter son stylo. La rentrée (commencer mal)!

Differentiated Learning

Accelerate

After all students have written the questions for **Activité 13**, ask accelerated students to do mini-dialogues in pairs; one student asks the question and the other responds.

Decelerate

Have these students listen to the mini-dialogues presented by the advanced students and treat it as a listening activity. Encourage them to write down what they learned about the experience of each teen (Alexandre, Julie, etc.) at the amusement park.

Learning Styles

Auditory Learners

Have someone in class read aloud the cues for **Activités 12–13** to help these students.

RESOURCES

 Workbook 12–13

 Listening Activity 2

 Drill & Practice Games

Reference Desk

1. The **passé compose** with **avoir** was introduced in Level 1 in **Unité 8** and reviewed in Level 2 in **Unité 2**.
2. A classic way to teach or review **être** verbs is to draw a house with people coming, going, arriving, leaving, going out, coming in, being born, dying, climbing, falling, remaining, entering, returning home. (Your artistic students can provide a drawing for you to use.)
3. MR. and MRS. P. VANDERTRAMP is a mnemonic device used to recall all 16 verbs that take **être** in the **passé composé.** Only 13 of those verbs are presented here, as those are the ones students have seen previously introduced in the **Rencontres culturelles** dialogues. Students learn **tomber** and **mourir** in **Unité 8**.
4. Consider writing the mnemonic device on the board every day until students can recall all 16 verbs, if that is your goal, or give an extra credit quiz to get students to remember them all.

Expansion

Have students write two statements about what someone did, each on a separate note card. One sentence should be an activity done at home and the other outside of the home. Collect the cards and mix them up. Then put students in groups of four. Give each group eight note cards. One member of each group reads the sentences, then calls on group members to say if the person stayed home or not. Groups exchange note cards with those of another group when they are done.

Révision: *Passé composé* with *être*

 1.2

emcl.com
WB 12–13
LA 2
Games

Do you remember how to make past tense sentences using the verb **être**? What two parts make up a sentence in the **passé composé**? What is different with past participles used with **être**? See if you can complete the sentences below correctly.

1. Océane est allé_ à Paris. A. **–s**
2. Lucas et Léo sont parti_ à 13h30. B. **–es**
3. Martine et Amélie sont rentré_ tôt. C. **–e**

If you couldn't answer the questions or do the activity, then read the summary below.

Certain verbs form their **passé composé** with the helping verb **être**. Most verbs that use **être** in the **passé composé** *express motion or movement* of the subject from one place to another. Note that the ending of the past participle of the verb agrees in gender and in number with the subject.

Elles **sont arrivées** à huit heures. *They arrived at 8:00.*

Here are the verbs you've already learned that use the helping verb **être**, along with their past participles. In addition to the agreement of the past participles, note the position of negative expressions and how to form questions using inversion.

Verb	Past Participle	Passé Composé
aller	**allé**	Ils ne **sont** jamais **allés** à Cannes.
arriver	**arrivé**	J'y **suis arrivé(e)** il y a deux heures.
descendre	**descendu**	**Est**-elle **descendue** à Nice de Paris?
devenir	**devenu**	Marame **est devenue** médecin.
entrer	**entré**	Nous **sommes entrés** dans la discothèque.
monter	**monté**	Elle **est** déjà **montée** dans sa chambre?
partir	**parti**	Florianne, à quelle heure **es**-tu **partie**?
rentrer	**rentré**	**Êtes**-vous **rentrés** avant minuit?
rester	**resté**	Nous n'y **sommes** pas **restés**.
retourner	**retourné**	Anne **est retournée** en France.
revenir	**revenu**	Je ne **suis** plus **revenu(e)**.
sortir	**sorti**	Kate, **es**-tu **sortie** avec tes amis?
venir	**venu**	Éric n'**est** pas **venu** à la soirée.

PASSÉ COMPOSÉ WITH ÊTRE:
The answers are: 1. C; 2. A; 3. B

Essential Instruction

1. Have students answer the questions and do the quiz in the top yellow section. Depending on how well they do, proceed to the practice activities or review thoroughly.
2. Ask students to find examples of inversion and negation in the sample sentences in the second yellow box.
3. Do **Activité 14** orally as a class to make sure students are paying attention to agreement of the past participle.
4. Have students work on **Activité 15** in pairs.

14 Complétez!

1.2, 5.1

*Lisez l'histoire de la classe de Mlle Merrick qui est allée à Paris. Complétez les phrases avec la forme convenable d'**être** et le participe passé du verbe entre parenthèses.*

1. Le premier jour à Paris, le groupe... tôt parce qu'il y avait beaucoup à voir et à faire à Paris. (*partir*)
2. Tous les élèves... en haut de la tour Eiffel pour prendre de belles photos de Paris et des monuments. (*monter*)
3. La prof, Mlle Merrick, ... voir une amie française à midi. (*aller*)
4. Sonia et moi, nous... dans le Louvre pour voir la *Joconde*. (*entrer*)
5. Benoît... avec nous. (*venir*)
6. Vers 20h00, Sonia et moi, ... à la recherche d'un bon restaurant pas cher. (*sortir*)
7. Morgane et toi, vous... à l'hôtel, mais pourquoi? (*rester*)

15 Samedi!

1.1, 1.2, 1.3

Dites où tout le monde est allé samedi. Choisissez une expression de la liste.

la discothèque	le festival	l'aquaparc	le complexe sportif	la MJC	la soirée

1. les copains et moi

2. tu

3. Sylvaine et Guillaume

4. Fatima

5. les ados

6. je

Differentiated Learning

Accelerate

Have these students tell a story about one of the numbered items in **Activité 15.** The sentence from the activity can be their beginning or ending.

Decelerate

Slower-paced students may benefit from **Drill and Practice Games** designed for ***T'es branché?***, verb games online, or activities available at stores that sell educational materials.

Special Needs Students

Dyslexia

Conjugation can be challenging for these students. Allow them to use their own charts and notes when doing the activities.

Answers

1. est parti
2. sont montés
3. est allée
4. sommes entré(e)s
5. est venu
6. sommes sorti(e)s
7. êtes resté(e)s

1. Les copains et moi sommes allés au festival.
2. Tu es allé(e) à la discothèque.
3. Sylvaine et GUillaume sont allés à la MJC.
4. Elle est allée à l'aquaparc.
5. Ils sont allés à la soirée.
6. Je suis allé(e) au complexe sportif.

Expansion

Ask each student to write down the names of five cities they would like to visit in the United States. Collect the information, then make a list of all the cities. Distribute the list to each pair of students. Students take turns asking and telling if they have been to these cities, for example, **Es-tu allé(e) à Boston?** The partner answers **Oui, j'y suis allé(e)** or **Non, je n'y suis pas allé(e).** When pairs are done, place a map of the U.S. on the bulletin board. Ask students randomly if they have gone to the cities on the list. Assign a kinesthetic or AD(H)D student to place a thumb tack on each city visited by someone in the class. (The pronoun **y** was introduced in **Unité 8** of Level 2.)

Communication

Interpersonal: Paired Practice

To practice the **passé composé** of **avoir** and **être** verbs, have students work in pairs to prepare a dialogue about one day or a trip during summer vacation. Encourage students to write cues in English to help them remember what to say so they don't read their dialogues, but actually perform them for the class.

Answers

16

1. a grandi
2. a joué
3. a arrêté
4. est partie
5. est allée
6. ont quitté
7. a découvert
8. a fait
9. a vu
10. est arrivé
11. sont allés

1. Romain est resté souvent à la maison.
2. Audrey a découvert un festival...
3. Audrey est allée au zoo...
4. Audrey est partie faire du ski...
5. Romain a visité le musée...
6. Audrey a couru dans le parc.
7. Audrey est montée dans la grande roue.
8. Romain est allé au ciné-club.

Reference Desk

By now students may have questions about the different French verbs for leaving, for example, **quitter** used in **Activité 16**, which means "to leave someone or something." Here are some more to clear up: **partir** (*to leave*), **sortir** (*to go out*), **retourner** (*to return to where you started*), **rentrer** (*to go home or back to where you're living*), **s'en aller** (*to go away*).

Communication

Interpersonal: Cooperative Groups

Have students pretend they are in **la cour** at school after summer break talking to their friends. Their task is to find out what everyone in their group did during summer vacation and ask follow-up questions to make their dialogues as long as possible. It is up to each group if they want to tell true or made-up stories or a combination. The students not presenting have to write down if the story by each student is all true or all or partially imagined. Vote on the best "fooler" in class.

16 La vie de Karim

1.2, 1.3, 5.1

Complètez l'histoire de Karim en mettant les verbes au passé composé. Attention à utiliser le bon auxiliaire (avoir ou être).

1. Karim... dans un petit village. (*grandir*)
2. Il y... au football avec des amis. (*jouer*)
3. Mais à Nice, il.... (*arrêter*)
4. Un jour la mère de Karim... du village. (*partir*)
5. Sa mère... à Nice avant les autres membres de sa famille. (*aller*)
6. Ils... leur maison avec la piscine. (*quitter*)
7. À Nice, Karim... les supermarchés. (*découvrir*)
8. D'abord, il... de Léo. (*faire la connaissance*)
9. Ensuite, il... Élodie au ciné-club. (*voir*)
10. Ce soir, il... chez Léo et Élodie. (*arriver*)
11. Lui et ses amis... voir un film. (*aller*)

17 Les jumeaux

1.1, 1.2, 1.3, 5.1

Audrey aime les activités en plein air et son frère, Romain, préfère les activités à l'intérieur. Dites qui a fait chaque activité pendant les vacances. Attention si le verbe prend "avoir" ou "être."

MODÈLES

sortir avec des copines
Audrey est sortie avec des copines.

passer des heures à la médiathèque
Romain a passé des heures à la médiathèque.

1. rester souvent à la maison
2. découvrir un festival de jazz dans la rue Malherbe
3. aller au zoo voir les gorilles et les pandas
4. partir faire du ski à la montagne
5. visiter le musée d'histoire
6. courir dans le parc
7. monter dans la grande roue
8. aller au ciné-club

Essential Instruction

1. Model the **passé composé** by explaining what you did yesterday or last weekend or during vacation. Encourage students to ask you questions about your experience.
2. For students needing more practice, have them say where certain people went, and then say what they did there, for example, **Maxime est allé à l'aéroport. Il a voyagé en Europe.**

Révision: Imperfect Tense  1.2

emcl.com
WB 14–16
Games

When do you use the imperfect tense rather than the **passé composé**? Can you figure out which verbs in the paragraph below would be in the imperfect?

Julie put a novel and her MP3 player in her bag and changed into her swimsuit. She got in the car and drove for 15 minutes. It was a sunny day at the beach. Many people were sunbathing. Others swam.

If you need help, read the summary below.

The **imparfait** is another tense used to talk about the past. You use the **imparfait** to describe how people or things were and to describe what used to happen or what people used to do in the past.

Karim **collectionnait** des cartes de football. *Karim collected soccer cards.*

To form the imperfect, add the endings **–ais, –ais, –ait, –ions, –iez,** and **–aient** to the stem of the present tense **nous** form.

faire Imperfect stem: *fais* (from *nous fais~~ons~~*)			
je	**fais**ais	nous	**fais**ions
tu	**fais**ais	vous	**fais**iez
il/elle/on	**fais**ait	ils/elles	**fais**aient

À quoi **jouais**-tu à l'âge de cinq ans? *What did you play at the age of five?*
Je **faisais** semblant d'être un super-héros. *I pretended to be a superhero.*

The verb **être** has an irregular stem in the imperfect: **ét–**.

Vivianne **était** une princesse pour Mardi Gras. *Vivianne was a princess for Mardi Gras.*

IMPERFECT TENSE: The imperfect tense is used to describe people, things, or conditions as they were or used to be, or habitual repeated actions. In the English paragraph, these verbs would be in the imperfect: **Il faisait du soleil. Beaucoup de gens bronzaient. D'autres nageaient.**

RESOURCES

 **Workbook 14–16**

 **Drill & Practice Games**

Reference Desk

1. **The imparfait** was introduced in **Unité 4** of Level 2. If you did not do the Oral History project on p. 215 of Level 2 last year, you might consider having students do it in this unit.
2. Point out that the endings **–ais**, **–ait**, and **–aient** all sound alike.
3. Verbs that end in **–cer** have a cedilla under the final **c** when it precedes an **a**; however, the cedilla does not appear in the **nous** and **vous** forms, for example, **ils commençaient** but **nous commencions.**
4. Verbs that end in **–ger** have an **e** after the **g** and before the endings in all forms except for **nous** and **vous**, for example, **il mangeait** but **nous mangions.**
5. Other verbs with spelling changes in the present tense form the imperfect regularly, for example, **je préférais**, **j'achetais**, and **je nettoyais.**
6. Verbs that end in **–ier** have **–ii** in the **nous** and **vous** forms, for example, **vous étudiiez.** These require a longer vowel sound.
7. **Falloir**, **neiger**, and **pleuvoir** have only an **il** form. In the imperfect they are **il fallait**, **il neigeait**, and **il pleuvait.**
8. When expressing a past idea, these verbs are generally in the imperfect, not the **passé composé**: **adorer**, **aimer**, **avoir**, **connaître**, **être**, **penser**, **pouvoir**, **savoir**, and **vouloir.**

Differentiated Learning

Decelerate

Let these students know which verbs they will need to put in the **passé composé** on the quiz so that they have a chance to do well and don't get frustrated.

Learning Styles

Kinesthetic Learners

Have the students chant: **ais, ais, ait, ions, iez, aient heh!** It is a jingle that quickly teaches the endings of the imperfect.

Special Needs Students

Dyslexia

These students may benefit from having an oral quiz on the **passé composé** with **avoir** and **être**, rather than a written one.

Answers

18

1. Quand Fatouma et Hélène étaient petites, elles jouaient à la poupée.
2. Quand Diane et moi étions petit(e)s, nous faisions des châteaux de sable.
3. Quand Myrian était petite, elle jouait du piano.
4. Quand tu étais petit(e), tu jouais à la marelle.
5. Quand Richard était petit, il collectionnait les coquillages.
6. Quand j'étais petit(e), j'allais à l'aquaparc.
7. Quand Sophie et toi étiez petit(e)s, vous couriez.

Communication

Presentational: Cooperative Groups

Ask students to bring in a picture from a magazine or the Internet, for example, a family eating in a restaurant or some other activity. Collect the images, then put the students in groups. Give each group a picture that elicits a lot of descriptive sentences in the imperfect. For example: **Les Lenoir étaient dans un restaurant. Il y avait le père, la mère, et deux enfants. Ils mangeaient ensemble. Ils prenaient des pâtes. Le repas était délicieux.** Finally, post all the pictures. A representative from each group reads their story, and the rest of the class matches the description to the right image.

Culture

Products: Activity

Singing songs that use the **imparfait** is a good way to solidify comprehension of this tense. The popular French singer, La Grande Sophie, sings **"On savait."** The song recounts what it is like growing up. Another option is Joe Dassin's **"Le petit pain au chocolat,"** which recounts a love story that starts in **une pâtisserie.** Make copies of the song lyrics, leaving blanks for all the verbs in the imperfect for students to fill in.

The imperfect is used to describe:

Use	Example	
People or things as they were or used to be	Mon grand-père **était** médecin.	*My grand-father was a doctor.*
Conditions as they were or used to be	Il n'y **avait** pas d'arbres.	*There were no trees.*
Actions that took place repeatedly, regulary, or habitually in the past	Nous **allions** souvent à l'aquaparc.	*We often used to go to the waterpark.*

18 Les activités enfantines

1.2, 1.3

Dites ce que tout le monde faisait quand ils étaient petits.

MODÈLE

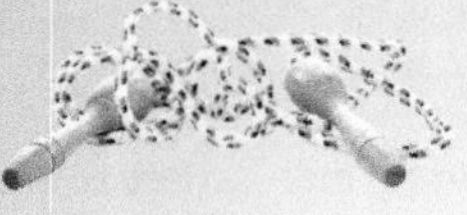

Marame
Quand Marame était petite, elle sautait à la corde.

1. Fatoumata et Hélène

2. Diane et moi

3. Myriam

4. toi

5. Richard

6. moi

7. Sophie et toi

COMPARAISONS

What is an example of a past tense verb formed with one word in English? Does it express a past tense completed action (like **passé composé**) or a habitual or repeated action (like the imperfect)?

4.1

COMPARAISONS: "I saw the movie Saturday" and "I read the blog this morning" are examples that have one verb form in the past; however, in these two examples these verbs are more like the **passé composé** than the imperfect. Both "I saw" and "I read" in this instance describe something that happened once in the past. To make the sentence express an idea like the imperfect, you could say, "I saw the movie every Christmas" and "I read the blog every day last year."

Essential Instruction

1. Reviewing the **passé composé** and the **imparfait** at the beginning of every class as a warm-up activity will help to keep the forms fresh in students' brains.
2. The students might find it helpful to think of the **passé composé** and the **imparfait** as a team that works together to express actions in the past; they complement each other. The **passé composé** is akin to a photo that freezes an action in the past, whereas the **imparfait** is more like a movie that shows continuous and repeated actions. Encourage students to write an opening scene for a movie. Post the stories that are in the **passé composé** on the right wall of the classroom, those that use only the **imparfait** on the left wall of the classroom, and those that use both tenses on the back wall of the classroom.
3. Do **Activité 18** as a class, and ask students to work on **Activité 19** with a partner.

19 Un accident de voiture  1.1, 1.2, 1.3, 5.1, 5.2

Un accident de voiture a eu lieu. Le conducteur responsable est parti. Vous êtes le seul témoin (witness). Téléphonez à la police et répondez à leurs questions.

1. Où étiez-vous quand vous avez vu cet accident?
2. Quelle heure était-il?
3. Est-ce qu'il pleuvait?
4. Il y avait combien de voitures, de conducteurs et de passagers?
5. Les deux conducteurs sont-ils partis?
6. Comment est arrivé l'accident?
7. Quel âge a le conducteur?
8. Qu'est-ce qu'il faisait quand l'accident est arrivé?
9. La conductrice a-t-elle eu mal?
10. Son fils va bien?

Révision: The Imperfect and the *passé composé*  1.2

emcl.com
WB 17–18
Games

If you wrote a sentence that used both the imperfect and the **passé composé**, do you remember which one you would use to interrupt a continuous action? If you don't remember, read the summary below.

You have learned two past tenses in French, the imperfect and the **passé composé**. These two tenses are not used in the same way.

The imperfect describes how people or things were in the past, what happened regularly, or a condition that existed at some time in the past.

En été, Laure et Awa **couraient** au bord de la mer.	*During the summer, Laure and Awa ran on the seashore.*
Moi, je **préférais** rester à la maison.	*Me, I preferred staying home.*

The **passé composé** indicates a single, completed action.

Un jour, nous **sommes allés** à la plage.	*One day, we went to the beach.*
Mamy **a ramassé** des coquillages avec nous.	*Grandma picked up sea shells with us.*

IMPERFECT TENSE AND THE *PASSÉ COMPOSÉ*: If you are describing a continuous action, that part of the sentence would be in the imperfect; anything that interrupted that action would be in the **passé composé**.

RESOURCES

 **Workbook 17–18**

 **Drill & Practice Games**

Answers

19 *Possible answers:*

1. J'étais devant un magasin/je marchais dans la rue/je conduisais ma moto, etc.
2. Il était 13h15.
3. Non, il faisait beau.
4. Il y avait deux voitures, un camion rouge et blanc conduit par un homme seul, et un monospace vert conduit par une femme et son enfant.
5. Non, ils sont toujours là (mais le conducteur du camion va partir).
6. Le camion a heurté le monospace à une intersection.
7. Il a une trentaine d'années.
8. Je pense qu'il parlait sur son portable.
9. Oui, elle a dû recevoir un choc, elle a mal à la tête.
10. Oui, apparemment, il va bien.

Reference Desk

There are many online activities to help with the difference between the **imparfait** and the **passé composé.**

Game

Machine à écrire

Divide the class into two teams, then assign at least one letter or accent mark to each student. Start the game by giving one team a subject pronoun and an infinitive in French. This team must quickly spell out loud the correct form of the verb in the imperfect tense. For example, if you say **il/neiger**, students must spell **neigeait.** If done correctly, the team earns a point. Then the other team gets its turn at a word. Whenever a team fails, its rival gets a chance to spell the same word and win another point. If students are having trouble with a verb, write it on the board, erase it, then put the item back on the list.

Differentiated Learning

Accelerate

Students who have mastered the **imparfait** might enjoy making a story out of one of the images in **Activité 18.**

Decelerate

As a class, write a short story in English in the past that shows repeated actions and habitual conditions. Using the criteria on p. 42, decide whether each verb should be written in French in the **passé composé** or the **imparfait.** Pair up advanced students with slower-paced students to write only the verbs in French.

Answers

20 *Possible paragraph:*

Pablo Picasso était déjà artiste quand il est venu à Paris en 1901. Il a fait la connaissance de Georges Braques, en 1907. Les deux artistes ont inventé le Cubisme. Ils décomposaient leurs sujets en formes géométriques. En 1910, Picasso est allé en Provence, où il a travaillé dans un grand atelier. Il était révolté contre le fascisme en Espagne quand il a fait son chef d'œuvre *Guernica* en 1936. Le tableau est devenu un symbole de la Résistance pendant la Deuxième Guerre Mondiale.
En 1948, Picasso a commencé à travailler avec la céramique. En 1957, le musée d'art moderne à New York a organisé une exposition de son œuvre. Plus de 100.000 visiteurs sont venus admirer....

Reference Desk

Pablo Picasso is the subject of **Activité 20** because he was mentioned in the culture reading about PACA on p. 32. Although born in Spain, he lived much of his life in Paris and southern France.

Games

Quand je voyagerai....

Put students in teams. Have each team choose two locations, such as **l'Italie**, **la Tunisie**, or **Paris**, from a bag or bowl. Each group races to write sentences about what they will do when they go there, for example, **Quand j'irai en Italie, je verrai la tour de Pisa.** Award points for correct sentences.

Quand le professeur est entré....

Tell students you will be going into the hallway for two minutes, and that when you come back, they have to be in the process of doing something. Also, they must observe what everyone else is doing. When you come back in the classroom, ask students what everyone was doing when you entered, and have them respond with a sentence in the **imparfait** and the **passé composé**, for example, **Monique dessinait un cheval au tableau quand vous êtes entré(e) dans la salle de classe.**

To tell a story, use the imperfect to give background information and to describe circumstances in the past. The imperfect answers the question, "How were things?" Use the **passé composé** to express what events took place only once in the past. The **passé composé** answers the question, "What happened?"

Tu **étais** en ville.	*You were in town.*
Un accident de voiture **a eu** lieu.	*A car accident happened.*

The imperfect and the **passé composé** are often used in the same sentence to describe an ongoing action that was interrupted by another action. Use the imperfect to express the background condition or ongoing action and the **passé composé** to describe the completed action.

Vous **aviez** peur pour la conductrice; donc, vous **avez téléphoné** à la police.	*You were afraid for the driver; therefore, you called the police.*

COMPARAISONS

Which English sentence shows an interrupted action? **4.1**

Kyle **was reading** when his mom **came home**.

We **were jumping up** and **raising** our arms when the song **was playing**.

20 La vie de Pablo Picasso

1.2, 1.3, 3.1, 5.1

Pablo Picasso était, selon beaucoup de critiques, l'artiste le plus important du XXème siècle. Utilisez les notes suivantes pour raconter les événements importants de sa vie.

1901: Pablo Picasso/être déjà artiste quand/venir à Paris
1907: il/faire la connaissance de Georges Braques
les deux artistes/inventer le Cubisme
ils/décomposer leurs sujets en formes géométriques
1910: Picasso/aller en Provence où il/travailler dans un grand atelier
1936: il/être révolté contre le fascisme en Espagne quand il/faire son chef-d'œuvre *Guernica*
le tableau/devenir un symbole de la Résistance pendant la Deuxième Guerre Mondiale
1948: il/commencer à travailler avec la céramique
1957: le musée de l'art moderne à New York/organiser une exposition de son œuvre
plus de 100.000 visiteurs/venir admirer ses tableaux, ses objets d'art, et ses céramiques

Le Château de Vauvenargues, résidence de Picasso.

COMPARAISONS: The first sentence shows an interrupted action. All the verbs in the second sentence would be put in the **imparfait** in French sentences.

Essential Instruction

1. Tell students what you did over the weekend, speaking in the two tenses, and using lots of drama to emphasize the verbs. Have students retell your story in the **vous** form using the same exaggeration. Then have them write it in the third person singular form.
2. Pair up advanced students with those who are slower-paced to complete **Activité 20.**
3. Depending on your students' comprehension of the grammar topic, you may want to read the story in **Activité 21** in your own voice at a slower pace before having students listen to the recording. The script is located in the front pages of this Annotated Teacher's Edition. Make sure students understand why they made a mistake by showing them the script after they've done the listening activity.
4. Do **Activité 22** as a class and **Activité 23** as written practice.

21 La journée de Mme Aknouch

1.1, 1.2

*Écrivez les numéros 1–6 sur votre papier. Écoutez l'histoire. Ensuite, dites si chaque phrase est vraie (**V**) ou fausse (**F**).*

1. Mme Aknouch n'a pas d'enfants.
2. Elle a travaillé aujourd'hui.
3. Elle a fait du footing au complexe sportif.
4. Elle a fait les courses.
5. À l'école sa fille jouait à cache-cache avec ses copains.
6. Amina et sa mère ont pris le métro pour rentrer.

22 La soirée

1.2, 1.3, 5.1

Dites ce que tout le monde faisait quand l'actrice est arrivée à la soirée. Choisissez une expression de la liste.

danser jouer du piano discuter du film toucher un tableau manger des hors-d'œuvres chanter profiter du buffet

MODÈLE Pierre
Pierre mangeait des hors-d'œuvre quand l'actrice est arrivée.

1. Mlle Duchamp
2. M. et Mme Laforêt
3. Serge et moi
4. M. Dumont
5. tu
6. Mme Declerc
7. Pierre

23 Un super-héros

1.2, 1.3, 5.1

Complétez l'histoire suivante en utilisant le passé composé et l'imparfait. Puis devinez le nom du super-héros.

Il y (avoir) un homme qui (venir) d'une autre planète. Il (avoir) les cheveux noirs et il (être) beau. Il (trouver) un travail de reporter dans une grande ville. Il (porter) des lunettes et un costume quand il (travailler) au bureau. Quand il y (avoir) un crime, il (mettre) vite un costume rouge et bleu. Il (être) très fort, mais il (devenir) moins fort quand il (être) près d'une pierre (*stone*) verte. Il (aimer) Loïs Lane. Un jour, Loïs (tomber) des chutes du Niagara, et il l' (aider). Elle (découvrir) son identité. Ils (s'aimer) beaucoup et ils (se marier).

Answers

1. F
2. F
3. V
4. V
5. F
6. F

1. Mlle Duchamp jouait du piano.
2. M. et Mme Laforêt dansaient.
3. Serge et moi discutions du film.
4. M. Dumont chantait.
5. Tu touchais un tableau.
6. Mme Declerc profitait du buffet.
7. Pierre mangeait des hors-d'œuvres.

23

...avait...venait...avait...était...a trouvé...portait...travaillait...y avait... mettait...était...devenait...était... aimait...est tombée...a aidée...a découvert...s'aimaient...se sont mariés.

Differentiated Learning

Accelerate

Ask these students to write an activity similar to **Activité 23**, a story with verbs in parentheses. Collect them, then pass them out to students needing extra practice.

RESOURCES

Communicative Activities

Answers

24 *Activities will vary.*

25 *Activities will vary.*

26 *Activities will vary.*

Reference Desk

1. You may want to read the model **récit personnel** together as a class, then consider why each verb is in that tense before doing **Activité 27** as a class.
2. If students don't do **Activité 27** correctly, provide remedial practice on the **passé composé** (including preceding direct object agreement) and the **imparfait.** Or, provide another **récit personnel** to study together.
3. An effective **organigramme** to use for describing an event is a sequencing chart. To make a template of one for students, draw three boxes at the top of the page with arrows to the right between them, then continue until the page is full.

Expansion

If you are collaborating with another Level 3 class, or a class in a French-speaking culture, you may want students to conduct the poll with those students, then make comparisons between their own class and the other class. You might include polling of what activities are for boys, and which ones are for girls in the French-speaking culture, to speculate on why there may be such differences between the cultures. If you have a website for your class, consider posting the results for **Activité 24**, as well as the projects in **Activités 25–26**.

À vous la parole

Question centrale: Comment la vie des Francophones évolue-t-elle avec le temps?

24 Quand j'avais dix ans....

1.2, 1.3, 5.1, 5.2

Interpersonal/Presentational Communication

Faites un sondage auprès de vos camarades de classe pour déterminer leurs passe-temps préférés quand ils avaient dix ans. Faites une grille comme celle de dessous et écrivez les réponses de dix élèves. Ensuite, partagez vos résultats avec la classe en expliquant quelles étaient les activités les plus populaires.

MODÈLE **A: Qu'est-ce que tu faisais quand tu avais dix ans?**
B: Je jouais aux jeux vidéo.

Nom	Activité
Abdou	Il jouait aux jeux vidéo.
Manon	Elle jouait à la poupée.

Résumé possible:

À l'âge de dix ans, quatre garçons jouaient aux jeux vidéo. Une fille jouait à la poupée....

Communiquez!

25 Une famille francophone

Interpretive/Presentational Communication

Faites des recherches sur une famille francophone. Ça peut être la famille de votre correspondant(e), la famille royale belge, la famille Rainier de Monaco, ou une famille en ligne qui partage ses photos ou vidéos. Créez un document qui décrit cette famille (les membres, âges, passe-temps, professions, vacances, etc.). Ensuite, chaque personne dans la classe va présenter oralement la famille sur laquelle il ou elle a fait des recherches. Finalement, vous allez discuter de ce que vous avez appris des familles francophones.

1.2, 1.3, 2.1, 2.2, 3.2, 5.2

26 À la découverte de Nice

Interpretive/Presentational Communication

Avec vos camarades de classe, préparez un site web dédié à Nice et au tourisme. Tout le monde va choisir un rôle et travailler en équipe pour: créer la page d'accueil, trouver des photos, écrire les adresses de sites intéressants, écrire une critique de restaurant, etc. Incluez dans les documents: les plages de Nice, la vieille ville, le musée Matisse, le musée Chagall, l'arrière-pays niçois, le Carnaval, les monuments, une liste de bons restaurants, une liste de bons hôtels.

1.2, 1.3, 3.1, 3.2

Essential Instruction

1. Depending on time, you may want to do one, two, or all three of the **À vous la parole** activities on this page. Another option is to have students choose the one that most interests them.
2. The sample Personal Narrative is a bit above your students' ability level, but it gives them something to strive toward.
3. Work with students to help them pick an appropriate topic for their ability level: either a narrative that describes an event (easiest); explores feelings (more difficult); or leads to a personal discovery (most difficult).

Stratégie communicative

Personal Narrative  1.1, 1.2

Un récit personnel est un essai écrit, en général, à la première personne (**je**). L'auteur raconte un moment particulier de sa vie, et expose souvent ses sentiments, ses découvertes, ou ses expériences intimes. Lisez le récit ci-dessous et dites si ce récit personnel (1) décrit un événement, (2) explore des sentiments sur quelque chose qui s'est passé, ou (3) mène à une découverte personnelle.

Il y a des évènements et des rencontres qui changent toute une vie. Ma vie a changé l'année de mes dix-huit ans. J'étais encore au lycée, en terminale, et j'allais passer mon bac. J'étudiais la langue de Shakespeare depuis maintenant six ans. L'anglais me fascinait. Je regardais tous les films possibles et imaginables anglais et américains en version originale, je lisais le dictionnaire français-anglais, je tenais un journal en anglais où j'écrivais tous les mots que j'apprenais dans mes lectures. Je n'étais pas encore allée en Angleterre ou en Amérique mais j'en rêvais secrètement. L'année de mon bac j'ai eu l'opportunité d'aller avec ma classe deux semaines dans une famille d'accueil en Angleterre. Ma famille était une famille nucléaire avec six enfants. Le père était professeur de français et de religion et la mère prof d'anglais. Chaque jour nous parlions tous ensemble, parents et enfants, de la langue et de la culture anglaise dans le salon, dans la cuisine, et à table. J'ai trouvé ces conversations fascinantes. Un jour, le père de ma famille d'accueil m'a invitée à son lycée où il m'a demandé de parler de la France et surtout de répondre aux nombreuses questions de ses élèves et c'est comme ça que j'ai découvert ma vocation pour l'enseignement. Aujourd'hui, je fais le plus beau métier du monde: je suis prof et tous les jours je partage avec les autres ma langue et ma culture, et c'est un grand bonheur.

27 Le passé composé ou l'imparfait?  1.2, 1.3

En écrivant un récit, vous devez choisir correctement le temps des verbes. Dans ces phrases écrites par d'autres élèves, conjuguez les verbes en choisissant le bon temps (tense).

1. Je/J'... mon meilleur ami au skatepark. (faire la connaissance de)
2. Après cela, je... mes camarades de classe. (ne... plus insulter)
3. Pour mon neuvième anniversaire, ma grand-mère... un gâteau en forme d'un terrain de foot. (me servir)
4. Enfin, je/j'... que j'... plus sportive que mes cousins. (réaliser, être)
5. Alors, j'... que le prof... m'aider. (apprendre, vouloir)

28 Je choisis un thème.  1.2, 1.3

Pour trouver un sujet pour votre récit personnel, remplissez un organigramme avec des idées. Pour trouver des idées, vous pouvez regarder des photos, faire une liste d'objets personnels qui sont importants, ou lire d'autres récits personnels en ligne. Quand vous avez un thème intéressant, écrivez votre récit personnel.

 **Search words: souvenirs d'enfance, souvenirs d'adolescence**

RESOURCES

 **Pre-test**

 ***Leçon* Quiz**

Answers

 27

1. J'ai fait la connaissance de
2. n'ai plus insulté
3. m'a servi
4. j'ai réalisé; étais
5. ai appris; voulait

28 *Paragraphs will vary.*

Expansion

This activity demonstrates the importance of pre-writing or brainstorming before undertaking a composition. It would be helpful to write a short class **récit personnel** together to model the process. Find out which of the three types (description of an event, exploration of feelings tied to a personal story, or description of a personal discovery) interests the most students, and write that one as a class. Students will see that the more they add to their pre-writing outline, the easier it will be for them to do the actual writing.

Differentiated Learning

Accelerate

Students may be interested in publishing their **récits** online.

Decelerate

These students may not be able to write their own **récit.** Other options for them include a story in which they provide the correct verb tense and verb forms, a cartoon that they describe by answering questions you have written, or changing personal pronouns to the third person.

RESOURCES

e-visual 3

Workbook 1–3

Flash Cards

Listening Activity 1

Drill & Practice Games

Reference Desk

1. Point out that **le mariage** is a **faux ami** in this context; it means "wedding."
2. A wedding anniversary is **un anniversaire de mariage**.
3. Students learned several **domaines** and **secteurs** on p. 512 of **Unité 9** in the Level 2 textbook. You may want to review these with the class.
4. Describe to students the two types of French weddings before they do **Activité 1**.

Vocabulaire actif

Le mariage et le travail

1.2

Emma se marie avec Théo.

la demoiselle d'honneur

le garçon d'honneur

la bague de fiançailles

les alliances (f.)

le gâteau de mariage

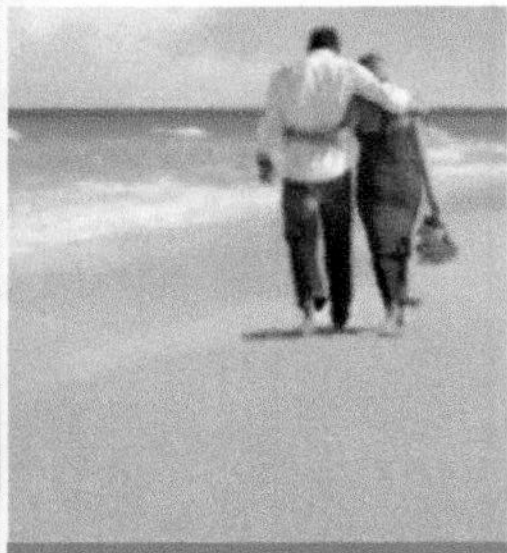
le voyage de noces

Vous voulez travailler....

Avocats Laterne

pour un cabinet d'avocat

Boiron

dans un laboratoire de recherches

Agrifruits

en plein air

pour une PME (Petite et Moyenne Enterprise)

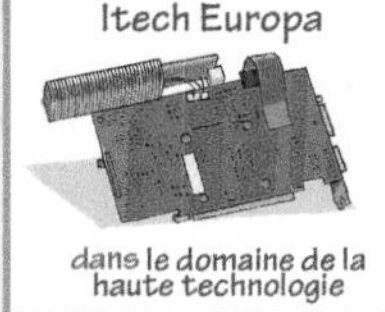

dans le domaine de la haute technologie

chez Airbus

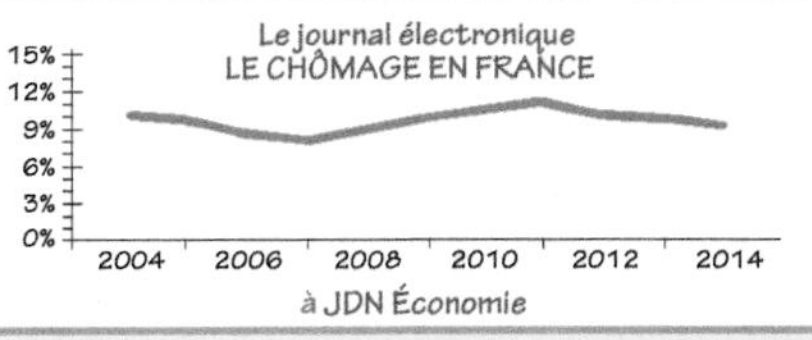

à JDN Économie

Essential Instruction

1. Play the audio for both groups of words.
2. Write a short love story together on the board.
3. Ask students where they would like to work, or conduct a class poll.

Pour la conversation  1.2, 1.3, 2.1, 5.1

How do I say I don't care?

> **Je m'en fiche.**
> *I don't care.*

How do I say where I'd like to work?

> **J'aimerais bien travailler** dans un laboratoire de recherches.
> *I'd like to work in a research laboratory.*

Et si je voulais dire...?

la lune de miel	*honeymoon*
la pièce montée	*wedding cake*
le témoin	*witness to the ceremony*
le vin d'honneur	*reception*
se fiancer	*to get engaged*
une entreprise	*company*
monter une enterprise	*to set up a company*
un entretien	*job interview*

1 Jean-Pierre et Marie-France vont se marier.  1.2, 1.3, 2.1, 5.1

Lisez l'histoire du mariage de Jean-Pierre et Marie-France. Puis, répondez à la question qui suit.

Jean-Pierre était amoureux de Marie-France. Il lui a demandé de se marier avec lui. Elle a accepté la bague de fiançailles que Jean-Pierre lui a offert. Ils ont décidé de se marier à la mairie. Ils y sont allés avec la demoiselle d'honneur, la sœur de Marie France, et le garçon d'honneur, le cousin de Jean-Pierre. Ils ont invité 89 amis et membres de leur famille à la réception, qui a eu lieu dans un restaurant. On a servi les invités du saumon et du steak. Le gâteau de mariage était violet et rose. Le lendemain, Jean-Pierre et Marie-France sont partis en voyage de noces, destination Tahiti!

Est-ce que Jean-Pierre et Marie-France ont respecté les traditions françaises? Justifiez votre réponse.

2 Le mariage de Chloé et Pierre

Regardez la scène et répondez aux questions.  1.2, 2.1

1. Où est tout le monde?
2. Qui vient de se marier?
3. Que porte la mariée?
4. Elle a quels bijoux?
5. Où sont assis la demoiselle d'honneur et le garçon d'honneur?
6. Que font les invités?
7. Qu'est-ce qu'ils vont manger à la fin du repas?

Differentiated Learning

Accelerate
Have these students use each of the words and expressions in **Et si je voulais dire...?** in original sentences. Then have them research **les pièces montées** and give creative names to the photos of the cakes that they find.

Decelerate
Pair each of these students with an advanced student, who listens to the slower-paced student read the story aloud. The advanced student can answer all the other student's questions about meaning and pronunciation.

Multiple Intelligences

Visual-Spatial
Ask these students to draw either the previous scenes at the church and city hall or the honeymoon.

Answers

Ils ont respecté les traditions culturelles (fiançailles, cérémonie civile, réception, voyage de noces), mais ils n'ont pas respecté la tradition de se marier à l'église.

1. Les gens sont à un repas de mariage.
2. Un homme et une femme viennent de se marier.
3. La mariée porte une belle robe blanche.
4. Elle porte un collier en perles, une bague de fiançailles, et une alliance.
5. Ils sont assis à la table des mariés.
6. Ils attendent de pouvoir manger.
7. Ils vont manger une pièce montée (un gâteau de mariage).

Reference Desk

1. Point out that **Je m'en fiche** is familiar French.
2. After students have read the story in **Activité 1** silently, discuss the answer to the critical thinking question as a class.
3. After doing **Activité 2** orally, ask students to write a narrative about the wedding, expanding on the story by saying what happened before and after the action in the illustration. You may want each student to have his/her story peer edited before handing it in to you.

Culture

Practices: Information

In France, a bride and groom must be married at **la mairie** in a civil ceremony. They then have the option of having a church service. **Le vin d'honneur** is the reception immediately following one or both ceremonies; this is described more in detail on p. 53.

Answers

3

1. R
2. E
3. R
4. E
5. E
6. E
7. E

1. Inès aimerait travailler pour une PME.
2. Maxime aimerait travailler dans un laboratoire de recherches.
3. Mathilde aimerait travailler dans le domaine de la haute technologie.
4. Julien aimerait travailler pour un cabinet d'avocats.
5. Julianne aimerait travailler chez Airbus.
6. Nicolas aimerait travailler à JDN Économie.

1. Clara
2. un collier de perles
3. Hervé
4. presque cent
5. à la Guadeloupe
6. Parce Clara commence son travail.

Reference Desk

1. You may want the class to brainstorm vocabulary related to a church ceremony and a reception before they listen to the audio in **Activité 3.**
2. If you aren't sure students know what types of companies **Airbus** and **JDN Économie** are, review with them before completing **Activité 4.** Airbus is a line of airplanes made by a European consortium of countries. **JDN Économie** is an online magazine.
3. **Activité 5** is another comprehensible input paragraph like **Activité 1** on p. 49.

3 Le mariage de Claudia et Philippe

1.1, 1.2

Écrivez les numéros 1–7 sur votre papier. Écrivez ***E*** *si la phrase décrit la cérémonie à l'église ou* ***R*** *si la phrase décrit la réception.*

4 Où on aimerait travailler

1.2, 1.3, 3.1, 5.1

Dites où tout le monde aimerait travailler en choisissant une expression de la colonne.

MODÈLE Jacques a besoin d'argent de poche (*pocket money*) et son oncle a une petite entreprise de construction.
Jacques aimerait travailler pour une PME.

1. Inès est secrétaire et cherche un nouveau travail.
2. Maxime finit ses études à la faculté des sciences pharmaceutiques.
3. Mathilde a des idées pour créer la nouvelle génération de smartphones.
4. Julien aime le droit.
5. Julianne a de l'expérience comme designer d'avions.
6. Nicolas a étudié le marché international.

une PME
chez Airbus
un cabinet d'avocats
JDN Économie
un laboratoire de recherches
le domaine de la haute technologie

5 Au téléphone

1.1, 1.2, 5.1

Lisez la conversation entre Mme Garnier et sa sœur Gabriella, qui habite en Australie, et qui n'a pas pu venir pour le mariage de sa nièce.

Mme Garnier: Je t'envoie des photos. Clara était très belle dans sa robe de mariée.
Gabriella: Tu lui as prêté des bijoux?
Mme Garnier: Le collier de perles de maman et le bracelet de diamants qu'Hervé m'a donné pour notre anniversaire de mariage l'année dernière.
Gabriella: Il y avait combien d'invités à la réception?
Mme Garnier: Presque cent.
Gabriella: Ils sont partis où pour leur voyage de noces, Clara et Lucas?
Mme Garnier: Ils voulaient aller à la Guadeloupe.
Gabriella: Ils reviennent quand?
Mme Garnier: Le 15 septembre. Clara commence à travailler pour un journal en ligne le 17.

1. Comment s'appelle la mariée?
2. Elle avait quels bijoux de sa mère?
3. Comment s'appelle le mari de Mme Garnier?
4. Il y avait combien d'invités à la réception?
5. Où le couple va-t-il en voyage de noces?
6. Pourquoi est-ce que le couple revient le 15 septembre?

Essential Instruction

1. Before doing **Activité 4**, explain that **aimerait** is the conditional tense. You may want to review the formation of the conditional.
2. Have students take turns playing the roles of Mme Garnier and Gabriella in **Activité 5.** Then put students in pairs to answer the questions.
3. Have students listen to the dialogue on p. 51 and then answer the questions. Do **Activité 6** as a class.

Rencontres culturelles

emcl.com WB 4

Élodie va assister à un mariage.

    1.2

Mots-clé **Noce** (du latin *nuptiae*, "mariage"). Au début du XIIème siècle, "la noce" signifiait l'union spirituelle d'un homme avec le Christ. Au XIIIème siècle, "la noce" représentait l'heureuse célébration qui suit un mariage, avec par exemple un festin (gros dîner), de la musique, et une danse.

Élodie parle à son cousin, Mathieu, qui va bientôt se marier.

Mathieu: Crois-moi, Élodie! Le mariage c'est une vraie entreprise: la réception, la liste des invités, le choix du garçon et de la demoiselle d'honneur. Et mettre d'accord ma mère et ma belle-mère, ça demande beaucoup de diplomatie.
Élodie: Et Sophie?
Mathieu: Elle s'en fiche! Il n'y a qu'une chose qui l'intéresse: notre voyage de noces en Italie! Ombrie et Toscane… je ne te raconte pas le nombre de châteaux et d'églises que nous devrons visiter!
Élodie: Et après?
Mathieu: Je finis cette année à Centrale et après j'aimerais bien travailler dans un laboratoire de recherches sur les nanotechnologies. J'ai une piste à Grenoble, j'y ai déjà fait un stage… ils sont intéressés.
Élodie: Et si on t'offrait le poste, vous déménageriez?
Mathieu: Oui, il faudrait aussi que Sophie change de travail ou qu'elle se fasse muter dans la région….
Élodie: Et le bébé?
Mathieu: On aimerait en avoir un très vite.
Élodie: Eh bien, j'aurai le rôle de ma vie: marraine!

6 Élodie va assister à un mariage.

Répondez aux questions.  1.1, 1.2

1. Élodie va assister au mariage de qui?
2. Comment s'appelle la mariée?
3. Où vont-ils en voyage de noces?
4. Où Matthieu aimerait-il travailler?
5. Élodie sera la marraine de qui?

Extension **Quand on vous dit "mariage," vous pensez à quoi?** 

Un journaliste interviewe un couple dans une joaillerie où ils achètent leurs alliances.

Journaliste: Quand on vous dit "mariage," vous pensez à quoi?
Elle: La robe, la bague de fiançailles, les alliances, la cérémonie à l'Église… ce qui fait rêver quoi!
Lui: La réception, le voyage de noces….
Elle: À la joie de ma mère, à mon père la larme à l'œil….
Lui: Mettre d'accord ma mère et ma belle-mère, bonjour l'ambiance! Si c'était à refaire, je me pacserais… plus vite fait, moins de cérémonial, et donc moins de problèmes….

Extension Comparez l'attitude de la femme et de l'homme vis-à-vis du mariage.

RESOURCES

 **Dialogue Video**

 **Workbook 4**

Answers

 6

1. son cousin
2. Sophie
3. en Italie
4. dans un laboratoire de recherches à Grenoble
5. du premier bébé

Extension

La femme voit les préparatifs du mariage comme un rêve, et l'homme comme beaucoup de responsabilités.

Reference Desk

1. The expression **se faire muter** means "to get oneself transferred," while **avoir une piste** means "to have an *in*." Students will learn the definition "ski slope" for piste in **Unité** 4.
2. **L'École Centrale** is **une grande école** for business students; it is located in Paris. Graduates of schools such as this often hold important positions in politics, government, business, etc.
3. Students may be interested to look up the uniform of the **École Polytechnique**, another **grande école**.
4. While France is often a romantic destination for American couples, the French often go to Italy.

Expansion

Cut up each part in the dialogue and put all the parts of the dialogue in an envelope. Ask students, working in pairs, to put the dialogue in order. Tell them the easiest place to start is with the questions.

Differentiated Learning

Accelerate

Ask your advanced students to find an example of the future and conditional in the main dialogue. Have pairs of these students prepare the **Extension** dialogue and present to the rest of the class from memory. Let the class know ahead of time the general topic of the conversation and then discuss what they didn't understand when they heard the dialogue.

Decelerate

Have these students find a wedding present for Mathieu and Sophie online, based on what they know about their life together.

Special Needs Students

Auditory Impairment

Allow these students to read the dialogue while they are viewing it so that they have a better chance of comprehending the main ideas.

RESOURCES

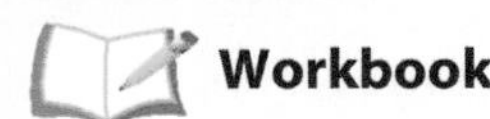

Workbook 5

Reference Desk

1. **Les classes préparatoires aux grandes écoles** (**CPGE**) are affililated with the Ministry of Education, while **les grandes écoles** depend on other ministries such as agriculture, culture, defense, industry, justice, and health.
2. The first **grandes écoles** were created during the 18th century.
3. According to the Ministry of Education, **une grande école** is an "**établissement d'enseignement supérieur qui recruit ses élèves par concours et asure des formations de haut niveau.**"

Points de départ

Pre AP

emcl.com
WB 5

Question centrale
Comment la vie des Francophones évolue-t-elle avec le temps?

L'enseignement supérieur en France

1.2, 2.1, 5.1

L'enseignement supérieur français est un système qui comprend les grandes écoles*, les universités, et des écoles spécialisées privées*. Tout étudiant ayant obtenu son bac peut s'inscrire à l'université. Cependant, l'accès aux grandes écoles se fait sur concours*. Les établissements d'enseignement supérieur privés possèdent chacun leurs propres* conditions d'entrée: concours, dossier*, obtention préalable* d'une licence* ou d'un master universitaire.

Les classes préparatoires* préparent aux concours. Ces classes proposent deux années d'un enseignement général intensif, soit à dominante littéraire, soit à dominante mathématique et scientifique.

Tous les grands secteurs d'activités ont leur école: l'administration a l'ENA (École nationale d'administration); les finances ont HEC (École des hautes études commerciales); pour les sciences, l'École Polytechnique; l'éducation, les Écoles Normales supérieures; l'armée, l'École Spéciale militaire de Saint-Cyr. Toutes ces écoles supérieures sont rattachées à différents ministères*, par exemple Polytechnique est rattachée au ministère de la Défense.

Search words: classes préparatoires aux grandes écoles, ena, hec, école polytechnique, écoles normales supérieures, école spéciale militaire

grande école *elite school;* **privé(e)** *private;* **concours** *competitive exam;* **propres** *own;* **dossier** *selection on merit;* **préalable** *prerequisite;* **licence** *B.A.;* **soit... soit** *either... or;* **préparatoires** *preparatory;* **ministères** *cabinets/departments*

COMPARAISONS

Quelles universités américaines ressemblent aux grandes écoles?

4.2

L'École des beaux-arts à Paris prépare des carrières dans la création photo, le design, ou le graphisme.

Mon dico des grandes écoles

Hypokhâgne: *première année de classe préparatoire (du grec* hypo *qui veut dire "en-dessous")*
Khâgne: *deuxième année ou lettres supérieures*
Taupins: *surnom donné à ceux qui vivent enfermés dans les bibliothèques, au milieu des livres.*
X: *désigne à la fois les élèves et l'École Polytechnique elle-même*

Mots-clé

Étudiant (apparaît en 1260). Il est en concurrence avec *escolier* (aujourd'hui *écolier)* jusqu'à la fin du XVIIème. **Étudiante** n'apparaît dans son sens actuel qu'à la fin du XIXème siècle; auparavant, elle désignait la petite amie de l'étudiant.

Essential Instruction

1. Review with students what they already know about higher education in France.
2. Have students look at the websites of the **grandes écoles** in the first culture reading.
3. Compare weddings in France and North Africa. Find an acceptable video of each one online.
   Search words: mariage maroc vidéo
4. After students have read the culture paragraphs, make true statements about the readings and ask students if they relate to 1, 2, or 3.

Le mariage: fête civile et fête religieuse  1.2, 2.1, 5.1

Le marié signe le registre d'état civil à la mairie.

Aujourd'hui, en France, 240.000 couples se marient et 140.000 se pacsent chaque année. Le mariage est une cérémonie qui doit d'abord être civile. Ensuite, les mariés peuvent décider d'avoir une cérémonie religieuse ou non.

La cérémonie civile se passe à la mairie devant un officier d'État civil qui enregistre l'échange de consentement entre le futur époux et la future épouse. Si c'est l'unique cérémonie, on y échange les anneaux qui symbolisent l'union et l'autorité civile remet aux époux le livret de famille* qu'ils signent et qu'ils doivent conserver*. Les naissances des enfants et les décès* seront par la suite inscrits au livret de famille.

Dans un pays majoritairement catholique, la cérémonie religieuse a lieu à l'église. Elle peut donner lieu à une simple bénédiction ou à une messe. Les jeunes mariés cherchent aujourd'hui à personnaliser la cérémonie: décoration florale de l'église, choix des textes, et surtout choix des chants et des musiques.

La cérémonie du mariage est généralement suivie d'un réception. En soirée, un repas de mariage est servi aux invités. Le repas, assis, peut comprendre: une entrée, un poisson, une viande, un plat d'accompagnement, du fromage, et des desserts, dont notamment* le gâteau de mariage. On y boit aussi des vins excellents et du champagne. Le dîner est souvent suivi d'une animation musicale qui permet de danser. C'est le moment où les mariés reçoivent des cadeaux généralement choisis sur une liste de mariage.

 Search words: **mairie mariage civil (+ nom de la ville), cérémonie de mariage vidéo**

livret de famille *family record book;* **conserver** *to keep;* **décès** *death;* **notamment** *notably*

Les mariages au Maghreb

La future mariée teintée de henné.

En Afrique du nord, le mariage est une cérémonie culturelle et religieuse, qui comporte* plusieurs rituels. La cérémonie du henné* est une façon de préparer une jeune femme musulmane à sa vie de femme mariée, et aux responsabilités qu'elle comporte. Cette fête se déroule* sept jours avant le mariage, chez les parents de la future mariée, en soirée et uniquement entre femmes. On teint le corps de la future mariée de henné, dans le but de lui porter chance dans son mariage.

comporte *entails;* **henné** *henna;* **se déroule** *takes place*

Reference Desk

Here is some additional vocabulary to use when discussing weddings in France: **l'unique cérémonie** (*the only ceremony*); **le repas assis** (*a sit-down meal as opposed to a buffet*); **suivi de** (*followed by*); **en soirée** (*in the evening*).

Differentiated Learning

Adapt

Ask questions that elicit the main ideas from the culture readings, for example, What do students need to provide when applying to **une grande école**? Which wedding ceremony is required, the one at the church or city hall?

Special Needs Students

Reading Difficulties

Provide an outline of the readings or a cloze exercise that focuses on the main ideas of the culture sections.

Answers

7

1. l'ENA: à Strasbourg; HEC: à Paris; l'École Polytechnique: à Paris; les Écoles Normales supérieures: à Paris, à Cachan, à Lyon; l'École Spéciale militaire de Saint-Cyr: à Guer
2. l'armée: l'École Spéciale militaire de Saint-Cyr; le commerce: HEC; les sciences et techniques: l'École Polytechnique; l'éducation: les Écoles Normales supérieures; l'administration: l'ENA
3. *Answers will vary.*
4. *Answers will vary.*

À discuter
Answers will vary.

Communication

Interpersonal: Paired Practice

Have pairs of students prepare dialogues during different stages of a relationship: first date, engagement, wedding preparations, the photographer taking pictures, reception, honeymoon, birth of first child, and 25th wedding anniversary. Have each pair present their dialogue, and ask the rest of the class to identify where each pair is in their relationship.

Le gâteau de mariage est traditionnellement une pièce montée (*tiered cake*) faite de choux à la crème (*cream puffs*).

COMPARAISONS

Êtes-vous déjà allé(e) à un mariage civil ou religieux aux États-Unis? Comparez-le aux mariages français.

4.2

7 Activités culturelles

1.2, 1.3, 3.1, 3.2, 5.1

Complétez les activités suivantes.

1. Faites des recherches pour montrer où se trouvent les grandes écoles mentionnées.
2. Si je veux faire carrière dans..., quelle école dois-je choisir?
   - l'armée
   - le commerce
   - les sciences et techniques
   - l'éducation
   - l'administration
3. Faites une liste de choses à planifier pour une fête de mariage religieuse.
4. Composez un menu de dîner de mariage en vous aidant d'Internet. Choisissez:
   - une entrée
   - un poisson
   - une viande
   - un plateau de fromages
   - des desserts

À discuter

Comment est-ce que le mariage représente un rite de passage?

Essential Instruction

1. The first and second culture activities would appeal to lower-ability students because they can easily find the answers in the readings. The third and fourth option would be more appropriate for the higher-ability students.
2. Put a student who has worked on each activity in a group to share what he/she has learned.
3. Meet as a class to debrief.
4. Have students read the wedding invitation; then, answer the questions in **Activité 8** as a class.

Du côté des médias

Pre AP   1.2, 5.1

Interpretive Communication

Lisez le faire-part de mariage ci-dessous.

Mme Albert et M. et Madame Lucas
sont très heureux
de vous annoncer le mariage de leurs enfants :

Laetitia et Sébastien

qui, après 5 ans de réflexion, se décident enfin !

Ils vous attendent avec impatience
le samedi 16 juin 2012 pour fêter cet événement.

Célébration à 15h30
Mairie de Fontenay aux Roses
75 rue Boucicaut
92260 Fontenay aux Roses

Réception à partir de 18 heures
Restaurant la Forestière
1 avenue du Président Kennedy
78100 Saint-Germain en Laye

Laetitia Brochant et Sébastien Lacroix
9 rue Victor Hugo
92260 Fontenay aux Roses
Tel : 01 53 50 60 82
lbrochant@orange.fr

8 Le faire-part de mariage de Laetitia et Sébastien

  1.2, 1.3

Répondez aux questions.

1. Comment s'appelle la future mariée? Le futur mari?
2. Où est-ce que le couple va se marier?
3. Dans quelle ville a lieu la réception?
4. Quelle est la date du mariage?

Answers

 8

1. Laetitia Brochant et Sébastien Lacroix
2. à la mairie de Fontenay aux Roses
3. à Saint-Germain en Laye
4. le samedi 6 juin 2012

Culture

Practices: Activity

In the United States on a traditional invitation the parents of the bride are listed as hosts. Who is listed on the wedding invitation in the textbook? What kind of a wedding is it going to be, religious, or civil, or both? (Civil, **la mairie**, without a mention of a church.) What element of humor renders the invitation less formal? (.. **se décident enfin!**) How do you know that the young couple is not traditional? (The bride is keeping her name.) What does **à partir 18 heures** mean? (from six o'clock on)

Differentiated Learning

Accelerate

Have these students write their own wedding invitation, perhaps for Barbie and Ken, or a famous couple from history or current events.

Decelerate

Ask these students to find three French wedding invitations online and explain to the class how they are different from the one in the textbook.

Special Needs Students

Dyslexia

These students often benefit from reading aloud or following along as they listen to others read. Either read the wedding announcement aloud or pair them with another student who reads it aloud. Allow these students to answer one or two questions about the text to boost their confidence.

Answers

Activities will vary.

Reference Desk

1. The section **La culture sur place** is intended to provide active cultural experiences for students through investigation and developing relationships with Francophones. This spirit of inquiry will help francophone culture come alive for students. To see the six different types of activities to be found in this section, go to p. T46 of the front pages of this Annotated Teacher's Edition.
2. A reproducible blackline master of the chart is available in the **Copy Masters** ancillary.

La culture sur place

Question centrale: Comment la vie des Francophones évolue-t-elle avec le temps?

La culture ado

Introduction et Interrogations

Est-ce que la culture est surtout une idée nationale (la culture française)? Y-a-t-il aussi une culture des enfants, une culture des adolescents? Dans cette **Culture sur place**, vous allez examiner la culture des ados.

9 Première Étape: Réfléchir

1.2, 1.3

*Recopiez cet organigramme sur une feuille de papier. Dans la première colonne, écrivez ce que vous savez déjà des adolescents en France. Ces connaissances (*knowledge*) peuvent venir de vos expériences personnelles ainsi que de ce programme. Dans la deuxième colonne, écrivez ce que vous voulez savoir des ados français, sous forme de questions. N'écrivez rien dans la troisième colonne pour l'instant.*

Ce que je SAIS	Ce que je VOUDRAIS SAVOIR	Ce que J'AI APPRIS

10 Deuxième Étape: Rechercher

1.2, 1.3, 2.1, 3.2, 5.1

*Même s'il faut se souvenir que les blogues ne représentent qu'un point de vue, rechercher les intérêts des adolescents dans un autre pays francophone est facile aujourd'hui grâce à (*thanks to*) ces ressources en ligne.*

1. Accédez à une liste de blogues d'ados (jeunes âgés de 16 à 20 ans) francophones, par exemple, vous pouvez voir des profils sur skyrock.
2. Identifiez trois blogues intéressants.
3. Sur chaque blogue, examinez les photos, les liens, et les détails de la vie de l'auteur. Écrivez ce que vous apprenez de ces ados français sur votre organigramme dans la troisième colonne.

11 Faire l'inventaire!

1.2, 1.3, 2.1, 3.1, 4.2, 5.1

Avec votre partenaire ou avec toute la classe, répondez à ces questions.

1. Qu'est-ce que vous avez en commun avec les ados dont vous avez lu les blogues? Qu'est-ce que vous n'avez pas en commun? (Vous pouvez faire un diagramme Venn.)
2. Y avait-il beaucoup de différences parmi les trois blogues que vous avez lus? Beaucoup de similarités? Par exemple?
3. Est-ce que l'on peut vraiment identifier une culture à laquelle tous les ados français appartiennent? Pourquoi, ou pourquoi pas?
4. Vous pensez qu'il y a une "culture des adolescents" qui traverse les frontières nationales? Quels sont quelques aspects de cette culture, si elle existe?

Essential Instruction

1. Before assigning **Activité 9**, have students review previous chapters for information about adolescents in France. Filling in the first column together as a class will get students started on this personal graphic organizer.
2. Give students time to read some French blogs outside of class before doing **Activité 10**.
3. Conduct a debriefing of the pairs or class as a whole to make sure all students benefit from the points of view of others.
4. Point out the difference between the stem for the imperfect and the conditional.

Structure de la langue

Révision: Conditional Tense  1.2

Do you remember how to say "I would like a ticket"? What tense is that? Does this tense describe reality? What are the endings of this tense that are added to the stem? How do you get the stem? If you can't answer these questions, read the summary below.

The **conditionnel** is a tense used to tell what people *would* do or what *would* happen.

Caro **aimerait** travailler dans un laboratoire de recherches. — *Caro would like to work in a research laboratory.*

To form the conditional of regular **–er** and **–ir** verbs, add to the infinitive the endings of the imperfect tense: **–ais, –ais, –ait, –ions, –iez, –aient**. For regular **–re** verbs, drop the final **e** from the infinitive before adding the imperfect endings.

Vendriez-vous votre bague de fiançailles? — *Would you sell your engagement ring?*

Je **choisirais** Paris pour mon voyage de noces. — *I would choose Paris for my honeymoon.*

Some irregular French verbs have an irregular stem in the conditional, but their endings are regular.

Infinitive	Irregular Stem	Conditional	Examples
aller	**ir-**	j'**irais**	Tu **irais** à Saint-Paul de Vence?
s'asseoir	**assiér-**	je **m'assiérais**	Papa **s'assiérait** dans son fauteuil.
avoir	**aur-**	j'**aurais**	Nous **aurions** une décapotable.
courir	**courr-**	je **courrais**	Marc **courrait**-il dans le marathon?
devoir	**devr-**	je **devrais**	Vous **devriez** étudier pour l'interro.
être	**ser-**	je **serais**	**Serais**-tu un comptable?
faire	**fer-**	je **ferais**	Ils ne **feraient** pas du ski alpin.
falloir	**faudr-**	il **faudrait**	Il **faudrait** faire le ménage.
pleuvoir	**pleuvr-**	il **pleuvrait**	Il **pleuvrait** avant notre arrivée.
pouvoir	**pourr-**	je **pourrais**	On **pourrait** faire une soupe?
recevoir	**recevr-**	je **recevrais**	Les Cheval **recevrait** l'Italienne.
savoir	**saur-**	je **saurais**	Tu **saurais** les solutions.
venir	**viendr-**	je **viendrais**	**Viendrais**-tu au concert avec moi?
voir	**verr-**	je **verrais**	Marie **verrait** toute l'Europe.
vouloir	**voudr-**	je **voudrais**	Nous **voudrions** nous habiller bien.

CONDITIONAL TENSE: The French sentence would be: "Je voudrais un ticket." It is an example of the conditional tense, which doesn't describe reality, rather what "might" happen. To form this tense, add the endings **–ais, –ais, –ait, –ions, –iez,** or **–aient** to the infinitive for regular verbs.

RESOURCES

 **Workbook 6–8**

 **Drill & Practice Games**

Reference Desk

1. As a memory aid, students might like to think of "Mr. W. (Would) Conditional" since the conditional is translated by the word "would" in English.
2. Here is a list of some other irregular verbs in the conditional: **j'achèterais, je m'appellerais, je deviendrais, j'emmènerais, je me lèverais, je nettoierais, je reviendrais.**
3. In the conditional, **devoir** means "should" or "ought" and **pouvoir** means "could."
4. The conditional was introduced in the Level 2 textbook on p. 492 of **Unité 9.**

TPR

Make a set of note cards with the name of one verb tense (**P** for present, **PC** for **passé composé**, **I** for **imparfait**, **F** for **futur**, or **C** for **conditionnel**) on each card. Give a card to each student. Then read short stories that contain examples of each tense. As you read the texts, have students hold up their card for the entire class to see each time they hear the verb tense on their card. At the beginning, it is a good idea to pause for a few seconds after each verb.

Differentiated Learning

Decelerate

Have these students listen to other students' points of view first if they are reluctant to share their own opinions in **Activité 11.** Be sure to include these students in the discussion at some point.

Special Needs Students

Linguistically Challenged

Give these students a worksheet that asks them to break down the production of the regular and irregular conditional by listing its parts before using it:

Verb: **Avoir/elles**

Stem: **aur-**

Sentence: **À Nice elles auraient besoin d'un maillot de bain.**

The sentence needs to prove the student understands the meaning of the verb.

Answers

12 *Possible answers:*

1. Noah pourrait acheter un pantalon pour homme et un pull beige.
2. Khaled et moi pourrions acheter deux pantalons, deux polos, et deux pulls.
3. Laure et Milo pourraient acheter un bonnet en laine et une cravate en soie.
4. Tu pourrais acheter une robe rouge, un collier de diamants, un pantalon gris, une cravate, et une chemise blanche.
5. Vous pourriez acheter un pantalon gris, une paire de chaussettes noires, un polo blanc, une cravate, et des boucles d'oreilles en perles.
6. Quentin pourrait acheter un polo de toutes les couleurs, un pull beige, dix paires de chaussettes noires, deux colliers de diamant, et une jupe bleue.

Critical Thinking

Comparisons

Ask your students what these expressions mean in English: **j'aimerais, j'irais**, and **je serais.** Then ask them to explain what they use in English to express "I would (do something)" to indicate what would happen. They should say that, in English, "would" is used before a verb.

Communication

Presentational: Cooperative Groups

Put students in small groups. Then write this question on the board: **Si vous gagniez à la loterie, qu'est-ce que vous feriez?** The first student asks the person on his/her left the question, changing to the pronoun **tu**. He/she gives two or three responses, then asks the next student in the circle, and so on. Finally, each student presents what someone in the group would do, changing the pronoun again, this time to **il** or **elle**.

The conditional is often used to make suggestions or to make a request more polite.

À ta place, j'**irais** à la réception avec le garçon d'honneur.	*If I were you, I would go with the best man to the reception.*
Tu **devrais** lui téléphoner. Tu **voudrais** le faire maintenant?	*You should call him. Would you like to do it now?*

12 Un nouveau poste

1.2, 1.3, 2.2, 5.1

Les personnes ci-dessous cherchent un nouvel emploi. Que pourraient-elles acheter pour aller à leur entretien avec l'argent qu'elles ont?

MODÈLE Jeanne: 165€
Jeanne pourrait acheter une jupe bleue et une chemise blanche.

1. Noah: 274€
2. Khaled et moi: 432€
3. Laure et Milo: 143€
4. toi: 511€
5. vous: 312€
6. Quentin: 616€

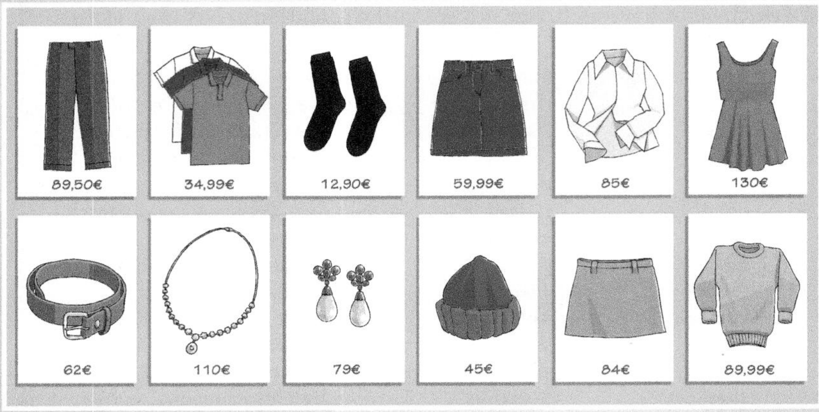

COMPARAISONS

Which sentence would not be in the conditional in French?
When I was a child, I **would go** to my grandma's after school.
Jeremy **would like** to order now.

4.1

COMPARAISONS: The first sentence would not be in the conditional in French because it is simply an indirect statement expressing a past idea and would take the imperfect in French.

Essential Instruction

1. Place pairs of expressions in the imperfect and conditional side-by-side on the board, for example, **Chloé gagnait, Chloé gagnerait.** If students have difficulty, prepare a worksheet and ask them to circle the expressions in the conditional. You may find that students also need this practice with the conditional and the future.
2. Put students in groups to do **Activité 12**, and in pairs to do **Activité 13**.
3. Now that students have had practice with the conditional, do **Activité 14** as a class.

Communiquez!

13 Le mariage

1.2, 5.1, 5.2

Interpersonal Communication

Posez des questions à votre partenaire au sujet de son mariage idéal. Puis, changez de rôles.

MODÈLE à quel âge/se marier
A: **À quel âge est-ce que tu te marierais?**
B: **Je me marierais à 28 ans.**

1. combien de personnes/inviter
2. que/porter
3. qui/choisir comme demoiselle d'honneur ou garçon d'honneur
4. que/offrir comme alliance
5. où/avoir lieu la réception
6. où/aller pour ton voyage de noces

Où aimerais-tu aller pour ta lune de miel?

À Tahiti, et toi?

14 Les conseils

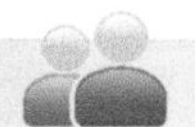  

1.2, 5.1, 5.2

Vos amis ont beaucoup de problèmes. Donnez-leur des conseils en accord avec la situation de chacun. Utilisez le conditionnel dans vos réponses.

MODÈLE A: J'ai perdu le portable de mon frère.
B: **À ta place, je lui achèterais un nouveau portable.**

1. J'ai eu 7 sur 20 à mon contrôle d'anglais.
2. Je suis toujours en retard pour mon premier cours.
3. J'ai très faim et soif.
4. J'ai besoin d'argent pour aller au concert.
5. Je me dispute avec mes parents parce que j'oublie de faire mes corvées.
6. Je suis fâché(e) quand je fais le plein parce que l'essence coûte chère.
7. Je vais faire du camping, et je n'ai pas de sac de couchage.
8. C'est l'anniversaire de Colette le 4 octobre, et je ne sais pas ce que je peux lui offrir.

Differentiated Learning

Accelerate

Have these students write a story that uses the conditional, for example, about a student who wins **un billet d'avion gratuit** and is planning his or her trip.

Decelerate

Slower-paced students can contribute to an extension of **Activité 14** by thinking up other scenarios for their partner to comment on.

Multiple Intelligences

Intrapersonal

Give these students, working in pairs, a problem situation to solve together, for example, **"Tu n'as pas eu une invitation pour le prom."** Students come up with original solutions, for example, **"Je ferai une publicité sur Internet pour trouver quelqu'un de m'accompagner."** Students share their problems and solutions with the class. Ask for other solutions from the rest of the class.

Answers

13 *Answers for A:*

1. Combien de personnes est-ce que tu inviterais?
2. Qu'est-ce que tu porterais?
3. Qui choisirais-tu comme demoiselle d'honneur ou garçon d'honneur?
4. Qu'offrirais-tu comme alliance, une alliance en argent ou en or?
5. Où aurait lieu la réception?
6. Où irais-tu pour ton voyage de noces?

14 *Possible answers for B:*

1. À ta place, je suivrais des cours particuliers.
2. À ta place, je mettrais une alarme dans ta chambre, sur ton smartphone, et sur ton ipod.
3. À ta place, je prendrais un goûter.
4. À ta place, je passerais à la banque.
5. À ta place, j'essayerais de faire mes corvées tout de suite en rentrant de l'école.
6. À ta place, je prendrais les transports en commun plus souvent.
7. À ta place, j'en emprunterais un.
8. À ta place, j'irais au centre commercial pour voir plusieurs magasins.

TPR

Pair the following high-frequency conditional expressions with a gesture: **Je devrais** (Wag your finger); **Je pourrais** (Show your muscles); **J'aimerais** (Tap your heart twice). Then say several sentences that use these verbs and ask the class to show you the appropriate gesture.

Expansion

For **Activité 13**, ask students to extend the activity for asking questions about their partner's career, the city they plan to live in, the number of children they'll have, whether they'll have a cat or dog. Or, have them extend the conversation by having Speaker A give a different response, **"À ta place, je me marierais à 32 ans. Je pense que 28 est trop jeune."**

RESOURCES

 Workbook 9

 Drill & Practice Games

Answers

1. Si tu dormais, tu aurais plus d'énergie.
2. Si elle allait à Versailles, elle apprendrait beaucoup de choses sur l'histoire de France.
3. Si tu rangeais tes vêtements, tu la trouverais.
4. S'ils faisaient le plein, ils pourraient conduire.
5. Si vous suiviez des leçons de guitare, vous pourriez jouer la musique rock et former un groupe.
6. S'ils préparaient une choucroute garnie, ils pourraient manger.
7. Si je suivais un cours particulier, je pourrais faire mes devoirs de maths.

Game

Funny Sentences

Divide the class into two teams. One half of the class will write **si** clauses on note cards, for example, **Si j'avais beaucoup de temps....** The other half of the class writes result clauses on note cards, for example **je danserais le tango.** Gather all the cards and put them in two piles. Ask for volunteers to take a card from each pile and read the sentence aloud. Many of the sentences will be nonsensical.

Révision: Conditional Tense in Sentences with *si*  1.2

emcl.com
WB 9
Games

"If I were president, I would build homes for the homeless and working poor." What tense is used in the first clause in the French equivalent? What tense is used in the second clause?

If you don't remember, read the summary below.

Use the conditional tense along with **si** and the imperfect tense to tell what would happen if something else happened or *if* some condition contrary to reality were met.

si + imperfect	conditional

S'il ne **pleuvait** pas, tu **pourrais** nager. — *If it wasn't raining, you could go swimming.*

Nous **aurions** plus d'argent si nous étions avocats. — *We would have more money if we were lawyers.*

The phrase with **si** and the imperfect can either begin or end the sentence.

15 Des changements   1.2, 1.3, 5.2

Dites comment la vie des personnes suivantes serait différente si elles faisaient les changements indiqués.

MODÈLE Je ne suis pas en forme. (*faire des promenades au parc*)
Si tu faisais des promenades au parc, tu serais en forme.

1. Je suis fatigué(e). (*dormir*)
2. Virginie ne connaît pas la vie des rois et reines français. (*aller à Versailles*)
3. Tu ne peux pas trouver ta tablette dans ta chambre. (*ranger tes vêtements*)
4. Mohammed et Lucie ne peuvent plus conduire. (*faire le plein*)
5. Marina et moi, nous ne pouvons pas former un groupe de rock. (*suivre des leçons de guitare*)
6. Les ados ont faim. (*préparer une choucroute garnie*)
7. Je ne sais pas faire ce problème de maths. (*suivre un cours particulier*)

CONDITIONAL TENSE WITH *SI*: In the "if" clause the imperfect tense is used; it is followed by the conditional tense. However, the order of clauses is interchangeable.

Essential Instruction

1. Have students try to answer the questions in the yellow top section. Tell them to read the grammar summary if they don't remember.
2. Project some **si** clauses on the board and see if students can match them to conditional choices on the right.
3. Ask students to write some personal conditional statements that use **si**, or ask a personal question addressing another student.
4. After doing **Activité 16**, see if students can extend the activity with other cues.
5. Review the near future before reviewing the future tense.

Si je gagnais à la lotterie, je ferais le tour du monde!

16 Avec un partenaire

Interpersonal Communication

Que feriez-vous dans les situations suivantes? À tour de rôle, posez des questions à votre partenaire.

MODÈLE gagner à la loterie
A: **Si tu gagnais à la loterie, que ferais-tu?**
B: **Si je gagnais à la loterie, j'achèterais une voiture de sport.**

1. aller à la MJC
2. voir un accident de voiture
3. perdre ton smartphone
4. faire la connaissance de ton acteur préféré
5. recevoir un billet d'avion gratuit
6. visiter un parc d'attractions
7. faire les courses au marché

Révision: Future Tense
Future Tense after *quand*

emcl.com
WB 10–13
LA 2
Games

The future tense consists of only one word. To form the future tense, use the same stem as that of the conditional tense (the infinitive for **-er** and **-ir** verbs or the infinitive minus the **-e** for **-re** verbs). The future endings are **-ai**, **-as**, **-a**, **-ons**, **-ez**, and **-ont**.

assister			
j'	**assisterai**	nous	**assisterons**
tu	**assisteras**	vous	**assisterez**
il/elle/on	**assistera**	ils/elles	**assisteront**

Vous **assisterez** au mariage de Manon? — *Will you attend Manon's wedding?*

Non, nous **voyagerons** au Maroc. — *No, we'll be traveling to Morocco.*

As with the conditional, some irregular French verbs have an irregular stem in the future, but their endings are regular. Note that for all verbs, the future stem ends in **-r**.

C'est elle qui **fera** un stage à JDN Économie? — *Is she the one who will do an internship at JDN Économie?*

RESOURCES

Workbook 10–13

Listening Activity 2

Drill & Practice Games

Answers

16 *Answers for B will vary.*

1. A: Si tu allais à la MJC, que ferais-tu?
2. A: Si tu voyais un accident de voitures, que ferais-tu?
3. A: Si tu perdais ton smartphone, que ferais-tu?
4. A: Si tu faisais la connaissance de ton acteur préféré, que ferais-tu?
5. A: Si tu recevais un billet d'avion gratuit, où irais-tu?
6. A: Si tu visitais un parc d'attractions, que ferais-tu?
7. A: Si tu faisais les courses au marché, qu'achèterais-tu?

Reference Desk

1. **Aller** + infinitive is used to express events that will occur in the immediate future, while **le futur** is used for events that will take place in the more distant future, for example, **dans dix ans, pendant les grandes vacances**, etc.
2. Many verbs with spelling changes in the present keep them in the future: **j'achèterai, j'emmènerai, je nettoierai**, etc. However, **préférer** does not change in the future: **je préférerai.**

Critical Thinking

Analysis
Ask students why the conditional and future tenses appear in the same lesson. What do they have in common? (Both share the same stem.) Then ask them how many sounds are in the future endings (only four). Finally, write the conjugation of a verb in the future. Circle the endings and ask what irregular verb the endings resemble (**avoir**).

Differentiated Learning

Accelerate
Ask students to change a list of near future statements to the future tense. Then have them write six sentences of their own in the near future and work with slower-paced students who may need help putting them in the future tense.

Decelerate
If these students cannot learn all the future endings, have them master the **je** and **tu** forms for conversation.

Multiple Intelligences

Visual-Spatial
Have these students make an album that illustrates what they would do if they won the lottery, using images from the Internet or drawing their own pictures.

Answers

1. Jérémy n'assistera pas au mariage, mais il ira à la réception.
2. J'assisterai au mariage et j'irai à la réception.
3. Paul et Zohra assisteront au mariage et iront à la réception.
4. Jérémy et toi n'assisterez pas au mariage, mais vous irez à la réception.
5. Nadine n'assistera pas au mariage, et elle n'ira pas à la réception.
6. Zohra et moi assisterons au mariage et irons à la réception.
7. Tu n'assisteras pas au mariage, mais tu iras à la réception.

1. C
2. C
3. F
4. F
5. C
6. F
7. C
8. F

Reference Desk

"**Quand Futur Futur**" is a mnemonic device to help students remember that **quand** and **lorsque** clauses are in the future in a future sentence.

Communication

Presentational: Cooperative Groups

Have students work in small groups to prepare a time capsule (**une capsule témoin**) that shows teens in 2090 what life was like for teens in the U.S. in 2012. They should include 10–12 objects in their capsule and write a description to post online with photos of the objects they chose: **Quand les ados de 2090 ouvriront la capsule témoin, ils verront *The Hunger Games* sur DVD....**

Expansion

Have students make horoscopes for the signs of the Zodiac for this month or next month, for example, **Les sagitaires voyageront.**

Another use of the future tense is to tell what will happen *when* something else happens in the future. Here is the order of tenses in these sentences with **quand**:

Quand Anne **dira** oui, Salim **se mariera** avec elle.
When Anne says yes, Salim will marry her.

quand + future	future
lorsque (*when*) + future	future
aussitôt que (*as soon as*) + future	future
dès que (*as soon as*) + future	future

Lorsque Salim **achètera** sa bague de fiançailles, Anne **cherchera** sa robe de mariée.
When Salim buys the engagement ring, Anne will look for a wedding dress.

Aussitôt que Salim **sera** ingénieur, il **travaillera** chez Airbus.
As soon as Salim is an engineer, he'll work for Airbus.

Dès que Salim et Anne **se marieront**, ils **déménageront** à Toulouse.
As soon as Salim and Anne marry, they will move to Toulouse.

17 Le mariage d'Anne et Salim

1.1, 1.2

Voici la liste des invités au mariage de Salim et Anne à Saint-Paul de Vence. La deuxième liste indique qui ira à la réception. Dites qui assistera au mariage et à la réception.

MODÈLE **Hervé assistera au mariage, mais il n'ira pas à la réception.**

1. Jérémy
2. moi
3. Paul et Zohra
4. Jérémy et toi
5. Nadine
6. Zohra et moi
7. toi

Le mariage		La réception	
Zohra	✔	Zohra	✔
toi		toi	✔
Nadine		Nadine	
Paul	✔	Paul	✔
Hervé	✔	Hervé	
moi	✔	moi	✔
Jérémy		Jérémy	✔

18 Le conditionnel ou le futur?

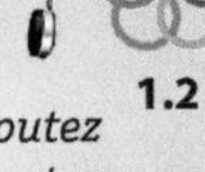

1.2

*Écrivez les numéros 1–8 sur votre papier. Écoutez les phrases suivantes. Écrivez **C** si la phrase est au conditionnel et **F** si la phrase est au futur.*

COMPARAISONS

In what way is the future tense in English different from the future tense in French? What tense is used in each clause of the following sentence? When I'm in Paris, I will visit the Louvre.

4.1

COMPARAISONS: The future tense in English is a compound tense ("You will succeed in college"), whereas the future tense in French is expressed in one word. In the example sentence, the "when" clause is in the present in English (unlike in French), even though the second clause is in the future tense.

Essential Instruction

1. Do **Activité 17** as a class.
2. Have students ask you questions about your future. When a question is too personal, you may say, **"Question suivante?"**
3. Before doing **Activité 18**, review with students what the endings of the conditional and future sound like so that they can be successful. It will be helpful to remind students that although the first person singular future and conditional seem to sound the same, the other endings are easier to distinguish. The conditional has a predominant long "a" sound.
4. Students can work in pairs to complete **Activités 19–20.**

Communiquez!

Quand j'aurai 25 ans, je me marierai avec toi!

19 Nos avenirs

1.2, 5.1, 5.2

Interpersonal Communication

Que ferez-vous quand vous aurez 25 ans? À tour de rôle, posez des questions à votre partenaire.

MODÈLE que/faire le weekend
A: **Quand tu auras 25 ans, qu'est-ce que tu feras le weekend?**
B: **Quand j'aurai 25 ans, j'irai au complexe sportif pour faire du sport.**

1. où/habiter (dans un appartement ou une maison)
2. dans quelle ville/habiter
3. où/travailler
4. que/faire comme passe-temps
5. où/aller pendant les vacances

20 Qu'est-ce que tu feras demain?

1.2, 5.1, 5.2

À tour de rôle, posez des questions à votre partenaire.

MODÈLE se lever
A: **Dès que tu te lèveras, qu'est-ce que tu feras?**
B: **Dès que je me lèverai, je m'habillerai.**

1. prendre ton petit déjeuner
2. arriver au lycée
3. entrer dans la cantine
4. quitter l'école
5. rentrer chez toi
6. dîner
7. faire tes devoirs

Answers

19 *Answers for B will vary.*

1. ...où habiteras-tu, dans un appartement ou dans une maison?
2. ...dans quelle ville habiteras-tu?
3. ...où travailleras-tu?
4. ...que feras-tu comme passe-temps?
5. ...où iras-tu pendant les vacances?

20

1. A: Dès que tu prendras ton petit-déjeuner, qu'est-ce que tu feras?
   B: Dès que je prendrai mon petit-déjeuner, ...
2. A: Dès que tu arriveras au lycée, qu'est-ce que tu feras?
   B: Dès que je arriverai au lycée, ...
3. A: Dès que tu entreras dans la cantine, qu'est-ce que tu feras?
   B: Dès que j'entrerai dans la cantine, ...
4. A: Dès que tu quitteras l'école, qu'est-ce que tu feras?
   B: Dès que je quitterai l'école, ...
5. A: Dès que tu rentreras chez toi, qu'est-ce que tu feras?
   B: Dès que je rentrerai chez moi, ...
6. A: Dès que tu dîneras, qu'est-ce que tu feras?
   B: Dès que je dînerai, ...
7. A: Dès que tu feras tes devoirs, qu'est-ce que tu feras?
   B: Dès que je ferai mes devoirs, ...

Communication

Interpersonal: Paired Practice

Ask students to prepare a dialogue in which they discuss with a classmate what things they are going to do during the next **grandes vacances.** Once students have presented their dialogues, ask them to write eight statements about what they remember of their classmates' plans.

Special Needs Students

Social Anxiety

Approach individually and discretely the students who have anxiety issues to see if they have any questions about **Activité 17**. Some may prefer to respond to taped questions at home rather than speak in class.

AD(H)D

Help these students do **Activités 19–20** by dividing the tasks into parts. Review the formation of the future for each of the verbs and help them add relevant vocabulary to complete the sentences. Work with the students one sentence at a time rather than asking them to complete the exercise on their own.

Speech Impairment

Pair students with patient partners who understand that they should not finish sentences for students who have speech difficulties.

RESOURCES

Communicative Activities

Answers

21 *Answers will vary.*

22 *Possible answers:*

Alec va probablement travailler dans un laboratoire de recherches médicales.

Angèle va probablement travailler à JDN économie.

Saloua va probablement travailler en plein air dans le domaine de la haute technologie.

Reference Desk

If students enjoy **Activité 22**, ask them to find **une petite annonce** online for a job they would like now or in the future.

Blended Instruction

Consider using blended instruction, a combination of in-class learning and computer-mediated instruction or learning opportunities. Ask students to complete activities on the computer, using their cell or smartphone, or other emerging technology. This will allow students to one their tech skills and become more independent learners. Schedule routine Internet and e-book learning in class and in the lab.

Culture

Practices: Information

Often in the United States the bride and groom prepare a special choreographed first dance. In France, a video program of the couple from infancy to wedding day is often shown.

À vous la parole

Question centrale: Comment la vie des Francophones évolue-t-elle avec le temps?

1.1, 1.2, 1.3, 2.1, 3.2, 5.1, 5.2

21 Les mariages français et américains

Interpretive/Presentational Communication

Avez-vous déjà assisté à un mariage américain? Si non, trouvez une vidéo d'un mariage américain sur Internet. Ensuite, regardez une vidéo d'un mariage français sur Dailymotion.fr, Vimeo, ou YouTube. Expliquez ce qui se passe sur la vidéo du mariage français à votre partenaire. Puis, remplissez un diagramme Venn comme celui de droite.

Les mariages américains | Les mariages dans les deux pays | Les mariages français

Search words: dailymotion, vimeo

22 Où est-ce qu'ils vont travailler?

1.2, 1.3, 5.1

Interpretive Communication

Lisez les profiles des jeunes gens suivants. Ensuite, dites où chacun d'entre eux va probablement travailler.

Alec

Salut! Je m'appelle Alec et, j'ai 26 ans. Je suis en deuxième année d'études de pharmacologie à l'université Blaise Pascal. J'ai fait des études de biologie à l'université pendant 5 ans avant de commencer mon Master. Je devrais obtenir mon diplôme à la fin de l'année.

Angèle

Bonjour à tous! Moi, c'est Angèle. J'ai 23 ans. J'ai passé mon bac GEA (gestion des entreprises et des administrations), puis j'ai commencé une formation en Économie et Gestion à l'université. Je ne voulais pas vraiment travailler dans une entreprise, alors j'ai commencé une Prépa (école préparatoire) en journalisme pour joindre l'école de journalisme de Toulouse. Dans deux ans, je veux rejoindre le Journal du Net Économie, car je connais des personnes qui y travaillent.

Saloua

Salut les potes! Je m'appelle Saloua, et j'ai 21 ans. Je viens de commencer une formation technique en électricité à CFORPRO. Je ne veux pas joindre une entreprise et travailler dans un bureau. Je voudrais faire des études sur le terrain, c'est-à-dire à l'extérieur, comme installer des panneaux solaires.

Essential Instruction

1. Information to include in **Activité 21** is what the bridal party and guests are wearing, how the tables are decorated, what kind of music is selected, what food is served, and of particular interest what kind of "animation" has been prepared.
2. Have students write **une petite annonce** for their ideal job.
3. Read the author biography. In **Rencontre avec l'auteur** there is always a critical thinking question to come back to.
4. Have students share their personal experiences when they respond to the **Pré-lecture** question.
5. The graphic organizer is available in the **Copy Masters** ancillary. You may want to go over the answers after listening to recorded audio.

Lecture thématique

Les petits enfants du siècle

Rencontre avec l'auteur 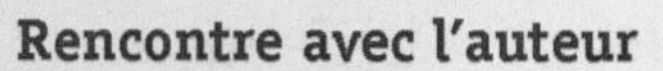  1.2, 2.1, 3.1, 5.1

Christiane Rochefort (1917–1998) a publié son premier roman à succès à l'âge de 41 ans, *Le repos du guerrier* (1958), qui est devenu un film. C'est en 1961 que *Les petits enfants du siècle* a été publié. Ce roman raconte la vie d'une petite fille, Josyane, qui grandit (*grows up*) dans la banlieue de Paris dans les années d'après-guerre (*post-war years*). Souvent poétique, son écriture (*writing*) traite (*deals with*) souvent de l'exploitation des enfants et des femmes. Rochefort a reçu deux prix littéraires prestigieux. De quelle façon *Les petits enfants du siècle* est-il une étude psychologique d'une enfant maltraitée (*mistreated*)?

Pré-lecture

À quel âge avez-vous commencé à faire des corvées à la maison pour aider vos parents?

Stratégie de lecture  1.3, 3.2

Setting

Dans la fiction, le cadre spatio-temporel regroupe tous les détails qui déterminent le lieu et l'époque où se situe l'action. Mais il y a aussi le milieu (*setting*) social, politique, moral, et psychologique que les personnages (*characters*) traversent. Alors que vous lisez le texte ci-dessous, recherchez tous les éléments qui déterminent le milieu dans lequel (*in which*) le personnage de Josyane évolue (*evolves*), et remplissez l'organigramme ci-dessous.

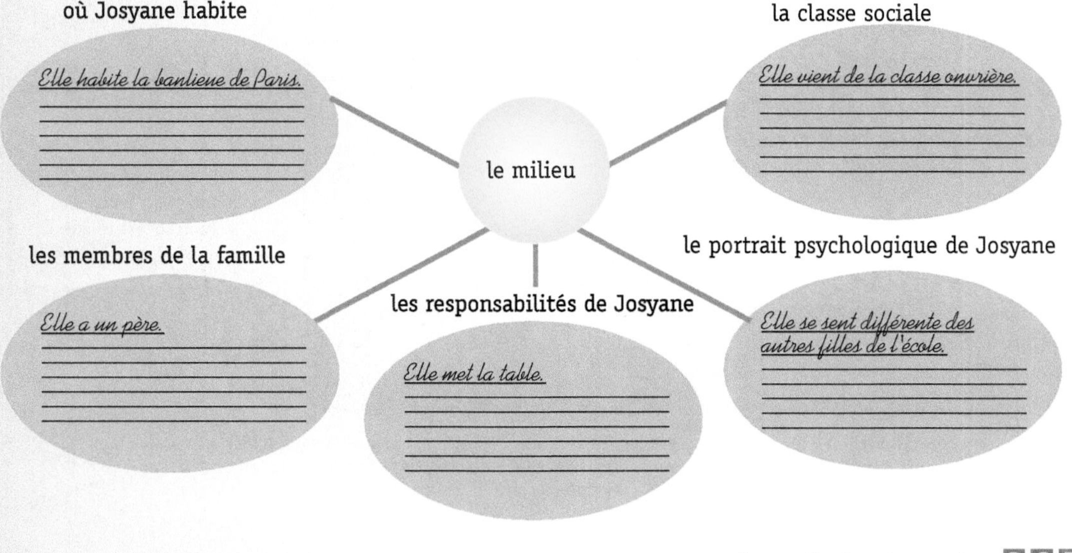

Answers

Pré-lecture
Answers will vary.

Stratégie de lecture
où Josyane habite: Elle habite dans un appartement avec trois chambres, dans une cité. Il y a une salle de bains, une cuisine-salle de séjour. Ils ont une machine à laver.
la classe sociale: Son père et sa mère travaillent dans une usine.
les membres de la famille: son frère Patrick, ses frères jumeaux, sa mère
les responsabilités de Josyane: Elle s'habille. Elle met le couvert. Elle va à l'école. Elle prépare le petit déjeuner pour ses frères, elle les emmène à l'école et les ramène à la maison. Elle fait les courses. Elle fait la vaisselle. Elle fait ses devoirs.
le portrait psychologique de Josyane: Sa mère est malade, alors elle a beaucoup de responsabilités pour aider à s'occuper de ses frères.

Reference Desk

1. Students make a connection to literature in this section. Each reading section contains a strategy, a pre-reading question, during-reading questions, and a post-reading question.
2. In the **Rencontre avec l'auteur**, students find a brief biography of the writer.
3. In the **Stratégie**, students learn a literary term that they will apply to the selection.
4. Christiane Rochefort challenged the rosy picture of economic development and social progress **d'après-guerre** by illustrating the negative aspects of France's rapid modernization in *Les petits enfants du siècle* (1961). Considered **un roman réaliste**, it won **le Prix Populiste** in 1962. Rochefort's first novel, ***Le repos du guerrier***, caused a scandal with its realistic use of language. She also wrote ***Les stances à Sophie*** (1963) and ***Une rose pour Morrison*** (1966).

Differentiated Learning

Accelerate
Students with high-level reading skills should be able to read the excerpt and complete the **Stratégie de lecture** independently. After they have filled it in, check their work for completeness and accuracy.

Decelerate
Play the recording of the reading to lower-ability students, and stop several times to verify global comprehension. Sample questions could be: What is this passage about? Who is telling the story? Who were the members of her family and what were they like? What jobs did she have to do? What did she like to do? Point out information they can insert in their **organigramme**.

Multiple Intelligences

Intrapersonal
Students might best understand the broad sense of setting by analyzing a popular TV show and focusing on the social, political, moral, and psychological conditions as they define one main character. Have each student read a description to group members, who then try to guess the name of the show.

Answers

Pendant la lecture

1. Ils lui ont dit qu'elle ne faisait pas les choses comme il faut.
2. quatre enfants
3. Parce qu'elle peut manger et n'a pas besoin de travailler.

Reference Desk

The **Outils de lecture** provides another tool to help students understand the selection. Give them a couple examples of how to read using context clues to decode new vocabulary.

Expansion

You may want your students to write the answers to the **Pendant la lecture** questions, designed to help them determine the main points of the story.

Outils de lecture  1.1, 1.2

Reading in Context

Vous allez sans doute trouver des mots et expressions que vous ne connaissez pas quand vous lisez en français. C'est une bonne idée de les analyser en contexte, c'est-à-dire (*that is to say*), de trouver le sens (*meaning*) des autres mots d'une phrase et de considérer la progression des idées. Comme ça, vous pouvez mieux deviner (*guess*) le sens des nouveaux mots. Essayez de lire cet extrait (*selection*) sans utiliser le glossaire du dessous.

C'était un dimanche au début de l'hiver. Mes parents... étaient heureux, mais ils avaient besoin d'argent. Les Allocations Familiales* arriveraient donc au bon moment.

Je naquis*... le 2 août. C'était ma date correcte, mais je faisais rater les vacances à mes parents, en les retenant* à Paris tout le mois d'août, alors que l'usine, où travaillait mon père, était fermée. Je ne faisais pas les choses comme il faut.

J'étais pourtant* en avance pour mon âge: Patrick avait à peine* pris ma place dans mon berceau* que je me montrais capable, en m'accrochant* aux meubles, de quitter la pièce dès qu'il se mettait à pleurer. Au fond je peux bien dire que c'est Patrick qui m'a appris à marcher.

Quand les jumeaux* firent leur arrivée* à la maison, je m'habillais déjà toute seule et je savais poser sur la table les couverts et le pain, en me mettant sur la pointe des pieds.

—Et dépêche-toi de grandir*, disait ma mère, pour que tu puisses m'aider un peu.

Elle était déjà malade quand je la connus. Elle ne pouvait pas aller à l'usine plus d'une semaine de services, aller acheter le pain, pousser les jumeaux dans leur double landau*, le long des blocs, pour qu'ils prennent l'air, et surveiller* Patrick, qui était en avance lui aussi, malheureusement. Il n'avait même pas trois ans quand il mit un petit chat dans la machine à laver. Cette fois-là, quand même, papa lui donna une bonne gifle*: on n'avait même pas fini de payer la machine.

Je commençais à aller à l'école. Le matin je préparais le déjeuner pour les garçons, je les emmenais à la maternelle, et j'allais à l'école. À midi, on restait à la cantine. J'aimais la cantine, on s'assoit* et les assiettes arrivent toutes remplies. C'est toujours bon ce qu'il y a dans des assiettes qui arrivent toutes remplies. Les autres filles en général n'aimaient pas la cantine, elles trouvaient que c'était mauvais. Je me demande ce qu'elles avaient à la maison.

Pendant la lecture
1. Qu'est-ce que les parents de Josyane ont dit à leur fille?

Pendant la lecture
2. Il y a combien d'enfants dans cette famille?

Pendant la lecture
3. Pourquoi est-ce que Josyane aimait la cantine de l'école?

Allocations familiales *welfare*; **naquis** *was born*; **retenant** *holding them back*; **pourtant** *though*; **à peine** *barely/hardly*; **berceau** *cradle*; **m'accrochant** *holding on*; **jumeaux** *twins*; **firent leur arrivée** *made their appearance*; **grandir** *grow up*; **landau** *baby stroller*; **surveiller** *look after*; **gifle** *slap*; **s'assoit** *s'assied*

Essential Instruction

1. Ask the students to read the passage for understanding, using context clues to figure out new vocabulary.
2. Play the recording of the selection, pausing to answer the **Pendant la lecture** questions.
3. All students should complete the first activity in **Activités d'expansion**, which is always based on the **organigramme** they filled out as they read.

Le soir, je ramenais* les garçons et je les laissais* dans la cour, à jouer avec les autres. Je montais prendre les sous* et je redescendais aux commissions*. Maman faisait le dîner, papa rentrait et ouvrait la télé, maman et moi nous faisions la vaisselle, et ils allaient se coucher. Moi, je restais dans la cuisine, à faire mes devoirs.

Maintenant, notre appartement était bien. Avant, on habitait dans le treizième*, une sale* chambre avec l'eau sur le palier*. Quand le quartier avait été démoli, on nous avait mis ici, dans cette Cité. On avait reçu le nombre de pièces auquel nous avions droit selon le nombre d'enfants. Les parents avaient une chambre, les garçons une autre. Moi, je couchais avec les bébés dans la troisième. On avait une salle de bains, où on avait mis la machine à laver, et une cuisine-salle de séjour, où on mangeait. C'est sur la table de la cuisine que je faisais mes devoirs. C'était mon bon moment: quel bonheur* quand ils étaient tous couchés, et que je me retrouvais seule dans la nuit et le silence! Le jour, je n'entendais pas le bruit*, je ne faisais pas attention; mais le soir j'entendais le silence. Le silence commençait à dix heures: les fenêtres s'éteignaient*, les radios se taisaient*, les bruits, les voix*, et, à dix heures et demie, c'était fini. Plus rien. Le désert. J'étais seule, en paix*. Je me suis mise à aimer mes devoirs peu à peu. J'aurais bien passé ma vie à ne faire que des choses qui ne servaient à rien.

Pendant la lecture
4. Quels services est-ce que Josyane rendait à sa mère?

Pendant la lecture
5. Comment était le vieil appartement de Josyane? Combien de pièces y avait-il dans le nouvel appartement?

Pendant la lecture
6. Que représentaient les devoirs, le soir, pour Josyane?

Pendant la lecture
7. Quel est l'opinion de Josyane à propos des devoirs?

ramenais *walked back;* **laissait** *would leave;* **sous** l'argent; **commissions** *errands;* **treizième** *thirteenth district of Paris;* **sale** *dirty;* **palier** *landing;* **bonheur** *happiness;* **bruit** *noise;* **s'éteignaient** *turned off;* **se taisaient** *would turn quiet;* **la voix** *voice;* **en paix** *at peace*

Post-lecture

D'où vient l'attitude de Josyane envers elle-même?

23 Activités d'expansion

1.2, 1.3, 5.1, 5.2

Complétez les activités suivantes.

1. Utilisez les informations de votre organigramme pour écrire un paragraphe qui décrit le milieu du roman *Les petits enfants du siècle* et ce qu'il révèle de Josyane.
2. Mettez les événements du roman en ordre chronologique. Écrivez "1" pour la première phrase, "2" pour la deuxième phrase, etc.
3. Vous êtes la concierge (*superintendent*) de l'immeuble où habite Josyane. Vous vous inquiétez parce qu'elle a trop de responsabilités pour son âge. Écrivez une lettre à l'assistante sociale qui s'occupe de votre HLM.

Le monde visuel

Immeuble, rue Croulebarbe, Paris, c. 1957. Albert Édouard. Musée national d'Art moderne, Centre Georges Pompidou. Don de Famille Albert en 2009.

RESOURCES

Pre-test

***Leçon* Quiz**

Answers

Pendant la lecture

4. Elle allait chercher les enfants à l'école et allait faire les courses.
5. Son vieil appartement était très sale et ils avaient une chambre. Il y avait quatre pièces (trois chambres et une cuisine-salle de séjour).
6. Les devoirs représentaient la tranquillité, une rupture des corvées de la journée.
7. Ils ne servent à rien mais elle aime la paix qu'ils lui donnent.

Post-lecture

Possible answer: Elle vient de son expérience.

1. *Paragraphs will vary.*
2. 1. Josyane est née.; 2. Elle s'occupe de son petit frère Patrick.; 3. Les jumeaux sont nés.; 4. La mère de Josyane était malade.; 5. Josyane aide sa mère avec les bébés.; 6. Josyane va à l'école.; 7. La famille de Josyane change *d'appartement.*
3. *Letters will vary.*

Reference Desk

Le monde visuel is intended to connect students to art. Share with students this paragraph: L'architecte français Édouard Albert (1910–1968) est connu pour ses bâtiments (*buildings*) en acier (*steel*) et en aluminium. Le dessin d'un architecte est une interprétation visuelle et spatiale de ses idées. Pour représenter cet immeuble parisien, Albert se sert des lignes pour rendre une idée concrète, facile à visualiser pour les clients et les amateurs d'art. Le tracé en ligne est un style d'art en deux dimensions, montrant les contours et les ombres (*shading*). Ici qu'est-ce qui a des lignes ou des bords (*edges*) visibles? Ce dessin est "de l'art" en terme de beauté ou de fonction?

Differentiated Learning

Accelerate

Point out that **Je naquis** uses **le passé simple**, a literary tense. Make a list of sentences using regular and irregular verbs in **le passé simple** and ask students to put them in **le passé composé**.

Decelerate

These students may need to work with a partner to complete **Activité 1** in the **Activités d'expansion.** If it's something they are incapable of doing, even with help, have them just turn in answers to the **Pendant la lecture** questions.

Multiple Intelligences

Offer the students a choice of activities based on their learning style. **Activité 1** might appeal most to the Intrapersonal learners. **Activité 2** might intrigue the Logical-Mathematical learners, while **Activité 3** might engage the Interpersonal learners the most. Offer the Visual-Spatial learners the option of finding artwork that portrays Josyane's world.
Search words: **bridgeman art library**

Answers

Activities will vary.

Reference Desk

1. The **Connexions par Internet** activity connects students to an educational subject matter such as sociology, architecture, literature, math, art, career planning, or music.
2. The **Communautés en ligne** activity is intended to help students build online francophone communities.
3. **Passez à l'action!** is an activity for the whole class, often suggesting roles and tasks for students.
4. The type of **Faisons le point!** activity on p. 69 will be found in all uneven units; this model is designed to get students to reflect on the Essential Question. Another model begins in **Unité 2** and is always found in the even units.

Expansion

Activité A: You may want to model a paragraph about family, childhood, or marriage in France, then encourage students to research a different francophone country or region.
Activité B: Share your **formation en français** experiences abroad with the class.
Activité C: Make sure each student has a role; you may want to create groups for each bulleted task.

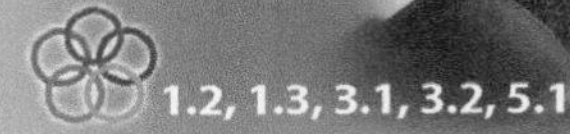

Projets finaux

A Connexions par Internet: La sociologie

1.2, 1.3, 3.1, 3.2, 5.1

Presentational Communication

Écrivez une petite composition sur la famille, l'enfance, ou le mariage dans un pays francophone. Vous devriez d'abord faire des recherches sur votre sujet en ligne. Parlez des traditions. Puis, notez les changements dans les familles, l'enfance, ou le mariage dans la société contemporaine. À quelles influences est-ce que vous attribuez ces changements? Commencez votre composition avec une définition de la sociologie et une phrase d'introduction.

B Communautés en ligne

1.2, 1.3, 3.2, 5.1, 5.2

Étudier à l'étranger pour perfectionner votre français/Interpersonal Communication

Vous voulez devenir un citoyen du monde, alors vous avez pris la décision d'étudier à l'étranger pour perfectionner votre français. Si vous voulez faire un programme d'échange pendant que vous êtes au lycée, cherchez un programme comme AFS ou un autre programme d'immersion. Si vous préférez participer à un tel programme à l'université, cherchez le *Junior Year Abroad Program* d'une université. Ensuite, écrivez 6-10 questions pour un(e) élève ou étudiant(e) qui est revenu(e) après un séjour à l'étranger via le programme que vous avez choisi. Vous pouvez trouver cette personne en ligne ou écrire un mail au programme qui vous mettra en contact avec quelqu'un. Finalement, discutez de ce que vous avez appris en petits groupes.

C Passez à l'action!

1.2, 1.3, 3.2, 5.1

Une MJC chez nous/Presentational Communication

Le gouvernement français a décidé d'aider votre ville à établir une MJC parce que les élèves de votre communauté ont montré un fort intérêt dans la langue et la culture françaises. Comme ça vous aurez un programme d'immersion: vous parlerez français pendant toutes les activités comme le ciné-club, les sports, les leçons de musique, etc. Votre MJC aura comme modèle une vraie MJC française.

Votre groupe va faire des recherches et trouver une MJC en France qui servira de modèle. Les autres équipes vont:

- choisir les activités
- faire de la publicité
- prendre des photos des ados en train de faire les activités
- créer une page d'accueil sur Internet
- écrire une lettre pour inviter tous les Francophones de votre région

Essential Instruction

1. Read through the **Projets finaux** and brainstorm with students the various tasks related to each project. If you only have time for students to do one activity, let them pick the one that appeals to them. Provide a detailed rubric so students know in advance how they will be graded.
2. A graphic organizer is available in the **Copy Masters** ancillary for **Faisons le point!** Ask students to include the page number where they can find the information as they review the Unit and to evaluate what they remember. Pair slower-paced students with a more advanced student to complete **Activité D**.

D Faisons le point!

 1.2, 1.3, 2.1, 2.2, 3.1, 4.1, 5.1

Faites un diagramme comme celui de dessous et remplissez-le pour montrer vos connaissances concernant la question suivante: Comment la vie des Francophones évolue-t-elle avec le temps? Un exemple a été fait pour vous.

Question centrale: Comment la vie des Francophones évolue-t-elle avec le temps?

Leçon A **Rencontres culturelles: Qu'est-ce qui est nouveau dans la vie d'Élodie?**	**Élodie commence à participer à la culture adolescente. Elle fait partie d'une bande de copains et elle a un nouveau petit ami.**
Leçon A **Extension: Comment est-ce que Julie communique avec ses amis?**	
Leçon A **Points de départ: Modes de vie…: Qu'est-ce que les jeunes français ont en commun?**	
Leçon A **Points de départ: Les MJC: Que sont les MJC?**	
Leçon A **L'argot des ados: Quel est un exemple du langage des adolescents?**	
Leçon A **Du côté des médias: Comment est-ce que les jeunes Français se rencontrent?**	
Leçon B **Rencontres culturelles: Qu'est-ce que Karim a arrêté de faire quand il a déménagé à Nice? Qu'est-ce qui était nouveau pour lui à Nice?**	
Leçon B **Extension: Qu'est-ce qui est nouveau dans les vies de Mme Duhamel et Mme Laforge?**	
Leçon B **Points de départs: La famille: De quelle manière les familles françaises ont-elles changé?**	
Leçon B **Points de départ: La Francophonie: Comment est-ce que les valeurs des jeunes gens en Afrique changent leurs pays?**	

Differentiated Learning

Accelerate

Allow these students, working in a group, to devise their own final project based on unit content.

Decelerate

Have students revisit the **Contrat de l'élève** and self-assess how well they know the unit content.

Answers

D

Leçon A: Julie utilise les réseaux sociaux sur Internet.; Ils aiment tout ce qui est audiovisuel et numérique.; Les MJC sont des lieux de rencontre pour les jeunes.; "Un mec" est un terme d'argot pour un garçon.; Ils utilisent le courrier du coeur.

Leçon B: Karim a arrêté le foot.; Les supermarchés étaient quelque chose de nouveau pour lui.; Elles ont divorcé.; Il y a moins de mariages et plus de PACS.; Les jeunes Africains sont influencés par le monde moderne.

Critical Thinking

Evaluate

Ask students to evaluate their learning by:

1. Saying what they can do now. ("I can tell a story in the past tense using the **passé composé** and the **imparfait**.")
2. Saying what they need to review. ("I still confuse my future and conditional irregular stems.")
3. Making a list of questions to ask you or the class before the unit exam.

RESOURCES

Listening Activity
Synthèse

Answers

A

1. G
2. B
3. A
4. C
5. F
6. E
7. D

B

Conversations will vary.

Reference Desk

1. The **Évaluation** section quizzes students on these skills: listening, speaking, writing, and culture. It lets each student know what he/she needs to practice more or review thoroughly before the unit test.
2. The **Évaluation de compréhension auditive** is based on scripts that usually combine unit vocabulary and grammar.
3. The **Évaluation orale** provides paired speaking practice. Sometimes you may want to vary it by playing one of the roles yourself and choosing different partners before putting students in pairs.

Évaluation Pre AP

emcl.com
LA *Synthèse*

A Évaluation de compréhension auditive 1.1, 1.2

Interpretive Communication

Les vacances

Écrivez les numéros 1–7 sur votre papier. Ensuite, écoutez l'histoire, et écrivez la lettre qui correspond à l'endroit où les personnes feront les activités suivantes pendant les vacances.

1. Caroline	A. le ciné-club
2. Serge	B. le skatepark
3. Amélie et Amadou	C. le festival de musique
4. Jacques	D. la discothèque
5. Martine	E. le complexe sportif
6. Yasmine et Julien	F. le cours particulier
7. Chloé	G. la MJC

B Évaluation orale 1.1, 1.2, 1.3, 5.1, 5.2

Interpersonal Communication

Avec un partenaire, jouez les rôles de deux ados qui sont à la MJC.

Vous voulez savoir si votre copine a fait la connaissance d'un nouveau copain.	→ Dites que c'est vrai.
Demandez son prénom.	→ Dites comment votre copain s'appelle.
Demandez où votre copine l'a rencontré.	→ Dites où vous avez rencontré votre copain.
Demandez comment il est.	→ Décrivez votre copain. Dites ce que vous avez découvert de lui. (Peut-être qu'il aime quelque chose que vous aimez aussi.)
Dites que ce serait bien de le présenter à votre bande de copains.	→ Dites que vous proposez d'organiser une soirée pour le présenter à vos copains.
Dites que vous aimeriez le connaître.	→ Demandez ce que votre ami(e) aimerait faire ce soir.
Proposez une activité pour ce soir.	→ Acceptez ou refusez.

Essential Instruction

1. Have students read through the answers in **Activité A** before listening to the questions. Replay the audio as needed. Some students, especially those with auditory difficulties, will benefit from seeing the script.
2. For **Activité B**, ask students to brainstorm vocabulary, functions, and structures they need to know to complete the dialogue. Then assign partners to create the dialogue. Select several pairs to present.
3. You may want to put the class in five small groups to complete **Activité C**, then have each group present their comparisons to the class.
4. All students should complete **Activité D** because there's a proficiency writing section on the unit test; assign **Activités E–F** to those students who need a visual cue or who are creative.

C Évaluation culturelle

 1.2, 3.2, 4.2

Vous allez comparez les cultures francophones à votre culture aux États-Unis. Vous aurez peut-être besoin de faire des recherches sur la culture américaine.

1. **Les modes de vie des adolescents**
   Comparez les modes de vie des adolescents francophones et américains. Quelles sont les similarités et les différences des deux groupes? Est-ce qu'il y a une "culture ado" qui rassemble (*gathers*) ces deux groupes?
2. **Les MJC**
   Où est-ce que vous vous retrouvez avec vos amis? Aimeriez-vous avoir une MJC avec des activités pour les ados? Ça existe déjà dans votre communauté? Qu'est-ce que les MJC françaises offrent? Qu'est-ce qu'une MJC américaine devrait offrir pour plaire (*please*) aux ados américains?
3. **Les familles**
   Faites un sondage auprès de vos camarade de classe pour savoir au sein de quel type de famille (nucléaire, monoparentale...) vos amis vivent. Comparez les pourcentages à ceux des familles françaises.
4. **Classes préparatoires et grandes écoles**
   Si un ado voulait travailler pour la Banque de France un jour, qu'est-ce que vous lui conseilleriez? Si vous vouliez vous inscrire à ou Duke, qu'est-ce que vous devriez faire?
5. **Le mariage**
   Quels genres de cérémonies de mariage existent en France? Laquelle est la plus populaire en France? Et aux États-Unis? Comparez aussi les réceptions de mariage en France et aux États-Unis.

D Évaluation écrite

 1.3, 2.1, 5.1

*Écrivez un faire-part de mariage pour un couple français à Nice. N'oubliez pas d'inclure (*include*):*

- le nom du couple et de leurs parents
- la date et l' endroit de la cérémonie et de la réception
- l'adresse de l'église et du restaurant où la réception aura lieu
- l'adresse où on envoie son RSVP

E Évaluation visuelle

 1.3, 2.1, 3.1, 5.1

Écrivez un paragraphe qui décrit le mariage d'Albert et Claudette. Décrivez ce que vous voyez à la cérémonie et imaginez ce qui se passera après, pendant la réception. Dites depuis combien de temps Albert connaît Claudette et où ils travaillent. Parlez de leurs rêves pour l'avenir (future).

F Évaluation compréhensive

 1.3, 5.1

Créez une histoire avec six illustrations: dessinez une famille en vacances sur la Côte d'Azur. Montrez les activités de cette famille. Vous devrez décider quelle sorte de famille c'est. Les enfants ont moins de dix ans et aiment les jeux d'enfants.

Reference Desk

1. The **Évaluation culturelle** asks students to make comparisons between francophone and American cultures.
2. The **Évaluation écrite** is intended to build writing proficiency.
3. The **Évaluation visuelle** is designed for visual learners who do best with a visual prompt.
4. The **Évaluation compréhensive** is designed for those students who have a desire to be creative with unit content. Sometimes it works to pair an artist with a good writer to complete this activity. These students could do this activity instead of **Activité D**.

Game

Jeopardy!
Create categories of questions: vocabulary, culture, grammar, speaking in French (perhaps answering questions), potpourri. Place the questions on your board so that the easiest one in each category comes first and the most difficult one comes last; give each question a point value that is visible to students (10–50). Divide the class into two teams. The first player picks a category and a point value. The team with the highest number of points, once all the questions have been asked, is the winner.

Differentiated Learning

Accelerate
Have these students do **Activité E** or **F** in addition to **A–D**.

Special Needs Students

Auditory Impairment
Allow students with hearing difficulties to listen to **Activité A** several times. You may also want to read the questions which will give them ample time to process the information.

Multiple Intelligences

Intrapersonal
Ask these students to share with the class or a small group how their view of francophone life has changed or expanded after studying **Unité 1**.

RESOURCES

Listening Pre-test D

***Unité* Test**

Reference Desk

Remind the students that the **Leçon** where each vocabulary word can be found is indicated in red.

Game

Les définitions

Put students in two teams. Read a definition for one of the unit's new vocabulary words. A designated player from each team races to the board to write the word. Whichever one writes the word correctly earns a point for his/her team. Here are some definitions to get you started: 1. **une bague de mariage** (**une alliance**); 2. **un parc où on joue dans l'eau** (**un aquaparc**); 3. **un groupe de copains** (**une bande**); 4. **un enfant qui a moins d'un an** (**un bébé**); 5. **l'endroit où les avocats travaillent** (**le cabinet d'avocats**); 6. **un groupe qui se rencontre pour voir des films** (**un ciné-club**); 7. **un endroit où on fait toutes sortes de sports** (**un complexe sportif**); 8. **aller très vite à pied** (**courir**); 9. **s'installer dans une nouvelle maison** (**déménager**); 10. **la jeune femme qui aide son amie pendant sa cérémonie de mariage** (**la demoiselle d'honneur**)

Vocabulaire de l'Unité 1  1.2

absolument absolutely *A*
les **alliances (f.)** wedding rings *C*
l' **aquaparc (m.)** water park *A*
assister (à) to attend *C*
aussitôt que as soon as *C*
la **bague: bague de fiançailles** engagement ring *C*
une **bande** group of friends *A*
le **bébé** baby *C*
un **cabinet: cabinet d'avocats** law firm *C*
le **ciné-club** film club *A*
collectionner to collect *B*
un **coquillage** seashell *B*
comme: c'est comme ça que.... that's how.... *B*
le **complexe: complexe sportif** sports center *A*
la **complicité** complicity *A*
courir to run *B*
le **cours: cours particulier** private class *A*
déménager to move *C*
la **demoiselle d'honneur** bridesmaid *C*
détester to detest *A*
la **discothèque** nightclub *A*
l' **enfance (f.)** childhood *B*
enfantin(e) childish *B*
une **entreprise** business, company *C*
être: être affolé(e) to panic *A*; **être fâché(e)** to be angry *A*
une **famille: famille monoparentale** single-parent family *B*; **famille nucléaire** nuclear family *B*; **famille recomposée** blended family *B*
faire: faire semblant (de) to pretend (to) *B*; **Tu ferais bien de.....** You would do well to.... *A*
se **faire: se faire muter** to get reassigned *C*
fiche: elle s'en fiche she doesn't care *C*
le **festival** festival *A*
le **garçon: garçon d'honneur** best man *C*
s' **inquiéter** to worry *A*
intéressé(e) interested *C*
jouer: jouer à cache-cache to play hide-and-seek *B*; **jouer à la marelle** to play hopscotch *B*; **jouer à la poupée** to play with dolls *B*; **jouer aux billes** to play marbles *B*; **jouer aux petites voitures** to play with toy cars *B*
un **laboratoire: laboratoire de recherches** research laboratory *C*
lorsque when *C*
une **marraine** godmother *C*
mettre: mettre d'accord to get people to agree *C*
la **MJC** community center *A*
les **nanotechnologies (f.)** nanotechnology *C*
la **peine: ce n'est pas la peine** it's not worth it *A*
une **piste** lead *C*
un **poste** job position *C*
une **PME (petite et moyenne entreprise)** small business *C*
une **princesse** princess *B*
se **quitter** to leave one another *A*
ramasser to pick up *B*
la **réception** reception *C*
un **regret** regret *B*
le **sable** sand *B*
sauter to jump *B*; **sauter à la corde** to jump rope *B*
le **skatepark** skateboard park *A*
la **soirée** evening out *A*
sourire to smile *A*
un **sourire** smile *A*
un **super-héros** superhero *B*
un **timbre** stamp *B*
le **voyage: voyage de noces** honeymoon *C*

Learning Styles

Auditory Learners

These students benefit from saying and spelling the vocabulary words out loud. Pair similar students and have them work together to review the vocabulary in this way.

Unité 2 Les rapports personnels

Reference Desk

The photos show two of the topics in this unit: the kitchen and French cuisine; and fashion, a topic of dinner conversation.

Reference Desk

If a **jour férié** falls on a Friday or Monday and people have a three-day weekend, the French often say, **"On fait le pont."** An extended weekend is also called **un weekend prolongé**.

Citation

"C'est dans le rapport à autrui que l'on prend conscience de soi…"

It's in our relationships with others that we become aware of ourselves.

—Michel Houellebecq, écrivain européen

Essential Instruction

After the students read the quotation, have them discuss if it's true that we become aware of ourselves solely in interacting with others. Some students will raise the issue that you can learn a lot about yourself doing activities alone.

Unité 2

Les rapports personnels

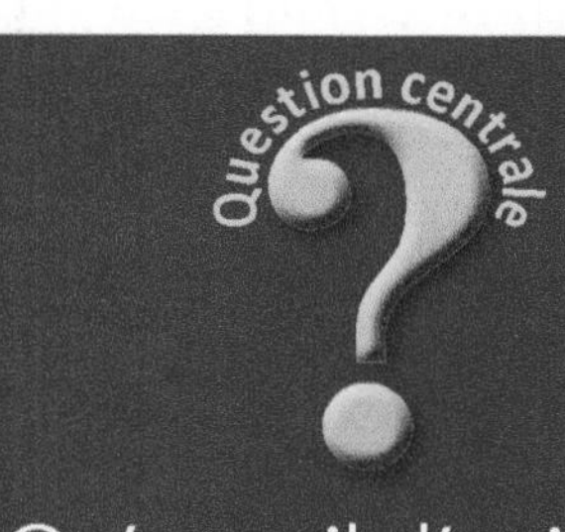

Qu'y a-t-il d'universel dans les rapports entre les gens?

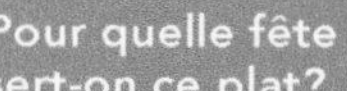

Comment s'appelle ce dessert?

Contrat de l'élève

Leçon A I will be able to:

- talk on the phone, invite someone, and respond affirmatively to an invitation.
- talk about Christmas Eve in France and **l'Aïd el-Fitr** in North Africa.
- use interrogative pronouns and direct object pronouns.

Leçon B I will be able to:

- ask for help, respond to a request for help, and ask someone to pass me something.
- talk about French cuisine and a famous cooking school.
- use indirect object pronouns and **C'est** vs. **il/elle est**.

Leçon C I will be able to:

- express what I can't keep myself from doing, say someone is right, and ask what someone is talking about.
- talk about dining etiquette in France.
- use the relative pronouns **qui** and **que** and the relative pronouns **ce qui** and **ce que**.

Reference Desk

With the **Question centrale**, students are asked to examine their relationships and compare them to those in the francophone world.

Differentiated Learning

Accelerate

Ask students who are seeking more of a challenge to conduct the review of the **Contrat de l'élève** with the rest of the class.

Decelerate

Review the **Contrat de l'élève** with students. Reassure them that in addition to learning these new concepts, they will be doing a thorough review of the basics that they learned in Level 1. Encourage them to think that this year will be the year that they will succeed even more than before.

RESOURCES

e-visual 4

Workbook 1–3

Flash Cards

Listening Activity 1

Drill & Practice Games

Reference Desk

1. Traditionally, **le réveillon** was the meal served after midnight mass on Christmas Eve and New Year's Eve. Now in France masses are said at 10:00 P.M. (**la messe anticipée**), so the meal is served earlier in the evening.
2. Although there are traditional dishes corresponding to our turkey at Thanksgiving, the fare will vary according to regional specialties. In addition to **les toasts aux œufs de lump**, **les verrines** are very popular for appetizers. **Le gigot** (*lamb*) is a favorite main course in some families. For dessert, **vacherin glacé** is popular. If time allows, have students use the search words **verrine** and **vacherin glacé** for photos and recipes.
3. Even the French take short cuts when it comes to cooking and entertaining. Use the search word **Picard** to find an interactive website of the chain of stores that sells frozen herbs, sauces, main courses, and desserts.

Culture

Products: Information

"**Une lettre au Père Nöel**," sung by Patrick Bruel, recounts the expectations of a child writing to **le Père Nöel** with reflections about the passage of time.
Search words: une lettre au père nöel patrick bruel

Vocabulaire actif

emcl.com
WB 1–3
LA 1
Games

Le réveillon de Noël

1.2, 5.1

Le menu

Essential Instruction

1. Have the students guess what each dish is by looking at the photos on the page or larger, more vivid photos of these foods online.
2. Ask students what traditional American dishes would correspond to each category (appetizer, first course, main course, and dessert) in their home.
3. Review with students the order of courses.
4. The activities in the Lombard home on Christmas are in chronological order

Noël Chez les Lombard

Les Lombard accueillent leurs invités.

M. Lombard range leurs manteaux.

Chloé embête son frère dans la cuisine.

Il les emmène au salon.

Mme Lombard sert le repas.

Les Lombard mettent les cadeaux pour leurs enfants sous le sapin de Noël.

Pour la conversation 1.1, 1.2

What do I say when I phone someone?

› **Je ne te dérange pas?**

I'm not bothering you?

How do I invite someone?

› **Vous aimeriez** la soirée du réveillon avec nous?

Would you like to come spend Christmas Eve with us?

How do I respond affirmatively to an invitation?

› **Pourquoi pas? On n'a rien de prévu.**

Why not? We don't have anything planned.

How do I say a proposal works for me?

› **Ça tombe bien.**

That works out well.

Et si je voulais dire...?

une truffe	*truffle*
un plateau de fruits de mer	*seafood platter*
un homard	*lobster*
une langouste	*rock lobster*
une fougasse	*lattice-shaped bread popular in Provence*
une brioche	*slightly sweet bread*

Reference Desk

1. Useful expressions for phoning in French include **Allô** (*Hello*); **Ça sonne.** (*It's ringing.*); **C'est de la part de qui?** (*Who is calling?*); **Ne quittez pas, s'il vous plaît.** (*Stay on the line please.*); **Je vous le/la passe.** (*Let me get him/her for you.*); **Je peux laisser un message?** (*Can I leave a message?*); **Vous pouvez rappeler plus tard.** (*You can call back later.*)
2. **Accueillir** means "to welcome." **L'accueil** can refer to a reception desk where one can get information. On the Internet **accueil** is the home page.
3. **Un sapin** is a pine tree.
4. Students learned **ranger** (*to arrange, to pick up*) in Level 2, **Unité 3. Ranger la cuisine** means "to clean the kitchen." **Ranger les placards** means "to straighten up the closets," whereas **ranger les manteaux** has the sense of "to put the coats where they belong."
5. **Une bête** means "a beast," but it can also mean an insect or bug. Hence, "to bug someone" is **embêter quelqu'un. Ma bête noire** is the thing that you dread or hate.
6. **Servir** is an irregular **-ir** verb that is conjugated like **partir**.

Communication

Interpersonal: Paired Practice

Put students in pairs to have a phone conversation about Christmas. Student A calls Student B and invites him/her to **le réveillon**, explaining what will be served at dinner for all courses except dessert. Student B accepts the invitation and offers to bring dessert. Invite a couple pairs of students to present their dialogue in front of the class. Challenge advanced students to sit back-to-back with their partner.

Differentiated Learning

Accelerate

Have the accelerated students research photos of the foods in **Et se je voulais dire...?** Have them select a recipe and make a shopping list to prepare it for their family.

Decelerate

Have these students face each other when doing the phone conversation in the **Communication** activity. This will facilitate their comprehension of what their partner is saying.

Answers

1

1. des toasts aux œufs de lump, des huîtres, une salade verte, du canard, des mandarines, une bûche
2. Léa a accueilli ses grands-parents, rangé leurs manteaux, et elle leur a servi l'appéritif.
3. Elle était très occupée à l'université.
4. Oui.
5. Ils ont mis des cadeaux sous le sapin.
6. demain matin

2 4., 7., 2., 5., 3., 6., 1.

Reference Desk

Point out that the subject line of the e-mail literally means "Christmas—you are missing to me," or more colloquially, "Christmas, I miss you."

1 Absente à Noël

1.2, 5.1

Lisez le mail de Léa à sa grande sœur, qui n'habite plus à la maison. Puis répondez aux questions suivantes.

À: Élodie @ orange.fr
Cc:
Sujet: Noël – tu me manques!

Salut, Élodie!

Je sais que tu as beaucoup à faire à l'université à New York. C'est dommage que tu n'aies pas été là pour Noël. Maman et Papa ont préparé un bon repas pour le réveillon de Noël—des toasts aux œufs de lump, des huîtres, une salade verte, du canard. Et comme dessert il y avait des mandarines et une bûche, bien sûr! Pour une fois je ne les ai pas embêtés pendant qu'ils préparaient tout. En fait, je les ai aidés. J'avais beaucoup de responsabilités. J'ai accueilli papi et mamie, j'ai rangé leurs manteaux, je les ai emmenés au salon, et je leur ai servi l'apéritif. Heureusement, ils ont mis des cadeaux pour moi sous le sapin de Noël! Je vais les ouvrir demain matin. Et toi, tu as bien mangé chez ton ami? Téléphone-nous bientôt!

Je t'embrasse,
Léa

1. Qu'est-ce que les parents de Léa ont servi pour le réveillon de Noël?
2. Comment Léa a-t-elle aidé ses parents?
3. Pourquoi est-ce qu'Élodie n'est pas venue?
4. Est-ce que la famille de Léa a passé la fête en famille?
5. Qu'est-ce que les invités ont fait?
6. Quand est-ce que Léa va ouvrir ses cadeaux?

2 Le réveillon de Noël

1.2, 1.3

Mettez les événements pour le réveillon de Noël en ordre chronologique.

1. M. et Mme Gaillot mettent les cadeaux pour leurs enfants sous le sapin de Noël.
2. M. Gaillot range les manteaux des invités.
3. La belle-mère de Mme Gaillot l'aide dans la cuisine.
4. M. Gaillot invite ses parents et son oncle.
5. M. et Mme Gaillot emmènent leurs invités au salon.
6. Mme Gaillot sert le repas.
7. Les Gaillot les accueillent à la porte le soir du réveillon.

Essential Instruction

1. After reading the e-mail, have students answer it as Léa's big sister Élodie who no longer lives at home. In the e-mail, they will describe the American Christmas meal Élodie had in her exchange family's home in New York.
2. Have students work in pairs to do **Activités 2** and **3**.
3. Do **Activité 4** as a class.

Communiquez!

3 Invitations

1.1, 1.2, 5.1, 5.2

Interpersonal Communication

À tour de rôle, invitez votre partenaire qui va dire s'il ou elle a quelque chose de prévu ou pas.

Tu voudrais venir au concert ce soir?

Oui, je n'ai rien de prévu.

MODÈLE le ciné-club jeudi soir
A: **Tu voudrais m'accompagner au ciné-club jeudi soir?**
B: **Oui, je n'ai rien de prévu.**
ou
Non, désolé(e), j'ai quelque chose de prévu.

1. l'aquaparc cet été
2. le complexe sportif mercredi après-midi
3. la MJC mardi soir
4. le festival de musique le 14 décembre
5. la discothèque samedi soir
6. la soirée de Léo le 31 décembre

4 À table!

1.1, 1.2, 5.1

Dites ce que Mme Gaillot a servi comme....

1. apéritif
2. hors-d'œuvre
3. plat principal
4. dessert

Special Needs Students

AD(H)D/Dyslexia/Linguistically Challenged
Allow students who have difficulty with concentration, reading, or language to write out their lines phonetically on note cards and use the note cards when they present.

Multiple Intelligences

Visual-Spatial
Ask these students to make **le menu** for the meal in **Activité 4.** Pass out the menu to the class before doing the exercise.

Answers

3 *Answers B will vary.*

1. A: Tu voudrais m'accompagner à l'aquaparc cet été?
2. A: Tu voudrais m'accompagner au complexe sportif mercredi après-midi?
3. A: Tu voudrais m'accompagner à la MJC mardi soir?
4. A: Tu voudrais m'accompagner au festival de musique le 14 décembre?
5. A: Tu voudrais m'accompagner à la discothèque samedi soir?
6. A: Tu voudrais m'accompagner à la soirée de Léo le 31 décembre?

1. des toasts aux œufs de lump
2. du foie gras et des huîtres
3. de la dinde aux marrons
4. une bûche de Noël et des mandarines

Expansion

Students can expand **Activité 3** by using the following expressions: To accept: **Volontiers! C'est une très bonne idée! Pourquoi pas? Oui, ça me dit!** To decline: **Malheureusement, je ne peux pas. Dommage.**

Answers

5

1. le 24 décembre
2. les invités
3. M. Dupont
4. au salon
5. des mandarines
6. les enfants/Guy et Martine

6 *Answers will vary.*

5 Un réveillon traditionnel!

1.1, 1.2, 5.1

Écrivez les numéros 1–6 sur votre papier. Écoutez la description du réveillon de Noël chez les Dupont. Ensuite, écrivez un mot ou une expression pour répondre aux questions que vous entendez.

6 Questions personnelles

1.2, 1.3, 4.2, 5.1

Répondez aux questions.

1. Quand est-ce qu'on sert la dinde chez toi?
2. As-tu déjà mangé du canard? des côtes de chevreuil? des mandarines? des huîtres?
3. Qu'est-ce que tu mets sur les toasts?
4. Qu'est-ce que tu fais pour accueillir tes amis quand ils te rendent visite?
5. Quels cadeaux est-ce que tu vas offrir à ta famille cette année?
6. Est-ce que tu as quelque chose de prévu pour samedi soir?

Une assiette d'huîtres.

J'ai goûté au magret de canard, mais je n'aime pas.

Essential Instruction

1. Listen to the first description in **Activité 5** together as a class. Model an appropriate answer because students are not used to writing open-ended answers to listening questions.
2. After students have completed **Activité 6** in pairs, call on students at random to answer questions 1–6.
3. Play the video of the dialogue for the class. After finding out where the holes in their comprehension are, read the dialogues aloud, selecting three students for the roles.
4. Ask students the questions in **Activité 7**.

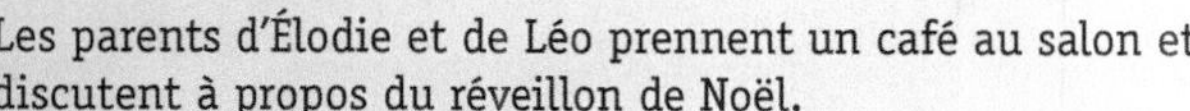

Rencontres culturelles

emcl.com
WB 4

Une invitation

1.1, 1.2, 2.1, 5.1

Les parents d'Élodie et de Léo prennent un café au salon et discutent à propos du réveillon de Noël.

Mère: Bon, tu es d'accord, mais qui est-ce qu'on invite pour le réveillon?
Père: Appelle les Martin... je suis sûr qu'ils n'ont rien de prévu.
Mère: C'est un peu tard, non? On est quand même à cinq jours du réveillon.
Père: Écoute, tu leur dis qu'on improvise quelque chose....
Mère: Et s'ils disent qu'ils ont déjà accepté une invitation?
Père: Eh bien, on passera le réveillon en famille... vas-y, appelle, je te dis!

(La mère d'Élodie et de Léo téléphone à Amélie Martin.)

Mère: Allô? Amélie, je ne te dérange pas? C'est pour le réveillon de Noël, vous faites quelque chose?
Amélie: Non....
Mère: Vous aimeriez venir passer la soirée du réveillon avec nous?
Amélie: Pourquoi pas? On n'a rien de prévu... mais vous, vous n'avez rien accepté de votre côté?
Mère: Non... puisque je vous invite... on avait envie d'une soirée un peu tranquille, en petit comité.
Amélie: Ça tombe bien, alors! C'est moi qui fais les toasts. J'insiste!
Mère: C'est gentil. Au 24, alors!

7 Une invitation

1.2, 1.3

Répondez aux questions.

1. Pourquoi est-ce que la mère d'Élodie et de Léo téléphone à Amélie?
2. Qui a l'idée de téléphoner aux Martin?
3. Si les Martin n'acceptent pas l'invitation, que va-t-il se passer?
4. La mère d'Élodie et de Léo prévoit (*foresees*) quelle sorte de soirée?
5. Qu'est-ce que Mme Martin offre de préparer?
6. La soirée, c'est pour fêter quelle fête?

RESOURCES

 **Dialogue Video**

 **Workbook 4**

Answers

1. pour l'inviter pour le réveillon de Noël
2. le père d'Élodie
3. La famille d'Élodie passera le réveillon en famille.
4. une petite soirée tranquille
5. les toasts
6. le réveillon de Noël

Reference Desk

Help students understand words and expressions they haven't seen before:

1. **À propos de** is used with **discuter**; it can also be used with **parler**.
2. **Ils n'ont rien de prévu** means "They have nothing planned."
3. **On est quand même à cinq jours du réveillon** means "But **le réveillon** is still five days away." Ask students to give additional examples of the **à** + time/distance formula.
4. **Puisque** means "since." However, in the sentence **Puisque je vous invite**... it can be translated as "That's why we are inviting you."
5. **En petit comité** means "in a small group."
6. **Au 24 alors** means "We'll see you on the 24th."

Differentiated Learning

Accelerate

Have accelerated students make a cloze activity based on the new vocabulary in the dialogue that the slower-paced students can fill in.

Special Needs Students

Social Anxiety

These students may appreciate reading one of the roles in the dialogue with you privately since performing in front of a group might be too stressful for them.

Answers

Extension

Elle se plaint que ses invités sont difficiles. Oui.

Reference Desk

Give the advanced students you want to read the **Extension** dialogue this list of new vocabulary: **le Saint-Sylvestre** (*New Year's Eve*); **gras** (*fatty*); **à ce rythme-là** (*at that rate*); **le menu minceur** (**mince** means "thin," so this menu is low calorie); **se plaint** (*is complaining*); **être du même avis** (*to be of the same opinion*).

Extension **Une autre fête: Le réveillon de la Saint-Sylvestre**   1.1, 1.2, 5.1

Le 27 décembre, M. et Mme Laurent parlent d'une fête qui s'approche.

M. Laurent: Tiens regarde, j'ai préparé un carton d'invitations pour le réveillon.

Mme Laurent: Très joli... tu le tires sur papier ou tu l'envoies aux Roland par Internet?

M. Laurent: Par Internet, chérie... Comme dit ton fils "pensez à économiser la planète." Et qu'est-ce que tu vas servir?

Mme Laurent: Tu sais, les Roland sont difficiles: pas trop gras pour lui, pas de viande pour elle, pas trop de sucre pour les deux...

M. Laurent: À ce rythme-là, ce n'est pas un menu de réveillon qu'il faut préparer mais leur proposer le menu minceur de leur cure de thermalisme.

Extension De quoi est-ce que la mère se plaint? Pourquoi? Son mari est-il du même avis?

1.1,1.2, 5.1

Essential Instruction

1. Have students read the first culture reading to themselves. Then ask them the comprehension questions.
2. Ask students to design **une bûche de Noël** and vote on the top three.
3. Make a classroom list of the different types of holidays that your students celebrate at home.

Points de départ

emcl.com WB 5

Le réveillon de Noël

1.2, 2.1, 4.2

Question centrale: Qu'ya-t-il d'universel dans les rapports entre les gens?

En France, le réveillon de Noël du 24 décembre est aussi important, sinon* plus, que le jour de Noël lui-même. La soirée se passe* généralement en famille, contrairement au réveillon du nouvel an (nuit de la Saint-Sylvestre), qui réunit plutôt les amis. Le soir du réveillon, on dîne en famille, contrairement au jour de Noël, où toute la famille (grands-parents, oncles, tantes, etc.) se réunit pour le déjeuner. Le repas du réveillon est un vrai festin*. On mange souvent des toasts aux œufs de lump, des huîtres, du saumon fumé, et de la dinde aux marrons. En dessert, on sert un gâteau spécial, une bûche de Noël.

Le réveillon est un vrai moment de fête.

La France étant un pays de tradition catholique, certaines familles assistent à la messe de minuit. Les enfants mettent leurs chaussons* sous le sapin de Noël avant d'aller se coucher. Selon leur âge, ils pensent que le père Noël y déposera des cadeaux, qu'ils trouveront à leur réveil*, le 25 décembre.

Search words: noël en france

sinon *if not;* **se passe** *is spent;* **festin** *feast;* **chaussons** *slippers;* **à leur réveil** *upon waking*

Produits

La bûche de Noël est un gâteau en forme de bûche (*log*). Traditionnellement, elle est à base de crème au beurre (*butter cream*), mais depuis plusieurs années on peut trouver une version glacée (*iced*). La bûche de Noël existe en plusieurs parfums: vanille, praliné, chocolat, ou café. Le pâtissier la décore avec des Pères Noël, des haches (*axes*), des scies (*saws*), des lutins (*elves*), etc. en sucre. Cette tradition existe dans de nombreux pays francophones comme en France et en Belgique.

1.2, 2.2

COMPARAISONS

Quelles sont vos traditions familiales pour les fêtes?

4.2

RESOURCES

Workbook 5

Reference Desk

Over 600,000 Jews in France celebrate the 8-day Festival of Lights that falls in December. The date is dictated by the Hebrew calendar. There is a series of rituals that are performed during the celebration; some are family-based, and others are celebrated communally. Many families exchange small gifts each night. Fried foods are eaten to remember the importance of oil during the festival of Hanukkah. Here are some terms to share with the class: **juif/juive** (*Jewish*); **le Sabbat** (*Sabbath*); **la Ménorah** (*Menorah*); **la prière** (*prayer*); **kasher** (*kosher*); **une bougie** (*candle*); **une galette aux pommes de terre** (*latke*); **une toupie** (*dreidel*, or *spinning top*).

Differentiated Learning

Accelerate

Ask these students to write a culture reading, similar to "**Le réveillon de Noël**," about **une fête** that their family celebrates.

Learning Styles

Kinesthetic Learners

Students who love to cook might like to make a **bûche de Noël** for the class. Consider using a design a student made.

Multiple Intelligences

Musical-Rhythmic

Have these students organize a songbook of French holiday music. There are non-religious options for songs if Christmas carols pose a problem in your school.

Answers

8 *Answers will vary.*

La Francophonie

Les fêtes au Maghreb

À la fin du mois sacré du Ramadan, on fête la rupture (la *id al-fitr* en arabe, "fête de la rupture") du jeûne*. C'est la fête de l'Aïd. Elle s'accompagne de tout un cérémonial: il y a le don* de rupture du jeûne (la *Zakat el-Fitr*), la prière, le repas avec les dattes, la présentation des vœux* à la famille et aux amis.

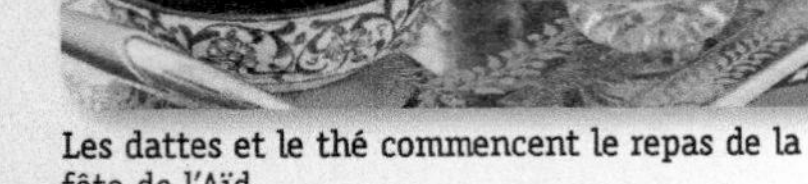

Les dattes et le thé commencent le repas de la fête de l'Aïd.

Au Maghreb, c'est la tradition de préparer des gâteaux aux amandes ou à la pistache. Les enfants et les maris aident les femmes en amenant les immenses plateaux* remplis de pâtes dans les boulangeries de quartier qui louent leurs fours. L'acte le plus important de la fête est le don aux pauvres de la communauté. Les enfants reçoivent de l'argent et des cadeaux.

En France, avec cinq millions de Musulmans, cette fête devient importante. Dans les grandes villes (Paris, Lyon, Lille, Marseille, par exemple), elle donne lieu à de grands rassemblements* (parfois plus de 10.000 personnes). À Paris, la Mairie de Paris ouvre l'Hôtel de Ville de Paris aux Musulmans et à tous ceux et celles qui veulent partager cette fête. La fête de l'Aïd a pris une dimension nationale. C'est aussi une occasion de lutter contre l'islamophobie.

Search words: ramadan, aïd el-fitr

jeûne *fasting;* **don** cadeau; **vœux** *wishes;* **plateaux** *trays;* **rassemblements** *gatherings*

Mots-clé

Fête (du latin *festa*, 1050). Le mot renvoie d'abord à un contexte religieux avant de désigner une rupture avec la vie quotidienne (XIIème), puis une commémoration (XIVème). Il désigne toute occasion de débauche surtout dans **faire la fête** (1880); il apparaît dans les années 1960 dans une expression où il désigne une menace: **ça va être ta fête**.

8 Activités culturelles

1.3, 3.2, 4.2

Faites les activités suivantes.

1. Comparez les plats servis pour le réveillon de Noël en France et en Amérique. Servez-vous d'un organigramme Venn.
2. Faites un dessin qui montre la tradition du jour de Noël pour les enfants en France et dans votre pays.
3. Trouvez la date de l'Aïd el-Fitr cette année.
4. Consultez l'Internet sur les événements en France pour voir comment est célébrée l'Aïd el-Fitr cette année.
5. Trouvez en ligne une recette pour un couscous ou un gâteau d'Aïd el-Fitr. Cochez les ingrédients que vous avez à la maison et faites une liste des ingrédients qu'il vous faut acheter. Vous allez servir 12 personnes.

Ce dessert est une bûche de Noël.

Essential Instruction

1. Ask a student to point out on a world map where **le Maghreb** is located.
2. Read **Les fêtes au Maghreb** with your students.
3. Discuss the importance of Islam in France. Have students brainstorm what they already know about **le Maghreb** and Islam.
4. Assign one or more of the **Activités culturelles.** You may want to assign one activity per group, combining 3 and 4 into one activity.
5. Discuss the **Perspectives** on p. 85.
6. Put students in pairs to read the realia and complete **Activité 9.**

Perspectives

1.2, 2.1

"Avant d'aller faire la prière rituelle à la mosquée, nous distribuons la *Zakat el-Fitr*, l'aumône donnée aux pauvres par acte de générosité et de compassion. Ce don purificateur permet aux personnes pauvres de ne pas avoir faim et représente une libération de la mendicité (*begging*) en ce jour sacré." Selon ce Musulman, quel est le but de la *Zakat el-Fitr*?

Du côté des médias

Pre AP

1.2, 2.1

Interpretive Communication

Lisez l'introduction et la liste des jours fériés en France.

Jours fériés en France

La France compte 11 jours fériés qui correspondent à des fêtes civiles ou religieuses. Il y a des jours fériés fixes et des jours fériés mobiles. Le 1er mai, c'est la fête du travail, elle donne l'obligation à tous de ne pas travailler tout en étant payé. Le Vendredi Saint est un jour férié supplémentaire dans les départements de la Moselle, du Bas et du Haut-Rhin et en Guadeloupe, Martinique, et Polynésie française.

France	2012	2013	2014
Jour de l'an	1 jan	1 jan	1 jan
Lundi de Pâques	9 avril	1 avril	21 avril
Fête du Travail	1 mai	1 mai	1 mai
8 Mai 1945	8 mai	8 mai	8 mai
Jeudi de l'Ascension	17 mai	9 mai	29 mai
Lundi de Pentecôte	28 mai	20 mai	9 juin
Fête Nationale	14 juillet	14 juillet	14 juillet
Assomption	15 août	15 août	15 août
La Toussaint	1 nov	1 nov	1 nov
Armistice	11 nov	11 nov	11 nov
Noël	25 déc	25 déc	25 déc

Done

9 Les jours fériés en France

1.3, 3.2

Faites les activités suivantes.

1. Comptez les fêtes civiles.
2. Comptez les fêtes religieuses.
3. Comptez les jours fériés fixes.
4. Choisissez un jour férié et faites des recherches sur Internet; puis, faites une présentation en classe.

Answers

9

1. 5
2. 6
3. 8
4. *Answers will vary.*

Perspectives
Answers will vary.

Critical Thinking

Comparisons

Have students compare the holidays in France with those of the United States. How do they differ? French people are very focused on the month of May because there are more holidays than in other months. It is unofficially called **le mois à trous** (*the month of holes*). If a holiday falls on a Monday, they will have a three-day weekend. Ask the students to look at this year's calendar. Is this a good year for French holidays in May? Which holiday schedule would you prefer?

Expansion

Have your students visit the website for **Éducation Nationale**. They will choose a school zone and examine the school holiday schedule. Have them put each vacation date on a calendar for this academic year. Then ask them to add the holidays as seen on p. 85. How many days a year do French students **not** attend class out of the total number of school days?

RESOURCES

 Workbook 6–8

 Listening Activity 2

 Drill & Practice Games

Structure de la langue

emcl.com
WB 6–8
LA 2
Games

Révision: Interrogative Pronouns  1.2

See if you can write a question for each answer below, using interrogative pronouns.

1. Amélie est la personne qui a invité des amis à dîner.
2. Il y a un bouquet sur la table.
3. Elle a invité M. et Mme Dumont.
4. Amélie a fait la cuisine avec sa fille.
5. Elles se sont servies des recettes de la mère d'Amélie.

If you were unable to come up with some of the questions, then read the grammar summary below to review.

Interrogative pronouns are used to ask for information. The pronoun you use depends on whether you are referring to a person or a thing and on whether the pronoun is the subject, direct object, or object of a preposition.

	Subject	Direct Object	Object of Preposition
People	qui qui est-ce qui	qui (+ inversion) qui est-ce que	qui
Things	qu'est-ce qui	que (+ inversion) qu'est-ce que	quoi

Use **qui**, **qui est-ce qui**, or **qu'est-ce qui** as the subject of the verb.

Qui mange les huîtres? — *Who is eating oysters?*
Qui est-ce qui mange les huîtres? — *Who is eating oysters?*
Qu'est-ce qui est sous le sapin de Noël? — *What's under the Christmas tree?*

Use **qui**, **qui est-ce que**, **que**, or **qu'est-ce que** as the direct object of the verb.

Qui invites-tu? — *Whom are you inviting?*
Qui est-ce que tu invites? — *Whom are you inviting?*
Qu'achètent-ils? — *What are they buying?*
Qu'est-ce qu'ils achètent? — *What are they buying?*

Use **qui** or **quoi** as the object of a preposition.

À qui est-ce que tu téléphones? — *Whom are you calling?*
De quoi as-tu envie comme cadeaux? — *What do you want for presents?*

INTERROGATIVE PRONOUNS:
1. Qui a invité des amis à dîner?
2. Qu'est-ce qu'il y a sur la table?
3. Qui est-ce qu'elle a invité?
4. Avec qui Amélie a-t-elle fait la cuisine?
Avec qui est-ce qu'Amélie a fait la cuisine?
5. De quoi se sont-elles servies?
De quoi est-ce qu'elles se sont servies?

Essential Instruction

1. For your logical-sequential thinkers this chart is self-explanatory. **Qui** and **que**, interrogative pronouns, are used to refer to people and things. Other students will learn better from the examples.
2. For students of different learning styles, try using manipulatives like a Barbie and Ken. Ask the class these questions: **Qui va épouser Ken? Qui est-ce qui va épouser Ken? Qu'est-ce qui se passe aujourd'hui? Qui invitent-ils au mariage? Qui est-ce qu'ils n'invitent pas? Que reçoivent-ils comme cadeaux? Qu'est-ce qu'ils reçoivent comme cadeaux? Avec qui Barbie va-t-il passer son voyage de noces? Avec quoi Ken coupe le gâteau?**

10 Ramadan

1.2, 1.3

Complétez la phrase avec l'expression interrogative convenable.

1. ... fête le Ramadan? Les Musulmans fêtent le Ramadan.
2. ... est-ce qu'on fête le Ramadan? On fête le Ramadan avec sa famille et ses amis.
3. ... les enfants reçoivent? Ils reçoivent des cadeaux et de l'argent.
4. ... les Musulmans aident pendant le Ramadan? Ils aident les gens pauvres.
5. ... on prépare à la fin du Ramadan? On prépare de délicieux gâteaux à la fin du Ramadan.
6. ... il y a dans les gâteaux? Il y a souvent des amandes.
7. ... prépare les gâteaux? Les mères préparent tous les gâteaux, mais les autres membres de la famille les aident.
8. ... est-ce qu'on parle le jour de *l'Aïd-el-Fitr?* On parle du délicieux repas.

11 Le réveillon de Noël chez les Lagarde

1.1, 5.2

Votre ami vous a envoyé des photos du réveillon sur son smartphone. Utilisez une des expressions interrogatives ci-dessous pour poser des questions. Votre partenaire va jouer le rôle de votre ami et vous répondre.

qu'est-ce qui | qui | de quoi | qu'est-ce que | à qui | qui est-ce que

MODÈLE

accueillir les invités
Qui accueille les invités?

1. ranger les manteaux

2. emmener les grands-parents au salon

3. embêter

4. être sur la table

5. servir

6. téléphoner

7. parler

Differentiated Learning

Accelerate/Decelerate

Pair a high-ability student with a lower-ability student to complete **Activités 10** and **11.** Often students have a way of explaining concepts to their peers that are more effective than our charts. In addition, lower-ability students will not be afraid to ask questions of their partners as they might of their teacher.

Multiple Intelligences

Intrapersonal

Ask these students to write questions that use the interrogative pronouns. Collect the questions and distribute them to the other students, who will write a paragraph that answers all the questions. If students are uncomfortable talking about their own lives, they can imagine that the questions address a celebrity or historical figure of their choice.

Answers

1. Qui (est-ce qui)
2. Quand
3. Qu'est-ce que
4. Qui est-ce que
5. Qu'est-ce qu'
6. Qu'est-ce qu'
7. Qui (est-ce qui)
8. De quoi

1. Qui range les manteaux?
2. Qui emmène les grands-parents au salon?
3. Qui embête le chef dans la cuisine?
4. Qu'est-ce qui est sur la table?
5. Qui sert? Qu'est-ce qu'on sert?
6. Qui téléphone?
7. Qui parle?

RESOURCES

Workbook 9–10

Drill & Practice Games

Answers

1. A
2. A
3. B
4. B
5. A
6. B
7. A
8. A

Reference Desk

1. In the Level 2 textbook, students learned the direct object pronouns **me**, **te**, **nous**, and **vous** first (**Unité 5A**), followed by **le**, **la**, **l'**, **les** (**Unité 5B**, where the concept of direct object pronouns in the **passé composé** was also first introduced).
2. You may want to go over the content of the yellow box together as a class as students often need reinforcement with direct object pronouns.

12 Qui et quoi à Noël?

1.1, 1.2

Écoutez les réponses suivantes. Ensuite, choisissez la question correspondante.

1. A. Qu'est-ce que tu vas manger en hors-d'œuvre?
   B. Qui est-ce que tu vas manger en hors-d'œuvre?
2. A. Que va-t-il mettre dans les assiettes?
   B. Qui va-t-il mettre dans les assiettes?
3. A. Qu'est-ce qui va offrir des cadeaux?
   B. Qui est-ce qui va offrir des cadeaux?
4. A. De quoi vas-tu préparer?
   B. Que vas-tu préparer?
5. A. De quoi ta mère va-t-elle avoir besoin?
   B. Qu'est-ce que ta mère va servir?
6. A. Qu'est-ce qui va être invité?
   B. Qui est-ce qu'on va inviter?
7. A. Pour qui vas-tu préparer la bûche de Noël?
   B. De qui vas-tu parler?
8. A. Qui va accueillir ta famille?
   B. Que va accueillir ta famille?

Révision: Direct Object Pronouns: *me, te, le, la, nous, vous, les*

1.2

emcl.com
WB 9–10
Games

Do you remember where to place direct object pronouns in a sentence? Why is there an **–e** on the past participle in the exchange below?

-Marie, tu as bu la limonade?
-Oui, je l'ai bue.

If you weren't able to answer the questions above, then read the grammar summary to review direct object pronouns.

Direct object pronouns answer the question "who" or "what" and replace direct objects. **Le**, **la**, and **les** may refer to either people or things; **me**, **te**, **nous**, and **vous** refer only to people.

	Masculine	Feminine	Before a Vowel Sound
Singular	me te le	me te la	m' t' l'
Plural	nous vous les	nous vous les	nous vous les

DIRECT OBJECT PRONOUNS: Direct object pronouns are placed in front of the verb of which they are the object. In the **passé composé**, the past participle agrees with the preceding direct object, here **la limonade**, so an **–e** has to be added to show that the word is feminine.

Essential Instruction

1. After students listen to each recorded statement using interrogative pronouns, pause the recording and choose the correct answer as a class. Explain why the other choice is wrong.
2. To review direct object pronouns, write some questions on the board and ask for volunteers to say which pronoun is needed in the response. Then discuss placement of the pronouns in the present tense, near future, and **passé composé**.
3. Complete **Activité 13**, calling on students at random. If they have difficulty, use classroom objects as manipulatives to practice the direct object pronouns **le**, **la**, **l'**, and **les**.

These pronouns come right before the verb of which they are the object. The sentence may be affirmative, interrogative, negative, or have an infinitive.

Désolé! Vous **m'**attendez?	*I'm sorry! Are you waiting for me?*
Non, nous ne **t'**attendons pas, mais Camille t'attend.	*No, we aren't waiting for you, but Camille is.*
Les cadeaux? Où **les** mets-tu?	*The presents? Where are you putting them?*
Je vais **les** mettre sous le sapin de Noël.	*I'm going to put them under the Christmas tree.*

In the **passé composé**, the past participle agrees in number and in gender with the preceding direct object pronoun.

Les huîtres? Tu **les** as achetées?	*The oysters? Did you buy them?*
Non, mais le foie gras, je **l'**ai acheté.	*No, but the goose liver pâté, I bought it.*

13 Sandrine met le couvert pour la fête.

Sandrine met la table pour le réveillon de Noël. Utilisez les pronoms d'objet direct et les expressions ***à gauche de, à droite de, entre, sur, au-dessus de,*** *etc. pour dire où elle met chaque chose.*

MODÈLE les assiettes
Elle les met entre les fourchettes et les couteaux.

1. la nappe
2. les fourchettes
3. les cuillers
4. le verre de Diane
5. le couteau d'Éric
6. les serviettes
7. le poivre
8. la tasse de Diane
9. le bol d'Éric

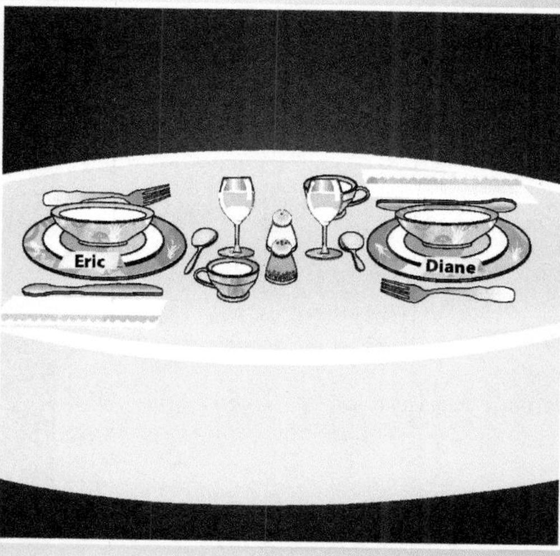

Answers

13

1. la nappe: sur la table
2. les fourchettes: à gauche des assiettes
3. les cuillers: au-dessus des assiettes
4. le verre de Diane: au-dessus de la petite cuiller
5. le couteau d'Éric: à droite de son assiette
6. les serviettes: à droite des couteaux
7. le poivre: sur la table
8. les petites assiettes: sur les grandes assiettes/sous les bols

Reference Desk

1. When there are two verbs in a sentence, the direct object pronoun goes before the second verb, the infinitive.
2. Ask students how you can tell if **l'** is referring to a masculine or feminine subject. By adding an ***e*** on **vu**, we can see that: **Je l'ai vue**. *I saw her.*

Culture

Practices: Information

In some families, the forks and spoons are inverted when placed on the table to show the monogram on the silver. The bread is put on the tablecloth not on a bread plate. Except in certain provinces, like Normandy and Vendée, butter is not served with bread. There is a small object, which varies in size and shape, called a **porte-couteau**, upon which the knife rests between courses. Students may need reminding that the fork goes on the left ("fork" has four letters and so does the word left), and the knife and spoon go on the right ("knife" and "spoon" have five letters and so does the word right). A glass designated for water is a **un verre à eau**. A glass of water is a **verre d'eau**. (See p. 114 for more information.)

Answers

14 *Possible answers:*

1. A: Qui t'attends après les cours?
   B: ...m'attend après les cours.
2. A: Qui comprend bien la chimie?
   B: ...la comprend bien.
3. A: Qui a vu la prof en ville vendredi soir?
   B: ...l'a vue vendredi soir.
4. A: Qui a mis la table hier soir?
   B: ...l'a mise hier soir.
5. A: Qui appelle ton ami le soir?
   B: ...l'appelle le soir.
6. A: Qui sait les noms de tous les états des États-Unis?
   B: ...les sait.
7. A: Qui va chercher des tennis ce weekend?
   B: ...va en chercher.
8. A: Qui nous invite à ta soirée?
   B: Léo et moi t'invitons à ma soirée.
9. A: Qui écoute toujours ta mère?
   B: ...l'écoute toujours.

15

1. Yasmine l'a appelée à neuf heures moins cinq.
2. Yasmine ne vous a pas appelés, mais vous l'avez appelée à huit heures trente-deux et à midi.
3. Yasmine l'a appelé à cinq heures et demie.
4. Yasmine ne l'a pas appelée, mais Manon l'a appelée à sept heures.
5. Yasmine ne nous a pas appelés, mais nous l'avons appelée à neuf heures et à neuf heures huit.
6. Yasmine les a appelés à neuf heures moins cinq et à onze heures onze.
7. Yasmine ne m'a pas appelé(e), mais je l'ai appelée à neuf heures.
8. Yasmine ne l'a pas appelé(e), mais Bruno l'a appelée à midi.

Reference Desk

Before students complete **Activité 15**, make sure they understand the "x" indicates Yasmine called that person and the "T" indicates who made a call to her.

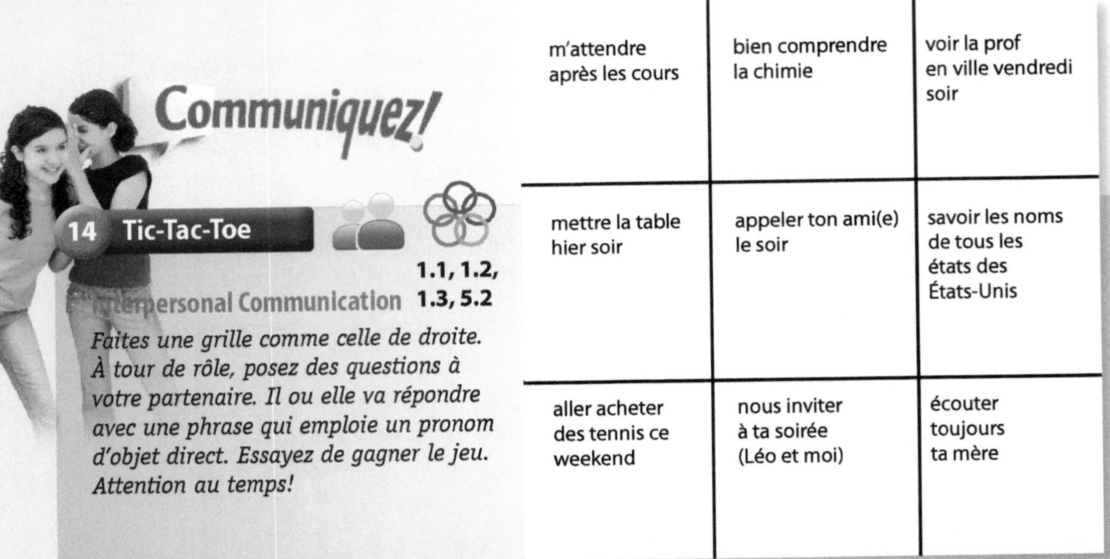

14 Tic-Tac-Toe

1.1, 1.2, 1.3, 5.2

Interpersonal Communication

Faites une grille comme celle de droite. À tour de rôle, posez des questions à votre partenaire. Il ou elle va répondre avec une phrase qui emploie un pronom d'objet direct. Essayez de gagner le jeu. Attention au temps!

m'attendre après les cours	bien comprendre la chimie	voir la prof en ville vendredi soir
mettre la table hier soir	appeler ton ami(e) le soir	savoir les noms de tous les états des États-Unis
aller acheter des tennis ce weekend	nous inviter à ta soirée (Léo et moi)	écouter toujours ta mère

15 Allô!

1.2, 1.3

Dites qui Yasmine a appelé (x) et qui l'a appelée (T).

MODÈLE Noah
Yasmine ne l'a pas appelé, mais Noah l'a appelée à neuf heures huit.

1. Simone
2. Bruno et toi
3. Thomas
4. Manon
5. Noah et moi
6. Khaled et Simone
7. moi
8. Bruno

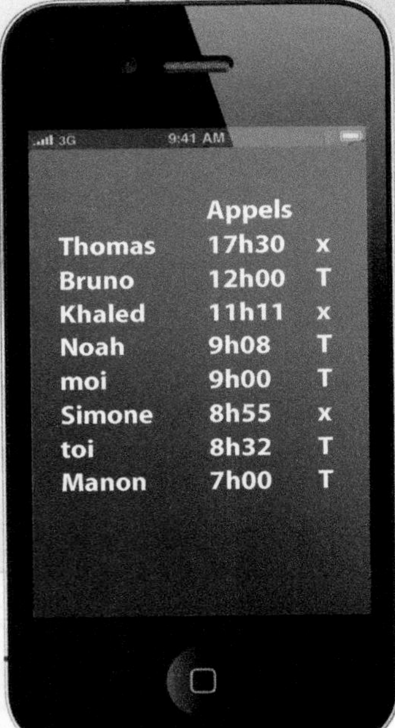

Essential Instruction

1. Play a quick game of Tic-Tac-Toe on the board to review the rules. Have students use the grid to take turns asking questions of their partner. The other student responds with a sentence that uses a direct object pronoun.
2. Do **Activité 15** as a class to make sure students understand the symbols on the phone.
3. You may want students to select an activity of their choice. Students who can follow instructions online may like to do **Activité 16**.

Activité 17 would be fun for students who really enjoy culture. Students with interpersonal skills may enjoy **Activité 18** the best.

À vous la parole

16 Une carte de vœux

 1.3

Presentational Communication

Envoyez une carte de vœux par Internet à un(e) ami(e), un parent, ou à votre prof à l'occasion d'une fête qui approche. Écrivez un message. Envoyez la carte en suivant les instructions du site web.

 **Search words: dromadaire, cybercartes, cartes de vœux virtuelles**

17 L'abécédaire des pays maghrébins

 1.3, 3.2

Presentational Communication

Pour chaque lettre de l'alphabet, écrivez un mot ou une expression sur le thème du Maghreb. Considérez ces thèmes: l'Islam, la cuisine, la géographie, les gens célèbres, les passe-temps. Pour chaque mot ou expression, donnez une définition. Vous pouvez commencer avec les exemples ci-dessous.

A: ***Aïd-el-Fitr:*** fête à la fin du Ramadan quand les musulmans offrent un don aux gens pauvres et font un festin

B: **Bourguiba**, Habib: élu président de la république de la Tunisie en 1957

C: **Couscous:** un plat typique servi avec de la viande et des légumes

18 Viens à la fête!

1.1, 2.1, 5.1, 5.2

Interpersonal Communication

Avec un partenaire, jouez les rôles d'un hôte ou d'une hôtesse qui invite des amis pour célébrer la Saint-Sylvestre.

Differentiated Learning

Accelerate

Ask these students to make up an original Tic-Tac-Toe game to practice direct object pronouns. Pass them out to pairs of students who need more practice.

Decelerate

Before these students do **Activité 14**, tell them there will be two questions in the near future, two in the **passé composé**, and five in the present.

RESOURCES

 **Communicative Activities**

Answers

16 *Activities will vary.*
17 *Activities will vary.*
18 *Activities will vary.*

Reference Desk

The second activity, **L'abécédaire**, might be fun to do in teams as a challenge to see if the students can complete the whole alphabet with a term for each letter.

Blended Instruction

Consider using blended instruction, a combination of in-class learning and computer-mediated instruction or learning opportunities. Ask students to complete activities on the computer, using their cell or smartphone, or other emerging electronic technology. This will allow students to hone their tech skills and become learners that are more independent. Schedule routine Internet and e-book learning in class and in the lab.

Communication

Interpersonal: Paired Practice

Write student names on the board, for example: (1) Théo et Luc (2) Sylvie (3) moi (4) Robert (5) Chloé et Marie-Alix. Students ask their partner if they saw these people at the game, for example, **Est-ce que tu as vu la prof au match?** The other student responds, for example, **Non, je ne l'ai pas vue.** Finally, have each pair take turns writing down their dialogues to check for correct agreement in the **passé composé**.

RESOURCES

Pre-test

***Leçon* Quiz**

Answers

1. /ɥ/
2. /w/
3. /ɥ/
4. /w/
5. /ɥ/
6. /ɥ/

Reference Desk

The symbols used to express sounds come from the International Phonetic Alphabet.

Expansion

To practice the loss of accentuation in a response after a question, have students give an answer to these questions: (1) **Tu pourrais me donner un coup de main? (Te donner un coup de main? Avec plaisir!)** (2) **Tu pourrais me passer le chinois? (Te passer le chinois? Avec plaisir!)** (3) **Tu pourrais ouvrir cette boîte? (Ouvrir cette boîte? Avec plaisir!)**

Prononciation 1.1

Emphasis within a Sentence

- Within a sentence, a clause, or another word group, only the last word is accentuated, with the last vowel slightly longer than the others.

MODÈLES Je suis fatigu**é**.
Je suis fatigu**é** d'attendre mon am**i**.

Une invitation pour le réveillon

*Dans les phrases suivantes, accentuez la dernière syllabe du dernier mot de chaque proposition (*clause*).*

1. Voilà l'invita**tion** que je pro**pose**. (2 exemples)
2. Comme tu **vois**, c'est tout **simple**. (2 exemples)
3. On va l'envo**yer** par Inter**net**. (2 exemples)
4. Je peux en faire une **autr**e pour le me**nu**, si tu **veux**. (3 exemples)
5. Pas du **tout**, la même serait très **bien**, à mon a**vis**. (3 exemples)

Des dialogues dans la cuisine

Vous allez entendre les dialogues suivants deux fois. La deuxième fois, vous entendrez uniquement la question. Répondez.

1. Tu pour**rais** me donner un coup de **main**? — Te donner un coup de **main**? Avec plai**sir**!
2. Tu pour**rais** me passer le poi**vre**? — Te passer le poi**vre**? Avec plai**sir**!
3. Tu pour**rais** ouvrir cette **boîte**? — Ouvrir cette **boîte**? Avec plai**sir**!

The Semi-Consonants /ɥ/ et / w/

- The sound **/w/** appears in **oui**. The sound **/ɥ/** appears in **nuit**.

Louis, demande-lui!

Répétez les phrases en faisant attention aux sons **/w/** *(oui) et* **/ɥ/** *(nuit).*

1. (standard) Louis, et la soirée? Je ne sais pas, moi, demande-lui!
2. (familier) Louis, et la soirée? Je ne sais pas, moi, demande-lui!

Écoutons les sons /ɥ/ et /w/

Écrivez **/w/** *si vous entendez un son comme dans* **oui**, *et* **/ɥ/** *si vous entendez un son comme dans* **nuit**.

Essential Instruction

1. Have students create more examples like the first model. Project the models that are correct, and put students in groups to repeat them.
2. Model #1 in **Activité B** with a student volunteer, then put students in pairs to practice all three sentences.
3. Replay the audio for **Activité D** as often as is needed.
4. Use manipulatives to introduce the vocabulary on p. 93.

Leçon B

Vocabulaire actif

emcl.com
WB 1–3
LA 1–2
Games

Les ustensiles (m.) et les formes (f.)

1.2

Donnez-moi le machin....

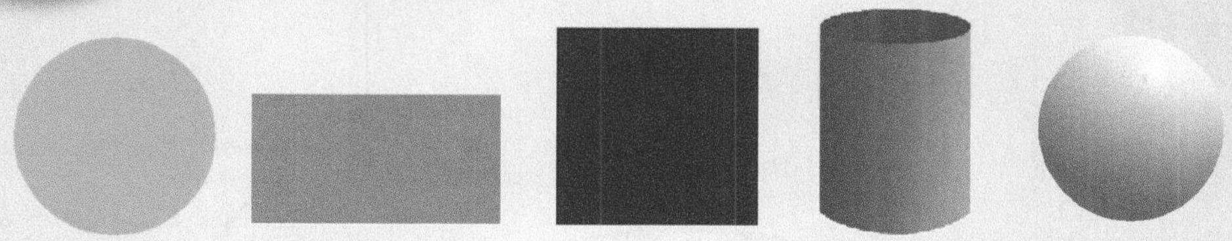

rond

rectangulaire

carré

cylindrique

sphérique

conique

cubique

en forme de poire

C'est [H] comme ça.

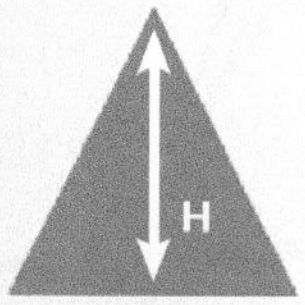

haut

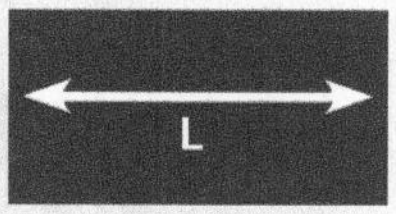

long

large

C'est en....

plastique

métal

tissu

bois

RESOURCES

e-visual 5

Workbook 1–4

Flash Cards

Listening Activities 1–2

Drill & Practice Games

Reference Desk

1. A synonym for **un machin** is **un truc**.
2. You may want to ask students to make a list in French of all the objects they can think of that have each shape. Collect the lists, then ask the class **la forme** of several objects from the list.
3. Encourage students to have fun writing a short dialogue in which they exaggerate the height, length, or width of an object or animal, for example, a fish they caught, a snake they saw, a birdhouse they built, a sandwich they made.
4. Point out that **large** is a false cognate, or **faux ami**, because it means "wide" not "large."

Learning Styles

Kinesthetic Learners

While doing **Activité A**, have students tap the syllables, with the last syllable tapped more emphatically as they say the words.

Special Needs Students

Auditory Impairment

Before listening to **Activité D** as a class, eliminate extraneous noise by closing the door to help hearing-impaired students concentrate and focus on the recorded activity. If possible, supply these students with earphones.

Reference Desk

1. The kitchen items students need to know are illustrated.
2. The verbs to use with these utensils are boxed.
3. Additional kitchen verbs include: **faire cuire** *(to cook)*; **faire chauffer** *(to heat)*; **faire griller** *(to grill)*; **faire bouillir** *(to boil)*; **racler une carotte** *(to peel a carrot)*; **peler une pomme** *(to peel an apple)*; **verser** *(to pour)*; **ajouter** *(to add)*.
4. **Un coup** in **Pour la conversation** is used idiomatically in many French expressions. Here are a few to share with students: **avoir un coup de chance** *(to have a bit of luck)*; **avoir un coup de pompe** *(to feel tired suddenly)*; **boire un coup** *(to have a drink)*; **donner un coup de pied** *(to kick)*; **être dans le coup** *(to be with it)*; **jeter un coup d'œil** *(to glance)*; **sur un coup de tête** *(to do something impulsively)*.

Communication

Interpersonal: Paired Practice

To use the **Pour la conversation** vocabulary, put students in pairs to prepare a dialogue. Student A asks for help with something. Student B accepts; refuses (giving a reason); or hesitates, asking for more information. Together, the pair determines a time and place to meet if Student B ultimately accepts.

Une cuisine bien équipée

emcl.com
WB 4

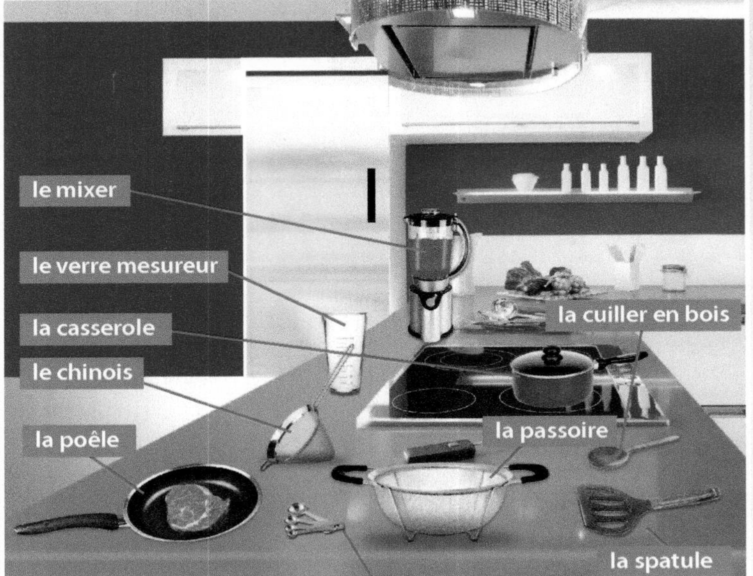

le mixer: Ça sert à **mélanger** les ingrédients.
la cuiller en bois: Ça sert à **remuer** la sauce.
la casserole: Ça sert à **chauffer** la soupe.
la poêle: Ça sert à **cuire** les steaks.
le verre mesureur: Ça sert à **mesurer** l'eau.
le chinois: Ça sert à **filtrer** les herbes.
la spatule: Ça sert à **racler** la sauce.

Pour la conversation   1.1, 1.2, 5.2

How do I ask for help?

› **Tu pourrais me donner un coup de main?**
Could you give me a hand?

How do I accept a request for help?

› **Avec plaisir.**
With pleasure.

How do I refuse a request for help?

› **Je crains que non.**
I'm afraid I can't.

How do I hesitate to a request for help?

› **Ça dépend.**
That depends.

How do I ask someone to pass me something?

› **Tu peux me passer** la passoire?
Can you pass me the strainer?

Et si je voulais dire...? 

une marmite	*cooking pot*
un moule	*baking pan*
un rouleau à pâtisserie	*rolling pin*
griller	*to grill*
refroidir	*to chill*
rôtir	*to roast*

Essential Instruction

1. Have the students listen to the audio recording of the new vocabulary words and expressions, while you hold up each item that you have brought from home.
2. Put all kitchen objects on a table. Have students stand around the table. Ask them to pass the utensils to you: **Ariane, tu peux me passer une cuiller à mesurer?**
3. Have students read **Activité 1** silently at their desks.
4. Students can work on **Activité 2** in pairs.

1 On fait un gâteau.   1.2

Pour son club de scouts, Amélie doit trouver les objets suivants dans la cuisine. Faites une liste des ustensiles. Puis, devinez ce qu'elle va préparer.

Trouvez d'abord six fruits rouges dans votre frigo. Coupez-les. Faites fondre (*melt*) cinq grammes de beurre dans une poêle. Ajoutez les fruits. Faites cuire pendant dix minutes en remuant de temps en temps. Pour faire la pâte (*crust*), mettez 300 grammes de farine (*flour*) dans un machin conique en métal; avec un machin en forme d'une grande tasse, ajoutez 50 grammes de sucre. Ajoutez 150 grammes de beurre. Mettez la vanille dans un objet en forme d'une petite cuiller et ajoutez. Vous aurez besoin d'un objet cylindrique pour étaler (*spread out*) la pâte. Faites chauffer le four. Mettez les fruits dessus la pâte. Faites cuire au four à 180°C pendant 35 minutes.

2 Donnez-moi....  1.1, 5.2

Demandez l'objet illustré.

MODÈLE **Donnez-moi le machin cubique en plastique!**

1. 

2. 

3. 

4. 

5. 

6. 

7. 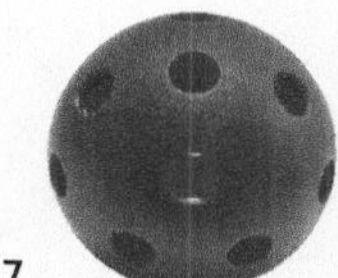

Answers

Ustensiles: une poêle, une cuiller en bois, un chinois, un verre mesureur, une cuiller à mesurer, une passoire; Elle va préparer une tarte.

1. Donnez-moi le machin rectangulaire en plastique!
2. Donnez-moi le machin cylindrique en bois!
3. Donnez-moi le machin rectangulaire en papier!
4. Donnez-moi le machin conique en plastique!
5. Donnez-moi le machin long et rond en bois!
6. Donnez-moi le machin cubique en plastique!
7. Donnez-moi le machin sphérique en plastique!

Expansion

You may want to have students read back each sentence of the text to you in **Activité 1** as you manipulate objects and use gestures to show the cooking process in the text.

Differentiated Learning

Accelerate

Ask these students to find and label images that show their understanding of the **Et si je voulais dire...?** vocabulary words.

Expand

Ask students to think of other objects with these shapes and bring them into class the next day. For additional practice, students can do **Activité 2** again, but using the new objects.

Learning Styles

Auditory/Kinesthetic Learners

Allow these students to come up to the front of the class and select the kitchen objects that you name. You might ask them also to use gestures to show their understanding of the verbs in the box on the vocabulary presentation page, for example, **"Faites chauffer la soupe."**

Answers

3

1. Passe-moi l'objet en coton/soie.
2. Passe-moi l'objet en bois.
3. Passe-moi l'objet en plastique.
4. Passe-moi l'objet en laine.
5. Passe-moi l'objet en soie.
6. Passe-moi l'objet en métal.

1. Ça sert à cuire les steaks. C'est une poêle.
2. Ça sert à cuire la sauce. C'est une casserole.
3. Ça sert à rincer les légumes. C'est une passoire.
4. Ça sert à racler la sauce. C'est une spatule.
5. Ça sert à mesurer les liquides. C'est un verre mesureur.
6. Ça sert à mélanger les ingrédients. C'est un mixeur.

Reference Desk

Students learned **le velours**, **le coton**, **la soie**, and **la laine** in **Unité 6C** on p. 341 of the Level 2 textbook. You may want to review these vocabulary words with students before they complete **Activité 3**.

Game

Qu'est-ce que c'est?

Put a kitchen object or another object students know the name for in a pillowcase. Ask for a student volunteer who will reach in and feel the object. He/she will describe it first, then identify it, for example, **"C'est conique, petit, et en métal. C'est un chinois."** Repeat until you have reviewed all the kitchen utensils introduced in this lesson.

3 Passez-moi l'objet.... 1.1, 5.2

Demandez qu'on vous passe l'objet en décrivant de quoi il est fait.

bois velours métal coton plastique soie laine

MODÈLE  **Passe-moi l'objet en velours.**

1.  2.  3.  4. 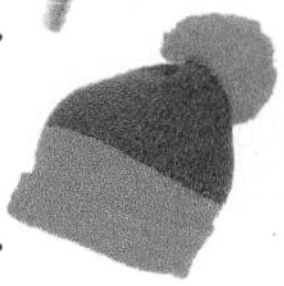 5. 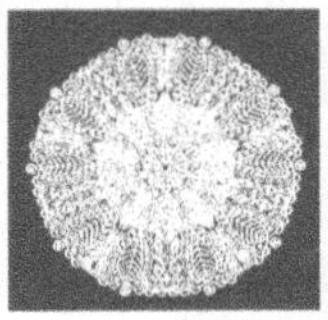 6.

4 Ça sert à quoi? 1.1, 1.2

Dites à quoi l'ustensile sert et comment il s'appelle.

mélanger les ingrédients chauffer la sauce cuire les steaks mesurer les liquides remuer les ingrédients rinser les légumes racler la sauce

MODÈLE **Ça sert à remuer les ingrédients. C'est une cuiller en bois.**

1.  2.  3.  4.  5.  6.

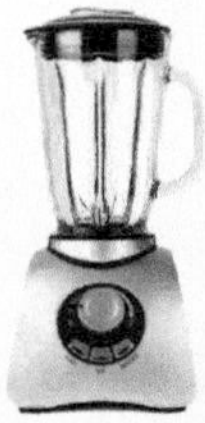

Essential Instruction

1. Do **Activité 3** as a class; bring other objects from home for students to describe. Call on students at random as this activity is quite easy.
2. Ask for student volunteers to do each item of **Activité 4**. If you have brought these objects to class, have the student hold the object while responding in front of the class.
3. Have students listen to the audio recording to complete **Activité 5**. You may want to ask students to shout out the correct answer.
4. If you prefer, call on students to answer the questions in **Activité 6** rather than having student pairs communicate.

5 À quoi ça sert?

1.1, 1.2

Écrivez les numéros 1–6 sur votre papier. Écoutez les descriptions suivantes. Ensuite, choisissez l'objet qui correspond à la définition.

A. le chinois	B. le mixer	C. la spatule
D. la passoire	E. la casserole	F. le verre mesureur

6 Questions personnelles

1.1, 1.2, 5.1

Répondez aux questions.

1. De quels ustensiles est-ce que tu te sers pour préparer ton plat préféré? C'est quoi?
2. Quand tu fais la cuisine, te sers-tu d'un verre mesureur ou est-ce que tu préfères deviner combien d'ingrédients il faut ajouter (*add*)?
3. En quoi est ton verre mesureur, en plastique ou en verre?
4. À qui est-ce que tu donnes un coup de main dans la cuisine en général?
5. Quelle forme a ton clavier? Ton CD? Ton écran de portable?

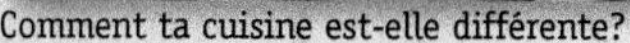

Comment ta cuisine est-elle différente?

Answers

1. D
2. A
3. F
4. C
5. B
6. E

6 *Answers will vary.*

Culture

Products: Information

There is a drinking song that you may or may not want to teach.
Search words: **boire un petit coup**

Boire un petit coup, c'est agréable
Boire un petit coup, c'est doux
Mais il ne faut pas rouler dessous la table
Boire un petit coup, c'est agréable
Boire un petit coup, c'est doux

Differentiated Learning

Expand

Divide the class into three groups. Have students in Group A search online for the menus of the top restaurants in Paris. They will select a restaurant, and choose three **entrées**, three **plats principaux**, and three **desserts**, which they will transfer to a menu that they have decorated. Students in Group B will search online for menus of the top **brasseries** in Paris. They will select a restaurant and choose three **entrées**, three **plats principaux**, and three **desserts**, which they will transfer to a menu that they have decorated. Students in Group C will visit the websites of the three top pastry stores in Paris. On poster board, they will make an advertisement for a shop of their choosing, labeling selected photos of pastries. Have groups display their final products.

Search words: **pierre hermé**, **café lenôtre**, **gérard mulot**

RESOURCES

 Dialogue Video

 Workbook 5

Answers

1. le père de Léo
2. le père de Léo
3. Léo
4. le père de Léo
5. la mère de Léo

Reference Desk

1. Ask students to scan the dialogue to find the French equivalents of these words and expressions: (1.) That smells good; (2.) ruin the sauce; (3.) I'm going then…; (4.) Can you give me a hand?; (5.) Here (it is); (6.) Nothing's ever where it should be; (7.) I put it there to help you proceed.
2. Vocabulary expressions that students may not know in the second dialogue include: **une molette** (*cutting wheel*); **mord(re)** (*cuts into, to cut into*); **un ouvre-boîte** (*can opener*); **le Moyen Âge** (*Middle Ages*).

Culture

Products: Information

Have students work in pairs to figure out what each proverb means: **Trop de cuisiniers gâtent la sauce./Il faut manger pour vivre, et non pas vivre pour manger./Après grand banquet petit pain./L'appétit vient en mangeant.**

Rencontres culturelles

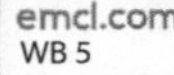

On fait la cuisine.

Le père d'Élodie et de Léo prépare le dîner avec l'aide de son fils.

Léo: Hum… ça sent bon ici!
Père: Bon ben, pas touche… tu vas me faire rater la sauce.
Léo: Ah bon eh bien, je m'en vais alors….
Père: Non, non, reste là… tu pourrais me donner un coup de main?
Léo: Mais avec plaisir.
Père: Tu peux me passer la passoire?
Léo: Tiens!
Père: Non, ce n'est pas ça.
Léo: C'est quoi alors?
Père: Tu sais bien, elle est ronde et conique, un peu plus étroite que celle-là, en métal et haute comme ça. Ça sert à filtrer les herbes.
Léo: Il n'y a rien qui ressemble à ça….
Père: Mais si tu vois bien ce que je veux dire…. Oh, ça s'appelle comment déjà?

(La mère de Léo entre dans la cuisine.)

Mère: Un chinois! Il est devant toi… posé sur la casserole dans laquelle tu vas verser la sauce.
Père: Toujours la même chose: rien n'est jamais à sa place.
Mère: Moi qui l'avais posé là pour t'avancer….

7 On fait la cuisine.

Identifiez la personne.

1. Cette personne fait la cuisine parce qu'on invite des amis pour le réveillon de Noël.
2. Cette personne a besoin d'un chinois.
3. Cette personne a du mal à trouver un ustensile.
4. Cette personne décrit l'ustensile.
5. Cette personne a voulu avancer la préparation du repas.

Extension **Leïla rend un service à son frère.**

Leïla et son frère Khaled sont dans la kitchenette.

Khaled: Tu pourrais me donner un coup de main? Il faut juste que tu ouvres ces boîtes.
Leïla: Oui, comment?
Khaled: Avec un… j'oublie le nom. C'est un machin en métal, avec deux poignées recouvertes de plastique blanc, une petite molette avec des dents qui mord le métal.
Leïla: Il faut acheter un ouvre-boîte électrique pour Maman pour Noël. C'est le Moyen Âge ici!

Extension De quoi est-ce que Khaled a besoin? Comment est la cuisine de sa mère?

Essential Instruction

1. Do #1 in **Reference Desk** with the class.
2. Check comprehension by doing **Activité 7**.
3. Show the filmed dialogue.
4. Have students read the culture reading silently, then ask easy comprehension questions.

Points de départ

Pre AP

emcl.com
WB 6

Question centrale
Qu'ya-t-il d'universel dans les rapports entre les gens?

La cuisine française

Longtemps la cuisine a occupé une part importante du budget des familles françaises et aussi une part importante de leur temps. Mais, vous pouvez voir dans les graphiques ci-dessous que cela a changé. Même si les femmes restent majoritairement celles qui font la cuisine (75%), les hommes participent de plus en plus à la préparation des repas (44%).

La paëlla est un bon plat espagnol à servir à ses invités.

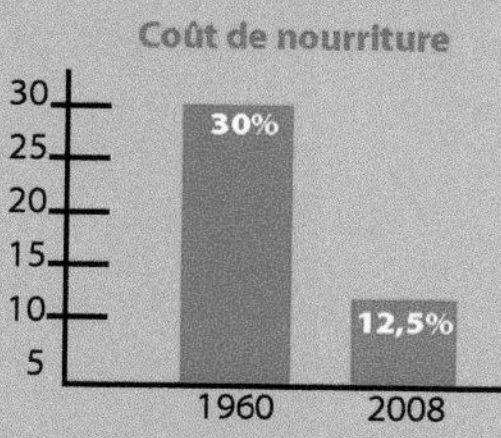

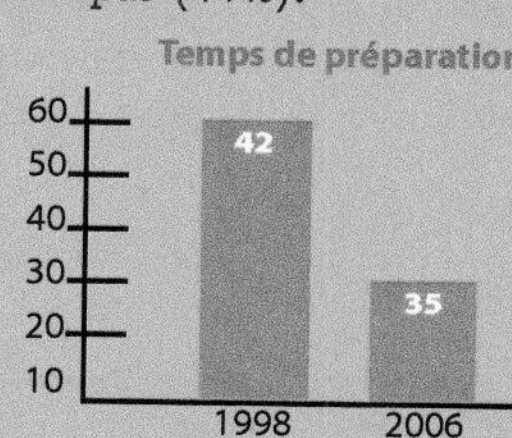

Dans la majorité des familles, la préparation des repas a beaucoup changé. On ne cuisine plus, on "assemble" les ingrédients déjà préparés: des pâtes, des viandes, de la volaille* avec des sauces et des assaisonnements* souvent pré-cuisinées. Et la gastronomie traditionnelle à base de plats mijotés*, ou de plats au four, est en forte diminution, par manque de temps. Désormais*, la cuisine est rapide (steak, poisson grillé, pâtes) et plus diététique (légumes cuits à la vapeur*, salades composées sucrées-salées, salades de fruits au lieu des desserts traditionnels).

La cuisine du plat unique est aussi de plus en plus populaire: ici ce sont les influences italienne (la pizza), espagnole (la paëlla), maghrébine (couscous), et asiatique (cuisine au wok) qui ont modifié les habitudes gastronomiques des Français.

Ce qui domine dans la pratique gastronomique des Français, c'est une grande liberté: on mélange des ingrédients d'origines différentes, on détourne* les techniques de cuisson venues d'ailleurs, on associe des genres culinaires variés.

Search words: recettes, faire les courses en ligne, cuisine française

volaille *poultry;* **assaisonnements** *seasonings;* **mijotés** *simmered;* **Désormais** *From now on;* **cuits à la vapeur** *steamed;* **détourne** *diverts*

Mots-clé

Cuisine vient du bas-latin: *cocina*, 1155. Dès son origine, il a le sens du lieu où l'on cuisine et l'art de cuisiner. Il désigne surtout un espace spécifique dans les milieux nobles et bourgeois; il est inconnu du monde paysan et ouvrier jusqu'à la fin du XIXème siècle.

COMPARAISONS

Dans votre famille, est-ce que vous "assemblez" les ingrédients la plupart du temps ou est-ce que vous prenez le temps de cuisiner? Qu'est-ce que vous mangez qui n'est pas considéré "américain"?

4.2

RESOURCES

Workbook 6

Reference Desk

1. The eating habits of the French have changed radically in the last twenty years. McDonalds, called **Macdo**, has 1,200 restaurants in France.
2. The supermarket chain **Carrefour** sells fresh and frozen food, paper goods, clothing, makeup, in short, everything you would find in an American large grocery store chain. The supermarkets are not open on Sunday with a few exceptions such as the three Sundays preceding Christmas.
3. Outside markets are very popular on the weekends. However, despite changes to traditional shopping imposed by households with two working partners short on time, every day you hear **"Il faut aller chercher du pain chez le boulanger."**

Communication

Interpersonal: Paired Practice

Ask students to find out from their parents or guardians the percentage of the household budget that is spent on food and the time taken by the cook in the family to prepare meals during the week. The next day, ask students to interview ten classmates to get this information. Have them tabulate the results and make a graph to show comparable U.S. results to the French graphs.

Critical Thinking

Comparisons

Have students compare a French fast-food restaurant with an American equivalent. Some ideas: **Flunch**, **Pizza del Arte**, **Brioche Dorée**, **Planétalis**, **Pomme de Pain**, **Restaumarché**.

Answers

8 *Activities will vary.*

Perspectives
Answers will vary.

Pour la formation (*professional preparation*) culinaire, une destination prestigieuse est **Le Cordon Bleu**, avec ses 30 écoles à travers (*throughout*) le monde. Son but est de partager et répandre (*to spread*) la culture et l'art de vivre à la française qui remontent (*dates back*) au moyen âge. Ses enseignants sont des chefs de la gastronomie de niveau international. Les étudiants acquièrent (*acquire*) des connaissances théoriques et une expérience pratique. Une fois nommés chefs, ils travaillent dans les meilleurs restaurants et hôtels du pays et du monde.

Les apprentis chefs du Cordon Bleu apprennent à faire de la haute cuisine.

 **Search words: cordon bleu paris**

 **1.2, 2.1, 5.1**

8 Activités culturelles

 **1.3, 2.1,2.2, 3.2**

Faites les activités suivantes.

1. Écrivez un paragraphe dans lequel vous expliquez les deux graphiques.
2. Voici ce qui caractérise aujourd'hui la cuisine française; illustrez chaque phrase par un exemple de repas.
   - On ne cuisine plus, on assemble.
   - On fait une cuisine à base de cuisson rapide.
   - On fait une cuisine avec un plat unique.
   - On mélange les ingrédients d'origine géographique différentes.
3. Faites une carte qui montre où se trouvent les 30 écoles Cordon Bleu.
4. Écrivez un dialogue qui emploie une expression du dico gastronomique. Vous devriez montrer que vous comprenez le sens de l'expression.

Perspectives

"La cuisine est devenue ludique, mais elle est aussi une pratique multiculturelle et traduit un esprit d'accueil et d'ouverture." Pourquoi ce chef est-il pour les changements récents de la cuisine française?

Mon dico gastronomique

Il a mangé du lion. *Il a une énergie incroyable.*
Il s'est mis à table. *Il a avoué.*
Je ne suis pas dans mon assiette. *Je ne me sens pas bien.*
Ne me raconte pas de salades. *N'essaie pas de m'embrouiller avec des mensonges.*

Essential Instruction

1. Ask students to read silently the text in the **Produits** box about **Le Cordon Bleu.**
2. Using the computer, on the **Le Cordon Bleu** website, have students decide, if given a scholarship, what diploma they would want to earn, and where in the world they would choose to study.
3. Have students choose a cultural activity to do in **Activité 8** based on their interest.
4. Divide the class into three groups. Each one is responsible for presenting one of the main paragraphs in the **Du côté des médias** reading.
5. For a bit of fun, show a clip from *Julie and Julia* where Julia Child attempts to learn French cooking.
   Search words: meryl streep, new julie & julia clip, cooking class
6. Do **Activité 9** as a class.

Du côté des médias

Lisez l'article du site du Cordon Bleu à Paris.

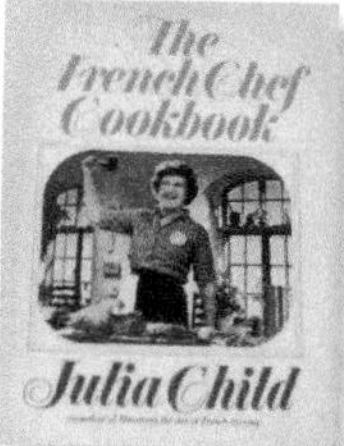

Le Cordon Bleu est fier de vous annoncer la sortie en France du film *Julie & Julia* inspiré de l'ouvrage du même nom.

Le livre, qui était à l'origine un blog, retrace l'histoire de Julie Powell, secrétaire trentenaire, qui décide de prendre une année sabbatique pour réaliser en 365 jours les 524 recettes du livre *Mastering the Art of French Cooking* de la célèbre chef américaine Julia Child, diplômée de l'école Le Cordon Bleu Paris en 1951.

Julia Child a été l'une des premières femmes à mettre en valeur les techniques culinaires françaises enseignées à l'école Le Cordon Bleu Paris auprès du grand public américain par le biais d'émissions de télévision et de nombreux ouvrages. Julia Child a reçu la Légion d'Honneur en 2000 et la Médaille Présidentielle de la Liberté en 2003. Le projet de Julie Powell présente Julia Child comme un modèle à suivre pour les nouvelles générations de chefs et d'amateurs culinaires enthousiastes.

Devant le succès rencontré par le livre *Julie & Julia*, Columbia Pictures a produit le film avec en tête d'affiche, Meryl Streep dans le rôle de Julia Child, Amy Adams dans le rôle de Julie Powell et Stanley Tucci dans le rôle de Paul Child. Le succès du film aux États-Unis a permis au livre de Julia Child, *Mastering the Art of French Cooking,* de devenir un best-seller près de 50 ans après sa parution originale.

9 Le Cordon Bleu présente *Julie et Julia.*

*Indiquez si chaque phrase est vraie (**V**) ou fausse (**F**). Corrigez les phrases fausses.*

1. *Julie & Julia* est d'abord un blogue, puis un livre, finalement un film.
2. Le but de Julie est de préparer 250 recettes du Cordon Bleu.
3. Julia Child est connue seulement pour les recettes de ses livres.
4. Amy Adams joue le rôle de Julia Child dans le film.
5. *Mastering the Art of French Cooking* est devenu un best-seller après la sortie du film.

Answers

1. V
2. F; 524 recettes
3. F; Julia Child est connue pour ses émissions de télévision et pour avoir reçu des prix.
4. F; Meryl Streep joue le rôle de Julia Child.
5. V

Reference Desk

Julia Child's TV show "The French Chef," along with her opus *Mastering the Art of French Cooking*, are credited with changing the way Americans relate to food. During her heyday, 96 U.S. stations aired her TV show. She was awarded the prestigious Peabody Award in 1964 and an Emmy Award in 1966; in the 1970s and 1980s she made frequent appearances on "Good Morning America." Not everyone was a fan of Julia Child. Critics complained that she did not wash her hands enough and put too much fat in her dishes. One letter said, "You are quite a revolting chef, the way you snap bones and play with raw meats." Julia Child would have turned 100 in 2012. Her original entire kitchen, where her TV show was filmed, is now located at the Smithsonian in Washington, D.C.

Culture

Products: Activity

Students who like to cook can make Julia Child's recipe for the French baguette or onion soup for all to taste. It took almost a year "and 284 pounds of flour" for Julia Child to develop the master bread recipe made with American ingredients. These recipes are available online.

Differentiated Learning

Decelerate

Show an excerpt from the movie *Julie and Julia* or a segment of Julia Child's TV show to help these students understand the realia reading.

Learning Styles

Auditory Learners

These students may like to participate in a Julia Child sound-alike contest. Film these students, and allow their classmates to vote on the best interpretation of her voice and cooking style.

RESOURCES

 Workbook 7–9

 Drill & Practice Games

Answers

1. Elle lui demande si elle est libre pour le réveillon de Noël.
2. Il propose de leur dire de venir chez eux.
3. Elle lui offre de faire les toasts.
4. Léo lui donne un coup de main.
5. Oui, il lui ressemble un peu.
6. La mère de Léo lui montre où il se trouve.

Reference Desk

While **lui** means "to him" or "to her," and **leur** means "to them," in a sentence like **Je lui fais un gateau** it means "for him/her." Indirect object pronouns are often used with verbs of communication, such as **proposer à lire à**, **écrire à**, **téléphoner à**, **dire à**, **parler à**. Sometimes the *to* is implied: **Je lui ai dit la vérité**, "I told (to) her the truth."

Structure de la langue

emcl.com
WB 7–9
Games

Révision: Indirect Object Pronouns: *me, te, lui, nous, vous, leur*

1.2

Do you remember how indirect object pronouns different from direct object pronouns? Are they placed differently too? What are some verbs that take indirect object pronouns?

If you can't answer the questions above, then read the grammar summary below to review.

	Masculine or Feminine	Before a Vowel Sound
Singular	me te lui	m' t' lui
Plural	nous vous leur	nous vous leur

These pronouns come right before the verb of which they are the object. The sentence may be affirmative, interrogative, negative, or have an infinitive.

Tu peux **me** donner un coup de main? Non, je ne **te** donnerai pas un coup de main.	*Can you give me a hand?* *No, I won't give you a hand.*
Vous offre-t-il un cadeau? Oui, il **nous** offre des machins en bois.	*Is he offering you a gift?* *Yes, he is offering us some things made of wood.*

Unlike direct objects, indirect objects do not agree in number and gender with the past participle in the **passé composé**.

Laure et Lise? Tu **leur** as téléphoné? Lise, oui. Je **lui** ai téléphoné.	*Laure and Lise? Did you phone them?* *Lise, yes. I phoned her.*

10 Invitation et préparatifs

  1.3

*Répondez aux questions sur les deux premiers dialogues en utilisant **lui** ou **leur**.*

1. Pourquoi est-ce que la mère d'Élodie et de Léo téléphone à Amélie Martin?
2. Qu'est-ce que le père propose de dire aux Martins?
3. Qu'est-ce qu'Amélie offre à son amie?
4. Qui donne un coup de main à son père dans la cuisine?
5. Est-ce que le machin que le père cherche ressemble à une passoire?
6. Qui montre au père où se trouve le chinois?

INDIRECT OBJECT PRONOUNS: Indirect object pronouns are saying "to me," "to you," "to her," for example. No, like direct object pronouns, indirect object pronouns are also placed before the verb of which they are the object. Some verbs that take indirect object pronouns include **donner**, **parler**, **montrer**, **téléphoner**, **ressembler à**.

Essential Instruction

1. Before the students write out their answers for **Activité 10**, ask them to find the expressions beginning with **à** or **aux** which will be replaced by **lui** or **leur.** You may want them to write a paragraph using the answers to the questions. Remind students to add a title to their paragraph.
2. Review the kitchen utensils using the e-visuals.
3. You may want students to do **Activité 11** orally first, then in writing.

11 Les cadeaux de mariage

1.3

L'année dernière beaucoup d'amis et de couples qu'Isabelle connaît se sont mariés. Voici la liste des cadeaux qu'elle leur a offert. Dites ce qu'elle a offert à chaque personne ou couple.

MODÈLE

Sabrina et Édouard
Isabelle leur a offert une passoire et un chinois.

1. Olivier
2. Fred et Julie 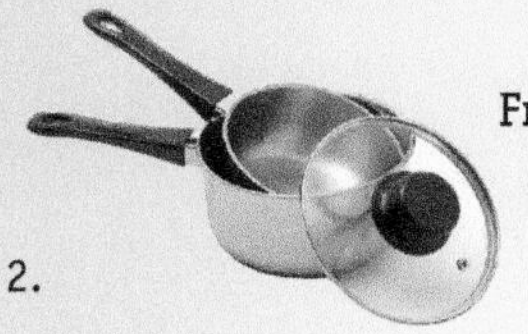
3. Bruno et toi 
4. Assia 
5. Djamel et Leïla 
6. Mamadou et Lamina 
7. Éric et moi 
8. toi 
9. Chloé 
10. moi 
11. Jamila et Théo 
12. Abdel-Cader 

Answers

1. Olivier leur a offert un bol en verre.
2. Fred et Julie leur ont offert des casseroles.
3. Bruno et toi leur avez offert des cuillers en bois.
4. Assia leur a offert deux verres mesureurs.
5. Djamel et Leïla leur ont offert des poêles.
6. Mamadou et Lamina leur ont offert des tasses.
7. Éric et moi leur avons offert des serviettes.
8. Tu leur as offert un mixer.
9. Chloé leur a offert des fourchettes et des couteaux.
10. Je leur ai offert des assiettes.
11. Jamila et Théo leur ont offert une spatule.
12. Abdel-Cader leur a offert des verres.

Reference Desk

As in the United States, French couples register wedding gifts they would like to receive by creating **une liste de mariage**, but this is a relatively new phenomenon. You may want students to do the culture activity below.

Culture

Products: Activity
Have students imagine they and their friends are 28 years old and couples are starting to marry. Have them find appropriate wedding gifts for five friends and make a list of what they would buy and what each gift would cost.
Search words: **fête du mariage galeries lafayette le catalogue cadeau, printemps maison, printemps chambre, printemps salon, printemps cuisine**

Differentiated Learning

Expand
Have students extend their responses in **Activité 11** with **parce que**, giving a reason why the gift will be appreciated. Example: **Isabelle leur a offert une passoire et un chinois parce qu'ils adorent faire des pâtes.**

Accelerate
Ask these students also to do **Activité 11** in the present. Remind students that **offrir** is conjugated like **parler**.

RESOURCES

 **Workbook 10–11**

 **Drill & Practice Games**

Answers

12

1. lui
2. leur
3. vous
4. te
5. m'
6. nous

Reference Desk

In the activity **Les fêtes**, the first two sentences follow the pattern from the previous exercises. The students will look for **à** + person and replace with **lui** or **leur**. For the rest of the sentences, the students have to search for the clues that indicate the pronoun replacement. **Tu *nous* montres...** leads to **Je *vous* montre...**, for example. Before asking the students to complete this activity, do a few sample replacements of pronouns other than **lui** and **leur** to assure their success.

12 Les fêtes

 1.1, 1.2

Complétez chaque dialogue avec un pronom indirect.

1. -Qu'est-ce que tu vas offrir à ta mère pour la Fête des mères?
   -Je vais... offrir un foulard en soie.
2. -Vous allez remercier vos grands-parents pour vos cadeaux de Noël?
   -Nous... avons déjà écrit.
3. -Tu nous montres tes photos de Noël?
   -Non, je ne... montre pas mes photos de Noël.
4. -C'est mon anniversaire dimanche.
   -Je... dis "Bon anniversaire" alors.
5. -Qu'est-ce que ton père t'a envoyé de Québec pour ta fête?
   -Il... a envoyé un CD québécois et un blouson en cuir.
6. -Vous allez... téléphoner pour nous dire quand aura lieu votre soirée?
   -Je peux vous dire maintenant même que c'est le 14 février.

Révision: *C'est* vs. *il/elle est*

 1.2

emcl.com
WB 10–11
Games

Which expression above do you use with a proper or modified noun? Which one do you use with an adjective or stress pronoun?

If you can't answer the questions above, then read the grammar summary below to review.

Both **c'est** and **il/elle est** can mean "it is" as well as "he/she is." The expression that you use depends on what follows the verb **être**.

C'est Kenji Tanaka.
C'est un ado.
Il est japonais.
C'est un élève diligent?
Oui, c'est lui!

C'EST vs IL/ELLE EST: C'est takes both a proper or modified noun. **Il/Elle est...** is followed by an adjective or stress pronoun.

Essential Instruction

1. Complete **Activité 12** as a class.
2. The rule is very straightforward for **c'est** vs. **il/elle est**; still, students have difficulty internalizing it. To practice the concept, do a chain exercise. Put students in small groups. In each group, the first student introduces a teen: **C'est Marie. Elle est grande et sympa.** Marie will respond, **C'est moi?** The first person will respond, **Oui, c'est toi.** Then Marie will introduce a student using the same pattern, but different adjectives, until everyone in the group has had a turn. This activity also works as a whole-class activity.
3. Play the audio recording for **Activité 13** and discuss any errors students make.
4. Students can do **Activité 14** in pairs.

C'est....		
+ proper noun + modified noun + stress pronoun + adjective referring to previous idea	**C'est** Christiane Rochefort? **C'est** un écrivain français. Oui, **c'est** elle. Et son roman, **ce n'est pas** difficile.	*Is it Christiane Rochefort?* *She's a French writer.* *Yes, it is she.* *And her novel, it isn't difficult.*
Il/Elle est....		
+ adjective + profession + nationality + previously mentioned person or thing	**Il n'est pas** bon marché. **Elle est** metteur en scène. **Il est** sénégalais. Où est le magasin? **Il est** là-bas.	*It isn't cheap.* *She is a director.* *He is Senegalese.* *Where is the store? It is over there.*
Il est....		
+ main idea of a sentence	**Il est** nécessaire d'étudier pour le bac.	*It is necessary to study for the bac.*

13 C'est qui?

1.1

Écrivez les numéros 1–6 sur votre papier. Écoutez les descriptions. Puis, choisissez la personne décrite.

A. Kristen Stewart
B. Hillary Rodham Clinton
C. Dany Boon
D. Donald Trump
E. Claude Monet
F. Natasha St-Pier

14 Des Francophones célèbres

1.1

*Choisissez **C'**, **Il**, ou **Elle** pour compléter les descriptions. Finalement, devinez à qui correspond chaque description en choisissant un nom de la liste.*

Natasha St-Pier   Toulouse-Lautrec   Audrey Tautou   Tahar Ben Jelloun   Marie-Antoinette   Jeanne d'Arc

1. ... est une actrice. ... est française. ... est attachante dans le rôle d'Amélie Poulain, la serveuse de Montmartre.
2. ... est un homme marocain. ... est un écrivain célèbre qui parle du racisme. ... est lui qui a écrit un livre pour sa fille.
3. ... est une chanteuse canadienne. ... est elle qui chante des chansons romantiques. ... est jolie femme.
4. ... est un artiste petit. ... est lui qui habitait à Montmartre. ... est nécessaire de connaître ses affiches des cabarets et des théâtres de son quartier.
5. ... est une jeune femme courageuse. ... est elle qui a combattu contre les Anglais pendant la guerre de Cent ans.
6. ... est une reine de l'histoire de France. ... était une belle femme riche.

Answers

1. D
2. C
3. A
4. E
5. F
6. B

1. C'; Elle; Elle; C'est Audrey Tatou.
2. C'; C'; C'; C'est Tahar Ben Jelloun.
3. C'; C'; C'; C'est Natasha St-Pier.
4. C'; C'; Il; C'est Toulouse-Lautre.
5. C'; C'; C'est Jeanne d'Arc.
6. C'; C'; C'est Marie-Antoinette.

Communication

Interpersonal: Cooperative Groups

Have each student write a description of a celebrity on a notecard. Collect the notecards and distribute several to each group. Each student in the group reads a description and the other students try to guess his/her identity.

Differentiated Learning

Accelerate

Have these students prepare an original dialogue that uses indirect object pronouns, and present it with their partner to the class.

Decelerate

Write all the answers that will be used in **Activité 12** on the board for these students, but out of order.

RESOURCES

Communicative Activities

Answers

All activities will vary.

Reference Desk

Blended Instruction

Consider using blended instruction, a combination of in-class learning and computer-mediated instruction or learning opportunities. Ask students to complete activities on the computer, using their cell or smartphone, or other emerging electronic technology. This will allow students to hone their tech skills and become learners that are more independent. Schedule routine Internet and e-book learning in class and in the lab.

Before putting students in partners to do **Activité 15**, ask them to brainstorm vocabulary that they have learned for the following categories: **cuisine**, **école**, **maison**, **camping**, and **voyage.** Write the vocabulary on the board for students to refer to as they create their **devinettes**.

À vous la parole

Question centrale

Qu'ya-t-il d'universel dans les rapports entre les gens?

15 Devinettes

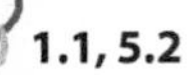

1.1, 5.2

Interpersonal Communication

À tour de rôle avec votre partenaire, pensez à un objet, par exemple, quelque chose qu'on a typiquement dans la cuisine, à l'école, ou dans votre chambre. Donnez des indices à votre partenaire, mais seulement un à la fois. Si votre partenaire devine après avoir reçu le premier indice, il ou elle marque trois points; après le deuxième indice, il ou elle marque deux points; après le troisième indice, il ou elle marque un point. Le premier à marquer dix points gagne. Suivez le modèle.

MODÈLE

Vous:	Je pense à un objet dans la cuisine. Il est long comme ça.
Partenaire:	C'est une casserole?
Vous:	Non. C'est un objet en métal.
Partenaire:	C'est un mixer?
Vous:	Non. Ça sert à faire cuire les steaks.
Partenaire:	C'est une poêle?
Vous:	Oui. Tu marques un point.

16 J'enrichis mon vocabulaire.

Il y a beaucoup d'expressions françaises dans le dictionnaire anglais. Certaines sont utilisées dans le contexte de la cuisine et de la restauration. Faites huit phrases en anglais qui utilisent des mots de la liste ci-dessous. Vous devez montrer que vous comprenez bien le sens du mot ou de l'expression.

Pas acceptable: I ordered à la carte.
Acceptable: I paid more ordering à la carte—first, a plate of snails for 12 euros, then a spinach soufflé that cost 15.

à la carte	crème de la crème	au gratin
à votre santé	hors-d'œuvre	haute cuisine
charcuterie *(food, not place)*	entremets	chef
connoisseur	gourmand	maître d'hôtel
cordon bleu	gourmet	RSVP

1.2, 1.3, 5.1

17 Chef du Cordon Bleu

1.3, 5.1

Presentational Communication

D'abord, trouvez une recette simple en ligne. Ça peut être une recette française, martiniquaise, maghrébine, etc. Vous allez filmer votre préparation comme pour une émission de cuisine. Montrez les ingrédients à vos spectateurs, puis chaque étape de la préparation. Montrez votre vidéo à la classe. Apportez votre plat en classe pour vos camarades de classe.

Search words: recettes + nationalité, par exemple, recettes marocaines

Essential Instruction

1. Have the entire class do **Activité 15** in pairs.
2. Ask students to choose **Activité 16** or **17**.
3. Give an example of circumlocution in English before students read the paragraph in **Stratégie communicative.**
4. Have students complete **Activités 18** and **19** in pairs.

Stratégie communicative 

Using Circumlocution

Vous voulez dire quelque chose en français mais vous ne connaissez pas le mot exact. La meilleure solution est de définir le mot en faisant des phrases avec des mots que vous connaissez déjà. Cette technique s'appelle la circonlocution; elle vient de deux mots latins et signifie "parler autour". Il est important de pratiquer la circonlocution lorsque nous apprenons une langue étrangère. Elle vous permet d'enrichir vos conversations en français. Voici un petit truc très utile pour parler d'un object dont vous ne connaissez pas le nom; identifiez sa forme, de quoi il est fait, et quand et où il est utilisé, par exemple: **S'il vous plaît, je cherche un objet conique en métal pour la cuisine qui sert à filtrer les herbes. (un chinois)**

18 Vous pouvez m'aider? 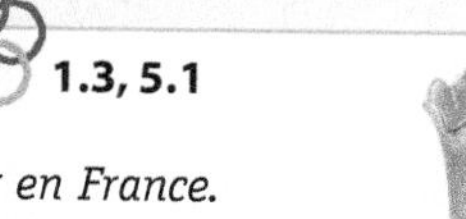 1.3, 5.1

Imaginez que vous venez de vous installer en France. Vous avez besoin de beaucoup de choses pour votre nouvel appartement. Le problème c'est que vous ne connaissez pas le nom de tous ces objects. Essayez de décrire les objets ci-dessous selon le modèle. Utilisez le vocabulaire de la Leçon B.

MODÈLE

(un porte-stylos)

C'est un objet cylindrique en métal. Ça sert à ranger les stylos.

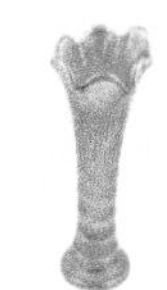
1. (un vase)

2. (une louche)

3. (un entonnoir)

4. (une boîte à mouchoirs)

5. (un grille-pain)

6. (un couvercle)

19 Devinez!  1.1, 2.1, 5.1, 5.2

*Utilisez des gestes (**Il est haut/long/large comme ça.**) pour commencer un jeu avec votre partenaire. Votre partenaire doit identifier l'objet dont vous faites la description. S'il ou elle ne peut pas le deviner tout de suite, donnez plus de détails, par exemple, **On s'en sert à l'école.** Vous pouvez également préciser sa forme et en quoi il est fait. Voici quelques suggestions:*

une trousse | une calculatrice | un sac à dos | une raquette de tennis | un gant de toilette

MODÈLE **C'est un objet rond ou carré que l'on porte au bras gauche en général. Il (une montre) indique l'heure. Il permet de ne pas être en retard.**

Answers

1. C'est un objet haut en verre. Ça sert à mettre des fleurs.
2. C'est un objet long en métal. Ça sert à servir la soupe.
3. C'est un objet cylindrique en métal. Ça sert à filtrer le lait.
4. C'est un objet rectangulaire en bois. Ça sert à mettre des mouchoirs en papier.
5. C'est un objet rectangulaire en plastique. Ça sert à préparer des toasts.
6. C'est un objet rond en terre. Ça sert à couvrir les casseroles.

19 *Answers will vary.*

Reference Desk

1. Here is some useful vocabulary for students to learn/review before completing **Activité 18: un récipient** (*container*); **un appareil** (*appliance*); **un ustensil** (*utensil*); **en tissu** (*made of fabric*). You may want students to add the location (**dans le salon**, **garage**) where the object is generally used.
2. Challenge each student to think of additional objects to describe to expand **Activité 18.**

Game

L'objet mystérieux

Tape a secret vocabulary word on the back of each student. Students will walk around the room asking questions about the secret word, trying to guess what it is. **L'objet est grand ou petit? Il est rond? On s'en sert dans la cuisine?**

Differentiated Learning

Adapt

Write out descriptions of other objects, and have students identify them in writing. They may need to use their French-English dictionary.

Special Needs Students

Linguistically Challenged/Behavior Problems/ Speech Impairment

These students would benefit from working in a group with you to complete **Activité 19.**

RESOURCES

 **e-visual 6**

 **Workbook 1–4**

 **Flash Cards**

 **Listening Activities 1–2**

 **Drill & Practice Games**

Reference Desk

1. Put the following terms on the board: **le socialisme**, **l'entraîneur**, **réaliser**, **champion**, **la candidature.** Ask students what expressions these new words are related to, whether they're nouns or verbs, and to guess what they might mean. For students interested in increasing their vocabulary, one strategy is to learn other words related to a new vocabulary word.
2. A lot of American citizens might bristle at the word **socialiste**, but in France and Europe socialism is an important political option.
3. Explain why **réaliser** is a **faux ami**.

Communication

Interpersonal: Paired Practice

To practice the expressions in **L'art de la conversation** and **Pour la conversation**, have students work in pairs to prepare a dialogue about topics discussed at their dinner table. Ask students to expand and include many points of view from the various family members.

Culture

Perspectives: Information

High fashion in France has a world-wide reputation, and the French created the term **haute couture**. The fashion houses where this luxurious apparel is created must adhere to strict rules, such as their work must be done by hand, and they must not exceed a certain number of employees.

Leçon C

Vocabulaire actif

emcl.com
WB 1–4
LA 1–2
Games

L'art de la conversation   1.1, 1.2, 5.1

la politique

C'est bientôt **les élections présidentielles.** Les Français vont-ils **voter** pour **le candidat** du **parti politique socialiste** cette année?

les médias

On **passe** le nouveau **hit** de Faudel à la radio.
Ce **blogueur** suit les manifestations à Paris.

la mode

Pour le **prêt-à-porter** femmes, on remarquera la **longueur des jupes** cette saison.
Le **look tradi** sera à la page.

le sport

Sylvain **s'est entraîné** au **club** pour le **championnat d'athlétisme.**
Il a gagné **une médaille.**

le cinéma

On passe une comédie **dramatique** au Gaumont. **Réalisé** par Noémie Lvovsky, le film *Camille redouble* a été **tourné** en France et a reçu deux **récompenses.**

l'économie

À cause de l'**endettement** des pays, le **PNB** de l'Europe a **baissé.**
La hausse du **taux d'inflation réduit la valeur** des **revenus.**

Essential Instruction

1. Introduce the new vocabulary with the e-visuals for this lesson.
2. Tell students they will listen to news on the radio. Play the recording twice with textbooks closed. The third time, play the recording, stopping at specific points to ask students to identify what is being discussed.
3. Have students listen again, this time with their books open. Make sure students understand each bolded word.
4. Have students listen to the three expressions in **Pour la conversation** with their books open. Ask them to respond to the last question.
5. You might have pairs of students read each mini-dialogue in **Activité 1**, then turn to the class to identify the **thème**.

Pour la conversation  

1.1, 5.2

How do I express I can't stop myself from doing something?

> **Je ne peux pas m'empêcher de** penser aux gens qui souffrent dans le monde.
> *I can't help but think about the people who are suffering in the world.*

How do I say that someone is right?

> Élodie **a raison.**
> *Elodie is right.*

How do I ask about dinner table topics?

> Et à votre table, **vous parlez de quoi**?
> *And at your dinner table, what do you talk about?*

Et si je voulais dire...? 

le scrutin, le bulletin	*ballot*
un électeur, une électrice	*voter*
le dirigeant	*leader*
un programme électoral	*political platform*
une crise économique	*economic crisis*
un défilé de mode	*fashion show*
une station de radio	*radio station*

1 Thèmes de conversation  1.1,1.2

Indiquez le thème des conversations suivantes.

la politique   l'économie   la mode   le sport   le cinéma   les médias

1. -C'est une co-production franco-canadienne.
   -De vrais serveurs jouent les rôles principaux, pas des vedettes.
2. -Tu as remarqué la longueur des manteaux cette saison?
   -Oui, ça me fait penser aux années 1950.
3. -Tu suis les manifestations à Paris?
   -Oui, je lis le blogue d'un blogueur qui y participe.
4. -Tes parents soutien le parti socialiste?
   -Oui, ils tendent à le soutienir cette fois-ci.
5. -L'endettement change notre mode de vivre.
   -Le gouvernement va augmenter les impôts (*taxes*), c'est sûr!
6. -Il a gagné ses deux courses (*races*) au championnat de France indoor.
   -Il se prépare pour ça depuis des mois.

En politique européenne, on se rénit au Parlement pour prendre de nouvelles mesures écologiques.

Answers 

1

1. le cinéma
2. la mode
3. les médias
4. la politique
5. l'économie
6. le sport

Reference Desk

Here is some useful supplemental vocabulary about politics: **une campagne électorale** (*political campaign*); **un challenger** (*challenger*); **un movement populaire** (*grassroots movement*); **le/la perdant(e)** (*the loser*); **une urne** (*voting box*).

Critical Thinking

Comparisons

The French are known for their skills in **la polémique**, or argument, practicing it even at the dinner table. Ask students if their families get into heated discussions at the dinner table. What topics are the most controversial?

Game

Dinner Topics

Divide the class into two teams. The first player of the first team picks a card; the cards contain the six topics, or themes, from page 108. The player has 20 seconds to state a sentence that pertains to the topic. If it is accepted by the teacher, the player earns a point for his or her team.

Differentiated Learning

Accelerate

Have students learn the **Et si je voulais dire...?** and supplemental vocabulary from **Reference Desk** to create a radio or television broadcast.

Learning Styles

Visual Learners

Have these students create a campaign poster for a real or imaginary political candidate.

Multiple Intelligences

Visual-Spatial

Ask these students to find clips online about the six topics, or themes: politics, the media, fashion, sport, cinema, and the economy in France. Have them play the clips for the class. While they watch, students write down a theme for each one. You may want to award points for those students who can even grasp some of the details in the clips.

Answers

2

1. inflation
2. endettement
3. candidat
4. voter
5. PNB
6. revenu
7. look
8. prêt-à-porter
9. passe
10. médailles
11. sortie

1. Il a des questions sur la politique et l'économie.
2. Ils sont endettés.
3. Ce qu'est le PNB.
4. Ils participent aux discussions en classe.
5. PNB
6. Si elle peut lui proposer des livres, magazines ou blogues.

2 Complétez!

1.1, 1.2

Complétez les phrases en choisissant un mot ou une expression de la liste.

endettement PNB médailles revenu voter look
prêt-à-porter passe sortie candidat inflation

1. L'... diminue la valeur du dollar ou de l'euro.
2. Quand une personne doit (*owes*) beaucoup d'argent à une banque ou quand un pays doit de l'argent à un ou plusieurs autres pays, ça s'appelle l'....
3. Pour les élections présidentielles américaines, il y généralement un... républicain et démocrate.
4. À l'âge de 18 ans, on peut....
5. La valeur de toute l'activité économique d'un pays s'appelle le....
6. L'argent qu'on gagne (*earn*) quand on travaille s'appelle le....
7. Connais-tu quelqu'un qui a un... BCBG?
8. Dans les défilés de mode (*fashion shows*), les mannequins portent des vêtements haute couture (*high fashion*) et non de....
9. On... le nouveau hit d'Adèle à la radio.
10. Aux Jeux Olympiques, Shaun White a gagné deux... d'or.
11. J'attends la... du film *Tintin*, basé sur la BD belge.

3 La politique et l'économie

1.1, 1.2

Lisez la lettre que Gabriel écrit à sa tante à propos de son cours d'économie, puis répondez aux questions.

Salut Tata!

J'espère que tu pourras m'aider avec mes difficultés au lycée en ce moment parce que tu es forte en politique et en économie. Comment peut-on savoir si l'endettement dans les pays occidentaux en ce moment va causer une crise? Moi, je ne comprends même pas ce qu'est le PNB, ou comment les revenus d'un pays changent la situation globale. Je veux vraiment dire à mon prof: "Vous parlez de quoi, exactement?" Mais certains de mes camarades entrent dans la discussion, alors je me sens vraiment bête. Quels livres ou magazines ou blogues me proposes-tu? Je voudrais mieux comprendre la politique et l'économie, et je dois le faire vite!

Grosses bises à tous,
Gabriel

1. Pourquoi est-ce que Gabriel écrit à sa tante?
2. Qu'est-ce qui se passe dans les pays occidentaux (*Western*) en ce moment?
3. Qu'est-ce que Gabriel ne comprend pas?
4. Quelle est la compréhension des autres élèves?
5. Qu'est-ce que Gabriel demande à sa tante?

Essential Instruction

1. Do **Activités 2** and **3** as a class. Ask students to read the letter silently at their desks.
2. For **Activité 4** have students work in pairs. When finished, each person shares one thing in small groups that he/she can and cannot help doing.
3. After listening to **Activité 5**, make sure students understand any incorrect answers.
4. Have students complete **Activité 6** as written homework for a change. The next day ask for volunteers to answer the questions orally without looking at their homework.

4 Je ne peux pas m'empêcher de....

 1.1, 1.2

Dites que vous pouvez ou que vous ne pouvez pas vous empêcher de faire chaque chose.

MODÈLE manger de la glace
Je ne peux pas m'empêcher de manger de la glace.
ou
Je peux parfois m'empêcher de manger de la glace.

1. manger du chocolat
2. faire du shopping
3. jouer aux jeux vidéo
4. surfer sur Internet
5. envoyer des textos
6. prendre de la pizza
7. regarder des films
8. téléphoner à mes copains

Ma sœur ne peut pas s'empêcher de rater la dinde!

5 De quoi parle-t-on?

  1.1, 1.2

Écrivez les numéros 1–6 sur votre papier. Écoutez les histoires et les descriptions. Ensuite, choisissez la catégorie à laquelle chacune correspond.

A. le cinéma B. la mode C. la politique D. l'économie E. les médias F. le sport

6 Questions personnelles

 1.2, 3.1, 4.2

Répondez aux questions suivantes.

1. Chez toi, on parle de quoi à table? Est-ce qu'il y a certains sujets que tu évites?
2. Est-ce que tu suis la politique intérieure? Et la politique internationale? À ton avis, est-ce que les hommes et femmes politiques ont souvent raison?
3. On passe souvent les chansons de tes musiciens préférés à la radio?
4. As-tu déjà gagné une médaille? Dans quel sport?
5. Es-tu un blogueur ou une blogueuse? Si oui, quels sont tes thèmes?
6. Quels films est-ce qu'on passe au cinéma ce weekend?

Differentiated Learning

Accelerate

Have students listen to a **France Info** broadcast and make a list of the general topics.

Decelerate

Allow slower-paced students to read the scripts as they listen to **Activité 5**.

Answers

1–8. Je peux m'empêcher de... + *infinitif*./Je ne peux pas m'empêcher de... + *infinitif*.

1. C
2. F
3. A
4. D
5. E
6. B

6 *Answers will vary.*

Expansion

To extend **Activité 4**, ask each student to write two new cues. Project the new cues for the pairs to see and use.

RESOURCES

Dialogue Video

Workbook 5

Answers

1. Léo et Élodie
2. Ce n'est pas correct devant les invités.
3. Léo et Élodie
4. Ils étaient aussi idéalistes.
5. le sport et le cinéma

Reference Desk

1. **La politique… ne fait jamais grève** means that politics never ceases or goes on strike.
2. Ask students to give you the verb for **le réveillon.** (**réveillonner**)
3. The forms of **souffrir** in the present tense are: **souffre**, **souffres**, **souffre**, **souffrons**, **souffrez**, **souffrent.** It follows the pattern of **offrir.**
4. **Tuer** is a regular -**er** verb.
5. **Invahi** is the past participle of **invahi** (*to invade*).
6. The expression **en guerre** means "at war."
7. Ask students the name of Tolstoy's opus. (***La guerre et la paix***)

Rencontres culturelles

emcl.com
WB 5

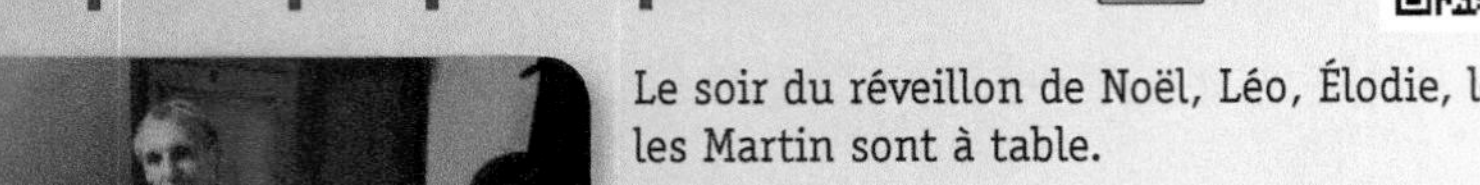

On ne parle pas politique à table!

1.1, 1.2, 3.1, 5.1

Le soir du réveillon de Noël, Léo, Élodie, leurs parents, et les Martin sont à table.

Mère: J'ai déjà dit: on ne parle pas politique à table le jour du réveillon quand même! Pensez à nos invités....

Léo: Mais la politique, maman, elle, ne fait jamais grève.

Élodie: Et pendant que nous réveillonnons, moi je ne peux pas m'empêcher de penser aux gens qui souffrent dans le monde.

Léo: Élodie a raison. Les dictatures tuent, des territoires sont envahis, même les démocraties emprisonnent et usurpent les droits des hommes.

Élodie: Ce qui me donne le plus de soucis, ce sont les sans-abris....

Léo: N'oublie pas les prisonniers politiques et les nations en guerre.

Mère: Oh là là! Oui, c'est vrai que tout le monde n'a pas la chance de se retrouver autour d'un bon repas comme nous, dans la paix. Qu'en penses-tu, mon chéri?

Père: Ah, nos enfants ont récupéré notre idéalisme de jeunesse! Il faut les encourager!

(Il s'adresse aux Martin.)

Et à votre table, vous parlez de quoi?

M. Martin: Plutôt du sport ou du cinéma, mais pas si passionnément!

7 On ne parle pas politique à table!

1.3

Répondez aux questions.

1. Qui veut parler politique à table?
2. Pourquoi est-ce que la mère de Léo et d'Élodie ne veut pas qu'on parle politique à table?
3. Qui parle le plus passionnément?
4. Comment étaient les parents d'Élodie et de Léo quand ils étaient jeunes?
5. Quels sont les sujets de conversation chez les Martin?

Essential Instruction

1. Have student volunteers read the main dialogue aloud; then play the audio, and finally show the video.
2. Ask the class the questions in **Activité 7.**
3. Have three advanced students enact the scene in the **Extension** dialogue for the rest of the class. Students should be able to understand the general topic of conversation. Ask an advanced student to answer the **Extension** question.

Extension **Les médias**   **1.1, 1.2, 2.2, 3.1**

Les Gagnon sont à table pour le dîner.

Papa: Qu'est-ce qu'on entend, c'est la radio ou ton lecteur MP3?
David: C'est une émission qui passe à la radio, sur mon lecteur MP3.
Papa: Ah, la radio à diffusion numérique! On peut dire au revoir aux émissions de qualité!
David: Mais qu'est-ce que tu dis? Au contraire, la qualité de la réception est inouïe, on peut l'écouter à toute heure où qu'on se trouve!
Papa: Tout dépend, la diffusion sur même fréquence empêche l'accès aux petites radios indépendantes. Donc, comme je l'ai dit, la fin des meilleures stations de radio!
Maman: En tout cas, numérique ou non, mangez au lieu de discuter, ça refroidit!

Extension Selon le père de David, quels sont les inconvénients de la diffusion numérique?

1.1, 1.2, 2.2, 3.1

Answers

Extension

Elle ne donne pas accès aux meilleures stations.

Reference Desk

Here are some vocabulary words from the **Extension** conversation that students might not know: **la diffusion numérique** (*digital broadcasting*); **inouï/e** (*incredible, unheard of*); **Ça refroidit!** (*It's getting cold!*).

RESOURCES

Workbook 6–7

TPR

Ask a student to set the table according to the wishes of another student. The student may be directed to set the table correctly or to do so with novel commands. Repeat this process with other students.

Expansion

Have students share the table manners they were taught. Students may especially like to hear this from their classmates from other cultures.

Communication

Interpersonal: Cooperative Groups

Designate a table in the classroom as a dining room table. Have students in groups prepare a short dialogue that highlights one of these concepts from the culture reading: French punctuality, offering the hostess a gift, serving the main dish, place settings, host putting guests at ease, a safe or an unsafe topic of conversation. The rest of the class tries to figure out what culture point is being shown.

Points de départ

emcl.com
WB 6–7

Question centrale

Qu'ya-t-il d'universel dans les rapports entre les gens?

Manières de table

1.2

Quand vous êtes invité à 20h30, vous pouvez arriver dans la demi-heure qui suit l'heure d'invitation. Si vous apportez un petit cadeau, ça peut être des fleurs, du vin, ou des chocolats. Si vous invitez et vous recevez ces cadeaux, les fleurs doivent être mises dans un vase, le vin offert aux invités, les chocolats proposés au moment du café. Si vous recevez un livre ou un autre cadeau, vous devez l'ouvrir et le laisser visible.

On commence toujours à servir par le couvert le plus éloigné*. Dans la tradition française, la lame* du couteau regarde toujours vers l'intérieur. Les couverts qui ne sont pas plats se placent les dents vers le haut pour les fourchettes, et côté bombé* pour les cuillers.

Un beau couvert donne de l'appétit.

La France produit beaucoup de vin pour consommation à l'intérieur et à l'extérieur du pays. Le vin fait partie des repas au quotidien et en particulier lorsqu'il y a des invités. Chaque vin est alors choisi avec attention pour accompagner chaque plat. Il existe plus de 40 verres à vin différents suivant les vins et leur origine.

Le devoir de l'hôte est de mettre à l'aise* ses invités. Les Français adorent débattre*, mais il y a des sujets dont on ne parle pas, comme l'argent. La politique peut enflammer* la soirée, et elle n'est pas toujours soulevée*. La conversation sur le dernier film qu'on a vu le dernier livre qu'on a lu, la musique qu'on écoute, la série télé qu'on regarde, le sport qu'on pratique ou dont on est fan est toujours appréciée. Elle permet d'opposer les jugements. Toute conversation est un affrontement*, un débat d'idées. La France est le pays qui a inventé la polémique*. Il faut savoir aussi que tout ça est un jeu.

Search words: chocolatier paris, fleuriste paris

éloigné *far away;* **lame** *blade;* **bombé** *rounded;* **mettre à l'aise** *make (guests) confortable;* **débattre** *to debate;* **enflammer** *to fuel;* **soulevé(e)** *raised;* **affrontement** *clash;* **polémique** *controversy*

Mots-clé

Manière (de l'ancien adjectif français *manier* (1119), "que l'on fait fonctionner à la main" (1140), mais aussi "habile,"(1155), et "bien dressé" (d'un faucon, vers 1175). Il s'est séparé de *main* pour ne retenir que habile pour désigner la façon d'être, d'agir, et de se comporter. C'est cette acceptation liée au comportement en société sous la forme plurielle (les bonnes et mauvaises manières, 1662) qui est la plus courante.

COMPARAISONS

Quels sont les sujets de conversation chez vous à table quand vous avez des invités? Sont-ils différents des sujets de conversation quotidiens? Y-a-t-il des sujets dont les Américains évitent de parler pendant les repas?

4.2

Essential Instruction

1. After students read **Manières de table**, have them make a list of points to remember regarding being a guest at a French home.
2. Ask students what to do in this situation: **Vous êtes invité(e) chez une famille française. Qu'est-ce que vous offrez?**
3. After they read the **Produits** box, students can research the Paris wine tasting of 1976 (The Judgement of Paris).
4. Call on individual students to read the situations in **Activité 8.** Divide the class into pairs and have each set of pairs draw a number (1–4). This represents the activity they will complete. Pairs can exchange numbers if they wish. One pair in each group presents their project.

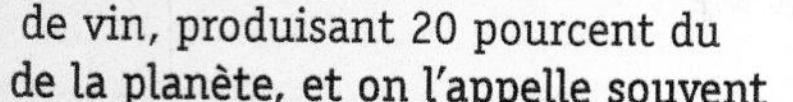

On produit du **vin** en France depuis l'ère de la Grèce antique. La France est le premier producteur mondial de vin, produisant 20 pourcent du vin de la planète, et on l'appelle souvent "le pays du vin." Il y a plus de 3,400 vins en France.

1.2, 2.2

8 Activités culturelles

1.3, 2.2, 4.2

Complétez les activités suivantes.

1. Vous voulez impressionner votre hôte parisien avec une boîte de bons chocolats. Cherchez un bon chocolatier à Paris. Expliquez votre choix et le prix à votre partenaire.
2. Le père de votre correspondant français a invité un collègue à dîner. Sa femme veut le servir d'abord.
3. Faites une liste de sujets que vous pouvez soulever au dîner avec un collègue.
4. Faites la liste des manières de table américaines et comparez-les aux manières françaises avec un organigramme venn.

À discuter

Avec vos copains, vous parlez de quels sujets à table?

Une boîte de chocolats est toujours un bon cadeau à offrir à ses hôtes.

Answers

8 *Activities will vary.*

À discuter
Answers will vary.

Culture

Products: Information
French wines are highly regarded throughout the world. They are, however, in fierce competition with Spanish, Australian, Chilean, and Argentinean wines.

Differentiated Learning

Decelerate
These students may be interested in presenting a dialogue that shows what teens talk about when they dine together, for example, **au fast-food.**

Answers

Du côté des médias
Answers will vary.

Expansion

Have students design a T-shirt with a motto that shows a value important to them.

Du côté des médias

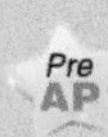

1.2, 1.3, 3.1

Interpretive Communication

Lisez la page d'accueil du site **Judo Club Sorquais**. *Faites quatre phrases pour montrer votre compréhension des valeurs mentionnées ou dessinez un tee-shirt.*

Code moral du judo

Le Judo véhicule des valeurs fondamentales qui s'imbriquent les unes dans les autres pour édifier une formation morale.

Le respect de ce code est la condition première, la base de la pratique du Judo.

L'amitié
C'est le plus pur des sentiments humains.

Le courage
C'est faire ce qui est juste.

L'honneur
C'est être fidèle à la parole donnée.

La modestie
C'est parler de soi-même sans orgueil.

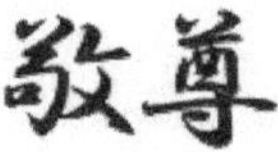

Le respect
Sans respect aucune confiance ne peut naître.

Le contrôle de soi
C'est savoir se taire lorsque monte la colère.

La politesse
C'est le respect d'autrui.

La sincérité
C'est s'exprimer sans déguiser sa pensée.

Essential Instruction

1. Have students who play sports share their values or the values of their team or coach.
2. Ask them to prioritize the values from the realia on a list of one to eight, one being the most important value in their lives to eight being the least.
3. Have students complete **Activité 9**. If they have difficulty connecting with family members who do not live with them, encourage them to interview a teacher or the parent of a friend.
4. Consider doing **Activité 10** as a class if finding a Francophone proves difficult. Local universities, churches, or community centers may have names of people who would volunteer to be interviewed. If a guest cannot visit the class, consider an interview via an Internet video service.

La culture sur place

Question centrale

Qu'ya-t-il d'universel dans les rapports entre les gens?

Les préférences culinaires

Introduction et Interrogations

Dans cette unité vous allez penser à votre expérience personnelle en matière de cuisine et aussi élargir vos connaissances.

9 Première Étape: Réfléchir 1.3, 2.1, 3.2, 5.1

Répondez par écrit aux questions suivantes.

1. Quel est votre repas préféré?
2. Quel est le repas préféré des adultes avec qui vous habitez (vos parents ou vos gardiens)? Y a-t-il des différences entre vos préférences, vos goûts, et les leurs?
3. Parlez avec deux membres de votre famille qui n'habitent pas avec vous: un [...] un de votre âge (comme un cousin) et un plus âgé (comme un grand-parent). Qu'est-ce qu'ils préfèrent manger?

Formulez quelques hypothèses—pourquoi est-ce que ces différences ou similarités existent?

10 Deuxième Étape: Rechercher  1.3, 2.1, 2.2, 3.2, 5.1, 5.2

Interviewer un(e) Francophone, individuellement ou en groupe. Le sujet de votre interview concerne les repas et les générations.

1. Faites une liste de questions à lui poser.
2. Préparez une présentation orale qui récapitule (*summarizes*) votre interview. Comparez les réponses de votre participant avec vos propres préférences vis-à-vis des repas.

11 Faire l'inventaire!  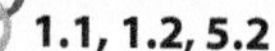 1.1, 1.2, 5.2

Discutez des questions suivantes en classe.

1. Est-ce qu'il y avait des thèmes à travers les différentes présentations? Par exemple?
2. Comment est-ce que les descriptions de la cuisine recueillies lors des interviews individuelles sont-elles similaires ou différentes des descriptions générales de l'unité?
3. Est-ce que vous pensez que les généralisations sont nécessaires pour comprendre une culture? Pourquoi, ou pourquoi pas? Et les expériences individuelles?
4. Est-ce que vous préférez étudier des généralisations ou "vivre la culture"?

Answers

All activities will vary.

Differentiated Learning

Expand

Before assigning **La culture sur place**, review the vocabulary for breakfast, lunch, snack, and dinner to prepare students to answer the questions in **Activité 9**. For **Activité 10,** if the students have no access to a Francophone, they might ask their questions on a French blog. In **Activité 11,** students are asked to decide if it is more valuable to generalize about a culture or to experience it first-hand. This discussion aligns closely with the Essential Question running throughout the unit: whether or not there is a universal thread that links us all together.

RESOURCES

 Workbook 8–9

 Drill & Practice Games

Answers

1. qui
2. qui
3. que
4. que
5. que
6. qui
7. qu'
8. qui
9. qui

Reference Desk

1. Students learned the relative pronouns **qui** and **que** in Level 2, **Unité 7**, p. 381.
2. Students should understand that if something is relative it means that it depends on a context for its meaning. This instruction is true for **qui** and **que** since as relative pronouns what they mean depends on their direct antecedent. Students should look to the dependent clause for clues. If there is no subject in the dependent clause, **qui** must be used. If there is a subject, then **que** is the choice: **L'homme *qui* parle.... L'homme *que* je connais....**

Communication

Interpersonal: Cooperative Groups

Put students into small groups and have each group write sentences about their teachers. The rest of the class tries to identify the teacher. For example, **C'est la prof qui conduit une BMW. Le sport que ce prof préfère est le rugby.**

Structure de la langue

emcl.com WB 8–9 Games

Révision: The Relative Pronouns *qui* and *que* 1.1, 1.2

The relative pronouns **qui** and **que** connect two clauses in a complex sentence. The pronouns **qui** and **que** introduce a dependent clause that describes a preceding person or thing, called the antecedent.

Qui is used as the subject of the dependent clause. The verb that follows **qui** agrees with the antecedent.

J'ai voté pour François Hollande, **qui** était le meilleur candidat, à mon avis.	*I voted for François Hollande, who was the best candidate, in my opinion.*
Le parti politique les Verts, **qui** veut protéger l'environnement, manifeste à Paris.	*The Green political party, which wants to protect the environment, is demonstrating in Paris.*

Que is used as the direct object of the dependent clause.

L'athlète **que** j'admire le plus a gagné une médaille aux Jeux Olympiques.	*The athlete whom I admire the most won a medal in the Olympics.*
Le championnat **qu'**on regarde est aussi à la télé.	*The championship that we are watching is also on TV.*

When the dependent clause is in the **passé composé**, the past participle of the verb agrees in gender and in number with the antecedent of **que**.

Les robes **qu'**on a vu**es** à Paris étaient longues.	*The dresses we saw in Paris were long.*

12 Dans les médias

1.1, 1.2

*Choisissez **qui** ou **que** pour compléter les phrases suivantes.*

1. Les élections présidentielles,... ont eu lieu cette année, ont coûté cher.
2. Le candidat... était socialiste a gagné.
3. Le problème... je vois pour l'Europe, c'est l'endettement.
4. Le PNB de la Chine,... tout le monde regarde, n'a pas baissé.
5. Le look tradi... les mannequins portent cette année est dans tous les magazines de mode.
6. L'athlète... s'est entraîné le plus a gagné le championnat d'athlétisme.
7. La médaille... il a gagné est dans sa chambre.
8. On passe une nouvelle comédie... est une co-production franco-américaine.
9. Le blogueur,... aime bien Audrey Tautou, dit qu'elle est très bien dans ce rôle.

Le président de la compagnie, qui est parti le mois dernier, s'est installé à New York.

Essential Instruction

1. Review **qui** and **que** by writing sentences about students on the board.
2. Ask the students to read each sentence in **Activité 12**, inserting **qui** or **que**. Correct the sentences, explaining in each case why the pronoun was appropriate.
3. Before completing **Activité 13**, do some practice sentence combinations that resemble those they will hear. Put these sentences on the board and discuss why **qui** or **que** is the correct choice.
4. Point out the example of **ce qui** in the dialogue on p. 112, and write on the board: **Ce que je désire, c'est que vous fassiez vos devoirs.** Then review the model examples on p. 119.

13 Qui ou que? Là est la question!   1.1, 1.2

*Écrivez les numéros 1–8 sur votre papier. Écoutez les deux phrases. Puis, écrivez le pronom relatif **qui** ou **que** que vous utiliseriez pour faire une seule phrase.*

emcl.com
WB 10–11
Games

The Relative Pronouns *ce qui* and *ce que* 1.1, 1.2

You just reviewed that the relative pronouns **qui** and **que** always have a definite antecedent. But if the antecedent is not specific or if it is unknown, use **ce qui** or **ce que**.

Ce qui (*what*) is used as the subject of the dependent clause.

Ce qui est un problème, c'est l'endettement.	*What is a problem is the debt.*
Le candidat sait **ce qui** est important.	*The candidate knows what is important.*

Ce que (*what*) is used as the direct object of the dependent clause.

Ce que nous voulons, c'est un nouveau look.	*What we want is a new look.*
Ce qu'on remarquera cette année, c'est la longueur des jupes.	*What we'll notice this year is the length of skirts.*

COMPARAISONS

How would you express these linking words in English?

Montre-moi **ce que** tu as dessiné.
Le gouvernement ne réduit pas son endettement, **ce qui** sera un problème.

4.1

COMPARAISONS: **Ce que** is best translated with "what," and **ce qui** with "which":
"Show me what you drew."
"The government is not reducing its debt, which will be a problem."

RESOURCES

 **Workbook 10–11**

 **Drill & Practice Games**

Answers

1. qui
2. que
3. qui
4. qui
5. que
6. qui
7. qui
8. qui

Reference Desk

1. Students may need to be reminded that in #5 of **Activité 14**, **se passer** means "to happen." **Se** is not the subject, but rather it is part of the pronominal verb.
2. Do your students know that not all flowers are created equal in France? White lilies and chrysanthemums are reserved for funerals, red roses for lovers, and yellow flowers have the connotation of infidelity. Be careful when offering these flowers to your hostess. Advise students to ask the **fleuriste** for suggestions.

Differentiated Learning

Accelerate

Ask these students to give the French equivalents of these sentences: 1.) Here is what I bought. 2.) Tell me what you learned in school today. 3.) I don't know what they are discussing. 4.) We don't know that verb, which is a problem. 5.) To know French table manners is what I want.

Special Needs Students

AD(H)D/Dyslexia/Linguistically Challenged

For many of these students, a grammatical explanation will not lead to comprehension. Understanding that **ce qui** and **ce que** mean *what* in English will help. Give them ample opportunities to practice oral and written examples. Giving students short but frequent quizzes will ensure that they are learning.

Answers

14

1. Ce que
2. Ce qu'
3. ce que
4. Ce qu'
5. ce qui
6. Ce que
7. Ce que
8. Ce que

1. Ce qui est le plus important pour Max, c'est le problème de l'inflation. Ce qu'il trouve le moins important, c'est le problème de l'endettement.
2. Claire: le problème de l'inflation... le problème du chômage
3. Nicole: le problème du chômage... le problème de l'endettement
4. Thomas: le problème de l'endettement... le problème de l'inflation
5. Abdel: le problème de la pollution... le problème de l'endettement
6. Anne: le problème du chômage... le problème de la pollution

14 Le réveillon d'Élodie et Léo

1.1, 1.2

*Complétez les phrases suivantes avec **ce qui** ou **ce que**.*

1. ... la mère d'Élodie et Léo connaît bien, c'est les manières à table.
2. ... elle dit à ses enfants est direct: "On ne parle pas politique à table."
3. Elle n'aime pas... ses enfants disent devant les Martin.
4. ... Élodie n'aime pas, c'est voir les sans-abris.
5. Léo n'aime pas... se passe dans beaucoup de pays.
6. ... les enfants cherchent, ce sont des solutions aux problèmes contemporains.
7. ... le père des ados pense, c'est que ses enfants ont hérité de son idéalisme et celui (*that*) de sa femme quand ils étaient jeunes.
8. ... les Martin aiment, c'est la passion de la discussion.

15 La politique

1.2, 1.3

Dites ce qui est le plus important pour chaque personne et ce qu'il ou elle trouve le moins important selon les informations données dans la grille. Le plus grand chiffre indique le problème le plus important pour la personne.

	l'endettement	la pollution	le chômage	l'inflation
Noah	3	2	1	4
Anne	2	1	4	3
Nicole	3	1	4	2
Max	1	3	2	4
Thomas	4	2	3	1
Abdel	1	4	2	3
Claire	2	3	1	4

MODÈLE Noah
Ce qui est le plus important pour Noah, c'est le problème de l'endettement. Ce qu'il trouve le moins important, c'est le problème du chômage.

1. Max
2. Claire
3. Nicole
4. Thomas
5. Abdel
6. Anne

Ce que je ne comprends pas, c'est ton désintérêt de la politique!

Essential Instruction

1. Do **Activité 14** as a class.
2. Ask the students to add their names to the chart in **Activité 15** saying, **Ce qui est le plus important pour moi c'est**..., and **Ce que je trouve le moins important, c'est....et pourquoi**. Students can work in pairs.
3. Before starting the game in **Activité 16** you might want to do a comprehensive review of the lesson vocabulary. **Activité 16** can serve as a good review for the **Leçon** Quiz.
4. For **Activité 17** consider having interested groups video tape their presentations.
5. Have all students complete **Activité 18** as written homework.

À vous la parole

Qu'ya-t-il d'universel dans les rapports entre les gens?

16 Vous parlez de quoi?

1.1, 1.3, 5.2

Presentational Communication

Pour vous préparer à jouer ce jeu, faites une liste de vocabulaire pour chaque thème indiqué dans l'activité "On discute à table." Il y a deux équipes. Le premier joueur de l'Équipe 1 et le premier joueur de l'Équipe 2 vont au tableau. Quand le prof propose un thème, les joueurs ont une minute pour écrire tous les mots et expressions de vocabulaire qu'ils savent sur ce thème. Le joueur avec la liste la plus longue gagne un point pour son équipe.

1.1, 5.2

17 On discute à table!

Interpersonal Communication

Imaginez que "On discute à table!" est une nouvelle émission de télé-réalité. L'objectif est de parler le plus longtemps possible sur un thème proposé par l'animateur (le professeur). L'animateur va donner un thème de la liste ci-dessous à votre groupe. Vous allez pratiquer avec vos camarades de classe. Ensuite, discutez autour d'une table devant la classe sur ce même thème. Pendant votre présentation, vous pouvez vous servir d'une liste de vocabulaire. Le groupe qui parle le plus longtemps gagne le jeu.

Thèmes possible:

l'art
le cinéma
l'économie
l'environnement
les fêtes francophones
les médias (livres, musique, etc.)
la politique
le sport
la technologie
la mode

18 Mon dîner chez....

1.3, 2.1

Presentational Communication

Imaginez que vous venez de dîner chez une famille française. Quand vous rentrez, vous écrivez à propos de votre expérience dans votre journal intime. Mentionnez le cadeau que vous avez offert et la réaction de la famille. Parlez du repas: Qu'est-ce qu'on vous a servi, et dans quel ordre? De quoi avez-vous parlé? Pour terminer, évaluez votre hôte ou hôtesse.

RESOURCES

Communicative Activities

Answers

All activities will vary.

Reference Desk

Blended Instruction

Consider using blended instruction, a combination of in-class learning and computer-mediated instruction or learning opportunities. Ask students to complete activities on the computer, using their cell or smartphone, or other emerging electronic technology. This will allow students to hone their tech skills and become more independent learners. Schedule routine Internet and e-book learning in class and in the lab.

Differentiated Learning

Expand

In **Activité 18** the journal entry might be all about the **faux-pas** the guest made at the dinner party, including the choice of flowers as a hostess gift.

Answers

Stratégie de lecture

Box 2. Les mauvais résultats scolaires du fils.
Box 3. Les différentes attentes entre le père et le fils pour l'avenir scolaire du fils.
Box 4. Les difficultés qu'a le père à imposer son autorité à son fils.

Reference Desk

Sacha Guitry was born in Saint Petersburg, Russia, in 1885. His father, Lucien Guitry, was a well-known actor. In fact, Sacha started performing on stage at the age of 5. He knew he was going to be an artist so he did not take his studies seriously. In the 1920s, Guitry wrote 124 plays (some written in fewer than three days), more than 30 books, and he later fell in love with film, directing 33 movies. During the occupation by the Nazis, he was accused of accepting favors from the enemy. He wrote a tribute to Maréchal Pétain entitled *1929–1942-From Joan of Arc to Philippe Pétain*. After the war, because of his suspected collaboration, he was imprisoned for two months and absolved in 1947. His career, however, never recovered from this accusation. Guitry was married five times and is known for his witty and caustic remarks on love and marriage. He died in 1957 in Paris and is buried in the Montparnasse cemetery.

Lecture thématique Pre AP

Deux couverts

Rencontre avec l'auteur   1.2

Sacha Guitry (1885–1957) est un homme de théâtre et de cinéma. Il a écrit 124 pièces de théâtre qui sont encore souvent jouées en France. Son style est basé sur le dialogue et il crée des mondes avec un langage original. Ses pièces sont souvent centrées sur les problèmes quotidiens. Dans *Deux couverts*, une comédie en un acte, un père voudrait dîner avec son fils. Qu'est-ce qu'il veut fêter?

Pré-lecture

Préférez-vous dîner en famille ou avec vos amis?

Stratégie de lecture  1.2, 1.3, 4.2

Generational Conflict

Dans un texte littéraire, un conflit, ou une crise, est une lutte entre deux forces opposées. Un type de conflit est la lutte entre deux personnages de générations différentes, par exemple, une mère et une fille, ou un grand-père et son petit-fils. Lisez l'extrait (*excerpt*) de la pièce de théâtre et trouvez dans le dialogue quels sont les conflits qui existent entre le père et son fils. Un exemple a été fait pour vous.

Fils	Père	Description du conflit
"J'ai été avec des camarades...."	"Et tu n'as pas pensé à moi... tu ne t'es pas souvenu que j'attendais ici le résultat."	La perte de temps que le fils a occasionnée à son père, et son impolitesse
"En géographie, il m'a demandé quels étaient les principaux fleuves de l'Australie!!! Comment veux-tu savoir ça!"	"À plusieurs reprises, cet hiver, mon petit, je t'ai proposé de t'appliquer davantage...."	
"Oui... je ne connais rien de plus bête que ce truc-là!"	"Oui, seulement, moi, je ne m'en fiche pas du baccalauréat!"	
"...et tu crois que je vais rester de seize à vingt-trois ans sans profiter de la vie?..."	"Tu me laisseras le soin, je te prie, de diriger ton instruction et ton éducation jusqu'à ta majorité."	

Essential Instruction

1. Have students listen to **Rencontre avec l'auteur** to learn about Sacha Guitry and follow along in their books. How many plays did he write? What was a theme running through many of his works?
2. As students each answer the **Pré-lecture** question, tally the results in two columns on the board: **en famille** and **avec des amis**. Encourage students to give a reason.
3. Present the **Stratégie de lecture** to students so that as they read the play they can be looking for these examples of intergenerational conflict.
4. Read and discuss the definition of irony in **Outils**. Ask for examples of dramatic irony found in *Romeo and Juliet* or a French movie you have shown in class.
5. Read through the **Pendant la lecture** questions before reading or listening. If students get a question wrong, make sure they understand the relevant passage before moving on.

Outils de lecture  1.1, 1.2

Irony

L'ironie fait la différence entre l'apparence et la réalité. L'ironie dramatique révèle une information dont le lecteur ou les spectateurs sont conscients, mais pas les personnages. À la fin de la pièce, pourquoi est-ce ironique quand le père dit "...tu vas voir que je ne dîne pas seul! D'ailleurs... regarde... deux couverts..."? Quel personnage ignore que Pelletier va dîner seul?

Le Valet: Monsieur, Marie voudrait savoir pour quelle heure est le dîner.
Pelletier: Je me le demande!... Sept heures!... Est-il possible de faire attendre ainsi des enfants... et des parents!... Que voulez-vous, nous dînerons sitôt que monsieur Jacques sera là!...
Le Valet: C'est à cause des perdreaux*...
(On sonne)
Pelletier: Elle peut les mettre!... Allez ouvrir... enfin!... C'est toi?...
(Jacques entre.)
Jacques: Oui, Papa!
Pelletier: Eh! Bien?
Jacques: Recalé*!
Pelletier: Oh!... Embrasse-moi tout de même!
(Jacques embrasse son père.)
Pelletier: Mon pauvre petit!... Oh!... Et... quand l'as-tu su?
Jacques: Que j'étais recalé?
Pelletier: Oui...
Jacques: À... cinq heures et demie.
Pelletier: À cinq heures et demie?
Jacques: Oui, Papa...
Pelletier: Oh! Ce n'est pas possible?
Jacques: Mais si, Papa, pourquoi?
Pelletier: Oh!... Tu sais l'heure qu'il est?
Jacques: Oui, il doit être six heures...
Pelletier: Non, mon petit, non... il est sept heures cinq!... Et j'attends depuis quatre heures!
Jacques: Je te demande pardon, Papa.
Pelletier: D'où viens-tu?
Jacques: Je... j'ai été... heu...
Pelletier: Où as-tu été?
Jacques: J'ai été avec des camarades...
Pelletier: Oui, mais, où... où as-tu été?

Pendant la lecture
1. Qui est-ce que le père attend?

Pendant la lecture
2. Jacques a-t-il réussi au bac?

Pendant la lecture
3. Le père attend depuis quand?

perdreaux *partridges;* **Recalé** *Held back (educ.)*

Answers

Outils de lecture
Jacques

Pendant de lecture
1. Le père attend son fils.
2. Non, il n'a pas réussi au bac.
3. Le père attend depuis quatre heures.

Reference Desk

Consider these strategies for reading the play: (1) Divide the play into sections and include both choral and individual readings. (2) Read stage directions and **Pendant la lecture** questions before reading, and encourage students to predict what will happen next. (3) Ask students to visualize the characters and contemplate the setting. (4) Provide a focus or final question to contemplate while reading. This acts both as a learning and comprehension check.

Differentiated Learning

Accelerate
Have these students work together to explain how Guitry's play is about **les problèmes quotidiens**. They can present their findings to the rest of the class.

Decelerate
Divide the reading into small sections. Play each section and ask questions to test basic understanding. Who are the characters? Why was the father waiting? Where was the son? When the students demonstrate this basic understanding, they can answer the questions in the margins. Ask them to find the lines that justify their answers. Continue reading the play in small sections. Encourage students to find evidence in the text.

Answers

Pendant la lecture

4. Oui, il a mangé un snack avec son ami.
5. Il dit que les questions étaient stupides.
6. Il lui a conseillé de travailler diligemment.
7. Non.

Jacques: Nous avons été prendre quelque chose....

Pelletier: Vous avez été prendre quelque chose!!! C'est superbe! Et tu n'as pas pensé à moi... tu ne t'es pas souvenu que j'attendais ici le résultat....

Jacques: Si, Papa... mais le temps a passé si vite!

Pelletier: Je ne trouve pas! *(Un temps.)* Assieds-toi, ne reste pas debout*. Et, pourquoi as-tu été recalé?

Jacques: Ils m'ont posé des questions stupides!

Pelletier: Ça m'étonne*! Peut-être t'ont-elles semblées stupides parce que tu les ignorais! Quelles sont les questions auxquelles tu as mal répondu?

Jacques: D'abord, il m'a posé en histoire une question que je n'avais jamais étudiée....

Pelletier: À qui la faute*?

Jacques: Alors, comme je n'ai pas su répondre... il a fait le malin*, et il m'a demandé sur un ton vexant si je savais au moins quel avait été le héros de la bataille d'Arc....

Pelletier: Et tu as répondu?

Jacques: J'ai répondu en rigolant: Jeanne d'Arc!

Pelletier: Oui, eh bien, je trouve la réponse plus stupide que la question! En géographie?

Jacques: En géographie, il m'a demandé quels étaient les principaux fleuves de l'Australie!!! Comment veux-tu savoir ça!

Pelletier: En l'apprenant*! Je ne vois pas d'autre moyen! À plusieurs reprise, cet hiver, mon petit, je t'ai proposé de t'appliquer davantage... tu ne me semblais pas au point... mais, chaque fois que je t'en ai fait l'observation, tu m'as juré* que tout "allait très bien..." et ma foi, tu avais fini par me donner ta confiance!... Enfin, c'est fait, c'est fait! Je ne m'exagère pas la gravité de cette aventure, bien sûr... ce n'est pas un désastre, mais c'est un avertissement*, et je te conseille de donner un bon coup de collier* cet été afin d'être prêt, afin d'être complètement prêt en octobre prochain. C'est bien en octobre, n'est-ce pas, que tu repasses*?

Jacques: Oui, on peut se représenter en octobre.

Pelletier: Comment, on peut? Qu'est-ce que ça veut dire?

Jacques: Heu... ben....

Pelletier: Parle....

Jacques: Ben, ça veut dire que j'aimerais autant ne pas repasser....

Pelletier: Qu'est-ce que tu dis?

Pendant la lecture
4. Jacques a-t-il déjà mangé? Avec qui?

Pendant la lecture
5. Quelle était l'attitude du fils quand on l'a interrogé?

Pendant la lecture
6. Quel conseil le père a-t-il donné au fils?

Pendant la lecture
7. Le fils veut-il repasser le bac?

---

debout *standing;* **Ça m'étonne.** *I'm astonished.;* **faute** *fault;* **faire le malin** *was a smart alec;* **En l'apprenant.** *By learning it.;* **as juré** *swore;* **avertissement** *warning;* **bon coup de collier** *good effort;* **repasses** passes un examen pour la deuxième fois

Essential Instruction

1. Play the recording in its entirety and ask basic comprehension questions.
2. Play the recording again, stopping at intervals to furnish supplementary vocabulary, ask, and answer questions.
3. Allow your high-ability students to work in small groups to answer the questions **Pendant la lecture.**
4. Work with your lower-ability students to help them understand the reading. See footnote p. 123.

Jacques:	Oui, quoi… j'aimerais mieux en rester là. Moi, je m'en fiche du baccalauréat!
Pelletier:	Ah! Oui?
Jacques:	Oui… je ne connais rien de plus bête que ce truc-là!
Pelletier:	Allons donc?
Jacques:	Ah! La, la!
Pelletier:	Oui, seulement, moi, je ne m'en fiche pas du baccalauréat!
Jacques:	Ça, c'est autre chose!
Pelletier:	Oui, et c'est même une chose qui a son importance! Mais tout de même, je ne serais pas fâché de savoir pourquoi tu te fiches du baccalauréat!
Jacques:	Oh! C'est bien simple… je me suis aperçu* aujourd'hui que tous les idiots avaient été reçus!
Pelletier:	Vraiment?
Jacques:	Oui!
Pelletier:	Et les élèves intelligents ont tous été refusés?
Jacques:	Oui!
Pelletier:	Exemple: toi!
Jacques:	Oui.
Pelletier:	C'est admirable!
Jacques:	Moi, je les connais, Papa, les camarades de ma classe! Il y en a deux, tiens… Rondel et Debacker, ils ont eu le maximum de points… eh! Bien, je n'ai jamais rencontré deux types plus bêtes! Il n'y a pas moyen de causer* avec eux cinq minutes!
Pelletier:	Mais, mon enfant, la vie ne se passe pas en conversations! Tu as d'étranges idées sur l'intelligence…. Les deux camarades dont tu parles n'ont peut-être pas ton toupet*, ton bagout et ton exubérance… ce sont sans doute des enfants réfléchis et sérieux….
Jacques:	Ils sont abrutis*, tout simplement! Quand on pense qu'ils ont refusé Mareuil!
Pelletier:	Mareuil? Qui est Mareuil?
Jacques:	Mareuil, tu sais bien, que je t'ai amené un matin, à déjeuner….
Pelletier:	Oui, oui, parfaitement. C'est ce jeune homme qui a inventé un aéroplane.
Jacques:	C'est ça! Eh! Bien, ils l'ont recalé parce qu'il ne savait pas qui avait succédé à Pépin-le-Bref! Je me demande un peu à quoi ça peut servir de savoir qui a succédé à Pépin-le-Bref, pour un type qui veut être aviateur! Veux-tu que je te dise, Papa… je suis sûr que Mareuil a du génie*!

Pendant la lecture
8. Selon Jacques, qui a réussi au bac?

Pendant la lecture
9. Pourquoi a-t-on recalé Mareuil?

je me suis aperçu j'ai réalisé; **causer** parler; **toupet** *nerve*; **abrutis** *dazed, dumb*; **génie** *genius*

Answers

Pendant la lecture

8. Jacques pense que seulement les idiots ont réussi au bac.
9. On a recalé Mareuil parce qu'il ne savait pas une réponse évidente à une question d'histoire.

Differentiated Learning

Accelerate/Decelerate
Have students keep a list of clues in the scene that indicate the story takes place sometime in the past.

Learning Styles

Auditory Learners
Have these students work in pairs to read the play to each other. This will imprint the sound of the words in their mind.

Special Needs Students

Dyslexia/AD(H)D
Make copies of the play to distribute to these students so that they can underline, highlight, and write comments and translations to help them break down this long excerpt into smaller parts.

Answers

Pendant la lecture

10. Jacques a seize ans.
11. Parce que sans le bac, le fils n'aura pas un bon métier.

Critical Thinking

Comparisons

Ask students to read the poem "**Le Cancre**" by Jacques Prévert and compare the attitude of Jacques to the student in the poem.

Pelletier: Je n'ai jamais dit le contraire!... D'ailleurs, il ne s'agit pas de ton ami Mareuil en ce moment, il s'agit uniquement de toi!... Il est possible que ton camarade ait du génie... mais, sans vouloir te désobliger*, comme jusqu'à présent, toi, tu ne me sembles avoir de dispositions géniales pour aucune branche, tu me laisseras le soin*, je te prie, de diriger ton instruction et ton éducation jusqu'à ta majorité.

Jacques: Ah! Non!

Pelletier: Comment "Ah! Non!"? Est-ce que tu perds la tête?... Je ne discute pas avec toi, en ce moment... je te renseigne simplement!

Jacques: Je peux tout de même te répondre!

Pelletier: Parle-moi autrement, je te prie! Vas-y... réponds... je t'écoute!

Jacques: J'ai seize ans, n'est-ce pas... or à vingt ans, il faudra que je fasse mon service militaire... et tu crois que je vais rester de seize à vingt-trois ans sans profiter de la vie?

Pelletier: Ne crie pas, c'est inutile! Je n'ai pas l'intention de t'empêcher de profiter de la vie!

Jacques: Est-ce qu'on peut profiter de la vie, quand on travaille!

Pelletier: Oh! Oui, petit malheureux!

Jacques: Mon intention est d'interrompre dès aujourd'hui, mes études!

Pelletier: Ton intention!!!

Jacques: Oui!

Pelletier: Oui, eh! bien, ma volonté à moi est que tu les termines comme je l'entendrai!

Jacques: Mais, Papa, laisse-moi t'expliquer...

Pelletier: Non, assez! À moi, de parler maintenant! J'ai vu le fond de ta pensée, et tu m'as fait connaître ton intention! Tu n'as rien à m'expliquer. Tu vas maintenant connaître ma pensée et ma décision! Si tu dois avoir un jour du génie, mon enfant, ton baccalauréat n'en empêchera pas l'éclosion*... mais si toute ta vie tu dois rester un cancre*, tu auras du moins la possibilité d'entrer aux Postes et Télégraphes, étant bachelier! *(Temps.)* Si par malheur, tu refusais d'obéir, je me séparerais de toi! *(Un temps.)* Ainsi, j'ai passé quinze années de ma vie à me priver de bien des choses pour te donner une éducation aussi forte que ma tendresse, et voilà le fruit de mes peines! Est-ce que tu te rends compte de ce que j'ai fait pour toi?

Jacques: Oui, quoi... tu as....

Pendant la lecture
10. Quel âge a le fils?

Pendant la lecture
11. Pourquoi le père veut-il que son fils repasse son bac?

désobliger *to offend;* **soin** *care;* **n'en empêchera pas l'éclosion** *won't prevent the birth (of your genius);* **cancre** *dunce (educ.)*

Essential Instruction

1. Have the students find pieces of evidence in the text that illustrate the conflict the father has in disciplining his son.
2. Ask students to make a list of the ways in which the son manipulates, threatens, alarms, and confuses the father.
3. Ask students to point out the classic ways the son justifies himself. Have they ever said the same things? "The test was stupid." "None of my friends did well." Discuss whether or not Guitry drew an accurate portrayal of a teen boy.

Pelletier: Oh! Non, ne me dis pas que j'ai fait ce qu'ont fait les autres pères.

Jacques: Tu t'es privé?

Pelletier: Oui... mais tu ne t'en es jamais aperçu! Nous ne sommes pas si riches que tu crois! Nous ne sommes pas riches. Tu es très élégant... tu t'habilles très bien... moi, c'est tout fait! Je ne me plains pas... je l'ai voulu... et je ne le regrette pas encore.... Ah! Mon petit bonhomme, tu ne t'es rendu compte de rien! Ta mère est morte deux ans après ta naissance... il y a quatorze ans de cela, comprends-tu?

Jacques: Quoi?

Pelletier: Quoi? J'avais trente-six ans, mon petit, et j'en ai cinquante, à présent! J'étais jeune... je ne le suis plus! J'ai vieilli* pour toi... je me suis consacré* entièrement* à toi! Écoute bien... deux fois j'ai dû me remarier... la première fois, tu étais trop petit... la seconde fois, tu étais trop grand... Penses-y de temps en temps!
(Un temps.)

Jacques: *(regarde la pendule et se lève.)* Au revoir, Papa....

Pelletier: Quoi?

Jacques: Au revoir, Papa!

Pelletier: Où vas-tu?

Jacques: Je dîne chez Mareuil... et il est sept heures et demie....

Pelletier: Ah! Tu dînes chez Mareuil....

Jacques: Oui, Papa... ça t'ennuie*?

Pelletier: Du tout, mon enfant, du tout... c'est tout naturel... ça doit être sûrement naturel!

Jacques: Et toi?

Pelletier: Moi? Oh! Mon petit, ça se trouve bien... je ne dîne pas seul!

Jacques: Ah!

Pelletier: Oui... regarde toi-même! *(Il ouvre la porte de la salle à manger.)* Tu vois! Tu peux lire le menu... tu vas voir que je ne dîne pas seul! D'ailleurs... regarde... deux couverts!

Jacques: *(vexé.)* Au revoir, Papa... à demain....

Pelletier: À demain, mon petit.... *(Jacques embrasse son père et sort.)* Et il me fait la tête! *(Et après avoir pensé qu'il pourrait peut-être téléphoner à Madame Blandin—et, après y avoir renoncé, Pelletier entre dans la salle à manger, en disant:)* Émile, vous pouvez servir!

Pendant la lecture
12. Qu'est-ce que le père a fait pour son fils?

Pendant la lecture
13. Pourquoi le père ment-il?

J'ai vieilli *I've gotten old;* **je me suis consacré** j'ai sacrifié; **entièrement** complètement; **ça t'ennuies** *do you mind*

Answers

Pendant la lecture

12. Le père a tout sacrifié pour son fils.
13. Parce ce qu'il ne veut pas que son fils se sente coupable.

Differentiated Learning

Expand

Have students find instances in the script where the father is trying to make the son feel guilty. According to the father, why didn't he remarry? What is the irony in the father's words "**et je ne le regrette pas encore**" when referring to his son?

RESOURCES

Pre-test

***Leçon* Quiz**

Answers

Post-lecture

Pelletier est un bon père parce qu'il fait des sacrifices pour son fils. Pelletier est un mauvais père parce qu'il n'est pas assez autoritaire envers son fils.

Le monde visuel

Le style de l'arrière-plan est un peu impressionniste. Le sujet frappe l'œil car il est peint avec des touches plus nettes et mieux définies que le paysage de l'arrière-plan, ce qui crée un contraste.

19 *Activities will vary.*

Communication

Presentational: Cooperative Groups

Arrange students into two heterogeneous groups, the prosecution and the defense. The students will work cooperatively to write arguments for both sides to determine if Pelletier was a good father or not. A representative from each side will play the role of the lawyers, and the remaining students will be in the jury box. The students are authorized to embellish details and use lots of drama.

Post-lecture  1.3

Pelletier est-il un bon ou mauvais père? Pourquoi?

Le monde visuel  1.2

Dans ce tableau, Jules Ernest Renoux (1863–1932) a peint un petit garçon de manière réaliste, sur un arrière-plan de style différent. L'interprétation artistique des paysages d'arrière-plan en peinture a changé à travers l'histoire de l'art. Au XVIème siècle, on peut voir derrière la *Joconde*, de Léonard de Vinci, un arrière-plan qui annonce la peinture de paysage. Au XVIIIème siècle, Claude Lorrain a essayé de peindre ses paysages d'arrière-plan de manière plus réaliste que les peintres de son époque. Mais au XIXème siècle, les peintres voulaient plutôt montrer des impressions de paysage. Quel est le style dans lequel est peint le paysage d'arrière-plan dans ce portrait du fils de Renoux? Qu'est-ce qui frappe l'œil en premier, le sujet ou le paysage? Selon vous, pourquoi une telle juxtaposition du portrait réaliste et d'un paysage de style différent?

Portrait de Marcel Renoux vers 13 ou 14 ans, c. 1912. Jules Ernest Renoux. Collection privée.

19 Activités d'expansion  1.3, 5.2

Complétez les activités suivantes.

1. Écrivez un paragraphe dans lequel vous expliquez les conflits entre le père et son fils dans cette pièce. Servez-vous des informations de votre grille.
2. Jouez le rôle du père et écrivez une lettre que vous allez glisser (*slip*) sous la porte de la chambre de votre fils qui explique ce que vous voulez pour lui et pourquoi.
3. Imaginez que le père et le fils dînent ensemble et discutent de l'avenir du fils. Écrivez le dialogue pour cette scène entre le père et le fils.

Essential Instruction

1. Students interested in art should always try to answer the questions in **Le monde visuel**.
2. Assign **Activité 19** #1 as written homework. Have students refer to the **Stratégie de lecture** on p. 122.
3. Offer a choice of the other two activities in **Activité 19**.
4. Challenge your drama students to act out a section of ***Deux couverts***.
5. For the **Projets finaux**, have students choose **A** or **B. Activité C** offers an opportunity for all students. Consider the different jobs students can fill: researchers, photographers, graphic designers, typists, editors, and taste testers!

Answers

All activities will vary.

T'es branché?

Projets finaux

A Connexions par Internet: L'éducation civique

1.2, 1.3, 3.1, 3.2

Presentational Communication

Allez faire des recherches en ligne sur un sujet politique qui vous intéresse.

1. Préparez une liste de quatre partis politiques en France. Pour chacun, dites ce qu'ils sont pour et contre.
2. Écrivez une petite biographie d'un homme ou d'une femme politique. Référez-vous aux quelques suggestions ci-dessous.

Search words: **charles de gaulle, georges pompidou, françois mitterand, jacques chirac, nicolas sarkozy, françois hollande, christine lagarde**

B Communautés en ligne

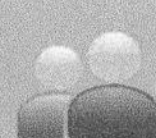

1.3, 3.1, 3.2, 4.2

Dans les médias/Presentational Communication

Faites un profil du paysage médiatiques des États-Unis. Vous pouvez parler des best-sellers, des émissions de télé et des films populaires, et des blogueurs célèbres. Préparez des commentaires qui montrent votre compréhension des médias actuels et ce que vous pensez de ces médias. Ensuite, envoyez votre document à une classe francophone, une autre classe de français américaine, ou postez votre document en ligne. Demandez à vos lecteurs de préparer un document semblable avec leurs réactions sur les médias là où ils habitent. Finalement, comparez les deux documents.

C Passez à l'action!

1.3, 3.1, 3.2

Un livre de recettes/Presentational Communication

Avec votre classe, préparez un livre de recettes francophones. Chaque groupe choisit des pays ou régions qui l'intéressent le plus, et cherche par exemple des recettes de provinces française, des recettes maghrébines, québécoises, belges, ou antillaises. Cherchez des recettes en ligne sur des sites francophones. Puis, écrivez ces recettes en anglais.

Le cari créole se prépare avec de la viande ou du poisson, des lentilles, du thym, du curcuma, du gingembre, et des oignons.

Differentiated Learning

Accelerate

These students may welcome the challenge inherent in working on **Activité A.**

Decelerate

Have these students write a paragraph about the ideal father before answering the **Post-lecture** question. They should use adjectives and give examples. Review some adjectives with them before they write.

Answers

Answers will vary.

D Faisons le point! 1.3

Remplissez l'organigramme pour montrer vos connaissances de cette unité.

Je comprends	Je ne comprends pas encore	Mes connexions

What did I do well to learn and use the content of this unit?	What should I do in the next unit to better learn and use the content?
How can I effectively communicate to others what I have learned?	What was the most important concept I learned in this unit?

Essential Instruction

1. **Activité D** is designed to help students become independent learners. They should fill in the grid as they review **Leçons A**, **B**, and **C**. They can consider this assignment a way of personally assessing what they know and what they need to study before the Unit Test.
2. Have students write you a letter outlining what they would like you to help them with before the final assessment. Students love writing notes, so this may be the non-threatening way for them to ask you for help.
3. Students should all do **Activités A** and **B** to help prepare them for the Listening and Speaking portions of the Unit Test.
4. For **Activité C**, have groups draw a number from a hat to select an activity. All students with the same number work together, then present their determinations to the class.

Évaluation

Pre AP

emcl.com LA *Synthèse*

A Évaluation de compréhension auditive

1.1, 1.2

Interpretive Communication

Une fête

*Écrivez les numéros 1–6 sur votre papier. Écoutez Laure parler d'une fête dans sa famille. Puis, écrivez **V** si la phrase est vraie et **F** si la phrase est fausse.*

B Évaluation orale

1.1, 5.2

Interpersonal Communication

*Téléphonez à votre partenaire. Demandez si vous le/la dérangez et s'il ou elle peut vous donner un coup de main dans la cuisine pour préparer la soirée du nouvel an que vous organisez. Votre partenaire va vous dire ce qu'il ou elle est en train de faire, et s'il ou elle peut venir. Utilisez quelques expressions de la section **"Pour la conversation."***

C Évaluation culturelle

3.1, 3.2, 4.1, 4.2 ,5.1

Vous allez comparer les cultures francophones à la culture américaine. Vous aurez peut-être besoin de faire des recherches sur la culture américaine.

1. **Les grandes fêtes**
   Comment est-ce que les Français passent le réveillon de Noël? Qu'est-ce qu'ils mangent? Qui est-ce qu'ils invitent? Qu'est-ce qui se passe le lendemain pour les enfants? Dites comment les Américains fêtent Noël. Si vous et votre famille fêtez Noël, vous pouvez parler de vos expériences personnelles. Si vous ne célébrez pas Noël mais une autre fête (Ramadan, Hanoukka, Kwanza, etc.), expliquez ce que vous faites.
2. **La cuisine française**
   Expliquez comment la cuisine française a changé. Comment est-ce que les Français préparent leurs repas maintenant? Quelles influences internationales est-ce qu'on remarque dans la cuisine française? Comment est-ce que la cuisine américaine ressemble à la cuisine française? Où est-ce qu'on peut apprendre l'art de la cuisine française traditionnelle en France et chez vous?
3. **Les expressions gastronomiques**
   Si un Français ou une Française vous dit, "Je ne suis pas dans mon assiette" et "Ne me raconte pas de salades," qu'est-ce qu'il ou elle veut dire? Faites une liste d'expressions gastronomiques en anglais, par exemple," "You're full of beans" and "You're just buttering me up."
4. **Les bonnes manières à table**
   Comparez les bonnes manières à table en France avec celles (*the ones*) que vos parents vous ont apprises.
5. **Le vin**
   Quel pays est le premier producteur mondial de vin? Est-ce que l'on produit du vin dans votre région? Combien de vins différents produit-on aux États-Unis? Quel est le rang (*ranking*) des vins américains?
6. **L'art de la conversation à table**
   De quoi est-ce qu'on évite de parler à table en France? Et chez vous?

RESOURCES

Listening Activity
Synthèse

Answers

A

1. F
2. V
3. F
4. V
5. V
6. F

Communication

Interpersonal: Paired Practice

For **Activité B** have students use their mobile phones as props. Ask them to embellish the conversation using any expressions that they have learned to create an interesting, realistic conversation. You may want to time the dialogues and reward pairs with the longest or most accurate dialogues.

Interpersonal: Cooperative Groups

Put students in 6 heterogeneous groups. A student from each group will draw a card with a number from one to six. That number is the activity that they are assigned to complete. Write the number down for your records. The student groups are to compare French and American cultures by doing one of the six activities. Encourage students to share the responsibility for the end product and to build on each member's strengths to complete the activity.

Differentiated Learning

Accelerate/Decelerate

By grouping the students heterogeneously, it is anticipated that the lower-ability students will benefit from working with stronger language students and feel free to ask questions they might not feel comfortable asking you.

Special Needs Students

Linguistically Challenged

These students may feel inferior to other students due to their language skills. Let them share their experiences and knowledge in **Activité C** about life in the United States.

Reference Desk

1. For **Activité D** have students review vocabulary for possible menus in **Leçon A** pp. 76–77, 83–84 and **Leçon B** p. 99.
2. For ideas regarding manners and gifts for the host, see **Leçon C** p. 114, and for conversation topics see **Leçon C** pp. 108–109, 112–113, and 121.

D Évaluation écrite

1.3, 2.1, 4.1

Vous êtes un journaliste américain à Paris. Un collègue français vous a invité chez ses parents pour le réveillon de Noël. Écrivez un article dans lequel vous parlez:

- de ce que vous avez offert à votre hôte
- de ce qu'on vous a servi
- des bonnes manières à table que vous avez observées (En France, on....)
- des sujets de conversation

E Évaluation visuelle

1.3, 2.1

Écrivez un paragraphe en français sur la fête illustrée ci-dessous en répondant aux questions.

1. Quelle est la date?
2. C'est quelle fête?
3. Qu'est-ce qui s'est passé ce soir-là chez les Roussin? Imaginez!
4. Qui a mis ses chaussons sous le sapin de Noël?
5. Qu'est-ce que les enfants vont ouvrir demain matin?

F Évaluation compréhensive

1.3, 2.1

Créez une histoire avec six illustrations: dessinez une famille et leurs invités à table. Montrez un conflit.

Essential Instruction

1. Let the high-ability, self-directed learners proceed at their own pace while completing **Activités D**, **E**, and **F.** When they finish, check their work. Have them collaborate to make a jeopardy game with categories and questions for the class to review unit content.
2. Help average to low-ability students structure their review.
3. By responding to the questions in **Activité E**, students will have drafted a paragraph. You may want to allow time for peer-editing.
4. Storyboard templates are available online to help with **Activité F**.

Vocabulaire de l'Unité 2  1.2

à: à cause de because of C; **à la page** in fashion C; **à propos de** about A; **à sa place** in its place B; **à table** at the (dinner) table C
accueillir to welcome A
s' **adresser (à)** to address (someone) C
un **apéritif** drink and food offered before the meal A
l' **athlétisme (m.)** athletics C
autour de around C
avoir: avoir la chance (de) to have the opportunity (to) C
baisser to decrease C
un **blogueur, une blogueuse** blogger C
une **bûche de Noël** yule log A
ça: ça tombe bien that works out well A
le **candidat** candidate C
le **championnat** championship C
chauffer to heat (up) B
le **club** club C
un **côté: de votre côté** as for you A
des **côtes (f.) de chevreuil** venison chops A
un **coup de main** (helping) hand B
craindre: Je crains que non. I'm afraid not. B
cuire to cook B
les **démocraties (f.)** democracies C
dependre (de) to depend (on) B
déranger to bother A
les **dictatures (f.)** dictatorships C
la **dinde aux marrons** turkey with chestnuts A
dramatique dramatic C
les **droits (m.) de l'homme** human rights C
l' **économie (f.)** economy C
écouter: écoute… listen… A
les **élections (f.) présidentielles** presidential elections C
embêter to annoy A
emprisonner to imprison C
en: en bois wooden B; **en guerre** at war C; **en métal** made of metal B; **en petit comité** with a few friends A; **je m'en vais** I'm going B
encourager to encourage C
l' **endettement (m.)** debt C
s' **entraîner** to practice (sports) C
envahi(e) invaded C
étroit(e) narrow B
faire: faire grève to go on strike C
filtrer to filter B
le **foie gras** goose liver pâté A
les **formes (f.)** shapes B
la **hausse** increase C
les **herbes (f.)** herbs B
le **hit** hit *[inform.]* C
un **hors-d'œuvre** appetizer A
des **huîtres (f.)** oysters A
l' **idéalisme (m.)** idealism C
improviser to improvise A
une **invitation** invitation A
la **jeunesse** youth C
large wide B
la **longueur** length C
le **look tradi** traditional look C
le **machin** thing B
un **magret de canard** duck breast A
des **mandarines (f.)** mandarin oranges A
une **médaille** medal C
les **médias (m.)** media C
mélanger to mix B
mesurer to measure B
la **mode** fashion C
les **nations (f.)** nations C
les **œufs de lump (m.)** lumpfish roe A
la **paix** peace C
le **parti politique socialiste** socialist political party C
passer: passer à la radio to play on the radio C; **on passe…** … is playing (at the movies) B
passionnément passionately C
personnel, personnelle personal A
le **PNB (Produit National Brut)** GNP (Gross National Product) C
la **politique** politics C
posé(e) set down B
poser to put down B
pour: pour t'avancer to help you B
pouvoir: ne pas pouvoir s'empêcher (de) cannot help (but) C
le **prêt-à-porter** ready-to-wear C
prévu(e) planned A
un **prisonnier, une prisonnière** prisoner C
puisque since A
quand: quand même after all A; regardless C
que whom C
racler to scrape, to scrub B
les **rapports (m.)** relationships A
rater to mess up B
réalisé(e) (par) directed (by) C
une **récompense** award C
récupérer to recapture C
réduire to reduce C
remuer to stir, to toss B
le **réveillon de Noël** Christmas Eve celebration A
réveillonner to celebrate Christmas/New Year's Eve C
des **revenus (m.)** income C
le **sapin de Noel** Christmas tree A
la **sauce** sauce B
le **saumon: saumon fumé** smoked salmon A
servir (à) to be used (for) B
si so C
le **souci** worry C
souffrir to suffer C
le **taux d'inflation** inflation rate C
des **territoires (m.)** territories C
le **tissue** fabric A
des **toasts (m.)** canapés A
tomber: tomber bien to fall well A
tourné filmed C
tranquille calm, quiet A
tuer to kill C
universel, universelle universal A
les **ustensiles (m.)** utensils B
usurper to usurp C
la **valeur** worth C
verser to pour B
voter to vote C

Shapes… see p. 93
Utensils… see p. 94

RESOURCES

Listening Pre-test D

***Unité* Test**

Reference Desk

1. Remind students that the **Leçon** where each vocabulary word can be found is indicated in red.
2. Have students find the vocabulary words that are related to these words: **long, la dette, la prison, la tranquillité, l'univers, le vote, la passion, un champion, un drame, l'idéal, national.**

Game

Panique!
This review game offers lots of flexibility. Use it here for reviewing vocabulary with a focus on antonyms. Divide the class into two teams. Choose one helper from each side. The helpers will count points for the opposite side. Prepare a list of antonyms from the unit vocabulary: **hausser/baisser, froidir/chauffer, blasé/dramatique,** etc. Call out a word; all students write its antonym. Call time. Helpers circulate and count the number of correct responses. Spelling counts! Teams receive one point for every correct response. The team with the most points wins.

Differentiated Learning

Expand
To review vocabulary, give students small white boards. Ask a question about the vocabulary: **Comment s'appelle le grand repas avant Noël? Quel est l'équivalent français du *GNP* ?** After someone offers a response, write the word or expression on the board for reinforcement. A student could also lead the activity.

RESOURCES

Listening
Units 1-2

Answers

1. B

1. D
2. C
3. D

Reference Desk

1. The **Bilan cumulatif** is based on the French Language and Culture AP exam prepared by the College Board. It assesses students' proficiencies in the Interpersonal, Interpretive, and Presentational modes of communication. Students are also asked to demonstrate their understanding of the products, practices, and perspectives of the target cultures.
2. The Print Text section consists of a variety of authentic print materials such as articles and correspondence. A multiple choice question follows the text.
3. The Audio Text is a professional recording, usually a dialogue. Encourage students to preview and skim the questions before listening. They should then answer the multiple choice questions.

Unité 2 Bilan cumulatif 

I. Interpretive Communication: Print texts  1.2

Lisez ce reportage sur les activités des familles d'aujourd'hui, puis répondez à la question.

La MJC près de chez vous

Dans la société actuelle où les familles sont si occupées entre le travail, l'école, et la vie à la maison, il est bon de savoir qu'il y a des endroits dans sa communauté pour les enfants. En France, l'engagement à la promotion de la vie active et familiale est clair par le grand nombre de Maison des Jeunes et de la Culture. Cette association populaire, financée par le gouvernement, sert de lieu d'accueil pour tous et propose une variété d'activités sportives et de loisir qui rendent les ados heureux.

On peut tout faire à la MJC. Par exemple, à ma MJC, on organise du sport; des clubs, par exemple, le ciné-club, tout dans un cadre rassurant. Les adolescents peuvent participer au cours de théâtre ou aux sorties en ville. On peut faire de la danse, de la musique, ou peindre. On peut suivre des cours individuellement ou en groupes.

1. Cette MJC n'offre pas....
   A. d'activités pour les ados
   B. de cours des finances personnelles pour adultes
   C. de ciné-club
   D. de cours de théâtre

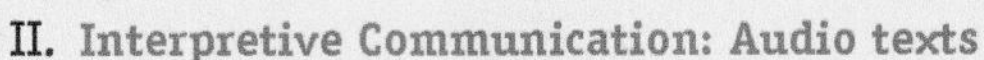

II. Interpretive Communication: Audio texts   1.2

Écoutez le dialogue suivant deux fois, puis complétez les phrases.

1. Cette conversation a lieu entre....
   A. deux amies
   B. une femme et sa mère
   C. une Française et sa demoiselle d'honneur
   D. une fiancée américaine et une organisatrice de mariage française
2. L'objectif principal de cette entrevue est de/d'....
   A. aider Victoria à choisir sa demoiselle et son garçon d'honneur
   B. permettre à Victoria de comprendre son futur mari
   C. prendre connaissance des traditions françaises sur le mariage
   D. sélectionner un gâteau de mariage bien français
3. Dans le contexte de l'interview, Victoria aurait tendance à poser une question prochainement sur....
   A. le travail en France
   B. le rôle du garçon d'honneur
   C. la cathédrale de Chartres
   D. des destinations pour un voyage de noces spécial

III. **Interpersonal Writing: E-mail Reply**  **1.3, 5.2**

*Vous allez écrire une réponse à un message électronique. Il faut répondre à toutes les questions et donner des détails à propos du sujet du message. Écrivez formellement. N'oubliez pas d'écrire une salutation au début et une formule de politesse (*closing*) à la fin de votre message.*

C'est un message électronique du propriétaire de la boutique Espace Cuisine à Montréal. Vous lui avez écrit parce que vous préparez une grande réunion de famille pour célébrer les 90 ans de votre grand-mère. Donc, vous avez besoin d'acheter du matériel de cuisine et de louer de la vaisselle.

De: Philippe Bourdon
Objet: Organisation d'une fête et matériel nécessaire

Monsieur ou Madame,

Merci de votre demande de renseignements. Nous sommes en effet spécialistes du matériel de cuisine. Nous vendons toutes les grandes marques de la profession et aux meilleurs prix. Nous louons aussi de la vaisselle et du matériel. Vous pouvez commander chez nous tout ce que vous désirez pour compléter votre batterie de cuisine et faire que votre projet soit un franc succès. Mais pour mieux vous conseiller, dites-nous quels outils de préparation et ustensiles vous manquent et si vous envisagez de faire de la pâtisserie. Vous devriez aussi préciser le nombre de couverts, et les plats et boissons que vous comptez servir. Nous sommes prêts à vous aider à bien fêter les 90 ans de votre grand-mère.

Dans l'attente de vous lire, veuillez agréer, chère Madame, /cher Monsieur l'expression de nos sentiments distingués.

Philippe Bourdon
Espace Cuisine
3640 avenue St-Denis
Montréal

IV. **Presentational Writing: Persuasive Essay**  **1.3, 2.1, 4.2**

Expliquez les manières de table en France et aux États-Unis et dites pourquoi elles sont importantes ou pas importantes dans la vie contemporaine.

Reference Desk

1. The E-mail Reply is a free response test section that helps students develop their interpersonal writing skills.
2. The Presentational Writing section asks students to write a persuasive essay.

Reference Desk

In the Speaking section of the assessment, students are asked to participate in a conversation or make a cultural comparison using their presentational speaking skills.

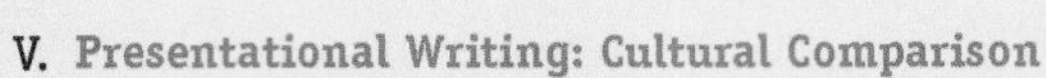

V. Presentational Writing: Cultural Comparison  **1.3, 2.1,2.2, 4.2**

Vous êtes étudiant américain en France. Pendant la fête de Noël, vous vous trouvez loin de votre propre famille. Alors, votre meilleure amie française vous a invité à passer cette fête chez elle près de Lyon. C'est le 26 décembre et vous venez de passer la fête avec trois générations de sa famille. Vous avez même aidé la famille à préparer le repas du réveillon. Parlez de votre expérience: tout ce que vous avez fait et ce que vous avez mangé, et comparez les traditions françaises avec les traditions de chez vous ou de votre communauté.

Unité 3 La Francophonie

Reference Desk

In **Unité 3** students will learn to appreciate the heritage of the French language in the world. You may remind students that French is an international language spoken as an official language or one of the official languages in 33 countries around the world. This unit focuses on Quebec, Tunisia, and Senegal.

Reference Desk

Habib Bourguiba (1903–2000) is revered as the Father of Tunisia. He led Tunisia's fight for independence from France, which was achieved on March 20, 1956. He served as President of Tunisia from 1957–87. Habib Bourguiba studied law and political science at the Sorbonne before returning to Tunisia to practice law and become politically active. He was a moderate president whose policies earned women the right to vote, banished polygamy, and urged the removal of the veil. His domestic policies strengthened Tunisian industry and tourism. The per capita income and literacy rates rose during his term of office.

Citation

"La langue française constitue l'appoint à notre patrimoine culturel, enrichit notre pensée, exprime notre action, contribue à forger notre destin intellectuel et à faire de nous des hommes à part entière."

The French language defines our cultural heritage, enriches our thinking, expresses our action, contributes to the formation of our intellectual destiny so as to set us apart from all of humanity.

—Habib Bourguiba, Chef de l'État tunisien

À savoir

Il y a environ 220 millions de personnes qui parlent français dans le monde.

Essential Instruction

1. Recall with students that **la francophonie** refers to countries throughout the world where French is spoken.
2. Put students in teams to try to name as many francophone countries as they can.
3. Distribute a list of the francophone countries, and have the teams count up how many they were able to name and which ones they missed. If possible use a list that differentiates countries where French is an official language, and those where it is not.
4. Preview with students the **Contrat de l'élève** to give them an overview of the unit.
5. Challenge students to guess the answers to the questions in the photos: **Où se situe cette mosquée?** and **Comment s'appelle cette habitation au Sénégal?**

Unité 3

La Francophonie

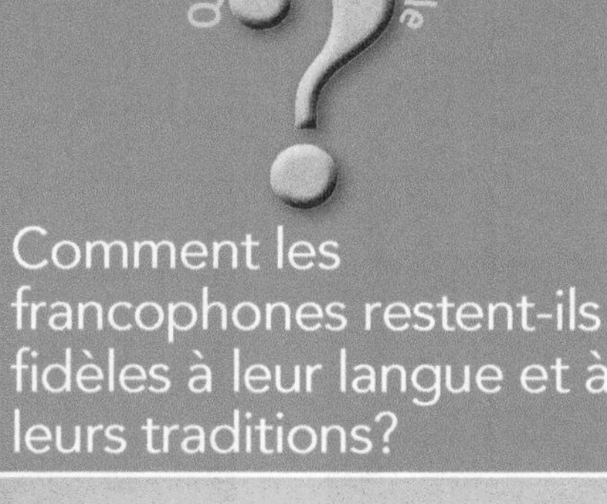

Comment les francophones restent-ils fidèles à leur langue et à leurs traditions?

Comment s'appelle cette habitation au Sénégal?

Contrat de l'élève

Leçon A I will be able to:

- say where my ancestors came from and where they settled.
- discuss the goals and services of the **Alliance française**, French immigration to Quebec, and Quebec immigration to New England.
- use the pronouns **y** and **en** and put two object pronouns in a sentence.

Leçon B I will be able to:

- start a fairy tale.
- discuss Tunisia, North African immigration to France, and North African stories.
- use reflexive verbs.

Leçon C I will be able to:

- respond to an introduction, say where I grew up, and give a compliment.
- discuss subsidized housing, government payments to families, and talk about Senegal.
- use the comparative and superlative of adverbs.

Expansion

1. To set the tone for the appreciation of the French language, have students search the song **"La Langue de Chez Nous"** by Yves Duteil, which is a tribute to **la langue française**.
2. Discuss the lyrics and sing the song as a class.
3. Put students in groups and have them record their own rendition of the song.
   Search words: la langue de chez nous, yves duteil, paroles

Differentiated Learning

Decelerate

Using the map distributed in class to list francophone countries, ask students to write down the name of each continent where French is spoken. Then have them find to which continent Quebec, Tunisia, and Senegal belong.

Learning Styles

Visual Learners

Show images of various places in the world (the Eiffel Tower, a market in Dakar, the Great Wall of China, Buckingham Palace, the Egyptian pyramids, a restaurant in Vietnam, etc.), and ask students what city or country each image represents and if it is a francophone country.

RESOURCES

 e-visual 7

 Workbook 1–3

 Flash Cards

 Listening Activities 1–2

 Drill & Practice Games

Reference Desk

1. When names of family members contain the adjective **grand**, this adjective is used figuratively and refers to a length of time, not size. To make it easier for students to remember which generation **grand-oncle** and **grand-tante** refer to, point to their similarity with **grand-père** and **grand-mère**, just like "grandfather" and "grandmother" in English. The word **arrière** is added to the previous generation. To refer to family members from a generation farther back than one's great grandparents, the French use the adjective **arrière** over and over, just like Americans use the adjective "great."
2. The singular form of **aïeux** is **aïeul** which is pronounced /ajœl/, a good tongue twister!

Game

Moi aussi!

Student A starts the game selecting a family member: **"J'ai une arrière-grand-mère qui s'appelle Joëlle."** Student A throws a tennis ball to Student B who quickly must answer, **"Quelle coïncidence! Moi, j'ai un arrière-grand-père qui s'appelle Joël."** Student B throws the ball to Student C who says, **"J'ai une cousine germaine qui s'appelle Joëlle."** The game continues using any family members that students can think of in masculine and feminine forms. The teacher must keep the game going quickly.

Leçon A

Vocabulaire actif

emcl.com
WB 1–3
LA 1–2
Games

Ma famille et où elle s'est installée

1.2, 5.1

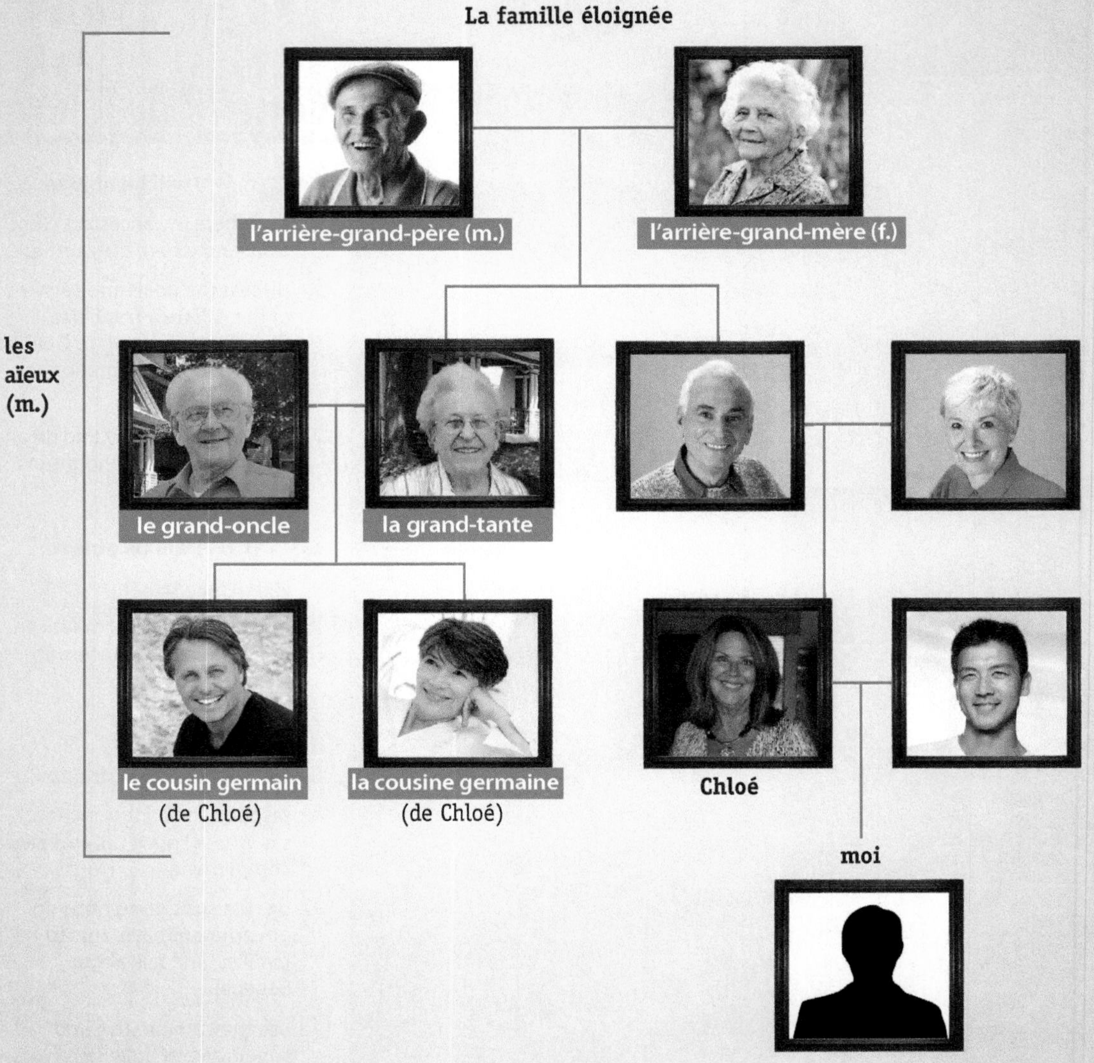

La famille éloignée

les aïeux (m.)

l'arrière-grand-père (m.)

l'arrière-grand-mère (f.)

le grand-oncle

la grand-tante

le cousin germain (de Chloé)

la cousine germaine (de Chloé)

Chloé

moi

Essential Instruction

1. Bring photos of your family or find photos of celebrities online. Present the photos as your family members providing their names, ages, and occupations. Feel free to embellish or add bizarre information.
2. Ask students the names of their relatives.
3. Give students a map of the United States. Have them draw their family tree on the map, labeling the family members as seen in **Ma famille et où elle s'est installée**; they should name as many people as they can, in as many states as they can. Then ask who has a family member in such and such state.
4. Have the students examine the list of states. Ask them why the names of some states are preceded by **dans**, others **en**, and still another by the preposition **à**.

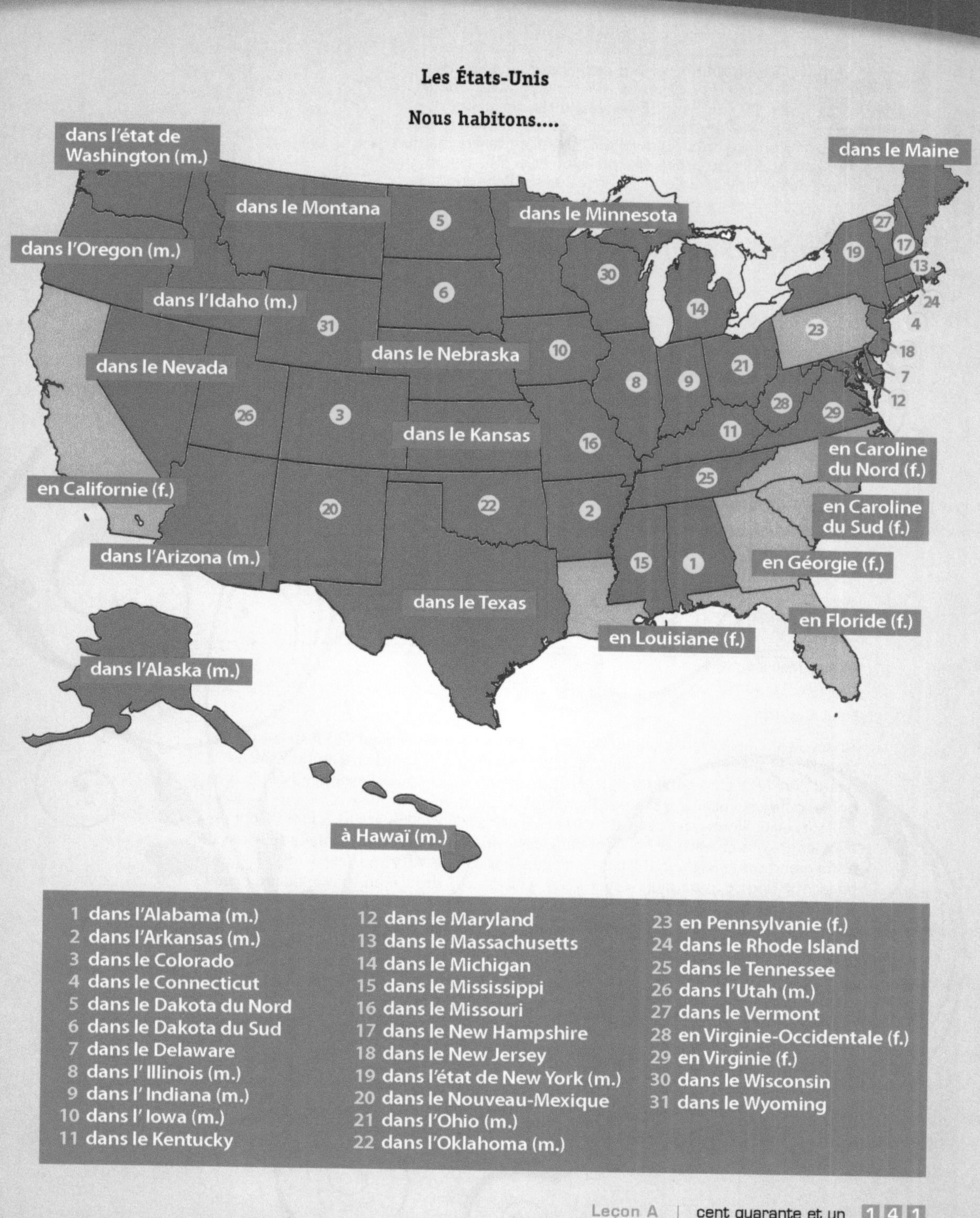

Connections

Human Geography

Work with social studies teachers to track genealogies and migration movements in the United States throughout different periods (from the Colonial to present).

Reference Desk

1. In Level 1, Unit 10A, p. 525, we have introduced the prepositions before cities, countries, and continents as follows:
   to = à *(aller à, vivre à, etc.)*
   à + name of city *(à Dakar)*
   au + masculine name *(au Canada)*
   en + feminine name *(en Afrique)*
   aux + plurals *(aux États-Unis)*
2. In Level 3, we are introducing another preposition, *dans*, to stress "being within" rather than "going to". This does not exclude the basic rule using *à*, even with the verbs *habiter* and *s'installer*, but adds a nuance for Level 3 students:
   "in" (in the sense of inside, within)= *dans/en*
   dans + article + masculine state *(dans le Minnesota, dans l'Illinois)*
   en + feminine state *(en Californie, en Louisiane)*
3. Note that most countries which begin with a vowel are feminine. (exceptions are *l'Iran, l'Irak, L'Israël*).
   This is not true of American states: all states beginning with a vowel are masculine: *l'Arizona l'Illinois, l'Idaho, l'Oregon, l'Alaska*. So with the preposition to (*à* and its derivatives, and *en*), we would have to say:
   Je vais au Minnesota. Tu vas en Idaho, en Oregon, etc.

Differentiated Learning

Accelerate

Tell students that the preposition **dans le** used before masculine states is interchangeable with **au: J'habite dans le Nebraska. Nous sommes au Nebraska.** The only exception is masculine nouns that start with a vowel, and thus are treated as feminine nouns: **dans l'Idaho** is interchangeable with **en Idaho.**

Learning Styles

Visual Learners

These students should rewrite the list of states grouping them in the following columns: **dans, dans l'état de, en**, and **à**. They will be able to remember which prepositions are used with which states by seeing the list in their minds.

Auditory Learners

Students may learn best by repeating the names of the states and their prepositions three times each.

Answers

1

1. aux États-Unis
2. à Seattle; dans l'état de Washington
3. grand-père Félix
4. la sœur de Félix; en Californie
5. le frère de Romane et Félix
6. la fille d'Alexis; en Californie
7. dans le Névada
8. son grand-oncle Raymond; Il habite trop loin.

Culture

Products: Information

You might like to show scenes from the award-winning movie ***Le Bonheur de Pierre***, a comedy about a contemporary immigrant, a French professor from Paris who inherits an inn in Canada. With his wife, he leaves France for a small village in Quebec. Instead of the idyllic life they seek, they find nothing but problems created by the local mayor.

Search words: le bonheur de pierre

Mots-clé

C'est au XVIème siècle qu'est apparue la forme moderne du mot **aïeux**, tiré du latin *avus, aviolus, aiol*. Ce sont les poètes classiques qui lui ont donné cette belle orthographe, afin de le faire rimer avec "cieux," "Dieu," "glorieux," etc. Aujourd'hui même, ce terme marque le respect et la nostalgie du passé. L'expression "Oh mes aïeux!" exprime l'incrédulité, et insinue que les ancêtres seraient choqués.

Pour la conversation

1.1, 1.2

How do I say where my ancestors came from and settled?

› **Mes aïeux sont arrivés de** Bretagne et **se sont installés** au Québec.

My ancestors arrived from Brittany and settled in Quebec.

Et si je voulais dire...?

la descendance	*descent, lineage*
le droit de garde	*custody*
la marraine	*godmother*
le parrain	*godfather*
descendre de	*to be descended from*

1 Un long voyage

1.2, 5.1

Lisez le mail de Sandrine à son frère au Québec, puis répondez aux questions.

À: Cédric
Cc:
Sujet: Mon long voyage

Salut, Cédric!

Tu vas bien? Quel voyage pour rendre visite à toute notre famille qui s'est installée aux États-Unis! J'ai atterri à Seattle, dans l'état de Washington. D'abord on a rendu visite au grand-père Félix qui y habite. Il s'y est installé quand il s'est remarié avec Sandy. Puis, on a pris la route pour aller voir sa sœur, Romane. Il a fallu que l'on traverse l'Oregon car elle est toujours en Californie, avec son autre frère Alexis. La fille d'Alexis, Michèle, habite tout près, mais les enfants de Michèle habitent dans le Nevada. Encore de la route! Tu te souviens de notre grand-oncle Raymond? Il habite maintenant dans le Maryland. Trop loin! Cela faisait beaucoup trop de route, alors je ne l'ai pas vu! C'est à toi de lui rendre visite quand tu iras à ta conférence à Baltimore.

Bises,
Sandrine

1. Où est-ce que Sandrine va pour voir ses aïeux?
2. Où habite la première personne qu'elle voit?
3. Comment s'appelle-t-il?
4. Qui est Romane? Où s'est-elle installée?
5. Qui est Alexis?
6. Qui est Michèle? Elle habite dans quel état?
7. Où habitent les enfants de Michèle?
8. Qui est-ce que Sandrine ne voit pas? Pourquoi?

Essential Instruction

1. Students will listen to **Pour la conversation** and **Et si je voulais dire...?** Ask students, **"Savez-vous où sont arrivés vos aïeux et où ils se sont installés?"**
2. Students will read **Un long voyage** to each other, alternating sentences. They will then complete questions 1 through 8 together.
3. For **Activité 2** students will work in pairs using the family tree to ask the question **Qui est...?** and respond. **Qui est Rose? C'est mon arrière-grand-mère.** They will add detail: **C'est mon arrière-grand-mère qui était professeur dans une petite école en Pennsylvanie en 1900.**
4. In pairs, students will complete **Activité 3.**

2 C'est qui? 1.2, 1.3

Imaginez que vous êtes Jean-Luc. Identifiez chaque membre de votre famille selon le modèle.

MODÈLE

Étienne
C'est mon cousin germain.

3 Les états américains

3.1

Indiquez l'état pour chaque capitale.

MODÈLE Baton Rouge
La capitale de la Louisiane est Bâton Rouge.

1. Albany
2. Harrisburg
3. Santa Fe
4. Salt Lake City
5. Columbia
6. Oklahoma City
7. Atlanta
8. Richmond
9. Pierre
10. Raleigh
11. Tallahassee
12. Honolulu
13. Montpelier
14. St. Paul

Le Capitole à Bâton Rouge

Answers

Rose: C'est mon arrière-grand-mère.
Pierre: C'est mon arrière-grand-père.
Hugo: C'est mon grand-oncle.
Maude: C'est ma grand-tante.
Philippe: C'est mon grand-mère.
Cécile: C'est ma grand-mère.
Étienne: C'est mon cousin germain.
Marguerite: C'est ma cousine germaine.
Sylvie: C'est ma mère.
Thibault: C'est mon père.

1. La capitale de l'état de New York est Albany.
2. La capitale de l'état de la Pennsylvanie est Harrisburg.
3. La capitale de l'état du Nouveau Mexique est Santa Fe.
4. La capitale de l'état de l'Utah est Salt Lake City.
5. La capitale de l'état de la Caroline du sud est Columbia.
6. La capitale de l'état de l'Oklahoma est Oklahoma City.
7. La capitale de la Géorgie est Atlanta.
8. La capitale de la Virginie est Richmond.
9. La capitale du Dakota du sud est Pierre.
10. La capitale de la Caroline du nord est Raleigh.
11. La capitale de la Floride est Tallahassee.
12. La capitale d'Hawaï est Honolulu.
13. La capitale du Vermont est Montpelier.
14. La capitale du Minnesota est St Paul.

Culture

Products: Information

On the theme of family members, ***Tatie Danielle*** is a film classic about a cranky aunt who lives life her way. Students may enjoy watching scenes from this comedy that can be found online.
Search Words: tatie danielle

Differentiated Learning

Accelerate

Have students do **Activité 2** again, replacing the persons in the activity with their own family members, and adding their godparents using vocabulary from **Et si je voulais dire...?**

Learning Styles

Kinesthetic Learners

1. Project Jean-Luc's family on a screen. Two students with fly swatters will go to the screen and try to tap the picture of the family member you name faster than the other: **C'est la mère de Jean-Luc.**
2. Project the map of the United States. Using the same flyswatter technique, call out a state. Students must tap it and use **dans**, **en**, or **à** with the state. Teacher: **le Tennessee!** Student: **dans le Tennessee.**

Answers

4

1. Mes grands-parents se sont installés dans le Texas.
2. Ma petite cousine s'est installée dans l'Arizona.
3. Mon cousin s'est installé dans l'Alaska.
4. Mon arrière-grand-mère et sa fille se sont installées dans l'Illinois.
5. Ma tante s'est installée dans le Massachussetts.
6. Mon cousin germain s'est installé dans l'état de Washington.

5

Script can be found in the front pages of the Annotated Teacher's Edition.

1. V
2. F
3. F
4. F
5. V
6. F

6 *Answers will vary.*

Communication

Interpersonal: Paired Practice

In pairs, students will ask and answer questions for **Activité 4.** Student A: **Où a déménagé ta grand-tante?** Student B: **Ma grand-tante a déménagé ....** Roles will be reversed so that student B forms the questions and student A responds. Expand the exercise by adding the question **pourquoi?** Example: **Ma grand-tante a déménagé en Virginie parce que mon grand-oncle cherchait du travail.**

Interpersonal: Paired Practice

Pair students to ask questions about the states. There may be multiple answers to some questions.

Où peut-on trouver les vedettes de cinéma?
Où est-ce que la Déclaration de l'Indépendance a été écrite?
Où se trouve le centre de commerce et la Bourse?
Où peut-on trouver les casinos?
Où est-ce que Thomas Jefferson a vécu?
Où peut-on trouver des surfeurs?
Où parle-t-on français?
Où peut-on trouver de très bonnes pêches?

4 Où se sont-ils installés?

1.3

Après l'ouragan (hurricane) Katrina à la Nouvelle-Orléans, beaucoup de membres de la famille de Joséphine ont déménagé. Jouez le rôle de Joséphine et dites où ils se sont installés.

MODÈLE ma grand-tante/Iowa
Ma grand-tante s'est installée dans l'Iowa.

1. mes grands-parents/Texas
2. ma petite cousine/Arizona
3. mon cousin/Alaska
4. mon arrière-grand-mère et sa fille/Illinois
5. ma tante/Massachussetts
6. mon cousin germain/l'état de Washington

5 Qui sont vos aïeux?

1.1, 1.2, 5.1

Interpretive Communication

*Écrivez les numéros 1–6 sur votre papier. Écoutez la discussion entre le prof d'histoire et ses élèves. Ensuite, indiquez si les phrases sont vraies (**V**) ou fausses (**F**).*

1. Le professeur a demandé à ses élèves de faire des recherches sur un site généalogique en ligne.
2. L'arrière-grand-mère et l'arrière-grand-père d'Annie se sont rencontrés au Québec.
3. La famille de Roger vient d'Italie.
4. La famille de Roger s'est installée dans le Michigan où ils étaient forgerons.
5. Chase a de la famille en Louisiane.
6. Une partie de la famille de Melissa habite à Hawaï.

6 Questions personnelles

1.2, 1.3, 5.1

Répondez aux questions.

1. Comment s'appellent votre arrière-grand-père et votre arrière-grand-mère?
2. Est-ce que vous connaissez ou avez connu votre grand-tante ou grand-oncle? Où habitent/habitaient-ils?
3. D'où sont arrivés vos aïeux? En quelle année? Comment sont-ils venus?
4. Avez-vous voyagé dans d'autres états? Si oui, lesquels?
5. Quels états voudriez-vous visiter? Pourquoi?

Essential Instruction

1. Students will do **Où ont-ils déménagé?** in pairs.
2. Students will listen to **Qui sont vos aïeux?** answering **vrai** or **faux** 1 through 6.
3. For **Activité 6** put students in groups of three and have them ask each question to one another to practice using the vocabulary in context.
4. Students will listen to **Les ancêtres de Justin** and individually answer questions 1 through 7 on p.146.

Rencontres culturelles

emcl.com
WB 4

Les ancêtres de Justin    1.1, 1.2, 5.1

Léo et son ami américain, Justin, se parlent au cercle de conversation de l'Alliance française de Nice.

Léo: Tes ancêtres sont venus de France? C'est incroyable! Tu en es sûr?

Justin: Absolument. Mon père a fait des recherches généalogiques sur l'histoire de notre famille: il me les a montrées. C'est passionnant.

Léo: Et alors?

Justin: Eh bien, mes aïeux sont arrivés de Bretagne et se sont installés au Québec sur l'île d'Orléans. Mon ancêtre devait être forgeron. Mais il en a profité pour changer de métier. Il s'est occupé de mécanique. Ils étaient très pauvres. La vie était très difficile.

Léo: Mais ils ne sont pas restés?

Justin: Plusieurs générations y ont vécu. C'est en 1929 avec la grande crise qu'ils sont venus tenter leur chance aux États-Unis. Ils se sont installés dans le Maine.

Léo: C'était une manière de garder le contact avec la Francophonie.

Justin: Si tu veux! Pour mon arrière-grand-père, c'était surtout le moyen de trouver du travail! Mon arrière-grand-père a travaillé sur les bateaux comme pêcheur et mon arrière-grand-mère travaillait dans une conserverie. Après, ça a été mieux....

Léo: Et ton grand-père, il vit toujours dans le Maine?

Justin: Mon grand-père a compris que le Maine allait devenir très touristique alors, il a ouvert un petit restaurant, puis un hôtel, sur Mount Desert Island; maintenant ce sont des cousins qui le tiennent.

Léo: Et tout ce temps tu ne m'as rien dit!

Un forgeron.

Le Maine.

RESOURCES

 Dialogue Video

 Workbook 4

Reference Desk

1. **L'Île d'Orléans** is located 3.1 kilometers east of Quebec City in the Saint Lawrence River. It was one of the first outposts of **La Nouvelle France** settled in the 17th century. In 1535, the explorer Jacques Cartier originally called it **Bacchus** for the grapevines he found there. Later it was named in honor of the Duc d'Orléans, son of King François Ier. A large percentage of French Canadians can trace their ancestry to the early settlers who lived on the island. It is often called **Le Berceau de l'Amérique Française**, the cradle of French America. See pp. 148, 150–151.
2. Many believe the name **Québec** comes from the Algonquin word meaning "narrow passage or strait."
3. In French, one says **à Québec** to refer to the city of Quebec, but **au Québec** to refer to the province of Quebec.
4. The word **forgeron** (*blacksmith*) comes from the verb **forger**, which means "to shape or form a piece of metal."

Expansion

Put students in groups and ask them the following question: **Comment les photos à la page 145 correspondent-elles à la lecture "Les ancêtres de Justin"?** You may give each group a few minutes of discussion time and then share answers with the class.

Differentiated Learning

Accelerate

Students may answer the **Questions personnelles** by pretending that they belong to a well-known American family such as the Kennedys, the Lincolns, etc.

Special Needs Students

Auditory Impairment

Allow students with auditory impairment to follow the script while the recorded dialogue plays.

Answers

7 *Possible answers:*

1. Le père de Justin a fait des recherches généalogiques pour mieux connaître ses ancêtres.
2. Les aïeux de Justin se sont installés au Québec sur l'île d'Orléans.
3. Justin pense que son ancêtre était forgeron.
4. La grande crise de 1929 a poussé la famille de Justin à venir s'installer aux États-Unis.
5. L'arrière-grand-père de Justin était pêcheur.
6. L'arrière-grand-mère de Justin travaillait dans une conserverie.
7. Le grand-père de Justin vit dans le Maine.

Extension

Il cherche des documents civils de ses ancêtres pour faire un arbre généalogique de sa famille.

7 Les ancêtres de Justin

  **1.1, 1.3**

Utilisez chacune des expressions suivantes dans une phrase pour montrer votre compréhension du dialogue et du vocabulaire.

MODÈLE l'Alliance française
Justin et Léo sont à l'Alliance française, une organisation associée à la promotion de la langue et la culture françaises.

1. des recherches généalogiques
2. l'île d'Orléans
3. forgeron
4. la grande crise de 1929
5. pêcheur
6. une conserverie
7. le Maine

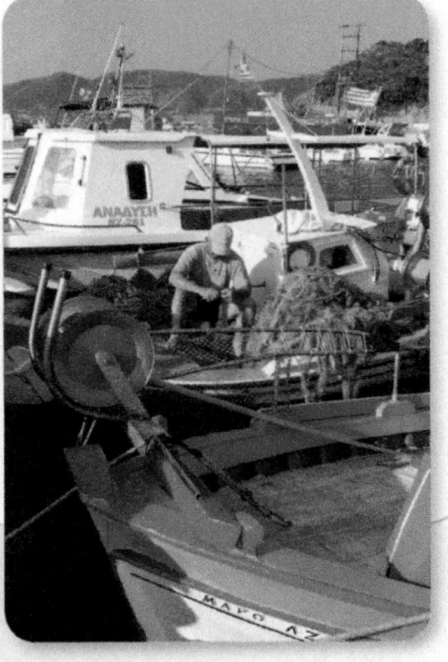

Extension **Un projet de famille**   **1.1, 1.2, 5.1**

Alexis interrompt son père qui travaille sur son ordinateur.

Alexis: Mais qu'est-ce que tu cherches là?
Père: Là, je suis sur le site des archives départementales: on y trouve tous les actes officiels.
Alexis: C'est-à-dire?
Père: Eh bien, les actes de naissance, les changements de propriété, les changements d'état civil, différents types de contrats....
Alexis: Et avec ces documents, on remonte loin?
Père: Pour notre famille, je les ai presque tous retrouvés. Je suis remonté jusqu'à la Révolution française.
Alexis: Alors cet arbre généalogique, on le voit quand?
Père: Bientôt... patience....

Extension Qu'est-ce que le père d'Alexis cherche sur Internet? Ses recherches l'aident à faire quoi?

1.1, 1.2, 5.1

Essential Instruction

1. Have students answer **Activité 7** in pairs. Ask several pairs to give an answer for each question in order to get students used to the repetition of the correct syntax associated with each group of words.
2. Ask students with theatrical inclination to volunteer to read the **Extension** dialogue as a skit.
3. Have the students read **L'Alliance française** individually or in pairs. You may ask them to summarize each paragraph in one sentence in French or English.
4. The following are comprehension questions that can be asked orally, or done in student pairs:
En quelle année l'Alliance française a-t-elle été fondée et par qui?
Quels sont les objectifs de l'organisme?
Quel est le plus grand centre de l'Alliance française aux Etats-Unis?
Combien d'étudiants participent aux programmes dans le monde entier?
Quels sont les programmes organisés par l'Alliance française?

Points de départ

Pre AP

emcl.com
WB 5

Question centrale

Comment les Francophones restent-ils fidèles à leur langue et à leurs traditions?

L'Alliance française  1.2, 2.1

Fondée en 1883, sous l'égide* de Paul Cambon, et avec des membres du comité fondateur aussi prestigieux que Ferdinand de Lesseps, Louis Pasteur, Jules Verne, et Ernest Renan, l'Alliance française est une association qui a pour objectif de participer au rayonnement* de la culture française et à l'enseignement de la langue française.

L'Alliance française compte environ 1.000 comités répartis dans 135 pays. Elle accueille plus de 500.000 étudiants à travers* le monde. Les Alliances françaises organisent des conférences, des programmes de cinéma, des concerts, et des représentations théâtrales. Elles coopèrent aussi avec de nombreuses associations artistiques locales.

L'Alliance française des États-Unis est l'une des plus importantes antennes*; elle a été créée en 1902. On trouve des Alliances françaises à travers tous les États-Unis, aussi bien sur la côte Est que dans le Wyoming, l'Idaho, le Kansas, ou encore en Floride et en Californie. Le French Institute-Alliance française de New-York est le centre le plus important aux USA.

 **Search words: alliance française de nice, alliance française usa**

égide *umbrella;* **rayonnement** *influence;* **à travers** *throughout;* **antennes** *branches*

Mots-clé

Au début, le mot **alliance** désigne le phénomène religieux et le caractère psychologique du lien par mariage entre deux grandes familles. Ce terme évolue à une union par engagement mutuel et développe un sens juridique et politique au XIIIème siècle.

COMPARAISONS

Comment est-ce que les États-Unis participent au rayonnement de l'anglais et de la culture américaine?

 **Search words: voice of america**

 4.2

1.2, 2.2

Produits

L'Alliance française offre des **examens agréés** (*approved*) par la Chambre de Commerce et d'Industrie de Paris (CCIP). Donc, si vous vous intéressez à travailler dans les affaires (*business*), pour une compagnie française ou une compagnie américaine avec une succursale (*branch*) en France, vous pouvez vous inscrire à l'Alliance française pour vous préparer.

RESOURCES

 **Workbook 5**

Game

Qui est-ce?

Divide the class in two teams. Each team must find the name of one famous French person (scientist, entertainer, philosopher, etc.) that starts with each letter of the alphabet from A–Z. Give them fifteen minutes to find as many persons as possible. You may allow them to repeat letters or not.

Differentiated Learning

Accelerate

High-ability students will listen to **Extension** p. 146, **Un projet de famille**, and answer the question prior to looking at the script.

Decelerate

Students will visit the **Alliance française** website for the city of Nice and the **French Institute-Alliance française de New-York** website. They will compare the two centers in terms of cultural events, classes for adults and children, and diplomas offered.

Multiple Intelligences

Musical-Rhythmic

Ask students to write a song that explains what the **Alliance française** is, who founded it, where the centers are located, and what activities they offer.

Reference Desk

The French-Canadian accent varies from the continental French accent, as our American accent is different from the British. You may want to find online and show the video "**Cours de Québécois Saguenéen**" to expose the students to the sound of French spoken in Canada, and to learn a few more French-Canadian expressions as an extension of **Mon dico québécois.**
Search words: **cours de quebecois saguenean**

Expansion

The following are comprehension questions that can be asked orally or done in student pairs:
En quelle année a été fondé le Québec et par qui?
D'où proviennent les premiers colons venus de France?
Les "filles du Roi" étaient les filles de quel roi? Pourquoi ont-elles émigré?
Qui était Félix Leclerc? De quelles nationalités étaient les personnes venues s›installer à l'île d'Orléans au XXe siècle?
Les habitants de quelles régions de la Nouvelle France sont-ils venus s›installer en Nouvelle Angleterre? À quelle époque?
Dans quelle industrie ont-ils commencé à travailler?
Dans l'état du Maine, quel est le pourcentage de la population qui parle français actuellement à la maison?
Comment sait-on que la recherche des ancêtres québécois est importante aujourd'hui?

L'immigration française: de l'île d'Orléans au Québec

C'est avec Samuel de Champlain que commence l'aventure coloniale française au Québec. Il fonde la ville de Québec en 1608 et fait venir les missions religieuses. Mais c'est vers 1630 que commencent les premières grandes migrations. Plus de mille colons* arrivent de Bretagne, de Normandie, d'Anjou, puis 770 filles du Roi* sont envoyées pour agrandir l'empire colonial. Les conflits militaires amènent 1.200 hommes supplémentaires du Dauphiné, de Ligurie, et de Savoie.

L'île d'Orléans, proche de* Québec, aujourd'hui reliée* par un pont, est le berceau* de peuplement* de la Nouvelle France. Sainte Famille, le village le plus ancien, a été fondé en 1661. C'est sur cette île qu'est enterré* Félix Leclerc (1914–1988), l'un des plus grands chanteurs québécois.

Dans les années 1960–1970, les immigrants francophones au Québec venaient principalement d'Haïti et du Vietnam; aujourd'hui, la majorité des immigrants viennent de France, de Belgique, et du Maghreb.

Search words: île d'orléans tourisme, île d'orléans familles souches, île d'orléans québec région

colons *settlers;* **filles du Roi** *King's Daughters (group of young and single women sent to* **la Nouvelle France** *to get married to the settlers and have children);* **proche de** *close to;* **reliée** *connected;* **berceau** *cradle;* **peuplement** *populating;* **enterré** *buried*

Mon dico québécois

Qu'est-ce que ça mange ça? *Qu'est-ce que ça signifie?*
J'ai ben de la misère avec ça. *Je supporte cela difficilement.*
Ça m'a coûté une beurrée. *Ça m'a coûté cher.*
Ça n'a pas d'allure ton affaire. *Ça n'a pas de sens.*
T'es rendu végétarien maintenant? *Tu es devenu végétarien?*

La ville de Québec montre la présence française en Amérique.

Au début de la colonisation, les Québecois habitaient dans la "Nouvelle France."

Essential Instruction

1. Distribute a map of **Québec** to your students. Then project the map of North America from **Unité 10** Level 1 (p. 516). Help your students locate **l'île d'Orléans** and **la Nouvelle France.**
2. Now ask students to find where **la Nouvelle Angleterre** is located, and see if they all knew it is a region of the United States, not Canada.
3. You may ask students to brainstorm what other states or regions in the United States have a francophone (linguistic or cultural) heritage.
4. Divide the class in two groups. One group will read **L'immigration française: de l'île d'Orléans au Québec,** the other **La Nouvelle Angleterre.**

1.2, 2.1

La Francophonie

La Nouvelle Angleterre

On estime* à 900.000 le nombre de Francophones en Nouvelle Angleterre. Ce sont les descendants des Québécois et des Acadiens qui, sans travail, sont venus s'y installer entre le milieu du XIXème siècle et la Seconde Guerre mondiale. Ils travaillent tout d'abord dans l'industrie textile; leurs descendants sont maintenant journalistes, avocats, commerçants, etc. Il existe aujourd'hui 500 organisations qui s'occupent de la recherche des ancêtres québécois. Dans le Maine, on estime que 5% de la population parle français à la maison.

Un documentaire récent, ***Réveille***, montre une réapparition de l'intérêt des immigrés de Québec et de leurs enfants de la Nouvelle Angleterre pour la langue française et l'héritage québécois.

1.2, 2.2

Search words: réveil activités culturelles, waking up french

estime *estimates*

Le parc national de l'Acadie dans le Maine a été découvert par Samuel de Champlain.

8 Activités culturelles

1.3, 3.2

Complétez les activités suivantes.

1. Identifiez les professions de Ferdinand de Lesseps, Louis Pasteur, Jules Verne et Ernest Renan.
2. Faites la carte d'identité de l'Alliance française:
   - Siècle de création
   - Nombre de pays
   - Nombre de comités
   - Activités
3. Trouvez l'Alliance française la plus proche de chez vous et faites une liste d'activités ou de programmes qui vous intéressent.
4. De quelles régions venaient les premiers colons du Québec? Situez-les sur une carte de France.
5. Faites une liste des noms de famille français des habitants de l'Île d'Orléans et de la Nouvelle Angleterre.

Perspectives

"Étant une personne qui apprécie la sagesse *(wisdom)*, la tradition, et la richesse qui sortent de notre passé, il me faut être 'branché' dans le monde francanadien. De nos jours, *'C'est une pinotte!'* Les médias sociaux, Radio Canada, et d'autres ressources en ligne comme ToutCanadien.com rendent cette connexion à portée de main (*within reach*) à tout moment." Comment est-ce que cet américain avec des ancêtres québécois profite des médias canadiens pour enrichir sa vie aux États-Unis?

Answers

8

1. Ferdinand de Lesseps: diplomate et entrepreneur; Louis Pasteur: scientifique; Jules Verne: écrivain; Ernest Renan: écrivain et historien
2. siècle de création: 19ème; nombre de pays: 135; nombre de comités: 1.000; activités: conférences, cinéma, concerts, théâtre
3. *Answers will vary.*
4. de Bretagne, de Normandie, d'Anjou; au nord-ouest de la France
5. *Examples*: Arrivé, Aubin, Beaudoin, Chrétien, Charpentier, Dufresne, Fontaine, etc.

Perspectives

Il utilise des ressources en ligne.

Reference Desk

Les voyageurs and **les coureurs des Bois** were hearty, daring fur traders in the 17th and 18th centuries, who left Quebec and Montreal and headed westward in search of beaver pelts. They would be gone for months at a time, travelling thousands of miles, paddling ten to twelve hours a day in birch bark canoes. These adventurers set up outposts along the waterways of the United States. Many of our cities bear French names due to their presence. These colorful merchants were known for their dress, music, and folklore.

Communication

Interpersonal: Cooperative Groups

Put students into five groups. Each group will draw a card from 1 to 5, corresponding to the numbered activities in **Activités culturelles**. Each group will collaborate to complete the activity. Students working on the first activity should expand it to include a brief biography of each person listed. All groups will share their work with the class.

Differentiated Learning

Decelerate

Give students a map of North America and have them circle **la Nouvelle France** and **la Nouvelle Angleterre** in different colors. Have them write **le Québec** under **la Nouvelle France**, and ask them to research when the region changed its name. Finally, ask students to make a list of the American states that make up the region of **la Nouvelle Angleterre**.

Multiple Intelligences

Naturalist

These students will research the canoes, hunting instruments, and animals hunted by the **voyageurs** and **les coureurs des bois**.

Musical-Rhythmic

Students will teach two songs of the **voyageurs**, "**Alouette**" and "**À la Claire Fontaine**," to the class.

Visual-Spatial

Students will make a chart of the trading posts and routes travelled by the **voyageurs.**

Communication

Presentational: Cooperative Groups

Assign online research to groups of students. Each group chooses a place featured in the brochure and finds more photos and information. Then each group prepares a short presentation for the class as if they were tour guides.

Du côté des médias

Pre AP 1.2

Interpretive Communication

Lisez la brochure sur l'île d'Orléans.

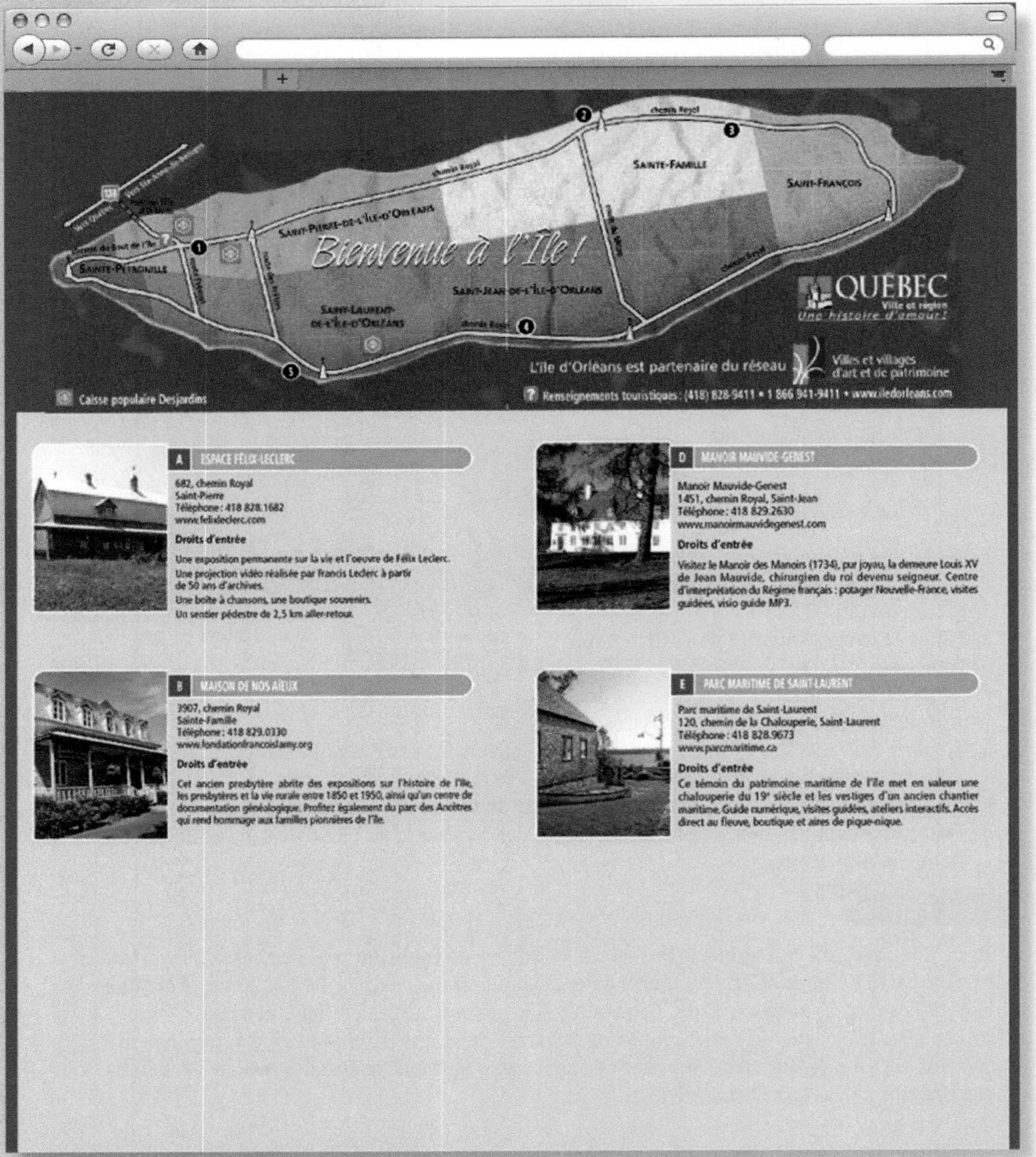

Sainte-Pétronille

Saint-Pierre-de-l'Île-d'Orléans

Sainte-Famille

Saint-François

Saint-Jean-de-l'Île-d'Orléans

Saint-Laurent-de-l'Île-d'Orléans

chemin Royal

Bienvenue à l'Île !

QUÉBEC Ville et région *Une histoire d'amour!*

L'île d'Orléans est partenaire du réseau Villes et villages d'art et de patrimoine

Renseignements touristiques : (418) 828-9411 • 1 866 941-9411 • www.iledorleans.com

Caisse populaire Desjardins

A ESPACE FÉLIX-LECLERC

682, chemin Royal
Saint-Pierre
Téléphone : 418 828.1682
www.felixleclerc.com

Droits d'entrée

Une exposition permanente sur la vie et l'oeuvre de Félix Leclerc.
Une projection vidéo réalisée par Francis Leclerc à partir de 50 ans d'archives.
Une boite à chansons, une boutique souvenirs.
Un sentier pédestre de 2,5 km aller-retour.

D MANOIR MAUVIDE-GENEST

Manoir Mauvide-Genest
1451, chemin Royal, Saint-Jean
Téléphone : 418 829.2630
www.manoirmauvidegenest.com

Droits d'entrée

Visitez le Manoir des Manoirs (1734), pur joyau, la demeure Louis XV de Jean Mauvide, chirurgien du roi devenu seigneur. Centre d'interprétation du Régime français : potager Nouvelle-France, visites guidées, visio guide MP3.

B MAISON DE NOS AÏEUX

3907, chemin Royal
Sainte-Famille
Téléphone : 418 829.0330
www.fondationfrancoislamy.org

Droits d'entrée

Cet ancien presbytère abrite des expositions sur l'histoire de l'île, les presbytères et la vie rurale entre 1850 et 1950, ainsi qu'un centre de documentation généalogique. Profitez également du parc des Ancêtres qui rend hommage aux familles pionnières de l'île.

E PARC MARITIME DE SAINT-LAURENT

Parc maritime de Saint-Laurent
120, chemin de la Chalouperie, Saint-Laurent
Téléphone : 418 828.9673
www.parcmaritime.ca

Droits d'entrée

Ce témoin du patrimoine maritime de l'île met en valeur une chalouperie du 19e siècle et les vestiges d'un ancien chantier maritime. Guide numérique, visites guidées, ateliers interactifs. Accès direct au fleuve, boutique et aires de pique-nique.

Essential Instruction

1. Have students work in pairs to read **Du côté des médias.** The students will condense into one to two sentences the importance of each of the four tourist sites highlighted in the brochure.
2. Students will prioritize which sites they would personally like to visit in descending order and state why.
3. Students will continue in pairs to read the tourist brochure **l'Île d'Orléans.** They will do the corresponding activities, 1 through 4.
4. As an extension to the fourth activity, have the students find lodgings and restaurants for their visit to the island.
   Search words: mrc île d'orleans, tourisme île d'orleans

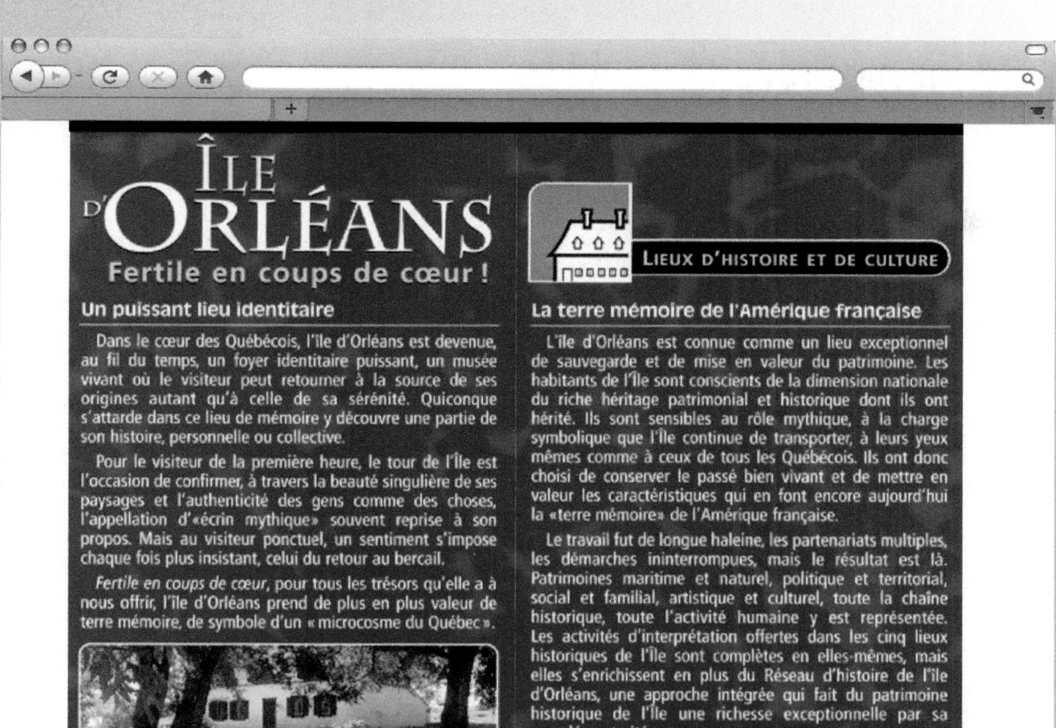

ÎLE D'ORLÉANS

Fertile en coups de cœur !

Un puissant lieu identitaire

Dans le cœur des Québécois, l'île d'Orléans est devenue, au fil du temps, un foyer identitaire puissant, un musée vivant où le visiteur peut retourner à la source de ses origines autant qu'à celle de sa sérénité. Quiconque s'attarde dans ce lieu de mémoire y découvre une partie de son histoire, personnelle ou collective.

Pour le visiteur de la première heure, le tour de l'Île est l'occasion de confirmer, à travers la beauté singulière de ses paysages et l'authenticité des gens comme des choses, l'appellation d'«écrin mythique» souvent reprise à son propos. Mais au visiteur ponctuel, un sentiment s'impose chaque fois plus insistant, celui du retour au bercail.

Fertile en coups de cœur, pour tous les trésors qu'elle a à nous offrir, l'île d'Orléans prend de plus en plus valeur de terre mémoire, de symbole d'un « microcosme du Québec ».

LIEUX D'HISTOIRE ET DE CULTURE

La terre mémoire de l'Amérique française

L'île d'Orléans est connue comme un lieu exceptionnel de sauvegarde et de mise en valeur du patrimoine. Les habitants de l'Île sont conscients de la dimension nationale du riche héritage patrimonial et historique dont ils ont hérité. Ils sont sensibles au rôle mythique, à la charge symbolique que l'Île continue de transporter, à leurs yeux mêmes comme à ceux de tous les Québécois. Ils ont donc choisi de conserver le passé bien vivant et de mettre en valeur les caractéristiques qui en font encore aujourd'hui la «terre mémoire» de l'Amérique française.

Le travail fut de longue haleine, les partenariats multiples, les démarches ininterrompues, mais le résultat est là. Patrimoines maritime et naturel, politique et territorial, social et familial, artistique et culturel, toute la chaîne historique, toute l'activité humaine y est représentée. Les activités d'interprétation offertes dans les cinq lieux historiques de l'Île sont complètes en elles-mêmes, mais elles s'enrichissent en plus du Réseau d'histoire de l'île d'Orléans, une approche intégrée qui fait du patrimoine historique de l'Île une richesse exceptionnelle par sa complémentarité.

9 Île d'Orléans

1.3, 3.2

Complétez les activités suivantes.

1. Faites une liste des adjectifs et des noms qui décrivent l'île d'Orléans.
2. Imaginez que vous travaillez à l'office du tourisme de l'île d'Orléans. Indiquez aux touristes qui vous appellent comment rejoindre les lieux à la page 150 à partir de Québec sur la route 138.
3. Faites des recherches sur les cinq sites mentionnés plus haut et choisissez un site à visiter. Dites pourquoi il vous intéresse.
4. Organisez votre visite de l'île d'Orléans.

Answers

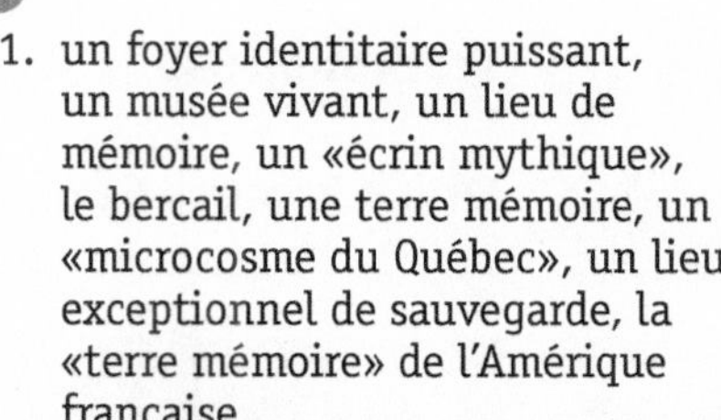

9

1. un foyer identitaire puissant, un musée vivant, un lieu de mémoire, un «écrin mythique», le bercail, une terre mémoire, un «microcosme du Québec», un lieu exceptionnel de sauvegarde, la «terre mémoire» de l'Amérique française
2. 1. L'espace Félix Leclerc: Traversez le Pont de l'Île d'Orléans et tournez à gauche sur le chemin Royal.; 2. La Maison de nos aïeux: Traversez le Pont de l'Île d'Orléans, tournez à gauche sur le chemin Royal, c'est sur votre gauche juste après la route du Mitan.; 3. La Seigneurerie Mauvide Genest: Traversez le Pont de l'Île d'Orléans, tournez à gauche sur le chemin Royal, passez la route du Mitan et continuez tout droit.; 4. Le parc maritime: Traversez le Pont de l'Île d'Orléans et continuez tout droit sur la route Prévost. Puis, tournez à gauche sur le chemin Royal et continuez tout droit.
3. *Answers will vary.*
4. *Answers will vary.*

Culture

Practices: Information

Une érablière, also called **cabane à sucre**, is a place where artisans produce maple syrup. As they compete against industrialization, these old-fashioned artisans are slowly disappearing. There is one traditional **érablière** left in **l'Île d'Orléans**. **Québecois** typically eat maple syrup cold with cream and bread, in yogurt, over ice cream, fruit, pancakes or French toast, and even use it as a base for broth or gravy.

Differentiated Learning

Accelerate

Students will make a brochure for their state or their hometown using the same format as found on pp. 150–151.

Decelerate

Have students collaborate to make a map of Canada, contrasting with different colors the provinces considered Francophone, Anglophone, and bilingual. They should label key cities in each province. Each group will present their poster or visual to the classroom.

Special Needs Students

AD(H)D

Students with short attention spans may benefit from focusing on one tourist site at a time from the **Du côté des médias** brochure, and listing essential elements described in each paragraph.

RESOURCES

Workbook 6–9

Drill & Practice Games

Reference Desk

1. **Y** replaces prepositional phrases beginning with **à**, **chez**, **dans**, **derrière**, **devant**, **en**, and **sur**. When the noun following **à** is a person, the indirect object pronouns **lui** and **leur** are used.
2. Here are additional verbs followed by **à** + a thing: **s'intéresser à**, **s'habituer à**, **résister à**, **obéir à**, **répondre à**, **assister à**.
3. Point out the elision when using the pronoun **y** in negative sentences and with reflexive verbs: **Mme Martin n'y voyage plus avec son mari. Je m'y repose souvent.**
4. You may want to review the four uses of **en** with your students.
5. Students may be interested in learning idiomatic expressions such as **J'en ai marre!** *(I'm fed up!)* and **Je n'y arrive pas!** *(I can't do this!)*
6. In the **passé composé** there is no preceding direct object agreement: **J'en ai écrit trois.**

TPR

Throw a ball to a student as you say a sentence in French that requires a pronoun replacement. The student will return the ball to you as he/she restates the sentence with a pronoun. **Paul, Tu vas aller au cinéma avec Charles? Oui, je vais y aller avec Charles.** The ball adds an element of surprise since students don't know when it will be their turn.

Communication

Interpersonal: Paired Practice

Partners will ask each other if he/she would like pleasant or unpleasant things, using the pronoun **en**.

Structure de la langue

emcl.com
WB 6–9
Games

Révision: The Pronouns *y* and *en*

1.2, 1.2

Do you remember how to answer the questions below affirmatively, replacing what's underlined with the correct pronoun?

1. Vas-tu <u>au cinéma</u> le weekend?
2. Tu as <u>un dictionnaire français-anglais</u>?
3. Tu aimes manger <u>de la pizza</u>?
4. Voudrais-tu aller <u>en France</u>?

If you are unable to answer these questions, read the grammar summary below.

The pronouns **y** and **en** are placed before the verb of which they are the object in sentences that are affirmative, interrogative, negative, or have an infinitive.

À Paris? Non, nous ne voudrions pas **y** aller.	*To Paris? No, we wouldn't like to go there.*
Des oranges? Oui, j'**en** ai pris une.	Oranges? *Yes, I had one of them.*

Pronoun	Replaces	Examples	
y	preposition + place	Ta grand-tante était en Arizona? **Y** est-elle restée? Elle va **y** déménager.	*Your great-aunt was in Arizona?* *Did she stay there?* *She's going to move there.*
y	certain verbs, such as **penser à**, **réfléchir à** + name of thing	Son idée? Tu **y** penses?	*Her idea? Are you thinking about it?*
en	**de** + expression	Du vélo? **En** faites-vous en famille? Oui, nous **en** faisons ensemble. Mais nous n'**en** faisons pas pendant la semaine. Tu veux **en** faire avec nous samedi?	*Biking? Do you do it with your family?* *Yes, we do it together.* *But we don't do it during the week.* *Do you want to do it with us on Saturday?*

In an affirmative command, **y** or **en** follows the verb and is attached to it by a hyphen. In the **tu** form of **–er** verbs, the affirmative imperative adds an **s** before the pronoun **y** or **en.** In a negative command, **y** or **en** precedes the verb.

Prends-**en**!	*Take some!*
Mais n'**en** prends pas trop!	*But don't take too much/many.*

THE PRONOUNS y AND en: The affirmative answers using the pronouns **y** and **en** are:
1. J'y vais le weekend.
2. J'en ai un.
3. J'aime en manger.
4. Je voudrais y aller.

Essential Instruction

1. To review the pronoun **y,** refer to p. 439 in Level 2 of ***T'es branché?*** Then give students 10 sentences in which they replace expressions with the pronoun **y**. You may want to recycle the unit's vocabulary on p.141. **Paul habite *en Pennsylvanie*. Paul y habite. Paul veut habiter *en Virginie*. Paul veut y habiter.**
2. Remind students that **lui** and **leur** are used to replace expressions containing the preposition **à** followed by a person, whereas **y** is used to replace the pronoun **à** plus the name of a place or a thing. **Je parle *à Paul*. Je lui parle. Je vais *à Paris*. J'y vais.**
3. To review the pronoun **en**, refer to p. 386 in Level 2 of ***T'es branché?*** Remind students that **en** replaces places in sentences using a verb followed by the preposition **de.** Give students 10 sentences in which they replace expressions with the pronoun **en.**

Communiquez!

10 Tu penses à...?

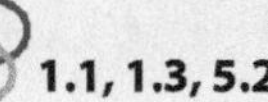

1.1, 1.3, 5.2

Interpersonal Communication

À tour de rôle, demandez à votre partenaire s'il ou elle pense aux sujets suivants. Répondez affirmativement ou négativement avec ***y****.*

MODÈLE les activités que tu faisais quand tu étais petit(e)
A: **Tu penses aux activités que tu faisais quand tu étais petit(e)?**
B: **Oui, j'y pense de temps en temps.**
ou
Non, je n'y pense pas.

1. les cadeaux de Noël que tu vas offrir
2. les questions que tes profs posent en classe
3. l'avenir
4. les informations à la télé
5. les amis que tu invites à ta fête
6. les problèmes de la vie contemporaine
7. les vacances

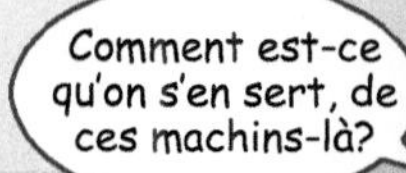

11 Vous vous en servez?

1.1, 5.2

Dites si tout le monde se sert de chacun des ustensiles suivants dans la cuisine. Répondez en utilisant ***en****, et soyez logique!*

MODÈLES Vous vous servez d'une cuiller en bois pour remuer la sauce?
Oui, nous nous en servons pour remuer la sauce.

Marianne se sert d'un bol pour préparer des steaks?
Non, elle ne s'en sert pas pour préparer des steaks.

1. Vous vous servez d'un chinois pour filtrer les herbes?
2. Madeleine se sert d'une poêle pour faire un gâteau?
3. Les sœurs Delattre se servent d'un verre mesureur pour mesurer le lait?
4. Tu te sers d'une cuiller en bois pour mesurer le sucre?
5. Jacques et Karim se servent d'un mixer pour faire des frites?
6. Je me sers d'une casserole pour faire chauffer la sauce?
7. Nous nous servons d'une passoire pour rincer les pâtes?

Answers

1. A: Tu penses aux cadeaux de Noël que tu vas offrir?
   B: J'y pense.../Je n'y pense pas.
2. A: Tu penses aux questions...?
   B: J'y pense.../Je n'y pense pas.
3. A: Tu penses à l'avenir...?
   B: J'y pense.../Je n'y pense pas.
4. A: Tu penses aux informations...?
   B: J'y pense.../Je n'y pense pas.
5. A: Tu penses aux amis...?
   B: J'y pense.../Je n'y pense pas.
6. A: Tu penses aux problèmes...?
   B: J'y pense.../Je n'y pense pas.
7. A: Tu penses aux vacances...?
   B: J'y pense.../Je n'y pense pas.

1. Oui, nous nous en servons pour filtrer les herbes.
2. Non, elle ne s'en sert pas pour faire un gâteau.
3. Oui, elles s'en servent pour mesurer le lait.
4. Non, je ne m'en sers pas pour mesurer le sucre.
5. Non, ils ne s'en servent pas pour faire des frites.
6. Oui, tu t'en sers pour faire chauffer la sauce.
7. Oui, vous vous en servez pour rincer les pâtes.

Reference Desk

In everyday speech, the negative particule **ne** in negative sentences with **y** and **en** may be omitted: **J'y pense pas. T'en as pas?**

Communication

Interpersonal: Paired Practice

Pair students to do **Activités 10** and **11**. One student will hold the book and the other will do the writing. The person with the book will read the question. The person responding can look at the question if necessary in order to answer. For the next item, students will trade responsibilities.

Differentiated Learning

Decelerate

Low-ability students will need to break down the pronoun replacement lesson into smaller steps. They will benefit from a set of sentences featuring only the pronoun **y**. They should underline the words to be replaced, then rewrite the sentences using **y**. Next, they should do a series of sentences with pronoun replacements using **en**, again underlining the words they intend to replace.

Multiple Intelligences

Musical-Rhythmic

To help auditory learners with switching from declarative to negative sentences with object pronouns, encourage them to do **Activité 10** and **Activité 11** by paying attention to the number of syllables it takes to answer a question in the declarative form. Then let them know that sentences in the negative are simply sentences in the declarative form with two more syllables: **J'y pense (2)**, **Je n'y pense pas (4)**, **Nous nous en servons (5)**, **Nous ne nous en servons pas (7)**, etc.

RESOURCES

 **Workbook 10–11**

 **Drill & Practice Games**

Answers

Script can be found in the front pages of the Annotated Teacher's Edition.

1. y
2. en
3. y
4. en
5. y
6. y
7. en
8. en

Reference Desk

1. To help students remember the order of object pronouns, create one or two sentences they can learn by heart such as **Je donne des bonbons aux enfants à la maison. Je leur y en donne.**
2. Help students remember that **y** always comes before **en** by stressing that the pair **y en** sounds like the sound a donkey makes in French: "**hi-han**."

12 De petites conversations

 1.1, 1.2

Interpretive Communication

*Écrivez les numéros 1–8 sur votre papier. Écoutez les questions et indiquez si vous répondriez avec **y** ou **en**.*

Révision: Double Object Pronouns

 1.2

emcl.com
WB 10–11
Games

Imagine there is a new student in your French immersion school. Answer her questions affirmatively, replacing what's underlined with two pronouns.

1. Tu me montres la cantine?
2. Pourrais-tu me prêter ton stylo?

If you can't answer these questions, read the grammar summary below.

When there are two pronouns in one sentence, their order before the verb in a declarative sentence is:

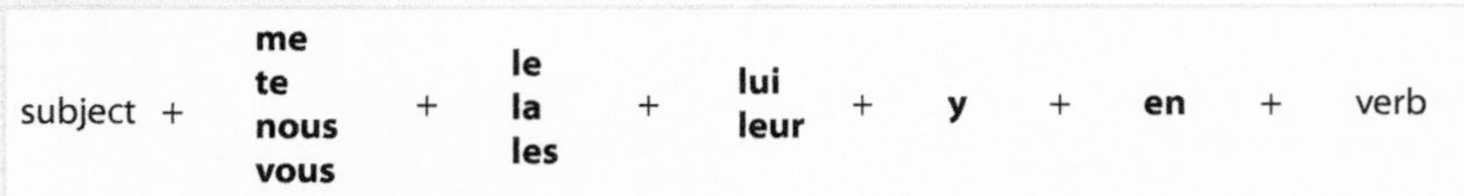

subject +	me te nous vous	+	le la les	+	lui leur	+	y	+	en	+	verb

These pronouns come right before the verb of which they are the object in sentences that are affirmative, negative, interrogative, or have an infinitive. They also precede the verb in a negative command.

Quand as-tu vu mes cousins germains en ville?	*When did you see my first cousins in town?*
Je ne **les y** ai pas vus hier.	*I didn't see them there yesterday.*
Les vacances d'été? Je **leur en** ai parlé au téléphone.	*Summer vacation? I talked to them about it on the phone.*
Vous allez inviter vos cousins germains chez vous?	*Are you going to invite your first cousins to your house?*
Oui, je vais **les y** inviter.	*Yes, I'm going to invite them there.*
Non! Ne **m'en** parle pas!	*No! Don't talk to me about it!*

DOUBLE OBJECT PRONOUNS: These are the affirmative answers to the questions:
1. Je te la montre.
2. Je pourrais te le prêter.

Essential Instruction

1. As a bell-ringer activity, do a quick review of **y** and **en** by having students listen to **De petites conversations** answering questions 1 through 8.
2. Re-acquaint students with the position of the pronouns by asking them questions: **Tu aimes le chocolat? Tu l'aimes?; Chris connaît Sara? Il la connaît?; Vous mangez des frites en classe de français? Vous y en mangez?** Students must respond with pronouns.
3. Ask students, "Which sounds better: **me le** or **le me**," or ask "**le moi** or **moi le**?" Invariably the students will choose the correct order by ear.
4. Review pronoun positions in the affirmative and negative commands.
5. In pairs, students will ask and answer the questions in **Logique ou non?**

In an affirmative command, the order of pronouns is:

verb	+	le la les	+	lui leur	+	moi toi nous vous	+	y	+	en

Je donne l'invitation à ta grand-tante?
Oui, **donne-la**-lui!

Should I give the invitation to your great-aunt?
Yes, give it to her!

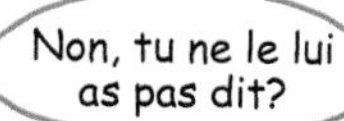

COMPARAISONS

Verbs can be transitive or intransitive. A transitive verb takes a direct object; an intransitive verb does not require a direct object. Are the verbs in the sentences below transitive or intransitive?

1. Chelsea **is eating** at the café.
2. Zach **sees** Chelsea.
3. Zach **writes** Chelsea a text message.

 4.1

13 Logique ou non?

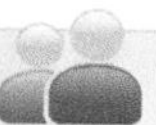  1.2, 1.3

Si la question est logique, répondez affirmativement. Si non, répondez négativement. Faites attention au temps du verbe. Utilisez des pronoms dans vos réponses. Attention à l'ordre.

MODÈLES Tu lis le conte de fées à ton petit-cousin?
Oui, je le lui lis.
ou
Non, je ne le lui lis pas.

1. Est-ce que votre frère ou votre sœur conduit une auto tamponneuse au supermarché?
2. Avez-vous acheté la nouvelle Renault décapotable pour le président des États-Unis?
3. Vos camarades de classe vont-ils donner leurs smartphones à leurs parents?
4. Est-ce que vous offrirez des cadeaux à vos parents pour leur anniversaire de mariage?
5. Simon et toi, vous avez parlé au prof de vos devoirs?
6. Votre meilleur ami rend son livre de poche au président de la France?
7. Votre grand-mère va donner des euros à son chien?

COMPARAISONS: In sentence #1, "is eating" is used intransitively. In sentences #2-3, "sees" and "writes" are used transitively because these verbs take direct objects ("Chelsea" and "a text message").

Answers

1. Non, il/elle n'y en conduit pas.
2. Non, je ne la lui ai pas achetée.
3. Non, il ne vont pas les leur donner.
4. Oui, je leur en offrirai.
5. Oui, nous lui en avons parlé.
6. Non, il ne le lui rend pas.
7. Non, elle ne va pas lui en donner.

TPR

This activity can be done by individual students or in pairs depending on the size of your class.

1. For a pronoun review, prepare by writing a series of sentences in the affirmative, negative, declarative, or commands. Cut the sentences into the different words. Paper clip the words of the sentence into packets.
2. Pair students and ask them to clear their desks. Give each pair of students a packet.
3. Have them unscramble the words and make a sentence. Students will write their sentence on the classroom board.
4. When students are done, or when you say **"Changez,"** students may exchange their packet with another pair of students. At the end of the exercise, ask students to write the sentences on the board.

Connections

Music
"**Je te le Dis Quand Même**" by Patrick Bruel, and **"Belle, belle belle"** by Claude François are popular songs which feature object pronouns.
Search words: paroles je te le dis quand même, paroles belle belle belle

Differentiated Learning

Accelerate
Tell advanced students that in the negative the particles **ne...pas** always surround the conjugated verb, but the pronouns always precede the verb they refer to. Have them add **ne...pas** in parenthesis on the object pronouns charts on pp. 154 and 155.

Learning Styles

Auditory Learners
Students will repeat a series of sentences containing double object pronouns many times to record the sound of the pronoun combinations in their memory.

Multiple Intelligences

Visual-Spatial
Students will create a chart with columns for each of the following pronoun types: direct, indirect, **y**, **en**, and stress pronouns. At the top of each column they will indicate what type of noun the pronouns replace (person, thing, place) and write an example for each category.

RESOURCES

Communicative Activities

Answers

A: add *Je donne* to form questions.
1. B: Oui, donne-les-lui!
2. B: Non, ne la lui donne pas!
3. B: Oui, donne-les-leur!
4. B: Non, ne le lui donne pas!
5. B: Oui, donne-le-lui!
6. B: Non, ne les leur donne pas!
7. B: Oui, donne-les-leur!
8. B: Non, ne la lui donne pas!

Reference Desk

Blended Instruction

Consider using blended instruction, a combination of in-class learning and computer-mediated instruction or learning opportunities. Ask students to complete activities on the computer, using their cell or smartphone, or other emerging electronic technology. This will allow students to hone their tech skills and become more independent learners. Schedule routine Internet and e-book learning in class and in the lab.

Connections

Music

Jean-Jacques Goldman wrote a song, "**Je te Donne**," that stayed on the charts in France for months. It is a bilingual English-French song that is easy to sing, and imprints the pronoun word order in students' memory through repetition.

Search words: **je te donne paroles**

À vous la parole

Question centrale: Comment les Francophones restent-ils fidèles à leur langue et à leurs traditions?

Communiquez!

14 Des cadeaux de Noël pour les enfants à l'hôpital

1.1, 1.2, 5.2

Interpersonal Communication

Avec votre partenaire, jouez le rôle du Père Noël et de son assistant(e) à l'hôpital. L'assistant(e) demande au Père Noël à quel enfant on doit donner chaque cadeau. Le Père Noël doit répondre logiquement.

MODÈLES
les cartes de foot au garçon de 8 ans
A: **Je donne les cartes de foot au garçon de 8 ans?**
B: **Oui, donne-les-lui!**

A: **Je donne le collier en argent à la fille de 2 ans?**
B: **Non, ne le lui donne pas!**

1. les jeux-vidéo au garçon de 15 ans
2. la poupée à la fille de 16 ans
3. les robes de princesse aux petites filles de 5 ans
4. le costume d'un super-héros au garçon de 17 ans
5. le ballon de foot au garçon de 12 ans
6. les B.D. aux garçons de 3 ans
7. les DVD des contes de fées aux petites filles de 6 ans
8. la corde à sauter à la fille de 17 ans

Essential Instruction

1. Before beginning **Activité 14** have students brainstorm, with books closed, the kinds of gifts that children and adolescents like to receive.
2. **Activité 15** should be assigned in advance so that students can research their family origins with their relatives.
3. **Les familles souches de l'Île d'Orléans** is a computer-assisted activity.

15 D'où viennent vos aïeux?

 1.3

Presentational Communication

Faites une présentation dans laquelle vous:

- dites lesquels de vos ancêtres ont quitté leur pays d'origine et le nom de ce pays
- donnez la date de leur voyage si vous la connaissez
- dites comment ils ont voyagé (en bateau? en avion?)
- expliquez où ils se sont installés
- dites pourquoi ils s'y sont installés

Peut-être qu'il faudra que vous parliez à vos parents ou grands-parents pour vous renseigner sur l'histoire de votre famille. Servez-vous de cartes pour montrer les pays, les états, ou les provinces en question pendant votre présentation.

16 Les familles souches de l'île d'Orléans

 1.3, 3.2

Interpretive and Presentational Communication

L'île d'Orléans était la terre d'accueil de 300 familles souches (*founding*) canadiennes qui ont immigré de France pendant le XVIIème siècle. Les noms de famille comprennent Pichet, Drouin, Goulet, Noël, Rousseau, Gagnon, Gosselin. Choisissez un des projets ci-dessous à compléter.

A. Trouvez les dates pour le fondateur d'une famille et écrivez une phrase sur sa vie, par exemple: **Il est né en Bretagne, date inconnue, et il est mort à X, en 1788, dans la Nouvelle France.**

 Search words: **ancestry canada**

B. Trouvez l'arbre généalogique d'une de ces familles et parlez du point de vue d'un membre de la famille toujours vivant, par exemple: **Mon arrière-grand-père était X, né à Sainte-Famille en 1903 et mort à Québec en 1975.**

 Search words: **arbre généalogique québec + nom de famille**

C. Faites une liste de 60 de ces familles souches de l'île d'Orléans en ordre alphabétique. Indiquez avec un * les noms de famille qu'on trouve toujours au Québec.

 Search words: **familles souches île d'orléans**

Answers

15 *Presentations will vary.*

16 *Research will vary.*

Critical Thinking

Analysis

Have students research the meaning of **souche**. What is the literal meaning of the word? (*stump of a tree*) How is it used when referring to genealogy? (It has the sense of "born and raised.") What political implications does **souche** have in France today? (It creates a "we vs. they" atmosphere of native French vs. foreigners.)

Special Needs Students

Social Anxiety

You may have students who do not know much about their family origins, or who find the questions invasive. You might propose that they research a well-known family like the Kennedys.

At-Risk Students

Be attentive to the fact that some students may not have Internet at home. Make sure you provide a time and space for students to do online research at school.

AD(H)D

Giving students with attention difficulties too many topic choices can inhibit their forward momentum. Meet with them individually to help them choose a topic that fits their interests and skills.

Answers

 *Research will vary.*

Reference Desk

Canada is one of the countries with the most immigrants and also the most political refugees. The country welcomes approximately 250,000 permanent immigrants each year. It is the second destination of immigrants after the United States.

Communiquez!

17 L'immigration au Canada

 1.3, 1.3, 3.1, 3.2

Interpretive and Presentational Communication

Allez sur le site réservé à l'immigration du gouvernement canadien. Recherchez les formulaires et guides de demandes d'immigration au Canada aujourd'hui. Cliquez sur "français." Renseignez-vous sur une des trois possibilités suivantes:

A. Visiter le Canada de façon temporaire
B. Immigrer au Canada de façon permanente
C. Parrainer (*sponsor*) une la famille

Une fois vos recherches finies, formez un groupe avec les élèves qui ont fait des recherches sur la même catégorie que vous. Mettez vos informations en commun et présentez vos recherches à la classe.

 **Search words: citizenship and immigration canada**

Des immigrés maghrébins à Toronto.

Essential Instruction

1. Explain that each Canadian province has its own particular laws for short and long-term stays.
2. In **Activité 17** have students imagine that they are considering a long-term stay in Canada to study French, and they need to find out what is required for entry into the country.
3. Have students compare the immigration laws in the United States to those of Canada.
4. For the pronunciation exercises on p. 159, play **A**, **B**, **C**, and **D** separately. Replay each section several times to give students practice repeating the intonation.

Prononciation 1.1

Rising and Falling Intonation in Commands

- In commands, the voice descends abruptly on the last syllable. In longer commands, the voice rises in the first group of words and falls abruptly at the end of the sentence.

Des phrases impératives

Répétez chaque phrase. Faites attention à la descente de la voix à la fin de la phrase.

1. Fais entrer ta grand-tante!
2. Fais entrer ta petite cousine!
3. Fais entrer ton arrière-grand-mère!

Jacqueline fait du babysitting.

Répétez la phrase déclarative, suivie de la phrase à l'impératif. Faites attention à l'intonation.

1. Il faut fermer la porte. — N'oubliez pas de fermer la porte!
2. Il faut lui donner son dîner. — N'oubliez pas de lui donner son dîner!

Open and Closed Vowels

- In the following pairs, the first vowel is open and the second closed. The sounds can be found in the words underneath. Listen carefully for the distinction in the vowel sounds in the pairs of words.

/ɛ - e /	/o - ɔ/	/ø - œ/
faites – été	mot – mort	heureux – bœuf

Les aïeux

Répétez les phrases suivantes. Faites attention aux sons des voyelles.

1. Vos aïeux sont français, et les nôtres sont anglais.
   /o/ /ø/ /ɛ/ /e//e//o/ /ɛ/
2. Notre aïeul est anglais, et le vôtre est japonais!
   /o/ /œ/ /ɛ/ /ɛ/ /e/ /o/ /ɛ/

D Pendant deux heures

Répondez affirmativement à la question d'après le modèle que vous entendez; utilisez l'expression "pendant deux heures."

MODÈLE Tu as travaillé jeudi?
Oui, j'ai travaillé pendant deux heures.

RESOURCES

Pre-test

***Leçon* Quiz**

Answers

Script can be found in the front pages of the Annotated Teacher's Edition.

1. Oui, j'ai regardé la télé pendant deux heures.
2. Oui, j'ai joué (au foot) pendant deux heures.
3. Oui, j'ai porté un blouson pendant deux heures.
4. Oui, j'ai décoré ma chambre pendant deux heures.

Differentiated Learning

Decelerate

Students can collaborate to make a poster featuring the English and French lyrics of the national anthem "**O Canada.**" They should decorate the borders of the poster with symbols of the entire country such as a maple leaf, **fleur de lys**, hockey stick, and pictures of Montreal and Quebec.

Adapt

Before doing **Activité 17**, ask students to think of the reasons why someone might want to emigrate to Canada (work, studies, etc.). Then have students brainstorm what kind of questions a potential immigrant may have to answer on an application to the Canadian government.

Multiple Intelligences

Musical-Rhythmic

Ask these students to present the Canadian national anthem "**O Canada,**" integrating the words and the music in a slideshow presentation where each page features a line of music and a photo of Canada.

RESOURCES

 e-visual 8

 Workbook 1–3

 Flash Cards

 Listening Activity 1

 Drill & Practice Games

Reference Desk

1. Supplementary vocabulary to write a fairy tale:
   Personnages: un fantôme, **une sorcière** (*witch*), **le roi** (*king*), **la reine** (*queen*)
   Actions: tomber amoureux de (*to fall in love with*), **jeter un sort** (*to cast a spell*), **se venger de** (*to avenge oneself from*), **bannir de** (*to banish from*), **tuer** (*to kill*), **se transformer en** (*to be transformed in*)
   Éléments: une baguette magique (*wand*), **du poison**, **le feu** (*fire*)
   Lieux: un chemin, **le château hanté**, **une rivière**, **une chaumière** (*a small rural house*)
   Essentiels: Il était une fois (*once upon a time*), **en ce moment-là** (*at that time*), **d'abord** (*first of all*), **ensuite** (*then*), **puis** (*then*), **finalement**, **tout d'un coup** (*all of a sudden*)
2. Definition of genres:
   Un conte de fees is a short story that typically features characters such as fairies, elves, trolls, dwarfs, giants, or gnomes who have the ability to use magic or enchantments.
   Une fable is a fictional story, in prose or verse, featuring animals and mythical characters that have human characteristics.
   Une ballad is a poem set to music.

Vocabulaire actif

Les contes francophones 1.2

Essential Instruction

1. The picture of the young boy with the book in his hands presents the theme of storytelling: **un conte de fées**, **une fable**, **une histoire vraie**, and **une ballade**.
2. Put these terms on the board. Ask students to tell you what stories they heard as children that would be classified under these categories. Write their examples under each heading.
3. Ask students to define each genre. What are the differences among them? Which do they prefer?
4. Have students name elements in a fairy tale in English. Give them the equivalent words in French that they will copy in their notebooks.
5. Using these elements, ask students to look at the comic strip on p. 161 and tell the story of **Blanche Neige**.
6. Listen to **Pour la conversation** and **Et si je voulais dire...?**
7. Students will repeat these terms, then add them to their vocabulary list.

Expansion

Play excerpts of Walt Disney's ***Blanche-Neige et les Sept Nains*** for the students. They should understand a lot since they know the story and the articulation is clear.
Search words: walt disney's snow white and the seven dwarfs french

L'histoire de Blanche Neige

emcl.com
WB 3

Blanche Neige ne se méfie pas de la magicienne.

Les amis de Blanche Neige sont rusés.

La magicienne a joué un tour à Blanche Neige.

Le prince a déjoué le tour de la magicienne.

Pour la conversation   1.1

How do I start a fairy tale?

› **Il était une fois** un petit garçon, Fahim.
Once upon a time there was a little boy, Fahim.

Et si je voulais dire...? 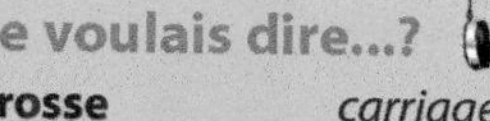

un carrosse	*carriage*
un crapaud	*toad*
un grimoire	*magic book*
un ogre	*ogre*
un pays lointain	*far-away country*
une potion magique	*magic potion*

Differentiated Learning

Accelerate
Have your high-ability students write the fairy tale ***Blanche-Neige*** using the comic strip as a guide.

Decelerate
Have students find the translation in French of the titles of popular fairy tales of their youth. They will present their findings to the class who will guess the titles in English. **Cendrillon** is Cinderella.

Answers

1

1. Ce n'est pas aussi sérieux qu'elle pensait.
2. Elle lui lisait des histoires.
3. Elle a appris à se méfier des personnes qui pourraient lui jouer un mauvais tour.
4. des magiciens, des fées, et des animaux
5. de lui envoyer ses livres

2

1. une fille qui se méfie du loup
2. une histoire vraie
3. une fable
4. des magiciens, des fées, et des animaux
5. un animal rusé
6. un conte de fées
7. une pièce de théâtre
8. une histoire vraie

Game

Un conte de fée

Divide the students into two teams. Each team will huddle to choose a fairy tale and organize three scenes from it, which they will act out. The other teams must name the fairy tale (1 point) and describe what is happening in each scene (3 points). One point will be deducted for any English spoken.

1 Un cours pour la future prof

1.2

Lisez la lettre de Valérie à sa mère, puis répondez aux questions.

Salut Maman!

J'espère que tout va bien pour toi et Papa. On dit qu'il faut se mettre aux choses sérieuses à la fac, mais non! Tu ne vas pas croire ce que nous lisons ce semestre. Tu te souviens de toutes les histoires que tu me lisais quand j'étais petite, où j'ai appris qu'il fallait me méfier des personnes qui me joueraient peut-être un mauvais tour? Maintenant ce sont les textes du cours. On les analyse pour voir s'ils sont toujours d'actualité pour les élèves d'école primaire. Tu savais déjà, tous les soirs qu on passait ensemble à lire, que ces histoires de magiciens, de fées, d animaux allaient me servir à la fac? Peux-tu m'envoyer tous mes vieux livres?

Bises,
Valérie

1. Quelle impression a Valérie de la fac?
2. Que faisait la maman de Valérie quand elle était petite?
3. Valérie a appris une leçon quand elle était jeune. Laquelle?
4. Qui étaient les personnages dans les livres de son enfance?
5. Que demande Valérie à sa mère?

2 La lecture

1.2

Choisissez la définition de la liste qui correspond aux définitions suivantes.

une histoire vraie | une ballade | une fable | un conte de fées | un poème | une pièce de théâtre | une fille qui se méfie du loup (*wolf*) | un animal rusé

MODÈLE "Ce soir, c'est tout le Québec que j'invite chez-nous"
C'est un poème québécois.

1. le Petit Chaperon Rouge
2. *La vie de Marie Curie*
3. "Le lièvre (*hare*) et la tortue (*tortoise*)"
4. "John Henry"
5. le loup dans "Le Petit Chaperon Rouge"
6. "Cendrillon"
7. *Roméo et Juliette*
8. *La vie de Thomas Jefferson*

Essential Instruction

1. Students will work in pairs to do **Activité 1**. They will alternate reading each sentence aloud of Valerie's letter, and answer the questions.
2. Bring students together to share their answers.
3. Do **La lecture** as a class activity. Challenge the students to expand their answers:
Le Petit Chaperon Rouge est un conte de fées qui raconte l'histoire d'une petite fille qui se perd dans la forêt et qui rencontre un loup.

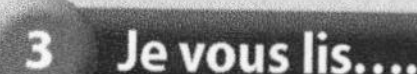

3 Je vous lis....

 1.1

Jouez le rôle de la maîtresse d'une école primaire et dites ce que vous lisez aux enfants selon le modèle. Choisissez un mot ou une expression de la liste.

poème conte de fées fable histoire pièce histoire vraie roman

MODÈLE 

Les enfants, aujourd'hui je vous lis une histoire.

1. 

2. 

3. 

4. 

5. 

6. 

7. 

Answers

1. Les enfants, aujourd'hui, je vous lis une pièce de théâtre.
2. ... un conte de fée.
3. ... une histoire vraie.
4. ... un conte de fée.
5. ... une fable.
6. ... une histoire vraie.
7. ... une pièce de théâtre.

Communication

Interpersonal: Paired Practice

Students will be placed in pairs. They will stand with their books open to p.163. One student in the pair will point to a picture of a literary genre and the other, following the formula, will say "**Les enfants, aujourd'hui je vous lis....**" They will alternate who points to a picture and who speaks. At your discretion, you will call "**Changez**" and they will form new partners to continue the exercise. As an alternative, they may change the exercise to say "(student name) **aujourd'hui je te lis....**"

Special Needs Students

Behavior Problems

To some students, telling fairy tales might seem childish and not a serious subject. They need to be reminded that these are excellent ways of self-expression that will bring out their creativity.

Linguistically Challenged/Social Anxiety

These students can be placed with higher-ability students in learning groups. When doing presentational activities, they can be given roles that correspond to their abilities. For example, the stronger students in a play might assume the lead role, and those who are less comfortable can have minor parts. All should cooperate equally in the writing of the activity, however.

Answers

Script can be found in the front pages of the Annotated Teacher's Edition.

1. D
2. C
3. A
4. B
5. E

5 *Answers will vary.*

Communication

Interpersonal: Paired Practice
Presentational: Cooperative Groups

In pairs, students will interview each other alternately asking and answering the questions in **Questions personnelles**.
In larger groups, or in front of the class, they will introduce their partner, sharing information about literary preferences that they learned by asking the questions.

"Voici Jean. Quand il était petit, ses parents lui lisaient des contes de fées."

TPR

Make up a story and have students each draw an element in a frame to make a comic strip. Example:

Il était une fois, une princesse qui était petite comme une souris.

Il y avait un ogre qui aimait chasser les princesses. Le prince était un peu myope, alors, il n'a pas vu l'ogre entrer dans sa maison.

L'ogre a enlevé la princesse.
Le roi était inconsolable.
Le prince est allé voir le magicien qui l'a transformé en rat.

Le prince-rat est allé chez l'ogre et a repris la princesse.
Le roi a acheté des lunettes pour le prince.

4 Une princesse rusée

1.1, 1.2

Interpretive Communication

Écoutez le conte de fées, puis choisissez la lettre de la partie qui complète la phrase.

1. Il était une fois...
2. D'habitude, la princesse...
3. Elle aimait...
4. Le magicien a...
5. Mais il n'a pas réussi parce que...

A. marcher dans la forêt.
B. joué un mauvais tour.
C. se préparait dans la salle de bains avant de faire une promenade.
D. une princesse qui habitait dans un château.
E. la princesse a mis des cordes aux arbres pour se rappeler du chemin.

5 Questions personnelles

1.1, 1.2

Répondez aux questions.

1. Quelles sortes d'histoires est-ce que tes parents te lisaient quand tu étais petit(e)?
2. Quel est ton conte de fées préféré? En existe-t-il une version cinématographique? Est-ce que tu préfères lire ou regarder cette histoire?
3. Aimes-tu lire des histoires vraies? Si oui, sur quels sujets ou sur qui?
4. Quelles sortes de textes est-ce que tu dois lire pour tes cours de littérature au lycée?
5. Qui est ton magicien préféré—Merlin, Harry Potter, ou Mickey Mouse dans *Fantasia*?
6. Si tu pouvais jouer un tour, qu'est-ce que tu ferais?

Essential Instruction

1. Before the students listen to **Une princesse rusée**, have them skim the choices of answers. This is good training for future language exams where questions give valuable cues to the main idea of the listening or reading passage.
2. The same strategy can be applied to the reading **Un conte maghrébin.** Students should peruse the questions for **Activité 6** before listening to the story.
3. After listening to **Un conte magrébin**, ask questions for general comprehension, including the questions on p. 166. Have students identify typical "little sister remarks" that they find in the dialogue. Examples: **"Je n'ai pas faim." "....je vais tout lui dire."**

Rencontres culturelles

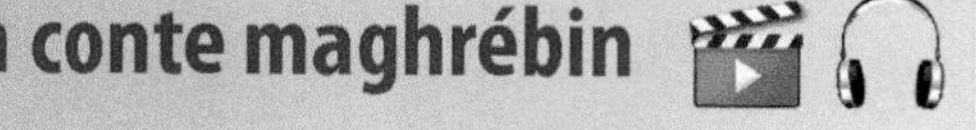

Un conte maghrébin

   1.1, 1.2, 5.2

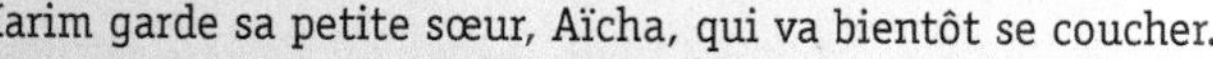

Karim garde sa petite sœur, Aïcha, qui va bientôt se coucher.

Karim: C'est prêt... tu viens? Tu t'es lavé les mains?
Aïcha: Je n'ai pas faim....
Karim: Ah non, tu ne vas pas commencer! Je t'ai préparé une soupe comme tu l'aimes....
Aïcha: Je n'aime pas la soupe.... Il y a une heure j'ai mangé un yaourt. Et maman m'a fait un bon goûter....
Karim: D'accord, alors vas te coucher tout de suite!
Aïcha: Tu vas te faire disputer par maman si je ne me brosse pas les dents: je vais tout lui dire.
Karim: Bon ça suffit: tu te brosses les dents et tu vas te coucher.
Aïcha: Qu'est-ce que tu me lis comme histoire?
Karim: Je te raconte **"L'élève du magicien."** Tu l'aimes, n'est-ce pas?
Aïcha: Je l'adore.
Karim: Il était une fois un petit garçon, Fahim. C'était un enfant très intelligent. Sa mère l'avait envoyé chez un maître qu'on lui avait conseillé, loin, dans la montagne. Mais pendant que les autres élèves apprenaient, lui devait s'occuper des travaux de la ferme, pour payer ses études. Il passait très peu de temps en classe, mais il arrivait à apprendre si vite que son maître avait commencé à se méfier de lui. Mais Fahim sera plus rusé, et découvrira même que son maître est un magicien.
Aïcha: Et après?
Karim: La suite demain....
Aïcha: Moi, je la connais. Il apprendra les mêmes choses que le magicien et comme ça il pourra déjouer ses mauvais tours.... Bonne nuit!

Le mot **maître** a plus ou moins trois sens: celui d'instructeur (maître d'étudiants), celui de dominateur (maître d'esclaves), et celui de propriétaire (maître de maison). Il reflète en fait les deux facettes de l'autorité: positive si elle est éducative ou protectrice, mais négative si elle est dominatrice.

RESOURCES

 **Dialogue Video**

 **Workbook 4**

Reference Desk

L'élève du Magicien: Un conte du Maghreb is an illustrated fairy tale for children written in 2007 by Nora Aceval, a French author born in Algeria. The hero, Fahim, whose name means "the cunning one," lives with his mother in a poor and rural region of Algeria. Determined to give her son an education, Fahim's mother sends him to a boarding school, where he learns that his schoolmaster is in fact a magician who transforms his students into mules. Eventually, Fahim will learn the importance of knowledge, honesty, and justice.

Learning Styles

Visual Learners
Have students illustrate a storyboard of **Un conte maghrébin** with captions.

Auditory Learners
These students will benefit from having access to the recording so that they can repeatedly hear the French as they are reading it. Listening helps them make the association with the written word.

Kinesthetic Learners
Have these students mime the story as the audio is being played.

Answers

Script can be found in the front pages of the Annotated Teacher's Edition.

1. garde
2. de soupe
3. se brosser les dents
4. un petit garçon
5. un magicien
6. déjouer les mauvais tours

Extension

Ils sont stricts.

Expansion

Have students create a dialogue in pairs or groups of three, where a parent/parents interview a potential babysitter. Students should stress the parental values they are portraying, and the potential babysitter could be an ideal or terrible fit. The dialogue may be realistic or comical.

6 Un conte maghrébin

1.3

Complétez les phrases suivantes.

1. Karim... sa petite sœur, Aïcha, qui doit se coucher bientôt.
2. Elle ne veut pas..., même si d'habitude elle l'aime.
3. Elle veut... avant de se coucher ou elle va tout dire à sa maman.
4. Fahim est... qui travaille dur à la ferme de son école.
5. Il découvre que son maître est....
6. Fahim apprend à... du magicien.

Extension **Le babysitting**

1.1, 1.2

Coralie fait du babysitting chez les Darras.

Mme Darras: On ne va pas rentrer très tard, avant minuit.
M. Darras: N'oubliez pas de lui faire réciter ses leçons avant le dîner.
Coralie: Je peux la laisser regarder la télévision un petit moment?
Mme Darras: Non, juste sa leçon de chinois. Le DVD est dans le salon.
Coralie: J'y veillerai.
Mme Darras: Pour le dîner, il faut qu'elle mange un légume, un yaourt, et un fruit.
M. Darras: Il faut qu'elle se brosse les dents avant de se coucher....
Mme Darras: ... et qu'elle se couche à 20h30.
Coralie: Entendu. Bonne soirée!

Extension Comment sont les parents envers leur enfant?

1.3

Essential Instruction

1. After listening to **Un conte maghrébin**, students may answer questions 1 through 6.
2. Play the **Extension** dialogue without having students see the script, and see if they can answer the question. Then play the dialogue again while allowing them to follow the script. Encourage students to give specific examples to illustrate their answer.
3. Read the passage **La Francophonie** to the students, stopping to ask comprehension questions.
4. In the computer lab, have students research **la Tunisie** using the search words provided. They are to learn where it is located, what kind of government it has, languages spoken, major industry, and what there is to see and do.
5. Students will report their findings using a graphic organizer of their choice.
   Search words: graphic organizer

Points de départ

emcl.com
WB 5

La Francophonie

1.2, 3.1, 5.1

La Tunisie

La Tunisie est le plus petit des trois pays du Maghreb. Elle compte aujourd'hui un peu plus de dix millions d'habitants, et sa capitale est Tunis. La plus grande partie de la population vit sur la côte, à Gabès, Bizerte, Sfax, et Sousse.

Protectorat* français à partir de 1883, la Tunisie devient indépendante en 1956. Habib Bourguiba devient le premier Président d'une république qui se caractérise par un pouvoir détenu par* un parti unique, le Néo-Destour.

La Tunisie a toujours accordé une place importante à l'éducation; elle lui consacre 21% de ses ressources. Aujourd'hui, presque 80% de la population est alphabétisée* et 70%, garçons et filles à égalité, est scolarisée*. Plus de 20.000 étudiants fréquentent l'université dont* 30% des professeurs sont des femmes.

Search words: bonjour tunisie, tunisie tourisme, actualités tunisie, gouvernement tunisie

Protectorat *Protectorate;* **pouvoir détenu par** *power held by;* **alphabétisée** *literate;* **scolarisée** *sent to school;* **dont** *among which*

Des étudiantes discutent de la lecture pour le cours de sciences po.

L'université de Tunis Carthage est l'une des meilleures universités de Tunisie.

RESOURCES

Workbook 5

Reference Desk

1. Tunisia measures almost 64,000 square miles in area, approximately the size of the state of Wisconsin. It has an estimated population of fewer than 10.7 million. The median age is 30.5. Its name is derived from the capital Tunis located in the northeast.
2. 98 per cent of the population of Tunisia is Arab or Berber, one per cent European, mostly French and Italian. Islam is the state religion although Tunisia has a secular culture which is tolerant of other religions. The language is called **Derja**, which is a blend of Tunisian and Arabic. Many people speak French, but it is not an official language.
3. The climate in the north is rainy and mild in winter, and hot and dry in summer. The south has a desert climate.

Differentiated Learning

Accelerate

High-ability students will listen to **Le babysitting** and answer the question about the dialogue. They will then compare Coralie's babysitting rules to those they had as children.

Decelerate

Students will write in French a list of rules that their parents used to give their babysitter when they were young. If they did not have a babysitter, they should imagine what rules their parents would have given a babysitter.

Critical Thinking

Comparisons

1. Ask students to research the five biggest groups of immigrants in the United States. Have them choose one group and research social, economic, political, or racial issues attributed to this particular group.
2. Ask students to compare their research with what they have learned about **Maghrébins** immigrants in France. They should do more in-depth research and may focus on one or two particular issues, for example, immigration status, health care, education, jobs, and voting blocks.

L'immigration maghrébine en France 2.1, 5.1

On compte aujourd'hui trois générations d'immigrés d'origine maghrébine en France (immigrés, enfants, et petits-enfants). Elles représentent entre 3,5 millions et 6 millions de personnes, soit 5% de la population française. Les plus nombreux sont les immigrés d'origine algérienne (900.000), puis marocaine (450.000), et enfin tunisienne (220.000). Aujourd'hui l'immigration est d'abord une immigration de regroupement familial (50%) et dans une moindre mesure* économique (13%). L'asile* politique représente 16% des demandes; il est donc plus important que l'immigration sur le plan économique.

Construite en 1926, la mosquée de Paris représente l'importance de la culture maghrébine en France.

Près de 8% des jeunes de moins de 18 ans en France sont d'origine maghrébine. Ils sont surtout concentrés dans la région parisienne où ils représentent 12% de la population. Parmi* les étudiants venant étudier en France, un quart des étudiants étrangers est originaire de la Tunisie, du Maroc, ou de l'Algérie.

Certains immigrés retournent souvent à leurs pays d'origine. Quand ils reviennent en France, ils apportent des vêtements, des objets d'art, des tissus, et d'autres choses de leurs pays d'origine. Il y a des Maghrébins qui ouvrent des restaurants où on sert des spécialités de leurs pays maghrébins, et vendent des épices, des tissus, des produits artisanaux, et autres au public français et maghrébin.

moindre mesure *lesser extent;* **asile** *asylum;* **parmi** *among*

Produits

Il y a beaucoup de **restaurants maghrébins** en France où on sert le couscous et d'autres plats d'Algérie, de Tunisie, et du Maroc. Certaines spécialités de la région sont la pastilla, la chorba, la brick, le tajine, et les gâteaux arabes. Trouvez des photos de ces plats en ligne. 1.2, 2.2

COMPARAISONS

Y-a-t-il des immigrés dans votre communauté ou votre lycée? D'où viennent-ils? 4.2

Mots-clé

Immigrer (1840) est emprunté (*is borrowed*) du latin *immigrare* qui signifie "venir dans." Il vient de *migrare* qui signifie changer de résidence. Les mots **immigré** et **immigration** apparaissent vers 1770.

Essential Instruction

1. Students will read **L'immigration maghrébine en France** noting the statistics for Algerians, Moroccans, and Tunisians.
2. They will look at the photo of the mosque in Paris and research the location of other large mosques in France.
3. Students will read **Les contes maghrébins** and work in groups to answer **Activités culturelles**.

COMPARAISONS

Les contes maghrébins  1.2

Quelles histoires enfantines vous a-t-on lu es quand vous étiez petit(e)? 4.2

La nature imaginative et poétique de l'âme* berbère* et arabe a donné naissance* à une littérature de contes très variée. On distingue des contes religieux qui attribuent aux saints d'extraordinaires miracles, comme "Lalla Mimouna," histoire d'une femme vertueuse dont la détermination d'apprendre la prière pour connaître Dieu lui donne le pouvoir d'arrêter un navire* et de marcher sur l'eau.

Il y a aussi des contes plaisants* et humoristiques comme le héros comique le plus populaire de l'Orient, Joha, à la fois malin* et naïf. Il joue des tours à ses concitoyens*, leur dit des vérités* pas bonnes à entendre. Joha s'appelle Bechkerker dans l'Aurès algérien, Brozi et Moussa dans le Riff marocain, BenChekran, l'ivrogne, ou Bou Hamar, l'homme à l'âne dans les tribus arabes. Ces anecdotes ont un rôle moralisateur.

Il y a aussi de nombreux contes d'animaux, notamment* en Kabylie: le chacal*, le hérisson*, ou le lièvre* sont des héros familiers pleins de ruse*. Quant aux* contes merveilleux, ils doivent être racontés le soir, selon la tradition, sous peine de* devenir méchant ou d'avoir des enfants méchants. Enfin il existe de nombreux contes dont le récit est proche de celui des contes occidentaux: Le Petit Poucet (*Tom Thumb*) devient Mqidech ou Haddidouan, celui qui lutte* contre l'ogresse (Ghoula en arabe, Teriel en kabyle).

 **Search words: contes maghrébins, l'élève du magicien**

âme *soul;* **berbère** *Berber;* **a donné naissance** *gave birth to;* **navire** *ship;* **plaisants** *nice;* **malin** *clever;* **concitoyens** *fellow citiyens;* **vérités** *truths;* **notamment** *notably;* **chacal** *jackal;* **hérisson** *hedgehog;* **lièvre** *hare;* **ruse** *trick;* **Quant aux** *As for;* **sous peine de** *under the threat of;* **lutte** *fight*

La tajine de poulet au citron est un plat principal servi dans les restaurants tunisiens en France.

7 Activités culturelles  1.3, 3.1, 3.2, 4.2

Complétez les activités suivantes.

1. Choisissez une ville tunisienne: Sousse, Gabès, Sfax, Bizerte, ou Tunis. Faites des recherches sur cette ville et présentez-la à votre classe.
2. Dites à quoi correspondent ces pourcentages sur la Tunisie:
   • 21% • 80% • 70% • 30%
3. Faites un graphique en secteurs (*pie chart*) montrant le nombre d'immigrés en France d'origine marocaine, algérienne, et tunisienne.
4. Trouvez une recette pour un plat tunisien et faites votre liste d'achats.
5. Identifiez ces personnages de contes maghrébins:
   • Lalla Mimouna • Joha • Mqidech

À discuter

Qu'est-ce que vous pensez des immigrés qui gardent les traditions de leurs pays d'origine? Est-ce que votre famille observe des traditions d'un pays différent de celui où vous habitez? Quelle est l'origine de ces traditions?

Answers

1. *Answers will vary.*
2. 21%: les ressources de la Tunisie consacrées à l'éducation; 80%: la population alphabétisée; 70%: la population qui fait des études; 30%: les professeurs d'université femmes en Tunisie
3. immigrés d'origine marocaine: 450.000; d'origine algérienne: 900.000; d'origine tunisienne: 220.000
4. *Answers will vary.*
5. Lala Mimouna: une femme vertueuse; Joha: un héros comique; Mqidech: le Petit Poucet

À discuter
Answers will vary.

Critical Thinking

Comparisons

Maghrébin folk heroes are either religious or humorous people, or animals with extraordinary abilities. To what would these characters correspond in American culture? What is the effect of Walt Disney and contemporary television characters on our folklore?

Search words: **lives of saints**, **walt disney**, **the simpsons**, **saturday morning television**

Connections

Folklore

There is a direct link between American and African folklore characters, notably Brer Rabbit, who has been linked to African and Cherokee cultures. Have students research popular folk stories in the United States, and the cultural groups they come from.

Search words: **uncle remus**, **brer rabbit**, **american folk tales**

Learning Styles

Visual Learners

These students will draw or find pictures of the major characters in Maghrebin folklore.

Multiple Intelligences

Mathematical-Logical

Students who enjoy graphs and charts will work to create a graph that illustrates the statistics found in the reading **L'immigration maghrébine** and present their visual to the class.

Musical-Rhythmic

Students will research Maghrebin music. They will identify the instruments used and play recordings for the class.

Answers

8 *Activities will vary.*

Reference Desk

It was in Tunisia where the upheavals of the Arab Spring started in 2010, where the first demonstrations and revolutions led to the resignation of the president. Viewed as a progressive North African country, Tunisia has been an example to other Arab nations aspiring to democratic rights and privileges, such as Egypt, Lybia, Bahrain,Yemen, and Syria. Tunisian people seek better economic opportunities and more progressive rights for women.

Du côté des médias

Pre AP 1.2, 5.1

Interpretive Communication

*Lisez les informations sur les manifestations (*events*) en Tunisie pendant l'année.*

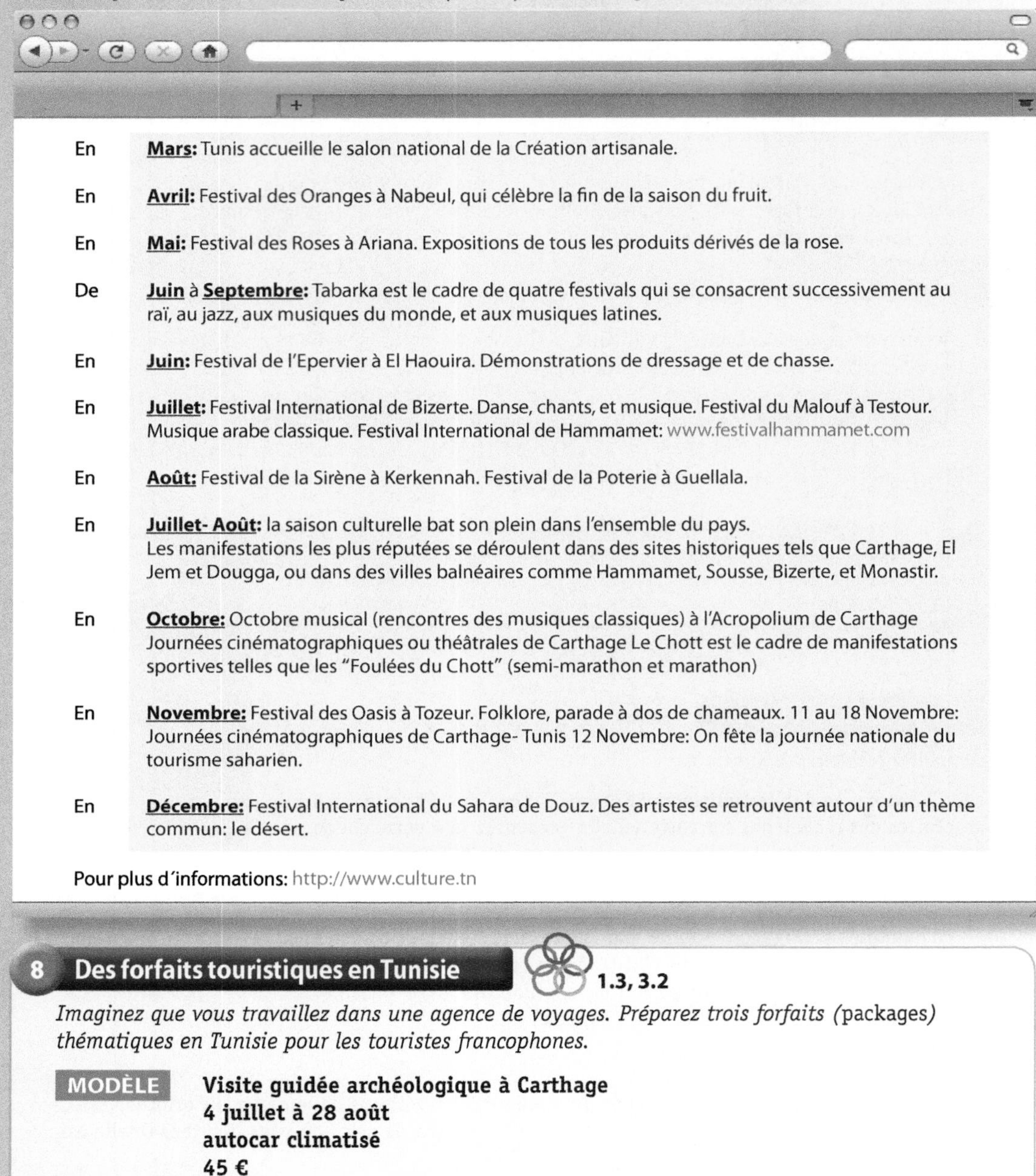

En **Mars:** Tunis accueille le salon national de la Création artisanale.

En **Avril:** Festival des Oranges à Nabeul, qui célèbre la fin de la saison du fruit.

En **Mai:** Festival des Roses à Ariana. Expositions de tous les produits dérivés de la rose.

De **Juin** à **Septembre:** Tabarka est le cadre de quatre festivals qui se consacrent successivement au raï, au jazz, aux musiques du monde, et aux musiques latines.

En **Juin:** Festival de l'Epervier à El Haouira. Démonstrations de dressage et de chasse.

En **Juillet:** Festival International de Bizerte. Danse, chants, et musique. Festival du Malouf à Testour. Musique arabe classique. Festival International de Hammamet: www.festivalhammamet.com

En **Août:** Festival de la Sirène à Kerkennah. Festival de la Poterie à Guellala.

En **Juillet- Août:** la saison culturelle bat son plein dans l'ensemble du pays. Les manifestations les plus réputées se déroulent dans des sites historiques tels que Carthage, El Jem et Dougga, ou dans des villes balnéaires comme Hammamet, Sousse, Bizerte, et Monastir.

En **Octobre:** Octobre musical (rencontres des musiques classiques) à l'Acropolium de Carthage Journées cinématographiques ou théâtrales de Carthage Le Chott est le cadre de manifestations sportives telles que les "Foulées du Chott" (semi-marathon et marathon)

En **Novembre:** Festival des Oasis à Tozeur. Folklore, parade à dos de chameaux. 11 au 18 Novembre: Journées cinématographiques de Carthage- Tunis 12 Novembre: On fête la journée nationale du tourisme saharien.

En **Décembre:** Festival International du Sahara de Douz. Des artistes se retrouvent autour d'un thème commun: le désert.

Pour plus d´informations: http://www.culture.tn

8 Des forfaits touristiques en Tunisie

1.3, 3.2

*Imaginez que vous travaillez dans une agence de voyages. Préparez trois forfaits (*packages*) thématiques en Tunisie pour les touristes francophones.*

MODÈLE **Visite guidée archéologique à Carthage**
4 juillet à 28 août
autocar climatisé
45 €

Essential Instruction

1. Students will read **Du côté des médias** and work in pairs to do **Des forfaits touristiques en Tunisie.**
2. They will also examine the festivals and cultural offerings in Tunisia and identify corresponding events in the United States. For example, the **Festival des Roses** would be a counterpart to our Rose parade. The events do not have to be identical to be used as comparisons.
3. As a review of reflexive verbs, students will tell you what they do to get ready for school. This will serve as a review of **se lever, se laver, se brosser les dents, se peigner, se maquiller,** and **s'habiller**.
4. Ask a student to conjugate one of these verbs on the board as a review.
5. Give examples of reflexive verbs in affirmative and negative sentences as well as affirmative and negative commands.

Structure de la langue

emcl.com
WB 6–10
LA 2
Games

Révision: Reflexive Verbs  1.1, 1.2

See if you remember the reflexive pronouns by completing the sentences below with the correct pronoun.

1. Alice... prépare pour la journée.
2. Je... dépêche chaque matin.
3. Les Duval... amusent au parc d'attractions.
4. Tu... brosses ou tu... peignes?

A. te
B. se
C. s'
D. me

Answer the questions affirmatively.

5. À quelle heure vous levez-vous, Pierre et Jean?
6. T'es-tu brossé les dents avant l'école?
7. Martine et Jacques vont-ils s'entendre bien avec leur nouveau beau-père?

If you have trouble with 1–7 above, be sure to read the grammar summary below to review reflexive verbs.

Reflexive verbs describe actions that the subject performs on or for itself. Reflexive pronouns (**me**, **te**, **se**, **nous**, **vous**) are used with reflexive verbs and represent the same person or thing as the subject. In affirmative and negative declarative sentences or questions, the reflexive pronoun comes directly before the verb.

Note the forms of the reflexive verb **se méfier** below.

se méfier			
je	**me méfie**	nous	**nous méfions**
tu	**te méfies**	vous	**vous méfiez**
il/elle/on	**se méfie**	ils/elles	**se méfient**

Pourquoi est-ce que tu **t'inquiètes**? *Why are you worrying?*
Je ne **m'inquiète** pas. Je **m'amuse** beaucoup! *I'm not worrying. I'm having a lot of fun!*

To make a negative sentence, put **ne** in front of the reflexive pronouns and **pas** after the verb.

Nous **ne nous habillons pas** en jean aujourd'hui. *We aren't wearing jeans today.*

REFLEXIVE VERBS:
The correct reflexive pronouns are: 1. B; 2. D; 3. C; 4. A. The answer to the questions are: 1. Je me lève à....; 2. Oui, je me suis brossé les dents avant l'école. 3. Oui, ils vont bien s'entendre avec leur nouveau beau-père.

Differentiated Learning

Accelerate
Have students make a slideshow presentation entitled "**Ma Journée**" featuring photos of themselves performing reflexive verb activities. Encourage students to use costumes and props to add interest, and not spare the drama!

Decelerate
Students would benefit from a worksheet that breaks down each form of a reflexive verb into discrete parts: explanation and application. By taking them through a step-by-step review of the affirmative, negative, and affirmative and negative commands, they will be less apt to mix up the forms.

RESOURCES

 **Workbook 6–10**

 **Listening Activity 2**

 **Drill & Practice Games**

Reference Desk

1. Pronominal verbs are divided into three categories: reflexive (**se laver**), reciprocal (**se parler**), and none of the above (**se passer, s'enfuir**).
2. Some verbs may be either reflexive or non-reflexive; that is, the subject may perform an action on itself (reflexive), or on someone or something else (non reflexive). For example: **Michèle se lave** (reflexive), but **Michèle lave le chien** (non reflexive).
3. Verbs such as **se lever** and **s'inquiéter** are irregular, and have accent modifications when conjugated in the present tense. An **accent grave** modifies the last syllable for all pronouns but the **nous** and **vous** forms. Conjugating these verbs on the board will give you the classic "shoe verb" design.

TPR

Ask students to form an **accent grave** with their right arm. To do that, the elbow dips and the fingers point upward to make an **accent grave**. Make sure the students' arms are not making an **accent aigü**. You must do the exercise in front of them but in reverse. Conjugate the verb **se lever**. Students will raise their arms to add the accent for the **je**, **tu**, **il**, **elle**, **ils** and **elles** forms. They will lower their arms for the **nous** and **vous** forms. Conjugate **se promener** in the same way.

The students will "get the feel" for the position of the accent marks by doing this maneuver.

Reference Desk

1. Show students that changes in verb forms from affirmative to negative commands are done for the sake of euphony. For example, ask them which of these sounds more like a command, **Te réveilles!** or **Réveille-toi!** They will most likely agree that the second verb sounds better, and is easier to say. Therefore, **Ne te réveille pas!** flows better than **Ne réveille-toi pas!**
2. In the **passé composé**, reflexive verbs agree with the preceding direct object. Example: **Nous *nous* sommes lavés.**
3. However, when the body part follows the verb, the subject does not agree with the reflexive verb because it is no longer the subject but rather the part of the body that undergoes the action. In the sentence **Nous nous sommes lavé la figure**, only the face got washed, so the second **nous** is demoted to an indirect object.
4. The reflexive verbs **s'asseoir**, **se plaindre**, and **se souvenir** do have irregular past participles: **assis**, **plaint**, and **souvenu**.

Notice that the form and placement of reflexive verbs change in command forms.

Use	Explanation	Example	
affirmative command	reflexive pronoun after the verb	Laure, **dépêche-toi**!	*Laure, hurry up!*
negative command	reflexive pronoun before the verb	Ne **t'inquiète** pas!	*Don't worry!*

The **passé composé** of reflexive verbs is formed with **être.** Notice the rules for using reflexive verbs in the **passé composé.**

Rule	Example	
reflexive pronoun is placed before **être**	Pourquoi **t'es**-tu **couché**?	*Why did you go to bed?*
past participle agrees in gender and number with the subject	Elle ne **s'est** pas **réveillée** tard ce matin.	*She didn't wake up late this morning.*
no agreement of the past participle if a direct object follows the verb	Elles **se sont brossé** les dents après le dîner.	*They brushed their teeth after dinner.*

Blanche neige ne s'est pas méfiée de la méchante magicienne.

COMPARAISONS

Some verbs can be made reflexive in French by adding the reflexive pronoun **se**.

Jacques parle à Océane.
Océane parle à Jacques.
Ils **se parlent**.

In the second sentence, how is the reflexive idea expressed in English?

4.1

COMPARAISONS: **Ils se parlent** can be expressed in English as "They talk to each other;" "Each other" expresses a reciprocal action between two or more persons or things.

Essential Instruction

1. Have students do **On s'entraîne!**, paying attention to agreement.
2. Review the affirmative and negative imperative of reflexive verbs by having students transform simple sentences into commands.
3. Write sentences with reflexive verbs on the board, and have students transform them in the **imparfait** and **passé composé.**
4. Pair a high and low-ability student together to collaborate on the activity **L'élève du magicien.**
5. Students will complete **Le bal** individually.

9 On s'entraîne!

 1.2, 1.3

Dites si les personnes suivantes s'entraînent au stade, au fitness, à la piscine, ou au complexe sportif; le complexe sportif propose roller, footing, et vélo.

MODÈLE Marcel nage.
Il s'entraîne à la piscine.

1. Marc et moi, nous courons.
2. Sophie et Florence plongent.
3. Jérémy et Saïd font du vélo.
4. Les footballeurs jouent au foot.
5. Mlle Dumont et toi, vous faites de l'aérobic.
6. Tu fais du footing.
7. Je fais du yoga.
8. L'équipe de rugby fait du rugby.
9. Sabine fait du roller.

10 L'élève du magicien

 1.1

Racontez ce conte maghrébin en utilisant les verbes réfléchis entre parenthèses au présent, au passé composé, à l'imparfait, ou à l'infinitif.

Dans ce conte, il (1. s'agir) d'un petit garçon intelligent qui (2. s'appeler) Fahim. Fahim (3. adorer) faire ses devoirs. C'était un bon élève. Un jour, il (4. se lever) tôt et (5. s'habiller) de son meilleur pantalon et de sa meilleure chemise parce qu'il allait voyager à sa nouvelle école. Il (6. s'inquiéter) parce qu'il n'avait jamais quitté son village. Il (7. se rendre) à sa nouvelle école qui (8. se trouver) loin de son village. Quand il y est arrivé, ses nouveaux camarades de classes (9. se présenter). Ils (10. s'entendre) bien avec Fahim. Mais le maître était strict. Un jour, il a dit à Fahim qu'il devait (11. s'occuper) des travaux de la ferme pour payer ses études. Il (12. ne plus s'amuser) parce qu'il préférait étudier. Un jour, Fahim a réalisé que son maître (13. être) magicien. Qu'est-ce qui est arrivé? Fahim a appris à déjouer les mauvais tours du magicien parce qu'il était plus rusé que lui!

11 Le bal

1.1

Interpretive Communication

Écrivez les numéros 1–5 sur votre papier. Écoutez l'histoire et écrivez une réponse courte à la question que vous entendez.

Answers

1. Nous nous entraînons au stade.
2. Elles s'entraînent à la piscine.
3. Ils s'entraînent au complexe sportif.
4. Ils s'entraînent au stade.
5. Vous vous entraînez au fitness.
6. Tu t'entraînes au complexe sportif.
7. Je m'entraîne au fitness.
8. Elle s'entraîne au stade.
9. Elle s'entraîne au complexe sportif.

1. s'agit
2. s'appelle
3. adorait
4. s'est levé
5. s'est habillé
6. s'inquiétait
7. s'est rendu
8. se trouvait
9. se sont présentés
10. s'entendaient
11. s'occuper
12. ne s'amusait plus
13. était

11

Script can be found in the front pages of the Annotated Teacher's Edition.

1. une jolie robe rose
2. Elle s'est lavée et s'est maquillée.
3. au château
4. Elle a dansé.
5. le prince

Reference Desk

Help students handle reflexive verbs easily by reminding them to focus on the subject and verb agreement first. Teach them that **se dépêcher** is no different than **aimer**; you need to conjugate the verb in the right tense, then add the reflexive pronoun right before the verb. For example, **"Je suis allé(e)...."** is very similar to **"Je (me) suis dépêché(e)."**

Special Needs Students

Linguistically Challenged
Before undertaking written activities, these students would benefit from doing the first three examples of any exercise one on one with their teacher, so that they feel confident about how to proceed.

Multiple Intelligences

Verbal-Linguistic
These students would enjoy retelling the story of **L'élève du magicien** as a fairy tale beginning with **"Il était une fois..."**

Bodily-Kinesthetic
These students would be perfect to pantomime scenes from the story as it is narrated.

RESOURCES

Communicative Activities

Answers

All activities will vary.

Reference Desk

Blended Instruction

Consider using blended instruction, a combination of in-class learning and computer-mediated instruction or learning opportunities. Ask students to complete activities on the computer, using their cell or smartphone, or other emerging electronic technology. This will allow students to hone their tech skills and become more independent learners. Schedule routine Internet and e-book learning in class and in the lab.

À vous la parole

Communiquez!

12 Un conte maghrébin à la radio

Presentational Communication

Trouvez un conte maghrébin en ligne. Lisez le conte et transformez-le en script pour une émission de radio. Vous aurez besoin d'un narrateur ou d'une narratrice, d'un animateur ou d'une animatrice qui introduit l'émission, et d' acteurs pour jouer les rôles avec leurs voix. Si vous voulez, créez aussi des bruitages (*sound effects*). Enregistrez (*Record*) votre émission pour la classe.

Search words: contes maghreb, contes et légendes de tunisie/algérie/maroc

13 Les immigrés célèbres en France

1.1, 1.3

Interpretive and Presentational Communication

Dans la liste ci-dessous, vous trouverez les noms des immigrés célèbres ou d'autres célébrités françaises dont les parents étaient immigrés. Recherchez si l'arrivée d'un(e) immigré correspond à une vague (*wave*) d'immigration en France, et expliquez pourquoi la personne que vous recherchez est célèbre.

Yves Montand, Albert Uderzo, Louis de Funès, Pablo Picasso, Isabelle Adjani, Faudel, Basile Boli, Amin Maalouf

Search words: les immigrés en France, immigration en France historique

Communiquez!

14 La nouvelle Tunisie

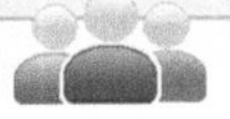

1.1, 3.1, 3.2

Interpretive Communication

Récemment beaucoup de choses ont changé en Tunisie. Faites des recherches sur un des thèmes suivants. Ensuite, faites une présentation en groupe où chaque membre présente un thème différent.

A. la révolution du jasmin ou la révolution de la dignité
B. le président en 2010 et en 2012
C. la grève générale
D. la révolte de Sidi Bouzid
E. le caravane de la libération

Essential Instruction

1. Have students draw cards with the numbers 13, 14, or 15. The number on the card will place them in groups corresponding to the number of the activity in **Communiquez!** that they will work on together.
2. For the activity **Un conte de fées,** students of various learning styles and talents can be grouped together to collaborate on creating a fairy tale.
3. There are various formats to choose from: video, slideshow presentation, large storyboards with captions, to name a few.*
4. Students can write an original story using characters from their daily lives, or retell a classic tale.
5. Time on task can be divided into: brainstorming, rough draft, editing, correcting by teacher, and then creating the story in a format of their choice.

*Search words: **launchpadtoys/toontastic, puppet-pals for online storytelling programs**

Stratégie communicative

Using Transitions in a Story 1.1

Pour raconter une histoire, il est nécessaire de faire une liste des personnages et des événements principaux. Utilisez des adjectifs, des adverbes, et les pronoms relatifs **qui** et **que** pour faire de belles et longues phrases. Pour finir, créez une harmonie entre descriptions et événements en utilisant des adverbes et des locutions conjonctives. Combien en connaissez-vous dans la liste suivante? Cherchez dans le dictionnaire les mots que vous ne connaissez pas.

d'abord/au début/au commencement
avant, après
dès que
plus tard
pendant que
tandis que
pendant ce temps, en attendant
en même temps
ensuite/par la suite
finalement/enfin/à la fin

15 Un conte de fées 1.2, 1.3, 3.1, 3.2

Écrivez un conte de fées, par exemple, un conte bien connu avec un milieu moderne, ou un conte de l'écrivain français Charles Perrault tels que **"La Belle au bois dormant," "Le Petit Chaperon** rouge," ou encore "Cendrillon," qui se terminent différemment de l'original. (Vous pouvez aussi surfer le net et découvrir d'autres contes pour enfants, par exemple, des contes du Sénégal).

16 On rédige! 1.3

Maintenant faites lire votre conte à votre partenaire et corrigez le sien *(his or hers)* en suivant les directives ci-dessous:

	Les accords entre les verbe et leurs sujet sont corrects.
	Les adjectifs sont placés au bon endroit.
	Il est clair de qui ont parle.
	Toutes les phrases sont reliées entre elles.
	Chaque mot est écrit correctement.
	Les signes de ponctuation sont bien utilisés.

Pour finir, publiez votre conte en ligne ou préparez un document avec tous les contes de la classe.

RESOURCES

Pre-test

Leçon Quiz

Answers

15 *Writings will vary.*

16 All boxes should be checked by student.

Expansion

1. To prepare students for this activity, ask them to think of well-known fairy tales, and summarize them in French in logical main action lines, using for example: **D'abord**..., **puis**..., **en même temps**, **ensuite**..., **enfin**..., etc.
2. Suggested criteria for the fairy tales:
Must be written in the **passé composé** and the **imparfait**.
Must be all original work, no computer translation or plagiarism.
Will contain the following elements:
A struggle between good and evil
A beautiful and appealing hero or heroine
A colorful ogre or monster
A negative consequence from not following orders
A task to complete
A happy ending

Special Need Students
Linguistically Challenged
Students who have difficulty expressing themselves verbally often have imaginative thoughts but do not easily understand how to express those complex thoughts simply and in a logical manner. Help those students think of storytelling in terms of events that follow each other. Ask them first to list a series of events they would like to use in their stories, then to arrange those events in consecutive actions by writing simple sentences and adding a transition word in front of each one. They should add details and images last.

RESOURCES

 e-visual 9

 Workbook 1–4

 Flash Cards

 Listening Activity 1

 Drill & Practice Games

Reference Desk

1. **Une copropriété** is a condominium where there is a collective ownership and board of directors.
2. If you rent, you are **un(e) locataire.** If you own the property, you are **un(e) propriétaire**.
3. In French Polynesia, a traditional house is called **un faré.**
4. **Mr. Bricolage** is a home improvement chain of stores. The website offers photos of various tools and how-to videos which would serve as listening comprehension exercises. **Search words: mr bricolage**

Vocabulaire actif

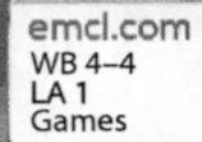

Le logement et le bricolage

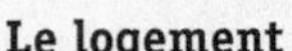

Le logement

Essential Instruction

1. Have students listen to **Le logement.**
2. Ask students **"Où habites-tu?"** using the new vocabulary.
3. Students will listen to **Nos projets de bricolage**.
4. Explain to students what an **HLM** is and ask if there are any collective housing projects in their community.

Dans un HLM

une cité

Nos projets de bricolage

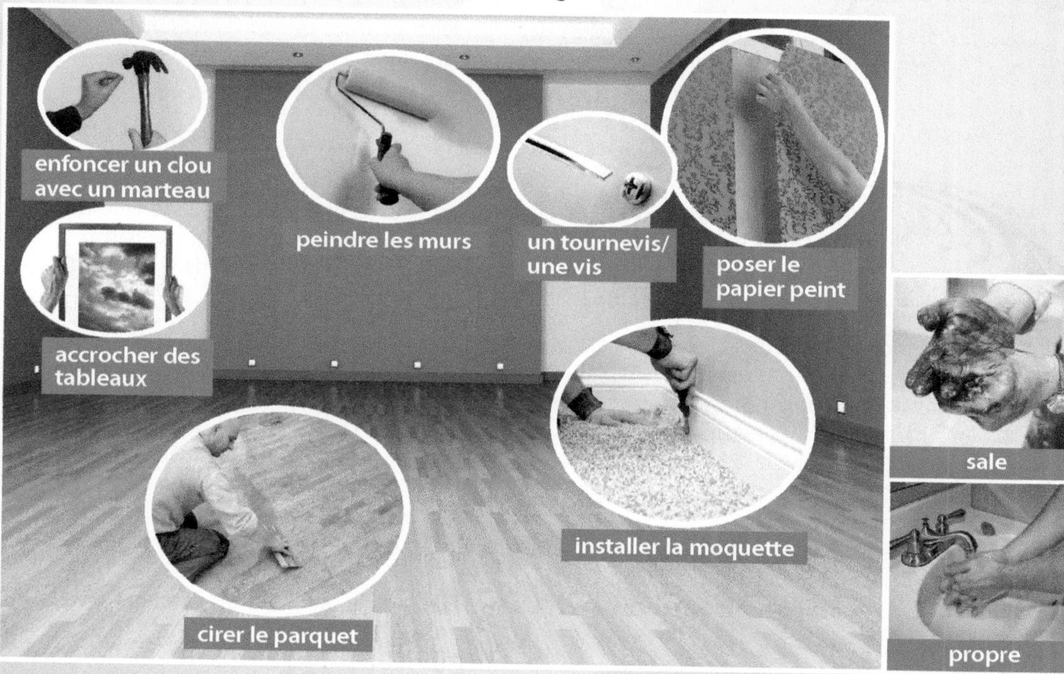

TPR

Place a hammer, nail, screw, wax, paintbrush, piece of carpet, and a picture frame on a table. Ask students to do novel commands: "Take the paint brush and paint my desk." "Take the wallpaper and put it under the hammer." You may want to use plastic toy tools.

Connections

Music

"Nettoyage de Printemps," a song by Gilbert Laffaille, lists all of the repair work the singer did to prepare for his love to move in. The song also features many pronominal verbs and useful daily vocabulary.

Search words: **nettoyage de printemps gilbert lafaille**

Expansion

Ask students to imagine how to redo their bedroom. They should make a list of tools and materials needed by visiting the **Mr. Bricolage** website.

Learning Styles

Kinesthetic Learners

This unit is ideal to involve kinesthetic learners in vocabulary presentations. Have those students mime do-it-yourself activities as you introduce vocabulary.

Special Needs Students

At-Risk Students

Students with difficult living situations may not be comfortable talking about their housing. Instead of asking them where they live, present short scenarios and ask them where these people might live. For example: **Pierre a 20 ans. Il est célibataire. Il n'a pas beaucoup d'argent. Où habite-t-il?; Martha Stewart veut habiter en France pendant l'été. Quelle habitation va-t-elle choisir?**

Answers

1

1. Je vous propose une maison individuelle.
2. Je vous propose une résidence secondaire.
3. Je vous propose une ancienne ferme.
4. Je vous propose une maison mitoyenne.
5. Je vous propose une villa.

Reference Desk

State that **Cela a été fait** is a combination of two verb forms. Which ones? Explain that this is a form of the **passé surcomposé**, a hybrid form of the **passé composé** of **être** + past participle of another verb to express the passive voice: "That has been done."

Game

Devinettes

There are many words for a dwelling. Put students in teams and see which team can look up the meaning of the following terms the fastest: **demeure**, **domicile**, **foyer**, **gîte**, **habitation**, **logement**, **cabane**, **cabanon**, **bastide**, **bungalow**, **chalet**, **pavillon**, **bicoque**, **mas**, **masure**, **échoppe**, and **buron.** They must add the appropriate article, **le** or **la**. Then expand the game to include **devinettes.** Students will give definitions for others to identify. **Une maison dans la montagne? C'est un chalet.**

Pour la conversation  

1.1, 5.1

What do I say when I'm introduced to someone?

› **Très heureux/heureuse.**

Pleased to meet you.

How do I say where I grew up?

› **J'ai grandi dans** un HLM qui n'était pas très propre.

I grew up in a subsidized apartment building that wasn't very clean.

How do I give a compliment?

› **On dirait que** cela a été fait par un professionnel!

One would say it was done by a professional!

Mots-clé À l'origine, le mot **bricolage** avait un sens presque péjoratif (*derogative*). Issu du mot "bricole," qui est une petite chose sans valeur, le bricolage était l'action de réparer des choses sans valeur. Aujourd'hui, c'est une activité professionnelle ou de loisirs importante si l'on considère la popularité des magasins et émissions de bricolage pour aider les particuliers.

Et si je voulais dire...?

un agent immobilier	*real estate agent*
un logement	*lodging*
un pavillon	*single-family house*
une résidence	*appt./condo building*
un terrain à bâtir	*building lot*

1 Agent immobilier  1.2, 5.1

Jouez le rôle d'un agent immobilier et suggérez des logements pour les personnes en fonction de leurs préférences ou de leurs besoins. Choisissez un logement parmi ceux de la liste.

studio · maison individuelle · ancienne ferme · villa · résidence secondaire · maison mitoyenne

MODÈLE J'ai 60 ans, et je ne travaille plus. Je vis seule dans une maison individuelle trop grande pour une personne. Mes revenus sont modestes, mais je n'ai pas besoin d'habiter dans un HLM. Je n'ai pas beaucoup de meubles. J'aimerais vivre en ville.
Je vous propose un studio.

1. Nous avons trois enfants, deux filles et un garçon. Donc, nous avons besoin de trois chambres. Mon mari et moi, nous travaillons en banlieue. Nous prenons la voiture pour aller au travail, nous aimerions avoir un garage.
2. Nous habitons en appartement pendant la semaine, mais ma famille et moi, nous voudrions un deuxième logement à la campagne. Nous aimons nager et faire des randonnées.
3. Il me faut un grand jardin à la campagne pour tous mes animaux. Mon mari et moi, nous aimons beaucoup bricoler.
4. Je préfère ma chambre au premier étage et la cuisine au rez-de-chaussée. Je n'ai pas besoin d'une maison individuelle, c'est trop grand pour moi.
5. Ma famille et moi, nous recherchons une maison au bord de la mer pour les vacances d'été.

Essential Instruction

1. Have the students listen to the vocabulary for **Pour la conversation.**
2. Ask students to think of a sentence that would precede each recorded remark. ***Je vous présente M. Labec.* "Ah, oui, très heureux/heureuse!";*"Tu as fait ce travail*? On dirait que cela a été fait parun professionnel."**
3. Select students to read aloud the sentences in **Agent immobilier.** The class will choose the appropriate housing option.
4. Pair students to do **Nos projets de bricolage.**
5. Change partners to do **À l'agence immobilière.**

2 Nos projets de bricolage

 1.2

Complétez les phrases avec un mot ou une expression de la liste.

un marteau | les peint | poser le papier peint | un tournevis | accroche des tableaux | la moquette | propre | nettoyer | les vis

Les jeunes de la cité ont peint les murs de la ville.

1. Des jeunes ont fait des graffiti sur les murs extérieurs de notre maison, alors les on....
2. Pour enfoncer un clou, il faut....
3. Nous voulons enlever... qui est sale dans les chambres et mettre du parquet.
4. On a peint les murs. Maintenant on....
5. Notre fille n'aime pas les murs blancs de sa chambre; donc, on....
6. Pour réparer les meubles cassés, il nous faut serrer (*tighten*)... avec....
7. Les murs de la cuisine sont sales; il faut les....
8. Après tout notre travail, notre maison est beaucoup plus....

3 À l'agence immobilière

1.1, 1.2, 5.2

Interpersonal Communication

*Un agent immobilier (*real estate agent*) parle au téléphone avec une cliente qui cherche un logement. Avec votre partenaire, jouez les rôles de l'agent et de la cliente. Si vous êtes la cliente, vous devez choisir la bonne phrase de la liste.*

-Je sais peindre et poser le papier peint.
-C'est encore mieux! Je peux voir l'appartement aujourd'hui?
-Ça me conviendrait parfaitement. Je n'ai pas peur de travailler avec mes mains.
-Bonjour, Monsieur! Je m'appelle Mlle Delacroix. Je viens de déménager ici, et je cherche un logement.
-Non, pas du tout. J'aime une ambiance vivante, mais pas trop la nuit.
-C'est que... j'ai grandi loin d'ici, et je ne connais personne. J'aimerais connaître mes voisins dans un immeuble en ville, mais pas trop grand.

L'agent: Allô! Ici M. Rivard.
La cliente: (1.)
L'agent: Très heureux. Vous désirez habitez en ville ou à la campagne?
La cliente: (2.)
L'agent: Ah bon. Mais bricoler, vous aimez ça?
La cliente: (3.)
L'agent: Et les passants, ça vous dérange?
La cliente: (4.)
L'agent: J'ai une idée. Il y a un immeuble en ville, pas trop grand, près de la rue commerçante, mais il y a quelques problèmes avec les appartements. On va baisser le prix pour les locataires qui feront les réparations eux-mêmes. Qu'en pensez-vous?
La cliente: (5.)
L'agent: Je ne vous ai pas dit, mais l'immeuble est tout près du métro.
La cliente: (6.)
L'agent: Disons à 15h30. Je vous enverrai l'adresse par mail. À bientôt, Mlle!

Answers

1. les peint
2. un marteau
3. la moquette
4. accroche des tableaux
5. pose le papier peint
6. les vis, un tournevis
7. nettoyer
8. propre

1. Bonjour, Monsieur! Je m'appelle Mlle Delacroix. Je viens de déménager ici, et je cherche un logement.
2. C'est que... j'ai grandi loin d'ici, et je ne connais personne. J'aimerais connaître mes voisins dans un immeuble en ville, mais pas trop grand.
3. Je sais peindre et poser le papier peint.
4. Non, pas du tout. J'aime une ambiance vivante, mais pas trop la nuit.
5. Ça me conviendrait parfaitement. Je n'ai pas peur de travailler avec mes mains.
6. C'est encore mieux! Je peux voir l'appartement aujourd'hui?

Differentiated Learning

Accelerate
Students will visit the site of an **agence immobilière** and read descriptions of apartments and houses for sale to use as a template. They will make a facsimile of a listing for the apartment or house they live in, illustrated with photos. Square footage will be converted to square meters.

Decelerate
Students will visit the site of an **agence immobilière** and read descriptions of apartments and houses for sale. They will select three residences that they would like to buy, copy their photo and listing, and record why each house appeals to them.

Answers

1. Nous pourrions cirer le parquet.
2. ... poser un nouveau papier peint.
3. ... accrocher des tableaux.
4. ... enfoncer des clous dans le bois.
5. ... installer une nouvelle moquette.

5

Script can be found in the front pages of the Annotated Teacher's Edition.

1. A
2. D
3. B
4. F
5. C
6. E

6 *Answers will vary.*

Communication

Interpersonal: Paired Practice

Have students prepare their answers to **Questions personnelles.** Each student will then stand and pass from student to student asking and answering questions 1–3 until they have interacted with all of their classmates, time permitting.

Interpersonal: Cooperative Groups

Students will be divided in two to three groups, depending on class size, to participate in a discussion of questions 4 and 5 of **Activité 6**.

4 Les frères Jarreau: Réparations et Décorations

 1.1, 1.3

Il y a un problème avec les logements suivants. Dites ce que votre compagnie pourrait faire pour trouver une solution.

poser un nouveau papier peint	peindre le mur	accrocher des tableaux
enfoncer des clous dans le bois	installer une moquette	cirer le parquet

MODÈLE  **Nous pourrions peindre le mur.**

1. 
2. 
3. 
4. 
5. 

Communiquez!

5 Comment réparer?

  1.1, 1.2

Interpretive Communication

Écrivez les numéros 1–6 sur votre papier. Écoutez les descriptions suivantes. Choisissez la solution à chaque problème de logement.

A. peindre les murs
B. accrocher des tableaux
C. poser de nouveaux papiers peints
D. nettoyer et cirer le parquet
E. acheter une résidence secondaire
F. se servir d'un marteau et enfoncer des clous

6 Questions personnelles

 1.2, 1.3

Répondez aux questions.

1. Où voudrais-tu habiter—dans une villa, une maison mitoyenne, un immeuble, une maison individuelle, ou une ancienne ferme?
2. Quand tu pars en weekend ou en vacances, où séjournes-tu (*where do you stay*)?
3. Est-ce que tes parents aiment bricoler? Si oui, qu'est-ce qu'ils ont fait dans votre maison? Les as-tu déjà aidés?
4. Quels problèmes est-ce que tu associes avec les cités? Pourquoi est-ce que ces difficultés existent? Si tu pouvais changer quelque chose, que changerais-tu pour éliminer ces problèmes?
5. Est-ce qu'il y a des graffiti dans votre école? Quelle solution proposes-tu?

Essential Instruction

1. Have students do **Les frères Jarreau: Réparations et Décorations**
2. Students will listen to **Comment réparer?** and answer A through F.
3. Pair students to improvise scenes in **Le premier appartement d'Adja.**
4. After listening to **Le premier appartement d'Adja**, ask comprehension questions that make students dig into the passage for the answers.
5. Students will work in pairs to answer questions in **Activité 7.**

Rencontres culturelles

emcl.com
WB 5

Le premier appartement d'Adja

1.1, 1.2, 5.2

Élodie et sa mère rendent visite à une employée de sa mère, Adja, qui est d'origine sénégalaise.

Mère: Élodie, je te présente Adja.
Élodie: Très heureuse.
Mère: Dis, tu aimes ton nouvel appartement?
Adja: Pour moi c'est un château. Tu sais, j'ai grandi dans un HLM qui n'était pas très propre.
Mère: Quel travail tu as fait! Tu as tout fait le plus rapidement possible.
Adja: Le plus difficile, ça a été de poser le papier peint.
Mère: On dirait que cela a été fait par un professionnel! Tu bricoles mieux que moi. Finalement tu as tout repeint?
Adja: Oui, vous arrivez juste pour m'aider à poser les tableaux.
Élodie: Justement, nous avons apporté un marteau et des clous pour vous aider.

7 Le premier appartement d'Adja

Interpersonal Communication

1.3, 5.2

Jouez les scènes suivantes avec votre partenaire. Servez-vous du nouveau vocabulaire du dialogue et de votre imagination.

1. Au bureau il y a trois jours, Adja et la mère d'Élodie prennent rendez-vous.
2. À la maison ce matin, la mère d'Élodie suggère que sa fille l'accompagne chez Adja.
3. Dans la voiture, Élodie et sa mère discutent de leur visite chez Adja.

Extension **Le nouvel appartement de Michèle**

1.1, 1.2

Un peintre entre dans le salon de Michèle.

Peintre: Alors, dites-moi un peu ce que vous voulez faire....
Michèle: Pas de papier peint, de la peinture blanche partout, et vous me faites enlever la moquette. Elle est si sale!
Peintre: Qu'est-ce qu'il y a dessous?
Michèle: Soulevez, là....
Peintre: Des parquets de Versailles!
Michèle: Tout l'appartement est comme ça! Alors la moquette, *out*!
Peintre: Mon frère cire les parquets.
Michèle: Ça tombe bien. Vous avez sa carte?

Extension Pourquoi est-ce que Michèle est contente d'avoir cet appartement?

1.3

Differentiated Learning

Accelerate

High-ability students will do the **Extension** in pairs and answer the corresponding question.

Decelerate

Low-ability students will work with you to read the **Le premier appartement d'Adja**. This will give you an opportunity to help them in a small group to improve their comprehension and pronunciation.

RESOURCES

Dialogue Video

Workbook 5

Answers

7 *Skits will vary.*

Extension

Parce que l'appartement a de beaux parquets.

Reference Desk

The word **papier peint** refers to a paper-based material brought from China in the 18th century; it is used to decorate walls. Despite its name, it is not hand painted; it is printed. The **papier peint** is different from the traditional **tapisserie** which involved a thicker, cloth-based fabric.

RESOURCES

 Workbook 6

Reference Desk

1. The French refer to several **HLM** buildings as **un parc HLM**. This designation, which brings to mind the elements of a natural space, is preferred over **une cité** which too often denotes filth and poverty associated with urban living.
2. In the 1980s, French singer Renault brought attention to the social issues associated with subsidized housing with his song "**Dans mon HLM**." You might show students the song on video, but we recommend not showing the lyrics, which contain some slang and inappropriate expressions. The students will not understand the lyrics if they hear them, but it is best not to draw attention to them in writing and/or teach them. Renault is a very positive figure who has used his fame to deliver social messages.

Points de départ

emcl.com
WB 6

Question centrale: Comment les Francophones restent-ils fidèles à leur langue et à leurs traditions?

Les HLM 1.2, 2.1, 3.1, 5.1

Créés en 1894, les HLM (habitation à loyer* modéré) sont un système d'immeubles qui offre des appartements à bon marché. La construction des HLM est limitée, et seul un français sur cinq peut bénéficier de ce type de logement. Ce sont les plus défavorisés*, souvent les immigrés ou les familles nombreuses, qui y habitent. Les étudiants peuvent aussi bénéficier des avantages offerts par les HLM. Autrefois réservés aux banlieues, on construit* depuis 1981 des HLM en centre-ville parmi d'autres immeubles où habite une population différente, afin d'intégrer les résidents à la population du quartier. Aujourd'hui, les Français font pression sur le gouvernement pour construire d'avantage de HLM.

 **Search words: logement social, banlieue parisienne**

défavorisés *underpriviliged;* **construit** *builds*

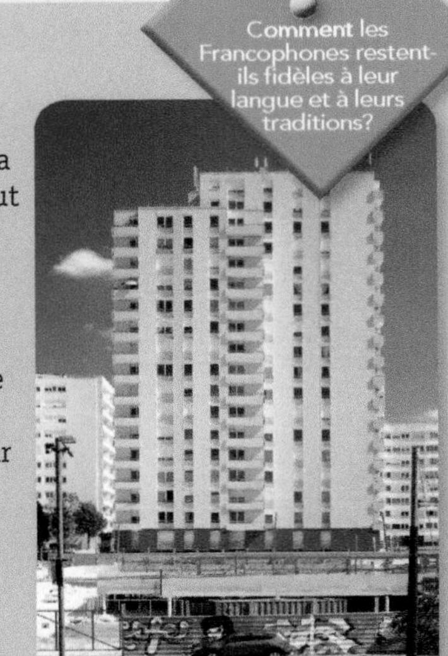

En France, un HLM peut avoir de 4 à 30 étages.

COMPARAISONS

Existe-t-il des logements de type HLM dans ta communauté? Où sont-ils? Comment sont-ils?

Les allocations familiales 1.2, 2.1, 3.1, 5.1

Toute personne résidant en France, parente de deux enfants, française ou non, peut bénéficier des allocations familiales*. La famille reçoit une somme d'argent de l'état pour l'aider avec les frais* liés à la nourriture, aux vêtements, et au logement. Les allocations familiales sont un revenu supplémentaire versé à toutes les familles nombreuses quel que soit* leur revenu. De la même manière, les familles françaises bénéficient d'une réduction d'impôts* qui augmente avec le nombre d'enfants. À partir du troisième enfant, la mère ou le père peut bénéficier d'un congé* parental sans perte* de salaire pendant un an. Quant aux* femmes qui ont élevé au moins trois enfants sans travailler, elles bénéficient d'une retraite* car élever des enfants est aussi considéré comme un travail à part entière*.

 **Search words: caf allocation familiale**

allocations familiales *welfare;* **frais** *costs;* **quel que soit** *whatever;* **impôts** *tax;* **congé** *leave from work;* **perte** *loss;* **quant aux** *as for;* **retraite** *retirement;* **à part entière** *full-fledged*

Essential Instruction

1. In the computer lab, have students listen to **Les HLM.** You might want to have students repeat certain words after they have heard the recording.
2. Next, ask students to record themselves reading that paragraph and then listen to themselves.
3. Put students in different groups and have them listen to either **Les allocations familiales** or **Le Sénégal.**
4. Each group will need to summarize the text they heard.

La Francophonie

 1.2, 2.1

Le Sénégal

Le Sénégal est un pays de l'Afrique de l'Ouest. Il doit son nom au fleuve qui le traverse. Les habitants sont les Sénégalais. Il existe six langues nationales différentes dont la plus importante est le wolof; ce plurilinguisme* explique que le français soit* la langue officielle. Le Sénégal compte 16 millions d'habitants, et sa capitale est Dakar; l'autre grande ville est Saint-Louis, l'ancienne capitale.

Ancienne colonie française, indépendante depuis 1960, le Sénégal est une république semi-présidentielle. Le Sénégal fait partie des pays les plus industrialisés avec la présence de nombreuses compagnies multinationales françaises et américaines. L'économie sénégalaise est dominée par la pêche et le tourisme. L'essor* du tourisme s'explique par le développement de réserves et parcs naturels qui couvrent* huit pour cent du territoire. Le Sénégal compte six parcs nationaux et une trentaine de réserves naturelles. Le Sénégal accorde une grande place à la culture dans son développement. Voici une liste des personnalités qui contribuent au rayonnement* de la culture sénégalaise et de la culture francophone dans le monde.

Écrivains	Léopold Sédar Senghor, Cheikh Hamidou Kane, Boubacar Boris Diop, Birago Diop, Aminata Sow Fall, Mariama Bâ
Artistes	Ousman Sow, Babacar Touré
Metteurs en scène	Ousman Sembène, Safi Faye
Musiciens	Youssou N'Dour, Viviane Ndour, Ismael Lô
Styliste (mode)	Oumou Sy

 **Search words: tourisme sénégal, gouvernement du sénégal**

plurilinguisme *multilingualism;* **soit** *is;* **essor** développement; **couvrent** *cover;* **rayonnement** *influence*

La tradition orale constitue une grande partie de l'identité Sénégalaise. Birago Diop a fait l'une des premières tentatives de préserver l'oralité (*oral tradition*) des griots traditionnels en publiant *Les Contes d'Amadou Koumba* en 1947.

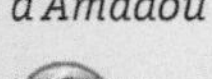 **Search words: conte-moi** 2.2

Les réserves naturelles du Sénégal protègent les animaux en voie de disparition.

Connections

Nature

Have students research the endangered species in Senegal. What are they, and why is their existence threatened?

Special Needs Students

Social Anxiety

Discussing where your students live might be stressful to some if they are living in subsidized housing, commuting between divorced parents, or living with extended family members. If you sense this might be true for some of your students, you could invite the class to answer the question about where they are living by using a fanciful lodging from the options listed in the **Game** on p.178.

Answers

8

1. *Drawings will vary.*
2. *Answers will vary.*
3. Situation géographique: Afrique de l'Ouest; Langues: wolof, français, et 4 autres langues africaines; Régime politique: république semi-présidentielle; Capitale: Dakar; Ressources naturelles: parcs nationaux et réserves naturelles
4. *Answers will vary.*

Perspectives
dans l'ombre et les arbres; la religion animiste; oui; Il pense que l'âme des morts est dans la nature.

1.2, 2.1

✲ *Le logement traditionnel au Sénégal*

Traditionnellement, les Sénégalais habitent dans des concessions, formées d'un groupe de cases ou de maisons. Le style de ces cases varie quelquefois selon l'ethnie* et surtout selon la situation géographique des peuples. La case bambara est la plus typique non seulement au Sénégal mais dans toute l'Afrique. C'est une habitation circulaire avec un toit en chaume*.

ethnie *ethnic group;* **chaume** *thatch*

On voit beaucoup de cases bambara dans les villages du Sénégal.

8 Activités culturelles

1.3, 2.1, 3.1, 3.2, 5.1

Complétez les activités suivantes.

1. Faites un dessin de cinq ou six appartements dans un HLM au même étage. Dans chaque appartement, écrivez le nom de famille, leur origine, et le prénom et l'âge de chaque membre de la famille que vous imaginez comme résidents.
2. Recherchez combien le gouvernement français donne cette année selon le nombre d'enfants par famille, et déterminez le montant d'allocations familiales que touche une famille avec:
   - deux enfants qui ont 4 et 6 ans
   - quatre enfants qui ont 10, 12, 14, et 17 ans
   - six enfants qui ont 6, 8, 12, 16, 17, et 18 ans
3. Faites la carte d'identité du Sénégal:
   - Situation géographique
   - Langues
   - Régime politique
   - Économie
   - Capitale
   - Ressources naturelles
4. Faites des recherches sur un(e) Sénégalais(e) célèbre et présentez cette personne à la classe.

Perspectives

1.2, 2.1

Dans son poème "Souffles," le poète sénégalais Birago Diop dit: "Ceux qui sont morts ne sont jamais partis:/Ils sont dans l'Ombre qui s'éclaire/Et dans l'ombre qui s'épaissit./Les Morts ne sont pas sous la Terre:/Ils sont dans l'Arbre qui frémit,/Ils sont dans le Bois qui gémit...." Où vont les morts, selon Diop? Ses idées appartiennent à quelle religion? Basé sur ce qu'il croit, est-ce qu'il voudrait sauvegarder l'environnement? Pourquoi, ou pourquoi pas?

Des habitations typiques d'un village sénégalais.

Essential Instruction

1. As a bell-ringer activity, put the following terms on the board and ask students to define them: **un HLM**, **les allocations familiales**, **une famille nombreuse**, **une réduction d'impôts**, **le plurilinguisme**, **Dakar**, **des griots.**
2. Students will work in teams to answer **Activités culturelles** questions 1 and 2, p.184. Students will answer question 3 from **Activités culturelles** p.184 individually.
3. Assign the reading **Guide touristique Sénégal** for an in-class activity.
4. Students will collaborate to make a list from the reading of attractions offered to a tourist visiting Senegal.

Du côté des médias Pre AP 1.2

Lisez le paragraphe sur le Sénégal touristique.

» **Guide touristique senegal:**

Situé dans une zone transitoire entre l'Afrique Equatoriale verdoyante et le désert du Sahara, le Sénégal offre une version presque complète de tous les écosystèmes du continent africain. Vous pouvez découvrir les grands fauves dans l'est du pays, les dauphins pourchassant les pirogues dans les lagons, les mangroves du delta de Siné-Saloum, les lacs de sel rose, les plages de sable blanc et les baobabs. L'architecture est aussi très diversifiée, il y a des hôtels ultramodernes, des mosquées et des huttes de terre. Pour les aventuriers, de belles promenades à dos de chameaux et des rallyes dans le désert vous raviront. La musique bien sûr rythme la vie quotidienne des sénégalais et de façon incessante. Á cause de sa diversité, comprendre le Sénégal n'est pas facile et trouver le temps de tout voir l'est encore moins. A courte distance de l'atmosphère frénétique de Dakar, la capitale du Sénégal, l'île de Gorée est une oasis de tranquillité. De nos jours, les palais aux murs ocres sommeillent sous leurs guirlandes de bougainvillées et l'ombre douce des palmiers s'étend sur les rues désertes. Ce patrimoine mondial de l'UNESCO recèle un sombre héritage: autrefois c'était un centre de commerce des esclaves. Pour en savoir plus, deux musées exposent le détail poignant de ce passé.

Ce guide touristique est fourni par notre partenaire opodo voyagez plus loin

9 Guide touristique Sénégal

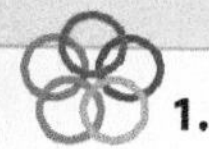

1.2, 1.3

Choisissez une des activités suivantes.

1. Faites un collage avec des vues du Sénégal.
2. Dessinez et colorez l'une des scènes décrites dans le paragraphe.

Answers

9 *Activities will vary.*

Expansion

Ask students to find images and information about **l'Île de Gorée** and its relationship to slavery. This would be a good time to remind students why there are francophone countries in Africa, and how **la francophonie**, which is now a positive term that focuses on cultural and linguistic diversity, bears the origin of painful roots.

Learning Styles

Visual Learners

Students will collaborate to do **Activité 9**, making a collage of different aspects of Senegal that transmit the essence of the country: its natural resources, industry, music, wildlife, its cities, and villages.

Multiple Intelligences

Naturalist

Students interested in nature will research Senegal's six national parks and thirty nature preserves to answer the question, "What is Senegal committed to doing to preserve the wildlife of its country?"

Mathematical-Logical

What are the current economic challenges facing the people of France today?

Intrapersonal

In **Perspectives**, the Senegalese poet Birago Diop suggests that our dead are always with us, embedded in nature. Students will read the poem "**Souffles**" and answer the question posed about the poet's commitment to the environment as evidenced in his work.

Answers

All activities will vary.

Expansion

Use the following questions as a springboard for class discussion.

1. **Est-ce que l'organisation que vous avez choisie répond aux besoins que vous considérez importants pour les immigrés? Pourquoi ou pourquoi pas?**
2. **Quelles sont les responsabilités des organisations humanitaires envers les immigrés?**
3. **Quelles sont les responsabilités d'un pays d'accueil envers ses immigrés? Y a-t-il des limites?**
4. **En considérant la pyramide, quels besoins n'ont pas été satisfaits? Comment pourrait-on répondre à ces besoins-là?**

La culture sur place

Les besoins des immigrés

Introduction et Interrogations

Tous les immigrés arrivent d'un pays et s'installent dans un autre pays, mais leurs expériences ne sont pas identiques. Dans cette *Culture sur place*, considérons les besoins des immigrés. De quoi ont-ils besoin? Quel est le lien entre leurs besoins et leurs expériences? Qu'est-ce que les organisations humanitaires dans leur pays d'accueil pourraient leur donner?

10 Première Étape: Réfléchir

1.3

Nous allons d'abord penser aux besoins des immigrés qui s'installent dans un nouveau pays.

1. Avec un partenaire, faites une liste de ce dont les immigrés pourraient avoir besoin en s'installant dans un nouveau pays. Écrivez en français, et utilisez un dictionnaire si nécessaire.
2. Organisez votre liste dans un organigramme selon les cinq types de besoins: ⟶
3. Une fois finie, partagez votre liste avec deux autres étudiants ou avec la classe.

La pyramide des besoins d'Abraham Maslow

- besoins d'épanouissement*
- besoins d'estime
- besoins affectifs
- besoins de sécurité
- besoins primaires

**self-actualization*

11 Deuxième Étape: Rechercher

1.3, 3.1, 3.2

Maintenant, avec votre partenaire, recherchez les buts d'une des organisations humanitaires dédiées (*dedicated*) aux besoins des immigrés. Ces organisations aident les immigrés en Belgique.

- Croix-Rouge de Belgique
- Défense des Enfants International
- Mentor-Escale
- Les Amis d'Accompagner
- Caritas International Belgique
- Mouvement Convivial (ou "Convivium")

En utilisant un site tel que www.donorinfo.be ou www.google.be, faites des recherches sur l'organisation que vous avez choisie. Cochez dans votre graphique les aides que les immigrés peuvent recevoir de la part de cette organisation.

Essential Instruction

1. Present **Activité 10**. Explain the mechanics of the exercise, making certain that the students understand how to proceed.
2. Explain the correspondence between **Activités 10** and **11**. Each organization listed has a specific focus. Students will choose or be assigned an organization to research. For example, **Mentor-Escale** is dedicated to offering social and educational education to the exiled averaging 16–17 years old.
3. In their search, students may discover other organizations that they would like to add to the list of support for immigrants.
4. Have students read the **Révision** and take the mini-test to see what they recall.
5. Review **plus...que**, **moins...que** and **aussi...que**, as well as the irregular forms of **bien**, **beaucoup**, and **peu**.

Structure de la langue

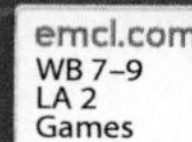

Révision: Comparisons with Adverbs

1.1

Can you tell which sentence uses an adverb, and which one uses an adjective?

1. C'est une voiture rapide.
2. La voiture circule rapidement.

See if you can complete the following sentences in the comparative:

3. Je conduis... que ma sœur. *(bien)*
4. Alain travaille... en classe que moi. *(peu)*
5. Tu joues au foot... que Sylvie. *(beaucoup)*

If you got any wrong in 1-5, be sure to read the grammar summary below to review the comparative of adverbs.

Comparisons using adverbs are formed in the same way that comparisons with adjectives are formed.

plus + adverb + **que**	Tu as fini **plus** rapidement **que** moi! (+)	*You finished faster than me!*
moins + adverb + **que**	Adja voyage **moins** souvent **que** sa sœur. (-)	*Adja travels less often than her sister.*
aussi + adverb + **que**	Aïcha peint **aussi** rapidement **qu'**un professionnel. (=)	*Aïcha paints as quickly as a professional.*

When making comparisons, some adverbs have irregular forms.

Adverb	Comparative	Example	
bien (*well*)	**mieux** (*better*)	Chantal pose **mieux** le papier peint **que** lui.	*Chantal puts on wallpaper better than he does*
beaucoup (*a lot, much*)	**plus** (*more*)	David travaille **plus qu'**Antoine.	*David works more than Antoine.*
peu (*little*)	**moins** (*less*)	Ils nagent **moins que** tes amis.	*They swim less than your friends.*

COMPARAISONS

Madison makes **good** drawings.
She draws **well**.

It is useful to be able to distinguish between adjectives and adverbs. Which sentence above uses an adverb, and which an adjective?

4.1

ADVERBS: Sentence #1 uses the adjective **rapide**. In sentence #2 **rapidement** is an adverb. The ending **–ment** is like **–ly** (*actively, carefully*) in English. The answers for 3–5 are: 3. mieux ; 4. moins ; 5. plus.

COMPARAISONS: The second sentence uses an adverb; adverbs modify verbs; "well" modifies the verb "draws." The first sentence uses an adjective; adjectives modify nouns; "good" modifies the noun "drawings." Remember, adjectives describe nouns, whereas adverbs describe verbs.

RESOURCES

Workbook 7–9

Listening Activity 2

Drill & Practice Games

Reference Desk

1. To help students form correctly the comparative with adverbs, remind them that just like **ne... pas** always surrounds the verb in a simple sentence unless an adverb is irregular, **plus/aussi/moins...que** always surrounds the adverb in a comparative sentence.
2. For practice, pair students and ask them to form comparative sentences using adverbs about their classmates. For example, **Jack court plus rapidement que Jil.** Caution students not to provide any negative attributes.

Differentiated Learning

Accelerate

Have students compare themselves now to what they could do when they were seven. They are to write as many comparisons as they can, using regular and irregular adverbs. Award a small token to the student who wrote the most comparisons correctly.

Decelerate

These students will need a structured review of adjectives and adverbs. They need to see, side by side, how adjectives and adverbs are formed and used in sentences. Insist on where adjectives are placed, versus adverbs, as placement plays the most important role in comparative sentences. Give sample sentences with adjectives and others with adverbs, then have students figure out where the **plus...que** goes.

Answers

1. La France a gagné la Coupe du Monde plus souvent que les Pays-Bas.
2. L'Uruguay... moins souvent que l'Allemagne.
3. L'Allemagne... plus souvent que la France.
4. La République de Corée... moins souvent que les Pays-Bas.
5. L'Italie... plus souvent que l'Angleterre.
6. La Suède... moins souvent que l'Argentine.
7. Le Brésil... plus souvent que la Turquie.
8. L'Argentine... plus souvent que le Portugal.

1. mieux
2. moins mal
3. plus souvent
4. moins sérieusement
5. aussi souvent
6. moins souvent
7. plus
8. plus tard

Script can be found in the front pages of the Annotated Teacher's Edition. Abdoulaye travaille le plus sérieusement.

Reference Desk

The **FIFA** is a **franglais** acronym for **la Fédération Internationale de Football Association**. Since 1930, it has gathered national soccer teams every four years to compete for the World Cup. The **FIFA**, which started with 13 teams, now encompasses more than 200 countries.

12 La coupe du monde de la FIFA

1.1, 1.2

Voici le classement des pays qui ont gagné une place à la Coupe du Monde de football depuis 1986. Comparez les gagnants.

1ère place: Espagne, Italie, Brésil, France, Brésil, Allemagne, Argentine
2ème place: Pays-Bas, Allemagne, France, Brésil, Italie, Argentine, Allemagne
3ème place: Allemagne, Turquie, Croatie, Suède, Italie, France
4ème place: Uruguay, Portugal, République de Corée, Pays-Bas, Bulgarie, Angleterre, Belgique

MODÈLE l'Espagne/l'Italie
L'Espagne a gagné la Coupe du Monde moins souvent que l'Italie.

1. la France/les Pays-Bas
2. l'Uruguay/l'Allemagne
3. l'Allemagne/la France
4. la République de Corée/les Pays-Bas
5. l'Italie/l'Angleterre
6. la Suède/l'Argentine
7. le Brésil/la Turquie
8. l'Argentine/le Portugal

13 Une enquête pour un Français et une Américaine

1.1, 1.2

Tristan habite en France et sa cousine Kelsey habite aux États-Unis. Kelsey a envoyé une enquête à son cousin français pour voir comment il vit. Complétez les phrases avec la forme comparative appropriée. Utilisez l'adverbe indiqué.

	Tristan	Kelsey
1. De quels sports fais-tu bien?	foot et tennis	basket et softball
2. Combien de fois par semaine vas-tu au café?	3–4	0–1
3. Combien d'heures étudies-tu chaque soir?	3	1–1.5
4. Combien de films américains regardes-tu chaque mois?	2	2
5. Combien de fois par an voyages-tu?	3	1
6. Combien de corvées fais-tu à la maison?	1	3
7. À quelle heure arrives-tu au lycée?	8h00	7h15

1. Tristan joue... au foot que Kelsey. (*bien*)
2. Kelsey joue... au softball que Tristan. (*mal*)
3. Tristan va... au café que Kelsey. (*souvent*)
4. Kelsey étudie... que Tristan. (*sérieusement*)
5. Tristan regarde des films américains... que Kelsey. (*souvent*)
6. Kelsey voyage... que Tristan. (*souvent*)
7. Tristan travaille... à la maison que Kelsey. (*peu*)
8. Tristan arrive au lycée... que Kelsey. (*tard*)

Communiquez!

14 Qui est le meilleur élève?

1.1, 1.2

Écoutez le paragraphe qui compare Abdoulaye et Étienne. Dites quel élève travaille le plus sérieusement, Abdoulaye ou Étienne.

Essential Instruction

1. Ask students to respond orally to the questions for **Activité 12.** Allow them time to write each answer in their notebooks.
2. Pair students to do **Activité 13.**
3. Personalize this activity by asking two of your own students to respond to the same questions. The class will compare these two students using the same format as in the activity.
4. Students will listen to **Qui est le meilleur élève?** to decide if the answer is Abdoulaye or Etienne. Ask students to justify their answer by recalling what they learned about each student.
5. After a review of the superlative of adjectives, use **Activité 15** as the basis for a debate. One half of your class will assume the role of chauvinist Americans and the other chauvinist French. Each side will argue that their country is better than the other in the categories 1 through 9.

Révision: Superlative of Adverbs

1.1, 1.2

emcl.com
WB 10–11
Games

Can you tell which sentence uses the comparative and which the superlative of adverbs?

1. Mon ami fait du ski nautique plus souvent que toi.
2. Je conduis le plus prudemment dans ma famille.

What grammatically correct sentence can you make with the parts below?

3. /le plus/Julien et/en classe/Annick/parlent

If you cannot do 1–3, read the grammar summary below.

The superlative of adverbs is formed in the same way as the superlative of adjectives.

le + **moins/plus** + adverb	Mon frère loue une résidence secondaire le plus souvent.	*My brother rents a second home the most often.*

Adverbs that are irregular in the comparative are also irregular in the superlative.

Adverb	Superlative	Example	
bien	le mieux	Qui peint **le mieux**?	*Who paints the t?*
beaucoup	le plus	Lise nettoie **le plus** dans sa famille.	*Lise cleans the most in her family.*
peu	le moins	C'est moi qui étudie **le moins** dans la classe.	*I'm the one who studies the least in class.*

15 Les Français ou les Américains?

1.1

Après plus de deux années d'études de français, vous connaissez bien la France et les Français. Dite si, selon vous, les Français ou les Américains font les activités suivantes ***le plus + adverbe****.*

MODÈLE **Selon moi, les Français discutent le plus passionnément.**
ou
Selon moi, les Américains discutent le plus passionnément.

1. protéger l'environnement attentivement (*attentively*)
2. passer les vacances tranquillement (*peacefully*)
3. travailler efficacement
4. parler joliment
5. se saluer (*greet*) affectueusement
6. vivre simplement
7. s'habiller bien
8. voyager souvent
9. dîner tard

SUPERLATIVE OF ADVERBS: Sentence #1 uses the comparative and sentence #2 the superlative of adverbs. The reordered sentence is: **Julien et Annick parlent le plus en classe.**

RESOURCES

Workbook 10–11

Answers

Subjects of answers will vary.

1. ... protègent l'environnement le plus attentivement.
2. ... passent les vacances le plus tranquillement.
3. ... travaillent le plus efficacement.
4. ... parlent le plus joliment.
5. ... se saluent le plus affectueusement.
6. ... vivent le plus simplement.
7. ... s'habillent le mieux.
8. ... voyagent le plus souvent.
9. ... dînent le plus tard.

Expansion

Show pictures of different means of transportation and ask students to decide which one is **le/la plus/moins rapide**, **le/la meilleur(e) marché**, or **le/la meilleur(e) ou le/la pire pour l'environnement.** You could choose an elephant, horse, moped, bicycle, car, train, jet, rocket, or car models.

TPR

Ask students to bring in a toy car or truck. Each student will pit his/her toy against another student's in a race to see which one goes faster, more slowly, or as quickly. This exercise can be expanded to ask who has the better car, the faster car, and the slower car so as to juxtapose the comparative and superlative forms of adjectives and adverbs.

Learning Styles

Auditory Learners

Have students clap or tap a particular rhythm as they say the superlative sentences as found in the adverb chart and in corrected activities.

Visual-Spatial

Since these students tend to think in images, have them make a poster that illustrates the comparative and superlative regular and irregular adverbs.

Multiple Intelligences

Mathematical-Logical

Have students create a template for the comparative and superlative forms of adjectives and adverbs, with examples. This visual can be posted on the wall for reference.

RESOURCES

Communicative Activities

Answers

All activities will vary.

Reference Desk

Blended Instruction

Consider using blended instruction, a combination of in-class learning and computer-mediated instruction or learning opportunities. Ask students to complete activities on the computer, using their cell or smartphone, or other emerging electronic technology. This activity will allow students to hone their tech skills and become more independent learners. Schedule routine Internet and e-book learning in class and in the lab.

À vous la parole

Question centrale: Comment les Francophones restent-ils fidèles à leur langue et à leurs traditions?

Communiquez!

16 Dans mon HLM

1.1, 1.3, 5.2

Interpersonal Communication

Deux locataires, qui viennent de s'installer dans le même HLM, parlent de l'état de leurs appartements et de leurs projets pour les rénover (*renovate*). Avec un partenaire, jouez les rôles de ces deux locataires et parlez de ces sujets:

A. votre famille
B. l'étage où se trouve votre appartement
C. l'état de votre appartement (sale? propre?)
D. combien de pièces vous avez
E. la couleur de vos pièces
F. les changements de couleurs des murs, papier peint, moquette, etc. que vous comptez faire
G. les tableaux que vous voulez poser aux murs

Communiquez!

17 Mon logement de rêve

1.1, 1.3, 5.2

Presentational Communication

Trouvez une habitation en France où vous voudriez vivre. Imprimez les photos qui sont disponibles. Ensuite, écrivez un paragraphe sur les changements que vous voudriez faire, en parlant des meubles ou appareils électroménagers, tapis ou moquettes, tableaux ou objets d'art, papier peint ou peinture, etc. Si vous préférez, vous pouvez dessiner votre habitation et montrez comment vous l'avez décorée.

Search words: acheter maison, immobilier france

Essential Instruction

1. To review vocabulary from **Leçon C**, ask students what kinds of renovations can be expected on an apartment. Write key phrases on a board or project them on a screen.
2. Pair students and have them prepare a script for **Activité 16.**
3. Assign **Activité 16** to be performed as a skit before the class.
4. Assign **Activité 17** as individual homework.
5. Have students work in groups for **Activité 18.** Give specific roles to different students based on their abilities and skills.
6. Prepare a date ahead of time to showcase art for **Activité 19.** In addition to printing an image, you may ask students to write a paragraph describing the image, mentioning the artist, the art movement, or their reaction and reason for choosing this art. Students with culinary interest might enjoy preparing a typical Senegalese dish.

Answers

All activities will vary.

Communiquez!

18 Un nouveau HLM

1.3, 2.1, 5.1

Presentational Communication

Imaginez que vous êtes architecte et que le gouvernement français vous paie pour dessiner un nouveau HLM en centre-ville parmi d'autres immeubles qui ne sont pas subventionnés (*subsidized*) par l'état. Faites un dessin. Pensez à ce que vous proposez pour les enfants, les ados, les personnes handicapées, et les personnes âgées de ce HLM. Finalement, présentez votre dessin et répondez aux questions de la classe.

Communiquez!

19 Une galerie sénégalaise

1.3, 3.1, 3.2

Interpretive and Presentational Communication

Transformez votre salle de classe en une galerie sénégalaise. Imprimez en couleurs des tableaux d'artistes sénégalais. Accrochez aussi des poèmes sénégalais entre les tableaux. Pendant que vous travaillez, écoutez de la musique sénégalaise traditionnelle ou moderne. Vous pouvez inviter les autres classes de langue (espagnol, allemand, chinois...) et aussi de sciences humaines et sociales (*social studies*) à visiter votre galerie.

Sculpture africaine en cuivre.

Une peinture sénégalaise sur coton.

Special Needs Students

Behavior Problems

Activité 19 is a collaborative exercise for those who like working in a team to transform their classroom into Senegal through its art and music. Students who are easily distracted when there is less structure should not be left without a specific task to perform. Be sure to give them a responsibility in which they can take on a leadership role.

Search words: **spirit of senegal**

Social Anxiety

For **Activité 16** and **Activité 18**, students with a difficult housing situation might not want to share their personal experience; however, they might want to contribute their thoughts, feelings, and knowledge to generate a list of concerns associated with subsidized housing in their region or country.

Answers

Rencontre avec l'auteur
Le rituel du deuil (*mourning*).

Pré-lecture
Answers will vary.

Stratégie de lecture
"Des initiés ont lu le Coran. "La religion officielle du Sénégal est musulmane.
"En général, c'est le petit frère qui hérite de l'épouse laissée par son aîné." La tradition du Sénégal est que si un homme marié meurt, son frère épouse la veuve (*widow*).
"Je te préfère à l'autre, trop légère, trop jeune. / "Et tes femmes, Tamsir?" Tamsir, comme l'était Modou, est polygame; la polygamie est acceptée dans certaines régions du Sénégal.
"J'égrène mon chapelet." La religion officielle du Sénégal est musulmane.
"l'une de tes épouses fait des travaux de teinture*, l'autre vend des fruits, la troisième inlassablement tourne la manivelle* de sa machine à coudre." Le Sénégal est un pays peu modernisé et il y a beaucoup de métiers artisanaux.

Connections

Music

Jean Ferrat in his song **"La Femme est l'avenir de l'homme"** speaks to the role of women in modern society. Have students outline the images of these women presented in the song vis-à-vis the treatment of Mariam Bâ in Senegalese society. Students may want to use the same chart in **Stratégie de lecture** to analyze the song as well.

Lecture thématique 

Une si longue lettre

Rencontre avec l'auteur   1.2

Mariama Bâ (1929–1981) est née au Sénégal. Elle est élevée par ses grands-parents maternels à la mort de sa mère dans un univers musulman traditionnel. Après de brillantes études, elle devient institutrice, métier qu'elle exercera pendant 12 ans. Mère de neuf enfants, mariée trois fois, elle décide de se consacrer à la cause des femmes et s'engage dans des associations féministes. Elle lutte pour les droits des femmes et contre la polygamie. En 1979, elle publie *Une si longue lettre* qui devient très vite un grand succès. Il s'agit d'une lettre de confidences à une amie sur sa vie de femme, et sur le comportement de son beau-frère. À partir de la lecture de cet extrait, qu'apprenez-vous de la culture sénégalaise?

Pré-lecture  1.3

Si vous deviez écrire une lettre de confidences, que souhaiteriez-vous raconter de votre vie et à qui?

Stratégie de lecture 1.2, 1.3, 2.1

Making Cultural Inferences

Lorsque vous lisez un texte, vous en tirez (*draw*) naturellement des conclusions. Cela s'appelle faire des inférences. Quand un texte donne des indications culturelles, comme dans la lecture qui suit sur le Sénégal, vous faites des inférences culturelles. Au cours de la lecture, inscrivez dans la colonne de gauche d'un tableau comme celui de dessous les indices textuels concernant la culture sénégalaise. Dans la colonne de droite, expliquez les renseignements que ces citations fournissent (*furnish*). Un exemple vous est donné.

Textual clue	Cultural inference
C'est "le quarantième jour de la mort de Modou," le mari de la narratrice.	Au Sénégal, on célèbre le quarantième jour après la mort d'un membre de la famille.
"Des initiés ont lu le Coran."	

Essential Instruction

1. To prepare students to read an excerpt from **Une si longue lettre** they will listen to the **Rencontre avec l'auteur** with Mariama Bâ. From what they learn about the author, what can they expect to read?
2. Ask students if they would ever write **une lettre de confidences.** To whom would it be written? Who would be the most understanding, a parent, an adult mentor, or a friend? What are the risks of writing a personal letter? What would be the reason to do so?
3. Students will complete the **Stratégie de lecture** as they read the extract.
4. Asks students to answer the **Pendant la lecture** questions after listening to the recording, or pause where there is a question to monitor their comprehension as you go through. Students can work on the questions in pairs or small groups and then share their findings with the class.

Outils de lecture  1.1, 1.2

Gender Criticism

Il existe plusieurs études critiques d'un texte littéraire, par exemple l'analyse des liens (*ties*) entre un récit de la vie personnelle de l'auteur (critique biographique), ou l'analyse des personnages d'un roman selon la psychologie moderne (critique psychologique). La critique de genre s'intéresse à l'identité de l'homme et de la femme en littérature, et à comment ces images reflètent ou rejettent les paramètres sociaux traditionnels qui ont freiné (*put brakes on*) l'égalité entre l'homme et la femme.

***Retour du marché*, 2005. Cécile Delorme.**

J'ai célébré hier, comme il se doit, le quarantième jour de la mort de Modou. Je lui ai pardonné. Que Dieu exauce* les prières* que je formule quotidiennement pour lui. Des initiés ont lu le Coran. Leurs voix ferventes sont montées vers le ciel. Il faut que Dieu t'accueille parmi ses élus, Modou Fall!

Après les actes de piété*, Tamsir est venu s'asseoir dans ma chambre dans le fauteuil bleu où tu te plaisais*. En penchant* sa tête au dehors, il a fait signe à Mawdo; il a aussi fait signe à l'Imam de la mosquée de son quartier. L'Imam et Mawdo l'ont rejoint. Tamsir parle cette fois. Ressemblance saisissante* entre Modou et Tamsir, mêmes tics de l'inexplicable loi de l'hérédité. Tamsir parle, plein d'assurance; il invoque (encore) mes années de mariage, puis conclut*:" Après ta 'sortie' (du deuil*), je t'épouse. Tu me conviens* comme femme et puis, tu continueras à habiter ici, comme si Modou n'était pas mort. En général, c'est le petit frère qui hérite de l'épouse laissée par son aîné. Ici, c'est le contraire. Tu es ma chance. Je t'épouse. Je te préfère à l'autre, trop légère, trop jeune. J'avais déconseillé ce mariage à Modou."

Quelle déclaration d'amour pleine de fatuité* dans une maison que le deuil n'a pas encore quitté. Quelle assurance et quel aplomb tranquilles! Je regarde Tamsir droit dans les yeux. Je regarde Mawdo. Je regarde l'Imam. Je serre* mon châle noir. J'égrène mon chapelet*. Cette fois, je parlerai.

Ma voix connaît trente années de silence, trente années de brimades*. Elle éclate*, violente, tantôt sarcastique*, tantôt méprisante.

Pendant la lecture
1. Depuis combien de temps Moudou est-il mort?

Pendant la lecture
2. Comment sait-on que la narratrice est pieuse?

Pendant la lecture
3. Qui est venu s'asseoir dans la chambre de la narratrice?

Pendant la lecture
4. Que propose Tamsir?

Pendant la lecture
5. Pourquoi Tamsir ne s'intéresse-t-il pas à l'autre femme de Modou?

Pendant la lecture
6. Comment est-ce que la narratrice se sent après avoir entendu la proposition de Tamsir?

---

exauce *grants;* **prière** *prayer;* **piété** *piety;* **où tu te plaisais** que tu aimais; **En penchant** *In leaning;* **saissante** *striking;* **conclut** *concludes;* **le deuil** *mourning;* **Tu me conviens** *You suit me;* **fatuité** *self-conceit;* **serre** *pull closer;* **J'égrène mon chapelet** *I touch my strings of beads while praying;* **brimades** *vexations;* **éclate** *explodes;* **tantôt sarcastique** *sometimes sarcastic;* **méprisante** *scornful*

Answers

Pendant la lecture
1. depuis quarante jours
2. Elle prie beaucoup pour son mari.
3. Tamsir, le frère de Modou, l'Imam, et Mawdo
4. Il voudrait épouser la narratrice.
5. Elle est trop jeune et mince pour lui.
6. Elle se met en colère.

Expansion

Use the images brought by students from **Activité 19**, and ask them to imagine that each painting represents a scene from the novel ***Une si longue lettre*** that the excerpt does not describe. Have them choose a painting and narrate a very short story of what might have happened in the novel. This game can be played before or after the reading.

Diffentiated Learning

Accelerate

High-ability students will be able to listen to the passage and pass directly to the **Pendant la lecture** and **Post-lecture** questions. After they have finished this assignment, ask them to make a family tree of Mariama Bâ's family with notes about each person drawn from the story.

Decelerate

Low-ability students will appreciate you working with them, one on one or in a group, to break the passage down into smaller sections, explaining vocabulary and structure and helping them answer the **Pendant la lecture** and **Post-lecture** questions.

Special Needs Students

Auditory Impairment

For students who have difficulty hearing, make arrangements for them to use earphones to listen to the recording, or be placed near the source of the broadcast.

Answers

Pendant la lecture

7. Un acte d'amour et de foi, c'est aussi un choix.
8. trois; des petits travaux

Post-lecture

Possible answer:

La narratrice est une femme d'une cinquantaine d'années, obéissante à la tradition de sa culture. Après la mort de son mari, elle remet en question ses croyances. Ce qui est remarquable dans cette transformation est que la femme change d'opinion après trente ans.

Le monde visuel

Possible answer:

Les couleurs sont vives, les dimensions sont plates, il n'y a pas de reliefs ou même d'ombres.

19 *Activities will vary.*

Communication

Interpersonal: Cooperative Groups

In groups, students will discuss the picture **"Les Femmes qui Marchent à la file"** from **Le monde visuel** as an example of primitive art, and as a metaphor of the life of women in Senegal. They will need to compare it to other Senegalese art pieces which have been presented in class.

—As-tu jamais eu de l'affection pour ton frère? Tu veux déjà construire un foyer neuf sur un cadavre chaud. Alors que l'on prie pour Modou, tu penses à de futures noces. Ah! oui: ton calcul, c'est devancer* tout prétendant* possible, devancer Mawdo, l'ami fidèle qui a plus d'atouts* que toi et qui, également, selon la coutume, peut hériter de la femme. Tu oublies que j'ai un cœur, une raison*, que je ne suis pas un objet que l'on se passe de main en main. Tu ignores ce que se marier signifie pour moi: c'est un acte de foi* et d'amour, un don total de soi à l'être que l'on a choisi et qui vous a choisi. Et tes femmes, Tamsir? Ton revenu ne couvre ni leurs besoins ni ceux de tes dizaines d'enfants. Pour te suppléer* dans tes devoirs financiers, l'une de tes épouses fait des travaux de teinture*, l'autre vend des fruits, la troisième inlassablement* tourne la manivelle* de sa machine à coudre*. Toi, tu te prélasses en seigneur vénéré*, obéi au doigt et à l'œil. Je ne serai jamais le complément de ta collection....

Pendant la lecture

7. Pour la narratrice, qu'est-ce que c'est que le mariage?

Pendant la lecture

8. Combien de femmes Tamsir a-t-il? Que font-elles pour contribuer aux finances de la maison?

---

devancer *to forestall;* **prétendant** *suitor;* **atouts** *asset;* **raison** *mind;* **foi** *faith;* **don** cadeau; **suppléer** *to provide;* **teinture** *dyeing;* **inlassablement** sans fatigue; **manivelle** *crank;* **machine à coudre** *sewing machine;* **tu te prélasses en seigneur vénéré** *you lounge around like an honored lord*

Post-lecture  1.3

Comment décririez-vous la narratrice? Que pouvez-vous dire de la femme que la narratrice était dans le passé, et de celle qu'elle est devenue? Qu'est-ce qui rend cette transformation remarquable?

Le monde visuel  1.2, 3.1

Cécile Delorme (1946–) est une artiste française qui passe beaucoup de temps en Afrique. Le tableau, à la page 193, Sénégalaises, montre la vie des femmes, qui marchent à la file (*in single file*) en revenant du marché, presque comme dans un défilé de mode. Le style est naïf, c'est-à-dire pas réaliste en ce qui concerne l'architecture, l'anatomie, et la perspective. L'art naïf est souvent marqué par une simplicité, de petits détails, et une coloration brillante. Quels aspects de l'art naïf sont visibles dans ce tableau? Soyez précis.

19 Activités d'expansion  1.3, 4.2, 5.2

1. Écrivez un paragraphe dans lequel vous parlez de la vie traditionnelle des femmes au Sénégal. Servez-vous des informations de votre grille.
2. Imaginez que Tamsir n'arrête pas de proposer le mariage à la narratrice. Avec un partenaire, jouez le rôle des protagonistes. Tamsir donne ses raisons pour le mariage, et la narratrice refuse avec ses propres raisons.
3. Imaginez que la narratrice est votre correspondante. Écrivez-lui une lettre dans laquelle vous lui donnez des conseils.
4. Analysez la place de la femme dans une culture que vous connaissez bien, et comparez-la à la vie traditionnelle des femmes au Sénégal.
5. Comparez la vie d'un personnage du texte avec votre vision de la vie.

Essential Instruction

1. **Activité 20** challenges students to draw inferences from the reading about Mariama's life to use as a basis to write an essay, dramatic scene, letter, a cultural analysis, or a personal philosophy statement. Give the students a choice of activity, or assign one or more to them. The pre-writing outline should be done in class under your supervision so that they write a thoughtful, well-structured piece of writing.
2. For **les Projets finaux,** ask groups to select **A** or **B** as their final project. Reserve a day in the lab or class for them to work. Have each group present its project to the class.
3. For **C** form groups with a balance of extroverts and quieter students. Encourage students to film their work in advance, which gives them the opportunity to redo it if they are not pleased with the first try.

T'es branché?

Projets finaux

A Connexions par Internet: L'anthropologie

1.2, 1.3, 3.1, 3.2

Presentational Communication

L'anthropologie culturelle est l'étude des variations culturelles entre les hommes et les sociétés humaines grâce à la collecte de données concernant l'impact des processus économiques et politiques mondiaux sur les **réalités culturelles locales.** Les anthropologues utilisent différentes méthodes: observations, interviews, et enquêtes. Faites des recherches sur les Berbères. Imaginez que vous êtes au Maghreb et que vous étudiez les berbères. Préparez un sondage pour mieux connaître ces gens. Quelles réponses anticipez-vous aprés vos rechenches?

Les Berbères sont les descendants des premiers habitants d'Afrique du Nord.

B Communautés en ligne

3.2, 5.2

L'Alliance française/Interpersonal Communication

Trouvez l'Alliance française la plus proche de chez vous et choisissez un cours auquel vous pouvez vous inscrire ou un événement culturel auquel vous voudriez assister. Expliquez à votre partenaire pourquoi ce cours ou cet événement culturel vous intéresse.

C Passez à l'action!

1.3

Projet: Un conte de fées/Presentational Communication

Avec quelques camarades de classe, préparez des scènes pour un conte de fées de Charles Perrault ou un conte maghrébin. Décidez qui va introduire le conte, qui va être le narrateur/la narratrice, qui va jouer les rôles des personnages, qui va préparer le décor, et qui va écrire les invitations.

Answers

All activities will vary.

Game

Le jeopardy

Create a jeopardy board by making a table with six columns across and five rows down. On the far left column write point values. Across the top, choose categories from the chapter: **Vocabulaire**, **Grammaire**, **Francophonie**, **Culture**, etc. Write five questions for each category. Divide students in groups of four or five to play.

Differentiated Learning

Accelerate

For **Passez à l'action!**, students will do the project as indicated, or your more adventurous students may be given random words by the class, approved by the teacher, that they must integrate into their fairy tale.

Decelerate

Meet with low-ability students to describe what is involved in project **A** and **B.** Help students decide what to select, and make a plan of action. They will need to see an example of what the final project should look like. For **C**, find time to help them brainstorm their fairy tale, assign roles, and write the story. The more guidance they receive, the more successful they will become. These fairy tales can be done with the help of online programs.

Search words: **show me**, **launchpadtoys/toontastic**, **puppet-pals**

Answers

D

Leçon A: Il fait des recherches sur Internet.; avec l'Alliance française; la langue française et leurs ancêtres québécois; Il utilisent des ressources en ligne.; l'espace Félix Leclerc, la Maison de nos Aïeux, le Manoir Mauvide Genest, et le parc Maritime de Saint-Laurent et de l'Île d'Orléans

Leçon B: Karim lit *L'élève du magicien* à sa sœur.; Les maghrébins immigrés en France créent des commerces qui permettent aux Français de profiter d'objets artisanaux et de la cuisine du Maghreb.

Leçon C: Il écoute peut-être Youssou N'Dour, Viviane Ndour, et Ismael Lô.

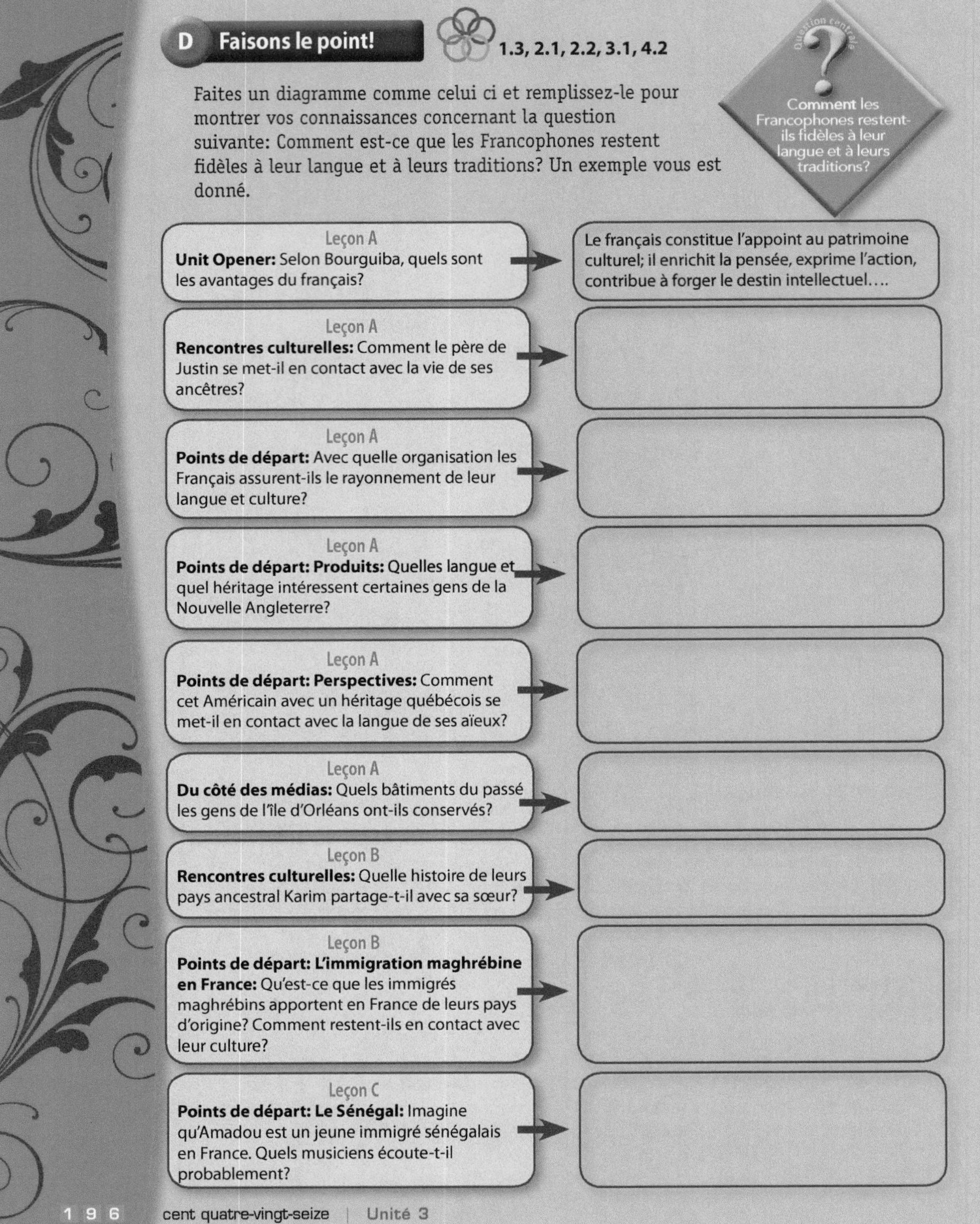

D Faisons le point! 1.3, 2.1, 2.2, 3.1, 4.2

Faites un diagramme comme celui ci et remplissez-le pour montrer vos connaissances concernant la question suivante: Comment est-ce que les Francophones restent fidèles à leur langue et à leurs traditions? Un exemple vous est donné.

Leçon A **Unit Opener:** Selon Bourguiba, quels sont les avantages du français?	Le français constitue l'appoint au patrimoine culturel; il enrichit la pensée, exprime l'action, contribue à forger le destin intellectuel....
Leçon A **Rencontres culturelles:** Comment le père de Justin se met-il en contact avec la vie de ses ancêtres?	
Leçon A **Points de départ:** Avec quelle organisation les Français assurent-ils le rayonnement de leur langue et culture?	
Leçon A **Points de départ: Produits:** Quelles langue et quel héritage intéressent certaines gens de la Nouvelle Angleterre?	
Leçon A **Points de départ: Perspectives:** Comment cet Américain avec un héritage québécois se met-il en contact avec la langue de ses aïeux?	
Leçon A **Du côté des médias:** Quels bâtiments du passé les gens de l'île d'Orléans ont-ils conservés?	
Leçon B **Rencontres culturelles:** Quelle histoire de leurs pays ancestral Karim partage-t-il avec sa sœur?	
Leçon B **Points de départ: L'immigration maghrébine en France:** Qu'est-ce que les immigrés maghrébins apportent en France de leurs pays d'origine? Comment restent-ils en contact avec leur culture?	
Leçon C **Points de départ: Le Sénégal:** Imagine qu'Amadou est un jeune immigré sénégalais en France. Quels musiciens écoute-t-il probablement?	

Essential Instruction

1. Conduct a guided review of the unit using the chart **Faisons le point!**
2. For each entry on the left, have students find the answers in the unit.
3. Lead an expanded discussion of the questions. Assign a class participation point every time a student contributes to the conversation.
4. For **Évaluation de compréhension auditive,** have students write down the answer. Replay each sentence for students who missed the correct answer.
5. Give students a few minutes to prepare before they do the dialogue for **Évaluation orale.** They will flip a coin to see who plays the American and who plays the immigrant. You may also give students a sheet that lists expectations you have regarding their conversation (length, vocabulary control, grammar accuracy, etc.).

Évaluation 

emcl.com
LA *Synthèse*

A Évaluation de compréhension auditive   1.1, 1.2

Interpretive Communication

*Écoutez la conversation entre Amina et Ahmed, qui décrit un conte de fées. Ensuite, indiquez si les phrases sont vraies (**V**) ou fausses (**F**).*

1. Amina lit un conte contemporain.
2. Le héros du conte s'appelle Jean et habite dans une belle villa.
3. La cité où le héros habite est très propre.
4. L'arrière-grand-père africain du héros est magicien.
5. L'ancêtre a donné un couteau magique au père de David.
6. La cité sera belle et propre.
7. Sa sœur pense que le conte d'Ahmed est bête.

B Évaluation orale  1.1, 5.2

Interpersonal Communication

Avec un partenaire, jouez les rôles d'un(e) immigré(e) et d'un(e) Américain(e) qui se sont inscrit(e)s dans un cours de français à l'Alliance française à New York. Dans votre conversation:

L'Américain(e) se présente et demande de faire sa connaissance.	L'immigré(e) donne son nom à l'Américain(e).
L'Américain(e) demande à l'immigré(e) où il/elle a grandi (pas l'Amérique).	L'immigré(e) dit dans quel pays il ou elle a grandi.
L'Américain(e) demande où la famille de l'immigré(e) s'est installée.	L'immigré(e) répond.
L'Américain(e) demande si toute la famille de l'immigré(e) est venue en Amérique.	L'immigré(e) dit lesquels de ses parents sont venus en Amérique et lesquels sont restés dans son pays d'origine.

RESOURCES

 **Listening Activity**
Synthèse

Answers

Script can be found in the front pages of the Annotated Teacher's Edition.

1. V
2. F
3. F
4. V
5. F
6. F
7. F

B *Conversations will vary.*

Game

Les Frères Parker

Create a template for a game board that you can use for each chapter. Have one die per board and enough game pieces for each student. You will want to have 20–30 spaces. Write questions from the unit on cards, and put the cards face down in a pile in the middle of the board. Students will roll the die, move their game piece the number of spaces corresponding to the die, and answer a question from the pile. Students may refer to their books if necessary.

Special Needs Students

Linguistically Challenged

These students will need more help preparing for their dialogues. Help them be less self-conscious presenting the dialogue to the class by giving them an opportunity to rehearse it with their partner ahead of time.

AD(H)D

These students will need help organizing their review of the **Unité.** Encourage them to use their flash cards to practice vocabulary, review their exercises and activities, and meet with you to answer any lingering questions.

Answers

All activities will vary.

Reference Desk

Any of the **Évaluation** activities can be used as an assessment tool. Include additional visual prompts similar to those in **Activité E**, which are particularly helpful for students with difficulty processing language.

Communication

Interpersonal: Cooperative Groups

Have students in small groups sit in a circle. Each student spends one minute writing down information he or she remembers from the chapter according to a topic you call out. Call time and have the paper passed to the student on the right. The next student reviews and edits what is written, if necessary, and adds more ideas. After the ideas have been exhausted, call time and have students review in their groups. Students then verify the information from the book.

C Évaluation culturelle

2.1, 3.1, 3.2, 4.2, 5.1

Vous allez comparer les cultures francophones à votre culture aux États-Unis. Vous aurez peut-être besoin de faire des recherches sur la culture américaine.

1. **L'Alliance française**
   Expliquez ce que l'Alliance française offre en général. S'il y a une Alliance française dans votre région, présentez son programme et dites de quelles activités ou cours vous profiteriez.
2. **L'immigration**
   Faites un résumé des vagues migratoires de la France vers le Québec et du Québec vers les États-Unis. Existe-t-il une présence francophone dans votre région? Si oui, qu'est-ce que vous pouvez remarquer? Quelles traces sont toujours visibles?
3. **La Tunisie**
   Comparez la Tunisie aux autres pays du Maghreb. On y parle quelles langues? C'est une ancienne (*former*) colonie de quel pays? La Tunisie est-elle plus ou moins libérale que le Maroc et l'Algérie? De quelles façons? Et comment compareriez-vous les États-Unis par rapport à ses voisins, le Canada et le Mexique?
4. **Les étudiants maghrébins**
   Des étudiants venant étudier en France, combien sont originaires du Maghreb? D'où viennent les étudiants étrangers qui étudient dans les universités américaines?
5. **Les subventions du gouvernement**
   De quelles aides pouvez-vous bénéficier en France pour le logement et pour élever vos enfants? Quelles aides existent aux États-Unis?
6. **Les contes maghrébins**
   Qu'est-ce qui est universel dans les contes pour enfants que vous connaissez? Quels aspects des contes maghrébins sont uniques?
7. **Le logement traditionnel au Sénégal**
   Comparez le logement traditionnel au Sénégal avec les logements traditionnels aux États-Unis, par exemple, ceux des Native Americans.

D Évaluation écrite

1.3

*Votre famille vient de déménager. Vous avez acheté une maison en ligne et vous trouvez qu'il y a beaucoup de choses à faire. Écrivez à vos grands-parents québécois. Expliquez les problèmes qu'il y a avec la maison et qui fai t quoi pour la rénover (*renovate*).*

On doit réparer le plafond du salon.

Essential Instruction

1. Number cards from 1 to 7, enough for every member in the class.
2. Students will draw a card that will indicate which topic they will work on in **Évaluation culturelle**.
3. Organize the students into groups according to their randomly chosen topic.
4. Provide a rubric and a list of vocabulary and structures to include.
5. Have them identify pages in their book and sources online that will help them complete their evaluation. They should include a visual when they present their topic to the class.
6. For **Évaluation écrite** insist that the students take 10–15 minutes to outline their essay before starting to write.
7. Provide a storyboard to each student in which they will draw a cartoon-story, one event for each box. This will be the writing prompt for the **Évaluation compréhensive**.

E Évaluation visuelle 1.3

Votre famille vient d'immigrer aux États-Unis. Dites où tous les membres de votre famille se sont installés.

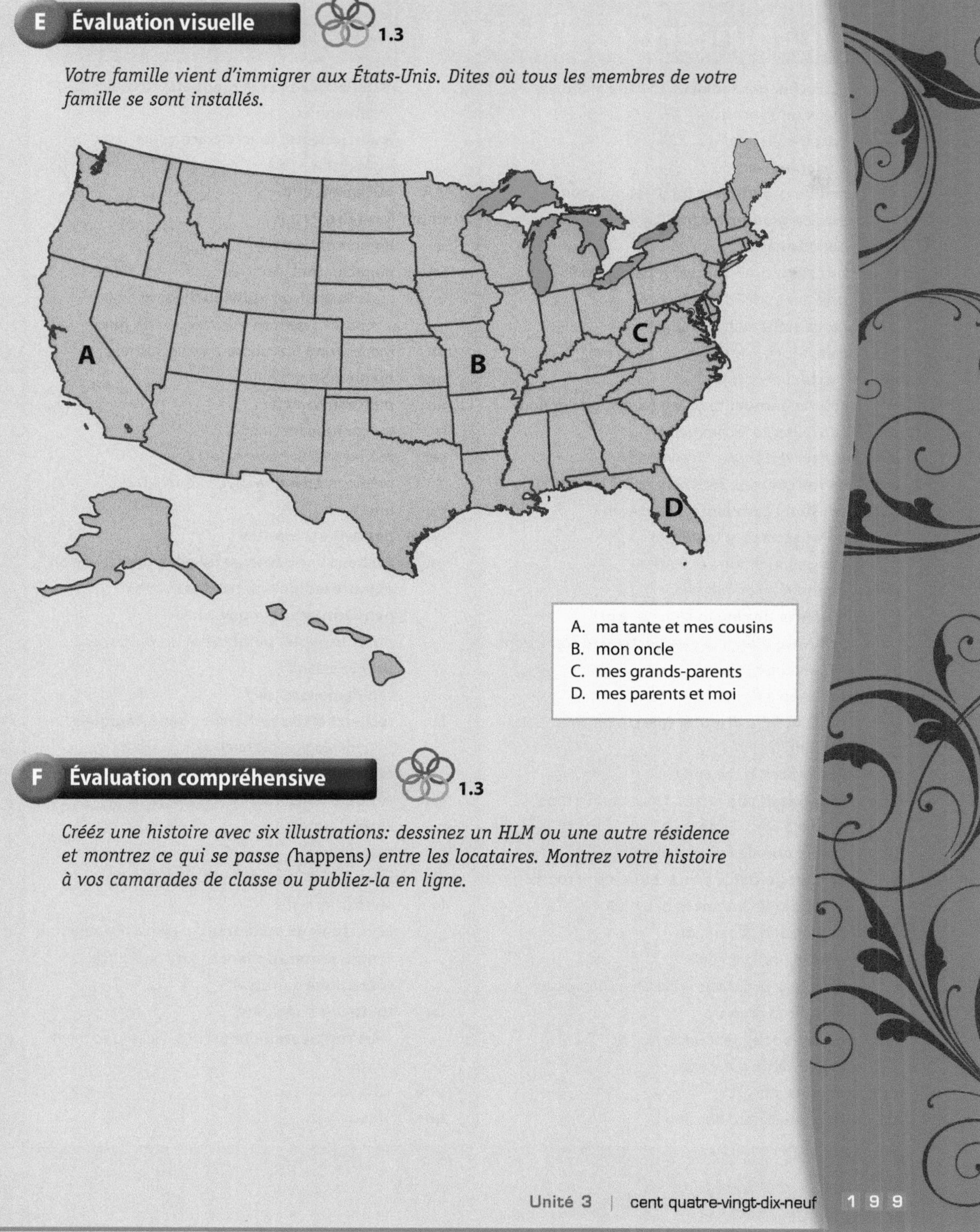

F Évaluation compréhensive 1.3

*Créez une histoire avec six illustrations: dessinez un HLM ou une autre résidence et montrez ce qui se passe (*happens*) entre les locataires. Montrez votre histoire à vos camarades de classe ou publiez-la en ligne.*

Answers

All activities will vary.

Game

Les prépositions

To review the prepositions associated with American states, and prepare students to complete **Évaluation visuelle**, ask them to stand up on their chairs. Call out a state, for example, *Minnesota*. Point to a student randomly. He or she should state the correct preposition associated with it, in this case, **dans le Minnesota**. If the student is correct, he or she will remain standing. If incorrect, he or she will be asked to sit down. Play the game until there is only one student left, or a certain amount of time has passed. For a variation, you may divide the class in two or three groups, and assign one student to call out names of states.

Learning Styles

Kinesthetic Learners

Create flash cards with information lines on the topics seen in the unit mentioned in **Évaluation culturelle**, 1–7. Have your kinesthetic learners sort these cards correctly under the appropriate categories. This will help them see what topics they know, and what still needs to be studied.

Auditory Learners

Before preparing the activities, these students should discuss with a partner what each topic is about, what vocabulary words they can associate to it, and what cultural information they remember from their research or in-class participation.

RESOURCES

 **Listening Pre-test D**

 ***Unité* Test**

Reference Desk

There is a high correlation between retaining information and getting enough sleep. We often encourage students to get enough sleep before an exam, but it would serve them well to consistently get enough rest every night to increase their productivity and memory retention. Discuss this issue and other wellness practices with your students.

Vocabulaire de l'Unité 3  1.2

	accrocher des tableaux to hang paintings *C*
les	**aïeux (m.)** ancestors *A*
un(e)	**ancêtre** ancestor *A*
	ancien(ne) old *C*
l'	**arrière-grand-mère (f.)** great-grandmother *A*
l'	**arrière-grand-père (m.)** great-grandfather *A*
une	**ballade** ballad *B*
le	**bricolage** do-it-yourself repairs *C*
	bricoler to do DIY projects *C*
	ça: ça suffit that's enough *B*
	cela it *C*
un	**cercle** circle, group *A*
	cirer le parquet to polish hardwood flooring *C*
	conseiller to recommend *B*
une	**conserverie** canning company *A*
un	**conte: conte de fées** fairy tale *B*
le, la	**cousin(e) germain(e)** first cousin *A*
	déjouer un tour to undo a spell *B*
	éloigné(e) distant, extended *A*
un(e)	**employé(e)** employee *C*
	enfoncer un clou to hammer a nail *C*
	être: être d'origine (+ adjective) to come from (+ country) *C*
une	**fable** fable *B*
se	**faire: se faire disputer (par)** to get in trouble (with) *B*
	finalement in the end *C*
une	**fois: Il était une fois....** Once upon a time (there was).... *B*
la	**Francophonie** French-speaking world *A*
	garder: garder le contact to keep in touch *A*; **garder un enfant** to babysit *B*
une	**génération** generation *A*
les	**graffiti (m.)** graffiti *C*
	grand(e): la grande crise Great Depression *A*
	grandir to grow up *C*
le	**grand-oncle** great uncle *A*
la	**grand-tante** great aunt *A*
une	**histoire** story *B*
un	**HLM** subsidized housing *C*
	installer: installer la moquette to install carpeting *C*
	jouer: jouer un tour to place a spell on *B*
	juste just *C*
	justement fittingly *C*
un(e)	**locataire** tenant *C*
le	**logement** housing *C*
un(e)	**magicien(ne)** magician *B*
une	**maison: maison individuelle** single-family house *C*; **maison mitoyenne** row house *C*
un	**maître, une maîtresse** master, mistress *B*
une	**manière** way *A*
un	**marteau** hammer *C*
la	**mécanique** mechanics *A*
se	**méfier (de)** to be wary (of) *B*
	même: même que that *[inform.]* *B*
un	**mur** wall *C*
un(e)	**passant(e)** passer-by *C*
un	**pêcheur, une pêcheuse** fisherman, fisherwoman *A*
	peindre les murs to paint the walls *C*
	pendant: pendant que while *B*
	poser le papier peint to put up wallpaper *C*
	propre clean *C*
	rapidement quickly *C*
la	**recherche: des recherches généalogiques** genealogical research *A*
	repeindre to repaint *C*
une	**résidence secondaire** second home *C*
	rusé(e) cunning *B*
	sale dirty *C*
un	**studio** studio apartment *C*
la	**suite** (the) rest *B*
	tenir: tenir un restaurant to own a restaurant *A*
	tenter: tenter sa chance to try one's luck *A*
	touristique touristy *A*
un	**tournevis** screwdriver *C*
	très: Très heureux/heureuse. Pleased to meet you. *C*
une	**villa** villa *C*
une	**vis** screw *C*

Essential Instruction

The alphabetical listing of vocabulary words is an excellent reference for students, but it may not be the best way for them to learn. Encourage them to group the words into similar topics to support their learning. Encourage them also to create a sentence, whether orally or in writing, using each vocabulary word correctly.

Unité 4 Préparatifs de départ

Reference Desk

In **Unité 4, Préparatifs de départ**, students learn about winter vacations in the alpine regions of France and in tropical **la Réunion.** We learn that four out of ten French people take off to a destination for winter break, so let's join them!

Reference Desk

The accompanying quotation tells us that to really love a country we must savor its food, drink, and song. To set the tone, in the opening photos we see the Alps and a celebration of **Carnaval** in Annecy.

Citation

"Pour bien aimer un pays il faut le manger, le boire et l'entendre chanter."

To really like a country, you must eat it, drink it, and hear it sing.

—Michel Déon, écrivain, dramaturge, et académicien français

À savoir

Quatre Français sur dix partent en vacances d'hiver.

Essential Instruction

1. Looking at a map of France, ask students to guess where one would go skiing for winter break.
2. Find in the **unité** where the opening photo of **Carnaval** was taken. What is the equivalent of **Carnaval** in the United States?
3. Students will review the **Contrat de l'élève** to gain an overview of what they will learn in **Unité 4.**

Unité 4

Préparatifs de départ

Question centrale

?

Qu'est-ce qu'on doit connaître de sa destination pour réussir son voyage?

Dans quelle ville fête-on ce carnaval?

Comment s'appelle cette montagne?

Contrat de l'élève

Leçon A I will be able to:

- ask for an opinion and respond appropriately.
- discuss **la Réunion**, **Chamonix**, **le Mont Blanc**, and **les Alpes**.
- use the present participle and negative expressions.

Leçon B I will be able to:

- say what I must do, tell someone they'll have an opportunity to do something, and say what I was expecting.
- discuss the **Savoie** region of France, **les classes de neige**, and Annecy.
- review **savoir** and **connaître** and use the subjunctive of regular and irregular verbs after **il faut que**.

Leçon C I will be able to:

- say I'm going to do a different activity and tell someone to avoid injury.
- discuss ski resorts in France and volunteer tourism in Francophone countries.
- use the subjunctive after impersonal expressions.

Reference Desk

1. The charming city of Annecy is a popular year-round tourist destination. It is known as "The Venice of France" because of the Thiou canal running through **la vieille ville.** Visitors can take a cruise on **Le Lac d'Annecy**, rent a paddleboat or canoe, or run, bike, or walk along the lake's paved paths.
2. Annecy is well known for its annual **Festival international du film d'animation.**

Special Needs Students

AD(H)D

As you begin the unit, check to make sure that these students have their notebooks and other items they will need for class. Help them organize their notebooks, designating specific pages for the new vocabulary, structure, and culture of the unit.

RESOURCES

 e-visual 10

 Workbook 1–4

 Flash Cards

 Listening Activity 1

 Drill & Practice Games

Reference Desk

Expressions with **faire** were introduced in Level 1, **Unité 8** p. 404 and revisited in Level 2, **Unité 1** p. 48.

Vocabulaire actif

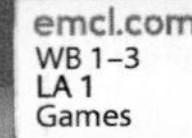

Les activités en plein air

Essential Instruction

1. Have students illustrate the vocabulary in their notebooks for **Les activités en plein air**, **Pour la conversation**, and **Et si je voulais dire...?**
2. Play **Pour la conversation** and **Et si je voulais dire...?** three times before asking the students to repeat. By delaying oral production, students have time to internalize the sounds, thereby reinforcing their French accent and minimizing the influence of their native language.
3. Brainstorm other **faire** expressions used to describe sports in order to reactivate students' memories. Utilize choral repetition of **faire** in **présent** and **passé composé**.
4. For **Activité 1,** read Florence's letter to the students and ask the comprehension questions one through five. Students should have their books closed but may take notes on what they hear.
5. Reread the letter, this time with students following in their books. Discuss any questions that pose problems.

Pour la conversation 

1.1, 1.2

emcl.com
WB 4

How do I ask someone's opinion?

> **Chamonix te dit?**
> *How do you feel about Chamonix?*

How do I react positively to someone's opinion?

> **Sans aucun doute.**
> *Without a doubt.*

> **Je suis persuadé(e).**
> *I'm convinced.*

How do I react negatively to someone's opinion?

> **Je vois les choses un peu différemment.**
> *I see things a bit differently.*

Et si je voulais dire...? 

aller à la chasse	*to go hunting*
se balader	*to go walking*
faire du surf	*to surf*
faire du rafting	*to go whitewater rafting*
faire du VTT	*to mountain bike*
visiter les gorges	*to visit gorges and canyons*

Communiquez!

1 Ah, le plein air!   1.2, 5.1

Interpretive Communication

Lisez le mail que Florence envoie à sa copine. Puis, répondez aux questions.

À: Emma
Cc:
Sujet: Il faut que tu viennes ici!

Salut, Emma!

Nous (ma tante, mon oncle, et ma cousine) sommes à Chamonix, et comme c'est chouette le plein air. Je suis persuadée que les Alpes, c'est le plus bel endroit du monde. Bien sûr que j'ai fait une randonnée équestre et que j'ai fait des sauts à ski, mais j'ai aussi essayé deux activités pour la première fois. On a dit, "Tu aimes l'aventure, n'est-ce pas?" et moi j'ai répondu, "Mais oui! Sans aucun doute." Hier j'ai fait de l'escalade, et puis ce matin j'ai fait du saut à l'élastique, et ça, c'est la meilleure activité de toutes! Alors, Chamonix te dit pour les prochaines vacances?

Bises,
Florence

1. Avec qui voyage Florence?
2. Quel est le plus joli endroit selon Florence?
3. Quelles activités est-ce que Florence a faites avant d'essayer quelque chose de nouveau?
4. Quelle nouvelle activité est-ce que Florence préfère?
5. Qu'est-ce que Florence propose à Emma?

Answers

1. avec sa tante, son oncle, et sa cousine
2. les Alpes
3. une randonnée équestre et des sauts à ski
4. du saut à l'élastique
5. d'aller à Chamonix avec elle pour les prochaines vacances

Expansion

Students work in small groups. Each group receives a set of three to four pictures of people, items, and pastimes based on winter sports and activities with which they are familiar. Instruct students to create a story based on the pictures. Call upon each group to present the story collectively with each successive student repeating the previous sentence(s) before adding the next sentence of the story.

Differentiated Learning

Accelerate
Students write a response to Florence's letter in which they propose a winter ski vacation for the following year. They must say where they would like to go and what activities they would like to do. Encourage them to elaborate by adding reasons for their choices.

Decelerate
Students will research the village of **Chamonix** as a potential winter vacation site. They will write in French the activities they would like to do.

Answers

2

2. A: Fais-tu du parachutisme ascensionnel?
   B: J'ai fait du..../Je n'ai jamais fait de..../Je fais souvent du....
3. A: Fais-tu des sauts à ski?
   B: J'ai fait des..../Je n'ai jamais fait de..../Je fais souvent des....
4. A: Fais-tu de la plongée sous-marine?
   B: J'ai fait de la..../Je n'ai jamais fait de..../Je fais souvent de la....
5. A: Fais-tu de l'escalade?
   B: J'ai fait de l'..../Je n'ai jamais fait d'..../Je fais souvent de l'....
6. A: Fais-tu des randonnées équestres?
   B: J'ai fait des..../Je n'ai jamais fait de..../Je fais souvent des....
7. A: Fais-tu du saut à l'élastique?
   B: J'ai fait du..../Je n'ai jamais fait de..../Je fais souvent du.....
8. A: Fais-tu du ski nautique?
   B: J'ai fait du..../Je n'ai jamais fait de..../Je fais souvent du....
9. A: Fais-tu du ski de fond?
   B: J'ai fait du..../Je n'ai jamais fait de..../Je fais souvent du....

Reference Desk

Before doing **Activité 2**, provide students with additional review and practice of the **passé composé** of **faire** with negatives. Choral repetition of the negative response will help set the pattern: **"Je n'ai jamais fait de..."** Remind students that the negative expression uses **de** or **d**.

Communication

Interpersonal: Paired Practice

Pair students to complete **Activité 2.** Students expand their answers by adding an extension using **parque que**, **quand**, **avec**, and/or a place. For example, **"J'ai fait de la planche à voile *quand j'étais dans le Colorado avec mes amis.*"** Put these words on the board as a reminder.

Communiquez!

2 Les activités en plein air

  1.1, 5.2

Interpersonal Communication

À tour de rôle, demandez à votre partenaire s'il ou elle fait l'activité sur la photo. Votre partenaire va répondre selon le modèle.

MODÈLE A: **Fais-tu de la planche à voile?**
B: **J'ai fait de la planche à voile une fois.**
ou
Je n'ai jamais fait de planche à voile.
ou
Je fais souvent de la planche à voile.

1. 
2. 
3. 
4. 
5. 
6. 
7. 
8. 
9. 

Essential Instruction

1. As a bell-ringer activity, create some **devinettes** based on the vocabulary. For example, **C'est une excursion où on monte à cheval.** Put the **devinettes** on cards with answers and let students read them to the class.
2. Do **Activité 3** with the class as a whole. After each response, ask more questions to keep the students speaking.
3. Have students read questions one through five silently before doing **Activité 4.** Replay any statement that the students do not understand.
4. For **Activité 5**, have students write their answers to the questions. When finished writing, everyone circulates to ask and answer each other's questions as if at a "mocktail" party. Students could record the answers of five different classmates, then report back to the class.

3 Précisez!

3.1

Dites ce que les personnes indiquées feront pendant les vacances selon les indications. Choisissez une expression de la liste.

de la planche à voile | du jet-ski | des randonnées équestres
du parachute ascensionnel | de l'escalade | des sauts à ski | du kayak

MODÈLE Mathis et Cédric passent beaucoup de temps à la plage.
Pendant les vacances, ils feront de la planche à voile.

1. Awa aime passer du temps à la campagne avec son cheval.
2. Marc et moi, nous aimons nos scooters de mer.
3. Nasser aime faire du ski alpin.
4. Gabrielle et Bruno aiment descendre les rochers (*rocks*).
5. Abdoulaye aime voler (*fly*) comme un oiseau.
6. Tu aimes ton petit kayak vert.

4 La Réunion, je kiffe!

1.1, 1.2

Interpretive communication

*Écrivez les numéros 1–5 sur votre papier. Écoutez Stéphane décrire sa vie à la Réunion. Écrivez **V** si la phrase que vous lisez est vraie et **F** si elle est fausse.*

1. Stéphane fait des sports d'hiver à la Réunion.
2. Il fait de la planche à voile avec des copains.
3. La randonnée équestre est une activité qu'il fait avec sa classe.
4. Stéphane ne sait pas faire de l'escalade.
5. Stéphane aime faire du saut à l'élastique le weekend.

5 Questions personnelles

1.3, 5.1

Répondez aux questions.

1. Préfères-tu les activités en plein air?
2. Qu'est-ce que tu aimes faire en été? en hiver? en automne? au printemps?
3. Un voyage à la montagne te dit? Pourquoi, ou pourquoi pas?
4. Quelles activités en plein air as-tu déjà essayées? Lesquelles est-ce que tu ne voudrais pas essayer?
5. Comment est-ce que tes choix sont différents de ceux de tes amis?

J'aimerais essayer le saut à l'élastique, mais j'ai un peu peur.

Answers

1. Pendant les vacances, elle fera des randonnées équestres.
2. ..., nous ferons du jet-ski.
3. ..., il fera des sauts à ski.
4. ..., ils feront de l'escalade.
5. ..., il fera du parachute ascensionnel.
6. ..., tu feras du kayak.

Script can be found in the front pages of the Annotated Teacher's Edition.

1. F
2. V
3. V
4. F
5. V

5 *Answers will vary.*

Expansion

Students adopt **une station de ski** in France or in Québec and track the weather conditions on the slopes for **le ski alpin** and **le ski du fond** for one week. They create a graph showing the snowfall in inches and temperatures in Fahrenheit.

Game

Vive le sport!

Do this fast-paced game to practice vocabulary. Distribute a set of five to six vocabulary flash cards to each student featuring winter sports vocabulary as well as sports that they have learned in the past. At your signal have them play charades, acting out each sport for a partner. Call time after one minute. The partners with the most correct guesses win the game.

Multiple Intelligences

Naturalist

The theme of mountains and an island will appeal to students who are interested in the world and the environment.

Visual-Spatial

Encourage these students to make a poster of a map of France and **la Réunion** with symbols of the winter and summer sports that are offered there.

Special Needs Students

Social Anxiety

There will be some students, because of their economic situation, who have never been on vacation, let alone been skiing or to an island. Encourage all students to use their imaginations to think about trips or vacations they hope to take in the future.

RESOURCES

Dialogue Video

Workbook 5

Answers

1. la Réunion
2. Chamonix
3. Chamonix
4. la Réunion
5. la Réunion

Reference Desk

1. **La Réunion** is a French island and department located in the Indian Ocean, east of Madagascar. It has a population of approximately 800,000.
2. **Piton de la Fournaise** (*Peak of the Furnace*) is a volcano located on the eastern side of **la Réunion**. Residents refer to it as **le Volcan**, and it is currently one of the most active volcanoes in the world.

Critical Thinking

Analysis

What kinds of volcanoes are there? Why are some volcanoes extinct, some dormant, and some active? Are there any volcanoes in the United States? If so, what kind of volcanoes are they?

Rencontres culturelles

emcl.com
WB 5

Les prochaines vacances

1.2

Élodie, Léo, et leurs parents planifient un voyage.

Père: Alors, Léo, Chamonix te dit?

Léo: Sans aucun doute... ça me tente de passer des vacances tout schuss....

Mère: Bon eh bien, nous avec Élodie, on voit les choses un peu différemment....

Élodie: Autrement dit, oui, au sommet, mais pas dans les Alpes.

Mère: On aimerait moins froid, plus humide, et plus chaud.

Élodie: Et plus près de la mer....

Léo: Alors pas Chamonix, mais plutôt les Alpes du Sud: le ski avec vue sur la mer?

Père: Mais non, tu n'y es pas du tout! Ce n'est pas ça qu'elles veulent! Moi, j'ai trouvé: c'est une île avec un volcan et du soleil, n'est-ce pas?

Mère: En y réfléchissant bien, ça pourrait être ça.

Élodie: Oui, en y regardant de plus près, ça doit être ça.

Léo: Ah, d'accord! Elles veulent nous faire le coup de la Réunion! Qu'est-ce qu'on peut y faire?

Élodie: On peut nager, faire des randonnées équestres, visiter le Piton de la Fournaise... aucun de nous ne s'ennuiera.

Léo: Je suis persuadé qu'on s'amusera. Alors, on part quand?

6 Les prochaines vacances

1.1, 1.2

Identifiez l'endroit dont on parle: Chamonix ou la Réunion.

1. Il y a de belles plages.
2. On y voit des montagnes.
3. On peut y faire du ski alpin.
4. Il y fait chaud et du soleil.
5. On peut y faire des randonnées équestres.

Essential Instruction

1. As a bell-ringer, put **au bord de la mer** and **dans les montagnes** on the board. Have students brainstorm activities that can be done in each place.
2. Have students skim the questions in **Activité 6** before listening with books closed. Then have them answer the questions.
3. Explain that **En y réfléchissant** means "(While) thinking it over... " The –**ant** ending is –*ing* in English. **Parlant**=*speaking*, **finissant**=*finishing*. This foreshadows the lesson on p. 214.
4. Before playing **Extension**, ask students to imagine differences of opinion that families might have when planning a vacation.
5. Play **Extension**. Put two columns on the board, **Client** and **Cliente**. Have the students cite from the text the conflicting points of view of the two travelers.

Extension **À l'agence de voyages**  1.1, 1.2, 1.3

Dans une agence de voyages, une agente essaie d'aider un jeune couple.

Agente: Reprenons depuis le début. Vous êtes sûr que vous voulez partir ensemble?
Client: Sans aucun doute!
Agente: Bon, alors, il va falloir vous mettre d'accord.
Client: On est vraiment désolés, mais moi, je préfère la mer, et elle, la montagne.
Agente: Proche ou loin?
Cliente: Plutôt loin.
Client: Mais pas trop loin....
Agente: Les Antilles vous disent?
Les clients: Oui!!
Agente: Seuls, je veux dire... vous deux, ou en groupe?
Cliente: On pourrait essayer en groupe.
Client: Il me semble que ça serait mieux juste nous deux.
Agente: Ah non, vous n'allez pas recommencer!

Extension Pourquoi est-ce que la région proposée par l'agente marche pour le client et la cliente? Pourquoi est-ce que l'agente est frustrée avec ce couple?

1.1, 1.2, 1.3

Answers

Extension

Parce que le paysage est varié et réunit le goût de chaque personne.; Ils n'ont pas le même avis.

Expansion

Your students have just won the lottery and have the option to travel to **La Réunion**, **la Corse**, **Chamonix**, and **Le Mont Blanc**. Have students research flights, the route, number of stops, and pricing for each of these destinations, all leaving from their hometown. How many hours would it take to get to each destination? What are the high, low, and shoulder season prices for each destination? What is the difference in price for economy and first class? The purpose of this exercise is for students to make a personal connection with these destinations, and to be aware of how they would have to travel to get there.

Search words: **discount airfare sites**

Differentiated Learning

Accelerate

High-ability students continue the dialogue in **Extension** until the **client** and **cliente** have arrived at a compromise or an impasse about their future trip.

Decelerate

Have students write a short **resumé** of the **Extension** conversation in English, explaining each point of view. They can cite liberally from the text but must transform the dialogue from first person to third.

RESOURCES

Workbook 6

Communication

Presentational: Cooperative Groups

Students work in small groups to write two lists of reasons: one for using **un agent de voyage** and one for planning a trip themselves. Have groups write their lists on large pieces of paper and then post these around the room. Once completed, students take a tour of the lists and discuss the most frequently cited reasons for both situations.

Points de départ

emcl.com
WB 6

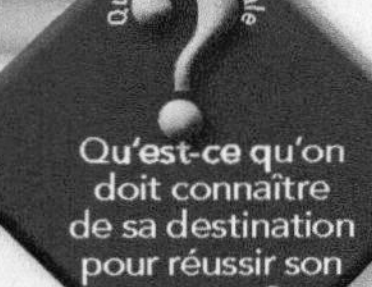

La Francophonie

1.2, 2.1

La Réunion

L'île de la Réunion est un département français située dans l'Océan Indien à côté de Madagascar. C'est une île volcanique, très montagneuse. Elle abrite* l'un des volcans les plus actifs du monde, le de la Fournaise. Avec 800.000 habitants, l'île a une population métissée*: elle est composée principalement de descendants d'esclaves venus d'Afrique et d'Inde, amenés* dans l'île pendant la colonisation au XVIIème siècle pour cultiver le café et les épices*, de descendants des colons blancs, et aussi d'immigrés venus de Chine. Sa capitale est Saint-Denis.

L'agriculture est importante pour l'économie. À côté de la canne à sucre* se sont développées les cultures maraîchères* et fruitières. Mais c'est le tourisme qui aujourd'hui est la première activité économique de l'île.

Les musiciens ont contribué à populariser les deux rythmes réunionnais: le *maloya*, proche du blues, qui est issu* de chants et de danses d'esclaves noirs, et le *séga*, qui regroupe des danses et musiques créoles populaires. Au XIXème siècle, le poète français Charles Baudelaire a séjourné* quelque temps à l'île de la Réunion, qui lui a inspiré des poèmes tels que "À une dame créole."

Search words: île de la réunion voyage, île de la réunion vacances, visite virtuelle réunion

abrite *is home to;* **métissée** d'ethnies mixtes; **amenés** brought; **épices** *spices;* **canne à sucre** *sugar cane;* **maraîchères** *of garden produce;* **issu** *comes from;* **séjourné** voyagé

Mon dico réunionnais (4.1)

Comen i lé?	*Comment ça va?*
Siouplé	*S'il vous plait.*
Nou sar dansé.	*On va danser.*
Mi aim à ou.	*Je t'aime.*
la kaz	*la maison*

Un champ de canne à sucre et de cocotiers à la Réunion.

Essential Instruction

1. Have students locate **La Réunion**, **la Corse**, **Chamonix**, and **Le Mont Blanc** using the maps in their textbooks.
2. Students read the three selections in **Points de départ**. Using a graphic organizer of their choosing, they note the population, industry, culture, famous people, and additional important details of each location.
3. Ask the students to compare orally the three destinations using the above categories.

✲ *Une autre île francophone: La Corse*  1.2

La Corse est une île de la mer Méditerranée où on parle français et corse. Considérée une région française, elle est composée de deux départements: la Corse-du-Sud et la Haute-Corse. Surnommée *"Île de Beauté,"* on peut y trouver de belles plages, des vues panoramiques montagneuses*, une bonne cuisine de terroir*, et des espaces naturels grâce à un parc marin international, des réserves naturelles, et le Parc naturel régional de Corse. Les activités principales de la Corse sont l'agriculture et le tourisme.

montagneuses *mountainous;* **terroir** *rural flavor*

Le drapeau corse.

Bonifacio, une ville de la Corse, est située sur des falaises.

Chamonix et le Mont Blanc  1.2

Chamonix, petite ville de 10.000 habitants, est considérée la commune la plus haute d'Europe. Elle doit ce titre à la présence sur son territoire du sommet le plus haut d'Europe, le Mont Blanc (4.810 m). C'est un atout* touristique considérable car le Mont Blanc est le troisième site naturel le plus visité au monde. Il possède un sentier* de randonnées le plus populaire d'Europe qui fait le tour du Mont Blanc (170 km). C'est aussi de Chamonix que part le téléphérique* de l'aiguille* du Midi qui monte à 3.777 m. La Mer de Glace*, la Vallée Blanche, et le Lac Blanc sont d'autres atouts touristiques à Chamonix.

Chamonix est devenue la capitale des amateurs d'alpinisme et des sportifs de haute montagne. Elle abrite l'École Nationale de Ski et d'Alpinisme spécialisée dans la formation des guides de haute montagne qui ont leur association et leur compagnie à Chamonix. Roger Frison-Roche pour ses récits* littéraires, Gaston Rebuffat pour ses films, et René Desmaison pour ses exploits en sont parmi les plus célèbres des guides.

 **Search words:** **centres d'intérêts touristiques à chamonix, information sur chamonix, chamonix mont blanc, forfaits de ski chamonix**

atout *asset;* **sentier** chemin; **téléphérique** *cable car;* **aiguille** le sommet; **glace** *ice;* **récits** contes

Expansion

Have students research the origins of **le drapeau de la Corse,** then compare it to **le drapeau de la Sardaigne** (Sardinia). Locate Sardinia on a map. How are the two flags similar yet different? Encourage students to describe in French what they see on each flag.

Multiple Intelligences

Musical-Rhythmic

Encourage students to search for the best rendition of "**Ti Fleur Fanée**," the unofficial national anthem of **La Réunion**, and samples of **La Maloya** and **la Sega** to play for the class.

Naturalist

Encourage students interested in nature and the environment to investigate **La Réunion**, **la Corse**, **Chamonix**, and **Le Mont Blanc** from the point of view of natural resources, agriculture, or local food specialties that are unique to the regions. They may be especially drawn to **Piton de la Fournaise**, since it is one of the most active volcanoes in the world.

Linguistic

Have students investigate the political culture of **La Réunion** to understand how the music became intertwined with political thought.

Answers

7

1. Situation: Département français dans l'Océan Indien; Économie: l'agriculture, le tourisme; Nombre d'habitants: 800.000 ; Art: musique *(maloya, séga)*, poésie (Baudelaire); Capitale: Saint-Denis
2. *Possible answers*: haute, naturel, visité, populaire, touristique, célèbre
3. *Map should include*: la France, l'Italie, l'Allemagne, l'Autriche, la Suisse, la Slovénie
4. la gentiane ou l'edelweiss, le chamois ou la marmotte
5. *Answers will vary*.

Communication

Presentational: Cooperative Groups

Divide the students into small groups. Prepare a list of national and/or regional parks and then transfer the names of the parks to index cards, one per card. Have groups randomly choose a card. Each group researches advice for visitors to that park and then presents their findings in French as if they were addressing a group of francophone visitors. Encourage the rest of the class to ask questions. Small groups could also present to each other for practice before presenting to the whole group.

Les Alpes  1.2

Italie, France, Suisse, Allemagne, Autriche, Slovénie—les Alpes s'étendent* principalement sur ces six pays et comptent plus de 80 sommets de plus de 4.000 mètres. C'est une barrière de 1.200 km qui s'étend de la Méditerranée au Danube. La plus grande ville des Alpes est Grenoble (500.000 habitants).

La faune et la flore alpines sont très protégées grâce aux nombreux parcs régionaux ou nationaux qui occupent le massif; le plus connu en France est le Parc de la Vanoise. La gentiane, l'edelweiss pour la flore, le chamois*, et la marmotte pour la faune sont les symboles des Alpes.

Search words: hautes alpes stations de ski, site officiel du parc de la vanoise

s'étendent *spread;* **chamois** *mountain goat;* **marmotte** *marmot*

Le chien du Saint-Bernard est une race de grands chiens de montagnes qui a sauvé beaucoup de gens égarés (*lost*) dans les Alpes ou de survivants d'avalanches.

COMPARAISONS

Quels parcs régionaux ou nationaux existent dans votre région? Qu'y a-t-il à voir?

 4.2

7 Activités culturelles  1.2, 1.3, 3.1, 3.2

Faites les activités suivantes.

1. Faites la carte d'identité de l'île de la Réunion.
   - Situation
   - Économie
   - Nombre d'habitants
   - Arts
   - Capitale
2. Faites une liste d'adjectifs qui décrivent Chamonix.
3. Faites une carte qui montre les Alpes dans chaque pays d'Europe.
4. Citez deux symboles des Alpes:
   - une fleur
   - un animal
5. Planifiez un séjour de quatre jours en Corse. Prenez des notes en recherchant ce qu'il y a à y faire et voir: gastronomie, excursions, randonnées, festivals, etc.

Le Mont Blanc est la plus haute montagne dans les Alpes.

Essential Instruction

1. In the computer lab, teams collaborate to complete questions one through four of **Activité 7.** These questions should not take a long time to do, and they can be corrected in class.
2. Have students read the questions and answers in **Du côté des médias** and to make a list of words that are new or that they would need to look up in order to understand the reading. Use synonyms, antonyms, or explanations in French to define. Encourage those students who understand the words to play the role of teacher and to provide a definition or meaning.

Perspectives 1.2

Dans son poème "Parfum exotique," Charles Baudelaire dit de la Réunion:

"... le parfum des verts tamariniers*,
Qui circule dans l'air et m'enfle* la narine*,
Se mêle dans mon âme au chant des mariniers*."

Par quel sens est-ce que Baudelaire ressent de la nostalgie pour la Réunion en retournant en France?

tamariniers *tamarind trees;* **enfle** *swell up;* **narine** *nostril;* **marinier** *sailor;* **ressent** *feels*

La station téléphérique de l'Aiguille du Midi, à Chamonix.

Du côté des médias   1.2, 1.3

Interpretive Communication

Lisez la FAQ sur la Réunion. Écrivez un contrôle sur ces informations pour votre partenaire.

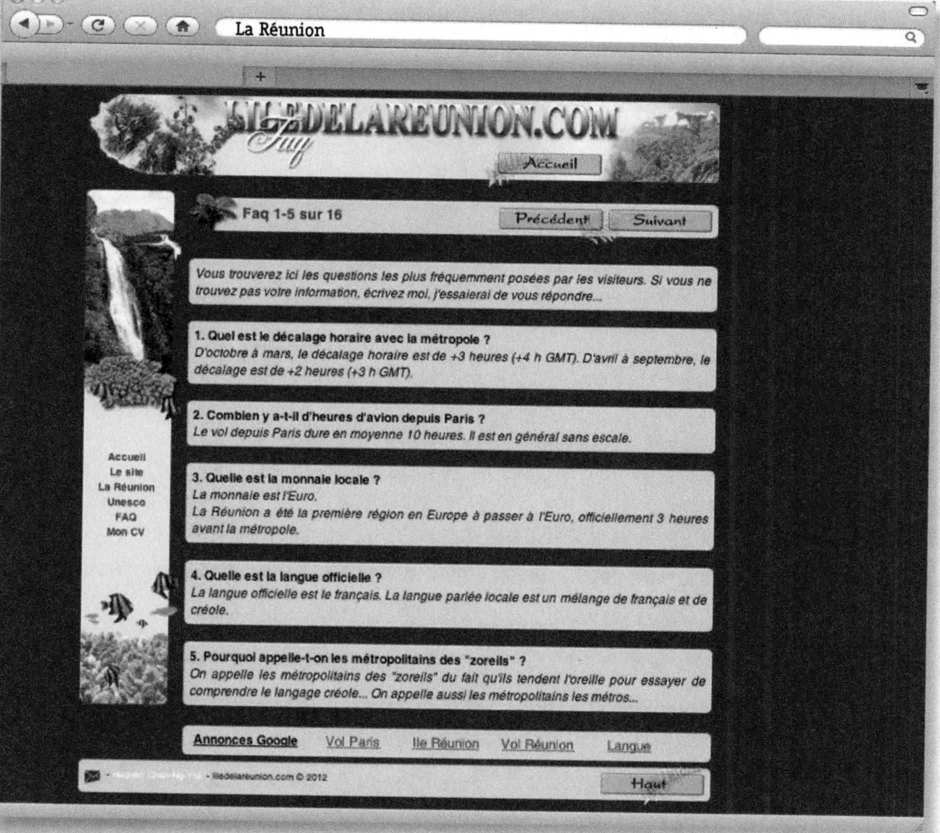

La Réunion

ILEDELAREUNION.COM

Faq

Accueil

Faq 1-5 sur 16 — Précédent — Suivant

Vous trouverez ici les questions les plus fréquemment posées par les visiteurs. Si vous ne trouvez pas votre information, écrivez moi, j'essaierai de vous répondre...

1. Quel est le décalage horaire avec la métropole ?
D'octobre à mars, le décalage horaire est de +3 heures (+4 h GMT). D'avril à septembre, le décalage est de +2 heures (+3 h GMT).

2. Combien y a-t-il d'heures d'avion depuis Paris ?
Le vol depuis Paris dure en moyenne 10 heures. Il est en général sans escale.

3. Quelle est la monnaie locale ?
La monnaie est l'Euro.
La Réunion a été la première région en Europe à passer à l'Euro, officiellement 3 heures avant la métropole.

4. Quelle est la langue officielle ?
La langue officielle est le français. La langue parlée locale est un mélange de français et de créole.

5. Pourquoi appelle-t-on les métropolitains des "zoreils" ?
On appelle les métropolitains des "zoreils" du fait qu'ils tendent l'oreille pour essayer de comprendre le langage créole... On appelle aussi les métropolitains les métros...

Accueil
Le site
La Réunion
Unesco
FAQ
Mon CV

Annonces Google — Vol Paris — Ile Réunion — Vol Réunion — Langue

iledelareunion.com © 2012 — Haut

Answers

Perspectives
Answers will vary.

Du côté des médias
Answers will vary.

Reference Desk

GMT stands for Greenwich Mean Time (**l'heure moyenne de Greenwich**). France is on CET (Central European Time or **l'heure d'Europe centrale**) which is GMT + 2 during the summer and GMT + 1 the rest of the year.

Differentiated Learning

Accelerate

High-ability students should make a trivia game based on the information found in the chart of **Du côté des médias.** In addition, have them answer the question in **Perspectives** based on the Baudelaire poem "**Parfum exotique.**"

Decelerate

Have students analyze why **le chien du Saint-Bernard** is physically adept at saving lost skiers and victims of avalanches. When did this tradition start and by whom? Students should do their research in French and in English, and then present their findings to the class.

RESOURCES

 Workbook 7–9

 Drill & Practice Games

Reference Desk

Attention should be given to **-ger** verbs. For example, since the **nous** form of **nager** is **nageons**, the present participle will be **nageant.** The verbs **être, avoir**, and **savoir** have irregular stems because using the **nous** form and adding **-ant** would be difficult to say. Point out that the present participle can be used as an adjective as in **La Belle au Bois Dormant.**

TPR

Prepare a set of cards on which are written two infinitives such as **parler** and **manger.** Call out the two verbs. Students must act out the two activities simultaneously and say what they are doing by conjugating the first verb, and expressing the second as a present participle. **Je parle en mangeant./Nous parlons en mangeant.**

Expansion

To practice forming present participles, put students into groups of four or five. Give each group a worksheet that has six incomplete sentences, for example, **Fabrice fait ses devoirs....** Each group writes as many logical completions as possible using present participles. For example, **Fabrice fait ses devoirs (en téléphonant, en mangeant une pizza, en prenant le bus au lycée).** You could turn this activity into a game. Give the teams a time limit. At the end of that time, the team that finishes with the most correct and logical sentences wins.

Structure de la langue

emcl.com
WB 7–9
Games

Present Participle

 1.1

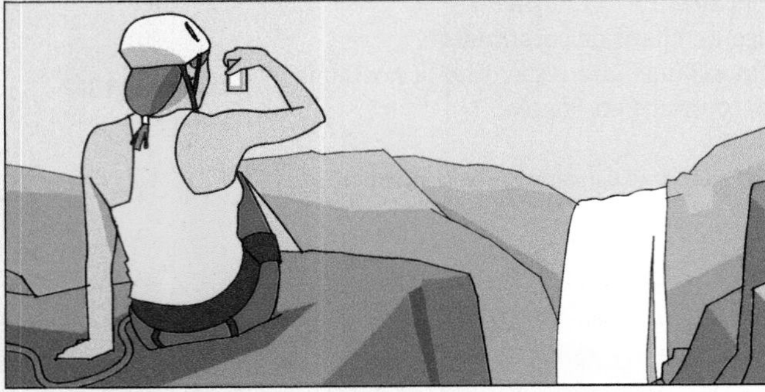

De quoi Marie-Alix prend-elle une photo en faisant de l'escalade?

The present participle is a verb form that ends in **–ant.** This ending corresponds to the suffix *–ing* in English. To form the present participle, add **–ant** to the stem of the present tense **nous** form of the verb.

Verb	Nous Stem	Present Participle
faire	fais-	**faisant**
attendre	attend-	**attendant**
finir	finiss-	**finissant**
aller	all-	**allant**
partir	part-	**partant**

COMPARAISONS

What is another function of the present participle in English? Is this also possible in French?

The teacher woke the *sleeping* student.
Le prof a réveillé l'élève **qui dormait**.

4.1

The three verbs indicated below have irregular present participles.

Irregular	Present Participle
avoir	**ayant**
être	**étant**
savoir	**sachant**

The preposition **en** usually precedes the present participle. **En** means "while," "upon," "in," or "on" if the two actions in the sentence take place at the same time.

En voyant la neige, mon frère a voulu faire de la luge. — *Upon seeing the snow, my brother wanted to go sledding.*

En means "by" if a cause-and-effect relationship is expressed.

C'est **en écoutant** le prof que tu pourras réussir à ton examen. — *By listening to the teacher, you will pass the test.*

COMPARAISONS: In the English sentence, "sleeping" is acting as an adjective. In French, the use of the present participle as an adjective is more limited, for example, you might find it in poetry and songs.

Essential Instruction

1. Show the formation of the present participle and the three exceptions.
2. With white boards or in their notebooks, have students write the present participle of infinitives you call out.
3. Give students a lot of oral drill so that they can produce the present participle easily.
4. Form pairs and have the students complete **Activité 8** and **Activité 9**, alternating statements and questions.

Communiquez!

8 Les activités des jeunes

1.1, 1.2

Interpretive Communication

Abdel-Cader a fait un sondage pour savoir ce que ses camarades de classe font pour s'amuser en plein air. Dites combien d'ados font chaque activité.

MODÈLE jouer au baseball
Quinze ados s'amusent en jouant au baseball.

Comment les ados s'amusent-ils en plein air?

32—piqueniquer dans un champ
20—nager dans un lac
15—jouer au baseball
11—faire une randonnée équestre
8—se promener dans la forêt
7—faire du saut à l'élastique
6—faire de la planche à voile
1—prendre la flore en photo

9 Qu'est-ce que tu fais en…?

Interpersonal Communication

Avec un(e) partenaire, posez des questions sur ce que vous faites pendant que vous faites d'autres choses. Puis répondez aux questions. Suivez le modèle.

1.1, 1.2, 5.2

MODÈLE écouter ton lecteur MP3/faire les corvées
A: **Est-ce que tu écoutes ton lecteur MP3 en faisant les corvées?**
B: **Oui, j'écoute mon lecteur MP3 en faisant les corvées. Et toi?**
A: **Moi, je chante en faisant les corvées.**

1. parler au téléphone/conduire
2. se détendre/lire un roman
3. manger/étudier
4. envoyer des textos/écouter le prof
5. surfer sur Internet/dîner avec tes parents
6. s'amuser/faire du shopping
7. finir tes devoirs/regarder la télé
8. écouter de la musique/faire du sport
9. regarder la télé/faire tes devoirs
10. faire des sauts à ski/savoir que tu pourrais avoir un accident

Answers

8

Trente-deux ados piqueniquent dans un champ.
Vingt ados nagent dans un lac.
Quinze ados jouent au baseball.
Onze ados font une randonnée équestre.
Huit ados se promènent dans la forêt.
Sept ados font du saut à l'élastique.
Six ados font de la planche à voile.
Un ado prend la flore en photo.

9 *Answers B will vary.*

1. A: Est-ce que tu parles au téléphone en conduisant?
2. A: Est-ce que te détends en lisant un roman?
3. A: Est-ce que tu manges en étudiant?
4. A: Est-ce que tu envoies des textos en écoutant le prof?
5. A: Est-ce que tu surfes sur Internet en dînant avec tes parents?
6. A: Est-ce que tu t'amuses en faisant du shopping?
7. A: Est-ce que tu finis tes devoirs en regardant la télé?
8. A: Est-ce que tu écoutes de la musique en faisant du sport?
9. A: Est-ce que tu regardes la télé en faisant tes devoirs?
10. A: Est-ce que tu fais des sauts à ski en sachant que tu pourrais avoir un accident?

Connections

Music

Have students sing "**En Passant par la Lorraine**," a classic children's song featuring present participles. As a cloze activity, students will fill in the blanks with the words they hear.
Search Words: en passant par la lorraine

Differentiated Learning

Accelerate

Have students plan a ski vacation leaving from Paris. They should plan to take the train to a ski resort of their choice in France. Which train do they take? Can they get a student discount? What is the cost in dollars?
Search Words: voyages-sncf

Decelerate

For students to practice a few troublesome verbs, have them fill out a worksheet with the following headings: **Infinitif**, **Nous: Présent**, **Participe présent**, **Traduction**

Adapt

Ask students to think of other ways that they multitask, using the format of **Activité 9**.

RESOURCES

 Workbook 10

 Listing Activity 2

 Drill & Practice Games

Reference Desk

Negatives are introduced in Level 1, **Unité 10**, **Leçon B**, pp. 538–539 and reviewed in Level 2, **Unité 1**, **Leçon A**, p. 14.

Connections

Music

Edith Piaf's song **"Non, Je ne Regrette Rien"** is a gold mine of negatives.

Search Words: non je ne regrette rien

Révision: Negation  1.1

emcl.com
WB 10
LA 2
Games

See if you can tell what the sentence below means in English and how you form a negative sentence in French.

Je n'achète rien pour mon voyage à Chamonix.

If you can't do those two things, read the grammar summary below.

To make a verb negative, put **ne (n')** before the verb and **pas**, **plus**, **jamais**, **rien**, or **personne** after it in the present tense.

Élodie? Chamonix **ne** la tente **pas**.	*Élodie isn't interested in Chamonix.*
Elle **ne** va **jamais** à la Réunion.	*She never goes to Reunion.*

In the near future, the negative expression is sandwiched around the conjugated form of **aller**.

Je **ne** vais **plus** me plaindre.	*I'm not going to complain anymore.*

In the **passé composé**, **ne (n')** precedes the helping verb and **pas**, **plus**, **jamais**, or **rien** follows it. **Personne**, however, follows the past participle.

Élodie **n'a rien** dit à son frère.	*Élodie didn't say anything to her brother.*
Léo **n'a** parlé à **personne** des vacances.	*Léo didn't talk to anyone about vacation.*

The expressions **ne (n')... personne** and **ne (n')... rien** may also be used as subjects. In this case, **personne** or **rien** begins the sentence and **ne (n')** is in its usual position.

Personne ne voulait skier, sauf Léo.	*No one wanted to ski, except for Léo.*

NEGATION: The English meaning of the sentence is: "I'm buying nothing for my trip to Chamonix." To form a negative with **ne... rien**, put the **ne** (n') before the verb and the **pas** after the verb. Other negative expressions that work the same way in the present tense are **ne... pas**, **ne... jamais**, **ne... plus**, and **ne... personne**. If you don't remember how to make a sentence negative in the near future or passé composé, review the examples on this page.

Essential Instruction

1. Because of the complexity of the negatives, do **Activité 10** with the students.
2. Compare negative sentences in English with their equivalent in French to examine word order.
3. Continue the complaint of the dog in the photo. What else would he say if he could?

10 Au parc d'attractions

1.2

Comparez les deux illustrations. Puis répondez aux questions en suivant le modèle.

MODÈLE Qui avait une consultation avec la voyante?
À 19h00, quelqu'un avait une consultation avec la voyante, mais à 21h00 personne n'avait de consultation avec la voyante.

1. Qui a acheté des tickets?
2. Il y avait du popcorn au snackbar?
3. On pouvait gagner un animal aux jeux d'adresse?
4. Les ados se sont amusés?
5. Un enfant attendait de faire un tour de manège?
6. Jacques et Annie ont fait un tour de grande roue?

Other Negative Expressions

emcl.com
WB 11–12
Games

Koffi n'aime que les activités dangereuses.

RESOURCES

Workbook 11–12

Drill & Practice Games

Answers

1. À 19h00, Léo a acheté des tickets, mais à 21h00 personne n'a acheté de tickets.
2. À 19h00, il y avait du popcorn au snackbar, mais à 21h00 il n'y en avait plus.
3. À 19h00, on pouvait gagner un animal aux jeux d'adresse, mais à 21h00 on ne pouvait plus rien gagner.
4. À 19h00, les ados se sont amusés, mais à 21h00 personne ne s'est amusé.
5. À 19h00, un enfant attendait de faire un tour de manège, mais à 21h00 personne n'attendait de faire un tour de manège.
6. À 19h00, Jacques et Annie ont fait un tour de grande roue, mais à 21h00 personne n'a fait un tour de grande roue.

Expansion

Write the affirmative expressions **souvent**, **toujours**, **quelqu'un**, and **quelque chose** on the board. Ask students to name the negative expressions that are the opposite of these expressions. They should name **ne (n')...jamais**, **ne (n')...plus**, **ne (n')...personne**, and **ne (n')...rien**. Next, have students write a question for each of the expressions, for example, **Tu regardes souvent les films étrangers?** Finally, students exchange their questions with a partner who answers each one in writing using an appropriate negative. Make sure to model your expectations before students start writing, in order to check comprehension and to model the level of language that you want them to use.

Multiple Intelligences

Visual-Spatial/Mathematical-Logical
These students would benefit from making a chart of the negatives with their corresponding word order.

Special Needs Students

Linguistically Challenged
Provide these students with a lot of guided practice to master each negative. Worksheets and oral drill will help them succeed.

Dyslexia
Assist students with negation by using colored paper to make negative sentences with **ne...plus** to help them see the pattern.

Reference Desk

In a sentence with both a conjugated verb form and an infinitive, **personne** follows the infinitive, for example, **Marc ne peut voir personne ce weekend parce qu'il est malade.** **Personne** may also be used after a preposition, for example, **Je ne téléphone à personne après 10 heures du soir.**

Communication

Interpersonal: Paired Practice

Print seven to ten negative sentences. Cut up each sentence and put the words in an envelope. Divide the students into groups of two or three and ask them to reconstruct the words into meaningful, grammatically correct sentences. Put the corrected sentences on the board or provide an answer key for students to check as the groups finish.

Connections

Music

Sing **"A la pêche aux Moules"** as an example of a song featuring negatives.

The expression **ne (n')... que** (*only*) is often used instead of the adverb **seulement**, which has the same meaning. This expression restricts or limits choices. **Ne (n')** precedes the verb, or the helping verb in the **passé composé**, and **que** comes before the word or expression it describes.

Salim **ne** fait **que** des activités en plein air.	*Salim only does outdoor activities.*
En vacances il **ne** fait **que** des sports nautiques.	*On vacation he only does water sports.*

The negative expression **ne (n')... ni... ni...** means "neither... nor." **Ne (n')** precedes the verb, or the helping verb in the **passé composé**, and each **ni** comes directly before the word or expression it describes.

Djamel **ne** veut essayer **ni** le jet ski **ni** le saut à ski.	*Djamel wants to try neither the jet ski nor ski jumps.*
Il **n'**aime **ni** la montagne **ni** la mer.	*He likes neither mountains nor sea.*

Ni... ni...ne (n') may begin a sentence. In this case, each **ni** precedes the word or expression it describes and **ne (n')** is in its usual position.

Ni Hélène **ni** moi **n'**irons à la campagne.	*Neither Hélène nor I will go to the countryside.*
Ni nos parents **ni** nos amis **ne** pouvaient nous persuader.	*Neither our parents nor our friends were able to persuade us.*

The negative expression **ne (n')... aucun(e)** may be used as an adjective or a pronoun and means "no," "not any," or "not one." As an adjective, **aucun(e)** agrees in gender with the noun following it. **Ne (n')** precedes the verb, or the helping verb in the **passé composé**. **Aucun(e)** comes after the verb, or the past participle in the **passé composé**, and before the noun it describes.

Je **n'**ai **aucun** doute que tu t'amuseras!	*I have no doubt that you will have fun*

Aucun(e) may also begin a sentence. In this case, it precedes the word or expression it describes and **ne (n')** is in its usual position.

Aucun de nous **ne** s'ennuiera.	*None of us will be bored.*

COMPARAISONS: Although not a hard and fast rule, it often works to put "only" in front of the word it modifies. In the example sentence, "only" modifies the verb "to like." In French, there is no confusion in where to place **ne... que**, unlike in English. "Only" is a tricky word because where it is placed can change the meaning of a sentence, as in this example:
I spoke to him only yesterday. (*only* meaning "recently")
I only spoke to him yesterday. (*only* meaning speaker spoke to no one else)

COMPARAISONS

What is the position of "only" in English sentences?

Nous **n'**aimons **que** les desserts au buffet.

We *only* like desserts at the buffet.

4.1

Essential Instruction

Have the students complete **Activité 11** orally before writing the exercise.

11 L'anniversaire de Chloé

1.1

Vous voulez acheter une carte-cadeau pour Chloé pour son anniversaire. Mais ce n'est pas facile! Dites qu'elle n'aime ni la première chose ni la deuxième. Puis, généralisez en disant ce qu'elle n'aime pas.

MODÈLE

Chloé n'aime ni les boutiques ni les grands magasins. Elle n'aime aucun magasin de vêtements.

1. 

2. 

3. 

4. 

5. 

6. 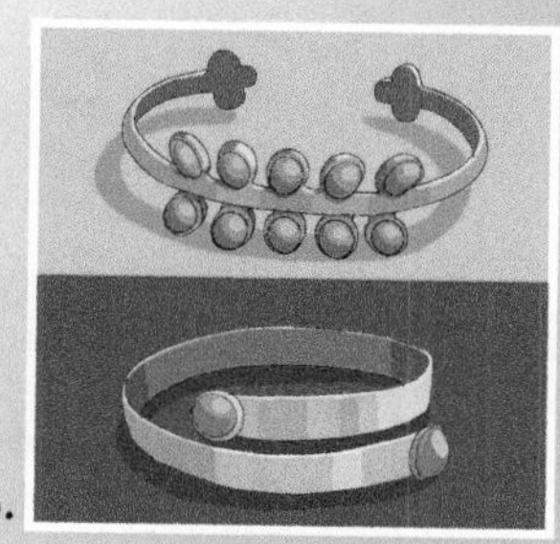

Answers

1. Chloé n'aime ni les restaurants mexicains, ni les restaurants italiens. Elle n'aime aucun restaurant.
2. Chloé n'aime ni les films d'aventures, ni les comédies romantiques. Elle n'aime aucun film.
3. Chloé n'aime ni les romans, ni les contes. Elle n'aime aucun livre.
4. Chloé n'aime ni les glaces, ni les gâteaux. Elle n'aime aucun dessert.
5. Chloé n'aime ni le foot, ni le hockey. Elle n'aime aucun sport.
6. Chloé n'aime ni les bracelets en argent, ni les bracelets en or. Elle n'aime aucun bracelet/bijou.

Connections

Humor

Here are some jokes to share with the class.

1. **J'ai perdu mon chien, dit Madame Dupont à sa voisine. Faites passer une annonce. Ça ne sert à rien, il ne sait pas lire.**
2. **Quel est l'animal qui mange avec sa queue? Réponse : Tous. Aucun n'enlève sa queue pour manger.**
3. **Savez-vous que votre chien aboie toute la nuit? Oh, ça ne fait rien, il dort toute la journée!**

Expansion

Put students in pairs. Student A plays the role of a salesperson who wants to sell student B articles from the store. Student B plays the role of a person impossible to please. Then have students reverse roles. **Madame, j'ai des gants en laine et en coton. Ah non! Je n'aime ni la laine, ni le coton.**

Special Needs Students

Dyslexia/Linguistically Challenged

For **Activité 11**, breaking the negative responses down into simple chunks might help. Have the students work with you or a strong partner. The partner starts with a question, for example, "**Claire aime les boutiques et les magasins?**" The student responds, "**Non, ni les boutiques, ni les magasins.**" Finally, encourage them to say, "**Aucun magasin!**" From there move to the full response when they are ready.

Answers

12

1. Yann n'y a passé qu'une semaine.
2. Il n'a fait que des activités en plein air.
3. Il n'a acheté que des tee-shirts.
4. Il n'a fait de shopping que dans des boutiques bon marché.
5. Il n'a essayé que les plats français.

13

Script can be found in the front pages of the Annotated Teacher's Edition.

1. oui
2. non
3. oui
4. oui
5. oui
6. non
7. non
8. oui

14

1. A: Est-ce que tu voyages dans les états du Midwest ou de la Côte Est?
   B: Je ne voyage ni dans les états du Midwest ni dans les états de la Côte Est.
2. A: Est-ce que tu lis des fables ou des contes de fées?
   B: Je ne lis ni des fables ni des contes de fées.
3. A: Est-ce que tu fais des projets de bricolage ou de design?
   B: Je ne fais ni des projets de bricolage ni des projets de design.
4. A: Est-ce que tu sers des hors-d'œuvres ou des desserts à tes invités?
   B: Je ne sers ni hors-d'œuvres ni desserts à mes invités.
5. A: Est-ce que tu te sers d'une poêle ou d'une casserole pour préparer tes repas?
   B: Je ne me sers ni d'une poêle ni d'une casserole.
6. A: Est-ce que tu parles de politique ou de sport à table?
   B: Je ne parle ni de politique ni de sport.
7. A: Est-ce que tu rencontres tes amis à la MJC ou au club de fitness?
   B: Je ne rencontre mes amis ni à la MJC ni au club de fitness.
8. A: Est-ce que tu fréquentes les discothèques ou les festivals?
   B: Je ne fréquente ni les discothèques ni les festivals.

12 Des vacances à la Réunion

1.1

Yann a passé ses vacances à la Réunion. Quand il raconte ses exploits, il exagère toujours. Corrigez ses phrases selon les indices données.

MODÈLE "J'ai voyagé avec dix amis." (*deux amis*)
Yann n'a voyagé qu'avec deux amis.

1. "J'ai passé un mois à la Réunion." (*une semaine*)
2. "J'ai fait beaucoup d'activités culturelles." (*en plein air*)
3. "J'ai acheté des cadeaux de luxe pour ma famille." (*tee-shirts*)
4. "J'ai fait du shopping dans les meilleures boutiques." (*bon marché*)
5. "J'ai essayé tous les plats réunionnais." (*français*)

13 Questions simples

1.1, 1.2

Interpersonal Communication

*Écrivez les numéros 1–8 sur votre papier. Écoutez les mini-dialogues. Puis, écrivez **oui** si la personne mentionnée fait du sport dont on parle ou **non** si elle n'en fait pas.*

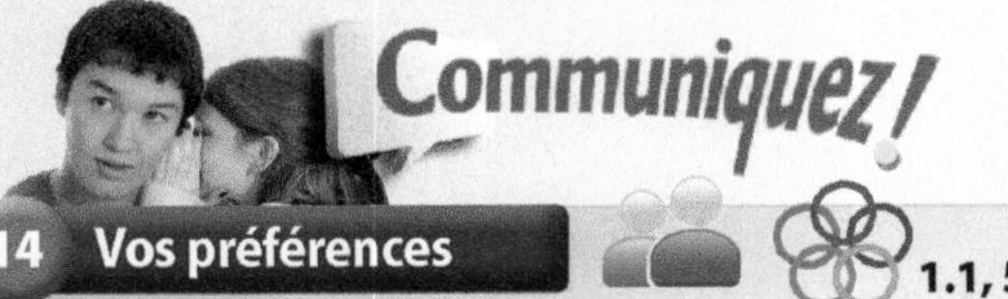

14 Vos préférences

1.1, 5.2

Non, je ne vais faire ni sauts à ski, ni sauts à l'élastique!

Interpersonal Communication

À tour de rôle, posez des questions sur vos préférences. Puis répondez.

MODÈLE faire des recherches généalogiques ou scientifiques
A: **Est-ce que tu fais des recherches généalogiques ou scientifiques?**
B: **Je ne fais ni des recherches généalogiques ni des recherches scientifiques. Et toi?**
A: **Moi, je ne fais que des recherches généalogiques.**

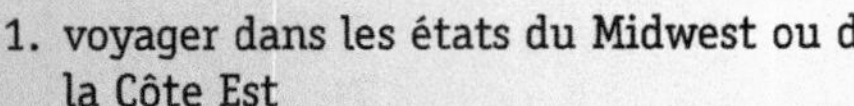

1. voyager dans les états du Midwest ou de la Côte Est
2. lire des fables ou des contes de fées
3. faire des projets de bricolage ou de design
4. servir des hors-d'œuvre ou des desserts à tes invités
5. te servir d'une poêle ou d'une casserole pour préparer tes repas
6. parler de politique ou de sport à table
7. rencontrer tes amis à la MJC ou au club de fitness
8. fréquenter les discothèques ou les festivals

Essential Instruction

1. Before completing **Activité 12** in pairs, practice oral and written examples of **ne...que** word order in the **passé composé**.
2. Students listen to **Activité 13**, then answer questions one through eight. Stop the recording after each mini-dialogue to expand and ask comprehension questions to encourage students to speak more.
3. Complete **Activité 14** with students. Expand by asking them why or why not.
4. Students work in groups of three or four to do **Activité 15**. Have the groups present their conversation to the class.
5. To complete **Activité 16**, students circulate to interview each other, as if at a party. Debrief the students on what they learned about their classmates. Have them use percentages. **Combien d'élèves entre vous a fait de l'escalade?**

À vous la parole

Communiquez!

Question centrale: Qu'est-ce qu'on doit connaître de sa destination pour réussir son voyage?

15 On va où pour les vacances?

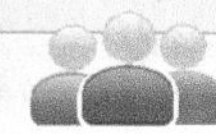  1.1, 1.2, 5.2

Interpersonal Communication

Avec deux camarades de classe, jouez les rôles de trois amis qui discutent des vacances d'hiver. Chaque personne suggère une destination, et les autres demandent ce qu'il y a à voir et faire. Prenez une décision basée sur les intérêts du groupe. Finalement, décidez qui va faire des recherches en ligne (restaurants, musées, endroits à visiter, etc.), qui va trouver l'hôtel et les billets d'avion, et qui va s'occuper des activités.

Communiquez!

16 Activités en plein air

  1.3, 5.2

Interpersonal and Presentational Communication

Interviewez dix camarades de classe pour savoir quelles activités de plein air ils ont déjà faites. Remplissez un tableau comme celui de dessous. Puis, présentez les résultats de votre enquête.

	1	2	3	4	5	6	7	8	9	10
faire une randonnée équestre	✓		✓	✓			✓		✓	✓
faire de la planche à voile										
faire du saut à l'élastique										
faire du saut à ski										
faire de l'escalade										
faire du ski de fond										

MODÈLE

A: **As-tu déjà fait une randonnée équestre?**
B: **Oui, j'ai fait des randonnées équestres.**
ou
Non, je n'ai jamais fait de randonnées équestres.

Sommaire: Quatre élèves n'ont jamais fait de randonnées équestres.

Multiple Intelligences
Verbal-Linguistic

Give students a chance to discuss their results to **Activité 16** with multiple partners. Set a timer. Students discuss, and when the timer rings they switch partners. The goal at the end of several rounds is to share what kinds of differences or similarities they discovered.

RESOURCES

Communicative Activities

Answers

All activities will vary.

Reference Desk

Blended Instruction

Consider using blended instruction, a combination of in-class learning and computer-mediated instruction or learning opportunities. Ask students to complete activities on the computer, using their cell or smartphone, or other emerging electronic technology. This will allow students to hone their tech skills and become more independent learners. Schedule routine Internet and e-book learning in class and in the lab.

Communication

Interpersonal: Paired Practice

Students write their name in the middle of a piece of paper. In each of the four corners they write a different place they would like to go for a winter vacation. When finished, have them exchange papers with a partner. The partner takes some time to write several questions regarding each destination: Why this particular place? With whom would they travel? What would they like to see and do there? When done writing, students ask each other their questions and jot down short responses. Expand the activity by having pairs work with another set of partners to share what they learned about their partner's vacation preferences.

Answers

All activities will vary.

Reference Desk

Encourage students to think of advertising campaign slogans with which they are familiar. Does your region encourage tourists to visit? Is there a slogan associated with its advertisements? For example, Minnesota is known as "The land of 10,000 lakes." "It's good being first!" reinforces the fact that Delaware was the first state to ratify the constitution, and Idaho's ads say, "Great potatoes. Tasty destinations."

17 Un design et un slogan pour les Alpes

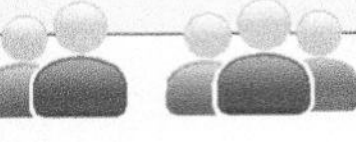

1.3, 3.2

Presentational Communication

Vous êtes chargé(e) de créer un design et un slogan pour une campagne de publicité pour les Alpes en France. Considérez les attractions, les activités, et les symboles de la région. Vous pouvez travailler avec un(e) partenaire ou en groupe.

18 Gagnez une semaine à Chamonix!

1.3

Interpretive and Presentational Communication

Imaginez que vous travaillez pour l'Office du Tourisme de Chamonix. Votre tâche est de faire un budget pour une promotion où deux groupes (un couple et une famille de gagnants) vont passer une semaine de vacances à Chamonix. Vous devez rechercher combien coûtera:

- le logement
- les repas dans les restaurants
- les activités
- la location de l'équipement

Écrivez un rapport dans lequel vous donnez des options pour le logement, les repas, les activités, et la location de l'équipement avec les prix. Finalement, créez une brochure ou un site Web où vous partagez cette promotion avec le public.

Search words: chamonix, forfait ski chamonix

Chamonix en été.

Essential Instruction

1. Students work in the computer lab for **Activités 17** and **18.**
2. For students collaborating on **Activité 17**, require that they create a list of specific attractions, activities, and symbols of the region. In doing their research, they might discover other aspects to include in their overview of the Alps. Their slogan might be a jingle.
3. **Activité 18** will require online research of an ideal vacation in **Chamonix**. Have students find templates for brochures into which they can copy photos, menus, activities, and ski package prices.
4. Have students repeat the sentences in **Activité A** and **Activité B** after the speaker. Have them reflect on the pattern. Model the pronunciation in **Activité C** and then do **Activité D**. Play **D** several times if there are students who cannot hear the difference in intonation.

Prononciation 

Intonation in Questions with Two Options 1.1

- When asking about two options, intonation rises steeply for the first choice and descends for the second.

 **L'intonation montante et descendante**

Répétez chaque phrase.

1. On part avec tes parents ou pas?
2. Tu préfères la mer ou la montagne?
3. On va à Chamonix ou à la Réunion?

 **Qu'est-ce que tu préfères?**

Posez la question alternative sur les éléments suggérés, en commençant par "Qu'est-ce que tu préfères...?"

MODÈLE faire du ski ou du snowboard
Qu'est-ce que tu préfères: faire du ski ou du snowboard?

1. faire une randonnée équestre ou une randonnée à pied
2. manger une pizza ou une omelette
3. aller à la boutique ou au centre commercial
4. mettre une chemise ou un pull

Pronounced /ə/

- Especially in groupings of two or more syllables, the sound **/ə/** should have the same length and intensity of the other vowels and not be pronounced like an **e** in English.

 **Le son /ə/**

Répétez les phrases.

1. C'est la première fois que je vais faire du ski!
2. Je pars pour une semaine.
3. Je me demande s'il fera beau!

 **Quelle voyelle entendez-vous?**

Écrivez ***E*** *si vous entendez le son dans* ***je*** *ou* ***regarde*** *et* ***É*** *si vous entendez le son dans* ***rentrée*** *ou* ***marcher****.*

RESOURCES

 **Pre-test**

 ***Leçon* Quiz**

Answers

Script can be found in the Audio Program Manual.

1. Qu'est-ce que tu préfères: faire une randonnée équestre ou une randonnée à pied?
2. Qu'est-ce que tu préfères: manger une pizza ou une omelette?
3. Qu'est-ce que tu préfères: aller à la boutique ou au centre commercial?
4. Qu'est-ce que tu préfères: mettre une chemise ou un pull?

1. E
2. E
3. É
4. É
5. E

Expansion

For additional intonation practice, provide students with a list of statements that they will change to yes/no questions by altering their intonation similar to **Activité A**. Include a section similar to **Activité B** with either/or options. Allow students to work in small groups. Monitor their practice and come back to whole group repetition to insure correct pronunciation.

Special Needs Students

Social Anxiety

Group responses give students with social anxiety issues a chance to practice speaking French in a safe way. Make sure that these students know that they do not have to speak loudly in choral responses. Even if they mouth the words, they will get benefit from the exercise.

Speech Impairment/Linguistically Challenged

For extra practice with pronunciation and speaking in general, encourage students to listen to any of the recorded activities or culture paragraphs and then select one to read out loud every day. Another option is for them to sing French songs daily. It is a non-stressful way to internalize pronunciation.

RESOURCES

e-visual 11

Workbook 1–3

Flash Cards

Listening Activity 1

Drill & Practice Games

Reference Desk

1. Skiers in Europe need to know the color symbols of the different slopes to make sure that they select trails that correspond to their ability: **vert** (**piste facile**); **bleu** (**piste de difficulté moyenne**); **rouge** (**piste difficile**); **noir** (**piste très difficile**). **Le plan de pistes de ski** is indispensible for getting to know the layout of the slopes and trails. Skiers find out about ski conditions by consulting **le bulletin d'enneigement** and **le risque d'avalanches.**
2. The term **les fesses** means a bottom, rear end, or (colloquially) buns. A **tire-fesses** is a rope tow that a skier straddles to get to the top of a hill. **Une fessée** means a spanking.

Leçon B

Vocabulaire actif

emcl.com
WB 1–3
LA 1
Games

À la station de ski

1.2

Sur les pistes

un tremplin de saut à ski

un moniteur/une monitrice

un télésiège

une piste

FORFAIT-SKI
Carte de libre accès aux pistes
Prénom: Khalid
Nom: Issam
Validité: journée
OFFICIEL

un forfait de ski

Les vêtements de ski

un masque de ski

un bonnet

les gants (m.)

un fuseau de ski

les chaussures (f.) de ski

un bâton de ski

les skis (m.)

Essential Instruction

1. Begin by asking students if they have ever skied or snowboarded. Where did they go? Did they take lessons?
2. Explain that **Leçon B** continues the winter sports theme, concentrating on skiing in the French Alps.
3. Have students listen to the vocabulary in **Activité A** several times without repeating.
4. Replay the vocabulary, allowing them to repeat.
5. Play **Pour la conversation**, stopping after each line to comment.
6. Have students work in pairs to do **Activité 1**, answering questions one through five.

Pour la conversation   1.1

How do I say what I must do?

› **Il faut que** je revienne en skiant correctement.

I must return skiing correctly.

How do I tell someone he or she will have the opportunity to do something?

› **Tu auras l'occasion d'**apprendre.

You will have the opportunity to learn.

How do I say I was expecting something?

› Ça, **je m'y attendais!**

I was expecting that!

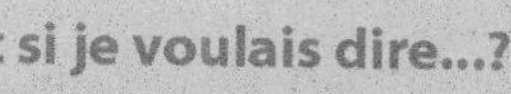 

Et si je voulais dire...?

des après-ski (m.)	*snow boots*
un remonte-pente	*ski-tow*
le ski nordique	*cross-country skiing*
un tire-fesses	*T-bar*
faire du patin à glace	*to ice-skate*

Communiquez!

1 Je m'y attendais!  1.2, 1.3

Interpretive Communication

Lisez le blogue d'Alexis qui a fait un séjour de sports d'hiver. Puis, répondez aux questions.

J'avais une semaine de vacances, et j'ai décidé de la passer à Chamonix. Pourquoi? Parce que j'adore les activités en plein air et la neige, mais je dois apprendre à skier correctement. J'ai acheté un forfait ski, et je me suis inscrit dans un cours avec un moniteur. J'avais l'intention de louer les skis et les bâtons, parce que j'avais dans ma valise tout le reste—mon bonnet, mes gants, mes chaussures de ski, et mon fuseau. En sortant du train, j'ai réalisé que ma valise n'y était plus. Ah ça, je ne m'y attendais pas! Ça coûte cher, les vêtements de ski!! Est-ce que quelqu'un a vu une valise bleue dans le train pour Chamonix le weekend dernier?

1. Pour quelle raison Alexis part-il à Chamonix?
2. Quels préparatifs a-t-il fait à l'avance?
3. Qu'est-ce qu'il comptait louer?
4. Quel problème a-t-il eu?
5. Qu'est-ce qu'Alexis cherche?

Answers

1. Il a une semaine de vacances.
2. Il a acheté un forfait de ski, et s'est inscrit à un cours.
3. des skis et des bâtons de ski
4. Il a perdu sa valise.
5. Quelqu'un qui a vu sa valise bleue dans le train.

Communication

Interpersonal: Paired Practice

Have students role-play a skier at a resort buying a lift pass, renting equipment, and buying a few chic ski outfits. The salesperson will ask pertinent questions to help the skier purchase **le nécessaire.** Level 1, **Unité 6**, **Leçon A**, p. 277 introduced students to shopping vocabulary and expressions.

Differentiated Learning

Accelerate

Have students write **un blogue** recounting a day of skiing in **Chamonix.** They must describe what they wore, what they did, and where they ate.

Decelerate

Have students illustrate the new vocabulary words in their notebooks. They may have to go online to find pictures of rope and T-bar tows.

Answers

2

1. station de ski
2. skis
3. bâtons
4. télésiège
5. forfait
6. tremplins de sauts à ski
7. moniteur
8. gants
9. bonnet

3 *Possible answers:*

Image 1: Cette personne a mis des skis, des chaussures et un fuseau de ski, un manteau et des gants.

Image 2: Cette personne a mis des skis et des bâtons de ski, des gants, des chaussures de ski, un fuseau de ski, un manteau et un bonnet.

Image 3: Cette personne a mis des skis et des bâtons de ski, des gants, des chaussures de ski, un fuseau de ski, et un gros pull-over léger.

Image 4: Cette personne a mis des skis et des bâtons de ski, des gants, des chaussures de ski, un fuseau de ski, et un pull-over léger.

4

1. gants
2. moniteur, monitrice
3. bonnet
4. tremplin de sauts à skis
5. bâtons
6. un ski
7. télésiège
8. fuseau de ski

Reference Desk

1. Additional vocabulary words associated with winter activities: **les randonnées nocturnes** *(nighttime hikes)*; **les balades à raquettes** *(snowshoe walks)*; **la luge** *(sledding)*; **la motoneige** *(snowmobiling)*; **le VTT sur neige** *(all-terrain vehicles on snow)*.
2. Websites for large ski resorts often include videos in French and webcam feeds that would interest students. These could be used for a variety of activities. Research **le Val de Thorens**, **La Plagne**, and **Alpe d'Huez**.

2 Faire du ski

1.2

C'est bientôt la saison des sports d'hiver. Une agence de voyage offre des conseils à ses clients, mais des mots ont disparu sur son site Web. Retrouvez les mots manquants (missing).

Si vous voulez faire du ski, vous devez aller dans une (1). Avant de partir sur les pistes de ski, vous devez vous équiper: louez des (2) et des (3). Avant de pouvoir prendre le (4) qui vous emmène en haut de la piste, achetez un (5) pour toute la semaine. C'est moins cher que de payer à la journée. Les (6) sont pour les skieurs avec beaucoup d'expérience. Demandez à un (7) ou une monitrice ses conseils. Il fait froid, donc n'oubliez pas vos (8) et votre (9) de ski.

Communiquez!

3 Sam et Nayah sont prêts à skier!

1.1, 5.2

Presentational Communication

À tour de rôle, décrivez ce que chaque personne porte dans les illustrations suivantes. Votre partenaire va deviner qui vous décrivez.

MODÈLE **Cette personne a mis des gants....**

4 Sur les pistes

1.2

Complétez la phrase avec un mot ou une expression.

1. Si on a froid aux mains, il faut acheter de meilleurs....
2. Si on ne sait pas skier, on peut apprendre avec un... ou une....
3. Si on a froid à la tête, il faut mettre un... bien chaud.
4. Un skieur qui fait de très longues distances part d'un....
5. Un skieur tient (*holds*) les... dans ses mains.
6. On attache la chaussure de ski à....
7. On monte en haut des pistes avec un....
8. Pour faire du ski on peut mettre un pantalon ou un....

Essential Instruction

1. Ask students to refer to the **Vocabulaire actif** as you read each sentence in **Activité 2**. Have them write down the missing vocabulary.
2. Have students do **Activité 3** in pairs. As an extension of this activity students can alternate describing a scene and drawing it. For example, **Nayah fait du ski nordique. Sam est tombé dans la neige.**
3. Have students change partners to work with someone new to complete **Activité 4** and **Activité 6.**
4. For **Activité 5** students listen and respond in writing.
5. Have students integrate the answers to **Activité 7** either in the form of **un blogue** or a letter to a friend.

5 La classe de neige

 1.1, 1.2

Interpretive Communication

Écrivez les numéros 1–6 sur votre papier. Écoutez ce que chacun des enfants emporte en classe de neige. Puis, choisissez le mot qui n'est pas mentionné.

1. un bonnet, des gants, un blouson, des bottes de ski
2. un fuseau de ski, des lunettes de ski, des gants, de la crème solaire, un bonnet
3. des chaussures de ski, des bâtons de ski, un forfait
4. un fuseau de ski, un pull, une écharpe, un bonnet, des skis
5. un bonnet, un fuseau de ski, une écharpe, des chaussures de ski, un masque de ski
6. des skis, des bâtons, un forfait, des chaussures

La station de ski de Val Thorens, dans les Alpes de Savoie.

6 Vous aurez l'occasion de....

  1.1, 5.1, 5.2

Interpersonal Communication

À tour de rôle, suggérez une destination et des activités pour les vacances.

MODÈLE ma famille/la Tunisie
A: **Ma famille et moi, on ne sait pas où passer les vacances.**
B: **Pourquoi pas aller en Tunisie? Vous aurez l'occasion de nager et de bronzer au bord de la mer.**

1. mes cousins/Montréal
2. ma tante/la Normandie
3. mes amis/l'Alsace
4. mon père/la Bretagne
5. ma bande de copains/la côte d'Azur
6. mes camarades de classe/Lyon
7. ma mère/la Martinique
8. mon frère/Grenoble

7 Questions personnelles

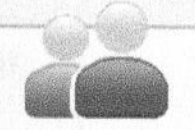  1.2, 1.3

Répondez aux questions.

1. As-tu déjà fait du ski? Où? Combien de fois?
2. Qu'est-ce qu'on peut louer dans une station de ski?
3. Quels vêtements et accessoires faut-il emporter?
4. Pourquoi est-ce qu'on aime faire du ski, à ton avis? À quoi est-ce qu'on s'attend?
5. Est-ce qu'on peut faire du ski près de chez toi, ou dans la région? Sinon, où sont les stations de ski dans votre région? Est-ce qu'il y a de meilleures pistes dans d'autres régions?

Answers

Script can be found in the front pages of the Annotated Teacher's Edition.

1. des gants
2. un fuseau de ski
3. un forfait
4. un pull
5. un bonnet
6. des bâtons

6 *Possible answers:*

1. B: Pourquoi pas aller à Montréal? Vous aurez l'occasion de visiter des festivals.
2. B: Pourquoi pas aller en Normandie? Vous aurez l'occasion d'admirer les falaises et de visiter des musées.
3. B: Pourquoi pas aller en Alsace? Vous aurez l'occasion de manger dans de bons restaurants et de visiter des cathédrales.
4. B: Pourquoi pas aller en Bretagne? Vous aurez l'occasion de faire du bateau, de pêcher des poissons, et de profiter des crêperies traditionnelles.
5. B: Pourquoi pas aller sur la Côte d'Azur? Vous aurez l'occasion de bronzer sur les plages et de rencontrer des célébrités.
6. B: Pourquoi pas aller à Lyon? Vous aurez l'occasion de faire du shopping, de visiter des petits musées, et de manger dans des petits restaurants.
7. B: Pourquoi pas aller à la Martinique? Vous aurez l'occasion de bronzer sur la plage, de faire du scooter des mers et de faire des randonnées dans la forêt.
8. B: Pourquoi pas aller à Grenoble? Vous aurez l'occasion de faire du shopping en ville et de visiter des centres de recherche scientifique.

7 *Answers will vary.*

Differentiated Learning

Accelerate

Have students write a descriptive paragraph about the photo of **la station de ski de Val Thorens** and research where it is located, and what "**La Folie Douce**" might mean in terms of skiing at **le Val de Thorens**.

Decelerate

As a guided practice, work with low-ability students in small groups to do **Activité 4** and **Activité 6.** They will appreciate the additional help in writing since these two exercises require vocabulary recall and writing skills.

RESOURCES

 **Dialogue Video**

 **Workbook 4**

Answers

8 *Possible Answers:*

1. Léo est informatif.
2. Élodie est désorganisée.
3. Léo n'est pas surpris.
4. Léo est le plus sportif.
5. Léo ou (et) Élodie est (sont) serviable(s).

Extension

Elles ne vont pas mettre toutes leurs affaires dans la même valise.

Reference Desk

École du ski français (**ESF**) is a federation of ski schools founded in 1937. The ski instructors pass competitive tests for national diplomas. From 1945 to today, the school has grown from 200 students in 41 schools to 17,000 students in 250 schools. 2,000 students a year pass 800,000 tests for skiing skill. The children's school, called **Piou Piou**, trains children as young as three to ski. The levels for children are: **flocon** (*snowflake*) **première**, **deuxième**, **troisième étoile**, **étoile de bronze**, and **étoile d'or.** There are courses for adolescents and adults in all modes of skiing.

Game

Devinettes

Divide students into two teams. Give each team different pictures of vocabulary items. Students from the opposite team must ask questions about ski clothing, ski equipment, and types of winter sports in an effort to guess which picture the team has chosen to use. For example, **"Est-ce que c'est quelque chose qu'on porte?" "C'est un sport?"**

Rencontres culturelles

emcl.com
WB 4

Les classes de neige

1.1, 1.2, 5.2

Élodie fait sa valise pour aller au ski.

Élodie: Cette fois il faut que je rentre à la maison en skiant correctement.

Léo: Tu auras l'occasion d'apprendre... les classes le matin, le ski l'après-midi, et moi avec les parents le week-end. Il y a 450 kilomètres de pistes à Combloux!

Élodie: Et les moniteurs?

Léo: Ils sont sympa.... Dis, le weekend tu veux faire du snowboard?

Élodie: Tu connais Megève? On ira aussi faire un peu de shopping.

Léo: Ça, je m'y attendais! Tu as vérifié que tu n'as rien oublié? Tes gants? Ton pantalon de ski? Ton bonnet? Tes lunettes?

Élodie: De toute façon, les skis, les chaussures, on loue tout sur place... Bon eh bien, il n'y a plus qu'à partir... il faut que je sois plus organisée! Au fait, tu n'as pas vu mon billet de train...?

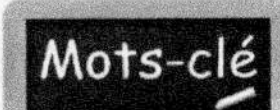

Valise (de l'italien *valigia* en1558). Au départ, le mot valise désigne un sac en cuir qui se porte en croupe (comme dans les westerns) avant de devenir un bagage rectangulaire porté à la main (1876). Valise a donné *dévaliser*, c'est-à-dire prendre à quelqu'un tout ce qu'il a sur lui.

8 Les classes de neige 

Formez des phrases en disant qui a les attributs suivants Élodie ou Léo?

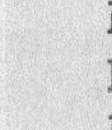

1.1, 1.2, 1.3

1. informatif/informative
2. désorganisé(e)
3. pas surpris(e)
4. le plus sportif/la plus sportive
5. serviable (*helpful*)

1.2, 1.3

Extension **Préparations pour un voyage en avion**

Deux sœurs se préparent pour un voyage en avion.

Maeva: Dis, j'ai hâte de voir Mamy et Papy.

Faustine: Moi de même. Bon, comment on fait?

Maeva: Moi, je n'ai pas confiance, je ne mets pas toutes mes affaires dans la même valise.

Faustine: Tu n'as pas confiance en qui?

Maeva: On a un changement de vol, il y a toujours le risque qu'une valise se perde. Comment on fait avec les médicaments?

Faustine: Mets-les dans ton sac à main.

Extension Quelle solution Maeva et Faustine ont-elles trouvée pour arriver chez leurs grands-parents avec l'essentiel?

1.2, 1.3

Essential Instruction

1. Present the information about the **École du ski français.** Show some online video clips of various **écoles du ski**, notably **Meribel.** The students see what a ski resort looks like, and they can watch students ski from beginners to advanced.
2. For **Activité 8**, have students listen to the dialogue **Les classes de neige** and answer the questions.
3. Have students locate **la Savoie** on the map of France noting its major cities of Chambéry and Annecy.
4. The students will read **"La Savoie"** noting its location, economy, festivals, local food specialties, and ski resorts.
5. Have them use the same topics to describe their town or locale.

Points de départ 

emcl.com
WB 5

Question centrale
Qu'est-ce qu'on doit connaître de sa destination pour réussir son voyage?

La Savoie 1.2, 2.1, 2.2, 5.1

La Savoie est devenue une province française en 1860. C'est une région frontalière* avec l'Italie, à laquelle elle est reliée par des cols* et par des tunnels dont le tunnel du Mont Blanc.* C'est un paysage de montagnes avec les Alpes, des lacs (Lac du Bourget, Lac d'Annecy), et des vallées (vallée de la Tarentaise, vallée de l'Arc).

La Savoie comprend deux départements, la Savoie et la Haute Savoie. Ses habitants sont les Savoyards. Les deux principales villes sont Chambéry et Annecy. Son économie est tournée vers l'imagerie*, les industries du sport et des loisirs, l'énergie solaire, et la photovoltaïque.* C'est aussi le berceau* du groupe de grande distribution* Carrefour.

Terre de culture, la Savoie abrite de nombreux festivals comme le festival du film d'animation à Annecy, référence mondiale pour les professionnels de l'animation. Terre de gastronomie, ses spécialités sont les fromages de beaufort, le reblochon, et la tomme. Terre de tourisme, c'est le royaume* du ski avec le plus grand domaine skiable* d'Europe et ses très nombreuses stations dont la plus ancienne est Chamonix. Ces stations sont souvent reliées entre elles pour constituer d'immenses domaines skiables* comme celui des Portes du soleil (Avoriaz, Morzine, Les Gets, etc.) avec ses 650 kilomètres de pistes.

 **Search words: savoie mont blanc, visiter la savoie, vacances savoie**

---

frontalière *border;* **col** *pass;* **imagerie** *print-making;* **photovoltaïque** *photovoltaic;* **berceau** *cradle;* **grande distribution** *retail;* **royaume** *realm;* **domaine skiable** *ski areas*

Produits

La raclette savoyarde est un plat avec du fromage à raclette et du jambon. Autrefois, on mangeait la raclette au coin de la cheminée, mais ces jours-ci il existe un appareil pour la préparation de la raclette. Trouvez des photos en ligne. Aimeriez-vous y goûter? **1.2, 2.2, 3.2**

COMPARAISONS

Comment pouvez-vous définir la "terre de culture," "la terre gastronomique," et la "terre de tourisme" dans votre région? **4.2**

La raclette est délicieuse sur les pommes de terre!

RESOURCES

 **Workbook 5**

Reference Desk

La photovoltaique (*photovoltaic*) literally means light (*photo*) and electricity (*voltaic*). Photovoltaic cells generate electricity from sunlight or other light sources. This technology is used to convert solar energy to usable power.

Connections

Gourmet/Gourmand

Students who love to cook can research recipes for **la raclette savoyarde**, **la fondue**, and **pommes de terre dauphinoise**. They might try to find **beaufort**, **le reblochon**, and **la tomme** cheeses in specialty cheese stores or organize a tasting for their family.

Multiple Intelligences

Naturalist

Students interested in nature could explore the Alpine region. How high are the mountain ranges? What do they look like in winter and summer? What animals can survive the rugged winters? How is the vegetation in the mountains different from that on the plains?

Visual-Spatial

Encourage students to make a chart of the Alps noting the major ski resorts, cities, lakes, and valleys so that they can envision the areas as they are discussed.

Bodily-Kinesthetic

What are the different options in a ski school from beginner to off-trail skiing? What are the most dangerous kinds of skiing? Which ones would they like to try?

Communication

Interpersonal: Cooperative Groups

Arrange students in heterogeneous groups composed of high and low-ability students. Using **Les classes de neige** as a point of reference, have them create the ideal three-week ski school experience. Where would they choose to go? How would they get to their destination? What ski classes would they like to take? What educational courses would help them to prepare for their ski adventure? Have each group report their findings to the whole class.

Annecy 1.2, 5.1

Annecy est une charmante petite ville. Les visiteurs aiment flâner* dans les rues pavées de la vieille ville médiévale en regardant les maisons fleuries près des canaux. Du château d'Annecy on peut voir le lac d'Annecy, un beau lac propre, où on peut faire du bateau, du ski nautique, et même louer des pédalos*.

Search words: lac d'annecy, accueil ville annecy

flâner *to stroll;* **pédalo** *pedal boat*

Annecy est connue pour son carnaval vénitien.

Les classes de neige 2.1, 2.2, 5.1

Les établissements scolaires ont la possibilité d'organiser chaque année des classes de neige. Les élèves partent aux sports d'hiver ensemble. Le séjour peut durer d'une à trois semaines. Lors des classes de neige, il s'agit de combiner loisirs et travail en classe. C'est l'occasion de mettre en place des projets qui concilient plaisir de la neige et démarche* éducative.

Search words: blogue classes de neige, vidéo classes de neige, photos classes de neige

démarche *undertaking*

1.2, 2.1, 5.1

La Francophonie: La récréation

À Saint-Martin

À Saint-Martin, une île dans la mer des Antilles où l'on parle français, on trouve deux sortes d'activités principales appelées "bleu" et "vert." La catégorie "vert" offre beaucoup d'activités pour les gens qui aiment la nature. La catégorie "bleu" est pour les fanas des sports aquatiques comme la plongée sous-marine, la planche à voile, le ski nautique, ou le scooter des mers.

Search words: saint-martin accueil, office de tourisme de l'île de st martin, bienvenue à saint martin tourisme, visiter saint-martin

COMPARAISONS

Où peut-on faire des sports aquatiques près de chez vous?

4.2

Marigot est une ville de Saint-Martin très fréquentée par les touristes.

Essential Instruction

1. Have students find photos of **la ville d'Annecy** in summer and winter and then decide if they are "**blanc**" because they prefer winter or snow sports, "**vert**" if they like to hike in the woods, or "**bleu**" preferring to engage in water sports. Having declared their preference, have them make a list of activities in which they would like to participate. Students can also be a blend of colors.
2. In the same vein, have students read **La francophonie** and proceed in the same manner choosing "**bleu**," "**vert**," or both.
3. For **Activité 9**, offer students the choice of items one, three, or four. All students do item two.
4. Complete **Activité A** together or in small groups.

Answers

All activities will vary.

Reference Desk

To help students with the reading, here are some words that they might not know: **l'entretien** (*maintenance*); **l'encadrement** (*training staff*); **les attentes** (*the expectations*); **une charte** (*a charter, document*); **l'hébergement** (*lodging*); **les glisses** (*refers to any sport such as skiing, surfing, windsurfing*).

9 Activités culturelles

1.3, 3.2

Faites les activités suivantes.

1. Faites une présentation PowerPoint™ sur la Savoie comme "Terre de culture," "Terre de gastronomie," ou "Terre de tourisme."
2. Situez les endroits mentionnés sur une carte de la Savoie.
3. Faites un album photos sur la ville d'Annecy. Écrivez des légendes qui décrivent ce qu'on voit.
4. Trouvez un blogue, une vidéo, ou des photos d'élèves français en classe de neige. Contactez-les et posez-leur quelques questions sur leurs expériences.

On fait la raclette avec un appareil à raclette et du bon fromage de Savoie.

À discuter

Votre classe planifie un séjour pour combiner loisirs et travail en classe. Que proposeriez-vous comme destination, mode de transport, logement, activités?

Du côté des médias

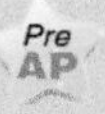

1.2, 5.1

Interpretive Communication

Lisez la brochure ci-dessous sur ce qu'on peut trouver en Savoie au Mont Blanc.

Le dico des stations

Pour vous guider dans la jungle des labels, appellations, dénominations, classifications...
Savoie Mont Blanc vous propose ce petit dico.
Bon choix... et bon séjour !

NORDIQUE FRANCE

Station labellisée « Nordique France » proposant un domaine nordique exceptionnel en termes de longueur, d'entretien, avec pistes de skating et d'alternatif, encadrement pour l'initiation, le perfectionnement et l'accompagnement.

LABEL FAMILLE PLUS MONTAGNE

Afin de mieux répondre aux attentes des parents et des enfants en vacances à la montagne, les stations de Savoie et Haute-Savoie, membres du Label Famille Plus Montagne se sont engagées dans une charte de qualité, mettant en valeur des critères stricts d'accueil, d'activités, d'animations, d'équipements et d'hébergements.

STATION DE SKI ADAPTÉ

Plus de 30 sites sont accessibles aux personnes en situation de handicap. Ces stations ont dû répondre à un double critère : la capacité de leur école de ski à proposer la pratique du handi-ski et l'accessibilité du site et de ses hébergements. L'ensemble de ces informations ont été validées au cours de visites sur place.

SITE NORDIQUE

Station Nordique offrant un accueil de qualité, des pistes variées bien préparées et sécurisées.

STATION GRAND DOMAINE

Station permettant d'accéder skis aux pieds à un domaine relié.

VILLAGE DE CHARME

Station adhérant à la charte des Villages de Montagne ou village authentique sans construction moderne avec des espaces naturels préservés et proposant l'ensemble des activités de montagne (ski alpin, fond, raquettes, traineaux à chiens, sentiers pédestres...) ou autres activités hors-ski.

STATION NOUVELLES GLISSES

Station disposant d'espaces sécurisés spécifiques aux nouvelles glisses et de moniteurs pour l'initiation et le perfectionnement.

STATION CLUB

Station alliant le modernisme, commodités pour tout le ski, accès aisés à de nombreux loisirs et animations nocturnes.

Differentiated Learning

Accelerate

High-ability students read **De côté des médias** and answer the questions on p. 232.

Decelerate

Have students make a report to the class about **la federation française de ski** in which they explain what the categories are for the ski teams (**ski alpin, ski de fond, biathlon, saut à ski, combiné, nordique, ski freestyle, snowboard, disciplines non-olympiques**) and show a picture of each.

Answers

1. Label famille plus montagne
2. Village de charme
3. Station club
4. Station de ski adapté
5. Site nordique
6. Nordique france
7. Station nouvelle glisse
8. Station grand domaine

Reference Desk

For additional information, photos, and videos visit the **Champagny-en-Vanoise** website.

10 Le dico des stations

1.2, 3.2

Retrouvez les labels qui correspondent à ces stations de ski.

1. station qui répond particulièrement aux attentes des parents et des enfants
2. station dans un cadre villageois authentique avec des espaces naturels préservés
3. station moderne, offrant de nombreux loisirs et animations le soir
4. station adaptée aux besoins des personnes handicapées
5. station spécialisée dans un accueil de qualité
6. station qui offre une variété de pistes et assure la sécurité de ses skieurs
7. station spécialisée dans la nouvelle glisse
8. On n'a pas besoin d'enlever ses skis pour aller de cette station au village intégré.

Le village de Campagny-en-Vanoise en Savoie.

Piste de ski dans le Mont-Blanc.

Essential Instruction

1. Have students take the mini-quiz to see what they remember of the "to know" verbs.
2. Using white boards or their notebooks, have students practice the forms of **savoir** and **connaître** in the **présent**, **imparfait**, **futur**, **conditionnel**, and **passé composé**.
3. Write incomplete sentences on the board for which the students will supply the verb: **Tu______Paul. Il _______faire du ski alpin.** This can be an oral and written exercise.

Structure de la langue

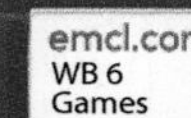

Révision: Savoir vs. Connaître

1.1

See if you can choose the right verb to complete each sentence and then summarize when to use each verb.

1. Je... que je suis en retard pour ma leçon de ski. (sais, connais)
2. Marc... cette station de ski. (sait, connaît)
3. Tu... le moniteur? (sais, connais)
4. Nous... faire des sauts à ski. (savons, connaissons)

Check your answers at the bottom of the page. If you got any wrong, read the grammar explanation to review how to form these verbs and when to use them.

Savoir and **connaître** both mean "to know." However, they each have specific contexts in which they are used.

Savoir		
• factual information • how to do something	Je **sais** où se trouve la piste. Les moniteurs **savent** faire du snowboard.	*I know where to find the slope.* *The instructors know how to snowboard.*
Connaître		
familiar/acquainted with people, places, things	Khaled **connaît** bien l'île de la Réunion.	*Khaled knows the island of Reunion well.*

Connaissez-vous mon ami Marc? — *Do you know my friend Marc?*
Il **sait** faire du ski de fond. — *He knows how to cross-country ski.*

The present tense forms are:

Savoir: sais, sais, sait, savons, savez, savent

Connaître: connais, connais, connaît, connaissons, connaissez, connaissent

The irregular past participle of **savoir** is **su**. The irregular past participle of **connaître** is **connu**.

Usage Tip

Connu is often used as an adjective: **Connu en France, le chanteur canadien y a vendu 500.000 albums.**

SAVOIR vs. CONNAÎTRE: The answers are: 1. sais; 2. connaît; 3. connais; 4. savons.
Savoir is used with factual information and to state how to do something.
Connaître is used to express familiarity with people, places, and things.

RESOURCES

Workbook 6

Drill & Practice Games

Reference Desk

1. **Savoir** plus an infinitive means "to know how to do something," "to be savvy."
2. **Connaître** often implies knowing something well (**Il connaît bien la cuinsine italienne**), from which we have the word **connaisseur**. **Connaître** is never followed by an infinitive. **Connaître par cœur** means "to know by heart."
3. **Reconnaître** (literally *to know again)* is "to recognize."
4. To help students remember the circumflex over the **aît** form, explain that "when **aît** get together they raise the roof," the roof being the circumflex. This is true for all forms of **connaître.**
5. Sometimes the French seem to say "shaypa" for **Je ne sais pas.**
6. As a filler in a conversation the French say, **"Tu sais? Vous savez?"**

Communication

Interpersonal: Cooperative Groups

In groups, students write as many sentences as they can with the two verbs "to know" in a timed practice. The group with the most correct answers wins.

Expansion

Les Bronzés Font du Ski is a slapstick French film from 1979 about some friends who go skiing together. Show a clip of one of the scenes with the volume off. Ask students what the people are doing, what they are wearing, and what the problems are. Replay the clip with the volume up as a listening exercise and to enjoy the film. **Search words: les bronzés font du ski**

Differentiated Learning

Deccelerate

Students might need to practice in English the two meanings of "to know" before being comfortable choosing between **savoir** and **connaître.** Ask them to write sentences using the verb "to know" to express familiarity with a person, place, or concept, and sentences using the verb "to know" to express informational knowledge or how to do something.

Accelerate

Challenge students who understand the distinction between **savoir** and **connaître** to make a chart for the class with examples in French and English.

RESOURCES

Workbook 10

Listening Activity 2

Drill & Practice Games

Answers

1. Tu sais écrire des chansons.
2. Les élèves de Mlle Choffrut connaissent les contes de fées maghrébins.
3. Éric et toi savez quand le festival aura lieu.
4. Je connais les tableaux de Monet.
5. Tu connais les monuments de Paris.
6. Élise et moi connaissons l'histoire de Cendrillon.
7. Les profs d'histoire savent quand la Révolution française a commencé.
8. Mamy sait où acheter le meilleur camembert.
9. Nous savons faire du ski alpin.

Reference Desk

Explain that English has a subjunctive as well. Many forms are the same as in the indicative so it is not as obvious. Here are a few examples.
Statements contrary to fact: If I were king, I would eliminate homework.
Wishful thinking: He wishes she were here with him.
Certain conjunctions: He wrote it down *in order that* he (might) remember.

11 Savoir ou connaître?

1.3

*Utilisez les indices ci-dessous pour faire des phrases avec les verbes **savoir** ou **connaître**.*

MODÈLE Simon/se servir du télésiège
Simon sait se servir du télésiège.

je/Megève
Je connais Megève.

1. tu/écrire des chansons
2. les élèves de Mlle Choffrut/contes de fées maghrébins
3. Éric et toi/quand le festival aura lieu
4. je/les tableaux de Monet
5. tu/les monuments de Paris
6. Élise et moi/l'histoire de *Cendrillon*
7. les profs d'histoire/quand la Révolution française a commencé
8. Mamy/où acheter le meilleur camembert
9. nous/faire du ski alpin

The Subjunctive of Regular Verbs after *il faut que*

1.1

emcl.com
WB 10
LA 2
Games

Il faut qu'Hamza mette des gants ou des lunettes de soleil aujourd'hui?

Verb forms in both English and French depend on the tense (time of the action) and the mood (attitude of the speaker) they reflect. You already know three moods in French: the indicative, used to state certainty or fact; and the imperative, used to give a command; and the conditional, used to state a condition. The fourth mood is called the subjunctive. This mood is used to express necessity, doubt, uncertainty, possibility, wish, feeling, or emotion.

In French the subjunctive usually appears after **que (qu')** in a dependent clause.

Essential Instruction

1. As a bell-ringer activity ask students what they know (**savoir**) about skiing. Ask them what ski areas they know (**connaître**).
2. Have partners take turns doing **Activité 11.** Correct the exercise in class.
3. Introduce the concept of the subjunctive. Explain that the subjunctive is always introduced by **que** in a dependent clause, and that it appears after certain verbs and conjunctions that they will learn in **Unité 4.**
4. Explain the formation of regular –**er**, –**ir**, and –**re** verbs.
5. Practice **il faut que** + subjunctive orally. Use whiteboards for written practice.
6. Introduce the verb **falloir** and its form for **présent**, **future**, **passé composé**, and **imparfait**.

Expansion

With whiteboards do an extensive drill of the forms of **il faut que** followed by regular verbs in the subjunctive. Put students in teams for competition to add some interest.

Il faut **acheter** un fuseau de ski. — *It is necessary to buy ski pants.*

Il faut que vous **achetiez** un fuseau de ski. — *You must buy ski pants. (It is necessary that you buy ski pants.)*

To form the subjunctive of most verbs, drop the **–ent** of the present tense **ils/elles** form and add the ending **–e**, **–es**, **–e**, **–ions**, **–iez**, or **–ent**, depending on the corresponding subject. Here are the subjunctive forms of regular **–er**, **–ir**, and **–re** verbs.

	tenter	finir	attendre
que je (j')	**tente**	**finisse**	**attende**
que tu	**tentes**	**finisses**	**attendes**
qu'il/elle/on	**tente**	**finisse**	**attende**
que nous	**tentions**	**finissions**	**attendions**
que vous	**tentiez**	**finissiez**	**attendiez**
qu'ils/elles	**tentent**	**finissent**	**attendent**

The subjunctive in French can be expressed by the present, future, conditional, or an infinitive in English.

Il faudra que vous **écoutiez** la monitrice. — *You'll have to listen to the instructor.*

Il faut que tu m'**attendes** sur la piste de ski. — *You must wait for me on the ski slope.*

Il faut qu'on **assiste** à un cours avant de faire du parachute ascensionnel. — *It's necessary to attend a course before going parasailing.*

Spelling Tip

Note that the **nous** and **vous** subjunctive forms are exactly like those for the imperfect. For **–er** verbs, the spelling of the other pronouns is the same as in the present tense.

COMPARAISONS

What do these two sentences have in common?

You must *be* on time.
Il faut que tu *soies* à l'heure.

COMPARAISONS: Both sentences use the subjunctive of the verb "to be." Note that in a regular indicative sentence, you would say, "You *are* on time." But the mandate implied in the expression above ("You must") triggers the subjunctive in English.

Differentiated Learning

Accelerate

Have students write a series of logical and bizarre sentences using **il faut que.** Students will circulate around the room making statements. The person who hears the statement will respond either **"Moi, je suis tout à fait d'accord"** or, to disagree, **"Même pas dans tes rêves."**

Special Needs Students

AD(H)D/Dyslexia/Linguistically Challenged

Help students with problems learning language to break down the verb conjugations into smaller parts. Starting with the verb **tenter**, let them conjugate this verb and many other **–er** verbs until they understand the pattern. Next, follow the same strategy with the **–ir** verb **finir** and finally the **–re** verb **attendre.** Learning in bite-size pieces can reduce frustration and confusion.

Answers

1. Il faut que tu trouves ton billet de train.
2. Il faut que tu loues des skis et des bâtons.
3. Il faut que tu achètes un forfait ski.
4. Il faut que tu skies sur la piste facile.
5. Il faut que tu assistes à un cours avec un moniteur.
6. Il faut que tu goûtes les spécialités de la région.
7. Il faut que tu finisses tes devoirs.
8. Il faut que tu attendes ta famille à la gare.

Script can be found in the front pages of the Annotated Teacher's Edition.

1. non
2. non
3. non
4. oui
5. oui
6. non
7. oui

1. Il faut qu'il étudie.
2. Il faut que tu manges des légumes.
3. Il faut que tu utilises ta carte-cadeau cinéma.
4. Il faut que vous téléchargiez la chanson en ligne.
5. Il faut qu'il reste au lit.
6. Il faut qu'ils se rendent au complexe sportif.
7. Il faut que tu achètes un cadeau.
8. Il faut que vous l'attendiez devant la salle de classe.

Reference Desk

Remind students that verbs ending in **–ier** have **–ii** in the **nous** and **vous** forms of the subjunctive, for example, **Il faut que vous étudiiez chaque soir**.

Connections

Music

Jean-Jacques Goldman sings "**Pas Toi**" which features the subjunctive of **faire**, **être**, and **apprendre.** It could be used as a cloze exercise where students fill in vocabulary and verbs in the subjunctive.

12 Les classes de neige

1.1

Dites à Élodie ce qu'elle doit faire pour réussir son séjour à Combloux. Choisissez un verbe de la liste.

apporter louer acheter goûter attendre assister à skier trouver finir

MODÈLE ton fuseau et tes gants
Il faut que tu apportes ton fuseau et tes gants.

1. ton billet de train
2. des skis et des bâtons
3. un forfait de ski
4. sur la piste facile
5. un cours avec un moniteur
6. les spécialités de la région
7. tes devoirs
8. ta famille à la gare

Communiquez!

13 Une leçon de ski

1.1

Écrivez les numéros 1–7 sur votre papier. Écoutez les conseils de la monitrice. S'il faut que les enfants fassent quelque chose, écrivez ***oui****; s'il ne faut pas qu'ils fassent quelque chose, écrivez* ***non****.*

14 Que faire?

1.3

*Dites ce qu'il faut faire dans les situations suivantes. Commencez vos phrases avec "****Il faut que…****" et choisissez une expression de la liste.*

manger des légumes utiliser ta carte-cadeau cinéma étudier
télécharger la chanson en ligne se rendre au complexe sportif
l'attendre devant sa salle de classe rester au lit acheter un cadeau

1. Sébastien n'a pas réussi à ses trois derniers contrôles en sciences physiques.
2. J'ai commencé à manger un dessert après le dîner, et maintenant je grossis!
3. Mes parents ne me donnent pas d'argent pour aller au cinéma!
4. Jonathan et moi, nous voulons écouter la nouvelle chanson de Natasha St-Pier.
5. Étienne a la grippe.
6. Manon et Khaled veulent faire du roller.
7. C'est l'anniversaire de mon meilleur ami.
8. Julien et toi, vous voulez parler à votre copain.

Essential Instruction

1. To review skiing vocabulary, ask students **devinettes: Qui vous aide à apprendre à skier? (un moniteur, une monitrice); Nommez trois vêtements que vous portez quand vous faites du ski, Quel document vous permet de faire du ski à la station du ski? (un forfait); Donnez un synonyme de patiner? (faire du patinage); Comment pouvez-vous monter en haut de la montagne? (en tire-fesses, en télésiège); Que portez-vous pour protéger vos yeux quand vous skiez?**
2. Have students write **Activité 12**.
3. Do **Activité 13** with students. Have them write a sentence, then check spelling and pronunciation as a group. Continue until all sentences are completed.
4. Complete **Activités 14** and **15** in pairs.
5. Present the subjunctive of **aller**, **faire**, **pouvoir**, **savoir**, and **vouloir** orally first so students hear the sound and the rhythm of each verb form.
6. Have students copy each verb in their notebooks or onto flash cards.

15 Phrases affirmatives ou négatives

1.3

Faites des phrases avec il faut que ou il ne faut pas que, selon la situation.

1. Tu voudrais faire une randonnée équestre. (*choisir un cheval sympa*)
2. Clara et ses amies comptent faire du ski alpin ce weekend. (*apporter leurs maillots de bain*)
3. Ethan et moi, nous avons envie d'aller au cinéma. (*acheter* Pariscope)
4. Je fais des recherches généalogiques. (*parler à mon arrière-grand-mère*)
5. Maxime et Sébastien voudraient voir la grande statue de la Liberté. (*se rendre au Vermont*)
6. Aïcha aimerait maigrir. (*manger moins de chocolat*)
7. Zoé et toi, vous n'aimez pas les crêpes. (*dîner à la crêperie*)
8. Les ados veulent s'amuser. (*se rencontrer au cabinet du dentiste*)

1.1

The Subjunctive of Irregular Verbs

You have learned how to form the subjunctive of regular verbs. However, several verbs have irregular forms in the subjunctive. Below are some standard verbs for which you should learn the subjunctive forms.

Verbs such as **aller**, **faire**, **pouvoir**, **savoir**, and **vouloir** have irregular stems but regular endings in the subjunctive.

emcl.com
WB 11
Games

Spelling Tip

Note that the **nous** and **vous** forms of **aller** and **vouloir** use the infinitive stem.

	aller	faire	pouvoir	savoir	vouloir
que je (j')	**aille**	**fasse**	**puisse**	**sache**	**veuille**
que tu	**ailles**	**fasses**	**puisses**	**saches**	**veuilles**
qu'il/elle/on	**aille**	**fasse**	**puisse**	**sache**	**veuille**
que nous	**allions**	**fassions**	**puissions**	**sachions**	**voulions**
que vous	**alliez**	**fassiez**	**puissiez**	**sachiez**	**vouliez**
qu'ils/elles	**aillent**	**fassent**	**puissent**	**sachent**	**veuillent**

Il faut que vous **alliez** à la station de ski de Combloux. *You must go to the ski resort at Combloux.*

Verbs such as **boire**, **croire**, **devoir**, **prendre**, **recevoir**, **venir**, and **voir** have regular endings in the subjunctive but irregular stems in the **nous** and **vous** forms.

RESOURCES

Workbook 11

Drill & Practice Games

Answers

1. Il faut que tu choisisses un cheval sympa.
2. Il ne faut pas qu'elles apportent leurs maillots de bain.
3. Il faut que vous achetiez *Pariscope*.
4. Il faut que je parle à mon arrière-grand-mère.
5. Il ne faut pas qu'ils se rendent au Vermont.
6. Il faut qu'elle mange moins de chocolat.
7. Il ne faut pas que vous dîniez à la crêperie.
8. Il ne faut pas qu'ils se rencontrent au cabinet du dentiste.

Game

Il le faut!

Divide the class into two teams. Write seven pronouns across the board in any order. Call the first seven students from Team A to the board; each student stands under a pronoun. Call out an irregular verb. Students write a sentence beginning with **Il faut que** that incorporates their pronoun, for example, **(vous) Il faut que vous sachiez à quelle heure le train part.** The team earns a point for each correct sentence. If all seven sentences are correct the team remains for another round. If not, Team B comes to the board. The team with the most points wins.

Differentiated Learning

Accelerate

Have stronger students create a list of behaviors that all students must exhibit in order to succeed, for example, **Il faut qu'on ait de bonnes notes.** Challenge them to use as many irregular verbs as possible.

Decelerate

Have students create a set of flash cards for each of the irregular verbs. Encourage them to add a sentence using each irregular verb in a complete sentence starting with **Il faut que/qu'...**

Expansion

Students make an **à faire** list of things to be done before leaving on a ski vacation. They use **il faut que** plus the subjunctive. The challenge is a minimum of 15 sentences. When students read their sentences to the class, ask **"Pourquoi? A quelle heure? Avec qui?"** to get them to elaborate.

Answers

1. Il faut que vous buviez du chocolat chaud.
2. Il faut que je prenne mes lunettes de soleil.
3. Il faut que nous fassions du snowboard.
4. Il faut que j'aille les chercher à la gare.
5. Il faut que tu saches te servir du télésiège.
6. Il faut qu'elle voie la monitrice de ski.
7. Il faut que nous apprenions à mieux skier.

Reference Desk

Visualizing the verbs on p. 238 as boot verbs helps reinforce the written differences found in their conjugations. Choral repetition reinforces the spoken forms. Write the conjugations with single forms (**je**, **tu**, **il/elle**) on the left and plural forms (**nous**, **vous**, **ils/elles**) on the right and draw a boot around the forms excluding **nous** and **vous**.

Expansion

Brainstorm a list of the regular and irregular verbs the students know. Write these on the board for easy reference. Use a koosh ball to practice subjunctive verb forms. Say an infinitive and a subject pronoun. Throw the ball to a student who must conjugate the verb with **il faut que**. That student must then say an infinitive and subject pronoun, and throw the ball to another student.

	boire	croire	devoir	prendre	recevoir
que je (j')	**boive**	**croie**	**doive**	**prenne**	**reçoive**
que tu	**boives**	**croies**	**doives**	**prennes**	**reçoives**
qu'il/elle/on	**boive**	**croie**	**doive**	**prenne**	**reçoive**
que nous	**buvions**	**croyions**	**devions**	**prenions**	**recevions**
que vous	**buviez**	**croyiez**	**deviez**	**preniez**	**receviez**
qu'ils/elles	**boivent**	**croient**	**doivent**	**prennent**	**reçoivent**

	venir	voir
que je	**vienne**	**voie**
que tu	**viennes**	**voies**
qu'il/elle/on	**vienne**	**voie**
que nous	**venions**	**voyions**
que vous	**veniez**	**voyiez**
qu'ils/elles	**viennent**	**voient**

The verbs **avoir** and **être** have both irregular stems and endings in the subjunctive.

	avoir	être
que je (j')	**aie**	**sois**
que tu	**aies**	**sois**
qu'il/elle/on	**ait**	**soit**
que nous	**ayons**	**soyons**
que vous	**ayez**	**soyez**
qu'ils/elles	**aient**	**soient**

Il faut que j'aille un peu plus vite....

16 À la station de ski

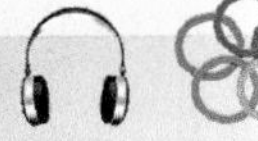

1.1

*Dites ce que les personnes suivantes doivent faire en faisant des phrases avec **il faut que**.*

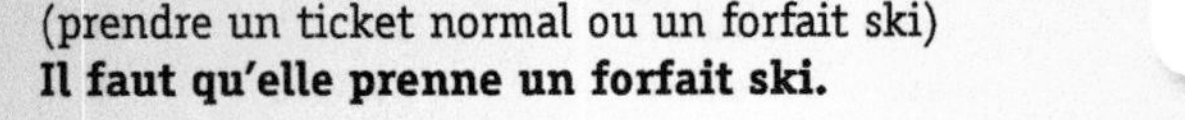

MODÈLE Julie ne veut pas payer cher pour skier. (prendre un ticket normal ou un forfait ski)
Il faut qu'elle prenne un forfait ski.

1. Vous venez de faire du ski et vous avez froid. (boire du chocolat chaud ou du coca)
2. Il fait du soleil et je ne vois pas bien. (prendre mon bonnet ou mes lunettes de soleil)
3. Il ne reste plus de skis à louer pour nous. (faire du snowboard ou de la planche à voile)
4. Mes amis viennent en train. (aller les chercher à la gare ou au centre commercial)
5. Tu veux monter en haut de la piste. (savoir se servir du télésiège ou des bâtons)
6. Clara aimerait s'inscrire dans un cours de ski. (voir son prof de français ou la monitrice de ski)
7. Nous ne skions pas bien. (rester dans le chalet ou apprendre à mieux skier)

Essential Instruction

1. Continue the presentation of irregular subjunctive by conjugating each irregular verb as before. After hearing the verb several times, students will repeat each verb after you.
2. Have students copy each verb in their notebooks or onto flash cards. Writing and saying the verb conjugations aloud reinforces how each verb changes in the **nous** and **vous** forms.
3. With whiteboards, practice these verbs singular to plural until students have mastered them.
4. Do **Activité 16** as a whole-class activity.
5. Students do **Activité 17** in pairs. Circulate to monitor their work.

17 On prend une décision importante.

 1.2

*Aidez tout le monde à choisir la meilleure solution. Faites des phrases avec **il faut que**.*

MODÈLE Koffi a vu un bon film et il veut le revoir, mais sa grand-mère l'attend.

A. voir le film et ne pas aller chez sa grand-mère
B. aller chez sa grand-mère et ne pas voir le film pour la deuxième fois aujourd'hui
Il faut que Koffi aille chez sa grand-mère et il ne faut pas qu'il voie le film pour la deuxième fois aujourd'hui.

1. Marc et moi, nous avons beaucoup de corvées à faire, mais on veut aller au complexe sportif.
   A. faire vos corvées avant d' aller au complexe sportif
   B. aller au complexe sportif puis faire vos corvées
2. Louis a un contrôle de français demain.
   A. étudier et savoir comment utiliser le subjonctif
   B. jouer aux jeux vidéo et ne pas étudier
3. Mes parents m'ont dit qu'ils me donneraient de l'argent si j'arrête d'être méchant avec mon frère.
   A. ne plus être méchant avec ton frère et acheter un cadeau à ton frère avec l'argent
   B. ne plus être méchant envers ton frère et acheter un scooter avec l'argent
4. Sandrine et Karim ont très soif, mais au musée on ne peut rien boire dans les salles d'exposition.
   A. boire un coca au café et ne pas voir les tableaux
   B. boire un coca au snack-bar du musée et voir les tableaux
5. Tu voudrais faire du ski en France.
   A. aller à Combloux et Megève
   B. aller à Paris et Lyon
6. Amadou et toi, vous avez gagné un séjour à Paris pour cinq nuits.
   A. savoir quels monuments visiter en parlant à votre prof de français et faire du shopping avant le voyage
   B. planifier votre visite sans consulter votre prof de français et faire du shopping à Paris

Answers

1. Il faut que vous fassiez vos corvées avant d'aller au complexe sportif.
2. Il faut qu'il étudie et sache comment utiliser le subjonctif.
3. Il ne faut plus que tu sois méchant avec ton frère et il faut que tu lui achètes un cadeau avec l'argent.
4. Il faut qu'elles boivent un coca au snack-bar du musée et il faut qu'elles voient les tableaux.
5. Il faut que tu ailles à Combloux et Megève.
6. Il faut que vous sachiez quels monuments visiter en parlant à votre prof de français et il faut que vous fassiez du shopping avant le voyage.

Connections

Cuisine

Have students find the recipe for **la raclette** and **la fondue savoyarde.** They transform the instructions from the command to **il faut que vous...** For example, if the recipe states "**Mélangez les ingredients,**" students change the sentence to read "**Il faut que vous mélangiez les ingrédients.**" Students could use this format to present a cooking show.

Communication

Interpersonal: Paired Practice

Students work in pairs to practice the irregular forms on pp. 237 and 238. The goal at the end of a given amount of time is for students to help each other to become subjunctive specialists.

Learning Styles

Auditory Learners

These students need to repeat these verbs aloud.

Visual Learners

These students have to *see* the words to understand them. Verb charts and flash cards are helpful.

Special Needs Students

AD(H)D/Dyslexia

Students with learning difficulties need to take one verb at a time and write it down in order to analyze the stem and how the verbs change for **nous** and **vous.** Consider giving them short quizzes on only one or two verbs so that learning all of them at once does not seem impossible.

Multiple Intelligences

Bodily-Kinesthetic/Musical-Rhythmic

Repetition of the conjugations helps students feel the beat: **que je fasse**, **que tu fasses**, **qu'il fasse**, **que nous fassions...** Have students tap their hands as they say each verb to feel the change in syllables.

Communicative Activities

Answers

All activities will vary.

Reference Desk

1. **Combloux**, a popular ski resort with approximately 2,000 residents, is a commune in the **Haute-Savoie** in southeastern France. **Combloux** is ideally located 2.5 miles from **Megève** and 19 miles from **Chamonix-Mont-Blanc**.
2. Many people believe that **fondue** originated in Switzerland. Frugal peasants would take their pieces of leftover hardened cheese, melt them, and add garlic, wine, and other ingredients to produce **fondue**.
3. The distinctive dish of rich melted cheese, potatoes, and other vegetables is called **la raclette** and has its origins in the Swiss Alps. It was the traditional hearty meal of farmers and shepherds.

Blended Instruction

Consider using blended instruction, a combination of in-class learning and computer-mediated instruction or learning opportunities. Ask students to complete activities on the computer, using their cell or smartphone, or other emerging electronic technology. This will allow students to hone their tech skills and become more independent learners. Schedule routine Internet and e-book learning in class and in the lab.

À vous la parole

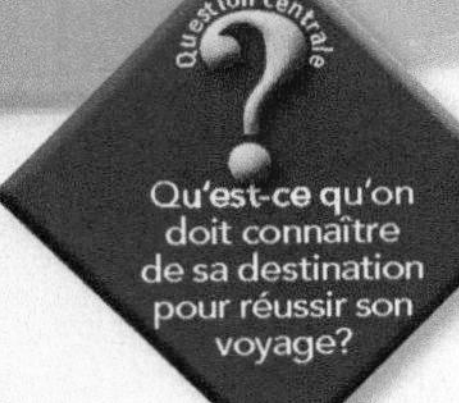

18 Les classes de neige

1.1, 5.2

Interpersonal Communication

Votre classe part bientôt en classe de neige à Combloux. Vous êtes en train de faire votre valise, mais vous pensez que vous avez oublié quelque chose. Vous avez laissé votre liste à l'école, donc vous téléphonez à un(e) ami(e). Parlez de ce que vous avez hâte de faire, de ce qu'il faut que vous emportiez, et renseignez-vous sur l'heure à laquelle il faut que vous vous rendiez à la gare.

19 La raclette et la fondue savoyardes

1.3, 3.2

Interpretive and Presentational Communication

Votre prof, qui est responsable des classes de neige, vous a parlé de ces deux spécialités, la raclette et la fondue de Savoie. Ce soir, votre dernier soir à Combloux, vous avez goûté ces deux spécialités. Faites des recherches pour trouver un restaurant et des recettes. Votre prof vous demande de faire une présentation sur ce que vous avez appris. Incluez des vidéos, des photos, une critique du restaurant, et les appréciations de vos camarades de classe.

Communiquez!

20 Un stage à l'Office du Tourisme d'Annecy

1.3, 3.2

Interpretive and Presentational Communication

Vous faites un stage (*internship*) à l'Office du Tourisme d'Annecy. On vous demande de créer une application pour smartphone pour inciter les touristes de venir à Annecy. Avec un groupe de camarades de classe, incluez les sites à voir, les activités, l'histoire de la ville/région, et la gastronomie. Il faut que vous trouviez des images ou des vidéos pour votre présentation.

Essential Instruction

1. Provide a rubric listing your expectations and evaluation points for **Activités 18**, **19**, and **20**.
2. For **Activités 19** and **20**, in addition to the option of using a slide show program, students can find easy-to-use templates online. **Search words: tripwow** and **trip advisor** for travelogue templates
3. Have students write **Activité 21**.
4. Have groups of three complete **Activité 22** and then present to another group.

Stratégie communicative

How-to Writing  1.3

Un mode d'emploi explique, par exemple, comment télécharger une chanson, écrire une recette, monter une étagère (*assemble a bookshelf*) ou une tente. Suivez ces quelques conseils pour donner des instructions:

- Écrivez les consignes (*instructions*) le plus simplement et clairement possible.
- Classez-les de manière logique.
- Familiarisez-vous avec votre public. Est-ce que vos lecteurs connaissent bien le sujet?
- Utilisez des supports visuels.

Testez vos consignes auprès d'un ou d'une camarade de classe. Les consignes sont-elles claires et faciles à comprendre? Votre camarade est-il ou est-elle perdu(e)? Manque-t-il une étape?

21 Comment télécharger une chanson  1.3

Remettez les consignes dans l'ordre de réalisation et réécrivez chaque consigne en utilisant **il faut que** + **subjonctif** selon l'exemple suivant:

MODÈLE Démarrer l'ordinateur.
Il faut que vous démarriez l'ordinateur.

1. Téléchargez votre chanson préférée.
2. Fermez le logiciel.
3. Démarrez l'ordinateur.
4. Ouvrez le logiciel.
5. Naviguez sur le site.
6. Synchronisez votre MP3.
7. Cliquez avec la souris.
8. Payez.

22 Préparatifs de voyage 1.3

Presentational Communication

Pensez à une destination où vous vous êtes rendu(e) ou où vous aimeriez vous rendre un jour. Imaginez que vous avez un site sur cette destination. Donnez à vos lecteurs quelques conseils et astuces *(wise tips)* concernant la préparation d'un voyage là-bas. Utilisez **il faut que** + **subjonctif**. Voici quelques éléments à garder en tête: les vêtements à emporter, l'insecticide ou la crème solaire, le type de chaussures; les cartes, les musées, l'hôtel; et des suggestions sur les restaurants.

Answers

3. Il faut que vous démarriez l'ordinateur.
5. Il faut que vous naviguiez sur le site.
7. Il faut que vous cliquiez avec la souris.
4. Il faut que vous ouvriez le logiciel.
8. Il faut que vous payiez.
1. Il faut que téléchargiez votre chanson préférée.
6. Il faut que vous synchronisiez votre MP3.
2. Il faut que vous fermiez le logiciel.

Presentations will vary.

Reference Desk

Discuss **Stratégie communicative**. Model how the strategies for writing to a specific audience can be applied to **Activités 18**, **19**, and **20** on p. 240.

Differentiated Learning

Accelerate
Students may work at their own pace completing the above exercises. When they have finished, encourage them to offer help to those still working.

Decelerate
These students would benefit from you working with them to define the tasks in each activity, to discuss how to research information, and what format they should use to present it. Assign deadlines for each step, and arrange to check students' work. Some of these students, although not strong in French, will have excellent computer skills and benefit from using those.

RESOURCES

e-visual 12

Workbook 1–3

Flash Cards

Listening Activity 1

Drill & Practice Games

Reference Desk

1. Most modern telemark skis resemble today's alpine skis. However, they are different in that the heel of the telemark skier's boot is not attached to the ski in a rigid binding. Because of this, the skier has more flexibility and can kneel into turns, thus creating a deep, smooth turn.
2. **Se faire vacciner** means "to get oneself vaccinated."
3. **Une pièce d'identité**, the national identity card, (***Carte nationale d'identité sécurisée*** or ***CNIS***) is a document issued by the French government. It looks like a driver's license because it is a laminated plastic card bearing the photograph, name, and address of the holder. It is valid for ten years.

Vocabulaire actif

Sports d'hiver et préparatifs de départ

Sports d'hiver

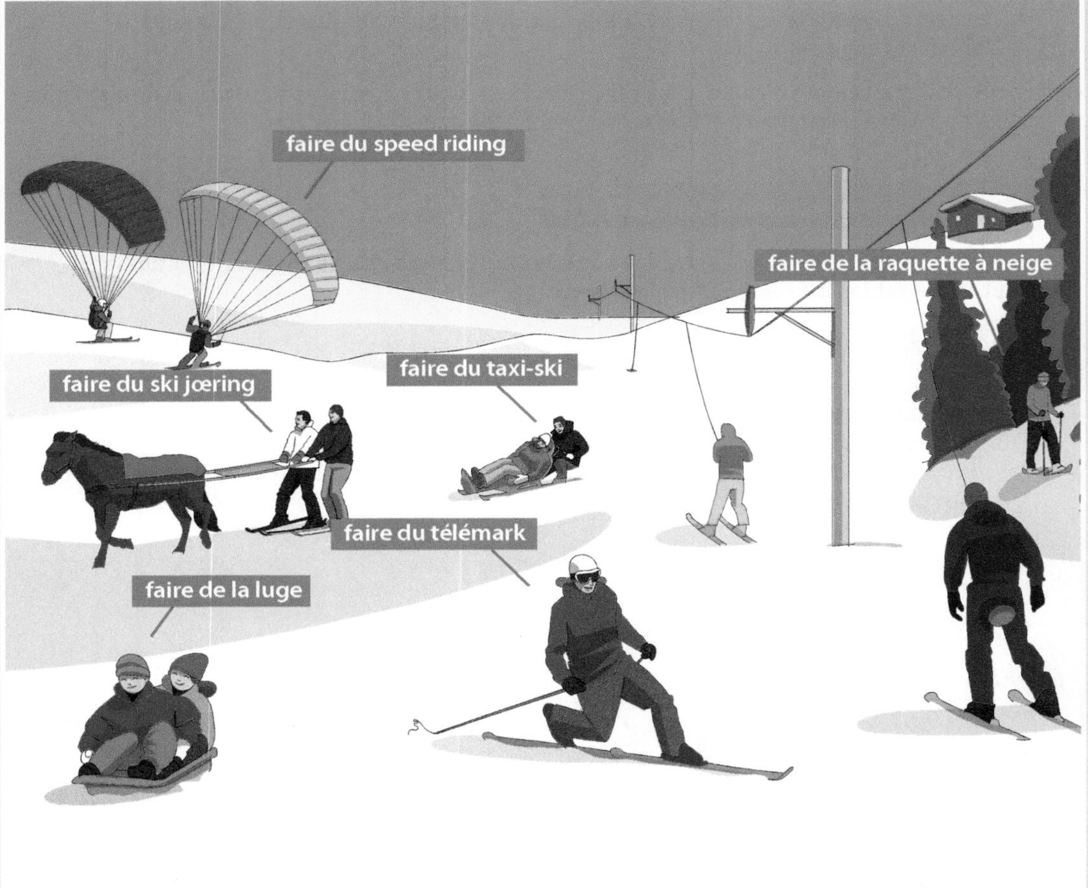

Essential Instruction

1. Have students look at the picture of the **Sports d'hiver** and identify each vocabulary word.
2. Ask students to listen to **Avant de voyager** and **Pour la conversation** three times before repeating.
3. Have students answer the question "**Qu'est-ce qu'il faut faire avant de voyager?**" orally using **Il faut que** + the verbs on p. 243.
4. Ask students to prioritize what **sports d'hiver** they would like to do, in descending order from the most interesting to the least.

Avant de voyager

Pour la conversation 

1.1, 5.1

How do I say I'm doing something different (from the others)?

> **Vous ferez ce que vous voulez, moi c'est** balade sur le domaine.
>
> *Do what you want, but for me it's a walk on the property.*

How do I tell someone it's important not to hurt himself or herself?

> **Il est important que** tu ne te foules pas la cheville ou que tu ne te casses pas le poignet!
>
> *It's important you don't sprain your ankle or break your wrist.*

Et si je voulais dire...? 

un alpiniste	*climber*
en règle	*in order*
périmé(e)	*expired*
valable	*valid*
annuler	*to cancel*
escalader	*to climb*
faire de l'alpinisme	*to mountain climb*
s'informer sur	*to get information on*

Communication

Interpersonal: Cooperative Groups

1. Arrange students in mixed-ability groups. Captains from each group select a card from each of four piles.
2. Place cards face down. On the cards in one pile write weather conditions like **Il fait un temps de chien**, **Il neige constamment**; **Il pleut à verse**... In the second pile provide a selection of characters: **Jean le malin**, **Marie la belle**, "**Grand Pied**," **Neige Blanche**, **le Monstre des Alpes**... The third pile is verbs: **chanter faux**, **skier comme un(e) professionnel(le)**, **pleurer tout le temps**... The fourth pile features random terms: **un bonnet de nuit**, **des chaussettes noires**, **trois petites roses**...
3. Have students create a skit using these terms plus at least one verb in the subjunctive. Allow 15 minutes to prepare before presenting.

Differentiated Learning

Accelerate

Have students pretend to be nervous parents. Have them make a list of things that their children should remember to do when the parents are away on a skiing trip. They must use **Il est important que** + their advice.

Decelerate

Have students research what **une carte d'identité française** looks like, where they can procure one, and how much it costs.

Special Needs Students

Social Anxiety/At-Risk Teens

Students who have never traveled might find this lesson difficult to imagine. Continue to encourage them to think that a trip like this could be in their future.

Answers

Serge et moi faisons de la raquette à neige.
Marie-Alix et Océane font du télémark.
M. Dupin fait du ski joering.
David et Yasmine font du taxi-ski.
Malika fait de la luge.
Mes amis et moi faisons du ski alpin.

1. B
2. A
3. D
4. G
5. E
6. F
7. C

Reference Desk

1. Vaccinations suggested for **le Sénegal** are: Hepatitis A and B, Typhoid, Meningococcus, Polio, Rabies, Measles, Mumps, Rubella, and Tetanus-Diphtheria.
2. Vaccinations for **la Réunion** are: Hepatitis A and B, Typhoid, Yellow Fever, Measles, Mumps and Rubella, and Tetanus-Diptheria.
3. **Ski jœring** is a mix of skiing and equestrianism. The term comes from the Norwegian word **skikjøring** meaning "ski driving." This sport has been practiced as far back as 2500 BC. The horse wears a harness with a flap for the skier to hold as the skier is pulled as if waterskiing.
4. Off-trail skiing is skiing in the backcountry on slopes that have not been groomed. They are not monitored by ski patrol nor maintained by a ski resort.

1 Quels sports d'hiver?

1.2

Indiquez les sports d'hiver qu'on fait.

2 Les préparatifs de départ

1.2

Répondez à la question en trouvant la phrase qui correspond aux préparatifs de départ des Lamire.

A. M. et Mme Lamire ont obtenu des passeports pour leurs enfants Lina et Lucas.
B. Pendant des mois, M. et Mme Lamire et leurs enfants ont planifié un voyage au Sénégal.
C. Le matin de leur départ, les Lamire ont vérifié qu'ils avaient tous leurs documents et essentiels.
D. Les Lamire n'ont pas dû obtenir de visas.
E. Le soir avant leur départ, les Lamire ont fait leurs valises.
F. Ils vont passer un bon séjour au Sénégal!
G. Les Lamire ne vont pas attraper (*catch*) de maladies.

1. Les Lamire ont choisi une destination et ont surfé sur Internet pour se renseigner. Qu'est-ce qu'ils ont fait ensuite?
2. M. et Mme Lamire avaient déjà des passeports pour les voyages internationaux, mais pas pour qui?
3. Les Lamire vont passer moins de trois mois au Sénégal; si on y passe plus de trois mois, il faut un visa. Donc, ont-ils des visas?
4. Mme Lamire a téléphoné au consulat de France, qui lui a conseillé de se faire vacciner. Est-ce qu'ils vont tomber malades au Sénégal?
5. Les Lamire ont acheté un couteau Suisse, de la lotion anti-moustique, et d'autres choses pour leur voyage. Où est-ce qu'ils ont mis leurs affaires?
6. Les Lamire ont besoin de chèques de voyage, de cartes de crédit, de passeports, d'un appareil photo, et d'un permis de conduire pour M. Lamire. Est-ce qu'ils ont oublié quelque chose?
7. À quoi est-ce que les Lamire s'attendent?

Essential Instruction

1. To review the **sports d'hiver** vocabulary, have students answer **Activité 1** orally.
2. Ask partners to complete **Activité 2**.
3. Play **Activité 3**. Students will identify whether the statement is about preparing for a trip or about a trip itself. Stop after each sentence to ask them what words gave them the clue to the answer.
4. Assign **Activité 4** in small groups. Have students share what they learned about their classmates' preferences and previous travel experience.

Communiquez!

3 On part où?

 1.1

Interpretive Communication

*Écrivez les numéros 1–8 sur votre papier. Puis, écrivez **oui** si la phrase décrit des préparatifs de voyage ou **non** s'il ne s'agit pas d'un voyage.*

4 Questions personnelles

1.2, 1.3

Répondez aux questions.

1. Quels sports d'hiver préfères-tu?
2. Quels préparatifs est-ce que tu dois faire si tu pars en voyage à la montagne en hiver?
3. Quels préparatifs est-ce que tu dois faire si tu pars en voyage au bord de la mer en été?
4. Avant de partir, qu'est-ce que tu mets sur ta liste pour vérifier que tu n'as rien oublié?
5. As-tu déjà été obligé(e) d'obtenir un passeport ou un visa? Pour aller où?

Answers

Script can be found in the front pages of the Annotated Teacher's Edition.

1. oui
2. non
3. non
4. oui
5. oui
6. oui
7. oui
8. oui

4 *Answers will vary.*

Game

La guerre de trois

Prepare a collection of visuals and/or flash cards of the vocabulary in **Vocabulaire actif**. Make sure to have as many as you have students. You may have to pull from the other **Leçons** in **Unité 4**. Have students count off by threes to form three teams. The teams form three lines in front of the teacher at the front of the room. Show a visual or flash card to the first three students. The first student to identify it correctly sits down. The first team with all of its members seated wins.

Differentiated Learning

Accelerate

Ask students to research and compare the number of tourists who elect to travel to **le Sénégal** and **la Réunion**. Have them find which ski resorts in France are the most popular for families and for single people.

Decelerate

Have students find pictures of people participating in the different **sports d'hiver**. Have them report to the class and tell which ones seem to be the most popular among French people. Are these the same sports we do in the United States at ski resorts like Aspen or Breckenridge?

RESOURCES

 **Dialogue Video**

 **Workbook 4**

Answers

1. une balade sur le domaine
2. Il accompagnera sa femme.
3. Léo
4. Elle s'est foulé la cheville en faisant de la luge.
5. Ils iront au Vietnam; ils feront du bénévolat.

Extension

Ils vont faire du bénévolat à Madagascar et aider à reconstruire des maisons.

Reference Desk

1. Madagascar is an island in the Indian Ocean east of Mozambique. It is the fourth largest island in the world with approximately 16.9 million inhabitants. The official languages are French and Malagasy. Five percent of all animal and plant species are found in its terrain. It is a haven for snorkelers and divers due to its 450 kilometers of barrier reefs.
2. **Je ne m'étais pas encore foulé la cheville.** Explain that this is the **plus-que-parfait** of **se fouler la cheville**. **Ça va les chevilles?** is an expression that the French would use when someone is bragging. In English, we say someone gets a swollen head. In French, people who are full of themselves have swollen ankles or **les chevilles qui enflent**.
3. WWOOF (Worldwide Opportunities on Organic Farms) is a network of international organizations that place volunteers on organic farms in 99 countries around the world.

Rencontres culturelles

emcl.com WB 4

Un weekend en famille

 1.1, 1.2, 5.2

Élodie, Léo, et leurs parents passent le weekend à Combloux.

Mère: Vous ferez ce que vous voulez, moi c'est balade sur le domaine.
Léo: Il faudrait que tu essaies le ski de fond!
Mère: J'ai hâte d'essayer.
Léo: Moi, de toute façon, c'est snowboard. Et toi, papa?
Père: Il se pourrait que j'accompagne ta mère....
Élodie: Quoi, tu vas abandonner le hors-pistes... Oh, c'est beau l'amour!
Léo: Tu te souviens quand on faisait de la luge?
Élodie: Là tu en faisais avec nous, maman.
Mère: Oui, mais je ne m'étais pas encore foulé la cheville!
Léo: C'est du passé: maintenant il faut que tu t'y remettes. L'année prochaine, c'est notre voyage bénévolat au Vietnam. Il est important que tu ne te foules pas la cheville ou que tu ne te casses pas le poignet!

Mots-clé **Snowboard** est un exemple du franglais. Faites une liste de 15 mots franglais. Ensuite, classez-les par catégorie, par exemple, la technologie, les sports, et le business.

5 Un weekend en famille

Répondez aux questions.

1. Qu'est-ce que la mère d'Élodie et de Léo veut faire à Combloux?
2. Qu'est-ce que leur père fera?
3. Qui va faire du snowboard?
4. Qu'est-ce qui est arrivé (*happened*) à la mère d'Élodie et de Léo la dernière fois?
5. Où la famille va-t-elle passer ses vacances l'année prochaine? Qu'est-ce qu'ils feront?

1.2, 1.3

Extension **Projet de woofing**

 1.1, 1.2

Des amis se rencontrent au café pour parler de leur voyage pour faire du bénévolat humanitaire.

Virginie: On est tous d'accord pour Madagascar?
Hugo: Oui, mais il faut qu'on trouve à woofer tous ensemble.
Mathieu: Là, sur le site, il y a deux offres, l'une au centre de l'île, l'autre au sud.
Virginie: Mais c'est pour faire quoi?
Mathieu: Celle du centre, il faudrait qu'on aide à entretenir des réseaux d'irrigation. Je préfère l'autre. Ce n'est pas très précis pour le sud, mais il semble qu'ils souhaitent des volontaires pour reconstruire des maisons de terre.
Hugo: Eh bien, c'est très bien. L'année dernière, on a joué aux agriculteurs, cette année, on fera de la maçonnerie. Tout le monde mérite une belle maison durable.
Virginie: Je vais travailler avec des gants....
Mathieu: Mais tu n'auras pas le temps de te faire des manicures!

Extension La bande d'amis choisit quel projet? Où?

 1.3

Essential Instruction

1. Listen to **Un weekend en famille** and then ask the questions in **Activité 5.**
2. Discuss Madagascar and the WWOOF project.
3. Listen to **Extension** and discuss the accompanying question in small groups.
4. In the computer lab, students read **Les stations du ski**. Assign each of the 12 ski resorts to groups of students. Teams research their **station de ski** and make a PR presentation of their resort, selling it as the best.

Points de départ 

emcl.com
WB 5

Question centrale: Qu'est-ce qu'on doit connaître de sa destination pour réussir son voyage?

Les stations de ski 1.2

C'est le goût pour les sports d'hiver qui a été à l'origine du développement d'immenses domaines skiables* dans les Alpes et d'un réseau de stations très attirantes*. C'est à Chamonix qu'ont d'ailleurs* été organisés les premiers Jeux Olympiques d'hiver en 1924.

On peut aller jusqu'à 200km/h en faisant du Speed Riding.

À côté des stations de ski historiques créées autour d'un village comme Chamonix, Saint-Gervais, La Clusaz, Villars de Lans ou Megève, il existe des stations nées de toute pièce* comme Courchevel, L'Alpe d'Huez, ou Les Deux Alpes, et enfin celles nées de la révolution des loisirs comme Les Arcs, Avoriaz, ou Serre-Chevalier. L'ensemble des domaines skiables des Alpes propose au total plus de 6.000 kilomètres de pistes de ski avec des domaines reliés* intégralement entre eux comme Les Trois Vallées avec ses 338 pistes qui couvrent 600 kilomètres.

À côté du ski alpin, l'offre sportive des stations s'est beaucoup développée: du snowboard au monoski en passant par le speed riding, la raquette à neige, le ski freestyle, ou le ski de randonnée.

Search words: **ski france, ski mont blanc, ski info france, ski combloux, contamines montjoie, photo (+ speed riding, raquette à neige, ski freestyle, ski de randonnée)**

---

attirantes *attractive*; **domaines skiables** *ski areas*; **d'ailleurs** *moreover*; **née de toute pièce** *developped from nothing*; **reliés** *connected*

Produits

Les épreuves des Jeux Olympiques ou de **championnat du monde de ski alpin** se divisent en deux catégories: les épreuves plus techniques telles que le slalom et le slalom géant, et les épreuves de vitesse pure comme le Super-G et la descente.

Normalement, les Français gagnent entre 1 et 11 médailles pour les J.O. d'hiver.

RESOURCES

Workbook 5

Reference Desk

Grenoble hosted the 1968 Winter Olympics. These were the first games to be broadcast in color; the first to require gender testing for female athletes; and the first time East and West Germany sent two separate teams. Jean-Claude Killy swept the men's Alpine events (three gold medals), and American figure skater Peggy Fleming won the United States' only gold medal in the entire competition.

Connections

Sociology

Madagascar has a ceremony called **Famadihana**, or moving of the bones. Every seven years the bodies of relatives are exhumed, new shrouds are wrapped around their bodies, and relatives dance with them. Ask students to research **Famadihana.** Why do family members come together to participate in this ceremony?

Culture

Practices: Information

Fédération Française du ski was founded in 1924. Its mission is to oversee the activities of ski clubs in France and regulate Olympic and non-Olympic ski competitions. Search words: **ffs, fédération française du ski**

Differentiated Learning

Accelerate

Ask volunteers to learn the **Extension** dialogue and present it to the class. The class answers the **Extension** question.

Multiple Intelligences

Naturalist

Madagascar offers a treasure of natural wonders such as rainforests, deserts, and barrier reefs. What would your naturalists want to study if they visited the island?

Visual-Spatial

Ask students to make a topographical map of Madagascar showing its cities and major points of interest.

Answers

6

1. **Chamonix**, Saint-Gervais, La Clusaz, Villars de Lans, Megève; Courchevel, L'Alpe d'Huez, Les Deux Alpes; Les Arcs, Avoriaz, Serre-Chevalier
2. *Photos will vary.*
3. *Answers will vary.*

À discuter
Answers will vary.

Reference Desk

1. **Le Burkina Faso** is a landlocked country in West Africa. Its capital is Ouagadougou. It has over 15 million inhabitants and is approximately 105,900 square miles in size.
2. The Republic of Mali measures over 480,000 square miles and has a population of 14.5 million people. Its capital is Bamako. Agriculture and fishing are its major industries. Some of Mali's prominent natural resources include gold, uranium, and salt. French is the official language of **le Mali.**
3. The Republic of Benin in West Africa is approximately 110,000 square miles in size. Its capital is Porto-Novo. There are over nine million inhabitants, the majority of whom live on its southern coastline on the Bight of Benin. The official language is French. Native languages such as Yoruba and Fon are also spoken.

 1.2, 2.1

Les voyageurs volontaires en pays francophones

"Engagez-vous:" c'est le thème de la campagne qui cherche à attirer les jeunes vers des initiatives solidaires aussi bien dans le domaine du tourisme qu'en développement local dans des pays francophones comme le Burkina Faso, le Sénégal, le Mali, et le Bénin. Un bon moyen pour les jeunes Français de faire l'expérience de la différence en participant à des actions d'entrepreneuriat solidaire, d'aide humanitaire, ou d'aide en milieu scolaire.

De nombreuses associations françaises aident les enfants du Sénégal.

 **Search words: voyages des bénévoles, bénévolat humanitaire**

COMPARAISONS

Quelles sont les organisations bénévoles de votre ville ou région?

6 Activités culturelles

 1.3, 3.2

Faites les activités suivantes.

1. Nommez....
   - des stations créées autour d'un village
   - des stations nées de rien
   - des stations issues de la société des loisirs
2. Trouvez une photo pour chacun des sports suivants:
   - monoski
   - speed riding
   - raquette à neige
   - ski freestyle
   - ski de randonnée
3. Trouvez des exemples d'initiatives solidaires en ligne. Quels sont les pays francophones concernés?

Le monoski.

À discuter

Où est-ce que vous aimeriez faire du travail bénévole ou humanitaire? Pourquoi est-ce que cet endroit a besoin d'aide?

Essential Instruction

1. Work in the computer lab to review winter sports with **Activité 6.**
2. Brainstorm a list of benevolent organizations in your community. What is their mission?
3. Students read **Les voyageurs volontaires en pays francophones** and learn about volunteer projects in third world countries available to young French people. Use the search words for more information.
4. **À discuter** gives students an opportunity to discuss their volunteering preferences. What do they do in their school, church, or community to give of their time and talent and why?

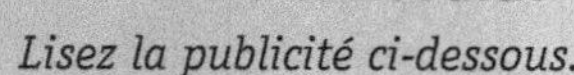

Du côté des médias

  1.2

Lisez la publicité ci-dessous.

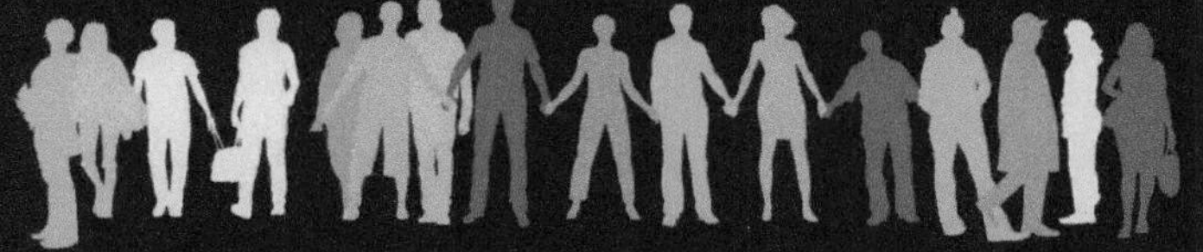

7 Les volontaires internationaux d'échange et de solidarité

  1.2, 1.3

Répondez aux questions.

1. Qui sont les volontaires internationaux?
2. Quelle qualité principale attend-on d'eux?
3. Quels sont les pays concernés?
4. Qu'est-ce que ces pays attendent des volontaires?
5. Quelle est la justification du slogan de l'affiche—"Pour un engagement volontaire, solidaire et responsable"?

Answers

1. des lycéens, des étudiants, des jeunes diplômés, des professionnels, ou des retraités
2. Ils ont envie de s'engager pour aider les autres.
3. les pays du Sud (Amérique Centrale, du Sud, Afrique, Asie, etc.)
4. une rencontre et des échanges qui vont permettre une solidarité internationale
5. *Possible answers:* volontaire: on n'est pas payé; solidaire: pour aider les gens qui souffrent; responsable: on échange de vraies compétences

Connections

Music

"Quand on n'a que l'Amour," the final song of the hit Broadway musical *Jacques Brel is Alive and Well and Living in Paris*, features negatives. It also presents an optimistic message about the force of love as a power for social change.

Search words: quand on n'a que l'amour, jacques brel

Expansion

Put students in small groups to create an ad or poster for a volunteer organization that exists or might exist in their school. Brainstorm what makes the ad on p. 249 informative and visually interesting. Groups present their final product to the class. Display the projects around your school.

Differentiated Learning

Accelerate/Decelerate

High and low-ability language students work in pairs or groups to read the ad for **Les volontaires internationaux d'échange et de solidarité**. Then have students go directly to the interactive website to learn more about the organization. Have them answer the questions in **Activité 7**.

Special Needs Students

Linguistically Challenged

Have students copy the **Activité 7** questions into their notebooks leaving space for notes and answers for each one. As you work with these students, encourage them to look for cognates within the ad as a way of reinforcing the number of words that they already know. Remind them that **attendre** means "to wait for" but **attendre quelque chose de quelqu'un** means "to expect something of someone."

Answers

All activities will vary.

Communication

Interpersonal: Paired Practice

One student plays the director of volunteers for a humanitarian organization interviewing the other student who plays a potential participant. The director asks this person why he or she wants to work for the cause, where the candidate would like to work, and what skill he or she can offer to the organization. The candidate must make the case for his or her candidacy.

Connections

Music

"**La Chanson Pour l'Auvergnat**," sung by Georges Brassens, relates the impact that an act of kindness can have on the life of a less fortunate person. It aligns nicely with the theme of volunteerism and humanitarian efforts. Note the imagery of "**quand dans ma vie il faisait faim.**"

La culture sur place

Question centrale: Qu'est-ce qu'on doit connaître de sa destination pour réussir son voyage?

Les voyages volontaires

Introduction et interrogations

Dans la *Leçon C*, on vous a informé sur les voyages volontaires qui attirent les jeunes Français. Votre but est de définir le volontarisme pour vous et vos camarades de classe. Comment est-ce que vous voulez aider les autres? Que signifient les mots "bénévole" et "humanitaire" pour vous?

8 Première Étape: Réfléchir

1.3, 3.1, 5.1

Pensez à vos préférences et à vos expériences. Qu'est-ce vous aimez (ou aimeriez) faire comme travail bénévole ou humanitaire? Quelques idées:

- construire ou réparer une maison
- travailler avec des jeunes ou des personnes âgées
- enseigner l'anglais
- préserver l'environnement
- fournir de l'eau propre
- autre chose

Trouvez deux ou trois camarades de classe qui ont les mêmes intérêts que vous. Faites des recherches sur Internet pour identifier une communauté où ce genre de travail ferait le plus grand bien.

9 Deuxième Étape: Préparer

1.3, 5.1

*Imaginez que vous voulez commencer votre projet bénévole ou humanitaire dans un autre pays avec vos partenaires, mais vous avez besoin d'un bienfaiteur (*benefactor*) pour vous donner de l'argent. Préparez une présentation pour ce bienfaiteur. La présentation doit inclure:*

- une description de votre projet (ou, quand, comment, qui, etc.)
- une description des objectifs de votre projet (pourquoi; résultats attendus)
- une liste de provisions ou ressources pour le projet
- une liste des bénéficiaires du projet (à qui s'adresse le projet; combien de personnes devraient pouvoir en bénéficier)

10 Faire le point!

1.1, 5.2

Discutez de ces questions en classe.

1. Quels sont les différents centres d'intérêt qui existent dans votre classe vis-à-vis (*regarding*) du travail bénévole ou humanitaire?
2. Si on faisait les projets proposés par votre classe, où irait-on? Qu'est-ce qu'on y ferait?
3. Comment est-ce que vous définiriez les mots "volontarisme," "bénévole," et "humanitaire" aujourd'hui?

Essential Instruction

1. For **Activité 8**, organize students into groups according to their preference for doing volunteer or humanitarian projects. Groups research online what work they could do and where it would have the most impact.
2. For **Activité 9**, encourage students to find mission statements of volunteer organizations to help structure the presentation of the project.
3. Ask a class scribe to record students' remarks for questions one and two of **Activité 10** and categorize them under the headings **bénévole** and **humanitaire**. Make sure to ask students to define **volontairisme**, **bénévole**, and **humanitaire**.
4. Remind the students that the expressions listed on p. 251 introduce the subjunctive in the same way **il faut que** does.

Structure de la langue

emcl.com
WB 6–8
LA 2
Games

The Subjunctive after Impersonal Expressions

1.1

You know that the subjunctive is used after the expression of necessity **il faut que**. There are other impersonal expressions that are followed by the subjunctive. These expressions give an opinion about someone or something specific. Here are some of these impersonal expressions.

il est nécessaire que	*it is necessary that*
il est important que	*it is important that*
il est indispensable que	*it is indispensable that*
il est essentiel que	*it is essential that*
il est possible que	*it is possible that*
il est impossible que	*it is impossible that*
il est bon que	*it is good that*
il est surprenant que	*it is surprising that*
il est utile que	*it is useful that*
il vaut mieux que	*it is better that*
il se pourrait que	*it is possible that*

Il est essentiel que tu **aies** un passeport. — *It is essential that you have a passport.*

Il est nécessaire que vous vous **renseigniez** au consulat.t — *It is necessary that you get informed at the consulate.*

Il est possible que vous **puissiez** réserver à l'avance. — *It is possible that you can reserve in advance.*

Il est bon qu'elle **se fasse vacciner.** — *It is good that she is getting a shot.*

Il est bon que je fasse du ski alpin.

COMPARAISONS

What mood is this sentence in in English? In French?

It is important that you *be* healthy.
Il est important que tu **soies** en forme.

4.1

COMPARAISONS: In a regular sentence in English, you would say "You are healthy," so this use of "be" indicates the subjunctive mood; the subjunctive is triggered by the expression "It is important," just as in the French sentence, which is also in the subjunctive.

RESOURCES

Workbook 6–8

Listening Activity 2

Drill & Practice Games

Reference Desk

1. Point out to the students that in the example **Il est bon qu'elle se fasse vacciner**, only the verb immediately following **que** is in the subjunctive. The second verb remains in the infinitive.
2. Ask students to guess the meaning of **il vaut mieux que** and **il est surprenant que**. The other expressions are similar to English.

Differentiated Learning

Accelerate
Have students work in teams to write as many sentences in the subjunctive as they can in five minutes using the **il est...que** expressions.

Decelerate
Ask students to do the same exercise as **Accelerate** but under your watchful eye.

Special Needs Students

At-Risk Students
Be sensitive to the fact that some of these students might be receiving direct aid from charitable organizations that the class has identified in their community.

AD(H)D/Linguistically Challenged
These students need to know that although there are new expressions that are followed by the subjunctive, the verbs that they have learned do not change. Reassure them that the majority of these expressions are very easy to guess.

Answers

11 *Answers B will vary.*

1. A: Il est possible que tu reçoives 18 sur 20 sur ton contrôle sur le subjonctif?
2. A: Il est possible que tu voyages en France un jour?
3. A: Il est possible que tu skies à Combloux cette année?
4. A: Il est possible que tu te foules la cheville en skiant?
5. A: Il est possible que tu finisses tous tes devoirs ce soir?
6. A: Il est possible que tu discutes de l'économie à table ce soir?
7. A: Il est possible que tu apprennes le chinois un jour?
8. A: Il est possible que tu ailles à une soirée ce soir?
9. A: Il est possible que tu fasses le tour du monde?

12 *Possible answers:*

1. Il est utile que je me renseigne en surfant sur Internet.
2. Il est bon que je planifie ce que je vais voir.
3. Il est nécessaire que je réserve une chambre d'hôtel.
4. Il vaut mieux que je vérifie que j'ai assez de vêtements dans ma valise.
5. Il est important que je mette de la crème solaire.
6. Il est indispensable que je fasse enregistrer mes bagages.
7. Il est essentiel que je parle français.
8. Il est possible que j'aille à Casablanca.
9. Il est bon que je sache dire "s'il te plaît" et "merci" en arabe.
10. Il vaut mieux que je boive du thé à la menthe *(mint)* quand on nous recevra.
11. Il est possible que je voie les souks.

Reference Desk

Casablanca is the economic and cultural capital of Morocco with a population over 3,000,000. It is the largest city in the Maghreb. Casablanca was founded in the seventh century and ruled by the Spanish and Portuguese from 1580 to 1640. It is the largest port in North Africa. The Hassan II mosque is the fifth largest mosque in the world, and its architecture is a mix of Moroccan and French styles.

Communiquez!

11 Possible ou impossible?

1.1, 1.2

Interpersonal Communication

À tour de rôle, demandez à votre partenaire si les situations suivantes sont possibles. Il ou elle va répondre oui ou non.

MODÈLE assister à un mariage cet été

A: **Il est possible que tu ailles à un mariage cet été?**
B: **Oui, il est possible que j'aille à un mariage cet été. Et toi?**
A: **Non, il est impossible que j'aille à un mariage cet été parce que je vais travailler.**

1. recevoir 18 sur 20 sur ton contrôle sur le subjonctif
2. voyager en France un jour
3. skier à Combloux cette année
4. se fouler la cheville en skiant
5. finir tous tes devoirs ce soir
6. discuter de l'économie à table ce soir
7. apprendre le chinois un jour
8. aller à une soirée ce soir
9. faire le tour du monde

12 Mon voyage au Maroc

1.1, 1.2

Vous allez voyager au Maroc. Choisissez une expression de la liste pour former une phrase au subjonctif.

Il est nécessaire que	Il est essentiel que	Il vaut mieux que	Il est utile que
Il est bon que	Il est important que	Il est indispensable que	Il est possible que

MODÈLE avoir un passeport
Il est nécessaire que j'aie un passeport.

1. se renseigner en surfant sur Internet
2. planifier ce que je vais voir
3. réserver une chambre d'hôtel
4. vérifier que j'ai assez de vêtements dans ma valise
5. mettre de la crème solaire
6. faire enregistrer mes bagages
7. parler français
8. aller à Casablanca
9. savoir dire "s'il te plaît" et "merci" en arabe
10. boire du thé à la menthe (*mint*) quand on nous recevra
11. voir les souks

Essential Instruction

1. Randomly pair students to do **Activités 11** and **12.**
2. Circulate among the students to answer questions, correct pronunciation, and to keep them on task.
3. Have students do the listening comprehension practice in **Activité 13.** After they have finished, ask them additional questions about the images A through G for additional oral practice.

Communiquez!

13 Notre séjour au Sénégal

1.1, 1.2

Interpretive Communication

Écrivez les numéros 1–7 sur votre papier. Écoutez les phrases, puis choisissez l'image qui correspond.

A. 

B. 

C. 

D. 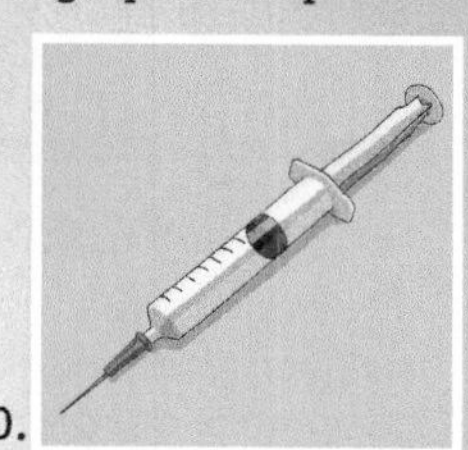

E. 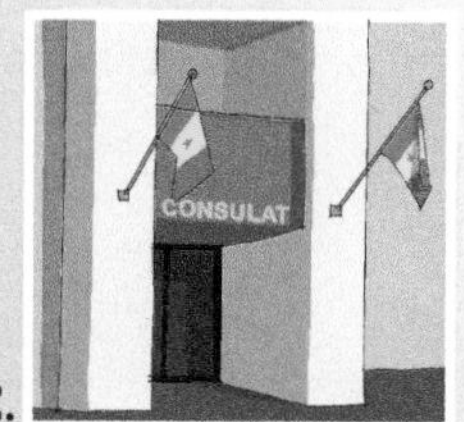

F. 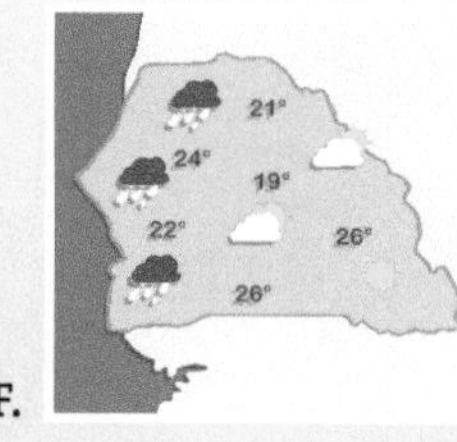

G. 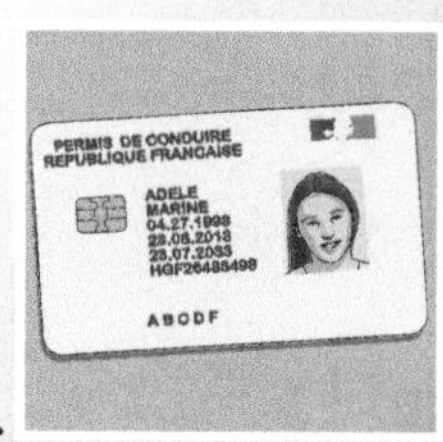

Communiquez!

14 Des situations

1.1, 5.2

Il est important qu'on s'inscrive pour aider cette association!

Interpersonal Communication

Avec deux camarades de classe, dites ce qu'il faut faire dans chaque situation. Utilisez les expressions de la liste suivante.

il est nécessaire que il faut que il est indispensable que il est important que il est essentiel que il vaut mieux que

MODÈLE organiser une fête d'anniversaire pour Nicolas

A: **Pour organiser une fête d'anniversaire pour Nicolas, il est important que j'invite tous ses copains.**
B: **Il est important que je lui achète un cadeau qu'il aime.**
C: **Il est indispensable que je prépare un gâteau d'anniversaire.**

1. protéger l'environnement
2. réussir à l'école
3. être bon élève ou bonne élève
4. faire du babysitting
5. avoir de bons amis
6. trouver un travail intéressant
7. être en forme
8. être heureux/heureuse

Differentiated Learning

Accelerate

Students go online to find visuals like photos or clip art, or they use their own drawings to make flash cards of situations in which the **il est... que** expressions could be used. They lead a review for the class. For example, they might find an advertisement of a mother helping her son: **Il est bon que la mère aide son fils.**

Decelerate

Students use white boards to do a guided ten-minute review of regular and irregular verbs in the subjunctive before doing **Activités 13** and **14.** Encourage them to use online practice programs.
Search words: conjuguemos

Answers

Script can be found in the front pages of the Annotated Teacher's Edition.

1. A
2. C
3. B
4. D
5. E
6. F
7. G

14 *Possible answers:*

1. Pour protéger l'environnement, il vaut mieux que mes parents conduisent une voiture hybride/ il est nécessaire qu'on recycle les bouteilles en plastique/il faut que le gouvernement fasse marcher les usines avec des éoliennes./
2. Pour réussir à l'école, il faut que chacun étudie sérieusement/il est important qu'on ait de bonnes notes /il est indispensable que les profs aident les élèves./
3. Pour être bon élève ou bonne élève, il vaut mieux que j'écoute le prof/il est indispensable que je fasse tous mes devoirs/il est essentiel que je ne sois pas souvent absent(e)./
4. Pour faire du babysitting, il est essentiel que j'aime les enfants/il est important qu'on sache donner les premiers secours/il vaut mieux qu'on soit organisé./
5. Pour avoir de bons amis, il est important qu'on sache écouter les autres/il vaut mieux que je ne sois pas jaloux (jalouse)/il faut que je sois honnête./
6. Pour trouver un travail intéressant, il est nécessaire que je cherche un travail tous les jours/il vaut mieux que tu aies un bon diplôme/il vaut mieux qu'il y ait peu de chômage./
7. Pour être en forme, il est indispensable que nous fassions du sport régulièrement/ il faut que les gens mangent sainement/ il est important que les parents apprennent aux enfants à bien manger./
8. Pour être heureux/heureuse, il est nécessaire qu'on soit sympa/il est important qu'on ait une famille et des amis/ il est nécessaire qu'on puisse poursuivre ses rêves./

RESOURCES

Communicative Activities

Answers

All activities will vary.

Reference Desk

Blended Instruction

Consider using blended instruction, a combination of in-class learning and computer-mediated instruction or learning opportunities. Ask students to complete activities on the computer, using their cell or smartphone, or other emerging electronic technology. This will allow students to hone their tech skills and become more independent learners. Schedule routine Internet and e-book learning in class and in the lab.

À vous la parole

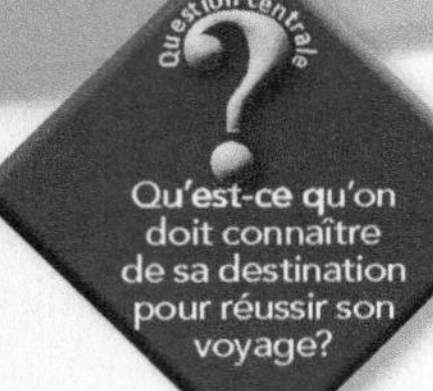

15 Les stations de ski

1.3

Presentational Communication

Créez une carte avec les stations de ski des Alpes qui sont mentionnées dans cette unité. Pour chaque station de ski, ajoutez un repère (*marker*) et une photo ou une vidéo. Écrivez un petit paragraphe qui décrit chaque station de ski.

Communiquez!

16 Théo à l'hôpital

1.1, 1.3, 5.2

Presentational Communication

Pendant la classe de neige, votre camarade de classe Théo s'est cassé la jambe en skiant. Un hélicoptère l'a ramené (*took back*) à Nice, où il est maintenant à l'hôpital. Créez un blogue où vous lui dites ce qui se passe pendant les cours et à la station de ski de Megève. Choisissez un camarade de classe pour jouer le rôle de Théo, qui va répondre aux messages.

Communiquez!

17 Les sports d'hiver

1.3

Presentational Communication

Créez un projet dont le but est d'informer les gens sur les sports d'hiver. Pour chaque sport:

- Faites une description qui comprend les risques
- Faites une liste de l'équipement nécessaire
- Donnez les meilleurs endroits où on peut pratiquer ces sports dans votre région, en France, ou au Canada

Essential Instruction

1. Consider assigning **Activités 15**, **16**, and **17** to students according to their learning styles and personalities.
2. **Activité 15** may appeal to visual learners and those with an artistic bent.
3. **Activité 16** is an interactive activity for students who like collaborating on projects. Your extroverts could transform this activity into a play in which Théo is skiing, falls, breaks his leg, and is transported back to Nice.
4. **Activité 17** is perfect for logical-sequential learners who like lists and statistics presented in an organized format.
5. Have students complete **Stratégie de lecture** after reading the poem. It serves as the framework for a class discussion of the structure and themes of the poem.
6. Have students identify the poem's mythical allusions.

Lecture thématique

Pre AP

Heureux qui, comme Ulysse, a fait un beau voyage

Rencontre avec l'auteur  1.2

Joachim Du Bellay (1522–1560) était un poète de la Renaissance française qui a fait ses études dans un collège humaniste. Il a écrit son recueil (*collection*) de poèmes *Les regrets* pendant un long séjour en Italie, destination de beaucoup de jeunes Français et artistes qui voulaient voir la grandeur de l'Italie antique et les chefs-d'œuvre de la Renaissance. En 1533, avec Ronsard, il a fondé un groupe de poètes, la Pléiade, dont le but était de définir de nouvelles règles poétiques. Il est mort très jeune, à 37 ans, et on l'a enterré à Notre-Dame. Son poème le plus célèbre est celui que vous allez lire. Le poète est-il content à Rome ou est-ce qu'il a des regrets?

Pré-lecture 1.3

Quel voyage est-ce que vous voudriez faire?

Stratégie de lecture  1.2,1.3

Structure, Meaning, and Theme

Ce poème est un sonnet en alexandrins avec deux quatrains et deux tercets; un quatrain est une strophe (*stanza*) avec quatre lignes, tandis qu'un tercet en a trois. Dans ces quatre strophes, le poète développe un thème. Remplissez l'organigramme avec l'idée centrale de chaque strophe; au centre mettez le thème du poème.

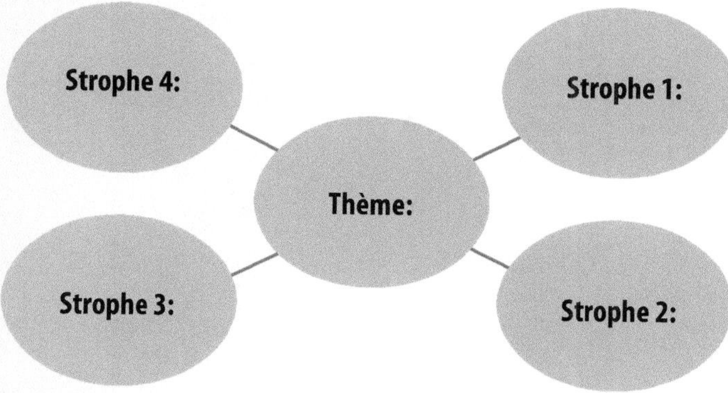

Outils de lecture  1.1, 1.2, 1.3

Allusions

Une allusion est une référence à une personne, événement, objet, ou œuvre de l'histoire ou de la littérature. Du Bellay se sert de deux allusions classiques. Vous les trouverez dans les deux premières lignes du poème. Recherchez ces deux allusions mythiques. Comment est-ce qu'elles renforcent son idée d'un "beau voyage"?

Answers

Rencontre avec l'auteur
L'auteur semble avoir des regrets.

Pré-lecture
Answers will vary.

Stratégie de lecture
Possible answers.
Thème: les voyages
Strophe 1: Les voyages ouvrent l'esprit.
Strophe 2: Le poète a la nostalgie de sa maison.
Strophe 3: Le poète préfère son pays aux merveilles du monde.
Strophe 4: Le poète se rappelle son univers qui lui manque.

Outils de lecture
Possible answers.
L'auteur fait allusion au grand voyage d'Ulysse, et à la conquête de la Toison d'or.

Reference Desk

La Pléiade is a name ascribed to a group of 16th century French Renaissance poets whose principal members were Pierre de Ronsard, Joachim du Bellay, and Jean-Antoine de Baïf. These poets sought to integrate classical literary styles like the ode and sonnet, and celebrate the beauty of the French language.

Special Needs Students

Social Anxiety
When pairing students for this activity, make sure that those with social anxiety can work with someone with whom they feel comfortable. Rather than asking them to perform for the class, you may want to ask them to speak in front of another pair of students or just for you.

Linguistically Challenged
For students who are new to French poetry, preview difficult vocabulary and expressions and translate difficult lines into English. Once they understand the poem, they will be more willing to participate in class discussions. Make a copy of the poem for each of them so that they can write notes and comments.

Answers

Pendant la lecture

1. Ulysse /les voyageurs
2. Ulysse/celui qui a voyagé
3. hélas
4. à sa maison (son pays, son village)
5. l'ardoise
6. à Rome
7. dans les pays de la Loire, chez lui

Post-lecture

Pour le poète, les grands sites de la Rome antique sont moins importants que les petits paysages de son pays natal.

Reference Desk

Joachim Du Bellay was living in Italy when he wrote "**Heureux qui Comme Ulysse.**" He thinks of his beloved region of Anjou, a former province in the Loire valley.

Communication

Interpersonal: Cooperative Groups

1. Distribute the lyrics to Brassens's "**Heureux qui Comme Ulysse.**" Select a rendition on the Internet to show to your students.
2. Listen once. Students underline difficult words.
3. Complete **Activité 18** number two in heterogeneous groups.
4. Discuss common points of the two poems. What elements has Brassens added to the poem to personalize it for him? Which area of France corresponds to "**la douceur angévine**" for Brassens? (**La Provence**) What is **la Camargue** noted for? (horses and cowboys)

1.2

Heureux qui, comme Ulysse, a fait un beau voyage,
Ou comme cestuy-là*, qui conquit* la toison*,
Et puis est retourné, plein d'usage et raison,
Vivre entre ses parents le reste de son âge!

Quand reverrai-je, hélas*, de mon petit village
Fumer la cheminée, et en quelle saison
Reverrai-je le clos* de ma pauvre maison,
Qui m'est une province, et beaucoup davantage*?

Plus me plaît le séjour* qu'ont bâti* mes aïeux,
Que des palais Romains le front audacieux,
Plus que le marbre* dur me plaît l'ardoise* fine:

Plus mon Loir gaulois*, que le Tibre* latin,
Plus mon petit Liré, que le mont Palatin,
Et plus que l'air marin* la doulceur* angevine*.

Pendant la lecture
1. Qui a fait un beau voyage?

Pendant la lecture
2. Qui est retourné "plein d'usage et raison"?

Pendant la lecture
3. Quel mot indique le regret?

Pendant la lecture
4. À quoi pense le poète?

Pendant la lecture
5. Quel matériel vient de sa région, le marbre ou l'ardoise?

Pendant la lecture
6. Où sont le Tibre et le mont Palatin?

Pendant la lecture
7. Où est-ce que le poète préfère vivre, à Rome ou dans les pays de la Loire?

---

cestuy-là celui-là (Ancien français); **conquit** *conquered;* **toison** *Golden Fleece;* **hélas** *alas;* **clos** *property;* **séjour** *dwelling;* **bâti** *built;* **marbre** *marble;* **ardoise** *slate (used on roofs in Loire Valley);* **gaulois** *gallic, or French;* **Tibre** *Tiber* (fleuve à Rome); **air marin** *sea air;* **doulceur** *sweetness;* **angevine** *from, or of Angers area*

Post-lecture

1.3

Les sites classiques de Rome sont-ils plus ou moins importants pour le narrateur que les sites de chez lui?

Essential Instruction

1. Play the poem, books closed; have students guess what the poem is about. Take note of words students recognized. Put these expressions on the board for later.
2. Play the poem a second time, books open, stopping after each **strophe** to answer the questions in the margin.
3. Compare the allusions to Rome and Anjou. Determine which location is more important to the narrator. (**Post-Lecture**)
4. Work in groups to answer **Activité 18**, numbers one and three.
5. Discuss the theme of **nostalgie**. Ask students how they feel when they are away from home, friends, and family. Put ideas on the board for students to copy and use in their journal entry in **Activité 18**, number three.

Le monde visuel  1.2, 3.1

Ulysse découvre Astyanax caché dans le tombeau d'Hector, c. 1654–1656. Sébastien Bourdon. Collection privée.

Sébastien Bourdon (1616–1671), peintre français, a peint *Ulysse découvre Astyanax caché dans le tombeau d'Hector* dans le style classique. Ce mouvement s'intéressait aux sujets classiques de la tradition grecque et romaine comme les histoires d'Ulysse, roi d'Ithaca, leader dans la guerre de Troie, et voyageur par excellence pour ses aventures en revenant de la guerre. Les classiques aimaient la proportion, les couleurs vives, et la formalité. Ils peignaient leurs sujets dans les vêtements de leur époque, souvent parmi des urnes et des piliers (*pillers*). La composition de ces tableaux est souvent symétrique. Quelles sont les caractéristiques classiques de ce tableau?

18 Activités d'expansion  1.3, 3.1, 5.1

Faites les activités suivantes.

1. Quel est le thème du poème? Comment est-ce que Du Bellay le développe? Citez les expressions du poème qui soutiennent votre point de vue. N'oubliez pas de mentionner comment le poète organise ses idées. Servez-vous de l'organigramme que vous avez rempli.
2. Imaginez que vous êtes Élodie des *Rencontres culturelles*. Écrivez un passage dans votre journal où vous parlez de votre nostalgie pour votre maison, votre chambre, votre famille, et votre bande de copains pendant que vous êtes en classe de neige.

 Search words: **vidéo georges brassens heureux qui comme ulysse**

3. Explorez comment le chanteur Georges Brassens a développé sa chanson "Heureux qui comme Ulysse" et comparez-la à l'original de Du Bellay.

Georges Brassens.

RESOURCES

 **Pre-test**

 ***Leçon* Quiz**

Answers

Le monde visuel
Les proportions sont réalistes, la symétrie équilibrée met en valeur chaque élément de la scène; les couleurs vives font un contraste avec les couleurs sombres.

1. *Possible answers*: Le thème: les grands voyages; le poète contraste le pays visité au pays natal du voyageur; Le poète fait usage de constructions grammaticales de comparaison: plus...que; l'organisation des idées: Strophe 1: les voyages apportent la sagesse et il est bon de rentrer à la maison.; Strophe 2: Le poète est en voyage et sa maison lui manque.; Strophe 3: Le poète compare son village aux grands lieux touristiques qu'il visite.; Strophe 4: Le poète insiste que son village lui plaît davantage que Rome.
2. *Answers will vary*.
3. *Answers will vary*.

Reference Desk

Humanism sees man as the measure of all things. It emphasizes the enjoyment of life on earth, the pursuit of beauty, and a return to the classic literature of Greece and Rome. In the Renaissance, the emphasis is on the enjoyment of life on earth rather than the strict medieval monastic view in which life is only a preparation for heaven.

Differentiated Learning

Accelerate
Students read **Le monde visuel** and prepare a presentation of the painting ***Ulysse découvre Astyanax caché dans le tombeau d'Hector*** to the class. What is the style of painting? Who are the people in the scene and what are they doing? What emotion does the painter convey?

Decelerate
Have students research the mythology of Ulysses, (Odysseus), Helen, Hector, and Astyanax. Ask them to present the story as a fairy tale, news commentary, or an historical event.

Answers

All activities will vary.

Reference Desk

Ridan (**né** Nadir Kouidri) was born in France in 1975. He is of Algerian descent, and the difficult life of Arab immigrants in France is a recurring theme in his music. His stage name, Ridan, is Nadir in **verlan.** His popular single "**Heureux qui comme Ulysse**" appeared on his second album, "**L'Ange de Mon Démon**" (2007) which is a blend of reggae, ska, rap, electro, and song.

T'es branché?

Projets finaux

A Connexions par Internet: La littérature

1.2, 1.3, 3.1, 3.2

Presentational Communication

Dans cette unité vous avez lu le poème "Heureux qui, comme Ulysse, a fait un beau voyage" par Du Bellay. Regardez le dessin animé de Ridan et son interprétation du poème. Ensuite, créez un storyboard où vous dessinez votre propre vidéo du poème qui en montre votre interprétation.

Search words: ridan heureux qui comme ulysse vidéo

B Communautés en ligne

3.1, 3.2

Le chien du Saint Bernard/Interpretive Communication

Visitez un club pour les passionnés du chien du Saint Bernard pour trouver les réponses à ces questions:

- Quelle est la devise du chien du Saint Bernard?
- Comment est-il physiquement?
- Comment décrit-on son caractère?
- Il est connu pour quels exploits?
- Il a quels problèmes de santé?
- Il est la vedette de quels films?
- Il faut payer combien pour avoir un chien du Saint Bernard?

Search words: chien du saint bernard

C Passez à l'action!

1.3, 3.1, 3.2, 5.1, 5.2

Le woofing: un voyage bénévole/Presentational Communication

Créez un document qui décrit ce qu'est le woofing. Faites une carte qui montre dans quels pays francophones on peut faire du woofing. Faites une liste de dix projets qui vous intéressent. Avec votre classe, choisissez parmi tous les projets, un projet que vous pourriez sponsoriser. Contactez l'organisation bénévole pour savoir s'ils préfèrent recevoir de l'argent ou du matériel. Organisez une collecte auprès de votre lycée.

D Faisons le point!

1.3

Servez-vous de l'organigramme que votre prof va vous donner. Remplissez-le avec vos connaissances.

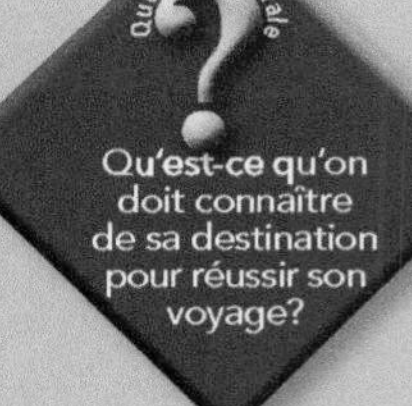

Essential Instruction

1. Have students read **Projets finaux** (**A**, **B**, or **C**) and create groups according to their preferred project. Provide a rubric that indicates your expectations and point values.
2. Make sure that students have access to the computer lab since not all of them have Internet access or computers at home.
3. For **Activité D**, p. 258, distribute copies of the graphic organizer located in the **Copy Masters** supplement. Impress upon students that filling in this form will give them an overview of what they know and what they need to study.
4. Have all students complete **Activité B** p. 259 as a vocabulary review.

Évaluation

Pre AP

emcl.com LA Synthèse

A Évaluation de compréhension auditive

1.1, 1.2

Interpretive Communication

On part à la montagne.

*Écrivez les numéros 1–7 sur votre papier. Écoutez Armelle et Amadou discuter de leur projet de vacances à la montagne. Ensuite, indiquez si les phrases que vous entendez sont vraies (**V**) ou fausses (**F**).*

B Évaluation orale

1.1, 5.2

Interpersonal Communication

Jouez les rôles de trois ados français qui planifient un voyage à Combloux.

A: Proposez Combloux.
B: Demandez ce qu'on peut y faire.
C: Dites ce que vous y avez fait la dernière fois.
B: Dites que vous ne savez pas faire du ski alpin.
A: Dites-lui qu'il ou elle peut apprendre d'un moniteur et parlez d'autres choses qu'il ou elle aura l'occasion de faire à Combloux.
B: Dites qu'il faut que vous reveniez en skiant correctement cette fois.
C: Dites-lui qu'il est important qu'il ou qu'elle ne se foule pas la cheville avant le mariage de sa sœur en mars.
A: Demandez si vos amis sont persuadés qu'il faut y aller.
B-C: Répondez.

C Évaluation culturelle

3.2, 4.2, 5.1

Vous allez comparer les cultures francophones à la culture américaine. Vous aurez peut-être besoin de faire des recherches sur la culture américaine.

1. **La Réunion et Hawaï**
   Comparez les îles de la Réunion et d'Hawaï en matière de géologie, population, activité économique, situation géographique.
2. **Les Alpes, le Mont Blanc, et les stations de ski**
   Cette région de la France peut être comparée à quelle région américaine? Pourquoi? Et dans cette région américaine, comment est la flore? Et la faune? Sont-elles comparables à la Savoie?
3. **La Savoie**
   Quels attributs font une "terre de culture," "terre gastronomique," et "terre de tourisme" de cette région? De votre région?
4. **Les classes de neige**
   Qu'est-ce qui se passe en classe de neige? Avez-vous l'occasion de voyager et de participer à un sport alors que vous êtes au lycée? Si non, qu'est-ce que vous proposeriez au directeur ou à la directrice de votre lycée pour vivre un séjour semblable (*similar*)?

RESOURCES

Listening Activity *Synthèse*

Answers

Script can be found in the front pages of the Annotated Teacher's Edition.

1. V
2. F
3. V
4. V
5. V
6. F
7. V

B *Activities will vary.*

C *Activities will vary.*

Reference Desk

The activities in **Évaluation** require students to synthesize the information that they have learned in this unit. Provide time to review vocabulary prior to completing **Activitiés B** and **C.**

Differentiated Learning

Accelerate

Encourage students preparing to take the AP exam to do **Activité A** individually and prepare **Activité B** in groups of three to present in front of you.

Decelerate

Have students work in pairs to do two out of the five options in **Activité C.**

Special Needs Students

AD(H)D

These students may have difficulty organizing their materials and their time. Help students to create a schedule for their **Projet final.** Work with them to establish due dates for their part of the project. Schedule check-in meetings to discuss resources, process, and progress.

Answers

All activities will vary.

Expansion

To prepare to write **Activité D**, have small groups do some brainstorming. List reasons to participate in **un voyage humanitaire**, think of expressions used to give one's opinion, and come up with questions one might ask to get information about a trip to Africa or the Antilles. Remind students that one way to give an opinion is to use the impersonal expressions they learned on p. 251.

5. **Les voyageurs volontaires**
Existe-t-il des organisations bénévoles dans votre ville ou région? Quelles sont-elles? Les avez-vous déjà aidées? Quels pays francophones ont besoin d'aide? À quoi est-ce que vous pourriez contribuer dans ces endroits?

D Évaluation écrite

Vous avez écrit une lettre à votre cousin pour lui proposer d'aller faire du ski dans les Alpes. Il vous répond en vous proposant un voyage différent: un voyage humanitaire en Afrique ou aux Antilles. Dites ce que vous en pensez, et demandez-lui plus de renseignements. Dites ce que vous êtes prêt(e) à faire.

E Évaluation visuelle

Décrivez ce qu'on fait à cette station de ski.

F Évaluation compréhensive

Créez une histoire avec six illustrations: dessinez une semaine de classes de neige dans les Alpes. Écrivez des légendes qui expliquent votre histoire ou racontez les aventures des ados à votre groupe.

Essential Instruction

1. Assign **Activité D** as an in-class activity. Give students ten minutes to write an outline of what they want to say. Circulate to answer questions. The input students get before they write helps to reduce the number of corrections needed later. Immediate feedback provides the input they need to do a good job.
2. **Activité E** could be done in the computer lab. If equipment is available, have students record their description of the scene.
3. Divide the class into small groups to complete **Activité F.** Provide paper for the group's six illustrations. This activity can be done as a competition. Set a time limit; allow groups to work and when time is called, have them post their drawings. Have students take a museum walk to view the final products and vote on the best representation. Decide with the class what judging criteria will be used.

Vocabulaire de l'Unité 4  1.2

abandonner to abandon *C*
s' **attendre (à)** to expect (something) *B*
avoir: avoir l'occasion (de) to have the opportunity (to) *B*
aucun(e) any, none, no one *A*; **aucun de nous ne (+ verb)** none of us (+ verb) *A*
un **bâton de ski** ski pole *B*
le **bénévolat** volunteer work *C*
se **casser**: **se casser le poignet** to break one's wrist *C*
les **chaussures (f.): chaussures de ski** ski boots *B*
une **classe: classe de neige** ski class *B*
le **consulat** consulate *C*
correctement correctly *B*
de: de toute façon in any case *B*
différemment differently *A*
dire: (noun) te dit? How do you feel about (noun)? *A*
le **domaine** property *C*
emporter to take (away) *C*
en upon, while *A*; **en skiant** while skiing *B*; **en y réfléchissant bien** on second thought *A*; **en y regardant de plus près** on a closer look *A*
s' **ennuyer** to get bored *A*
faire: faire de la luge to go sledding *C*; **faire de la planche à voile** to wind surf *A*; **faire de la raquette à neige** to go snowshoeing *C*; **faire de l'escalade** to rock climb *A*; **faire des sauts à ski** to go off ski jumps *A*; **faire du saut à l'élastique** to bungee jump *A*; **faire du ski de fond** to cross-country ski *A*; **faire du ski joering** to skijor *C*; **faire du snowboard** to snowboard *B*; **faire du speed riding** to speed ride *C*; **faire du taxi-ski** to take a ski-taxi ride *C*; **faire du telemark** to telemark ski *C*; **faire le coup (à quelqu'un)** to play a trick (on someone) *A*; **faire sa valise** to pack *B*; **faire une randonnée équestre** to go on a trail ride *A*; **faire un séjour** to stay *C*
se **faire: se faire vacciner** to get a shot *C*
un **forfait de ski** ski pass *B*
se **fouler: se fouler la cheville** to sprain an ankle *C*
un **fuseau de ski** ski pants *B*
les **gants (m.)** gloves *B*
le **hors-piste** off-piste skiing *C*
humide humid *A*
il: il est essentiel que it's essential that *C*; **il est indispensable que** it's indispensable that *C*; **il est important que** it's important that *C*; **il est surprenant que** it's surprising that *C*; **il est utile que** it's useful that *C*; **il se pourrait que** it's possible that *C*; **il vaut mieux que** it's better that *C*
une **île** island *A*
un **masque: masque de ski** ski goggles *B*
un **moniteur, une monitrice** instructor *B*
ne: ne (n')... aucun(e) no, none, not any, not one *A*; **ne (n')... ni... ni** neither... nor *A*; **ne (n')... que** only *A*
obtenir to obtain *C*
l' **office (m.) de tourisme** tourist office *C*
organisé(e) organized *B*
le **passé** past *C*
un **passeport** passport *C*
persuadé(e) convinced *A*
une **pièce: pièce d'identité** identification *C*
une **piste (de ski)** (ski) slope *B*
planifier to plan *A*
les **préparatifs (m.) de départ** travel preparations *C*
se **renseigner** to get information *C*
la **Réunion** Reunion *A*
sans aucun doute without a doubt *A*
seulement only *A*
le **ski** ski *B*; **ski de fond** cross-country skiing *A*
le **snowboard** snowboarding *C*
le **sommet** peak *A*
une **station: station de ski** ski resort *B*
sur: sur place on the premises *B*
un **télésiège** ski lift *B*
tout(e): tout schuss full throttle *A*
un **tremplin de saut à ski** ski jump *B*
tu: tu n'y es pas du tout you don't get it *A*
le **Vietnam** Vietnam *C*
un **visa** visa *C*
un **volcan** volcano *A*

RESOURCES

 **Listening Pre-test D**

 ***Unité* Test**

Game

Pictionnaire

Play Pictionary to review vocabulary from **Unité 4**. Divide the class into groups of five. In advance prepare five sets of index cards with vocabulary from p. 261. The fifth player becomes **l'arbitre** (*the ref*). He or she chooses a card from the list and shows it to the two players who draw. The first partner to guess the word correctly wins the round. For round two, the ref shows a new card to the other players whose turn it is to draw.

Differentiated Learning

Accelerate

Encourage students to make word groups of the vocabulary, for example, ski clothing, equipment, subjunctive, verbs, and expressions. As students review, have them add more terms to their lists.

Decelerate

Students might opt to use flash cards or online tools to review vocabulary. They could work in groups to quiz each other.

Special Needs Students

At-Risk Students

Students with weak study skills might need help getting organized to review for the test.

Dyslexia

Encourage these students to jot down grammar charts, vocabulary, or cultural information onto their test when they receive it. As they work their way through the test, they can refer to their notes.

RESOURCES

 Listening Units 3-4

Answers

1. D

Script can be found in the front pages of the Annotated Teacher's Edition.
1. B
2. B
3. D

Reference Desk

1. The **Bilan cumulatif** is based on the French Language and Culture AP exam prepared by the College Board. It assesses students' proficiencies in the Interpersonal, Interpretive, and Presentational modes of communication. Students are also asked to demonstrate their understanding of the products, practices, and perspectives of the target cultures.
2. The Print Text section consists of a variety of authentic print materials such as articles and correspondence. A multiple-choice question follows the text.
3. The Audio Text is a professional recording, usually a dialogue. Encourage students to preview and skim the questions before listening. They should then answer the multiple-choice questions.

Unité 4 Bilan cumulatif 

I. Interpretive Communication: Print texts  1.1, 1.2

Lisez ce reportage sur les initiatives en France aujourd'hui, puis répondez à la question.

Les jeunes et le bricolage? Certains d'entre eux ont anticipé une opportunité incroyable de créer une petite société qui offrirait des services de réparation, d'entretien et de rénovation dans les condos, HLM, maisons individuelles et maisons mitoyennes. Ils offrent toutes sortes de projets de bricolage—peindre les murs, poser le papier peint, accrocher des peintures, changer la moquette ou installer du parquet en bois.

1. Selon cet article, cette initiative s'est créée parce que....
   A. c'est une affaire familiale de père en fils
   B. le gouvernement encourage les jeunes à être créatifs
   C. le bricolage n'est pas très à la mode avec les jeunes
   D. les jeunes sont des entrepreneurs.

II. Interpretive Communication: Audio texts  1.1, 1.2

Écoutez le dialogue deux fois, puis répondez aux questions en choisissant la lettre correcte.

1. Où est-ce que Nora et Bruno vont faire du ski?
   A. dans les Vosges
   B. en Savoie
   C. dans les Pyrénées
   D. en Italie
2. Quand ils ont planifié le voyage, qu'est-ce qu'ils ont décidé de faire avant de partir?
   A. réserver un condo
   B. obtenir des forfaits de ski
   C. acheter des billets de train
   D. A, B, et C
3. Qu'est-ce qui est vrai en ce qui concerne Bruno?
   A. Il sait bien faire du ski alpin.
   B. Il a déjà goûté à la raclette savoyarde.
   C. Il veut faire du taxi-ski et de la luge.
   D. Il n'a ni skis ni bâtons, mais il compte les louer sur place.

III. Presentational Writing: Persuasive Essay  1.3

Vous allez écrire un essai persuasif basé sur une source que vous allez lire d'abord. Votre but est de présenter les différents points de vue soulevés par la source, puis de donner votre propre point de vue. Utilisez des exemples précis de la source pour soutenir votre point de vue.

Essential Instruction

1. Have students skim the questions before completing **Activité I.**
2. Ask students to do the same before listening to the dialogue in **Activité II.** Have them listen and write down their answers. Give immediate feedback.
3. Read the instructions together for **Activité III.** Make sure the students understand what is required of them.
4. Have pairs read the blogs and administration's response to the issue on p. 263. Encourage the students to work together to understand each person's point of view before completing their own essay.

Votre thème:  1.2, 1.3

En 2011, l'Union Européenne célèbre l'Année européenne du bénévolat et du volontariat. Malgré la générosité des gens qui voudraient aider, on trouve souvent que les associations utilisent une partie des aides qu'elles reçoivent des personnes pour couvrir les frais de logement, de nourriture et même les salaires de leurs employés. Des jeunes protestent contre cela et affirment que leurs paiements profitent aux riches. Qu'en pensez-vous?

Lisez les réponses d'un blogue à ce sujet:

Lina:
Bonjour à tous! Je suis étudiante et j'aimerais rejoindre une mission éco-volontaire au Sénégal pour un mois. Mais on me demande 2.000 euros (sans compter le billet d'avion!). C'est trop pour mon budget! Je ne comprends pas pourquoi on doit payer pour travailler! Je voudrais simplement apporter mon aide et ma motivation en échange du logement. On veut nous persuader qu'il faut avoir de l'argent pour aider les gens qui n'en ont pas! C'est absurde!

Jonathan:
Oui, moi aussi, je me demande pourquoi il faut payer pour participer dans le bénévolat humanitaire. Bien sûr, de nombreux projets ont besoin d'argent pour exister. Et nous, en participant, on gagne. Mais si c'est l'aide des personnes volontaires qui doit couvrir la nourriture et le logement, ce n'est pas possible. C'est dommage qu'il ne soit pas plus facile de partir aider juste pour aider comme le dit Lina.

Maël:
Le bénévolat? C'est un business. Faites attention! On vous offre le rêve, mais à un prix! Comme ça les associations peuvent sélectionner des volontaires ou éliminer des gens qui veulent profiter de vacances pas chères. Oui, certaines missions privées (surtout celles qui cherchent à sauver des animaux) coûtent beaucoup. Mais est-ce que c'est nous qui devons payer pour aider? Et sait-on véritablement où va l'argent que nous donnons?

Suzanne:
Vous avez parfaitement raison. C'est triste qu'on doive payer pour travailler. Il y a des millions de gens qui souhaitent sincèrement aider dame nature. Mais si nous avons à payer aussi cher, c'est trop décourageant. Comme vous, j'aimerais connaitre des associations pour lesquelles je n'aie qu'à payer mon billet d'avion.

Admin:
Bonjour à tous! Je tiens à vous rappeler que dans un monde parfait, toute personne devrait avoir la possibilité de participer (et d'être logée et nourrie) dans un projet bénévole sans payer un centime, ou peut-être juste le voyage. Mais ce n'est pas aussi simple. La structure économique des missions varie, et il y a toujours un coût. Certaines associations reçoivent de l'aide gouvernementale et d'autres dépendent des dons du public ou des fondations. Il y en a d'autres qui sont plus commerciales ou financées par une formule touristique. Il ne faut pas non plus penser que les associations qui demandent un paiement ne sont pas sérieuses. Parfois, il n'est pas nécessaire de voyager loin de votre communauté locale pour apporter de l'aide. L'important, c'est de trouver une activité qui corresponde à vos moyens et de vous engager pour la protection de la planète.

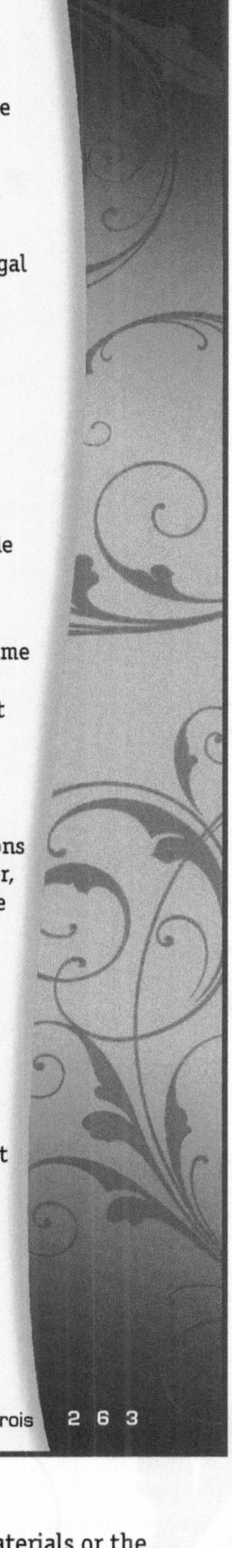

Differentiated Learning

Accelerate/Decelerate
Group the students heterogeneously to discuss the blog responses before proceeding to the writing.

Special Needs Students

Dyslexia
You may want to give dyslexic students the opportunity to read the paragraphs in advance. Give them extra time to answer questions.

At-Risk Students
These students often lack the materials or the setting they need to successfully prepare for tests at home. If possible, arrange for some guided study during class.

AD(H)D
Taking the tests in segments to avoid dealing with too much information at once might take some of the stress away from testing.

Expansion

Add another character to the conversation dialogue. This person will play the role of a third colleague. He or she will have a different place in mind to take the class and offer information and activities to do in that region. At the end of the dialogue, the most convincing party will have gained the approval of all.

IV. Interpretive Speaking: Conversation 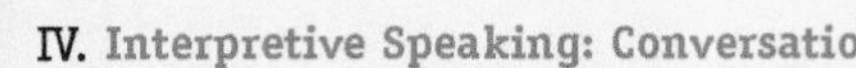 1.1, 1.2, 1.3, 5.2

Vous allez avoir une conversation avec Marc, un collègue qui enseigne dans la même école que vous. Ensemble, vous allez parler des préparatifs pour la classe de neige de l'hiver prochain. Suivez les indications suivantes.

Marc: Le directeur de l'école m'a demandé de vous aider à planifier la classe de neige. Il faut réserver le séjour bien à l'avance. L'Italie? La Suisse? Qu'en pensez-vous?

Vous: **Parlez des stations que vous connaissez en Savoie et de vos préférences.**

Marc: Vous avez raison. Pas besoin d'aller trop loin pour trouver de la neige. Je vais m'occuper de l'hébergement, des billets de train et des cours de ski.

Vous: **Demandez ce que les élèves doivent emporter dans leurs valises.**

Marc: Nous aurons l'occasion d'en parler lors des réunions avec les parents d'élèves. N'oublions pas l'importance de l'assurance médicale pour tout le monde!

Vous: **Rappelez au collègue que vous avez peur des accidents sur la piste.**

Marc: Rassurez-vous! Les moniteurs vont nous accompagner. Nous ne faisons pas de ski hors-piste! Mais, avez-vous des idées pour des cours?

Vous: **Parlez des activités scolaires et culturelles que vous pouvez ajouter au programme.**

Marc: Ça vous dit de fêter la fin de la semaine avec un repas spécial pour tout le groupe au chalet?

Vous: **Suggérez qu'on prépare des spécialités savoyardes.**

Marc: Nous mettrons des photos sur le blogue du voyage. Je ne m'attendais pas à avoir tant à faire pour organiser un tel voyage. Heureusement que vous êtes bien organisé(e)!

Essential Instruction

Give students a few minutes to read the questions before listening/viewing the dialogue. Remind them to use the instructions in bold print to help them structure their responses to the comments.

Unité 5 Comment se renseigner en voyage

265

Reference Desk

1. The Principality of Monaco is smaller than Central Park in New York. Its 30,000 inhabitants live in this Mediterranean tourist resort town whose major income is derived from casinos. With no income tax, and low business taxes, it is a haven for individuals and corporations. The principality is a constitutional monarchy. Prince Albert II is its head of state.
2. Monte Carlo is the administrative district of Monaco. The Monte Carlo casino, the **Hôtel de Paris**, the **Café de Paris**, and the **Salle Garnier**, home of the Monte Carlo opera, are its most famous tourist attractions. Sports fans enjoy the Formula One Monte Carlo Grand Prix, the Monte Carlo Rally, and the Rolex Masters Tennis tournament.

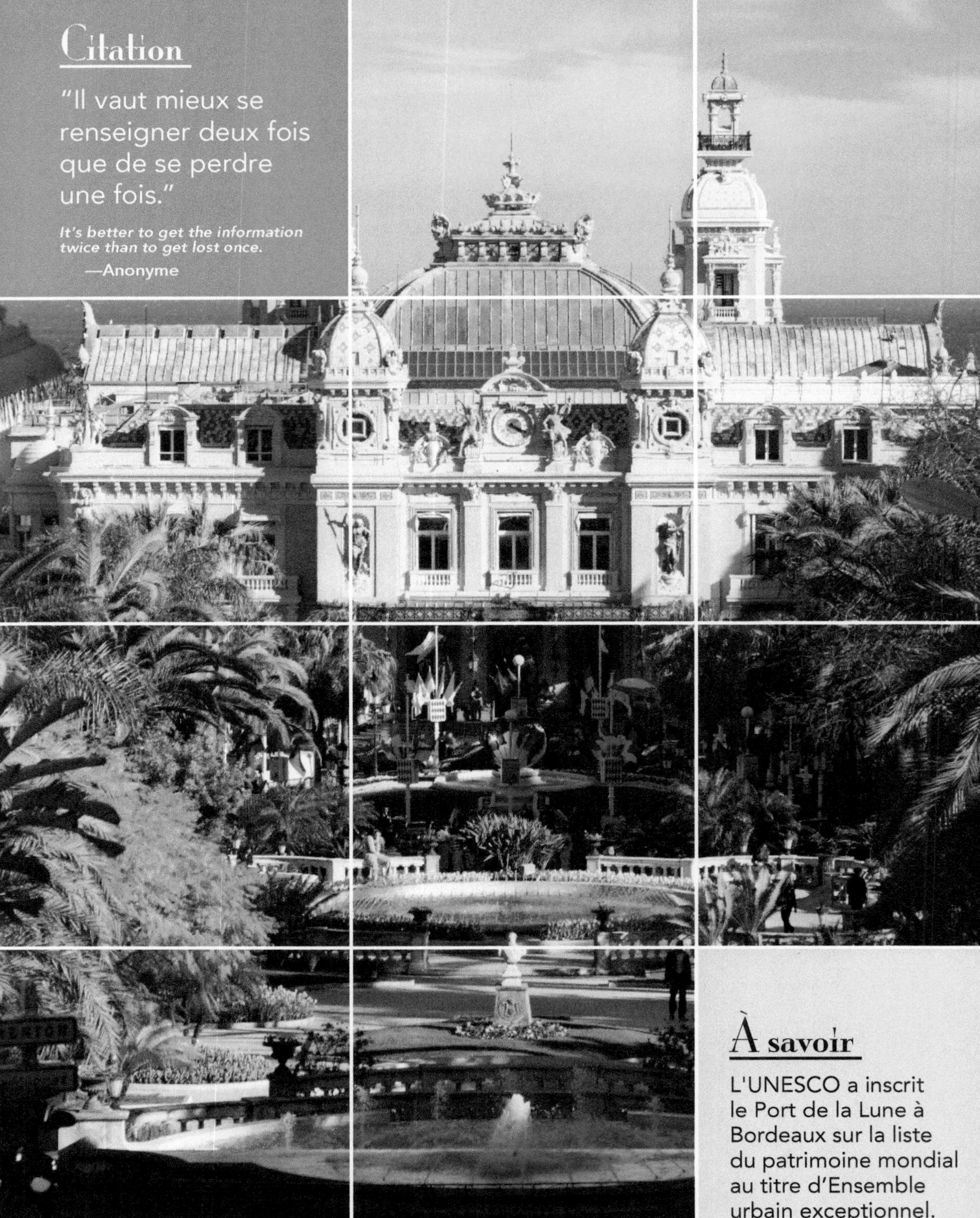

Citation

"Il vaut mieux se renseigner deux fois que de se perdre une fois."

It's better to get the information twice than to get lost once.

—Anonyme

À savoir

L'UNESCO a inscrit le Port de la Lune à Bordeaux sur la liste du patrimoine mondial au titre d'Ensemble urbain exceptionnel.

Essential Instruction

1. Introduce the unit theme of travel. Ask students where they have traveled or would like to travel. In traveling to a French-speaking country, what skills are needed to survive? (**Question centrale**) What travel situations require good language skills?
2. How does the **citation** relate to the theme of this **Unité**?
3. Review the **Contrat de l'élève**. What do students know about Monaco, Dijon, and Cannes? In this unit, they learn about these cities and also acquire travel skills needed for booking a hotel and ordering in a restaurant. The uses of the subjunctive are expanded.

Unité 5

Comment se renseigner en voyage

Reference Desk

Port de la Lune, a major port of exchange and commerce since the 16th century, is the name of the port of Bordeaux. The name is derived from the city's seal which features a crescent moon.

De quelles compétences ai-je besoin en voyageant?

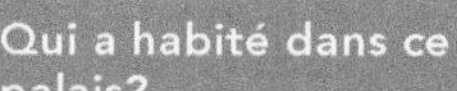

Qui a habité dans ce palais?

Cette jeune fille vient de quelle famille princière?

Contrat de l'élève

Leçon A **I will be able to:**

- find out information about my stay in a hotel.
- talk about Monaco, and hotels in France.
- use the subjunctive after expressions of wish, will, and desire.

Leçon B **I will be able to:**

- ask about specialties in a restaurant and what is served with a dish.
- talk about Dijon and the region of Bourgogne.
- use the subjunctive after expressions of emotion, and doubt or uncertainty.

Leçon C **I will be able to:**

- Express what I am or am not in the mood for, relate someone else's opinion, ask for an opinion, and express disagreement.
- talk about the French film industry, the Cannes festival, and the **César** awards.
- review the interrogative adjective **quel** and use the interrogative pronoun **lequel**.

Multiple Intelligences

Mathematical-Logical

Have students search the official website of the Principality of Monaco and share statistics about the relative size of Monaco compared to areas in the United States. How many residents are there, and what attractions does Monaco offer for tourists?

Visual-Spatial

Ask these students to add Monaco, Dijon, and Cannes to a map of France, using symbols to indicate their principal products.

RESOURCES

e-visual 13

Workbook 1–3

Flash Cards

Listening Activity 1

Drill & Practice Games

Reference Desk

Here is some additional vocabulary that might interest your students: **un bon rapport qualité prix** (*good value for the money*); **a deux pas de la mer** (*close to the sea*); **une chambre nickel** (*an immaculate room*); **dans un joli cadre** (*in a lovely setting*); **descendre à l'hôtel** (*to stay at the hotel*); **un très bon accueil** (*a very good welcome*); **le personnel serviable** (*an attentive staff*); **les peignoirs** (*bathrobes*); **un surclassement** (*an upgrade*).

Communication

Interpersonal: Cooperative Groups

Have students create a travel site review about their stay at the **Hôtel Belle Plage**, integrating the vocabulary from **A l'hôtel** and from the **Reference Desk.** They may choose to be positive or negative, but they must support their opinion with examples.

Vocabulaire actif

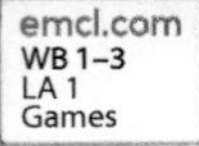

À l'hôtel

1.2, 5.1

Les prestations (f.) et le confort

Hôtel Belle Plage

34 allée de l'Hypocampe-06230 Villefranche-sur-Mer

Nos services

Bienvenus à l'hôtel Belle Plage. Pour votre bien-être total, notre hôtel vous offre les services et prestations suivantes:

l'ascenseur (m.)

un service blanchisserie

un centre de remise en forme

un centre d'affaires

Nos chambres

Pour vous garantir un séjour agréable, chacune de nos chambres est équipée de (d'):

une clé électronique

un coffre-fort

une connexion Wifi

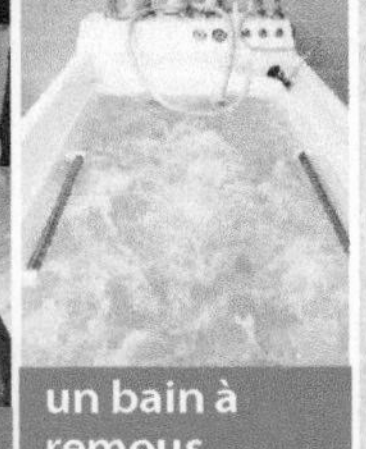
un bain à remous

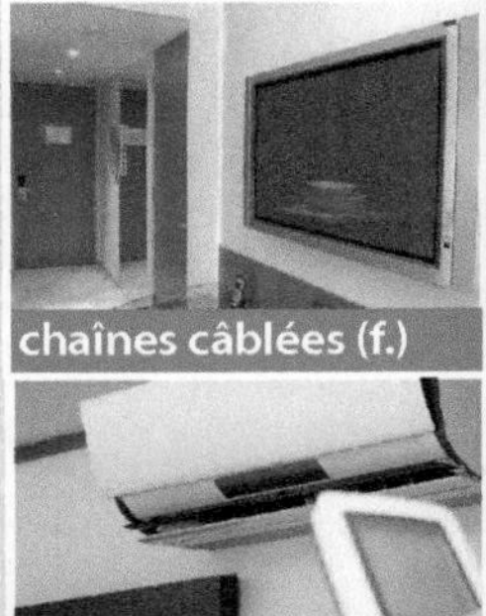
chaînes câblées (f.)

la climatisation

un service de chambre

Essential Instruction

1. Ask students what amenities (**les prestations**) they think are essential in a quality hotel. What is the difference between **une demi pension** and a standard hotel stay?
2. Put the vocabulary for **Leçon A** on the board. What words do the students recognize? Ask them to define each term in French.
3. Play the vocabulary and have students repeat.
4. Ask students to explain in French what responsibilities and services are associated with a **concierge.**
5. Explain how the verb **vouloir** introduces the subjunctive in the sentence, **"Je voudrais que vous me donniez quelques precisions."**

Dans le hall/le lobby

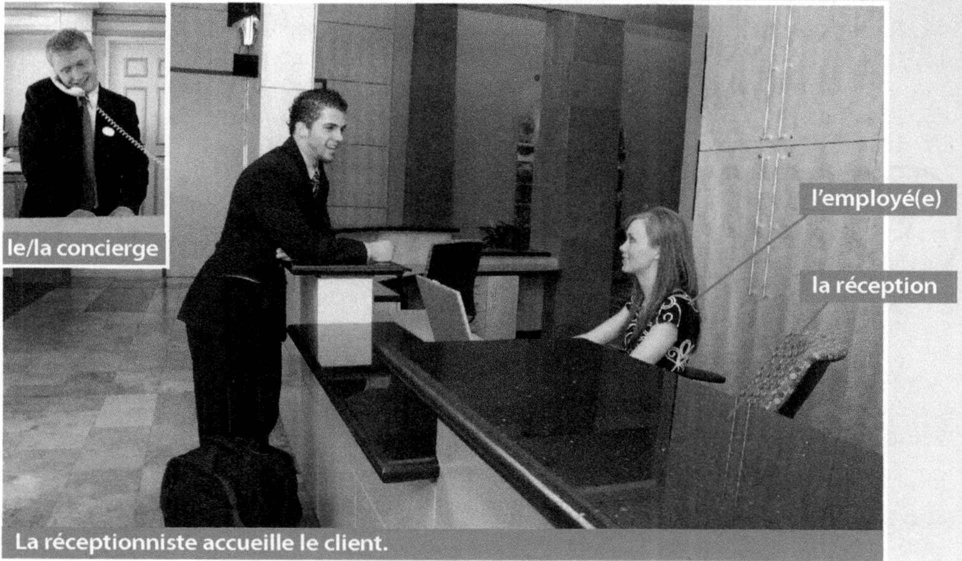

La réceptionniste accueille le client.

Pour la conversation  

1.1, 1.2

How do I ask for information?

> **Je voudrais que vous me donniez quelques précisions sur** les prestations de l'hôtel.
>
> *I would like you to give me some specific information about the amenities of the hotel.*

Et si je voulais dire...? 

en demi-pension	*with breakfast and one meal*
un club de vacances	*vacation club*
en pension complète	*with all meals*
une étoile	*one star (low rating)*
une pension de famille	*family-run hotel*
tout-compris	*everything included*

Communication

Interpersonal, Presentational: Cooperative Groups

Students work in small groups to role-play tourists booking a room in a hotel. They create a dialogue in which the travelers ask questions about the hotel's amenities, and the concierge answers giving details. Express services and room rates in euros. Challenge students to use as many vocabulary words from **Leçon A** as possible.

Differentiated Learning

Accelerate

Have students compare the amenities of the **Hôtel Belle Plage** (Villefranche-sur-Mer) with the **Hôtel Belle Plage** (Cannes). What **prestations** does the hotel in Cannes offer that are not listed in the vocabulary from the **Leçon**? What is the price of a single and double room in euros? Which hotel do they prefer and why?

Decelerate

Ask students to report to the class about categories of hotels in France and make a chart that illustrates the meaning of each of the star ratings. Have them include how the red *Michelin Guide* rates hotels and restaurants.

Multiple Intelligences

Bodily-Kinesthetic

Have students pantomime vocabulary from **Leçon A** for the class as a fast review.

Answers

1

1. réceptionniste
2. une clé (électronique)
3. connexion wifi
4. coffre-fort
5. la climatisation
6. chaînes cablées
7. bain à remous
8. service blanchisserie
9. concierge

Script can be found in the front pages of the Annotated Teacher's Edition.

1. le réceptionniste
2. une vieille clé
3. dans un coffre-fort
4. à la piscine
5. un sèche-cheveux
6. du service de chambre

3 *Answers will vary.*

Communication

Interpersonal: Paired Practice

Have students interview each other in **Activité 3** as a basis for conversation. Encourage them to ask follow-up questions like "**Pourquoi?**" and "**Quand?**" Circulate to monitor their conversations and answer questions. When students are finished, debrief each group.

Game

Ça y est

Arrange students in teams of five or six. Place a set of French vocabulary words written on individual cards in the center of each group, face up. Give the clues listed in **Activité 1.** Students scramble to be the first to identify and hold up the appropriate vocabulary card. The team that finds the card first yells **"Ça y est!"** and earns a point.

1 À l'hôtel

1.2, 5.1

Complétez les phrases.

1. En arrivant dans le hall de l'hôtel, les clients vont parler au....
2. Il donne... au client pour la porte de sa chambre.
3. Il y a des ordinateurs disponibles avec... compris dans le service.
4. On peut laisser ses bijoux ou son passeport dans le... à la réception.
5. Quand il fait chaud, on voudrait une chambre avec..., surtout aux Antilles.
6. Pour regarder la télé, beaucoup d'hôtels donnent accès à des....
7. Les hôtels de luxe ont souvent un... avec massage pour se détendre.
8. Dans les hôtels de luxe, le... vous permet de nettoyer les vêtements.
9. Quand on a faim, le... peut vous renseigner sur les restaurants du quartier.

2 Un bon ou un mauvais hôtel?

1.1, 1.2, 5.1

Interpretive Communication

Écrivez les numéros 1–6 sur votre papier. Écoutez Élise décrire son expérience dans un hôtel de Monaco. Écrivez une courte réponse pour répondre à chaque question, par exemple, "à la réception."

1. Qui n'était pas sympa?
2. Quelle sorte de clé a-t-on offert à Élise?
3. Où a-t-elle mis son passeport?
4. Où est-elle allée chaque matin?
5. Qu'est-ce qu'il y avait dans la salle de bains?
6. De quel service a-t-elle profité à midi et le soir?

3 Questions personnelles

1.1, 1.3, 5.1

Répondez aux questions.

1. Es-tu jamais allé(e) à l'hôtel?
2. L'hôtel avait-il une piscine? Un centre de remise en forme? Le service de chambre?
3. Tu as besoin de quelles prestations dans un hôtel?
4. Quelle chaînes câblées est-ce que tu préfères?
5. Aimes-tu la climatisation en été?
6. Comment serait ton hôtel idéal?
7. Où voudrais-tu descendre dans un hôtel?

Moi, j'ai besoin de la connexion Wifi à l'hôtel!

Essential Instruction

1. Students listen to **Activité 2** and answer questions 1–6. Play the recording again if they have questions.
2. Have students listen to **Un hôtel à Monaco** with books closed, and then have them volunteer details they remember from the conversation between Léo and Justin.
3. Students read the text and complete the sentences in **Activité 4.**
4. Read **Extension** to the students with books closed. Ask listening comprehension questions.
5. Have students read the two dialogues in pairs.

Rencontres culturelles

emcl.com WB 4

Un hôtel à Monaco

    1.1

Léo et Justin veulent réserver une chambre à Monaco.

Léo: La déscription de l'hôtel et les photos sont plutôt bien, mais c'est un peu cher.

Justin: Mais c'est Monte Carlo! Moi, je trouve qu'ils sont très imprécis sur les prestations.

Léo: Ah! Tu es bien américain: toujours le côté pratique.

Justin: Je te laisse la poésie des lieux monégasques et la vue imprenable sur la mer....

Léo: Tu veux qu'on leur téléphone?

Justin: Oui, je vais le faire avec mon accent américain! *(Au téléphone, Justin parle au réceptionniste.)* Bonjour, je voudrais que vous me donniez quelques précisions sur les prestations de l'hôtel.... Merci. Au revoir.

Léo: Alors?

Justin: Ils ont le Wifi, des chaînes câblées, il y a un jacuzzi dans la chambre, et on peut prendre le petit déjeuner dans la chambre sans payer le supplément.

Léo: Parfait! Réservons!

4 Un hôtel à Monaco

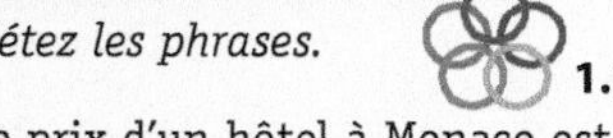 

Complétez les phrases. 1.2

1. Le prix d'un hôtel à Monaco est....
2. Justin voudrait se renseigner sur... de l'hôtel.
3. (prénoms) ... est plus pratique que....
4. Selon Justin, Léo s'intéresse à....
5. Les prestations de l'hôtel comprennent (*include*)....

Extension Les prestations désirées

  1.1, 1.2

Clément et Laurence aident leurs parents à chercher un bon hôtel pour leurs vacances en famille.

Clément: Bon alors, si toi tu veux le bain à remous, moi je veux les chaînes câblées et une connexion Wifi.

Laurence: Tu ne vas quand même pas passer ton temps en vacances à regarder le sport à la télé!

Clément: Si, pendant que toi et maman serez au centre de remise en forme!

Laurence: Pour la connexion Wifi d'accord: pas besoin de passer des heures à attendre un ordinateur libre au centre d'affaires.

Clément: Vérifie quand même qu'il y ait la climatisation dans cet hôtel.

Laurence: À Saint-Pierre et Miquelon, on n'en aura pas besoin!

Clément: Mais, Maman et Papa ont changé d'avis et préfèrent aller à Saint-Louis au Sénégal.

Extension Quelles prestations désirent Laurence et Clément? Où vont-ils passer leurs vacances? Avec qui? 1.1, 1.2

RESOURCES

 **Dialogue Video**

 **Workbook 4**

Answers

1. un peu cher
2. les prestations
3. Justin, Léo
4. la vue sur la mer et les lieux monégasques
5. le Wifi, les chaînes cablées, un bain à remous (jacuzzi) et le service de chambre.

Extension

Ils veulent un bain à remous, des chaînes cablées, une connexion Wifi, et la climatisation. Ils vont passer leurs vacances à Saint-Louis (au Sénégal) avec leurs parents.

Reference Desk

1. **Saint-Pierre et Miquelon**, located 25 km southwest of Newfoundland, is France's oldest overseas territory. Jacques Cartier declared it a French possession in 1536. There are eight islands although only two are inhabited. The language is French and the religion is Catholic.
2. **Saint-Louis au Sénégal**, established by French traders in 1659, is the capital of the **Saint-Louis** region and former capital of **Sénégal.** It is called **"la Venise africaine"** because of its river delta location. **Saint-Louis** is known for its tourism, sugar production, and fishing.

Differentiated Learning

Accelerate

Students write a dialogue between two friends booking a hotel in a ski region or at a beach resort. They express conflicting opinions as to what they want to do before arriving at a consensus.

Decelerate

Students search online to select two hotels: a five and a three-star hotel in the Villefranche-sur-Mer-Nice-Cannes area. Have them compare the amenities, proximity to the sea, and prices for each, and create a chart comparing the two. They should express cost in euros.

Special Needs Students

AD(H)D/Dyslexia/Linguistically Challenged

To assist students who have difficulty concentrating, reading, or with language, give them two or three lines from the dialogue on separate index cards. Allow them to work in groups and ask them to be responsible only for the three lines of dialogue on their cards. Organize a group presentation.

RESOURCES

Workbook 5

Reference Desk

1. Biarritz is a luxury resort town on the Bay of Biscay only 18 km from Spain. In the 18th century it became a health spa for the rich and famous. Tourists enjoy its golden-sand beaches, surfing, and its casino.
2. **Le Cheval Blanc de Courcheval** offers 34 lavishly-appointed rooms and suites. An enormous glass stallion adorns the courtyard.
3. Accor Hotel Group is comprised of Ibis, Novotel, and Sofitel hotel chains. There are over 4,200 hotels and 145,000 employees in 90 countries on five continents.

Points de départ

Pre AP

emcl.com
WB 5

Question centrale
De quelles compétences ai-je besoin en voyageant?

La tradition hôtelière française

1.2, 3.1

Même si la France et Paris sont les lieux les plus visités au monde, aucun hôtel français ne pouvait revendiquer* officiellement le terme de palace avant 2010. Le label "Palace" n'est officiel que depuis cette année-là en France. Seuls quelques hôtels sont classifiés comme étant des palaces aujourd'hui: à Paris, le Plaza Athénée; l'Hôtel du Palais à Biarritz; et le Cheval Blanc à Courchevel. Bien qu'hôtels de légende, le Ritz ou le Crillon à Paris, Le Negresco à Nice et le Carlton à Cannes, ou encore l'Eden Roc à Antibes ne bénéficient pas encore de cette appellation de palace.

L'Hôtel du palais est situé sur la plage de Biarritz.

À côté de cette hôtellerie de luxe, il existe de grands groupes hôteliers en France comme le groupe Accor, avec la chaîne d'hôtels Sofitel (200 hôtels) qui se veut* représentative de l'art de vivre à la française dans le monde entier.

Toujours dans le souci* de valoriser* cette tradition d'accueil et d'art de vivre, le réseau Relais et Châteaux valorise une hôtellerie installée dans des demeures* historiques où il s'agit de donner aux hôtes* le sentiment de vivre un moment d'histoire au présent: châteaux et gentilhommières*, pavillons de chasse à la campagne, hôtels particuliers* dans les villes. Une attention particulière est apportée à la gastronomie.

Search words: relais châteaux, gentilhommières france, sofitel, (nom de l'hôtel) + (nom de ville)

revendiquer *claim;* **se veut** *wants to see itself;* **souci** *preoccupation;* **valoriser** *to promote;* **demeures** *residences;* **hôtes** *guests;* **gentilhommières** *mansions in the country;* **hôtels particuliers** *mansions in the city*

Un pavillon de chasse dans l'Avenois.

COMPARAISONS

Est-ce que vous pouvez nommer, ou trouver, un hôtel de luxe à New York et Los Angeles?

4.2

Essential Instruction

1. Have students describe a luxury hotel. Do they know of any in the United States? Would they prefer to stay in a luxury hotel or in an historic chateau? Why?
2. As students read **La tradition l'hôtelière française**, have them locate each palace-hotel on the map of France.
3. In the computer lab, students visit the Accor and Sofitel websites to familiarize themselves with these hotel chains.
4. Ask students what they know of Monaco, the Grimaldi family, and Grace Kelly before reading **La Francophonie: Monaco**.
5. In the computer lab, students extend their understanding of the readings by using the search words at the end of each section.
6. Have students visit the websites for Campanile and the hotel chains Mercure, Ibis, and Novotel to learn about hotel chains for the budget-minded traveler.

La Francophonie: Monaco

1.2, 3.1

Son rocher*, son célèbre circuit* automobile en pleine ville, son port de plaisance*, son casino, et sa famille princière* ont fait la réputation de Monaco, qu'on appelle parfois Monte Carlo du nom d'un de ses quartiers. Cette principauté* indépendante de 1,5 km2 et de 30.000 habitants est située sur la côte méditerranéenne entre les villes françaises de Nice et Menton. Monaco constitue une véritable enclave sur le territoire français.

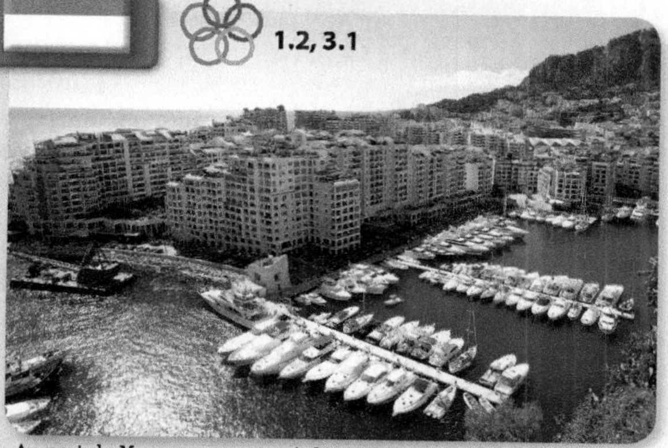

Au port de Monaco on peut voir les yachts de nombreuses célébrités internationales.

L'histoire de Monaco est liée à l'histoire de la famille Grimaldi, originaire de Gênes, qui s'empare* de la ville au XIIIème siècle et qui règne* toujours sur la principauté. Monaco est liée* à la France par une union douanière*.

Ville touristique, elle doit sa réputation, d'abord à la fin du XIXème siècle et au début du XXème siècle à l'aristocratie des princes russes*, puis dans les années 1950 à Hollywood dont les stars deviennent les habituées* du lieu. C'est ainsi que le Prince Rainier épouse Grace Kelly, star hollywoodienne des années 1950, égérie* d'Alfred Hitchcock. Aujourd'hui, Monaco est la patrie* de la jet set financière, sportive, et artistique.

Le Prince Rainier III et la Princesse Grace de Monaco.

La famille Grimaldi, avec ses princesses Caroline et Stéphanie, son prince Albert, aujourd'hui Prince régnant*, a largement contribué à l'image glamour et à l'image "jetseteuse" de Monaco.

Fille aînée* du prince Rainier III et de Grace de Monaco, Caroline de Monaco a eu trois enfants de son défunt* mari Stefano Casiraghi: Andrea, Charlotte, et Pierre. Dix ans plus tard, elle se remarie et a une autre fille, Alexandra de Hanovre. Sa sœur, Stéphanie de Monaco, a eu plusieurs mariages et divorces, et trois enfants: Louis et Pauline Ducruet, et Camille Gottlieb. Comme la génération princière* est reconnue uniquement dans l'union du mariage, la petite Camille n'est pas considérée une princesse.

Search words: monaco site officiel

rocher *rock*; **circuit** *racetrack*; **port de plaisance** *marina*; **princière** *princely*; **principauté** *principality*; **s'empare** *seize*; **règne** *reigns*; **liée** *linked*; **union douanière** *customs agreement*; **russes** *Russian*; **habituées** *regular visitors*; **égérie** *muse*; **patrie** *homeland*; **Prince regnant** *reigning prince*; **aînée** *older*; **défunt** mort; **princière** *princely*

Reference Desk

Grace Kelly, born in Philadelphia in 1929, began her acting career at the age of 20. She was nominated for an Academy Award for Best Supporting Actress in *Mogambo* (1953) and won an Academy Award for Best Actress for *A Country Girl* (1954). She starred in the Alfred Hitchcock films *Dial M for Murder* (1953), *Rear Window* (1953), and *To Catch a Thief* (1955). Kelly retired from acting in 1956 at age 26 to marry Rainier III, Prince of Monaco. She died in 1982, the result of an automobile accident.

Differentiated Learning

Accelerate

Have students read **La tradition hôtelière française** in the computer lab. Have them visit the websites for each of the eight palaces mentioned in the first paragraph of the reading. Ask them to locate each on the map of France, and list in descending order the ones they prefer and tell why. Have them evaluate them for price, amenities, and location.

Decelerate

Have students make a family tree of the Grimaldi family using the information from the reading. Have them research each family member online including Prince Albert and his new wife, Charlene. Why is it important that this couple has descendants?

Answers

5

1. Paris: le Plaza Athénée; Biarritz: l'Hôtel du Palais; Courchevel: le Cheval Blanc
2. *Answers will vary.*
3. *Answers may include more than the following:* Enfants: Andréa Casiraghi, Charlotte Casiraghi, Pierre Casiraghi; Père: Stefano Casiraghi; Mère: Caroline Grimaldi; Grand-père maternel: Rainier III Grimaldi; Grand-mère maternelle: Grace Kelly; Arrière-grand-père paternel: Pierre de Polignac; Arrière-grand-mère paternelle: Charlotte Grimaldi; Arrière-grand-père maternel: John Kelly; Arrière-grand-mère maternelle: Margaret Majer
4. Alfred Hitchcock a lancé la carrière de Grace Kelly, qui était une de ses actrices fétiches. Grace Kelly a tourné dans *Fenêtre sur cour*, *Le crime était presque parfait*, et *La main au collet*, réalisés par Hitchcock.
5. *Answers will vary.*

À discuter
Answers will vary.

Reference Desk

1. The English word hotel stems from the word **hôte** (host). Originally, **hôtel** referred to a house which was open to frequent visitors. **L'Hôtel Carnavalet** in Paris was the 17th century private residence of the Marquise de Sévigné and her family. **Un hôtel garni** is a hotel without a restaurant. **Une auberge** is an inn. **Une auberge de jeunesse** is a youth hostel.
2. The Princess Grace Foundation is named in honor of Grace Kelly, the wife of Prince Rainier III of Monaco. The organization was established in 1984, two years after Kelly's death, to recognize promising artistic talent in theater, dance, film, playwriting, and choreography, through scholarships granted to talented young artists.

1.2, 2.1, 5.1

Le Bal de la Rose, qui a lieu chaque printemps à Monaco, réunit la famille Grimaldi et des grands noms du monde du spectacle. C'est un grand rendez-vous mondain (*fashionable*), créé en 1954 par la Princesse Grace. Les bénéfices du bal sont reversés à la Fondation Princesse Grace, une œuvre de bienfaisance (*charity*) au service des personnes en difficulté, des enfants défavorisés (*disadvantaged*), d'autres actions humanitaires et aussi philanthropiques et artistiques.

Monaco en phénicien (*Phoenician*) signifie "l'Unique." Les gens qui y habitent sont des Monégasques.

5 Activités culturelles

1.3, 3.2

Faites les activités suivantes.

1. Associez un palace à chacune de ces villes:
   - Paris
   - Biarritz
   - Courchevel
2. Allez sur le site de l'hôtel Sofitel le plus proche de votre ville et trouvez des exemples de ce qui évoque l'art de vivre "à la française."
3. Faites l'arbre généalogique d'Andrea Casiraghi, fils de Caroline Grimaldi, qui remonte à son arrière-grand-père.

Search words: monte carlo arbre généalogique

4. Retrouvez les liens cinématographiques entre Grace Kelly et Alfred Hitchcock.
5. Recherchez la fondation du Prince Albert. Est-ce que vous la soutiendriez? Justifiez votre réponse.

Search words: fondation prince albert Monaco

À discuter

Imaginez que chaque élève de votre classe gagne une semaine gratuite dans un hôtel français de son choix. Faites une enquête pour voir dans quel hôtel et dans quelle ville vos camarades de classe iraient.

Andrea, Charlotte, et Pierre Casiraghi.

Essential Instruction

1. Arrange students into four groups. One student from each group draws a number, 1, 2, 3, 4, or 5. In the computer lab, students complete the task corresponding to their number in **Activité 5.** They present their final work to the class.
2. Pair students in groups of high and low ability to do **Activité 6.** Preview words that might give them difficulty.
3. Have students identify four American luxury hotels and compare them to four luxury hotels in France in terms of ambiance, price, and amenities. What are the hotel chains in the United States that would be on par with Accor and Sofitel?

Du côté des médias   1.2

Interpretive Communication

Lisez les statistiques suivantes sur le tourisme international à Monaco.

Tourisme Monaco

Chiffre d'affaires de l'hôtellerie et de la restauration monégasque
Le chiffre d'affaires de l'hôtellerie et de la restauration monégasque a augmenté de 8,4% cette année et affiche 493.472.800 euros H.T contre 455.421.462. Ces résultats consolident le mouvement de reprise du secteur de l'industrie du tourisme de la Principauté. Le taux d'occupation moyen augmente de 5%.

Durée moyenne de séjour
La durée moyenne de séjour dans l'hôtellerie monégasque demeure inchangée à 3 nuitées. Les quatre principales nationalités des touristes séjournant dans les hôtels de la Principauté sont, par ordre d'importance, les Français, les Italiens, les Britanniques, et les Américains du Nord. Ces marchés représentent 57% de l'ensemble des nuitées hôtelières.

Tourisme non hébergé
Le nombre de touristes visitant Monaco au cours de la journée est estimé de 4,5 à 5 millions chaque année. D'après l'Enquête de Satisfaction, cette évaluation sera revue à la hausse.

Capacité hôtelière
Elle s'élève à 2.535 chambres. La Grande Hôtellerie représente désormais 96% de l'ensemble de l'hébergement marchand de la Principauté.

Tourisme de loisir
Le tourisme de loisir représente plus de 80% de la fréquentation hôtelière.

Croisières
Avec 235 escales, les croisières engendrent l'arrivée de 321.820 passagers, soit une croissance respective de 24% et de 36%. Les passagers sont principalement originaires de l'Union Européenne (53%) et d'Amérique du Nord (36%).

6 Le tourisme international à Monaco  1.3

Faites les activités suivantes.

1. Faites un graphique en barres qui montre le chiffre d'affaires (*sales figures*) de l'hôtellerie (*hotel industry*) à Monaco en comparant cette année à l'année précédente.
2. Sur une carte du monde, indiquez Monaco avec son drapeau. Avec une ficelle (*string*) montrez les pays qui visitent la Principauté.
3. Faites un graphique en barres qui montre la nationalité des passagers en croisière (*taking a cruise*) qui passent par Monaco.

Answers

6 *Activities will vary.*

Expansion

Encourage advanced students to work together to read and study **Du côté des médias.** Have them identify and define new or difficult words and expressions from each section and then summarize what they learn. They could work with the strong math students in the class to prepare and present the information to the other students.

Differentiated Learning

Adapt
Assign students one of the following events according to their interests: the Formula One Monte Carlo Grand Prix, the Monte Carlo Rally, the Rolex Masters Tennis tournament, or the Rose Ball. How is each event organized? When does it occur? Who are the famous people associated with the events in the last three years?

Multiple Intelligences

Visual-Spatial
Encourage these students to create a publicity brochure with photos and descriptions for one or more hotels.

Mathematical-Logical
Have these students organize the statistical information from **Du côté des médias** in a graphic organizer and lead a class discussion of tourism in Monaco.

RESOURCES

 Workbook 6–9

 Listening Activity 2

 Drill & Practice Games

Reference Desk

Review the conjugation of **préférer**. Remind students of the rule for accent mark change. As a visual way of remembering, the accents look like sleet in the **nous** and **vous** forms, and like eyebrows in all other forms.

Expansion

Use word puzzles to practice the subjunctive. Create sentences with verbs in the subjunctive. Cut up the words and put each sentence into an envelope. There should be as many sentences as there are pairs of students. Place an envelope on each student's desk. Pairs of students travel from one desk to another reconstructing the sentences and copying the sentences into a notebook. Ask them to scramble the words before putting them back into the envelope for the next pair of students. At the end, have students put the sentences on the board.

Structure de la langue

emcl.com
WB 6–9
LA 2
Games

The Subjunctive after Expressions of Wish, Will, or Desire 1.2

In French the subjunctive usually comes after **que** in a dependent clause. As you have learned, various impersonal expressions are followed by the subjunctive. Verbs that express wish, will, or desire also take the subjunctive. Use the subjunctive after one of these verbs when the wish, will, or desire concerns someone other than the subject.

aimer *to like, to love*	J'**aimerais que** cet hôtel **offre** une connexion Wifi.	*I would like this hotel to offer wireless Internet.*
désirer *to want*	Léo **désire que** vous lui **montriez** le centre d'affaires de l'hôtel.	*Leo wants you to show him the hotel's business center.*
exiger *to require*	Nous **exigeons que** la chambre **ait** la climatisation.	*We require that the room have air conditioning.*
préférer *to prefer*	Elle **préfère que** tu lui **donnes** quelques précisions sur l'hôtel.	*She prefers that you give her some details about the hotel.*
souhaiter *to wish, to hope*	Vous **souhaitez qu'**il y **ait** un coffre-fort pour votre collier?	*Do you hope that there is a safe for your necklace?*
vouloir *to want*	Maman **veut que** je **voie** le concierge.	*Mom wants me to see the concierge.*

COMPARAISONS

In the following pairs of sentences, what verbs are in the subjunctive tense? (There's one per pair.)

The math teacher requires that we be on time.
Zach usually comes late.
We are in Denver.
I wish we were in Paris.

4.1

COMPARAISONS: In the first pair, "be" is in the subjunctive because the indicative would use "are" instead. In the second pair, "were" is in the subjunctive because the thought does not indicate reality.

Essential Instruction

1. With white boards, have students conjugate verbs in the subjunctive. Mix regular and irregular verbs that they have previously learned until they demonstrate mastery.
2. Verbs of wishing, willing, and desiring are followed by the subjunctive provided there is a subject change. Ask students to suggest verbs they know from these categories.
3. Present the verb chart and have students answer the **Comparaisons** question.
4. Do **Activités 7** and **8** as guided practice with the students.

7 L'agenda de Didier

1.1

Dites avec qui Didier voudrait aller aux destinations suivantes.

MODÈLE

tu
Didier veut que tu ailles au festival de musique avec lui.

1. Julie et toi

2. je

3. Cédric

4. Marina et moi

5. ses cousins

6. tu

8 Phrases logiques

1.3

Faites sept phrases logiques en utilisant un mot ou une expression de chaque colonne.

je (j')	aimer		le réceptionniste	indiquer où se trouvent les meilleurs restaurants
tu	préférer		la concierge	lui réserver une chambre
Awa	exiger		la chambre	avoir un coffre-fort
le client	souhaiter	**que**	l'employé	être près du métro
Saskia et moi	vouloir		vous	lui offrir une clé électronique
Abdel et toi	désirer		l'hôtel	aller au centre d'affaires
Laure et Laïla				profiter du centre de remise en forme

Answers

1. Didier veut que Julie et toi alliez au complexe multisport avec lui.
2. Didier veut que j'aille à la MJC avec lui.
3. Didier veut que Cédric aille en discothèque/à la soirée avec lui.
4. Didier veut que Marina et moi allions au cinéma avec lui.
5. Didier veut ses cousins aillent à l'aquaparc avec lui.
6. Didier veut que tu ailles à la soirée/en discothèque avec lui.

8 *Possible answers:*

1. J'aime que le réceptionniste m'offre une clé électronique.
2. Tu préfères que la concierge t'indique où se trouvent les meilleurs restaurants.
3. Awa exige que la chambre ait un coffre-fort.
4. Le client souhaite que l'employé lui réserve une chambre.
5. Saskia et moi voulions que vous profitiez du centre de remise en forme.
6. Abdel et toi désirez que l'hôtel se trouve près du métro.
7. Laure et Leïla préfèrent que vous alliez au centre d'affaires.

Communication

Interpersonal: Cooperative Groups

To practice the new use of the subjunctive, divide the class into small groups. Ask half of the groups to imagine what the principal of their school wishes, wants, demands, or requires that students do in order to have a great school and a great school experience. Ask the other half of the groups to imagine what students wish, want, demand, or require that the administration and teachers do to create a great school and a great school environment. Each group creates a list of sentences. Remind students that they must use the subjunctive. Put an administrator group with a student group and have them share their ideas. Collect their lists.

Learning Styles

Kinesthetic Learners

These students may need to write out the verbs to ingrain them in their minds.

Multiple Intelligences

Musical-Rhythmic

These students would benefit from oral drill. Encourage them to find the rhythm of the verbs as they conjugate them.

Special Needs Students

Linguistically Challenged

Consider offering a special session to re-teach the subjunctive in small groups. These students might be confusing the subjunctive with the indicative. Flash cards and online practice will help them learn.

Answers

9 *Possible answers:*

1. A: Comment tu trouves la musique à la radio?
   B: J'aimerais qu'elle soit plus variée. Et toi?
2. A: Comment tu trouves les émissions sur CBS?
   B: J'aimerais qu'elles soient moins longues.
3. A: Comment tu trouves la cantine du lycée?
   B: J'aimerais qu'il y ait plus de légumes.
4. A: Comment tu trouves les devoirs pour le cours d'histoire?
   B: J'aimerais qu'ils soient moins difficiles.
5. A: Comment tu trouves le temps qu'il fait aujourd'hui?
   B: *Answers will vary.*
6. A: Comment tu trouves les émissions de télé-réalité?
   B: J'aimerais qu'elles passent moins souvent.

10

Script can be found in the front pages of the Annotated Teacher's Edition.

1. B
2. G
3. C
4. A
5. E
6. H
7. D
8. F

Reference Desk

Consider doing choral repetition of the subjunctive forms for the irregular verbs **être**, **avoir**, **aller**, **faire**, **vouloir**, **pouvoir**, and **prendre** in order to help students commit these forms to memory.

9 On se parle. 1.1, 5.2

Interpretive Communication

À tour de rôle, demandez-vous comment vous trouvez les personnes et les choses indiquées. Donnez vos opinions en utilisant l'expression ***J'aimerais que***.

MODÈLE le directeur du lycée
A: Comment tu trouves le directeur du lycée?
B: J'aimerais qu'il soit moins strict. Et toi?
A: J'aimerais qu'il n'aille pas à la cantine tous les jours.

1. la musique à la radio
2. les émissions sur CBS
3. la cantine du lycée
4. les devoirs pour le cours d'histoire
5. le temps qu'il fait aujourd'hui
6. les émissions de télé-réalité

Communiquez!

10 Souhaits de vacanciers   1.1, 1.2

Écrivez les numéros 1–8 sur votre papier. Écoutez les souhaits des vacanciers. Puis, choisissez l'image qui y correspond.

A. 

B. 

C. 

D. 

E. 

F. 

G. 

H. 

Essential Instruction

1. Students complete **Activité 9** with a variety of partners. Have them change partners to ask and answer the prepared questions using the pattern provided. This exercise could also be written.
2. Have students listen to the remarks and choose the appropriate image for **Activité 10**.
3. For **Activité 11**, give students the option of preparing a dialogue to be presented live in class, or filming the dialogue. Students might like to write the dialogue as a commercial for the hotel.
4. Go to the computer lab to complete **Activité 12** using the search words provided. Ask students to list reasons why Monaco is a destination for all kinds of travelers.

À vous la parole

11 Une réservation

1.1, 5.1, 5.2

Interpersonal Communication

Avec un partenaire, jouez les rôles d'un(e) réceptionniste et d'un client qui se parlent au téléphone. Le client voudrait se renseigner sur les prestations de l'hôtel; il en est satisfait, alors il réserve une chambre. Le/la réceptionniste donne une liste des prestations, et demande au client les dates de son séjour, son nom, s'il prendra le petit déjeuner dans sa chambre, et comment il voudrait régler.

12 Un hôtel à Monaco

1.3, 3.2

Interpretive/Presentational Communication

Imaginez que vous êtes à Paris et que vous voudriez passer trois jours à Monaco. Pour vous, l'argent n'est pas un problème, mais vous voulez savoir combien vous dépenserez à l'avance. Remplissez une grille comme celle de dessous avec les informations et les montants (*amounts*) que vous trouverez en ligne. Faites un budget pour chaque jour. Finalement, discutez avec vos camarades de classe: Ce genre de vacances en vaut-il le prix? Est-ce que Monaco est une destination pour tout le monde?

Jour 1	Détails	Prix
Train Paris-Monaco		
Hôtel		
Visite du palais		
Déjeuner		
Musée Océanographique		
Grand Prix		
Dîner		

Search words: **monaco site officiel, musée océanographique de monaco, monaco grand prix, hôtel monaco, sncf, palais monaco**

RESOURCES

Communicative Activities

Answers

All activities will vary.

Reference Desk

The Oceanographic Museum of Monaco was inaugurated in 1901 by Prince Albert I. It is a museum of marine science as well as an aquarium featuring 90 pools containing 4000 species of exotic fish. There is a shark lagoon that was recently added. Jacques Cousteau was director of the museum for many years. Exotic Garden is a botanical garden opened in 1933. It features 1000 species of succulents and cacti. Below the garden there are prehistoric caverns.

Blended Instruction

Consider using blended instruction, a combination of in-class learning and computer-mediated instruction or learning opportunities. Ask students to complete activities on the computer, using their cell or smartphone, or other emerging electronic technology. This will allow students to hone their tech skills and become more independent learners. Schedule routine Internet and e-book learning in class and in the lab.

Multiple Intelligences

Naturalist

Ask students interested in animals and plant life to investigate the Oceanographic Museum and Exotic Garden as well as the sea life in the Mediterranean.

Intrapersonal

The history of the accession of the Grimaldi family in Monaco to the throne as well as Monaco's unusual political standing in the world would interest students who enjoy history and politics.

Bodily-Kinesthetic

Encourage these students to explore the careers of Prince Albert III and Princess Charlene as Olympic athletes.

RESOURCES

 Pre-test

 *Leçon* Quiz

Answers

Script can be found in the Audio Program Manual.

1. I
2. I, INT
3. F
4. I, INT

1. S
2. R
3. F

Reference Desk

1. **Le style relâché** was introduced and practiced in Level 2, **Unité 4**, **Leçon A**.
2. Remind students that speakers often drop the **je** as well as the **ne** in **Je ne sais pas.** The result sounds like **"chez pas."**

Prononciation 1.1

Pauses and Intonation in a Sentence

- Commas add pauses at the beginning, in the middle, or at the end of a sentence. In French, the intonation goes up on the word before the comma at the beginning of a sentence (**détachement initial**). In the middle of a sentence, the intonation stays neutral before the comma (**détachement interne**). At the end of a sentence, the intonation goes down on the word before the comma (**détachement final**).

 **Le détachement initial, interne, final**

Répétez les phrases, en faisant attention au détachement initial, interne, et final.

1. Écoutez, nous, on prend du poisson.
2. À mon avis, ça sera très bien!
3. Bienvenue, Messieurs-Dames, à La Belle Époque!
4. Il n'y a pas grand-chose, sur cette carte!
5. Je n'aime pas le poisson, moi.
6. Ici, c'est un très bon restaurant.

B Détachement initial, interne, ou final?

*Écoutez les phrases. Indiquez le type de détachement que vous entendez, en écrivant **I** pour chaque détachement initial, **INT** pour chaque détachement interne, ou **F** pour chaque détachement final.*

The Sound /ə/

- Native French speakers tend to cut out certain sounds, especially the pronunciation of the sound **/ə/.** Generally, the **/ə/** is pronounced when it falls between three or more pronounced consonants, but is dropped at the end of a word and between two pronounced consonants.

Pronounced: / C C ə C /	**Unpronounced: / C ə C /**
Il insistera.	Il bougera.

- The style in which one speaks greatly affects whether or not the **/ə/** is pronounced. The more relaxed the style is, the more often the **/ə/** is dropped.

C Prononciation du /ə/ interne

*Répétez les phrases suivantes, faisant attention de ne pas prononcer les **/ə/** en rouge.*

1. Je mets mon portefeuille dans mon vêtement.
2. Nous dînons simplement le dimanche.

D Style standard, familier, et relâché

*Écoutez et répétez les phrases. Notez combien de fois vous entendez le son **/ə/** pour chaque style.*

Standard	**Familier**	**Relâché**
1. Maintenant, je vais à la boulangerie.	Maintenant, je vais à la boulangerie.	Maintenant, je vais à la boulangerie.
2. Je ne veux pas acheter de bottes.	Je ne veux pas acheter de bottes.	Je ne veux pas acheter de bottes.

E Style standard, familier, ou relâché?

*Écrivez **S** si vous entendez le style standard, **F** si vous entendez le style familier, ou **R** si vous entendez le style relâché.*

Essential Instruction

1. Play Section **A** three times. Ask students to listen and note how the intonation changes after commas. Encourage students to use their finger to note how the voices rise and fall in the sentences.
2. Ask students to read the sentences aloud with you.
3. Do Section **B** and check answers. Replay the section again for those who could not hear the **détachements**. Provide additional sentences for students to practice.
4. Have students repeat **C** with you and then read the sentences aloud in groups and individually.
5. Before doing parts **D** and **E** explain that the term **style relâché** means relaxed style and is the opposite of carefully articulated speech. Have students write the answers for part **E** on whiteboards to hold up for you to see so that you can monitor who is having difficulty.
6. Be sensitive to students who find this exercise difficult and frustrating because they cannot hear the changes in intonation as well as others.

Leçon B

Vocabulaire actif

emcl.com
WB 1–3
LA 1
Games

Au restaurant bourguignon

1.2

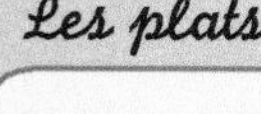

La viande

Les sauces

(servie sur le saumon, les langoustes, les lasagnes, les brocolis)

(servie sur les moules, les courgettes, les filets de sole, le lapin)

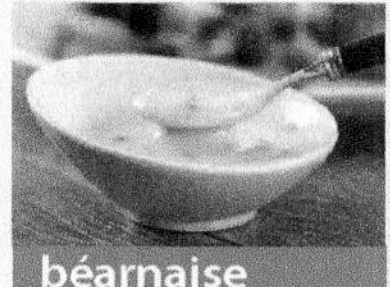

(servie sur le steak, le bœuf, l'agneau)

(servie sur la volaille, le bœuf, le poisson, les légumes)

(servie sur les œufs, la truite, les coquilles Saint-Jacques, les pommes de terre, les asperges)

Differentiated Learning

Expand

Have students find Burgundy on the map. Ask: When you hear the word Burgundy what comes to mind? What are its principal cities? What famous wine producers are located in Burgundy? What other well-known regional product comes from Dijon? Why would Joan of Arc not be fond of the Burgundians?

Learning Styles

Auditory Learners

Encourage these students to listen to and repeat the vocabulary in **Au restaurant bourguignon** multiple times.

Visual Learners

Ask visual learners to attach a different image to each picture in **Au restaurant bourguignon.** For example, a picture of a squirrel along with the **plat** labeled **le chevreuil** adds visual reinforcement to meaning.

RESOURCES

 e-visual 14

 Workbook 1–3

 Flash Cards

 Listening Activity 1

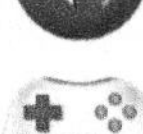 Drill & Practice Games

Reference Desk

1. **Sauce béchamel** is one of the five classic French sauces made by cooking butter and flour until it forms a "**roux**" which is then thinned with milk.
2. **Sauce marinière**, from Southern Italy, is made with tomatoes, garlic, herbs, and onions.
3. **Sauce béarnaise** is made by emulsifying butter in egg yolks and flavoring with herbs.
4. **Sauce hollandaise** resembles **béarnaise** but uses lemon juice instead of herbs.
5. Supplemental vocabulary: **le végétarisme** (*vegetarianism*); **végétarien(ne)** (*vegetarian*); **le végétalisme** (*veganism*); **végétalien(ne)** (*vegan*); **biologique, bio** (*organic*).

Critical Thinking

Categorize

Put these terms on the board **Produits Laitiers**, **Viandes Rouges**, **Volaille**, **Poissons**, **Légumes**, **Crustacés**. Have students list each vocabulary term under its appropriate category.

Culture

Perspectives: Information

Vegetariansim is not a large movement in France. French cuisine is heavily meat-based, but meat-free restaurants can be found across the country. French restaurants do include vegetarian options on the menu.

Answers

1

1. Elle a dîné au restaurant.
2. Non, parce qu'elle est végétarienne.
3. Parce que les parents de David ne savaient pas qu'elle est végétarienne.
4. Le bœuf bourguignon, parce que la sauce déguise le goût de la viande.
5. Il a commandé du chevreuil avec de la moutarde et des champignons.
6. Non, parce qu'une viande était suffisant pour elle.
7. Son père a pris du jambon persillé, et sa mère un steak avec une sauce béarnaise et des frites.

Reference Desk

1. Burgundy is a famous wine region in eastern France. There are 74,000 acres of vineyards, 100 different **appellations**, and 3,000 wine producers of 18 million cases of red and white wine per year. This wine region stretches 75 miles from Dijon to Macon. Some of the famous wines are produced in the **Côte d'Or**, **Côte de Nuits**, **Côte de Beaune**, and **Nuits-Saint-George** regions.
2. Dijon is famous for its mustards. Black currant mustard is one of its specialties. Famous mustard producers include **Maille**, **Amora**, and **Edmond Fallot**.
3. Only a few French verbs can be inverted in the first person singular (**faire, être, savoir,** and **pouvoir**). **Puis-je** from **pouvoir** is used to ask permission: **Puis-je savoir quelles sont les spécialités?**

Pour la conversation

1.1

How do I ask about restaurant specialties?

› **Puis-je savoir** quelles sont les spécialités?

May I find out the specialties?

How do I ask what a dish is served with?

› **Il est servi avec** de la moutarde?

Is it served with mustard?

Et si je voulais dire...?

le gibier	*game*
des paupiettes (f.)	*stuffed trout*
la poule au pot de truite	*boiled chicken with white sauce*
le canard à l'orange	*orange duck*
le cassoulet	*bean dish with goose meat and fat*
les cailles (f.) farcies	*stuffed quails*

1 Chère Maman

1.2, 1.3

Nayah est étudiante à Dijon. Lisez la lettre qu'elle a écrite à sa mère, puis répondez aux questions.

Chère Maman,

Mes études se passent bien. La famille de David m'a invitée à dîner au restaurant le weekend dernier, et j'ai mangé de la viande pour la première fois. Ses parents ne savent pas que je suis végétarienne, donc je n'avais pas le choix. J'ai pris la spécialité du restaurant—le bœuf bourguignon. La sauce à base de vin rouge était bonne et a déguisé le bœuf. David a commandé le chevreuil avec de la moutarde et des champignons. Il m'a offert de goûter, mais une viande c'était assez, alors j'ai dit non merci! Le père de David a choisi le jambon persillé, et sa mère un steak servi avec une sauce béarnaise et des frites.

Écris-moi vite.

Je t'embrasse,

Nayah

1. Qu'est-ce que Nayah a fait le weekend dernier?
2. Normalement, est-ce qu'elle mange de la viande? Pourquoi?
3. Pourquoi dit-elle qu'elle n'avait pas le choix?
4. Qu'est-ce que Nayah a commandé? Pourquoi?
5. Quel plat est-ce que son ami a pris?
6. Est-ce que Nayah a goûté au dîner de David? Pourquoi, ou pourquoi pas?
7. Qu'est-ce que les parents de David ont pris?

Essential Instruction

1. Present **Pour la conversation** vocabulary. Explain that Burgundy's abundant forests make it popular with hunters. Regional specialties feature game like quail, pheasant, deer, and rabbit.
2. Have students read **Activité 1**. Ask them what clues indicate that Nayah is a girl.
3. Students do **Activité 1** in pairs, answering questions 1–7.
4. Treat **Activité 2** as a guessing game. Put the animal choices on the board. Read the clues to the students. Expand the format to include the other lesson vocabulary.
5. Explain the preparation of each sauce. Have students answer **Activité 3** referencing the vocabulary on p. 281.

2 La viande  1.2

Faites correspondre chaque description à la viande de la liste.

faisan bœuf porc veau chevreuil lapin

1. un animal rose
2. un animal qui vole
3. une jeune vache
4. un petit animal avec de longues oreilles qui saute (*jumps*)
5. un grand animal qu'on peut chasser (*hunt*) en automne
6. un animal qu'on utilise pour faire des hamburgers et des steaks

3 Quelle sauce ce soir?  1.2, 5.1

Indiquez avec quelle sauce chaque viande ou légume est servi.

MODÈLE  **Les moules sont servies avec la sauce marinière.**

1. 
2. 
3. 
4. 
5. 
6. 
7. 
8. 
9. 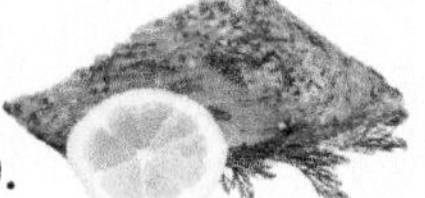
10. 
11. 

Answers

1. porc
2. faisan
3. veau
4. lapin
5. chevreuil
6. bœuf

1. Le steak est servi avec la sauce béarnaise.
2. Les œufs bénédicte sont servis avec la sauce hollandaise.
3. Le poisson est servi avec la sauce blanche/béchamel.
4. Le lapin est servi avec la sauce marinière.
5. Les pommes de terre sont servies avec la sauce hollandaise.
6. Le chevreuil est servi avec la sauce béarnaise.
7. Les asperges sont servies avec la sauce hollandaise/blanche.
8. Les langoustes sont servies avec la sauce béchamel.
9. Le saumon est servi avec la sauce béchamel.
10. Les courgettes sont servies avec la sauce blanche/béchamel.
11. Le poulet est servi avec la sauce blanche.

Reference Desk

1. **La chasse** means "hunting," **chasser** means "to hunt." **Un chasseur** is "a hunter."
2. **Le gibier** means "game." **Le gros gibier** is "big game" such as hunting for **sanglier** (*wild boar*), **cerf** (*stag*), **daim** (*fallow deer* from which we get suede), and **chevreuil** (*venison*). **Le petit gibier** is the general term for hunting fowl and small animals like **lièvre** (*hare*), **lapin** (*rabbit*), **perdrix** (*partridge*), and **faisan** (*pheasant*).

Differentiated Learning

Accelerate

Have students research restaurants in Dijon, then imagine that they own a restaurant. Have them create a menu featuring the specialties of the region with appetizing descriptions of each plate. They must include starters, main course, and dessert.

Decelerate

Have students find recipes for the five sauces listed in **Au restaurant bourguignon.** Ask students to do an imaginary cooking demonstration in class as if they had a cooking show. They will pantomime the cooking.

Learning Styles

Kinesthetic Learners

Encourage these students to cook samples of each sauce for the class.

Visual Learners

Ask these students to make a large chart of the Burgundy wine region, labeling the famous wines of each area.

Culture

Products: Activity

"Qui va à la chasse, perd sa place." What does this mean? Give examples in your daily life of how this expression might be relevant.

Answers

Script can be found in the front pages of the Annotated Teacher's Edition.

1. non
2. non
3. oui
4. non
5. oui
6. non
7. oui

5 *Answers will vary.*

Reference Desk

Here is some additional vocabulary that students might like to know: **jeter un coup d'oeil** (*to glance*); **comprendre** (*to include* as well as *to understand*); **maints plats** (*many dishes*); **il est très viande** (*the menu is mainly meat*); **les trompettes de la mort** (*a very popular mushroom which owes its name to its dark color*).

Game

Bingo

Using an online Bingo game generator, create boards featuring food terms and vocabulary. Students mark their cards if they have the word that you define in French.

Search words: **bingo game maker**

Communiquez!

4 Les plats cuisinés, délicieux!

1.1, 1.2

Interpretive Communication

Écrivez les numéros 1–7 sur votre papier. Puis, écoutez Stéphane décrire ses goûts culinaires. Enfin, écrivez ***oui*** *ou* ***non*** *pour répondre à la question que vous entendez.*

5 Questions personnelles

1.2, 1.3

Répondez aux questions suivantes.

1. Est-ce que tu vas souvent au restaurant? Quels restaurants préfères-tu: italiens, mexicains, ou chinois?
2. Préfères-tu choisir des plats avec ou sans viande? De quelle(s) viande(s) est-ce que tu ne manges pas? Et tes parents? Et tes amis?
3. Aimes-tu les plats servis avec une sauce? Si oui, lesquels?
4. Qu'est-ce que tu aimerais goûter dans un restaurant français?
5. As-tu jamais goûté du chevreuil? Si oui, c'était bon? Et le lapin?

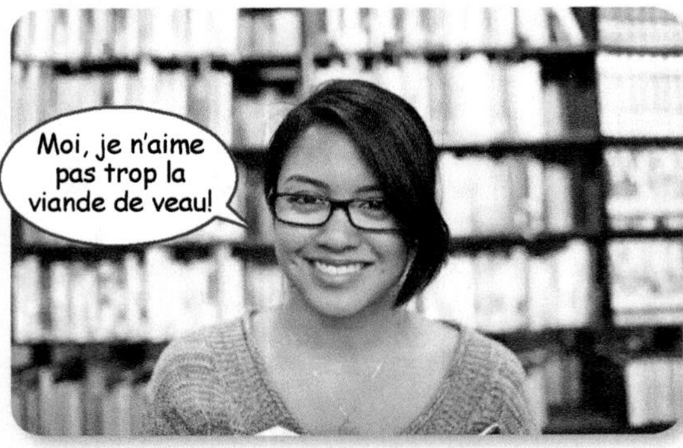

Essential Instruction

1. Students listen to **Activité 4** and answer **oui** or **non** on whiteboards. Have them show you their answer after each item for an immediate comprehension check.
2. In pairs, students interview each other as to their own food preferences by doing **Activité 5.**
3. Ask them to present their findings to a different partner before getting volunteers to report to the class. **Voici Marc. Il adore la cuisine mexicaine.**
4. Students listen to **Au restaurant dijonnais** with books closed, then tell you what they remember hearing.
5. Play the passage again as they follow in the book. Ask general comprehension questions.
6. Present the vocabulary from **Reference Desk** and answer any questions they may have before assigning **Activité 6.**

Rencontres culturelles

emcl.com
WB 4

Au restaurant dijonnais

1.1, 1.2, 5.2

Justin et Léo sont à table dans un restaurant à Dijon.

Le serveur: Bonjour, Messieurs. Avez-vous jeté un coup d'œil à la carte?

Justin: Oui, justement, puis-je savoir quelles sont les spécialités de la région?

Le serveur: Alors, la gastronomie de la Bourgogne comprend la moutarde et les escargots, bien entendu, mais aussi maints plats de viande et de poisson.

Léo: Il est très viande, mais il ne comprend pas toutes les dénominations.

Le serveur: D'accord, alors, le jambon persillé est fait avec du porc; le chevreuil sauce maison est servi avec des trompettes de la mort.

Justin: Les trompettes de la mort? Mon Dieu, qu'est-ce que c'est que ça?

Léo: Ce sont des champignons.

Le serveur: Oui, nous servons aussi du lapin, du faisan, mais personnellement je vous conseille un grand classique, le bœuf bourguignon!

Justin: Il est servi avec de la moutarde?

Le serveur: Non, mais la moutarde de Dijon, fermentée, accompagne très bien tous les plats.

Justin: Des escargots pour nous deux pour commencer, et pour moi, le bœuf bourguignon.

Léo: Je doute que les escargots aient bon goût. Pour moi, le jambon persillé seulement, s'il vous plaît. Je suis étonné que tu essaies les escargots!

Justin: À Rome, fais comme les Romains, et à Dijon, fais comme les Dijonnais!

6 Au restaurant dijonnais

1.1, 1.2

Identifiez la personne décrite.

1. Il explique ce que c'est, les trompettes de la mort.
2. Il explique les spécialités de la région.
3. Il voudrait goûter aux escargots.
4. Il sert beaucoup de plats de viande.
5. Il commande le bœuf bourguignon.
6. Il dit que son ami a besoin d'informations.
7. Il récite un proverbe.

RESOURCES

 **Dialogue Video**

 **Workbook 4**

Answers

1. Léo
2. le serveur
3. Justin
4. le serveur
5. Justin
6. Léo
7. Justin

Reference Desk

In addition to meaning "to understand," **comprendre** means "to include." **"La gastronomie de la Bourgogne comprend la moutarde et les escargots..." "Le service est compris?"**

Differentiated Learning

Accelerate

Ask students to work in groups of three to present **Activité 6** as if it were a scene from a movie.

Special Needs Students

AD(H)D/Dyslexia/Linguistically Challenged

Break down the dialogue into small sections. Ask these students basic comprehension questions in French to which they will respond in English. In this way, you will be able to determine their level of understanding. Rework the dialogue with them. Ask the same questions but this time have them reply in French.

Extension

Ils vont goûter à la cuisine des Antilles et du Sénégal.

Communication

Interpersonal: Cooperative Groups

Students write a dialogue similar to **Au restaurant dijonnais** and discuss their personal food preferences as well as what regional foods they would like to taste from **la Bourgogne**. Have them use these expressions: **Ça me dit**, **Ce plat me donne l'eau à la bouche**, **Je ne l'aime pas trop**, **Chacun à son goût**.

1. **Papilles (gustatives)** are taste buds.
2. **Tiep bou dienn**, the national dish of Senegal, is made of fish (sea bream and cod) and cooked with basil, onion, garlic, and vegetables to which a sauce of shrimp, and vegetables is added.
3. **Accras de morue**, a traditional snack food that supplements meals on the island of Saint Martin, is made of cod, garlic, chilies, cilantro, and onions.
4. **Couscous d'agneau** is a classic Moroccan dish made from lamb and vegetable dish and garnished with couscous.
5. **Saka-Saka**, is a Congolese word for cassava leaves which can only be found in the tropics. The dish is made with garlic, onion, green and sweet peppers, eggplant, and dried salted fish.

Extension **Des amis dînent au restaurant.**   1.2

Au restaurant, les amis regardent la carte et discutent des plats.

Amir:	Tiens, voici la carte; c'est un tour de la gastronomie de la Francophonie.
Charlotte:	Alors ce soir on voyage, j'ai peur qu'on n'ait plus envie de revenir....
Nicole:	Je sens que mes papilles sont en train de partir vers les Antilles!
Antoine:	Je voudrais goûter à la cuisine africaine.
Amir:	Il y a du *tiep*, c'est un plat de fête sénégalais.
Charlotte:	Qu'est-ce qu'il y a dedans?
Amir:	Du riz, du poisson, des aubergines, du piment.... C'est très bon!
Nicole:	Pour moi, des accras de morue.
Charlotte:	Je prendrais bien un bon couscous à l'agneau.
Antoine:	Moi je fais comme Amir.
Amir:	Pas très aventurier! Alors on va goûter le *saka-saka*. À toi de deviner ce qu'il y a dedans!

Extension La bande d'amis va goûter des plats de quelles régions ou pays francophones?

 1.2

Essential Instruction

1. Have students listen to **Extension** in the computer lab then research the recipes to identify their origins.
2. Play the dialogue again and ask volunteers to read the roles of the friends. Repeat with other students.

Points de départ 

emcl.com
WB 5

Question centrale
De quelles compétences ai-je besoin en voyageant?

Dijon et la Bourgogne

1.2, 2.1, 3.1

La Bourgogne est traversée par la Loire.

Dijon, capitale de la Bourgogne, a un passé prestigieux. C'est aujourd'hui le chef-lieu* du département de la Côte d'Or et de la région Bourgogne. L'agglomération dijonnaise* compte 340.000 habitants.

Dijon est l'ancienne* capitale du Duché de Bourgogne. Celui-ci a joué un grand rôle au XIV ème et XVème siècle alors qu'il recouvrait* les actuels Pays-Bas, la Belgique, le Luxembourg, le Palatinat en Allemagne et la Suisse, et les provinces de l'Alsace, de la Champagne, et de la Picardie. C'est le roi de France, Louis XI, qui a annexé l'État bourguignon en 1477 après la défaite* de Charles Le Téméraire.

Dijon au fil* des siècles s'est enrichi d'un riche patrimoine architectural dont témoignent* ses maisons à colombages*, ses beaux hôtels particuliers, et ses édifices religieux, églises et monastères* de style gothique qui charment les touristes.

Carrefour ferroviaire* depuis le XIXème siècle sur l'axe Paris-Marseille, Dijon est devenu un pôle économique important avec des industries dans les domaines électrique, mécanique, et électronique, mais aussi pharmaceutique et agro-alimentaire. Comme produits agro-alimentaires on peut citer la moutarde, le chocolat, le pain d'épices* et, la production de crème de cassis*. Avec l'ouverture* en décembre 2011 de la ligne TGV à grande vitesse entre le Rhin et le Rhône (le LGV), Dijon retrouve sa situation de plaque tournante* vers la Suisse, l'Allemagne et la Belgique, et vers le sud de l'Europe.

Search words: dijon tourisme, visiter dijon, dijon et sa région

chef-lieu *administrative center;* **agglomeration dijonnaise** *Dijon region;* **ancienne** *former;* **recouvrait** *extended;* **défaite** *defeat;* **au fil** *over;* **témoignent** *give evidence;* **maison à colombage** *half-timbered house;* **monastère** *monastery;* **carrefour ferroviaire** *rail hub;* **pain d'épice** *gingerbread;* **crème de cassis** *type of liquor made from black currants;* **ouverture** *opening;* **plaque tournante** *hub*

On peut voir **les trésors de l'art des Ducs de Bourgogne** dans l'ancien Palais des Ducs où se trouve le Musée des Beaux-Arts.

Search words: mba dijon

Le Palais des Ducs de Bourgogne à Dijon.

RESOURCES

Workbook 5

Reference Desk

Comparisons

Discuss national and regional American dishes. What foods do we associate with the South, the Eastern Seaboard, the Midwest, and the West Coast of the United States? Is our food purely American or a fusion of international cuisines? Give examples.

Expansion

In the lab, have students read **Dijon et la Bourgogne**. Make this a game to see how fast the students can find the following terms: **Les nonettes**,(*spice bread*); Fabrice Gillotte (famous chocolate maker from Dijon). **Les Trois Glorieuses** (famous wine festival and auction in Beaune), **Hospices de Beaune** (hospital for the poor opened in 1443), **Salle des pôvres** (the great hall of the **Hospices de Beaune**), **mba Dijon** (**Musée de Beaux Arts**), **crème de cassis**, and listed search words.

Special Needs Students

Social Anxiety

Many students have a very limited experience tasting foods with exotic ingredients. Continue to encourage them to be open to new tastes and dishes.

Dyslexia

Since **Dijon et la Bourgogne** is a longer reading, consider letting students with reading difficulties know in advance. Give them a copy of the reading and encourage them to read and mark the text with questions, vocabulary, or paraphrases.

Answers

7

1. *Answers will vary.*
2. *Possible answers:* la "Tour de Bar" en est le bâtiment le plus ancien; les "cuisines ducales", cuisines du duché; la Tour de la Terrasse (aujourd'hui Tour Philippe le Bon), tour de 52 mètres; la Place Royal, grande place du Palais; le 'Castrum', rempart élevé au IIIème siècle contre les invasions barbares.
3. *Answers will vary in time:* Dijon, Besançon, Belfort, Montbéliard, Mulhouse; branche Ouest: Dijon, Besançon, Belfort, Montbéliard, Mulhouse (branche Est)
4. 3envies, Amora, Delouis, Dijona, Edmond Fallot, Grey Poupon, Maille, Émile Noël, Parfum des Oliviers, Pléniday, Reine Dijon, Seau Baby, etc. (*Students give four.*)

Perspectives
Answers will vary.

Culture

Products: Information
Mustard is a popular condiment found on tables along with salt and pepper in modestly priced French restaurants. It is a staple in many recipes including the classic vinaigrette salad dressing, composed of three parts oil to one part vinegar to which one can add fine herbs. Mustard is used to emulsify the oil and vinegar in the vinaigrette.

Expansion

Have students inventory the kinds of mustards available in their local grocery store. What are the brands? How many of them are produced in France? What are the common ingredients found in these mustards?

La moutarde de Dijon est une moutarde forte qui existe en plusieurs variétés. Avant le XIVème siècle, le centre de la préparation de la moutarde était à Paris, mais depuis la Bourgogne s'en est fait une spécialité. C'est un produit que la France exporte aussi. 2.1

Quelle marque (*brand*) de moutarde est-ce que vous achetez? Avez-vous jamais goûté à la moutarde de Dijon? 4.2

7 Activités culturelles

1.3, 3.2

Faites les activités suivantes.

1. Dessinez la carte de l'ancien Duché de Bourgogne entre le XIVème et le XVème siècle.
2. Faites une liste de cinq choses intéressantes à voir au Palais des Ducs, avec des descriptions.
3. Faites une liste des destinations qu'on peut visiter sur la nouvelle ligne à grande vitesse Rhin-Rhône.
4. Trouvez quatre marques qui sont attachées à la moutarde de Dijon.

Perspectives

1.2

"En raison du superbe réseau de canaux navigables en bateau en Bourgogne, ma famille et moi, on a loué une péniche (*barge*). Quelle belle vue de cette magnifique région de France avec ses villages pittoresques et sa campagne verdoyante (*verdant*)! On s'est arrêté dans plusieurs villages où on a fait du vélo, flâné, fait les touristes, les courses et du shopping pour des souvenirs.... J'ai un très bon souvenir de la Bourgogne à cause de cette expérience en bateau." Selon cette vacancière, qu'est-ce qu'un voyage en péniche en Bourgogne offre aux touristes?

La moutarde de Dijon a une réputation mondiale.

Search words: la bourgogne fluviale, comment visiter la bourgogne en bateau

Péniches sur un fleuve de Bourgogne.

Essential Instruction

1. Assign partners to work in the computer lab on the activities in **Activité 7** according to their interest and ability.
2. After reading **Perspectives**, have students find a barge company online that offers travel to northern and southern Burgundy. Ask them to select a specific boat from each route and compare prices, sites, and accommodations.
3. Have students read **Du côté des médias**. Ask comprehension questions: On what days is the cooking school open? What are three adjectives that describe the recipes? How long is each class? What are two options for tasting the recipes? They cite their answers from the text.
4. Students choose an activity in **Activité 8**; for the second one, they might opt to film a commercial for the cooking school.

Du côté des médias  1.2, 5.1

Interpretive Communication

Lisez les informations suivantes pour un cours de cuisine à Dijon.

Le Menu

En 1h30, apprenez à préparer un repas complet de A à Z ou découvrez trois recettes autour d'un thème.

Avec l'aide de nos Chefs professionnels, réalisez des recettes élaborées inventives et toujours faciles à reproduire chez soi autour des produits de saison.
A vous de jouer !

Ce cours est destiné a être dégusté sur place dans le cadre d'un repas convivial à partager avec tous les participants du cours. Cependant, si vous le souhaitez, vous pouvez également emporter ce repas pour une dégustation chez vous !

Toute réservation sur internet doit être effectuée 48h avant la date du cours de cuisine choisi. Pour les réservations de dernière minute, contactez notre centrale de réservation au +33 (0)892 700 558 (0.34€ la mn)
Basse saison : de janvier à mars et d'octobre à décembre
Du lundi au samedi : de 9h30 à 13h et de 14h à 18h
Dimanches et jours fériés : de 10h à 16h
Haute saison : d'avril à septembre
Du lundi au samedi : de 9h30 à 18h30
Dimanches et jours férié : de 10h à 18h

8 L'Atelier des Chefs 1.3

Faites les activités suivantes.

1. On vous accepte pour l'Atelier des Chefs. Écrivez le message que vous avez reçu sur Internet.
2. Préparez une annonce à la radio pour l'Atelier des Chefs; vous avez 20 secondes.

Answers

8 *Activities will vary.*

Game

Que veut dire...?

Ask students to write down what they think the following idioms mean in English. The person with the closest renditions wins: **La moutarde me monte au nez.** (*I am getting angry.*); **mettre son grain de sel** (*to add one's two cents*); **C'est du beurre.** (*It is easy.*); **tomber dans les pommes** (*to faint*); **arriver comme un cheveu sur la soupe** (*something that happens at a bad time*).

Differentiated Learning

Adapt

There are many options for touring Burgundy, from organized excursions to cycling, barge travel, and even by hot air balloon. There are many things to do as well, such as cultural visits, cooking schools, wine tasting, and camping, just to name a few. Give your students a generous imaginary budget and have them organize a one-week itinerary traveling through Burgundy. Ask them to list hotels, restaurants, and the activities they do during their stay.

Learning Styles

Visual Learners

Have students create visuals for each of the expressions used in the game. They could visualize the French expressions on one side and the English equivalents on the other and add the written form to both. Use these to expand vocabulary and/or to decorate the classroom.

RESOURCES

Workbook 6–10

Drill & Practice Games

Reference Desk

1. Remind students that the indicative indicates fact, and the subjunctive is subjective, expressing opinion, wishes, desires, and emotions. If they understand that concept, they will be able to understand how the subjunctive is used.
2. Explain that these subjective expressions are followed by the subjunctive provided there is a subject change.
3. When verbs of emotion have no subject change, they are often followed by **de.** Contrast: **Je suis contente d'aller avec toi. Je suis contente que tu ailles avec moi.**

Structure de la langue

emcl.com
WB 6–10
Games

The Subjunctive after Expressions of Emotion 1.1

You have already learned that the subjunctive is used in a dependent clause after the expression **il faut que**; after certain impersonal expressions; and after expressions of wish, will, or desire. The subjunctive is also used after expressions of emotion (such as happiness, sadness, surprise, fear, anger). Use the subjunctive after one of the following expressions of emotion when the emotion concerns someone other than the subject.

être content(e) que	to be happy that
être heureux/heureuse que	to be happy that
être triste que	to be sad that
être désolé(e) que	to be sorry that
être fâché(e) que	to be angry that
être étonné(e) que	to be surprised that
avoir peur que	to be afraid that
regretter que	to be sorry that
s'inquiéter que	to worry that
Ça me surprend que….	It surprises me that….
Ça m'embête que….	It bothers me that….
C'est dommage que…	It's too bad that….

Ça me surprend que vous **mangiez** du chevreuil.	*It surprises me that you are eating venison.*
Je suis étonné que le veau **coûte** si cher!	*I'm surprised that the veal costs so much!*
Karim est fâché qu'il n'y **ait** pas de lapin au restaurant.	*Karim is mad that there isn't any rabbit at the restaurant.*
Le serveur a peur que nous n'**aimions** pas le faisan.	*The waiter is afraid that we don't like the pheasant.*
C'est dommage qu'on ne **serve** pas de bœuf bourguignon.	*It's a shame that beef bourguignon isn't served.*

Essential Instruction

1. With their books closed, ask students to suggest expressions of emotion that you will write on the board. Add to the list the expressions from the lesson that they did not mention.
2. Using these expressions, have students make sentences using the subjunctive.
3. In pairs, have students do **Activité 9**. Assign students to put the sentences on the board for correction.
4. Students change partners to play Tic-Tac-Toe in **Activité 10**.

9 Des phrases logiques

1.1

Faites des phrases logiques en combinant les mots de la première colonne et les phrases de la deuxième colonne. Attention à l'emploi du subjonctif. Il y a plus d'une réponse possible. Suivez le modèle. Quand vous aurez fini, comparez vos phrases avec celles d'un(e) partenaire.

Isa est surprise qu'il y ait un cheveu dans sa salade.

MODÈLE Diane/contente Le veau est bon.
Diane est contente que le veau soit bon.

1. moi/étonné(e)	Le jambon persillé n'a pas bon goût.
2. Yannick/triste	Le restaurant coûte trop cher.
3. Djamel/content	Vos amis n'aiment rien sur la carte.
4. toi/avoir peur	Il y a un moustique dans l'assiette.
5. Nicole/désolée	Ton ami est en retard.
6. Marc et Nathan/heureux	Il y a des spécialités.
7. Laure et toi/tristes	Le service est compris.
8. Youssef et moi/étonnés	Les clients ne commandent pas de dessert.
9. le serveur/fâché	La sauce est mauvaise.

10 Tic-Tac-Toe du subjonctif

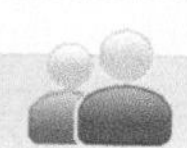

1.1

Prenez une feuille de papier. Avec un(e) partenaire, essayez de remplir votre grille de tic-tac-toe, chacun à votre tour, en faisant des phrases à l'aide des indices donnés. Vous pouvez aussi inventer votre propre grille.

MODÈLE

Je suis triste que tu veuilles chercher un autre hôtel.

avoir un bain à remous dans la chambre	vouloir chercher un autre hôtel	tu/m'attendre
le plat/être trop épicé	ne pas avoir assez d'argent	goûter le faisan
s'entendre avec le serveur	avoir la climatisation	aimer le dessert

Answers

9 *Possible answers:*

1. Je suis étonné(e) que le jambon persillé n'ait pas bon goût.
2. Yannick est triste que le restaurant coûte trop cher.
3. Djamel est content que le service soit compris.
4. Tu as peur que ton ami soit en retard.
5. Nicole est désolée que la sauce soit mauvaise.
6. Marc et Nathan sont heureux qu'il y ait des spécialités.
7. Laure et toi, vous êtes tristes que vos amis n'aiment rien sur la carte.
8. Youssef et moi sommes étonnés que les clients ne commandent pas de dessert.
9. Le serveur est fâché qu'il y ait un moustique dans l'assiette.

10 *Possible answers:*

1. Je suis très content(e) qu'il y ait un bain à remous dans la chambre.
2. Je suis désolé(e) que tu veuilles chercher un autre hôtel.
3. Je suis fâché(e) que tu ne m'attendes pas!
4. Nous sommes surpris que le plat soit trop épicé.
5. Ma mère est surprise que tu n'aies pas assez d'argent.
6. Nous sommes tristes que tu ne goûtes pas le faisan.
7. Nous sommes étonné(e)s que mon père s'entende avec le serveur.
8. Ma famille est fâchée qu'il n'y ait pas la climatisation.
9. Ma mère est triste que je n'aime pas le dessert.

Communication

Interpersonal: Paired Practice

Put students in pairs. Prepare a worksheet that describes a series of situations where they can respond, for example, **Les parents de mon ami disent qu'il ne peut pas prendre la voiture ce weekend** and **Le nouvel élève ne vous invite pas à sa boum.** Students take turns forming sentences using **je** or **nous**, an expression of emotion, and the subjunctive of the verb in the original sentence.

Differentiated Learning

Accelerate
Students may want to expand the exercises by writing a sentence about members of the class.

Decelerate
Give students a worksheet with expanded exercises for practice, or have them use online quizzes.
Search words: **quizlet**

Multiple Intelligences

Kinesthetic Learners
Encourage these students to write out verbs and subjunctive expressions.

Special Needs Students

AD(H)D
Help students with attention difficulties to break down the information about the subjunctive by reviewing the conjugation of regular and irregular verbs. They would benefit from a one-page chart used as an easy-reference when doing the exercises.

Answers

devions; donne; marche; puisse; devions; ait; coûte; veuille; envoyiez

Communication

Presentational: Cooperative Groups

After completing **Activité 11** have students work in mixed-ability groups to imagine this as a short skit. How might the rental agency's representative reply to the group's concerns about the apartment? Have the students write out each part and choose actors to present. Collect the written copy.

11 Une annonce trompeuse à Chamonix

1.3, 5.1

Julien et ses copains ont loué un appartement à Chamonix pour un weekend de ski. Il écrit à l'agence pour se plaindre. Complétez la lettre qu'il écrit en mettant les verbes entre parenthèses à la forme convenable.

Chamonix, le 14 janvier

Monsieur Dujardin,

Je regrette que mes amis et moi, nous (*devoir*) vous écrire, mais l'appartement que vous nous avez loué est loin de correspondre à votre annonce.

Nous voulions avoir une vue sur le Mont-Blanc. Mais nous avons été surpris de découvrir qu'aucune des fenêtres ne (*donner*) sur la montagne.

Ça nous embête que le bain à remous dans la salle de bains ne (*marcher*) pas. Je suis fâché que mes copains et moi, on ne (*pouvoir*) pas se reposer dans l'eau chaude après une journée de ski.

Nous avons demandé un appartement dans le domaine. Nous sommes étonnés que nous (*devoir*) prendre un bus pour aller à la station de ski.

C'est dommage qu'il n'y (*avoir*) pas de chaînes câblées dans le salon.

Cela nous surprend que cet appartement (*coûter*) si cher parce qu'il ne correspond pas du tout à votre annonce.

Je suis désolé qu'on ne (*vouloir*) pas revenir dans votre appartement. Nous souhaitons que vous nous (*envoyer*) deux cents euros.

Je vous prie d'agréer, Monsieur, nos salutations distinguées.

Julien Durouleaux

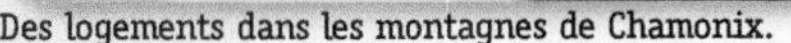

Des logements dans les montagnes de Chamonix.

Essential Instruction

1. Have students read the letter and complete the sentences in **Activité 11**.
2. In groups, have students respond to the letter as Monsieur Durouleaux. Challenge each group to use as many verbs in the subjunctive as possible.
3. Introduce the subjunctive after expressions of doubt or uncertainty. Explain that the indicative indicates a fact or certainty and the subjunctive shows emotion, opinion and, in this case, doubt and uncertainty.
4. Write the subjunctive/indicative expressions from the bottom of the chart on p. 293, mixing the two columns. Ask students to identify which expressions indicate doubt or uncertainty, and which ones express certainty.

emcl.com
WB 11
LA 2
Games

The Subjunctive After Expressions of Doubt or Uncertainty

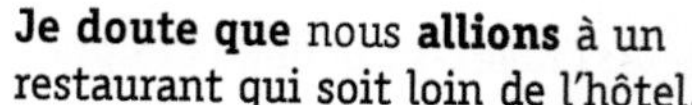

1.1

Je ne suis pas sûr que tu veuilles aller au cinéma avec moi, mais....

Another use of the subjunctive is after expressions of doubt or uncertainty. For example, the verb **douter** (*to doubt*) is followed by the subjunctive in the dependent clause.

Je doute que nous **allions** à un restaurant qui soit loin de l'hôtel.	*I doubt that we are going to a restaurant that is far from the hotel.*

When the verbs **penser** and **croire**, as well as certain expressions of certainty, are used negatively or interrogatively, they express doubt or uncertainty and are therefore followed by the subjunctive.

penser	**Penses-tu que** la sauce **soit** bonne avec du lait?	*Do you think that the sauce will be good with milk?*
croire	Non, **je ne crois pas qu'**elle **soit bonne**.	*No, I don't believe that it will be good.*
être sûr que	Le serveur, **est-il sûr qu'** on n'**ait** plus de poisson?	*The waiter, is he sure that they have no more fish?*
être certain que	Non, **il n'est pas certain que** vous **puissiez** en commander.	*No, he isn't certain that you can order it.*
être vrai que	**Est-il vrai que** tu **saches** faire toutes les sauces françaises?	*Is it true that you can make all the French sauces?*
être évident que	**Il n'est pas évident que** le chef **soit** français.	*It is not obvious that the chef is French.*

However, when **penser** and **croire**, as well as expressions of certainty, are in the affirmative or in the negative interrogative, they no longer express doubt and are followed by the indicative.

Ne crois-tu pas que cette sauce béarnaise **est** la meilleure?	*Don't you believe that this Béarnaise sauce is the best?*
Il est évident qu'on sert beaucoup de plats délicieux!	*It is obvious that they serve a lot of delicious dishes*

The following chart can help you determine the use of the subjunctive and the indicative.

Subjunctive	Indicative
Je doute que....	Je ne doute pas que....
Penses-tu que...?	Je pense que....
Je ne pense pas que....	Ne penses-tu pas que...?
Crois-tu que...?	Je crois que....
Je ne crois pas que....	Ne crois-tu pas que...?
Je ne suis pas sûr(e) que....	N'es-tu pas sûr(e) que...?
Je ne suis pas certain(e) que....	Je suis certain(e) que....
Es- tu certain(e) que...?	N'es-tu pas certain(e) que...?
Il n'est pas vrai que....	Il est vrai que....
Il n'est pas évident que....	Il est évident que....
Est-il évident que...?	N'est-il pas évident que...?

RESOURCES

Workbook 11

Listening Activity 2

Drill & Practice Games

Reference Desk

The charts help clarify the concept of the subjunctive with expressions of doubt and uncertainty. Students need time to think about what each expression conveys in the affirmative, negative, interrogative, and combinations of the three. Reinforce the logic of the subjunctive, even if students find it frustrating at first. Explain that this concept exists in other Latin languages so mastering the subjunctive in French will make the study of Spanish, for example, easier.

Game

Doute ou non?

Put students in pairs with whiteboards. Give them the options of **est en classe** or **soit en classe.** Mix expressions that are followed by the indicative and subjunctive. Students confer to write the correct response. Assign a point for each correct answer, for example, **Je doute que Paul...**or **Je suis certain que Paul...**

Differentiated Learning

Accelerate

Have students collaborate to write a short scene from a soap opera using as many expressions with the subjunctive as possible. Expressions of wishing, wanting, doubting, and fearing lend themselves to melodramatic pathos. Have groups present to the class.

Decelerate

Ask students to write flash cards of the indicative and subjunctive expressions in two colors, green for expressions followed by the indicative and red for those followed by the subjunctive. The color-coding might help them remember, especially if they are visual learners.

Answers

Affirmative answers will use the indicative, negative answers will use the subjunctive.

2. A: Croyez-vous que les études universitaires m'intéressent?
3. A: Croyez-vous que je prenne du café au petit-déjeuner?
4. A: Croyez-vous que je fasse du dessin?
5. A: Croyez-vous que je suive un cours d'art?
6. A: Croyez-vous que j'aille souvent au parc d'attractions?
7. A: Croyez-vous que je coure dans les marathons?
8. A: Croyez-vous que je m'entraîne au fitness?

1. Mme Delattre est sûre que la ville ouvre un centre d'accueil pour les sans-abri.
2. Le père de Mme Delattre n'est pas sûr que sa femme et lui puissent faire un don au centre d'accueil.
3. Les infirmiers ne croient pas que l'hôpital fasse assez pour combattre le SIDA.
4. Le directeur de l'hôpital croit qu'on enseigne bien aux patients le traitement pour le SIDA.
5. Théo et Clara sont certains que le racisme est un problème dans la société.
6. Leurs parents ne sont pas certains qu'une manifestation contre le racisme soit une bonne idée pour Théo et Clara.
7. Simon ne pense pas que son oncle boive trop d'alcool.
8. Sa tante pense que sa famille doit faire une intervention.

12 J'interviewe mes camarades de classe.

1.1, 1.2, 5.2

D'abord, répondez aux questions individuellement et gardez vos réponses. À tour de rôle, en groupes de trois, posez une question à vos partenaires basée sur les questions. Suivez le modèle. Si vos camarades de classe ne vous croient pas, montrez-leur vos réponses écrites.

MODÈLE
A: **Croyez-vous que j'aie peur des gros chiens?**
B: **Non, je ne crois pas que tu aies peur des gros chiens!**
C: **Moi, je crois que tu as peur des gros chiens!**
A: **C'est vrai. J'ai peur des gros chiens!**

1. Vous avez peur des gros chiens?
2. Les études universitaires vous intéressent?
3. Vous prenez du café au petit-déjeuner?
4. Vous faîtes du dessin?
5. Vous suivez un cours d'art?
6. Vous allez souvent au parc d'attractions?
7. Vous courez dans les marathons?
8. Vous vous entraînez au fitness?

13 Les problèmes dans la société

1.3

Formez des phrases en utilisant le premier verbe indiqué à l'indicatif et le deuxième verbe à l'indicatif ou au subjonctif.

MODÈLES

le directeur du lycée Victor Hugo/douter que le gouvernement/vouloir moderniser son école
Le directeur du lycée Victor Hugo doute que le gouvernement veuille moderniser son école.

les élèves/ne pas douter que le directeur/installer un nouveau labo de langues
Les élèves ne doutent pas que le directeur installe un nouveau labo de langues.

1. Mme Delattre/être sûr que la ville/ouvrir un centre d'accueil pour les sans-abri
2. le père de Mme Delattre/ne pas être sûr que sa femme et lui/pourvoir faire un don au centre d'accueil
3. les infirmiers/ne pas croire que l'hôpital/faire assez pour combattre le SIDA
4. le directeur de l'hôpital/croire qu'on/enseigner bien aux patients le traitement pour le SIDA
5. Théo et Clara/être certain que le racisme/être un problème dans la société
6. leurs parents/ne pas être certain qu'une manifestation contre le racisme/être une bonne idée pour Théo et Clara
7. Simon/ne pas penser que son oncle/boire trop d'alcool
8. sa tante/penser que sa famille/devoir faire une intervention

Essential Instruction

1. Ask a student to assume the role of teacher. As a review, ask him/her to explain the use of the subjunctive in expressions of doubt and uncertainty.
2. Students do **Activité 12** in groups of three.
3. Using whiteboards, students do sentences 1–8 in **Activité 13**, one at a time, then show their responses for each sentence. This way you can correct errors as they do the exercise and give immediate feedback.
4. Students work in pairs to do **Activité 14**. Before they begin, preview any terms that they might not know or remember.
5. Play **Activité 15**. Students write **D** or **C** according to the sense of the statement. If the class has problems, play each sentence again, writing out the statement on the board to explain.

14 L'environnement   1.1, 5.2

*À tour de rôle, posez les questions suivantes à votre partenaire. Mettez la forme correcte du verbe indiqué au subjonctif. Puis, donnez votre avis honnêtement, soit (*either*) à l'affirmatif avec l'indicatif, soit (*or*) au négatif avec le subjonctif.*

1. Penses-tu qu'on... prendre l'effet de serre au sérieux? (*devoir*)
2. Crois-tu que le Vélib... l'environnement? (*aider*)
3. Penses-tu que nous... venir au lycée à vélo ou à pied? (*devoir*)
4. Es-tu sûr(e) qu'il y... des animaux en voie de disparition? (*avoir*)
5. Est-il vrai qu'on... sauvegarder les espaces sauvages pour eux? (*devoir*)
6. Tu n'es pas certain(e) qu'on... arrêter les marées noires? (*pouvoir*)
7. Tu n'es pas sûr(e) que les panneaux solaires... bon marché? (*être*)
8. Est-il vrai que toi et ta famille, vous...? (*recycler*)
9. Est-il évident que les hommes politiques nous... sur les problèmes de l'environnement? (*écouter*)

Communiquez!

15 La cuisine, c'est bon!   1.1, 1.2

Interpretive Communication

*Écrivez les numéros 1–6 sur votre papier. Écoutez les phrases. Puis, écrivez **D** si vous pensez que la phrase exprime (*expresses*) un doute, ou **C** si vous pensez qu'elle exprime une certitude.*

Answers

1. doive
2. aide
3. devions
4. ait
5. doive
6. puisse
7. soient
8. recycliez
9. écoutent

15

Script can be found in the front pages of the Annotated Teacher's Edition.

1. D
2. C
3. C
4. C
5. D
6. D

Communication

Interpersonal: Cooperative Groups

Put students into small groups. Ask them to bring a magazine picture that can be described using the subjunctive after an expression of emotion. The first student describes his or her picture, for example, **Mme Bouquet est heureuse que sa fille lui téléphone.** The second student asks a question, for example, **Qu'est-ce que sa fille lui dit?** The first student responds. Have students extend their discussion as far as they can. The remaining students take turns describing their pictures with the person to their right.

Differentiated Learning

Adapt

Ask students to write a series of statements, which may or may not reflect their beliefs. Have them mingle with other students reading one of their remarks. The other student agrees (**Je crois que...**) or disagrees (**Je doute que...**), repeating the student's statement. The students reverse roles. One student might say "**Je déteste le chocolat.**" The other responds "**Je doute que tu détestes le chocolat.**" or "**Je veux aller au cinéma.**" The other student would say "**Je crois que tu veux aller au cinema.**"

Special Needs Students

Linguistically Challenged

Some students have difficulty understanding the difference between the indicative and the subjunctive as well as conjugating the verbs correctly. Providing a review of regular and irregular conjugations in both moods is essential each time the use of the subjunctive is expanded.

RESOURCES

Communicative Activities

Answers

All activities will vary.

Reference Desk

Blended Instruction

Consider using blended instruction, a combination of in-class learning and computer-mediated instruction or learning opportunities. Ask students to complete activities on the computer, using their cell or smartphone, or other emerging electronic technology. This will allow students to hone their tech skills and become more independent learners. Schedule routine Internet and e-book learning in class and in the lab.

À vous la parole

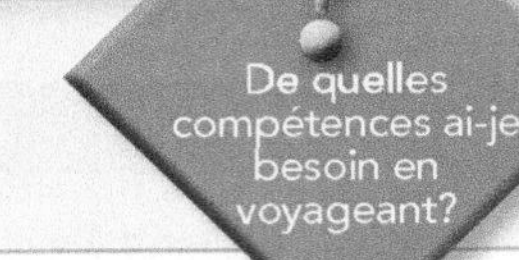

16 Au restaurant dijonnais

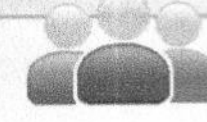

1.1, 1.2, 5.1, 5.2

Interpersonal Communication

Vous êtes dans un restaurant dijonnais avec un ami. Un(e) autre camarade de classe jouera le rôle du serveur ou de la serveuse. Pour la partie A, parlez avec votre ami(e) de ce que vous anticipez en utilisant des expressions comme **je regrette**, **je suis désolé(e)**, **j'ai peur que**. Après un certain temps, le serveur/la serveuse arrive et vous commandez un repas avec hors-d'œuvre, plat principal, dessert, et boisson. Pour la partie B, imaginez que le serveur/la serveuse vous a servi. Dites ce que vous pensez de la nourriture et exprimez un doute vis-à-vis (*regarding*) du dessert qui n'est pas encore arrivé.

17 Mon restaurant à Dijon

1.3, 5.1

Presentational Communication

Imaginez que vous ouvrez un restaurant américain à Dijon. Préparez le menu en français. N'oubliez pas d'inclure quelques spécialités régionales pour plaire à vos clients qui ne sont pas très aventuriers. Il faut aussi mettre les prix en euros et créér une couverture avec une image et un nom attrayant (*seductive*).

18 En péniche

1.3, 3.2

Interpretive/Presentational Communication

Vous voudriez mieux connaître la Bourgogne. Donc, vous planifiez un voyage en péniche dans la région. Préparez un document avec les villes que vous allez visiter et une liste de choses à faire et à voir à chaque destination. Incluez une carte qui montre où vous irez.

Search words: **la bourgogne fluviale, comment visiter la bourgogne en bateau**

Essential Instruction

1. Before doing **Activité 16** have students go online to find the menus of top restaurants in Dijon so that they include authentic appetizers, main courses, and desserts on their menus.
2. To help students brainstorm American specialties for their restaurant, have them visit American restaurants online from different regions of the United States.
3. For **Activité 18**, encourage students to be creative in their choice of format. They may want to make a commercial for television, a travelogue, or a multi-media presentation.
4. Have students listen with books closed as you read the sentences in **Activité 19**. Ask them to tell you where the statement was made.
5. For **Activité 20** students may choose, or be assigned, four of the ten options for a dialogue. Encourage them to make the dialogues realistic by weaving into the conversation as much vocabulary as they can.

Stratégie communicative 

Practical Conversations

Lorsque vous voyagerez dans un pays francophone, vous aurez besoin d'obtenir certains renseignements. Se souvenir de certaines expressions et de certains mots vous sera très utile au moment d'acheter un billet de train, de commander dans un restaurant ou dans un café, ou encore si vous avez besoin qu'on vous indique le chemin, par exemple.

19 Débuts de dialogues pratiques

 1.3, 5.1

Lisez les questions ou les phrases ci-dessous et précisez l'endroit où on pourrait les entendre.

1. Vous pourriez vérifier s'il y a assez d'huile?
2. Je voudrais que vous me donniez quelques précisions sur les prestations.
3. Je cherche un blouson en cuir noir.
4. Le bœuf bourguignon que vous avez préparé est délicieux.
5. Vous avez le dernier *Pariscope*?
6. Vous pouvez m'indiquer le chemin? Je cherche le musée d'Orsay.
7. Quelle sont les spécialités de la région?
8. Vous avez un forfait ski?

20 Je me renseigne en voyage.

  1.1, 5.1, 5.2

Avec votre partenaire, créez une conversation pour quatre endroits de la liste. Posez une question, demandez un service, ou renseignez-vous de manière générale.

1. une station-service
2. un marché
3. un kiosque à journaux
4. un guichet de cinéma
5. un hôtel
6. un restaurant en Normandie
7. une réception de mariage
8. un cercle de conversation à l'Alliance française
9. une gare
10. chez une famille française

La Gare de Lyon, à Paris.

Answers

19
1. à la station-service
2. à l'hôtel
3. au magasin/centre commercial
4. au restaurant/à une soirée
5. au kiosque à journaux/à la librairie
6. dans la rue
7. au restaurant
8. à la station de ski

20 *Conversations will vary.*

Reference Desk

Henri Gault, Christian Millau, and André Gayot are important names in the world of French cuisine. Restaurant critics and travel guide writers, they coined and promoted the term **nouvelle cuisine.** Have students research Gault, Millau, and Gayot to learn more.

Differentiated Learning

Expand

Ask students to go online to research the locations they will use as a basis for the conversation in **Activité 20.** This research will afford them more details for their dialogues. For example, photos of **une réception de mariage** found online will act as prompts for a dialogue.

Accelerate

Have pairs or small groups brainstorm vocabulary, verbs, and expressions needed for two of the destinations in **Activité 20**, then create a poster list of the expressions and display them around the room for the class to consult as they work on their own conversations.

Learning Styles

Visual Learners

Have students create a visual to complement each of the four dialogues they choose from **Activité 20** and then use them when they present the conversation.

RESOURCES

 e-visual 15

 Workbook 1–4

 Flash Cards

 Listening Activity 1

 Drill & Practice Games

Reference Desk

1. There are many different film **genres: un western, une comédie, un film d'horreur, un film de science-fiction, un film classique, un film d'aventures, un film d'action, un film policier** (*detective*), **un documentaire, un drame, une comédie musicale, un voyage dans le temps** (*time travel*).
2. Useful terms: **le premier rôle** (*leading male actor*), **le premier rôle feminin** (*leading female role*), **le second rôle** (*supporting actor*), **la vedette** (*star*), **le metteur-en-scène** (*director*), **une course-poursuite** (*car chase*). **Un(e) mordu(e)** comes from the verb **mordre** (*to bite*). A fan is someone who is bitten by a certain interest. **Un navet** (*a turnip*) is a bad film.

Vocabulaire actif

emcl.com
WB 1–3
LA 1
Games

Le cinéma   1.2

Tourner un film

www.premiere.fr/films

CINEMA

NOUVEAUTÉS CINÉMA/HORAIRES ET SALLES

Comme des frères
Comédie, couleur, 104 mns
Réalisé par: Hugo Célin
Avec: François-Xavier DEMAISON
Nicolas DUVAUCHELLE
Pierre NINEY
Mélanie THIERRY
Date de sortie: le 21 novembre

Résumé:
Depuis que Charlie est morte, la vie de Boris, Elie et Maxime n'est plus la même. Ces hommes de trois générations différentes, que tout sépare, ne savent comment faire face à cette tragédie. Mais comme Charlie le leur avait demandé, ils décident de faire un voyage ensemble en Corse. Et voilà qu'alors qu'ils ont perdu cette femme adorée, elle va changer leur vie pour toujours.

Notes et critiques:
Presse (24 critiques) *****
Internautes (3 avis) *****

Voir la bande-annonce

CINEMA

NOUVEAUTÉS CINÉMA/HORAIRES ET SALLES

>Cinéma>Horaires et salles

UGD Capitole
134 la Canebière
13001 Marseille

Le monde de Charlie
Pays de Production: États-Unis
Drame américain avec Logan Lerman, Emma Watson, Ezra Miller. Durée: 2h30
Titre original: The Perks of Being a Wallflower
13h45 (vo, sous-titré), 17h35 (vf, doublé)

Labels: les nouveautés (f.); la durée; le genre; un réalisateur, une réalisatrice; une sortie; la description; la critique; le cinéma; le titre; une version originale (V.O.); les sous-titres/sous-titré; Le film a été tourné en Corse.; le casting; une bande-annonce; une vedette; un long métrage; le doublage/doublé; la version française

Essential Instruction

1. Have students listen to the vocabulary **Le cinéma.** Ask them questions about the text using the vocabulary in the margins.
2. Have the students listen to **Pour la conversation** and the additional vocabulary.
3. Put the vocabulary from **Reference Desk** on the board and ask students to give examples of each genre. Ask students to name their favorite actors and directors, a film with a car chase, and **navets** that they have seen.
4. Expand the discussion to current television shows as well since they have the same elements and students are apt to watch televison more regularly.
5. Have students read **Activité 1.** Ask them questions 1–6.

Pour la conversation  1.1, 5.1

emcl.com
WB 4

How do I say what I'm not in the mood for?

> **Je ne suis pas trop d'humeur pour** une comédie dramatique.
>
> *I'm not in the mood for a dramatic comedy.*

How do I relate the opinion of someone else?

> **Il paraît que c'est** très drôle.
>
> *It appears it's very funny.*

How do I ask about someone's impressions?

> **Quelles sont** tes **impressions** du film?
>
> *What are your impressions of the movie?*

How do I express disagreement?

> **Je ne partage pas** ton **avis.**
>
> *I don't share your opinion.*

Et si je voulais dire...? 

un cascadeur	*stuntman*
la distribution	*the cast*
un figurant	*extra (actor)*
une représentation	*performance*
applaudir	*to clap*
huer	*to boo*

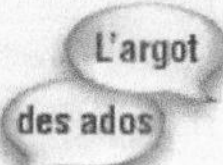

LE CINÉMA

le cinoche	*le cinéma*
un(e) mordu(e) du cinéma	*un fan*
un nanar	*un mauvais film*
un navet	*un mauvais film*
une star	*une vedette*

1 Une critique  1.2

Lisez la critique du film suivant, puis répondez aux questions.

Le chien de mon frère

2012. 2h10. Comédie française en couleurs.
La dernière grande comédie pour ceux qui aiment rire vient de sortir dans les salles. Allez voir ce film tout de suite. Le casting est très fort. Un long métrage par un réalisateur bien connu qui pourrait devenir un classique. Évitez la bande-annonce, qui en révèle trop sur les personnages et les événements. Si vous voulez voir une comédie, ou tout simplement rire de bon cœur, ne cherchez pas plus loin: *Le chien de mon frère* est ce qu'il vous faut. C'est un film touchant et drôle à la fois au sujet d'un chien adopté qui a un peu trop d'énergie. Vous partagerez mon avis. Je vous le promets.

1. Quelle est la durée du film?
2. Quand est-ce qu'il est sorti?
3. Que pense le critique de ce film?
4. Qu'est-ce qu'on ne doit pas faire?
5. Quand est-ce qu'on devrait choisir ce film?
6. Quelle est la description du film?

Answers

1. 2h10
2. Il vient de sortir.
3. Qu'il a un très bon casting et pourrait devenir un classique.
4. Regarder la bande-annonce.
5. Quand on veut rire.
6. Il s'agit d'un chien adopté qui a trop d'énergie.

Reference Desk

A number of French films have been remade into American films including *Three Men and a Baby* (***Trois hommes et un couffin***), *The Birdcage* (***La Cage aux folles***), *Father's Day* (***Les Compères***), *The Tourist* (***Anthony Zimmer***), *The Good Thief* (***Bob le flambeur***), *Dinner for Schmucks* (***Le Dîner de cons***), and many more.

Differentiated Learning

Accelerate

Have students go online to research current popular French films. Ask them to determine the percentage of foreign films to French films that are in the theaters and to identify the popular American actors in current films.

Search words: l'officiel des spectacles

Decelerate

Give students time in the computer lab to explore **allociné**. Ask them to list what American television series are playing in France. Have them select one, read ten critiques, then make a list of positive and negative expressions used by viewers. Low-ability students may enjoy this site, the result being that they read more French out of curiosity.

Special Needs Students

At-Risk Students

Discussing films can be a good hook to get these students involved. Young people enjoy going to movies and renting DVDs. Look for ways to engage them in conversations about topics that interest them.

Answers

1. le genre
2. le titre
3. la durée
4. le réalisateur
5. le casting
6. la description
7. le cinéma
8. la version

1. C'est la durée du film.
2. C'est le cinéma où passe le film.
3. C'est la version.
4. C'est la description du film.
5. C'est le genre du film.
6. C'est la critique du film.
7. Ce sont les sous-titres.
8. C'est le casting./Ce sont les vedettes.
9. C'est le réalisateur.

Reference Desk

Pariscope is an inexpensive weekly magazine listing events and happenings in Paris. One third of the listings are under **Cinéma** since this is such a popular pastime. **Salles** are listed alphabetically by neighborhood, and some theaters offer discounts on Mondays and Wednesdays. An important code to know is **V.O.** (films not dubbed in English). Other headings include: **Arts** for hours and locations of galleries and museums plus **Expositions**, **Théâtres**, **Musique**, **Enfants**, **Promenades et Loisirs**. Codes to be aware of are **tlj** (*every day*), **sf** (*except*), **ent** (*price*) and **tr** (*reduced price*).

2 Pariscope

1.2

Choisissez l'expression convenable de la liste suivante qui correspond à chaque expression indiquée dans le guide.

le genre · le réalisateur · le cinéma · le titre · la durée · la version · la description · le casting

C ASSOCIES CONTRE LE CRIME (2) France. Coul. (1h44) (3) Comédie policière (1) de Pascal Thomas (4) L'impétueuse Prudence enquête avec son époux sur la disparition d'une richissime héritière russe. Avec Agathe de la Boulaye, André Dussolier, Catherine Frot, Nicolas Marie, Eric Naggar, Linh-Dan Pham, Hervé Pierre, Bernard Verley. (5) **Nouvel Odéon 6e. Publicis Cinémas 8e. Gaumont Alésia 14e. Gaumont Parnasse 14e. Le Champlin-St Lambert 15e. Studio 28 18e.**

J L'ÂGE DE GLACE 4: LA DÉRIVE DES CONTINENTS (Ice Age: Continental Drift) États-Unis. Coul. (12-1h34). Animation, de Steve Martino, Mike Thurmeier. Le morcellement de la terre sépare nos héros des leurs et les fait dériver sur un iceberg. (6) **UGC Orient-Express 1er. L'Épée de bois 5e. Gaumont Champs-Élysées 8e** (3D). **UGC Ciné Cité Bercy 12e** (3D). **MK2 Bibliothèque 13e. Gaumont Aquaboulevard 15e. Studio 28 18e.** (7) (vo) (8)

3 C'est quoi ou c'est qui?

1.2

Identifiez la personne ou la chose.

MODÈLE Le film s'appelle *Bienvenue chez les Ch'tis.*
C'est le titre du film.

1. Le film commence à 14h00 et se termine à 15h45.
2. On passe le film au Gaumont.
3. C'est en français.
4. Il s'agit d'un facteur (*mail carrier*) qui déménage dans le nord de la France et vit des aventures.
5. C'est une comédie.
6. "C'est une comédie qui fait rire. Vous allez l'adorer."
7. Pour le public américain, il y a des mots écrits en anglais sur l'écran.
8. Dany Boon, Kad Merad, et Chloé Félix sont les acteurs dans le film.
9. Dany Boon a aussi tourné le film.

Essential Instruction

1. Have students do **Activité 2** and **Activité 3** in pairs.
2. Ask students to listen and respond to questions 1–6, **Activité 4**.
3. Put the desks in a circle and have students take turns asking the questions in **Activité 5**. Since this is such a popular topic, you should be able to expand the conversation and have a lively discussion about their personal taste in films.
4. Ask students to talk about their favorite television shows. Do they think there is a difference between television and movie stars? Do they pay attention to the name of the director of a film or television series? Do they prefer movies made from books like *Harry Potter* or *The Lord of the Rings*? Why or why not?

Communiquez!

4 Quel film on va voir?

1.2

Interpretive Communication

Écrivez les numéros 1–6 sur votre papier. Écoutez la conversation, puis écrivez un mot ou une expression pour répondre aux questions que vous entendez.

5 Questions personnelles

1.3

Répondez aux questions.

1. Est-ce que tu préfères voir les films au cinéma ou à la télé? Comment décides-tu quels films tu vas voir au cinéma?
2. Quels aspects d'un film sont importants dans ton choix—le genre, les acteurs, le réalisateur, ou autre chose?
3. Est-ce que tu regardes quelquefois des films étrangers (*foreign*)? Préfères-tu voir un film étranger avec des sous-titres ou doublé en anglais? Pourquoi?
4. Quelles différences y a-t-il entre tes goûts et les goûts de tes ami(e)s? Et entre les goûts des ados et les goûts des adultes que tu connais?
5. Quel est le dernier film que tu as vu? Quel film as-tu envie de voir bientôt? Pourquoi?
6. Quel(s) film(s) français ou en français as-tu vu(s)?

Answers

4 Script can be found in the front pages of the Annotated Teacher's Edition.

1. une comédie
2. Adam Sandler
3. Non, ils veulent rire.
4. non
5. la bande-annonce
6. non

5 *Answers will vary.*

Communication

Interpersonal: Paired Practice

Using **Activité 2** as a model, have students work with partners to recreate two ***Pariscope*** film listings. They can use French or American films but must include all of the categories. Once done, students work with another set of partners to discuss their films. They ask each other questions using the vocabulary in the box, for example, **Quel est le titre des films? C'est quel genre? Comment s'appelle le réalisateur?** If time, have students share with the rest of the class.

Differentiated Learning

Expand

In small groups, have students reminisce about the films and television shows they watched as children. What was the very first film they remember? What was the story about? What was their reaction to it? Have students report back to the class about the programs and films they discussed. Take a poll of their favorites.

Accelerate

Ask these students to learn the **Et si je voulais dire...?** and **L'argot des ados** vocabulary from p. 299 and create an activity to teach their classmates. Encourage them to create a dialogue to demonstrate the new expressions used in a realistic context as part of their activity.

Decelerate

Ask students who need extra time learning vocabulary to copy the expressions from **Et si je voulais dire...?** and **L'argot des ados** before the students do their introduction activity.

RESOURCES

 **Dialogue Video**

 **Workbook 5**

Answers

1. les films
2. La Coupole
3. réalisateur
4. synopsis, ex-chef d'orchestre soviétique
5. la bande-annonce
6. nanar, catastrophe

Communication

Interpersonal: Paired Practice

Have students write a dialogue between a parent and child discussing which movie they should go see. The conversation should point out the differences in generational tastes.

Game

De quoi s'agit-il?

Have students work in small groups to write a short synopsis of five popular films from their childhood to the present. Next, get them together to play a guessing game with the other groups in the class. **C'est l'histoire d'un ogre vert qui a, comme copain, un âne bavard.** (*Shrek*)

Rencontres culturelles

emcl.com WB 5

On va au multiplexe.

   1.1, 1.2, 5.2

Élodie et Karim consultent les films sur AlloCiné.

Élodie: Quel genre de film te dit?
Karim: Clique d'abord sur Accueil, pour voir les nouveautés.
Élodie: Tiens, *Le concert* passe à La Coupole! C'est d'un excellent réalisateur!
Karim: Ah oui? Lequel?
Élodie: Radu Mihaileanu. Et le casting est composé de vraies vedettes!
Karim: Je ne suis pas trop d'humeur pour une comédie dramatique, mais voyons le synopsis: "Un ex-chef d'orchestre soviétique est maintenant homme de ménage au Bolchoï. Au travail, il tombe sur un fax adressé au directeur: il s'agit d'une invitation à venir jouer à Paris. Il réunit ses anciens copains musiciens et les emmène tous à Paris…." Il paraît que c'est très drôle. Que disent les critiques?
Élodie: Les critiques donnent quatre étoiles, ça promet!
Karim: Bon, je veux bien. Prends les Ciné Chèques et allons-y.

(Après le film….)

Karim: Quelles sont tes impressions du film?
Élodie: J'ai éprouvé une émotion intense. C'est un vrai chef-d'œuvre!
Karim: Je ne partage pas ton avis, je suis plutôt blasé; le ton était plat, les actions stéréotypées, trop de pauses entre les dialogues à mon goût!
Élodie: N'as-tu donc pas apprécié la musique?
Karim: Laquelle?
Élodie: Celle du final, de Tchaïkovski!
Karim: Non, vraiment, c'est un nanar style Hollywood. Une vraie catastrophe!

6 On va au multiplexe.

  1.2

Complétez les phrases suivantes.

1. Karim et Élodie voient… sur AlloCiné.
2. Élodie suggère le film *Le concert*, qui passe à….
3. Le… est Radu Mihaileanu.
4. Le… indique qu'il s'agit d'un… qui emmène ses anciens copains musiciens à Paris.
5. Karim pense que le film est un… et une….

Essential Instruction

1. Have students watch the video **On va au multiplexe**. Ask general comprehension questions.
2. Students watch the video again and answer the questions 1–5 in **Activité 6.**
3. Write the terms **réactions positives** and **réactions negatives** on the board. Have students find the comments in the dialogue about the film that could be put into each category, for example, **"C'est d'un excellent réalisateur,"** or **"C'est un nanar style Hollywood."**
4. Place students into high and low-ability groups to read **Extension,** then have them answer the question about the dialogue. A short class discussion can follow.
5. Students work in the computer lab to research the actresses, director, and films mentioned in **Extension.**

Extension **Les criminelles**  1.1, 1.2

Alexandre et Simon sont à la FNAC dans le rayon DVD.

Alexandre:	Tu as acheté tout ça!
Simon:	Il y a une promotion, et en plus des titres géniaux.
Alexandre:	Lesquels?
Simon:	Criminelles... Brigitte Bardot, Catherine Deneuve, Jeanne Moreau, Isabelle Adjani, Isabelle Huppert....
Alexandre:	Dans quels films?
Simon:	Devine!
Alexandre:	Deneuve, *La sirène du Mississipi*; Moreau... le Truffaut... *La mariée était en noir*? Adjani, *Mortelle randonnée*; Bardot, *La vérité*; et Huppert... lequel? Elle a beaucoup joué les criminelles....
Simon:	Surtout chez Chabrol.
Alexandre:	Difficile... euh... je sais pas, moi....
Simon:	C'est un bon Chabrol! Viens chez moi, je te ferai une projection privée... ça sera la surprise....

Extension 1.3

Quel film est-ce qu'Alexandre n'arrive pas à deviner? Les garçons parlent de combien d'acteurs et de réalisateurs? Est-ce qu'Alexandre et Simon sont des cinéphiles? Expliquez.

Answers

Extension

Un film de Claude Chabrol.; 7; Oui, ils semblent connaître beaucoup de films.

Reference Desk

1. Brigitte Bardot (1934) made 47 films, recorded 50 songs, and became the iconic sex symbol of the 1950s and 1960s.
2. Catherine Deneuve (1943) won an Academy Award and **César** for ***Indochine*** and a **César** for ***Le Dernier Métro***. Her face was chosen to represent Marianne, the symbol of France, from 1985–89.
3. Jeanne Moreau (1928), an actress, singer, director, and screenwriter, was best known as the star of François Truffaut's classic film ***Jule et Jim***.
4. Isabelle Adjani (1955) was awarded the most **César** for best actress. She starred in the films ***Camille Claudel*** and ***La Reine Margot***.
5. Isabelle Huppert (1953) has made 90 films and appeared on television. Her famous films include ***Violette Nozière***, ***Le Pianiste***, and ***La Cérémonie***.
6. Claude Chabrol (1930–2010), known for his thrillers, was a prolific film director of the French new wave movement, **La Nouvelle Vague**.

Differentiated Learning

Accelerate

Students write a review of a movie or DVD that they have seen recently using the format of **Le cinéma**, p. 298.

Decelerate

Have students research five top French and American directors and make a chart with their names and the titles and dates of their five most successful films.

Special Needs Students

Visually Impaired/Auditory Impairment

These students may not go to movies often but can benefit from discussions about current films in terms of plot, vocabulary, and cast.

RESOURCES

Workbook 6

Communication

Interpersonal: Paired Practice

Have students work with a partner to define and give examples of **un film commercial** (*Twilight*, big studio, large budget) and **un film indépendant** (*500 Days of Summer*, Sundance Film Festival, small budget). They then can compare ideas with another set of partners. Finally, discuss the definitions as a class and make a list of favorites from both categories.

Points de départ

Pre AP

emcl.com WB 6

Question centrale: De quelles compétences ai-je besoin en voyageant?

Le Septième Art en France

1.2, 3.1

La France est l'une des grandes nations du cinéma: par son histoire avec l'invention du spectacle cinématographique et les débuts du cinéma, au goût, pour l'expérimentation des formes, depuis *Le voyage dans la lune* de Georges Méliès (1902) jusqu'à *The Artist* (2011); et par son public, car en France, le cinéma n'est pas seulement un divertissement*, c'est un art.

Le cinéma français est un cinéma d'inventeurs de formes: de ses débuts avec Georges Méliès et Abel Gance (*Napoléon*, 1927); du cinéma réaliste (Jean Renoir, *La bête humaine*, 1938) et poétique (Marcel Carné, *Les enfants du Paradis*, 1945); de la Nouvelle vague* avec Claude Chabrol (*Le beau Serge*, 1958), Jean-Luc Godard (*À bout de souffle*, 1959), et François Truffaut (*Jules et Jim*, 1961); des années 1960, avec Alain Resnais (*L'année dernière à Marienbad*, 1961), Jacques Demy (*Les parapluies de Cherbourg*, 1964), et Philippe de Broca (*L'homme de Rio*, 1964); jusqu'à l'époque contemporaine avec Jean-Pierre Jeunet (*Le fabuleux destin d'Amélie Poulain*, 2001), Sylvain Chomet (*Les triplettes de Belleville, 2002)*, Marjane Satrapi (*Persépolis*), et Laurent Cantet (*Entre les murs*, 2008).

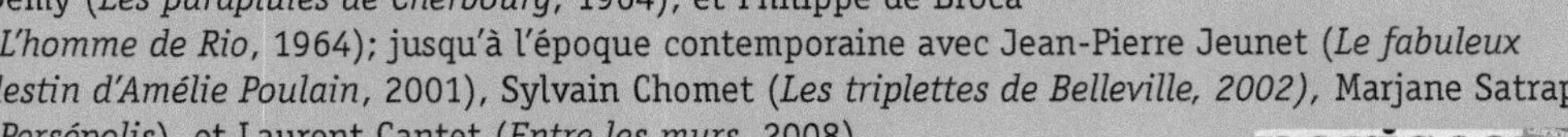

Les Triplettes de Belleville.

Mais le cinéma en France est aussi une pratique culturelle qui a son public: les cinéphiles* vont d'abord voir un film pour le réalisateur qui l'a fait et qui est considéré comme un auteur. Clint Eastwood et Woody Allen n'oublient jamais de rappeler que c'est en France qu'ils ont été d'abord reconnus comme de vrais auteurs.

Paris est la capitale mondiale de la cinéphilie. C'est la seule ville au monde où l'on puisse voir la même semaine 300 à 400 films dans 30 ou 40 langues différentes. Le premier acte d'un cinéphile parisien chaque mercredi matin, c'est d'acheter *Pariscope* ou de le consulter en ligne!

Pariscope magazine

Search words: georges méliès et le film "hugo"; la nouvelle vague; filmographie (+ nom du metteur en scène)

divertissement *entertainment;* **Nouvelle vague** *New Wave;* **cinéphile** fan du cinéma

Mots-clé

C'est un critique franco-italien, Ricciotto Canudo, qui a créé le terme **"le septième art,"** en 1923. Sur sa liste le cinéma vient après la poésie, la musique, le théâtre, les arts plastiques, l'éloquence (c'est-à-dire la rhétorique), et la danse.

Essential Instruction

1. Have students list **les sept arts** as shown in **Mots-Clés**.
2. Assign to groups of students the 15 films listed in **Le Septième Art en France.** Have each group present its film to the class by including the year it was made, the director, actors, plot, and awards. If you deem appropriate, have students watch trailers of these movies online.
3. Ask students to research and compare the awards for the Cannes Film Festival with the American Academy Awards.

 1.2, 2.1

Le cinéma a commencé en France en 1895 avec l'invention du **cinématographe** par Auguste et Louis Lumière, ou les Frères Lumière. **Leur premier film s'appelle** *Sortie d'usine*. **Le film à succès de Martin Scorsese**, *Hugo*, qui se passe dans les années 20, est un hommage au réalisateur français George Méliès.

COMPARAISONS

Est-ce que vous allez au cinéma pour voir l'œuvre du réalisateur, ou pour les acteurs? Quelles sont les autres raisons qui vous amènent à assister à une séance de cinéma?

 4.2

Le Festival de Cannes  1.2

Le Festival de Cannes est un festival du film international dont la première édition a eu lieu en 1946 avec des représentants de 21 pays. La récompense suprême de Cannes est la Palme d'Or: en plus de 60 ans le Festival aura couronné* un peu plus de 500 films. En 1946, ils étaient quelques centaines de participants, aujourd'hui ils sont 40.000 dont 4.000 journalistes, 500 photographes, 300 équipes de télévision, et 86 envoyés spéciaux pour la presse en ligne.

 **Search words: festival cannes**

aura couronné *will have crowned*

C'est au Palais des Festivals et des Congrès de Cannes que sont décernées les Palmes d'Or.

Parmi les prix décernés à Cannes sont **la Palme d'or**, **le Grand Prix**, et **le Prix du Jury**. Le prix le plus prestigieux est la Palme d'or pour le meilleur film de la compétition. Le Grand Prix récompense le film qui manifeste un esprit de recherche et le plus d'originalité. Le Prix du Jury récompense un film aimé par le jury.

1.2, 2.1

Le réalisateur reçoit le Prix du Jury pour son film *La Part des Anges*.

Communication

Interpersonal: Cooperative Groups

Have students discuss the **Comparaisons** question in small groups and report back to the class. Ask a scribe to tally the number of students who choose a film for the director or for the actors, and record on the board their reasons for going to the movies.

Differentiated Learning

Adapt

Put high and low-ability students in pairs. Have them select a movie, either a classic or a contemporary film, to discuss in the style of Roger Ebert and Gene Siskel. (You will have to explain that these were two movie critics who did not always agree on the quality of films.) One person finds it excellent while the other person is less enthusiastic. They may use **On va au multiplexe** as the template for their dialogue. Have them use the vocabulary and expressions from the lesson.

Multiple Intelligences

Visual-Spatial

Have students make a publicity poster for a French film. They must list actors and directors, and add viewer comments.

Verbal-Linguistic/Bodily-Kinesthetic

Have students act out improvised short scenes from popular movies; the other students guess the titles.

Answers

7 *Activities will vary.*

Perspectives
Answers will vary.

Game

Jeopardy
Make a Jeopardy board with these headings: **Vocabulaire**, **Expressions**, **Films**, **Acteurs**, **Réalisateurs.** Students play the game in teams making questions from the cues you give them. You can find Jeopardy game templates online.
Search words: **free flash jeopardy review generator**

Tim Burton accompagne Isabelle Hupert au festival de Cannes.

Les César 1.2, 2.1, 3.1

Ils ont été créés en 1976 sur le modèle des Oscar hollywoodiens. La compression en métal qui symbolise le César est due au sculpteur du même nom: César, qui a donné son nom à la récompense. Chaque année ils couronnent le meilleur du cinéma français mais ils élisent* aussi le meilleur film étranger. Les cinq principales récompenses sont le meilleur film, le meilleur réalisateur, la meilleure actrice, le meilleur acteur, et le meilleur scénario.

Meilleur film, les César ont leurs champions: *Le dernier métro* (1981) de François Truffaut et *Cyrano de Bergerac* (1991) de Jean-Paul Rappeneau avec 10 César chacun; *Le Prophète* de Jacques Audiard (9 César en 2010); *Providence* d'Alain Resnais (1978), et *Au revoir les enfants* de Louis Malle (1988): 7 César.

Les réalisateurs les plus récompensés sont Roman Polanski (3 César), Alain Resnais, Bertrand Tavernier, Jean-Jacques Annaud, Claude Sautet, et Jacques Audiard (2 César).

Meilleure actrice, elles sont plusieurs à avoir reçu plusieurs César: Jeanne Moreau (3), Romy Schneider (2), Annie Girardot (3), Catherine Deneuve (2), Isabelle Adjani (5, record absolu), Nathalie Baye (4), Isabelle Huppert (1). Meilleur acteur, ils sont peu nombreux à l'avoir reçu plusieurs fois: Michel Serrault (3), André Dussolier (3), Gérard Depardieu (2), Daniel Auteuil (2).

élisent *elect*

7 Activités culturelles

1.3, 3.2

Faites les activités suivantes.

1. Faites un axe chronologique sur les œuvres des inventeurs de formes dans le cinéma français.
2. Écrivez la description d'un film dans votre axe chronologique (#1). Vos camarades de classe écriront des descriptions pour les autres films.
3. Trouvez sur Internet les noms des films qui ont reçu la Palme d'or pour les cinq dernières années. Est-ce que les Américains ont eu l'occasion de les voir au cinéma?
4. Trouvez des photos de vedettes qu'on a prises au dernier Festival de Films de Cannes. Quelles vedettes hollywoodiennes y sont allées?
5. Trouvez qui a été récompensé lors de la dernière cérémonie des César.
   - Meilleur film
   - Meilleur réalisateur
   - Meilleur acteur
   - Meilleure actrice

Perspectives

Selon le Ministère des Affaires Étrangères français, le cinéma français est un "axe fort de la politique culturelle de la France à l'étranger." Pourquoi les Français sont-ils si fiers de leur cinéma et certains de son influence?

Essential Instruction

1. Have students outline the information in **Les César** using the categories **Meilleur Film, Les Réalisateurs, Meilleure Actrice, et Meilleur Acteur.**
2. Assign **Activité 7.** Discuss each task, explaining your expectations. When done, ask students to share their work with the class.
3. Have students read **Du côté des médias.**
4. Students do **Activité 8** by creating their own poster. They select a film and director that interest them, and write a commentary. Have students present their work to the class, explaining their choice of film.
5. Students can find posters from previous years online.
   Search words: **affiche officielle du festival de cannes**

Du côté des médias Pre AP  1.2

Interpretive Communication

Regardez l'affiche et lisez le paragraphe de dessous.

FESTIVAL DE CANNES | MARCHÉ DU FILM | CANNES COURT MÉTRAGE

Les affiches

L'Affiche officielle : L'affiche officielle du 62e festival de Cannes est inspirée d'un photogramme de l'Avventura (1960), chef d'oeuvre intemporel d'un maître du cinéma, Michelangelo Antonioni. Cette mystérieuse silhouette féminine, comme arrêtée dans son mouvement, semble ouvrir une fenêtre sur la magie du cinéma et invite au rêve. L'affiche a été créée par Annick Durban. Elle a développé une scénographie complète, des publications jusqu'aux décorations du Palais, qui vous sera dévoilée dans les semaines à venir. Crédit de l'affiche : L'Avventura - M. Antonioni. Société cinématographique Lyre - Cino del Duca ©AFFIF

8 L'affiche officielle de Cannes  1.3, 3.1, 5.1

Faites l'activité ci-dessous.

Pensez à un réalisateur ou à une réalisatrice que vous admirez. Choisissez une scène-clé de son œuvre et créez une affiche qui montre son style ou sa vision pour un concours d'affiches pour le Festival de Cannes. Préparez aussi un petit paragraphe pour expliquer votre affiche.

Answers

8 *Posters will vary.*

Reference Desk

Le Festival International du Film de Cannes (Festival de Cannes) is an annual film festival usually held in May. This prestigious festival is invitation-only and is an important showcase for European films. It was founded in 1946 with 16 countries presenting films. The festival previews new films of all genres, including documentaries. Its most prestigious award, **le Palme D'Or**, was created in 1955.

Differentiated Learning

Accelerate

Ask students to research the Cannes Film Festival at its official website, then present their findings to the class. What is the festival's mission? When does it take place? What film categories are judged? Who is the president of the jury? How many different countries are represented? Which American films are entered?

Decelerate

If **Du côté des médias** seems too difficult for your low-ability students, have them adapt it by finding reviews of a French film in French to attach to the **affiche.** They must translate the review for you into English to demonstrate their understanding.

Multiple Intelligences

Musical-Rhythmic

Musically oriented students may be interested in the film scores associated with popular French films. Encourage them to research films and choose one whose music appeals to them.

Answers

All activities will vary.

Communication

Interpersonal: Cooperative Groups

Students work in small groups to discuss the unit question, **De quelles compétences ai-je besoin en voyageant?** Have them list the skills needed for traveling, from booking a hotel and ordering in a restaurant, to taking public transportation, and interacting with people. A representative from each group writes their list on the board. This information serves as the **point de départ** for a discussion about travel survival skills and the importance of being aware of cultural differences.

La culture sur place

Question centrale: De quelles compétences ai-je besoin en voyageant?

Je fais le/la touriste  1.2

Introduction et Interrogations

Il y a 25 ans, organiser un voyage en Europe n'était pas facile. Il fallait trouver un hôtel, faire des réservations, se renseigner sur les restaurants et les monuments, et trouver les moyens de transport avec seulement les livres touristiques et le téléphone. Avec l'arrivée d'Internet, ces voyages sont devenus beaucoup plus faciles à organiser. Comment est-ce vous organiseriez un voyage avec vos connaissances et les ressources modernes?

9 Première Étape: Réfléchir  1.3, 5.1

*Écrivez les numéros 4, 3, 2, et 1 sur une feuille de papier. Que savez-vous de Dijon ou de Monte Carlo? Votre professeur va vous demander de faire des recherches sur l'une de ces villes. À côté du numéro "4" sur votre feuille de papier, écrivez 4 détails que vous connaissez de cette ville qui pourraient vous aider à planifier votre voyage. Par exemple, ces détails peuvent traiter (*address*):*

- du climat
- de la géographie et de l'agriculture (montagnes, plages, corniches, vignobles, etc.)
- des monuments
- des plats régionaux
- des événements culturels (festivals, concerts, matchs sportifs, expositions)

10 Deuxième Étape: Faire des recherches  1.3, 3.2

Maintenant, vous avez quatre détails. Avec le nom de votre ville et le mot "tourisme" utilisez un moteur de recherche sur Internet pour identifier:

1. **1 question** que vous vous posez toujours à propos de (*about*) votre ville et de votre voyage
2. **2 choses** que vous voulez définitivement voir ou faire pendant votre voyage
3. **3 choses** qui vous intéressent dans la ville

Une fois votre liste finie, partagez votre plan 4-3-2-1 avec un partenaire qui a un plan 4-3-2-1 pour l'autre ville.

11 Faire le point 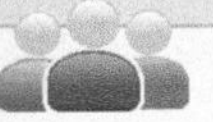  1.1, 1.2, 5.1

Discutez des questions suivantes en classe.

1. Pourquoi est-ce parfois une bonne idée de bien organiser à l'avance un voyage dans une ville étrangère?
2. Quand on part en voyage à l'étranger, certaines choses ne peuvent pas être organisées à l'avance. Lesquelles?
3. Est-ce que vous préférez que votre voyage soit bien organisé et planifié à l'avance, ou préférez-vous plutôt partir à l'aventure?
4. Qu'est-ce que la classe a appris de chaque ville?
5. Est-ce que vous recommanderiez un séjour dans la ville que vous avez choisie, ou dans celle de votre camarade? Pourquoi?

Essential Instruction

1. Students choose, or are assigned, a city for **Activités 9** and **10.** They use their books as reference, or search online.
2. For **Activité 11** use questions 1–5 for class discussion, or assign each question to a group who leads the discussion.
3. Review the forms of the interrogative adjective **quel.** For **Activité 12** ask students to form questions using a form of **quel.** You can show flash cards of vocabulary as cues for making questions.
4. To introduce forms of **lequel**, write a word on the board such as **le livre.** Then write **quel livre**? Now cross out the word **livre** and add **le** to **quel.** Students will see that **lequel** stands for a masculine singular word. Do the same for the other forms of **lequel.**
5. Redo **Activité 12** replacing the interrogative adjective with a form of **lequel.**

Structure de la langue

emcl.com
WB 7–8
Games

The Interrogative Adjective *quel*

 1.1

The interrogative adjective **quel** asks the question "which" or "what." **Quel** agrees with the noun it describes. **Quel** may precede the noun it describes or come directly before the verb **être**.

	Singular	Plural
Masculine	quel	quels
Feminine	quelle	quelles

Quelles seront les nouvelles sorties cette année? — *What will be the new releases this year?*

Quel genre de film aimerais-tu voir? — *What type of film would you like to see?*

12 Un jeu télévisé

 1.1

Vous participez à un jeu télévisé. On vous montre un indice et vous devez répondre par une question. Suivez le modèle.

MODÈLE la Tunisie, le Maroc, l'Algérie
Quels sont les pays du Magreb?

1. "Je me souviens."
2. Monte-Carlo
3. sauce servie avec le steak
4. le Luxembourg, la Belgique, la Suisse, la France
5. Paris, Marseille, Lyon
6. les César
7. le 1er janvier
8. la boucherie, la pâtisserie, la crémerie, l'épicerie
9. le Mont-Blanc
10. la Savoie

Quel est le jeu télévisé le plus populaire?

The Interrogative Pronoun *lequel*

 1.2, 4.1

emcl.com
WB 9–10
LA 2
Games

The interrogative pronoun **lequel** asks the question "which one(s)." It is often used to replace the interrogative adjective **quel** plus a noun. **Lequel** consists of two parts: the definite article and **quel**. Both parts agree in gender and in number with the noun they replace.

RESOURCES

 **Workbook 7–10**

 **Listening Activity 2**

 **Drill & Practice Games**

Answers

1. Quelle est la devise du Québec?
2. Quelle est la capitale de Monaco?
3. Quelle est la sauce béarnaise?
4. Quels sont les pays francophones en Europe?
5. Quelles sont les plus grandes villes de France?
6. Quels sont les prix du festival de Cannes?
7. Quel est le premier jour de l'année?
8. Quels sont les petits magasins d'alimentation?
9. Quelle est la plus haute montagne d'Europe?
10. Quelle est la région d'où vient la fondue?

Communication

Interpersonal: Cooperative Groups

For practice asking questions using **quel**, put students in small groups of four or five. Prepare a set of notecards, writing a profession on each one, for example, **un acteur**. The first student in each group draws a card and identifies his or her profession. The other students in the group think of an interview question using a form of **quel** to ask the first student, for example, **Quel est le titre de votre dernier film?** After each student has asked a question, the second student draws another profession card and the activity begins again.

Differentiated Learning

Accelerate

Ask high-ability students to assume the role of the teacher and re-explain the grammar lesson. Give them time to organize their presentation and find examples.

Decelerate

To practice interrogative words, use words whose gender is obvious (**la fille**, **le garçon**, **la tante**, **l'oncle**...) to practice forms of **quel** and **lequel**. In some instances, working with new or unfamiliar vocabulary, low-ability students may fail to use the correct form of **quel** or **lequel** because they do not know the gender of the word.

TPR

To give students practice selecting the appropriate form of **lequel**, prepare a list of sentences that can logically be followed by a question using **lequel**, for example, **L'acteur a gagné un prix prestigieux.** Read each sentence for the class. After each sentence, have students hold up a sheet of paper with **lequel**, **laquelle**, **lesquels** or **lesquelles** on it to identify which form they would select if asking a question. When students have selected the correct form of **lequel**, say the question that would logically follow the sentence you read so students can check their answer, for example, **Lequel est-ce que l'acteur a gagné?**

Expansion

To practice interrogative adjectives and pronouns orally say, "**Je préfère la glace au chocolat.**" Ask students to form questions using forms of **quel et lequel. Quelle glace préférez-vous? Laquelle préférez-vous?** Students then can work with a partner using the same format.

	Singular	Plural
Masculine	lequel	lesquels
Feminine	laquelle	lesquelles

Quel film sera le meilleur, *Cyrano de Bergerac* ou *Au revoir, les enfants*? — *What film will be the best,* Cyrano de Bergerac *or* Au revoir, les enfants*?*

Lequel sera le meilleur? — *Which (one) will be the best?*

A form of **lequel** may be the subject or direct object of a sentence or the object of a preposition. **Lequel** can refer to both people and things.

De tous les cinémas, **lesquels** sont les moins chers? — *Of all the theaters, which ones are the least expensive?*

On a vu beaucoup de bandes-annonces avant le film. **Laquelle** préfères-tu? — *They're showing a lot of previews before the film. Which one do you like?*

Avec **lequel** de ses copains Karim est-il allé au cinéma? — *With which one of his friends did Karim go to the movies?*

A form of **lequel** may be used as a one-word question.

Nous avons vu un long métrage. **Lequel**? — *We saw a full-length film. Which one?*

Several forms of **lequel** contract when they are preceded by **à** and **de**. Note the forms that change below.

	lequel	lesquels	lesquelles
à	auquel	auxquels	auxquelles
de	duquel	desquels	desquelles

Il y a trois cinémas près de l'hôtel. **Auquel** allons-nous? — *There are three movie theaters near the hotel. To which one are we going?*

Martine vient de rentrer du cinéma. Ah bon? **Duquel**? — *Martine just returned from the movie theater Really? From which one?*

COMPARAISONS: It's harder to have a dangling preposition in French because the preposition becomes part of the pronoun in **auquel**, **auxquels**, or **auxquelles**. Some English teachers want you to avoid dangling prepositions for more formal writing. You can do that with the sentence above by rephrasing it: "To which one do you want to speak?"

COMPARAISONS

In which language is it more difficult to have a dangling preposition?
Voici quatre profs. **Auquel** voudrais-tu parler?
Here are two teachers. **Which one** do you want to speak **to**?

Essential Instruction

1. Review the contractions using **de** + **le**, **la**, and **les**, and **à** + **le**, **la**, and **les**.
2. Give ample oral examples how these contractions are used with **lequel**.
3. Do **Activités 13** and **14** with the students. Have students write out each sentence in their notebooks.
4. Have students listen to the questions in **Activité 15** and answer **A** through **G.** Replay each question until you are sure the students understand each one.

13 La chambre d'Alima

 1.2

Complétez la phrase avec la forme convenable de "lequel."

MODÈLE **Voici l'ordinateur sur lequel Alima surfe sur Internet pour trouver des concerts.**

1. Voici les cahiers dans... Alima fait ses devoirs pour son cours d'histoire.
2. Voici la souris avec... Alima ouvre les logiciels.
3. Voici le lit dans... Alima dort tard le samedi matin.
4. Voici la copine avec... Alima regarde un film d'aventures.
5. Voici les feuilles de papier sur... Alima écrit sa composition de littérature.
6. Voici la chambre dans... Alima se repose après les cours.
7. Voici les stylos avec... Alima écrit les invitations à sa fête d'anniversaire.

14 Plus de renseignements!

  1.1, 1.2

Interpersonal Communication

Votre ami vous parle de ce qu'il compte faire ce weekend. Demandez-lui plus de renseignements.

MODÈLE Demain soir, j'aimerais aller *au cinéma*.
Ah bon? Auquel?

1. Je vais voir le deuxième film *d'un nouveau réalisateur*.
2. J'aime *les genres de films* qu'il tourne.
3. Je pense que mes amis et moi, nous allons aller *au stade* pour regarder un match de foot.
4. *L'équipe* que je préfère gagne presque toujours.
5. Nous mangerons *au fast-food américain*.
6. Après ça, je vais voir *une exposition*.
7. Finalement, je me servirai *de la recette de ma grand-mère* pour faire un bon dîner.

15 Quel cinéma?

  1.1, 1.2

Écrivez les numéros 1–7 sur votre papier. Écoutez les questions. Choisissez la réponse logique.

A. Je préfère celle avec Dany Boon.
B. La meilleure bande-annonce est celle de *Amélie*.
C. J'ai choisi de voir un documentaire.
D. Le meilleur film? C'est *Intouchables*!
E. Je préfère Gérard Depardieu et Juliette Binoche.
F. Sans aucun doute, c'est Steven Spielberg.
G. Je veux voir un film drôle samedi soir.

Answers

1. lesquels
2. laquelle
3. lequel
4. laquelle
5. lesquelles
6. laquelle
7. lesquels

1. À bon? Lequel?
2. À bon? Lesquels?
3. À bon? Auquel?
4. À bon? Laquelle?
5. À bon? Auquel?
6. À bon? Laquelle?
7. À bon? De laquelle?

Script can be found in the front pages of the Annotated Teacher's Edition.

1. G
2. D
3. A
4. B
5. E
6. F
7. C

Game

Tout se transforme!

Challenge teams of students to write a list of as many **quel** + noun expressions as they can think of on white boards, then transform the **quel** expressions into appropriate forms of **lequel.** Score each task separately to determine the winners.

Differentiated Learning

Accelerate/Decelerate

In the computer lab, have students do online practice exercises with forms of **lequel.**

Search words: **columbia edu**, **exercises with lequel**

Special Needs Students

Linguistically Challenged/AD(H)D/Dyslexia

This information may seem like a lot to learn at one time. Students would benefit from a worksheet that breaks down the information into small sections with written exercises for each part.

RESOURCES

Communicative Activities

Answers

All activities will vary.

Reference Desk

Blended Instruction

Consider using blended instruction, a combination of in-class learning and computer-mediated instruction or learning opportunities. Ask students to complete activities on the computer, using their cell or smartphone, or other emerging electronic technology. Doing this allows students to hone their tech skills and become more independent learners. Schedule routine Internet and e-book learning in class and in the lab.

À vous la parole

Communiquez!

16 Pariscope

1.3, 5.1

Presentational Communication

Écrivez la description d'un film que vous aimeriez créér ou voir, comme ci-dessous. Incluez la date du film, la durée, le genre, et le cinéma à Paris où vous voudriez que la première ait lieu. N'oubliez pas les noms des acteurs qui joueront les rôles principaux.

> **C ASSOCIÉS CONTRE LE CRIME** France. Coul. (12-1h44). Comédie policière, de Pascal Thomas. L'impétueuse Prudence enquête avec con époux sur la disparition d'une richissime héritière russe. Avec Agathe de la Boulaye, André Dussolier, Catherine Frot, Nicolas Marie, Eric Naggar, Linh-Dan Pham, Hervé Pierre, Bernard Verley. **Nouvel Odéon 6e. Publicis Cinema 8e. Gaumont Alésia 14e. Gaumont Parnasse 14e. Le Champlin-St-Lambert 15e. Studio 28 18e.**

Communiquez!

17 Une interview à Cannes

1.2, 1.3, 3.2, 5.2

Interpretive/Interpersonal Communication

Vous êtes journaliste et vous vous rendez à Cannes pour le Festival. Vous devez interviewer une vedette du cinéma français. Pour vous préparer, faites des recherches sur une des vedettes ci-dessous (ou une autre vedette française qui vous intéresse). Travaillez avec un partenaire qui fait des recherches sur la même vedette. L'un de vous va jouer le rôle du journaliste, et l'autre va jouer le rôle de la vedette.

Search words: **isabelle adjani, danny boon, vincent cassell, gérard depardieu, jean dujardin, isabelle hupert, audrey tautou**

Communiquez!

18 Les titres des films américains

1.2, 1.3, 3.2, 5.2

Interpretive/Presentational Communication

Recherchez les titres français des films que vous aimez. Ensuite, faites une liste en français de vos dix films préférés et partagez-la avec vos camarades de classe. Affichez votre liste dans la classe.

Essential Instruction

1. Students will find ample online resources to do **Activité 16**. Encourage them to invent a film, and select famous actors to play roles in their production.
   Search words: **ugc**, **roger ebert suntimes**, **allociné**
2. **Activité 18** will appeal to your dramatic students.
3. In making a list of their top ten films for **Activité 19**, make sure students research the name of the American film in French.
4. Students will listen to the biography of Fernand Raynaud. What American comic actors might be on par with him? Do they know what vaudeville is and how it might correspond to the **Folies Bergères** during World War II?
5. What television shows today feature comedy sketches? How are they structured?

Lecture thématique 

La quarantaine

Rencontre avec l'auteur  1.2

Jean-Marie Gustave Le Clézio

Jean-Marie Gustave Le Clézio (1940–) est un auteur qui s'inspire souvent des pays lointains. Il décrit l'environnement de ces endroits de manière sensorielle... les sons, les saveurs, les images.... (Vous pouvez découvrir son écriture en lisant la page 346 de ce manuel.) Inspiré par l'histoire de son grand-père maternel et son grand-oncle Léon, Le Clézio crée des narrateurs qui font un voyage en mer qui est interrompu par *La quarantaine* du titre. Mais c'est aussi l'histoire d'Arthur Rimbaud, célèbre poète français. Ses poèmes réapparaissent au long de la narration et le roman se termine avec le narrateur contemporain à Marseille, retraçant les derniers pas de Rimbaud. Dans la sélection que vous allez lire, quelle coïncidence touche le narrateur?

Pré-lecture  1.1

Quel ancêtre voudriez-vous connaître? Pourquoi? Partagez avec votre partenaire oralement.

Stratégie de lecture  1.2

Epistolary Novels

Un roman épistolaire est constitué d'une série de documents tels des lettres, des pages de journal intime ou des articles de journaux. Récemment, ces romans incluent des documents électroniques tels des courriels et blogues. Dans *La quarantaine*, Le Clézio se sert fréquemment de pages de journaux intimes pour raconter les histoires de ses divers narrateurs. Remplissez la grille ci-dessous en indiquant les thèmes qu'il aborde et comment il les traite à la page du journal intime de fin août 1980 à Marseille. Deux exemples ont été faits pour vous.

Sujets	Traitement
1. souvenir d'enfance: Rimbaud	une anecdote
2. désir: retracer les pas de Rimbaud	une comparaison (*simile*)
3.	

Outils de lecture  1.1, 1.2

Sensory Details

Les détails sensoriels sont des mots et des expressions qui décrivent l'apparence, le son, l'odeur et la sensation tactile d'une chose. L'utilisation d'éléments sensoriels est une caractéristique d'une bonne description écrite. Au fur et à mesure de votre lecture, faites une liste des sens auxquels Le Clézio se réfère dans cette sélection, et donnez un exemple pour chacun.

Differentiated Learning

Expand

1. Have students read "Le bateau ivre" by Arthur Rimbaud.
2. Have a group of students prepare a short presentation of Arthur Rimbaud prior to reading this excerpt, and another group prepare a presentation of Le Clézio.

Answers

Rencontre
Possible answer.
Il se rend compte que Rimbaud a tout abandonné comme Léon, son grand-oncle.

Pré-lecture
Answers will vary.

Stratégie de lecture
Possible answers:
3. arrivée à Marseille: *identification de la saison, détail sensoriel "une odeur d'incendie"*; 4. exploration de l'hôpital: *description, actions du narrateur*; 5. rencontre avec un Arabe: *description physique, de ses actions*; 6. imaginer Rimbaud à Marseille: *questions*; 7. nostalgie de Léon et Suryavati: *description d'un sentiment*

Outils de lecture
Possible answers.
le toucher: *l'air brûlait, l'ombre fraîche*; l'odeur: *comme une odeur d'incendie*; la vue: *ses grands murs de béton blanc; Son visage est émacié...; la taie laiteuse du ciel; une mince peau*; l'ouïe: *« Allah Kerim ! »*
le goût: *je goûtais à l'ombre*

Reference Desk

1. Arthur Rimbaud (1854-1891) was a handsome, precocious but rebellious boy whose teacher opened up the world of literature for him by letting him borrow books from his personal library. Rimbaud came to denounce the poets who came before him, referring to their **"vieillerie poétique."** He had a passionate but explosive amorous relationship with Verlaine. Rimbaud became a vagabond, traveling the world. Verlaine called him **"l'homme aux semelles de vent."** He developed a tumor in his leg and died in Marseille where he had gone to get treatment. Rimbaud said **"Il faut être absolument moderne"** and **"Je sais aujourd'hui saluer la beauté."** Paul Claudel saw stages in Rimbaud's development: first, revolt; then he saw him as a "voyant"; finally, he referred to his "mystérieuse douceur."
2. Le Clézio found in Rimbaud a vagabond traveler like himself.

Answers

Pendant la lecture

1. à Rimbaud.
2. le grand-oncle du narrateur.
3. retourner sur les lieux de Rimbaud.
4. 9h00; Il ressent la chaleur du temps.
5. pour les prisonniers.
6. au site de l'hôspital où Rimbaud a séjourné.
7. un homme arabe, il écoute de la musique.
8. de Rimbaud.
9. de son grand-oncle Léon et son amante.

Critical Thinking

Application

Before studying this except, have students imagine situations when one can be "en quarantaine" (sickness, political asylum, etc.)

Comparisons

Have students expand their English vocabulary by finding words in the English dictionary that come from the glossed French vocabulary: **caché** (*cache*); **sentir** (*sentiment, sentimentalism, sentimentality, sentimentalize*); **errer** (*errant, errantry*); **terrestre** (*terrestrial, terrigenous*); **vêtu** (*vestments*). (A good tip to give students is to add an "**s**" after "ê" to figure out word meanings by comparing them to English words, for example, **la forêt**/*forest*.)

Marseille, fin août 1980

C'est à lui que je pense, encore. Je m'en souviens, j'avais dix ou onze ans, ma grandmère m'avait parlé de ce qui s'était passé, ce soir-là, dans le bistrot de Saint-Sulpice, elle m'avait lu des passages du *Bateau ivre*, je lui ai demandé : « Mais ton Rimbaud, est-ce que c'est comme un oncle pour moi ? » Je croyais qu'on l'avait caché*, chassé*, juste parce qu'il était un voyou*, qu'il était parti en abandonnant tout le monde, comme Léon.

Alors j'ai voulu aller sur le dernier lieu où il avait vécu, comme on va sur un caveau* de famille. Pour voir ce qu'il avait vu, sentir ce qu'il avait senti*. C'était encore le plein été à Marseille. À neuf heures du matin, à la descente du train, l'air brûlait, il y avait sur la ville comme une odeur d'incendie*...

Au bout de la rue, jouxtant* l'ancienne prison des bagnards* transformée en archives ou en musée, l'hôpital dresse* ses grands murs de béton* blanc coulés* sur la poussière de la démolition. Il ne subsiste plus rien de l'ancien hôpital. J'ai erré* sans but dans les couloirs, dans ce qui reste du jardin entre deux parkings. J'ai lu l'inscription : « Ici, le poète... termina son aventure terrestre*. » L'amphithéâtre Arthur-Rimbaud. Dans la salle des pas* perdus, un Arabe vêtu* d'un jogging-pyjama, pieds nus dans des sneakers blancs, écoute son transistor. Son visage est émacié, creusé* par la souffrance*. Il porte lui aussi une petite moustache, et ses cheveux sont coupés très court, comme un bagnard. Il écoute sa musique, et son regard est doux, rêveur, comme s'il était loin d'ici, dans les Aurès. « Allah Kerim ! »

Et lui, l'autre, a-t-il boitillé* jusqu'aux grands platanes* de l'entrés, appuyé sur sa béquille*, pour s'asseoir à l'ombre* fraiche ? A-t-il marché, appuyé au bras d'Isabelle, en se mordant la lèvre pour ne pas crier, jusqu'au bout du jardin, pour regarder la mer au loin, entre les toits de la ville et les collines, confondue* à la taie laiteuse* du ciel ?

C'était le même été, il y a de cela quatre-vingt-neuf ans, quand Léon et Suryavati se sont effacés* de la mémoire des Archambau, comme s'ils entraient dans un autre monde, de l'autre côté de la vie, séparés de moi par une mince peau qui les rend invisibles. Ils n'ont jamais été aussi près de moi qu'en cet instant.

Pendant la lecture
1. À qui pense le narrateur?

Pendant la lecture
2. Qui est Léon?

Pendant la lecture
3. Qu'est-ce que le narrateur voudrait faire?

Pendant la lecture
4. Quelle heure est-il? Qu'est-ce que le narrateur ressent?

Pendant la lecture
5. On a bâti l'hôpital pour quelle partie de la population?

Pendant la lecture
6. Où va le narrateur?

Pendant la lecture
7. Qui voit-il? Que fait cet homme?

Pendant la lecture
8. De qui parle le narrateur?

Pendant la lecture
9. Le narrateur se souvient de quel ancêtre?

caché *hidden*; **chassé** *chased out*; **un voyou** *bad character*; **un caveau** tombeau; **sentir** *to feel*; **incendie** *fire*; **jouxtant** *adjoining*; **un bagnard** prisonnier; **dresser** *to set up, erect*; **le béton** le ciment; **coulé(e)** *poured*; **errer** *to wander*; **terrestre** sur la planète Terre; **creusé** *lined*; **la souffrance** *suffering*; **un pas** *step*; **vêtu de** habillé de; **boitiller** *to walk with a limp*; **un platane** sorte d'arbre; **une béquille** *crutch*; à l'ombre *in the shade*; **confondu(e)** *fused with*; **la taie laiteuse** *milky pillowcase*; **s'effacer** *to be erased*

Essential Instruction

1. Have students take turns reading the selection aloud.
2. Ask students to read the selection again silently and try to answer the **Pendant la lecture** questions in their head.
3. Then have students fill out the graphic organizer and list of sensory details.
4. This is the last section of the novel; ask students what themes and storylines Le Clézio is wrapping up here and what thoughts and feelings his Rimbaud pilgrimage leads the narrator to in the last paragraph.

J'avais faim. Je me sentais libre. Je respirais l'air torride, je goûtais à l'ombre légère des grands platanes centenaires*. En quittant l'hôpital, j'ai acheté une boule de pain chez Paniol, et j'ai redescendu la longue rue qui serpente* jusqu'à la gare.

centenaire qui a 100 ans environ; **serpenter** *to wind, meander*

Pendant la lecture

10. Pourquoi le narrateur va-t-il quitter Marseille?

Post-lecture  1.2, 2.2, 3.1

La visite à Marseille est-elle une réussite pour le narrateur? Si oui, pourquoi?

Le monde visuel

Très jeune, Georges Rouault (1871-1958) a fait un apprentissage avec un vitrier, qui lui a appris à faire de la peinture sur verre. À partir de 1902, il a peint des aquarelles et gouaches aux couleurs vives. Il est devenu en plus un dessinateur et un graveur notable. Rouault était novateur par ses sujets, son utilisation des couleurs, par ses techniques et les mediums qu'il choisissait. Classé souvent comme fauviste ou expressionniste, Rouault voulait toujours rester indépendant. Les Fauves aimaient les couleurs intenses et s'inspiraient de l'instinct, tandis que les Expressionnistes aimaient déformer la réalité pour provoquer une réaction émotionnelle chez les spectateurs; ces derniers s'inspiraient d'une vision subjective. Pourquoi certains critiques appelaient Rouault un Fauve ou un Expressionniste?

 **Search words:** **la collection georges rouault centre georges pompidou, blogs cinéma**

La ville, 1912. Georges Rouault. Collection privée.

19 Activités d'expansion

Faites les activités suivantes.

1. Écrivez une composition qui explique les sujets du journal intime d'août 1980 à Marseille et la façon dont Le Clézio a choisi de les traiter.
2. Écrivez une histoire contemporaine en vous servant de mails comme documents. N'oubliez pas d'insérez des détails sensoriels.
3. Recherchez la fin de la vie d'Arthur Rimbaud. Puis, relisez le texte de Le Clézio et écrivez un paragraphe dans lequel vous expliquez comment vous comprenez mieux la sélection.
4. Choisissez un poème de Rimbaud. Apprenez-le, ou au moins une strophe, par cœur. Présentez les vers à haute voix en groupe. Discutez en groupe des sujets et des thèmes de Rimbaud.

 **Search words:** **poèmes Rimbaud, lisez poèmes rimbaud en ligne**

Answers

Pendant la lecture

10. Il a l'impression qu'il a rencontré ceux qu'il cherchait.

Le monde visuel

En considérant *La ville*, Rouault est un Fauve par ses couleurs vives; et un Expressionniste par sa coloration, ses bâtiments qui semblent bouger et par les plans colorés qui représentent la terre.

Reference Desk

Rouault is considered one of the great artists of the 20th century. His grandfather taught him the essentials of painting. Then, he studied in Élie Delaunay's and Gustave Moreau's studios, after taking night classes in **les arts décoratifs**. His first paintings showed "**une humanité misérable**," with subjects such as prostitutes and clowns. Throughout his life, he was part of a Christian artistic community, and drew inspiration from religious topics. Although he exhibited with **les Fauves**, his technique was different and sometimes his coloration was more muted and somber. Critics often link his work to medieval mosaics and frescoes. Upon his death, Rouault's family bequeathed a lot of his art to the State.

Differentiated Learning

Expand

Have each student present an engraving of Rouault's in small groups and discuss the artist's subject and techniques.

Learning Styles

Visual Learners

These students may enjoy making a "stained glass" design **d'après Rouault** using colored tissue paper. Affix the artwork to an exterior window to let the light shine through.

Answers
All activities will vary.

Projets finaux

A Connexions par Internet: Le cinéma

1.3, 3.1, 3.2

Interpretive/Presentational Communication

Imaginez que vous suivez cours de cinéma à l'université. Le prof mentionne "la Nouvelle Vague," mais vous ne savez pas exactement ce que c'est. Faites des recherches en ligne pour pouvoir donner une définition, préciser l'époque, et faire une liste des grands réalisateurs et de leurs meilleurs films. Avec un groupe de camarades de classe, faites une présentation devant un la classe, chaque élève se chargeant d'une catégorie de recherche.

B Communautés en ligne

3.1, 3.2, 5.2

Notre blogue cinéma/Interpretive Communication

Lisez quelques critiques de films en français en vous servant des "search words" ci-dessous. Ensuite, avec vos camarades de classe, créez un blogue sur le cinéma. Chaque élève écrit une critique d'un film français ou américain. Partagez le lien de votre blogue avec d'autres classes de français et avec les Francophones que vous connaissez. Demandez-leur d'ajouter leurs critiques au blogue.

Search words: allociné blogs, blogs cinéma

C Passez à l'action!

1.3, 3.1, 3.2, 5.1, 5.2

On tourne un film.

Avec vos camarades de classe, planifiez un film sur un thème de *T'es branché?* Par exemple, vous pouvez faire un film sur un sujet dans *Points de départ* ou sur un thème ou une histoire des *Lectures thématiques*. Il faut prendre beaucoup de décisions: Qui va devenir le réalisateur? Qui écrit ou adapte le scénario? Qui s'occupe de la mise en scène (*setting*)? Qui joue les rôles? Qui s'occupe des costumes? etc.

D Faisons le point!

1.3

Faites un diagramme comme celui de droite et remplissez-le pour montrer vos connaissances concernant la question centrale. Un exemple a été fait pour vous.

Essential Instruction

1. Assign **Projets finaux A**, **B**, and **C** to all students individually or in groups. As an alternative, you may decide to let them choose their activity. In any event, all the completed work will be shared with the class.
2. **Projet D** can be done during a class period. This class time will give you the opportunity to give individual attention to students who might need extra help. When students have completed the assignment, use this **diagramme** as a tool for review and a basis for conversation.

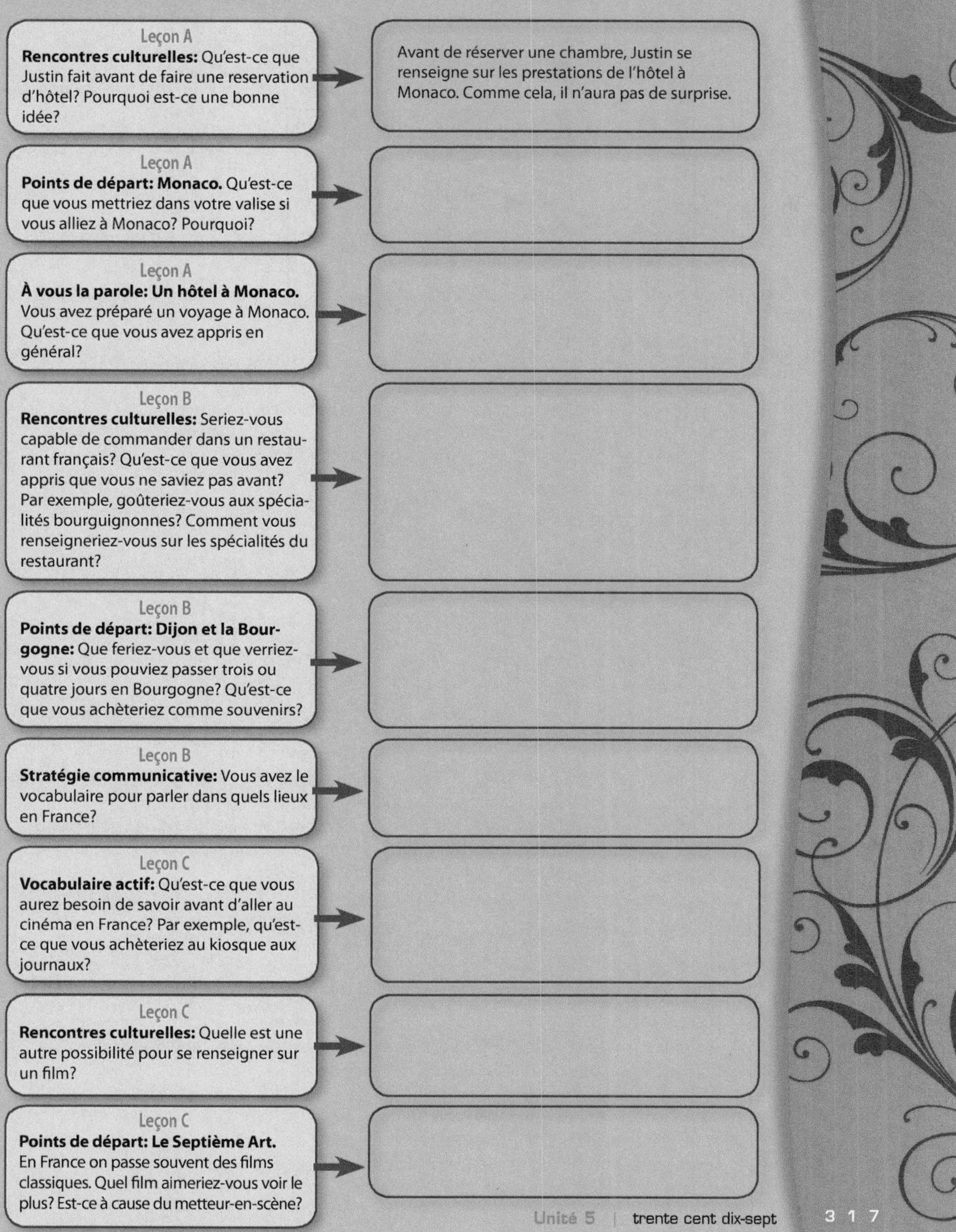

Leçon A **Rencontres culturelles:** Qu'est-ce que Justin fait avant de faire une reservation d'hôtel? Pourquoi est-ce une bonne idée?	Avant de réserver une chambre, Justin se renseigne sur les prestations de l'hôtel à Monaco. Comme cela, il n'aura pas de surprise.
Leçon A **Points de départ: Monaco.** Qu'est-ce que vous mettriez dans votre valise si vous alliez à Monaco? Pourquoi?	
Leçon A **À vous la parole: Un hôtel à Monaco.** Vous avez préparé un voyage à Monaco. Qu'est-ce que vous avez appris en général?	
Leçon B **Rencontres culturelles:** Seriez-vous capable de commander dans un restaurant français? Qu'est-ce que vous avez appris que vous ne saviez pas avant? Par exemple, goûteriez-vous aux spécialités bourguignonnes? Comment vous renseigneriez-vous sur les spécialités du restaurant?	
Leçon B **Points de départ: Dijon et la Bourgogne:** Que feriez-vous et que verriez-vous si vous pouviez passer trois ou quatre jours en Bourgogne? Qu'est-ce que vous achèteriez comme souvenirs?	
Leçon B **Stratégie communicative:** Vous avez le vocabulaire pour parler dans quels lieux en France?	
Leçon C **Vocabulaire actif:** Qu'est-ce que vous aurez besoin de savoir avant d'aller au cinéma en France? Par exemple, qu'est-ce que vous achèteriez au kiosque aux journaux?	
Leçon C **Rencontres culturelles:** Quelle est une autre possibilité pour se renseigner sur un film?	
Leçon C **Points de départ: Le Septième Art.** En France on passe souvent des films classiques. Quel film aimeriez-vous voir le plus? Est-ce à cause du metteur-en-scène?	

Answers

D

Leçon A: *Answers will vary.*; Monaco est une principauté très touristique et très chère.

Leçon B: *Possible Answers*: Les spécialités françaises ont beaucoup de sauces et de viandes pas communes.; *Answers will vary.*;Dans toutes les régions, y compris à la montagne où il y a des stations de ski.

Leçon C: Il est bon d'acheter *Pariscope* pour connaître le synopsis, le casting, le réalisateur, le genre, la durée, et la critique du film.; On peut consulter les sites Internet.; *Answers will vary.*

Expansion

Pair students of equal linguistic ability. Break down **Activité D** by lesson, and assign a different lesson to each group to allow them to focus and write more meaningful responses.

Differentiated Learning

Accelerate

High-ability students can do the **Projets finaux** on their own with minimal intervention. Challenge them to complete the assignment from memory without looking up any information from the unit.

Decelerate

You may want to complete the **diagramme** with students in a small group. They may understand the gist of each question but may have difficulty expressing themselves. Allow them to work individually, in pairs, or in groups, and to look up any information that they do not remember. Ask them to make a list of elements they do not understand.

Adapt

Consider giving students the option of creating their own project. Make sure that you provide them with guidelines so that they are aware of your expectations.

RESOURCES

Listening Activity
Synthèse

Answers

Script can be found in the front pages of the Annotated Teacher's Edition.

1. V
2. F
3. V
4. F
5. V
6. V
7. F

Game

Jeu de vitesse

Divide your class in two teams. Give the class ten to fifteen minutes to write down as many things as they can think of that could go wrong to make a hotel experience a terrible one. The team which has come up with the longest list after the time allotted wins the game.

Évaluation

emcl.com LA *Synthèse*

A Évaluation de compréhension auditive

1.1, 1.2

Interpretive Communication

Un hôtel à Dijon

*Écoutez Aude et Rachid discuter de leur réservation dans un hôtel en Bourgogne. Ensuite, écrivez **V** si les phrases sont vraies ou **F** si elles sont fausses.*

1. Le couple a choisi un hôtel en Bourgogne parce qu'il y a beaucoup de sites à visiter et la cuisine est bonne.
2. Ils ont aimé leur hôtel à Monaco.
3. Rachid a appelé pour s'assurer qu'il y avait un restaurant dans l'hôtel.
4. L'hôtel a un réceptionniste mais pas de concierge.
5. Les spécialités du restaurant sont les escargots et le bœuf bourguignon.
6. Aude aime le lapin à la moutarde.
7. L'hôtel offre une piscine et un centre de remise en forme.

B Évaluation orale

1.1, 1.3

Interpersonal Communication

*Avec un partenaire, jouez les rôles d'un(e) étudiant(e) américain(e) qui planifie un voyage à Dijon ou à Monte Carlo (**A**), et d'un(e) étudiant(e) américain(e) qui vient de rentrer de cette destination (**B**). **L'étudiant(e) A** pose des questions sur la cuisine, le climat, et ce qu'il y a à voir et à faire. **L'étudiant(e) B** lui donne des renseignements. Finalement, les étudiants décident quel film ils vont voir ensemble ce weekend.*

C Évaluation culturelle

1.3, 2.1, 2.2, 3.2, 4.2, 5.1

Vous allez comparer les cultures francophones à votre culture aux États-Unis. Vous aurez peut-être besoin de faire des recherches sur la culture américaine.

1. **Les hôtels**
   Quels types d'hôtels existent en France? Aux États-Unis? Dans quelles chaînes d'hôtels êtes-vous déjà descendu(e)? Où aimeriez-vous aller en France? Dans quel type d'hôtel? Avec quelles prestations?
2. **Les produits et les gens célèbres**
   Pour quels produits Monaco est-elle connue? Quelles personnes sont liées à Monaco? Quels sont les produits et personnes célèbres de votre région? Quelles sont les différences ou les similarités avec Monaco?

Essential Instruction

1. Have students skim the questions before taking the aural comprehension test **Un hôtel à Dijon**.
2. For **Evaluation orale**, give partner A and B index cards with the prompts for conversation. Allow them a few minutes to prepare.
3. In the computer lab, students will do **Evaluation culturelle**, 1–7.
4. In writing the **Evaluation écrite**, students will embellish the dialogue with pertinent details such as the name of the restaurant, type of cuisine, names of the two diners, and their relationship to each other.
5. Using the picture as a prompt, the students will discuss what film they want to see.
6. Using a storyboard format, students will create a story with each box illustrating a specific vacation activity. Students who say that they cannot draw are welcome to use stick figures or make photo collages.

3 **Une capitale régionale**
Qu'est-ce que vous savez sur l'histoire de Dijon? Pour quels produits cette ville est-elle connue? Comparez la capitale bourguignonne avec la capitale de votre région, province, ou état.

4. **Le Septième Art**
Quelles sont les indications culturelles qui indiquent que le cinéma est important en France? Pourquoi les Français disent-ils que le cinéma est un art? Comparez l'attitude des Français envers le cinéma et l'attitude des Américains que vous connaissez.

5. **Les César et les Oscars**
Quels réalisateurs français et américains ont reçu le plus de récompenses? Quelles vedettes françaises et américaines ont reçu le plus de récompenses?

D Évaluation écrite

 1.1, 1.3

Écrivez un dialogue qui a lieu dans un restaurant français pour un serveur/une serveuse et deux clients.

E Évaluation visuelle

  1.1, 5.2

Avec un(e) partenaire, jouez les rôles d'un(e) ado qui sait quel film il/elle voudrait voir et d'un(e) autre ado qui appelle son ami(e) pour voir s'il/elle est libre et voudrait voir un film ce weekend.

F Évaluation compréhensive

 1.3

Créez une histoire avec six illustrations: dessinez un couple en vacances à Monaco. Montrez et décrivez ce qu'ils font et voient.

Differentiated Learning

Accelerate
Challenge high-ability students to write a pastiche of the comic scene **Les croissants.** It can take place in a ski resort, at the beach, in a restaurant, in a hotel, at school, or any other environment of their choosing which is classroom appropriate.

Decelerate
Low-ability students would benefit from a study day in class in which they can systematically review the content of the unit lessons. It would afford you time to have a free-question day so that they can ask for help on any topic no matter how basic.

Special Needs Students

AD(H)D
Provide students with a structured, step-by-step guideline for doing the **Evaluation.**

At-Risk Students
Some students do not have the proper atmosphere at home for study, or are working after school until late. Time in class to study would be very beneficial.

RESOURCES

Listening Pre-test D

***Unité* Test**

Expansion

To help students memorize the vocabulary, and to help them remember how each word is used, ask them to classify the new vocabulary words in four columns listing nouns, verbs, adjectives, and prepositions. Ask your stronger students to expand those lists and find derivatives of some of those words, for example: **une catastrophe** is a noun; students can find that the adjective is **catastrophique**.

Vocabulaire de l'Unité 5  1.2

accueil home page *C*
les **actions (f.)** actions *C*
adressé (à) addressed (to) *C*
agréable pleasant *A*
apprécier to like *C*
l' **ascenseur (m.)** elevator *A*
auquel, auquelle to which *C*
un **bain: bain à remous** whirlpool bath *A*
une **bande-annonce** film trailer, preview *C*
bien: bien entendu of course *B*
blasé(e) blasé *C*
la **Bourgogne** Burgundy *B*
bourguignon(ne) from, of Burgundy *B*
c'est: c'est dommage que… it's too bad that… *B*
ça: ça promet it sounds promising *C*
le **casting** casting *C*
une **catastrophe** catastrophe *C*
un **centre: centre d'affaires** business center *A*; **centre de remise en forme** fitness center *A*
chacun(e) each (one) *A*
une **chaîne: chaîne cablée** cable channel *A*
un **chef: chef d'orchestre** conductor *C*
un **classique** classic *B*
un(e) **client(e)** guest *A*
un **coffre-fort** safe *A*
une **compétence** skill *A*
composé(e) (de) made up (of) *C*
comprendre to include *B*
un(e) **concierge** concierge *A*
le **confort** comfort *A*
une **connexion: connexion Wifi** wireless internet connection *A*
consulter to consult *C*
la **critique** review *C*; **les critiques (m., f.)** critics *C*
les **dénominations (f.)** denominations *B*
la **description** description *A*
les **dialogues (f.)** dialogues *C*
dijonnais(e) from, of Dijon *B*
un **directeur, une directrice** director *C*
le **doublage** dubbing *C*
doublé(e) dubbed *C*
douter to doubt *B*
la **durée** duration, length *C*
duquel, duquelle from which *C*
électronique electronic *A*
une **émotion** emotion *C*
éprouver to feel *C*
équipé(e) equipped *A*
une **étoile** star *C*
être: être certain que to be certain that *B*; **être étonné que** to be surprised that *B*; **être évident que** to be obvious that *B*
exiger to require *A*
le **faisan** pheasant *B*
un **fax** fax *C*
fermenté(e) fermented *B*
le **final** finale *C*
garantir to guarantee *A*
la **gastronomie** gastronomy *B*
le **goût** taste *B*; **à mon goût** for my taste *C*
le **hall** lobby *A*
un **homme: homme de ménage** janitor *C*
l' **humeur (m.): je ne suis pas trop d'humeur pour** I'm not in the mood for *C*
imprécis(e) vague *A*
imprenable unobstructed *A*
une **impression** impression *C*
intense intense *C*
le **jambon: jambon persillé** ham and porc dish made with chopped parsley *B*
jeter un coup d'œil (à) to glance (at) *B*
un **lieu** place *A*
le **lobby** lobby *A*
long, longue: un long métrage feature film *C*
maints many *B*
mon: mon Dieu my god *B*
monégasque from, of Monaco *A*
le **multiplexe** multiplex cinema *C*
un **nanar** flop *C*
les **nouveautés (f.)** new releases *C*
paraître: il paraît que it appears that *C*
parfait(e) perfect *A*
partager to share *C*
une **pause** pause *C*
personnellement personally *B*
plat(e) flat, lifeless *C*
plutôt quite *A*
pratique practical *A*
des **précisions (f.)** specific information *A*
les **prestations (f.)** amenities *A*
quelques a few, some *A*
un **réalisateur, une réalisatrice** movie director *C*
regretter to be sorry *B*
un(e) **Romain(e)** Roman *B*
la **sauce: sauce béarnaise** Béarnaise sauce *B*; **sauce béchamel** béchamel sauce *B*; **sauce blanche** white sauce *B*; **sauce hollandaise** hollandaise sauce *B*; **sauce marinière** white wine sauce *B*
servi(e) served *B*
un **service** service *A*; **service blanchisserie** laundry service *A*; **service de chambre** room service *A*
souhaiter to hope, to wish *A*
une **sortie** release *C*
sous-titré subtitled *C*
les **sous-titres (m.)** subtitles *C*
soviétique Soviet *C*
stéréotypé(e) stereotypical *C*
un **style** style *C*
suivant(e) following *A*
le **synopsis** movie synopsis *C*
tomber: tomber sur to discover accidentally *C*
le **ton** tone *C*
tourner un film to shoot a movie *C*
les **trompettes de la mort (f.)** trumpet of the dead mushrooms *B*
le **veau** veal *B*
une **vedette** star *C*
la **viande** meat *B*
une **version: version originale (V.O.)** original version *C*
vrai(e) real *C*
le **Wi-Fi** wireless internet *A*

Essential Instruction

Use whiteboards to review vocabulary. Give students a category and see how many vocabulary words they can write in a timed game. Categories could include but not be limited to: **cuisine**, **hôtel**, **cinéma**, **émotions**, **subjonctif**, and **argot.** Accept any correct French words, not just the ones from the current lesson.

Unité 6 On se débrouille en France.

Reference Desk

1. **Se débrouiller** means "to manage" or "to get along." It has the sense of figuring out how to do something you need to do.
2. **Être débrouillard** means "to be resourceful."
3. The largest bank in France is the French Post Office, which offers banking services in addition to its traditional functions. Well-known retail banks with branch offices throughout France are: **Crédit Agricole**, **BNP Paribas**, **Société Générale**, **Caisse d'Epargne**, **Banque Populaire**, and **Crédit Mutuel**.
4. A bookstore is called **une librairie**. France boasts 2,500 bookstores. The French government offers grants and interest-free loans to potential bookstore owners. Unlike in the United States, e-book sales account for only a small percentage of the consumer publishing market.

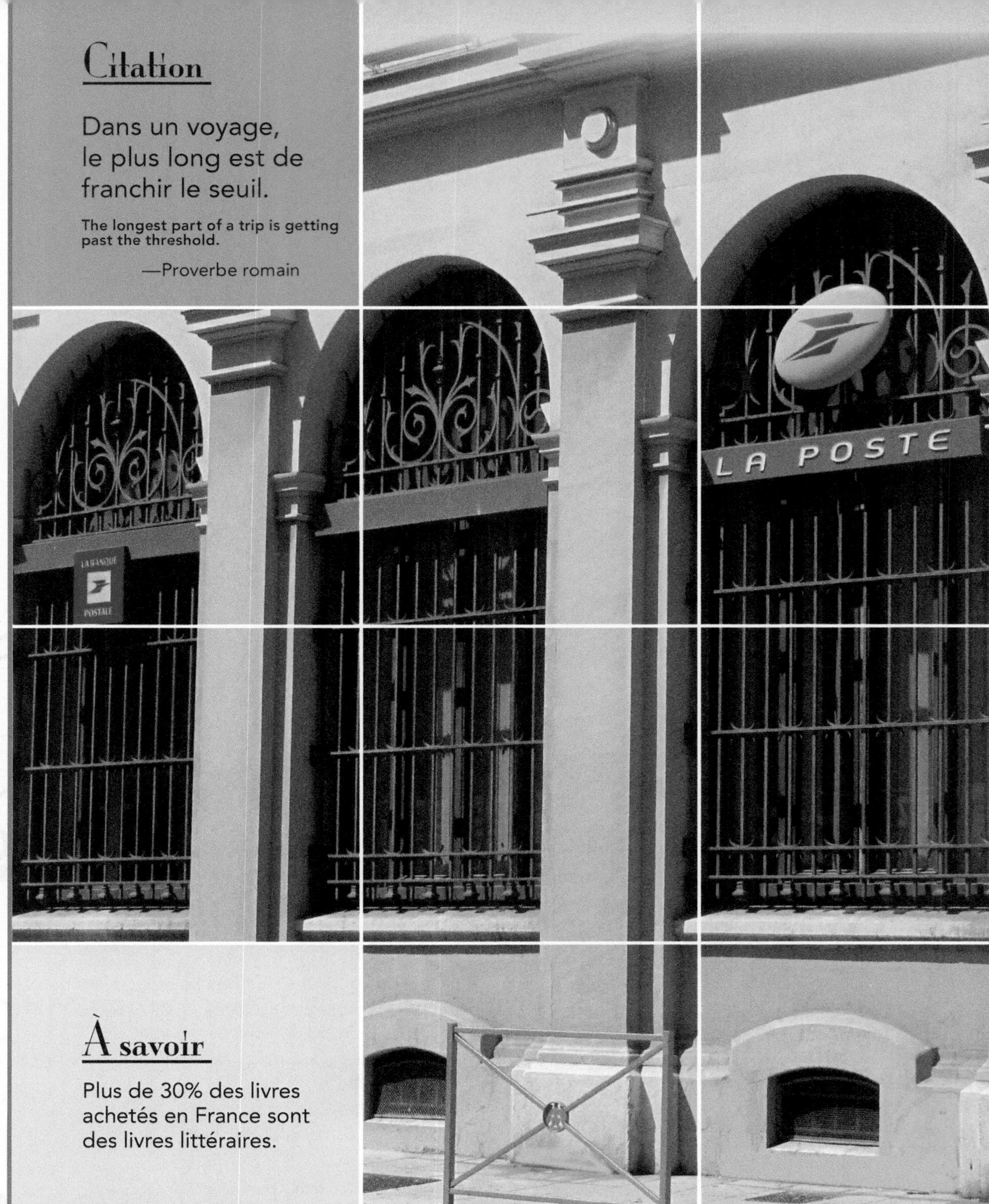

Citation

Dans un voyage, le plus long est de franchir le seuil.

The longest part of a trip is getting past the threshold.

—Proverbe romain

À savoir

Plus de 30% des livres achetés en France sont des livres littéraires.

Essential Instruction

1. Ask how many students have a bank account. Which banks in their town are national banks and which are local? What are the well-known credit cards used in the United States?
2. In this **Unité** students continue to learn travel survival skills by acquiring vocabulary needed to open a bank account, write a French check, and send money.
3. Students also learn about the reading habits of the French and how to talk about their own reading preferences.

Unité 6

On se débrouille en France.

Comment s'intégrer à une autre culture?

Ce logo représente quelle institution française?

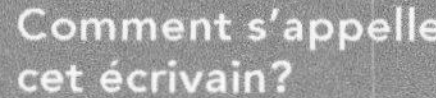

Contrat de l'élève

Leçon A I will be able to:

- open a bank account and make a promise.
- discuss French banks and how best to get money while staying in Europe.
- use the future tense in sentences with **si** and **quand**.

Leçon B I will be able to:

- ask what a book is about and say I'll never be able to decide.
- discuss French reading habits and the Nobel prize-winning author **Le Clézio**.
- use verbs + **de** + nouns and the relative pronoun **dont**.

Leçon C I will be able to:

- say what I need and specify items.
- discuss the services of the French post office.
- use demonstrative adjectives and demonstrative pronouns.

Reference Desk

1. Shakespeare and Company is an iconic **librairie** in the **5e arrondissement** very near **la cathédrale de Notre-Dame.** The store is located in a 17th century building that was a former monastery and part of Notre Dame. Ex-patriot Sylvie Beach opened the store in 1919 and ran it until her death in 1951. Georges Whitman became the bookstore's next owner, and his daughter helps manage it today. The **librairie** is a center for Anglophone writers and artists and fosters an exchange between French and English literature.
2. Shakespeare and Company is a destination place for aspiring young writers who often live upstairs and work as booksellers downstairs in the store. Future additions to the store may include a **café**, an underground cinema, and an exhibition space for a **mélange** of arts and showings.

Special Needs Students

At-Risk Students

Many students come from families who do not use checking and saving account services and might not qualify for credit cards. Be sensitive to this possibility when discussing money and banking.

Multiple Intelligences

Mathematical-Logical

Ask students to report to the class about the relative size of the large retail banks listed in the **Reference Desk.**

Visual-Spatial

Have students make flash cards of the logos of the large retail banks (including **la Poste**) to identify them when traveling.

RESOURCES

e-visual 16, 17

Workbook 1–2

Listening Activity 1

Drill & Practice Games

Reference Desk

Additional vocabulary for your students: **un carnet de chèques** (*checkbook*); **un compte-chèques** (*checking account*); **les frais supplémentaires** (*additional charges*); **le taux d'intérêt** (*interest rate*); **déposer sur un compte** (*to deposit money*)

Culture

Products: Information

Carte bancaire is the debit and credit card most widely used in France. It allows the owner to withdraw cash where the **CB** logo is displayed. Using this card, there is no service fee at any ATM in France. These cards are "smart cards" because there is a microchip embedded in the card rather than a magnetic strip. To use the card, you must have a PIN that you enter for every transaction.

Vocabulaire actif

emcl.com
WB 1–2
Games

À la banque et à la fac

1.2, 5.1

À la banque

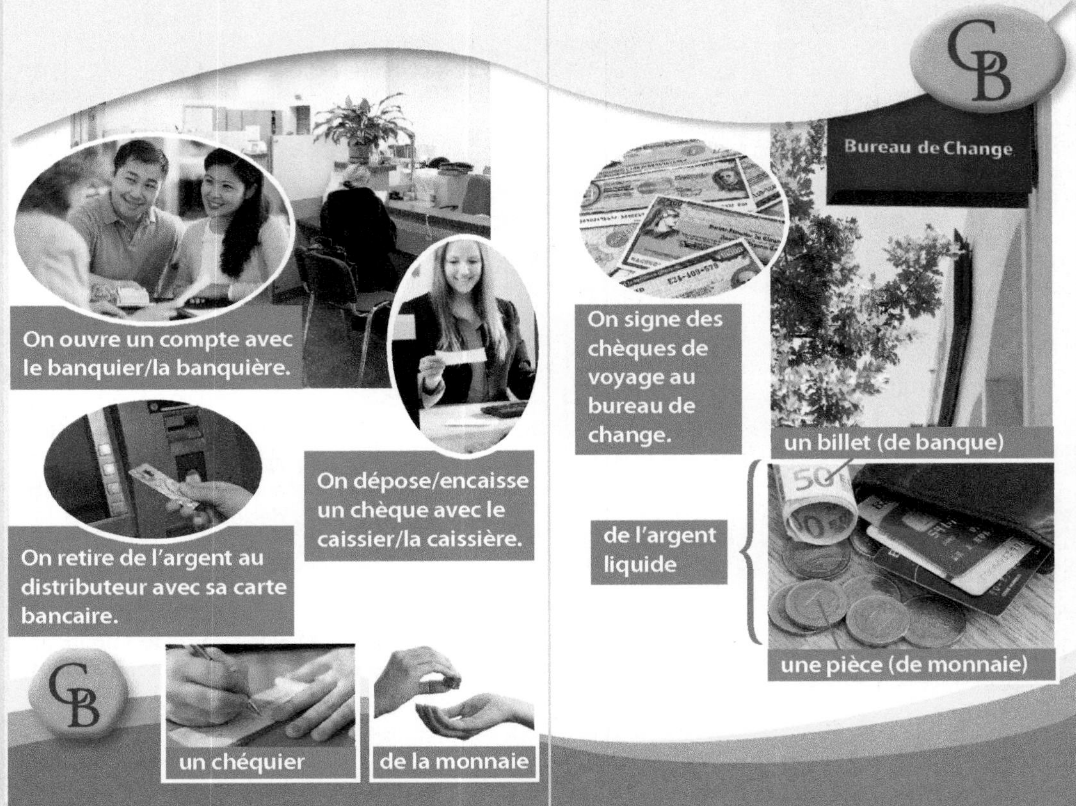

Essential Instruction

1. Put the vocabulary for **Leçon A** on the board. Which words do the students recognize? Ask them to define each term in French.
2. Have students listen to the recording of the vocabulary several times before repeating.
3. Make note of the verbs **ouvrir**, **déposer**, **encaisser**, **retirer**, and **obtenir** used with the banking functions pictured. To check comprehension, begin the expression and let students complete it, for example, **On ouvre un...**, **On depose...**
4. Encourage students to group the vocabulary into word families to help them memorize meaning, for example, **la banque**, **le banquier**, **la banquière** and **la caisse**, **le caissier**, **la caissière**.
5. Ask students if they were to major (**se spécialiser en**) in a subject at the **Université de Toulouse** what would it be and why?

À la fac

emcl.com
WB 3–4
LA 1
Games

Pour la conversation   1.1, 1.2

What do I say at the bank to open an account and get a debit card?

› **Je voudrais ouvrir un compte et obtenir** une carte bancaire.

I would like to open an account and obtain a debit card.

How do I make a promise?

› **C'est promis!**

It's a promise!

Et si je voulais dire...?

un code confidentiel	*PIN*
un crédit	*credit*
une dette	*debt*
un emprunt	*loan*
une hypothèque	*mortgage*
un virement automatique	*automatic payment*

Reference Desk

1. Toulouse is the fourth largest city in France after Paris, Lyon, and Marseille. It is the center of high-tech industries, notably aerospace, electronics, biotechnology, and information technology. Airbus has its headquarters, and assembles many of its planes, in Toulouse.
2. The **Université de Toulouse**, established in 1229, is divided into three separate universities.
3. **Infographie** is the science of presenting complex information in an understandable visual form, for example, a color-coded subway map of London, or color-based charts of the periodic table of elements.
4. **Génie civil** is civil engineering. **L'ingénieur** is derived from the term for engineering, **la génie**.
5. Since education is nationalized in France, tuition at public universities is quite low. For example, in 2012 undergraduate tuition was **174€** in some institutions. Private universities can cost up to **8900€** a year.

Expansion

Have students research Toulouse: its location, nickname (**La Ville Rose**), and its gourmet **spécialités: cassoulet**, **garbure** (*a hearty soup*), **saucisse de toulouse** (*sausage*), **and crouquants** (*crisp biscuits with almonds*).

Multiple Intelligences

Mathematical-Logical

Students who enjoy science and technology might envision studying in Toulouse. Have them research the website.

Visual-Spatial

Encourage students to find photos of the city, its churches, museums, its square, **le Capitole**, etc., and to make a poster of the key sites.

Search words: **toulouse**, **wikitravel**

Answers

1

1. un compte
2. un chéquier
3. banquier
4. chèques
5. signer
6. l'argent liquide
7. bureau de change

Script can be found in the front pages of the annotated Teacher's Edition.

1. B
2. D
3. A
4. C
5. E
6. G
7. F

Expansion

Put the following popular expressions on the board. Let students guess their equivalent meaning in English. Give points for each correct answer. **Il n'a pas un rond** and **Il est fauché** both mean "He is broke." **Vouloir le beurre et l'argent du beurre.** (*Can't have your cake and eat it too.*) **Jeter de l'argent par la fenêtre.** (*Throw money out the window.*)

1 Une visite à la banque

1.2, 5.1

Complétez les phrases suivantes.

1. Awa a besoin d'ouvrir... à la banque.
2. Elle voudrait avoir... pour faire des chèques et pour retirer de l'argent au....
3. À la banque, elle se présente au... pour ouvrir un compte.
4. Elle a des... de voyage, mais elle voudrait de l'argent liquide, c'est-à-dire des... et des....
5. Le caissier demande à Awa de... ses chèques de voyage.
6. Au guichet, Awa reçoit de..., des euros en billets et en pièces de monnaie.
7. Avant de partir en voyage en Angleterre, Awa retourne à la banque et va au... pour échanger des euros en livres (*British pounds*).

Communiquez!

2 Nouveau compte en banque!

1.1, 1.2, 5.1

Interpretive Communication

Écrivez les numéros 1–7. Écoutez Jonathan décrire son expérience dans une banque en France. Faites correspondre la phrase que vous entendez à la bonne image.

A.

B.

C.

D.

E.

F.

G.

Essential Instruction

1. Read the clues from **Activité 1** and have students write the answers on whiteboards for immediate correction.
2. Have students listen to the recording from **Activité 2** to find the picture which corresponds to the statement. Afterward, ask students additional questions about the photos to get them speaking.
3. Review the vocabulary on p. 325 before having the students do **Activité 3**.
4. Arrange students in pairs to interview each other using questions from **Activité 4**. Upon completion, have students circulate to ask other members of the class any two questions from the list.
5. Have students report back by telling what they learned about their classmates, first to a different partner, then to the class.

3 Quelles études?

1.2, 1.3, 5.1

Dites où les étudiants se sont inscrits pour suivre les études qui les intéressent.

MODÈLE Johann s'intéresse aux affaires publiques.
Il s'est inscrit à sciences po.

1. Karine veut être médecin.
2. Marco souhaite étudier les philosophies de Freud et Jung.
3. Océane voudrait devenir juge un jour.
4. Abdoulaye s'intéresse à la chimie.
5. Juliette voudrait étudier les œuvres des grands peintres européens.
6. Julien compte devenir ingénieur.
7. Naya voudrait travailler pour une grande compagnie internationale.
8. Abdel-Cader aimerait devenir metteur en scène.

4 Questions personnelles

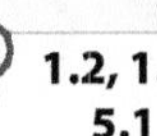

1.2, 1.3, 5.1

Répondez aux questions.

1. As-tu déjà ouvert un compte en banque? Si oui, pourquoi?
2. Est-ce que tu préfères dépenser ton argent ou le mettre à la banque?
3. As-tu une carte bancaire? Si oui, quand est-ce que tu t'en sers?
4. Est-ce que tu connais quelqu'un qui collectionne des pièces de monnaie?
5. Est-ce que tu as déjà utilisé des chèques de voyage?
6. Quand est-ce que tu vas avoir besoin d'un bureau de change?
7. Quand tu sors avec des ami(e)s, qui paie? Est-ce que tu as toujours de l'argent liquide sur toi? Et tes ami(e)s?
8. Si tu allais à l'université, tu t'inscrirais dans quelle faculté? Pourquoi?
9. Qu'est-ce que tu comptes devenir un jour?

Answers

1. Elle s'est inscrite à la fac de médecine.
2. Il s'est inscrit à la fac de psychologie.
3. Elle s'est inscrite à la fac de droit.
4. Il s'est inscrit à la fac de chimie-biochimie.
5. Elle s'est inscrite à la fac d'histoire de l'art.
6. Il s'est inscrit à la fac de génie-civil.
7. Elle s'est inscrite à la fac de gestion-économie d'entreprise.
8. Il s'est inscrit à la fac d'infographie.

4 *Answers will vary.*

Reference Desk

1. The three largest French banks, based on their total assets in 2013, are: **BNP Paradis**, **Crédit Agricole SA**, and **Société Générale**.
2. *Great Place to Work* polled 500 salaried employees in 2012 to decide the top ten best places to work in France. Here are the top five: 1) PepsiCo France, 2) Microsoft France, 3) Mars Pet Care and Food France, 4) Davidson Consulting (**enterprise de conseil**), and 5) Leroy-Merlin (**distributeur d'articles de bricolage et de jardinage**)

Differentiated Learning

Accelerate

Ask small groups to create an original skit among a bank employee and some travelers asking questions about the bank's services. Students should use the vocabulary from the lesson and **Et si je voulais dire...?** Ask them to research websites of French banks for additional information.

Search Words: **crédit agricole**, **bnp paribas**, **la banque postale**

Decelerate

Have students graph the euro to dollar ratio for any five-day period. How would a gift costing 50 euros on the first day of a trip rise or fall in price for an American paying by credit card in dollars? What are the denominations of euro bills and coins? Find pictures of each.

RESOURCES

 **Dialogue Video**

 **Workbook 5**

Answers

1. ouvrir un compte en banque
2. oui
3. que ce n'est pas compliqué
4. demain matin
5. l'infographie
6. Il veut être réalisateur de films.

Reference Desk

1. Students may not know the meaning of some expressions. **Ce n'est pas évident** has the special meaning of "It is not easy." **Être coupable** is the opposite of **être innocent. En trois jours** means "It takes three days," whereas **dans trois jours** means "three days from now." **Avant de** + infinitive is the equivalent of *before + ing*. **Avant de parler** = *before speaking*.
2. John Lasseter is the chief creative officer of Walt Disney Animation Studios. He is known for the three *Toy Story* films and the *Cars* films.
3. **Je n'ai que cours l'après-midi**. Remind the students that **ne...que** means "only" and **un formateur** means "a trainer;" **une formation** means "training."

Rencontres culturelles

emcl.com
WB 5

La banque et la fac

   1.1, 1.2

Justin voudrait ouvrir un compte à la banque.

Justin: Les finances en France, pour moi ce n'est pas évident....
Léo: Tu verras, quand tu iras à la banque.... Non, ce n'est pas compliqué.
Justin: Mais combien faut-il de papiers? Vous adorez les certificats, les autorisations... on a toujours l'impression d'être coupable! Qu'est-ce que je dis au banquier?
Léo: "Je voudrais ouvrir un compte et obtenir une carte de crédit." Tu auras ta carte de crédit en trois jours.
Justin: Trois jours? Avant de pouvoir retirer de l'argent liquide au distributeur automatique? Mais qu'est-ce que je vais devenir?!
Léo: Demain matin, tu as cours à quelle heure?
Justin: Si je me souviens bien, je n'ai que cours l'après-midi.
Léo: C'est parfait! Si on y va à 11h00, tu auras ton compte à midi. Au fait, tu es content de ton cours d'infographie?
Justin: Oh, oui, en ce moment on travaille sur la lumière, le réglage, le positionnement... c'est génial!
Léo: Tu es notre futur John Lasseter. Tu réalises quand ton premier *Toy Story*?
Justin: Je ferai mieux que ça... je vous ferai entrer dans le monde de la quatrième dimension graphique!
Léo: Ça existe?
Justin: Je n'en sais rien! En tout cas, je le ferai!
Léo: Quand tu finiras ton premier film, tu m'inviteras à la première?
Justin: C'est promis!

5 La banque et la fac

  1.2

Répondez aux questions.

1. Que doit faire Justin?
2. Est-ce que Justin pense que c'est compliqué d'ouvrir un compte à la banque?
3. Que dit Léo pour le rassurer?
4. Quand Justin va-t-il à la banque?
5. Qu'est-ce que Justin étudie?
6. Qu'est-ce que Justin veut faire dans l'avenir?

Essential Instruction

1. Have students skim the questions before watching the video "**La banque et la fac**," then close their books.
2. After the video, ask students to recall any details they remember about the dialogue. Put the details on the board.
3. Have students watch the video again, this time following along in the text. Turn the volume down and play the video again. Have students watch for mannerisms as the friends talk. Students do **Activité 5** with a partner.

Extension **Au Salon Studyrama**   1.1, 1.2

Ludovic et Manon parlent au formateur à l'École des Arts graphiques.

Manon: Les formations en arts graphiques, c'est un cursus de 2, 3 ou 4 ans?

Formateur: Ça dépend... vous avez des formations courtes en deux ans avec des BTS en deux ans en communication visuelle, et ensuite, vous pouvez faire un diplôme supérieur des arts appliqués dans une école spécialisée; ou alors vous choisissez une école d'art et de graphisme, puis vous vous spécialisez en 3ème cycle, option multimédia.

Ludovic: Et si on suit ce cursus on pourra faire ensuite tous les métiers liés à l'infographie?

Formateur: Oui, après ça dépend de vous, de vos choix....

Manon: Ça veut dire quoi?

Formateur: Ça veut dire qu'il y a énormément de secteurs.

Ludovic: Par exemple?

Formateur: Les services de communication d'entreprises, les agences de publicité, les sociétés de commerce en ligne, les maisons d'édition, le secteur de la presse, les jeux en ligne, mais aussi le cinéma et la télévision, l'animation....

Ludovic: Tant mieux! Et on gagne combien?

Formateur: Au début 1.500 euros par mois... après ça peut monter très vite. Ça dépend de votre talent!

Extension Qu'est-ce que les deux jeunes gens apprennent de la profession qui les intéresse en parlant avec le formateur?

1.2

Answers

Extension

Ils apprennent les différents cursus de formation, les différents diplômes, et les différents métiers qu'on peut faire avec.

Reference Desk

1. **La faculté** is a component of a university dedicated to teaching and research in a certain discipline. **La Faculté de Droit** is the law school, for example. The dean is the administrative head of a specific school. Students refer to **la faculté** as **la fac**. Most students say that they are **à la fac** rather than **à l'université**.
2. Offer this additional vocabulary for a discussion about students' futures: **école technique** (*trade school*), **faire un stage** (*to do an internship*), **s'engager dans le militaire** (*to enlist or join the military*).

Differentiated Learning

Accelerate

Have high-ability students read **Extension** in pairs then write questions about the conversation. In larger groups, have them ask and answer classmates' questions.

Decelerate

While the high-ability students work on **Extension**, work with low-ability students to have them read "**La banque et la fac**" for pronunciation, or have them read the dialogue in **Extension** as a group.

Special Needs Students

AD(H)D/Linguistically Challenged

To assist students who have difficulty concentrating, reading, or with language, give them two or three lines from the dialogue on separate index cards. Have students work in groups and ask them to be responsible for only the lines that are on their cards. Organize a group presentation.

Dyslexia

To make the reading easier, have students cover the dialogue, revealing only one line at a time.

RESOURCES

Workbook 6

Reference Desk

1. Many non-European credit cards lack a **puce**, the microchip found in most French credit cards. Without this piece it usually doesn't pose a problem for travelers in restaurants or cafés or when purchasing items in stores. However, it can be difficult to use these cards to purchase metro tickets, at train ticket stations, or for **Vélib** public bicycles. (**Vélib** bicycle subscriptions can be purchased online.)
2. **BMO**, **Banque de Montréal** has 321 branches in the United States.

Points de départ

Pre AP

emcl.com
WB 6

La Francophonie: Les banques

En France

1.2, 3.1

Le système bancaire français est très centralisé. Il est dominé par cinq groupes: La BNP Paris-Bas (Banque nationale de Paris et des Pays-Bas), le groupe Crédit agricole avec le Crédit Lyonnais, et la Société générale, la Banque populaire, la Caisse d'Epargne appelées la BPCE, et la Poste. C'est un secteur qui emploie plus de 500.000 personnes. Les Banques forment le troisième employeur privé* de France.

Certaines banques offrent des "cartes à puce*." Ces cartes bancaires contiennent un circuit intégré* qui transmet de l'information à un négociant (marchand ou banquier). Le consommateur vérifie cette information à l'aide d'un code confidentiel. Ce système prévient* les fraudes.

Search words: **bnp paris-bas, crédit agricotle, credit lyonnais, banques populaires, la caisse d'épargne, poste gérer votre argent**

Une succursale de la Banque Nationale de Paris, ou BNP.

employeur privé *private employer;* **carte à puce** *microchip bank card;* **circuit intégré** *circuit board;* **prévient** *prevents*

Au Canada

La Banque Royale du Canada, établie en Nouvelle-Écosse en 1864, est la plus grande banque du Canada. Elle sert 17 millions de clients, a plus de 80.000 employés, et plus de 1.200 succursales*. Cette entreprise opère aussi aux États-Unis et dans 50 autres pays du monde.

La Banque de Montréal, fondée en 1817, est la plus vieille banque du Canada. Avec plus de sept millions de clients et plus de 900 succursales, c'est la quatrième plus grande banque du Canada. Aux États-Unis, elle est connue sous le nom de BMO Harris Bank.

Search words: **banque royale du canada, banque de montréal, bmo harris**

succursale *branch*

Essential Instruction

1. Have students read **La Francophonie: Les banques** in the computer lab, then visit each major bank's website to learn about their services.
2. Have students find a photo of a **carte bancaire** online. What information is provided? Why is this card different from the credit cards in the United States?
   Search words: **images**, **carte bancaire**
3. After reading "**Au Canada**," have students compare **La Banque Royale du Canada** to **La Banque de Montréal** in terms of age, customers, and branches in Canada and abroad.
4. Students read **Retirer de l'argent en Europe** and make a list of the travel advice and new vocabulary they learned from the reading.
5. In high and low-ability teams, have students do **Activité 6** and **Perspectives** in the computer lab. Use this as a basis for class discussion.

Retirer de l'argent en Europe

1.2, 3.1

Autrefois, quand on voyageait en Europe, on utilisait des chèques de voyages ou convertissait* les devises* nationales dans un bureau de change. Aujourd'hui, la plupart des gens se servent de leur carte bancaire (de débit ou de crédit). Les achats par carte bancaire sont convertis au taux* de change interbancaire, qui est plus avantageux que dans un bureau de change. C'est une bonne idée d'emmener deux cartes, au cas où* l'une d'entre elles ne marche plus, soit endommagée* ou volée. C'est aussi une bonne idée de garder de l'argent liquide sur soi au cas où des magasins n'acceptent pas votre carte bancaire, votre carte de crédit, ou vos chèques de voyage. Toutefois, évitez les retraits* d'argent avec votre carte parce que les frais supplémentaires sont élevés*. Pour utiliser votre carte bancaire dans un distributeur automatique, votre banque personnelle doit être connectée au réseau* international Cirrus ou PLUS. L'avantage des chèques de voyage et des cartes bancaires est qu'ils peuvent être remplacés sous 24 heures en cas de perte* ou de vol*. Au cas où vous ayez besoin d'argent d'urgence, votre famille ou un ami peut faire un virement* automatique dans une banque européenne proche* de votre hôtel.

Search words: retrait bancaire, retrait étranger, cic

convertissait *converted;* **devise** *currency;* **au cas où** *in case;* **endommagée** *damaged;* **retrait** *withdrawal;* **élevés** *high;* **réseau** *network;* **perte** *loss;* **vol** *theft;* **virement** *transfer;* **proche** *close*

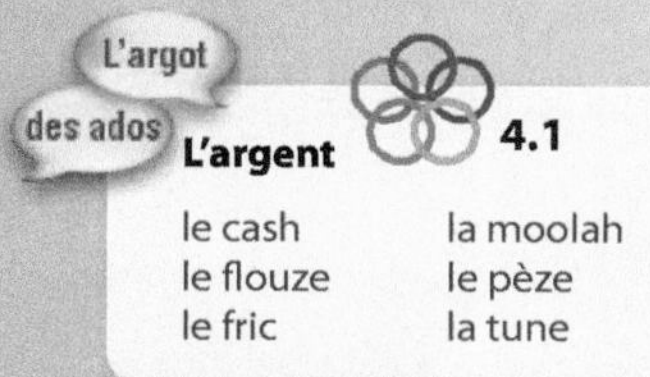

L'argent 4.1

le cash	la moolah
le flouze	le pèze
le fric	la tune

Si votre séjour en France dure plus longtemps, peut-être que vous déciderez de vous procurer **une Carte bleue**, une carte bancaire de débit, ou de crédit, utilisée par beaucoup de Français. C'était la première carte bancaire en France.

6 Activités culturelles

1.3, 3.1, 3.2, 5.1

Complétez les activités suivantes. Vous aurez besoin de visiter le site officiel des banques mentionnées dans Points de départ.

1. Vous voulez ouvrir un compte dans une banque parisienne. Trouvez les banques qui vous permettent d'ouvrir un compte en ligne.
2. Trouvez la banque avec la plus grande sélection de cartes.
3. Trouvez les banques qui facilitent (*offer*) la mobilité bancaire.
4. Écrivez un sketch qui utilise deux expressions argotiques pour "l'argent."

Perspectives

1.2

"J'étais auditrice libre à l'Université d'Aix-Marseille. Très vite, j'ai ouvert un compte à la banque du coin et j'ai demandé une carte bancaire que je pouvais utiliser aux restaurants, au cinéma, à la librairie, et dans d'autres magasins. Pour mon anniversaire et pour Noël, mes parents m'ont envoyé de l'argent par virement bancaire." Cette étudiante américaine a-t-elle eu une bonne ou mauvaise expérience avec sa banque en France?

Answers

6 *Answers will vary.*

Perspectives
Answers will vary.

Communication

Interpersonal: Paired Practice

Have students make flash cards with the banking terms that they have learned. On one side have students write the English and on the other side the French equivalent. In pairs, have them quiz each other on the terms French to English, English to French. Your more visual learners and artistic students might want to use images instead of the expressions in English. In addition to appealing to their particular learning style, this also eliminates interference from English.

Differentiated Learning

Accelerate

Have students research the latest statistics on the top five American banks. How do they compare in size, customers, and branches to the top five French banks?

Decelerate

Ask students to select a French or Canadian bank and make a publicity brochure featuring the services it offers. Have them go online and use the search words listed below the readings. They must include the logo in the brochure.

Special Needs Students

At-Risk Students

To some students from low-income families, the study of international banking might seem very remote to their current lifestyle. Encourage them to think that by continuing their education they could expand their career possibilities, and that living in Europe or working in banking could be in their future.

Answers

1. D
2. C
3. F
4. B
5. A
6. E

Game

Au hasard

Divide the class into two teams. Give one team yellow paper and the other green. Each member of the yellow team writes an interesting IF clause (name of person or thing + verb in present tense). The green team writes an interesting RESULT clause (name of person or thing plus verb in the future). After a short amount of time, have the students put their papers in yellow or green piles. Read one yellow IF clause adding **alors** and one green RESULT clause. As you read the sentences, you may have to edit them for correctness or appropriateness as needed. Students could also take turns choosing the slips once you have checked them.

Du côté des médias

1.2

Interpretive Communication

Trouvez l'information qu'il faut mettre auprès des lettres A–F.

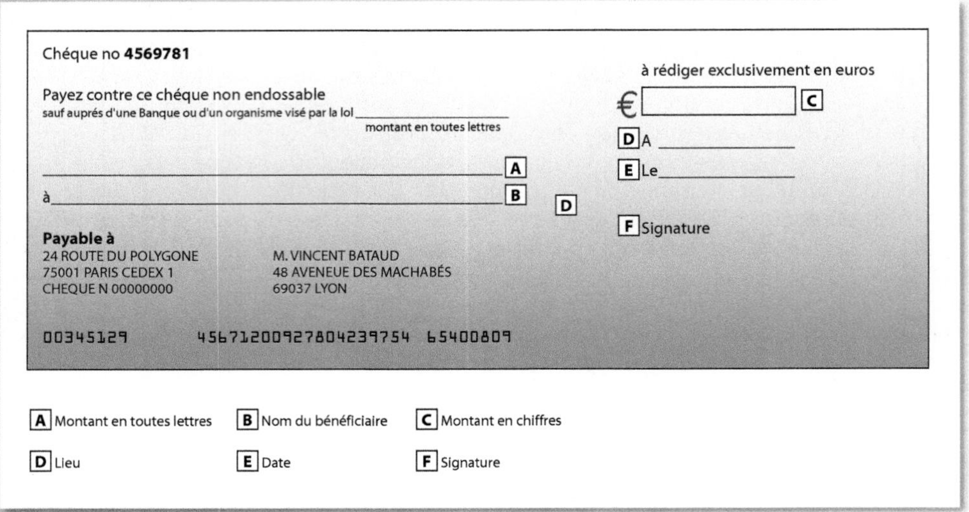

Chéque no **4569781**

à rédiger exclusivement en euros

Payez contre ce chéque non endossable
sauf auprès d'une Banque ou d'un organisme visé par la loi ________
montant en toutes lettres

€ ________ C

D A ________

E Le ________

________ A

à ________ B

D

F Signature

Payable à
24 ROUTE DU POLYGONE
75001 PARIS CEDEX 1
CHEQUE N 00000000

M. VINCENT BATAUD
48 AVENEUE DES MACHABÉS
69037 LYON

00345129 4567120092780423 9754 65400809

A Montant en toutes lettres
B Nom du bénéficiaire
C Montant en chiffres
D Lieu
E Date
F Signature

7 Un chèque bancaire

1.3

Donnez la lettre qui correspond à l'action mentionnée.

1. Vous écrivez "Paris."
2. Vous écrivez combien vous dépensez en toutes lettres.
3. Vous écrivez votre nom et prénom.
4. Vous écrivez combien vous dépensez en chiffres.
5. Vous écrivez le nom de la personne, du magasin, du restaurant, du supermarché, etc.
6. Vous écrivez la date d'aujourd'hui.

Essential Instruction

1. Have students examine the check from **le Crédit Mutuel** and compare it to a copy of a blank check that you provide.
2. What are the differences in format? How would writing the date be different?
3. Students do **Activité 7** as a class.
4. Have students go online to explore how to open a French bank account.
   Search words: **ex-pat**, **moving to France**, **opening a French bank account**
5. Explain to students that any sentence with a **si** clause is translated exactly as it is in English. Have students review the examples on p. 333.

Structure de la langue

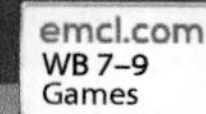

Future Tense in Sentences with *si*

To tell what will happen *if* something else happens or *if* some condition contrary to reality is met, use the future tense along with **si** and the present tense. Here is the order of tenses in these sentences with **si**.

si	+ present	**future**

Si Marame **trouve** du travail à Paris, elle **pourra** ouvrir un compte bancaire. — *If Marame finds work in Paris, she'll be able to open a bank account.*

Luc **signera** des chèques de voyage **s'il a** besoin. — *Luc will sign his traveler's checks if he needs them.*

With **si** and the present tense, you may also use the present tense or the imperative in the result clause.

si	+ present	**present**
si	+ present	**imperative**

Nous **pouvons** retirer de l'argent au distributeur **si** nous **voulons** acheter quelque chose. — *We can take money from the ATM if we want want to buy something.*

Si vous **voulez** faire une demande de carte bancaire, allez à la banque. — *If you want to request a debit card, go to the bank.*

RESOURCES

Workbook 7–9

Drill & Practice Games

Reference Desk

Point out that of the three sequences described on this page, the one with **si** and the present tense along with the future is the most common. **Si** meaning "whether" can take any tense.

Expansion

Give students a slip of paper and ask them to make a facsimile of the **Crédit Mutuel** check. Ask them to buy a pair of sunglasses from their favorite French store (which they will invent) for 60€ and to fill out the check with the amount. Have them draw the sunglasses on paper and explain why they made that choice.

Differentiated Learning

Decelerate

To visualize the correct tense placement in sentences with **si** clauses and to allow students to manipulate the structures, make a list of sentences using each of the three sequences described on this page. Cut the sentences up or put them on index cards. Include cards that have present, future, and imperative for the result clause, forcing students to choose the correct tense and explain why. For example, your cards might be: **Si je suis malade** (one card), **je serai absent/e demain** (one card), and **je suis absent/e demain** (one card). Have students manipulate the cards to create a logical and correct sentence. Model the different options for placement of the **si** clause.

Answers

8

1. Nous deviendrons hommes/femmes d'affaire si nous étudions l'économie.
2. Il deviendra metteur en scène s'il étudie l'histoire de l'art.
3. Tu deviendras banquier/banquière si tu étudies la gestion.
4. Ils deviendront chercheurs/chercheuses s'ils étudient l'infographie.
5. Elle deviendra médecin si elle étudie la médecine.
6. Vous deviendrez pilotes si vous étudiez l'aéronautique.
7. Ils deviendront vétérinaires s'ils étudient l'anatomie des animaux.

9 *All answers B will vary.*

1. A: Qu'est-ce que tu feras si tu vas en vacances?
2. A: ... si tu deviens riche?
3. A: ... si tu achètes un smartphone?
4. A: ... si tu passes du temps à la campagne?
5. A: ... si tu fais du camping?
6. A: ... si tu dînes dans un restaurant français?
7. A: ... si tu voyages à Paris?
8. A: ... si tu vas au parc d'attractions?
9. A: ... si tu vas à la Martinique?
10. A: ... si tu gagnes un billet d'avion gratuit?

COMPARAISONS

Does the phrase with **si**/*if* have to be at the beginning of the sentence in French or English?

4.1

8 Les professions

1.2

Dites ce que les personnes suivantes deviendront si elles étudient les matières indiquées.

chercheur/chercheuse médecin écrivain banquier
homme/femme d'affaires pilote vétérinaire metteur en scène

MODÈLE je/la chimie
Je deviendrai chercheur/chercheuse si j'étudie la chimie.

1. nous/l'économie
2. Hugo/l'histoire de l'art
3. tu/la gestion
4. Chloé et David/l'infographie
5. Marion/la médecine
6. Jules et toi/l'aéronautique
7. Samia/la littérature
8. Marie-Alice et Alex/l'anatomie des animaux

Communiquez!

9 Que feras-tu si...?

1.1

Interpersonal Communication

Avec un partenaire, parlez de ce que vous ferez dans chaque situation. Posez des questions, puis répondez-y.

MODÈLE sortir ce weekend
A: **Qu'est-ce que tu feras si tu sors ce weekend?**
B: **Si je sors ce weekend, j'irai au cinéma. Et toi, qu'est-ce que tu feras si tu sors ce weekend?**
A: **Je ferai du shopping si je sors ce weekend.**

1. aller en vacances
2. devenir riche
3. acheter un smartphone
4. passer du temps à la campagne
5. faire du camping
6. dîner dans un restaurant français
7. voyager à Paris
8. aller au parc d'attractions
9. aller à la Martinique
10. gagner un billet d'avion gratuit

COMPARAISONS: No, the phrase with **si**/*if* and the present tense can either begin or end the sentence in both languages.

Essential Instruction

1. Have students do **Activité 9** in class. They will need time to look up any needed vocabulary from the list on p. 325. Correct the exercises upon completion.
2. Arrange students randomly in pairs to do **Activité 10.** Debrief with the class as a whole the variations on each activity. Ask students to think of other situations and possible options.
3. Remind students that **quand** and **lorsque** are synonyms, and **aussitôt que** and **dès que** are also synonyms.
4. Go over the chart and examples with the students.

Future Tense after *quand*  1.2

emcl.com
WB 10–11
LA 2
Games

Another use of the future tense is to tell what will happen *when* something else happens in the future. Here is the order of tenses in these sentences with **quand:**

quand	+ future	**future**

Quand je **suivrai** le cours d'histoire de l'art, je **connaîtrai** tous les artistes importants!	*When I take the art history course, I will know all the important artists!*

You also use the future tense after the conjunctions **lorsque**, **aussitôt que**, and **dès que**.

Lorsqu'il y **aura** un projet en génie, nous **pourrons** travailler ensemble.	*When there is an engineering project, we can work together.*
Aussitôt que le prof **arrivera**, nous **passerons** notre examen de psychologie.	*As soon as the teacher arrives, we will take our psychology test.*
Tu me **diras** ton emploi de temps **dès que** tu le **sauras?**	*Will you tell me your schedule as soon as you know it?*

Note in the examples above that the phrase with **quand, lorsque**, **aussitôt que**, or **dès que** can either begin or end the sentence.

COMPARAISONS

What is the difference between the tenses used in the French and English examples above?

COMPARAISONS: When referring to future events, the French verb in each clause is in the future when **quand** is used, but in English the verb following "when" is in the present tense.

RESOURCES

 Workbook 10–11

 Listening Activity 2

 Drill & Practice Games

Reference Desk

If students understand the logic of the rule for "**Quand Future/ Future**" they will not find it difficult. In English we say, "When I go to town, I will buy milk." To the French, this is illogical since you are not in town now but you WILL be in town when you WILL buy the milk. Since both activities occur in the future, both verb tenses should be in the future.

Differentiated Learning

Accelerate

Have students write examples of these clauses in the future as they pertain to their personal lives.

Decelerate

Have students review the formation of the future tense of regular and irregular verbs so that they will be successful using the clauses with the future. Encourage them to use online practice sites to make it more enjoyable.

Multiple Intelligences

Visual-Spatial

Students can make a chart comparing **si** clauses and **quand** clauses in the future.

Answers

10

1. ...j'ouvrirai un compte.
2. ...fera une demande de carte de crédit.
3. ...auras de l'argent liquide.
4. ...voyageront au Canada.
5. ...donnera des pièces de monnaie et des billets à la caisse.
6. ...irons en Angleterre.

11

Script can be found in the front pages of the annotated Teacher's Edition.

1. C
2. A
3. E
4. B
5. D
6. H
7. F
8. G

12 *Conversations will vary.*

Game

Conjugons!

To review verbs, give students a whiteboard. Call out a subject and an infinitive, for example, **parler/tu**. Students write the verb in the future. Write the correct verb on the board. Students keep their own score. To add difficulty, give students a subject and verb in the present tense, which they write in the future. The student with the highest score is the **RDJ** or **Roi/Reine du Jour**.

Communication

Interpersonal: Cooperative Groups

For **Activité 13**, divide the class in two groups. The teacher asks the activity questions. A student from one team answers, then a student from the second team adds to what the first student said. Next, a student from the first team adds a new detail, or embellishes what has just been said. Continue until students can go no further. To continue, ask a new question and repeat the process.

10 À la Banque Centrale

1.2

Il n'y qu'une banque dans votre village, la Banque Centrale. Complétez les phrases sur les activités des clients à la banque.

1. Quand j'irai à la Banque Centrale, je.... (*ouvrir un compte*)
2. Maylis recevra une carte de crédit quand elle.... (*faire une demande de carte de crédit*)
3. Lorsque tu retiras de l'argent au distributeur, tu.... (*avoir de l'argent liquide*)
4. Les Dujardin utiliseront leur Carte bleue lorsqu'ils.... (*voyager au Canada*)
5. Quand vous signerez votre chèque, on vous.... (*donner des pièces de monnaie et des billets à la caisse*)
6. Nous demanderons des chèques de voyage quand nous.... (*aller en Angleterre*)

11 Quand je serai en France

1.1, 1.2

Interpretive Communication

Écrivez les numéros 1–8 sur votre papier. Écoutez les questions suivantes. Choisissez la lettre qui correspond à la meilleure réponse.

A. J'étudierai les sciences à la faculté de médecine.
B. Alors, je serai infirmier.
C. Quand j'aurai mon bac, j'irai à l'université.
D. Aussitôt que je serai en France, j'ouvrirai un compte bancaire.
E. Non, je travaillerai d'abord en Afrique.
F. Alors, j'utiliserai mes chèques de voyage.
G. Oh là là, qu'est-ce que tu es négatif! Et bien alors, j'appellerai mes parents au Canada.
H. Si je ne peux pas ouvrir de compte, j'utiliserai ma carte American Express®.

12 Le weekend prochain

1.1, 5.2

Interpersonal Communication

À tour de rôle, vous allez parler de ce que vous ferez le weekend prochain. Le but est de continuer la conversation aussi longtemps que possible. Suivez le modèle.

MODÈLE rentrer chez toi vendredi soir
A: **Qu'est-ce que tu feras lorsque tu rentreras chez toi vendredi soir?**
B: **Lorsque je rentrerai chez moi, je me détendrai.**

Essential Instruction

1. After the verb review, students do **Activité 11**. Ask them to translate the sentences into English to emphasize the difference between the two languages.
2. Students hear questions in **Activité 12** and select the correct response. Replay to reinforce listening comprehension.
3. Students work in pairs to do **Activité 14** then act out their dialogue for the class. Students may use cue cards.
4. For **Activité 15**, students work online to research where they want to pursue an internship.

À vous la parole

Question centrale
Comment s'intégrer à une autre culture?

Communiquez!

13 À la banque 1.1, 1.2, 5.2

Interpersonal Communication

Avec votre partenaire, jouez les rôles d'un(e) étudiant(e) américain(e) qui voudrait ouvrir un compte en France et d'un des employés de la banque.

Dites bonjour au client/à la cliente et proposez votre aide.	Dites que vous voudriez ouvrir un compte et que vous avez besoin d'un chéquier.
Dites que vous pouvez l'aider.	Répondez poliment.
Demandez son nom et adresse en France.	Donnez vos coordonnées.
Dites qu'il faut 50 euros pour ouvrir un compte.	Dites que vous avez des chèques de voyage en dollars.
Demandez-lui de les signer.	Dites que vous les avez déjà signés.
Donnez un chéquier au client/à la cliente.	Remerciez l'employé(e).

Communiquez!

14 L'apprentissage 1.2, 1.3, 3.2

Interpretive/Presentational Communication

Imaginez que vous avez décidé de ne pas aller à l'université. Vous préférez poursuivre (*pursue*) un apprentissage (*apprenticeship*). Choisissez une région de France et recherchez les possibilités. Finalement, écrivez deux petites annonces pour un apprentissage: une annonce du côté du demandeur (vous, l'apprenti) et une autre de la compagnie.

Search words: **apprentissage alsace, apprentissage bretagne, etc.**

RESOURCES

Communicative Activities

Answers

All activities will vary.

Reference Desk

Blended Instruction

Consider using blended instruction, a combination of in-class learning and computer-mediated instruction or learning opportunities. Ask students to complete activities on the computer, using their cell or smartphone, or other emerging electronic technology. This process will allow students to hone their tech skills and become more independent learners. Schedule routine Internet and e-book learning in class and in the lab.

Differentiated Learning

Accelerate

Encourage students to expand the dialogue in **Activité 14** to include a bit of polite chatter and more questions about banking to make the conversation between the client and the banker more interesting.

Special Needs Students

Social Anxiety

Offer options to students when presenting to the class. In addition to allowing them to record their presentation rather than deliver it live, allow them to sit rather than stand, or to use a prop that helps to ease performance anxiety.

Linguistically Challenged

It may be necessary to have a special session to help these students write dialogues in small groups. Students may be more open to help when working with others at their level.

RESOURCES

Pre-test

***Leçon* Quiz**

Answers

Script can be found in the Audio Program Manual.

1. v, d
2. r
3. l
4. r

1. oui
2. non
3. oui
4. oui
5. non

Reference Desk

L'enchaînement vocalique means that there is no linking, but rather continuous vowel sound. English speakers tend to pronounce words separately; for example, they say *a name* rather than *an aim*. On the other hand, French speakers link words giving the impression that they run together. Students might say /**dez arbr**/ but encourage them to say /**de zarbr**/ or /**kel ər**/ instead of the correct /**ke l ər** /.

Prononciation

Repeated Consonants Surrounding Falling /ə/ 1.1

- When two identical consonants surround the falling **/ə/**, both need to be pronounced in the same breath.

Les consonnes géminées par chute du /ə/

Écoutez les phrases, et répétez la deuxième.

1. Je voulais téléphoner.	Je voulais **t**e **t**éléphoner.
2. Il vient dormir.	Il vient **d**e **d**ormir.
3. Il faut lire.	Il faut **l**e **l**ire.
4. Max la réparerait.	I**l** **l**a répa**r**e**r**ait.

À l'écoute de deux consonnes identiques

Écoutez chaque phrase. Écrivez les consonnes répétées. Il peut y avoir deux exemples dans une phrase.

Nasal vowels

- Usually, the consonant **/n/** is not pronounced when the accompanying vowel is nasal, except in cases of liaison. However, liaison is impossible after nouns when a nasal vowel is followed by an initial vowel in the next word, for example: **Il met son argent‿à la banque**. This is called **l'enchaînement vocalique**.

L'enchaînement vocalique

Répétez ces exemples de l'enchaînement vocalique.

1. Il a‿un‿acc**en**t‿amusant.
2. Rendez-vous à la mais**on**‿à‿onze heures!
3. On devait aller tous les mat**ins**‿à la fac.

Trouvez l'enchaînement vocalique

Écrivez ***oui*** *si vous entendez l'enchaînement vocalique, ou* ***non*** *si vous ne l'entendez pas.*

Essential Instruction

1. For part **A**, have students compare the sentences before listening and notice how column two is different. Ask them to tap out the beats of the syllables pronounced in one breath.
2. Have students listen to both and repeat the second group of sentences.
3. For part **B**, play each sentence twice, if necessary, for students to hear the repeated consonants.
4. Read the sentences in part **C** several times so that students detect the sound of the liaison. Have them read the sentences after you.
5. Have students listen to part **D** and write **oui** or **non**, depending on whether or not they hear the **enchainement vocalique**.
6. Modify for students with hearing impairments or those who are linguistically challenged.
7. Students listen to the vocabulary and expressions on p. 339, then copy the terms in their notebooks with an English or French example of each genre.

Vocabulaire actif

emcl.com
WB 1–3
LA 1
Games

À la librairie   1.2

Je m'achète....

RESOURCES

 e-visual 18

 Workbook 1–3

 Flash Cards

 Listening Activity 1

 Drill & Practice Games

Reference Desk

1. **Un livre de poche** was created in 1953 by Henri Filipacchi. The **livre de poche** (*paperback*) is an inexpensive small-sized book, published at low cost in great quantities. Now publishers such as Flammarion, Presses de la Cîté, and Gallimard have niche markets producing **livres de poche.**
2. **Recueillir** (*to collect*) is an irregular verb conjugated like an –**er** verb. From that verb comes **un recueil** (*a collection*). **Une nouvelle** (*a short story*) is a **faux ami. Un manga** (*a Japanese comic*) covers a wide variety of subjects: action-adventure, comedy, science fiction, mystery, and romance to name a few. They are typically printed in black and white. The manga cartoons have international appeal.
3. Students might not know the following expressions: **un tome** (*a volume*); **un compte-rendu** (*a report*); **un récit** (*an account*); **vient de paraître** (*just published*); **il s'agit de** (*it is about*); **un bouquin** (*a book*).

Differentiated Learning

Accelerate

Encourage these students to create an activity to introduce or review the **Vocabulaire actif.** Include **Et si je voulais dire...?** if it suits your class. Ask them to visualize and personalize their activity to get the students involved and speaking.

Decelerate

Have students work with a partner to practice and review the new vocabulary. Encourage them to work with the electronic flash cards for additional practice.

Answers

1. d'avoir trop de lecture
2. 75 ans
3. un manga, un recueil de poésie, un roman de science-fiction, un roman policier, et des nouvelles
4. la poésie
5. Elle lui demande si elle doit lire autant dans son cours à elle.

Communication

Presentational: Paired Practice

Have students write a one-sentence description of one of their favorite books and use **Il s'agit de** to give a synopsis. Post the names of the favorite books and have students write their names on the ones that they have read or that could interest them. Have them share their preferences with a partner.

Pour la conversation   1.1

How do I ask what a book is about?

› **Ça parle de quoi?**

What's it about?

How do I say I'll never be able to decide?

› **Je n'arriverai jamais à** me décider!

I'll never be able to decide!

Et si je voulais dire...?

une critique littéraire	*literary critic*
un discours	*speech*
un essai	*essay*
une légende	*legend*
des mémoires (m.)	*memoirs*
un polar	*mystery novel*
une tragédie	*tragedy*

1 Le cours de littérature   1.2

Lisez la lettre de Sylvie à sa correspondante au Canada.

le 13 février
Cannes

Hélène,

J'aime bien lire, mais ça sert à quoi si on n'a jamais le temps de faire autre chose?! Quand j'aurai soixante-quinze ans et que je ne travaillerai plus, peut-être que j'aurai le temps de lire pour le plaisir. Mais là, vraiment, on exagère, tu ne trouves pas? Notre prof n'est pas raisonnable. Il exige que nous lisions un manga, un recueil de poésie, un roman de science-fiction, un roman policier, et combien de nouvelles? Moi, j'ai horreur de la poésie. Et toi, on te fait lire comme ça dans ton cours de littérature?

Amitiés,
Clara

1. De quoi est-ce que Clara se plaint?
2. Elle compte avoir le temps de lire quand elle aura quel âge?
3. Il faut qu'elle lise quelles sortes de textes?
4. Elle a horreur de lire quoi?
5. Qu'est-ce qu'elle demande à sa correspondante?

Essential Instruction

1. Review the vocabulary by describing a type of publication and having students guess the genre. Ask students questions, using **lire**, about their tastes in reading, how often, when, and where they do their reading.
2. Have students read **Activité 1** then answer questions 1–5. Ask if they felt that they, too, could complain about their assignments. Encourage them to do so **en français**!
3. In partners, ask students to collaborate to do **Activités 2** and **3**. Have them propose names of other authors and their genres.

2 Des écrivains francophones

 1.2

Dites ce que chaque écrivain écrit. Choisissez un genre de livre dans la liste ci-dessous.

MODÈLE Patrick Poivre-d'Arvor
Il écrit des articles et des livres.

articles livres recueils de poésie romans de science-fiction
pièces romans policiers nouvelles thriller

1. Jacques Prévert
2. Georges Simenon
3. Stiegg Larsson
4. Jules Verne
5. Samuel Beckett
6. Guy de Maupassant

3 La lecture, ça vous passionne?

 1.2, 5.1

Dites si vous lisez ou vous ne lisez pas les livres ci-dessous.

MODÈLES

Je lis des romans.
Je ne lis pas de dictionnaire.

pièce autobiographie roman de science-fiction roman policier
article mystère recueil de poésies nouvelle

1. 

2. 

3. 

4. 

5. 

6. 

7. 

8. 

Answers

2

1. Il écrit des recueils de poésie.
2. Il écrit des romans policiers.
3. Il écrit des thrillers.
4. Il écrit des romans de science-fiction.
5. Il écrit des pièces.
6. Il écrit des nouvelles.

3

1. Je lis des nouvelles./Je ne lis pas de nouvelles.
2. Je lis des romans de science-fiction./Je ne lis pas de romans de science-fiction.
3. Je lis des recueils de poésie./Je ne lis pas de recueils de poésie.
4. Je lis des articles./Je ne lis pas d'articles.
5. Je lis des romans policiers./Je ne lis pas de romans policiers.
6. Je lis des autobiographies./Je ne lis pas d'autobiographies.
7. Je lis des mystères./Je ne lis pas de mystères.
8. Je lis des pièces./Je ne lis pas de pièces.

Game

20 questions

Prepare cards with the **Vocabulaire actif** words, enough cards so that each group has a stack. Before playing, ask students to brainstorm questions they might ask to determine a **genre littéraire**, for example, **Ce genre raconte la vie de quelqu'un? Le sujet de l'histoire est aussi l'auteur?** Once the students have an idea of how to proceed, divide the class into groups of four or five. One student draws a card from the stack, then the questioning begins. Once 20 questions are asked, players may not ask any more, and the answer is revealed. If a player guesses correctly, he or she draws a card and play begins again.

Differentiated Learning

Accelerate

Have students write a review of one of their favorite books using the format found on an online shopping site.

Decelerate

Ask students to copy the vocabulary into their notebooks and add an example. If they write the vocabulary word **un best-seller**, for example, they will also list the name of a best-seller such as ***Le Hobbit***.

Special Needs Students

At-Risk Students

These students might be avid readers so talking about books could be a subject that would interest them.

Answers

4

Script can be found in the front pages of the Annotated Teacher's Edition.

1. F
2. NF
3. F
4. F
5. F
6. F
7. NF
8. NF

5 *Answers will vary.*

6 *Answers will vary.*

Communication

Interpersonal: Paired Practice

Have students work in pairs to do **Activite 6** then share what they discussed.

4 Ce que je lis

1.1, 1.2

Interpretive Communication

*Écrivez les numéros 1–8 sur votre papier. Écoutez Stéphanie interviewer des passagers à la gare du Nord sur ce qu'ils lisent dans le train. Écrivez **F** si on lit de la fiction, ou **NF** si on ne lit pas de fiction.*

Communiquez!

1.1, 1.2, 5.2

5 Qu'est-ce que tu es en train de lire?

T'es en train de lire une nouvelle?

Oui, c'est un recueil des nouvelles de Maupassant.

Interpersonal Communication

À tour de rôle, demandez à votre partenaire ce qu'il ou elle est en train de lire. Suivez le modèle.

MODÈLE

A: **Qu'est-ce que tu es en train de lire?**
B: **Je suis en train de lire un roman policier de Georges Simenon.**
A: **Ça parle de quoi?**
B: **Il s'agit d'un sans-abri qu'on retrouve dans la Seine, et Maigret trouve les réponses aux questions du mystère.**
A: **Tu le recommandes?**
B: **Mais oui! C'est passionnant.**

6 Questions personnelles

1.2,1.3

Répondez aux questions.

1. Préfères-tu lire de la poésie ou de la prose? Des romans ou des nouvelles? Pourquoi?
2. Tu offres des livres à tes amis et à tes parents pour leurs anniversaires? Si oui, quelles sortes?
3. Ce que tu lis en ce moment, ça parle de quoi?
4. Comment est-ce que tu te sers d'un dictionnaire, sur Internet ou à la bibliothèque?
5. Quels best-sellers as-tu lus? Qui les a écrits?
6. Selon toi, la littérature française parle de quoi?

Essential Instruction

1. Talk to students about what you are reading and your favorite genres. Have them share their ideas.
2. Listen to **Activité 4** and answer 1–8. Replay the recording if some students missed more than one or two questions.
3. Consider having your active readers do **Activité 5** in a small group. They could present to the class as a dialogue.
4. Ask students to complete **Activité 6** in pairs, then share with the class something they learned about their classmate's reading tastes.
5. Before watching **Des bouquins pour Justin**, ask students about the photo. Where are they? What are they looking at? Why do you think that they are there? What might the dialogue be about?
6. Have students watch the video with books closed. Ask volunteers to give a synopsis. Other students can add details.
7. Play the video again and ask general comprehension questions.
8. Students work in pairs to do **Activité 7**.

Rencontres culturelles

emcl.com
WB 4

Des bouquins pour Justin

   1.1, 1.2, 5.2

Justin cherche des livres à la librairie, avec l'aide de Léo.

Justin: Je n'arriverai jamais à me décider!
Léo: Bon, on commence par quoi? Tu voulais un roman de Le Clézio... achète le dernier!
Justin: Ça parle de quoi?
Léo: Ça s'appelle *Ritournelle de la faim*... tu sais comme dans le "Boléro" de Ravel, quelque chose qui revient. Il s'agit de l'enfance d'une fille dans les années 1930 qui abandonne l'imaginaire pour la réalité.
Justin: Ah, oui, et il me faut *Le... voleur d'ombres*, le dernier Marc Lévy... mon amie Heather adore ses drôles d'histoires d'amour.
Léo: Et n'oublie pas cette petite nouvelle d'Anna Gavalda, *L'Echappée belle.*
Justin: J'ai envie d'un manga. Que me conseilles-tu?
Léo: *Dreamland*, dont tu deviendras voyageur... je ne t'en dis pas plus.
Justin: J'ai lu quelque chose sur Mabanckou, l'écrivain congolais. Tu connais?
Léo: *Demain, j'aurai 20 ans?* Très drôle et plein de tendresse.
Justin: C'est un titre auquel j'aurais dû penser tout seul.
Léo: Pourquoi?
Justin: Demain j'aurai 20 ans! Ça tombe bien!

7 Des bouquins pour Justin

Donnez le titre et, quand c'est possible, le nom de l'auteur pour chaque livre décrit.

1. C'est un livre drôle écrit par un auteur congolais.
2. Une jeune fille échange l'imaginaire pour la vie réelle.
3. C'est une histoire d'amour amusante.
4. Le lecteur/la lectrice devient voyageur.
5. C'est une petite nouvelle.

1.2, 3.2

J.M.G. Le Clézio
RITOURNELLE DE LA FAIM
roman
nrf
GALLIMARD

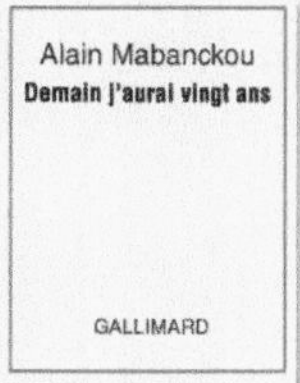

RESOURCES

 **Dialogue Video**

 **Workbook 4**

Answers

1. *Demain j'aurai vingt ans*. Alain Mabanckou.
2. *Ritournelle de la faim*. Jean-Marie Le Clézio.
3. *Le voleur d'ombres*. Marc Lévy.
4. *Dreamland.*
5. *L'échappée belle*. Anna Gavalda.

Reference Desk

1. Jean-Marie Gustave Le Clézio (born in 1940), known as J. M. G. Le Clézio, is a French-Mauritian professor and writer of over 40 works; he was awarded the 1963 **Prix Renaudot** for his novel ***Le Procès-Verbal***.
2. Joseph-Maurice Ravel (1875–1937) was a French composer of impressionist music on par with Claude Débussy.
3. Marc Lévy (born in 1961) has written ten novels that have been translated into over 40 languages and have sold over 23 million copies. He is the most well-known French author in the world.
4. Anna Gavalda (born in 1970) is a French writer of best-selling popular short stories and novels.
5. Alain Mabanckou (born in 1966 of Congolese origin) is a French novelist, journalist, and poet. His works offer insight into the people of modern Africa and those Africans who have immigrated to France.

Differentiated Learning

Accelerate

Assign more advanced students titles of books mentioned in the dialogue. Have them give a brief biography of the author and a synopsis of the book.

Answers

Extension

Answers will vary.

Reference Desk

1. Michel Tournier (born in 1924) is a French writer known for his original style who integrates Socrates, Plato, and German philosophers into his writing.
2. **BD** is short for **une bande dessinée.**
3. Françoise Sagan (1935–2004) was a French playwright, novelist, and screenwriter. Sagan wrote stories with strong romantic themes involving wealthy and middle-class characters. As a teenager she wrote ***Bonjour Tristesse***, which continues to be a classic today.
4. **Grand Corps Malade (GCM),** whose given name is Fabien Marsaud, was born in 1977. He derived his name from a diving accident that left him unable to walk. Through determination and therapy he regained his mobility. He is classified as a French slammer.

Extension **Lecteurs à la FNAC**  1.1, 1.2

Un journaliste interviewe des passants sortant de la FNAC.

Journaliste: Quel est votre meilleur souvenir de lecture?

Passante 1: Le premier livre que j'ai choisi seule... c'était *Vendredi ou les limbes du Pacifique* de Michel Tournier.

Passant 2: Ma mère m'avait offert *L'île au trésor* de Stevenson: je l'ai lu sans m'arrêter.

Passante 3: Là j'ai acheté *Ward*, je ne sais pas de quoi ça parle, je sais simplement qu'il s'agit d'un livre dans lequel l'auteur crée une langue et d'un pays dont il invente la littérature.

Passant 4: Ma première BD: Tintin, *Le secret de la Licorne*... ça reste pour moi le chef d'œuvre du genre.

Passante 5: Toutes les adolescentes de mon âge se souviennent de *Bonjour Tristesse*: je le relis chaque année, à la fin de l'été: vous avez remarqué? Toutes les adolescences finissent toujours à la fin de l'été: c'est drôle, non?

Passant 6: Moi, c'est quand j'écoute du slam: les textes du premier disque de Grand Corps Malade, *Midi vingt,* la vie à l'échelle d'une journée... vous en connaissez beaucoup de souvenirs comme ça.

Extension Quels titres suggérés par les passants vous intéressent? Pourquoi? Y a-t-il un livre que vous recommanderiez à un(e) ami(e)?

1.3

Frederick Werst
Ward
Ier et IIe Siècle
Seuil

Essential Instruction

1. Students read **Extension** and make a list of the titles and authors mentioned. Have them go online and write a synopsis of each one.
2. Students do **Extension** by filling in the titles of works that might interest them in the squares provided.
3. Have students write down the statistics in the passage **Les habitudes de lecture des Français** then compare, where possible, that information to American reading habits. The statistics will not line up perfectly but are meant to be a point of departure for a discussion of comparative reading habits.

Search words: reading habits of americans, pew internet

Points de départ

Pre AP

emcl.com
WB 5

Question centrale
Comment s'intégrer à une autre culture?

Les habitudes de lecture des Français

1.2, 2.1, 3.1

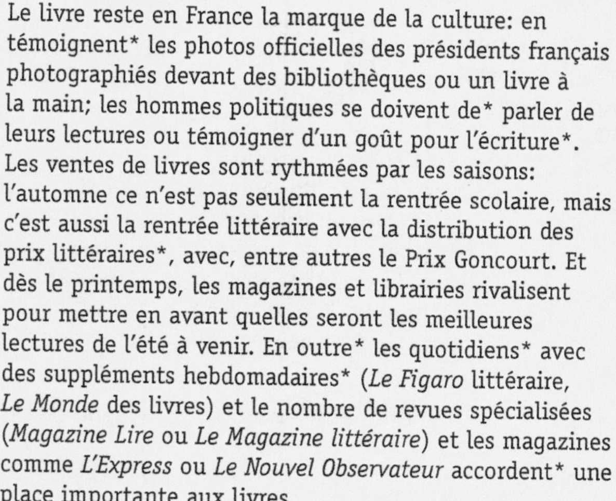

Le livre reste en France la marque de la culture: en témoignent* les photos officielles des présidents français photographiés devant des bibliothèques ou un livre à la main; les hommes politiques se doivent de* parler de leurs lectures ou témoigner d'un goût pour l'écriture*. Les ventes de livres sont rythmées par les saisons: l'automne ce n'est pas seulement la rentrée scolaire, mais c'est aussi la rentrée littéraire avec la distribution des prix littéraires*, avec, entre autres le Prix Goncourt. Et dès le printemps, les magazines et librairies rivalisent pour mettre en avant quelles seront les meilleures lectures de l'été à venir. En outre* les quotidiens* avec des suppléments hebdomadaires* (*Le Figaro* littéraire, *Le Monde* des livres) et le nombre de revues spécialisées (*Magazine Lire* ou *Le Magazine littéraire*) et les magazines comme *L'Express* ou *Le Nouvel Observateur* accordent* une place importante aux livres.

Les petites librairies sont plus fréquentées dans les petites villes de France que les grandes.

Quatre-vingt et un pour-cent des Français sont considérés comme lecteurs, et ils possèdent environ 170 livres par famille. Parmi ces lecteurs 80% ont un dictionnaire; 40% une encyclopédie; 68% des livres de cuisine; et 50% des romans, des essais ou des ouvrages* historiques. Si le nombre de gros lecteurs* augmente, le nombre de petits lecteurs* est en baisse*.

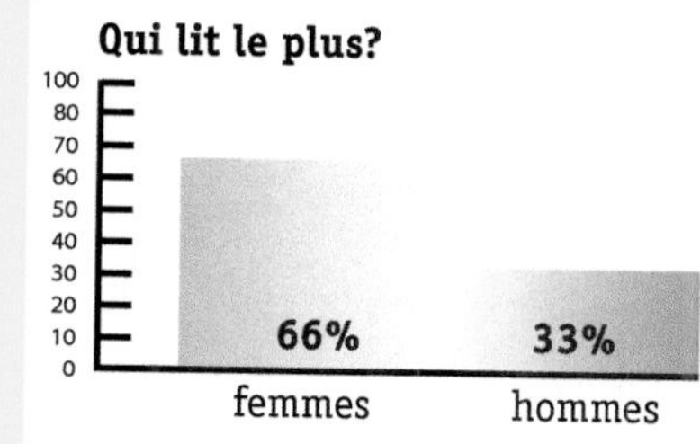

Search words: fnac France

témoignent *witness*; **se doivent de** *must*; **écriture** *writing*; **prix littéraire** récompense pour les écrivains; **En outre** *Moreover*; **quotidien** journal qu'on reçoit tous les jours; **hebdomadaire** un journal qu'on reçoit une fois par semaine; **accordent** donner; **ouvrage** livre, œuvre; **gros/petit lecteur** *heavy/light reader*; **être en baisse** diminue

2.1

Produits

En France on aime **les émissions de télé littéraires** telles que "Un livre, un jour" (France 3), "Des mots de minuit" (France 2), "Ça balance à Paris" (Paris Première), et "Le Cercle" (Canal +). La première émission de télé où on a discuté les livres a été "Lectures pour tous," de 1953 à 1968.

COMPARAISONS

Comparez la place du livre dans la société française et dans la société américaine.

4.2

RESOURCES

Workbook 5

Communication

Interpersonal: Paired Practice

Have students interview each other using the questions from **Lecteurs à la FNAC: Quel est ton meilleur souvenir de lecture? Le premier livre que tu as choisi seul(e)? Ton premier BD?** Consider expanding the survey to include questions about their current reading, popular magazines, favorite song lyrics, and Internet sites.

Critical Thinking

Analysis

How has online shopping changed the purchasing habits of Americans? What factors have led to the demise of small bookstores in the United States?

Differentiated Learning

Accelerate

Have students compare the book purchasing practices of the French and Americans. From where do the majority of French and Americans buy their books? What literary magazines in the United States correspond to those magazines mentioned in the article?

Decelerate

Students make true and false statements from the reading **Les habitudes de lecture des Français**, then ask their classmates who answer either **vrai** or **faux.**

Special Needs Students

Linguistically Challenged

Spend some time teaching pre-reading techniques before asking students to read difficult passages. Encourage them to skim for information, look for cognates, and read without looking up every word in the dictionary.

Reference Desk

1. **Amener** means "to bring someone to a place." **Amenez vos amis! Emmener** is "to take someone away from a place." Have students remember the word "men" in the two verbs as a reminder that these verbs are used with people. The verbs **apporter** and **emporter** are used with objects: **Apporte-moi un stylo**. Bring me a pen. **Pizza à emporter.** Pizza take-out.
2. **L'île Maurice**, officially the Republic of Mauritius, is an island nation in the Indian Ocean about 1,200 miles off the African coast.
3. The word **le pays** can mean region or country. If one is **dépaysé**, one could feel disoriented and not in one's country.
4. **Un colon** is a colonist who establishes **une colonie**.

Communication

Interpersonal: Cooperative Groups

Have students discuss **Perspectives** in small groups. One student takes notes on the discussion. Combine groups to share their findings in a whole-class discussion.

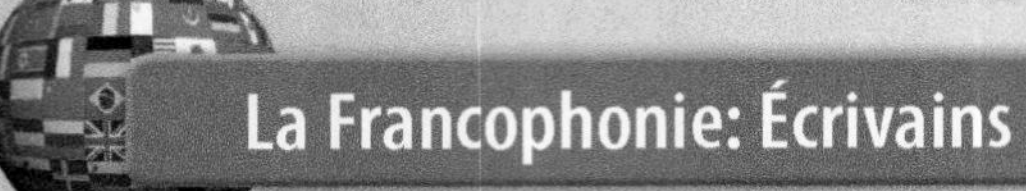

1.2, 3.1

✲ France

COMPARAISONS

Est-ce que la France ou les États-Unis a reçu plus de prix Nobel pour la littérature?

4.2

Prix Nobel de Littérature en 2008, Jean-Marie Gustave Le Clézio, né à Nice en 1940, est un écrivain nomade ou voyageur. Il commence à écrire très jeune: ainsi dès l'âge de sept ans il écrit sur le bateau qui l'emmène avec sa mère de l'île Maurice au Nigéria. Son premier roman *Le Procès-verbal* (1963) le rend célèbre à 23 ans. Son écriture s'inspire de son expérience et de ses voyages: l'Île Maurice de ses origines familiales (*Le Chercheur d'or* et *La Quarantaine*, en 1985 et 1995), et l'Afrique de son enfance (*Onitsha*, 1991). De la vie qu'il a partagée avec Indiens dans la jungle panaméenne* pendant quatre ans (1970–1974), il tire *La Fête chantée*, *La Relation de Michoacán*, et *Le Rêve mexicain*. Les origines de sa femme l'amèneront* également* au Maroc dont *Désert* (1980) est l'exploration poétique, épique, et historique. Homme de la frontière* (*Étoile errante*, *Ritournelle de la faim*), il a très tôt compris que le dépaysement de soi* était une garantie de la sauvegarde de son identité et de sa vérité*.

Search words: prix nobel littérature, association des lecteurs de j.-m. g. le clézio

panaméenne de Panama; **amèneront** *will bring*; **également** *as well, equally*; **frontière** *border*; **dépaysement de soi** *self-transcendence*; **vérité** *truth*

✲ À la Guadeloupe

Maryse Condé a aussi beaucoup voyagé. Née en Guadeloupe, elle a étudié les Lettres Classiques à la Sorbonne à Paris, puis elle a vécu en Afrique dans plusieurs pays. Elle vit maintenant aux États-Unis et à la Guadeloupe. Comme romancière*, elle explore des questions fondamentales de race, de sexe, et de culture. Elle a reçu le Grand Prix Littéraire de la Femme pour *Moi, Tituba, sorcière, Noire de Salem* (1986). Ce roman est l'histoire d'une femme née au 17ème siècle d'une esclave noire et d'un colon blanc. Élevée par une vieille sorcière* antillaise, elle arrive à confronter la souffrance et à réclamer* son identité. Un autre roman connu de Maryse Condé est *Histoire de la femme cannibale* (2005). Il s'agit d'une femme née en Guadeloupe mais qui a vécu en France, en Afrique, aux États-Unis, et au Japon. Ce roman montre que l'identité n'est pas seulement une affaire de géographie, mais aussi de cœur.

Search words: moi tituba sorcière, victoire, les saveurs et les mots; maryse condé vidéo

romancière femme qui écrit des romans; **sorcière** *witch*; **reclamer** *to reclaim*

Essential Instruction

1. On the world map, point out the locations where the authors lived or traveled as mentioned in the two readings. Show photos of the two authors to personalize the readings.
2. Have students do numbers 1 and 2 of **Activité 8.** They should go online to complete numbers 3 and 4.
3. Combine high and low-ability students in small groups to answer the questions in **Activité 9.**

8 Activités culturelles

 1.2, 1.3, 3.2

Faites les activités suivantes.

1. Dites à quoi ces pourcentages correspondent selon la lecture:
   - 81%
   - 50%
   - 80%
   - 68%
   - 40%
2. Faites une carte du parcours (*travel*) de Le Clézio tel qu'il est décrit dans la présentation.
3. Lisez une critique d'un livre de Le Clézio et présentez-la dans vos propres mots.
4. Faites une liste de six titres de Maryse Condé et dites où chacun a lieu.

Perspectives

Le Clézio a dit: "L'artiste est celui qui nous montre du doigt une parcelle du monde." Est-ce vrai de tous les écrivains que vous connaissez? Selon vous, c'est le sentiment d'un voyageur ou d'un écrivain?

Du côté des médias

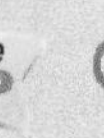

 1.2, 5.1

Interpretive Communication

Lisez les informations dans le tableau ci-dessous.

Poids des principaux secteurs d'édition dans les ventes des éditeurs (2010, en valeur et en quantité)

Œuvres Littéraires vendues en France	Chiffre d'affaires (en%)	Ex. vendus (en%)
Livres scolaires	10	8
Parascolaires/Pédogogie, formation des enseignants	3	5
Sciences et techniques, médecine, gestion	4	1
Sciences humaines et sociales	8	4
dont droit	*3*	*1*
Religion	1	1
Ésotérisme	0,3	0,3
Dictionnaires et encyclopédies	4	5
dont encyclopédies en fascicules	*2*	*3*
Romans	24	25
Théâtre, poésie	0,3	0,5
Documents, actualité, essasis	4	3
Jeunesse	14	20
Album de bandes dessinées	6	6
Mangas, comics	2	**3**
Beaux arts	4	2
Loisirs, vie pratique, tourisme, régionalisme	14	13
Cartes géographicques, atlas	2	3
Ensemble	**100**	**100**

9 La lecture en France

Répondez aux questions.  1.2

1. Quels ont été les livres les plus vendus en France en 2010?
2. Qu'est-ce qui est plus populaire que les livres pour la jeunesse?
3. Quel a été le pourcentage du chiffre d'affaire pour les livres scolaires et parascolaires (*extracurricular*)?
4. Est-ce que les Français achètent plus de livres sur les sciences et techniques, la médecine, et la gestion (*business management*) ou sur les sciences humaines (*humanities*) et sociales?
5. Quels livres ont été les moins vendus en 2010?

Answers

 8

1. 81%: le pourcentage des Français qui sont considérés comme lecteurs; 50%: le pourcentage des lecteurs français qui lisent des romans, des essais, ou des ouvrages historiques; 80%: le pourcentage des lecteurs français qui ont un dictionnaire; 68%: le pourcentage des lecteurs français qui ont des livres de cuisine; 40%: le pourcentage des lecteurs français qui ont une encyclopédie
2. *Answers will vary.*
3. *Answers will vary.*
4. *Answers will vary.*

Perspectives
Answers will vary.

 9

1. les romans
2. les romans
3. 13%
4. les sciences humaines et sociales
5. les livres sur l'ésotérisme

Reference Desk

Jean-Marie Le Clézio was awarded the **Prix Nobel de littérature** in 2008. Maryse Condé has received over 15 awards, such as the most distinguished **Prix de l'Académie Française** (1998) and the **Grand Prix du roman métis** (2010). Amongst other distinctions, she was crowned **Chevalier de l'ordre de la Légion d'honneur** (2004) and **Grand officier de l'ordre national du Mérite** (2010).

Differentiated Learning

Accelerate
Have students do a timed writing, answering the questions in **Perspectives**.

Decelerate
Have students do the second activity of **Activité 8**, making a map of the places that Le Clézio and Maryse Condé have lived, as described in the reading passage.

Special Needs Students

AD(H)D/Dyslexia/Linguistically Challenged
To students with learning challenges, long reading passages in French seem daunting. Break down the readings into smaller sections. Ask students basic comprehension questions in French that they can answer in English. In this way, you will be able to determine their level of understanding. Afterward, ask the same questions in French.

RESOURCES

 Workbook 6–7

 Listening Activity 2

 Drill & Practice Games

Answers

1. On parle du recueil de poésie.
2. On parle du mystère.
3. On parle du roman policier.
4. On parle de la nouvelle.
5. On parle du roman de science-fiction.
6. On parle du livre de poche.
7. On parle du manga.
8. On parle du thriller.

Reference Desk

1. Students copy the verbs + **de** + nouns into their notebooks. Suggest different ways of remembering the expressions with **de**. **Avoir besoin de** means "to need," but it is easier to remember if they think of "to have a need of."
2. **Plaindre** means "to pity." If you pity yourself, **se plaindre de**, you complain. The majority of the verbs + **de** + noun may be followed by an infinitive: **J'ai besoin de lait. J'ai besoin d'acheter du lait.**

Structure de la langue

emcl.com
WB 6–7
LA 2
Games

Révision: Verbs + *de* + Nouns

 1.1

Many verbs and verbal expressions in French are followed by **de** and a noun. They include:

avoir besoin de	*to need*
avoir envie de	*to want, to feel like*
avoir peur de	*to be afraid of*
être amoureux/amoureuse de	*to be in love with*
être au courant de	*to be informed of*
être content(e) de	*to be happy about*
se méfier de	*to beware of*
s'occuper de	*to take care of*
parler de	*to speak/talk about*
se plaindre de	*to complain about*
rêver de	*to dream about*
se servir de	*to use*
se souvenir de	*to remember*

Il **a envie d'une glace.** — *He wants an ice cream.*

Il **se plaignait de l'édition de poche** qu'il a lue la semaine dernière. — *He was complaining about the paperback he read last week.*

10 Club de lecture

 1.1

Dites de quels livres des participants à des clubs de lecture parlent.

MODÈLE

On parle du dico électronique.

recueil de poésie — livre de poche — roman policier — dico électronique — mystère — manga — roman de science-fiction — thriller — nouvelle

1. 

2. 

3. 

4. 

5. 

6. 

7. 

8. 

Essential Instruction

1. Review **se plaindre de** and **se servir de.** Remind students that **se souvenir de** is conjugated like **venir**.
2. Students work in study teams to learn the **de** + noun expressions. Use class time to memorize. Give a small bonus-point quiz as motivation to learn them in class.
3. Allow students time to prepare **Activité 10** before doing the exercise orally.
4. Present the relative pronoun **dont.** Give students a sentence to help them memorize, for example, **Le livre dont j'ai besoin coûte cher, L'ami dont la soeur est malade s'appelle Roger. Je n'ai pas vu le film dont il m'a parlé.**

The Relative Pronoun *dont*  1.1

emcl.com
WB 8–9
Games

You know how to combine two shorter sentences into a longer one by using the relative pronouns **qui** and **que**. The word **dont** is also a relative pronoun, used to connect two clauses in a complex sentence. **Dont** (*about which/whom, of which/whom*) replaces **de** plus a noun and is used with the verbs and verbal expressions that are followed by **de** and a noun that you reviewed on page 348.

dont	=	**de**	+	noun

In the following examples, note how **dont** always comes directly after its antecedent to join the two separate sentences into one.

C'est un manga. Ma sœur m'a parlé de ce manga.	*It is a manga. My sister talked to me about this manga.*
C'est un manga **dont** ma sœur m'a parlé.	*It is a manga about which my sister talked to me.*
J'ai trouvé l'anthologie de poésie. J'avais besoin de l'anthologie de poésie.	*I found the poetry anthology. I needed the poetry anthology.*
J'ai trouvé l'anthologie de poésie **dont** j'avais besoin.	*I found the poetry anthology that I needed.*

The relative pronoun **dont** means "whose" in sentences where **de** indicates relationship or possession.

J'ai lu une nouvelle d'un écrivain sénégalais. Le père de l'écrivain est américain.	*I read a short novel by a Senegalese writer. The father of the writer is American.*

RESOURCES

 **Workbook 8–9**

 **Drill & Practice Games**

Reference Desk

1. **Dont** must always be expressed in French, even if its English equivalent is omitted.
2. **Dont** may refer to people or things.
3. The meaning of **dont** varies depending on context. In relative clauses, **dont** is used instead of **qui** or **que** with **de** expressions.
4. When **dont** means "whose," it replaces **de** and a noun. If used with **la façon**, it means "in which."

Differentiated Learning

Decelerate

Some students may need extra practice combining sentences with **dont.** A worksheet that combines two sentences using the relative pronouns **qui**, **que**, and **dont** would be helpful.

Answers

11

1. Karim n'a pas fini le roman policier dont il s'est plaint.
2. Marie-Alix a acheté le recueil de nouvelles dont elle avait besoin pour sa classe d'anglais.
3. M. Legrand a vu le recueil de poésie dont il se méfie du site en ligne.
4. Maman m'a offert un best-seller dont mon frère lui a parlé comme cadeau.
5. À la librairie, j'ai vu une nouvelle édition de poche d'un roman de Le Clézio dont je me servirai pour ma composition.
6. En classe les élèves lisent une anthologie de littérature dont ils sont contents.
7. C'est un roman de science-fiction très intéressant dont je me souviens bien.

Communication

Interpersonal: Cooperative Groups

Give students a cloze exercise featuring **qui**, **que**, and **dont.** Have them fill in the blanks, then join two other students to compare answers. They must agree on what is correct. Encourage them to explain their choice to the group. Put the answers for each trio on the board. Compliment them by saying **Chapeau!**

J'ai lu une nouvelle d'un écrivain sénégalais **dont** le père est américain. — *I read a short novel by a Senegalese writer whose father is American.*

Dont means "in which" after the expression **la façon.**

La façon **dont** Le Clézio écrit est fascinante. — *The way in which Le Clézio writes is fascinating.*

COMPARAISONS

4.1

Does **dont** refer to people or things in French? In English, what does "whose" refer to?

Voici la fille dont le père est venu au lycée.
Here is the girl whose father came to school.
Voici le restaurant dont le chef est italien.
This is the restaurant whose chef is italian.

11 Combinez les phrases!

1.3

*Combinez les deux phrases pour en faire une avec **dont**. Suivez le modèle.*

MODÈLE Léo a acheté le dico. Il avait besoin d'un dico.
Léo a acheté le dico dont il avait besoin.

1. Karim n'a pas fini le roman policier. Il s'est plaint du roman policier.
2. Marie-Alix a acheté le recueil de nouvelles. Elle avait besoin du recueil pour sa classe d'anglais.
3. M. Legrand a vu le recueil de poésie en ligne. Il se méfie du site.
4. Maman m'a offert un best-seller comme cadeau. Mon frère lui a parlé du best-seller.
5. À la librairie, j'ai vu une nouvelle édition de poche d'un roman de Le Clézio. Je me servirai de la nouvelle édition de poche pour ma composition.
6. En classe les élèves lisent une anthologie de littérature. Ils sont contents de cette anthologie.
7. C'est un roman de science-fiction très intéressant. Je me souviens bien de ce roman.

La glace, c'est le goûter dont Mme Morot a envie.

COMPARAISONS: *Whose* can be used for people or things in both French and English.

Essential Instruction

1. Do **Activité 11** as pair work. Ask volunteers to share their answers. Encourage students who did not do well to ask questions for further clarification.
2. Students listen to **Activité 12** and answer questions 1–7. Play each one again and have the students identify the clue that gave them the answer.
3. Have students write the answers to **Activité 13** in their notebooks and refer to the picture for cues. Expand the conversation by asking open-ended questions about the picture. For example, you could ask how many days Mme Laforge plans to stay at the hotel.

Communiquez!

12 Dans le cours de littérature

1.1, 1.2

Écrivez les numéros 1–7 sur votre papier. Écoutez les phrases. Puis, écrivez le genre de livres dont tout le monde se sert pour son cours de littérature.

Communiquez!

13 À l'Hôtel Beauséjour

1.2

Identifiez les personnes dont on parle.

MODÈLE Ses enfants s'appellent Véro et Marc.
La personne dont les enfants s'appellent Véro et Marc est M. Gaillot.

1. Sa valise est très grande.
2. Sa tablette est rouge.
3. Sa robe est longue.
4. Son fils est fatigué.
5. Sa femme est bavarde.
6. Elle met des bijoux dans le coffre.
7. Sa fille est énergique.

Answers

Script can be found in the front pages of the annotated Teacher's Edition.

1. une nouvelle
2. un recueil de poésie
3. un manga
4. un best-seller
5. un dictionnaire
6. un roman policier
7. un roman de science-fiction

1. La personne dont la valise est trop grande est Mme Laforge.
2. La personne dont la tablette est rouge est M. Leforestier.
3. La personne dont la robe est longue est Mlle Bobard.
4. La personne dont le fils est fatigué est M. Gaillot.
5. La personne dont la femme est bavarde est M. Bobard.
6. La personne qui met des bijoux dans le coffre est l'employée.
7. La personne dont la fille est énergique est M. Gaillot.

Communication

Interpersonal: Cooperative Groups

To personalize using **dont**, put students into mixed-ability groups of four or five. Announce a topic and write it on the board, for example, **une fête dont vous vous souvenez bien.** Students in each group take turns relating a holiday that they remember well and adding a specific detail, for example, **La fête dont je me souviens bien est Noël, 2012. J'ai reçu un cadeau exceptionnel!** After a couple of minutes, change the cue on the board. The next student in line to speak begins with the new cue. Other cues that you might use include: **un truc dont vous n'avez pas envie, un cours dont vous êtes content/e** and **une personne dont vous avez fait la connaissance cette année.**

Differentiated Learning

Accelerate

Have students look at the picture and tell a story about the people at the hotel, inventing details about each character.

Decelerate

Ask students to write you a letter in which they ask questions or suggest ways that they can learn better. Students might find this approach less threatening. Assure them that this will not influence their grade but may result in them getting the help they need.

Multiple Intelligences

Visual-Spatial/Logical-Mathematical

Have students collaborate to make a poster for the class which explains the use of **qui**, **que**, and **dont** with examples.

RESOURCES

Communicative Activities

Answers

All activities will vary.

Reference Desk

Blended Instruction

Consider using blended instruction, a combination of in-class learning and computer-mediated instruction or learning opportunities. Ask students to complete activities on the computer, using their cell or smartphone, or other emerging electronic technology. This process will allow students to hone their tech skills and become more independent learners. Schedule routine Internet and e-book learning in class and in the lab.

À vous la parole

14 Des cadeaux pour mon anniversaire

1.3, 3.2

Interpretive and Presentational Communication

Vous aimez lire et vos parents voudraient vous acheter des livres en français pour votre anniversaire. Ils dépenseront environ 100 euros ou 130 dollars canadiens. Faites une liste des livres que vous voudriez lire. Dans votre liste, incluez le titre, le nom de l'auteur, une description de ce dont il s'agit, et le prix.

Search words: **(France) fnac**
(Québec) archambault

Communiquez!

1.3, 2.1, 3.2, 5.1

15 Grand Corps Malade, slameur

Interpretive and Presentational Communication

Fabien Marsaud, ou "Grand Corps Malade," son nom de slameur, est un slameur français qui a fait des albums. De son art il a dit, "Je viens du slam. C'est un art a capella, c'est un art live, il faut qu'il y ait un auditoire pour qu'il y ait du slam." En groupes, préparez une présentation sur lui qui inclue:

Grand Corps Malade

- une courte biographie
- une explication de ses thèmes
- un exemple de son art (vous donnerez les paroles à la classe, avec un glossaire)
- une critique de son art
- une évaluation: Est-ce de la poésie? Justifiez votre réponse.

Essential Instruction

1. Students do **Activité 14** in the computer lab.
2. Have students do **Activité 15** using the rubrics provided. Have them select one of his songs that is appropriate in terms of lyrics and teach it to the class. Students may opt to project an online video clip of **Grand Corps Malade** singing the song they selected, or they could make their own music video.
   Search words: grand corps malade paroles
3. In explaining the technique of writing a persuasive essay, have students read the **Modèle.** Ask them to identify the examples the writer uses to create a negative impression of the hotel.
4. Make sure the students understand the step-by-step process of writing a persuasive essay as outlined in **Activité 16.** Brainstorm possible subjects for their essay and vocabulary that would be helpful.

Stratégie communicative 

Writing a Persuasive Essay 1.2

Le discours argumentatif a pour objectif de convaincre, de persuader le lecteur. Vous devrez écrire un discours argumentatif afin de convaincre quelqu'un de lire ou de ne pas lire un livre, de voir ou de ne pas voir un film, ou de se rendre ou de ne pas se rendre à un certain endroit. Voici un exemple d'essai argumentatif. Est-ce que l'écrivain veut vous convaincre de rester ou de ne pas rester dans un hôtel de la gare?

Exemple:

Vous souhaitez rester dans un petit hôtel pas trop cher à proximité de la gare. L'hôtel de la gare est à deux pas de la gare et croyez-moi, il est difficile de l'oublier, surtout après une longue journée, car la suivante vous paraîtra encore plus longue.

Le soir, impossible d'ignorer les trains qui se succèdent. Mais, bon vous aviez choisi de rester près de la gare... vous saviez ce qui vous attendait. Par contre, c'était sans compter les jeunes du quartier que vous entendrez discuter au pied de l'immeuble, ou encore les étudiants de la fac sortant de la boîte au coin de la rue.

Un petit hôtel tout près de la Gare de l'Est.

Dans ces conditions, vous regretterez de ne pas avoir dépensé un petit peu plus d'argent pour la nuit, car impossible de lire votre guide et encore moins votre anthologie de poésie préférée. Et, vous serez si fatigué le lendemain après une nuit blanche que vous vous endormirez devant votre café. La journée en sera d'autant plus longue.

16 Mon discours argumentatif  1.3, 3.2

Suivez les étapes suivantes pour écrire votre discours argumentatif:

1. Choisissez un sujet et votre public. Le public que vous aurez choisi déterminera votre niveau de langue, familier ou standard.
2. Faites des recherches et classez vos arguments dans un organigramme.
3. Faites d'abord un brouillon (*rough draft*). Citations, faits, et statistiques peuvent constituer des points importants pour défendre votre point de vue. Commencez votre thèse par un fait, ensuite continuez avec deux paragraphes, et enfin concluez.
4. Demandez à un camarade de classe de revoir ce que vous avez écrit; acceptez ou rejetez ses remarques.
5. Mettez au propre et rendez votre épreuve finale à votre professeur.

RESOURCES

 Pre-test

 *Leçon* Quiz

Answers

 *Essays will vary.*

Reference Desk

Students may not know the meaning of these expressions: **un discours** (*a speech or address*); **un pas** (*a step*); **une nuit blanche** (*a sleepless night*); **mettre (quelque chose) au propre** (*to copy (something) out neatly*); **une épreuve** (*a paper*)

Differentiated Learning

Accelerate

High-ability students will be able to work independently to complete this assignment with a minimum amount of oversight on your part. Once you approve their choice of subject, let them work on their own.

Decelerate

Meet with low-ability students to explain the process of writing a persuasive essay. Have them show you their work as they complete steps 1–5. For step 3, have them show you their rough draft for your input before they start to write.

Special Needs Students

AD(H)D/Linguistically Challenged

Create deadlines for each step of the writing process and encourage students to write in simple sentences. Be available to make corrections and comments at every step to help them focus.

RESOURCES

 e-visual 19

 Workbook 1– 3

 Flash Cards

 Listening Activity 1

 Drill & Practice Games

Reference Desk

Here is some supplementary vocabulary needed to use the interactive website for **La poste: les outils pratiques** (*practical tools*); **offres, conseils pas à pas** (*step-by-step offers and advice*); **en outre mer** (*overseas*); **à l'étranger** (*abroad*); **formalités douanières** (*customs requirements*)

Vocabulaire actif

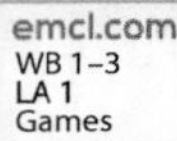

À la poste   1.2

Pour la conversation   1.1, 5.1

How do I say what I need?

› **Il me faut** une assez grande boîte....
I need a rather big box....

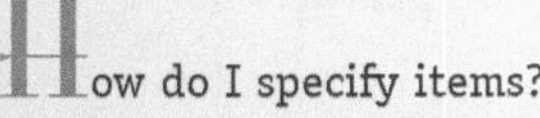

How do I specify items?

› **Quels sont ceux que** tu veux envoyer?
Which ones do you want to send?

› **Ceux que** j'ai achetés l'autre jour à la librairie.
The ones I bought the other days at the bookstore.

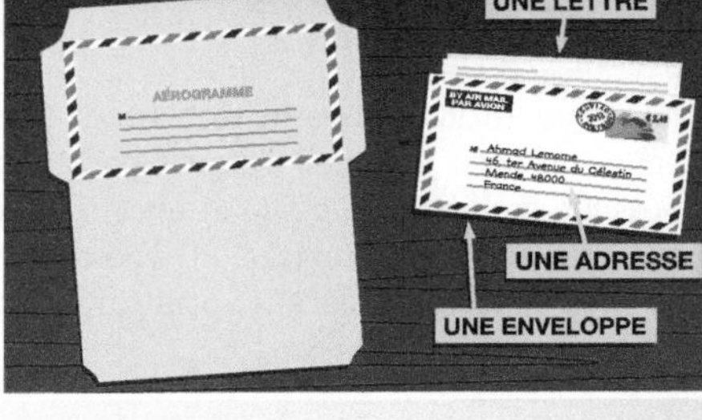

Et si je voulais dire...? 

le code postal	*ZIP code*
un compte chèque	*postal checking account*
le destinataire	*addressee*
le frais de port	*postal rate*
à destination de	*destined for*
en recommandé	*by registered mail*
par avion	*by airmail*

Lettre: *letre* (980) est issu du latin *littera* (lettre de l'alphabet) qui sous l'influence du grec *grammata* a pris le sens de missive puis d'ouvrage (*work*) écrit et, par suite, de littérature et, plus généralement, de culture et instruction. On parle de la "fac de lettres" pour se référer aux études de français.

Essential Instruction

1. Have students draw the vocabulary in their notebooks from **A la poste** and **Et si je voulais dire...?**
2. Tell students **il me faut = j'ai besoin de**.
3. Ask students what they think **ceux** means in **Ceux que j'ai achetés**...What gender is **ceux**? How do they know?
4. Describe a vocabulary word for students to guess: "**La personne qui va recevoir la lettre est**..."
5. Have students read **Activité 1** and answer the questions.
6. Have students do **Activité 2** using **Il me faut** and **J'ai besoin de** for each picture.

1 Ce que ma grand-mère m'a raconté

1.2

Lisez la composition que Louise a écrite à l'école primaire, puis répondez aux questions.

Pour cette composition sur la vie d'autrefois j'ai interviewé ma grand-mère. Elle m'a raconté comment elle avait rencontré mon grand-père. De tous endroits possibles, elle l'a rencontré à la poste! Elle allait souvent à la poste pour envoyer des lettres et des livres à sa sœur. On n'avait pas accès à Internet et aux mails comme aujourd'hui. Pendant que le postier pesait son colis, mon grand-père lui a demandé ce qu'elle lisait parce qu'il la trouvait belle. Elle lui a répondu qu'elle était en train de lire un roman policier de Georges Simenon. Ils ont découvert qu'ils aimaient tous les deux cet écrivain. Mon grand-père a demandé à ma grand-mère d'écrire un message sur son aérogramme qu'il allait envoyer à son frère dans l'armée. Elle a écrit l'adresse parce qu'elle écrivait mieux que mon grand-père. Après, mon grand-père a accompagné ma grand-mère jusqu'à chez elle. Elle a offert de lui prêter son roman, et ils ont décidé de se retrouver plus tard au café.

1. Où est-ce que les grands-parents de Louise se sont rencontrés?
2. Qui a raconté à Louise l'histoire de la rencontre de ses grands-parents?
3. Quel objet de la grand-mère de Louise est-ce que son grand-père a remarqué?
4. Qu'est-ce que les grands-parents de Louise envoyaient ce jour-là?
5. Pendant que le postier pesait le colis de sa grand-mère, qu'est-ce que son grand-père a demandé à sa grand-mère?

2 À la poste

Dites ce qu'il vous faut. 1.1

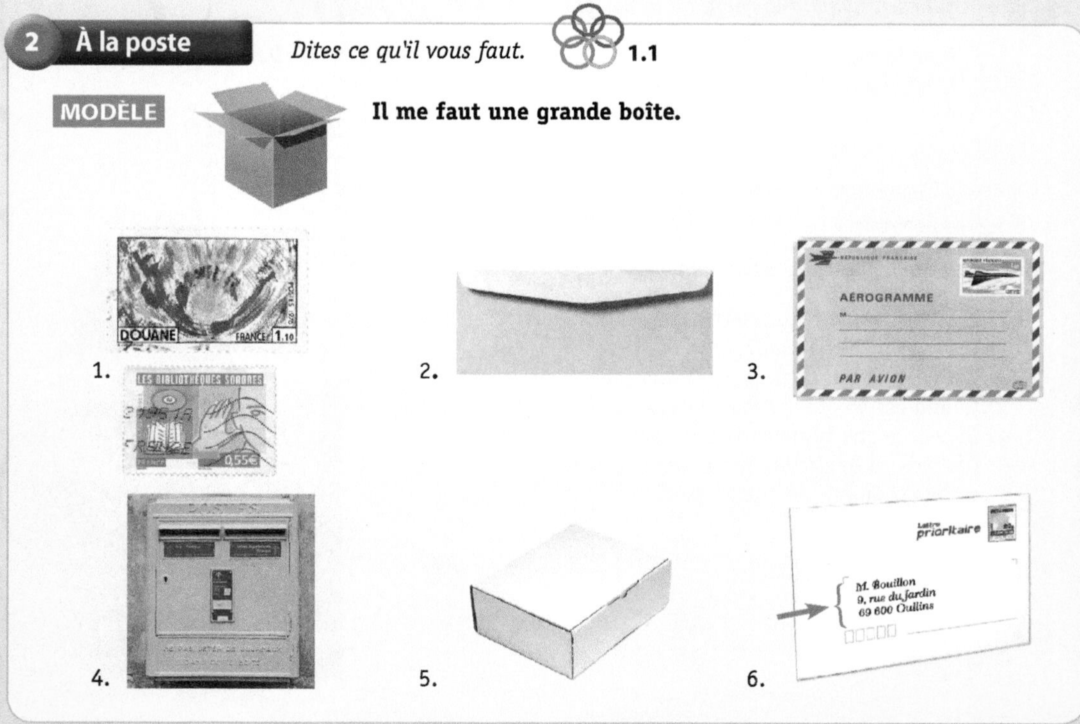

MODÈLE **Il me faut une grande boîte.**

1. 2. 3. 4. 5. 6.

Answers

1. à la poste
2. sa grand-mère
3. son roman
4. Elle envoyait un colis, il envoyait un aérogramme.
5. Il lui a demandé d'écrire un message et l'adresse sur l'aérogramme qu'il allait envoyer à son frère dans l'armée.

1. Il me faut des timbres.
2. Il me faut une enveloppe.
3. Il me faut un aérogramme.
4. Il me faut (trouver) une boîte aux lettres.
5. Il me faut une petite boîte.
6. Il me faut une adresse.

Communication

Presentational: Cooperative Groups

Have groups of three write out the conversation that they imagine took place between Louise's grandmother and grandfather the first time they met at **la poste.** Small groups present their conversations to another group for practice and then to the class. Collect the written work.

Differentiated Learning

Accelerate

Ask students to calculate the rate for sending a standard weight letter from Paris to **la Guadaloupe**. In addition, have them find the post office(s) that offer(s) the most services for the **code postal** 75012 in Paris.

Decelerate

Have students visit the site for **la Poste** and USPS to compare the services offered by each agency. Which post office offers the most services? Explain.

Search words: **poste france site officiel**, **united states postal service**

Adapt

Many students have never been to the local post office so they are unaware of the kinds of stamps, packaging, and other services available. Have them visit their local post office and write a short composition about what they saw.

Answers

3

1. envoyer
2. une enveloppe
3. l'adresse, timbres
4. postier
5. peser
6. affranchir

4

Script can be found in the front pages of the annotated Teacher's Edition.

1. D
2. C
3. E
4. F
5. A
6. B

5 *Answers will vary.*

Game

Devinez

Ask a volunteer to go to the board and draw a vocabulary word. The first student who recognizes the word must run to the board and write the word. As a variation, you could call out a vocabulary word and students have to draw it on their whiteboards, or you can draw the vocabulary word on the board, and students write the word on their whiteboards.

3 Clément va à la poste.

1.2

Complétez les phrases de Clément avec un mot de la liste.

envoyer l'adresse affranchir postier timbres une enveloppe peser

1. Je voudrais... une carte d'anniversaire au Canada.
2. Je mets la lettre dans... blanche.
3. J'écris... et je mets des....
4. Je donne la lettre au....
5. Je demande au postier, "Vous pouvez... mon colis?"
6. Il me donne le prix pour... mon colis.

Communiquez!

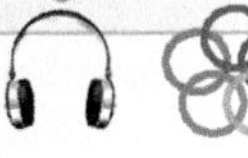

4 Le courrier

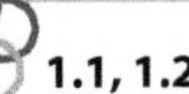

1.1, 1.2

Interpretive Communication

Écrivez les numéros 1–6 sur votre papier. Écoutez chaque phrase, puis choisissez la lettre qui correspond à la chose ou la personne indiquée.

A. la factrice B. l'adresse C. à la poste D. cette carte postale
E. le timbre F. l'affranchissement

5 Questions personnelles

1.3

Répondez aux questions suivantes.

1. Y a-t-il une boîte aux lettres dans ton quartier? Peux-tu y aller à pied?
2. Connais-tu ton facteur ou ta factrice?
3. Quand est-ce que tu vas à la poste?
4. Qu'est-ce que tu demandes au postier de faire?
5. Connais-tu quelqu'un qui collectionne des timbres? Si oui, de quels pays?

J'vais surtout à la poste pour affranchir mes lettres.

Essential Instruction

1. Have students do **Activité 3.** After correcting, ask questions to get students speaking, for example, For whom is the card? How old is your friend? Where does he or she live? What is in the package? How much did you pay for it?
2. Students listen to **Activité 4** and answer the questions A-D. Monitor the students to see who might be having difficulty.
3. Have students work in pairs to complete **Activité 5.** Afterward, ask the class these questions challenging them to add details.
4. Have students look at the picture of Justin and Léo. What do they want to do? What must they do to send the package?
5. Have students watch the video **À la poste** with books closed. Ask general comprehension questions about what Justin and Léo want to do.
6. Students read the dialogue and complete **Activité 6.** Ask students to read and answer questions.

Rencontres culturelles

emcl.com
WB 4

À la poste

   1.1, 1.2, 5.2

Léo et Justin sont à la poste.

Justin: Il me faut une assez grande boîte cartonnée comme cette boîte-ci pour envoyer mes livres.
Léo: Quels sont ceux que tu veux envoyer? J'ai des boîtes chez moi.
Justin: Ceux que j'ai achetés l'autre jour à la librairie du coin.
Léo: Alors, j'ai une boîte chez moi qui conviendrait....
Justin: En fait, j'ai aussi besoin d'une grande enveloppe pour les deux catalogues de la librairie.
Léo: Bon alors, on va chez moi pour tout préparer!
Justin: Et on revient après? La poste ferme à quelle heure?
Léo: À 18h00, mais on a le temps.
Justin: Et pour l'affranchissement....
Léo: Cet appareil ici fait très bien ça tout seul.

6 À la poste

  1.2

Complétez les phrases.

1. Léo et Justin sont à....
2. Justin voudrait acheter une grande... et une grande....
3. La poste ferme à....
4. Avant d'envoyer ses boîtes et son enveloppe, Justin va... pour chercher une boîte.
5. On ne va pas parler au postier; on va se servir d'un... qui fait....

Extension **Florence a besoin d'envoyer de l'argent.**

  1.1, 1.2

Florence est à la poste pour envoyer de l'argent aux États-Unis.

Florence: Bonjour, monsieur! Je voudrais envoyer de l'argent à un ami aux États-Unis, s'il vous plaît.
Postier: Bonjour, mademoiselle! Le moyen le moins cher est par mandat international.
Florence: Combien de temps cela prendra-t-il?
Postier: À peu près autant qu'une lettre. Cinq à sept jours.
Florence: Euh... y a-t-il un moyen plus rapide?
Postier: Bien sûr, le mandat express international. C'est un peu plus cher mais votre ami recevra votre paiement en deux jours.
Florence: Y a-t-il un moyen encore plus rapide?
Postier: Le plus rapide, sans compte bancaire postal, c'est un transfert Western Union. L'argent est disponible immédiatement!

Extension Finalement, Florence va se servir de quel service?

 1.3

RESOURCES

 Dialogue Video

 Workbook 4

Answers

6

1. la poste
2. boîte cartonnée, enveloppe
3. 18h
4. chez Léo
5. appareil, l'affranchissement

Extension

Elle va se servir du transfert Western Union.

Expansion

Lightly tape a large rectangular piece of paper on the board, which will serve as an envelope. Ask a series of students to do the following tasks as you cue them: write in the name of a **destinataire**, write an **adresse**, add a **code postal**, write "registered letter." Have a series of other students remove the envelope, pantomime weighing it, putting the envelope into a box, weighing the box, and finally putting the box in a mailbox. Have the rest of the class identify the action.

Differentiated Learning

Accelerate

Have students use the French post office website as a basis for writing a new dialogue about sending a letter or a package, or using their banking services. Encourage them to use details to make the dialogue interesting. They may want to use the **Extension** format as their template.

Search words: **poste france site official**

Decelerate

Have students read **Extension** and outline in French the various ways to send money abroad.

Special Needs Students

Linguistically Challenged/AD(H)D

Pairing these students with high-ability peers to read the dialogues might be helpful. They can ask their classmates basic questions that they may be too embarrassed to ask you. Working in groups also allows students to proceed at their own pace.

RESOURCES

Workbook 5

Reference Desk

Louis XI established the **relais de poste** for royal correspondence. The **chevaucheurs** were equestrians who traveled an average of 16 to 20 km before stopping at **relais** or staging posts to eat, rest, and change horses. In ensuing centuries, mail carriers and travelers stopped at these inns. They ate in **auberges** and slept in **gîtes**. With the onset of the rail system, mail delivery by horseback diminished. Today, many restaurants and hotels are called **relais**, evoking the romance of times past.

Expansion

Ask students to compare the presence of **la poste**, as described in the last paragraph of the reading, with the USPS in towns in the United States. Ask students if they can think of an equivalent of the **chevaucheurs** carrying mail on horseback from one post to the next (Pony Express).

Points de départ 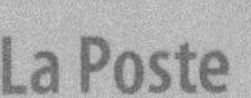 

emcl.com
WB 5

Question centrale
Comment s'intégrer à une autre culture?

La Poste 1.2, 3.1

La Poste est l'héritière des relais de poste créés par Louis XI en 1477, et de l'office des messagers royaux* créé en 1576. L'administration des postes en France date du XVIIème siècle et à cette époque, c'est le destinataire qui payait le port*. À partir de 1946, les PTT (Poste, télégraphe et télécommunication) regroupent* deux administrations: la poste et les télécommunications.

La poste se reconnaît par son logo bleu et jaune.

Aujourd'hui la Poste est un service public qui compte 17.000 points de contact et qui emploie 270.000 personnes. Elle compte 11 millions de clients pour ses activités bancaires. Elle achemine* 28 milliards de documents par an, et elle est le deuxième opérateur européen en courrier distribué et en chiffre d'affaires* sur le colis express* en Europe.

Un camion de poste.

Le bureau de poste est un des lieux symboliques de la continuité d'une vie administrative dans les plus petits villages et l'un des symboles de l'unité du territoire. La Poste est symbolisée par le facteur qui distribue le courrier, apporte les mandats*, les colis, et l'argent à domicile*. C'est un des personnages du service public le plus populaire.

 **Search words: la poste france, jour de fête jacques tati vidéo, bienvenue chez les ch'tis**

messagers royaux *royal messengers;* **port** *postage;* **regroupent** *group together;* **achemine** *route;* **chiffre d'affaires** *revenue;* **colis express** *express mail for packages;* **mandats** *money orders;* **à domicile** à la maison

Le Minitel: précurseur* d'Internet  1.2, 3.1

En 1982, la Poste propose un ordinateur, le Minitel, pour chaque maison. Le Minitel permet aux français de se brancher à un annuaire* électronique et à d'autres services. On pouvait ainsi acheter un bouquet de fleurs, faire des réservations (train, avion, théâtre...), voir les bulletins météo, et ainsi de suite*. L'invention de l'Internet a rendu le Minitel désuet*. Ce dernier a été amené à disparaître le 30 juin 2012.

précurseur *precursor;* **annuaire** *phone book;* **ainsi de suite** *and so on;* **désuet** *obsolete*

Essential Instruction

1. Have students read **La Poste** and outline the information under these categories: **l'historique, les services, et le symbolisme de la poste dans les petits villages.**
2. Students read **Le Minitel** and write a one-line definition of what the **Minitel** was.
3. Put the dates listed in **Activité 7** on the board. Have students supply the corresponding event.
4. Students do **Activités 2**, **3**, and **4** in the computer lab and then use this information to discuss services offered by **la poste française**.

COMPARAISONS

Quels problèmes a la poste américaine? Quel rôle avait Benjamin Franklin dans la création de poste américaine?

4.2

2.2

Produits

Deux films témoignent (*testify*) de la popularité du facteur français. Jacques Tati a immortalisé le facteur dans ***Jour de fête*** (1947) et ***Bienvenue chez les Ch'tis*** (2008), dont l'un des héros est facteur, a obtenu le plus grand succès cinématographique de tous les temps en France.

7 Activités culturelles

1.3, 3.1, 3.2

Complétez les activités suivantes.

1. Dites à quel événement ces dates correspondent:
   - 1477
   - 1576
   - 1946
   - 1982
   - 2012
2. Allez sur le site officiel de la Poste. Recherchez le code postal de ces villes: Colmar, Pau, Aix-les-Bains.

Search words: poste france site officiel

3. Allez sur le site officiel de la Poste. Nommez trois choses que vous pouvez voir au musée de la poste.
4. Allez sur le site officiel de la Poste. Comment est-ce que la Poste aide les gens qui visitent la France ou séjournent (*have a long stay*) en France?

À discuter

Quel est le rôle de la poste dans votre communauté? Dans votre vie?

Les facteurs et factrices se déplacent souvent à vélo en ville.

Differentiated Learning

Expand

Find online the excerpt "Jacques Tati flying mailman on a bicycle" and play it several times. The first time, play it for the comedic enjoyment. The second time, turn down the volume; stop the clip at pivotal points to ask students about the comedic action. The third time, play the clip and ask students to provide their own voiceover soundtrack.

Answers

1. 1477: Louis XI crée les relais de poste.; 1576: L'office des messagers royaux est créé par Louis XI.; 1946: La poste et les télécommunications sont réunis sous l'appellation les PTT.; 1982: La poste introduit l'ordinateur Minitel.; 2012: Le Minitel disparaît.
2. Colmar: 68000; Pau: 64000; Aix-les-Bains: 73100
3. *Answers will vary.*
4. *Answers will vary.*

Reference Desk

1. Jacques Tatie (1907–1982) was a comic actor, writer, and filmmaker. ***Jour de Fête*** recounts the efforts of a small-town postal worker who sets out to compete with what he thinks is the speed and efficiency of the United States Post Office. His endearing slapstick efforts to achieve "**rapidité**" are set against the backdrop of a small town in what the French refer to as "**la France profonde.**"
2. **Le Musée de la Poste** is located near **la Gare Montparnasse** in the **15e arrondissement de Paris.** Among its offerings are artifacts dealing with the work of postal workers, their uniforms throughout the ages, mailboxes, collections of stamps, postmarks, and cancellations applied by hand or machine.

Critical Thinking

Anaylsis

In what ways has the use of the Internet impacted the economic viability of the United States Post Office? How has France expanded the traditional services of the post office?

RESOURCES

Workbook 12–13

Answers

8

1. Découvrir nos offres mobiles; Tarifs; Envoyer et recevoir des colis; Collectionner
2. Send and receive mail/All offers–Step-by-step guide–Postage prices–Q&A–Calculate the effect of CO^2 by sending mail air or ground–Customer commitment–General conditions/Send and receive packages/Manage your money/Take advantage of our online services/Discover our mobile phone offers/Our practical services/Our fees/Our collections

Reference Desk

The word **philatélie** refers to the study of stamp production, stamp identification, and postal history. It does not necessarily mean stamp collecting.

Du côté des médias

1.2

Interpretive Communication

emcl.com
WB 12–13

Lisez cette page du site officiel de la Poste.

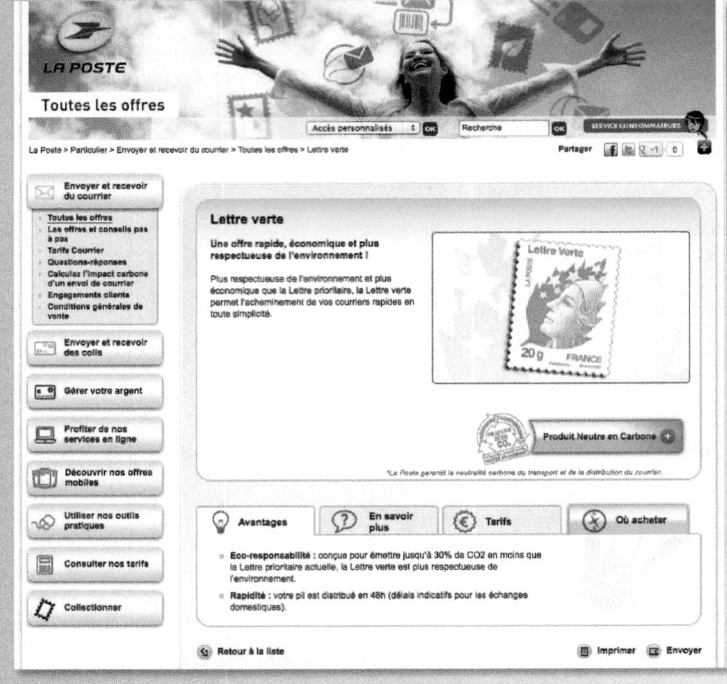

8 La Poste en France

1.2, 1.3, 5.1

Complétez les activités suivantes.

1. Dites où vous cliqueriez pour:
   - Acheter un smartphone
   - Trouver les prix pour les produits et services de la poste
   - Envoyer un colis
   - Acheter des timbres pour votre collection de timbres
2. Traduisez (*Translate*) la colonne à gauche (commençant avec "Envoyer et recevoir du courrier") en anglais pour les visiteurs qui parlent anglais.

Essential Instruction

1. In the computer lab, give students time to play with the interactive features of the **site official de la poste.** Put students in groups of three at a computer to complete **Activité 8** as a competitive timed exercise. A representative from each team puts the answers on the board. Score points for the first team done, and points for the best team's work.
2. For **Scénarios culturels**, divide students into groups. Have a representative from each group draw a number from one to five. Have the groups work to create a scene corresponding to the number drawn. If you have more than ten students, assign duplicate scenarios. Give students an appropriate amount of time to write, edit, and rehearse their scene before presenting it to the class. Encourage the students to embellish the scene to add interest.
3. Afterward, lead a discussion using the talking points in **Activité 10.**

La culture sur place

Question centrale
Comment s'intégrer à une autre culture?

Scénarios culturels

Introduction et Interrogations

Quand on voyage, on n'est pas toujours à l'aise dans toutes les situations. Quand il y a un moment de contact entre deux (ou trois ou quatre) cultures, les conflits sont inévitables. Cela ne veut pas dire que le résultat est forcément négatif. Comment vivre un scenario difficile dans une autre culture?

9 Première Étape: Répondre  1.1, 1.2, 5.1

Considérez chaque situation, ensuite pensez à votre réaction. Que feriez-vous? Décidez de votre réponse et faites un role-play avec un partenaire.

Scenario #1: À la banque ou vous avez une compte, vous voulez retirer de l'argent liquide. Vous donnez votre carte de crédit au banquier. Il vous dit que la carte est endommagée, et que vous ne pouvez pas l'utiliser. Que faites-vous? Que dites-vous au banquier?

Scenario #2: Vous avez besoin d'argent en France. Votre famille a un peu d'argent à vous envoyer, mais vous ne savez pas comment l'envoyer entre les deux localités. Où allez-vous pour vous renseigner? Que dites-vous?

Scenario #3: Vous faites la queue à la poste pour 45 minutes avec un colis à envoyer. Vous arrivez au postier, et il vous répond que vous vous êtes trompé de queue (*made the mistake of getting in the wrong line*). Il va vous falloir recommencer avec une nouvelle queue. Que faites-vous? Que dites-vous au postier?

Scenario #4: À un restaurant, vous commandez une carafe d'eau car vous avez très soif. Vous avez deux verres à votre place, et vous versez (*pour*) de l'eau dans un des deux verres. La serveuse arrive et vous gronde (*scold*) parce qu'elle dit que vous avez mis de l'eau dans le verre à vin. Quelle est votre réponse?

Scenario #5: En voyageant dans le sud de la France, vous prenez le train pour passer une journée dans une petite ville historique. La jolie petite ville n'a qu'une banque, et elle ferme de 12h00 à 14h00 pour le déjeuner. Malheureusement, vous avez besoin d'argent liquide pour acheter votre billet de train, la banque est fermée, et le train part à 14h00. Que faites-vous?

10 Faire le point!   1.3

Discutez les questions suivantes en classe.

1. Quel scénario était le plus difficile pour vous? Et le plus facile? Pourquoi?
2. Est-ce que ces scénarios pourraient se passer aux Etats-Unis aussi? Pourquoi ou pourquoi pas?
3. Y a-t-il d'autres scénarios difficiles dont vous voulez discuter?

Answers

All activities will vary.

Expansion

Have students expand on one of the scenarios in **Activité 9** by writing an e-mail to a friend or family member recounting the incident and explaining what they did to resolve it.

Learning Styles

Visual Learners

These students may want to create a backdrop for their scenario which represents the teller window or restaurant **décor**.

Kinesthetic Learners

These students will enjoy acting out the scenario.

Special Needs Students

Social Anxiety

Students who have trouble performing in front of others might be allowed to read their role rather than have to establish eye contact with the class.

Linguistically Challenged

Pair these students with high-ability students who can help them create the scenario.

RESOURCES

Workbook 6–7

Listening Activity 2

Drill & Practice Games

Answers

11 *All answers B will vary.*

1. A: Vous aimez cet ordinateur-ci ou cet ordinateur-là?
2. A: Vous aimez ce portable-ci ou ce portable-là?
3. A: Vous aimez ces chaussettes-ci ou ces chaussettes-là?
4. A: Vous aimez cette casquette-ci ou cette casquette-là?
5. A: Vous aimez ces chaussures-ci ou ces chaussures-là?
6. A: Vous aimez ce roman-ci ou ce roman-là?
7. A: Vous aimez cet accessoire-ci ou cet accessoire-là?

Reference Desk

To teach demonstrative pronouns, write **celui** on the board. Ask students if they see two words in **celui** (**ce** + **lui**). So **celui** refers to *this* masculine person or thing. The same is true for **ce + elle**, **ce + eux**, and **ce + celles**. Students see that each form is a composite of two words.

Structure de la langue

emcl.com
WB 6–7
LA 2
Games

Révision: Demonstrative Adjectives 1.1

Demonstrative adjectives point out specific people or things. **Ce**, **cet**, and **cette** mean "this" or "that"; **ces** means "these" or "those." Demonstrative adjectives agree with the nouns that follow them.

Singular			Plural
Masculine before a consonant sound	Masculine before a vowel sound	Feminine	
ce colis	**cet** aérogramme	**cette** lettre	**ces** catalogues

Ce colis est arrivé hier. — *This package arrived yesterday.*
J'irai à **cette** poste pour envoyer ma lettre. — *I will go to that post office to mail my letter.*

To make a clear distinction between who or what is closer to the speaker and who or what is farther away, add **-ci** after the noun to mean "this" or "these" or **-là** after the noun to mean "that" or "those."

Cette adresse-**ci** n'est pas correcte. — *This address is not correct.*
Je dois envoyer **cet** aérogramme-**là** à mes parents. — *I have to send that aerogram to my parents.*

Communiquez!

11 Des soldes au magasin 1.1

Interpersonal Communication

À tour de rôle, demandez ce que votre partenaire aime. Suivez le modèle.

ordinateur chemise casquette portable
roman chaussettes accessoire chaussures

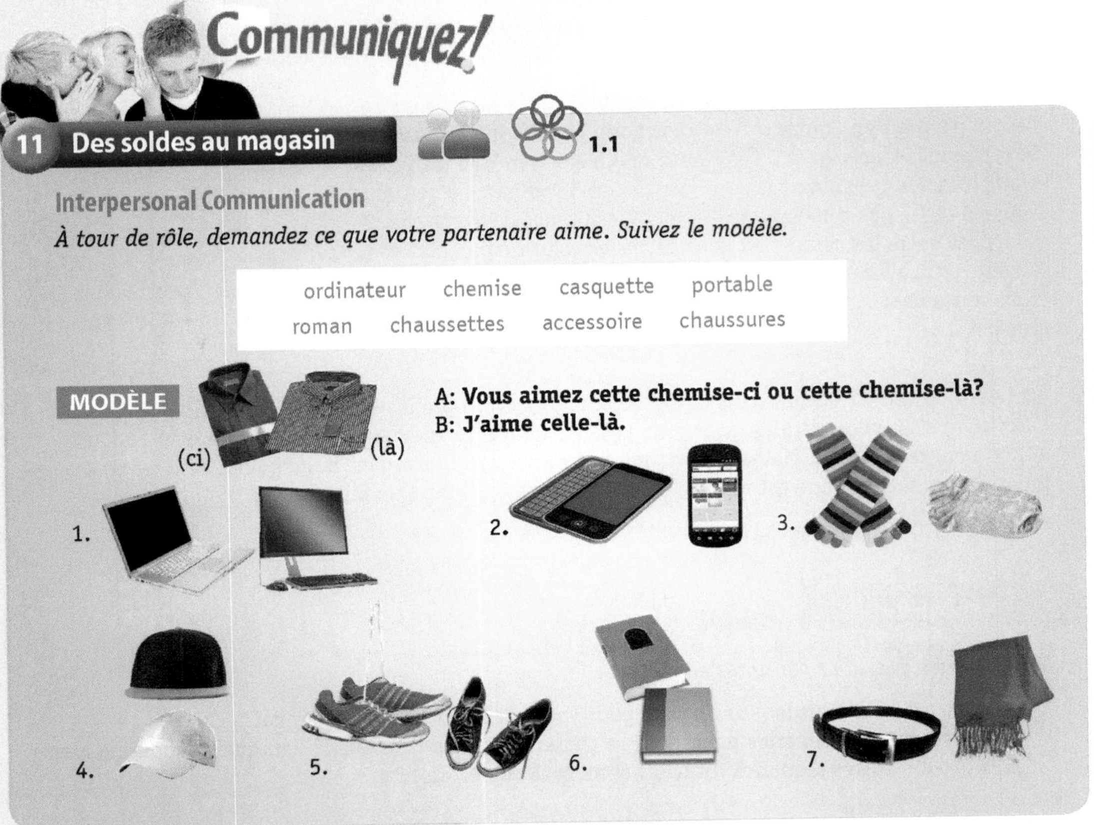

Essential Instruction

1. Review demonstrative adjectives. These words are reviewed in Level 2, **Unité 1**, **Leçon B.**
2. Introduce demonstrative pronouns. Use preferences as your context, for example, **Voici deux cahiers. Ce cahier-ci est rouge, et ce cahier-là est orange. Quel cahier préférez-vous? Celui-ci ou celui-là?** Continue until the pattern is set.
3. To check comprehension, first ask students to replace the word with the demonstrative adjective with its demonstrative pronoun. **Ce livre** is replaced by **celui**. Ask students to add **-ci** and **-là** to the demonstrative pronouns to show contrast.
4. For practice, have students draw two similar objects, then pose preference questions to another student. Use the same formula as in your introduction. **Voici deux cahiers. Ce cahier-ci est rouge, et ce cahier-là est orange. Quel cahier préfères-tu? Celui-ci ou celui-là?**
5. Pair students to do **Activité 11**, then change partners and repeat.

Demonstrative Pronouns  1.1, 1.2

emcl.com
WB 8–11
Games

The demonstrative pronoun **celui** points out specific people or things and is often used to replace the demonstrative adjective **ce** plus a noun. The form of **celui** agrees in gender and in number with the noun it replaces. The singular forms mean "this one," "that one," or "the one." The plural forms means "these," "those," or "the ones."

	Singular	Plural
Masculine	celui	ceux
Feminine	celle	celles

C'est **celui** qui envoie le colis qui doit payer. — *The one who sends the package has to pay.*

Il y avait beaucoup de lettres dans ma boîte aux lettres, même **celles** de mes voisins. — *There were a lot of letters in my mailbox even those of my neighbors.*

A demonstrative pronoun is never used alone in a sentence. It is followed by **–ci** or **–là**, **qui** or **que**, or **de**.

Add **–ci** or **–là** after a form of **celui** to indicate a choice, to clarify, or to single out. To point out who or what is closer to the speaker (*this one, these*), add **–ci;** to point out who or what is farther away (*that one, those*), add **–là.**

Quels facteurs y travaillent? **Ceux-ci** ou **ceux-là**? — *Which postal carriers work there? These or those?*

Les enveloppes blanches? Vous préférez **celles-ci** ou **celles-là**? — *The white envelopes? Do you prefer these or those?*

RESOURCES

 **Workbook 8–11**

 **Drill & Practice Games**

Reference Desk

Celui-ci or **celle-ci** may also mean "the latter." **Celui-là** or **celle-là mais** also mean "the former." A form of **celui-ci** always comes before a form of **celui-là** when both occur in the same sentence, for example, **D'où viennent tes copains Shelley et Martin? Celui-ci est français et celle-là est américaine.** Point out that in English we tend to use the reverse of this phrasing, saying "former" before "latter."

Differentiated Learning

Adapt

Ask students to select a series of articles from home to display at their desks. One half of the class is going to go to the flea market to look over the wares displayed on students' desks. Vendors will try to sell the students on their items by talking about this item and that item, or this one and that one. The teacher will be a customer also. Reverse the roles.

Special Needs Students

AD(H)D

Help students with attention difficulties break down the information about the demonstrative adjectives and pronouns by reviewing each one separately with examples. They would benefit from a one-page chart that could be used as an easy reference when doing the exercises.

Answers

12

Script is available in the front pages of the Annotated Teacher's Edition.

1. B
2. B
3. B
4. C
5. A
6. C

13

1. Avec celui-ci ou avec celui-là?
2. À celui-ci ou à celui-là?
3. Chez ceux-ci ou chez ceux-là?
4. À celle-ci ou à celle-là?
5. Ceux-ci ou ceux-là?
6. À celle-ci ou à celle-là?
7. Dans celle-ci ou dans celle-là?
8. Celles-ci ou celles-là?
9. Ceux-ci ou ceux-là?

Reference Desk

1. Before presenting **celui + qui** or **que**, review the use of the relative pronouns. Remind students that **qui** needs a verb and **que** needs a subject and a verb in the dependent clause.
2. **Celui qui** and **que**, and **celui de** are translated according to their antecedents just like in English.
3. Prepare oral examples for each concept. For example, you could put a CD on two students' desks. One could be popular and the other not. Ask a student which one he or she prefers: **Celui de Marie ou celui de Mark?** This question will anchor the concept of possession. Change the sentence to which CD he or she prefers: **Celui *qui* est sur la table de Marie**, or **Celui *que* je vois- là.**

Add **qui** or **que** after a form of **celui** for identification. Use **celui qui** as the subject and **celui que** as the object.

Les colis? **Ceux que** nous avons envoyés étaient les plus chers.	*The packages? Those that we sent were the most expensive.*
Celui qui habite près de la poste peut prendre le courrier.	*The one who lives near the post office can get the mail.*

Add **de** after a form of **celui** to express possession.

Simone a cherché son courrier et **celui de** ses parents aussi.	*Simone got her mail and her parents' too.*
Ces lettres-ci? Ce sont **celles de** Noah.	*These letters? They are Noah's.*

12 À la poste

1.1, 1.2

Écrivez les numéros 1–6 sur votre papier. Écoutez les phrases. Choisissez la réponse logique.

1. A. ceux-ci B. celle-là C. celui-là
2. A. de ceux-ci B. de celle-là C. celui-là
3. A. ceux-ci B. celles-là C. celui-là
4. A. ceux-ci B. celui-ci C. celle-ci
5. A. ceux-ci B. celui-ci C. celle-ci
6. A. ceux-ci B. celle-là C. celui-là

13 Une Américaine à Paris

1.2, 1.3

Vous voudriez mieux connaître Jennifer, une Américaine à Paris. Donc, vous posez des questions à son amie.

MODÈLE Jennifer travaille pour une compagnie à Paris.
Pour celle-ci ou pour celle-là?

1. Elle déjeune avec le directeur.
2. Elle va envoyer une carte postale à son ami américain.
3. Elle fait les courses chez les petits commerçants.
4. Elle va à une banque internationale.
5. Elle lit les mystères anglais.
6. Elle va assister à une première française d'un film.
7. Elle rêve de passer ses vacances d'hiver dans une station de ski.
8. Il lui faut des enveloppes.
9. Elle trouve les arts passionnants.

Essential Instruction

1. Students listen to the recording and do **Activité 12**, questions 1–6.
2. Pair students to do **Activité 13**. Upon completion, correct their work.
3. Have students change partners to complete **Activité 14**. Encourage them to ask follow-up questions like **pourquoi?**
4. Debrief the students by polling their preferences as an opportunity to expand conversation.

Communiquez!

14 Est-ce que je connais bien mon partenaire?

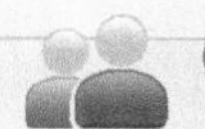  1.1, 1.2

Interpersonal Communication

À tour de rôle, posez des questions sur vos préférences pour mieux connaître votre partenaire.

MODÈLE les romans (*de Stephen Chbosky/de Stephen King*)
A: **Tu préfères les romans de Stephen Chbosky ou de Stephen King?**
B: **Je préfère ceux de Stephen King. Et toi?**
A: **Moi, je préfère ceux de Stephen Chbosky.**

1. les films (*de Brad Pitt/de Johnny Depp*)
2. les souvenirs (*d'enfance/d'adolescence*)
3. les contes (*du Maghreb/de l'Afrique*)
4. les voitures (*du Japon/de l'Italie*)
5. les tableaux (*des cubistes/des impressionnistes*)
6. la musique (*de la France/de l'Allemagne*)
7. les repas (*qu'on prépare à la maison/qu'on sert dans un restaurant français*)
8. les sports (*d'hiver/d'été*)
9. les maisons (*en banlieue/à la campagne*)
10. les CD (*de Taha/de St-Pier*)

Answers

1. A: Tu préfères les films de Brad Pitt ou de Johnny Depp?
   B: Je préfère ceux de .... Et toi?
   A: Moi, je préfère ceux de ....
2. A: Tu préfères les souvenirs d'enfance ou d'adolescence?
   B: Je préfère ceux d' .... Et toi?
   A: Moi, je préfère ceux d' ....
3. A: Tu préfères les contes du Maghreb ou de l'Afrique?
   B: Je préfère ceux du/de l'.... Et toi?
   A: Moi, je préfère ceux du/de l'....
4. A: Tu préfères les voitures du Japon ou de l'Italie?
   B: Je préfère celles du/de l'.... Et toi?
   A: Moi, je préfère celles du/de l'....
5. A: Tu préfères les tableaux des cubistes ou des impressionnistes?
   B: Je préfère ceux des .... Et toi?
   A: Moi, je préfère ceux des ....
6. A: Tu préfères la musique de la France ou de l'Allemagne?
   B: Je préfère celle de .... Et toi?
   A: Moi, je préfère celle de ....
7. A: Tu préfères les repas qu'on prépare à la maison ou qu'on sert dans un restaurant français?
   B: Je préfère ceux qu' .... Et toi?
   A: Moi, je préfère ceux qu'....
8. A: Tu préfères les sports d'hiver ou d'été?
   B: Je préfère ceux d' .... Et toi?
   A: Moi, je préfère ceux d' ....
9. A: Tu préfères les maisons en banlieue ou à la campagne?
   B: Je préfère celles .... Et toi?
   A: Moi, je préfère celles ....
10. A: Tu préfères les CD de Taha ou de St-Pier?
    B: Je préfère ceux de .... Et toi?
    A: Moi, je préfère ceux de ....

Communication

Interpersonal: Paired Practice

Arrange students in pairs to improvise a television interview. A television host interviews a famous celebrity about his or her preference in movies. The goal is to time how long they can keep the conversation going. Switch roles, change celebrities, and time again.

Differentiated Learning

Accelerate

Ask students to create a slide show presentation on demonstrative adjectives and pronouns to explain, step-by-step, what they are and how they are used, giving specific examples. Encourage them to use a realistic context. They are free to compare pop music, art, television programs, or movies to make it more interesting. At the end of the presentation they give a quiz.

Decelerate

Have students draw or find pictures of five things they like to eat and do not like to eat. They present their food preferences to the class using demonstrative adjectives and pronouns.

RESOURCES

Communicative Activities

Answers

All activities will vary.

Reference Desk

Blended Instruction

Consider using blended instruction, a combination of in-class learning and computer-mediated instruction or learning opportunities. Ask students to complete activities on the computer, using their cell or smartphone, or other emerging electronic technology. This will allow students to hone their tech skills and become more independent learners. Schedule routine Internet and e-book learning in class and in the lab.

À vous la parole

Communiquez!

15 Mon colis

1.3, 5.1

Presentational Communication

Vous avez un(e) correspondent(e) francophone. Prenez un colis et mettez-y les choses qui vous identifient, par exemple, un album, un jeu vidéo, des photos, une balle de baseball.... Apportez votre colis en classe et expliquez à vos camarades de classe la signification de chaque chose dans votre colis.

Communiquez!

16 J'envoie mon colis.

1.1, 5.2

Interpersonal Communication

Avec votre partenaire, jouez les rôles d'un(e) étudiant(e) américain(e) qui voudrait envoyer le colis de l'activité précédente et d'un postier/une postière qui l'aide à la poste. Mettez l'adresse du destinataire et votre adresse en France sur le colis.

Dites que vous voudriez envoyer ce colis, et donnez la destination.	→	Dites que vous allez le peser, puis indiquez le prix de l'affranchissement.
Dites qu'il vous faut des timbres pour six cartes postales à destination des États-Unis et trois aérogrammes.	→	Donnez le prix.
Payez.	→	Remerciez le/la client(e).

Essential Instruction

1. Have students bring in the objects mentioned in **Activité 15**. You may want them to bring two of the same things so that you can review demonstrative adjectives and pronouns. Students can explain that this hat is from Mexico and that one is from Texas, for example.
2. Give students time to prepare their oral presentation for **Activité 16**. Have students reverse roles to play both speakers.
3. Poll students as to how many have visited non-English-speaking countries. If you have immigrants in the classroom who did not understand English upon arrival, have them relate, if they are willing, how they felt before they learned to communicate.
4. Have students fill out the chart in **Stratégie de lecture** as they do their reading.
5. Give students examples of direct and indirect discourse in English. Contrast: **Il dit: "Tu es fou."** with **Il dit que tu es fou**.

Lecture thématique

Persepolis

Rencontre avec l'auteur   1.2

Marjane Satrapi (1969–), d'origine iranienne, est un écrivain et une réalisatrice qui vit maintenant à Paris. Elle a fait ses études au lycée français de Téhéran. Sa famille l'a envoyée en Europe en 1984, à l'âge de 14 ans, pour qu'elle échappe (*escape*) à la guerre en Iran. Elle a écrit *Persepolis*, une bande dessinée en quatre tomes, qui raconte son expérience. Ayant obtenu un grand succès avec *Persepolis*, Satrapi a adapté son œuvre autobiographique en long métrage d'animation en français. Vous allez lire une sélection de son troisième tome quand elle vit à Vienne avec une famille autrichienne (*Austrian*). Comment est-ce que Marjane s'intègre dans la culture européenne?

Pré-lecture  1.2

Avez-vous jamais visité un pays où l'on ne parle pas anglais? Si oui, qui a parlé pour vous? Comment vous êtes-vous débrouillé(e)?

Stratégie de lecture  1.2

Narrator and Narration

Un narrateur/une narratrice est le personnage qui raconte une histoire. Il ou elle détermine les informations que le lecteur/la lectrice aura sur les événements et les autres personnages. Pendant que vous lisez, remplissez un tableau comme celui de dessous avec les faits que vous apprenez de la narratrice dans les parties où elle narre, c'est-à-dire les parties qui ne sont pas des dialogues.

Ce que Satrapi décrit	Ce que j'apprends de la narratrice
sa matinée	Elle n'aime pas se réveiller tôt.

Outils de lecture  1.2

Direct and Indirect Reporting

Il y a deux façons de rapporter ce qu'un personnage dit, en utilisant le discours direct, ou le discours indirect. Dans le discours direct, un personnage peut dire "Je suis passionnée des bandes dessinées." L'auteur utilise des guillemets (*quotation marks*) ainsi que les mots directements énoncés par celui qui parle. Dans le discours indirect, il n'y a pas de guillemets, par exemple, Michèle a dit qu'elle est passionnée des bandes dessinées. Quelle forme de discours Satrapi utilise-t-elle dans l'extrait suivant?

Answers

Rencontre avec l'auteur
Possible answer: Elle participle aux activités et à la routine de ses amis.

Pré-lecture
Answers will vary.

Stratégie de lecture
Possible answers:
son réveil: Elle programme son réveil à 6h30.
son école: Elle n'y a pas d'amis.
son attitude: Elle justifie son exclusion.
sa famille d'accueil: Ils l'invitent tous les jours.
son allemand: Il est rudimentaire.
Les sujets de conversation: Elle parle de la guerre et de la mort avec ses amis, mais pas avec sa famille d'accueil.

Outils de lecture
L'auteur utilise le discours direct (bulles et narration) et le discours indirect (propos rapportés par le cousin).

Reference Desk

In **Pré-lecture**, brainstorm vocabulary for emotions and problems that one might feel in this situation, for example, **la peur**, **la frustration**, **la tristesse**, **la nostalgie**, **le chômage**, **l'hébergement**, **le travail**, and **l'argent**.

Differentiated Learning
Adapt
Have students listen to the interview with Marjane Satrapi talking about her movie ***Persepolis***. This interview will help make her come to life and will add interest to the reading. Consider showing the film trailer as a **point de départ** for further discussion.
Search words: **persepolis**, **exclusive marjane satrapi**, **movieweb**

Reference Desk

Students may not know the meaning of these expressions: **6h30 pile** (*6:30 on the dot*); **bosser travailler** (*familiar term*); **cultive-toi** (*get with it*); **connard** (*idiot* in very strong language); **Je me suis fait une raison.** (*I got used to it.*)

...

Essential Instruction

1. Ask students if they have ever been the "new kid" in school, at camp, or on the block. How does it feel?
2. Project **Tyrol** and **Les Pâtes.** Hide the words in the captions. Ask students to look at each frame and surmise what is happening by studying facial expressions and body language. Have them suggest dialogue.
3. Have students read **Tyrol** and **Les Pâtes**. Ask them to summarize the gist of each comic strip.
4. Explain the vocabulary and have students reread the cartoons for deeper meaning.
5. Ask students to cite examples from the story of how Marjane, the new girl at school, feels inside as she interacts with her classmates.

(suite)

* CHÉRIE

Culture

Perspectives: Information

Mikhaïl Bakunin is often referred to as the father of anarchist theory. He was a Russian revolutionist, philosopher, and believer in the theory of "collective anarchism." His most famous works are "God and the State" and "Statism and Anarchy."

Differentiated Learning

Accelerate

Have students write their own captions to the comic strips **Tyrol** and **Les Pâtes.** They may follow the original story or write their own.

Decelerate

Ask students to make a list of ways in which Marjane does not fit in with the others. They must cite examples from the text.

Special Needs Students

At-Risk Students

There may be students in your class who closely identify with the new girl in school. Students should be sensitive to the fact that being different, being new, and/or speaking another language can make a student feel isolated from others.

RESOURCES

 **Pre-test**

 ***Leçon* Quiz**

Answers

Pendant la lecture

1. avec Lucia
2. le bruit du sèche-cheveux de Lucia
3. la famille de Lucia
4. en français
5. en Europe francophone
6. de la guerre et de la mort
7. Il a fabriqué un cadre-photo pour elle.
8. une photo
9. Elle dit qu'elle est sa sœur.

Post-lecture

Possible answer:

Elle va retourner à Téhéran pour continuer ses études de lycée.

Le Monde visuel

Possible answer:

L'art de Satrapi est rude, elle n'utilise pas de couleurs. Elle montre l'exaspération du personnage principal en dessinant son visage furieux vu de l'intérieur du coussin; à l'école, elle lui dessine des yeux ronds et globuleux. Pour montrer la convivialité du repas, Satrapi dessine des visages souriants.

 17

1. *Answers will vary.*
2. Elle dit J'aime beaucoup le Tyrol.; Elle dit "Les Tyroliens sont très sympathiques. "
3. Dans les années 80, c'était l'époque de la Guerre Iran-Irak (1980–1988). La politique irakienne de Saddam Hussein voulant évoluer vers le modernisme et la laïcité et opposée à la puissance économique et militaire de l'Irak de l'Ayatollah Khomeini a envahi l'Irak. Cette guerre a été très longue et a causé énormément de morts et de dégâts économiques pour les deux pays. Elle s'est terminée par un cessez-le-feu mais sans victoire pour aucun pays. *Paragraphs will vary.*

Pendant la lecture

Lisez les questions avant de lire la bande dessinée. Après avoir lu l'histoire, répondez aux questions.

1. Avec qui est-ce que Marjane partage une chambre?
2. Qu'est-ce qui l'embête chaque matin?
3. Qui veut faire la connaissance de Marjane?
4. Le cousin de Lucia parle à Marjane en quelle langue?
5. Où a-t-il appris cette langue?
6. À table, comme au lycée, on ne parle pas de quels sujets?
7. Qu'est-ce que le parent de Lucia a fait pour Marjane?
8. Qu'est-ce qu'elle a mis dans le cadre?
9. Qu'est-ce que Marjane pense de Lucia maintenant?

Post-lecture  1.3

Basé sur ce que vous savez de la vie de Marjane, elle va où prochainement?

Le monde visuel  1.2, 1.3, 3.1

Satrapi a dessiné *Petropolis* elle-même. Comment décririez-vous son style—raffiné, primitif ou quelque chose d'autre? Comment a-t-elle montré son exaspération avec sa camarade de chambre? Son exclusion à l'école? La convivialité d'un repas partagé?

17 Activités d'expansion  1.3, 3.1, 3.2, 5.1

Faites les activités suivantes.

1. Écrivez un paragraphe dans lequel vous expliquez ce que vous savez de l'adolescence de Satrapi en Europe. Est-ce que Satrapi l'adulte utilise le discours direct, le discours indirect, ou une combinaison, pour rapporter l'autobiographie de sa vie? Expliquez aussi sa façon d'écrire une bande dessinée.
2. Changez les propos au discours indirect dans les bulles de la sélection au discours direct, par exemple: *Elle dit qu'elle a bien mangé. Elle dit, "J'ai bien mangé."*
3. Satrapi est née en 1969. Dans la sélection que vous avez lue, elle est adolescente. Qu'est-ce qui se passe en Iran à cette-époque là (environ 1983)? Faites des recherches en ligne. Ensuite, écrivez un paragraphe dans lequel vous expliquez pourquoi les parents de Marjane l'ont envoyée en Europe. Selon vous, ont-ils pris une bonne décision? Justifiez votre réponse.

Essential Instruction

1. Have students answer the questions based on the cartoon strips. Ask them supplementary questions to encourage conversation. You might inquire if they have ever been bothered in the morning by a parent or sibling. Can they relate to Marjane's challenge of making new friends?
2. Have students work online to do **Activité 17.** Question three may be the subject of a class discussion of political refugees not only in Marjane's experience, but also in the world today.
3. Have students do activity **D** together. Ask them to submit areas that they do not yet understand so that you can incorporate more instruction in those areas before the unit test.

Projets finaux

A Connexions par Internet: Le marketing

1.3, 3.1, 3.2, 5.1

Presentational Communication

Avec un ou deux partenaires, créez la page d'accueil d'une banque destinée aux jeunes français. D'abord, vous devrez décider quels services les jeunes recherchent. Quels messages attireraient les jeunes? Quel slogan choisiriez-vous? Comment s'appelle votre banque?

B Communautés en ligne

3.1, 3.2, 5.2

Les étudiants américains en France/Interpretive Communication

Beaucoup d'universités américaines et françaises offrent des échanges. Pour savoir si une telle expérience vous intéresserait, préparez cinq questions que vous voudriez poser sur les défis (*challenges*) de vivre et d'étudier en France. Ensuite, cherchez un blogue en ligne et contactez le blogueur/la blogueuse. Posez-lui vos questions. Discutez de ce que vous avez appris avec vos camarades de classe.

Search words: campus france, mon expérience d'étudiant en france

C Passez à l'action!

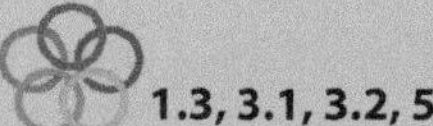
1.3, 3.1, 3.2, 5.1

Combattons l'analphabétisme!/Presentational Communication

Si vous et vos camarades de classe pensez que tout le monde a le droit de savoir lire, suivez ces étapes pour enquêter sur l'analphabétisme *(illiteracy)* dans le monde francophone, et proposez une solution.

- Faites une liste des pays francophones que vous avez étudiés, et cherchez le taux d'analphabétisme dans chaque pays.
- Choisissez un pays dans la liste.
- Trouvez une association avec laquelle vous pouvez travailler.
- Faites une collecte de livres dans votre école/communauté.
- Envoyez les livres à l'association.
- Peut-être qu'il faudra organiser une collecte de fonds pour payer l'expédition.

D Faisons le point!

1.1, 1.3

Remplissez le schéma que votre a prof va vous donner.

Question centrale: Comment s'intégrer à une autre culture?

Answers

All activities will vary.

Critical Thinking

Evaluation

Encourage the students to evaluate their learning in this unit. 1) Have them write the answer to the question, "What do I know now that I did not know before doing this unit?" 2) Ask them to evaluate what they still need to review. 3) Have them write a list of questions (that are not answered in the book) to ask the teacher before the unit exam.

Multiple Intelligences

Projets A, **B**, and **C** would appeal to students with different multiple intelligences. Give the students a choice of activities as a way of appealing to what they are interested in. For example, the Bodily-Kinesthetic/Visual-Spatial students might enjoy making a website or a commercial for a bank for young people. The intrapersonal students would like to do project **B**. Your Interpersonal/Logical-Mathematical students might be drawn to the third activity.

Special Needs Students

At-Risk Students/Behavior Problems/ Linguistically Challenged

These language students possess a variety of talents. Many can draw, others are adept in technology, some love photography. Expand the **Projets finaux** to include activities in which they can excel.

RESOURCES

Listening Activity
Synthèse

Answers

A Script can be found in the front pages of the Annotated Teacher's Edition.

1. V
2. V
3. F
4. F
5. V
6. V
7. V
8. F

B *Conversations will vary.*

Game

En vitesse!
As a bell-ringer game, give students five minutes to write as many words and expressions as possible that pertain to **la banque** and **la poste**. Tally the correct words to determine the **le roi** or **la reine du vocabulaire du jour**.

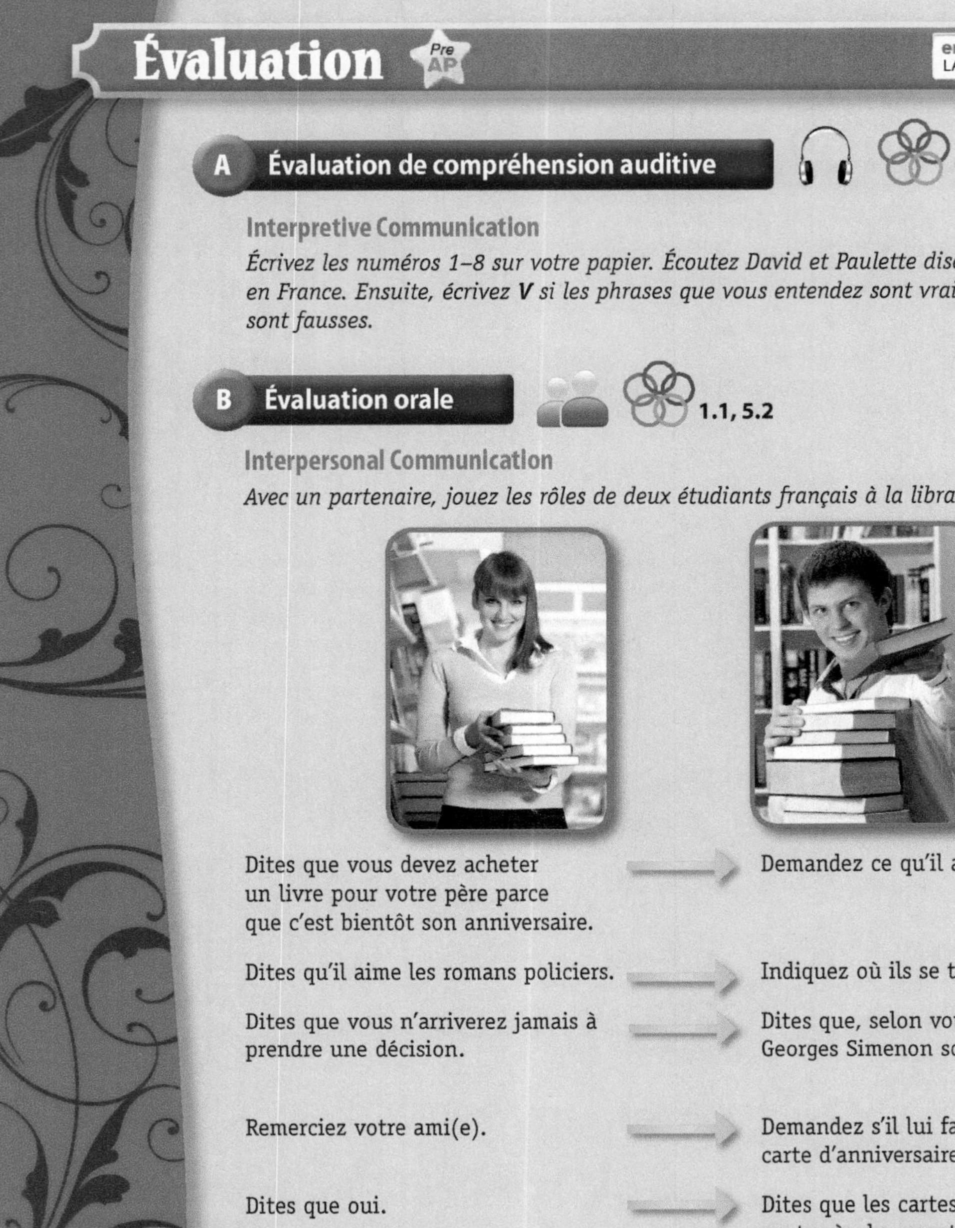

Évaluation

Pre AP

emcl.com
LA *Synthèse*

A Évaluation de compréhension auditive

1.1, 1.2

Interpretive Communication

*Écrivez les numéros 1–8 sur votre papier. Écoutez David et Paulette discuter de la poste en France. Ensuite, écrivez **V** si les phrases que vous entendez sont vraies, ou **F** si elles sont fausses.*

B Évaluation orale

1.1, 5.2

Interpersonal Communication

Avec un partenaire, jouez les rôles de deux étudiants français à la librairie À Tout Lire.

Dites que vous devez acheter un livre pour votre père parce que c'est bientôt son anniversaire.	→	Demandez ce qu'il aime lire.
Dites qu'il aime les romans policiers.	→	Indiquez où ils se trouvent.
Dites que vous n'arriverez jamais à prendre une décision.	→	Dites que, selon votre mère, ceux de Georges Simenon sont intéressants.
Remerciez votre ami(e).	→	Demandez s'il lui faut une carte d'anniversaire.
Dites que oui.	→	Dites que les cartes d'anniversaires sont près du comptoir.
Demandez à votre ami(e) s'il ou elle va venir fêter l'anniversaire de votre père.	→	Promettez de venir.

Essential Instruction

1. Have students listen to **Évaluation A.**
2. Pair students to do **Évaluation B.** Give class time to prepare their dialogue. Students may use a small cue card.
3. Have students choose a card marked one, two, three, or four, which will give them their assignment for **Évaluation C.** Tell them that they must organize their work to share with the class.
4. For **Évaluation D** students might want to write the response using a real e-mail format. Have them answer the question and add chatty conversation in the way they would if they were writing to a friend.
5. Give students a few minutes to jot down notes about the picture before they do **Évaluation E.** Then use the picture to get students speaking.
6. A storyboard format lends itself to **Évaluation F.** Remind students that they do not have to be a Picasso to draw figures.

C Évaluation culturelle

 1.3, 2.1, 2.2, 3.1, 3.2, 4.2, 5.1

Vous allez comparer les cultures francophones à votre culture. Vous aurez peut-être besoin de faire des recherches sur la culture américaine.

1. **Les banques**
   Quelles banques françaises peut-on trouver à Paris? Quelles banques canadiennes peut-on trouver à Montréal? Comment s'appellent les banques dans votre ville? Toutes ces banques sont-elles des banques nationales, régionales, ou internationales?
2. **Les habitudes de lecture**
   Comparez les habitudes des lecteurs français à celles des lecteurs américains. Est-ce que vos habitudes ressemblent plutôt aux habitudes des Français ou des Américains? Justifiez votre réponse.
3. **Jean-Marie Gustave Le Clézio**
   Le comité Nobel considère Le Clézio comme un "écrivain de nouveaux départs, de l'aventure poétique et de l'extase sensuelle, explorateur d'une humanité au-delà et en dessous de la civilisation régnante." Qu'est-ce qui peut illustrer ce résumé dans ce que vous avez appris sur Le Clézio?
4. **La Poste**
   Quels services est-ce que la poste française offre? Comment est-ce que la poste américaine est différente de la poste française?

D Évaluation écrite

 1.2, 1.3

Votre correspondant français vous a écrit un e-mail. Lisez-le et répondez en utilisant des pronoms démonstratifs.

Il faut que je lise un roman américain et que j'en fasse un résumé. Quels livres est-ce que tu me conseillerais?

Je voudrais t'envoyer un colis avec des choses typiques d'ici. Qu'est-ce que tu préférerais? Des choses à manger, à regarder, ou à écouter?

A+,

Khaled

E Évaluation visuelle

 1.3

Décrivez ce qui se passe à la poste.

F Évaluation compréhensive

Créez une histoire avec six illustrations qui montre un Américain en France qui visite la banque, la librairie, et, finalement, la poste.

 1.3

Answers

All activities will vary.

Reference Desk

1. You might want to have students take a learning styles test as they prepare to study for the final evaluation. Preview it to make sure that it is a good measurement tool. Search words: **learning styles test**
2. Consider evaluating students for part **A** on the work completed rather than on the quality of their speaking. Use this time period to give informal feedback and advice before the assessment.

Differentiated Learning

Adapt

Ask students to find a graphic organizer of their choosing featuring these question words: **Qui?**, **Que?**, **Comment?**, **Pourquoi?**, **Quand?**, **Avec qui?** During their pre-speaking or pre-writing preparation, have them fill out the graphic organizer. Doing this gives them the framework for organizing their ideas before oral and written evaluations.

Search words: **graphic organizer**, **enchanted learning**, **interactive graphic organizers**

Special Needs Students

Linguistically Challenged

For the **Évaluation orale**, make sure that students with linguistic challenges are given a partner who understands instructions well and will be supportive during the conversation.

RESOURCES

Listening Pre-test D

***Unité* Test**

Games

Pictionnaire
Play Pictionary to review vocabulary. Create a set of vocabulary flash cards and put them in a large envelope. Divide the class into two teams. One student selects a word and draws it on the board while teammates try to guess the word. Award one point for each word guessed correctly in an allotted amount of time. Include vocabulary from previous chapters to make the game more challenging.

Charades
Play Charades with unit vocabulary. Divide the class into two teams. One student acts out the word for teammates during a short time period. Award a point for each word guessed correctly. Include vocabulary from previous chapters to make the game more challenging.

Vocabulaire de l'Unité 6

1.2

un **aérogramme** air letter *C*
affranchir to stamp *C*
l' **affranchissement (m.)** postage *C*
un **appareil** machine *C*
l' **argent (m.): argent liquide** cash *A*
arriver: arriver à faire quelque chose to bring oneself to do something *A*
assez rather *C*
une **autobiographie** autobiography *B*
une **autorisation** permit *A*
avoir: avoir l'impression (de) to have the impression (of) *A*
le **banquier, la banquière** banker *A*
la **biochimie** biochemistry *A*
une **boîte** box *C*; **boîte aux lettres** mailbox *C*; **boîte cartonnée** cardboard box *C*
un **bouquin** book *[inform.]* *B*
le **bureau: bureau de change** foreign exchange counter *A*
c'est: c'est promis it's a promise *A*
le **caissier, la caissière** bank teller *A*
une **carte: carte bancaire** debit card *A*
un **catalogue** catalog *C*
celui, celle that/this one, the one *C*
un **certificat** certificate *A*
ceux the ones, these, those *C*
un **chèque** check *A*; **chèque de voyage** traveler's check *A*
un **chéquier** checkbook *A*
un **colis** package *C*
un **compte** account *A*
congolais(e) Congolese *B*
coupable guilty *A*
se **débrouiller** to get by *A*
se **décider** to make up one's mind *B*
déposer to deposit *A*
dernier, derniére: le dernier the latest *B*
une **dimension** dimension *A*
le **distributeur (automatique)** ATM *A*
dont about which/whom, of which/whom *B*
le **droit** law *A*
en: en ce moment at the moment *A*
encaisser to cash *A*
être: être amoreux/ amoreuse (de) to be in love (with) *B*; **être content(e) (de)** to be happy (about) *B*
évident obvious *A*
un **facteur, une factrice** mailman, mailwoman *C*
les **finances (f.)** finances *A*
futur(e) future *A*
le **génie civil** civil engineering *A*
la **gestion économique d'entreprise** economic business management *A*
graphique graphic *A*
l' **imaginaire (m.)** fantasy *B*
l' **infographie (f.)** computer graphics *A*
s' **intégrer (à)** to integrate (into) *A*
un **livre: livre de poche** paperback *B*
un **manga** manga *B*
la **médecine** medicine *A*
la **monnaie** change *A*
parler: parler de to be about *B*
peser to weigh *C*
une **pièce (de monnaie)** coin *A*; **pièce de théâtre** play *B*
la **poésie** poetry *B*
policier detective *B*
le **positionnement** positioning *A*
le **postier, la postière** postal worker *C*
une **première** première (of movie) *A*
la **psychologie** psychology *A*
réaliser to direct (movie) *A*
la **réalité** reality *B*
retirer to withdraw *A*
les **sciences (f.): sciences politiques (sciences po)** political science *A*
signer to sign *A*
la **tendresse** tenderness *B*
un **titre** title *B*

Reading material... See p. 339

Essential Instruction

Students should be able to recall the word or expression from English to French, and from French to English. They should be able to spell and pronounce the terms correctly. In reviewing vocabulary, have students define each term.

Unité 6 Bilan cumulatif 

I. Interpretive Communication: Print Texts  1.2

Lisez cet article sur les Français et l'argent aujourd'hui, puis répondez à la question.

Avec la dernière crise économique en Europe, beaucoup moins de touristes sont descendus dans les grands hôtels de la côte d'Azur en France et à Monaco. Évidemment, maintenant, les revenus des entreprises sont beaucoup moins importants. Pour répondre à la situation et pour encourager les touristes à profiter d'un séjour de plus longue durée sur la côte, les hôtels français et monégasques proposent des offres incroyables. Si on réserve une chambre dans un des hôtels participants, toutes sortes de prestations sans supplément sont disponibles, par exemple chambre avec climatisation, bain à remous, accès au centre d'affaires avec connexion Wifi et fax, et coffre-fort. En plus, le concierge de l'hôtel s'occupera de planifier les visites touristiques. On s'attend à ce que les revenus soient plus importants pour la saison à venir à cause de ces nouvelles prestations.

1. D'après le texte quel est le réflexe des entreprises en période de crise?
   A. de travailler différemment pour augmenter sa clientèle
   B. de faire semblant qu'il n'y a pas de problème
   C. de ne rien changer

II. Interpretive Communication: Audio Texts  1.1, 1.2

Madison va en France pour les vacances. Avec son amie Sidney, elle regarde les guides touristiques. Écoutez le dialogue suivant deux fois, puis complétez les phrases.

1. La conversation a lieu....
   A. dans un office de tourisme
   B. au téléphone
   C. au cinéma
   D. dans une librairie

2. Madison décide d'acheter....
   A. un magazine de cuisine
   B. rien
   C. deux livres de poche
   D. un guide sur les régions de France

3. Sidney suggère à Madison....
   A. qu'elle achète plusieurs guides
   B. qu'elle regarde un documentaire avec elle
   C. d'acheter ses livres à sa destination et d'aller voir un film au cinéma
   D. qu'elle rentre à la maison

RESOURCES

Pre AP Listening Units 5–6

Answers

1. A

Script can be found in the Audio Program Manual.

1. D
2. A
3. C

Reference Desk

1. The **Bilan cumulative** is based on the French Language and Culture AP exam prepared by the College Board. It assesses students' proficiencies in the Interpersonal, Interpretive, and Presentational modes of communication. Students are also asked to demonstrate their understanding of the products, practices, and perspectives of the target cultures.
2. The Print Text section consists of a variety of authentic print materials such as articles and correspondence. A multiple-choice question follows the text.
3. The Audio Text is a professional recording, usually a dialogue. Encourage students to preview and skim the questions before listening. They should then answer the multiple-choice questions.

Differentiated Learning

Accelerate/Decelerate

Have students skim the questions before reading the passage or listening to the dialogue. In this way, they have a sense of what it is about. Encourage students not to try to decode every word as they read or listen but work on understanding the gist of the passages.

Reference Desk

1. The E-mail Reply is a free response test section. Students develop their interpersonal writing skills.
2. The Presentational Writing section asks students to write a persuasive essay.

III. Interpersonal Writing: E-mail Reply  1.2, 1.3

*Vous allez écrire une réponse à un message électronique. Il faut répondre à toutes les questions et donner des détails à propos du sujet du message. Écrivez formellement. N'oubliez pas d'écrire une salutation au début et d'utiliser une formule de politesse (*closing*) à la fin de votre message.*

Vous êtes responsable d'une librairie qui se trouve à la rue de Rivoli à Paris. Vous répondez à Antony Talbot, écrivain américain, que vous avez invité à une discussion sur le futur du livre et qui cherche à mieux connaître les habitudes de lecture des Français.

De: Antony Talbot

Objet: Les Français et les livres

Cher Monsieur,

Je vous remercie de m'avoir invité à participer à la "Table ronde des auteurs" qui aura lieu au mois de mars à la librairie "Aux Quatre Coins" que vous organisez chaque année pour vos lecteurs pendant la semaine de la Foire du Livre à Paris. Je comprends qu'il y aura une conférence suivie d'une discussion où je présenterai mon nouveau roman *Livre fragile*, et parlerai du futur du livre. Afin de préparer cette rencontre, j'aimerais en savoir plus sur l'importance du livre dans la vie des Français. Quelles sont leurs préférences? Livres de cuisine? Romans policiers? Essais? Mangas? Y a-t-il des émissions littéraires à la télé ou à la radio? Je sais que les prix littéraires ont une grande importance en France, mais influencent-ils vraiment les lecteurs? Combien de titres vendez-vous par an? Je vous remercie d'avance de répondre à mes questions. Ces précisions me seront très utiles et me permettront de mieux connaître les goûts et les habitudes de vos lecteurs afin de préparer ma présentation.

Bien cordialement,

Antony Talbot
11 Oak Drive
Greenwich, CT 06830
USA

IV. Presentational Speaking: Cultural Comparison  1.2, 1.3

Vous êtes consultant en finances. Vous faites une présentation qui s'appelle "Comment vivre et voyager avec votre argent" à un groupe d'étudiants américains qui participeront à un échange en France. Leurs parents se rappellent l'époque où on était obligé de voyager en Europe avec des chèques de voyage, et la monnaie de plusieurs pays. Il faut leur expliquer que tout a changé et les renseigner sur comment organiser les finances de leurs enfants. Parlez de ce que leurs enfants doivent savoir pour ouvrir un compte et obtenir une carte bancaire. Les parents auront besoin de savoir comment ils peuvent envoyer de l'argent à leurs enfants.

Essential Instruction

1. Make copies of the **Bilan cumulatif III** and **IV** for students so that they can jot down notes. Students must answer every question posed in the e-mail, so they should number each question to make sure that they write a thorough response. In the same way, for the Presentational Speaking: Cultural Comparison, they need to outline their talking points.

Unité

7 Les arts francophones

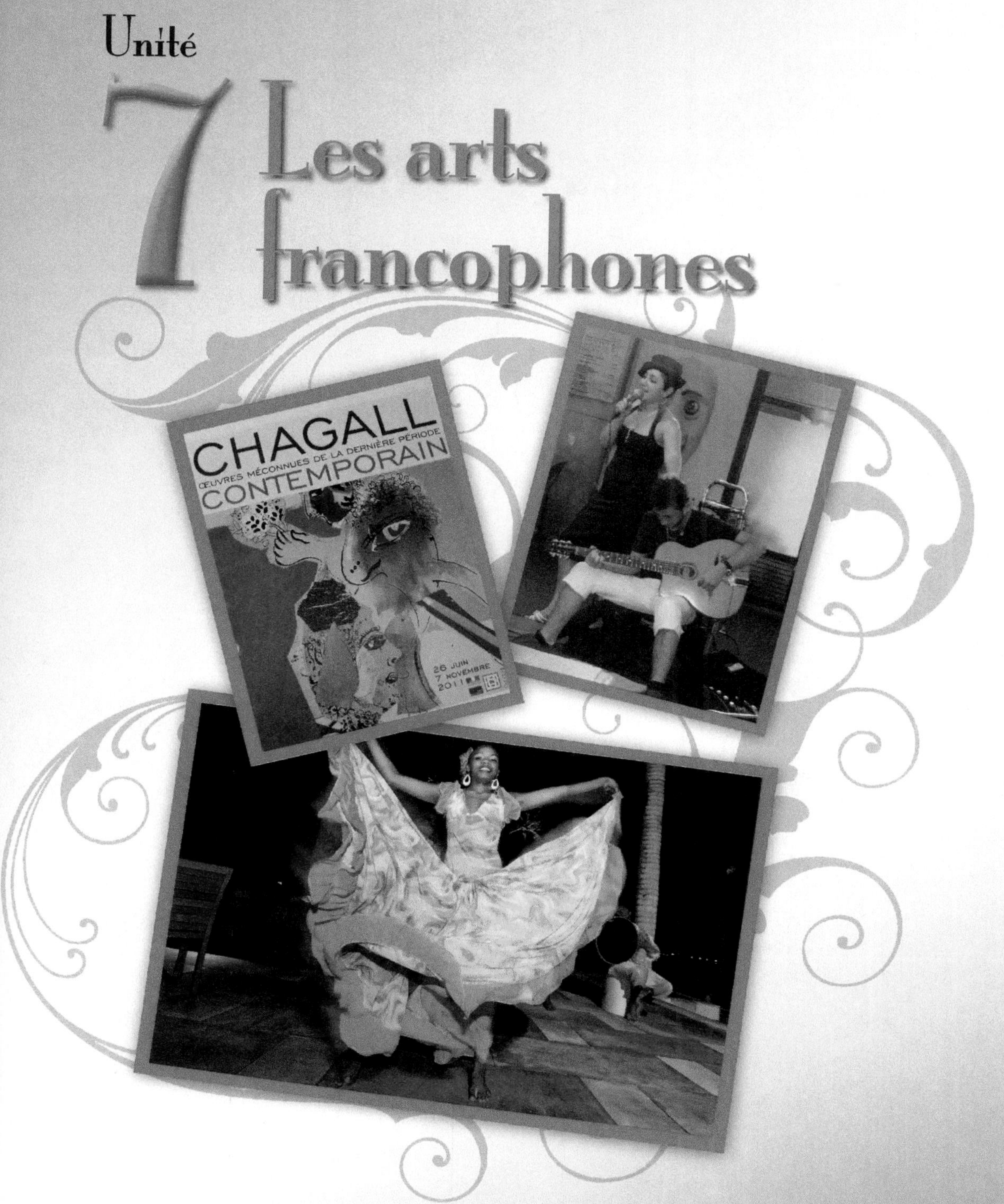

Reference Desk

1. Marc Chagall lived in Paris and is one of the most famous French immigrant painters along with Pablo Picasso. The 19th and 20th centuries were prolific artistic times in the **ville des arts**, and most artists emigrated there from all parts of the world to find fame, inspiration, kinship, and perhaps good cuisine.
2. Live music is a very common entertainment in French cities, not solely in Paris. Small villages continue to hold frequent festivals combining music, singing, and dance. **Le festival de musique** is a yearly music and art fest that spans several days in all cities of France. This tradition goes back to the Middle Ages when **troubadours** would bring the arts (music, singing, literature, poetry, theatre) alive to a people who did not necessarily have access to books and travels, the elite repertoire of fine arts, and philosophies.
3. This Maurician dancer is interpreting **le séga**. This musical dance is typical of the islands in the Indian Ocean and is influenced by African, Indian, and European rhythms. It is a good example of what creole culture is, as it has African origins yet does not exist in Africa.

Reference Desk

1. The photo represents a couple dancing swing. Swing is a North American dance form influenced by the Charleston and created from jazz and band music of the Harlem Renaissance in the United States in the 1920s.

Expansion

1. Students might want to share with the class their tastes in painting, music, and dance. Write three columns on the board, one for each art category, then poll students to find out if they know French or francophone painters, painting movements, singers, and dancers or dance styles.
2. Group students by art category, then assign each group a survey to write in French about their own tastes and those of their families.
3. Compile the three surveys into one with three section headings: **La peinture**, **La musique**, **La danse**, and give it to students as a class opener or homework the next day.

Citation

"L'art ne reproduit pas le visible, il rend visible."

Art doesn't reproduce what is visible; it makes things visible.

—Paul Klee, peintre suisse

À savoir

Trente-trois pour-cent des Français ont visité un musée au moins une fois au cours de l'année dernière.

Essential Instruction

1. Ask students how many French painters and writers they can name. Inquire if they can define classicism, impressionism, and surrealism.
2. Students will read sample poems from the Renaissance, 17th century, Romantic period, and the Surrealist movement of the 20th century.
3. Students will expand their mastery of the subjunctive using **pour que**, and learn the verb **plaire**.
4. Review the **Contrat de l'élève** to give students an overview of what they are going to learn.

Unité 7 Les arts francophones

Expansion

Ask students to bring pictures of paintings, singers and bands, and dancers they like, and have a short show-and-tell as a bell ringer.

Question centrale

Comment l'art est-il un reflet de la culture?

"Comment s'appelle ce chanteur?

De quel siècle date ce village?

Contrat de l'élève

Leçon A I will be able to:

- say when a painting was painted, and describe an artist's painting.
- discuss major art movements in France and traditional and contemporary art in West Africa.
- use adjectives to describe, and in comparative and superlative constructions.

Leçon B I will be able to:

- describe the development of an artist, say that an artist was successful, and describe an artist and his/her ability to connect with his or her audience.
- talk about music, singers, and groups from France and Quebec.
- use the verb **plaire**.

Leçon C I will be able to:

- describe how an artist raises themes, fits into a culture, and what he or she worked on; describe how a work of art takes a position; attribute new inventions to an artist.
- discuss **La Pléiade**, Romanticism and Victor Hugo, and Surrealism.
- use **pour** + **infinitif** and the subjunctive after **pour que**.

Multiple Intelligences

Visual-Spatial

This unit will be of special interest to these students since one of its themes is the visual artist. They can share with the class what they already know of different artists throughout the ages.

Musical-Rhythmic

Ask these students to do a preliminary review of popular music of France and Quebec by referencing the current top music, artists, and songs.

Word search: la fnac, archambault

Special Needs Students

At-Risk Students

Be sure to poll these students about their interest in art and music, as this unit might have great appeal for them.

RESOURCES

 e-visual 20

 Workbook 1–3

 Flash Cards

 Listening Activity 1

 Drill & Practice Games

Reference Desk

1. **Le Musée des Beaux-Arts de Lyon** is the municipal museum of Lyon housed in the former 17th century Benedictine convent. The collection spans art from ancient to modern times. The Egyptian collection is especially noteworthy.
2. **Un vernissage** is a private reception and viewing of an art exhibition before the opening to the public. Since there are many small art galleries in French cities and towns, this is a popular event among art lovers.

Vocabulaire actif

La peinture et les mouvements d'art

1.2, 5.1

La peinture

Musée des Beaux-Arts
20 Place des Terreaux. 69001 Lyon

un musée des beaux-arts: un musée dans lequel on peut trouver des peintures, des objets d'art, des sculptures, etc.

un atelier: pièce dans laquelle l'artiste travaille

un pinceau: une sorte de brosse pour appliquer des couleurs sur la toile

une toile: support sur lequel le peintre applique les couleurs

Pour la conversation

1.1, 1.2

How do I say when a painting was painted?

> *Les coquelicots* **a été peint en** 1873.
> *The Poppies* was painted in 1873.

How do I describe an artist's approach?

> **Avec ce tableau,** Renoir **recherche de plus en plus** les effets de lignes.
> *With this painting, Renoir is looking more and more into the effects of lines.*

> **Avec cette méthode**, Seurat **s'éloignait des** impressionnistes.
> *With this method, Seurat distanced himself from the Impressionists.*

How do I describe the colors used in a painting?

> **L'artiste a utilisé** le jaune pâle.
> *The artiste used pale yellow.*

Et si je voulais dire...?

une aquarelle	*watercolor*
un cadre	*frame*
un fusain	*charcoal*
un modèle	*model*
une palette	*palette*
graver	*to engrave*
poser	*to pose*

Essential Instruction

1. Students will listen to the recording of **La peinture et les mouvements d'art**.
2. Students will use a full page of their notebook to draw and label the vocabulary on p. 380.
3. Students will create a timeline or use another graphic organizer of their choosing to note the chronology of **Les movements d'art**, selecting a few key words to describe each one. They may choose to print a sample picture as an illustration of the style of the period. As students read about other movements, artists, and poets in this **Unité**, they will add that information as well.

Les mouvements d'art (m.)

 1.2, 5.1

emcl.com
WB 3
LA 1

La salle rococo (1730–1789)

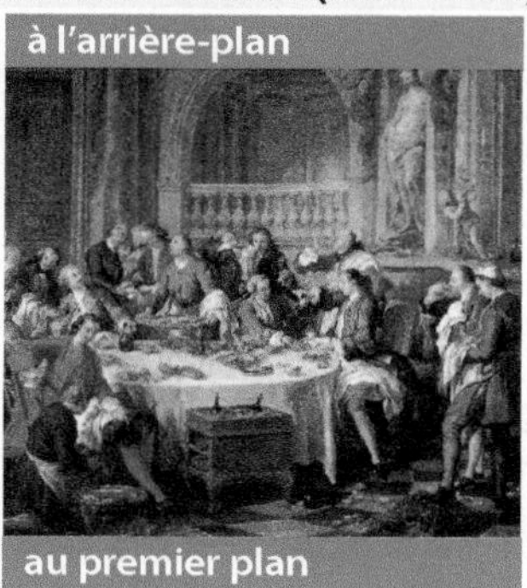
à l'arrière-plan
au premier plan

Le rococo: un mouvement qui naît après le déclin du mouvement baroque dans la seconde moitié du XVIIIème siècle; ses sujets sont surtout des aristocrates

La salle néo-classique (1760–1830)

une perspective en gros plan

Le néo-classicisme: l'art du XVIIIème au XIXème siècles qui se sert de la mythologie pour ses sujets; inspiré par la Rome antique

La salle romantique (1775–1850)

un paysage marin

Le romantisme: l'art du XVIIIème au XIXème siècles qui exprime l'idéal et les sujets exotiques

La salle réaliste (1830–1890)

Le réalisme: l'art du XIXème siècle qui montre les scènes de la vie courante, pas idéalisées

La salle impressionniste (1850–1900)

une fête champêtre en plein air

L'impressionnisme (m.): l'art du XIXème siècle qui note les impressions fugitives avec une touche rapide; les paysages sont souvent peints en plein air

Le néo-impressionnisme: une technique qui oppose des petites touches de peinture de couleurs primaires et des couleurs complémentaires; c'est l'œil qui les mélange

La salle expressionniste (1888–)

une nature morte

L'expressionnisme (m.): un mouvement dont peintres montrent une vision émotionnelle et subjective du monde

Communication

Interpersonal: Cooperative Groups

Assign groups of students to find names of painters to fit in each of the six art movements introduced on this page.

Differentiated Learning

Accelerate

Students will visit the website of the **Le Musée des Beaux-Arts de Lyon**. They will make questions for the class on the details of operation, rules of the visit, and key pieces of art in the museum's collection. The class will then visit the website and answer the questions they have created.

Decelerate

Have students present to the class the names of three famous artists from each listed art movement who are not featured in the lesson, with a sample picture of each.

Answers

1 *Possible answers:*

1. Il n'a pas été impressionné par ce qu'il a vu.
2. l'art qui représente quelque chose
3. dans un atelier
4. Ils s'intéressaient à ces œuvres d'art.
5. non

1. un pinceau
2. la toile
3. un atelier
4. en plein air
5. une peinture
6. à l'arrière-plan, au premier plan
7. une nature morte
8. un paysage
9. une fête champêtre

Game

Appuyez sur le buzzer!
First ask students to go to the board one by one and write a vocabulary word you dictate. You should use the vocabulary from the word bank of **Activité 2.** You will then read the sentences from this **Activité.** Students will refer to the vocabulary on the board to select the term that completes each sentence. The first person who buzzes in (using an imaginary buzzer) with the correct term gets a point.

1 Un jour au musée des beaux-arts

1.2, 5.1

Lisez le blogue d'un étudiant, puis répondez aux questions.

Bon d'accord, je ne suis pas un spécialiste de l'art, mais cette exposition ne m'a pas impressionné! Tous les tableaux se ressemblent: des couleurs sombres, pas de couleur vive, pas de paysage, pas de nature morte, pas de portrait, juste des lignes. Il est évident que le peintre n'a pas besoin de travailler en plein air pour capturer ses sujets. Un atelier lui suffit! Pourquoi a-t-il créé ces peintures? Je ne pourrais pas le dire. J'ai observé les autres visiteurs, et ils semblaient s'intéresser aux œuvres d'art, mais je ne comprends pas pourquoi! Je préfère l'art qui représente quelque chose. Les nouvelles techniques, les nouvelles méthodes, et les effets de lignes—à quoi ça sert? J'ai quitté cette exposition pour en voir une autre sur la bande dessinée, un art que je peux comprendre.

Théo

1. Quelle est la réaction du blogueur aux tableaux qui sont exposés?
2. Préfère-t-il l'art moderne ou l'art qui représente quelque chose?
3. D'après le blogueur, où travaille le peintre?
4. Quelle était la réaction des autres visiteurs du musée?
5. Qu'est-ce que le blogueur a aimé de sa visite au musée des beaux-arts?

2 La peinture française

1.2, 5.1

Complétez les phrases avec un mot ou une expression de la liste.

un atelier — une peinture — un pinceau — la toile — en plein air
un paysage — à l'arrière-plan — une fête champêtre — une nature morte — au premier plan

1. L'artiste-peintre utilise... pour étaler (*spread*) les couleurs sur la toile.
2. Le peintre met des couleurs vives sur....
3. Quand l'artiste travaille à l'intérieur, il est dans....
4. Un artiste qui peint dehors (*outside*) travaille....
5. L'œuvre au mur du musée s'appelle un tableau ou....
6. Les images qui semblent être à une certaine distance sont... et celles qui semblent être plus proche sont....
7. Une représentation de fruits, de fleurs, ou d'objets est....
8. Une scène avec une rivière au premier plan et des montagnes à l'arrière-plan est....
9. Une peinture du XVIIIème siècle avec des gens dans un jardin s'appelle....

Essential Instruction

1. Students, in pairs, will read Théo's letter (**Activité 1**) to each other and answer the questions that follow.
2. Upon completion, ask volunteers to read the answers aloud. Ask students to justify their response by citing the line in the letter that provides the specific information.
3. Students will identify the negative remarks Théo makes about art.
4. Pair high and low-ability students in teams to do **Activité 3**. Project a picture of **Le Canal du Loing** and ask volunteers to describe it.
5. Students will listen to **Quel beau tableau!** to answer the **vrai** and **faux** questions. Ask students what details they remember from the recording.
6. Have students skim the **Questions personnelles** and point out anything they do not understand.
7. Students will circulate, asking and answering these questions of each other.

3 Un tableau impressionniste

 1.2, 5.1

Complétez le paragraphe sur Le canal du Loing *par Alfred Sisley en vous servant d'un mot de la liste.*

en plein air · peinture · perspective · premier plan · paysage · peint · toile · l'arrière-plan

Cette... est par Alfred Sisley, un peintre impressionniste anglais du XIXème siècle. Sur la... il met des couleurs sombres. Il ne travaille pas dans un atelier, mais.... Le tableau, c'est essentiellement un..., qui montre la terre (*earth*) et la végétation. Ce n'est ni un portrait ni une nature morte. Au... on voit quelques arbres. Au centre, il y a une maison. À... on voit le ciel (*sky*) dans son immensité. Avec ce tableau, Sisley recherche un effet de.... Sisley a... ce tableau en 1892 quand il habitait dans cette région.

The Loing Canal, 1892. Alfred Sisley.

Communiquez!

4 Quel beau tableau!

  1.1, 1.2

Interpretive Communication

*Écrivez les numéros 1–7 sur votre papier. Écoutez Pablo et Chloé parler peinture. Ensuite, indiquez si les phrases que vous entendez sont vraies (**V**) ou fausses (**F**).*

5 Questions personnelles

  1.2, 1.3

Répondez aux questions.

1. Est-ce que tu fais de la peinture? Si oui, qu'est-ce que tu aimes peindre?
2. Est-ce que tu as déjà visité un musée des beaux-arts? Quelles peintures as-tu aimées?
3. Est-ce que tu suis un cours d'art maintenant? Qu'est-ce que tu étudies?
4. Comment s'appelle ton artiste préféré(e)?
5. Travaille-t-il ou travaille-t-elle dans un atelier ou en plein air?

Answers

peinture; toile; en plein air; paysage; premier plan; l'arrière-plan; perspective; peint

Script can be found in the front pages of the Annotated Teacher's Edition.

1. V
2. F
3. F
4. F
5. V
6. V
7. F

5 *Answers will vary.*

Expansion

1. Ask students where the closest fine arts museum is located in their community. How large is the collection and what famous works are featured?
2. Poll how many students think that representational art is the true art form, and how many prefer abstract art. Ask them to explain why.

Differentiated Learning

Accelerate

Ask students to write a **blogue** similar to Théo's letter in which they discuss a piece of art they love or do not like at all.

Decelerate

Students can find and print examples of **un fusain**, **une aquarelle**, **une nature morte**, and **un paysage.** They will add the name of the artist, and explain how the techniques are different. This step could be done in English since the objective is to get them to connect personally with works of art.

Multiple Intelligences

Visual-Spatial

Have students find an impressionist painting that resembles **Le Canal du Loing**. Students will identify what themes and techniques the two art works have in common. Ask if they have any of their own art that they would like to share with the class.

RESOURCES

Workbook 4

Reference Desk

1. **Un canotier** has two meanings: a person who goes boating, and a straw oval hat adorned with a ribbon. We see both the boaters and their hats in Renoir's painting **Déjeuner des canotiers**.
2. The meaning of **propre** depends on the context. Before a noun, it means "own" as in **mes propres mains** (*my own hands*); after a noun, it means "clean" as in **mes mains propres** (*my clean hands*). In the reading we see yet another meaning, that of "typical" as in **propres au peintre**.
3. The suffix **âtre** adds "ish" to a color, thus **rougâtre** means "reddish."
4. Gustave Caillebotte (1848–1894) was a photographer, art collector, and painter associated with the impressionist movement although his paintings had more of a photographic, realistic style. **La Grande Jatte** (*the big basin*) is an island in the Seine just outside of Paris.

Rencontres culturelles

emcl.com
WB 4

Quelques grands maîtres de la peinture française

1.2

On vous présente quatre tableaux de grands maîtres de la peinture française. Ces tableaux ont été peints au XIXème siècle.

Les coquelicots, 1873. Claude Monet.

Claude Monet a peint *Impression, soleil levant* en 1872. Ce tableau donne son nom à un nouveau mouvement artistique: l'impressionnisme. Monet a peint de nombreux paysages, notamment* des scènes de bateaux sur l'eau, qui sont parmi ses œuvres les plus caractéristiques. Il peignait en plein air sur un bateau qu'il avait transformé en atelier. Il étudiait les nuances de l'atmosphère et de la lumière sous les touches de pinceau. *Les coquelicots* (1873) montre un paysage de collines, sur lesquelles un champ de fleurs s'épand* tel une mer jusqu'à l'horizon; ce tableau représente un pas* supplémentaire de l'artiste vers l'abstraction, tendance qui se retrouvera dans ses célèbres *Nymphéas* de Giverny. Au premier plan, on voit deux femmes avec leurs enfants traversant les hautes herbes* par une journée d'été. Mais ces personnages ont peu de détails et leur expression ne se voit pas. Pour Monet, qui finira par abandonner la figure humaine*, l'homme n'était qu'une partie de la nature. Selon ses propres* mots, le maître de l'impressionnisme a voulu saisir l'éphémère*: "Ce que je ferai ici aura au moins le mérite de ne ressembler à personne, parce que ce sera l'impression de ce que j'aurai ressenti*, moi tout seul."

notamment *namely*; **s'épand** *spreads*; **pas** *step*; **herbes** *grass*; **figure humaine** *human figures*; **propres** *own*; **éphémère** *fleeting moment*; **j'aurai ressenti** *I will have felt*

Bal du moulin de la Galette, 1876

Pierre Auguste Renoir s'éloigne du mouvement impressionniste pour rechercher une expression plus réaliste par des effets de lignes, des contours, et des contrastes. Dans le *Bal du moulin de la Galette* (1876), les lignes diagonales prolongent* le champ de vision de la table aux personnages de l'arrière-plan, alors que les couleurs vives et les contours nets des objets de la table, inanimés, contrastent avec les couleurs pastelles et les touches plus impressionnistes des personnages. L'effet recherché est une atmosphère d'éclatement*, de spontanéïté, et de fête. Il s'agit ici d'une fête champêtre moderne qui regroupe les amis et proches* du peintre: sa fiancée, Aline Charigot, au premier plan à gauche; puis à droite son ami Gustave Caillebotte. Dans ce tableau on retrouve l'amour de la vie populaire et de la sensualité propres* au peintre, et les femmes typiques de Renoir: le visage rond, la peau blanche, les joues rougeâtres*, la forme ronde. Le paysage, les arbres aux touches lumineuse et floues*, le canot*, rappellent les caractéristiques de l'impressionnisme, mais les nature mortes et l'importance des personnages distinguent Renoir de Monet. Avant sa mort, Renoir aura peint à peu près six mille tableaux, un record avant Picasso.

prolongent *extend*; **éclatement** *bursting*; **proche** *close friend or relative*; **propre** *typical*; **rougeâtre** *reddish*; **floues** *blurry*; **canot** bateau

Essential Instruction

1. Ask students to read **Rencontres culturelles** as a class activity or an independent assignment. Ask which sentences are not clear to them.
2. For each reading, students can fill out a grid: **Artiste-peintre**, **Mouvement pictural**, **Titres de(s) tableau(x) Techniques**, **Citations**, **Remarques supplémentaires**. This will help them to organize the information about each painter.
3. Ask open-ended questions to get students to comment on each painting: Who and what do they see in each painting? What is happening? What time of day might it be?

Un dimanche après-midi sur l'île de la Grande Jatte, 1886. Georges Seurat.

Georges Seurat est un peintre pointilliste, connu surtout pour son tableau d'un taille inouïe* *Un dimanche après-midi sur l'île de la Grande Jatte* (1886). Il s'agit d'une scène de plein air au bord de la Seine lors* d'une belle journée d'été. Le sujet comprend une quarantaine de personnages s'abritant à l'ombre * au premier plan, par une journée ensoleillée*. L'œuvre montre la bourgeoisie qui se livre* à ses loisirs… promenade, voile, pêche. L'art de Seurat est le résultat de recherches scientifiques sur les couleurs et les théories de la vision. Sur cette toile il a posé de petites touches séparées de couleurs pures qui se confondent* à une certaine distance. On appelle cette technique le "pointillisme" ou le "néo-impressionnisme." Elle se distingue de l'impressionnisme qui recherche la sensation changeante de la lumière, plutôt que les images figées*. Seurat a dit, "Les littérateurs et les critiques voient de la poésie dans ce que je fais. Non, j'applique ma méthode, et c'est tout." Seurat a exercé une influence indéniable sur Gauguin, Van Gogh, et Pissarro, mais aussi sur les fauves, les cubistes, et les futuristes.

inouïe *unbelievable;* **lors** pendant; **s'abritant à l'ombre** *sheltered by the shade;* **ensoleillée** *sunny;* **se livre** *gives itself to;* **se confondent** *merge;* **figées** *stilted, stiff*

Terrasse du café le soir, 1888. Vincent Van Gogh.

Vincent Van Gogh, un Néerlandais qui a passé ses dernières années dans le sud de la France, a réalisé ce tableau à Arles, une ville provençale, en septembre 1888. Il s'agit d'une terrasse de café en pleine nuit. Dans ce tableau, Van Gogh utilise des couleurs chaudes au premier plan, pour donner de la profondeur* à la perspective. Le blanc des tables du café dirige* l'œil vers la partie obscure du tableau. À l'arrière-plan, les bâtiments sont sombres, mais le ciel étoilé d'un bleu vif qui remplace le noir de la nuit est le centre d'attention de cette peinture, qui se veut* tranquille et non opprimante*. Les personnages dans la rue ajoutent* à la tranquillité du lieu. On retrouvera le sujet de la nuit étoilée chez Van Gogh dans *Nuit étoilée sur le Rhône* et *Nuit étoilée*. Dans une lettre adressée à sa sœur Wilhelmina, le peintre a dit: "Cela m'amuse énormément de peindre la nuit sur place. Autrefois on dessinait et peignait le tableau le jour d'après le dessin. Mais moi je m'en trouve bien de peindre la chose immédiatement." Son usage de couleur arbitraire souligne* ses sentiments fort, la raison pour laquelle Van Gogh est désigné précurseur* de l'expressionisme.

profondeur *depth;* **dirige** *direct;* **se veut** *is meant to be;* **opprimante** *oppressing;* **ajoutent** *add;* **souligne** *underlines;* **précurseur** *forerunner*

Game

C'est quel artiste?
Prepare images of paintings that represent art movements and artists presented thus far in this **Unité.** Write the names and vocabulary words of those painters, art movements, and paintings on the board for quick reference. Then show students one image at a time and have them guess what painting it is, give the name of the artist, and also the art movement associated with it. Students may work as a class or in teams. For a twist, you may show students images they have not seen before but that belong to the artists that have been introduced in this **Unité.** A step up would be to show paintings of artists they have not discussed and try to fit them into the art movements they have learned.

Differentiated Learning

Accelerate
Have students compare the following Van Gogh paintings: **Terrasse du café le soir** with **Nuit étoilée sur le Rhône** and **Nuit étoilée.** They should compare and contrast the paintings in terms of technique, color, and theme.

Special Needs Students

AD(H)D/Dyslexia
These students might be discouraged at first by the length of the readings and the technical writing. Breaking down each passage into smaller sections will make the readings seem more manageable.

Visually Impaired
Make modifications for students who do not see well or are color-blind since this lesson is so visual.

At-Risk Students/Behavior Problems
Some of your students have never been exposed to art as children. This activity is an opportunity to enlarge their view by personalizing the art.

Answers

6

Monet: 1. l'impressionnisme; 2. les changements de l'atmosphère et de la lumière; 3. oui; 4. saisir l'éphémère, ce qui passe
Renoir: 1. l'impressionnisme; 2. aux hommes et aux atmosphères de fête; 3. avec des formes rondes et des couleurs blanches et roses; 4. lumineuse, floue, très gaie
Seurat: 1. la bourgeoisie; 2. Elles font une promenade, de la voile, se repose; sur une plage; 3. plutôt scientifique car c'est une méthode par laquelle le peintre pose des touches séparées de couleur pure; 4. un après-midi de repos pour la bourgeoisie
Van Gogh: 1. la Provence; 2. Il met des couleurs chaudes au premier plan pour donner de la profondeur au tableau.; 3. Car il utilise les couleurs de façon arbitraire pour évoquer des sentiments forts.

6 Quelques grands maîtres de la peinture française

1.2, 1.3

Répondez aux questions suivantes.

Monet

1. Comment s'appelle le mouvement que Monet a créé?
2. Qu'est-ce qu'il étudiait de son bateau-atelier?
3. Comment est-ce qu'il a peint les personnes dans *Les coquelicots*?
4. Quel était le but de Monet dans *Les coquelicots*?

Renoir

1. Renoir faisait partie de quel mouvement?
2. Si ce tableau représente l'œuvre du peintre, à quoi s'intéressait-il comme sujet, à la nature comme Monet ou à autre chose?
3. Comment sont peintes les femmes?
4. Comment est l'ambiance du tableau?

Seurat

1. Seurat représente quelle classe sociale dans son chef-d'œuvre?
2. Qu'est-ce que ces personnes sont en train de faire? Où?
3. Comment est sa méthode, plutôt artistique ou scientifique? Expliquez.
4. Quel est le sujet de ce tableau?

Van Gogh

1. Van Gogh est associé à quelle région de la France?
2. Comment est-ce que l'artiste se sert de la perspective?
3. Pour quelle raison principale est-ce qu'on associe Van Gogh à l'expressionnisme?

On peut admirer les peintures de Monet, Renoir, Seurat, et Van Gogh au musée d'Orsay.

Essential Instruction

1. Arrange students in groups of high and low ability to answer **Quelques grands maîtres de la peinture française**.
2. Use these four groups of questions as a basis for a class discussion of these artists and their works. If possible, have larger prints of each painting.
3. Assign students to research one of the eight artists featured in **l'impressionnisme** for a brief presentation the following day. They will print one famous painting to use as a visual as they present their artist and the painting. Display the prints in the classroom.

Points de départ 

emcl.com
WB 5

Question centrale: Comment l'art est-il un reflet de la culture?

L'impressionnisme 1.2, 3.1

L'impressionnisme était un mouvement de la seconde moitié du XIXème siècle. Les peintres exprimaient* dans leurs tableaux les impressions que les objets et la lumière suscitent. Les impressionnistes aimaient peindre en plein air, pas dans un atelier. Les peintres de ce mouvement sont Claude Monet, Pierre-Auguste Renoir, l'Américaine Mary Cassatt, Camille Pissarro, Berthe Morisot, Edgar Degas, l'Anglais Alfred Sisley, et Frédéric Bazille.

Search words: **impressionnisme france, (nom de l'artiste) + impressionnisme, mouvements artistiques france**

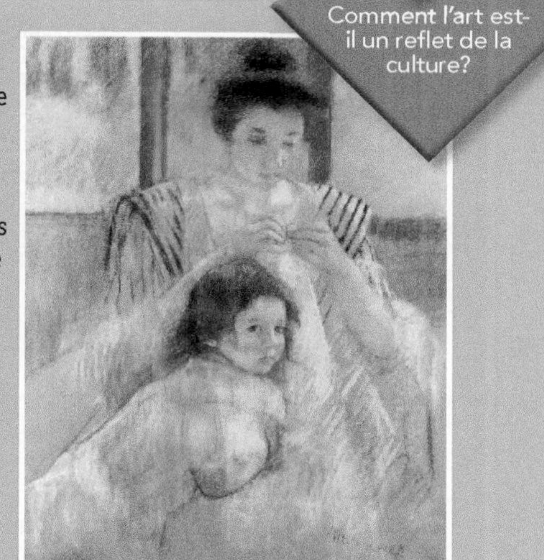

Mère et enfant, 1897. Mary Cassatt.

exprimant *expressed;* **suscitent** *spark*

Produits

Impression, soleil levant (1872) est le tableau de Monet qui a donné le nom "impressionnisme" à ce nouveau mouvement artistique.

Impression, soleil levant, 1872. Claude Monet.

COMPARAISONS

Est-ce que le mouvement impressionniste aux États-Unis est venu avant ou après l'impressionnisme en France? Qui sont les maîtres de l'impressionnisme américain?

4.2

RESOURCES

Workbook 5

Connections

History

Review with students historical periods or dates associated with each art movement presented on p.381. Ask them to find out what happened in world history during those periods. You may team up with the history teacher to reinforce knowledge they have acquired in history class.

Differentiated Learning

Accelerate

Students will answer the two-part **Comparaisons** question.

Multiple Intelligences

Visual-Spatial

Have students make a collage of impressionist paintings with titles of their works.

Critical Thinking

Analysis

Have students do a critique of **le néo-impressionnisme** and **l'expressionnisme** in groups by comparing and contrasting two paintings. You may give them paintings to choose from for each movement, or let them select their own.

Le néo-impressionnisme  1.2, 1.3

Le pin, St-Tropez, 1909. Paul Signac.

Le néo-impressionnisme a suivi l'impressionnisme entre 1885 et 1915. Les peintres néo-impressionnistes peignaient par petite touches*, par points de ton* pur juxtaposés*. Un autre nom de ce mouvement est le pointillisme ou le postimpressionnisme. Les peintres de ce mouvement se nomment* des pointillistes, dont les plus grands sont Georges Seurat et Paul Signac.

 Search words: **néo-impressionnisme, post-impressionnisme, (nom de l'artiste) + néo-impressionnisme, mouvements artistiques france**

touche *stroke;* **ton** *shade of color;* **juxtaposés** *side by side;* **se nomment** s'appellent

Le tableau ***Un dimanche après-midi sur l'île de la Grande Jatte*** (1886) est devenu le sujet du music-hall *Sunday in the Park with George* en 1984, un siècle après l'œuvre de Seurat. Le créateur, Sondheim, a pour thème de montrer les tourments de l'artiste qui crée de l'art.

 Search words: **sunday in the park with george you tube**  2.2

L'expressionnisme/Le fauvisme 1.2

Vase à bone sur une table. Matisse (1869–1954).

L'expressionisme était surtout un mouvement artistique du début du XXème siècle. Ce sont des artistes allemands qui en sont à l'origine. Les peintres expressionnistes utilisent une intensité de l'expression et souvent des couleurs vives. Le précurseur de ce mouvement est Vincent Van Gogh. Dans ce groupe il faut aussi mentionner les fauves qui ont créé le fauvisme. Les fauves comme Maurice de Vlaminck et André Derain touchent* par moments à l'expressionnisme. Il ne faut surtout pas oublier les contributions d'Henri Matisse.

 Search words: **expressionnisme europe, fauvisme, vlaminck, derain, matisse, mouvements artistiques france**

touchent *reach*

Essential Instruction

1. In the computer lab students will read the passages on **Le néo-impressionnisme** and **L'expressionnisme/Le fauvisme** using the search words provided.
2. How do these movements differ? Who are the key artists? If they could own one painting, which one would they select and why?
3. Ask students to read **L'Afrique de l'ouest.** They will keep this question in mind: What are the differences between African art and the European paintings you have studied? Find examples of how **le cubisme**, notably the art of Pablo Picasso, has been directly influenced by African art.
Search words: **cubism, african art, masks**

La Francophonie: L'art

✲ Dans L'Afrique de l'ouest 1.2

L'art africain traditionnel est essentiellement composé de produits artisanaux*. L'artisanat correspond à la fabrication d'objets, principalement en bois ou en bronze, tels des masques, statues, armes, ou d'autres objets traditionnels comme des poteries ou encore les vêtements. Ces arts sont considérés des Arts premiers. Ils sont à l'image des thèmes ou scènes de la vie de tous les jours de groupes ethniques particuliers, telles les statues tribales Ashanti du Ghana, ou Bambara du Mali. Il en est de même* pour la fabrication d'instruments de musique: les congas* en bois et peau de chèvre*, les balafons*, les cloches*, reflètent un lien entre l'expression artistique et la nature dans les cultures africaines.

La peinture africaine a toujours été décorative, privilégiant* les bas-reliefs plutôt que les représentations bidimensionnelles* propres aux cultures occidentales*. De l'art traditionnel, dit "naïf," aux formes géométriques simples et aux couleurs primaires, à l'art populaire qui donne de nouvelles formes aux matériaux naturels (fresques, portraits, posters), la peinture africaine contemporaine reflète l'évolution et les contradictions des réalités urbaines. La peinture africaine est à l'origine des grands mouvements occidentaux tels le cubisme (Pablo Picasso), le néo-impressionnisme, et la peinture murale. Il est important de comprendre les liens indissociables entre l'Afrique et l'Occident dans la peinture moderne, car bien souvent, les peintres africains contemporains s'inscrivent dans les mouvements occidentaux de peinture, tel Chéri Samba, peintre Congolais, dont l'art figuratif a été exposé à Paris et à New York.

Search words: l'art africain traditionnel, produits artisanaux africains, peintres africains, chéri samba

produits artisanaux *crafts;* **Il en est de même** *It is the same;* **conga** *drum-like instrument;* **peau de chèvre** *goat skin;* **balafon** *xylophone-like instrument;* **cloches** *bells;* **privilégiant** *favoring;* **bidimensionnelle** *two-dimensional;* **occidentales** *Western*

L'art africain est connu pour ses sculptures et objets artisanaux.

Le Nid dans le nid, 1996. Chéri Samba.

Reference Desk

Chéri Samba is a famous contemporary Congolese painter. In his art he uses pictural codes of **bande dessinée** and language (French, English, Lingala dialect) to create an art form that represents social, political, and cultural aspects of modern life in Africa.

Connections

Art History

Compare and contrast several examples of Native American art with samples of tribal art of Africa.

Differentiated Learning

Adapt

Students will collaborate to make a collage of pictures of statues, masks, and other artifacts of the Ashani, Bambara, and Ghanian tribes to be displayed in the classroom.

Multiple Intelligences

Musical-Rhythmic

Here are three activities which might appeal to students interested in music: 1) Students might be interested in watching clips of "Sunday in the Park with George." 2) They also might enjoy the song "Into the Woods" (available online) to show how Stephen Sondheim playfully treats this theme. 3) Students could play for the class the song "Starry, Starry Night" and explain how this song relates closely to Vincent Van Gogh's life.

Visual-Spatial

Students will explain the technique of pointillism and demonstrate how it is achieved by painting a simple object through a series of colorful dots.

Search words: **pointillism, art talks, george seurat**

Answers

7

1. *Answers will vary.*
2. *Answers will vary.*
3. réalisme, impressionnisme, néo-impressionnisme, fauvisme, cubisme
4. *Mère et enfant*, Mary Cassatt: Musée d'Orsay, Paris; *Impression, soleil levant*, Claude Monet: Musée Marmottan, Paris; *Le pin, St-Tropez*, Paul Signac: Musée Puschkin, Moscou; *Un dimanche après-midi sur l'île de la Grande Jatte*, Georges Seurat: Art Institute, Chicago
5. *Answers will vary.*
6. *Answers will vary.*
7. *Answers will vary.*

Perspectives
Answers will vary.

Reference Desk

Students might be interested to know that most European major art movements have origins in African and Oriental art. Impressionism and its corollaries (**le néo-impressionisme, l'expressionisme**, **le fauvism**, etc.) reacted against the European tradition of classical theories, a phenomenon typical of 19th century art and literature. These artists of different origins often traveled and sought new ideas abroad. Post-Impressionist Paul Gauguin created an art style greatly influenced by the African primitivism he discovered in his numerous travels to French Polynesia. Likewise, expressionists Henri Matisse and Pablo Picasso's particular usage of expressive colors and asymmetrical compositions were inspired by African art.

7 Activités culturelles

1.3, 3.1, 3.2

Complétez les activités suivantes.

1. Faites des recherches et décrivez un tableau impressionniste, néo-impressionniste, ou expressionniste que vous aimez beaucoup. Vous pouvez choisir un tableau de la section *Points de départ*.
2. Regroupez dans un album les tableaux qui montrent le développement et l'évolution de l'impressionnisme à l'expressionnisme/fauvisme à travers les œuvres de peintres français. Pour chaque tableau, incluez une légende avec le titre, le nom de l'artiste, le style, et l'année de son exécution.
3. Faites une chronologie (*time line*) qui montre les périodes artistiques en France ainsi que leurs dates:
   - impressionnisme
   - réalisme
   - fauvisme
   - cubisme
   - néo-impressionnisme
4. Recherchez dans quels musées les tableaux des artistes cités précédemment sont exposés aujourd'hui. Attention: ils ne sont pas tous à Paris.
5. Recherchez combien coûte un Monet, un Renoir, ou un Degas. Est-ce que la valeur de leurs tableaux augmente ou diminue?
6. Recherchez deux peintres contemporains d'Afrique de l'Ouest et notez:
   - leur nom et pays d'origine
   - leur style de peinture (couleurs, formes, matériau de travail, etc.)
   - un tableau particulier (nom et description)
7. Trouvez un exemple d'art contemporain populaire en Occident influencé par les cultures africaines.

Perspectives

Au début, les impressionnistes ont beaucoup été critiqués parce qu'ils osaient (*dared*) modifier les standards de l'époque: des tableaux détaillés, peints en ateliers, représentant des paysages ou des scènes d'événements historiques. Après avoir vu le tableau *Impression, soleil levant* de Monet, un critique l'a critiqué, ainsi que les tableaux de ses amis, en nommant leur collection "L'exposition des impressionnistes." Quelle est la réputation des impressionnistes maintenant? Pourquoi est-ce que ce critique ne pouvait pas apprécier les tableaux impressionnistes? Pourquoi est-ce que les goûts artistiques changent avec le temps?

Essential Instruction

1. Before assigning **Activités culturelles**, give the students a clear understanding of what each activity requires and your expectations.
2. Assign the odd-numbered activities to be done individually.
3. Arrange students of high and low ability in groups to do the even-numbered activities. Devise a system of accountability so that each student works equally on the assignment.

Answers

8 *Paragraphs will vary.*

Reference Desk

Students will most likely know Vincent Van Gogh as the brilliant artist gone mad who cut off his left earlobe. But they might also be interested to know that the same odd genius whose paintings sell at auctions for millions of dollars only sold one painting while he was living. You may assign students to search the name of that painting (**Vignoble Rouge à Arles** (**Montmajour**))for extra credit.

Du côté des médias

Lisez les informations sur les expositions.

Flash-back: été 1912, Cologne accueille l'exposition événement "Sonderbund", à la gloire du modernisme européen.

Avec cinq cent soixante-dix-sept toiles et cinquante-sept sculptures, les cent soixante-treize artistes invités (Cézanne, Gauguin, Picasso ou Van Gogh en tête) incarnent l'avant-garde artistique de l'époque, du post-impressionnisme à l'expressionnisme allemand.

Le Wallraf-Richartz Museum célèbre le centenaire de cette "mission moderne," à travers une fidèle reconstitution regroupant cent des chefs-d'oeuvre initialement exposés.

Informations pratiques sur 1912–Mission Moderne- Le centenaire de l'exposition Sonderbund **dans l'onglet agenda.**
En savoir plus sur le lieu: Wallraf-Richartz Museum

8 L'exposition Sonderbund en flash-back

Votre prof va vous donner une carte postale. Imaginez que vous avez assisté à cette exposition. Écrivez une carte postale qui:

- dit où vous êtes.
- décrit ce que vous avez vu.
- explique l'importance de cette exposition historiquement.

Differentiated Learning

Accelerate

Students will write an essay answering the question posed in **Perspectives.** They must give precise examples to support their point of view.

Decelerate

Have students read **Du côté des médias.** Ask them questions to assure that they understand the meaning of the reading. Assign **L'exposition Sonderbund en flash-back.**

Answers

9

1. pointilliste
2. réflexion, librettiste
3. 1984
4. Pulitzer
5. Playwrights Horizon, Inc., New York City, James Lapine

Reference Desk

Le Théâtre du Châtelet was built between 1860–62 for dramatic performances. Today it is known for operettas, ballet, and contemporary musicals. It is home to the **Orchestre de Paris**. Stephen Sondheim, born in 1932, is an American composer-lyricist who has won seven Tony awards for the lyrics of his songs, and a Pulitzer Prize for "Sunday in the Park with George."

Du côté des médias

1.2

Lisez l'article sur la production Sunday in the Park with George *au Châtelet-Théâtre.*

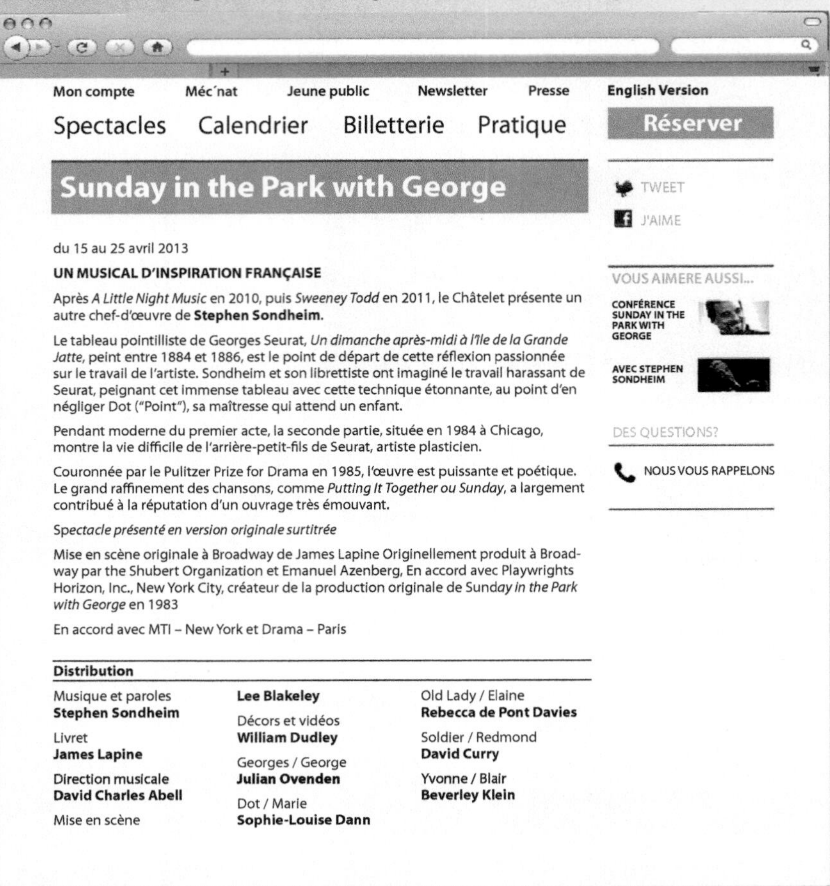

Mon compte | Méc'nat | Jeune public | Newsletter | Presse | English Version

Spectacles | Calendrier | Billetterie | Pratique | Réserver

Sunday in the Park with George

du 15 au 25 avril 2013

UN MUSICAL D'INSPIRATION FRANÇAISE

Après *A Little Night Music* en 2010, puis *Sweeney Todd* en 2011, le Châtelet présente un autre chef-d'œuvre de **Stephen Sondheim**.

Le tableau pointilliste de Georges Seurat, *Un dimanche après-midi à l'île de la Grande Jatte*, peint entre 1884 et 1886, est le point de départ de cette réflexion passionnée sur le travail de l'artiste. Sondheim et son librettiste ont imaginé le travail harassant de Seurat, peignant cet immense tableau avec cette technique étonnante, au point d'en négliger Dot ("Point"), sa maîtresse qui attend un enfant.

Pendant moderne du premier acte, la seconde partie, située en 1984 à Chicago, montre la vie difficile de l'arrière-petit-fils de Seurat, artiste plasticien.

Couronnée par le Pulitzer Prize for Drama en 1985, l'œuvre est puissante et poétique. Le grand raffinement des chansons, comme *Putting It Together ou Sunday*, a largement contribué à la réputation d'un ouvrage très émouvant.

Spectacle présenté en version originale surtitrée

Mise en scène originale à Broadway de James Lapine Originellement produit à Broadway par the Shubert Organization et Emanuel Azenberg, En accord avec Playwrights Horizon, Inc., New York City, créateur de la production originale de Sunday *in the Park with George* en 1983

En accord avec MTI – New York et Drama – Paris

Distribution

Musique et paroles
Stephen Sondheim

Livret
James Lapine

Direction musicale
David Charles Abell

Mise en scène
Lee Blakeley

Décors et vidéos
William Dudley

Georges / George
Julian Ovenden

Dot / Marie
Sophie-Louise Dann

Old Lady / Elaine
Rebecca de Pont Davies

Soldier / Redmond
David Curry

Yvonne / Blair
Beverley Klein

TWEET

J'AIME

VOUS AIMERE AUSSI...

CONFÉRENCE SUNDAY IN THE PARK WITH GEORGE

AVEC STEPHEN SONDHEIM

DES QUESTIONS?

NOUS VOUS RAPPELONS

9 Sunday in the Park with George

1.2

Complétez les phrases.

1. *Un dimanche après-midi à l'île de la Grande Jatte* est un tableau... de Seurat.
2. L'œuvre est une... passionnée sur le travail de l'artiste, notamment Seurat et son....
3. La seconde partie a lieu en... à New York.
4. *Sunday in the Park with George* a gagné le... *for Drama* en 1985.
5. ... a écrit la musique et les paroles, et... est responsable de la mise en scène.

Essential Instruction

1. Students will read the article **Du côté des médias** about "Sunday in the Park with George."
2. Ask students questions about the text, which will require them to cite specific information from the article.
3. Students will finish the sentences in **Activité 9**.
4. Have students watch the clip online "It's Hot Up Here" where the actors create a **tableau vivant** of the painting.
5. This video will bring to life Seurat's painting. Before doing **Révision: Agreement and position of adjectives**, test what students recall of adjective formation and placement by asking them to brainstorm a list of random adjectives that describe **un homme**. Ask volunteers to go to the board and write descriptions of **un homme**. This exercise will give you an idea of how in depth you need to review adjectives.

Structure de la langue

Révision: Agreement and Position of Adjectives

1.2

French adjectives usually follow the nouns they describe.

C'est une peinture **expressionniste.** — *It's an expressionist painting.*

To form a feminine adjective, all you often have to do is add an **–e** to the masculine adjective.

Voilà une scène **intéressante.** — *There is an interesting scene.*

The following groups of adjectives have irregular feminine forms.

	Masculine	Feminine
no change	moderne	moderne
-eux→ -euse	paresseux	paresseuse
-er→ -ère	dernier	dernière
double consonant + **-e**	bon	bonne

Some adjectives are invariable and don't change, even when modifying something feminine: **orange**, **marron**, **super**, **sympa**, **bon marché**.

Some masculine adjectives have irregular forms in the feminine: **blanc→ blanche**, **frais→ fraîche**, **long→ longue**.

The adjectives **beau**, **nouveau**, and **vieux** have irregular feminine forms as well as irregular forms before a masculine noun beginning with a vowel sound.

Masculine	Masculine before a Vowel Sound	Feminine
beau	bel	belle
nouveau	nouvel	nouvelle
vieux	vieil	vieille

Some short, common adjectives precede the nouns they describe. These are the BANGS adjectives that express beauty, age, number, goodness, and size:

Beauty: **beau, joli**

Age: **nouveau, vieux, jeune**

Numbers: **premier, deuxième**

Goodness: **bon, gentil, mauvais**

Size: **grand, petit, court, long, gros**

RESOURCES

Workbook 6–9

Drill & Practice Games

Game

Les adjectifs
Ask students to shout out as many adjectives as they know. You will write the masculine form on the board for the students to use as reference. A student will start with the sentence **Jean est un garçon.** Point to another student who will add an adjective from the word bank: **Jean est un beau garçon.** Point to another student who will add another adjective to that sentence: **Jean est un beau garçon intelligent.** Continue asking students to add adjectives so that the sentence becomes very long. When a given student cannot remember the whole sentence, the game starts over, this time with a feminine subject like Marie. If you want to challenge them, create the next sentence with the subject **Jean et Marie.** This change will require students to use verbs and adjectives in the plural.

Differentiated Learning

Decelerate
Give students a worksheet with common vocabulary and target adjectives, such as **un train/lent** or **un professeur/bon.** They are to combine the adjectives and the nouns using the correct form and position. Give the students an answer sheet so that they can correct their work as they go along.

Special Needs Students

Auditory Impairment
The distinction among forms of the irregular adjectives can seem very subtle to students with hearing difficulties. Accentuate the differences when you speak so that they can see how your mouth changes according to the pronunciation.

Dyslexia
The spelling of irregular adjectives can present a special challenge for dyslexic students. Spell them out in rhythm. For example, the troublesome spelling of **vieille** is easier to learn if each letter is given a beat. **V-I-E-I-L-L-E.**

RESOURCES

Workbook 6–10

Drill & Practice Games

Answers

1. C'est une nouvelle toile japonaise.
2. C'est un joli portrait réaliste.
3. C'est un petit musée de beaux-arts impressionniste.
4. C'est un grand tableau expressionniste.
5. C'est une vieille fête champêtre française.
6. C'est une mauvaise nature morte sombre./C'est une mauvaise et sombre nature morte.
7. C'est un bon peintre moderne.

Reference Desk

1. Remind students that the final **s** in **plus** and **moins** is silent.
2. Emphasize that, just like in English, the adjectives good and bad in French are irregular. We do not say "gooder" or "badder."
3. Assure students that the more often they say aloud these adjectives with nouns, the better their ear will be tuned to what is correct so that they will not have to depend on charts and rules.

10 L'art   1.3

Formez des phrases avec deux adjectifs selon le modèle.

MODÈLE peinture/beau/française
C'est une belle peinture française.

1. toile/nouveau/japonais
2. portrait/réaliste/joli
3. musée de beaux-arts/impressionniste/petit
4. tableau/grand/expressionniste
5. fête champêtre/français/vieux
6. nature morte/mauvais/sombre
7. peintre/moderne/bon

Révision: Comparative of Adjectives

 1.2

emcl.com
WB 10
Games

Use the following constructions to compare people and things in French:

plus (*more*)	+	adjective	+	**que** (*than*)
moins (*less*)	+	adjective	+	**que** (*than*)
aussi (*as*)	+	adjective	+	**que** (*as*)

The adjective being compared agrees in gender and in number with the first noun in the comparison.

Les couleurs sont **aussi sombres** dans ce tableau **que** dans cet autre tableau. — *The colors are as dark in this painting as in the other (one).*

The comparative of **bon/bonne** is **meilleur/meilleure**.

Ce tableau est **meilleur** que l'autre.

Essential Instruction

1. Ask a volunteer to be the teacher and explain the formation and placement of adjectives.
2. Students will do **Activité 10.** Correct each sentence, one at a time, offering an explanation to students who did not do the sentence correctly.
3. Review the chart for **plus**, **moins**, and **aussi... que**, reminding the students that the adjective agrees in gender and number with the first noun in the comparison.
4. Compare two students who will stand in front of the class. Whisper to one to be happy and the other sad. **Qui est plus heureux que l'autre? Qui est moins heureux? Qui est plus triste?** Continue the process with other adjectives such as **fâché**, **ennuyé**, **fatigué**, and **surpris.** The students, on cue, will mime the emotions for the class. Add another student to the group to demonstrate **aussi...que**.
5. Do **Comparez les HLMs!** as a class activity to give students immediate feedback.
6. Give examples of the superlative of adjectives preceding and following the noun and ask students to deduce the rule for formation.

11 Comparez les HLMs!  1.3

Comparez ces deux HLM. Utilisez les indices donnés et les adjectifs entre parenthèses.

1. Le HLM au premier plan... le HLM à l'arrière-plan. (*propre*)
2. L'ado qui porte le tee-shirt orange... l'ado en bleu. (*diligent*)
3. Les enfants... les passants. (*vieux*)
4. Les enfants... leurs parents. (*énergique*)
5. Jeanne... son frère. (*sportif*)
6. La sculpture du HLM au premier plan... celle du HLM à l'arrière-plan. (*laid*)
7. L'ambiance du HLM au premier plan... celle du HLM à l'arrière-plan. (*accueillant*)

Révision: Superlative of Adjectives  1.2

emcl.com
WB 11–12
LA 2
Games

Use the superlative construction to say that a person or thing has the most of a certain quality compared to all others.

le/la/les + **plus** + adjective	Le musée d'Orsay est le musée impressionniste **le plus célèbre**.

Both the definite article and the adjective agree in gender and in number with the noun they describe. Remember that if an adjective precedes a noun, its superlative form also precedes it. If an adjective follows a noun, so does its superlative form.

Le Louvre est **le plus grand** musée d'art. — *The Louvre is the biggest art museum in Paris.*

The superlative of **bon(s)** is **le/la/les meilleur(s)**.

À mon avis, c'est **le meilleur** tableau du musée. — *In my opinion, it's the best painting in the museum.*

RESOURCES

 Workbook 11–12

 Listening Activity 2

 Drill & Practice Games

Answers

1. ... est plus propre que...
2. ... est moins diligent que...
3. ... sont moins vieux que...
4. ... sont plus énergiques que...
5. ... est moins sportive que...
6. ... est moins laide que...
7. ... est plus accueillante que...

Expansion

Project or make a large copy of Seurat's painting **Un Dimanche[....]** Ask volunteers to describe the figures in the painting as if they knew them. For example, for the woman on the right with the parasol: "**Voici Madame DuPont. Elle a cinquante ans et elle adore sortir le dimanche avec son mari. Ce matin, ils se sont disputés parce que son mari, Rufus, ne voulait pas aller au parc.**" They will continue to describe what she is wearing (using as many adjectives as possible), what she is looking at, what she is thinking, how many children she has, what their names are.... This exercise will encourage students to be imaginative as they describe each person.

Differentiated Learning

Adapt

Students will brainstorm names of popular pop stars, actors, well-known athletes, competitive high school sports teams, and heroes from history, which you will write on the board. Ask a student to compare them. Hopefully the class will not all share the same opinion, and this will lead to a spirited discussion. Continue the process comparing other elements.

Special Needs Students

Behavioral Problems

When asked to make comparisons, some students may take the opportunity to ridicule classmates. You may want to limit comparisons to historical figures, celebrities, and stores and restaurants around town rather than students in school.

Multiple Intelligences

Visual-Spatial

Enlist these students to make sketches of people and things that can be used for comparisons.

Answers

1. La tour Eiffel est le monument le plus célèbre.
2. Le Louvre est le plus ancien musée.
3. La Joconde est l'œuvre du Louvre la plus connue.
4. Le quartier Latin est le plus vieux quartier.
5. les Champs-Élysées est l'avenue la plus large.
6. La place de la Concorde est la plus grande place.
7. Notre-Dame est la plus belle cathédrale.
8. Le jardin des Tuileries est le plus joli jardin.

Script can be found in the front pages of the Annotated Teacher's Edition.

1. F
2. O
3. F
4. O
5. O
6. O
7. O

Game

Qui est...?

Practice using the superlative of adjectives by playing this game with the class. Ask students to throw out the names of 10 famous personalities (celebrities, politicians, historical figures). Write the names of those persons on the board. Then give out one adjective. Students will make a sentence combining that adjective and a person from the board, for example, **Lady Gaga est la chanteuse la plus bizarre.** If students still need practice with the position of adjectives in superlative constructions, choose all adjectives that follow the noun for the first six sentences, then give out adjectives that are placed before the noun. If students are comfortable with those constructions, mix and match them.

12 Je connais Paris!

1.3

Formez des phrases au superlatif en utilisant les indices donnés.

MODÈLES le musée d'Orsay/fréquenté/musée impressionniste
Le musée d'Orsay est le musée impressionniste le plus fréquenté.

le musée d'Orsay/grand/musée impressionniste
Le musée d'Orsay est le plus grand musée impressionniste.

1. la tour Eiffel/célèbre/monument
2. le Louvre/ancien/musée
3. la *Joconde*/connu/œuvre du Louvre
4. le quartier Latin/vieux/quartier
5. les Champs-Élysées/large/avenue
6. la place de la Concorde/grand/place
7. Notre-Dame/beau/cathédrale
8. le jardin des Tuileries/joli/jardin

La *Joconde* est le tableau le plus connu au Louvre.

Communiquez!

13 Les plus grands peintres!

1.1, 1.2

Interpretive Communication

*Écrivez les numéros 1–7 sur votre papier. Écoutez les phrases. Ensuite, indiquez si chaque phrase que vous entendez représent un fait (**F**) ou une opinion (**O**).*

Après la tour Eiffel, le Sacré-Cœur est le plus haut monument de Paris.

Curieusement, le pont Neuf est le pont le plus ancien de Paris.

Essential Instruction

1. Students will work together to write **Activité 12** in their notebooks.
2. Ask students to create five original superlative sentences to share with the class.
3. After students complete **Les plus grands peintres**, correct their work. Replay each statement and ask if the students agree with the opinions stated.
4. As a light activity, ask students to describe **La Joconde** physically. Then ask open-ended whimsical questions such as her name, where she lives, what she ate for breakfast, and the name of her parents, to get students talking.
5. Read with students **Activités 14**, **15**, and **16** to explain what is expected in each activity. If time is not an issue, assign all three to each student. If there is not time for students to do all three, ask them which one they would like to do, and with whom.

À vous la parole

Communiquez!

14 Au musée des beaux-arts

1.1, 1.2, 5.2

Interpersonal Communication

Jouez les rôles d'un(e) ado qui visite un musée avec son père ou sa mère. L'exposition n'intéresse pas du tout l'ado qui commence par critiquer les deux premiers tableaux qu'il/elle voit. Ce sont des peintures que son père ou sa mère adore. Le parent a alors une idée: il emmène son ado voir un tableau qu'il ou elle est sûr que son fils ou sa fille va aimer. Ils discutent alors de la peinture en détail. Ils parlent du mouvement, de ce que le peintre a mis au premier plan, au centre, et à l'arrière-plan, des couleurs, et de ce qui se passe dans le tableau.

Communiquez!

15 Un calendrier artistique

1.3, 3.2, 5.1

Presentational Communication

Créez un calendrier artistique en vous servant d'un outil en ligne. Pour chaque mois, mettez l'image d'une peinture française. Pour chaque peinture, écrivez une courte description en français (50 mots maximum) qui identifie le mouvement, le peintre, la date, le titre, et les caractéristiques de l'œuvre de qui sont visibles sur le tableau.

Search words: **calendar maker**

Communiquez!

16 Le musée du quai Branly

1.1, 1.2, 3.2, 5.1

Interpretive/Presentational Communication

Le musée du quai Branly a des objets d'art de l'Afrique, de l'Asie, de l'Océanie, et des Amériques. Imaginez que vous faites un stage (*internship*) au musée et que vous êtes chargé(e) de créer une application pour Smartphone qui décrive 15 objets de la collection africaine. Pour votre objet préféré, enregistrez (*record*) un commentaire. Ecrivez un texte simple.

Search words: **musée du quai branly promenades à la carte**

RESOURCES

Communicative Activities

Answers

All activities will vary.

Reference Desk

Blended Instruction

Consider using blended instruction, a combination of in-class learning and computer-mediated instruction or learning opportunities. Ask students to complete activities on the computer, using their cell or smartphone, or other emerging electronic technology. This process will allow students to hone their tech skills and become more independent learners. Schedule routine Internet and e-book learning in class and in the lab.

Multiple Intelligences

Bodily-Kinesthetic/Verbal-Linguistic

These students will be attracted to the first activity, which allows their dramatic juices to flow in a play scenario.

Visual-Spatial

These students most likely will be interested in the second activity, making an artistic calendar in which they can create an attractive visual presentation of the art they have studied.

Mathematical-Logical

These students would elect to do the third option, organizing in a systematic way a presentation of 15 art objects with explanations.

RESOURCES

Pre-test

***Leçon* Quiz**

Answers

Script can be found in the Audio Program Manual.

1. M
2. A
3. A
4. M
5. A

D

deux (phrases numéro 1 et 3)

Reference Desk

1. This pronunciation lesson is one of the most important since it addresses a most confusing issue: when to pronounce the **h** in French. Students need to know that the **h** comes in two varieties: silent (**muet**) and aspirant (**aspiré**).
2. Students must never make the liaison for the following common words: **Le Havre**, **le haricot vert**, **le haut**, **le héros**, **la hâte**, **le hibou**, **la honte**, **le hockey**, **le hall**, and **le homard**. It is like fingernails on a blackboard to the French.
3. Tell students that the **le** or **l'** before the noun provide the clue as to how to pronounce the word. If they see **le**, they should take a breath before saying the word that follows whereas **l'** can be pronounced as if it were part of the word.

TPR

Invert your fist so that the back of the hand is facing down. Open your fingers quickly as if to let go of a butterfly. This is the movement for a nasal sound.

Prononciation 1.1

Pronouncing the Letter "h"

- Sometimes the letter "h" is pronounced, and sometimes it is not.

Exemples: un$_{n}$‿hôtel: liaison du "n"

les$_{z}$‿hommes: liaison du "s"

une histoire: enchaînement consonantique

Note the pronunciation of the letter "h" in the examples below.

Exemples: en⁀haut

les⁀Halles

L'artiste

Répétez les phrases suivantes. Faites attention à la prononciation des mots qui commencent avec un "h."

1. Cet$_{t}$‿homme est un peintre.
2. Il habite la⁀haute montagne, dans un$_{n}$‿hôtel.
3. Les$_{z}$‿hommes du village l'admirent.

Vous entendez le "h" muet ou aspiré?

*Écrivez **M** (muet) si vous n'entendez pas le "h," et **A** (aspiré) si vous l'entendez.*

1. Il est de bonne humeur.
2. C'est le héros du livre.
3. Quelle est la hauteur de la tour Eiffel?
4. Cette histoire est incroyable.
5. Regarde vers le haut!

The Nasal and Non-Nasal "n"

- Sounds represented by the letter "n" can be nasal or non-nasal.

La nasalisation et la dénasalisation

Répétez les phrases et expressions avec des exemples de la prononciation de "n." Des exemples de nasalisation sont suivis d'exemples de dénasalisation.

1. Il peint – Ils peignent
2. Il craint – Ils craignent
3. Le bain – Il se baigne

Nasal ou pas nasal?

Écrivez le nombre de phrases que vous entendez qui n'ont pas de son nasal.

Essential Instruction

1. Before playing the pronunciation exercises, explain the difference between the mute and aspirant **h** with examples. Tell students that if the article before the word beginning with an **h** is **le** or **la** instead of **l'** that is the clue that the **h** is to be breathed not elided.
2. Play part **A** several times for pronunciation practice.
3. Part **B** will test if students can distinguish words with the **h muet** and **h aspiré**. Play the recording several times so that students hear the difference. Have them repeat the sentences.
4. Explain that **a**, **e**, **i**, **o**, **u** before an **n** or **m** has a nasal sound. This would explain why the third person singular of **craindre** and **peindre** are nasal and the plural forms are not.
5. Students will listen to the contrast between the singular and plural of these verbs in part **C**, and take the test in part **D**.

Vocabulaire actif

emcl.com
WB 1

La musique  

Le jazz

Le swing

La salsa

La pop

Multiple Intelligences

Musical-Rhythmic

Students who are musical will enjoy this theme of French and American music and artists. Have them expand on the explanation of these genres. Ask them to think of more examples.

Special Needs Students

At-Risk Students

Watch for interest on these students' part about musical groups. This may be a way of getting them more engaged in learning.

RESOURCES

 e-visual 21

 Workbook 1–4

 Flash Cards

 Listening Activity 1

 Drill & Practice Games

Reference Desk

1. **Le Casino de Paris**, built by the Duke de Richelieu in 1730, is not a gambling establishment as its name might suggest but rather a performance venue. Throughout the centuries it has served as a site to show fireworks, and later as an arena to watch wrestling. By 1914 the casino became a music hall where one could watch light entertainment in a luxurious setting for not a lot of money. Famous performers such as Mistinguett, Maurice Chevalier, and Josephine Baker have headlined there. Serge Gainsbourg and Jean Ferrat are among the famous singers who have appeared in concert. Currently, the casino serves as a venue for comedians, pop singers, and musicals.
2. Josephine Baker (1906–1975), although born in the United States, was the most famous African-American singer, actress, and dancer in France. She often performed at **Le Casino de Paris.** In addition to her illustrious career on stage, she also was a spy in the French Resistance, and received the **Légion d'Honneur** award from the hands of President Charles de Gaulle.

Critical Thinking

Analysis

Have students investigate why Paris in the 1920s was the heyday for black Americans. Who were the key performers and where did they appear?

Reference Desk

Ricardo Santana is a Cuban guitarist and lead singer in the group **la Nueva Esperanza** (*the New Hope*). His music is a combination of fusion, jazz, and salsa. Melissa (born in 1985) is a French R&B singer with Algerian (Kabyle) roots. She started her musical career with Maniac from Norway. Her first album, "**Avec tout mon amour**," and two singles, "**Elle**" and "**Cette Fois**," have made her a popular international artist.

emcl.com
WB 2–4
LA 1
Games

Au concert

DICTIONNAIRE DE LA MUSIQUE:

un auteur-compositeur-interprète: artiste qui écrit les paroles, compose la musique, et chante la chanson, par exemple, Serge Gainsbourg

un album concept: album où les chansons forment une histoire, surtout populaire dans les années 60 et 70 dans la musique rock britannique

une chanson réaliste: chanson dramatique de l'entre-guerres, interprétée par une femme, sur des thèmes dramatiques, par exemple, les chansons d'Édith Piaf

une chanson poétique: chanson dont les paroles ressemblent à un poème et qui fait ressentir une émotion, par exemple, "Le Temps des cerises" d'Yves Montand

une chanson engagée: chanson qui parle d'un problème de la société, par exemple, "Le déserteur" de Boris Vian

Essential Instruction

1. Ask students about their musical tastes. Are there any students who play instruments in the band or orchestra or sing in the choir? How many students play musical instruments for pleasure? Do they ever go to concerts? Which ones?
2. Students will copy into their notebooks the vocabulary for the different types of French music.
3. As a class make a timeline of the dates for **le jazz**, **le swing**, **la pop**, and **la salsa**.
4. Students will listen and repeat the expressions and vocabulary in **Pour la conversation** and **Et si je voulais dire...?**
5. As an aural exercise, put the terms in the word bank from **Les définitions** on the board. Read the eight incomplete sentences to the students who will have their books closed. Students will write down the missing word. Have them read aloud the completed sentences.

Pour la conversation   1.1

How do I describe the development of an artist?

> **Il passe de** la caricature **à** la chanson engagée.

He moves from caricatures to political issue songs.

How do I say that an artist was successful?

> **Ses chansons** du temps qui passe et des amours tristes **lui ont valu d'immenses succès.**

His songs of passing time and sad love were valued as immense successes.

How do I describe an artist's emphasis?

> Brel **c'est le goût pour** la musique populaire.

Brel is about a taste for popular music.

How do I describe an artist's ability to connect with his or her audience?

> Elle **a séduit** plusieurs générations **qui se sont reconnues dans** le lyrisme intimiste de ses textes.

She seduced several generations who saw themselves in the intimate lyricism of her texts.

Et si je voulais dire...? 

un air	*tune*
un chœur	*choir*
un morceau	*composition*
la musique de chambre	*chamber music*
un opéra	*opera*
diriger	*to conduct*

1 Les définitions  1.2

Complétez les phrases suivantes avec un mot ou une expression de la liste.

réaliste · mélodie · un album concept · la pop · interprète · paroles · compositrice · compositeur · poétique

1. Un CD avec une idée thématique s'appelle....
2. Une chanson... offre une représentation de la vraie vie.
3. La personne qui compose la musique est le... ou la....
4. Un... chante les chansons des autres avec sa propre (*own*) interprétation.
5. Les chansons ont une musique et des....
6. Par définition, ... est écoutée par un grand nombre de personnes.
7. Une chanson... a des paroles lyriques.
8. Tout le monde connaît la... de "Frère Jacques."

Answers

1. un album concept
2. réaliste
3. compositeur, compositrice
4. interprète
5. paroles
6. la pop
7. poétique
8. mélodie

Reference Desk

In the **Dictionnaire de la Musique** we find five definitions of musical terms with examples of French artists. Students will find corresponding Anglophone artists who could be put in these categories.

Connections

Music

Students may enjoy watching ***Les choristes***, a story about a music teacher in a French boarding school who transforms an unruly group of students into singers.

Multiple Intelligences

Visual-Spatial

Ask students to design a CD cover of one of the French artists featured in this lesson.

Musical-Rhythmic

Students can make a music video of one of the popular French singers from this unit.

Linguistic

Students will present lyrics of a classic or popular French song that they like. They will explain briefly what the song is about and why they endorse it.

Answers

2 *Best matches:*

1. le jazz
2. la pop
3. un auteur
4. une chanson engagée
5. une chanson
6. un interprète
7. une chanson poétique
8. un auteur-compositeur-interprète
9. le swing
10. la salsa

3 *Answers will vary.*

Communication

Presentational: Paired Practice

Students will take opposing views about purchasing music. One view would be the preference of buying music of artists recorded in concert rather than in a studio because the music captures the essence of the artist in performance. The opposing view would be that the sound quality of the studio is far superior to that recorded at a concert. Open up this debate to the class as a whole.

Culture

Products: Activity

Ask students to write on little pieces of paper the letters A through E. In a "blind listening test" play five popular French songs, each one identified by one of these letters. Students will decide which song is their top favorite down to the least popular based on what they heard. The little papers allow them to change the listing of their preferences by rearranging the cards. Reveal to students the name of the artist and song which correspond to each letter.

2 Moi, je connais la musique!

1.2, 5.1

Associez un mot ou une expression de la liste avec les indices ci-dessous.

la salsa · le swing · le jazz · la pop · la mélodie · un interprète · une chanson engagée · une chanson poétique · un auteur · un auteur-compositeur-interprète

1. la Nouvelle-Orléans, Duke Ellington, Louis Armstrong, les boîtes de Paris
2. les Beatles, les meilleurs hits de l'année, les Top 50
3. Adele, Lady Gaga, Taylor Swift
4. la politique, les idées pour changer une société, lutter pour une cause, les années 1960
5. les notes, le compositeur, la compositrice
6. le chanteur, la chanteuse de chansons popularisées par quelqu'un d'autre
7. les paroles, les poèmes, le lyricisme
8. Leonard Cohen, qui a écrit "Hallelujah" (interpreté par Jeff Buckley, k.d. lang, Rufus Wainwright, etc.)
9. Jimmy Dorsey et son orchestre, la Deuxième guerre mondiale (*WWII*)
10. musique pour la danse, exportation de la culture hispanique

3 Questions personnelles

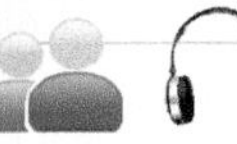

1.3, 5.1

Répondez aux questions suivantes.

1. Quel(s) type(s) de musique aimes-tu écouter? Et tes amis? Et tes parents? Et tes grands-parents?
2. Quels musiciens est-ce que tu admires? Pourquoi?
3. Est-ce que tu as déjà assisté à un concert? Si oui, de quelle sorte de musique?
4. Est-ce que tu joues d'un instrument? Si oui, duquel?
5. Tu aimerais devenir musicien/musicienne célèbre? Pourquoi, ou pourquoi pas?
6. Penses-tu que la mélodie soit la chose la plus importante dans une chanson?

Essential Instruction

1. Ask students to define the musical terms in **Moi, je connais la musique!** They may refer back to the readings for help.
2. In pairs, students will complete **Activité 2**. Can they add more terms and artists to each list?
3. In small groups, students will ask and answer questions pertaining to their musical taste in **Questions personnelles.**
4. Ask students what they answered for each **Question personnelle** to generate a discussion about various musical tastes. Take advantage of expanding on this activity because music is so much a part of students' lives.
5. Pair students to answer **Qu'est-ce que tu préfères?** Debrief students as to their preferences. Some students will not care for any of the choices. If so, they can use **ne...ni...ni: Je n'aime ni le pop, ni la world, ni le hip-hop.**
6. Students will do **Activité 5.** Be sure that they understand each question.

4 Qu'est-ce que tu préfères?

1.1, 1.2, 5.2

Interpersonal Communication

À tour de rôle, demandez ce que votre partenaire préfère.

MODÈLE A: **Préfères-tu la pop, la world, ou le hip-hop?**
B: **Je préfère le hip-hop.**

1. la pop, la world, le hip-hop
2. les chansons réalistes, poétiques, ou engagées
3. les interprètes ou les auteurs-compositeurs-interprètes
4. le jazz, la musique classique, le rock, la musique alternative
5. les chansons engagées ou les chansons romantiques
6. les paroles ou la composition musicale
7. le swing ou la salsa

5 Ce que j'écoute

1.1, 1.2

Écrivez les numéros 1–6 sur votre papier. Écoutez Amina et Antoine discuter de leurs interprètes préférés. Puis choisissez la réponse qui correspond aux questions posées.

1. Qu'est-ce qu'Amina écoute?
   A. une chanson d'Édith Piaf
   B. une chanson de Serge Gainsbourg
   C. une chanson de Jacques Brel
2. Pourquoi écoute-t-elle cet artiste?
   A. Parce qu'elle est triste.
   B. Parce qu'elle adore cet auteur et interprète.
   C. Parce qu'elle aime la musique classique.
3. Quel auteur-compositeur-interprète Antoine préfère-t-il?
   A. Boris Vian
   B. Serge Gainsbourg
   C. Charles Aznavour
4. Qui aime Charles Aznavour?
   A. Antoine
   B. Amina
   C. Antoine et Amina
5. Comment sait-on que Charles Aznavour est un bon auteur-compositeur-interprète?
   A. Parce qu'il écrit de belles chansons.
   B. Parce qu'on l'a nommé "Artiste de variétés du siècle."
   C. Parce qu'Amina l'a vu en concert et pense qu'il chante bien.
6. Qu'est-ce qu'Amina sait faire?
   A. danser le swing
   B. jouer du saxophone
   C. créer des albums concept

Answers

4 *Answers will vary.*

5

Script can be found in the front pages of the Annotated Teacher's Edition.

1. C
2. B
3. B
4. C
5. B
6. A

Communication

Interpersonal: Cooperative Groups

When it comes to music, your students have well-defined opinions about what they like and don't like. Let students pretend that they have to propose five American singers for the International Music Awards. Encourage them to have a lively discussion of their musical favorites. Here are some expressions they might like to use: **Je trouve ça nul**, **Je ne peux pas supporter ....**, **Je suis fan de ....** or **C'est du bonheur**.

Differentiated Learning

Adapt

Continuing the theme of musical preferences that we saw in **Qu'est-ce que préfères**, students will track the music award winners in France for the last five years. How many were French, American, and British?

Search words: nrj awards

RESOURCES

Workbook 5

Reference Desk

1. Boris Vian helped introduce the American jazz greats Duke Ellington and Miles Davis to France. He was best known for his reactionary literature and pessimistic view on the desperation of human existence. His most famous book, ***J'irai cracher sur vos tombes***, tells the story of struggling Black Americans in the United States in the post-slavery South.
2. An artist, a rebel, a pariah, Serge Gainsbourg attracted controversy when he rewrote the French national anthem with a reggae tune.
3. Charles Aznavour was first noticed by legendary singer Édith Piaf.
4. Supplemental music vocabulary: **la batterie** (*drums*), **la caisse claire** (*snare drum*), **la guitare basse, electrique, ou acoustique,** and **le synthé** (**synthésiteur**). **Désacordé** means an instrument is out of tune. **Chanter faux** means "to sing out of tune," whereas **chanter juste** means "to sing in tune." **Chanter en playback** means "to lip synch."

Communication

Presentational: Cooperative Groups

Divide the class into five teams. Assign one of the five musical artists (Vian, Gainsbourg, Azanavour, Brel, and Barbara) to each group. Each group's task is to select one song from the artist to teach the class. They will listen to clips of songs online to make their selection. Students will provide the lyrics and a glossary of terms. Two class periods might be needed to select the song and prepare the lyrics. These songs could be sung as a bell-ringer activity every day, or for brain breaks between exercises.

Rencontres culturelles

emcl.com
WB 5

Les grands auteurs-compositeurs-interprètes français

1.2

On vous présente cinq auteurs-compositeurs-interprètes de la chanson française.

C'est **Boris Vian** (1929–1959) qui va donner le tempo (celui du swing et du jazz) et la couleur sonore* (celle de sa trompette) à l'après-guerre*. Ingénieur, écrivain, journaliste, peintre, il est surtout fou* de musique, de jazz, et de chanson en général. Dans son seul album *Chansons possibles et impossibles*, 1956, il passe de la caricature ("J'suis snob") à la chanson engagée ("La java des bombes atomiques," et "Le Déserteur"). Réputé pour son militantisme provocateur*,"Le déserteur" est probablement la chanson de Vian la plus connue, dont on a fait un album par la suite.

sonore *sound-effect;* **après-guerre** *post-war (WWII);* **fou** *crazy about;* **provocateur** *agitated*

Serge Gainsbourg a été très populaire chez les jeunes.

Serge Gainsbourg (1928–1991) qui ne cachera* jamais son admiration pour Boris Vian, fait partie de la même lignée*: jongleur* de mots, curieux de sonorités* venues d'ailleurs* (jazz, mambo, reggae, new wave, rap) et ne s'attachant à aucun genre* pour mieux réussir dans chacun. Tout lui réussit: la chanson réaliste ("Le poinçonneur des lilas"), la chanson poétique ("La Javanaise," "Je suis venu vous dire que je m'en vais"), la pop ("Poupée de cire, poupée de son"), l'album concept (*Histoire de Melody Nelson*) qui influencera aussi bien Air que Beck ou Jarvis Cocker, et la provocation politique (avec une version de *La Marseillaise* en reggae).

Mais Serge Gainsbourg est aussi l'auteur-compositeur d'un nombre impressionnant de succès interprétés pour nombre d'entre eux par des femmes: Vanessa Paradis, Brigitte Bardot, Jane Birkin (sa muse), Isabelle Adjani, Anna Karina, Catherine Deneuve, Juliette Greco, et Françoise Hardy.

cachera *hide;* **lignée** tradition; **jongleur** *juggler;* **sonorité** *sound, tone;* **d'ailleurs** *from elsewhere;* **ne s'attachant à aucun genre** *belonging to no specific genre*

Charles Aznavour.

Charles Aznavour (1924–), lui aussi l'auteur-compositeur d'un nombre important de chansons à succès interprétées par Edith Piaf, Frank Sinatra, Liza Minnelli, et Dianne Reeves, est surtout l'interprète du temps qui passe et des amours tristes qui lui ont valu d'immenses succès: "Tu t'laisses aller," "Il faut savoir," "La Mamma," "For Me Formidable," "La Bohême," "Emmenez-moi," "Désormais," "Hier encore," "Comme ils disent." Ajouter à cela que Charles Aznavour est un formidable *homme de scène**, élu* par *Time Online* et *CNN "Artiste de variétés du siècle,"* rassemblant* plus de 100.000 spectateurs sur le site des Plaines d'Abraham en 2008 à Québec. Enfin Charles Aznavour a joué au cinéma dans plus de 50 films.

homme de scène *performer;* **élu** *chosen;* **rassemblant** *gathering*

Essential Instruction

1. Make copies of the readings in **Rencontres culturelles** so that students can underline and add notes.
2. Have students take turns reading aloud about each artist. This is an opportunity for you to add comments and play a bit of each song or selections of songs for them to hear.
3. At the end of each section, ask students to volunteer what they remember about each artist.
4. Pair students to do **Activité 6**. Use these questions and answers as a basis for a class discussion about these classic singers. Which of the artists, in students' opinion, could be a popular singer in today's music market?
5. Other **chanteurs engagés** that you might consider introducing to students include Georges Brassens, Serge Reggiani, Michel Berger, Daniel Balavoine, Renaud, and Francis Cabrel.

Jacques Brel (1929–1978) est lui aussi auteur-compositeur-interprète. Il est d'origine belge. Brel c'est la puissance lyrique du texte*, le goût pour la musique populaire dans les mélodies et une interprétation très dramatique. Parmi ses grands succès, "La valse à mille temps," "Bruxelles," et "Jef," appartiennent* de cette esthétique réaliste et populaire alors que "Le Moribond," "Ne me quitte pas," "Quand on a que l'amour," "Le Plat Pays," et "Les Vieux," sont d'un lyrisme plus intimiste et musicalement plus économe*. Reste le Brel critique social, celui des "Bourgeois," des "Flamandes," ou encore des "Bigotes," et de "Ces gens-là."

puissance lyrique du texte *lyrical power of the text;* **appartiennent** *belong;* **économe** *frugal*

Barbara (1930–1997) est la chanteuse qui a séduit plusieurs générations qui se sont reconnues* dans le lyrisme intimiste de ses textes, l'émotion très personnelle qui s'en dégage*, la mélodie piano comme une confidence. Pianiste chantante, elle passe de longues années à chanter dans les cabarets de la rive gauche. De cette relation particulière avec le public, elle écrira une chanson: "Ma plus belle histoire d'amour c'est vous" que le public lui renvoie en miroir au cours de ses concerts. "Dis, quand reviendras-tu?," "Nantes," "Göttingen," "Pierre," "Le mal de vivre," "La solitude," "Une petite cantate," "Au bois de Saint-Amand," "La Dame brune," "Marienbad," mais aussi "L'Aigle noir," "L'homme en habit rouge" forment comme un récit de vie dans lequel chacun, chacune choisit son parcours*.

reconnues *recognized;* **s'en dégage** *comes out;* **parcours** chemin

6 Des auteurs-compositeurs-interprètes français

1.3

Répondez aux questions.

Boris Vian

1. On associe Boris Vian à quels genres de musique?
2. Qu'est-ce qu'il faisait comme métier?
3. Comment s'appelle sa chanson d'un soldat?

Serge Gainsbourg

4. Serge Gainsbourg chantait quelles sortes de chansons?
5. Il a été maître de quels genres de musique?

Charles Aznavour

6. Charles Aznavour se concentre sur quels thèmes principaux (citez-en deux)?
7. À part chanteur, qu'est-ce qu'il fait comme métier?

Jacques Brel

8. Comment est-ce que Jacques Brel interprétait ses chansons?
9. On peut associer quels titres à son pays d'origine?
10. Comment était sa musique?

Barbara

11. Barbara préférait quel instrument de musique?
12. Où a-t-elle commencé sa carrière?
13. Quel était son rapport avec le public?

Answers

6

1. la chanson engagée
2. Il était ingénieur.
3. "Le déserteur"
4. des chansons de tous les genres
5. la chanson réaliste, la chanson poétique, la pop, l'album concept
6. le temps qui passe, les amours tristes
7. acteur de cinéma
8. Il était très dramatique.
9. "Bruxelles, " "Flamandes"
10. lyrique et populaire
11. le piano
12. dans les cabarets de Paris
13. Elle était très proche de son public.

Reference Desk

Barbara (1930–1997) was *the* French singer who symbolized the generation of cabaret musicians. She had a special connection with her public. Barbara addressed her original song **"Ma plus belle histoire d'amour, c'est vous"** to her fans. For the French, her passing also meant the death of an entire generation and music genre.

Expansion

Students will listen to the lyrics of "If we only have love" in English and **"Quand on n'a que l'amour"** in French. They will decide which rendition is more powerful to them and why. Ask if this song could be considered **une chanson engagée.** Why or why not? What is the theme? How does the repetition of **Si** or If add to the drama and intensity of the concluding verse?
Search words: jacques brel is alive and well and living in paris

Differentiated Learning

Accelerate
Serge Gainsbourg has been considered a **"provocateur."** What in his life and works would justify this title? Explain by providing examples.

Decelerate
How would the song **"Le déserteur"** be considered **une chanson engagée**?

Special Needs Students

Hearing Impaired Students
Although they will not be able to enjoy the music as fully as other students, these students can still enjoy the lyrics as poetry.

Social Anxiety/At-Risk Students
Students who have not been raised to appreciate different singing styles may, at first, be turned off by those of Aznavour and Piaf. Encourage them to develop new tastes in music.

RESOURCES

Workbook 6

Reference Desk

Édith Piaf (1915–1963) was a French singer who started her career singing in the streets, thus her alternative name "**la môme**" (*the kid*). Piaf's music told tales of love lost, pathos, and sorrow. Her classic songs that became her trademark are "**La Vie en rose**," "**Non, je ne regrette rien**," "**Milord**," and "**l'Accordéoniste**."

Communication

Presentational: Paired Practice

Students will compare the lyrics of "**La Marseillaise**" to Gainsbourg's "**La Marseillaise**" in reggae. They will answer these questions: What changes did Gainsbourg make that have provoked and infuriated so many French people when the song was released? Do you think that a national anthem should be tampered with? Student pairs will report back to the class on their findings.

Points de départ

emcl.com
WB 6

Question centrale: Comment l'art est-il un reflet de la culture?

La chanson française 1.2

C'est une des caractéristiques de la chanson française: le chanteur fait tout. Il écrit les paroles (auteur), il compose la musique (compositeur), et bien sûr il chante ses propres textes et ses propres musiques (interprète). Le phénomène a commencé après la Seconde Guerre mondiale dans les clubs de Saint-Germain des Prés de Paris, et il demeure important: de Charles Trenet et Boris Vian à Vincent Delerm, de Barbara à Émilie Simon, de Jacques Brel et Charles Aznavour à Bénabar et jusqu'aux slameurs comme Grand Corps Malade, sans oublier Serge Gainsbourg.

Search words: charles trenet, vincent delerm, émilie simon, bénabar, grand corps malade

2.2

"**La vie en rose**" est une chanson bien connue hors de (*outside of*) la France. Chantée par Édith Piaf en 1947, elle est vite devenue un hit. Beaucoup de chanteurs anglophones, tels que Louis Armstrong, Diana Krall, et KT Tunstall, l'ont fait connaître (*made it known*) par leurs fans. Écoutez la chanson en ligne.

Édith Piaf, chanteuse légendaire.

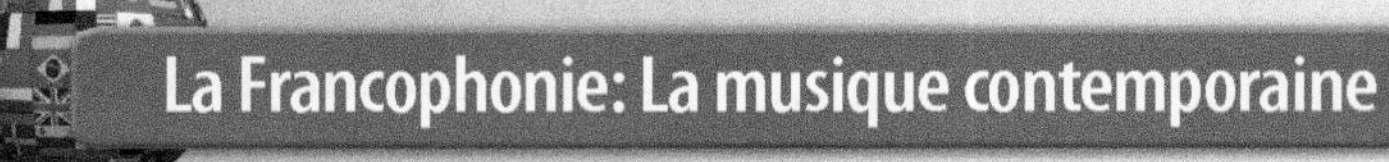

La Francophonie: La musique contemporaine 1.2, 3.1

En France

Ils sont aujourd'hui nombreux les héritiers* de cette tradition d'auteur-compositeur-interprète. Comme leurs prestigieux aînés*, ils sont passés par les caves*, les bars, les clubs, les petits festivals où se retrouvent les gens curieux et attentifs. Et ils revendiquent* tout l'héritage. Parmi les multiples descendants, en voici quelques représentants de divers genres, qui témoignent* de l'influence des plus grands de la chanson française, tout en observant une ouverture sur la scène internationale: Vanessa Paradis (jazz pop), Raphaël (pop), Calogéro (pop rock), Youssoupha (rap), et Melissa (R'n'B).

héritiers *heirs;* **aînés** *elders;* **caves** *basement music halls;* **revendiquent** *claim;* **témoignent** *pay witness to*

Le chanteur Raphaël a commencé sa carrière aux concerts de Vanessa Paradis et David Bowie.

Essential Instruction

1. In the computer lab, students will read all four sections of **Points de départ**. Ask students what the people listed in **Search words** have in common. Students will identify and listen to one popular song from each artist.
2. Teachers have suggested "**Romeo kiff Juliette**" is an appropriate video by **Grand Corps Malade**. Depending on the maturity level of your class, you may want to suggest a specific song from each artist.
3. In their notebooks, students will make a chart with the following headings: name of the artist, song they listened to, theme, orchestration, and their rating one to five, five being the highest.
4. They will continue the chart for **La Francophonie**, **en France**, and **Au Québec**.
5. This chart will provide the basis of a class discussion of French and French-Canadian music styles from yesterday and today.

 *Au Québec*

Vent du nord est un groupe folklorique québécois fondé en 2003. Certains de leurs chansons évoquent* l'influence celtique de l'Irlande et la Bretagne. Ils ont reçu de nombreux prix. Ils vont souvent en tournée. Leur premier album s'appelle *Maudite moisson!* Leur dernier est intitulé *Symphonique*. Ce groupe est bien connu, pas seulement au Canada, mais dans le monde entier.

Search words: vent du nord

évoquent *recall*

7 Activités culturelles

 **1.2, 1.3, 3.2**

Faites les activités suivantes.

1. Décrivez le grand chanteur français. Qu'est-ce que ça veut dire, "il fait tout"?
2. Trouvez le lieu associé avec les origines de cette tradition sur un plan de Paris.
3. Composez une playlist personnelle de vos chansons préférées d'un des chanteurs contemporains mentionnés ci-dessus.
4. Choisissez une chanson de Vent du nord ou d'un autre groupe ou musicien québécois sur Internet. Présentez-la à la classe; dites pourquoi vous l'aimez et faites-la écouter.

Perspectives

Le célèbre chanteur français Georges Brassens a dit, "Pourquoi philosopher alors qu'on peut chanter?" Que pense-t-il du rôle et de l'influence du chanteur français?

La musique québécoise est connue pour ses instruments traditionnels.

Answers

1. Il compose la musique, écrit les paroles, et chante la chanson.
2. Saint-Germain des Prés *(Show students on map.)*
3. *Answers will vary.*
4. *Answers will vary.*

Perspectives
Answers will vary.

Culture

Starmania is a **Franco-Quebécois** rock-opera created in 1978 by French artist Michel Berger and Quebec artist Luc Plamodon. It has reached such international success that it was remade in different countries. Tim Rice's *Tycoon* is an adaptation of the original French-Quebec work.

Differentiated Learning

Accelerate

Have students compare Jacques Brel's "**Les Vieux**" with Michel Sardou's "**Les Vieux Mariés.**" Although the theme is about old people, is the attitude toward them the same in both songs? Which is more melodic?

Decelerate

Compare the prices in euros of five of the same CDs sold in France and the United States. Convert euros to dollars using today's exchange rate.

Multiple Intelligences

Musical-Rhythmic

Have students work with you to organize a French karaoke day. For a minimum fee, karaoke classics of French popular singers are available online. Students could also make a karaoke program of songs of Raphaël and Vent du nord. The more students sing in French, the better their pronunciation becomes.

Answers

8

1. un groupe de musique créé par Coluche
2. Ils ont chanté la chanson des Restos du cœur.
3. Il lui a demandé d'écrire une chanson pour les Restos du cœur.
4. Il était comédien et acteur. Il se présente aux élections présidentielles de 1981. Il fait une grève de la faim pour protester contre la liberté d'expression. Il créé les restos du Cœur pour nourrir les sans-abri.

Reference Desk

Go online and find the lyrics to the song "**Les Restos du Cœur.**" Play it for your students and sing it with them.

Du côté des médias  1.2

Lisez la présentation de l'association "Les Restos du Cœur."

PRÉSENTATION DE L'ASSOCIATION "LES RESTOS DU CŒUR"

Fondés par Coluche en 1985, les Restos du Cœur sont une association française, sous le régime juridique de la loi de 1901, reconnue d'utilité publique et fondée sou le nom officiel de **"Les Restaurants du Cœur- les Relais du Cœur.**"

Ils ont pour but **"d'aider et d'apporter une assistance bénévole aux personnes démunies**, notamment dans le domaine alimentaire par l'accès à des repas gratuits, et par la participation à leur insertion sociale et économique, ainsi qu'à toute l'action contre la pauvreté sous toutes ses formes."

Durant la première campagne des Restos, l'hiver 1985-1986, ce sont 8,5 millions de repas qui ont été servis. À l'hiver 2006-2007, ce sont 81,7 millions de repas qui ont été distribués par l'association. Lors de cette 22e campagne, les Restos ont franchi la barre **d'un milliard de repas servis depuis leur création**.... En France, 3,7 millions de personnes gagnent moins de 645€ par mois (plus de 7 millions si l'on se réfère au seuil de pauvreté européen).

Même si vingt ans plus tard, les carences alimentaires les plus graves ont presque disparu, la pauvreté a pris un autre visage. Et les Restos ont toujours cruellement leur place.

Au-delà de l'aide alimentaire, les Restos du Cœur étendent depuis dix ans leurs actions à l'aide à la personne et à l'insertion. **Car pour sortir durablement de l'exclusion, un repas ne suffit pas.** Il faut aussi retrouver un emploi et avoir un toit.

La plus grande partie des ressources de l'association provient des donateurs et des concerts des Enfoirés. Elles sont complétées par des subventions des collectivités publiques, nationales, et européennes. Les Restos du Cœur sont très soucieux d'utiliser au mieux ces fonds publics et prives: les frais généraux sont réduits (moins de 10%) et les dépenses superflues éliminées.

En conséquence, plus de 90% des ressources sont consacrées aux actions de l'association. L'activité de l'association ne s'exerce que sur le territoire français métropolitain. Il n'existe aucune association agréée en dehors de l'Hexagone, car cela nécessiterait des structures beaucoup plus lourdes et donc plus onéreuses. Et, parce que les législations et les règles fiscales sont différentes, aucune association basée ou opérant a l'étranger ne relève de l'association française.

8 Les Enfoirés et les Restos du Cœur  1.2, 1.3, 3.2

Faites les activités suivantes.

1. Expliquez qui sont les Enfoirés.
2. Expliquez le lien entre les Enfoirés et les Restos du Cœur.
3. Lisez le témoignage de Jean-Jacques Goldman et la déclaration de Coluche sur son initiative. (Allez à la page d'ACCUEIL ou à la page LES ENFOIRES sur le sit en bas.) Qu'est-ce que Coluche lui a demandé de faire?
4. Allez plus loin: faites une recherche sur Internet sur Coluche. Quel était son métier? De quelle façon était-il engagé?

 **Search words: www.enfoires.com**

Essential Instruction

1. Ask students what financial aid and physical support would be needed to help the impoverished in the United States. What American organizations do they know of that are currently helping the homeless?
2. Students will read **Du côté des médias**. They will make a chart about **les Restos du Cœur.** They can use these headings: mission statement, key members, important dates and pertinent statistics, and new vocabulary to help them organize the information in the reading.
3. In groups, students will prepare the answers to the questions in **Activité 8** to be used in a class discussion of this benevolent group.
4. Students will sing the chorus of "**La Chanson des Restos du Cœur.**"
5. In the computer lab, students will listen to music by Raphaël and Vent du nord.

Regardez les albums de Raphaël et lisez les titres de ses chansons.

Une Nuit Au Châtelet

(2007)
Happe (Live 2006)
C'est Bon Aujourd'hui (Live 2006)
1900 (Live 2006)
Ceci N'est Pas Un Adieu (Live 2006)
Elisa (Live 2006)
Caravane (Live 2006)
Sur Mon Cou (Live 2006)
Les Petits Bateaux (Live 2006)
Saint-Etienne (Live 2006)
Des Mots (Live 2006)
Sur La Route (Live 2006)
Poste Restante (Live 2006)
Une Petite Cantate (Live 2006)
Et Dans 150 Ans (Live 2006)

Résistance A La Nuit

(2006)
1900 - Live
Au Temps Des Colonies - Live
C'est Bon Aujourd'Hui - Live
Caravane - Live
Ceci N'Est Pas Un Adieu - Live
Chanson Pour Patrick Dewaere - Live
Et Dans 150 Ans - Live
Funambule - Live
La Ballade Du Pauvre - Live
La Route De Nuit - Live
Les Petits bateaux - Live
Ne Partons Pas Fachés - Live
O Compagnons - Live
Peut Etre A-T-Il Rêvé - Live

Caravane

(2005)
Caravane
Ne Partons Pas Fâchés
Et dans 150 ans
C'est Bon Aujourd'hui
Chanson Pour Patrick Dewaere
Les Petits Bateaux
La Route De Nuit
Schengen
Peut-Etre A-T-Il Rêvé?
La Ballade Du Pauvre
Funambule

La Réalité

(2003)
O Compagnons
Sur La Route
Comme Un Homme A La Mer
Il Ira Loin
La Memoire Des Jours
Il Y A Toujours
Au Temps Des Colonies
Etre Rimbaud
1900
La Réalité
Des Mots
Suivez La Musique
Poste Restante
Une Journée Particulière

Hotel De L'univers

(2000)
Libre Service

9 Discographie de Raphaël

1.3, 3.2, 4.1, 4.2

Choisissez un album et donnez l'équivalent en anglais de ses titres pour un futur album en anglais.

Answers

9 *Answers will vary.*

Expansion

Ask students to search through Raphaël's discography and choose a song to present and explain to the class.

Differentiated Learning

Adapt

Students will watch music videos of Raphaël online. To locate them, type in the name of one of his albums. Excerpts of his music are also available on popular online stores. Questions to discuss: How would you characterize his music? Would this style be popular in the United States? Are there any American or British singers who are similar in style?

RESOURCES

Workbook 7–9

Listening Activity 2

Drill & Practice Games

Reference Desk

The indirect pronouns **me, te, lui, nous, vous, leur** are translated with the prepositions "to" or "for" in English. If students translate **il plaît** or **ils plaisent** as "it is pleasing" or "they are pleasing," the use of the indirect object with **plaire** will make sense. **Il me plaît** means "it is pleasing to me." It could be thought to be a synonym for **aimer.** Students should know that **Il a plu** can mean "it rained" or "it pleased." The context of the sentence should make the meaning obvious.

Communication

Interpersonal: Paired practice

Students will make a list of what they love, for example ice cream, horses, music, sports, and actors to name a few. One student will use **aimer. J'aime cette chanson.** The partner will use **plaire. Cette chanson me plaît.** Students will state what they like or love using **plaire** and **aimer.** They should use a minimum of 15 examples alternating between the two structures. Ask students to share what they wrote.

Structure de la langue

emcl.com
WB 7–9
LA 2
Games

Present Tense of the Irregular Verb *plaire* 1.1

The verb **plaire** (*to please*) is irregular. Only two of its present tense forms are frequently used: **il/elle/on plaît** and **ils/elles plaisent.** To express likes or dislikes, **plaire** is often used instead of **aimer. Plaire** takes an indirect object, using the pronoun **à** with a person or an indirect object pronoun.

Le jazz et le swing **plaisent** à mes grands-parents.	*Jazz and swing please my grandparents.*
Est-ce que la musique de Jacques Brel te **plaît**? Oui, sa musique me **plaît.**	*Do you like Jacques Brel's music?* *Yes, I like his music.*

The irregular past participle of **plaire** is **plu.**

Est-ce que cette chanson engagée vous a **plu**? Oui, elle nous a beaucoup **plu.**	*Did you like the protest song?* *Yes, we liked it a lot.*

COMPARAISONS

Le rock lui plaît. In the English version of this sentence, what are the subject and direct object? 4.1

COMPARAISONS: In the English version ("He/She likes rock"), the subject is "he" or "she" (the person doing the liking) and the direct object is "rock" (music), the thing that is liked. In French **le rock** is the subject (it does the "pleasing") and **lui** is an indirect object.

Essential Instruction

1. Review the form of the indirect objects.
2. Conjugate the verb **plaire** on the board. Students will repeat the verb after you. Underline the **il**, **elle**, **on**, and **ils**, **elles** forms as these are the most often used.
3. Write **Marc aime le chocolat suisse.** Change the sentence to **Le chocolat suisse lui plaît.** Explain that in the second example with **plaire**, Swiss chocolate is pleasing to him. Change the subject to read: **Marie aime le chocolate suisse.** Ask students to restate the sentence with **plaire. Le chocolat suisse lui plaît.** These French sentences are identical. Explain that the speaker can use **plaire** only if it is clear who (Marc or Marie) likes Swiss chocolate.
4. Write **Marc et Marie aiment le chocolat suisse.** Ask students to restate the sentence using **plaire.**
5. Students are now ready to do the interpersonal paired practice and **Ça plaît à Cassandre.**

Communiquez!

10 Ça plaît à Cassandre?

Interpretive Communication

À tour de rôle, demandez à votre partenaire si tel ou tel vêtement plaît à Cassandre ou ne lui plaît pas. Votre partenaire va répondre selon les indices donnés.

MODÈLES

A: **Le bonnet en laine plaît à Cassandre?**
B: **Oui, il lui plaît.**

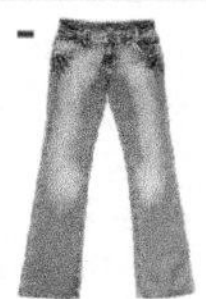

A: **Le pantalon rose plaît à Cassandre?**
B: **Non, le pantalon rose ne lui plaît pas.**

1. 

2. 

3. 

4. 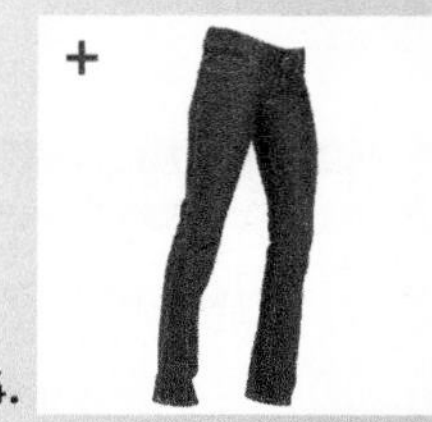

5. 

6. 

7. 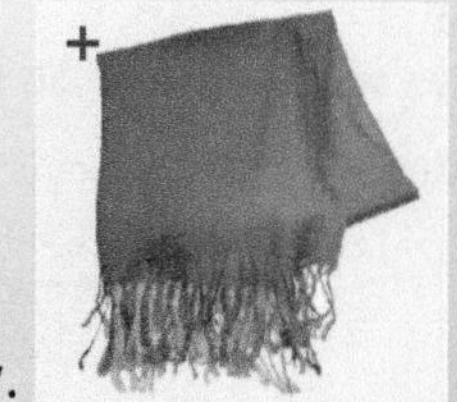

8. 

Answers

1. A: Le tee-shirt en couleur plaît à Cassandre?
   B: Oui, il lui plaît.
2. A: Les chaussures de tennis plaisent à Cassandre?
   B: Non, elles ne lui plaisent pas.
3. A: La robe en coton plaît à Cassandre?
   B: Non, elle ne lui plaît pas.
4. A: Le jean plaît à Cassandre?
   B: Oui, il lui plaît.
5. A: La ceinture noire plaît à Cassandre?
   B: Non, elle ne lui plaît pas.
6. A: La jupe noire et blanche plaît à Cassandre?
   B: Oui, elle lui plaît.
7. A: L'écharpe en lin plaît à Cassandre?
   B: Oui, elle lui plaît.
8. A: Le manteau bleu plaît à Cassandre?
   B: Non, il ne lui plaît pas.

Game

Aïe aïe aïe!

The difficulty with the verb **plaire** is that it requires an indirect construction. Students have to go through the mental exercise of rephrasing "I like this artist" with "This artist is pleasing to me." Put students in teams and give them a sentence in English, such as "**Nous aimons la pop.**" The team which can come up first with the correct construction "**La pop nous plaît**" scores a point. As the game progresses and students get more comfortable, add negative constructions and past tenses.

Differentiated Learning

Adapt

Students will make a list of painters and art movements they like and do not like using the verb **plaire.** Ask them to make sure that they use both third person singular and plural in their examples.

Answers

1. Le swing ne vous plaît pas, mais le hiphop vous plaît.
2. La musique folklorique et la pop lui plaisent.
3. Le jazz ne leur plaît pas, mais la pop leur plaît.
4. La musique classique nous plaît, mais le reggae ne nous plaît pas.
5. Le swing et la pop me plaisent.
6. Le hip-hop et le reggae ne lui plaisent pas.
7. La salsa ne nous plaît pas, mais le swing nous plaît.

1. A: Les émissions de musique te plaisent?
   B: Oui, elles me plaisent./Non, elles ne me plaisent pas.
2. A: Les sports d'hiver te plaisent?
   B: Oui, ils me plaisent./Non, ils ne me plaisent pas.
3. A: Les paysages te plaisent?
   B: Oui, ils me plaisent./Non, ils ne me plaisent pas.
4. A: Les devoirs de math te plaisent?
   B: Oui, ils me plaisent./Non, ils ne me plaisent pas.
5. A: Les cours de science te plaisent?
   B: Oui, ils me plaisent./Non, ils ne me plaisent pas.
6. A: Les peintures impressionnistes te plaisent?
   B: Oui, elles me plaisent./Non, elles ne me plaisent pas.
7. A: Les chansons romantiques te plaisent?
   B: Oui, elles me plaisent./Non, elles ne me plaisent pas
8. A: Les interprètes te plaisent?
   B: Oui, ils me plaisent./Non, ils ne me plaisent pas.
9. A: Les fêtes champêtres te plaisent?
   B: Oui, elles me plaisent./Non, elles ne me plaisent pas.
10. A: Les escargots te plaisent?
    B: Oui, ils me plaisent./Non, ils ne me plaisent pas.

Script can be found in the front pages of the Annotated Teacher's Edition.
1. + 2. + 3. + 4. - 5. - 6.-

Reference Desk

Before doing **Activité 11**, remind students that **Karim et toi** as a combined subject is **vous**, and **Annie et moi** as a combined subject is **nous**.

11 Un sondage sur les préférences de musique

 1.3

Voici les résultats d'un sondage que le Club de Musique a fait à la MJC. Qu'est-ce qui plaît à ses membres?

	+ = plaire – = ne pas plaire					
	Annie	Lindsay	moi	Karim	toi	Dylan
le swing	-	+	+	-	-	+
le jazz	-	-	-	+	+	-
la pop	+	+	+	+	+	+
le hip-hop	+	-	+	-	-	+
le reggae	-	-	-	+	+	+
la musique folklorique	+	+	-	-	-	+
la musique classique	+	-	+	+	+	-
la salsa	+	-	-	+	-	+

MODÈLES Karim: le jazz, la musique folklorique
Le jazz lui plaît, mais la musique folklorique ne lui plaît pas.

moi: le jazz, le reggae
Le jazz et le reggae ne me plaisent pas.

1. Karim et toi: le swing, le hip-hop
2. Lindsay: la musique folklorique, la pop
3. Dylan et Annie: le jazz, le hip-hop
4. Annie et moi: la musique classique, le reggae
5. moi: le swing, la pop
6. Lindsay: le hip-hop, le reggae
7. Lindsay et moi: la salsa, le swing

12 J'interviewe mon partenaire!

  1.1

À tour de rôle, demandez à votre partenaire si les choses suivantes lui plaisent.

MODÈLES les sports d'hiver
A: **Les sports d'hiver te plaisent?**
B: **Oui, les sports d'hiver me plaisent (beaucoup).**
ou
Non, les sports d'hiver ne me plaisent pas.

1. les émissions de musique
2. les sports d'hiver
3. les paysages
4. les devoirs de maths
5. les cours de science
6. les peintures impressionnistes
7. les chansons romantiques
8. les interprètes
9. les fêtes champêtres
10. les escargots

13 La musique qui leur plaît

  1.1, 1.2

Écrivez les numéros 1–6 sur votre papier. Écoutez les conversations. Puis, mettez un + si la personne aime la chose mentionnée dans la question, ou un – si elle ne l'aime pas.

Essential Instruction

1. Model the first and second sentence of **Activité 11.**
2. Pair students to do **Activité 12.** Encourage them to add words like **beaucoup**, **énormément**, or **pas mal** if they like the term. In the negative, they could add **pas du tout.**
3. Students will do **Activité 13** on whiteboards. They will hold up the answer for each listening comprehension item so that you can monitor how well they are doing.
4. Give students a choice of doing **Activité 14** or **15.**
5. All students should do **Activité 16**. Give them enough time to investigate each music website so they learn what French people listen to.

À vous la parole

14 Ma musique préférée

1.1

Interpersonal Communication

Avec un partenaire, parlez de votre musique préférée. Adaptez le dialogue ci-dessous.

A: Moi, j'adore les chansons de Jacques Brel.
B: Brel c'est le goût de la musique populaire.
A: À vrai dire, il passe de la musique populaire à la musique engagée.
B: Il a séduit plusieurs générations de Français et de Flamands.
A: Tu préfères quelles chansons de Brel?
B: J'aime beaucoup ses chansons romantiques telles que "Ne me quitte pas" et "Quand on n' a que l'amour." Et toi?
A: Moi, ce sont les chansons en français et en flamand que j'aime le plus.

15 Un podcast pour les Restos du cœur

1.3, 3.2

Presentational Communication

Les Restos du cœur est une association qui distribue des repas aux personnes dans le besoin. Imaginez que l'association organise un événement pour encourager les gens à faire un don. Pour cela ils organisent un concours (*contest*) de chanson. Ils vont choisir dix podcasts musicaux sur le site web. Peut-être qu'ils choisiront votre interprétation d'une chanson en français. C'est à vous de trouver une chanson, de la pratiquer, et de filmer votre groupe en train de la chanter. Avant de chanter, il faut que vous présentiez le chanteur et la chanson. N'oubliez pas de dire pourquoi vous avez choisi cette chanson pour le concours.

16 Ma playlist de chansons francophones

1.3, 3.2

Interpretive/Presentational Communication

Faites une playlist de 12 chansons chantées par des musiciens francophones en ordre de vos préférences. Il est possible que vous trouviez aussi des chansons de différentes époques. La première chanson de votre liste sera celle que vous aimez le plus.

Search words: nrj radio, victoires de la musique, le top 50, tops songs france, paroles (+ titre de la chanson ou le nom de l'artiste)

RESOURCES

Communicative Activities

Answers

All activities will vary.

Reference Desk

Blended Instruction

Consider using blended instruction, a combination of in-class learning and computer-mediated instruction or learning opportunities. Ask students to complete activities on the computer, using their cell or smartphone, or other emerging electronic technology. This process will allow students to hone their tech skills and become more independent learners. Schedule routine Internet and e-book learning in class and in the lab.

Differentiated Learning

Accelerate

In researching the music that students enjoy, have your high-ability students take their favorite song that they have heard thus far and make a music worksheet which features the lyrics, glossary, and a photo of the artist or artists. They will teach the class the song.

Decelerate

Students will visit **nrj.fr** or **la FNAC** to report on the current concerts given in Paris. Who are the groups, where are the venues, and what are the prices of the seats? Do these correspond to prices in the United States for similar groups?

Reference Desk

To prepare students for writing their essay, bring several objects to class and practice using the vocabulary of similarities and differences as a class or in pairs. You may have them compare simple objects such as an apple and a pear, or a CD and a cassette tape. The concrete visualization will help students practice the vocabulary so they can eventually use it for conceptual ideas.

Stratégie communicative

Write a Comparison-Contrast Essay 1.2, 1.3, 3.1, 3.2, 5.1

Comparer quelque chose c'est montrer les similarités qui existent entre deux choses. Contraster c'est montrer ce qui les différencie. Lorsque l'on écrit une rédaction, on compare et on contraste. C'est très simple, il y a deux manières d'organiser ses idées; vous pouvez comparer et contraster un élément à la fois (*point par point*) ou tout écrire sur le premier élément et ensuite passer au second (tout d'un bloc).

1. Choisissez deux tableaux ou deux artistes que vous comparerez et opposerez. Préparez un diagramme de Venn dans lequel vous montrerez les similarités et les différences qui existent selon les deux.

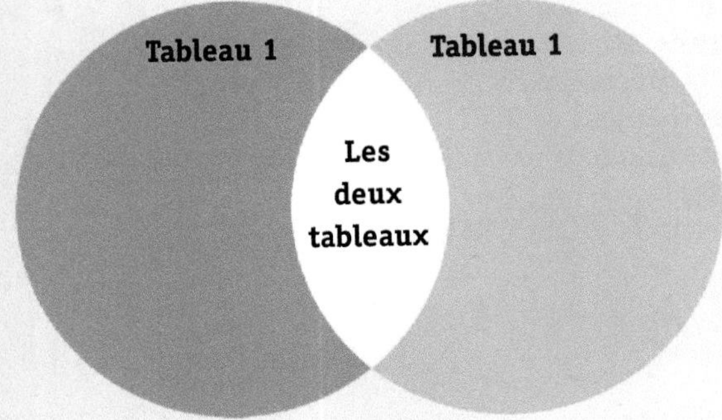

2. Complétez votre organigramme en utilisant les mots ci-dessous pour comparer et contraster:

Similarités	Différences
ressemble à	par contre
les deux	cependant
aussi	mais
également	bien que/qu'
(tout) comme	s'opposer: Les couleurs s'opposent.
comparé(e) à	pendant que
tel, telle: Elle est grande, telle sa mère.	contrairement à
le même, la même	en comparaison de: Il est triste, en comparaison de la fille.

3. Il est également utile d'utiliser le comparatif dans ce type de rédaction.

   Le tableau de Monet est plus joli que le tableau de Renoir en ce qui concerne l'atmosphère.

   Vous pouvez aussi comparer des noms en utilisant la structure suivante:

   Il y a autant de personnages dans le tableau de Renoir que dans l'autre, mais ceux du tableau de Renoir ont l'air plus heureux.

4. Remettez votre rédaction à un(e) camarade de classe. Il s'assurera que vous avez:
   - suivi le schéma d'organisation.
   - inclu une thèse et un fait sur le sujet.
   - inclu votre point de vue.
   - conclu.
5. Mettez au propre et publiez en ligne ou partagez votre rédaction avec votre classe.

Essential Instruction

1. Students can search online, or in art books, for two pieces of art that they would like to use for their comparison-contrast essay.
2. They will make copies of each, which will be handed in with their work.
3. Go over every term under the headings "similarities" and "differences." Remind students that **quoique** is a synonym for **bien que**. Both are followed by the subjunctive.
4. Pick two simple drawings and model a pre-writing comparison-contrast Venn diagram.
5. Allow one class period for pre-writing work so that you can circulate to explain, help, and correct their writing.
6. Students will listen and repeat the terms for **La littérature.**
7. Ask students to give you examples of works in the English language that they have read which correspond to each literary term.

Leçon C

Vocabulaire actif

emcl.com
WB 1–3
LA 1
Games

La littérature

1.2

Pour parler de la littérature

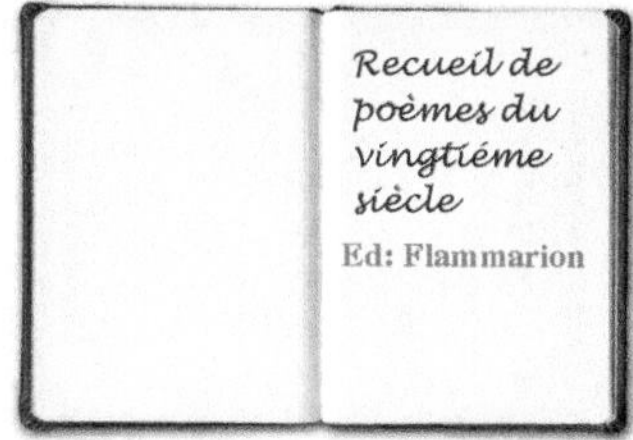

un recueil

un recueil: une collection de poèmes, par exemple *Paroles* par Jacques Prévert

la poésie: un genre littéraire qui utilise les images, les rimes, et les sonorités pour exprimer une idée ou un sentiment

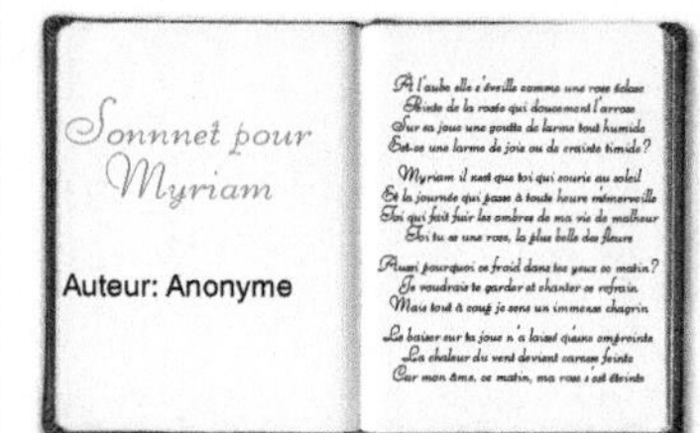

un sonnet (une strophe)

un sonnet: un poème de quatorze vers, composé de deux quatrains (quatre vers) et deux tercets (trois vers)

une strophe: ensemble de vers qui forment un paragraphe dans un poème

une fable

une fable: un récit imaginaire écrit en vers, avec une morale

une morale: une leçon dans une œuvre, par exemple: "Tout flatteur vit aux dépens de celui qui l'écoute" (Jean de La Fontaine)

la satire

la satire: une œuvre (pièce, texte, ou récit oral) critique et comique

Les écrivains

un poète
une femme poète

une romancière
un romancier

un dramaturge
une dramaturge

Differentiated Learning

Accelerate

Have students collaborate to make a presentation for the class on Molière, his life, and key works. Selecting one of his plays, they will act out a scene in English so that students can understand his style and wit. Suggest these works to students: ***Le Malade Imaginaire***, ***L'École des Femmes***, or ***Tartuffe***.

Decelerate

Students will present a fable of La Fontaine in English and then in French for the class. They will explain **la morale.**

Special Needs Students

At-Risk Students

Although not successful in school, some at-risk students are avid readers. Talking about books might be a subject that they would find interesting.

RESOURCES

 e-visual 22

 Workbook 1–3

 Flash Cards

 Listening Activity 1

 Drill & Practice Games

Reference Desk

Jean de La Fontaine (1621–1695) was the most important fabulist in French literature. He was part of a quartet of 17th century writers which included Racine, Boileau, and Molière. His fables were inspired in form and spirit from those of the classic poet Aesop who used animals as mouthpieces to deride vices such as greed, abuse of power, and vanity which were prevalent at the court of Louis XIV at Versailles.

Communication

Presentational: Cooperative Groups

Divide students into groups of four or five. Give them a short amount of time to write down names of English-language works and authors (sonnets, fables, satires, poets, novelists, and playwrights) that they have studied in other classes. Continue until the students have exhausted their memories. One group will be paired with another to exchange information to make one master list between them. A representative from each blended group will put their findings on the board under the categories listed above, using a different color marker to distinguish among the groups' work. Cross out duplications. Decide which group has added the most original entries to the list.

Reference Desk

1. Ode is a lyric poem often written to mark a specific occasion, to focus on a specific subject, or to convey intense emotion. There are varying forms for this genre.
2. Ballads are poems, often set to music, dating back to the time of wandering minstrels in medieval Europe.
3. Sonnet, whose name derives from the Italian for "little song," is a poem which presents a question or argument and resolves it in the final lines of the poem. Although the structure and rhyme scheme may vary, it is always 14 lines in length.
4. Fable is a literary form that tells a fictional story using animals as the mouthpiece and which terminates in a moral or lesson.

Connections

Literature

Students will use the structures in **Pour la conversation** to describe works that they are reading or have read in English or French class.

Le renard ment au corbeau et prend son fromage!

Anna doit se cacher jusqu'à l'aube pour cueillir la rose magique!

... et le brouillard touche le magicien qui demeure dans la vieillesse pour toujours.

Pour la conversation

1.1, 5.1

How do I describe how an artist raises themes?

› Ses *Amours* **donnent lieu à des variations sur les thèmes de** la plainte, du soupir, de l'aveu, et de la mélancolie.

His Amours *(book of poetry) gives rise to a variation of the themes of complaint, sighing, the confession, and melancholy.*

How do I describe how a work of art takes a position?

› **C'est une œuvre** politique **qui prend position sur** la guerre.

It's a political work that takes a position on war.

How do I describe the focus of an artist's work?

› La poésie **est la partie la plus volumineuse de l'œuvre de** Victor Hugo.

Poetry is the most voluminous part of Victor Hugo's work.

How do I attribute new inventions?

› **C'est à** Apollinaire **que l'on doit l'invention du** mot "surréalisme."

It's Apollinaire to whom one owes the invention of the word "surrealism."

How do I describe how an artist fits into a culture?

› **C'est une figure de la culture** populaire.

He is a figure of popular culture.

Et si je voulais dire...?

une ballade	*ballad*
une comparaison	*simile*
une explication de texte	*formal critique of literary selection*
le lyrisme	*lyricism*
une métaphore	*metaphor*
une ode	*ode*

Essential Instruction

1. Put the vocabulary from **Et si je voulais dire...?** on the board. Ask students to define the terms in English and give examples, where possible.
2. Before assigning **Mon cours d'anglais**, ask students to name a work of each of the writers listed in the word bank.
3. Students will work in pairs to do **Activités 1** and **2**.
4. Correct the exercises by asking students to read and supply the answer for each sentence.
5. Use these activities as a basis for a class discussion about what they are reading now for class or for leisure, and tell the class **de quoi il s'agit**.

1 Mon cours d'anglais

 1.2

Selon la phrase, choisissez l'auteur de la liste et complétez cette phrase: ***C'est l'écrivain américain(e)/anglais(e)/irlandais(e)....***

Emily Dickinson Mark Twain William Shakespeare Bram Stoker
Edgar Allen Poe Sir Arthur Conan Doyle Charles Dickens Jack London Harper Lee

1. Son héroïne, Scout, dont le père est avocat, demeure dans le sud des États-Unis; l'œuvre pour laquelle elle est connue est un roman qui prend position sur les droits des afro-américains.
2. Il aimait la satire et l'humour; son héros Huckleberry Finn a voyagé sur le fleuve Mississippi.
3. Il a écrit des recueils de nouvelles et des romans qui ont lieu en Alaska. Il aime décrire les paysages et les animaux sauvages.
4. Elle est demeurée en Nouvelle-Angleterre au XIXème siècle, et elle est connue pour sa poésie simple.
5. Il a écrit beaucoup de pièces comme *Roméo et Juliette* et des sonnets d'amour.
6. Son héros habite dans une ville où il y a souvent du brouillard; il travaille avec Docteur Watson.
7. Il est connu pour un conte de Noël avec le personnage Scrooge; la partie la plus volumineuse de son œuvre, ce sont des romans comme *Oliver Twist*.
8. C'est à lui qu'on doit l'invention des nouvelles fantastiques.
9. Son héros, un vampire, est en difficulté s'il voit l'aube.

2 Mon dico littéraire

 1.2

Choisissez un mot de vocabulaire de la liste pour remplacer les mots en italiques.

un recueil la poésie une fable satires sonnets une morale

1. Les bandes dessinées dans les magazines et journaux sont souvent des *critiques* politiques.
2. On peut lire des nouvelles ou des poèmes dans *un livre qui réunit ces textes.*
3. *Ce genre d'écriture* (*writing*) peut avoir des rimes ou peut être en vers libre (*free verse*).
4. À la fin d'*une histoire allégorique avec des animaux comme personnages* (*characters*), il y a souvent *une leçon.*
5. Shakespeare est connu pour ses *poèmes de 14 vers qui suivent une forme traditionnelle.*

Differentiated Learning

Accelerate

Ask students to present five **bandes dessinées** of the late Jacques Faizant, the journalist-illustrator and satirist of ***le Figaro*** newspaper, as an example of this genre of literature.

Answers

1. Harper Lee
2. Mark Twain
3. Jack London
4. Emily Dickinson
5. William Shakespeare
6. Arthur Conan Doyle
7. Charles Dickens
8. Edgar Alan Poe
9. Bram Stoker

1. satires
2. un recueil
3. la poésie
4. fable, morale
5. sonnets

Expansion

As a follow-up to **Activité 1**, ask students to formulate a short description of a popular American or French author they like. Have each student read his or her definition, and the class will try to find the artist described.

Answers

3

1. corbeau
2. renards
3. la vieillesse
4. mentir
5. cueillir
6. l'aube
7. brouillard
8. cache
9. demeure

4

Script can be found in the front pages of the Annotated Teacher's Edition.

1. F
2. V
3. V
4. V
5. F

5 *Answers will vary.*

Expansion

Bring a variety of books to class and have students sort them in French by genre.

3 Complétez!

1.2

Complétez les phrases.

1. Le... est un oiseau noir qui fait "crôa, crôa."
2. Les... sont des animaux roux qui habitent à la campagne et qui aiment manger les poules de la ferme.
3. Après la jeunesse et la cinquantaine (*middle age*), on arrive à....
4. Pinocchio aime....
5. Le Petit Chaperon Rouge (*Little Red Riding Hood*) veut... des fleurs avant de rendre visite à sa grand-mère.
6. Quand le soleil se lève, on appelle ça....
7. À Londres il y a souvent du... et il pleut souvent.
8. Un auteur peut montrer directement son message, mais on le... plus souvent.
9. Le jeune écrivain... dans un quartier où il y a beaucoup d'artistes et de musiciens.

Le brouillard indique qu'il s'agit d'un roman policier.

4 Ah, la poésie!

1.1, 1.2

*Écrivez les numéros 1–5 sur votre papier. Écoutez la conversation entre Manon et son père, puis indiquez si la phrase que vous entendez est vraie (**V**) ou fausse (**F**).*

5 Questions personnelles

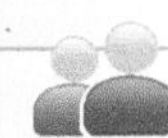

1.3

Répondez aux questions.

1. Quel est ton auteur préféré? Il ou elle écrit quel genre de littérature?
2. Qui te propose le plus souvent des livres?
3. Est-ce que la poésie te plaît? Pourquoi, ou pourquoi pas?
4. Préfères-tu les nouvelles avec une morale ou une intrigue (*plot*) intéressante?
5. Est-ce que tu comprends la satire politique de Stephen Colbert ou Jon Stewart?
6. Si tu allais écrire un texte et le publier (*publish*), quel en serait le genre? Pourquoi?

Essential Instruction

1. When you assign **Activité 3**, you may want to create a word bank for your students if you think that they will have difficulty with the exercise.
2. Students will be listening to the recording in **Activité 4.** Pause the recording after each statement to monitor how your students are doing.
3. Students will be placed into groups of high and low ability to interview each other using **Questions personnelles**. Tell them to take notes because they will be asked to share their answers with their classmates in a whole-class discussion.

Rencontres culturelles

emcl.com
WB 4

La poésie française  1.2, 3.1

Voici quelques poètes français et un exemple de leur poésie.

Pierre de Ronsard (1524–1585)

Ronsard ouvre la tradition de la poésie amoureuse. Ses *Amours* ("À Cassandre," 1552; "À Marie," 1555–1556; "À Hélène," 1578) donnent lieu à des variations sur les thèmes de la plainte, du soupir, de l'aveu, et de la mélancolie. Ils forment encore aujourd'hui un héritage culturel partagé. Voici quelques lignes de son sonnet "À Cassandre," qui se sert du thème *carpe diem*:

À Cassandre

...Tandis que vôtre âge fleuronne*
En sa plus verte nouveauté,
Cueillez, cueillez votre jeunesse:
Comme à cette fleur, la vieillesse
Fera ternir* votre beauté.

Avec le sonnet, Ronsard impose une forme poétique qui est la marque de fabrique de la poésie française de Ronsard jusqu'aux surréalistes, une "machine" à créer de nouveaux rapports entre les mots et finalement une nouvelle réalité.

plainte *complaint;* **fleuronne** *blooms;* **ternir** *tarnish*

Jean de La Fontaine (1621–1695)

C'est le plus populaire des écrivains, celui dont chacun* peut au moins réciter quelques vers "par cœur" ou reprendre l'une des célèbres morales. Jean de La Fontaine était un ami des bêtes et un écologiste avant l'heure*.

Les Fables, écrites entre 1668 et 1694, ont connu tout de suite un immense succès. Elles sont tout à la fois une œuvre politique qui prend position sur la guerre ("Le Lion" ou "Le Renard anglais"), contre l'esprit de conquête ("Le Paysan du Danube"), dénonce avec ironie et humour la vie de la Cour* avec ses flatteurs* ("Les Animaux malades de la peste"). Dans son œuvre philosophique il montre sa méfiance* sur la prétendue* supériorité de la race humaine, de "l'animal qu'on appelle homme" (*La Discorde*). C'est surtout une œuvre de moraliste qui voit l'homme esclave* de ses passions, de ses ambitions, et aussi de l'amour. Cette morale est passée dans le sens commun: elle dit que "nul n'est prophète en son pays" ou que "tel est pris qui croyait prendre". Lisez la fable suivante:

Le Corbeau et le Renard

Maître Corbeau, sur un arbre perché*,
Tenait en son bec* un fromage.
Maître Renard, par l'odeur alléché*,
Lui tint à peu près ce langage:
"Hé! bonjour, Monsieur du Corbeau.
Que vous êtes joli! que vous me semblez beau!
Sans mentir, si votre ramage*
Se rapporte à* votre plumage,
Vous êtes le Phénix des hôtes de ces bois*."

avant l'heure *before his time;* **Cour** *royal court;* **flatteurs** *people who flatter;* **méfiance** *suspicion;* **prétendue** *claimed;* **esclave** *slave;* **perché** *sitting in a tree;* **bec** *beak;* **alléchée** *tempted;* **ramage** *warbling;* **se rapporte à** *is in keeping with;* **bois** *woods*

continued...

RESOURCES

Workbook 4

Communication

Interpersonal: Cooperative Groups

Students in high and low-ability groups will select or be assigned a fable to dramatize. They will select simple costumes to represent the characters, create a backdrop, and present the fable in a dramatic reading. Before the performance, a student from the group will introduce the theme of the fable, explaining any vocabulary students may not understand. Give the students the option of filming the fable off-site if they prefer. Students who are shy might prefer using puppets.

Differentiated Learning

Accelerate

Have students compare Andrew Marvell's poem "To His Coy Mistress" to "**À Cassandra**" in terms of theme, tone, and the poet's art of persuasion.

Decelerate

Students will look online for an animated cartoon of "**Le Corbeau et le Renard**" which will render the poem easier to understand.

Learning Styles

Auditory Learners

These students would benefit from listening to recordings of the poem "**À Cassandra**" and the fable "**Le Corbeau et le Renard**" to aid in understanding.

Visual Learners

Have students make a cartoon strip of "**Le Corbeau et le Renard**" which advances the storyline frame by frame.

Critical Thinking

Analysis

Ask students to compare and contrast the two different pieces of writing on this page, using the tools taught previously in **Leçon A**.

"Le corbeau et le renard" de Jean de La Fontaine.

À ces mots le Corbeau ne se sent pas de joie;
Et pour montrer sa belle voix,
Il ouvre un large bec, laisse tomber* sa proie*.
Le Renard s'en saisit*, et dit: "Mon bon Monsieur,
Apprenez que tout flatteur
Vit aux dépens de celui qui l'écoute:
Cette leçon vaut bien un fromage, sans doute."
Le Corbeau, honteux et confus,
Jura, mais un peu tard, qu'on ne l'y prendrait plus*.

laisse tomber *let's fall/drops;* **la proie** *prey;* **s'en saisit** *seizes it;* **ne l'y prendrait plus** *would not trick him again*

Victor Hugo (1802–1885)

C'est le plus universel des écrivains français. Il a touché à tout: au roman, au théâtre, au pamphlet, à la satire, et bien sûr à la poésie.

La poésie est la partie la plus volumineuse de l'œuvre de Victor Hugo dont les principales sont *Les Orientales* (1829), *Les feuilles d'automne* (1831), *Les Chants du crépuscule* (1835), *Voix intérieures* (1837), *Les rayons et les ombres* (1840), et *Les Contemplations* (1856).

La poésie de Victor Hugo passe par le regard: un regard qui rend compte* du "spectacle du monde" avec ses merveilles* et ses pièges*; qui renvoie* à la mémoire, aux souvenirs de l'enfance; qui capte* aussi la simplicité du quotidien; qui cherche enfin à percer* le secret du visible, à trouver la lumière au-delà de* l'ombre et des profondeurs*.

Voici un poème qu'il a écrit après la mort* de sa fille:

Demain, dès l'aube

Demain, dès l'aube, à l'heure où blanchit* la campagne,
Je partirai. Vois-tu, je sais que tu m'attends.
J'irai par la forêt, j'irai par la montagne.
Je ne puis demeurer loin de toi plus longtemps.

Je marcherai les yeux fixés sur mes pensées*,
Sans rien voir au dehors, sans entendre aucun bruit,
Seul, inconnu, le dos courbé*, les mains croisées*,
Triste, et le jour pour moi sera comme la nuit.

Je ne regarderai ni l'or* du soir qui tombe,
Ni les voiles* au loin descendant vers Harfleur,
Et quand j'arriverai, je mettrai sur ta tombe
Un bouquet de houx* vert et de bruyère* en fleur.

Victor Hugo.

rend compte réalise; **merveille** *marvel;* **piège** *trap;* **renvoie** *takes you back;* **capte** *captures;* **percer** *to pierce;* **au-delà** *beyond;* **profondeur** *depth;* **blanchit** *whitens;* **pensée** *thought;* **courbé** *bent;* **croisées** *crossed;* **or** *gilding;* **voiles** *mists;* **houx** *holly;* **bruyère** *heather*

Essential Instruction

1. Play **"Demain, dès l'aube"** for the students. There are also excellent videos online.
2. Ask students to identify the verbs of movement and perception in the poem. Who is the speaker? List the words that suggest how the speaker feels. To whom is the speaker talking? What is the surprise at the end of the poem?
3. Students will read aloud Apollinaire's "**Automne.**" Ask them to find the description in the poem of **le paysan et son bœuf**, **le village**, **l'automne**, and **l'amour**. What images suggest a love that is no more?
4. Read the biography of Jacques Prévert and tell the students that they will be reading his poem "**Familiale**" toward the end of the lesson.

Guillaume Apollinaire (1880–1918)

C'est à Apollinaire que l'on doit l'invention du mot "surréalisme." Mais Apollinaire est d'abord celui qui a sorti le poète de la bibliothèque et qui a regardé le monde moderne qu'il avait sous les yeux: la publicité, les automobiles, les tramways, l'électricité. Pourtant la poésie d'Apollinaire puise* largement dans les grands thèmes de la poésie: amours de hasard*, regrets de jeunesse, fuite du temps*, sentiments contradictoires, souvenirs douloureux*, mélancolie, rejet du monde. *Alcools* (1913), *Calligrammes* (1918), *Poèmes à Lou* sont les recueils les plus célèbres d'Apollinaire.

Automne

Dans le brouillard s'en vont un paysan* cagneux*
Et son bœuf* lentement dans le brouillard d'automne
Qui cache les hameaux* pauvres et vergogneux*

Et s'en allant là-bas le paysan chantonne
Une chanson d'amour et d'infidélité
Qui parle d'une bague et d'un cœur que l'on brise*

Oh! l'automne l'automne a fait mourir l'été
Dans le brouillard s'en vont deux silhouettes grises

Paysage d'automne.

puise *draws from;* **hasard** *chance;* **fuite du temps** *passage of time;* **douloureux** *painful;* **paysan** fermier; **cagneux** *knock-kneed;* **bœuf** *ox;* **hameau** village; **vergogneux** *shameless;* **brise** *break*

Jacques Prévert (1900–1977)

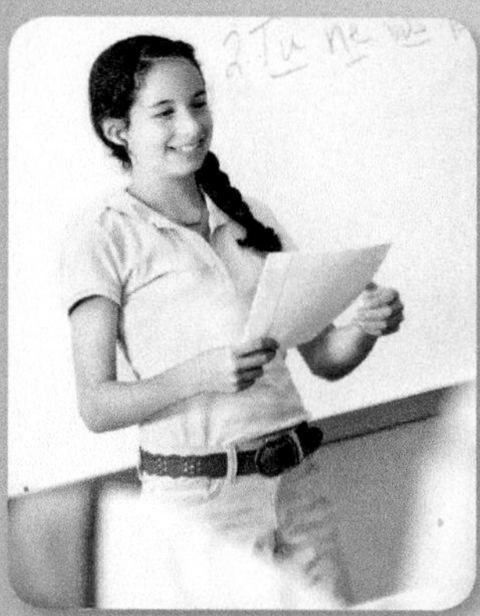
Tous les Français apprennent les poèmes de Jacques Prévert à l'école.

Jacques Prévert est un poète français très célèbre. Il fait partie du bagage poétique de tous les lycéens et est une figure de la culture populaire. Ses recueils se sont vendus à des millions d'exemplaires* et de nombreux collèges et lycées portent le nom de Jacques Prévert.

Qu'est-ce qui a fait le succès de Jacques Prévert? Sa poésie du quotidien, son hymne permanent à la liberté de penser et de parler, et bien sûr son style: jeux de mots, lieux communs, stéréotypes, inventions burlesques, jeux sur les sons, humour, Jacques Prévert cuisine sa poésie avec tous ces ingrédients. *Paroles* (1945), *Histoires* (1946), *Spectacle* (1951), *La pluie et le beau temps* (1955), et *Fatras* (1966) forment l'itinéraire poétique de Jacques Prévert.

Mis en musique par Joseph Kosma, les poèmes de Prévert ont été aussi popularisés par des interprètes comme Juliette Greco ("Barbara," "Je suis comme je suis") ou Yves Montand ("Les feuilles mortes") et chantés aussi en anglais. Vous pouvez lire un poème de Prévert dans la section *Lecture thématique.*

exemplaire *copy*

Reference Desk

Yves Montand (1921–1991) was a French singer and movie actor of Italian descent. He was discovered by Édith Piaf who incorporated him in her performances. His singing style could be compared to Frank Sinatra.

Communication

Interpersonal: Paired Practice

In partners, students will compare "**Demain, dès l'aube**" with "**Automne**" using the following headings: Title, Author, Theme, Speaker, and References to Nature. What do these poems have in common? How do they differ? Replicate the chart on the board, and ask each pair of students to share what they have discussed.

Connections

Drawing

Ask students to draw a picture to illustrate one of the poems presented on these pages.

Differentiated Learning

Accelerate

Give students an abbreviated outline of an **explication de texte**, and ask them to apply it to the poem of Victor Hugo or Guillaume Apollinaire.

Decelerate

Work in small groups with low-ability students to analyze the two poems. They will need help extracting the meaning.

Multiple Intelligences

Visual-Spatial

Students will find romantic paintings that would seem to illustrate the mood and setting of the poems by Hugo and Apollinaire.

Answers

1. des sonnets
2. de la vieillesse
3. "Les Fables de La Fontaine"
4. Il lui apprend que si on est fier, cela nous joue un tour.
5. des poèmes et des romans
6. le cimetière; Il va poser des fleurs sur la tombe de sa fille.
7. du surréalisme
8. l'amour, la jeunesse, le temps
9. la tristesse de l'automne et de l'amour qui finit
10. de l'humour
11. Il écrit des poèmes populaires sur les choses quotidiennes de la vie.

Connections

Music

Many students have seen the play or the movie ***Les Misérables***. What elements in this work would reflect the romantic desire to express feelings such as love, anger, revenge, and loyalty?

6 La poésie française

1.2, 1.3

Répondez aux questions suivantes.

Ronsard

1. Ronsard a écrit quelle sorte de poésie?
2. De quoi Ronsard avertit (*warns*) la jeune fille dans son poème?

La Fontaine

3. La Fontaine est surtout connu pour quel recueil?
4. Qu'est-ce que le renard apprend au corbeau?

Hugo

5. Qu'est-ce que Victor Hugo a écrit?
6. Quelle est la destination du sujet dans le poème? Qu'est-ce qu'il va y faire?

Apollinaire

7. Apollinaire faisait partie de quel mouvement littéraire?
8. Quels étaient ses thèmes?
9. Quel est le thème du poème "Automne"?

Prévert

10. Qu'est-ce que Jacques Prévert mettait dans sa poésie?
11. Pourquoi peut-on dire que les poèmes de Prévert touchent les étudiants?

Essential Instruction

1. As a bell-ringer activity, review the themes of the three poems in **Leçon C.**
2. Use the questions in **La poésie française** as the basis of an expanded class discussion of the three poetic styles.
3. Students will make a timeline from the 16th century to the present marking La Fontaine, Hugo, Apollinaire, and Prévert, or they can add to a previous timeline.
4. Have students draw a star. In the center they will write **la Pléiade.** Radiating from the star like beams of light students will write the names of the seven poets of this movement.
5. In the same vein, students will draw a heart. In the center they will write **le romantisme.** Radiating from the heart students will write the characteristics of romanticism: **le moi**, **l'émotion**, **la nature**, **l'imagination**, and **l'amour.**

Points de départ 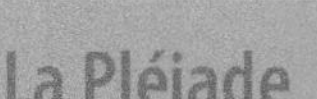 

emcl.com
WB 5

Question centrale

Comment l'art est-il un reflet de la culture?

La Pléiade

1.2, 3.1

Le village de Grignan, au sud de la France, date du XVIème siècle.

C'est au XVIème siècle que la Pléiade, un groupe de sept poètes, a vu le jour. La Pléiade va commencer un renouvellement* de la littérature française. Pierre de Ronsard, Joachim du Bellay, Jacques Peletier du Man, Rémy Belleau, Antoine de Baïf, Pontus de Tyard, et Étienne Jodelle veulent enrichir et défendre la langue et la littérature françaises par la redécouverte de la culture antique, et combattre l'ignorance populaire par l'art et la connaissance. *La Pléiade* désigne* le groupe des poètes, mais aussi leur mouvement poétique, dont la maxime* *carpe diem*, une expression latine, signifie* "Cueille le jour sans te soucier* de quoi demain sera fait." Cette règle morale est bien illustrée dans le poème "À Cassandre."

 **Search words: la pléiade, poèmes ronsard**

renouvellement *renewal;* **désigne** *designates;* **maxime** *saying;* **signifie** *means;* **soucier** *to worry*

COMPARAISONS

Il y a un grand nombre de poètes anglophones qui faisaient partie d'un groupe. Par exemple, il y avait les poètes américains noirs de la Renaissance de Harlem. Quel était leur but principal?

 4.2

Le romantisme de Victor Hugo

 1.2, 3.1

Victor Hugo était le chef du mouvement du romantisme. Les romantiques voulaient rompre* avec les strictes règles du classicisme et se concentrer sur les sentiments. Hugo a dit, "Tout est sujet, tout relève* de l'art; tout a droit de citer en poésie." Il se servait de tous les genres, écrivant des recueils de poésie, des romans, et des pièces, tout en s'engageant politiquement pendant toute sa vie. C'était l'homme du siècle.

 **Search words: le romantisme, victor hugo biographie, poèmes victor hugo**

rompre *to break from;* **relève** *rises up*

RESOURCES

 **Workbook 5**

Expansion

Students in groups will present one of the following poems: "**le Cancre**," "**La Grasse Matinée**," or "**Déjeuner du Matin**," from Prévert's collection ***Paroles***. Encourage students to watch online readings of these poems for pronunciation. They will make copies of the poems for the class. Students will read their poem to the class and explain how the main idea of the poem is expressed through the choice of language. The unifying question students will answer is: How do these three poems describe the struggles of everyday life?

Special Needs Students

Linguistically Challenged

Spend some time teaching pre-reading techniques before asking students to read difficult passages. Encourage them to skim for information, look for cognates, and read without looking up every word in the dictionary.

Reference Desk

1. To explain surrealism, ask students if they have ever had a weird dream that, while it was taking place, made perfect sense. It is only upon awaking, in the rational light of day, that the dream seemed bizarre. The surrealists tried to capture that unconscious reality of the dream and the unconscious for inspiration in their art.
2. The surrealist movement, under the leadership of André Breton, was composed of a group of artists, writers, and musicians. It was a revolt against rationalism and a celebration of the dream, the unconscious, and what is random, as a way to finding new truth. Recounting dreams, or writing whatever came into their head without censure, became the inspiration which lead to a new reality, a sur-reality. Dali's painting *Persistence of Memory* illustrates how the dream, the illogical juxtaposition of objects, creates a strong sensation in the viewer. Apollinaire's ***Calligrames*** is another example of this new expression.
3. Haiti, an island country in the Caribbean Sea, is the first black-led independent nation of Latin America. It gained independence in 1804 after a ten-year slave revolt. In 2004, former president Aristide was sent into exile by a **coup d'état**, and a provisional government was established. Michel Martelly became president in a democratic election in 2011.

Le surréalisme

1.2, 3.1

Le surréalisme est un mouvement littéraire et artistique né après la Première Guerre mondiale*. Le but de ces écrivains était de refuser toutes les constructions logiques de l'esprit, de valoriser* l'irrationnel, l'absurde, le rêve, le désir, et la révolte.

Search words: surréalisme littéraire, surréalisme artistique, calligrammes apollinaire

Première Guerre mondiale *World War I;* **valoriser** *promote*

Chez Apollinaire, l'idéal surréaliste se voit dans sa poésie, notamment ses **calligrammes**, des poèmes écrits en forme de dessins comme "La cravate."

Search words: apollinaire le miroir, calligrammes

La première Guerre Mondiale (Verdun) a drastiquement changé le mode de pensée de la société française.

La Francophonie: La poésie

1.2, 3.1

En Haïti

La tradition littéraire en Haïti est très riche. L'histoire d'Haïti est souvent le sujet de poèmes, écrits soit en français, soit en créole. James Noël, poète-écrivain, est considéré aujourd'hui comme une voix majeure de la littérature haïtienne. Il écrit en créole et en français. Voici l'un de ses poèmes:

Le nom qui m'appelle

Je suis celui qui se lave les mains
Avant d'écrire
Ne me demande pas comment je m'appelle
Je n'ai pas de nom
Je viens de là
De ce non-lieu qui cherche lune*
Pour s'exhumer* de son point d'ombre*
Un nom d'auteur me fait bien mal
Parce que poète
Ça m'est égal
Ni tapis rouge ne saura rendre
La justesse du sang* qui me fait
Passer
Pour un vitrier* qui vaut* sa mort
Je suis saigné*
Donc
Je me lave
Voilà mon nom qui vient de là

qui cherche lune *looking for the moon;* **s'exhumer** *disappear;* **son point d'ombre** *his shadow;* **sang** *blood;* **vitrier** *glazier;* **vaut** *deserves;* **saigné** *bled like an animal*

Essential Instruction

1. Students will investigate surrealism by using the search words provided in the textbook.
2. Ask students to define surrealism and to explain, from their reading, how and why it evolved.
3. Students will read **"Le nom qui m'appelle."** What is "the name" that calls the poet? Why does the poet wash his hands?
4. Have a class discussion about the fifth question, the vocation of the poet in James Noël's poem, using precise examples from the text.
5. Give students 15 minutes to answer the first three questions of **Activités culturelles**. If students are not familiar with ***Notre-Dame de Paris*** have them substitute ***Les Misérables***.
6. For the second question, ask students what English expressions might communicate the **carpe diem** attitude. ("You only live once," "It's now or never," "Go for it.")
7. Students will create a **calligramme** of their choosing and show it to the class. You might want to post them in the classroom.

7 Activités culturelles

1.1, 1.3, 3.1, 3.2, 5.1

Complétez les activités suivantes.

1. Associez un poète à chaque tendance littéraire:
   - la vie moderne
   - les sentiments amoureux
   - le thème *carpe diem*
   - le désir de valoriser l'irrationnel
2. Dites où vous avez déjà rencontré le thème du *carpe diem*—un poème, une chanson, un film, une émission de télé?
3. Même si vous n'avez pas lu *Notre-Dame de Paris* de Victor Hugo, vous en connaissez certainement certains détails. Remplissez ce schéma:
   - milieu
   - période
   - intrigue
   - conflit
4. Écrivez à votre tour un calligramme après avoir choisi un objet.
5. Parlez avec votre partenaire de ce que James Noël révèle de l' identité haïtienne dans son poème.

Perspectives

1.3

Dans son roman *Les Misérables*, Victor Hugo a dit, "On jugerait bien plus sûrement un homme d'après ce qu'il rêve que d'après ce qu'il pense." Ce sentiment reflète la philosophie de quel(s) mouvement(s) littéraire(s)?

Carpe diem fait partie du message de ce film américain.

Pour James Noël et de nombreux auteurs haïtiens, le héros doit être révolutionnaire.

Answers

1. James Noël; Victor Hugo; Ronsard/ Du Bellay/Pelletier du Man/Belleau/de Baïf/de Tyard/ Jodelle; Apollinaire
2. *Answers will vary.*
3. milieu: la cathédrale Notre-Dame de Paris; période: XVème siècle; intrigue: Un jeune poète écrit une pièce sans succès, mais observe une véritable histoire d'amour se dérouler devant ses yeux.; conflit: Le vilain Quasimodo enlève la belle Esmeralda et va être jugé.
4. *Conversations will vary.*
5. *Discussions will vary.*

Perspectives
du romantisme

Game

Le Cadavre Exquis
Surrealist artists would meet to play the parlor game **le cadavre exquis.** By randomly assembling words, new meaning can be achieved. The first sentence that was created by the surrealists was **"Le cadavre exquis boira le vin nouveau,"** thus the title. Start a sheet of paper for each row of students. This piece of paper will pass from student to student. Ask the first student, without thinking, to write an adjective. The paper is folded horizontally so that the second student cannot see what is written. The next student writes a noun, and folds the paper again. The third student writes an adverb, and folds the paper to cover the word, and the fourth student a verb. The paper is unfolded and the sentence is read aloud. Sometimes it makes no sense, but often there is a random logic.

Differentiated Learning

Accelerate
Students can research and write a response to the questions from the lesson: **"La Première Guerre Mondiale a dramatiquement changé la mode de pensée de la société française. Pourquoi?"**

Decelerate
Have students read a brief history of Haiti to answer these questions based on the lesson: Why does James Noël believe that the hero should be a revolutionary? What in the history of Haiti might lead him to this opinion?

Multiple Intelligences

Visual-Spatial
Students may want to investigate the work of two surrealistic painters, Magritte and Dali. Then they can make a collage of their own creation using photos and drawings of dissimilar objects to replicate the surrealistic style.

Answers

8 *Answers will vary.*

Expansion

Organize your own **Concours de poésie** with your class. Give students some guidelines and ask them to write a poem in French. They may choose a sonnet, an ode, or free verse. Have a vote and be sure to prepare prizes for the best poems. If possible, team up with another French teacher and plan this event across several classes. You may want to add categories or levels to encourage students of all abilities.

Du côté des médias Pre AP 1.2

Lisez le programme pour Poésie en liberté.

Prix Poésie en liberté

Le Prix poésie en liberté est un concours international de poésie en langue française. Il s'adresse aux jeunes de 15 à 25 ans de tous les pays. Il se déroule sur internet autour d'un sujet libre. Ce concours donne lieu à la parution annuelle d'une anthologie publiée depuis 2004 par les éditions Le Temps des Cerises.
Il est piloté par l'association "Poésie en liberté", sous l'autorité du ministère chargé de l'éducation, en collaboration avec le CRDP de Créteil, et avec le soutien du rectorat de l'académie de Créteil.

Modalités de participation au Prix poésie en liberté
Qui peut participer ?
Calendrier du Prix poésie en liberté
Télécharger le règlement du Prix poésie en liberté

EN SAVOIR PLUS

Sites à consulter

Poésie en liberté
Concours 2012, modalités de participation, règlement complet et archives
▸ Poésie en liberté

Éduscol
La poésie à l'école
Dossier à télécharger
▸ La poésie à l'école

Le Printemps des Poètes
Le Printemps des Poètes, association loi de 1901, coordonne la manifestation nationale en mars. Elle assume tout au long de l'année un rôle de centre de ressources permanent pour la poésie par l'information, le conseil, la formation et le soutien à la création.
▸ Le Printemps des Poètes

CRDP de l'académie de Créteil

Modalités de participation au prix Poésie en liberté

Le concours se déroule sur le site www.poesie-en-liberte.com
Le participant **envoie un poème inédit, en vers ou en prose, de 30 vers ou lignes, maximum**. La participation est limitée à un seul poème par candidat.
Un comité de lecture, composé des organisateurs, de professionnels de l'édition, de la culture, de l'éducation, de lycéens, d'étudiants et de poètes, établit un choix d'environ 300 textes qui sont soumis au jury.

Le jury est composé de onze lycéens et étudiants venus des quatre coins de la France et de l'étranger. S'ils le souhaitent, les lauréats de l'année précédente peuvent être membres du jury. Il est présidé par un poète assisté de deux organisateurs du concours.
Le jury établit le palmarès parmi ces textes. Il en propose une sélection pour l'anthologie annuelle du concours.

Qui peut participer ?

Le concours est ouvert :

- aux lycéens et étudiants en France
- aux lycéens des établissements français à l'étranger
- aux lycéens des pays francophones et non francophones
- aux étudiants jusqu'à 25 ans

Trois lauréats sont sélectionnés dans chaque catégorie :

- en seconde
- en première
- en terminale
- et parmi les étudiants

Deux palmarès spécifiques sont établis pour :

- l'enseignement agricole
- l'Île-de-France. Ce classement est organisé en partenariat avec le conseil régional. Il récompense un lycée francilien au titre de la meilleure participation ainsi que trois lycéens : seconde, première et terminale.

8 Poésie en liberté 1.3

Complétez les activités suivantes.

1. Écrivez un sommaire qui décrit le concours (*contest*), explique qui peut participer, et explique les règles.
2. Écrivez un poème pour ce concours.

Essential Instruction

1. Students will read **Prix poésie en liberté** in small groups and define the following terms: **Le Printemps des Poètes, Le Temps des Cérises, le CRDP de Créteil, un lauréat, un palmarès.**
2. They will complete **Poésie en liberté.**
3. Compare the **sommaires** of the different groups to decide which group wrote the most comprehensive summary.
4. Students will read **Académie Goncourt** in class. Preview any vocabulary or expressions that might give them trouble.
5. Have students answer the questions in **Le Goncourt des Lycéens.**
6. In correcting their work, students will cite the lines from the reading that gave them the information.

Lisez l'article sur le prix Goncourt des Lycéens.   1.2

Académie Goncourt

Accueil > Le Goncourt des Lycéens

Présentation

Le Prix Goncourt des Lycéens offre au public un choix défendu avec engagement et passion par de jeunes lecteurs à partir de la sélection de romans effectuée en septembre par l'Académie Goncourt.

Lancé en 1988 dans une dizaine de lycées bretons, ce prix, maintenant national, est organisé par la Fnac et le Ministère de l'Éducation Nationale, en coopération avec l'Académie Goncourt, pour donner aux jeunes l'envie de la lecture, le goût de l'écriture et du partage des idées.

Cinquante-deux classes de lycéens âgés de 15 à 18 ans, issus de seconde, première, terminale ou BTS, généralistes, scientifiques ou techniques, lisent et étudient en deux mois, avec l'aide de leurs professeurs et l'Association Bruit de Lire, la douzaine de romans de la sélection de rentrée de l'Académie .

La Fnac offre l'ensemble des livres dès la rentrée. Les classes et leurs professeurs sont ensuite invités à rencontrer les auteurs de la sélection.

À l'issue de ce marathon incluant lecture, fiches et débats, a lieu la première phase du vote (chaque région choisissant ses représentants et son tiercé de livres gagnants), à laquelle succède la finale à Rennes, berceau du Prix, en présence des représentants de l'Académie Goncourt.

À ce jour 17150 élèves ont été associés au prix et 37604 exemplaires de 216 romans contemporains différents ont été lus.

Le Goncourt des lycéens étant maintenant décerné quelques jours après le prix Goncourt proprement dit, il est rare aujourd'hui que les deux couronnent le même livre (ce qui s'était assez souvent produit dans le passé, d'Erik Orsenna en 1988 à Andreï Makine en 1995).

9 Le Goncourt des Lycéens   1.2

*Indiquez si la phrase est vraie (**V**) ou fausse (**F**). Changez les phrases qui sont fausses pour qu'elles soient vraies.*

1. Le Goncourt est un prix littéraire uniquement pour les lycéens.
2. Le prix des lycéens a débuté en Bretagne.
3. Le but du prix est de donner aux jeunes l'envie de la lecture, le goût de l'écriture, et du partage des expériences.
4. Chaque année, une douzaine de romans est considérée par des lecteurs adultes.
5. Plus de 39.000 exemplaires de 216 romans contemporains différents ont été lus jusqu'à présent.

Answers

9

1. V
2. V
3. V
4. V
5. F; Plus de 37.000 exemplaires de 216 romans contemporains différents ont été lus jusqu'à présent.

Reference Desk

1. **Académie Goncourt** was founded by Edmond de Goncourt (1822–1896) to encourage literature and reading. The **Prix Goncourt** is awarded yearly for best fiction.
2. Ask students to guess the name of the national award given to the best fiction in the United States, which would correspond to the **Prix Goncourt.** (Pulitzer Prize for fiction)

Special Needs Students

Linguistically Challenged/Dyslexia

The readings on pp. 426 and 427 are challenging. These students may feel overwhelmed at first. While the high-ability students are composing a poem, you might want to read these passages with students, paragraph by paragraph, asking general comprehension questions. In each paragraph, ask which words they think are important. What do they think the paragraph is about? Continue on to the next paragraph until readings are completed.

Answers

All activities will vary.

Reference Desk

Afin de is a synonym for **pour**, meaning "in order to," and may be used interchangeably. Both are followed by the infinitive.

La culture sur place

Question centrale

Comment l'art est-il un reflet de la culture?

La musique française  4.2

Introduction et Interrogations

Écouter de la musique est l'un des passe-temps favoris des adolescents dans le monde. Quel lien y a-t-il entre la musique que vous écoutez, et la musique préférée des jeunes en France?

10 Première Étape: Imaginer/Observer  2.2, 4.2

Écrivez trois hypothèses concernant la musique que les jeunes Français aiment. Aiment-ils écouter de la musique exclusivement en français, en anglais, ou bien dans d'autres langues? Les chansons populaires en France parlent de quoi? Les thèmes de la musique française ressemblent-ils à ceux de la musique américaine? Sont-ils un reflet de la culture française ou de la culture des jeunes?

11 Deuxième Étape: Rechercher  1.2, 3.1, 3.2, 5.1

Sur Internet, recherchez la chanson populaire en France.

1. Utilisez un outil de recherche et tapez les mots "Top 50 chanson," "Top 50 musique," "Top Tubes France," ou "Top Hits France."
2. Examinez la liste des chansons, surtout notez la langue et le pays de l'interprète. Combien de chansons est-ce que vous reconnaissez? Combien d'interprètes? Combien de chansons sont en français?
3. Avec l'aide de votre professeur, choisissez une chanson française de la liste.
4. Recherchez les paroles de la chanson avec l'aide d'un outil de recherche.
5. Lisez les paroles et essayez d'en comprendre le sens.
6. Écoutez la chanson ou regardez la vidéo si elle est disponible sur Internet.

12 Faire l'inventaire! 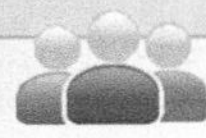  1.1, 4.2

Discutez des questions suivantes en classe.

1. Que pensez-vous de la chanson populaire parmi les jeunes en France?
2. Est-ce que vos hypothèses/observations étaient correctes? Pourquoi, ou pourquoi pas?
3. Comparez la musique populaire en France et chez vous. Est-ce que les chansons sont plutôt similaires ou différentes? Pourquoi, selon vous?
4. Que pensez-vous des paroles de la chanson française que vous avez choisie? Y a-t-il des chansons que vous connaissez sur le même thème en anglais? Comment s'appellent-elles?

Essential Instruction

1. Have students read through all the instructions to assure they understand the assignment.
2. For **Activité 10**, put students in groups to write hypotheses about French music.
3. For **Activité 11**, second question, suggest that the students create a chart with the headings **site**, **titre**, **artiste**, **pays** to identify the top ten songs from each website. Organizing the information will come in handy when discussing music tastes of young French people. As students collect data about songs, have them listen to samples online to find their favorites from which you will help them choose their key song.
4. Students will return to the same groups that they were in for step one, in order to complete **Activité 12**.
5. Review **pour** + infinitive to express purpose.
6. Students will do **Pour** + **infinitif** orally as a class activity. Ask them to generate more sentences with **pour** or **afin de**.

emcl.com
WB 6
LA 2
Games

Révision: *Pour* + infinitive  1.2

In sentences where the subject is the same in both clauses, use **pour** plus an infinitive to express "in order to."

Je suis allé(e) à la librairie **pour** trouver un recueil de Prévert.	*I went to the book store (in order) to find a collection by Prévert.*

13 Pour + infinitif  1.2, 1.3

*Faites des phrases avec **pour** + infinitif selon le modèle.*

pouvoir offrir un cadeau d'anniversaire · apprendre à jouer de la guitare · rester en forme · mieux apprécier les tableaux au musée · parler le français · faire du bricolage · faire du ski alpin · réveillonner avec sa famille

MODÈLE je/acheter une carte-cadeau
J'achète une carte-cadeau pour pouvoir offrir un cadeau d'anniversaire.

1. les étudiants américains/voyager en France
2. tu/suivre un cours d'art
3. Mégane et Sébastien/aller à la MJC
4. je/faire du sport
5. Saskia/faire une dinde aux marrons
6. Éric et toi/fréquenter les stations de ski
7. mes copains et moi/acheter un pot de peinture

COMPARAISONS  4.1

In English, what form of the verb is used after "in order to"?
Je lis **pour me renseigner**.
*I read **in order to be informed**.*

Myriam apprend le piano pour devenir chanteuse et interprète.

COMPARAISONS: Like in French, the infinitive form of the verb is used after "in order to."

RESOURCES

 **Workbook 6**

 **Listening Activity 2**

 **Drill & Practice Games**

Answers

 13

1. Ils voyagent en France pour parler le français.
2. Tu suis un cours d'art pour mieux apprécier les tableaux au musée.
3. Ils vont à la MJC pour apprendre à jouer de la guitare.
4. Je fais du sport pour rester en forme.
5. Elle fait une dinde aux marrons pour réveillonner avec sa famille.
6. Vous fréquentez les stations de ski pour faire du ski alpin.
7. Nous achetons un pot de peinture pour faire du bricolage.

Expansion

Ask students to prepare a list of sentences with **pour**, such as "**Je suis allé à la poste ce matin pour acheter des timbres.**" Group students and have them ask each other questions: "**Pourquoi est-ce que je suis allé à la poste ce matin?**" Other students will attempt to find the reason: "**Pour peser un colis? Pour rencontrer le postier? Pour arriver à l'école en retard?**" etc.

Differentiated Learning

Accelerate
Have students translate a French song they like. Remind them that they will be looking for equivalent expressions, not a word-for-word translation.

Decelerate
Pour + infinitive is a simple concept that low-ability students can master easily. Consider giving them a "feel good" quiz on the concept to boost their confidence and their average.

Multiple Intelligences

Musical-Rhythmic
Many of your students play a musical instrument. Encourage them to get the sheet music for a song in French that they like and perform the music in class or make a video of their performance.

Mathematical-Logical
Students who love analysis can graph comparative statistics about French and American taste in music. Have them investigate five years of **NRJ** music awards.

RESOURCES

 **Workbook 7–9**

 **Drill & Practice Games**

Expansion

With white boards, students will practice the regular and irregular subjunctive with **il faut**. You will say, "**aller/tu**," for example; students will make the sentence: **Il faut que tu ailles.** Write the answer on the board so that students can correct. As a variation, you can put students in pairs to write the verb and assign points for correct forms.

Subjunctive After *pour que*

emcl.com
WB 7–9
Games

 1.2

Les musiciens jouent beaucoup pour que la ville de Lyon les invite à leur festival.

You have already learned that the subjunctive is used after many different expressions.

Expressions	French	English
necessity	**Il faut que** tu **lises** la poésie de Ronsard.	*You need to read Ronsard's poetry.*
impersonal expressions	**Il est bon qu'**il **comprenne** la satire.	*It is good that he understand satire.*
wish, will, or desire	Notre prof **exige que** nous **étudiions** les sonnets.	*Our teacher requires us to study sonnets.*
doubt or uncertainty	**Croyez-vous qu'**Hugo **soit** plus intéressant qu'Apollinaire?	*Do you believe that Hugo is more interesting than Apollinaire?*
emotion	**Ça me surprend qu'**ils n'**aillent** pas lire les fables.	*It surprises me that they aren't going to read the fables.*

Pour que expresses a purpose. It is used with the subjunctive when the subject of the first clause is different from that of the second clause.

Je discute des fables avec Marco **pour qu'**il **puisse** comprendre les morales. — *I'm discussing the fables with Marco so that he can understand the morals.*

Maman a caché les cadeaux **pour que** les enfants ne les **voient** pas. — *Mom hid the gifts so that the children wouldn't see them.*

14 Les gens que je connais

1.2, 1.3

*Lisez la citation et la phrase qui suit. Ensuite, formez des phrases avec **pour que** selon le modèle.*

MODÈLE Ma tante: "Il faut que tu connaisses ton pays." Elle m'a inscrit à une visite guidée des châteaux de la Loire.

Ma tante m'a inscrit(e) à une visite guidée des châteaux de la Loire pour que je connaisse mon pays.

1. Maman: "Je voudrais que tu fasses les courses." Elle m'a donné 50 euros.
2. Ma grand-mère: "Il faut que je te parle chaque semaine." Elle m'a offert un portable.
3. Mon copain: "Je doute que tu sois engagé(e)." Il m'a donné le lien pour le site des Jeunes verts.
4. Ma cousine: "Il est essentiel que tu m'accompagnes au concert de rock." Elle m'a offert un billet de concert.
5. Mon oncle martiniquais: "Je veux que tu prépares une spécialité martiniquaise pour mon anniversaire." Il m'a expliqué comment préparer les accras de morue.

15 Pour vs. Pour que

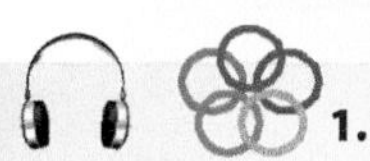

1.1, 1.2

Écrivez les numéros 1–5 sur votre papier. Écoutez les phrases. Choisissez la réponse logique.

A. Pour que tu me prêtes le recueil que tu as caché.
B. Pour mieux comprendre la prose de Victor Hugo.
C. Pour que tu apprécies ses poèmes simples.
D. Pour se rappeler de sa jeunesse.
E. Pour montrer que les gens dans leurs romans ne sont pas heureux.

16 La lecture

1.3

*Formez des phrases qui utilisent **pour que**.*

1. je/lire une fable de La Fontaine/mon neveu... apprendre la morale
2. ma mère/me prêter un roman de Le Clézio/je... pouvoir voyager sans quitter mon fauteuil
3. mon prof de littérature/nous montrer les caligrammes d'Apollinaire/nous... écrire des poèmes originaux
4. mon grand-père/me recommander "À Cassandre"/je... apprécier ma jeunesse

Differentiated Learning

Accelerate

Have students play a timed verb review game to add some challenge to an online verb review.
Search words: **conjuguemos**

Decelerate

Students may need to review the subjunctive if they have forgotten the formation and use. Giving them a one-page review sheet would help them see the big picture.

Multiple Intelligences

Visual-Spatial/Bodily-Kinesthetic

These students do well writing out the forms of the subjunctive because they often tell us that this is the way they learn the best.

Answers

1. Maman m'a donné 50 euros pour que je fasse les courses.
2. Ma grand-mère m'a offert un portable pour qu'elle me parle chaque semaine.
3. Mon copain m'a donné le lien pour le site des Jeunes verts pour que je sois plus engagé(e).
4. Ma cousine m'a offert un billet de concert pour que je l'accompagne au concert de rock.
5. Mon oncle martiniquais m'a expliqué comment préparer les accras de morue pour que je prépare une spécialité martiniquaise pour son anniversaire.

Script can be found in the front pages of the Annotated Teacher's Edition.

1. C
2. D
3. E
4. A
5. B

1. Je lis une fable de La Fontaine pour que mon neveu apprenne la morale.
2. Ma mère me prête un roman de Le Clézio pour que je puisse voyager sans quitter mon fauteuil.
3. Mon prof de littérature nous montre les caligrammes d'Apollinaire pour que nous écrivions des poèmes originaux.
4. Mon grand-père me recommande "**À Cassandre**" pour que j'apprécie ma jeunesse.

Game

Le jéopardy

Play Jeopardy to reinforce the difference between **pour** + infinitive and **pour que** + subjunctive. Write categories related to this unit (poetry, music, novels, singers, etc.). Prepare unfinished sentences such as: **Le chanteur Boris Vian a écrit** "**Le déserteur**" **pour....** If students produce a sentence grammatically correct and logical, they mark the points for the team. Divide the level of difficulty by verb tense, negative v. affirmative construction, and cultural content.

RESOURCES

Communicative Activities

Answers

All activities will vary.

Reference Desk

Blended Instruction

Consider using blended instruction, a combination of in-class learning and computer-mediated instruction or learning opportunities. Ask students to complete activities on the computer, using their cell or smartphone, or other emerging electronic technology. This process will allow students to hone their tech skills and become more independent learners. Schedule routine Internet and e-book learning in class and in the lab.

À vous la parole

Question centrale: Comment l'art est-il un reflet de la culture?

Communiquez!

17 J'interprète un poème. 1.2, 1.3, 3.1, 3.2, 5.1

Presentational Communication

Trouvez un poème francophone que vous aimez. Présentez ce poème devant votre classe. Soyez sûrs de (d'):

- choisir un poème de huit vers (*lines*) minimum.
- lire le poème plusieurs fois.
- chercher les mots que vous ne comprenez pas dans un dictionnaire.
- écrire une introduction qui donne le titre, le nom du poète, et le sujet ou le thème du poème.
- pratiquer devant un miroir.

Communiquez!

18 Je suis poète, et j'ai une licence poétique. 1.3

Presentational Communication

Quand un poète change la prononciation ou l'orthographe dans un poème pour des raisons artistiques, ça s'appelle la "licence poétique." Dans ce cas licence signifie "autorisation." Si les poètes avaient vraiment l'autorisation d'agir comme un vrai poète, que feraient-ils? Créez un poème qui énumère vos droits. Un exemple suit.

Je suis poète. Cette licence me permet de faire les actions suivantes:

- **de danser sous la pluie**
- **de crier sur le sommet de la colline**
- **de collecter de l'argent des gens qui n'utilisent pas la grammaire correctement**

Communiquez!

19 La poésie: Un conte numérique 1.3

Presentational Communication

Vous allez écrire un conte numérique en vous servant de six mots de vocabulaire de la liste de la *Leçon C*: **cueillir**, **la vieillesse**, **un corbeau**, **un renard**, **mentir**, **l'aube**, **demeurer**, **le brouillard**, **cacher**. Après l'avoir écrit, choisissez des images et de la musique pour embellir (*to embellish*) votre conte. Finalement, mettez votre conte en ligne avec ceux de vos camarades de classe.

Essential Instruction

1. Offer students the choice of tasks **17**, **18**, or **19**.
2. Students who select **17** might be interested in the poems in the collection ***Paroles*** because the language is simple and modern. They will find many of the poems recorded online.
3. Challenge students who select **18** to write 20 examples of poetic license using vocabulary and expressions that they have learned in previous chapters. They might want to make these examples into a children's reading book format with illustrations.
4. Students who choose **19** should be encouraged to use their own sketches and photos, music they create with digital software, or selections from their own music library to make the story more personable and entertaining.
5. Have students find photos of Prévert to get a sense of his no-nonsense personality. They will read his biography to learn more about him.
6. Students will reproduce the grid in **Stratégie de lecture** in their notebooks to fill out as they read.

Lecture thématique

Familiale

Rencontre avec l'auteur 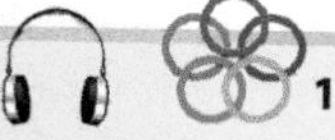 1.2

Jacques Prévert (1900–1977). Avec plus de 2,5 millions d'exemplaires vendus, *Paroles* (1945) est le recueil de poésie le plus lu en France. Il le doit à son langage émouvant (*moving*) et simple. Il le doit aussi au talent de Jacques Prévert dont la poésie est celle de la vie quotidienne, de l'humour, et de la facétie (*play on words*). Chaque poème est l'affirmation d'une exigence de liberté et proclame l'amour de la vie. Prévert y dénonce toutes les contraintes sociales. Qu'est-ce que le poète dénonce dans ce poème?

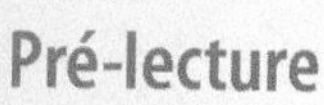 Pré-lecture  1.3

Aurez-vous envie de faire la même chose que vos parents?

Stratégie de lecture  1.1, 1.2

Develop a Theme

Dans ce poème, on aborde (*approach*) le thème du conformisme. Prévert dénonce le conformisme en juxtaposant une série d'actions sans lien ni transition. Pendant la lecture du poème, remplissez la grille avec les actions décrites. S'agit-il d'une famille conformiste ou non-conformiste? Les émotions des personnages sont-elles bouleversantes (*overwhelmed*) ou monotones? Comment réagissent (*react*) la mère et le père quand leur fils meurt? Notez l'effet des répétitions.

Actions	Signification
La mère fait du tricot	Une femme typique qui fait ce qu'elle a appris à faire; ce n'est pas le genre de mère qui pleure quand son fils part pour l'armée; elle accepte son sort comme quelque chose de "naturel."

Outils de lecture  1.2

Recognize Oxymorons

Un oxymore est une alliance de mots dont le rapprochement est inattendu (*unexpected*). L'oxymore fait coexister deux termes de sens contraires à l'intérieur d'une même expression, par exemple, "un silence éloquent." L'oxymore permet de donner une réalité à ce qui semble absurde. Comment le dernier vers du poème est-il un oxymore? Quelles idées s'opposent? Quel est le sens de ce vers? Quel est le message du poète?

Answers

Rencontre avec l'auteur
Prévert dénonce la désensibilisation sociale de la mort et la guerre.

Pré-lecture
Answers will vary.

Stratégie de lecture
"Le fils fait la guerre"
La juxtaposition avec la phrase précédente fait entendre que la guerre est une activité normale pour le fils, tout comme le tricot l'est pour la mère.
"Il [le père] fait les affaires" Le père a une responsabilité traditionnelle, chaque rôle des membres de la famille est vu comme une activité normale et de la même importance.
"Elle trouve ça tout naturel, la mère./ Il trouve ça tout naturel, le père" Les parents ont accepté leur situation sans réaction particulière. Ils sont désensibilisés.
"Il ne trouve absolument rien, le fils" Le fils fait son devoir de soldat comme un automate.
"Quand il aura fini la guerre [...]"
La vie de l'homme est une vie répétitive et impersonnelle.
"Le fils est tué il ne continue plus" La mort est décrite comme si elle n'avait pas de conséquences affectives, morales, psychologique.
"La mère et le père vont au cimetière" L'auteur ne parle pas des sentiments des parents. La mort et la vie sont traités de façon équivalente.
"Ils trouvent ça naturel le père et la mère"
Cette citation est un oxymore, car il est contre-nature qu'un enfant meure avant ses parents. Elle a un effet ironique.
"La vie continue [...]"
Le poète se sert des répétitions pour montrer que le conformisme social créé la désensibilisation de l'être humain.

Outils de lecture
La vie et la mort sont l'opposition par excellence dans le monde humain, leur rapprochement crée une continuité. Le message que donne l'auteur est que la société en temps de guerre voit la mort (et la guerre) comme un phénomène naturel qui n'a pas de conséquences particulière sur les gens. Cette perspective désensibilise l'homme.

Differentiated Learning

Accelerate
Ask students to find other examples of non-conformist ideas in poems they have studied previously in this chapter.

Decelerate
Distribute a list of poems that students can pick from to help them with **Activité 17.** You may want to give them more specific guidelines for the introductory paragraph. To prepare students to analyze the poem, ask them what a normal reaction is, in their opinion, for parents to have when their son or daughter is at war.

Answers

Pendant la lecture

1. La mère tricote, le fils est à la guerre.
2. Elle trouve cela normal: i.e.: Elle n'est pas choquée, elle n'a pas peur.
3. Il fait des affaires, il gagne de l'argent.
4. Il succédera à son père.
5. Il meurt à la bataille.
6. Sa mort ne change pas du tout leur vie. Ils continuent à faire leurs affaires, ils y ont simplement ajouté l'activité d'aller au cimetière.
7. au cimetière

Culture

Jacques Prévert was very involved in the surrealist movement because of its political message against social powers. Find the poem "**Quartier libre**" online and explain with the class why this poem could be considered surrealistic.

La mère fait du tricot*
Le fils fait la guerre
Elle trouve ça tout naturel la mère
Et le père qu'est-ce qu'il fait le père?
Il fait des affaires*
Sa femme fait du tricot
Son fils la guerre
Lui des affaires
Il trouve ça tout naturel le père
Et le fils et le fils
Qu'est-ce qu'il trouve le fils?
Il ne trouve rien absolument rien le fils
Le fils sa mère fait du tricot son père des affaires et lui la guerre
Quand il aura fini* la guerre
Il fera des affaires avec son père
La guerre continue la mère continue elle tricote*
Le père continue il fait des affaires
Le fils est tué* il ne continue plus
La mère et le père vont au cimetière
Ils trouvent ça naturel le père et la mère
La vie continue la vie avec le tricot la guerre les affaires
Les affaires la guerre le tricot la guerre
Les affaires les affaires et les affaires
La vie et le cimetière.

Pendant la lecture
1. La mère et le fils font quelles activités?

Pendant la lecture
2. Quelle est la réaction de la mère en voyant son fils en danger?

Pendant la lecture
3. Que fait le père?

Pendant la lecture
4. Que fera le fils dans l'avenir?

Pendant la lecture
5. Qu'est-ce qui arrive au fils?

Pendant la lecture
6. Comment est-ce que la mort de leur fils change la vie quotidienne des parents?

Pendant la lecture
7. Où vont la mère et le père?

fait du tricot *knits;* **aura fini** *will have finished;* **tricote** fait du tricot; **tué** *killed*

Essential Instruction

1. Read "**Familiale**" in an exaggerated, monotonous voice to the students, accelerating the pace for the last four lines. The students will listen with books closed.
2. Ask students what the theme is. What did they notice about the poetic style and word usage?
3. Students will read the poem aloud in unison. This will make them very aware of repetition and rhyme.
4. Reread the poem stopping to ask the questions in the margin.
5. Use the **Post-lecture** question as a basis of discussing **le train-train** of this family's life, which never seems to change despite tragedy.
6. In small groups, have students analyze "**Avant la défaite**" and answer the questions that follow.
7. Debrief all groups, paying special attention to the last two questions in the series which should lead to more class discussion.

Post-lecture  1.2

Qu'ajoute au thème de Prévert l'usage du présent comme temps grammatical?

Le monde visuel  1.2, 3.1

Soldat 1939. Walter Lichtenstein.

Walter Limot, né Walter Lichtenstein (1902–1984), était photographe en Allemagne avant d'immigrer à Paris en 1933 pour fuir (*flee*) le régime nazi. Là, il a contribué aux progrès techniques du cinéma français en travaillant avec de grands réalisateurs tels que Carne, Delannoy, Christian-Jacques Duvivier, et René-Clair. Il était expert en tout – trucages (les effets spéciaux), solarisations (technique par laquelle on utilise la chaleur naturelle sur le film pour créér des effets spéciaux), découpages (la façon dont on coupe le film pour créér des effets dramatiques), montages (le choix et l'arrangement des éléments visuels et auditifs pour créér un film). Dans cette photographie de la Deuxième Guerre Mondiale, Limot utilise des images fantômes (*ghost*) pour représenter la vie d'une sentinelle (soldat qui surveille l'ennemi) près d'un rail. Comment est-ce que cette photographie vous aide à comprendre ce que dit Prévert au sujet du fils dans le poème?

Answers

Post-lecture

L'usage du présent simple ajoute une monotonie au poème, un aspect d'interminabilité (cela ne finit jamais), ou d'atemporalité, sans début ou sans fin (contrairement à l'usage du passé).

Le monde visuel

Possible answer:

Cette photographie représente la mort comme une ombre qui saisit le soldat, mais à laquelle le soldat ne fait pas attention. Il est là sans prendre conscience que la mort est un danger, une fatalité; il l'accepte comme son propre reflet, comme les personnages du poème de Prévert l'acceptent.

Reference Desk

Jacques Prévert was very involved in the surrealist movement because of its political message against social powers.

Connections

History

Ask the history teacher to re-educate students on the main events and the progression of WWII in Europe and the United States. Then ask students to describe and compare the effects of the war on both continents.

Differentiated Learning

Accelerate

Students will write an essay about the collage of "**Avant la défaite**" as it relates to the theme of war.

Decelerate

Have students practice reading "**Familiale**" to later recite it for you. Encourage them to find an online poetry recitation to help with pronunciation and intonation. Have students describe their family routine and compare it to the routine described in the poem.

Learning Styles

Visual Learners

Project the poem and use two different color highlights to underline repetitions and oxymorons, or questions and answers, or use three colors and underline actions corresponding to each character.

Multiple Intelligences

Bodily-Kinesthetic

Students could make a dramatic video acting out the poem "**Familiale.**"

Answers

All activities will vary.

Game

Le Jéopardy
Review the cultural information taught in this unit by playing a Jeopardy game with the following categories: painters and their attributes, art movements and periods, music genres and artists, literary genres and periods, poets.

Projets finaux

A Connexions par Internet: La poésie

1.3, 3.1, 3.2

Presentational Communication

Écrivez un poème original. Peut-être que vous écrirez un calligramme ou un sonnet. Peut-être que vous voudriez écrire un poème qui ressemble à un des poèmes que vous avez lus dans cette unité. Publiez votre poème en ligne avec les autres poèmes de votre classe ou présentez-le dans un slam devant la classe. N'oubliez pas de donner un titre à votre poème et, si vous le publiez, de mettre votre nom en-dessous du titre.

Search words: comment faire un calligramme vidéo, cartable et récré

B Communautés en ligne

2.1, 3.2

La Fédération Française de Slam Poésie/Interpretive/Presentational Communication

Le slam est un phénomène mondial. La Fédération Française de Slam Poésie a comme but de "faire de la poésie un spectacle vivant" pour les poètes et les spectateurs. Faites des recherches en ligne pour trouver:

- la date d'origine de la ffdsp
- le nom du concours
- si la ffdsp est en contact avec les écoles
- les thèmes choisis par les poètes
- votre vidéo préférée

Search words: ffdsp, slamsncfconcours, le slam interscolaire, le grand slam de poésie, coupe du monde slam poésie vidéos

C Passez à l'action!

1.3

Pour soutenir les arts dans les écoles/Presentational Communication

Votre lycée au Québec a décidé de ne pas continuer les cours d'art et de musique pour des raisons budgétaires. Mais vous et vos amis aimez ces cours et certains de vos amis comptent travailler dans le domaine des arts un jour. Votre groupe a donc pris la décision de lutter contre ces changements. Vous avez pensé à tout: une lettre à l'éditeur de votre journal, une manifestation devant le lycée, une pétition signée par les élèves, un poème sur ce que cette perte (*loss*) représente, etc. Décidez qui dans votre groupe va s'occuper de quoi pour faire la lettre à l'éditeur, l'affiche qui indique la date et le lieu de la manifestation, le slogan, et un paragraphe qui explique l'importance des arts.

Essential Instruction

1. Assign or allow students to select the task for the **Projets finaux** according to their interests. Provide clear rubrics so that they understand your expectations.
2. If assigning students a poem, you might want to offer them more structure. A diamante poem, an acoustic poem, or a haiku may be less intimidating for students who struggle with language. Discuss these different types of poems and find templates online for students to emulate.
3. For the Slam poetry, students not only will identify their favorite video, but also will explain why.
4. Students will work in pairs of high and low-ability teams to complete **Faisons le point**! This activity will allow students to engage in a structured review.
5. Have a "Any question is OK" day where students can get help on even the most basic points without penalty.

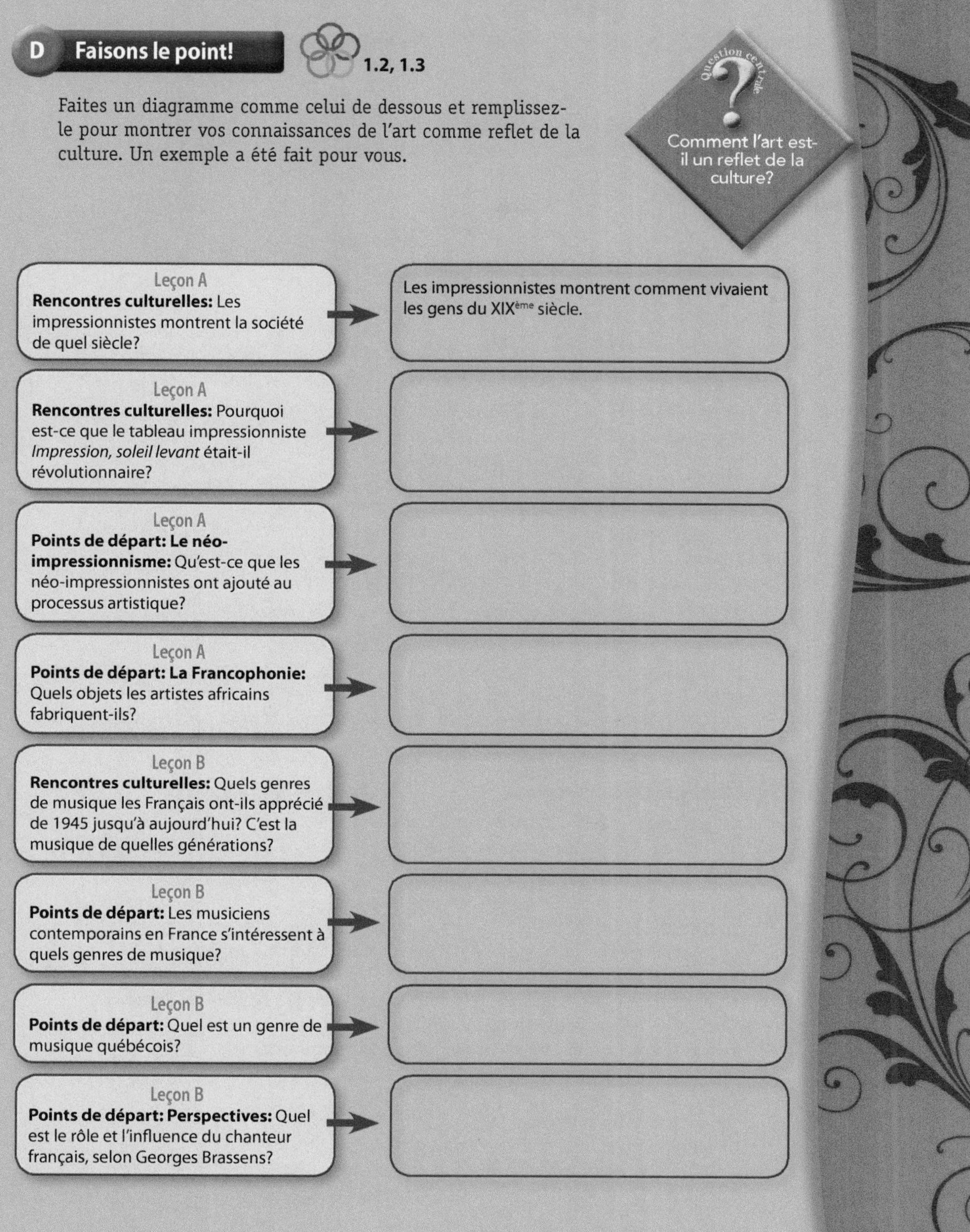

D Faisons le point! 1.2, 1.3

Faites un diagramme comme celui de dessous et remplissez-le pour montrer vos connaissances de l'art comme reflet de la culture. Un exemple a été fait pour vous.

Leçon A **Rencontres culturelles:** Les impressionnistes montrent la société de quel siècle?	Les impressionnistes montrent comment vivaient les gens du XIXème siècle.
Leçon A **Rencontres culturelles:** Pourquoi est-ce que le tableau impressionniste *Impression, soleil levant* était-il révolutionnaire?	
Leçon A **Points de départ: Le néo-impressionnisme:** Qu'est-ce que les néo-impressionnistes ont ajouté au processus artistique?	
Leçon A **Points de départ: La Francophonie:** Quels objets les artistes africains fabriquent-ils?	
Leçon B **Rencontres culturelles:** Quels genres de musique les Français ont-ils apprécié de 1945 jusqu'à aujourd'hui? C'est la musique de quelles générations?	
Leçon B **Points de départ:** Les musiciens contemporains en France s'intéressent à quels genres de musique?	
Leçon B **Points de départ:** Quel est un genre de musique québécois?	
Leçon B **Points de départ: Perspectives:** Quel est le rôle et l'influence du chanteur français, selon Georges Brassens?	

Answers

D

Leçon A: C'était le premier tableau abstrait de l'époque, Monet a utilisé des touches de pinceau plutôt que des tracés.; Ils ont ajouté un style de peintures avec des touches plus petites, des points, pour montrer une impression encore différente; des sculptures et des objets en bronze, des poteries, des armes, des vêtements, des instruments de musique

Leçon B: la chanson engagée (Boris Vian), et les auteurs-compositeurs-interprètes (Brel, Aznavour, Gainsbourg, Barbara), c'est la génération des cabarets; Ils conservent l'héritage de leurs prédécesseurs et sont à la fois influencés par la scène internationale (Raphaël, Youssoupha, Vanessa Paradis, Melissa); la musique folklorique (Vent du nord); Il a un rôle politique.

Leçon C: moralistes: XVIIème, romantiques: XIXème, critiques de la vie politique: XXème: qu'Haïti a une histoire faite de violence et de révolutions; du romantisme, parce que les sentiments pour lui reflètent une action politique plus que la pensée; le poème critique le conformisme social qui détruit les sentiments et le libre-arbitre des individus

Expansion

Pair students and have them choose one of the boxes to develop a detailed response.

Differentiated Learning

Accelerate/Decelerate

As students review the unit lesson by lesson, ask them to make a review sheet of information they still need to study, and details they have forgotten. Encourage them to develop their own personal style of study.

RESOURCES

Listening Activity
Synthèse

Answers

Script can be found in the front pages of the Annotated Teacher's Edition.

1. F
2. F
3. V
4. V
5. F
6. V
7. F
8. V

Connections

Art History

Ask students to present to the class one art movement in the United States and discuss its ties to political transformation (for example, the Harlem Renaissance, music in the 1960s, post-modernism, etc.).

Évaluation

emcl.com
LA *Synthèse*

A Évaluation de compréhension auditive

1.1, 1.2

Interpretive Communication
Deux artistes

*Écoutez Kevin et Annie discuter de leurs intérêts artistiques. Ensuite, indiquez si chaque phrase que vous entendez est vraie (**V**) ou fausse (**F**).*

B Évaluation orale

1.1, 5.2

Interpersonal Communication

À tour de rôle, jouez les rôles d'un(e) ado américain(e) et d'un(e) ado français(e). Avant de commencer, l'élève qui joue le rôle de l'ado américain(e) doit écrire des notes sur ce qu'il/elle sait d'un chanteur/d'une chanteuse américain(e) de son choix. L'élève qui joue le rôle de l'ado français(e) doit rechercher un chanteur ou une chanteuse français(e) pour ses notes.

Dans votre conversation, comparez vos artistes en ce qui concerne:

- leurs genres
- les albums ou les chansons qui leur ont valu d'immense succès
- le public qu'ils ont séduit (les ados? les adultes? leurs pays?)
- leurs thèmes

Finalement, choisissez un album de votre artiste à prêter à votre ami(e) et dites pourquoi il faut qu'il/elle l'écoute. Servez-vous des expressions dans Pour la conversation.

C Évaluation culturelle

1.3, 2.1, 2.2, 3.1, 3.2, 4.2, 5.1

Vous allez comparer les cultures francophones à votre culture. Vous aurez peut-être besoin de faire des recherches sur la culture américaine.

1. **L'impressionnisme**
   Qui sont les maîtres de l'impressionnisme en France? Comment ces peintres ont-ils transformé la façon de peindre? Quel impressionniste préférez-vous? Pourquoi? Qui sont les impressionnistes de l'école américaine? Lesquels aimez-vous? Pourquoi?
2. **L'art traditionnel**
   Comparez les objets traditionnels fabriqués en Afrique de l'Ouest aux objets fabriqués en Amérique par les Amérindiens.
3. **Les auteurs-compositeurs-interprètes contemporains**
   Qui sont les grands auteurs-compositeurs-interprètes contemporains en France et en Amérique? Comparez-les.
4. **Deux chansons célèbres**
   Comment s'appelle la chanson enregistrée par Édith Piaf qui est connue aux États-Unis? Expliquez pourquoi beaucoup de chanteurs l'ont enregistrée, selon vous. Nominez une chanson américaine à exporter en France. Justifiez votre choix.

Essential Instruction

1. When students do the listening comprehension passage, have them jot down notes about each character to help them answer the questions.
2. Students will prepare **B** and **C** in the computer lab. For part **C** they might want to make a chart to compare French and American artists.
3. For part **D** insist that the students spend 10 minutes making pre-writing notes about each point. Circulate to help students with their writing.
4. Students will review the expressions in **Pour la conversation** to help them write the description of the painting in part **E**.
5. Provide students a blank comic strip or storyboard to illustrate the fable of La Fontaine.

5. **La musique traditionnelle**
Quel est le nom du groupe folklorique québécois que vous connaissez maintenant? Connaissez-vous un groupe folklorique américain qui lui ressemble?
6. **Les groupes littéraires**
Pourquoi la Pléiade est-elle importante dans l'évolution de la littérature française? Quels groupes d'écrivains anglophones connaissez-vous?

D Évaluation écrite

1.3, 3.1, 4.2

Écrivez une composition sur un écrivain américain que vous admirez. Expliquez:

- le ou les genres qu'il ou elle aime.
- l'intrigue (*plot*) ou le thème d'une de ses œuvres.
- quand il ou elle a écrit cette œuvre.
- pourquoi vous aimez cette œuvre.

Servez-vous des expressions de *Pour la conversation*.

E Évaluation visuelle

1.3, 3.1, 3.2

Imaginez que vous devez écrire un paragraphe sur ce tableau. Expliquez:

- le mouvement auquel cette œuvre appartient (*belongs*).
- quand ce mouvement a eu lieu.
- qui est l'artiste.
- ce que le peintre recherche dans cette œuvre ou son œuvre en général.
- comment l'artiste s'éloigne des peintres qui l'ont précédé.
- ce qu'il a peint dans ce tableau.
- pourquoi vous aimez cette peinture ou pourquoi vous ne l'aimez pas.

Servez-vous des expressions de Pour la conversation.

F Évaluation compréhensive

1.3

Créez une planche de bande dessinée d'environ huit vignettes pour raconter ce qui se passe dans une autre fable de La Fontaine. Dessinez l'histoire et racontez-la avec des descriptions et des dialogues en utilisant vos propres mots.

Expansion

Ask students to write additional captions to their comics, and then give them feedback. After, have them embellish their work for a class or school exhibition on the famous work of La Fontaine.

Differentiated Learning

Accelerate
High-ability students can work independently to review for the evaluation.

Decelerate
Work with these students in groups or individually to help them structure their review. Many of these students have not yet developed study skills or do not have the time or place to study at home.

Special Needs Students

At-Risk Students
At this point, many of these students do not feel that they have a chance of succeeding. Break down tasks into smaller, measurable sections so that they could be successful in part if not in the whole evaluation.

RESOURCES

 **Listening Pre-test D**

 ***Unité* Test**

Game

Charades
Divide the class into two groups. Give them time to peruse the chapter for vocabulary and use the summative list on this page. Students will conspire to find words that the other team must pantomime. The goal is for a team to guess the word that is being acted out in whatever short time period you prefer. You can set the time according to the skill of the class.

Categories
Students will work in pairs to write from memory as many vocabulary words as they can remember for **Art**, **Musique**, **Écrivains**, and **Poésie**. Points will be awarded for the most words in each category. To make the game more challenging, assign a letter of the alphabet for each category. Give students time to correct their vocabulary. You can play the game again using the same categories, but this time, count only the words written perfectly.

Vocabulaire de l'Unité 7

 1.2

	à: à l'arrière-plan in the background *A*
un	**album: album concept** concept album *B*
	appliquer to apply *A*
un	**atelier** studio *A*
l'	**aube (f.)** dawn *C*
un	**auteur** author *B*
l'	**aveu (m.)** confession *C*
les	**beaux-arts (m.)** fine arts *A*
le	**brouillard** mist *C*
	cacher to conceal, to hide *C*
se	**cacher** to hide *C*
la	**caricature** caricature *B*
une	**chanson: chanson réaliste** chanson réaliste *B*
les	**coquelicots (m.)** poppies *A*
le	**corbeau** crow *C*
	cueillir to pick *C*
	de: de plus en plus more and more *A*
	demeurer to live *C*
	devoir to owe *C*
	donner: donner lieu à to give rise to *C*
un(e)	**dramaturge** playwright *C*
s'	**éloigner (de)** to distance oneself (from) *A*
	en: en gros plan in a close-up *A*; **en tournée** on tour *B*
l'	**expressionnisme (m.)** expressionism *A*
	expressionniste expressionist *A*
une	**fête: fête champêtre** garden party *A*
une	**figure** figure *C*
	immense immense *B*
l'	**impressionnisme (m.)** Impressionism *A*
un(e)	**impressionniste** Impressionist *A*
un	**interprète** performer *B*
	intimiste intimate *B*
l'	**invention (f.)** invention *C*
des	**lignes (f.)** lines *A*
le	**lyrisme** lyricism *B*
la	**mélancolie** melancholy *C*
la	**mélodie** melody *B*
	mentir to lie *C*
une	**méthode** method *A*
une	**morale** moral *C*
le	**néo-classicisme** neoclassicism *A*
	néoclassique neo-classic *A*
le	**néo-impressionnisme** Neo-impressionism *A*
	pâle pale *A*
la	**partie** part *C*
	passer: passer de… à to move from… to *B*
la	**peinture** painting *A*
un	**pinceau** paintbrush *A*
la	**plainte** complaint *C*
	plaire (à) to please *B*
un	**poète, une femme poéte** poet *C*
	poétique poetic *B*
	populaire popular *B*
	pour: pour que so that *C*
	prendre: prendre position (sur) to take a position (on) *C*
le	**réalisme** realism *A*
	rechercher to look for/into *A*
se	**reconnaître** to see oneself as *B*
un	**reflet** reflection *A*
le	**renard** fox *C*
le	**rococo** rococo style *A*
	rococo rococo *A*
un	**romancier, une romancière** novelist *C*
	romantique Romantic *A*
le	**romantisme** Romanticism *A*
la	**salsa** salsa music *B*
la	**satire** satire *C*
	séduire to seduce *B*
un	**sonnet** sonnet *C*
le	**sorcier** wizard *C*
le	**soupir** sighing *C*
le	**succès** success *B*
	sur: sur scène on-stage *B*
le	**surréalisme** surrealism *C*
le	**swing** swing music *B*
un	**texte** text *B*
les	**thèmes (m.)** themes *C*
une	**toile** canvas *A*
	valoir to be valued as/at *B*
des	**variations (f.)** variations *C*
la	**vieillesse** old age *C*
	volumineux, volumineuse voluminous *C*

Essential Instruction

1. Before playing vocabulary games, review the vocabulary list by giving definitions; students will guess the term. Describe characteristics of art and literary movements, and students will furnish the names.
2. Encourage low-ability learners to make vocabulary flash cards and work with study buddies to prepare for the test.

Unité

8 La France d'hier et d'aujourd'hui

441

Reference Desk

1. **La Conciergerie**, located on the **Ile de la Cîté**, served as the royal palace from the 10th to the mid-14th century. It became a prison in 1391. During the French Revolution, in 1793 and 1794, those suspected of opposing the revolution were detained there before being sentenced to death by the Revolutionary Tribunal. Over 2,600 prisoners left **La Conciergerie** to go to the guillotine. Marie-Antoinette was imprisoned there before her death.
2. **La Conciergerie** was known as "the antechamber to the guillotine." Tell students that **la tour bombec** was the torture chamber.

Citation

"La France est à refaire, mais elle sera toujours refaite."

France is to be remade, but she will always be remade.

—Aurélien Scholl, journaliste, auteur dramatique, chroniqueur, et romancier français (XIXème siècle)

À savoir

Après la chute de Napoléon 1er en 1814, Louis XVIII est remis sur le trône, et la France est encore gouvernée par un roi.

Essential Instruction

1. Ask students what they know about the French Revolution. Who were the king and queen at the time? When they think of Marie-Antoinette, what adjectives would they use to describe her? Can anyone cite the quotation attributed to her? (Note the source of the "Let them eat cake" quote is not verifiable and, if she did say it, some believe she was referring to **brioche** since there was no more bread.)
2. Tell students that **Unité 8** discusses the French Revolution.
3. Review the **Contrat de l'élève**.
4. Put students in groups. Have them try to list the 27 countries in the EU. Afterward, post a list of the countries to see which group listed the most.

Unité 8

La France d'hier et d'aujourd'hui

Comment le passé influence-t-il le présent?

Quel est ce bâtiment parisien?

Contrat de l'élève

Leçon A **I will be able to:**

- express obligation and say what I was made to do.
- talk about the last French king and queen, the **États généraux de l'Ancien Régime**, and the French declaration of citizens' rights.
- use expressions with **faire** and the construction **faire** + infinitive.

Leçon B **I will be able to:**

- say there is a lot of something and what I did in vain.
- talk about the institutions of the European Union.
- use expressions with **avoir** and the past infinitive.

Leçon C **I will be able to:**

- express my rights, discuss what I can afford, and say I want to discuss something in more detail later.
- talk about the rights of French citizens and their entitlement programs.
- use expressions with **être** and the pluperfect tense.

Reference Desk

1. The European Union is an economic and political union of 27 member states, established in 1992 by the Maastricht Treaty. The European Parliament governs the EU, and European Union citizens elect its members every five years.
2. For up-to-date information on the European Union, access its website.
   Search words: europa site officiel
3. The **citation** suggests that France is a country continuing to evolve. Two examples of dramatic changes over history are the French Revolution, which uprooted the centuries-old monarchy, and the admission of France into the European Union.

Differentiated Learning

Accelerate
Ask students to present the objectives and structure of the Treaty of Maastricht to the class.

Decelerate
Have students define the eurozone, list its members, and explain the basic tenets of the agreement.

Learning Styles

Visual Learners
Ask students to make a poster of the euro, including photos or drawings of the denominations of bills and coins.

Multiple Intelligences

Mathematical-Logical
Ask students to graph the ratio of the dollar to the euro in five-year increments from 1998 to the present. What are the challenges facing the euro today?

RESOURCES

 e-visual 23

 Workbook 1–3

 Flash Cards

 Listening Activity 1

 Drill & Practice Games

Reference Desk

1. **Ancien régime** was the political, economic, and social system from the 15th century to the Revolution. The clergy, nobles, and the rest of French society formed the three estates in order of importance. The third estate bore the tax burden for the other two.
2. **Les États généraux**, the general assembly of the three estates, met in 1789 to try to solve France's fiscal crisis. The effort failed because the clergy and the nobles wanted to maintain their status and power. The third estate, the commoners, met at a tennis court swearing not to disband until a constitution had been written.
3. **Citoyen/enne** was the term of address during the Revolution and the Reign of Terror.

Communication

Interpersonal, Presentational: Cooperative Groups

Have students work in groups to describe the pictures in **Activité 2** adding details, real or imagined, to tell a story about each one. Groups present their stories to the class.

Vocabulaire actif

emcl.com
WB 1–3
LA 1
Games

La Révolution française

1.2, 5.1

L'Ancien Régime: une référence au régime monarchique, du XVIème siècle au XVIIIème siècle, de la Renaissance à la Révolution, et ses institutions.

Les États généraux de l'Ancien Régime: des assemblées convoquées par le roi afin de traiter d'une crise politique ou financière; ils comprenaient le clergé, les aristocrates, les députés

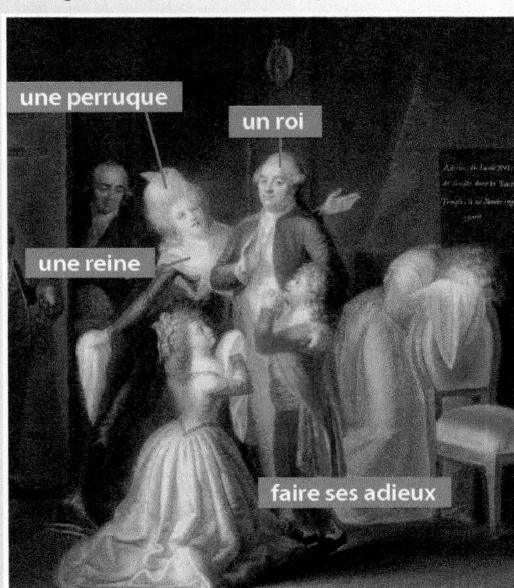

Pour la conversation

1.1,1.2

How do I express obligation?

> **Il était obligé de** faire venir les députés....
> *He was obligated to have the deputies come....*

How do express what I am made to do?

> **On te fait** étudier tout ça?
> *They make you study all that?*

Et si je voulais dire...?

la bourgeoisie	*middle class*
le dauphin	*king's successor*
la monarchie	*monarchy*
la noblesse	*nobility*
le royaume	*kingdom*
régner	*to rule, reign*
succéder à	*to succeed (king)*

Essential Instruction

1. Have students ask who, what, and where questions for the drawings in **La Révolution française**.
2. Have students listen to **La Révolution française** and **Pour la conversation**.
3. Define each term in **Et si je voulais dire...?** then ask students to provide the vocabulary word.
4. Students read **Activité 1** and answer the questions as a class.
5. Have students do the Interpersonal Activity above before doing **Activité 2**.

1 Nouveaux mots et expressions

 1.2, 5.1

Regardez les illustrations, puis répondez aux questions.

Caralie de Meaux

le président

le pape

Jean-Jacques

M. et MMe Delamain

le roi

les aristocrates

la reine

1. Qui est mort pendant la guerre?
2. Qui fait un discours au public français?
3. Que font M. et Mme Delamain?
4. Qui porte une perruque quand elle travaille?
5. Où habitent les aristocrates?
6. Qui écoute son public?
7. Où se réunit le clergé?
8. Qui aime danser?

2 Louis XVI

 1.1, 5.1

Lisez à haute voix les phrases suivantes en substituant les mots ou expressions en italique par des mots ou des expressions de vocabulaire appris dans cette leçon.

(1) *Le chef d'état et sa femme* sont emprisonnés en 1791. Louis XVI a (2) *présenté son point de vue* à l'Assemblée Nationale. Mais (3) *le clergé, les aristocrates, et les députés* n'ont pas aimé ce qu'il a dit. Le nouveau gouvernement (4) *l'a forcé* à passer ses derniers jours en prison. Condamné à (5) *être exécuté*, il (6) *a dit au revoir* à sa famille. Il (7) *a quitté la vie* brutalement sur la place de la Concorde.

Differentiated Learning

Accelerate
At the time of Louis XVI's execution, all of the gates of Paris were closed to block any outside intervention. Research who the revolutionaries feared and why. (Austrian forces, as Marie-Antoinette was a royal Austrian)

Decelerate
Have students make a drawing of **la cocarde** then explain what it is, who wore it, and why the choice of colors.

Multiple Intelligences

Musical-Rhythmic
Find songs of the revolution. Teach the class to sing **"Ça ira."**

Answers

1

1. Jean-Jacques
2. le président
3. Ils font leurs adieux à leur fils et leurs petits-enfants.
4. Caralie de Meaux
5. dans un château
6. le roi
7. au Vatican
8. la reine

1. le roi et la reine
2. donné un discours
3. les États généraux
4. l'a obligé
5. être guillotiné
6. a fait ses adieux
7. est mort

Connections

History
Have students make an **axe chronologique** of the events that lead to Louis XVI's death and the end of the monarchy. Encourage students to ask their social studies teachers for additional help.

Critical Thinking

Analysis
The king and queen were referred to as "**Le boulanger et sa femme.**" After the king died, the queen was called "**La veuve capet.**" Ask students why they referred to them that way.

Communication

Presentational, Interpersonal : Cooperative Groups
Have students work as a group to find the dramatic, gory, interesting facts about the guillotine, its inventor, victims, and locations and then present this short history along with illustrations.
Search words: **la conciergerie**

Answers

Script can be found in the front pages of the Annotated Teacher's Edition.

1. F
2. F
3. V
4. F
5. V
6. F

4

All answers B will vary.

1. A: Qui te fait lui rendre visite?
   B: ... me fait lui rendre visite.
2. A: Qui te fait faire le plein?
   B: ... me fait faire le plein.
3. A: Qui te fait étudier les maths?
   B: ... me fait étudier les maths.
4. A: Qui te fait sortir le weekend?
   B: ... me fait sortir le weekend.
5. A: Qui te fait faire la vaisselle?
   B: ... me fait faire la vaisselle.
6. A: Qui te fait tondre la pelouse?
   B: ... me fait tondre la pelouse.
7. A: Qui te fait nourrir ton chat ou ton chien?
   B: ... me fait nourrir mon chat ou mon chien.
8. A: Qui te fait t'habiller bien pour les fêtes?
   B: ... me fait m'habiller bien pour les fêtes.

5 *Answers will vary.*

Reference Desk

1. The **faire causative** (**faire** + infinitive) construction is used when one is not personally doing the action but is having it done: A builder builds a house but I am having the house built. **Je fais construire la maison**.
2. In a negative command object pronouns precede the form of **faire: Ne faites pas construire la maison par cet architect. Ne la faites pas construire par cet architecte.**
3. Examples of **faire** + infinitive that students might not know are: **faire bouillir l'eau** (*to boil water*) and **faire cuire** (*to cook*). See p. 456 for more uses of **faire**.
4. Making the verb reflexive has a sense of "getting yourself." For example, **Il s'est fait muter en France** means "He got himself transferred to France."

3 L'histoire de France

1.1, 1.2

Interpretive Communication

*Écrivez les numéros 1–6 sur votre papier. Écoutez Camille et sa mère parler de la Révolution française. Ensuite, indiquez si les phrases sont vraies (**V**) ou fausses (**F**).*

1. La mère de Camille a acheté un livre de maths à sa fille.
2. Camille est allée aux États généraux avec sa classe l'année dernière.
3. Camille a visité le château où le dernier roi et la dernière reine de France ont vécu.
4. Camille peut bien prononcer le verbe "guillotiner."
5. La mère de Camille est contente parce que sa fille s'est rappelée de l'histoire de la Révolution française.
6. Camille a remarqué les perruques que Marie-Antoinette portait.

4 Qui te fait...?

1.1, 1.2

Interpersonal Communication

À tour de rôle, demandez à votre partenaire qui lui fait faire les choses suivantes.

MODÈLE conduire au supermarché
A: **Qui te fait conduire au supermarché?**
B: **Ma mère me fait conduire au supermarché.**

1. lui rendre visite
2. faire le plein
3. étudier les maths
4. sortir le weekend
5. faire la vaisselle
6. tondre la pelouse
7. nourrir ton chat ou ton chien
8. s'habiller bien pour les fêtes

5 Questions personnelles

1.2, 1.3

Interpersonal Communication

Répondez aux questions.

1. Est-ce que tu aimerais vivre comme un aristocrate? Pourquoi, ou pourquoi pas?
2. Quels événements de l'histoire américaine est-ce que tu connais?
3. Quelle est ta réaction quand tes grands-parents font leurs adieux après une visite?
4. Qu'est-ce que tu es obligé de faire pendant le weekend?
5. Qui te fait faire des corvées à la maison?

Essential Instruction

1. Have students listen to the conversation in **Activité 4.** Tally how your students did to monitor their listening comprehension progress.
2. Explain **faire causative.** Do **Activité 5** with the class, putting each sentence on the board. Emphasize that **faire** is conjugated, and the second verb remains an infinitive.
3. Give students a few minutes to prepare their own answers for **Activité 6.** Ask individual students each of the questions before inviting them to interview each other.

Rencontres culturelles

emcl.com
WB 4

Une leçon d'histoire

   1.1, 1.2

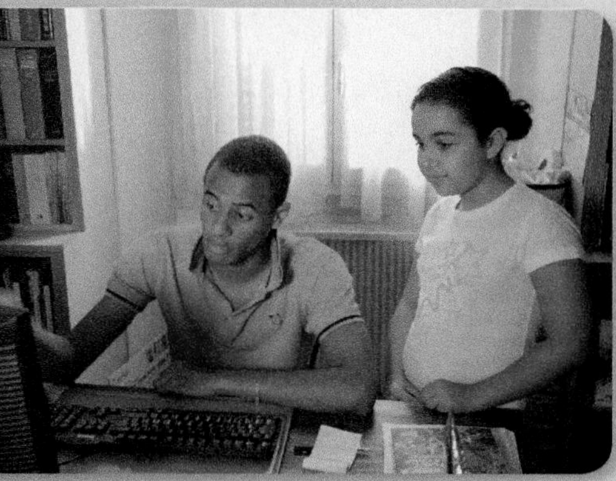

Karim travaille devant son ordinateur et sa petite sœur Aïcha vient lui parler.

Aïcha: C'est qui la dame avec une perruque?
Karim: D'abord, ce n'est pas une dame, c'est un monsieur.
Aïcha: C'est un monsieur? Qu'est-ce qu'il fait? Il s'est déguisé pour le Carnaval?
Karim: Non, il ne s'est pas déguisé! C'est le Roi de France, Aïcha.
Aïcha: Le Roi de France? Mais il est très vieux!
Karim: C'est Louis XVI, le dernier Roi de France avant la Révolution française.
Aïcha: Il fait un discours?
Karim: Là? Non, il assiste à l'ouverture des États généraux; il est obligé de faire venir les députés parce que le gouvernement n'avait plus d'argent. Là, il fait ses adieux à sa femme, Marie-Antoinette, et ses enfants.
Aïcha: Pourquoi? Il part en voyage?
Karim: Non, il va mourir. Il est condamné à être guillotiné.
Aïcha: Et après, qu'est-ce qui se passe?
Karim: Après, il y a Napoléon, il y a de nouveau des rois, de nouveau des révolutions, et puis il y a la République.
Aïcha: Et on te fait étudier tout ça?
Karim: Oui, jusqu'à la cinquième République.
Aïcha: Eh bien, moi, je sais toutes mes tables de multiplication!

6 Une leçon d'histoire

  1.2

Identifiez la personne décrite.

1. Cette personne porte une perruque.
2. Cette personne est mariée à Louis XVI.
3. Cette personne étudie l'histoire de France.
4. Cette personne sait toutes ses tables de multiplication.
5. Cette personne assiste à l'ouverture des États généraux.
6. Cette personne a été guillotinée.

RESOURCES

 **Dialogue Video**

 **Workbook 4**

Answers

1. Louis XVI
2. Marie-Antoinette
3. Karim
4. Aïcha
5. Louis XVI
6. Louis XVI

Communication

Interpersonal: Paired Practice

Have students practice **faire causative** in pairs. Prepare a worksheet for Student A with eight sentences expressing what certain people are doing: **Les voleurs parlent.** Prepare another worksheet for Student B, listing who is making the people on Student A's worksheet do the activity: **Les agents de police.** Student A reads the first sentence from the worksheet for Student B, who forms a new sentence using **faire** + infinitive: **Les agents de police font parler les voleurs.** Then ask Student A to replace **les voleurs** by a pronoun: **Les agents de police les font parler.**

Differentiated Learning

Adapt

Students make a list of all of the tasks their teachers, parents, and employers make them do, using the **faire causative.** For example, **"Mon professeur me fait parler français en classe."**

Decelerate

Work with students to skim and scan **Une leçon d'histoire.** Ask them to highlight and identify the historical figures and terms discussed in the conversation. Read the conversation together, helping students to understand difficult lines or passages. Ask them to read the conversation again before answering the questions in **Activité 6.**

Answers

Extension

Possible answer:
Parce que c'était un combattant pour la liberté, et il a été reconnu récemment.

Reference Desk

1. **On est dans l'actualité** means that we are talking about something that is happening now.
2. Aimé Césaire (1913–2008) was a French poet, author, and former mayor of Fort-de-France, Martinique. He is associated with the **la négritude**, a movement that strives to give young black people a sense of positive racial identity and pride. His writing has surrealistic traits.
3. **Le Panthéon**, located on the Left Bank, was originally built as a church dedicated to St. Genevieve, the patron of Paris. It now serves as a secular mausoleum containing the remains of distinguished French citizens.

Culture

Products: Information

The wig became popular during the reign of Louis XIII. This tradition continued into the 18th century. Men wore wigs which they powdered white. Women added tresses to their hair, weighted down with pomades and powders. This tradition was a symbol of aristocratic decadence and died out with the French Revolution. The romantics of the 19th century preferred natural, free-flowing hair.

Extension **La grande scène de l'histoire**  1.1, 1.2

Quatre élèves discutent à propos du choix d'un personnage historique à présenter en classe d'histoire.

Chloé:	D'abord, qu'est-ce qu'on veut faire passer comme message?
Amidou:	Oui, Chloé a raison, on ne va pas lancer des noms.
Samuel:	Il faut que le personnage ait un rapport avec la liberté....
Guillaume:	Une figure de combattant?
Amidou:	Oui, mais combattant de quoi?
Samuel:	Je ne sais pas, quelqu'un qui revendique la dignité pour son peuple, le respect de son identité!
Guillaume:	Et si on prenait Aimé Césaire?
Amidou:	Poète, résistant, homme politique....
Samuel:	Noir, martiniquais....
Chloé:	Et puis ça tombe bien, il vient d'entrer au Panthéon... on est dans l'actualité.
Amidou:	C'est lui qui a invité les autres peuples à "laisser entrez les peuples noirs sur la grande scène de l'Histoire."
Chloé:	Eh bien voilà, ça fait notre titre.

Extension Pour quelles raisons les élèves ont-ils choisi Aimé Césaire pour leur projet d'histoire?

1.3

Essential Instruction

1. Before showing the video, ask students to describe the people in the picture. Who are they and what are they doing?
2. Play the video. Have students watch with books closed. Ask general comprehension questions.
3. Have students listen to the dialogue and follow in their books.
4. As a class activity, have individual students read and answer the questions in **Activité 7**.
5. Ask students if they know of Aimé Césaire. What is the importance of **le Panthéon**?
6. Have students read the roles of the four speakers in **Extension**.
7. Provide students a short biography of Aimé Césaire to read in class. Have them work in pairs to answer the **Extension** question.
8. Discuss the poet and have the students read a sampling of his most famous poem, "**Cahier d'un retour au pays natal**."

Points de départ

emcl.com
WB 5

Comment le passé influence-t-il le présent?

Portrait de Louis XVI

1.2, 3.1

Louis XVI, roi de France.

Louis XVI (1754–1791) est le dernier Roi de France avant la Révolution française. Il succède à Louis XV. Conscient de l'état du Royaume, Louis XVI s'entoure de* personnalités réformatrices, en particulier en matière financière et économique. Mais, il s'oppose à la noblesse* qui ne veut pas de réformes ou renoncer à certains de ses privilèges.

C'est Louis XVI qui décide de soutenir la guerre d'indépendance américaine* pendant son règne et envoie le général La Fayette. La victoire des armées américaines appuyées* par les troupes royales aboutit* à la signature du traité de Versailles en 1783.

La convocation des États généraux (1789) pour résoudre la crise économique déclenche* la Révolution. Méfiant* pourtant* à l'égard de* la noblesse, Louis XVI se montre incapable d'accepter une évolution de la monarchie absolue vers une monarchie constitutionnelle. Il refuse de signer l'abolition des privilèges et la Déclaration des Droits de l'Homme. Prisonnier du peuple qui le ramène* de Versailles à Paris (1789) pour mieux le contrôler, sa fuite manquée* à Varennes (1791) et la menace* des armées royales européennes conduisent Louis XVI à la prison du Temple (1792). Déclaré "coupable de conspiration contre la sûreté* de l'État", il est guillotiné le 21 janvier 1793 sur l'actuelle place de la Concorde.

Search words: chronologie des rois de france, histoire de France, rois de France

s'entoure de *surrounds himself with;* **noblesse** *nobility;* **guerre d'indépendance américaine** *American Revolution;* **appuyées** *backed up;* **aboutit** *leads to;* **déclenche** *prompts;* **Méfiant** *suspicious;* **pourtant** *though;* **à l'égard de** *regarding;* **ramène** *brings back;* **fuite manquée** *failed escape;* **menace** *threat;* **sureté** *security*

1776
Déclaration d'indépendance des États-Unis

1781

Le marquis de Lafayette aide l'armée américaine à gagner la bataille de Yorktown

1783
Traité de Paris entre les États-Unis et la Grande-Bretagne

1789
Convocation des États-généraux

Prise de la Bastille, début de la Révolution française

Déclaration des droits de l'homme et du citoyen

1792

Louis XVI est mis en prison.

1793

Louis XVI est guillotiné.

Marie-Antoinette est guillotinée.

Produits

Jacques Prévert a écrit un poème **"Les belles familles"** sur les rois de France qui avaient le même prénom. Lisez-le en ligne et répondez à la question. Est-ce que le père et le fils de Louis XVI s'appelaient aussi Louis?

1.2, 2.1, 2.2

COMPARAISONS

Quels mots anglais, dérivés de *règne* et *regnum* (*reign*), ont plus ou moins le même sens?

4.1

RESOURCES

Workbook 5

Differentiated Learning

Accelerate
Aimé Césaire created the term **la négritude**. Have students define it and explain how it relates to the quotation in the reading.

Decelerate
Have students review the life and career of Aimé Césaire to justify why this Martiniquais merits a commemorative plaque placed in the Pantheon. Cite specific examples of achievements in his life.

Learning Styles

Visual Learners
Encourage students to find photos of Aimé Césaire and **le Panthéon** so that they can connect the images to the information about them.

Critical Thinking

Analysis

1. Why might one say that the American Revolution set the stage for the French Revolution? Explain.
2. Why did Louis XVI send financial and military support to the colonies? (To defeat France's enemy, England)
3. The Marquis de LaFayette played a major role in the American and French Revolutions. Explain with examples.
4. Louis XV led a lavish life style. He said **"Après moi, le déluge."** How did this attitude and life style affect the lives of Louis XVI and Marie-Antoinette?

Connections

Literature

Charles Dickens wrote *A Tale of Two Cities* which is a love story and a fictionalized historical account of the French Revolution. Consider playing excerpts of one of the versions of the movie to whet the students' appetite to read the entire novel. Clips are available online.

C'est en France qu'est née **la guillotine.** Le Docteur Guillotin voulait éviter la souffrance (*suffering*) pendant les exécutions. Pendant la Révolution, les exécutions par guillotine ont eu lieu sur la place de la Révolution (maintenant la place de la Concorde). C'est en 1977 qu'a eu lieu la dernière exécution par guillotine en France. **1.2, 2.2**

La guillotine.

COMPARAISONS

Les Français ont mis fin à la peine de mort (*capital punishment*) en 1981. Faites une liste de dix pays. Combien d'entre eux continuent d'appliquer la peine de mort? Et les États-Unis?

3.2, 4.2

Portrait de Marie-Antoinette

1.2, 3.1

Archiduchesse d'Autriche, fille de Marie-Thérèse d'Autriche et de l'Empereur François 1er, Marie-Antoinette (1755–1793) devient Reine de France en 1770 quand elle épouse Louis XVI. Elle aura quatre enfants dont le futur Louis XVII qui disparut dans des conditions mystérieuses pendant la Révolution.

De Marie-Antoinette, on a gardé la réputation d'une reine légère*, dépensière*, mêlée à* des intrigues politiques et amoureuses et à des affaires frauduleuses (l'affaire du collier de la Reine). Conservatrice, elle est peu favorable à l'Esprit des Lumières* et elle influence beaucoup le Roi dans son refus d'une évolution de la monarchie. Elle persuade le Roi de s'en remettre à une intervention des armées des Cours étrangères pour sauver le Royauté. Honnie* et calomniée*, celle qu'on surnomme alors "l'Autrichienne" est exécutée le 16 octobre 1793.

Marie Antoinette avant son exécution.

Search words: reines de france, marie-antoinette

légère *careless;* **dépensière** *quelqu'un qui dépense trop;* **mêlée** *involved in;* **Esprit des Lumières** *Ideas of the Age of Enlightenment;* **Honnie** *held in contempt;* **calomniée** *slandered*

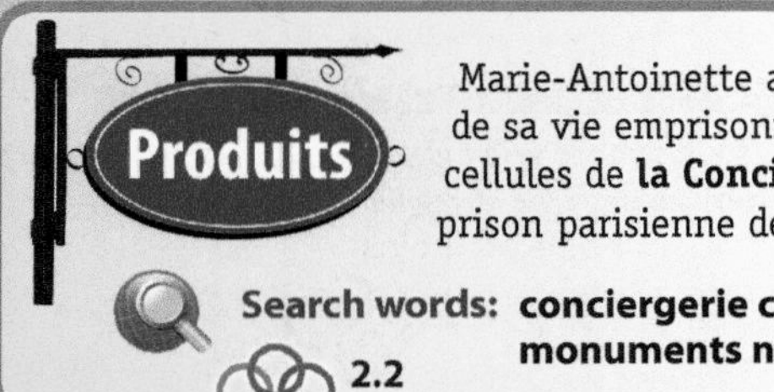

Marie-Antoinette a passé la fin de sa vie emprisonnée dans deux cellules de **la Conciergerie**, une prison parisienne de 1391 à 1914.

Search words: conciergerie centre des monuments nationaux

2.2

Aujourd'hui, la Conciergerie fait partie du palais de justice de Paris.

Essential Instruction

1. Have students make a timeline of the events from the American War for Independence to the death of Marie-Antoinette as featured in the textbook, if this has not yet been done.
2. Have them read and compare the portraits of the king with that of the queen and add additional dates to their timeline.
3. Ask students to read the poem **"Les belles familles"** and discuss the question.

Les États généraux

1.2, 3.1

Avant la Révolution française, la population était divisée en trois ordres: le clergé (qui avait le plus grand pouvoir), la noblesse (qui avait un peu moins de pouvoir), et le Tiers État* (qui avait un pouvoir minime). Le Tiers État est représenté par de députés aux états-généraux; une de leurs fonctions était de voter l'impôt. La dernière convocation des États généraux a eu lieu en 1789. Louis XVI les a invités en leur disant:

> "De par le Roi,
> Notre aimé et féal*.
> Nous avons besoin du concours de nos fidèles sujets* pour Nous aider à surmonter* toutes les difficultés où Nous Nous trouvons relativement à l'état de Nos finances, et pour établir*, suivant Nos vœux*, un ordre constant et invariable dans toutes les parties du gouvernement qui intéressent le bonheur* de Nos sujets et la prospérité de Notre royaume*...."

C'était la dernière convocation des États généraux. Elle représentait une révolution juridique: finalement, le groupe s'est proclamé Assemblée nationale et il n'y avait plus de rôle pour le roi.

Search words: états généraux de l'ancien régime

Tiers État *commoners;* **féal** *faithful (king);* **fidèles sujets** *faithful subjects;* **surmonter** *to overcome;* **établir** *establish;* **vœux** *wishes;* **bonheur** *happiness;* **royaume** *kingdom*

La *Déclaration des Droits de l'homme et du citoyen*

1.2, 3.1

Ayant aidé les Américains pendant la Révolution américaine, les Français étaient conscients de la *Déclaration d'indépendance des États-Unis* de 1776 et elle a influencé la *Déclaration des Droits de l'homme et du citoyen* qu'on a rédigée 13 ans plus tard. Elle énonce* des droits naturels individuels et collectifs du peuple français.

énonce *sets forth*

Produits

La ***Déclaration des Droits de la femme et de la citoyenne***, écrite par la féministe Olympe de Gouges en 1791, avait comme but d'appliquer les droits des hommes aux femmes. Malgré ses efforts vaillants pour faire accepter sa *Déclaration*, tout le monde n'était pas d'accord, et l'Assemblé a voté contre. Accusée d'être l'auteur d'une affiche offensive contre le gouvernement, elle a été guillotinée en 1793.

Search words: olympe de gouges

1.2, 2.2

Expansion

Assign students the following people and terms to augment their study of the French Revolution: **Charlotte Corday**, **La Fuite à Varennes**, **Robespierre**, **Marat**, **Danton**, **Les Girondins**, **la Tour Bonbec**, **L'Affaire du Collier**. Ask students to present a brief summary to the class with illustrations and anecdotes.

Game

Qui suis-je?

Play this game to review vocabulary and the lives of the famous people studied to date. Put students in small groups. Have each student draw a name from these choices: LaFayette, Dr. Guillotin, Jacques Prévert, Aimé Césaire, la Fontaine, Georges Seurat, to name a few. Each student goes in front of the rest of the group to answer **imparfait** and **passé composé** questions from members who try to discover his or her identity. The student in front of the group answers each question with a complete sentence, using the **imparfait** or the **passé composé**. The responders may be evasive but must be honest. After the identity of the first student is guessed, the second student goes in front of the group to answer questions, and so on.

Differentiated Learning

Expand

It is important to move students from the cliché of Marie-Antoinette as the one-dimensional, light-hearted, air-headed queen to seeing her personal evolution into a thoughtful, loving wife, mother, and sister. To do this, read "**La Dernière lettre de la Reine Marie-Antoinette**" with the class. It was written shortly before her execution.

Answers

7

1. 1770: Marie-Antoinette devient Reine de France.; 1754: naissance de Louis XVI; 1783: signature du traité de Versailles; 1789: convocation des États généraux; 1791: Louis XVI essaie de fuir à Vincennes.; 1792: Louis XVI est conduit à la prison du Temple.; 1793: Louis XVI est guillotiné le 21 janvier.; Marie-Antoinette est guillotinée le 16 octobre.
2. *Paragraphs will vary.*
3. *Possible answers*: Elle fait construire le Hameau de la Reine.; Elle ranime la mode et l'éclat à Paris avec ses spectacles et dîners.; Elle fait aménager des petits appartements; Elle crée un petit café pour les seigneurs et dames qui visitent le Palais; Elle invente un nouveau style de vie.; Elle accorde une protection aux musiciens.
4. *Answers will vary.*
5. *Answers will vary.*
6. *Answers will vary.*
7. *Possible answer*: Similarities: Both constitutions are similarly structured, with an introduction followed by a number of articles; Differences: The French declaration is narrated in the third person, claiming to report the words of the people of France. The American declaration is narrated in the first person, "We", without specifying to whom the "We" is referring.
8. Jasmine is the emblem of Tunisia. It is a white, pure and delicate flower, and symbolizes kindness and tolerance.

À discuter

Answers will vary.

Communication

Interpersonal: Cooperative Groups

Students work in groups to create an original crossword puzzle in French plus answer key. Have them focus on the people, events, and documents of the time of the French Revolution. Check puzzles for accuracy and have students correct errors. Groups exchange puzzles and solve them.
Search words: templates for crossword puzzles.

La Francophonie: Révolution

1.2

En Tunisie

En 2010–11, le peuple tunisien s'est révolté et a renversé* l'homme à la tête du régime, le Président Ben Ali. La Tunisie est ainsi devenue une démocratie en tenant ses premières élections libres en Octobre 2011. Cette révolution s'appelle la "révolution de jasmin." Essentiellement une révolution non-violente, la Révolution de jasmin a influencé les peuples dans d'autres pays arabes à se révolter aussi.

a renversé *overthrew*

7 Activités culturelles

1.3, 3.1, 3.2

Faites les activités suivantes.

1. Faites un axe chronologique de la vie de Louis XVI et Marie-Antoinette, indiquant à quoi correspondent ces dates: 1754, 1770, 1783, 1789, 1791, 1792, 1793.
2. L'histoire de La Fayette marque le début des relations amicales entre les États-Unis et la France. Faites des recherches sur cette amitié et présentez une petite histoire à la classe.

Search words: relations france états-unis, histoire des relations franco-américaines

3. Recherchez les modifications apportées par Marie-Antoinette à Versailles.
4. Marie-Antoinette est un personnage qui fascine le cinéma: faites des recherches sur les films français et américains où la reine apparaît. Choisissez en ligne un extrait à montrer à la classe.
5. Trouvez des tableaux de Marie-Antoinette et écrivez des légendes en-dessous qui décrivent sa vie.

Search words: élisabeth vigée le brun

6. Trouvez le tableau *Le Serment du Jeu de paume* par Jacques-Louis David en ligne et décrivez-le. Ou cherchez une autre image de la Révolution française, par exemple, l'exécution de Louis XVI ou la Prise de la Bastille, et décrivez-la.

Search words: serment du jeu de paume jacques-louis david, histoire-image

7. Faites un organigramme Venn sur la *Déclaration des Droits de l'homme et du citoyen* et la *Déclaration d'indépendance des États-Unis*. En quoi est le début du document français similaire et différent du début de la déclaration des droits américaine?
8. Recherchez pourquoi on appelle la révolution en Tunisie la Révolution de "jasmin."

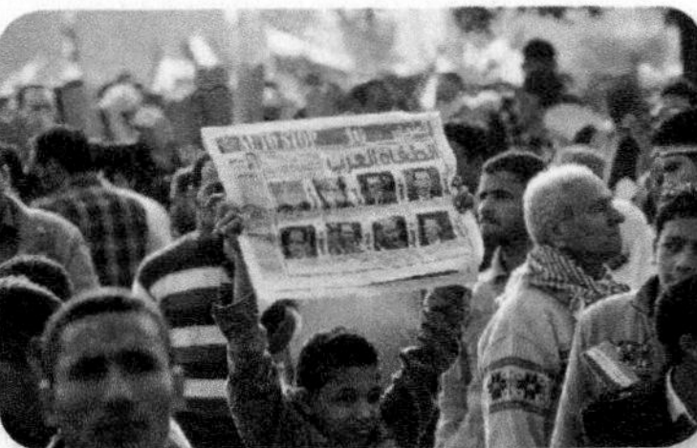

Pendant la Révolution de Jasmin.

À discuter

La Révolution française, était-elle inévitable, selon vous? Pourquoi, ou pourquoi pas?

Essential Instruction

1. Divide the class into four groups of varying abilities. Have students create a visual on a poster board of either **Les États généraux**, **La Déclaration des Droits de l'homme et du citoyen**, **La Déclaration des Droits de la femme et de la citoyenne**, or **En Tunisie.**
2. The visual should represent the group's subject symbolically and through words. Ask students to do additional research to add details to their visual. They present to the class.
3. In new groups, have students do one of the four tasks in **Activité 7**, then share their work with the class.
4. Have students write a one-sentence summary of each of the **Considérant** clauses from **Préambule.**
5. As a class discuss whether this document, idealistic as it is, has any "teeth" to enforce these tenets.
6. Have students do both activities in **Activité 8.**

Du côté des médias  1.2

Interpretive Communication

Lisez le préambule de la Déclaration universelle des droits de l'homme des Nations Unies.

Préambule

Considérant que la reconnaissance de la dignité inhérente à tous les membres de la famille humaine et de leurs droits égaux et inaliénables constitue le fondement de la liberté, de la justice et de la paix dans le monde.

Considérant que la méconnaissance et le mépris des droits de l'homme ont conduit à des actes de barbarie qui révoltent la conscience de l'humanité et que l'avènement d'un monde où les êtres humains seront libres de parler et de croire, libérés de la terreur et de la misère, a été proclamé comme la plus haute aspiration de l'homme.

Considérant qu'il est essentiel que les droits de l'homme soient protégés par un régime de droit pour que l'homme ne soit pas contraint, en suprême recours, à la révolte contre la tyrannie et l'oppression.

Considérant qu'il est essentiel d'encourager le développement de relations amicales entre nations.

Considérant que dans la Charte les peuples des Nations Unies ont proclamé à nouveau leur foi dans les droits fondamentaux de l'homme, dans la dignité et la valeur de la personne humaine, dans l'égalité des droits des hommes et des femmes, et qu'ils se sont déclarés résolus à favoriser le progrès social et à instaurer de meilleures conditions de vie dans une liberté plus grande.

Considérant que les Etats Membres se sont engagés à assurer, en coopération avec l'Organisation des Nations Unies, le respect universel et effectif des droits de l'homme et des libertés fondamentales.

Considérant qu'une conception commune de ces droits et libertés est de la plus haute importance pour remplir pleinement cet engagement.

8 La *Déclaration universelle des droits de l'homme* des Nations Unies

 1.3, 3.2

Faites les activités suivantes.

1. Faites un "word cloud" en soulevant les mots les plus importants de ce document.
2. Recherchez comment les Nations Unies font la promotion des droits de l'homme actuellement. Présentez un exemple à la classe.

 **Search words: l'onu et les droits de l'homme**

Answers

1. *Possible answer:* dignité, famille humaine, droits égaux, liberté, justice, paix, barbarie, conscience, libre, terreur, misère, protégés, révolte, tyrannie, oppression, essentiel, relations amicales, foi, droits fondamentaux, valeur, égalité, hommes, femmes, progrès social, meilleures, respect universel, libertés fondamentales, conception commune
2. *Presentations will vary.*

Reference Desk

The United Nations is an international organization founded in 1945. Its mission is to keep peace throughout the world; encourage friendly relations among member countries; work to eliminate hunger, disease and illiteracy; and be the harmonizing center to achieve these goals. There are currently 193 member states. The six official languages are: Arabic, Chinese, English, French, Russian, and Spanish.

Communication

Presentational: Cooperative Groups

In triads, students take a side to debate, as if in court. Should Marie-Antoinette be exiled, acquitted, or executed? Select one representative from each point of view to argue before the class who plays the jury. A vote to determine her fate follows the arguments.

Differentiated Learning

Accelerate

Have students research **la Révolution française** in more depth to lead the class in answering the question in **À discuter**.

Special Needs Students

Linguistically Challenged

Encourage students to read in English about the documents of the French Revolution to gain additional background. This reading will help them understand the passages in French.

Dyslexia

Give these students a study guide with key words to help them focus on the most important features of the readings.

RESOURCES

 **Workbook 6–7**

 **Drill & Practice Games**

Answers

1. M. Delattre fait ses adieux à sa femme.
2. Les enfants font semblant d'être des super-héros.
3. Les pilotes font grève.
4. Tu fais ta valise.
5. Saleh et moi faisons du ski de fond.
6. Coralie et Amadou font de la planche à voile.
7. Salim fait don de 10 euros.
8. Pierre et ses copains font partie d'un groupe de musiciens.

Reference Desk

1. Consider having students brainstorm categories for **faire** expressions they know, for example, weather, sports, household chores, pastimes, and miscellaneous. Have them write the category headings and list all of the **faire** expressions under the appropriate heading. In their miscellaneous category students might include expressions such as **faire du baby-sitting**, **faire le tour**, and **faire les devoirs**.
2. The "rules" governing the **imparfait** and the **passé composé** are guidelines. Context dictates tense selection. Words such as **d'habitude**, **de temps en temps**, and **souvent** are several of the cues for the **imparfait**. Expressions indicating a specific time, for example, **la semaine passé**, **hier**, and **pendant les vacances** often cue the **passé composé**.

Structure de la langue

emcl.com
WB 6–7
Games

Révision: Expressions with *faire*  1.1

The verb **faire** is one of the most frequently used verbs in French.

Tu **fais** un projet en histoire?	*Are you doing a history project?*

Faire is called a "building block" verb because it is used to form so many expressions in French. Some of the most common expressions with **faire** deal with various activities, the weather, shopping, and traveling. Here are some examples where **faire** is used in French but a different verb is used in English.

Louis XVI ne **faisait** pas **attention** aux besoins du peuple de la France.	*Louis XVI was not paying attention to the needs of the people of France.*
Louis XVI a **fait ses adieux** à sa famille.	*Louis XVI said good-bye to his family.*
C'était en janvier que Louis XVI est mort; il **faisait froid**.	*It was in January that Louis XVI died. It was cold.*

9 Qu'est-ce qu'ils font?  1.1

Dites ce que tout le monde fait en choisissant une expression de la liste.

faire semblant d'être un super-héros | faire grève | faire de la planche à voile | faire ta valise | faire ses adieux à sa femme | faire partie d'un groupe de musiciens | faire du ski de fond | faire don de 10 euros

1. M. Delattre

2. les enfants
3. les pilotes

4. tu

5. Saleh et moi

6. Coralie et Amadou

7. Salim

8. Pierre et ses copains

Essential Instruction

1. Use the chart **Révision: Expressions with faire** to launch a review of the verb.
2. Give students time to do **Activité 9** then correct the exercise in class.
3. Before assigning **Activité 10** ask why the **passé composé** was used in the first set of examples and the **imparfait** in the second. Review the differences in usage.
4. Have students write the questions for this exercise. Circulate to correct their work.
5. Ask students to generate other questions, using the same format, that they could ask someone using these two tenses. They can then use these questions to interview a partner.

10 Votre passé

 1.1

Interpersonal Communication

À tour de rôle, demandez à votre partenaire s'il ou elle a fait ou faisait les activités suivantes. Attention: il faut utiliser le ***passé composé*** *ou* ***l'imparfait****.*

MODÈLE faire du ski alpin/pendant les vacances d'hiver
A: **As-tu fait du ski pendant les vacances d'hiver?**
B: **Oui, j'ai fait du ski pendant les vacances d'hiver.**
ou
Non, je n'ai pas fait de ski pendant les vacances d'hiver.

faire du snowboard/quand tu avais dix ans
A: **Faisais-tu du snowboard quand tu avais dix ans?**
B: **Oui, je faisais du snowboard quand j'avais dix ans.**
ou
Non, je ne faisais pas de snowboard quand j'avais dix ans.

1. faire ton lit/quand tu avais cinq ans
2. faire la lessive/le weekend dernier
3. faire du scooter des mers/l'été dernier
4. faire un tour de montagnes russes/quand tu es allé(e) au parc d'attractions
5. faire de la gym/quand tu étais enfant
6. faire du shopping/pendant ton voyage
7. faire du patinage artistique/quand tu étais jeune

Faire + infinitive 1.2

emcl.com
WB 8–9
LA 2
Games

Differentiated Learning

Accelerate

Have students make an extended list of **faire** idioms to expand their vocabulary. Ask them to teach the class these expressions using gestures or memory aids.

Decelerate

The verb **faire** and its idioms are not difficult to learn. Consider giving your low-ability students a quiz so that they are successful. It should give "**un coup de pouce**" to their average.

Multiple Intelligences

Visual-Spatial

1. Ask students to draw the flag of the United Nations. Have them explain the significance of the colors and the specific map of the world the organization chose for the flag.
2. Explain where the United Nations is located in New York. Who designed the building? How is it organized? What is the name of our current ambassador?

RESOURCES

 **Workbook 8–9**

 **Listening Activity 2**

 **Drill & Practice Games**

Answers

 10

1. A: Faisais-tu ton lit quand tu avais cinq ans?
   B: Oui, je faisais mon lit quand j'avais cinq ans. /Non, je ne faisais pas mon lit....
2. A: As-tu fait la lessive le weekend dernier?
   B: Oui, j'ai fait la lessive le weekend dernier./Non, je n'ai pas fait la lessive ....
3. A: As-tu fait du scooter des mers l'été dernier?
   B: Oui, j'ai fait du scooter des mers l'été dernier./Non, je n'ai pas fait de scooter ....
4. A: As-tu fait un tour de montagnes russes quand tu es allé(e) au parc d'attractions?
   B: Oui, j'ai fait un tour de montagnes russes quand je suis allé(e) au parc d'attractions./ Non, je n'ai pas fait un tour ....
5. A: Faisais-tu de la gym quand tu étais enfant?
   B: Oui, je faisais de la gym quand j'étais enfant./ Non, je ne faisais pas de gym ....
6. A: As-tu fait du shopping pendant ton voyage?
   B: Oui, je j'ai fait du shopping pendant mon voyage./Non, je n'ai pas fait de shopping ....
7. A: Faisais-tu du patinage artistique quand tu étais jeune?
   B: Oui, je faisais du patinage artistique quand j'étais jeune./ Non, je ne faisais pas de patinage....

Reference Desk

To express who does an action in a causative construction, use **par** or **à** plus a noun or pronoun, for example, **Nous avons fait nettoyer le garage par les enfants.** The **par** or **à** phrase is replaced by an indirect object pronoun, for example, **Nous leur avons fait nettoyer le garage.**

Communication

Interpersonal: Paired Practice

To practice **faire** expressions in various tenses give pairs of students a note card with a sentence and a tense in parentheses, for example, **Claude ferait enregistrer ses bagages.** (**passé composé**) Student A reads the first sentence to Student B, who identifies the tense used, (conditional), and then changes the sentence to the tense in parentheses, for example **Claude a fait enregistrer ses bagages.** Partners exchange their card for a different one and switch roles. Pairs continue until they have practiced a sentence in each of the tenses being reviewed or until they have practiced with all of the cards.

To express the idea of having someone do something or having something done, use a form of the verb **faire** followed by an infinitive. Notice the differences in the following two sentences.

Jean **fait** une omelette.	*Jean makes an omelette.*
La reine **fait faire** une omelette.	*The queen has an omelette made (for herself).*

In the first sentence, Jean makes an omelet himself. In the second sentence, the queen has an omelet made for her by someone else (one of her cooks).

The form of **faire** can be in any tense.

M. Lebrun **a fait enregistrer** ses bagages.	*M. Lebrun had his luggage checked.*

When object pronouns are used, they precede the form of **faire.** There is no agreement between the past participle **fait** and a preceding direct object pronoun.

Les Français ont **fait guillotine**r Marie-Antoinette?	*Did the French (people) have Marie-Antoinette guillotined?*
Oui, ils **l'ont fait** guillotiner.	*Yes, they had her guillotined.*
Les députés des États généraux? Louis XVI **les a fait** venir.	*The deputies of the Estates General? Louis XVI made them come.*

In an affirmative command, object pronouns are attached with hyphens to the form of **faire.**

Faites-le faire un discours!	*Have him make a speech!*

COMPARAISONS

Explain how in French and English people say who does the action in sentences that use **faire + infinitif**.

Mme Charrier fait nettoyer le garage **par** ses enfants.
Mrs. Charrier has the garage cleaned **by** her children.

4.1

COMPARAISONS: In both French and English, the preposition **par** or "by" is used to indicate who does the action.

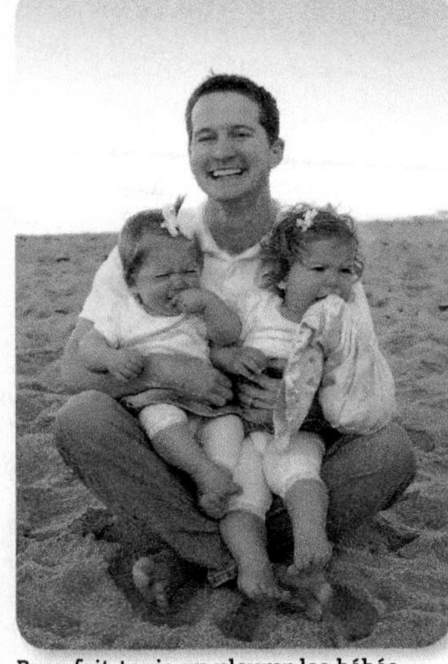
Papa fait toujours pleurer les bébés.

Essential Instruction

1. Review **faire causatif** using the explanation on p. 456 and referencing the exercise on p. 457.
2. Have students tell you what they have other people do for them; write the sentences on the board.
3. Ask them to translate the sentences to note that we usually use the verbs "have" or "make" in English.
4. Have students do **Activité 11** orally. Ask students for more examples of what travel arrangements M. Poux did for himself, and what his secretary organized for him.
5. To expand **Activité 11**, ask open-ended questions about M. Poux and his assistant. What is M. Poux's first name? How old is he? What is his assistant's name? Where is he going? What does he do for a living? What is in his suitcase? Accept silly answers as long as they are logical extensions of the questions. Ask a student to look up **un poux** or **un pou.**

11 Voyage d'affaires

M. Poux est un homme d'affaires important qui voyage beaucoup avec son assistante. Il fait une liste pour préparer son prochain voyage. D'après sa liste, est-ce qu'il fait les choses indiquées lui-même ou est-ce qu'il les fait faire par son assistante?

- *téléphoner à ma femme*
- *retirer de l'argent du distributeur*
- *trouver mon passeport*
- *acheter des billets de théâtre*
- *écrire mon discours*

- *réserver une chambre*
- *louer une voiture à Paris*
- *enregistrer mes bagages*
- *faire ma valise*
- *acheter les billets d'avion*

M. Poux trouve son passeport.

M. Poux fait louer une voiture à Paris.

1. 

2. 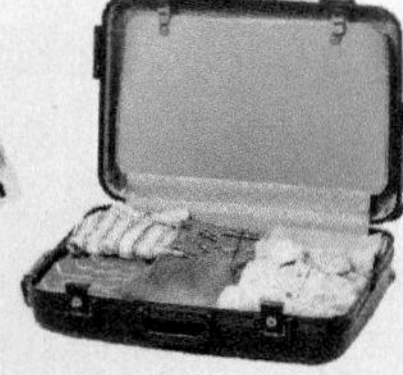

3. 

4. 

5. 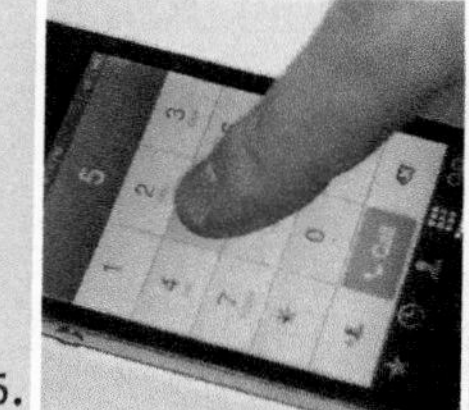

6. 

7. 

8. 

Answers

11

1. M. Poux fait acheter les billets d'avion.
2. M. Poux fait faire sa valise.
3. M. Poux achète des billets de théâtre.
4. M. Poux fait réserver une chambre.
5. M. Poux téléphone à sa femme.
6. M. Poux retire de l'argent au distributeur.
7. M. Poux fait enregistrer ses bagages.
8. M. Poux écrit son discours.

Communication

Interpersonal: Paired Practice

Have students write a role-play between M. Poux's assistant (from p. 457) and the agent at Avis France. In the dialogue, include a discussion of the types of cars available, rates, promotions, and options with and without a chauffeur. The assistant is very choosy and asks a lot of questions before reserving the car. This activity could be expanded to reserving airline tickets, booking a hotel, or making business-dinner reservations in a fine restaurant. Have students perform the role-play for the class.

Differentiated Learning

Decelerate

For extra practice create a handout of sentences, some using **faire** + infinitive, others showing the subject doing the action, for example, **Mme DuRose a fait arroser son jardin pendant qu'elle était en vacances. Mme DuRose arrose son jardin tous les matins.** Ask students to identify who is doing the action and to translate the sentences into English.

Adapt

Have students imagine they are rich and famous, then write at least ten things that they used to do, but now have done by others. **Quand j'avais vingt ans, je lavais la voiture une fois par mois. Maintenant je fais laver la voiture tous les jours par Jeeves.**

Answers

12

1. M. Legrand fait installer le four.
2. Maman et moi faisons poser le papier peint.
3. Les Dufour font repeindre la salle à manger.
4. Je fais planter des fleurs sur le balcon.
5. Nadine et Fatima font réparer le frigo.
6. Bruno et toi faites mettre le nouveau canapé dans le séjour.

13

1. B
2. A
3. D
4. E
5. C
6. F

Expansion

1. Ask small groups to add as many adjectives that end in **eux/euse, t/e,** etc. that they recall.
2. Consider a dictation inspired by the grammar exercises for **faire.** Read each sentence three times, first at natural speed, next more slowly giving students time to write, finally at normal speed so students can edit. Correct as a group. Post the corrected version or have volunteers write the sentences on the board.

12 L'immeuble

1.3

Le Clos Bellini a de nouveaux résidents qui font embellir leurs appartements par des bricoleurs professionnels. Dites ce qu'ils font.

MODÈLE tu/accrocher des peintures
Tu fais accrocher des peintures.

1. M. Legrand/installer le four
2. maman et moi/poser le papier peint dans le salon
3. les Dufour/repeindre la salle à manger
4. je/planter des fleurs sur le balcon
5. Nadine et Fatima/réparer le frigo
6. Bruno et toi/mettre le nouveau canapé dans le séjour

Les Dupré font réparer l'évier.

Communiquez!

13 Louis XVI et Marie-Antoinette

1.1, 1.2

Interpretive Communication

Écrivez les numéros 1–6 sur votre papier. Écoutez les phrases, et associez-les à la bonne illustration.

Essential Instruction

1. Students do **Activité 12** orally and then as a written exercise.
2. Play **Activité 13**, then have students talk about each illustration.
3. Have students choose one of the **A vous la parole** tasks.
4. For **Activité 14** have students watch clips of a **bateau mouche** tour. Students can focus on another monument along the Seine to vary the presentations, for example, **Notre-Dame**, **Le Musée d'Orsay**, **Le Louvre**, or the replica of the Statue of Liberty.
5. **Activité 15** will appeal to students interested in history and people committed to social causes.
6. For **Activité 16**, have students use the **Déclaration des Droits de l'homme** or the **Préambule** of the United Nations as a template.

À vous la parole

14 La Conciergerie

1.1, 3.2, 5.1

Interpretive/Presentational Communication

Vous êtes un nouveau guide pour une compagnie de bateaux-mouches à Paris. C'est à vous de développer le texte pour décrire la Conciergerie quand le bateau passe devant le monument et les touristes vous écoutent. Faites des recherches sur la Conciergerie et écrivez un texte qui décrive l'extérieur et explique ce qu'il y a à voir à l'intérieur. Votre gérante (*manager*) voudrait que vous parliez pendant 90 secondes. Finalement, enregistrez ou filmez votre présentation.

Search words: **conciergerie paris, conciergerie centre des monuments nationaux**

Communiquez!

15 La grande scène de l'histoire

1.3, 3.2, 5.1

Interpretive/Presentational Communication

D'abord, lisez le dialogue "La grande scène de l'histoire" (*Extension*) dans lequel des élèves français cherchent un personnage historique à présenter. Ensuite, choisissez une catégorie qui vous intéresse: l'environnement, les droits de l'homme, le féminisme, la protection des animaux, l'unification des pays européens, ou l'aide humanitaire dans les pays en crise. Ensuite, trouvez une personne francophone qui a eu une influence dans cette catégorie, par exemple, Jacques Cousteau, Brigitte Bardot, Bernard Kouchner, Olympe de Gouges, Jacques Delors, ou Toussaint Louverture. Ensuite, écrivez un dialogue similaire à celui de l'Extension. Finalement, enregistrez ou filmez votre présentation.

Search words: **la fondation brigitte bardot, médecins sans frontières, la declaration des droits de la femme et de la citoyenne, l'histoire de l'union européenne**

16 La Déclaration des Droits des adolescents

1.2, 1.3, 5.1

Interpersonal/Presentational Communication

Lisez le début de la *Déclaration des Droits de l'homme et du citoyen*. En groupes, écrivez le préambule pour une *Déclaration des Droits des adolescents*. Faites une version en anglais et donnez les deux documents à vos profs, au proviseur, aux profs de sport, et aux conseillers d'éducation de votre école avec votre signature et celles de vos camarades de classe.

RESOURCES

Communicative Activities

Answers

All activities will vary.

Reference Desk

1. **Bateaux mouches** are long multi-decked boats offering guided cruises on the Seine every hour during the day, and into the evening. Tourists may also choose lunch or dinner cruises. The name, **bateaux mouches**, refers to the area outside of Lyon called Mouche, where the boats are manufactured. **Bateaux mouches** are not the only tourist boats on the Seine, but they are the most identifiable by name.
2. Bernard Kouchner (co-founder of the Nobel Prize-winning **Médecins Sans Frontières**) is a politician and physician whose career is focused on his commitment to humanitarian causes throughout the world.
3. Jacques Delors (politician and economist) served as president of the European Commission in 1985. He was a proponent of budget reform, and he laid the foundation for a single market community that came to fruition in 1993.
4. Toussaint Louverture (1743–1803), the Black Napoleon, was the leader of the Haitian Revolution. He drove the French out of Haiti, and he created an independent black state where former slaves learned to be free, self-governing citizens.

Differentiated Learning

Accelerate

Students put the illustrations in **Activité 13** in chronological order, then use these to write a story about the fall of the royalty, including details that they have learned about the events of the French Revolution.

Decelerate

Have students do the **Accelerate** activity in small groups. Before beginning, work with them to order the pictures, and make a comprehensive pre-writing outline before beginning their composition.

RESOURCES

 Pre-test

 *Leçon* Quiz

Answers

Script can be found in the Audio Program Manual.

1. 2
2. 1
3. 1
4. 1

Expansion

To contrast the American and French "r," have students sing "Row, row, row your boat" once with an American "r" and then with a French "r." This should make them aware of the different position of the "r" in the mouth and be an amusing exercise as well.

Prononciation

Pronouncing the French /R/  1.1

- Remember, the letter "r" is pronounced differently than in English and is usually pronounced at the end of words, except in cases like "Monsieur" and verbs ending in **–er.**

A Je peux prononcer /R/!

Répétez les phrases suivantes.

1. Pardon, je suis encore en retard!
2. On regrette de devoir partir....
3. Pourquoi faut-il leur dire au revoir?

Mandatory Liaisons

- In general, liaison is mandatory in interior rhythmic groups. Look at the three liaisons in this sentence:

  Ils‿ont réservé dans‿un petit‿hôtel.

  Note the three final consonants that connect to the vowels or vowel sounds that follow.

  Note that "d" becomes /t/ before a vowel sound:

  Quand/ t /on écoute, on‿apprend beaucoup.

B Liaison obligatoire

Écoutez, puis répétez ces exemples de liaison obligatoire.

1. Il y a de nombreux‿exemples de petits‿appartements dans ce quartier.
2. C'est‿un excellent‿endroit et je suis tout‿à fait d'accord.
3. C'est un grand/ t /écrivain.
4. Il faut de grandes‿idées et de nouvelles‿attitudes!

C Comptez!

Écoutez les petits dialogues et, pour chaque phrase, mettez le nombre de liaisons que vous entendez.

1. —Tes amis ont trouvé de bonnes entreprises?
2. —Oui, ils en ont trouvé plusieurs.

3. —Ils ont posté des lettres de motivation?
4. —Oui, ils en ont posté plusieurs.

Essential Instruction

1. Contrast the French "r" and the American "r." In which part of the mouth is each "r" produced?
2. Continuing with **Pronunciation**, after listening and repeating the sentences in part A, ask individual students to read the sentences aloud.
3. Put several sentences requiring liaisons on the board. Ask a volunteer student to read a sentence.
4. Have students listen and repeat part B, and write the liaisons they hear in C.
5. Encourage students to reread the **Contrat de l'élève** on p. 443 to remind themselves what they will be learning in **Leçon B**.

Leçon B

Vocabulaire actif

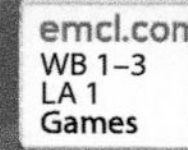

Le monde du travail

Alex cherche un emploi.

Alex trouve une petite annonce en ligne pour un poste qui l'intéresse.

Il rédige une lettre de motivation/de candidature.

Il accompagne son CV d'une photo.

Il envoie son CV à l'entreprise.

Il est convoqué pour un entretien.

L'emploi lui convient.

L'entreprise embauche Jean-Luc.

Il va travailler à plein temps, pas à mi-temps.

Abida fait un stage à TechMode.

Elle a signé un contrat avec le Chef du Personnel de la compagnie.

Elle met en pratique les connaissances acquises au cours de ses études universitaires.

Elle reçoit un salaire pendant sa formation en entreprise.

RESOURCES

e-visual 24

Workbook 1–3

Flash Cards

Listening Activity 1

Drill & Practice Games

Reference Desk

1. Other related terms and expressions include **une carrière** (*career*); **une demande d'emploi** (*job application*); **une description de poste** (*job description*); **la chasse a l'emploi** (*job hunting*); **les références** (*references*).
2. Job ads are found in the **Emplois** or **Carrières et Emplois** section of **les petites annonces.**

Differentiated Learning

Accelerate

Have students work in pairs and use circumlocution to practice the vocabulary. One student describes a word or expression without using the word until his/her partner guesses correctly. Model this first and encourage students to identify the word by saying, for example, **C'est une action** or **C'est ce qu'on fait avant de trouver un poste.**

Decelerate

Work with students to isolate the verbs used in each new expression, making sure that they practice the conjugations. Consider copying the images from **Le monde du travail** and asking the students to match the expression with the image. Work the pronunciation together.

Answers

1

1. à cause de l'économie
2. de rédiger une lettre de motivation pour un stage
3. Il a envoyé son CV.
4. Il a été embauché.
5. Il va commencer son stage payé.

Reference Desk

1. **Acquérir**, meaning "to acquire," is a challenging verb to conjugate. **J'acquiers**, **tu acquiers**, **il acquiert**, **nous acquérons**, **vous acquérons**, **ils acquièrent.** The future has a double *r*, **j'acquerrai**, and the past participle is **acquis.** Thus **les acquis** means what we acquire.
2. **Convoquer** is a synonym for **faire venir.** It has the sense of summoning someone.
3. **Gérer** means "to manage." **Un(e) gérant(e)** is "a manager," and **la gestion** means "management."

Pour la conversation

1.1

How do I indicate there is a lot of a certain item?

> **Il y a plein de** modèles....
> *There are a lot of models....*

How do I say I did something in vain?

> **J'ai beau** chercher des modèles pour la lettre de motivation....
> *I've been looking in vain for models for writing my cover letter....*

Et si je voulais dire...?

un apprentissage	*apprenticeship*
un atelier	*workshop*
un cadre	*executive manager*
les débouchés(m.)	*job openings*
un(e) gérant(e)	*manager*
la période d'essai	*trial period*
faire carrière	*to make a career*
occuper une fonction	*to occupy a position*
poser sa candidature	*put in one's application*

1 Tu imagines?

1.2

Lisez le mail de Romain à son frère au sujet d'un stage. Puis, répondez aux questions.

À: Olivier
Cc:
Sujet: On m'a pris!

Salut, Olivier!

Après avoir fait mes études à l'université, j'étais prêt à ne pas trouver de travail à cause de l'économie. Mais ma prof m'a proposé de rédiger une lettre de motivation pour un stage. Alors j'ai rédigé ma lettre, je l'ai envoyée avec mon CV accompagné d'une photo, et on m'a convoqué pour un entretien. On m'a pris! J'ai signé un contrat hier dans le bureau du Chef du Personnel, et je commence mon stage avec salaire dans quinze jours. Tu imagines? Et toi, comment vas-tu? Dans ton nouveau poste, est-ce que tu mets en pratique les connaissances acquises au cours de tes études universitaires?

À plus,
Romain

1. Pourquoi est-ce que Romain pensait qu'il ne trouverait pas de travail?
2. Qu'est-ce que sa prof lui a suggéré de faire?
3. Qu'est-ce que Romain a fait après?
4. Quel a été le résultat de son entretien?
5. Que va-t-il faire dans deux semaines?

Essential Instruction

1. Put the new vocabulary and expressions from **Le monde du travail** on the board. Define the term in French and ask for the equivalent term in English.
2. Play the recording as students follow in their books.
3. Have students listen to **Et si je voulais dire...?** Ask them to define the terms in French.
4. Students listen to **Activité 1** and answer the questions individually.
5. Arrange students in pairs to do **Activité 2** as a timed competition. Tally correct answers for each pair.
6. Have students listen to **Activité 3**, answering **oui** or **non** to the statements.
7. Review the questions for **Activitié 4.** Ask students to add questions that would be appropriate in discussing their work experience and future plans.
8. Ask students to circulate to ask and answer these questions. Encourage them to add details to have a more realistic conversation.

2 Je cherche du travail.

 1.2, 5.1

Choisissez une expression de la liste pour complétez les phrases suivantes. Attention: il est parfois nécessaire que vous vous serviez du subjonctif.

rédiger   se présenter   embaucher   mon CV
une annonce   mettre en pratique   plein temps   un contrat

MODÈLE Mes copains veulent que je recherche en ligne... qui m'intéresse.
Mes copains veulent que je recherche en ligne <u>une annonce</u> qui m'intéresse.

1. Mon prof souhaite que je... les connaissances acquises dans son cours.
2. Mon père préfère que je signe... avant de travailler.
3. Ma mère voudrait que mon père m'....
4. Mes grands-parents désirent que je... une lettre de motivation pour mon annonce préférée.
5. Ma mère exige que j'envoie... à TechMode.
6. Le Chef du Personnel de TechMode veut que je... à 10h15 pour un entretien.
7. Il souhaite que je travaille à....

3 Jeanne dans le marché du travail

  1.1, 1.2

Interpretive Communication

*Écrivez les numéros 1–6. Écoutez le parcours de Jeanne pour trouver un emploi. Si l'ordre des deux phrases est logique, écrivez **oui**; sinon, écrivez **non**.*

4 Questions personnelles

  1.3

Répondez aux questions.

1. Est-ce que tu travailles? Si oui, où? Depuis combien de temps?
2. As-tu déjà écrit un CV? Où l'as-tu envoyé? Avec ou sans photo?
3. Quels postes t'intéressent?
4. Voudrais-tu travailler à plein temps en été?
5. Quelles sont les connaissances que tu as acquises à l'école qui te préparent pour le monde du travail?

Differentiated Learning

Accelerate
Have students look for a job through a French newspaper's interactive site and make a help wanted list in French.
Search words: **offre d'emploi**, **le monde**

Decelerate
Have students write an e-mail back to Romain, congratulating him on his new job, asking for more details, and answering the questions he poses in the letter.

Answers

1. mette en pratique
2. un contrat
3. embauche
4. rédige
5. mon CV
6. me présente
7. temps plein

Script can be found in the front pages of the Annotated Teacher's Edition.

1. oui
2. non
3. oui
4. non
5. non
6. non

4 *Answers will vary.*

Critical Thinking

Analysis
Have students research and compare the current **taux de chômage** in France with that of the United States. Which is greater?
Search words: **institut national de la statistique et des études économiques**, **bureau of labor statistics**

Game

Allez-y!
To practice new vocabulary, prepare a set of note cards with a new word or expression on each one. Divide the class into two teams. Call the first player from each team to the front. Select the top card from the pile and read the word or expression that you want the players to use in a sentence. Say, "**Allez-y!**" to cue both players to write a sentence using that word or expression on the board. The student who uses the new vocabulary correctly in a sentence earns a point for his or her team. If both sentences are correct, both teams win a point. Play continues with the next two students, and the team with the most points at the end of the allotted time wins.

RESOURCES

 **Dialogue Video**

 **Workbook 4**

Answers

1. lettre de candidature
2. stage; Commission européenne
3. assistant
4. plein
5. plein de petits boulots

Reference Desk

1. Some vocabulary that students might not know: **rédiger un article** (*to write an article*); **un rédacteur** (*an editor*); **une redaction** (*an essay*); **jeter/lancer des fleurs** (*to compliment or praise someone enthusiastically*); **Tu as les chevilles qui enflent**! (*You are really full of yourself!*); **Il a de l'énergie à revendre.** (*He has so much energy he could sell it.*)
2. **Plein de beaucoup de** is a synonym for **beaucoup de.** Both partitive expressions are followed by **de** or **d'**. **Bien des** means "a lot of" and is always following **des** not **de**. A similar expression is **la plupart des** where **des** is always plural.

Rencontres culturelles

Karim fait une demande d'emploi.

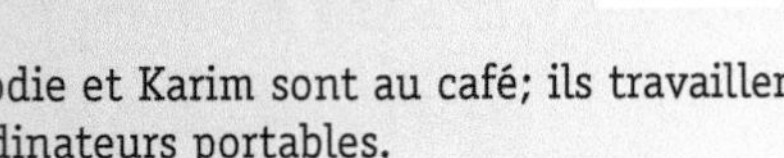

Élodie et Karim sont au café; ils travaillent devant leurs ordinateurs portables.

Élodie: Qu'est-ce que tu fais?

Karim: Je suis en train de rédiger une lettre de candidature pour un stage.

Élodie: Un stage cet été? Où ça?

Karim: Un stage d'assistant junior à Bruxelles.

Élodie: À la Commission européenne? À plein temps? Wahou!

Karim: Oui! Mais je dois commencer par rédiger la lettre de motivation.

Élodie: Regarde sur Internet, il y a plein de modèles, j'en suis sûre.

Karim: Après avoir trouvé un modèle pour le CV, j'ai beau chercher des modèles pour la lettre de motivation, ça doit quand même être *perso*....

Élodie: Ce n'est pas difficile avec toutes les qualités que tu as: tu écris bien, tu parles plusieurs langues, tu es sympa, tu t'intéresses aux autres, tu te débrouilles... tu as fait plein de petits boulots!

Karim: N'en jette plus! Tu vas me faire rougir....

5 Karim fait une demande d'emploi.

Complétez les phrases.

1. Karim doit écrire une....
2. Il aimerait faire un... à la... à Bruxelles.
3. C'est pour devenir un... junior.
4. Il travaillerait à... temps.
5. Selon Élodie, Karim a une bonne expérience parce qu'il a eu....

Essential Instruction

1. Have students watch the video **Karim fait une demande d'emploi** with books closed.
2. Ask students general comprehension questions.
3. Replay the video, asking students to pay attention to what Karim wants to do, where, and what document he needs to write.
4. Students listen to the recording and follow along in the text.
5. Ask what words or expressions students do not know from the context. Have them prepare the answers to **Activité 5**.
6. Have high and low-ability students work in pairs to read **Extension**. In addition to answering the **Extension** question, ask students to describe the other candidates.

Extension **On veut que quel candidat se présente pour un entretien?**

Au bureau Gabrielle et Jean-Pierre doivent choisir un candidat après réception des lettres de motivation.

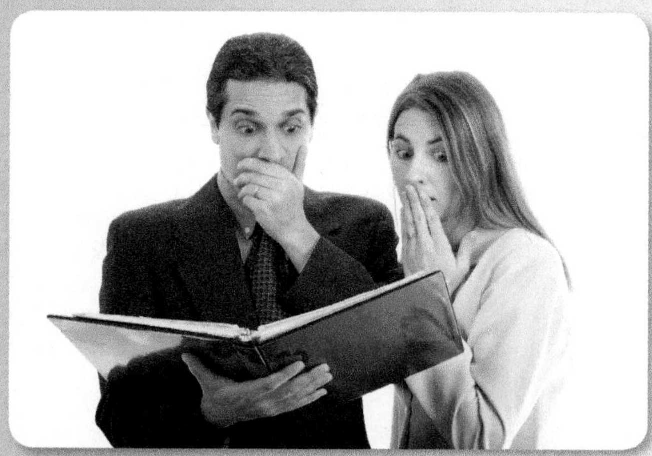

Gabrielle: Moi, j'en ai sélectionné trois: au moins eux, ils ont bien lu la petite annonce du site.

Jean-Pierre: Donc, ça fait cinq. Oui, moi aussi j'ai fait attention à ça: que la lettre de motivation réponde aux exigences du poste à pourvoir.

Gabrielle: Après, il y a les petits plus... parce que côté formation, ils ont à peu près tous le même profil.

Jean-Pierre: Toutes et tous des forts en langues....

Gabrielle: Oui, et puis comme on cherche un junior, l'expérience professionnelle, c'est plutôt limité.

Jean-Pierre: Moi, j'en ai un... il a été charpentier.

Gabrielle: Pas mal! Moi, j'en ai une qui a travaillé dans une unité de soins palliatifs.

Jean-Pierre: Dur... il y en a un, là, qui a une belle expérience... il a fait plein de boulots. Il a travaillé en Guinée, à Djibouti, en Tunisie... côté formation universitaire, il a un parcours plus chaotique.

Gabrielle: Pas grave, on le formera.

Jean-Pierre: On sent qu'il a de l'énergie à revendre... il ne doit demander que ça....

Gabrielle: Tu le convoques pour l'entretien.

Extension Quelles sont les qualifications du candidat que Gabrielle et Jean-Pierre choisissent pour l'entretien?

1.2

Extension

Il a travaillé en Guinée, à Djibouti, et en Tunisie.

Expansion

Have students monitor ***le Figaro*** and ***le Monde*** for a week to make a list of **les offres d'emploi**. Ask them to compare these to job offerings in an American large city paper. What are the similarities and differences?

Communication

Interpersonal: Paired practice

Have students work in pairs to read the **Extension** conversation aloud. Model pronunciation and expression before students practice. Ask students to switch roles. Choose volunteers to present to the class.

Differentiated Learning

Accelerate

Have students write **une lettre de motivation** for a job that they would like to do, outlining their interests and skills. Encourage students to look at online models of letters to get a sense of phrasing, just like the French do.

Decelerate

Have students write a brief description of a job they have done or would like to do, then describe the responsibilities using **il faut que**.

RESOURCES

Workbook 5

Reference Desk

Visit the European Union's official website and search the links in English or in French for activities geared to kids and teachers.

Points de départ

emcl.com WB 5

Question centrale: Comment le passé influence-t-il le présent?

Les institutions de l'Union européenne (UE) en quelques villes

1.2, 3.1

Bruxelles

C'est à Bruxelles que siège* **la Commission** et **le Conseil européen.**

La Commission européenne est le symbole de l'administration européenne. C'est une administration fédérale de 27.000 personnes environ. La Commission est d'abord la "gardienne des Traités" –à Rome en 1958, Bruxelles en 1967, Luxembourg en 1970, La Haye en 1986, Maastricht en1993, Amsterdam en 1999, Nice en 2003, et Lisbonne en 2009. Elle veille* à leur bonne application, et elle fait respecter l'intérêt général. Le président de la commission, nommé par le Conseil européen, nomme lui-même les commissaires (un par état membre). Leur mandat est de cinq ans. La Commission représente et défend les intérêts de l'UE dans sa globalité. Elle gère* et met en œuvre* la politique de l'UE. Ainsi elle propose de nouvelles lois, gère le budget, veille à l'application du droit, et représente l'UE auprès des autres nations.

Search words: **le site web official de l'union européenne, commission européenne, europa traité européens, histoire union européenne**

siège *sits;* **veille** *watches over;* **gère** *manages;* **met en œuvre** *carries out (to carry out)*

Le Conseil européen a été créé en 1974. Il réunit les chefs d'État et de gouvernement des pays membres de l'Union européenne. Il définit les grandes orientations*, décide des politiques à mettre en œuvre. Son rôle est de plus en plus important et consacre* la supériorité d'une union des États.

Search words: **conseil européen, siège du conseil européen**

1.2, 3.1, 3.2

grandes orientations *directions;* **consacre** *recognizes*

Strasbourg

C'est à Strasbourg que siège **le Parlement européen.** Il examine et adopte les lois. Il contrôle le fonctionnement des autres institutions et adopte le budget. Ses membres sont élus* au suffrage direct* par les citoyens de tous les États membres.

C'est le Parlement européen qui a le contrôle des dépenses.

Search words: **parlement européen europa, parlement européen toute l'europe**

élus *elected;* **suffrage direct** *direct vote*

Essential Instruction

1. Have students identify the location of the European Commission cities on a map.
2. Have students make a chart with the following column headings: **Institution**, **Pays**, **Mission**, **Remarques** to help organize the information on pp. 466–467 for a discussion.
3. In the computer lab, have students access the search words sites and add information to their list.
4. As a class, discuss the value of each institution. Is there a benefit to the fact that these institutions are located in separate countries?

Luxembourg

La Cour de justice des Communautés européennes se trouve à Luxembourg. Elle règle* les relations entre les Institutions européennes, les États, et les citoyens. Ses jugements dans le règlement* des conflits s'imposent à tous et le droit européen prime* sur le droit national.

Search words: **cours de justice curia**

règle *sets;* **règlement** *settlement;* **prime** *takes precedence*

Francfort

Francfort accueille la **Banque européenne** qui, depuis le Traité de Lisbonne, est devenue une institution indépendante à part entière, au même titre que la Cour de Justice ou le Parlement. Elle garantit la stabilité de l'euro.

Search words: **europa banque centrale européenne, toute l'europe banque centrale européenne**

Schengen ou l'espace Schengen

Ce petit village au bord de la Moselle est situé entre les frontières allemande, luxembourgeoise, belge, et française. Il est le symbole de **l'espace Schengen** qui regroupe tous les pays qui constituent un espace sans frontière intérieure et qui confient* la surveillance des frontières terrestres*, aériennes, et maritimes aux pays qui en sont limitrophes*.

Search words: **convention de schengen, toute l'europe l'espace schengen, carte espace schengen**

confient *entrust;* **frontière terrestre** *land border;* **limitrophe** *adjacent*

COMPARAISONS

Le traité North American Free Trade Agreement (NAFTA) entre le Canada, les États-Unis, et le Mexique fait penser à quel traité européen?

4.2

Mots-clé

Union est un mot emprunté au latin classique *unio* vers 1225. C'est en bas latin que *unio* a pris le sens de unité et union. Le mot désigne d'abord la jonction de plusieurs choses pour former un tout (1380); puis la concorde, la bonne entente entre plusieurs personnes; et enfin une liaison d'affection (XVème siècle).

Produits

Le drapeau de l'Union européenne est orné de 12 étoiles dorées disposées en cercle sur fond bleu, représentant la solidarité et l'union entre les peuples d'Europe. Il date de 1955.

2.2

Ce drapeau devant la Commission européenne de Bruxelles représente l'Union européenne.

Communication

Interpersonal: Cooperative Groups

The European Union has decided that there are too many institutions and needs to eliminate one. Put students in groups of five, each bearing a badge with the name of their institution. Have them prepare arguments as to why their commission is too important to be eliminated, and secondly suggest reasons why another institution should be cut. Students must passionately defend their own institution. Afterward, have the class debate the merits of each institution and vote one off the council.

Differentiated Learning

Accelerate

Ask students to write an argument for or against a change in the current North American Free Trade Agreement in which Canada, the United States, and Mexico would eliminate borders and share a common currency. Would this be a positive or negative change? Why?

Decelerate

Students make a map of the **Carte Espace Schengen** and present it to the class explaining the order of entry of the countries into the European Union by colors.

Multiple Intelligences

Musical-Rhythmic

Ask these students to lead the class in singing the National Anthem of Europe set to the music of Beethoven's "Ode to Joy."

Expansion

The Basques have large communities in Idaho. Why did they choose this area to live? What would be similar to their homeland?

Critical Thinking

Analysis
In what way can the Basque and the Bretons be compared to the Québécois? What do they have in common? (unique language, living within a larger country with a desire for their own identity)

La Francophonie: Institutions

1.2, 3.1

✲ Au Maghreb

Les pays maghrébins—la Tunisie, le Maroc, et l'Algérie—font partie de la Ligue arabe, ou La Ligue des États arabes. Fondée en 1945, la Ligue arabe a maintenant 22 pays membres. Son but est solidifier les relations entre pays membres et d'en surveiller* la collaboration. Elle doit aussi assurer la protection de leur indépendance et leur souveraineté, et, de façon plus générale, elle est censée* protéger les affaires et les intérêts des pays arabes.

C'est au Caire, en Égypte, qu'a été créée la Ligue Arabe.

surveiller *to watch over;* **censée** *supposed to*

La Francophonie: Citoyens de l'UE?

1.2, 3.1

✲ Les Basques

Euskadi est le nom d'une région autonome en Espagne où les citoyens sont des Basques. Les aspirations de cette communauté indépendante comprennent la représentation directe dans les institutions de l'UE, par exemple, le droit d'interjeter appel à* la Cour de Justice à Luxembourg. Même si la langue basque n'est pas une langue officielle dans l'UE, elle est reconnue comme minoritaire, tout comme le breton. Il y a aussi des Basques en France. Ils habitent dans le département des Pyrénées Atlantiques. Les Basques sont très attachés à leurs maisons, à la famille, et à la communauté. De nos jours, il y a des clubs gastronomiques où les hommes préparent des spécialités basques comme le cidre, l'agneau, le ragoût*, et le paprika. Un sport populaire Basque est la pelote.

La pelote basque.

interjeter appel à *to appeal to;* **ragout** *stew*

Essential Instruction

1. Have students read **la Francophonie: Institutions.** Ask them to make a chart comparing **La Ligue des États Arabes** with the United Nations charter. Where are these countries located? What are the common features? (Both were founded in 1945, and their mission statements are somewhat similar.)
2. Students read **Les Basques.** When did the Spanish Basques become autonomous? What languages might they speak?
   Search words: **euskadi**
3. Ask students to work in pairs to complete activity 1 of **Activités culturelles.** Compare responses with the whole class.
4. Have all students do activity 2.
5. Have students work in groups to do activity 3. Be sure the students play the game and take the quiz from the official website of the **Union Européene.**
6. Students work in small groups choosing activity 4 or 6. The groups present their results to the class.

 2.2

Le comité Nobel a décerné (*awarded*) **le prix Nobel de la paix** à l'UE en 2012 pour avoir "contribué pendant plus de six décennies à promouvoir la paix et la réconciliation, la démocratie, et les droits de l'homme en Europe."

6 Activités culturelles

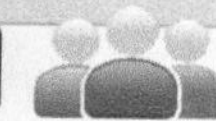  1.2, 1.3, 3.1, 3.2

Complétez les activités suivantes.

1. Retrouvez à quelles institutions de l'Union européenne appartiennent ces attributions:
   A. Ses jugements s'imposent à tous.
   B. Elle met en œuvre les politiques communautaires.
   C. Il définit les grandes orientations.
   D. Il constitue un espace sans frontière intérieure.
   E. Elle garantit la stabilité de la monnaie.
2. Faites un plan de l'Europe avec tous les pays membres. Indiquez les capitales et les langues qu'on y parle.
3. Sur le site officiel de l'Union européenne vous trouverez des jeux et quiz pour en apprendre plus sur l'UE. Jouez à ces jeux.

 Search words: **jeux et quiz strasbourg europe, coin des enfants jeux et quiz sur l'ue europa**

4. Formez huit groupes. Chaque groupe se charge de faire des recherches sur les spécificités d'un traité: Rome (1958), Bruxelles (1967), acte union européenne de Luxembourg (1970), La Haye (1986), Maastricht (1993), Amsterdam (1999), Nice (2003), Lisbonne (2009).
5. Organisez une visite dans une ville avec une institution européenne.
6. Recherchez ce que la Ligue arabe a fait ou a décidé de faire cette année ou l'année dernière.

Perspectives

Jacques Delors, ancien président de la Commission européenne, a dit, "Il me semble qu'à 27, à 30, ou 32 pays européens, nous pouvons avoir trois ambitions communes: un espace de paix active, un cadre pour le développement durable et une manière particulière de gérer-valoriser notre diversité culturelle." Qu'est-ce que Delors a prévu pour l'Union européenne? A-t-on réalisé ses ambitions?

Answers

1. A: La Cour de justice des Communautés européennes; B: La Commission européenne; C: le Conseil Européen; D: l'espace Schengen; E: la Banque européenne
2. *Answers will vary with time. Check the official site.*

3–6. *Activities will vary.*

Perspectives
Answers will vary.

Reference Desk

Jai alai is a ball game similar to Basque **pelota** in which a ball is bounced off walls in an enclosed court. It is a game that requires intense concentration and physical coordination, as the ball speeds have been clocked at 188 mph. This game is very popular in states such as Florida and Connecticut.

Differentiated Learning

Accelerate
Have students answer the question posed in **Perspectives** in a three-paragraph essay.

Decelerate
Encourage students to write a travel review page for the Internet for the city of Bilbao with a list of tourist attractions including the Guggenheim museum.

Learning Styles

Visual Learners
Encourage students to make a map of the Basque area indicating principal cities and ports. Students may enjoy reading the short book ***Ramuntcho***, a story of love and adventure written by Pierre Loti (1850-1923) and set in the Basque region.

Kinesthetic Learners
Have students explain **la pelote basque** to the class. How many people compose a team, what equipment is needed, and how is it scored?
Search words: **basque pelota**

Answers

1. 27
2. Genève
3. Espace Schengen
4. L'U.E. dispose de six pays détenteurs de la bombe atomique.
5. L'euro est la monnaie unique obligatoire de l'ensemble de l'U.E.

Communication

Interpersonal: Cooperative Groups

Have students work in small mixed-ability groups to create a list of 10 trivia questions (with answers) as a review of **Leçon B** so far. They should not copy the questions from **Du côté des médias** but should create their own questions covering the material studied so far. Collect each group's list and combine them to create a review game. Choose students to be the game hosts.

Du côté des médias

Pre AP 1.2

Interpretive Communication

Lisez les questions du quiz sur l'Union européenne.

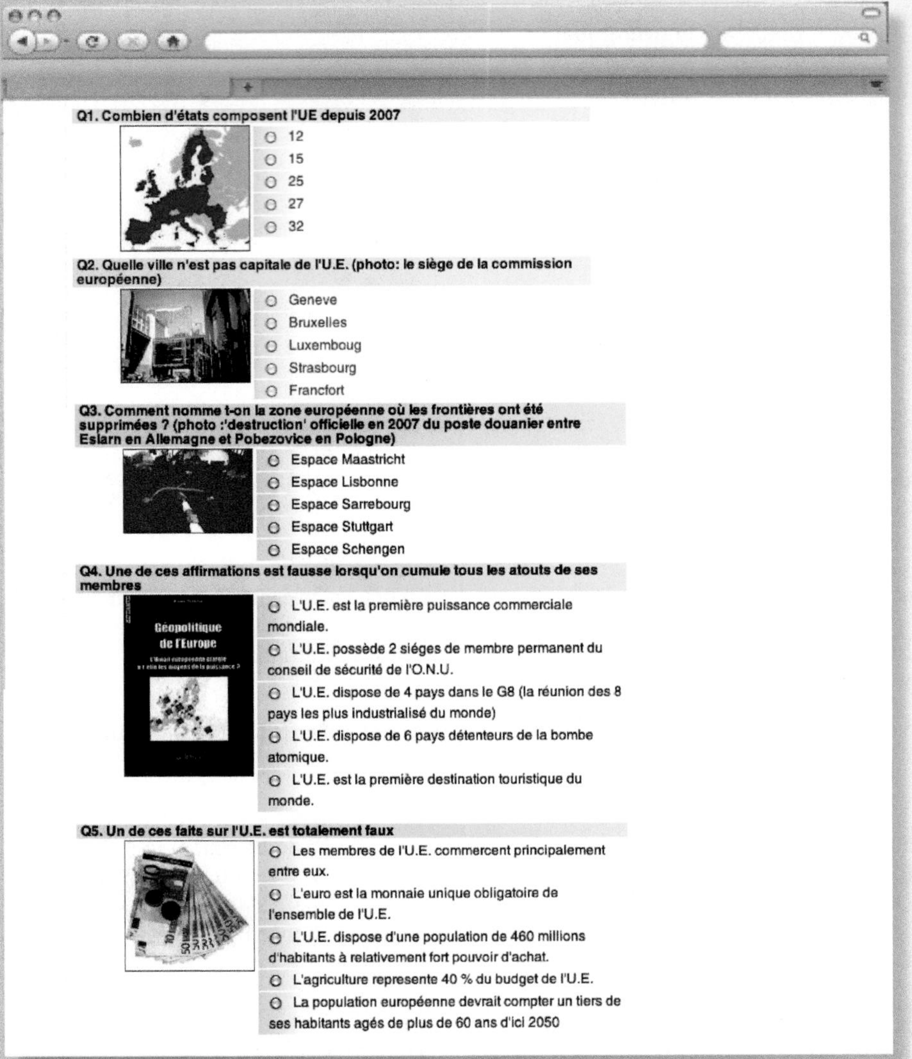

Q1. Combien d'états composent l'UE depuis 2007

- 12
- 15
- 25
- 27
- 32

Q2. Quelle ville n'est pas capitale de l'U.E. (photo: le siège de la commission européenne)

- Geneve
- Bruxelles
- Luxembourg
- Strasbourg
- Francfort

Q3. Comment nomme t-on la zone européenne où les frontières ont été supprimées ? (photo :'destruction' officielle en 2007 du poste douanier entre Eslarn en Allemagne et Pobezovice en Pologne)

- Espace Maastricht
- Espace Lisbonne
- Espace Sarrebourg
- Espace Stuttgart
- Espace Schengen

Q4. Une de ces affirmations est fausse lorsqu'on cumule tous les atouts de ses membres

- L'U.E. est la première puissance commerciale mondiale.
- L'U.E. possède 2 siéges de membre permanent du conseil de sécurité de l'O.N.U.
- L'U.E. dispose de 4 pays dans le G8 (la réunion des 8 pays les plus industrialisé du monde)
- L'U.E. dispose de 6 pays détenteurs de la bombe atomique.
- L'U.E. est la première destination touristique du monde.

Q5. Un de ces faits sur l'U.E. est totalement faux

- Les membres de l'U.E. commercent principalement entre eux.
- L'euro est la monnaie unique obligatoire de l'ensemble de l'U.E.
- L'U.E. dispose d'une population de 460 millions d'habitants à relativement fort pouvoir d'achat.
- L'agriculture represente 40 % du budget de l'U.E.
- La population européenne devrait compter un tiers de ses habitants agés de plus de 60 ans d'ici 2050

7 Quiz: L'Union européenne

1.2

Répondez aux questions sur le quiz.

Search words: quizz biz union européenne

Essential Instruction

1. As a review of the **L'union européenne**, have students take the small quiz in **Du côté des médias** and answer the questions for each section.
2. Ask students to work in pairs to brainstorm all of the **avoir** expressions that they remember.
3. Put the list of **avoir** expressions on the board and ask students to illustrate each one.
4. With white boards, have students practice conjugating **avoir** in all tenses and moods.
5. Ask students to make sentences with the **avoir** expressions. As a drill they must transform the sentences, singular to plural, and from one tense and mood to another.

Structure de la langue

emcl.com
WB 6–7
Games

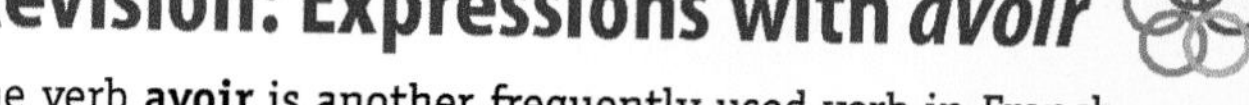

Révision: Expressions with *avoir* 1.1

The verb **avoir** is another frequently used verb in French.

J'**ai** un entretien demain pour un stage. *I have an interview tomorrow for an internship.*

Also called a "building block" verb, **avoir** is used in many expressions in French. Some of the most common expressions with **avoir** deal with age, physical ailments, or being hot/cold/hungry/thirsty/afraid. Can you think of others?

Marame **avait** vingt **ans** quand elle a travaillé à plein temps pour cette entreprise américaine. *Marame was 20 years old when she worked full-time for this American company.*

Je ne pourrais jamais travailler pour Air France parce que j'**ai peur** en avion! *I could never work for Air France because I'm afraid of flying!*

A new **avoir** expression is **avoir beau** plus an infinitive *(to do something in vain)*.

Nous **avons beau** chercher dans les petites annonces. *We've been trying in vain to find something in the want ads.*

8 Les gens de mon quartier

1.2

Faites des phrases qui décrivent les illustrations en vous servant d'une expression de la liste.

avoir de la chance · avoir hâte de partir en vacances · avoir l'air sérieux · avoir envie d'envoyer un texto · avoir lieu · avoir treize ans · avoir peur du vide · avoir raison · avoir faim

MODÈLE

le concert
Le concert a lieu le 16 mai.

1. M. et Mme Besnard

2. Diane

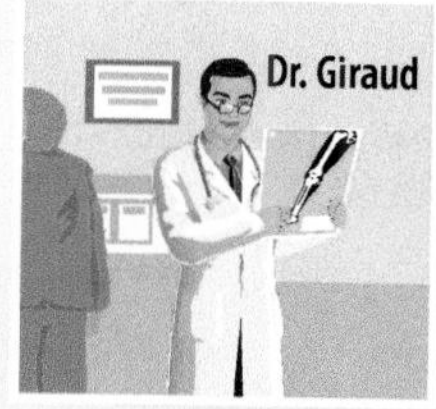

3. Docteur Giraud et toi

4. Timéo

5. je

6. Brigitte et Marie-Alix

7. Madiba

8. Maelis

RESOURCES

Workbook 6 –7

Drill & Practice Games

Answers

1. M. et Mme Besnard ont de la chance.
2. Diane a faim.
3. Docteur Giraud et toi avez l'air sérieux.
4. Timéo a raison.
5. J'ai envie d'envoyer un texto.
6. Brigitte et Marie-Alix ont hâte de partir en vacances.
7. Madiba a peur du vide.
8. Maelis a treize ans.

Communication

Interpersonal: Paired practice

Prepare a set of cards with sentences using an **avoir** expression in the present tense, for example, **Le concert a lieu vendredi le 13 avril à 19h00.** On the back of each card identify a different tense and show the new sentence, for example, **[passé composé] Le concert a eu lieu vendredi le 13 avril à 19h00.** Student A shows the side with the present tense sentence to his or her partner and names the new tense. Student B restates the sentence in the new tense. Student A verifies that it is correct then Student B shows his or her card and they repeat the process. When both students have completed a sentence, they exchange cards and move to a new partner. Continue until time is called.

Differentiated Learning

Accelerate

Ask students to write about historical events where people tried to do things in vain. Have them make a list of ten such endeavors. Sports figures and adventurers are prime examples.

Decelerate

Give students another opportunity to do well on a test of **avoir** expressions. Ask them to make flash cards of **avoir** expressions. Give them a "feel good" quiz on the expressions and conjugations of **avoir**. This quiz boosts their grade, helps them feel more invested in class, and gives them a firm foundation for this key French verb.

RESOURCES

 Workbook 8–11

 Listing Activity 2

 Drill & Practice Games

Answers

1. Marie-Antoinette a toujours eu besoin de s'amuser.
2. Elle n'a pas eu envie de quitter l'Autriche et sa famille.
3. Mais Louis, le fils du roi de France, a eu besoin de se marier avec elle.
4. Quand Louis XVI a eu/avait 16 ans, il s'est marié avec Marie-Antoinette.
5. Marie-Antoinette a eu de la chance parce qu'elle a eu de beaux enfants.
6. La prise de la Bastille a eu lieu le 14 juillet 1789 et tout a changé.

Reference Desk

Explain that **après avoir/être** + past participle is a mini **passé composé** without a subject and it follows the same rules of agreement as **passé composé**. Once students know if the verb is conjugated with **avoir** or **être**, this structure is very straightforward.

9 À la cour de France

 1.2

*Complétez les phrases avec la forme correcte du verbe **avoir** + **expression**. Attention au temps! L'histoire est au passé.*

avoir...	ans besoin de la chance lieu envie de

1. Marie-Antoinette... toujours besoin de s'amuser.
2. Elle n'... pas de quitter l'Autriche et sa famille.
3. Mais Louis, le fils du roi de France, ... de se marier avec elle.
4. Quand Louis XVI... 16 ans, il s'est marié avec Marie-Antoinette.
5. Marie-Antoinette... de la chance parce qu'elle a eu de beaux enfants.
6. La prise de la Bastille... lieu le 14 juillet 1789 et tout a changé.

Past infinitive

 1.1

emcl.com
WB 8–11
LA 2
Games

To say that one action in the past happened before another one, use the past infinitive. After the preposition **après**, add the helping verb **avoir** or **être** and the past participle of the main verb.

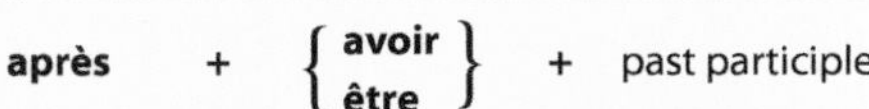

après + { avoir / être } + past participle

Après avoir convoqué Damien pour un entretien, le chef du personnel l'a embauché.

Après avoir trouvé une petite annonce, Thierry a envoyé son CV à l'entreprise.	*After finding a want ad, Thierry sent his résumé to the company.*
Après être arrivé en France, Abdel y a fait un stage en entreprise.	*After having arrived in France, Abdel interned at a French company there.*

Agreement of the past participle is the same as in the **passé composé.**

Après s'être présentée pour un entretien, Faustine a signé le contrat.	*After showing up for an interview, Faustine signed the contract.*

COMPARAISONS: In English both French sentences would be expressed thus: "Mom criticized me for **not having done** my chores." The negative word "not" is placed in front of "having," the auxiliary verb form used in the past infinitive, as in: "After not having gotten dressed," "After not having come to the concert," "After not having eaten," etc. Unlike in English, French has two ways to make the past infinitive negative.

COMPARAISONS

Both of the following sentences are correct in expressing the past infinitive in the negative in French. What is the rule in English?

Maman m'a critiqué pour **ne pas** avoir fait mes corvées.
Maman m'a critiqué pour **n'**avoir fait **pas** mes corvées.

4.1

Essential Instruction

1. Review the use of the **passé composé** and the **imparfait.**
2. Have students select the correct form of **avoir** in the appropriate tense for **Activité 10.**
3. Introduce the past infinitive with examples of **avoir** and **être** verbs.
4. Ask students to translate examples of the past infinitive from English to French to demonstrate the difference in wording.
5. Do **Activité 11** with them. Write the answers on the board to point out agreement.

10 Logique ou pas?

1.3

Faites des phrases logiques pour décrire l'histoire de Marie-France.

MODÈLE lire une petite annonce en ligne/envoyer son CV
Après avoir lu une petite annonce en ligne, Marie-France a envoyé son CV.

1. écrire sa lettre de motivation/trouver une petite annonce
2. recevoir une convocation pour un entretien/se présenter au Chef du personnel
3. signer un contrat/recevoir un offre de travail
4. s'installer dans son bureau/faire la connaissance des autres stagiaires
5. recevoir son premier chèque/travailler deux semaines
6. être embauché à plein temps/faire un stage

11 La vie de Marie-Antoinette

1.3

Regardez la chronologie de la vie de Marie-Antoinette. Écrivez des phrases avec l'infinitif passé et le passé composé pour décrire ce qui s'est passé.

MODÈLE **1755: Marie-Antoinette est née** (*was born*)
Elle vit en Autriche.

Après être née en 1755, Marie-Antoinette a vécu en Autriche.

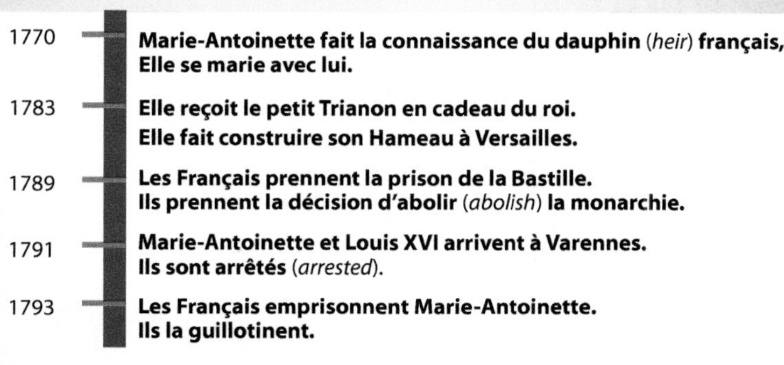

1770	**Marie-Antoinette fait la connaissance du dauphin** (*heir*) **français, Louis. Elle se marie avec lui.**
1783	**Elle reçoit le petit Trianon en cadeau du roi. Elle fait construire son Hameau à Versailles.**
1789	**Les Français prennent la prison de la Bastille. Ils prennent la décision d'abolir** (*abolish*) **la monarchie.**
1791	**Marie-Antoinette et Louis XVI arrivent à Varennes. Ils sont arrêtés** (*arrested*).
1793	**Les Français emprisonnent Marie-Antoinette. Ils la guillotinent.**

Differentiated Learning

Decelerate

To help students visualize the chronology of past events, use a timeline to emphasize the order of actions when a past infinitive is used. Encourage them to tell you which action came first. For example, with the sentence **Après m'être réveillé, je me lève**, students say **Alors, je me réveille puis je me lève.** Have them pinpoint these two actions on the timeline.

Answers

1. Après avoir trouvé une petite annonce, elle a écrit sa lettre de motivation.
2. Après avoir reçu une convocation pour un entretien, elle s'est présentée au Chef du personnel.
3. Après avoir reçu une offre de travail, elle a signé un contrat.
4. Après s'être installée dans son bureau, elle a fait la connaissance des autres stagiaires.
5. Après avoir travaillé deux semaines, elle a reçu son premier chèque.
6. Après avoir fait un stage, elle a été embauchée à plein temps.

1. Après avoir fait la connaissance du dauphin en 1970, Marie-Antoinette s'est mariée avec lui.
2. Après avoir reçu le petit Trianon en cadeau du roi, elle a fait construire son Hameau à Versailles.
3. Après avoir pris la prison de la Bastille, les Français ont pris la décision d'abolir la monarchie.
4. Après être arrivés à Varennes, Marie-Antoinette et Louis XVI ont été arrêtés.
5. Après avoir emprisonné Marie-Antoinette, les Français l'ont guillotinée.

Communication

Interpersonal: Paired Practice

Give student pairs two illustrations of people engaged in an activity featuring vocabulary they know. For example, give a team a photo of a woman cooking dinner. One student tells the other what they think will happen next: "**Après avoir préparé le dîner, Maman va appeler les enfants à table.**" The other student does the same with the second picture. The students copy down their sentences before passing their photos on to another pair and receiving two more. This process continues until all photos are discussed and sentences recorded. Circulate to check the quality of their work and make corrections.

Answers

12

Script can be found in the front pages of the Annotated Teacher's Edition.

1. I
2. I
3. L
4. L
5. L
6. L

13

All answers B will vary.

1. A: Qu'est-ce que tu as fait après t'être habillé(e)?
   B: Après m'être habillé(e) ....
2. A: Qu'est-ce que tu as fait après avoir fait les corvées?
   B: Après avoir fait les corvées ....
3. A: Qu'est-ce que tu as fait après avoir déjeuné?
   B: Après avoir déjeuné ....
4. A: Qu'est-ce que tu as fait après être sorti(e)?
   B: Après être sorti(e) ....
5. A: Qu'est-ce que tu as fait après avoir dîné?
   B: Après avoir dîné ....
6. A: Qu'est-ce que tu as fait après avoir fait la vaisselle?
   B: Après avoir fait la vaisselle ....

Reference Desk

The past infinitive is made negative in one of two ways: the negative may come before the past infinitive, for example, **Après ne pas avoir dormi, j'étais fatigué/e**, or **ne...pas** may surround **avoir** or **être**, for example, **Après n'avoir pas dormi, j'étais fatigué/e**.

12 Qu'est-ce qui s'est passé après?

1.1, 1.2

*Écrivez les numéros 1–6. Ensuite, écoutez les phrases. Si la phrase est logique, écrivez **L**. Sinon, écrivez **I** pour illogique.*

13 Samedi dernier

1.1, 1.2

Interpersonal Communication

À tour de rôle, demandez à votre partenaire ce qu'il ou elle a fait après avoir fait les activités ci-dessous.

MODÈLES se lever
A: **Qu'est-ce que tu as fait après t'être levé(e)?**
B: **Après m'être levé(e), j'ai pris mon petit déjeuner.**

faire ton lit
A: **Qu'est-ce que tu as fait après avoir fait ton lit?**
B: **Après avoir fait mon lit, j'ai rangé ma chambre.**

1. s'habiller
2. faire les corvées
3. déjeuner
4. sortir
5. dîner
6. faire la vaisselle

Essential Instruction

1. Do **Activité 12** with the students in a guided practice.
2. Have students listen to **Activité 13** and select the appropriate action.
3. Before doing **Activité 14** ask students to put the six verbs provided in the past infinitive forms.
4. Ask students to work with partners to do the interview questions.
5. As a whole-class activity, ask students to share what they said and give other examples.
6. For **Activité 15** students seeking a career in a certain field should research their chosen field online.
   Search words: **stepstone**
7. To write **une lettre de motivation** for **Activité 16**, encourage students to use online templates. They can fine tune their letter with your help.
   Search words: **modèles**, **conseils**, **exemples de la lettre de motivation**

À vous la parole

14 Un entretien d'information

1.3, 5.2

Presentational Communication

Un entretien d'information permet au candidat de trouver des informations sur le travail de son choix. Pour préciser, un entretien d'information permet au chercheur (*seeker*) d'emploi de trouver des informations sur un travail, un secteur d'activité, ou une entreprise en parlant avec des personnes qui travaillent dans ce domaine. Comme ce n'est pas un "vrai" entretien, il y a moins de stress. Un autre avantage est que vous créez un réseau de contacts (*network*). Faites une liste de boulots qui vous intéressent. Choisissez-en un. Préparez six questions au minimum que vous poseriez à quelqu'un qui connaît vos ambitions professionnelles ou qui travaille dans ce domaine.

15 J'écris une lettre de motivation.

1.3, 3.2

Presentational Communication

Imaginez que vous avez 24 ans et que vous cherchez votre premier boulot. Regardez des exemples de lettres de motivation en ligne. Finalement, préparez une lettre de motivation pour le poste de vos rêves.

Search words: modèle de lettre de motivation, lettre de motivation exemples

Communiquez!

16 Je fais passer un entretien.

1.1, 5.2

Interpersonal Communication

Avec un partenaire, jouez les rôles d'un gérant/d'une gérante d'entreprise et d'un candidat à un poste. Il faut que ce dernier ou cette dernière choisisse une profession ou trouve une petite annonce en ligne. Le gérant/la gérante lui pose des questions pour en savoir plus sur sa formation, ses qualifications, et ses objectifs professionnels. Enregistrez ou filmez l'entretien.

RESOURCES

Communicative Activities

Answers

All activities will vary.

Reference Desk

Blended Instruction

Consider using blended instruction, a combination of in-class learning and computer-mediated instruction or learning opportunities. Ask students to complete activities on the computer, using their cell or smartphone, or other emerging electronic technology. This process will allow students to hone their tech skills and become more independent learners. Schedule routine Internet and e-book learning in class and in the lab.

Differentiated Learning

Accelerate/Decelerate

Encourage the dramatic students to perform the interview in class. Ask the more reserved students to tape the interview for **Activité 17.** Consider mixing ability levels for both options.

Special Needs Students

AD(H)D

Work with these students to organize their ideas before writing **Activité 16.** Consider having a small study group to research the online templates and discuss and outline together what needs to be included in their letter.

RESOURCES

Pre-test

***Leçon* Quiz**

Connections

Business Education
Consider inviting the school's literacy teacher or a teacher from the business education department to come to class and share ideas for writing **résumés.** Doing this creates a link between the CV writing activity done in French class and the need students may have for a **résumé** in their own future.

Stratégie communicative 

Writing a Résumé  1.2, 1.3, 3.2, 5.1, 5.2

Tout d'abord trouvez un stage qui vous paraît intéressant. Ensuite, rédigez votre CV dans lequel vous décrirez votre parcours scolaire et vos centres d'intérêts. Le but du CV est de décrocher (*to land*) un entretien d'embauche. Imaginez que vous ayez déjà obtenu un diplôme universitaire avec la spécialité de votre choix. Le CV à la page 479 pourra vous servir de modèle.

Search words: **infostages, stages en entreprises, expériences professionelles pour jeunes diplômés, stage rémunérés, stages non rémunérés, expériences en entreprises, stagiaires, stages en entreprises**

Petites annonces stages

Assistant web designer/graphiste	**Me contacter**	**Paris**
Entreprise spécialisée dans la vente en ligne de bijoux et accessoires féminins cherche stagiaire pour webdesign/graphiste		
Stage rédacteur/rédactrice Internet	**Me contacter**	**Marseille**
Recherche stagiaire h/f pour rédaction et administration de contenu web pour un musée d'art		

Les étapes pour écrire un CV:

- Indiquez votre objectif professionnel clairement.
- Fournissez toutes les informations pour que le recruteur puisse vous contacter, y compris votre adresse e-mail.
- Incluez vos compétences et votre formation et expérience et les résultats universitaires s'ils sont bons.
- Rédigez. Le contenu doit tenir (*fit*) sur une page.

Essential Instruction

1. The **Stratégie communicative** is a challenging exercise for your high-ability students. Your lower-ability students can participate with modifications.
2. Students should investigate every term in **Search words** for the vocabulary needed to write a CV.
3. The **étapes pour écrire un CV** should be followed step by step.
4. The CV of Charlotte Hoffman serves as a clear example of how their CV should look.

MODÈLE

Charlotte Hoffman
Tel: 06.21.83.52.22

101 rue Paradis 13006 Marseille
charlotte.hoffman@iae-paris.com

22 ans
Candidate pour un poste de gestion de projet intranet nouvelle génération en apprentissage

Formation

–2011/2012 Master d'informatique 2- traitement de données, IAE Aix-en-Provence
–2010 Master 1- Science du Management, IAE Aix-en-Provence
Enseignements: Communication, Marketing, Stratégie, Économie, Anglais.
–2007 DUT GEA Option Petites et Moyennes Organisations, IUT de Marseille
–2005 Baccalauréat Economique option Mathématique Mention AB, Lycée Marcel Pagnol Marseille.

Connaissances acquises

Bilingue français-anglais, italien: réactualisable.
Informatique
Excellente culture web et grand intérêt pour les nouvelles technologies

Expériences professionnelles et associatives

Capgémini: analyse du besoin du client, conception, développement et intégration de produits et de solutions technologiques pour les systèmes d'informations

Emplois étudiants

Hôtesse de Caisse, Carrefour, Marseille, France
Vendeuse, Magasin de vêtements Zara, Marseille, France

Passetemps

Équitation (galop 6), footing, lecture

Reference Desk

A number of online job search sites in France offer a wide variety of information for jobseekers. Encourage students to read "**8 conseils simples pour un CV efficace et concis**" for suggestions.

Differentiated Learning

Accelerate

Have students research real or imagined summer internships. They might want to apply for a higher position in a job they already have. Encourage your students to re-invent themselves, if necessary, to make the CV believable.

Decelerate

Ask students to create a personal CV using Charlotte's as a template. Doing this gives them a solid format from which to work.

RESOURCES

e-visual 25

Workbook 1–5

Flash Cards

Listening Activity 1

Drill & Practice Games

Reference Desk

1. **Se faire soigner** means "to get oneself cared for."
2. **Se casser la cheville** means "to break an ankle." Students need to know that body parts are never expressed with a possessive adjective. We know it is her ankle by the pronoun **se.** This rule is true for reflexives like **se laver la figure** and not **se laver sa figure**.
3. **La Sécu** is a truncated word for **la sécurité sociale.** The same is true for **le kiné** which is short for **le kinésitérapeute**.
4. **On peut en discuter advantage. Davantage** means "more." Since **discuter** is followed by **de**, the replacement for the preposition is **en.**
5. Supplementary vocabulary: **un plâtre** (*a cast*); **un fauteuil roulant** (*a wheelchair*); **des béquilles** (*crutches*).

Vocabulaire actif

emcl.com
WB 1–2
LA 1
Games

L'assurance maladie et le débat

Qui a droit à l'assurance maladie?

Essential Instruction

1. Have students listen to **l'assurance maladie et le débat.**
2. Ask students to draw illustrations for Mme Tautou's accident on a makeshift storyboard in their notebooks and label each square.
3. Have students create a graphic organizer to display the expressions needed for a debate. They might want to draw two people debating and expressing opposing views by using dialogue balloons for each expression.
4. Students listen to **Pour la conversation** and **Et si je voulais dire...?**, then copy the terms in their notebooks for future reference.
5. Have students conjugate **prescrire** (like **écrire**) and **se sentir** in various tenses.

Une méthode de débat:  1.3

emcl.com
WB 3–5

1. Pour introduire votre position:
   A. Je suis pour/contre… pour deux raisons principales.
   B. Premièrement,….
   Deuxièmement,….
2. Pour répondre aux arguments de la première personne:
   A. Tu as raison. Je suis entièrement de ton avis.
   B. Tu as tort. J'ai un autre point de vue.
3. Pour répondre aux arguments de la deuxième personne:
   A. par contre - *on the other hand*
   au contraire - *on the contrary*
   cependant - *however*
   néanmoins - *nevertheless*
   évidemment - *evidently*
   d'ailleurs - *moreover*
   B. Je continue avec un deuxième argument.
   C. Une citation de… illustre….
   Les chiffres indiquent….
   Par exemple, j'ai une anecdote qui montre….

Pour la conversation   1.1, 5.1

How do I express that someone has a right?

› Mamy **a droit à** une voiture médicalisée….
Grandma has the right to medical transportation.

How do I express that someone can afford something?

› Elle **a les moyens de** payer un taxi normal.
She has the means to pay for a normal taxi.

How do I express I want to discuss something in more detail later?

› **On peut en discuter davantage plus tard.**
We can discuss it more later.

Et si je voulais dire…? 

un cabinet médical	*medical practice*
l'état de santé (m.)	*state of health*
une ordonnance	*prescription*
consulter	*to consult*
prescrire	*to prescribe*

Reference Desk

1. Supplementary vocabulary: **la chirugie** (*surgery*); **un(e) chirugien(ne)** (*a surgeon*); **une radio** (*an x-ray*); **une prise du sang** (*a blood test*); **guérir** (*to cure*). **Un toubib** is slang for doctor or medic.
2. **L'addition** refers to the bill in a restaurant and **la facture** to a billed statement.
3. Make sure students know the difference in English between complimentary and complementary. The latter is used for **assurance complémentaire.**
4. **Le moyen** means "the means," and **les moyens** implies financial means.

Expansion

Have students perform the following skit. A hypochondriac is visiting a doctor and complaining of many unusual ailments (using the **Et si je voulais dire…?** vocabulary and **avoir mal** expressions) only to find out that the doctor is a veterinarian. Have students play out the scene and improvise dialogue, or a have a narrator give stage directions to two students.

Differentiated Learning

Accelerate
Have students research the distribution of benefits of **la sécurité sociale.**
Search words: **sécurité-sociale française**

Decelerate
Ask students to write a simple composition of "**Une visite chez le médecin**" incorporating the vocabulary from **Et si je voulais dire…?**

Special Needs Students

Social Anxiety
For students who fear appearing in front of the class in a speaking role, suggest they act out skits under the direction of a narrator.

Answers

1. B
2. C
3. A
4. C
5. B

Script can be found in the front pages of the Annotated Teachers Edition.

1. Luc
2. Luc
3. Juliette
4. Luc
5. Juliette

3 *Answers will vary.*

Culture

Practices: Activity

Coluche reflects that "**À la sécurité sociale, tout est assuré sauf la pendule. Ça, on ne risque pas de la voler, le personnel a les yeux constamment fixés dessus.**" Explain.

Communication

Interpersonal: Cooperative Groups

Divide the class into two groups. Tell them that they are lawyers preparing the case for and against government health programs which will be argued before the Supreme Court. Give them time to make their case from their assigned point of view before conducting the debate. Consider assigning students in groups according to their personal point of view.

1 Les arguments

1.2

Complétez les phrases suivantes logiquement.

1. Une personne avec les moyens peut payer son traitement médical; ..., une personne pauvre sans assurance maladie ne peut pas.
   A. d'ailleurs B. par contre C. par exemple
2. Une personne pauvre a... droit aux services médicaux.
   A. au contraire B. contre C. néanmoins
3. Je ne veux pas en discuter maintenant, mais on peut en discuter... plus tard.
   A. davantage B. cependant C. d'ailleurs
4. Cette citation de l'article illustre la valeur du kiné, ... j'ai encore des doutes.
   A. deuxièmement B. d'ailleurs C. cependant
5. Mais non, tu as tort, je ne suis pas contre l'assurance maladie. ..., je suis pour.
   A. Tu as raison B. Au contraire C. Les chiffres

2 Quel débat!

1.2, 1.2

Interpretive Communication

Écrivez les numéros 1–5. Écoutez le débat entre Juliette et Luc sur l'assurance maladie. Puis, identifiez la personne décrite.

1. Cette personne commence avec deux arguments contre l'assurance maladie privée.
2. Il est important pour cette personne que les gens âgés puissent se faire soigner quand ils tombent malades.
3. Cette personne a un argument économique.
4. Cette personne pense que les abus par rapport à l'assurance maladie doivent être contrôlés.
5. Cette personne propose de continuer la conversation plus tard.

3 Questions personnelles

1.3

Interpersonal Communication

Répondez aux questions suivantes.

1. Dans un débat, est-ce que tu perds ou tu gagnes plus souvent?
2. Comment est-ce que tu préfères illustrer ta position, avec une citation, des chiffres, ou une anecdote?
3. À quoi est-ce qu'on devrait avoir droit, selon toi?
4. Es-tu pour ou contre l'assurance maladie pour tous?
5. Qu'est-ce qui se passe dans ton pays quand une personne malade n'a pas les moyens de se faire soigner?

Essential Instruction

1. Have students review the **Vocabulaire** and debate expressions on pp. 478–479 before doing **Activités 1**, **2**, and **3**.
2. Correct these exercises as a whole-group activity.
3. Students watch the **Rencontres culturelles** video with books closed. Ask what the dialogue was about, and have students give details they remember.
4. Have students listen to **Mamy a pris rendez-vous chez le kinésithérapeute** then read the dialogue aloud with a partner.
5. Have them write their answers to **Activité 4** on white boards showing you their answers each time.

Rencontres culturelles

emcl.com WB 6

Mamy a pris rendez-vous chez le kinésithérapeute.

   1.1, 1.2

Léo téléphone à sa sœur.

Léo: Tu ne viens pas?

Élodie: Non, je ne peux pas, je dois accompagner Mamy. Elle va chez le kiné. Elle m'a téléphoné parce qu'elle était tombée hier.

Léo: Mais tu n'as pas ton permis.... Tu y vas comment?

Élodie: T'inquiète pas. Mamy a droit à une voiture médicalisée pour l'emmener, ça lui coûte 2,40 euros....

Léo: Quoi? Mais Mamy, elle a les moyens de payer un taxi normal!

Élodie: Oui, c'est vrai, tu as raison. Mais c'est un service de la sécu et comme elle a des difficultés à marcher, elle y a droit....

Léo: Quel pays! Rien que des droits! Eh bien, moi, je suis contre... pas contre Mamy, mais contre ce système qui accorde la même chose à tout le monde: premièrement, ça coûte très cher à la collectivité et deuxièmement, il y a des choix dans la manière de se faire soigner qui dépendent de chacun.

Élodie: Et que chacun doit payer selon ses moyens, j'ai compris.

Léo: Oui, il y a des assurances individuelles pour ça.

Élodie: Je ne suis pas d'accord, mais on peut en discuter davantage plus tard. Maintenant je file!

4 Mamy a pris rendez-vous chez le kinésithérapeute.

  1.2, 1.3

Répondez aux questions.

1. Qu'est-ce qu'Élodie fait aujourd'hui?
2. Qu'est-ce qui est arrivé à sa grand-mère?
3. Qui va la soigner?
4. Comment est-ce qu'on va au cabinet du kinésithérapeute?
5. Qu'est-ce que Léo pense de l'assurance maladie pour tous? Pourquoi?

RESOURCES

 Dialogue Video

 Workbook 6

Answers

1. Elle doit accompagner sa grand-mère chez le kiné.
2. Elle est tombée.
3. le kinésithérapeute
4. en voiture médicalisée
5. Il pense que ça coûte cher à la collectivité, et que les gens ont le droit de choisir comment se faire soigner.

Culture

Practices: Information

When you call **le SAMU**, a French ambulance, the dispatcher takes down details of your problem and then sends out a private ambulance with a driver or, if necessary, a mobile intensive care unit. For less serious problems, **le SAMU** will dispatch a doctor for a house call. If you prefer to be taken to a particular hospital, you should mention this to the ambulance crew, as the usual procedure is to take you to the nearest one. In emergency cases (those requiring intensive care units), billing will be taken care of later. Otherwise, you need to pay in cash at the time you receive assistance.

Differentiated Learning

Accelerate

Have students write a three-paragraph position paper on their views of government-assisted health care. Ask them to research the question online and to cite examples from the research.

Decelerate

Ask students to work with a partner to create a list of pros and cons regarding government-assisted health care.

Multiple Intelligences

Mathematical-Logical

Ask students to find comparative statistics as to the number of people on welfare in the United States and France.

Special Needs Students

At-Risk Students

Students of all abilities may be receiving government benefits due to their low economic situation. Be sensitive to how this discussion could be a divisive issue in your class.

Answers

Extension

Hugo et Sophie

Reference Desk

1. **La collectivité** means the community or group as a whole.
2. The **y** in **Elle y a droit** replaces **à la voiture médicalisée**, which was stated previously in the dialogue.
3. **Emmener** means "to take someone somewhere" as **amener** means "to bring someone somewhere." **Emporter** and **apporter** are corresponding verbs meaning "to take" and "to bring" objects. In casual conversation the French use **amener** for people and things although it is not grammatically correct.
4. **Je file** is slang for **Je m'en vais** and has the sense of "I'm outta here."
5. **La prise en charge** means "coverage."
6. **La langue de bois** is double talk usually associated with politicians who talk and say nothing concrete.
7. **Le coup du fumeur** has the sense of "the smoker thing," as in the classic smoker argument people use.

Extension **Qui est pour? Qui est contre?**   1.1, 1.2

Au lycée, pendant le cours d'économie, les élèves participent à une discussion sur la prise en charge des dépenses sociales par l'État.

Prof: Bon, j'espère que vous avez préparé vos arguments. Qui commence?

Marielle: Moi. Moi, je suis pour la prise en charge des dépenses sociales par l'État. Premièrement, c'est une question de solidarité; deuxièmement, c'est une question de justice sociale....

Hugo: Bonjour la langue de bois! Moi, ce n'est pas tout à fait mon point de vue. Soyons concrets: si je fume toute ma vie et que j'ai un cancer, c'est la société qui est responsable et qui doit payer?

Théo: Évidemment, toujours le même exemple: le coup du fumeur. Par contre on peut aussi éduquer....

Caro: Entièrement de ton avis: c'est ça une société de solidarité, on fait progresser tout le monde en même temps.

Sophie: Certes. Néanmoins tout ça a un prix: qui paie?

Hugo: D'ailleurs, vous connaissez le montant du déficit des régimes sociaux? Quinze milliards d'euros....

Marielle: Qu'est-ce que c'est par rapport à un budget de mille milliards?

Théo: Si c'est le prix à payer pour conserver notre système... ce n'est pas cher payer!

Hugo: Eh bien moi, je préfèrerais qu'on me donne cet argent avec mon salaire et je ferai comme je veux. Ma santé, c'est mon choix.

Extension Quels élèves voudraient changer le système de l'assurance maladie en France?

1.2

Essential Instruction

1. For **Extension**, pair mixed-ability students to read the dialogue. Ask them to make two columns **pour** and **contre** and put the arguments of the students in the appropriate columns.
2. Have students answer the **Extension** question. Require that they cite the dialogue lines that support their answers.
3. As a class, have volunteers read **Les droits sociaux** aloud. Stop and outline on the board the principal tenets for **la solidarité collective** and **les préstations sociales**.
4. Have students research the **Search words** to add to notes taken in class.

Points de départ

Pre AP 

emcl.com
WB 7

Question centrale: Comment le passé influence-t-il le présent?

Les droits sociaux

 1.2, 3.1

Les Français manifestent contre les réformes sociales.

Issu* directement de la *Déclaration des Droits de l'homme et du citoyen* de 1789 et de la notion de "garantie sociale envers les citoyens malheureux," le modèle social français est celui de l'État-Providence. Il fait partie du programme du Conseil national de la Résistance, et il a été mis en place en 1945: il gouverne encore aujourd'hui la société française. Les Français y sont très attachés, et il est donc difficile à réformer. Il constitue aujourd'hui une véritable ligne d'affrontement* politique entre conservateurs qui veulent conserver l'État-Providence et réformateurs qui dénoncent l'État-Assistance.

Ce modèle est fondé sur le principe de la solidarité collective. Cette solidarité collective touche les domaines suivants: la protection sociale (chômage, invalidité*, retraite); la santé publique (sécurité sociale); l'éducation (gratuité du système éducatif jusqu'à l'université), et la politique familiale (allocations familiales, accueil garanti à l'école maternelle*). L'ensemble des prestations* sociales financées pour l'essentiel par les revenus du travail et de l'entreprise représentent aujourd'hui 2.000 milliards*.

Les prestations sociales sont de quatre types: les prestations de santé (maladie, invalidité, infirmité, accidents du travail); les prestations familiales (allocations selon le nombre d'enfants, congé de maternité*, congé parental, allocation logement); les prestations d'emploi (allocations chômage, allocations de préretraite); les prestations vieillesses (retraites* et pensions).

 Search words **ameli l'assurance maladie en ligne, le portail du service public de la sécurité sociale, école maternelle ministère de l'éducation nationale, prestations familiales, toutes les prestations**

issu *stemming from;* **affrontement** *confrontation;* **invalidité** *disability;* *école maternelle nursery school—pre-K;* **prestations** *benefits;* **milliard** *billion;* **congé de maternité** *maternity leave;* **retraites** *retirement*

RESOURCES

 **Workbook 7**

Communication

Interpersonal: Cooperative Groups

Divide students into groups. Have them research the viability of the French **sécu** in order to discuss "**le trou de la SS**," which is a term currently used for the deficit in funding for the French social security program. The discussion question is: Can France continue fiscally to be the **État-Providence** as in the past, or must she change? Follow with a whole-class discussion.

Differentiated Learning

Accelerate

Students write a short essay defending or denying extensive medical treatment for smokers who develop lung disease or cancer.

Decelerate

Ask students to create a word search of new vocabulary from the two readings for the class. Templates can be found online. Students can work on these word searches as a brain break between activities.

Special Needs Students

AD(H)D

It would be helpful to give these students a study sheet of basic content questions to answer while reading the dialogues.

Answers

1. 1789: date de la *Déclaration des Droits de l'homme et du citoyen;* 1945: L'État-Providence a été mis en place.
2. éducation: éducation; allocations familiales: politique familiale; invalidité: protection sociale; retraite: protection sociale; sécurité sociale: santé publique
3. A: prestations de santé; B: prestations familiales; C: prestations familiales; D: prestations familiales; E: prestations vieillesse; F: prestations d'emploi
4. *Answers will vary.*

À discuter

Answers will vary.

Critical Thinking

Comparisons

Put students into two teams to debate the **Comparisons** question. Both teams prepare their position and must give concrete reasons to support it. Each selects a debater who takes the side of the argument that his or her team prepared.

Moins de 20% des Français mettent leurs enfants à la crèche, préférant les élever eux-mêmes.

Mots-clé **Droit** est dérivé de *dreit* (842), issu du bas-latin *directum*, substantivation (*noun form*) de l'adjectif *directus*. Attesté au VIème siècle au sens général de justice, puis au VIIIème siècle au sens de règles ou d'ensemble des lois. Quelle est la signification de chacune de ces expressions qui incorpore le mot *droit?* *Je suis dans mon droit. J'y ai droit. Les droits et les devoirs.*

Pour les parents qui travaillent, **les crèches** s'occupent des bébés de deux mois et demi jusqu'à l'âge de trois ans. Les parents paient en fonction de leurs moyens.

2.2

COMPARAISONS

Quel système d'assurance, celui de votre pays ou celui de la France, est meilleur?

4.2

5 Activités culturelles

1.3, 3.1, 3.2, 4.2, 5.1

Complétez les activités suivantes.

1. Expliquez l'importance de ces dates en ce qui concerne l'État-Providence:
   - 1789
   - 1945
2. Indiquez à quel domaine appartiennent les protections sociales suivantes:
   - éducation
   - allocations familiales
   - invalidité
   - retraite
   - sécurité sociale
3. Indiquez les prestations auxquelles ces personnes ont droit en France:
   A. M. Dujardin a eu un accident de voiture et a mal au cou.
   B. M. et Mme Diop ont un bébé.
   C. M. et Mme Jussieu ont quatre enfants.
   D. M. Piedbœuf n'a pas les moyens de payer son loyer.
   E. Mme Chapelle a pris sa retraite.
   F. Mlle Hergy a perdu son emploi et elle a besoin d'argent pour vivre.
4. Comparez le système de protection sociale français et le système de protection sociale américain.

En France, on préfère l'aide à domicile aux institutions publiques.

À discuter

À votre avis, est-il plus facile d'élever (*raise*) ses enfants en France ou aux États-Unis?

Essential Instruction

1. Ask students to define **une crèche**, **une école maternelle**, and **une école élémentaire**.
2. Explain the vocabulary **démarches** (*the processes*) and **un annuaire malin** (*a clever directory*).
3. Have students work in triads to do **Activité 5**. Consider counting off by threes, putting the number ones in groups to complete activity 1, the twos in groups to complete activity 2, and the threes together for activity 3.
4. Offer activity 4 to a small group of students who present the information to the class. Have them include a visual list of the differences and/or similarities to augment their discussion.
5. Do **Activité 6** in the computer lab with all students searching the website and answering the questions.

Du côté des médias  1.2

Interpretive Communication

Lisez ces informations sur les écoles maternelles à Évry, en France.

Ecoles maternelles et élémentaires

- Inscrire mon enfant à l'école

Dès 3 ans, votre enfant a l'âge de faire ses premiers pas à l'école maternelle. A partir de 6 ans, il fait sa rentrée à l'école élémentaire. Pour l'inscrire, les démarches sont simples et entièrement gérées par la Ville. Pour les enfants nés en 2009, les inscriptions auront lieu du 13 février au 31 mai 2012 pour la rentrée scolaire de septembre 2012.

En savoir plus

- Les écoles d'Evry

Evry compte 17 écoles maternelles publiques et 21 écoles élémentaires publiques. Retrouvez toutes les coordonnées avec notre annuaire malin.

6 Écoles pour les enfants d'Évry  1.3

Complétez les phrases suivantes.

1. Ce site web accueille les parents qui habitent à....
2. Un parent peut inscrire son enfant dans une école maternelle quand l'enfant a... an(s).
3. Il ou elle va à l'école élémentaire à l'âge de... ans.
4. Il y a... écoles maternelles à Évry.
5. Il y a... écoles élémentaires publiques.

Answers

1. Évry
2. 3
3. 6
4. 17
5. 21

Communication

Presentational: Paired Practice

Encourage interested students to make a formal presentation to the class about Évry and its schools. Have them locate Évry on a map of France and include images from the website to enhance the presentation.

Differentiated Learning

Accelerate

Ask students to lead a class discussion of the question posed in **À discuter.** Have them examine government-sponsored education, medical, and social benefits of each country.

Decelerate

Give students the vocabulary terms from **la solidarité collective** and **les préstations sociales** and ask them to define each term in English.

Adapt

Ask where your students went to nursery school, kindergarten, and elementary school. What were their first memories of their schooling? Which school did they prefer? Is early education important now that there is educational television and the Internet? Would your students ever want to teach in any of these schools? Why or why not? Then have students write a short composition, "**Mes premiers souvenirs de l'école,**" based on this class discussion.

Answers

All activities will vary.

Reference Desk

Encourage students to consider the **Question centrale** as they complete **La culture sur place** activities.

La culture sur place

Question centrale: Comment le passé influence-t-il le présent?

La presse en danger

Introduction et Interrogations

La fameuse *Déclaration des Droits de l'homme et du citoyen* de 1789 est issue (*came out of*) directement de la Révolution française. Les révolutions récentes dans les pays tels que la Tunisie, l'Égypte, la Libye, et la Syrie soulignent l'importance des médias. Dans cette *Culture sur place*, nous allons discuter de la liberté de la presse et du danger qui est associé à cette liberté, surtout dans des situations comme les révolutions.

7 Première Étape: Réfléchir  1.2, 1.3, 3.2, 5.1

1. Pensez aux actualités que vous lisez, regardez, ou écoutez. Quand est-ce que les journalistes sont en danger quand ils font leurs reportages?
2. Regardez le **Baromètre de la liberté de la presse** sur le site "Reporters sans Frontières." Combien de reporters sont emprisonnés? Combien ont été tués?
3. Avec un partenaire, faites une liste de situations graves pour les reporters. Ensuite, répondez à ces questions avec votre classe:
   - Qu'est-ce que les journalistes peuvent faire pour minimiser le danger pendant qu'ils travaillent?
   - Qui est-ce qui décide des droits des journalistes à l'étranger? Y a-t-il un traité international?

8 Deuxième Étape: Étudier  1.3, 3.1, 3.2, 5.1

Lisez les objectifs de l'organisation "Reporters sans Frontières." Sur leur site, cliquez sur "Qui sommes-nous?/Présentation de Reporters sans frontières." Regardez la liste sous **Enquêter, agir, soutenir**. Faites un sommaire de ces idées.

9 Faire le point!   1.1, 1.3

Discutez des questions suivantes en classe.

1. Quel est le rôle du reporter sur la scène mondiale?
2. La liberté de la presse est-elle un droit inaliénable? Un journaliste a-t-il le droit de tout dire? Est-ce un droit universel? Pourquoi, ou pourquoi pas? Qu'est-ce que vous pensez de cette réalité?
3. Est-ce que la censure est toujours la même? Quelles sont quelques différences qui existent?
4. Est-ce que la censure entre dans votre vie? Comment? Comment est-ce que vous réagissez en général?
5. Est-il possible d'éliminer les "frontières," d'être un véritable "reporter sans frontières"? Pourquoi, ou pourquoi pas?

Essential Instruction

1. For **Activité 7**, have students research online names and nationalities of reporters who have been kidnapped or died in the line of duty. Using the questions provided, debate whether or not reporters should be in harm's way.
2. For **Activité 8**, have students do this summary individually or in partners.
3. For **Activité 9**, divide the class into three groups. Have group one prepare questions 1 and 2, group 2, questions 3 and 4, and group three, question 5. Require each group to research the answers and lead the class discussion on their topics.
4. Review **être**, then practice by throwing a soft ball to a student who conjugates **être** in the tense you indicate. Students may refer to tenses listed on the board.
5. Have students name the **être** expressions that they know; write them on the board.
6. Have students do **Activité 10**. Correct immediately afterward.

Structure de la langue

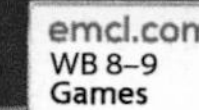

Révision: Expressions with *être*

1.1

The verb **être** is another frequently used verb in French.

Par contre, je **suis** pour la sécu médicale.	*On the other hand, I am for national health insurance.*

Also called a "building block" verb, **être** is used in a number of expressions in French where a different verb is used in English. You have already learned some common expressions with **être** that deal with agreeing with someone, giving the day/date, and saying that you are busy doing something.

Néanmoins, elle n'**est** pas **d'accord**.	*Nevertheless, she doesn't agree.*
Nous **sommes** dimanche.	*It's Sunday.*
Marc et Koffi **sont en train de** faire les corvées.	*Marc and Koffi are busy doing chores.*

To show ownership, use the expression **être à** (*to belong to*). A stress pronoun or a noun follows **être à**.

Pardon, monsieur! Ce portefeuille **est à** vous?	*Excuse me, sir! Is this wallet yours?*
Oui, merci! Il **est à** moi.	*Yes, thank you! It is mine.*

10 La fête d'anniversaire

1.1

Complétez chaque dialogue avec une expression de la liste. N'oubliez pas de conjuguer le verbe ***être*** *et d'accorder l'adjectif (masculin? féminin?), si nécessaire.*

être en train de | c'est | être en retard | être de | être au courant | être d'accord | être occupé | être chargé de | être prêt

MODÈLE —Christelle s'occupe des décorations?
—Oui, elle **est chargée des** décorations. Elle a choisi le thème "jardins" parce que l'anniversaire de Fatima est en mai.

1. —Quand est l'anniversaire de Fatima?
   —... le 14 mai.
2. —Qui enverra les invitations?
   —Les sœurs de Fatima... le faire maintenant.
3. —Fatima... Paris?
   —Non, sa famille vient du Maroc.
4. —La fête, ... à quelle heure?
   —À 18h30.
5. —Tu... à m'aider avec le gâteau d'anniversaire, Annie?
   —Oui, je suis déjà allée à l'épicerie.
6. —Christian, tu ne vas pas...?
   —Non, pas cette fois. Je serai à l'heure. C'est promis!
7. —Paul et Benoît, vous... de la fête pour Fatima?
   —Oui, nous venons d'acheter un cadeau et une carte d'anniversaire.
8. —Jacques et toi, vous... le 14 mai?
   —Non, nous sommes libres.
9. —La fête sera géniale!
   —Je....

RESOURCES

Workbook 8–9

Drill & Practice Games

Answers

1. C'est
2. sont en train de
3. est de
4. est
5. est prête
6. être en retard
7. êtes au courant
8. êtes occupés
9. suis d'accord

Communication

Interpersonal: Paired Practice

To practice using expressions + **être** in a variety of tenses, put students in pairs. Give each pair a note card with a sentence using a different expression and the tense that they are to change the sentence to, for example, **Nous étions en train d'étudier la presse française. (présent)**. Student A reads the sentence to Student B, who identifies the tense being used (**imparfait**) and then changes the sentence to the tense indicated, **Nous sommes en train d'étudier la presse française.** Have students exchange cards with another set of partners and change roles. Continue for the allotted time or until they have completed all of the cards.

Differentiated Learning

Accelerate/Decelerate

Have higher-ability students work with those who struggle with verb conjugations and adjective agreement. First, review **être** conjugations for a variety of tenses. Create a practice sheet for the coaches to use that checks comprehension of the meanings of the new **être** expressions and their use in realistic contexts.

Learning Styles

Visual Learners

Have these students create visuals representing each of the **être** expressions learned. Have them identify each expression on the back and ask them to assist you by using their visuals for review and practice.

RESOURCES

 **Workbook 10–13**

 **Listening Activity 2**

 **Drill & Practice Games**

Answers

1. Les bandes dessinées sont à Luc et moi.
2. Les sandales sont à Didier.
3. La tablette est à Mlle Magritte.
4. La casquette est à M. Delacroix.
5. Les recueils de poésie sont à Mme Leriche.
6. Les timbres sont à Solange.

Reference Desk

1. To help remember **plus-que-parfait**, suggest this jingle: P-Q-P is H-A-D since its translation is "had."
2. The **plus-que-parfait** and the **passé composé** contrast actions in the past. The **plus-que-parfait** is a "colder tense" than the **passé compose**; the action in the past happened before the past action of the **passé composé.** He *had written* the letter before he *saw* her. Writing the letter was over and done with before he saw her.

TPR

To practice distinguishing between verbs in the **imparfait** and the **plus-que-parfait**, have students make two cards each, one with "I" for the **imparfait**, and one with "P" for the **plus-que-parfait.** Read sentences that are in the imperfect or the **plus-que-parfait.** Ask students to hold up the appropriate card for the verb tense they hear.

11 Objets trouvés

1.1

À la fin de l'année scolaire, il y a beaucoup d'objets trouvés dans une boîte dans le bureau du proviseur. Dites-lui à qui est chaque objet.

MODÈLE

Karim

Le lecteur mp3 est à Karim.

Zakia

Les clés USB sont à Zakia.

1. Luc et moi

2. Didier

3. Mlle Magritte

4. M. Delacroix

5. Mme Leriche

6. Solange

Pluperfect Tense

1.1

emcl.com
WB 10–13
LA 2
Games

The **plus-que-parfait** (*pluperfect, past perfect*) is a tense used to tell what had happened in the past before another past action. It may be used to express "cause and effect." Like the **passé composé**, the **plus-que-parfait** consists of a helping verb and a past participle. To form the **plus-que-parfait**, use the imperfect tense of the helping verb **avoir** or **être** and the past participle of the main verb. Agreement of the past participle in the **plus-que-parfait** is the same as in the **passé composé**.

Camille s'est fait soigner à l'hôpital parce qu'elle était tombée sur la piste de ski!

Essential Instruction

1. Review possession with **être à** before doing **Activité 11** as a class activity.
2. Introduce the formation, translation, and use of the **plus-que-parfait.**
3. Review DR. MRS. P. VANDERTRAMP verbs conjugated with **être.**
4. Have students divide **Activité 12** with a partner; one does odds, the other does evens. Have students write the sentences before exchanging papers to correct. Students take turns reading their answers.

	répondre	tomber
j'	**avais répondu**	**étais tombé(e)**
tu	**avais répondu**	**étais tombé(e)**
il/elle/on	**avait répondu**	**était tombé(e)**
nous	**avions répondu**	**étions tombé(e)s**
vous	**aviez répondu**	**étiez tombé(e)(s)(es)**
ils/elles	**avaient répondu**	**étaient tombé(e)s**

Quand je suis rentré, j'ai rappelé à Ava de téléphoner au kiné. Mais, elle l'**avait** déjà **appelé**. Sa nièce **s'était déjà fait soigner**.

When I got home I reminded Ava to call the chiropractor. But, she had already called. Her niece had already received medical treatment.

12 Un été en France

1.3

Des élèves de votre classe de français sont restés avec des familles françaises pendant l'été. Dites ce qu'ils vous ont raconté.

MODÈLE Jamie/voir la *Joconde* au Louvre.
Jamie m'a dit qu'il avait vu la *Joconde* au Louvre.

1. vous/nager dans la mer Méditerranée
2. Heather et Amber/passer une semaine dans les Alpes
3. Zach/se promener sur les Champs-Élysées
4. tu/prendre une photo du château d'If à Marseille
5. Ashleigh/faire la connaissance des ados français
6. Justin et Tyler/prendre le métro souvent à Lyon
7. Madison/ne jamais s'ennuyer
8. Matt et Justin/aller à Cannes

COMPARAISONS

What do these examples of the **plus-que-parfait** in French and English express? **4.1**

Si tu avais écouté mes conseils!

If you had listened to my advice!

COMPARAISONS: These examples show that the **plus-que-parfait** can be used to express a wish about the past.

Answers

1. Vous m'avez dit que vous aviez nagé dans la mer Méditerranée.
2. Heather et Amber m'ont dit qu'elles avaient passé une semaine dans les Alpes.
3. Zach m'a dit qu'il s'était promené sur les Champs-Élysées.
4. Tu m'as dit que tu avais pris une photo du château d'If à Marseille.
5. Ashleigh m'a dit qu'elle avait fait la connaissance des ados français.
6. Justin et Tyler m'ont dit qu'ils avaient pris le métro souvent à Lyon.
7. Madison m'a dit qu'elle ne s'était jamais ennuyée.
8. Matt et Justin m'ont dit qu'ils étaient allés à Cannes.

Communication

Interpersonal: Cooperative Groups

Write a number for each subject pronoun on the board. Then write verbs on slips of paper and place them in lunch bags. Divide the class into groups and give each group a die and a bag of verb slips. Each student rolls the die, selects a verb slip from the bag, and makes a sentence with the **plus-que-parfait.** Once a verb is used, leave it out of the bag to prevent the verb being used again. Continue until each group has used all of the verbs.

Differentiated Learning

Decelerate

To visualize the difference between **passé compose** and **plus-que-parfait**, have students conjugate **avoir** in the **tu** form in present and, below it, in the imperfect. Across from the present, they write **parler** for **tu** in **passé composé**, and across from the imperfect, they conjugate **parler** for **tu** in the **plus-que-parfait.** Students see the correspondence between the verb forms, for example, **Tu *as*...Tu *as* parlé** and **Tu *avais*...Tu *avais* parlé.** Do this for a variety of verbs including those conjugated with **être.**

Adapt

Students write 10 sentences using the **plus-que-parfait**, **passé compose**, and the word **déjà**.
For example, **J'avais déjà mangé quand elle m'a invité au restaurant.**

Answers

Script can be found in the front pages of the Annotated Teacher's Edition.

1. D
2. B
3. A
4. F
5. E
6. C

14 *Answers will vary.*

Communication

Interpersonal: Cooperative Groups

Put students in groups of four or five to give alibis for their whereabouts at M. Montmorency's **château** when he was killed in the library at 11:00 P.M. Students take turns saying where they had been in the **château** before the murder, and where they had last seen the victim. For example, **J'avais flâné dans le jardin. J'avais vu M. Montmorency dans la salle à manger à 8h00.** Have a student play inspector Clouseau, interview the guests, and write up a report of the testimony of the group members.

13 Papy à l'hôpital

1.1, 1.2

Écrivez les numéros 1–6 sur votre papier. Écoutez le dialogue entre Chantal et son frère Théo. Ensuite, choisissez la bonne réponse à la question que vous entendez.

A. Oui, il l'avait mise dans son portefeuille avant de partir.
B. Elle s'était fait soigner par le kiné.
C. Il va rendre visite à son grand-père.
D. Il avait assisté à un concert en ville.
E. Elle était allée à l'hôpital avec Mamy.
F. Non, il avait déjà pris son dîner à la maison.

14 Qu'est-ce qui s'est passé avant...?

1.3

Pour chaque situation suivante, composez des phrases logiques au plus-que parfait indiquant ce qui a précédé. Pour chaque phrase qui n'est pas répétée par un autre groupe, votre groupe obtient un point.

MODÈLE Christine est allée en Europe.

- **Elle avait fait ses valises.**
- **Elle avait retiré de l'argent à la banque.**
- **Elle était allée à l'aéroport.**
- **Elle avait obtenu un passeport.**
- **Elle avait acheté des chèques de voyage.**

Monsieur Durand est arrivé en retard parce qu'il ne s'était pas réveillé assez tôt.

1. J'ai été embauché(e) à TechMode.
2. Ma famille et moi, nous avons fait du camping.
3. Marco et toi, vous avez donné un concert.
4. Tu es descendu(e) dans un hôtel à Paris.
5. Dikembe a écrit une composition sur Jacques Prévert pour son cours de littérature.
6. Latifa a gagné un marathon.
7. Malick s'est engagé en faveur de l'environnement.
8. Notre prof est devenu(e) prof de français.

Essential Instruction

1. Students listen to **Activité 13** and choose the best response to each question.
2. Have students make sentences about two events that happened in the past, one before the other, using the **plus-que-parfait** and the **passé compose**. Have a scribe write the sentences on the board.
3. Have students do **Activité 14** in pairs, then compare their answers with another duo.
4. For **Activité 15**, have students research medical services using the **Search words.** Have students identify by description the grandchildren speaking, their relationship to the grandmother, any directives the parents have given them to add interest.
5. **Activité 16** might tell the story of a trip your students made to the emergency room as they were growing up.
6. Students research the **Search words** online before writing **Activité 17**.

À vous la parole

Question centrale: Comment le passé influence-t-il le présent?

15 Mamy est malade.

 1.3, 5.1, 5.2

Interpretive/Presentational Communication

L'assurance maladie peut parfois payer les frais de transport en cas de maladie: domicile-hôpital, hôpital-domicile, domicile-lieu de traitement. La sécu est obligée de le faire avec une prescription médicale s'il y a des effets secondaires comme pour la chimiothérapie. Votre grand-mère souffre du cancer. Elle aura besoin de plusieurs traitements de chimiothérapie. Vos parents voyagent souvent; donc, c'est à vous, les petits-enfants, de trouver une solution. Votre grand-mère habite à Lyon. Écrivez un dialogue avec votre "frère" ou "sœur" qui parle du problème, de la solution, et explique qui va faire quoi. Enregistrez ou filmez votre dialogue.

 **Search words: vsl lyon, voiture médicalisée lyon**

Communiquez!

16 Une anecdote sur la santé

 1.3

Presentational Communication

Une anecdote est une petite histoire. Écrivez une anecdote sur quelqu'un de votre famille qui est tombé malade. Décrivez sa maladie et dites ce qui s'est passé quand il ou elle est allé se faire soigner dans un hôpital, une clinique, ou chez le kiné. Est-ce que l'assurance a payé? Enregistrez ou filmez votre présentation.

17 Entre la crèche et l'école primaire

 1.3, 4.2

Interpretive/Presentational Communication

Qui s'occupe des enfants entre la crèche et l'école primaire quand les parents travaillent? Faites une comparaison du système américain et du système français. Au lieu d'écrire un paragraphe, écrivez deux petites histoires ou conversations basées sur ce scénario: **Une mère et un père ont un fils de quatre ans. Ils travaillent tous les deux. Voici comment ils font pour s'occuper de leur enfant....**

 **Search words: jardin d'enfants, aide à domicile pour enfants de plus de 3 ans**

RESOURCES

 **Communicative Activities**

Answers

All activities will vary.

Communication

Interpersonal: Cooperative Groups

Students bring a photo depicting an activity in which they have participated. Put students in small groups. Each student describes what he or she did in the photo in the **passé composé**, then says two sentences in the **plus-que-parfait** that describe what he or she had done to prepare for that activity. For example, **"Samedi après-midi j'ai piqueniqué au zoo. Vendredi j'avais invité Claude. Samedi matin j'avais préparé des sandwichs."**

Reference Desk

Blended Instruction

Consider using blended instruction, a combination of in-class learning and computer-mediated instruction or learning opportunities. Ask students to complete activities on the computer, using their cell or smartphone, or other emerging electronic technology. This process will allow students to hone their tech skills and become more independent learners. Schedule routine Internet and e-book learning in class and in the lab.

Differentiated Learning

Accelerate

Give students two pages of a French novel featuring the **plus-que-parfait** among other tenses, and have them identify the tenses of the verbs.

Decelerate

Encourage these students to use online practice to master the **plus-que-parfait**. Small group practice is beneficial where they do a worksheet and check their answers.

Special Needs Students

Linguistically Challenged

Some students have difficulty learning this new tense because they still confuse the previous ones. A review of regular and irregular conjugations in both moods is essential each time a new verb tense is introduced.

Answers

Rencontre avec l'auteur
Possible answer: Il veut être savant, il est curieux, il est obstiné.

Pré-lecture
Answers will vary.

Stratégie de lecture
un savant; savoir;
raisonnable; raison; raisonner
félicité; félicitations; féliciter
traiter; traité; traitement, surtraitement
rouvrant; rouvert; réouverture
doute; douteux; indubitablement

Reference Desk

Before reading **l'extrait**, consider reviewing strategies for better reading comprehension: 1) Connect the topic with prior knowledge. 2) Ask questions while reading the text. 3) Visualize the content of the story. 4) Point out the most important facts in the text. 5) Draw conclusions that are not directly stated in the text. 6) Synthesize or combine information from the text with prior knowledge to create new ideas.

Lecture thématique

Pre AP

Le bourgeois gentilhomme Acte II, Scène IV

Rencontre avec l'auteur

1.2

Molière (1622–1673), pseudonyme pour Jean-Baptiste Poquelin, était un dramaturge classique du XVIIème siècle en France. Il a écrit des pièces pour le roi Louis XIV. Connu pour ses comédies de mœurs (*manners*), il a inventé une collection de "types," ou personnages stéréotypés comme le parvenu (*social climber*) M. Jourdain dans *Le bourgeois gentilhomme* dont vous allez lire un extrait. M. Jourdain voudrait se transformer en gentilhomme (*gentleman*) et pour y arriver il prend des maîtres pour l'instruire (*instruct*) et le former aux belles manières. Après avoir lu cet extrait, est-ce que vous pouvez faire un portrait de M. Jourdain? Quels sont les traits (*characteristics*) du parvenu?

Pré-lecture

1.3

Est-ce qui vous connaissez des gens qui ne sont pas contents de leur classe sociale? Qu'est-ce qu'ils font de comique?

Stratégie de lecture

1.1, 1.2

Word Families

Pour élargir votre vocabulaire, il est bon que vous appreniez des mots appartenant à la même famille linguistique. Si vous reconnaissez la racine (*root*) d'un mot, vous pouvez deviner ce que d'autres mots veulent dire. Pendant que vous lisez l'extrait de cette pièce célèbre, remplissez le tableau avec les mots que vous savez déjà et les nouveaux mots que vous allez rechercher dans le dictionnaire. Pour tous les mots de la deuxième et de la troisième colonne, indiquez aussi la partie du discours (*part of speech*). Donnez la définition de chaque mot dans la première et troisième colonne. Un exemple a été fait pour vous.

Mot de la pièce	Mot(s) que je connais déjà	Nouveaux mots que j'ai recherchés
Modèle: un gentilhomme: gentleman	**gentil** **gentillesse**	**gentiment (adv.):** kindly, nicely
un savant		
raisonnable		
félicité		
traiter		
rouvrant (*from* rouvrir)		
doute		

Essential Instruction

1. Students have already met Molière in **Unité 7.** Have them expand their appreciation of him by listening to the **Rencontre avec l'auteur.**
2. Discuss the question in **Pré-lecture.**
3. Have students read the **Pendant la lecture** questions before listening and discussing each section.
4. In pairs, have students fill out the **Stratégie de lecture** after reading each section. See who can add the most words to their list.

Outils de lecture  1.2

Dans un sens général, le cadre de l'histoire permet de situer le moment et le lieu d'une sélection littéraire. Dans ses pièces, Molière nous offre un vaste tableau de la France du XVIIème siècle. Qu'est-ce que vous remarquez de cette époque en lisant cet extrait?

Maître de Philosophie.	... Que voulez-vous apprendre?
Monsieur Jourdain.	Tout ce que je pourrai, car j'ai toutes les envies du monde d'être savant*; et j'enrage que mon père et ma mère ne m'aient pas fait bien étudier dans toutes les sciences quand j'étais jeune.
Maître de Philosophie.	Ce sentiment est raisonnable, *Nam sine doctrina vita est quasi mortis imago*. Vous entendez cela, et vous savez le latin sans doute.
Monsieur Jourdain.	Oui, mais faites comme si je ne le savais pas: expliquez-moi ce que cela veut dire.
Maître de Philosophie.	Cela veut dire que *Sans la science, la vie est presque une image de la mort.*
Monsieur Jourdain.	Ce latin-là a raison.
Maître de Philosophie.	N'avez-vous point quelques principes, quelques commencements des sciences?
Monsieur Jourdain.	Oh! oui, je sais lire et écrire.
Maître de Philosophie.	Par où vous plaît-il que nous commencions? Voulez-vous que je vous apprenne la logique?
Monsieur Jourdain.	Qu'est-ce que c'est que cette logique?
Maître de Philosophie.	C'est elle qui enseigne les trois opérations de l'esprit*.
Monsieur Jourdain.	Qui sont-elles, ces trois opérations de l'esprit?
Maître de Philosophie.	La première, la seconde, et la troisième. La première est de bien concevoir* par le moyen des universaux. La seconde, de bien juger* par le moyen des catégories; et la troisième, de bien tirer* une conséquence par le moyen des figures *Barbara, Celarent, Darii, Ferio, Baralipton*, etc.
Monsieur Jourdain.	Voilà des mots qui sont trop rébarbatifs*. Cette logique-là ne me revient point. Apprenons autre chose qui soit plus joli.
Maître de Philosophie.	Voulez-vous apprendre la morale?
Monsieur Jourdain.	La morale?

Pendant la lecture
1. Avec qui est-ce que M. Jourdain a une leçon?

Pendant la lecture
2. Qu'est-ce que M. Jourdain regrette de son enfance?

Pendant la lecture
3. Qu'est-ce que la phrase en latin exprime?

Pendant la lecture
4. M. Jourdain a-t-il quelques connaissances des sciences?

Pendant la lecture
5. Quelle est la première matière que le Maître propose?

savant *learned person;* **esprit** *mind;* **concevoir** *to conceive;* **juger** *to judge;* **tirer** *to pull out;* **rébarbatifs** *forbidding*

Answers

Outils de lecture

Possible answer: Les gens voulaient obtenir beaucoup de connaissances, ils avaient soif d'apprendre les nouvelles sciences.; Les hommes étaient influencés par des idées universelles.

Pendant la lecture

1. avec le Maître de philosophie
2. Il regrette que ses parents ne l'aient pas obligé à apprendre toutes les sciences.
3. Sans la connaissance, la vie est comme une image morte.
4. Oui, il sait lire et écrire.
5. la logique

Culture

Practices: Information

As a leitmotif, explain to students that Louis XIV was exceptionally proud of, if not vain about, his legs. It is not difficult to find paintings where his legs are prominently displayed. These should prove amusing to your students.

Differentiated Learning

Accelerate

Have students continue the chart on **Word Families** to add more words with their derivatives found in the play.

Decelerate

Ask students to read the biography of Molière. Have them explain to the class what the **Comédie Française** is, when and why it was established, and the tragic event that happened to Molière when he was performing ***Le Malade Imaginaire*** at the **Comédie Française.** (He died on stage during the performance.)

Answers

Pendant la lecture

6. Il rejette la logique (mathématiques), la morale (religieuse), la physique
7. l'orthographe

Reference Desk

1. King Louis XIV ruled as absolute monarch at Versailles, where Molière's actors entertained him. The importance of the court—20,000 strong—reached its height during his reign. While the Sun King forced nobles into financial dependence on the crown, he bestowed privileges on the **bourgeoisie**, whom he used to build his centralized bureaucracy. Bourgeois striving to rise above their social position gave Molière the idea for ***Le Bourgeois Gentilhomme***.
2. Molière borrowed characters, gestures, and comic routines from the Italian theater (**commedia dell'arte**). Most of his comic characters are excessive types whose passions are out of balance.
3. In 1670 Louis XIV ordered a Turkish ballet. The musician Lully along with Molière created the **comédie-ballet**, ***Le Bourgeois gentilhomme***, staged at the **Château de Chambord**. Molière played M. Jourdain, and Lully was the Grand Mufti. For the Court, the comedy was secondary to the dancing, music, and the Turkish extravaganza, which were the core of the play.

Maître de Philosophie. Oui.

Monsieur Jourdain. Qu'est-ce qu'elle dit cette morale?

Maître de Philosophie. Elle traite de la félicité, enseigne aux hommes à modérer leurs passions, et....

Monsieur Jourdain. Non, laissons cela. Je suis bilieux comme tous les diables; et il n'y a morale qui tienne, je me veux mettre en colère tout mon soûl, quand il m'en prend envie.

Maître de Philosophie. Est-ce la physique que vous voulez apprendre?

Monsieur Jourdain. Qu'est-ce qu'elle chante cette physique?

Maître de Philosophie. La physique est celle qui explique les principes des choses naturelles, et les propriétés du corps; qui discourt de la nature des éléments, des métaux*, des minéraux, des pierres, des plantes et des animaux, et nous enseigne les causes de tous les météores, l'arc-en-ciel*, les feux volants, les comètes, les éclairs, le tonnerre, la foudre*, la pluie, la neige, la grêle*, les vents et les tourbillons*.

Monsieur Jourdain. Il y a trop de tintamarre* là-dedans, trop de brouillamini.

Maître de Philosophie. Que voulez-vous donc que je vous apprenne?

Monsieur Jourdain. Apprenez-moi l'orthographe.

Maître de Philosophie. Très volontiers.

Monsieur Jourdain. Après vous m'apprendrez l'almanach, pour savoir quand il y a de la lune et quand il n'y en a point.

Maître de Philosophie. Soit. Pour bien suivre votre pensée et traiter cette matière en philosophe, il faut commencer selon l'ordre des choses, par une exacte connaissance de la nature des lettres, et de la différente manière de les prononcer toutes. Et là-dessus j'ai à vous dire que les lettres sont divisées en voyelles*, ainsi dites voyelles parce qu'elles expriment les voix; et en consonnes*, ainsi appelées consonnes parce qu'elles sonnent avec les voyelles, et ne font que marquer les diverses articulations des voix. Il y a cinq voyelles ou voix: A, E, I, O, U.

Monsieur Jourdain. J'entends tout cela.

Maître de Philosophie. La voix A se forme en ouvrant fort la bouche: A.

Monsieur Jourdain. A, A. Oui.

Pendant la lecture

6. Quelles autres matières est-ce que M. Jourdain rejette?

Pendant la lecture

7. Qu'est-ce que M. Jourdain décide d'apprendre?

arc en ciel *rainbow;* **tonnerre** *thunder;* **foudre** *lightening;* **grêle** *hail;* **tourbillons** *whirlwinds;* **tintamarre** *hullaballoo;* **voyelles** *vowels;* **consonnes** *consonants*

Essential Instruction

1. Have students listen to the play. Stop the recording at the end of each "lesson" (**la logique**, **la morale**, **la physique**, and **l'orthographe**), and ask for their reaction. Is M. Jourdain really learning something new?
2. Ask students to find words that reveal that M. Jourdain is a very emotional man. (**J'enrage**, **je suis bilieux**, **je veux me mettre en colère**.)
3. Encourage them to guess what **tintamarre** and **brouillamini** mean in context. (Confusion)

Maître de Philosophie.	La voix E se forme en rapprochant* la mâchoire* d'en bas de celle d'en haut: A, E.
Monsieur Jourdain.	A, E, A, E. Ma foi! oui. Ah! que cela est beau!
Maître de Philosophie.	Et la voix I en rapprochant encore davantage les mâchoires l'une de l'autre, et écartant* les deux coins de la bouche vers les oreilles: A, E, I.
Monsieur Jourdain.	A, E, I, I, I. Cela est vrai. Vive la science!
Maître de Philosophie.	La voix O se forme en rouvrant* les mâchoires en rapprochant les lèvres par les deux coins, le haut et le bas: O.
Monsieur Jourdain.	O, O. Il n'y a rien de plus juste. A, E, I, O, I, O. Cela est admirable! I, O, I, O.
Maître de Philosophie.	L'ouverture de la bouche fait justement comme un petit rond qui représente un O.
Monsieur Jourdain.	O, O, O. Vous avez raison, O. Ah! la belle chose, que de savoir quelque chose!
Maître de Philosophie.	La voix U se forme en rapprochant les dents sans les joindre* entièrement, et allongeant* les deux lèvres en dehors, les approchant aussi l'une de l'autre sans les joindre tout à fait: U.
Monsieur Jourdain.	U, U. Il n'y a rien de plus véritable: U.
Maître de Philosophie.	Vos deux lèvres s'allongent comme si vous faisiez la moue*; d'où vient que si vous la voulez faire à quelqu'un, et vous moquer de lui, vous ne sauriez lui dire que: U.
Monsieur Jourdain.	U, U. Cela est vrai. Ah! que n'ai-je étudié plus tôt, pour savoir tout cela?
Maître de Philosophie.	Demain, nous verrons les autres lettres, qui sont les consonnes.
Monsieur Jourdain.	Est-ce qu'il y a des choses aussi curieuses qu'à celles-ci?
Maître de Philosophie.	Sans doute. La consonne D, par exemple, se prononce en donnant du bout de la langue* au-dessus des dents d'en haut: DA.
Monsieur Jourdain.	DA, DA. Oui. Ah! les belles choses! les belles choses!

Pendant la lecture
8. Que dit M. Jourdain de cette "science"?

Pendant la lecture
9. M. Jourdain est-il un étudiant sérieux?

rapprochant *bringing closer;* **mâchoire** *jaw;* **écartant** *moving apart;* **rouvrant** *re-opening;* **joindre** *to join;* **allongeant** *extending;* **faisiez la moue** *were pouting;* **bout de la langue** *tip of the tongue*

Answers
Pendant la lecture
8. que c'est une vraie science
9. Non, il ne veut pas apprendre ce qu'il ne connaît pas, mais répéter ce qu'il connaît.

Reference Desk
Consider the verbs used in **le Maître de Philosophie** explanations of how M. Jourdain should hold his mouth and lips to form the vowel sounds: **écarter** (*to separate, move apart*); **rapprocher** (*to bring together*); **allonger** (*to lengthen*); **joindre** (*to join*); **appuyer** (*to press*). Review these verbs and then have the students follow the **Maître's** directions.

Differentiated Learning
Adapt
Show a clip of "**La leçon d'orthographe**" which shows the physical comedy and costuming of the scene.
Search words: le bourgeois gentihomme, act II, scene IV

Learning Styles
Visual Learners
Encourage these students to create a humorous drawing of M. Jourdain's head and face as he tries to pronounce the vowel sounds. Have the students identify the body parts mentioned in the scene: **la mâchoire, les dents, les lèvres, la bouche, la langue, le palais.**

Answers

Pendant la lecture

10. Il voudrait écrire un mot d'amour à une femme.
11. Il refuse de croire que la prose est le contraire de la poésie, que c'est un langage commun.

Reference Desk

The equivalent of "six of one, half a dozen of the other" is **bonnet blanc ou blanc bonnet**.

Maître de Philosophie.	L'F en appuyant les dents d'en haut sur la lèvre de dessous: FA.
Monsieur Jourdain.	FA, FA. C'est la vérité. Ah! mon père et ma mère, que je vous veux de mal!
Maître de Philosophie.	Et l'R, en portant le bout de la langue jusqu'au haut du palais*, de sorte qu'étant frôlée* par l'air qui sort avec force, elle lui cède, et revient toujours au même endroit, faisant une manière de tremblement: RRA.
Monsieur Jourdain.	R, R, RA; R, R, R, R, R, RA. Cela est vrai. Ah! l'habile* homme que vous êtes! et que j'ai perdu de temps! R, R, R, RA.
Maître de Philosophie.	Je vous expliquerai à fond toutes ces curiosités.
Monsieur Jourdain.	Je vous en prie. Au reste, il faut que je vous fasse une confidence. Je suis amoureux d'une personne de grande qualité, et je souhaiterais que vous m'aidassiez à lui écrire quelque chose dans un petit billet* que je veux laisser tomber à ses pieds.
Maître de Philosophie.	Fort bien.
Monsieur Jourdain.	Cela sera galant, oui.
Maître de Philosophie.	Sans doute. Sont-ce des vers que vous lui voulez écrire?
Monsieur Jourdain.	Non, non, point de vers.
Maître de Philosophie.	Vous ne voulez que de la prose?
Monsieur Jourdain.	Non, je ne veux ni prose ni vers.
Maître de Philosophie.	Il faut bien que ce soit l'un, ou l'autre.
Monsieur Jourdain.	Pourquoi?
Maître de Philosophie.	Par la raison, Monsieur, qu'il n'y a pour s'exprimer* que la prose, ou les vers.
Monsieur Jourdain.	Il n'y a que la prose ou les vers?
Maître de Philosophie.	Non, Monsieur: tout ce qui n'est point prose est vers; et tout ce qui n'est point vers est prose.
Monsieur Jourdain.	Et comme l'on parle qu'est-ce que c'est donc que cela?
Maître de Philosophie.	De la prose.
Monsieur Jourdain.	Quoi! quand je dis: "Nicole, apportez-moi mes pantoufles* et me donnez mon bonnet de nuit," c'est de la prose?

Pendant la lecture

10. Pourquoi M. Jourdain demande-t-il l'aide du Maître?

Pendant la lecture

11. Que dit M. Jourdain à propos de la prose?

palais *palate;* **frôlée** *brushed against;* **habile** *skillful;* **billet** lettre d'amour; **s'exprimer** *to express;* **pantoufles** *slippers*

Essential Instruction

1. Students continue listening to the scene up to the words: **"Je vous expliquerai à fond toutes ces curiosités."** Discuss difficult sections then replay.
2. In pairs, have students prepare the scene for a short performance.
3. Finish the scene. Ask why M. Jourdain is so intent on his lessons.
4. Note the comic effect of **que vous m'aidassiez**, and **que j'en susse rien.** The imperfect of the subjunctive is rarely if ever used except for comic effect.
5. Listen to the poetry-prose lesson. Why is the discussion of **la prose ou les vers** amusing?
6. Check comprehension: Why are the multiple renditions of the poem amusing? Do they make sense? What conclusion does M. Jourdain arrive at after this lesson? How do we know that M. Jourdain is still dazzled by the philosophy teacher? (He wants him to return.)
7. What example of prose reflects the simple no-nonsense life of M. Jourdain? (**pantoufles, bonnet de nuit**)

Maître de Philosophie.	Oui, Monsieur.
Monsieur Jourdain.	Par ma foi! Il y a plus de quarante ans que je dis de la prose sans que j'en susse rien, et je vous suis le plus obligé du monde de m'avoir appris cela. Je voudrais donc lui mettre dans un billet: *Belle Marquise, vos beaux yeux me font mourir d'amour*; mais je voudrais que cela fût mis d'une manière galante, que cela fût tourné gentiment.
Maître de Philosophie.	Mettre que les feux de ses yeux réduisent* votre cœur en cendres*; que vous souffrez nuit et jour pour elle les violences d'un....
Monsieur Jourdain.	Non, non, non, je ne veux point* tout cela; je ne veux que ce que je vous ai dit: *Belle Marquise, vos beaux yeux me font mourir d'amour.*
Maître de Philosophie.	Il faut bien étendre* un peu la chose.
Monsieur Jourdain.	Non, vous dis-je, je ne veux que ces seules paroles-là dans le billet, mais tournées à la mode, bien arrangées comme il faut. Je vous prie de me dire un peu, pour voir, les diverses manières dont on les peut mettre.
Maître de Philosophie.	On les peut mettre premièrement comme vous avez dit: *Belle Marquise, vos beaux yeux me font mourir d'amour*. Ou bien: *D'amour mourir me font, belle Marquise, vos beaux yeux*. Ou bien: *Vos yeux beaux d'amour me font, belle Marquise, mourir*. Ou bien: *Mourir vos beaux yeux, belle Marquise, d'amour me font*. Ou bien: *Me font vos yeux beaux mourir, belle Marquise, d'amour*.
Monsieur Jourdain.	Mais de toutes ces façons-là, laquelle est la meilleure?
Maître de Philosophie.	Celle que vous avez dite: *Belle Marquise, vos beaux yeux me font mourir d'amour*.
Monsieur Jourdain.	Cependant je n'ai point étudié, et j'ai fait cela tout du premier coup*. Je vous remercie de tout mon cœur, et vous prie de venir demain de bonne heure.
Maître de Philosophie.	Je n'y manquerai pas....

Pendant la lecture

12. Selon le Maître, laquelle des versions de la lettre est la meilleure?

réduisent *reduce;* **cendres** *ashes;* **ne... point** *none;* **étendre** *to extend;* **du premier coup** *at the first try*

Post-lecture  1.2

M. Jourdain est-il un étudiant doué? Pourquoi, ou pourquoi pas?

Answers

Pendant la lecture

12. la première

Post-lecture

Non, il n'est pas doué parce qu'il pense que rien n'est bon si ce n'est pas approuvé par un "maître", et il n'a pas de curiosité pour les choses nouvelles.

Reference Desk

1. **Un savant** can be a learned person or a scientist.
2. **L'esprit** means "mind," "spirit," and "wit." **Elle a de l'esprit** means "She is witty."
3. **Faire la moue** means "to pout." Ask students to say **moue** to see if their mouth indeed resembles a pout.
4. **Un billet de 5 euros** means a 5 euro bill. **Billet** refers to a ticket for the theater or for an airplane. **Billet** also means "letter." The word "billydoo," heard in country and western music, is a deformation of the word **billet–doux**, meaning "love letter."
5. **Pantoufles** means "slippers." **Un pantouflard** is a homebody who likes to stay in his house shoes.

Differentiated Learning

Expand

Have students search for images online of the various productions of ***Le Bourgeois Gentilhomme***. Have students collaborate to make a collage on a large poster board of the different interpretations of the play from the classic French 18th century staging to contemporary times. Ask what that suggests about the timelessness of the play. Is the message in the play as relevant today as it was then? Give examples.

Special Needs Students

Auditory Impairment

Pause the recording frequently so that students can process the French more slowly. Make sure that students with hearing problems use earphones or sit close to the source of the recording.

RESOURCES

Pre-test

Leçon Quiz

Answers

Le monde visuel

Cette photo représente bien le caractère superficiel et égoïste de M. Charon, qui est très fier, donc habillé de grands vêtements. Il aurait pu dire à Charon de se tenir grand et fier.

18 *Activities will vary.*

Reference Desk

J'ai le mot sur le bout de la langue is the equivalent of "I have the word on the tip of my tongue."

Critical Thinking

Analysis

Les Saveurs du Palais is a film about President Mitterand's cook at the **Elysée** palace in which the master chef prepares the president's favorite regional dishes. How is the title ***Les Saveurs du Palais*** a play on words? (**Palais** is a palate and a palace.)

Le monde visuel

1.2, 3.1

Serge De Sazo (1915–2012) est un photographe français d'origine russe. Il s'installe à Paris en 1922. Il devient soldat en 1942, et en 1944 il prend des photos de la Libération de Paris qui font le tour du monde et marquent sa renommée (*fame*). Dans la vie d'après-guerre, quand Paris se réanime, ses photos de cabaret, jazz, music-hall, et cinéma paraissent (*appear*) dans de nombreuses publications. Plus tard, il se consacre aux photos sous-marines. Sur cette photo on voit le célèbre acteur Jacques Charon jouer le personnage de M. Jourdain. Comment De Sazo rend-il hommage à la pièce de Molière? Pense-t-il que la manière dont "M. Jourdain" s'habille et se tient soit importante? Qu'est-ce qu'il aurait pu dire à Jacques Charon pour qu'il prenne une telle pose?

***"Jacques Charon dans* Le bourgeois gentilhomme,"** 1974. Serge De Sazo.

18 Activités d'expansion

1.3, 3.1, 3.2

Faites les activités suivantes.

1. Faites un sommaire de ce qui se passe dans cette scène en vous servant des mots de la grille que vous avez remplie.
2. Présentez une partie de la sélection devant la classe. Travaillez avec un groupe. Distribuez les rôles. Vous aurez besoin de deux acteurs, de quelqu'un qui s'occupe des costumes, quelqu'un qui s'occupe des lignes, quelqu'un qui joue le rôle du metteur en scène, et de quelqu'un qui joue le rôle du scénographe (*set designer*).
3. Faites le portrait d'un parvenu d'aujourd'hui. Écrivez une pièce, un poème, une histoire, ou une anecdote.
4. Trouvez le lien qui existe entre Molière et La Comédie-Française à Paris.
5. Faites des recherches sur un des sujets suivants pour mieux connaître la France au XVIIème siècle. Faites une présentation à la classe.
   - la vie à la cour de Versailles
   - le règne de Louis XIV
   - la journée de Louis XIV

   Search words: versailles site officiel

   - l'importance de la bourgeoisie au le XVIIème siècle
   - la vie de Molière
   - l'intrigue (*plot*) d'une autre pièce de Molière

Essential Learning

1. Discuss **Post-lecture** in small groups, then as a class.
2. Discuss costuming using the photo of Jacques Charon as an example. Compare this costume to paintings and drawings of courtiers at Versailles. Is this attire typical or exaggerated?
3. For **Activité 18**, have all students do number 1, the **sommaire**.
4. Assign mixed-ability partners for **Activité A**.
5. Consider assigning specific topics to partners according to interest or ability.
6. Discuss each question explaining what is required and the resources needed to complete the task.
7. Students do **B** and **C** or, in the interest of time, assign one of them. All work is shared with the class.
8. Give students a study day to complete part **D**. Be available to answer any questions or give additional instruction.

T'es branché?

Projets finaux

A Connexions par Internet: L'art oratoire

1.3

Interpersonal Communication

Avec un partenaire, choisissez l'un des thèmes ci-dessous. Il faut qu'une personne prenne la position pour l'argument et l'autre la position contre. Servez-vous du vocabulaire dans la *Leçon C*. Enregistrez ou filmez votre discours.

- Est-il important d'augmenter les impôts pour payer les cours d'art dans les écoles?
- Le gouvernement devrait-il payer pour la garde des enfants avant l'école primaire?
- Devrait-on avoir une assurance maladie pour tous aux États-Unis?
- Est-il important d'augmenter les impôts pour payer les programmes sportifs dans les écoles?

B Communautés en ligne

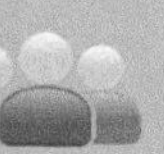

1.3, 2.1, 3.2

Europass/Presentational Communication

Europass aide les Européens à exprimer leurs compétences et qualifications pour trouver un emploi ou une formation. Faites des recherches sur Europass en ligne. Quels sont les cinq documents nécessaires à remplir? Quels documents doit préparer la personne qui cherche un travail? Quels autres documents sont nécessaires? Qui les prépare? On montre les cinq documents à qui? Quelles sont les principales fonctions des Centres nationaux Europass? Où se trouve le Centre national en France? Imaginez que vous êtes prof et que vous voulez que vos élèves se rendent compte que ce service existe. Faites une vidéo pour les informer sur Europass. Servez-vous de graphiques et de photos dans votre vidéo.

Search words: europass

C Passez à l'action!

1.3, 3.2

Passeport de langues Europass et mon portfolio/Presentational Communication

Pour chercher du travail en Europe, un employeur aura besoin de connaître vos compétences linguistiques. Cherchez un exemple d'un passeport de langues en ligne et préparez votre propre passeport linguistique. Mettez-le dans votre portfolio avec un enregistrement ou une vidéo d'une activité dont vous êtes fier/fière de *À vous la parole* de *l'Unité 8*.

Search words: europass passeport de langues

D Faisons le point!

1.3

Votre prof vous donnera un organigramme à remplir.

Answers

All activities will vary.

Reference Desk

The Europass comprises five documents: 1) CV, 2) Language passport, 3) Certificate Supplement, 4) Diploma Supplement, 5) Mobility. You can find descriptions of each in English and in French on the Europass website.

Differentiated Learning

Accelerate

Ask students to select another scene from ***Le Bourgeois Gentilhomme*** and present it dramatically to the class.

Multiple Intelligences

Musical-Rhythmic

Encourage students who enjoy music to listen to the overture to ***Le Bourgeois Gentilhomme*** by Jean-Baptiste Lully. How does this music reflect the grandeur of Versailles?

Bodily-Kinesthetic

Le Bourgeois Gentilhomme is classified a comedy-ballet. Why would the aspect of ballet interest Louis XIV?

Search words: **le roi qui danse**

RESOURCES

Listening Activity
Synthèse

Answers

A
Script can be found in the front pages of the Annotated Teacher's Edition.
1. la Révolution française
2. Bruxelles, voyage de classe
3. Commission européenne
4. petit salaire
5. assurance privée

B *Answers will vary.*

C *Answers will vary.*

Communication

Interpersonal: Cooperative Groups

Divide students into groups of four or five to review the **Contrat de l'élève.** Have them rate how well they know each topic by a system of stars, one star indicating needs review to five stars indicating mastery. Have students make a study list of topics needing more attention, and a list of those topics that can be left alone.

Évaluation

emcl.com
LA Synthèse

A Évaluation de compréhension auditive

1.1, 1.2

Interpretive Communication

Voyage scolaire

Écoutez Benoît et Margot discuter de leurs projets et voyages d'études. Ensuite, complétez la phrase avec un mot ou une expression convenable.

1. Margot a déjà étudié... dans son cours d'histoire l'année dernière.
2. Margot fait une excursion à... en....
3. Benoît voudrait faire un stage à la....
4. Si on l'embauche, il recevra un....
5. Margot doit faire une présentation sur l'....

B Évaluation orale

1.3, 3.2

Interpersonal Communication

Vous voulez gagner une bourse (scholarship) *pour faire des recherches sur l'Union européenne pour que vous puissiez l'expliquer aux Américains. Dites où vous voudriez aller pour comprendre les institutions de l'UE et décrivez le rôle de chacune.*

C Évaluation culturelle

1.3, 2.1, 3.1, 3.2, 4.2, 5.1

Vous allez comparer les cultures francophones à votre culture aux États-Unis. Vous aurez peut-être besoin de faire des recherches sur la culture américaine.

1. **Les révolutions**
   Expliquez comment la France change à la fin du XVIIIème siècle. Que veulent les Français? Comparez cette partie de l'histoire de France avec les débuts des États-Unis. Avant la Révolution américaine, qui gouvernait les colonies? Comment les Américains ont-ils changé leur destin?
2. **La guillotine et la peine de mort**
   Comment les Français exécutaient-ils les gens pendant la Révolution française? Cette méthode a duré jusqu'à quand? La France a-t-elle toujours la peine de mort? Et l'état dans lequel vous vivez?
3. **Les sièges du gouvernement**
   Expliquez où se trouvent les sièges des institutions européennes. Où se trouve le gouvernement fédéral américain? Quelles sont ses institutions?
4. **Les documents des droits humains**
   Comparez le début de la *Déclaration des Droits de l'homme et du citoyen* à cette partie de la *Declaration d'indépendance des États-Unis*.

Essential Instruction

1. Have students skim the questions before listening to **Activité A.**
2. For **Activité B**, give students time to prepare their oral work.
3. Have students research online information needed to complete **Activité C.** Assign one topic to be done thoroughly and the others in outline form.
4. Ask students to write a brief e-mail in **Activité D.** Have them refer back to the vocabulary on p. 480.
5. Have students fill out a graphic organizer using **Qui?**, **Que?**, **Où?**, **Pourquoi?**, **Quand?**, and **Comment?** as cues to help them write a composition about Marie-Antoinette imprisoned.
6. Students work in pairs to do **Activité E.**
7. Students use a storyboard to complete **Activité F** illustrating sympathetically or satirically the events toward the end of the 18th century. The description, which accompanies each frame, should reinforce whether they are royalist or revolutionary.

5. **L'assurance médicale**
Comparez l'assurance médicale en France avec l'assurance aux État-Unis. Comment les deux pays aident-ils leurs citoyens avec des soins gratuits? Qui sont exclus?

D Évaluation écrite

1.3, 3.2

Votre grand-mère est tombée. Vous voudriez qu'elle se fasse soigner. Écrivez un mail à son médecin qui:

- explique ce qui s'est passé
- décrit ses symptômes
- demande ce que vous devriez faire

E Évaluation visuelle

1.3

Décrivez qui c'est et où elle est. Expliquez les événements qui avaient eu lieu avant qu'on l'a arrêtée.

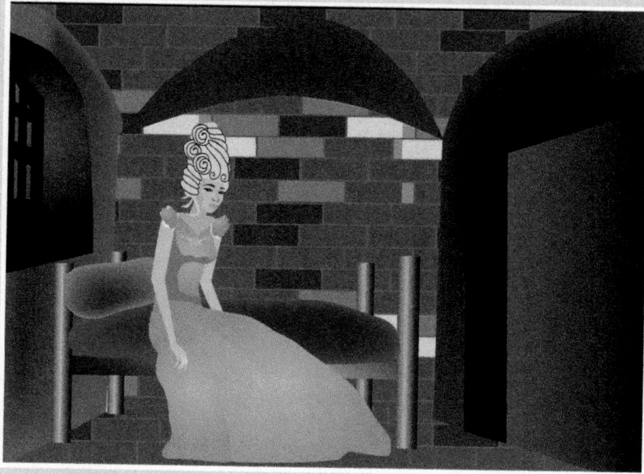

MODÈLE **On avait pris la Bastille, symbole de l'Ancien Régime....**

F Évaluation comprehensive

1.3

Créez six illustrations qui montrent l'histoire de France à la fin du XVIIIème siècle. Écrivez une description pour chaque image. Prenez le point de vue d'un personnage historique ou d'un citoyenne/d'une citoyenne dans la rue.

Answers

All activities will vary.

Reference Desk

Remind students to incorporate expressions + **être** and **plus-que-parfait** whenever possible and logical for **Activités E** and **F** as part of their review.

Communication

Interpersonal: Paired Practice

Have students work together to quiz each other orally and in written form on the vocabulary from the **Leçons** and the vocabulary list for **Unité 8**. They might want to assign categories for the vocabulary according to the themes of **histoire**, **assurances**, **emploi**, **verbes**, and **expressions**.

Differentiated Learning

Accelerate
High-ability students will be able to review the lessons in the **Unité** on their own.

Decelerate
While your high-ability students are working independently, organize a structured review of the **Leçons A**, **B**, and **C** for students who need more guided study. It is another opportunity to teach, study, and review skills with them.

RESOURCES

 **Listening Pre-test D**

 ***Unité* Test**

Vocabulaire de l'Unité 8  1.2

à: à mi-temps half-time *B*; **à plein temps** full-time *B*
accéder to access *C*
accorder to grant *C*
acquis(e) acquired *B*
une **anecdote** anecdote *C*
un(e) **aristocrate** aristocrat *A*
un(e) **assistant(e) junior** junior assistant *B*
l' **assurance (f.)** insurance *C*; **assurance maladie** health insurance *C*
au: au contraire on the contrary *C*; **au cours de** during, in the course of *B*
avoir: avoir beau to do (something) in vain *[inform.] B*; **avoir droit à** to be entititled to *C*; **avoir les moyens** to be able to afford, to have the means *C*; **avoir tort** to be wrong *C*
les **besoins (m.)** needs *A*
un **boulot** job *[inform.] B*
cependant however *C*
le **chef: chef du personnel** personnel manager *B*
chez: chez le kiné to the physical therapy office *C*
les **chiffres (m.)** figures, numbers *C*
la **chute** fall *A*
une **citation** quote *C*
un **citoyen, une citoyenne** citizen *A*
le **clergé** clergy *A*
la **collectivité** community, society *C*
la **compagnie** company *B*
complémentaire supplementary *C*
les **connaissances (f.)** knowledge *B*
un **contrat** contract *B*
un **CV** CV (Curriculum vitae) *B*
d'ailleurs moreover *C*
le **débat** debate *C*
se **débrouiller** to take care of things *B*
les **députés (m.)** deputies *A*
deuxièmement secondly *C*
des **difficultés (f.)** difficulties *C*
embaucher to hire *B*
entièrement completely, entirely *C*
un **entretien** interview *B*
un **état** state *A*
être: être à to belong to *C*; **être condamné(e)** to be condemned *A*; **être convoqué(e)** to be called *B*; **être obligé(e) (de)** to be obligated (to) *A*; **être perso** to be egotistical *[inform.] B*
des **factures (f.)** bills *C*
faire: faire ses adieux to bid farewell *A*; **faire un discours** to make a speech *A*; **faire un stage** to intern *B*
se **faire: se faire soigner** to seek (medical) treatment *C*
une **formation** education, training *B*
général(e) general *A*
gouverné ruled *A*
guéri(e) healed *C*
guillotiner to decapitate *A*
l' **hôpital (m.)** hospital *C*
illustrer to illustrate *C*
influencer to influence *A*
introduire to introduce *C*
le **kiné (kinésithérapeute)** physical therapist *C*
une **lettre: lettre de candidature** application letter *B*; **lettre de motivation** cover letter *B*
médical(e) medical *C*
médicalisé(e) medicalized *C*
mettre: mettre en pratique to put into practice *B*
mourir to die *A*
ne: N'en jette plus! Enough! Stop it! *[inform.] B*
néanmoins nevertheless *C*
on: on te fait they (one) make(s) you *A*
une **ouverture** opening *A*
par: par contre however, on the other hand *C*
partir: partir en voyage to take a journey *A*
se **passer** to happen *A*
un **permis (de conduire)** driver's license *C*
une **perruque** wig *A*
une **petite annonce** want ad *B*
la **peuple** people *A*
plein (de) a lot (of) *B*
une **position** position *C*
premièrement firstly *C*
le **présent** present *A*
privé(e) private *C*
une **qualité** quality *B*
rédiger to write *B*
la **rééducation** physical therapy *C*
un **régime** regime *A*
répondre to respond *C*
une **république** republic *A*
un **salaire** salary *B*
des **séances (f.)** sessions *C*
la **sécurité: sécurité sociale (sécu)** French national health and pension insurance *C*
des **soins (m.)** care, treatment *C*
un(e) **stagiaire** intern *B*
un **système** system *C*
une **table: table de multiplication** multiplication table *A*
tomber to fall *C*
un **traitement** treatment *C*
le **trône** throne *A*
wahou wow *B*

Essential Instruction

1. Encourage students to review the vocabulary through quizzing each other, flash cards, or rewriting the list.
2. Remind them that the letter behind the vocabulary word indicates the **Leçon** where it was featured.
3. Have students skim the questions for Parts I and II before the reading and listening evaluations to give them a sense of the gist of the offerings.
4. Students prepare for the Persuasive Essay by evaluating each point of view, making notes in the margins of remarks they want to incorporate in the essay.
5. Have them prepare a pre-writing outline to decide how to organize their essay in a logical way supported by clear examples. They must add their personal opinion about the subject, citing clear illustrations.

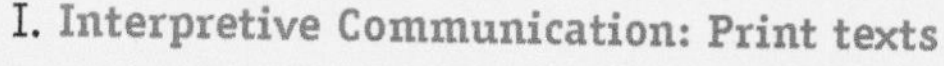

Unité 8 Bilan cumulatif 

I. Interpretive Communication: Print texts  1.2

Lisez cet article sur les jeunes gens qui viennent de finir leurs études universitaires. Puis répondez à la question.

À l'heure actuelle, il y a de plus en plus de jeunes diplômés sur le marché du travail. Par conséquent, il devient extrêmement difficile de trouver un stage de quelques mois en entreprise car la compétition est grande et féroce. C'est pourquoi aujourd'hui de nombreux jeunes partent en direction d'autres pays tels que les États-Unis pour tenter leur chance et obtenir une expérience professionnelle unique et perfectionner par la même occasion leur compétence en anglais.

1. D'après le texte, quelle difficulté la jeunesse française rencontre-t-elle aujourd'hui?
   A. **La nouvelle génération est très qualifiée mais a des difficultés à trouver des stages ou emplois.**
   B. Elle ne peut pas parler anglais.
   C. Les jeunes ne sont pas très compétitifs.
   D. Il est difficile d'obtenir un visa pour travailler à l'étranger.

II. Interpretive Coummunication: Audio Texts 1.1, 1.2

Écoutez le dialogue suivant deux fois, puis répondez aux questions.

1. La conversation a lieu....
   A. entre une Américaine et une Française
   B. entre une femme et son mari
   C. entre deux amies françaises
   D. entre une femme et sa sœur
2. Le sujet de conversation est....
   A. la vie de famille en Amérique
   B. le système médical en France par opposition au système américain
   C. le privilège de ne pas travailler au vingt-et-unième siècle
   D. le coût des médicaments en Amérique et en France
3. Les deux interlocuteurs....
   A. ne sont pas d'accord
   B. veulent vivre aux États-Unis
   C. n'aiment pas la sécu en France
   D. partagent le même point de vue sur l'assurance maladie

III. Presentational Writing: Persuasive Essay  1.2, 1.3

Vous allez écrire un essai persuasif basé sur une source que vous allez lire d'abord. Votre but est de présenter les points de vue soulevés (raised) *dans la source et de donner votre point de vue à la fin. Soutenez votre point de vue avec des exemples de la source ou de vos connaissances.*

Votre thème: L'élargissement de l'Union européenne: Trop, c'est trop? Êtes-vous pour ou contre d'autres élargissements de l'UE?

RESOURCES

 **Listening Units 7–8**

Answers

1. A

Script can be found in the front pages of the Annotated Teacher's Edition.

1. A
2. B
3. D

III *Compositions will vary.*

Reference Desk

1. The **Bilan cumulative** is based on the French Language and Culture AP exam prepared by the College Board. It assesses students' proficiencies in the Interpersonal, Interpretive, and Presentational modes of communication. Students are also asked to demonstrate their understanding of the products, practices, and perspectives of the target cultures.
2. The Print Text section consists of a variety of authentic print materials such as articles and correspondence. A multiple-choice question follows the text.
3. The Audio Text is a professional recording, usually a dialogue. Encourage students to preview and skim the questions before listening. They should then answer the multiple-choice questions.

Differentiated Learning

Decelerate

Low-ability students benefit from a study day in class where they can systematically review the content of the unit lessons. It would afford you time to have a free-question day where they can ask for help on any topic no matter how basic.

Special Needs Students

Linguistically Challenged

Simplify or reduce the scope of their tasks so that they can do well. You might want to put a ceiling of a "C" as their highest grade because of this modification.

AD(H)D

Provide students with more structure and step-by-step guidelines to help them when doing the **Evaluation.**

At-Risk Students

Some students do not have the proper atmosphere at home for study, or are working after school until late. Time in class to study would be very beneficial.

Answers

IV *Answers will vary.*

Reference Desk

In the speaking section of the assessment, students are asked to participate in a conversation or make a cultural comparison using their presentational speaking skills.

En 1951, il y avait six pays fondateurs de la Communauté européenne: l'Allemagne, la Belgique, la France, l'Italie, le Luxembourg, et les Pays-Bas. Entre 1963 et 2007, il y a eu cinq élargissements. En 2012, l'Union européenne compte 27 membres (pays adhérents). Cinq autres pays sont candidats: l'Islande, l'Ancienne République yougoslave de Macédoine, le Monténégro, la Serbie, et la Turquie; et trois pays sont candidats potentiels (l'Albanie, la Bosnie-et-Herzégovine, et le Kosovo). On peut bien se demander où s'arrêtent les frontières de l'Europe.

Des européens répondent:

Janine, 21 ans (Bordeaux): Moi, ce que j'aime c'est la possibilité de partir étudier en Europe, d'aller travailler et habiter où on veut. Quoi de mieux pour renforcer les liens et apprendre à se connaître?

Patrick, 28 ans (Dublin): L'Europe forme un bloc qui agit comme un contrepoids face à l'hégémonie d'autres blocs. Ensemble, nous sommes plus puissants face aux autres pays. Pour la sécurité de tous, l'union est importante.

Miguel, 34 (Barcelone): Si nous acceptons la Turquie, nous ouvrons nos portes au Proche et au Moyen Orient. La Turquie ne fait pas partie de l'Europe géographiquement.

Suzanne, 30 ans (Salzburg): Admettre la Turquie est un moyen d'aider au rapprochement de l'Occident et l'Orient.

Jason, 45 ans (Londres): On ne peut pas pousser la frontière de l'Europe jusqu'à l'infini! Nous commençons déjà à avoir énormément de problèmes concernant l'assimilation des immigrants, le chômage, la disparité économique entre pays riches et pays pauvres....

Victoria, 32 ans (Stockholm): On ne peut pas prévoir les conséquences bonnes ou mauvaises de l'élargissement de l'Union européenne. Mais l'important, c'est de prendre le temps de bien évaluer tous les candidats. Chaque pays doit respecter les droits de l'homme, les principes de liberté et de démocratie, et avoir des institutions et une économie stables. Sinon, on ne doit pas l'admettre. J'ai confiance dans le processus.

Sources: europa.eu, lexpress.fr, cidem.org

IV. Interpersonal Speaking: Conversation 1.2, 1.3

Vous avez une conversation avec votre petit frère qui suit le canevas ci-dessous.

Frère: Je dois présenter le portrait d'un peintre lundi prochain. Qu'est-ce que tu me conseilles?

Vous: **Dites-lui que les Impressionnistes ont changé les thèmes des tableaux et la manière de peindre. Donnez des exemples.**

Frère: Quel peintre impressionniste est-ce que tu préfères?

Vous: **Répondez, et expliquez pourquoi vous admirez cet artiste.**

Frère: Il faut que je choisisse un tableau aussi et que je le décrive.

Vous: **Recommandez une peinture et décrivez-la en le regardant. Identifiez le sujet et les couleurs. Expliquez ce qu'on voit au premier plan, au centre, et à l'arrière-plan. Dites que vous pouvez en discuter d'avantage ce soir.**

Essential Instruction

Ask students to prepare their responses for the speaking assessment. Put students in pairs and have them go through their conversation, switching roles when time is called. After the first round of conversations, ask them to reflect on what went well and what needed improvement. Discuss as a class. Have students switch partners and do the conversations again, incorporating the changes for improvement mentioned in the class reflection.

Unité

9 Récits de la vie contemporaine

505

Reference Desk

André Breton (1896–1966) was a French writer and poet. His treatise, "**Le Manifeste du surréalisme**," laid the groundwork for Surrealism.

Citation

"La plus grande faiblesse de la pensée contemporaine me paraît résider dans la surestimation extravagante du connu par rapport à ce qui reste à connaître."

The weakest point of contemporary thought seems to me to reside in the extravagant overestimation of the known with regard to what is left to be known.

—André Breton, écrivain et poète français

À savoir

Environ 50.000 étudiants français par an suivent des cours à l'étranger, et environ 250.00 étudiants internationaux suivent des cours en France.

Essential Instruction

1. Introduce the theme of the unit by having students discuss the **Citation** and the **À savoir** fact.
2. Ask if students would like to study in France, and if so, where and what?
3. Explain that in this **Unité** students will learn more about French education, the role of police in controlling crime, and the impact of social media on contemporary life.
4. Review the **Contrat de l'élève** and answer any questions.

Unité

9 Récits de la vie contemporaine

Quels sont les défis de la vie contemporaine?

Ces hommes travaillent pour quelle organisation?

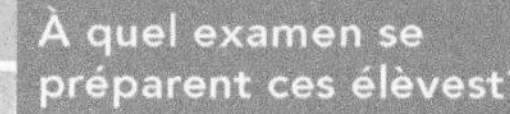

Contrat de l'élève

Leçon A I will be able to:

- express what I was incapable of doing and how someone looked.
- discuss the French educational system, including **le bac**.
- use the past conditional tense, including in clauses with **si**.

Leçon B I will be able to:

- say that I realized something.
- discuss the French police and crime.
- use possessive adjectives and possessive pronouns.

Leçon C I will be able to:

- ask when someone had an idea to do something, say what I was expecting.
- discuss teens and their connection to the Internet and social media.
- use indefinite adjectives and indefinite pronouns.

Reference Desk

Remind students that they already know the conditional tense. Ask them to tell you what they remember regarding conjugation and usage. Explain that they have already worked with if-clause sentences. Ask for some examples. Explain that they will expand their knowledge of both structures in this unit.

Differentiated Learning

Expand

Ask students in small groups to reflect on the **Question centrale.** Have them make a list of the challenges of contemporary life today. Ask students to share their list with you; put the items on the board. Circle any that relate to education, crime, or the Internet, as they will be studying these elements.

Special Needs Students

AD(H)D

Provide time for students with attention difficulties to organize their materials for the new unit. Have them prepare their notebook, binder, or folder ahead of time and ask them to decide what they no longer need. Assist them in setting up their binder with sections for vocabulary, structure, and culture notes, or any system that makes sense to them.

RESOURCES

 e-visual 26

 Workbook 1–4

 Flash Cards

 Listening Activity 1

 Drill & Practice Games

Reference Desk

1. Supplementary vocabulary: **gêné(e)** (*bothered*); **navré(e)** (*sorry*); **sidéré(e)** (*dumbfounded*); **ébloui(e)** (*dazzled*); **ravi(e)** (*delighted*); **hs** (**hors service**, *exhausted*).
2. **Décevoir** (*to disappoint, to disillusion*) is conjugated like **recevoir**. **Une déception** is "a disappointment."

Leçon A

Vocabulaire actif

emcl.com
WB 1–4
LA 1
Games

Ce que l'on évite et ce que l'on ressent

1.2, 5.1

Ce que Carla ressent face à un problème:

Ce que Léo a évité....

Essential Instruction

1. Show students illustrations from advertisements in magazines, or from classroom flash cards of people in different emotional states. Ask students to use **se sentir** + adjective in sentences to describe the people. Put the sentences on the board for the students to copy in their notebooks, underlining the adjectives.
2. Students listen to **La vie de Carla.** Add new adjectives from the recording to the list on the board.
3. Where possible, classify the adjectives with their opposites, for example, **encouragé(e)** ≠ **découragé(e)**.
4. Have students draw emoticons of happy, sad, and angry faces in their notebooks and write the adjectives under the appropriate headings.
5. Students listen to **Leo a évité** and draw and label the vocabulary in their notebooks.
6. Ask students to read **Activité 1** aloud.
7. As a whole class activity, have students answer the questions that follow.

fier
honteux
fâché
encouragé
découragé
attristé

fière
honteuse
fâchée
encouragée
découragée
attristée

Pour la conversation   1.1, 1.2

How do I express how someone looked?

› **Tu ne semblais pas** très bien.
You didn't seem very well.

How do I express what I was incapable of doing?

› **J'étais incapable de** décider quelle était la priorité....
I was incapable of deciding what the priority was.

Et si je voulais dire...? 

embarrassé(e)	*embarrassed*
soucieux, soucieuse	*worried*
être déçu(e)	*to be disappointed*
être dégoûté(e)	*to be disgusted*
passer un concours	*to take an exam*
refouler ses sentiments	*to repress one's feelings*

1 La première d'Ariane Azay!  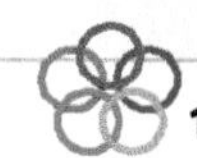 1.2, 5.1

Lisez ce blogue dans lequel une star explique ce qui s'est passé pendant une première.

Okay. Maintenant que tout le monde a vu les photos de la première. Voici les explications. J'ai trébuché et je suis tombée sur le tapis rouge. La grêle a commencé à tomber, alors que j'étais encore par terre (*on the ground*), et elle a abîmé (*ruined*) ma belle robe Chanel en soie. Je me suis foulé la cheville. Un bel inconnu m'a aidée à me lever. Et, non, je ne sais pas qui il est, et il est encore moins mon petit ami. Je déteste tous ces commérages. Après, je me suis fait bousculer par la foule, mais finalement j'ai pu entrer dans la salle du théâtre. Si ma chute (*fall*) vous a fait rire, vous devriez vous sentir honteux. Je ne suis pas fière de ce qui s'est passé mais les messages de tous mes fans m'ont encouragée, et je serai prête pour ma tournée qui commence le mois prochain.

Ariane

1. Que montrent les photos d'Ariane?
2. Qu'est-ce qui s'est passé pendant la première?
3. Qu'est-ce qu'elle portait ce soir-là?
4. Pourquoi est-ce qu'il y a eu des commérages?
5. Qu'est-ce qu'elle dit aux gens qui ont ri?
6. Qu'est-ce qu'elle va faire dans un mois?

Differentiated Learning

Accelerate

Have students write a blog from the point of view of a competing actress who does not like Ariane. Have her relate the incident of the fall on the red carpet from her negative point of view.

Decelerate

Ask students to draw a storyboard of the blog with captions in French describing each picture.

Answers

1. Elles montrent qu'elle est tombée.
2. Elle a trébuché, elle est tombée sur le tapis rouge, et un jeune homme l'a aidée à se relever.
3. une robe Chanel en soie
4. On dit que l'homme qui l'a aidée à se relever est son petit ami.
5. Qu'ils devraient se sentir honteux.
6. Elle va faire une bonne tournée.

Reference Desk

Fièr(e) is a good kind of pride as in "**Je suis fier de toi**" whereas **orgueilleux(se)** means proud in a negative sense as in "**Il est trop orgueilleux et ça m'énerve.**"

Critical Thinking

Application

Have students write five sentences each for **fièr(e)** and **orgueilleux(se)**, demonstrating that they understand the difference between the two "prouds."

Communication

Presentational, Interpersonal: Cooperative Groups

Students work in groups of three to transform the **Activité 1** blog into a dramatic scene. The narrator reads the introduction, setting the stage for the scene. A girl plays Ariane, and a boy the handsome stranger. Have students create dialogue that reflects the relationship between the two. Does the **bel inconnu** become someone more to her? Was Ariane too embarrassed to speak? Tune in to see!

Answers

2

1. Aïcha s'est sentie heureuse.
2. Les membres de la famille Lacombe se sont sentis attristés.
3. Anna et Sabrina se sont senties découragées/fâchées.
4. Nadège s'est sentie fière/heureuse/encouragée.

3

1. la grêle
2. les commérages
3. se faire bousculer
4. trébucher
5. se faire arrêter
6. la bagarre

Script can be found in the front pages of the Annotated Teacher's Edition.

1. V
2. F
3. F
4. V
5. V

Reference Desk

Weather review: **pleuvoir**, **il pleut**, **la pluie**, **neiger**, **il neige**, **la neige**, **geler**, **il gèle**, **la gèle**, **grêler**, **il grêle**, **la grêle**. A hailstorm is **une averse de grêle**.

Expansion

Encourage students to go online for an interactive review of weather expressions.
Search words: **quizlet, french weather expressions**

Communication

Interpersonal, Presentational: Cooperative Groups

Students work together to add as many reasons as they can think of as to why the people in **Activité 2** feel the way they do. As an example, students could write: **Nicolas s'est senti honteux parce qu'il a triché**. Correct in class.

2 Comment est-ce qu'ils se sont sentis?

 1.2

Dites comment les personnes suivantes se sont senties selon la photo. Choisissez un adjectif de la liste.

encouragé heureux honteux fier attristé découragé fâché

MODÈLE

Nicolas
Nicolas s'est senti honteux.

1. Aïcha

2. les membres de la famille Lacombe

3. Anna et Sabrina

4. Nadèje

3 Qu'est-ce qu'ils évitent?

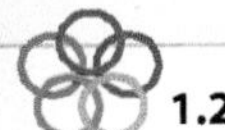 1.2

Complétez les phrases pour dire ce que les personnes évitent (de faire). Choisissez une expression de la liste.

les commérages la grêle se faire bousculer la bagarre trébucher se faire arrêter

1. Romain est rentré sous la pluie, mais il s'est senti heureux d'avoir évité....
2. Anaïs essaie d'éviter... parce qu'elle déteste quand on parle des autres.
3. Valérie évite la foule parce qu'elle ne veut pas....
4. M. Simon a évité de... parmi les jouets (*toys*) de ses enfants quand il est rentré du travail.
5. Sébastien a évité de... par l'agent de police après avoir perdu son permis de conduire.
6. Julien a évité... entre deux garçons fâchés.

Communiquez!

4 Une mauvaise journée

 1.1, 1.2

Interpretive Communication

*Écrivez les numéros 1–5 sur votre papier. Écoutez Sandrine et Ahmed discuter de la matinée de Sandrine. Ensuite, dites si les phrases que vous entendez sont vraies (**V**) ou fausses (**F**).*

Essential Instruction

1. Do **Activité 2** in groups. Have students refer to the adjective list in their notebooks and to add additional adjectives when describing the pictures.
2. Have students write **Activité 3**.
3. Use whiteboards to answer **Activité 4**. Replay any confusing statements.
4. Before playing the video, ask students if they have ever wanted to skip class. Watch the video with books closed.
5. Ask students if they can relate to Coralie's situation of being exhausted. When and why?
6. Students listen to the recording with books open.
7. To preview the past conditional tense (p. 516), ask what "**Si j'avais bossé...j'aurais évité tous ces ennuis**" probably means.
8. Students answer the questions for **Activité 5** in pairs.

Rencontres culturelles

emcl.com
WB 5

Élodie sèche ses cours.

   1.1, 1.2

Élodie parle à sa copine Coralie de sa journée.

Coralie: Lâcheuse! Tu m'as laissé seule dans le labo ce matin. Tu as séché tous tes cours?
Élodie: Écoute, il faut que je te raconte, je ne sais pas ce qui s'est passé....
Coralie: Oui, j'ai bien vu que tu ne semblais pas très bien.
Élodie: Oui, je me suis sentie très mal.
Coralie: Qu'est-ce qui t'es arrivé?
Élodie: Je suis arrivée à la maison, j'ai voulu commencer à travailler et j'étais comme tétanisée; incapable de décider quelle était la priorité.... J'étais paniquée; je me suis effondrée de fatigue.
Coralie: Et qu'est-ce que tu as fait alors?
Élodie: J'ai dormi... j'ai dormi pendant 18 heures!
Coralie: Dix-huit heures! Tu devrais être maintenant en pleine forme!
Élodie: À part le bac, qui me tourmente. Si j'avais bossé plus auparavant, j'aurais évité tous ces ennuis!

5 Élodie sèche ses cours.

  1.2, 1.3

Répondez aux questions suivantes.

1. Quand est-ce que Coralie a remarqué l'absence d'Élodie?
2. Qu'est-ce que Coralie a remarqué ce matin?
3. Comment se sentait Élodie une fois arrivée à la maison?
4. Elle a dormi combien de temps?
5. Qu'est-ce qui l'inquiète?

Le lycée de Coralie et d'Élodie.

RESOURCES

 Dialogue Video

 Workbook 5

Answers

1. Ce matin, au labo.
2. qu'Élodie ne se sentait pas bien
3. Elle était paniquée.
4. pendant 18 heures
5. le bac

Reference Desk

1. **Lâcheur(se)** means "coward." In Québec, the masculine form is spelled **lâcheux.** More vocabulary: **être tetanisé(e)** (*to be paralyzed*); **éffondré(e)** (*shattered, crushed*); **bosser** (*to work*).
2. Point out the difference between "**Qu'est-ce qui t'es arrivé**" and "**Je suis arrivée à la maison**" as seen in the dialogue.
3. **Discuter** is followed by **de** when referring to what is discussed: **Je discute *de* mes problèmes.**

Communication

Interpersonal: Paired Practice

Tell students to write as many excuses as they can think of about why they skipped class yesterday, plausible or not. Have students read them to you and to the class. Rate the excuses that are believable compared to those which would never work.

Differentiated Learning

Accelerate

Students write a short essay relating when and why they felt sad, discouraged, angry, or any other emotion they choose.

Decelerate

Ask students to make a list of expressions in **Élodie sèche les cours** that indicate she is not feeling up to par.

Answers

Extension

Non, parce qu'elle a réussi avec mention.

Reference Desk

Your students may want to know that **Ça va pas fort?** is familiar language for **Ça ne va pas bien? Se planter** is familiar for **se tromper. La session de rattrapage** is an organized tutoring session before retaking the **bac**.

Extension **Les résultats du bac**  

Abdel-Cader et Louisa parlent du bac qu'ils ont passé.

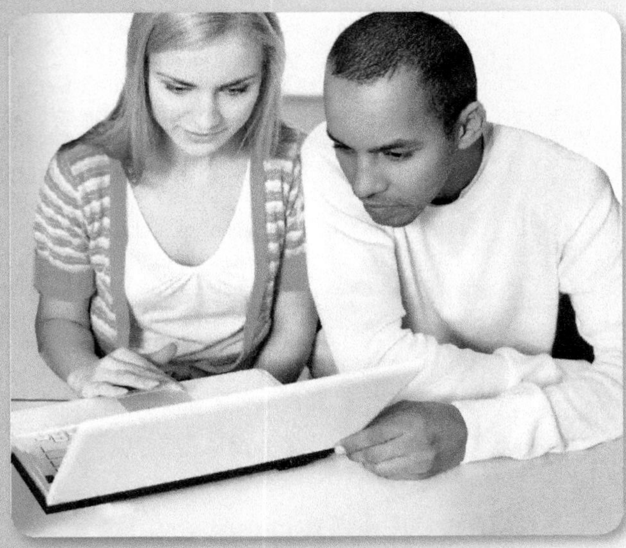

Abdel-Cader:	Ben alors, ça va pas fort?
Louisa:	En effet, je n'arrête pas de penser à la dernière épreuve du bac... je me suis complètement plantée!
Abdel-Cader:	Tu sais, on a tous cette impression à la fin des épreuves.
Louisa:	Non, vraiment, le sujet en histoire était beaucoup trop dur, je n'avais pas assez révisé. Je dois sérieusement me préparer pour la session de rattrapage.
Abdel-Cader:	Mais, tu sais, les résultats sont déjà en ligne. Tu ne les as pas consultés?
Louisa:	Non, j'ai trop peur de savoir.
Abdel-Cader:	Écoute, il vaut mieux affronter les problèmes. Regardons ensemble. Ben, tiens donc... regarde....
Louisa:	Gautier, Louisa... admise, mention passable! J'y crois pas!
Abdel-Cader:	Ben, toi alors, et avec mention!

Extension Louisa avait-elle besoin de s'inquiéter du bac? Pourquoi, ou pourquoi pas?

1.2, 1.3

Essential Instruction

1. Have students read **Extension.**
2. Ask students to state these expressions in another way: **Ça va pas fort**, **Je me suis plantée**, **les épreuves**, and **Je n'avais pas assez revisé.**
3. Ask general comprehension questions about the **Extension** dialogue, ending with the **Extension** question.
4. Have students rehearse and present the **Extension** dialogue in pairs.
5. The reading **Le système scolaire français** is challenging. Have students read the passage for general comprehension without consulting a dictionary.
6. For **Le système scolaire français**, ask students to record the detailed information, found in the first two paragraphs, in a graphic organizer.
7. For the remaining two paragraphs, students read the information and outline the areas of proposed reform of the French educational system.
8. Ask students to consult the **Search words** for more information.

Points de départ  emcl.com WB 6

Question centrale: Quels sont les défis de la vie contemporaine?

Le système scolaire français 1.2, 3.1

Le budget de l'éducation nationale représente le premier budget de l'état français, soit 2.000€ par habitant.

Le système scolaire français est divisé en trois niveaux: le primaire, le secondaire, et le supérieur. Il repose sur trois principes: l'école est obligatoire, laïque*, et gratuite. Il présente souvent deux visages et de nombreuses contradictions: il oppose public et privé (pour l'essentiel dominé par les établissements* religieux qui scolarisent* environ 16% des élèves); l'université et les grandes écoles qui forment les élites; l'enseignement général (survalorisé*) et l'enseignement professionnel (marginalisé*). Il existe aussi une préscolarisation à partir de trois ans (la plus élevée au monde mais une scolarisation moins longue que la moyenne* des pays développés); un taux de réussite* dans les formations courtes supérieur (à la moyenne de ces mêmes pays mais beaucoup plus faible dans les formations longues); un pourcentage de diplômes scientifiques supérieur à la plupart des pays développés mais un pourcentage de doctorat* inférieur à la moyenne européenne.

Le lycée international des Pontonniers à Strasbourg est un établissement d'enseignement secondaire.

Ce sont toutes ces contradictions qui expliquent que le système éducatif français qui doute de lui-même et de son efficacité* en dépit de* ses réussites, soit aujourd'hui conduit à mettre en œuvre* des réformes qui provoquent* un fort clivage* idéologique: réformes qui touchent la sélection; l'autonomie des établissements secondaires (en cours) et universitaires (réalisée depuis 2007); la gratuité des études dans l'enseignement supérieur (les étudiants paient environ 2.000€ par an); le calendrier scolaire (la semaine de quatre jours et un emploi du temps de 8h30 à 16h30 dans l'enseignement primaire); le temps de présence des enseignants dans les établissements (15 à 18 heures dans les lycées, 108 heures par an à l'université), l'articulation entre enseignement et vie professionnelle.

Mais la plus grande difficulté pour réformer tient aux Français eux-mêmes. Tous ont une idée précise sur ce qu'il faut faire, un mélange savant de conservatisme et de modernisation.

 Search words: **système éducatif français, budget du ministère de l'éducation, ministère de l'éducation nationale France**

COMPARAISONS

Quel est le ministère qui a le budget le plus important aux États-Unis?

4.2

laïque *secular*; **établissement** école; **scolarisent** *educate*; **survalorisé** *overrated*; **marginalisé** *marginalized*; **moyenne** *average*; **réussite** *success*; **doctorat** *Ph. D*; **efficacité** *efficiency*; **en dépit de** *despite*; **mettre en œuvre** *to carry out*; **provoquent** causent; **fort clivage** *strong division*

RESOURCES

Workbook 6

Critical Thinking

Comparisons

Ask students to make a chart comparing and contrasting the French and American school systems in terms of tuition, school calendar, teacher work hours, and career training.

Differentiated Learning

Accelerate

Ask students to write a short essay answering the question in **Comparaisons.** What does this suggest about the two countries' priorities?

Decelerate

Give students study questions to fill out as they read **Le système scolaire français** to help them understand the reading.

Multiple Intelligences

Intrapersonal

Ask students to research and comment on this: In France, education is under national control. Is this true in the United States? Explain.

Reference Desk

1. There are three categories of comments for students passing the **bac** on the first try: 1) **Mention Assez Bien**, 2) **Mention Bien**, 3) **Mention Très Bien.**
2. The three categories of the **Baccalauréat** are: 1) **Général**, consisting of the categories of **Économique et social** (ES), **Littéraire** (L), and **Scientifique** (S), 2) **Technologique: Sciences et technologies... de la gestion** (STG), **...industrielles** (STI), **...laboratoire** (STL), **...santé et du social** (ST2S), **...agronomie et du vivant** (STAV), **Techniques de la musique et de la danse** (TMD), and **Hôtellerie** and 3) **Professionnel**, which has 80 specialties.

Critical Thinking

Analysis

Ask students to explain the humor in the following quotations:

"Le bac, c'est comme la lessive: on mouille (*sweats*), **on sèche** (*can't come up with an answer*)**... et on repasse** (*takes the test again*)." Henri Troyat

"L'échec légendaire de Zola au bachot a réconforté beaucoup de candidats – qui n'étaient pas Zola." Tristan Bernard

Le baccalauréat

1.2, 2.1

Des élèves de lycée se préparent à la session du bac.

"Passe ton bac d'abord!"—cette expression qui a donné son titre à un film de 1978, reste dans son ensemble le mot d'ordre de la société française. Au point qu'un ministre de l'éducation avait fixé comme objectif de conduire 80% d'une classe d'âge au bac. Aujourd'hui, 64,8% des jeunes d'une classe d'âge ont leur bac.

Et tous les ans, c'est la même chose, en juin, toute la France passe le bac. C'est toute la famille qui se mobilise, qui partage le stress avant l'épreuve, qui s'angoisse* au moment de l'ouverture des sujets, qui soupèse* les chances de réussite et d'échec*, qui commente ou crie à l'injustice, enfin qui se réjouit* ou qui pleure au moment des résultats. Les résultats: 88,8% de réussite des élèves qui passent le bac. Sur 100 diplômés, 54 ont un bac d'enseignement général; 26, un bac technologique; et 20 un baccalauréat professionnel.

Search words: passer son bac, passer son bac vidéo, résultat bac (+ année), bac par correspondance

s'angoisse *anguish*; **soupèse** *feels the weight of*; **échec** contraire d'une réussite; **se réjouit** *is delighted*

Pour se préparer au baccalauréat, les étudiants français consultent les **annales du bac**; ce sont des sujets corrigés d'examens du baccalauréat d'années précédentes. On les trouve en ligne, ou sur des sites régionaux.

2.2

COMPARAISONS

Est-ce que vos frères, sœurs, et cousins ont dû passer un examen pour pouvoir obtenir un diplôme ou pour entrer à l'université? Si oui, était-ce facile ou difficile pour eux?

4.2

Bac de français

Annales 2012
Série ES/S

« Le roman et ses personnages »

Des élèves de lycée se préparent à la session du bac avec les *Annales*.

Mots-clé

École est un emprunté au latin classique *schola*, lui-même pris au grec *skholê*. Désigne en bas-latin, "la corporation," "la compagnie"; le grec renvoyant à jeu et à activité intellectuelle.

Mon dico scolaire

bachoter: *préparer un examen*
redoubler: *suivre le même cours ou année de scolarisation pour la deuxième fois*
l'école de la vie: *apprendre de l'expérience, pas d'un cours*

Essential Instruction

1. Ask students to explain the difference in structure between the SAT/ACT and the **bac**.
2. Explain the types of **bac**. Ask, if they had to take the **bac**, which category would they choose?
3. Have students read and take notes about **Le baccalauréat.** Ask how the **bac** is a family affair.
4. Ask students to add to their information by researching the **Search words.**
5. For **Activité 6**, have all students do tasks 1 and 2 and the **Perspectives** question.
6. Give students options to do one of the remaining three activities.
7. Have students read **Du côté des médias** and do 1 or 2 of **Activité 7**.

6 Activités culturelles

1.3, 3.1, 3.2

Complétez les activités suivantes.

1. Faites un dessin qui représente les trois niveaux du système scolaire en France.
2. Énumérez les principales contradictions du système scolaire français.
3. Comparez le système scolaire français et le système scolaire de votre ville ou état/province.
4. Créez une bande dessinée ou un dialogue qui montre les émotions dans une maison française où un ado va bientôt passer son bac.
5. Trouvez un lycée français en ligne et regardez leurs résultats au baccalauréat. Comparez les résultats avec ceux de l'école que votre partenaire a examinée.

Perspectives

Un homme de 45 ans voudrait passer son bac. Une jeune femme lui répond sur le blogue:

"Pour rien au monde je ne repasserais mon bac—stress, révisions de dernière minute, le vrai marathon! Mais l'avoir réussi m'a beaucoup aidée. J'ai maintenant le boulot de mes rêves. Alors, je vous conseille d'aller sur le site du CNED." Pourquoi est-ce que cette jeune femme essaie d'aider ce monsieur quand elle a eu une mauvaise expérience avec le bac?

Du côté des médias

1.2

*Lisez les informations tirées du (*pulled from the*) site web du Ministère de l'Éducation en France.*

Lycéens, vous souhaitez progresser en anglais?

Dans votre lycée ou un établissement à proximité, participez aux stages intensifs proposés gratuitement pendant les vacances scolaires d'hiver, de printemps, et d'été.

Inscrivez-vous: renseignez-vous auprès de votre établissement pour obtenir toutes les informations nécessaires (lieu du stage, modalités d'inscription, dates, etc.).

Enseignez l'anglais pendant les vacances scolaires

Vous êtes:

- enseignants
- assistants d'anglais
- étudiants étrangers
- locuteurs natifs
- assistants pédagogiques
- assistants d'éducation anglophones

Vous êtes intéressés pour participer aux stages d'anglais gratuits pour les lycéens ?

Déposez votre candidature sur la plateforme de recrutement des intervenants de langue anglaise

➢ *education.gouv.fr/recrutlangues*

Tous renseignements sur les stages d'anglais gratuits sont fournis par le lycée où est scolarisé l'élève: lieu du stage, modalités d'inscription, dates, etc.

1.3, 5.2

7 Stages intensifs d'anglais gratuits pour les lycéens pendant les vacances scolaires

Faites les activités qui suivent.

1. Vous êtes lycéen en France et vous voudriez suivre un stage intensif en anglais. Écrivez vos questions.
2. Vous êtes un(e) prof d'anglais américain(e) et vous aimeriez proposer un stage d'anglais intensif dans une école française. Écrivez votre CV ou une lettre de motivation.

Answers

6

1. *Drawings will vary.*
2. élémentaire, primaire, secondaire
3. *Answers will vary.*
4. *Comics will vary.*
5. *Answers will vary.*

Perspectives

Answers will vary.

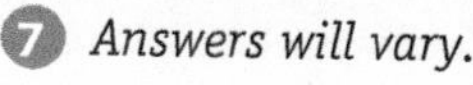

7 *Answers will vary.*

Connections

Music

"**Bac G**" by Michel Sardou is about a student taking a lower-ranking **bac** exam. In addition to the cultural value of the song, it could be used as a cloze listening activity since the lyrics contain commonly used vocabulary.

TPR

Have students prepare statements that are either **vrai** or **faux** based on the information about French education and **le bac.** Student A reads a statement to the class. If classmates think the statement is true, they go to one side of the room; if they think it is false, they go to the opposite side of the room. Student A reveals if the statement is true or false. If false, students propose how to correct it. Proceed to Student B who makes another statement and so on.

Differentiated Learning

Expand

Have students read blogs of French students writing about the **bac.** They could also find similar sites on their favorite social media.

Multiple Intelligences

Visual-Spatial

Encourage these students to create **une bande dessinée** for Activity 4 in **Activité 6** or create a series of posters advertising the importance of doing well on the **bac.** Have them imagine they work for the **Ministère d'éducation nationale.**

RESOURCES

 Workbook 7–9

 Drill & Practice Games

Communication

Interpersonal: Paired Practice

Give each pair of students a die: one dot corresponds to **je**, two dots, **tu**, three dots, **elle**, four dots, **nous**, five, **vous**, six, **elles.** Give them a list of regular, irregular, and reflexive verbs in the infinitive. Students roll a die and conjugate the verbs on the list, one by one, in the past conditional. Put a sample verb in each category on the board for reference. For future study, have students note the verbs that they missed.

Structure de la langue

Past Conditional Tense 1.1

M. Rivard aurait pu se faire arrêter.

The past conditional (**le conditionnel passé**) is a tense used to tell what would have happened in the past if certain conditions had been met. Like the **passé composé** and the **plus-que-parfait**, the past conditional consists of a helping verb and a past participle. To form the past conditional, use the conditional tense of the helping verb **avoir** or **être** and the past participle of the main verb. Agreement of the past participle in the past conditional is the same as in the **passé composé** and the **plus-que-parfait.**

	bosser	aller	se reposer
je/j'	**aurais bossé**	**serais allé(e)**	**me serais reposé(e)**
tu	**aurais bossé**	**serais allé(e)**	**te serais reposé(e)**
il/elle/on	**aurait bossé**	**serait allé(e)**	**se serait reposé(e)**
nous	**aurions bossé**	**serions allé(e)s**	**nous serions reposé(e)s**
vous	**auriez bossé**	**seriez allé(e)(s)(es)**	**vous seriez reposé(e)(s)(es)**
ils/elles	**auraient bossé**	**seraient allé(e)s**	**se seraient reposé(e)s**

Élodie **aurait bossé** plus auparavant. — *Élodie would have worked more before.*

Leïla ne **serait** pas **partie** du lycée sans son sac à dos. — *Leïla would not have left school without her backpack.*

Éric et son ami **se seraient dépêchés**. — *Éric and his friend would have hurried.*

COMPARAISONS

How is the past conditional formed in English? 4.1

I *would have worked* harder.
I *would have gone* before class.
I *would have rested* half an hour.

COMPARAISONS: In English, the past conditional tense is usually formed by using the conditional "would" followed by the auxiliary "have" plus the past participle of the verb that gives the meaning of what would have happened. The words "could," "should," "might," and "ought" already include a conditional meaning, so you cannot combine them with "would have," for example, there's Marlon Brando's famous line, "I could have been a contender."

Essential Instruction

1. Volunteers go to the board to write the conjugations of **avoir** and **être** in the conditional. Leave spaces after each verb.
2. Ask students what **j'aurais** means. (*I would have*) Ask them how to say "spoken" in French. If students suggest **parlé**, explain that **j'aurais parlé** means "I would have spoken." To each form of **avoir** on the board, add a past participle of a verb conjugated with **avoir** and explain the meaning. This activity demonstrates the modular of the tense.
3. Add past participles to the conditional of **être** on the board. Translate each verb as "I would have…" to train students to think of **je serais** like **avoir** rather than "I would be."
4. Ask students what **je me serais reposé** means. Students learn not to translate the auxiliary verb literally.
5. Students do **Activités 8** and **9** in class. Give immediate feedback.

8 Où serait-on allé?  1.1

Je serais allée au concert avec toi si tu étais venu me chercher.

Dites où tout le monde serait allé et ce qu'ils y auraient vu avec un billet d'avion gratuit pour la France.

le festival international du film | le Port de la Lune | la cathédrale | les châteaux de la Loire | le Parlement européen | le musée d'Orsay | les tableaux de Matisse

MODÈLE Brent/Bordeaux
Brent serait allé à Bordeaux; il y aurait vu le Port de la Lune.

1. Jennifer/Paris
2. Madison et moi, nous/Cannes
3. moi, je/Tours
4. Zach et toi, vous/Strasbourg
5. tu/Strasbourg
6. Nora et Ashley/Nice

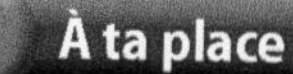

9 À ta place  1.1

Vous écoutez vos amis. Dites-leur ce que vous auriez fait à leur place.

suivre un cours avec un moniteur | rédiger une lettre de motivation | aller en ville | louer un vélo | se reposer | goûter la cuisine française | faire du ski nautique | choisir une salade | bosser plus auparavant

MODÈLE Zakia: "J'ai mangé de la pizza à la cantine."
À ta place, j'aurais choisi une salade.

1. Amélie: "Je n'ai pas réussi au bac."
2. Jean-Luc: "Je suis tombé en faisant du ski alpin."
3. Momo: "J'ai vu une petite annonce en ligne qui m'intéresse."
4. Sonia: "J'ai vu les châteaux de la Loire en voiture."
5. Dikembe: "Je suis allé sur la côte d'Azur et je n'ai rien fait."
6. Mamadou: "Je suis allé à Paris et j'ai mangé à McDo."
7. Sandrine: "J'ai travaillé avant de courir dans le marathon."
8. Renée: "Je n'ai rien fait mercredi après-midi."

Answers

1. Jennifer serait allée à Paris. Elle y aurait vu le musée d'Orsay.
2. Nous serions allé(e)s à Cannes. Nous y aurions vu le festival international du film.
3. Je serais allé(e) à Tours. J'y aurais vu les châteaux de la Loire.
4. Vous seriez allés à Strasbourg. Vous y auriez vu la cathédrale/le Parlement européen.
5. Tu serais allé(e) à Strasbourg. Tu y aurais vu le Parlement européen/ la cathédrale.
6. Elles seraient allées à Nice. Elles y auraient vu les tableaux de Matisse.

1. À ta place, j'aurais bossé plus auparavant.
2. ... j'aurais fait du ski nautique.
3. ... j'aurais rédigé une lettre de motivation.
4. ... j'aurais loué un vélo.
5. ... j'aurais suivi un cours avec un moniteur.
6. ... j'aurais goûté la cuisine française.
7. ... je me serais reposé(e).
8. ... je serais allé(e) en ville.

Game

Machine à écrire

To practice the forms of the past conditional, divide the class into two teams. Assign at least one letter or accent mark to each student. Start the game by giving one team a subject pronoun and an infinitive in French. Have students quickly spell out loud the correct form of the verb in the past conditional. Then, the other team tries to spell a word. If correctly spelled, the team gets a point. If there is an error, the rival team can try to spell it for a point. If necessary, assign a scribe to write the verb out on the board as it is being spelled.

Differentiated Learning

Accelerate/Decelerate

Have stronger students work as tutor partners with weaker students to review the conditional tense for **avoir** and **être** before moving on to the past conditional. To practice past conditional, give them a list of situations, for example, **Je suis arrivé/e à l'école en retard parce que je me suis levé/e tard,** then ask them to work together to write what they would have done in the subject's place: **À ta place, je me serais levé/e plus tôt.**

Expansion

Have students practice these verbs on line.
Search words: french verb practice, conjuguemos, quizlet

Answers

10 *B are possible answers.*

1. A: Je me suis promené(e) dans le jardin des Tuileries.
   B: À ta place, je ne me serais pas promené(e) dans le jardin des Tuileries, j'aurais fait les magasins.
2. A: Je suis allé(e) à l'arc de triomphe.
   B: À ta place, je ne serais pas allé(e) à l'arc de triomphe, je serais allé(e) à la tour Eiffel.
3. A: J'ai acheté des romans français.
   B: À ta place, je n'aurais pas acheté des romans français, j'aurais acheté des bandes dessinées françaises.
4. A: J'ai séjourné dans une auberge de jeunesse.
   B: À ta place, je n'aurais pas séjourné dans une auberge de jeunesse, j'aurais séjourné au Négresco.
5. A: J'ai fait du parachutisme ascensionnel.
   B: À ta place, je n'aurais pas fait du parachutisme ascensionnel, j'aurais fait du scooter des mers.
6. A: J'ai bronzé.
   B: À ta place, je n'aurais pas bronzé, je me serais baigné(e).

Reference Desk

1. The past conditional is also called the conditional perfect, and **le conditionnel passé.** Special translations of key verbs are: **devoir**, **j'aurais dû** (*I should have*); **pouvoir**, **j'aurais pu** (*I could have*); **vouloir**, **j'aurais voulu** (*I would have liked*); **être**, **j'aurais été** (*I would have been*).
2. Remind students that when the first verb is conjugated, the second is an infinitive: **J'aurais dû reviser.**

10 Un séjour en France

1.1, 5.2

Interpersonal Communication

Votre partenaire est allé à Paris. Dites-lui ce que vous auriez fait à sa place. Puis, échangez les rôles: vous êtes allé(e) sur la côte d'Azur. Votre partenaire vous dira ce qu'il ou elle aurait fait à votre place.

MODÈLES

(Paris)
visiter le musée du Louvre

A: **J'ai visité le musée du Louvre.**
B: **À ta place, je n'aurais pas visité le musée du Louvre. J'aurais visité le musée d'Orsay.**

(la côte d'Azur)
prendre des fruits de mer
A: **J'ai pris des fruits de mer.**
B: **À ta place, je n'aurais pas pris de fruits de mer. J'aurais pris de la ratatouille.**

1. Paris/se promener dans le jardin des Tuileries
2. Paris/aller à l'arc de triomphe
3. Paris/acheter des romans français
4. la côte d'Azur/séjourner dans une auberge de jeunesse
5. la côte d'Azur/faire du parachutisme ascensionnel
6. la côte d'Azur/bronzer

Essential Instruction

1. Review and drill the past conditional so that students can form it quickly and easily.
2. Have students work in partners to do **Activité 10.**
3. Ask students to put the answers on the board to correct.
4. Review the **plus-que-parfait**. Contrast it to the past conditional.
5. Explain the sequence of tenses: **Si +plus-que-parfait** + past conditional.
6. Do **Activité 11** as a whole-class activity.
7. Ask students to suggest more **si** clause combinations.

Past Conditional Tense in Sentences with *si*  1.1

emcl.com
WB 10
LA 2
Games

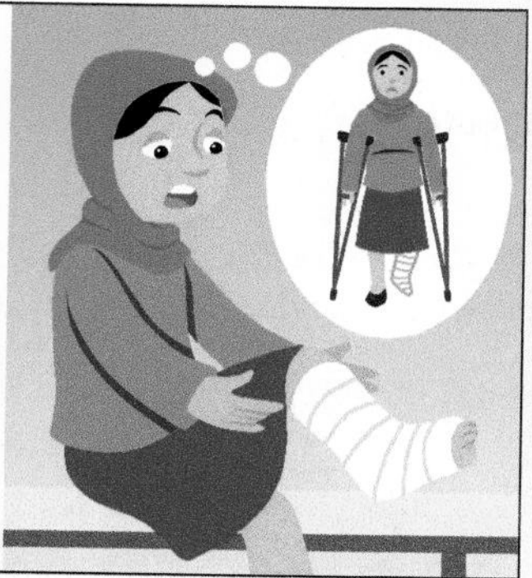

Si Alima n'avait pas trébuché, elle aurait évité tous ces ennuis.

COMPARAISONS

Is the use of the past conditional different in the English sentence from the French sentence?

Si tu avais lu l'article, tu aurais compris.

If you had read the article, you would have understood.

4.1

Use the past conditional tense along with **si** and the **plus-que-parfait** to tell what would have happened *if* something else had already happened or *if* some condition contrary to reality had been met.

si + plus-que-parfait	past conditional

Si je n'**avais** pas **trébuché**, je ne **me serais pas cassé** la jambe.	*If I hadn't tripped, I would not have broken my leg.*
Est-ce que tu **te serais senti** encouragée **s'**il t'**avait parlé?**	*Would you have felt encouraged if he had spoken to you?*

The phrase with **si** + **plus-que-parfait** can either begin or end the sentence.

11 La mauvaise journée d'Élodie  1.1

Dites ce qu'Élodie aurait ou n'aurait pas pu faire si elle avait agit différemment.

MODÈLE avoir une meilleure note
Si Élodie n'avait pas séché ses cours, elle aurait eu une meilleure note.

1. ne… pas se sentir mal
2. ne… pas être tétanisée
3. être capable de décider quelles étaient ses priorités
4. ne… pas paniquer
5. ne… pas dormir pendant 18 heures
6. éviter tous ces ennuis

Si Élodie n'avait pas séché ses cours, elle aurait pu sortir avec Karim ce soir.

COMPARAISONS: In both English and French sentences, the past conditional is only used in the result clause.

RESOURCES

 Workbook 10

 Listening Activity 2

 Drill & Practice Games

Answers

11 *Possible answers:*

1. Si Élodie avait bien étudié, elle ne se serait pas sentie mal.
2. Si Élodie n'avait pas commencé à travailler, elle n'aurait pas été tétanisée.
3. Si Élodie avait réfléchi, elle aurait été capable de décider quelles étaient ses priorités.
4. Si Élodie s'était préparée, elle n'aurait pas paniquée.
5. Si Élodie était restée à l'école, elle n'aurait pas dormi pendant 18 heures.
6. Si Élodie avait bossé plus, elle aurait évité tous ces ennuis.

Critical Thinking

Comparisons

Put a synopsis of **nous** forms of **avoir** on the board. In the first column conjugate **avoir** in the present, imperfect, future, and conditional. Translate each form. (*We have*, *We had*, *We will have*, *We would have*). Across from each simple tense, conjugate **avoir** in the **passé composé**, **plus-que-parfait**, **futur antérieur**, and the **past conditional** and translate each one. Doing this demonstrates how the first column simple tenses are used to form the second column compound tenses. It also shows their similarity to English. Repeat the process for **être** and reflexive verbs.

Differentiated Learning

Accelerate

Have students suggest if-clause combinations similar to **Activité 11** for class practice. They could use examples from French history and current situations.

Decelerate

Students need to be able to recognize and form the **plus-que-parfait** and the past conditional and differentiate between them. Additional worksheets, flash cards, and online practice are essential.

Special Needs Students

Dyslexia

For weaker readers, these two tenses are challenging. Have students note the *"v"* in **J'avais parlé**, and the *"r"* in **j'aurais parlé** to help differentiate between the two **avoir** tenses. The verb **être** is more distinguishable so the forms may be easier to recognize.

Communication

Interpersonal: Paired Practice

Students expand **Activité 10** by explaining why Student B would not do the activity Student A mentioned. For example, in the **modèle**, Student B would add: "**A ta place, j'aurais visité le Musée d'Orsay parce que j'adore les Impressionists.**" Have students alternate the roles.

Answers

12 Script can be found in the front pages of the Annotated Teacher's Edition.

1. B
2. A
3. F
4. C
5. E
6. D

13 *Answers will vary.*

Communication

Presentational: Paired Practice

Have one partner secretly write 10 original if clauses in the **plus-que-parfait**, using names of historical people or today's celebrities. The other student secretly writes result clauses using the same kind of subjects but in the past conditional. Then, they combine their sentences one by one. Have partners choose their five best sentences and share them with the class.

12 Et si et si! 1.2

Interpretive Communication

Écrivez les numéros 1–6 sur votre papier. Écoutez les descriptions des situations. Ensuite, faites correspondre la photo avec la phrase que vous entendez.

A. 

B. 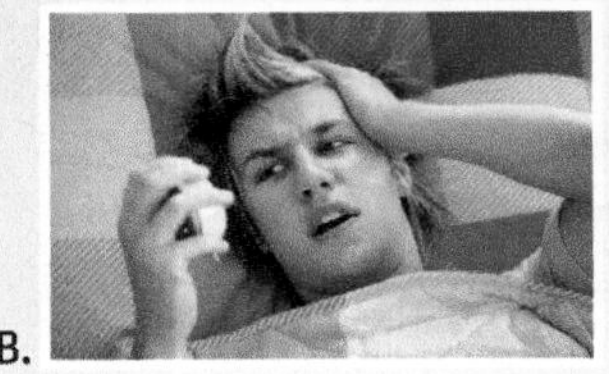

C. 

D. 

E. 

F. 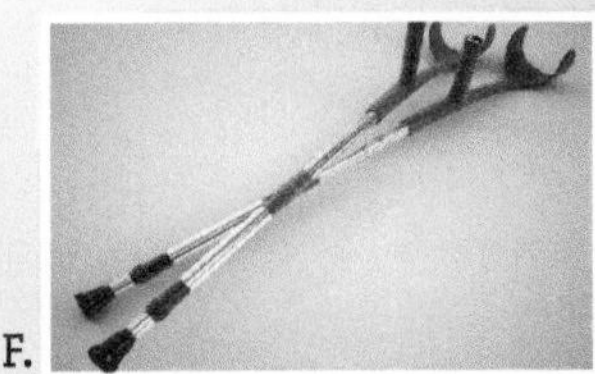

Communiquez!

13 Logique ou illogique? 1.1

Interpersonal Communication

À tour de rôle, formez huit phrases logiques ou illogiques avec les sujets et verbes de la liste. Suivez le modèle.

le prof/perdre de l'argent	Marina et moi/aller en ville
moi/gagner à la loterie	Abdel et Ben/trébucher
tu/voyager	Sophia et toi/se faire arrêter
ma mère/faire la cuisine	Julie et Chloé/sécher leurs cours

MODÈLES
A: **Si j'avais gagné à la loterie, j'aurais acheté une décapotable.**
B: **C'est logique!**

A: **Si le prof avait perdu de l'argent, il se serait senti encouragé.**
B: **C'est illogique!**

Essential Instruction

1. Before playing **Activité 12**, ask students to describe each photo adding as much real or imagined information as possible. For example, in the first picture, a student could say: "**Oh, là là, j'ai dû laisser toutes mes affaires à la bibliothèque!**"
2. Students do **Activité 13** in pairs then share their sentences with the class. The class then votes if their statements are logical or not.
3. Changing partners, have students complete **Activité 14.**

Communiquez!

14 Situations imaginaires

 1.1, 1.2

Interpersonal Communication

À tour de rôle, dites à votre partenaire ce que vous auriez ou n'auriez pas fait selon les situations imaginaires qui vous sont proposées.

MODÈLE avoir un accident
A. avoir peur B. téléphoner à vos parents C. quitter la scène

A: **Qu'est-ce que tu aurais fait si tu avais eu un accident?**
B: **Si j'avais eu un accident, j'aurais eu peur d'abord. Puis, j'aurais téléphoné à mes parents. Je n'aurais pas quitté la scène.**

1. avoir un examen d'histoire important à passer
   A. sécher le cours d'histoire B. étudier C. espérer le passer sans étudier
2. se fouler la cheville
   A. marcher avec des béquilles (*crutches*) B. demander à tes parents de t'emmener partout C. prendre rendez-vous chez le kiné
3. ne... pas gagner assez d'argent
   A. faire grève B. se plaindre C. essayer de trouver un nouveau job
4. tomber malade
   A. aller à l'école B. prendre de l'aspirine C. rester au lit
5. se réveiller très tard
   A. téléphoner à l'école B. manger des céréales C. prendre un taxi

Answers

14 *Possible answers:*

1. A: Qu'est-ce que tu aurais fait si tu avais eu un examen d'histoire important à passer?
   B: Si j'avais eu..., j'aurais étudié.
2. A: Qu'est-ce que tu aurais fait si tu t'étais foulé(e) la cheville?
   B: Si je m'étais foulé(e)..., j'aurais pris rendez-vous ....
3. A: Qu'est-ce que tu aurais fait si tu n'avais pas gagné assez d'argent?
   B :..., j'aurais essayé de trouver un nouveau job.
4. A: Qu'est-ce que tu aurais fait si tu étais tombé(e) malade?
   B: ..., je serais resté(e) au lit.
5. A: Qu'est-ce que tu aurais fait si tu t'étais réveillé(e) très tard?
   B: ..., j'aurais téléphoné à l'école.

Connections

Music

Maxime Leforestier wrote the song "**Mon Frère**" in which he relates that *if he had had* a brother, oh the things *they could have done* together. It is a perfect illustration of if clauses in compound tenses. It features vocabulary students know so it lends itself to a **dictée** as well as being an easy song to sing.

Differentiated Learning

Accelerate

Students, as soothsayers, write what would have happened in history if other things had occurred. **Si Louis XVI avaient accepté une monarchie constitutionnelle, il ne serait pas mort à la guillotine.**

Decelerate

Give students a worksheet of the compound tenses where they must conjugate regular, irregular, **avoir**, **être**, and reflexive verbs tense by tense to help gain mastery. Then, provide practice forming if clauses with the **plus-que-parfait**/past conditional combination. Give an extra-credit quiz on the material to motivate them to do well.

RESOURCES

Communicative Activities

Answers

All activities will vary.

Reference Desk

Blended Instruction

Consider using blended instruction, a combination of in-class learning and computer-mediated instruction or learning opportunities. Ask students to complete activities on the computer, using their cell or smartphone, or other emerging electronic technology. This process will allow students to hone their tech skills and become more independent learners. Schedule routine Internet and e-book learning in class and in the lab.

À vous la parole

Question centrale: Quels sont les défis de la vie contemporaine?

15 Mon album: Moments de ma vie

1.3

Presentational Communication

Choisissez six à huit photos ou faites six à huit dessins qui montrent des moments de votre vie quand vous avez vécu une émotion forte. Choisissez une émotion différente pour chaque image. Écrivez des légendes qui expliquent comment vous vous êtes senti(e) et pourquoi. Prenez une image de votre album et écrivez un récit qui décrit ce jour-là. C'est à vous de choisir de partager votre récit ou de le garder pour vous-même (*yourself*).

Communiquez!

16 Mon lycée en France

1.2, 1.3 , 3.2

Interpretive/Presentational Communication

Imaginez que vous allez faire votre terminale (*senior year*) dans un lycée français. Vous avez gagné une bourse (*scholarship*) qui paiera tout. C'est à vous de choisir la ville et le lycée. Selon vos critères (*criteria*), il faut que le lycée ait de bons résultats au bac parce que vous comptez aussi faire vos études universitaires en France. Il faut que vous vous assuriez que le lycée de votre choix prépare bien ses élèves aux études universitaires. Une fois que vous avez fait votre choix, présentez le lycée aux autres élèves: province, ville, voisinage, cours, etc.

Search words: lycée (+ ville), résultats du bac (+ année)

Communiquez!

17 Mes études universitaires en France

1.2, 1.3, 3.2

Interpretive/Presentational Communication

Vous voulez faire des études universitaires en France pour une année. Vous comptez vous inscrire comme auditeur/auditrice libre (*auditor*) pour pouvoir suivre des cours dans plusieurs facultés. D'abord, faites une liste de vos critères pour choisir une université (spécialisations offertes, situation, bibliothèques, etc.). Ensuite, trouvez une université qui répond à la plupart de vos besoins. Expliquez votre choix à la classe.

Essential Instruction

1. All students do **Activité 15.** They can use photos from advertisements or clipart online.
2. For use in pair work in **Activité 16**, have students find online potential schools they could attend and explain why they made their choice. Their decision should be based not only on successful test results, but also because of the region where the school is located.
3. For **Activité 17** students declare their field of study and justify how their choice of university will advance their education and training.
4. Explain the **liaisons défendues.** Mix examples of forbidden and permitted liaisons to test if the students can hear the difference.
5. Have students repeat part A after you, then have them read aloud the sentences in pairs.
6. Review masculine and feminine adjectives in part B.
7. Have students do the listening comprehension in part C.

Prononciation 1.1, 1.2

When Liaison Can't Be Made

- Note these examples of sentences in which liaison can't be made.

Subject group + verb group

Ma formation⁀était adaptée.

Linking with *et* and *ou*

Je parle anglais⁀et français.

Verb plus word that follows

Je vais étudier⁀en France.

Noun plus adjective that follows

Tu étais un étudiant⁀exceptionnel.

Je fais une demande d'emploi.

Répétez chaque phrase qui ne permet pas la liaison et trouvez la règle qu'on y associe.

1. Mes motivations⁀étaient très fortes.
2. J'ai une formation⁀internationale.
3. Je veux habiter⁀en Europe.
4. J'ai étudié les maths⁀et les langues.
5. Je suis le candidat⁀idéal!
6. J'accepte; je suis disponible en janvier⁀ou en février.

Distinguishing Feminine and Masculine

- To discern a feminine adjective, listen for the consonant that is pronounced when it is followed by an **–e**, for example, **Dominique est très surprise** indicates that the sentence is about a girl. With preceding direct objects, listen for the ending of the past participle, for example, **Tu l'as écrite?** This could refer to **une lettre**, for example, because the pronounced **–t** indicates the object is feminine.

Au féminin!

Répondez à la question au féminin singulier.

1. Vous êtes satisfaits?	Moi, non mais Chloé est très satisfaite.
2. Vous êtes bien couverts?	Moi, non, mais Dominique est très bien couverte.
3. Vous avez dit votre pensée?	Enfin, je l'ai dite!
4. Vous avez ouvert l'enveloppe?	Enfin, je l'ai ouverte!

Masculin ou féminin?

*Écrivez **M** si vous entendez un adjectif masculin ou une référence à un nom masculin. Écrivez **F** si vous entendez un adjectif féminin ou une référence à un nom féminin.*

RESOURCES

Pre-test

Leçon Quiz

Answers

Script can be found in the Audio Program Manual.

1. F
2. M
3. M
4. F

Expansion

To provide additional written practice and to test if your students are processing the difference between masculine and feminine adjectives, and liaisons, consider giving a dictation inspired by the pronunciation practice. Read each sentence three times, once at a natural speed and then once more slowly, giving them time to write. Read it again at normal speed so that they can edit. As a group correction activity, either project the paragraph on the board or have volunteers come up to write the sentences

Differentiated Learning

Expand

Provide a day in which students can practice the different liaisons in the computer lab.
Search words: french liaison practice

Learning Styles

Visual Learners

Point out to these students that the color red indicates letters that are not pronounced and that **liaisons** are not made in these situations. Provide additional practice using the same color patterns to add continuity to their learning.

RESOURCES

e-visual 27

Workbook 1–5

Flash Cards

Listening 1

Drill & Practice Games

Reference Desk

1. Remind students that to refer to religions, nationalities, and professions they have two options. To say "He is French" one can say **Il est français** (adjective) or **C'est un Français** (noun).
2. **S'apercevoir** and **se rendre compte** can be followed by **de + noun: Je me suis rendu compte *de* mon erreur.** Or when followed by a verb, **que** is used, as in the example from **Pour la conversation: Je me suis rendu compte *que* mon ordinateur n'est plus là.**

Vocabulaire actif

emcl.com WB 1–3

Comment décrire une personne

Une jeune fille d'origine....

emcl.com WB 1–3 LA 1 Games

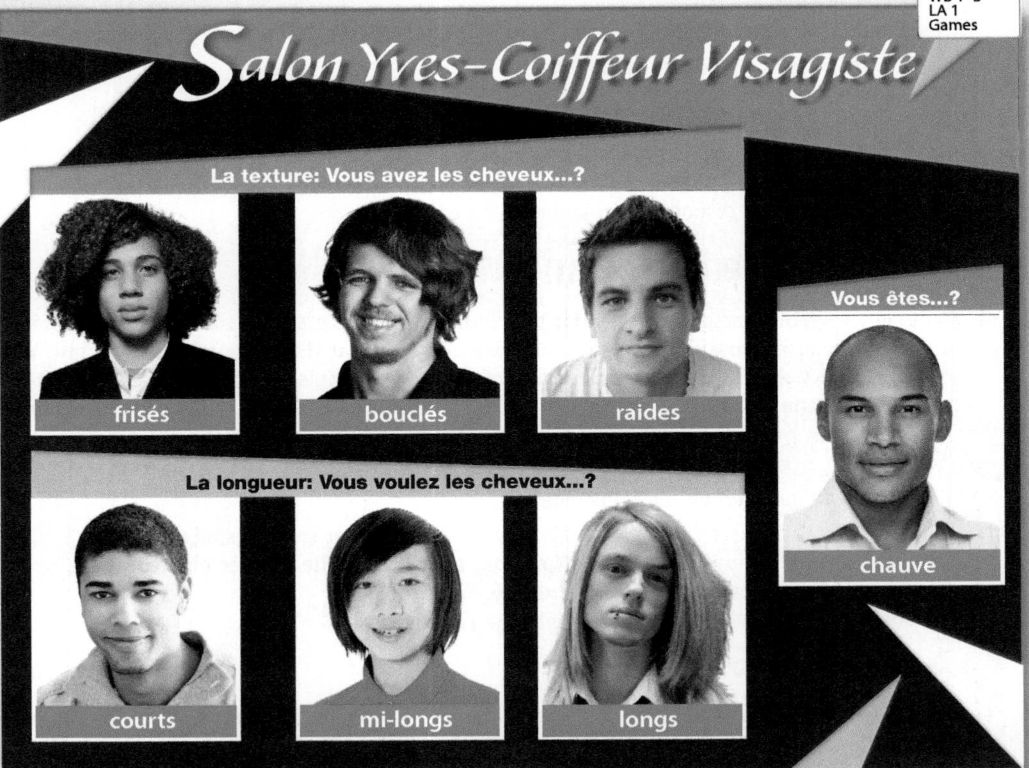

Essential Instruction

1. Play the recording of **Comment décrire une personne** and **Pour la conversation** twice. Have students repeat the second time.
2. Show students pictures of people whose physical description corresponds to the vocabulary. Ask students to describe the images using the new vocabulary words.
3. Ask students to describe celebrities who are in their twenties, thirties, forties, and fifties.
4. Have students copy the vocabulary into their notebooks, illustrating as many words as possible.

emcl.com
WB 4–5
LA 1
Games

CLUB FITNESS

Pour vous remettre en forme!

Vous êtes.... Devenez un homme...!

faible

fort

maigre

mince

gros

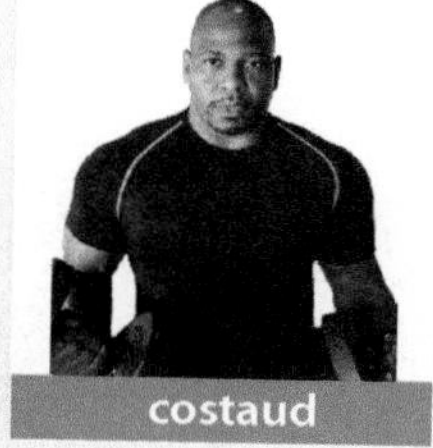
costaud

Une femme d'une... d'années

Pour la conversation   1.1

How do I ask if someone noticed something?

> **Tu ne t'es aperçu de rien?**
> *You didn't notice anything?*

How do I say that I realized something?

> **Je me suis rendu compte que** mon ordinateur n'était plus là.
> *I realized that my computer wasn't there.*

Et si je voulais dire...? 

affreux, affreuse	*frightful*
baraqué(e)	*large and sturdy*
élancé(e)	*slender, slim*
intello	*intellectual*
svelte	*slender*
trapu(e)	*stocky*
en plumetis	*light dress fabric*
en vichy	*gingham*

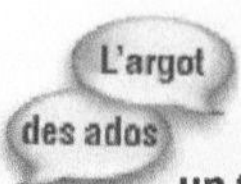

Les gens

un type	*guy*
un mec	*guy*
une nana	*girl*
une meuf	*chick*

Les enfants portent des vêtements....

à rayures

à carreaux

à pois

Communication

Presentational: Paired Practice

Give students a color photo of a person. Have them sit in such a way so as not to see their partner's picture. Student A describes the person to Student B who has to draw the person according to the description given. Then Student B gives the description of an image and Student A draws the person. Afterward, have each student show the original photo to the class. The partner then shows what he/she drew to see how closely the two resemble each other.

Differentiated Learning

Expand

Give students the name of a celebrity from one of the ethnic groups listed in the vocabulary section. Have students find a color photo of the person and present it to the class, describing the physical characteristics using as many adjectives as possible.

Multiple Intelligences

Visual-Spatial

Encourage these students to create posters to use in class to practice the new vocabulary. Ask them to use as many of the new words as possible. These can be funny but the physical attributes must be clear and easy to describe.

Answers

1. son cousin Johann
2. pour participer à un concours d'échecs
3. Il a la trentaine.
4. Il est muslcé et en forme.
5. une veste et une cravate à carreaux

2

1. africaine
2. vingtaine
3. courts et frisés, marron
4. mince
5. à rayures

Reference Desk

1. To say "in Paris," one can use **sur Paris** or more commonly **à Paris. Dans Paris** implies that it is in the city and not in the surrounding area.
2. To end a letter to a friend, one could write **grosses bises**, **gros bisous**, or **Je t'embrasse. Une bise** and **un bisou** mean a kiss. **Faire la bise** is to kiss on both cheeks. If you are not close but want to end a letter warmly, use **amicalement**.

Culture

Perspectives: Information

How many times to kiss on the cheek, and whom to kiss, varies from country to country. Have students make a chart of the country and the kisses.

Search words: kissing on the cheek

Expansion

Encourage students to go online and visit a quality salon in Paris to get tips on hair care, top hairstyles, and salon services. Ask them to write a short composition about what they have learned.

Search words: jean louis david, jacques dessange, coiffeurs pour homme

1 Le cousin scandinave de Nils

1.2

Lisez le mail que Nils a écrit à sa sœur, puis répondez aux questions.

À: Asta
Cc:
Sujet: Quelle coïncidence!

Chère Asta,

Tu ne vas pas croire, mais j'ai vu notre cousin Johann au Café des Artistes. Il est venu à Paris pour un concours d'échecs (*chess competition*). Il n'a ni écrit, ni téléphoné, pourtant il sait que je suis sur Paris. Comme il a changé! La trentaine, et il est évident qu'il fréquente un club de fitness. Il est musclé et semble en pleine forme. Avant, il était trop mince et ne faisait pas d'exercice. Mais, je l'ai reconnu tout de suite parce qu'il a le même sourire et toujours les mêmes grands yeux bleus. Ses cheveux sont toujours aussi longs et raides, comme dans le passé, mais moins blonds. Il était vêtu d'une veste et d'une cravate à carreaux. Il joue bien son rôle de champion d'échecs et intello!

Grosses bises,

N.

1. Qui est-ce que Nils a rencontré au café?
2. Pourquoi cette personne est-elle venue à Paris?
3. Quel âge a cette personne?
4. Comment est-elle maintenant physiquement?
5. Qu'est-ce qu'elle portait?

2 Décrivez Dikembe!

1.3

Complétez les phrases pour faire le portrait de Dikembe.

1. Dikembe est un beau jeune homme d'origine....
2. Il a une... d'années.
3. Il a les cheveux... et les yeux....
4. Physiquement, il est....
5. Il est vêtu d'une chemise....

Essential Instruction

1. Ask students to read **Activité 1.**
2. Give students time to answer the questions about the e-mail.
3. Ask students to read each question aloud. Ask for volunteers to answer.
4. Before assigning **Activité 2**, ask students to describe Dikembe using as many adjectives as possible.
5. Have students complete the description of Dikembe in **Activité 2**.
6. Expand the exercise by asking what he probably likes to do, where he lives, and how old he is exactly, to encourage the students to speak more.
7. Give students ample time to write the descriptions of the three people in **Activité 3**. Circulate to offer help.
8. Students do **Activité 4** in small groups.
9. After doing **Activité 4**, brainstorm the names of celebrities in many fields (sports, music, film, television) and put them on the board for reference. Make a guessing game to identify each one following the same format.

3 Descriptions  1.3

Décrivez les personnes ci-dessous en parlant de leur origine ethnique, leurs âges, leurs cheveux, leurs yeux, leurs corps, et ce qu'ils portent.

Gong

Henrik

Alima

MODÈLE **Mlle Aknouch est une jolie femme d'origine arabe. Elle a une trentaine d'années. Elle a de longs cheveux roux et les yeux verts. Elle est petite et mince. Elle est vêtue d'une robe à pois.**

Communiquez!

4 Devinettes    1.1, 1.2

Interpersonal Communication

*Écrivez les noms de dix personnes célèbres d'origines différentes. À tour de rôle, essayez de deviner l'identité des personnes sur la liste en posant des questions à votre partenaire. Il/Elle répondra par **oui** ou **non** uniquement.*

MODÈLE

A: **C'est un athlète?** B: **Oui.**
A: **Il a une vingtaine d'années?** B: **Oui.**
A: **Il est d'origine asiatique?** B: **Oui.**
A: **C'est Jeremy Lin?** B: **Oui.**

Answers

1. Gong est d'origine asiatique. Elle a une vingtaine d'années, elle a les cheveux raides, noirs et mi-longs, et les yeux marron. Elle porte une chemise à pois.
2. Henrik est une homme d'origine scandinave. Il a une trentaine d'années, il a les cheveux raides, blonds et courts, et les yeux bleus. Il porte une cravate et une chemise à rayures.
3. Alima est une femme d'origine arabe. Elle a une quarantaine d'années, elle a les cheveux bouclés, longs et roux, et les yeux verts. Elle porte une veste à carreaux.

4 *Answers will vary.*

Game

Qui est-ce?

Give students a piece of paper with the name of a student in class that day. Ask students to write a physical description of the person. Do a **divinettes** game where one student reads the description and the others guess the identity.

Differentiated Learning

Accelerate

Ask students to write a description of themselves now and in 50 years. They may illustrate each entry if they choose.

Decelerate

Students can practice physical description vocabulary online.
Search words: **quizlet, physical description, french**

Answers

Script can be found in the front pages of the Annotated Teacher's Edition.

1. F
2. D
3. C
4. B
5. E
6. A

6 *Answers will vary.*

Communication

Interpersonal: Cooperative Groups

Using **Activité 5**, divide students into groups of six and assign each a photo. Have them work to ascribe a name, physical description, and occupation to the person in the photo. They add what the person likes to do, hates to eat, name and kind of pets he or she owns, whatever they can add to create an interesting presentation to the class. As an extension, select two of the imaginary people described, and put them together in a situation where they have to have a conversation. Time how long the students can keep speaking. Repeat the process with others.

Communiquez!

5 Comment sont-ils?

1.1, 1.2

Interpretive Communication

Écrivez les numéros 1–6 sur votre papier. Ensuite, écoutez les descriptions des personnes. Finalement, choisissez la bonne photo.

A. 

B. 

C. 

D. 

E. 

F. 

6 Questions personnelles

1.1, 1.3

Répondez aux questions suivantes.

1. Quand tu fais la connaissance d'une personne, qu'est-ce que tu remarques d'abord?
2. De quelle origine es-tu? Et tes meilleurs amis?
3. Imagine que tu es au zoo avec ton ta petit(e) cousin(e) et que tu ne peux pas le la trouver. Quelle description donnerais-tu à l'agent de police?
4. As-tu des cousins qui sont plus âgés? Comment sont-ils?
5. Comment est ton meilleur ami ou ta meilleure amie?

Essential Instruction

1. Students listen to **Activité 5.**
2. Give students time to prepare answers to **Activité 6.** Ask a few students these questions as a whole-class activity and then have the students circulate to interview each other.
3. Ask students to look at the two photos in **Au voleur!** Where might Karim and Léo be? What probably happened to them?
4. Have students watch the video with books closed. Ask general comprehension questions about the story. Ask what details they remember hearing. Put their remarks on the board to verify later.
5. Play the recording as students follow in their books. Confirm or correct the statements you put on the board.
6. Have students play the roles of the two boys as they read their lines.
7. Have students fill out the **déclaration du vol** in class.

Rencontres culturelles

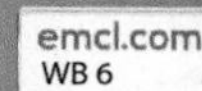

emcl.com
WB 6

Au voleur!

    1.2

Karim et Léo passent le temps au café.

Karim: Mais tu ne t'es aperçu de rien?
Léo: De rien! Absolument de rien!
Karim: Mais tu l'avais posé où? Quand même, un ordinateur ça se voit!
Léo: Là, sur la chaise! Il ne pouvait pas être plus visible.
Karim: Tu n'as vu personne s'approcher, passer à côté de toi?
Léo: Je lisais quand tu es allé au comptoir.... Il y avait un couple à la table devant, c'est tout. Tout d'un coup, je me suis rendu compte que mon ordinateur n'était plus là!
Karim: Ils ressemblaient à quoi?
Léo: À des gens qui flirtent, qui se racontent des histoires dans le blanc des yeux, qui s'occupent d'eux-mêmes quoi! Pas la tête à voler mon ordinateur.
Karim: Lui, tu l'as vu?
Léo: Lui, mince, les cheveux courts, une vingtaine d'années. Elle, très jolie, d'origine asiatique, cheveux longs, noirs, même âge. Elle était vêtue d'un très joli chemisier à pois rouges, façon Marilyn dans *Les Misfits*, très vintage.... Et toi, tu surveilles toujours ton ordinateur? Où est le tien?
Karim: Il est dans mon sac à dos, mais où est mon sac à dos? Il a disparu!
Léo: Désolé.... Si on remplissait une déclaration de vol au commissariat?
Karim: Il y en a un à deux rues d'ici.

7 Déclaration de vol

 1.3

Votre prof va vous donner une déclaration de vol à remplir. Remplissez-la pour Karim ou Léo.

RESOURCES

 **Dialogue Video**

 **Workbook 6**

Answers

 *Answers will vary.*

Reference Desk

1. Consider explaining to your students that **quand même** usually means "anyway." In this case, it is used as an expression of exasperation as in "Come on!" **Parler dans le blanc des yeux** is an intense conversation where people are speaking eye to eye. **Pas la tête à voler mon ordinateur** means "doesn't look like the type who would steal my computer."
2. **Le commissariat de police** is a police station that is open 24 hours a day. It houses the offices of **le commissaire de police** as well as other departments, police vehicles, and equipment.

Differentiated Learning

Expand
Have students write a police report based on the **declaration du vol.**

Multiple Intelligences

Visual-Spatial
Ask students to draw a police sketch of the alleged thieves.

Bodily-Kinesthetic
Encourage students to act out the robbery as it probably happened, using dialogue where appropriate.

Answers

8

1. au café
2. la chaise
3. lire
4. de devant
5. vingtaine
6. asiatique
7. volé
8. remplir une déclaration de vol

Extension

Elle aurait dû surveiller son sac.

Communication

Interpersonal: Paired practice

Divide the class into pairs with half of the pairs acting as the **policier** from the **Extension** conversation and half acting as the woman. Partners write a first-person monologue describing their character's experience. When done, put partners together, one woman and one **policier**, and have them read their monologues to each other. Ask for volunteers to read to the class. Collect the written copy.

8 Au voleur!

1.3

Complétez les phrases suivantes.

1. Karim et Léo passent le temps....
2. Léo a mis son ordinateur portable sur....
3. Il était en train de....
4. Il a vu un couple à la table....
5. Le jeune homme avait une... d'années.
6. La jeune fille était d'origine....
7. Le jeune homme et la jeune fille ont... les deux ordinateurs.
8. Karim et Léo vont au commissariat pour....

Extension **Au commissariat de police**

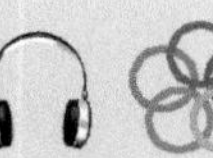

1.1, 1.2

Une femme parle à un policier.

Policier: Alors, qu'est-ce qui vous est arrivé?
Femme: Ça s'est passé dans le métro, très vite, entre deux stations.
Policier: Qu'est-ce qui s'est passé?
Femme: On m'a volé mon porte-cartes de crédit avec mon argent.
Policier: Vous l'aviez mis où?
Femme: Où vouliez-vous qu'il soit? Dans mon sac!
Policier: Oui, ça je m'en doute, mais il était dans une poche fermée par une fermeture éclair?
Femme: Non, mais il était bien au fond, je le mets toujours là et il ne m'est jamais rien arrivé....
Policier: Jusqu'à ce soir....
Femme: Je m'en suis rendu compte tout de suite.
Policier: Et vous vous souvenez de qui était autour de vous? Parce qu'on surveille une bande qui agit sur la ligne....
Femme: Ils étaient tout un groupe... comme d'habitude on était très serrés... jeunes, la vingtaine, plutôt grands, un d'entre eux était costaud, un très mince, avec les cheveux longs.
Policier: Et vous n'avez rien remarqué?
Femme: Serrés comme on était, vous croyez que je passais mon temps à surveiller mon sac? Vous, vous passez votre temps à surveiller le vôtre?
Policier: Moi je n'en ai pas! Mais vous, vous auriez dû!

Extension Comment est-ce que la femme aurait pu éviter le vol?

1.3

Essential Instruction

1. Ask students the questions orally in **Activité 8.**
2. Have students write the answers to the questions in their notebooks. Correct in class.
3. Invite your most dramatic students to read **Extension** as a scene.
4. Ask students to describe the woman's attitude and emotional state by citing examples from the text.
5. Have students work in pairs to answer the **Extension** question.
6. Ask students to give examples of how the woman could have avoided this problem, or do they think the theft was inevitable?
7. Students read **La sécurité publique** and outline the information.
8. They research the **Search words** and add more detail to their notes.
9. As a class discussion, answer the **Comparaisons** question.

Points de départ

emcl.com WB 7

La sécurité publique 1.2

Il existe deux forces qui assurent la sécurité publique: la police et la gendarmerie. La gendarmerie, créée en 1337, devenue gendarmerie nationale en 1791, est une force armée qui dépend du ministère de la Défense et du Ministère de l'intérieur. Elle est chargée de mission de police dans les campagnes et dans les zones autour des grandes villes. La gendarmerie assure la sécurité de 50% de la population et de 95% du territoire. Elle assure des missions d'enquêtes*, de maintien de l'ordre*, d'assistance et de secours*, de circulation routière* et de police militaire.

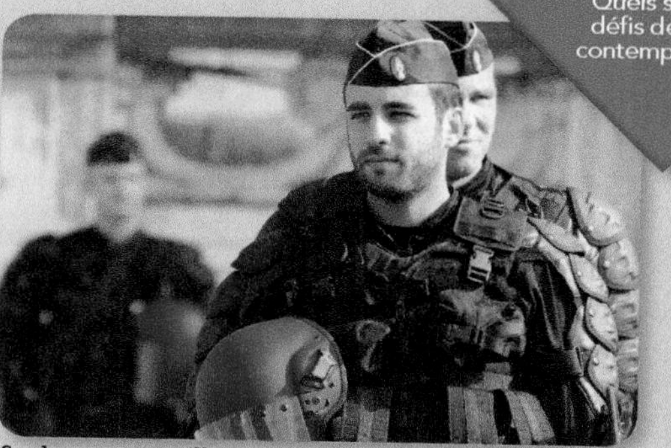
Ces hommes travaillent pour la gendarmerie nationale.

Search words: gendarmerie nationale, vidéos pour gendarmerie france

enquêtes *investigations;* **maintien de l'ordre** *maintaining order;* **secours** *help;* **circulation routière** *road traffic*

COMPARAISONS

Quelles forces assurent la sécurité publique aux États-Unis?

4.2

La police 1.2

Le rôle de la police est définie dans la Déclaration des droits de l'homme et du citoyen (1789) comme "force publique pour l'avantage de tous." Il existe deux sortes de police: la police nationale et la police municipale. Chacune de ces forces portent des uniformes différents. Les policiers municipaux sont placés sous l'autorité du maire de la ville: ils sont chargés d'assurer l'ordre et la sécurité, mais leur compétence est très limitée. En cas de crimes et de délits*, ils doivent se reporter à la police nationale ou la gendarmerie. Notamment, quand il s'agit de maintenir l'ordre et la protection civile, par exemple lors de manifestations ou d'attentats*, la police nationale déploie* les CRS (Compagnies républicaines de sécurité). Ces policiers ont la permission d'utiliser la force pour arrêter les émeutes*.

Ces hommes font partie de la police nationale.

Search words: préfecture de police de (+ nom de la ville)

délits *offenses;* **attentats** *murder attempts;* **déploie** *displays;* **émeutes** *riots*

RESOURCES

Workbook 7

Culture

Products: Information

Inspector Clouseau, who appears in the comedy *The Pink Panther*, is a famous caricature of a French detective. For a bit of levity, show the scene where Clouseau tries to reduce his French accent by mastering (or not) the sentence "I would like to buy a hamburger."
Search words: **la panthère rose-hamburger (français)**

Differentiated Learning

Accelerate

Have students write a list of advice tips on how to protect oneself while taking the Paris **Métro**.
Search words: **paris en toute sécurité**

Decelerate

Ask students to use the details in **Extension** to write a short police report of the metro robbery.

Culture

Products: Information

Papillon is a 1973 prison film based on the best-selling autobiography by French convict Henri Charrière. It is the story of a friendship of two convicts condemned to the French penal colony of Devil's Island. It stars Steve McQueen and Dustin Hoffman.

Communication

Presentational: Cooperative Groups

Have students work in small groups to prepare arguments for and against **la réinsertion sociale**, releasing prisoners back into society. A class discussion will follow debating these two points of view.

Les chiffres de la délinquance 1.2

Après avoir beaucoup augmenté depuis les années 1950, la délinquance (c'est-à-dire tous les délits, toutes les fautes, et tous les crimes) diminue depuis 2003.

Nombre de vols en 2008	
5.000 vols par jour	
Vols à main armée	6.107
Autres vols avec violence sans arme à feu*	100.526
Vols avec entrée par ruse	9.571
Cambriolages*	198.173
Vols liés* à l'automobile et aux deux-roues à moteur	640.400
Autres vols simples	581.600
Recels*	41.329
Total des vols	**1.847.305**

arme à feu *firearm;* **cambriolage** *robbery;* **liés** *linked;* **Recels** *Receiving stolen goods*

Une **déclaration de vol** est une fiche à remplir au commissariat de police quand on vous vole quelque chose. 2.1

Une prison célèbre se trouve au **château d'If.** Bâti comme une forteresse dans une île près de Marseille en 1524, ce château est devenu une prison. Ses cachots (*cells*) sont décrits dans *Le comte de Monte-Cristo* par Alexandre Dumas. 2.2

La prison du château d'If devient un lieu public après la première Guerre Mondiale (*WWI*).

De la prison à la réinsertion sociale 1.2

Pour la prison, il y a 84.000 incarcérations par an et 62.000 prisonniers. Six pour cent des prisonniers sont condamnés à des peines incompressibles* de 30 ans (il n'y a pas de prison à vie), peine maximale. Il n'y a pas d'application de la peine de mort*, qui a été supprimée en 1981. De plus en plus la justice française insiste sur la réinsertion sociale*, croyant qu'une justice répressive perpétue une société criminelle, alors que pour mieux combattre le crime, il faut mieux s'occuper de la société.

peines incompréhensibles *sentences without parole;* **peine de mort** *death penalty;* **réinsertion sociale** *rehabilitation*

Essential Instruction

1. Have students read **Les chiffres de la délinquance** and compare these statistics to those of the State of New York, which is close to the size of France.
2. Students complete all readings before doing **Activité 9.** Give students a choice of activities.
3. Online, have students research statistics about the American penal system to prepare for a class discussion of **À discuter.**

Mots-clé Le mot **police**, qui est d'abord écrit *pollice* (1250), est emprunté au latin *politia* qui désigne l'organisation politique, le gouvernement. Et ce même mot latin vient du grec *politeia* qui désigne un ensemble de citoyens. Il s'est séparé de la politique pour désigner l'ordre et le règlement établi dans une ville pour garantir la sûreté des habitants (1606) avant de passer de l'objet à la personne et aux institutions qui vont avec (1651).

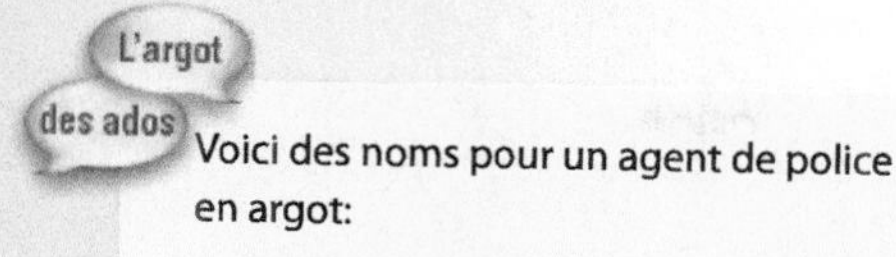

Voici des noms pour un agent de police en argot:

flic
poulet
poulaga

 **4.1**

9 Activités culturelles

 **1.3, 3.1, 3.2, 4.2**

Complétez les activités suivantes.

1. Dessinez le look (costume) de la gendarmerie et la police de Paris.
2. Préparez un organigramme qui montre les missions de la gendarmerie et de la police, surtout les différences.
3. Faites un tableau qui montre les types de crime, y compris les types de vols.
4. Faites un tableau qui montre les crimes aux États-Unis (avec les mêmes catégories mentionnées dans le texte) et comparez-le au tableau pour la France.

À discuter

Y a-t-il trop de gens emprisonnés aux États-Unis? Faites des recherches et discutez de vos conclusions avec vos camarades de classe. Croyez-vous à la réinsertion sociale? Pourquoi, ou pourquoi pas?

Cet agent de police travaille pour la police municipale.

Answers

 9

1. *Drawings will vary.* (**Gendarmerie** outfit has dark blue vest and pants, hat, high boots, and words GENDARMERIE in back of jacket. **Police** outfit has dark blue vest and pants, hat, light blue shirt, boots and words POLICE MUNICIPALE in back of jacket.)
2. Differences are: **Gendarmerie** belong to the national army; **police** is local and has less power.
3. Thefts with firearms; violent thefts without weapons; thefts with broken entry; robberies; auto thefts; petty thefts; buying stolen goods
4. *Answers will vary.*

À discuter
Answers will vary.

Critical Thinking

Analysis
The **CRS** is the riot branch of the French police force. What incidents in the last 10 years have made them feared and held in low esteem among ethnic groups in France?

Differentiated Learning

Expand
There are two films the students may want to watch which deal with imprisonment in France in times past: ***Le comte de Monte-Cristo*** and ***l'Homme dans le masque de fer***. Ask students to research and present the plots for both of these films, and explain how they relate to French history.

Adapt
Ask students to research a visit to **le château d'If**. Have them find information about the ferry, schedules, and prices. Encourage them to search videos to use in a presentation to the class.

Answers

10

1. *Un flic, Le Gendarme de Saint-Tropez, Les Keufs, Tendre poulet*
2. *Answers will vary.*
3. *Answers will vary.*

Connections

Music

The popular song "**Dans ma valise**" by Dorotheé features possessive adjectives with common vocabulary that is fun to sing and is a good learning and teaching tool.

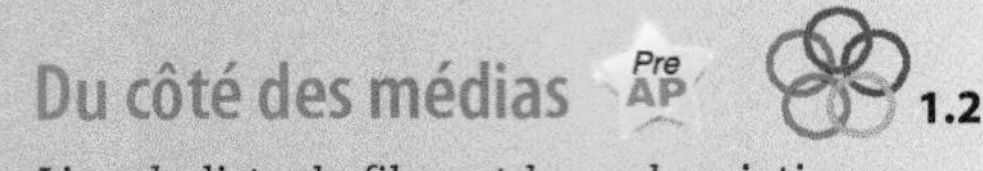

Du côté des médias

Pre AP 1.2

Lisez la liste de films et leurs descriptions.

FILMS CÉLÈBRES QUI FONT RÉFÉRENCE À LA POLICE OU À LA GENDARMERIE:

Tendre poulet (1977) de Philippe de Broca avec Philippe Noiret et Annie Girardot

Description: Comédie policière. Alors qu'elle poursuit une investigation sur des meurtres, Lise, commissaire de police, rencontre un ancien camarade de classe, Antoine. Crime et romance vont se mêler.

Les Keufs (1987) de Josiane Balasko avec Isaach de Bankolé

Description: Comédie policière. Mireille est une agente de police déguisée pour combattre la prostitution. Avec son partenaire Blaise, elle va s'acharner à libérer une jeune femme et son enfant.

Un flic (1972) de Jean-Pierre Melville avec Alain Delon et Catherine Deneuve

Description: Film d'action, policier, drame. Un gang attaque une banque. Le commissaire Édouard Coleman commence son enquête. Il s'aperçoit qu'il a plus en commun avec cette bande, car il est l'amant de la femme du chef du gang, Simon. Entre justice et loyauté, il s'ensuit une course qui vous laissera à bout de souffle.

Le Gendarme de Saint-Tropez (1964) de Jean Girault avec Louis de Funès, Michel Galabru, et Geneviève Grad

Description: La première d'une série de six comédies, Louis de Funès vous fera tordre de rire! Simple gendarme, Cruchot se laisse mener dans les mésaventures de sa fille qui ne cherche qu'un peu d'aventures dans sa vie, et en même temps découvrir une affaire de vol.

10 Films sur les flics

1.3, 3.2

Faites les activités suivantes.

1. Faites une liste de titres en ordre chronologique.
2. Avec un partenaire, recherchez chaque film et écrivez une phrase d'introduction pour chaque film.
3. Choisissez un clip disponible en streaming et regardez-le. Dites si vous recommanderiez le film ou pas. Justifiez votre décision.

Essential Instruction

1. Students read **À côté des médias** and answer **Activité 10.**
2. Have them go online and list from first to last the most popular in terms of awards won.
3. Ask students to write **Activité 11** before correcting as a whole-class activity.
4. Have students explain what is on their desk: **C'est mon livre, mon stylo, mon cahier.**
5. Ask students to look at a partner's desk and say: **C'est ton livre, ton stylo, ton cahier.**
6. Have them look at your desk and identify objects using **votre**, and so on.

Structure de la langue

emcl.com
WB 11
Games

Révision: Possessive Adjectives  1.1

As you have already learned, possessive adjectives express ownership or relationship. They agree in gender and in number with the nouns that follow them.

	Singular				Plural	
	Masculine				Feminine before a Consonant Sound	
my	**mon**		**ma**		**mes**	
your	**ton**		**ta**		**tes**	
his, her, its, one's, its	**son**	stylo	**sa**	trousse	**ses**	cahiers
our	**notre**	affiche	**notre**		**nos**	
your	**votre**		**votre**		**vos**	
their	**leur**		**leur**		**leurs**	

Ma grand-mère m'a dit qu'une fille avait volé **son** portefeuille. — *My grandmother told me that a girl had stolen her wallet.*

Remember that before a feminine singular word beginning with a vowel sound, **ma**, **ta**, and **sa** become **mon**, **ton**, and **son**, respectively.

Émilie s'est rendue compte que **son** amie ne venait pas. — *Émilie realized that her friend wasn't coming.*

11 Le vol à Lyon   1.3

Votre équipe de foot a voyagé à Lyon pour un match. Pendant le match, quelqu'un est entré dans votre monospace. Il a volé beaucoup de choses! Dites ce qu'il a volé et n'a pas volé.

MODÈLE Pierre: portable (*oui*)
Il a volé son portable.

Nadia: sac à dos (*non*)
Il n'a pas volé son sac à dos.

1. Fabrice: lecteur MP3 (*oui*)
2. Jérémy et moi: maillots de foot (*non*)
3. Malika: jeux vidéo (*oui*)
4. toi: veste (*non*)
5. Delphine et Nora: portefeuilles (*oui*)
6. moi: carte cadeau (*oui*)
7. Assane et toi: cahiers (*non*)
8. toi: bouteille d'eau minérale (*non*)
9. je: guide touristique de Lyon (*non*)

Que va-t-il se passer quand les joueurs retourneront à leur monospace?

RESOURCES

 **Workbook 11**

 **Drill & Practice Games**

Answers

1. Il a volé son lecteur MP3.
2. Il n'a pas volé nos maillots de foot.
3. Il a volé ses jeux vidéo.
4. Il n'a pas volé ta veste.
5. Il a volé leurs portefeuilles.
6. Il a volé ma carte cadeau.
7. Il n'a pas volé vos cahiers.
8. Il n'a pas volé ta bouteille d'eau minérale.
9. Il n'a pas volé mon guide touristique de Lyon.

Game

Cherchez l'objet!

Put students in small groups. Prepare a set of cards for each group. On each card paste the picture of an object and an owner's name. Each owner must have two possessions in the deck. For example, Pierre could own a camera and a pair of sandals. One student deals out all the cards. The first player asks another player if he or she has an object belonging to a person on one of the first player's cards, for example, **Jean, as-tu un objet de Pierre?** The interviewed player answers **oui** or **non.** If the answer is **oui**, the player being interviewed relinquishes the card to the first player. The first player earns a point for using the correct possessive adjectives in a sentence, for example, **J'ai son appareil-photo et sa paire de sandales.** If the first player forms an incorrect sentence, the card is returned to its original owner and the second player takes a turn.

Differentiated Learning

Accelerate

Set a timer and have students make a list of everything in their bedroom using **Il y a.**

Decelerate

Slide show presentations reinforce the possessive adjective and pronoun lessons. Have students use the **Search words** below to access a free clearinghouse of teaching approaches. They can watch these lessons for information and practice.
Search words: **share my lesson**

Multiple Intelligences

Visual-Spatial

Have students collaborate to make a poster of possessive adjectives to display in the classroom as reference.

RESOURCES

 Workbook 8–10, 12–13

 Listening Activity 2

 Drill & Practice Games

Connections

Spanish Language Speakers

Point out that **le mien**, **le tien**, **le sien** is comparable to **el mío**, **el tuyo**, **el suyo**.

Communication

Interpersonal: Paired Practice

Put students in small groups and distribute a picture of an object to each student, for example, **deux glaces** or **un couteau.** Students in each group exchange their picture with that of another student. Then students take turns returning the picture to its rightful owner, saying a sentence using a possessive pronoun, for example, **Ce sont les tiennes!** or **C'est le tien!** Students respond, **Oui, c'est le mien/la mienne** or **Non, ce n'est pas le mien/la mienne**.

Possessive Pronouns  1.1

emcl.com
WB 8–10, 12–13
LA 2
Games

A possessive pronoun replaces a noun plus a possessive adjective.

Thibault et moi, nous avions perdu nos lunettes. **Les siennes** étaient chez moi, **les miennes** chez lui.

Thibault and I lost our glasses. His were at my house, mine at his house.

The possessive pronoun is composed of two words, each of which agrees in gender and in number with the noun it replaces.

	Singular		Plural	
	Masculine	Feminine	Masculine	Feminine
mine	**le mien**	**la mienne**	**les miens**	**les miennes**
yours	**le tien**	**la tienne**	**les tiens**	**les tiennes**
his, hers, its, one's	**le sien**	**la sienne**	**les siens**	**les siennes**
ours	**le nôtre**	**la nôtre**	**les nôtres**	
yours	**le vôtre**	**la vôtre**	**les vôtres**	
theirs	**le leur**	**la leur**	**les leurs**	

Thomas et Lucas ont acheté des chemises à rayures comme **les miennes**, mais **les leurs** étaient plus chères.

Thomas et Lucas bought some striped shirts like mine but theirs were more expensive.

Combien coûtent **les vôtres**?

How much do yours cost?

COMPARAISONS  4.1

What is different about the possession expressed in the French and English sentences?

À qui est cette vidéo? Elle est à moi.
Whose video is it? It's mine.

COMPARAISONS: The French sentence uses **être à** + stress pronoun rather than a possessive pronoun. In English a possessive pronoun is used. Possessive pronouns are used more in English than in French.

Essential Instruction

1. Introduce possessive pronouns by comparing them with mine, yours, his... in English.
2. Review the forms. What do they notice is different with **notre** and **votre**, and **le nôtre** and **le vôtre**?
3. Ask students to identify things they own, first with a possessive adjective and then with the possessive pronoun. They say: **C'est mon cahier; C'est le mien; C'est mon stylo; C'est le mien.**
4. As a drill have them do the same exercise but pointing to another student's possessions (**C'est ton cahier. C'est le tien...**) so that they see the connection between the two possessive forms.
5. As a whole-class activity, ask students to do **Activité 12**, first orally, then as a written exercise. Write the answers on the board to correct.
6. Students do **Activité 13** in pairs.

12 Carla vient de déménager.

1.3

Toutes les affaires de Carla sont encore dans des cartons. Vous habitez l'appartement d'à côté et vous lui proposez de lui prêter ce dont elle a besoin.

MODÈLE "Je voudrais me laver les mains. Où est mon savon?"
Je te prête le mien.

1. "Je voudrais préparer un steak. Dans quel carton peut être ma poêle?"
2. "Il faut que je prenne une douche. Mon shampooing, il est où?"
3. "Je vais faire du footing. Qu'est-ce que j'ai fait de mes chaussettes blanches?"
4. "J'ai envie de me détendre. Où peuvent bien être mes magazines?"
5. "J'invite mes parents à dîner. Mes fourchettes sont dans quel carton?"
6. "J'aimerais écouter de la musique. Mon lecteur MP3 est où?"

Communiquez!

13 Je décris les gens que je connais.

1.1

Interpersonal Communication

À tour de rôle, décrivez les personnes que vous connaissez en vous servant des indices donnés.

MODÈLE mon meilleur ami/origine ethnique
A: **Mon meilleur ami est d'origine asiatique.**
B: **Le mien est d'origine arabe.**

1. ma meilleure amie/cheveux
2. mon cousin/physique
3. mes parents/âge
4. mon grand-père/yeux
5. ma grand-mère/cheveux
6. mon prof d'histoire/physique
7. ma tante/yeux
8. mon oncle/âge

Answers

1. Je te prête la mienne.
2. Je te prête le mien.
3. Je te prête les miennes.
4. Je te prête les miens.
5. Je te prête les miennes.
6. Je te prête le mien.

13 *Answers will vary.*

1. Ma meilleure amie a les cheveux .... La mienne ....
2. Mon cousin est .... Le mien ....
3. Mes parents ont .... Les miens ....
4. Mon grand-père a les yeux .... Le mien ....
5. Ma grand-mère a les cheveux .... La mienne ....
6. Mon prof d'histoire est.... Le mien ....
7. Ma tante a les yeux .... La mienne ....
8. Mon oncle a .... Le mien ....

Communication

Interpersonal: Cooperative Groups

Put students in small groups to practice possessive pronouns. Tell them they are on a trip and staying at a hotel with a friend. Prepare a worksheet with a list of items they were supposed to have packed. The first student in each group turns to the student on his or her right and states that he or she cannot find the first item on the list and asks to borrow the roommate's item. For example, **Dis, Tom, je ne peux pas trouver ma dentifrice. Est-ce que je peux t'emprunter la tienne?** The second student agrees. **Oui, je te prête la mienne.** Then, the second student plays the role of the borrower, the third student is the lender, and the dialogue continues.

Differentiated Learning

Accelerate

Students prepare a review lesson of possessive adjectives and pronouns to be presented to the class. They must make a worksheet for the students and must use manipulatives such as an apple, a book, a cell phone, a hat for their demonstration.

Decelerate

Have students use the online grammar review and practice sites to master how to express possession. Search words: **possessive adjectives, pronoun exercises french**

Answers

1. La mienne est plus belle que la sienne.
2. La mienne est plus nouvelle que la sienne.
3. La mienne est plus intéressante que la vôtre.
4. Les miens sont plus amusants que les tiens.
5. Le mien est plus dynamique que le tien.
6. La mienne est plus jolie que la sienne.
7. Les miens sont plus beaux que les leurs.
8. Les miennes sont plus grandes que les leurs.

15

Script can be found in the front pages of the Annotated Teacher's Edition.

1. Julien
2. Anne-Marie
3. Jean et Luc
4. M. et Mme Blanchard
5. Juliette et Sylvie Leblanc

Communication

Interpersonal: Cooperative Groups

Put students in groups of three. Ask them to secretly draw and color: 1) **une voiture de sport**, 2) **un livre**, 3) **des chaussures**, 4) **un chapeau**, 5) **une cravate**, 6) **un gâteau**, 7) **un fruit**, 8) **une calculatrice**, and 9) **une chemise**. In order, they show each other the first object and compare it to two others. The first student says: **Ma voiture de sport est rouge.** Looking at another student: **La tienne est noire.** Looking at the third, talking to the second student: **La sienne est rouge aussi.** The second student talks about the second object using this model. The third student talks about the third object, and it continues.

14 Richard se vante!

1.1

Richard écoute ses amis. Jouez le rôle de Richard, qui pense que ses affaires, animaux, et parents sont les meilleurs.

MODÈLE Julianne: "Abdel et Nicole ont deux beaux chiens."
Richard: **Les miens sont plus beaux que les leurs!**

1. André: "J'ai acheté une belle chemise à carreaux."
2. M. et Mme Diouf: "Thomas conduit une nouvelle voiture."
3. Solange: "Marc et moi, nous avons fait une vidéo très intéressante pour notre cours d'histoire."
4. Monique: "Mes parents sont très amusants!"
5. Joël: "Mon prof de français est dynamique!"
6. Océane: "Adja a une jolie sœur."
7. Abdoulaye: "Les Dumont ont de beaux chevaux."
8. Lucien: "Les Vaillancourt ont de grandes pièces."

15 C'est à qui?

1.2

Interpretive Communication

Écrivez les numéros 1–5 sur votre papier. Écoutez les mini-dialogues. Dites à qui appartient chaque chose; écrivez son prénom.

À qui est ce chien adorable?

Essential Instruction

1. In pairs, have students prepare and practice **Activité 14**. Randomly ask partners to do the dialogues. Ask them to add **"parce que"** and the reason why whatever they have is better.
2. Have students do **Activité 15** on whiteboards. They show you each answer to give you a sense of how they are doing.
3. Using the information from **Activité 16**, ask students to write a narrative police report of Suzanne Weiller's declaration.

À vous la parole

16 Une déclaration de vol

1.2, 5.1

Question centrale: Quels sont les défis de la vie contemporaine?

Résumez l'histoire de Suzanne Weiler à Paris par écrit en lisant sa déclaration de vol. Où le crime a-t-il eu lieu? Quand? À quelle heure? La victime est de quelle nationalité? Qu'est-ce qu'on lui a volé? Comment étaient les voleurs? Où a-t-elle rempli la déclaration de vol?

MINISTÈRE DE L'INTÉRIEUR ET DE LA SÉCURITÉ PUBLIQUE
DIRECTION GÉNÉRALE DE LA POLICE NATIONALE
RÉPUBLIQUE FRANÇAISE
Liberté Égalité Fraternité

Commissariat de Voie Publique
9, Rue Fabert
75007 PARIS
Tél.: 01 44 18 69 07
Fax: 01 44 18 33 87

CODE INSEE DU SERVICE	Dept	Commune	N° du Service
	75		

1 RÉCÉPISSÉ DE DÉCLARATION DE
- ❑ VOL À LA TIRE
- ❑ VOL À L'ÉTALAGE OU DANS UN TIROIR-CAISSE
- ❑ VOL DANS UN APPAREIL AUTOMATIQUE
- ❑ AUTRE VOL SIMPLE
- ❑ FILOUTERIE

2 L'an deux mil douze
le Vingt-quatre mars à Dix-sept heures quinze
Nous CRAVEAU Éric, Gardien de la Paix
__Officier X Agent de police Judiciaire, en fonction à Paris 7ᵉ
dressons procès-verbal de la plainte ci-dessous

3 PLAINTE (L'ÉTAT-CIVIL DU PLAIGNANT DOIT ÊTRE RÉLEVÉ SUR UNE PIÈCE D'IDENTITÉ OFFICIELLE)
SERVICE DE RÉCEPTION DE LA PLAINTE: 7ᵉ Arrdt — DATE ET HEURE: 17 heures 15
PRÉNOM, NOM, GRADE DU RÉDACTEUR: CRAVEAU Éric, Gardien de la Paix
(ÉVENTUELLEMENT NOM DE JEUNE FILLE SUIVI DU NOM D'ÉPOUSE ET PRÉNOMS)
Je soussigné(e) WEILER Suzanne
né(e) le 14/11/1995 à HOUSTON (Texas)
nationalité Américaine profession Étudiante
demeurant P.O. Box 1235 BROOKSHIRE, TEXAS 77423 USA
DÉPOSE PLAINTE CONTRE INCONNU POUR LES FAITS RELATES (REMPLIR LA RUBRIQUE VICTIME SI LE PLAIGNANT AGIT POUR LE COMPTE D'AUTRUI)

VICTIME	WEILER Suzanne
DATE ET LIEU DE NAISSANCE	14/11/95 HOUSTON TEXAS — NATIONALITÉ: Américaine
ADRESSE	P.O. Box 1235 BROOKSHIRE TEXAS 77423 USA
CODE POSTAL ET COMMUNE	TÉLÉPHONE
DATE EXACTE OU PRÉSUMÉE	24/03 vers 16 heures
NATURE DU JOUR	L M W J V X D In — ☐ VEILLE DE FÊTE LÉGALE OU CONGÉS SCOLAIRES — ☐ PÉRIODE DE FÊTE LÉGALE OU CONGÉS SCOLAIRES — ☐ JOUR DE FÊTE OU DE MANIFESTATION LOCALE
LIEU INFRACTION	75 PARIS 7ᵉ Métro La Tour Maubourg
NATURE DU LIEU	Métro
OBJETS VOLÉS	Un passeport de nationalité américaine au nom de WEILER Suzanne N° 131082315, une somme de 18 dollars américains, 180 dollars en chèques de voyage, et 30 euros, une MasterCard Gold et un permis de conduire de Texas avec photographie.
MODE OPÉRATOIRE PRÉCISIONS COMPLÉMENTAIRES	Deux individus de type méditerranéen d'environ une quinzaine d'années. L'un demande l'heure pendant que l'autre fouille dans le sac à dos.

RESOURCES

Communicative Activities

Answers

Où: Paris 7ème; Métro La Tour Maubourg; quand: le 24 mars 2012; heure: 17h15; nationalité de la victime: américaine; objets volés: passeport, 18 dollars, 180 dollars en chèques de voyage, 30 euros, une MasterCard Gold, un permis de conduire américain; description des voleurs: deux jeunes hommes d'une quinzaine d'année, d'origine méditérannéenne;déclaration remplie à: Paris, rue Fabert

Expansion

In pairs, have students prepare a dialogue in which a police officer interviews Suzanne to get all of the information about the robbery. The officer might ask, **Où habitez-vous? Quelle est votre nationalité?** Suzanne has to furnish the details of the robbery: time of day, where she was, how she felt. Encourage them to use the **Extension** dialogue on p. 530 as a guide.

Differentiated Learning

Accelerate
Have students write a scene of the robbery to be acted out. Ask them to embellish the dialogue with conversation between Suzanne and a friend, then the encounter with the two robbers, and finally the struggle that followed.

Decelerate
Students fill out a declaration inventing a minor crime committed against them adding who, what, where, and when information.

Answers
All activities will vary.

Reference Desk

Before doing **Activité 17**, remind students about the use of the **imparfait** and **passé composé** to describe past events. To help them decide if they need the **passé composé,** encourage them to ask the question, **Qu'est-ce qui est arrivé? Quelles étaient les circonstances?** acts as a cue for the **imparfait**.

Communiquez!

17 Je suis témoin.

1.1

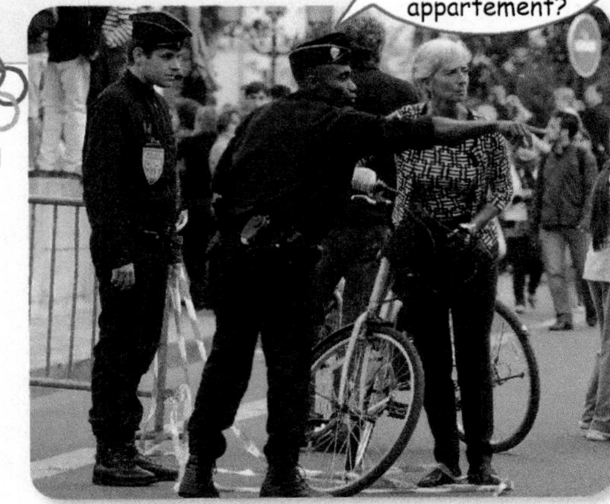

Interpersonal Communication

Avec un partenaire, jouez les rôles d'un témoin d'un cambriolage dans la maison de ses voisins et d'un agent de police qui pose beaucoup de questions. L'agent voudrait savoir:

- l'heure du crime
- une description du voleur: sa taille, son âge, ses cheveux, son origine ethnique, ses vêtements
- une description de la voiture du voleur, y compris le numéro de sa plaque minéralogique (*license plate*)

Communiquez!

18 Ce jour-là, je me suis rendu compte que....

1.3

Presentational Communication

Pour l'écrivain irlandais James Joyce, une "épiphanie" est une sorte de révélation, d'ordre quasi mystique qui marque un moment de votre vie et qui change tout. Choisissez un moment de votre vie quand vous vous êtes rendu compte de quelque chose d'important. Qu'est-ce qui a mené (*led*) à cette révélation? Comment a-t-elle changé votre attitude, vos buts, ou peut-être votre vie en général? Répondez à ces questions dans un récit personnel.

Communiquez!

19 Comment éviter les crimes sur Internet

1.3, 3.2

Interpretive/Presentational Communication

Avec des camarades de classe, faites une liste de règles pour vous protéger quand vous êtes sur Internet. Partagez les problèmes dont vous êtes au courant ou que vous avez vécus et donnez une solution pour chacun. Publiez votre liste et vos récits en ligne pour aider les autres élèves dans le monde francophone.

Essential Instruction

1. For **Activité 17**, encourage students to add physical descriptions of the suspects, what they saw being carried out of the house, and any other details to add some drama.
2. If **Activité 18** seems a bit too personal for some, ask them to think of an historic personage who had an epiphany which changed the course of his/her life. Joan of Arc and her voices would be a prime example.
3. For **Activité 19**, students can find security tips online to add to their list of precautions they created.
4. To expand on **Stratégie communicative**, demonstrate to students the use of a graphic organizer to organize the details of the story. Encourage them to weave into the drama what they imagine motivated Derek to visit France, how he earned the money, what he has in his suitcase, and other details to enhance the story.

Stratégie communicative

Telling a Story through Pictures  1.3

Vous allez raconter une histoire en regardant des illustrations. Dites de qui il s'agit, où l'action se déroule (*takes place*), ce qui se passe; donnez un maximum de détails. Pensez à ce qui a pu se passer avant, pendant, et après chaque scène. N'oubliez pas d'utiliser des conjonctions lorsque vous passez d'une scène à une autre. Par exemple, **Le lendemain Derek a pris un bus pour aller à l'aéroport.** L'histoire est racontée au passé. Pour la dernière scène, ajoutez un petit dialogue. Votre professeur vous dira s'il vous faudra raconter cette histoire par écrit ou oralement.

MODÈLE **Derek rêvait depuis longtemps de voyager à Paris. Quand il a finalement eu les moyens d'y aller, il a acheté un billet en ligne avec Air France et l'a imprimé chez lui. Il a beaucoup lu sur Paris; il veut surtout visiter le musée d'Orsay afin de voir les tableaux de Monet et des autres impressionnistes.**

RESOURCES

 Pre-test

 *Leçon* Quiz

Reference Desk

Before asking students to tell the story in **Stratégie communicative**, model a similar idea as a whole group activity. Choose several pictures and work as a group to create the story orally, reminding students of the **passé composé** and **imparfait** uses and the need for conjunctions to create continuity. Encourage them to add detail and interest. Write the story on the board as you proceed. Remind the students throughout the process that they will be doing a similar activity themselves.

Differentiated Learning

Accelerate

Encourage students to use dialogue and rich description to enhance their story. Have them go beyond the picture to give a personality to "the girl," explain where Derek and the girl might go for coffee afterward, and how much they both love Monet, for example.

Decelerate

In small groups, brainstorm phrases for students to use in their story, inspired by the illustration, which they will copy and incorporate. This process may keep students away from translators and dictionaries. Work with them in a step-by-step manner to write simple sentences for their story.

Reference Desk

Brainstorm vocabulary that students need to complete their story. Expressions for giving an opinion of a film, questions the boy might ask himself about the **bateaux mouches** tours on the Seine, and vocabulary for giving an opinion about a painting are examples of expressions to discuss.

Essential Instruction

1. After students have written their pre-writing outline independently or with your help, give them time in class to write the story. This process allows you one-on-one time with each student, helping them form their sentences, offering corrections, giving them instant feedback, and cutting your correcting time in half.
2. To prepare to teach the vocabulary for **Réactions et vêtements**, draw emoticons on the board for the following emotions: happy, sad, excited, depressed, and angry. Ask students to suggest vocabulary that they already know for each of these emotions. Have them copy what is written on the board into their notebooks.
3. Students listen to the **Réactions et vêtements** and add the new vocabulary to the list of emotions.
4. Ask students to draw the clothing from **Et si je voulais dire...?**
5. Play **Pour la conversation** and ask students to make more sentences with the expressions.

Leçon C

Vocabulaire actif

emcl.com
WB 1–3
LA 1
Games

Réactions et vêtements   1.2

Ces filles ressentent les sensations suivantes:

Abdoul a mis un jean délavé, une liquette, et des baskets (f.). Il a du charme, non?

Elle est complètement surprise.

Elle est tout à fait choquée.

Elle se sent vraiment accablée.

Elle est quand même frustrée.

Elle est surexcitée.

Elle se sent seule.

Pour la conversation   1.1

How do I ask when someone had an idea to do something?

> **Vous avez eu l'idée de** mettre votre vidéo sur YouTube tout de suite?

Did you have the idea to put your video on YouTube right away?

How do I say I didn't expect something?

> **Je ne m'y attendais pas....**

I didn't expect it.

Et si je voulais dire...? 

des bretelles (f.)	*suspenders*
des espadrilles (f.)	*rope-soled sandals*
des santiags (f.)	*cowboy boots*
un sweat à capuche	*hoodie*
courroucé(e)	*mad*
dépassé(e)	*over-excited*
survoltée(e)	*overwhelmed*

RESOURCES

 **e-visual 28**

 **Workbook 1–3**

 **Flash Cards**

 **Listening Activity 1**

 **Drill & Practice Games**

Reference Desk

1. **Surprise(e)** means "to be surprised." **Choqué(e)** means "to have a strong reaction to something."
2. **Les santiags** or **bottes de cowboy** originated in Spain, and then were introduced into Mexico. Today in the United States they are not only popular in Texas and Oklahoma, but are seen as fashion accessories everywhere.

Culture

Practices: Information

Mettre la ceinture et les bretelles (*to wear a belt and suspenders*) is an expression that denotes someone is super-cautious.

Differentiated Learning

Accelerate

Ask students to search online for more expressions denoting emotions and suggest them to the class.

Decelerate

Conjugate the verb **se sentir** with the students. Ask them to conjugate it in the present tense in all forms with various "emotion" vocabulary words to help students review adjective agreement in all forms.

Answers

1

1. Elle lui a dit que ça viendra.
2. des vidéos sur YouTube
3. très positive
4. Elle aurait emporté des shorts et vêtements d'été.
5. Il lui a demandé où elle a acheté ses baskets et sa liquette.

2

1. scandinave
2. grand et costaud
3. courts et bouclés
4. une chemise blanche, un jean délavé, et des baskets
5. charme

Reference Desk

1. One can say either **à Avignon** or **en Avignon**. The same is true for the city of Arles. Why? It is because Avignon was a separate state from France until the French revolution. Therefore, remembering this historical status, either form is correct.
2. The **Festival d'Avignon**, founded in 1947 by Jean Vilar, is held annually in July in the courtyard of the **Palais des Papes** and in other locations of the city. It is the oldest festival in France and draws directors, actors, and drama buffs from around the world.

Game

Vocabulaire 101!

Play this game to practice the new vocabulary. Prepare a set of note cards with a new word or expression on each one. Divide the class into two teams. Call the first player from each team to the front. Select the top card from the pile and read aloud the word or expression that you want the players to use in a sentence. Both players write a sentence on the board using that word or expression. The student who correctly uses the new word or expression in a sentence earns a point for his or her team. If both sentences are correct, both teams win a point. Then a different player from each team takes a turn.

1 Une lettre de France

Lisez la lettre que Charlotte a écrite à sa prof de français, puis répondez aux questions.

Madame,

Tout va bien ici à Avignon. Je suis un peu frustrée par mon français, mais vous m'avez dit que ça viendra, n'est-ce pas? La bonne nouvelle est que je ne me sens plus seule. J'ai eu l'idée de faire une vidéo avec d'autres filles et de la mettre sur YouTube. Je suis vraiment surexcitée par la réaction. Je ne m'y attendais pas! Depuis, on m'a invitée à en faire d'autres et je me suis fait plein d'amis maintenant.

J'étais un peu accablée par la chaleur (heat) les premiers jours parce que je n'avais pas pensé à emmener des shorts avec moi, juste un jean délavé et deux autres pantalons que je lave souvent. Il faut que je fasse du shopping! J'ai aussi fait la connaissance d'un garçon qui voulait savoir où j'avais acheté mes baskets et ma liquette. Philippe, c'est son nom, est très gentil et on sort ensemble très souvent.

En espérant que vous m'écrirez bientôt,

Jennifer

1. Qu'est-ce que la prof de Jennifer lui a dit pour l'encourager à propos de son français?
2. Que fait-elle avec d'autres ados?
3. Quelle était la réaction du public et la réaction de Jennifer face au succès de sa vidéo?
4. Comment est-ce qu'elle aurait fait sa valise différemment?
5. Comment a-t-elle fait la connaissance de Philippe?

2 Christian va en ville.

Complétez les phrases.

1. Christian est un type d'origine....
2. Physiquement, il est....
3. Il a les cheveux....
4. Aujourd'hui il porte....
5. Il a du..., non?

Essential Instruction

1. After students read **Activité 1**, ask the general comprehension questions.
2. Have students identify the various tenses and moods of verbs in the letter.
3. Ask students to describe what they think Charlotte and Philippe look like.
4. After students complete the sentences in **Activité 2**, ask them to expand on what Christian is like, what he likes to do, where he lives, and what he wants to do with his life.
5. Have students do **Activité 3** orally and then written.
6. Divide students into six groups. Ask them to write a short composition explaining who is in the picture you assigned to them, and explain why they are feeling the way they do.

3 Les réactions

1.3

Regardez les illustrations pour identifier les réactions des personnes. Choisissez un adjectif de la liste.

MODÈLE

M. Dugas

M. Dugas est complètement accablé.

accablé | seul | surpris | surexcité | choqué | frustré

1. M. et Mme Laroche

2. Mme Dufour

3. Matthieu

4. M. Carré

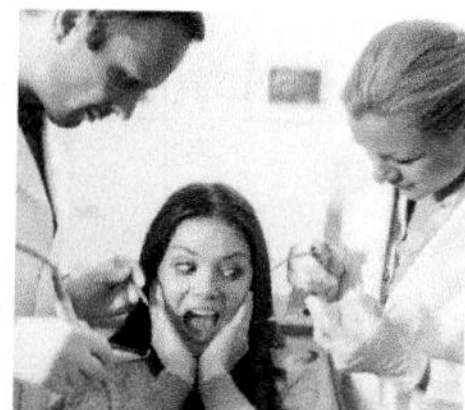

5. Isabelle

Les élèves sont choqués par les résultats du bac.

Answers

3

1. M. et Mme Laroche sont tout à fait surpris.
2. Mme Dufour est vraiment frustrée.
3. Matthieu se sent seul.
4. M. Carré est surexcité!
5. Isabelle est complètement choquée.

Communication

Presentational: Cooperative groups

Students collaborate to present a fashion show of current looks. They can consider "the Prep," "the Biker," or "the **Intello**" for example. There will be some students who will be the runway models wearing the outfits that various student narrators describe. **Search words: la redoute, la mode femme et homme**

Differentiated Learning

Accelerate

Have students pretend that they are Charlotte's French teacher and respond to her letter suggesting places in and outside of Avignon that she should visit.

Decelerate

Students can collaborate to make a collage of Avignon with captions about the historic places to visit. They should situate the city on the map. The goal is for them to promote Avignon to the class.

Answers

Script can be found in the front pages of the Annotated Teacher's Edition.

1. V
2. F
3. F
4. F
5. F

5 *Answers will vary.*

Communication

Interpersonal: Cooperative Groups

Create a grid. In the first column students write an emotion. In the second column they write a situation in which they feel that way, for example **accablé(e)... parce que j'ai raté un grand examen.** Have students walk around the room and ask one another "**Comment tu te sens?**" The other student responds with an emotion. The first student asks "**Pourquoi?**" and the second student responds with the reason. Then reverse the student roles.

Communiquez!

4 Quelle surprise!

1.1, 1.2

Interpretive Communication

*Écrivez les numéros 1–5 sur votre papier. Ensuite, écoutez la discussion entre Aminata et l'animateur M. Aknouch sur un concours (competition) vidéo. Finalement, indiquez si les phrases que vous entendez sont vraies (**V**) ou fausses (**F**).*

5 Questions personnelles

1.2, 1.3

Répondez aux questions.

1\. À quoi est-ce que tu ne t'y attendais pas à l'école cette année?
2\. Quels vêtements est-ce que les élèves à ton école portent en général?
3\. Aimes-tu le style des vêtements délavés?
3\. Qu'est-ce que tu fais quand tu vois un(e) élève qui est seul(e) à la cantine?
4\. Qu'est-ce qui te rends surexcité(e)? frustré(e)? accablé(e)?

Moi, les devoirs, ça me rend frustré!

Essential Instruction

1. Have students listen to **Activité 4** and answer **vrai** or **faux** to the statements.
2. Give students time to prepare **Activité 5.** In answering, require students to expand their answers with details.
3. Expand the exercise by asking more questions about the situations in their lives that make them feel certain ways.
4. Play **Actuellement sur YouTube**, books closed.
5. Ask students what they think the interview was about, who was speaking, and any details that they remember.
6. Students listen a second time with books open.
7. What do they think **Ils se sont déchainés; Quelques-unes ont complètement craqué** means?
8. What English words did they encounter in the dialogue?
9. Have students answer **Activité 6** as a whole-class activity.

Rencontres culturelles

emcl.com
WB 4

Actuellement sur YouTube

   1.1, 1.2

Un reporter interviewe Élodie au sujet de son hit sur YouTube.

Le reporter: Vous avez eu l'idée de mettre votre vidéo sur YouTube tout de suite?
Élodie: Non, pas du tout.
Le reporter: Ce groupe de garçons, où l'avez-vous rencontré?
Élodie: Au mariage de mon cousin.... Ce sont deux frères et un copain.
Le reporter: On les y avait invités pour chanter?
Élodie: Oui, mon cousin les avait vus chanter des gospels à l'église. Ils sont arrivés habillés comme sur la vidéo... jeans bleus délavés, liquettes, et baskets orange comme pour un show! En fait, j'ai appris par la suite qu'ils chantaient dans un chœur de gospel à Genève.
Le reporter: Et c'est après qu'ils ont fait le show?
Élodie: Pendant la soirée, ils se sont déchaînés, tous les trois! Un vrai show.... C'est là que j'ai commencé à les filmer et comme ils étaient très photogéniques, c'était plutôt agréable... en plus, je trouvais qu'ils avaient du talent et du charme.
Le reporter: Bref, c'est ça qui vous a décidé à les mettre sur YouTube?
Élodie: Oui, j'ai commencé à montrer la vidéo à mes copines; quelques-unes ont complètement craqué, et voilà comment la vidéo s'est retrouvée sur YouTube.
Le reporter: Vous avez dû être complètement surprise par le buzz et le succès.
Élodie: Surtout eux! Moi non plus, je ne m'y attendais pas, je n'avais pas fait ça pour ça: juste pour partager une petite émotion. Et maintenant, ils ont de vraies groupies!
Le reporter: Merci.

6 Actuellement sur YouTube

Identifiez les personnes décrites.

1. Cette personne a un hit sur YouTube.
2. Cette personne interviewe Élodie.
3. Ces personnes ont fait un show.
4. Cette personne s'est mariée.
5. Ces personnes ont craqué en voyant la vidéo.
6. Cette personne ne s'attendait pas au buzz et au succès de la vidéo.

1.2

RESOURCES

 Dialogue Video

 Workbook 4

Answers

1. Élodie
2. le reporter
3. deux frères et un copain d'Élodie
4. le cousin d'Élodie
5. les copines d'Élodie
6. Élodie

Reference Desk

Remind students that **actuellement** means "now," not "actually." The word "actually" can be translated as either **en réalité** or **en fait.**

Differentiated Learning

Expand

Assign parts of the dialogue to each student. Replay the recording so that they note pronunciation and intonation. Have them act out the scene.

Decelerate

To check understanding of the dialogue prepare a set of sentences that ask students to complete the idea in each one with an answer from the conversation, for example, **Élodie n'a pas eu l'idée de mettre son vidéo sur Youtube...(tout de suite)** or **Élodie a rencontré ce groupe de garcons...(au mariage de son cousin)**.

Answers

Extension

Answers will vary.

Communication

Interpersonal: Cooperative Groups

Have students write a dialogue of a phone conversation between **Jérémie et la jeune femme** in which they reconnect after so long. He asks her about her work, where she is living, and plans the next time they will see each other.

Extension **Ils se sont retrouvés sur Internet.**   1.1, 1.2

Alexandre skype avec son pote Jérémie.

Alexandre: Et, elle ressemble à quoi maintenant?
Jérémie: Les cheveux raides, longs maintenant, toujours aussi mignonne.
Alexandre: Et, elle fait quoi?
Jérémie: Elle vient de commencer à travailler en Allemagne dans une société internationale de services.
Alexandre: Tu l'as retrouvée comment?
Jérémie: J'ai commencé par Facebook, j'ai essayé Copains d'avant, j'ai fait un petit tour par Meetic....
Alexandre: Je ne pensais pas que tu tenais à elle à ce point!
Jérémie: Mais rien... pas de traces.... J'ai fini par m'inscrire sur LinkedIn, un site professionnel, et voilà comment j'ai finalement retrouvé sa trace... elle était là: photo très pro. Tu imagines le choc!
Alexandre: Bref, tu es de nouvel amoureux....
Jérémie: Je ne m'attendais quand même pas à ce que ça me fasse cet effet-là. Et elle m'a demandé de venir la voir en Allemagne pour Pâques!
Alexandre: Perdu, retrouvé. Quelle chance!

Extension Quelle est votre prédiction pour Jérémie et la jeune femme?

1.2

Essential Instruction

1. Have students read **Extension.**
2. Ask them to list the social media mentioned in the dialogue.
3. Have them write their prediction for the future encounters of **Jérémie et la jeune femme.**
4. Students work in triads to read **Internet et les réseaux sociaux chez les jeunes.** Ask them to paraphrase each paragraph noting important facts.
5. The third paragraph discusses the preferred Internet activities of adolescents. Have them use each verb listed in a sentence describing their own Internet use, for example, **Je télécharge des albums sur iTunes.**
6. Ask students to read **Produits** and visit the site **loisirs ados.** What does the site offer? Have they visited similar sites for American adolescents?

Points de départ

emcl.com
WB 5

Question centrale: Quels sont les défis de la vie contemporaine?

Internet et les réseaux sociaux chez les jeunes

1.2

À l'occasion d'un sondage* de mille jeunes, on a découvert que dix seulement n'étaient jamais allés sur Internet: ils avaient tous huit ans!

On compte aujourd'hui plus de 68% des familles qui ont au moins deux ordinateurs à la maison et la plupart des jeunes de plus de 11 ans se connectent seuls sur Internet; quant aux* jeunes de 15 ans, ils sont la moitié* à passer plus de trois heures en ligne par jour. Ils sont 75% à utiliser les messageries instantanées dont 90% au lycée et déjà 25% en école primaire. Quatre-vingt-onze pour cent des lycéens sont sur Facebook. Soixante pour cent des jeunes ont un profil sur Internet et 30% ont un blogue.

Près de la moitié des jeunes Français ont un ordinateur dans leur chambre.

Les élèves utilisent massivement le web pour leurs devoirs: c'est le lieu principal de recherche de l'information. Les activités préférées des jeunes sur Internet sont dans l'ordre: échanger, télécharger, jouer, s'informer, chercher, publier, acheter.

Les jeunes s'affranchissent* volontiers* des droits et des interdits*: pour la musique et la vidéo, avec la loi HADOPI contre le téléchargement illégal, ils ont recours désormais* au streaming, préféré au P2P.

Il existe une campagne de mise en garde* qui invite les jeunes à ne pas poster n'importe quoi* sur Internet et à ne pas publier la photo d'un ami, camarade, ou d'une connaissance sans son accord. Ils sont aussi conscients des risques sur Internet: 93% d'entre eux pensent que la prévention est importante.

Search words: **sondage ados internet, internet et les jeunes, internet et la musique, jeunes et médias numériques, jeunes réseaux sociaux, protéger son image sur le web**

sondage *survey*; **quant aux** *as far as*; **moitié** 50%; **s'affranchissent** *free themselves*; **volontiers** *readily*; **interdits** *restrictions*; **désormais** *from now on*; **mise en garde** *warning*; **n'importe quoi** *anything*

Produits 2.2

Le site **"loisirs ados"** invite les ados à chatter gratuitement sur leurs vies.

Mots-clé

Réseau vient de *rets* (1155), issu du latin *retis* pour désigner un filet. Réseau est le dérivé et le diminutif de *rets*. De petit filet, il devient filet (tissu formé de petites mailles) avant de prendre le sens abstrait de "ensemble de choses emprisonnant un individu." Utilisé en physiologie pour les nerfs, les vaisseaux au XVIIIème siècle, c'est au XIXème siècle que réseau prend le sens de "ensemble de personnes qui ont des liens entre elles."

RESOURCES

Workbook 5

Reference Desk

1. Supplementary vocabulary: **une page web** (*web page*); **un moteur de recherché** (*search engine*); **télécharger un fichier** (*download a file*); **cliquer sur un lien** (*click on a link*); **joindre un fichier à son message** (*attach a file*); **imprimer un document** (*print a document*); **la souris** (*mouse*); **le clavier** (*keyboard*); **une clé USB** (*memory stick*); **accéder à Internet** (*access the Internet*); **une adresse Internet** (*web address*); **le courrier électronique** (*e-mail*).
2. **HADOPI** is the acronym for the government agency created to administer the three strikes law passed in 2009. It stands for **Haute authorité pour la diffusion des oeuvres et la protection des droits sur internet.**

Communication

Presentational: Paired Practice

Ask students to recount how they use the Internet daily and which social network sites they prefer and why. Have them share their habits with a partner.

Differentiated Learning

Accelerate

Have students find online safety tips, then make a poster of this advice to display in the classroom.
Search words: **microsoft centre de sécurité, jeunesse et protection des mineurs**

Decelerate

Ask students to present the tenets of the **HADOPI** law.

Multiple Intelligences

Mathematical-Logical

Ask students to survey members of their class using the same categories as in the reading to compare the usage of the various social media and Internet by French and American youth.

Answers

 Answers will vary.

Perspectives
Answers will vary.

Expansion

Have students interview an older family member or friend about what life was like in the '60s, '70s, and '80s without the Internet. How did they communicate? What did they do to research information? Do they think that technology today, with all of its glitches, is truly a time saver and a way to better communication? Students can summarize their results of the interview and share them in a group discussion of "**La vie d'hier et d'aujourd'hui**."

Critical Thinking

Comparisons
Have students visit the websites featured in **Du côté des médias**. Have them make two columns. In the first column have them write the French websites listed in the chart, and in the second an American website of similar nature.

Communication

Presentational: Cooperative Groups
Have students search online French sites for music, lyrics, movies, and travel, and share them with the class.

7 Activités culturelles

 1.3

Complétez les activités suivantes.

1. Comparez votre rapport à Internet à celui des jeunes adolescents français.
2. Regardez l'ordre des activités des jeunes; faites une enquête dans la classe et comparez.
3. Faites une liste de vos activités préférées sur Internet dans l'ordre.
4. Écrivez une histoire avec une morale: la prévention sur Internet est importante. Ou bien, écrivez une liste des choses à ne pas faire.
5. Si vous avez un ou une amie francophone sur un média comme Facebook, racontez à la classe comment se passe ce contact.
6. Faites un graphique qui montre le profil digital des jeunes français.

Les jeunes Français passent jusqu'à deux heures par jour sur Internet.

Perspectives

"Écrire un blogue est une sorte de thérapie, me permettant de mettre des mots sur les maux. C'est un ami qui me soulage, me fait espérer et rêver." Pour quelles raisons est-ce que ce jeune blogueur écrit un blogue?

Du côté des médias

  1.2

Lisez la liste de ressources numériques (digital) ci-dessous.

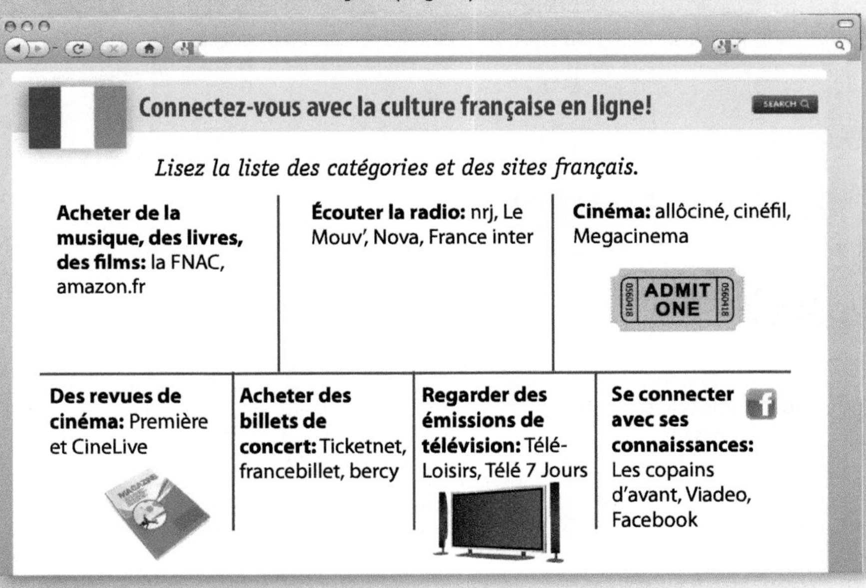

Connectez-vous avec la culture française en ligne!

Lisez la liste des catégories et des sites français.

Acheter de la musique, des livres, des films: la FNAC, amazon.fr	**Écouter la radio:** nrj, Le Mouv', Nova, France inter	**Cinéma:** allôciné, cinéfil, Megacinema

Des revues de cinéma: Première et CineLive	**Acheter des billets de concert:** Ticketnet, francebillet, bercy	**Regarder des émissions de télévision:** Télé-Loisirs, Télé 7 Jours	**Se connecter avec ses connaissances:** Les copains d'avant, Viadeo, Facebook

Essential Instruction

1. Have high and low-ability students work in pairs to complete three of the six tasks in **Activité 7**. Check to make sure all tasks are chosen. If there are some that are not selected, assign them as a group activity.
2. In small groups, as a game of speed, see which group can complete the tasks in **Activité 8** the fastest. Ask all groups to complete the exercise. Debrief them as to their findings.
3. Have students do **Activité 10** individually then select which of the two or three sites they prefer. Give them enough time to investigate the sites and write a justification for their preferences.

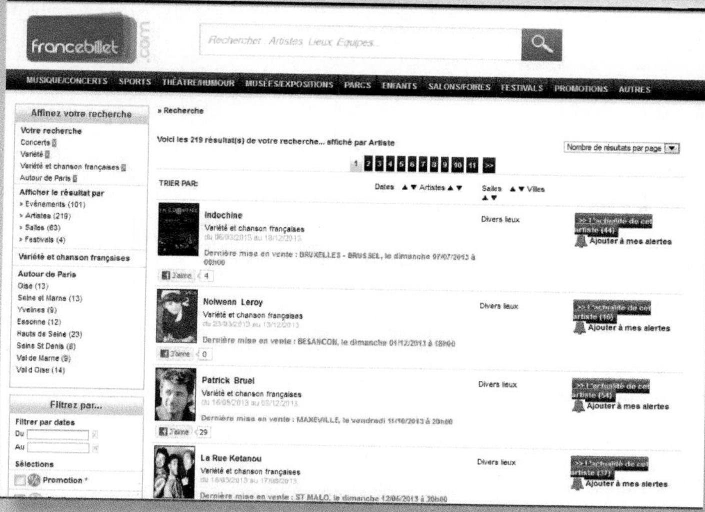

8 Sites Internet en France

3.2

Servez-vous des sites Internet mentionnés à la page 550 pour trouver:

- un CD en français que vous voudriez acheter
- un film en français que vous voudriez louer
- la chanson la plus populaire en France en ce moment
- un film américain qu'on passe en France cette semaine
- une revue d'un nouveau film français qui n'est pas un navet (*flop*)
- un concert auquel vous voudriez assister si vous étiez en France
- trois émissions de télé américaines à la télé en France actuellement
- quelques préférences d'un ado français tirées de (*pulled from*) son réseau social

9 Sites Internet

1.3, 3.2

Consultez trois liens à la page 550 et présentez-les à la classe.

10 J'évalue les sites.

1.3

Dites quel site vous préférez dans chaque catégorie. Justifiez vos choix.

1. Première ou CineLive
2. allôciné ou cinéfil
3. la FNAC ou amazon.fr
4. Les copains d'avant, Viadeo, ou Facebook
5. nrj, Mouv', ou Nova
6. Ticketnet ou francebillet
7. Télé-Loisirs ou Télé 7 Jours

Answers

8 *Answers will vary.*

9 *Answers will vary.*

10 *Answers will vary.*

Critical Thinking

Analysis

Students examine the American television shows currently shown in France. What impressions would the French have about our culture based on what they see through these programs?

Differentiated Learning

Accelerate

Using the websites provided, have these students compare current movies being shown in a French city of their choice with those currently shown in their hometown. Have them select a film showing in both countries. Is the title the same? What are the comparative prices of tickets? Can you reserve seats in both theaters? Are the reviews similar? Ask them to report back to the class.

Search words: **allô ciné, cinéfil**

Decelerate

Ask students to access radio sites to compare, selecting a genre such as rock, jazz, or pop and compare **les Palmarès** with the winners of the Grammys. How many artists overlap both charts?

Answers
All answers will vary.

Reference Desk

1. Indefinite adjectives refer to a general, not specific, person. **Aucun(e)** has a negative sense so **ne** must appear before the verb.
2. **N'importe quoi!** Is the equivalent of the sarcastic expression "Whatever!"

Connections

Music
"Tous les garçons et les filles" by Françoise Hardy features several indefinite adjectives plus vocabulary words students have already learned.

Communication

Interpersonal: Paired Practice
One student pretends to be a French student in a **lycée** in France who is being interviewed by an American student-reporter on daily life in France. Have them ask questions about their studies and preparing for the **bac.** Have students go online to get pertinent information about French school course of studies.

La culture sur place

Question centrale
Quels sont les défis de la vie contemporaine?

Les défis dans la Francophonie

Introduction et interrogations

Vous allez interviewer un(e) Francophone sur un sujet complexe et difficile: les défis de la vie contemporaine.

En groupe, choisissez un sujet pour une interview. Ensuite, contactez un de vos correspondants francophones.

Les trois sujets possibles:

1. Ses expériences personnelles (ou les expériences d'un membre de sa famille) avec le bac. (S'il n'est pas français, vous pouvez poser des questions sur l'équivalent du bac dans son pays.)
2. Ses interactions avec la police et le crime dans son pays.
3. Son usage du chat et du forum sur Internet et les risques de l'internet dans son pays.

11 Première Étape: Écrire des questions

1.3

Avec votre partenaire, écrivez une liste de questions à poser à votre correspondant francophone. Posez des questions faciles et générales, mais aussi des questions plus spécifiques. Écrivez au moins dix questions.

12 Deuxième Étape: Interviewer

1.1, 5.2

Complétez les activités suivantes:

1. Pendant l'interview, travaillez ensemble pour qu'une personne pose les questions et l'autre prenne des notes.
2. Après l'interview, résumez les réponses de votre ami(e) francophone dans une rédaction de 1-2 pages.
3. En classe, discutez avec les groupes qui ont choisi le même sujet que vous. Identifiez les points communs et les différences entre les interviews.

13 Faire l'inventaire!

1.1

Discutez des questions suivantes en classe après les interviews et les rédactions.

1. Est-ce que vos expériences se ressemblent?
2. Comment est-ce que la description des défis dans les interviews individuelles est différente des descriptions générales dans l'unité?
3. Est-ce que vous préférez étudier des généralisations ou baser vos recherches sur des expériences individuelles (anecdotes)?

Essential Instruction

1. **La culture sur place** activities are based on connecting with a French-speaking person in the community or online. If you do not know of any, you can find exchange schools in France.
Search words: **exchange between french and american schools, french embassy**
2. If time is an issue in establishing this exchange, for **Activités 11**, **12**, and **13**, students can interview you.
3. Review indefinite adjectives in **Structure de la langue** by asking students to translate the adjectives on the list from French to English to test recall.
4. Explain position and agreement of **aucun(e)**, **certain(e), and tout/tous/toutes(s)**, **n'importe quel(le)**, and **tel(le)**.
5. Ask students to make sentences with these adjectives.

Structure de la langue

emcl.com
WB 6-7
LA 2
Games

Révision: Indefinite Adjectives  1.1

Marion Cotillard ne s'habille pas avec n'importe quelle robe. Elle porte une robe Dior.

Indefinite adjectives are used to modify nouns in a non-specific sense. Like other adjectives, most indefinite adjectives agree in gender and in number with the nouns they describe. Here are some important indefinite adjectives to know; you have seen some of them before:

aucun(e)... ne (n')	*not one, no*
autre	*other*
certain(e)	*certain*
chaque	*each, every*
même	*same*
plusieurs	*several*
quelque	*some*
tout/tous/toute(s)	*all, every*

Nous avons eu l'idée de faire une vidéo avec **plusieurs** amis. — *We had the idea of making a video with several friends.*

Un **autre** ami n'aimait pas la vidéo. — *Our other friend didn't like the video.*

La plupart de means "most."

La plupart des ados français sont branchés. — *Most French teens are technologically savvy.*

Two additional indefinite adjectives are **n'importe quel/n'importe quelle** (*just any*) and **un tel/une telle** (*such a*).

Malik n'a pas mis **n'importe quel** jean. — *Malik didn't put on just any pair of jeans.*

Une **telle** chose n'arrivera jamais ici. — *Such a thing will never happen here.*

RESOURCES

 Workbook 6–7

 Listening Activity 2

 Drill & Practice Games

Expansion

Have students collaborate to write a letter to a French school requesting an exchange between an English class in France with a French class in the United States. Ask them to suggest a pen pal program as well as video exchanges.
Search words: french-american pen pals

Differentiated Learning

Accelerate
Have students imagine that they are going down the aisle of a grocery store, then write sentences using the indefinite adjectives as they refer to what they see: **Je veux acheter quelques pommes rouges parce qu'elles ont l'air délicieux.**

Decelerate
Ask students to copy the adjectives and examples into their notebooks. Have them write a sentence for each adjective listed.

Multiple Intelligences

Musical-Rhythmic
Ask students to search for French songs featuring the indefinite adjectives by putting each one in the search box.

Answers

14

1. chaque
2. plusieurs
3. tous
4. même
5. autre
6. telle
7. la plupart

15

1. Tous ses copains et toutes ses copines pourront venir.
2. Aucun de ces athlètes ne gagne de médaille.
3. Oui, elle peut acheter plusieurs vêtements.
4. Non, je ne garde pas le même portable, j'en achète un autre.

Expansion

Have students look at the picture of **les amis de Maeva**, then identify the beach in France where the young people are, the time of day, how they got to the beach, what they are going to have to eat, and how long they intend to stay. Have them write a conversation among four of them using as many indefinite adjectives as possible.

14 La journée de Maeva

1.3

Maeva a invité tous ses amis à la plage.

Complétez la description de ce que fait Maeva régulièrement. Utilisez les indices donnés entre parenthèses.

1. Maeva se lève... matin à 6h40. *(each)*
2. Pour le petit déjeuner, elle mange... tartines à la confiture. *(several)*
3. Elle va... les jours au club de fitness après les cours. *(every)*
4. Maeva achète toujours la... chose au supermarché: des yaourts, des pommes, du pain, du fromage. *(same)*
5. L'... jour, elle a rencontré Lucas au supermarché. *(other)*
6. Elle ne s'attendait pas à une...rencontre. *(such)*
7. Et, maintenant,... du temps, elle dîne avec Lucas. *(most)*

15 Des problèmes de maths: Solutions imprécises

1.3

Lisez chaque problème. Répondez à la question avec une phrase qui contient un mot ou une expression de la liste.

plusieurs   aucun(e)... ne (n')   tout   autre   même

MODÈLE Sophie et Max veulent acheter des poupées pour leur cousines. Ils ont 30€ et chaque poupée coûte 6€. Combien de poupées est-ce qu'ils achètent?
Ils achètent plusieurs poupées.

1. Laure veut inviter des copains à sa fête d'anniversaire. Ses parents lui disent qu'elle peut inviter cinq copains et cinq copines. Dans sa bande, il y a Michèle, Noah, Luc, Chantal, Céline, Anne, Dikembe, Martin, Lise, et Pierre. Combien de ses copains pourront venir? Combien de ses copines?
2. Pour gagner une médaille au marathon, il faut courir et finir en moins de cinq minutes par kilomètre. Claude a fait deux kilomètres en 12 minutes. Djamel a couru un kilometre en sept minutes. Stéphanie a couru trois kilomètres en dix-huit minutes. Combien de ces athlètes gagnent une médaille?
3. Fatima a besoin de nouveaux vêtements. Elle a 100€. Le manteau à carreaux coûte 145€. Le pantalon à rayures coûte 25€. La liquette coûte 12€, et la jupe côte 37€. Est-ce que Fatima peut acheter des vêtements?
4. Vous trébuchez et votre ordinateur portable tombe. Maintenant cet ordinateur ne marche plus. Pour le faire réparer, vous devez payer 600€. Pour acheter un nouvel ordinateur, vous devez payer 498€. Qu'est-ce que vous faites? Gardez-vous le portable original?

Essential Instruction

1. Drill the indefinite adjectives from English to French, and French to English.
2. Give students time to do **Activité 14.**
3. Have students put the sentences on the board for correction.
4. Ask various students to read the sentences in **Activité 15.**
5. Ask for volunteers to answer each math problem.
6. Have students examine each picture in **Activité 16** and respond with a form of **tel(le)**.

16 Je n'ai jamais vu....

Dites que vous n'avez jamais vu une telle chose ou personne.

MODÈLE

Je n'ai jamais vu un tel chœur.

1.

2.

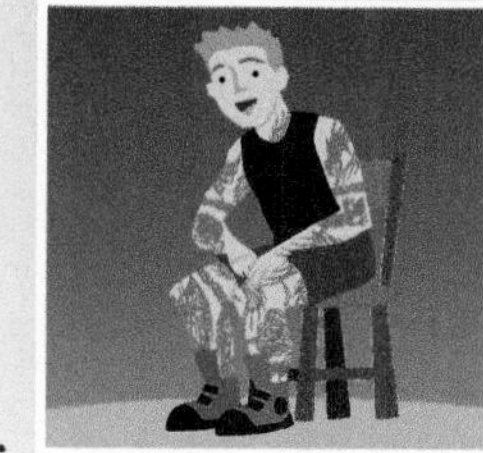
3.

4.

5.

6.

7.

Answers

16 *Possible answers:*

1. Je n'ai jamais vu une telle équipe/de tels joueurs.
2. ... une telle liquette.
3. ... de tels tatouages.
4. ... un tel cirque.
5. ... une telle fan.
6. ... une telle coiffure.
7. ... de telles baskets.

Communication

Interpersonal: Paired Practice

Students make up **Devinettes** to ask the class using indefinite adjectives. For example, they might say: **Chaque année, c'est le festival de théâtre en France en juillet.**

Differentiated Learning

Expand

Have students think of things in their lives that were amazing to see. Have them use the format in **Activité 16** to explain what they were and why they were so unusual. Have them present a picture or drawing as an illustration as they share what they wrote with the class.

Learning Styles

Visual Learners

Work with visual learners to create a chart summarizing the indefinite adjectives with gender and number changes: **aucun/e**, **certain/e**, and **tout/e.** After creating the chart, make sure to use these forms in a sentence context to reinforce pronunciation and spelling changes.

RESOURCES

Workbook 8–10

Drill & Practice Games

Reference Desk

Explain that pronouns replace a person or thing previously mentioned. **Aucun(e)**, **un(e) autre**, **tous (toutes) les deux** will agree with the word that was replaced whereas **la plupart des**, **plusieurs**, **quelqu'un**, and **quelque chose** are invariable.

Indefinite Pronouns

emcl.com
WB 8–10
Games

1.1

La plupart des vidéos de chats sur YouTube sont mignonnes.

Remember that a pronoun replaces a noun which has been mentioned before, or which is obvious in the context of the sentence. Therefore, indefinite pronouns refer to people or things without identifying them. Here are some important indefinite pronouns to know:

aucun(e)... ne (n')	*not one*
un(e) autre	*another*
la plupart	*most*
plusieurs	*several*
quelqu'un	*someone, somebody*
quelque chose	*something*
tous les deux	*both*

COMPARAISONS

What are the indefinite pronouns in this story?

Anna checked her social network to see if there were messages from her friends, but not one had responded to her last posting. She knew most were at the game, but several of them weren't going out tonight.

4.1

Tu as déjà mis une vidéo sur YouTube? Oui, **plusieurs**. — *Have you already put a video on YouTube? Yes, several.*

Tous les deux sont dans la vidéo. — *Both are in the video.*

To describe **quelqu'un** or **quelque chose**, use the adjective's masculine singular form preceded by **de**.

J'ai vu **quelqu'un de grand** derrière l'actrice dans cette vidéo. — *I saw someone tall behind the actress in this video.*

Il y avait **quelque chose d'épicé** dans ce plat! — *There was something spicy in this dish!*

Two other indefinite pronouns are **n'importe qui** (*anyone*) and **l'un(e)... l'autre** (*the one... the other*).

N'importe qui pourra voir votre vidéo sur Internet. — *Anyone will be able to see your video on the Internet.*

À leur mariage, ils étaient assis **l'un** près de **l'autre**. — *At their wedding, they were seated near each other.*

COMPARAISONS: The English indefinite pronouns are "not one," "most," and "several."

Essential Instruction

1. Ask for volunteers to answer the **Comparaisons** question.
2. Give the class time to do **Activité 17**. Have students respond orally and then have volunteers put the sentences on the board making sure to note where there is agreement.
3. Have students do **Activité 18** in pairs. Ask them to justify their remarks using **parce que**.

17 Un hit sur YouTube

Complétez chaque phrase pour résumer l'histoire de la vidéo d'Élodie. Utilisez un mot ou une expression de la liste.

aucun(e)... ne (n') | un(e) autre | la plupart | plusieurs | quelqu'un | quelque chose | tous les trois

1. Un garçon, son frère, et leur copain ont chanté au mariage du cousin d'Élodie. ... savaient chanter des gospels.
2. Ils portaient... d'orange ce soir-là.
3. ... des garçons ne portait un costume noir.
4. ... des invités ont aimé le show.
5. ... ados ont vu la vidéo qu'elle a filmé au mariage.
6. ... qui a regardé la vidéo 75 fois est une vraie groupie.
7. Est-ce qu'Élodie mettra... vidéo sur YouTube? Ça reste à voir!

18 Des descriptions

1.1

Interpersonal Communication

Avec un(e) partenaire, faites des remarques sur les personnes et les choses suivantes en utilisant ***quelqu'un*** *ou* ***quelque chose*** *et un adjective convenable.*

À mon avis, avoir un réseau social, c'est quelque chose de nécessaire.

MODÈLE Albert Einstein
A: **À mon avis, c'est quelqu'un d'intelligent.**
B: **Selon moi, c'est quelqu'un d'amusant.**

1. conduire sans mettre une ceinture de sécurité
2. Johnny Depp
3. être malade pendant les vacances
4. Heidi Klum
5. ton/ta meilleur(e) ami(e)
6. être diplômé(e)
7. le proviseur
8. se présenter pour une interview

Answers

1. Tous les trois
2. quelque chose
3. Aucun
4. La plupart
5. Plusieurs
6. Quelqu'un
7. une autre

18 *Possible answers:*

1. À mon avis, c'est quelque chose d'imprudent.
2. À mon avis, c'est quelqu'un de populaire.
3. À mon avis, c'est quelque chose d'embêtant.
4. À mon avis, c'est quelqu'un d'intéressant.
5. À mon avis, c'est quelqu'un de formidable.
6. À mon avis, c'est quelque chose de nécessaire.
7. À mon avis, c'est quelqu'un d'intelligent.
8. À mon avis, c'est quelque chose d'effrayant.

Game

Concentration

Ask students to write the **Unité 9** vocabulary and adjective list on index cards and make a corresponding card for each with the English translation or a picture on it. Put all cards face down. A student turns over two cards at random. If the cards match, he or she reads both cards and keeps the pair for a point. If the cards do not match, both are put back face down. Whoever makes the most matches wins.

Differentiated Learning

Accelerate

Ask students to write a portrait of a celebrity using **quelqu'un de** + adjective. Have them give examples from his or her life and explain why that judgment is valid.

Decelerate

Ask students to write sentences using each pronoun in a sentence. Encourage them to consult the sample sentences in the grammar presentation as a guide.

Answers

19

1. B
2. A
3. D
4. E
5. C

Communication

Interpersonal: Paired practice

Before doing **Activité 21**, have students work in pairs or small groups to answer these questions: 1) On which social media should one write a blog? 2) What should you talk about in your blog? 3) Why would others read your blog? When finished, have groups join another group to share their responses. Finally, discuss as a class.

19 On est branché!

1.1, 1.2

Interpretive Communication

Écrivez les numéros 1–5 sur votre papier. Écoutez les phrases. Faites correspondre la phrase à une image.

A.

B.

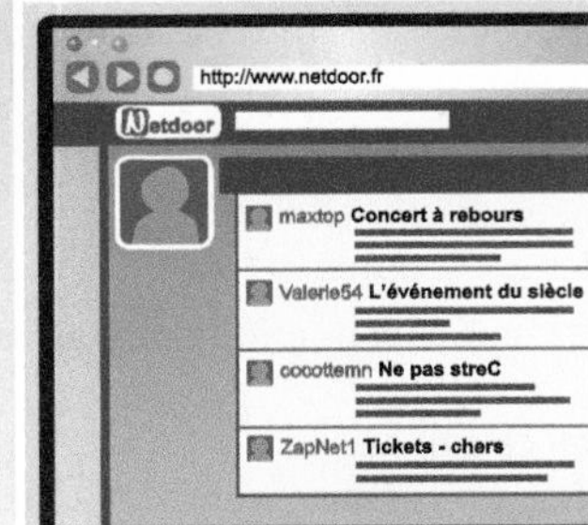

C.

D.

E.

Essential Instruction

1. For **Activité 19**, ask students to describe each of the pictures. Encourage them to invent details of each picture, ascribing a name to the people where relevant, explaining where they are, what they are doing, and why.
2. Have students do the listening comprehension questions. Monitor their answers.
3. Give students a choice of tasks for **À vous la parole**. Students electing **Activité 20** might want to combine their survey of their peers with those they find online. For **Activité 21** divide students according to their interests and have them write a short blog. Have them share with other students, asking for their comments and suggestions.

À vous la parole

20 Un sondage

1.3, 5.1, 5.2

Interpersonal/Presentational Communication

Avec quelques camarades de classe, créez un sondage sur l'utilisation de l'internet par les Américains de votre âge. Interviewez les ados des autres classes de français et recueillez les réponses. Finalement, publiez vos recherches en ligne pour que d'autres Francophones puissent lire vos résultats concernant les ados américains.

21 Nos blogues

1.3

Presentational Communication

Comme vous savez, il y a beaucoup de jeunes bloggeurs français. Avec vos camarades de classe, faites une liste de blogues qui intéresseraient les jeunes. Puis, formez des groupes pour chaque sujet de blogue et préparez une page d'accueil pour le blogue de votre groupe. À tour de rôle, écrivez un article pour votre blogue et demandez à des jeunes Francophones d'apporter leurs commentaires.

22 Interview

1.1

Regardez le sondage sur les "accros" (amoureux) des réseaux sociaux. Posez des questions à vos camarades pour trouver les pourcentages qui représentent les jeunes de votre classe ou de votre école.

RESOURCES

Communicative Activities

Answers

All activities will vary.

Reference Desk

Blended Instruction

Consider using blended instruction, a combination of in-class learning and computer-mediated instruction or learning opportunities. Ask students to complete activities on the computer, using their cell or smartphone, or other emerging electronic technology. This process will allow students to hone their tech skills and become more independent learners. Schedule routine Internet and e-book learning in class and in the lab.

Differentiated Learning

Accelerate/Decelerate

Use mixed-ability groups to create and administer the survey for **Activité 20.** Working as a team strengthens the stronger students' ability to communicate ideas in simplified French and provides practice in a comfortable learning context for weaker students.

Expand

Students who want to do more blogging might consider "Voices of Youth" found on the UNICEF website. According to the website, it is "a forum for the top international issues facing youth today. Allows young people to share their opinions and listen to the stories of others."

Answers

Rencontre avec l'auteur
Possible answer: Il y a des indications scéniques et les dialogues sont des petites conversations au discours direct.

Pré-lecture
Answers will vary.

Stratégie de lecture
Possible answer: généreux: 5; aimable: 4; religieux: 5; matérialiste: 1; rusé: 4

Culture

Products: Information

1. It is thought that ***Les Misérables*** could have inspired two popular television series. Richard Kimble in "The Fugitive" was modeled on Jean Valjean. Gerard, whose name sounded like Javert, relentlessly pursued Kimble. ***Les Misérables*** might also be the basis for Dr. Banner in "The Incredible Hulk," moving from town to town, being pursued by his own "Javert," journalist Jack McGee.
2. Some interesting facts: 1) ***Les Misérables*** is the source for 48 operas. 2) Victor Hugo wrote the longest sentence written in French in ***Les Misérables***; it is about 800 words long. 3) Victor Hugo liked to write while standing.

Lecture thématique

Pre AP

Les Misérables

Rencontre avec l'auteur

1.2

Victor Hugo (1802–1885) est poète, romancier, dramaturge, et dessinateur. Quand il meurt (*dies*), le pays lui rend hommage (*honors*) en organisant des funérailles nationales. Vous allez lire un extrait des *Misérables*, l'histoire de Jean Valjean, un ancien galérien (*forced labor prisoner*) qui a été emprisonné pour avoir volé du pain pour nourrir sa famille affamée (*starving*). La scène se passe en 1815. Juste après avoir été libéré, il se rend dans la ville de Digne où il reçoit l'hospitalité de l'évêque (*bishop*), monseigneur Myriel, qui l'accueille chez lui, lui donne à manger et un lit. Mais durant la nuit, Jean Valjean part en emportant les couverts en argent. Dans cet extrait, comment la scène se rapproche-t-elle (*approaches*) d'une scène de pièce de théâtre?

Pré-lecture

1.2

Est-ce que vous avez pardonné à quelqu'un? Était-ce facile ou difficile?

Stratégie de lecture

1.3

Characterization

La caractérisation d'un personnage de roman est la description des attributs physiques et moraux de ce dernier. Elle peut être indirecte, c'est-à-dire que l'auteur permet au lecteur de projeter un jugement subjectif sur un personnage, à travers ses paroles, ses pensées, ses gestes, et ses actions, ou de ce qui est dit de lui. La caractérisation directe est pour ainsi dire une image complète du personnage; le lecteur ne doit rien deviner.

Pour analyser le caractère de monseigneur Myriel, faites une grille comme celle de dessous. Pour chaque adjectif, choisissez le numéro qui exprime (*expresses*) le caractère de l'évêque ("5" indique qu'il montre le maximum de cette qualité). Mettez un X dans l'espace blanc approprié. Puis écrivez deux phrases avec chaque adjectif. Dans la première, faites une généralisation fondée sur la grille sur son caractère. Dans la deuxième, défendez votre généralisation avec un exemple du roman. À la fin de votre paragraphe, identifiez le type de caractérisation utilisé par Hugo.

	1	2	3	4	5
généreux					
aimable					
religieux					
matérialiste					
rusé					

Essential Instruction

1. Ask students what they know of Victor Hugo. Can they tell you the story of ***Les Misérables***? Who has seen the play or the movie? Who is their favorite character and why?
2. Listen to the **Rencontre avec l'auteur**.
3. Discuss the question of forgiveness posed in **Pré-Lecture.**
4. After reading the extract, students return to **Stratégie de lecture** to do the evaluation.
5. Put regular and irregular **passé simple** verbs on the board and ask students to guess the meanings.
6. Have students copy the irregular **passé simple** verbs in their notebooks and learn to identify them.
7. Play the first part of the extract with students following in their books. Answer the **Pendant la lecture** questions found in the margins.

Outils de lecture  1.2

Le passé simple

Le passé simple est un temps littéraire, utilisé dans l'œuvre de Victor Hugo. Il est important de pouvoir reconnaître les verbes conjugués à ce temps. Les verbes réguliers qui se terminent en **–er** ont les terminaisons suivantes: (**frapper**, *to knock*) **je frappai, tu frappas, il/elle/on frappa, nous frappâmes, vous frappâtes, ils/elles frappèrent.** Les verbes réguliers qui se terminent en **–ir** ont les terminaisons suivantes: (**accomplir**, *to accomplish*) **j'accomplis, tu accomplis, il/elle/on accomplit, nous accomplîmes, vous accomplîtes, ils/elles accomplirent.** Les verbes réguliers qui se terminent en **–re** ont ces terminaisons: (**répondre**, *to respond*) **je répondis, tu répondis, il/elle/on répondit, nous répondîmes, vous répondîtes, ils/elles répondirent.** Voici quelques verbes irréguliers au passé simple: (**avoir**) **il eut/ils eurent;** (**être**) **il fut/ils furent;** (**faire**) **il fit/ils firent.**

Jean Valjean, épisode des chandeliers. Anonyme. Édition des d'Eugène Hugues. Circa 1880.

Le lendemain, monseigneur Myriel déjeunait à cette même table où Jean Valjean s'était assis la veille*. Tout en déjeunant, monseigneur Bienvenu faisait gaîment remarquer à sa sœur qui ne disait rien et à madame Magloire qui grommelait* sourdement qu'il n'est nullement besoin d'une cuiller ni d'une fourchette, même en bois, pour tremper* un morceau de pain dans une tasse de lait.

—Aussi a-t-on ideé! disait madame Magloire toute seule en allant et venant, recevoir un homme comme cela! et le loger à côté de soi! et quel bonheur encore qu'il n'ait fait que voler! Ah mon Dieu! cela fait frémir* quand on songe*!

Comme le frère et la sœur allaient se lever de table, on frappa à la porte.

—Entrez, dit l'évêque.

La porte s'ouvrit. Un groupe étrange et violent apparut sur le seuil*. Trois hommes en tenaient un quatrième au collet*. Les trois hommes étaient des gendarmes; l'autre était Jean Valjean.

Un brigadier de gendarmerie, qui semblait conduire le groupe, était près de la porte. Il entra et s'avança vers l'évêque en faisant le salut militaire.

—Monseigneur…dit-il.

À ce mot Jean Valjean, qui était morne* et semblait abattu*, releva la tête d'un air stupéfait.

—Monseigneur! murmura-t-il. Ce n'est donc pas le curé*?

Pendant la lecture
1. Que font l'évêque et sa sœur le lendemain (après le départ de Jean Valjean)?

Pendant la lecture
2. Qui pense que monseigneur Myriel n'aurait pas dû accueillir Valjean?

Pendant la lecture
3. Qui est à la porte?

Pendant la lecture
4. Comment se sent Jean Valjean quand il revoit monseigneur Myriel?

Pendant la lecture
5. Monseigneur Myriel est-il fâché avec Jean Valjean? A-t-il une bonne raison d'être fâché avec lui?

la veille le soir d'avant; **grommelait** *muttered;* **tremper** *to dunk;* **frémir** *to shudder;* **quand on songe** quand on y réfléchit; **seuil** *threshold;* **en tenaient un quatrième au collet** *had a fourth (man) by the neck;* **morne** *glum;* **abbattu** *shattered;* **curé** *priest*

Answers

Pendant la lecture
1. Ils déjeunent.
2. madame Magloire
3. trois gendarmes et Jean Valjean
4. Il est choqué et se sent mal.
5. Il a une bonne raison d'être fâche car Valjean lui a volé ses couverts, mais il n'est pas fâché.

Expansion

To reinforce the idea that the **passé simple** is the equivalent of the **passé compose**, ask students to list all of the verbs in the **passé simple**, beginning with … **on frappa** continuing to the end of the page. (There are seven.) Have them write the equivalent **passé composé** next to each verb. Correct in class.

Differentiated Learning

Accelerate

Challenge students to write a two-paragraph story in the **passé simple**.

Decelerate

Give students a short list of irregular verbs in the **passé simple** to learn to recognize. Show them the similarities between the past participles and the beginning of many forms of the **passé simple**, for example, **Ils ont eu deux enfants. Ils eurent deux enfants. Elle a su que sa famille était partie**, and **Elle sut que sa famille….**

Multiple Intelligences

Musical-Rhythmic

Have students play the music from the scene between the bishop and Jean Valjean.

Visual-Spatial

Students may want to draw the **décor** of the scene.

Intrapersonal

Have students share examples of poems, novels, plays, and drawings of Victor Hugo.

Answers

Pendant la lecture

6. Il lui donne des chandeliers d'argent.
7. un honnête homme
8. C'est un homme qui aime Dieu. Il veut que Jean Valjean aime le bien plus que le mal.

Communication

Interpersonal: Cooperative Groups

Divide the class into small groups with group members each taking a role from the scene. Groups do a reading of the scene with volunteers presenting to the class.

—Silence! dit un gendarme. C'est monseigneur l'évêque.

Cependant monseigneur Bienvenu s'était approché aussi vivement* que son grand âge le lui permettait.

—Ah! vous voilà! s'écria-t-il en regardant Jean Valjean. Je suis aise de vous voir. Et bien mais! je vous avais donné les chandeliers* aussi, qui sont en argent comme le reste et dont vous pourrez bien avoir deux cents francs. Pourquoi ne les avez-vous pas emportés avec vos couverts?

Jean Valjean ouvrit les yeux et regarda le vénérable évêque avec une expression qu'aucune langue humaine ne pourrait rendre.

—Monseigneur, dit le brigadier de gendarmerie, ce que cet homme disait était donc vrai? Nous l'avons rencontré. Il allait comme quelqu'un qui s'en va. Nous l'avons arrêté pour voir. Il avait cette argenterie*....

—Et il vous a dit, interrompit l'évêque en souriant, qu'elle lui avait été donnée par un vieux bonhomme de prêtre chez lequel il avait passé la nuit? Je vois la chose. Et vous l'avez ramené* ici? C'est une méprise*.

—Comme cela, reprit le brigadier, nous pouvons le laisser aller?

—Sans doute, répondit l'évêque.

Les gendarmes lâchèrent Jean Valjean qui recula*....

Puis se tournant vers la gendarmerie *[l'évêque dit]*:

—Messieurs, vous pouvez vous retirer*.

Les gendarmes s'éloignèrent*.

Jean Valjean était comme un homme qui va s'évanouir*.

L'évêque s'approcha de lui, et lui dit à voix basse:

—N'oubliez pas, n'oubliez jamais que vous m'avez promis d'employer cet argent à devenir honnête* homme.

Jean Valjean, qui n'avait aucun souvenir d'avoir rien promis, resta interdit. L'évêque avait appuyé sur ces paroles en les prononçant. Il reprit avec une sorte de solennité:

—Jean Valjean, mon frère vous n'appartenez* plus au mal, mais au bien. C'est votre âme* que je vous achète; je la retire aux pensées noires et à l'esprit de perdition, et je la donne à Dieu.

Pendant la lecture
6. Qu'est-ce que l'évêque donne en plus à Valjean?

Pendant la lecture
7. Qu'est-ce que monseigneur Myriel veut que Valjean devienne?

Pendant la lecture
8. Pourquoi l'évêque est-il si généreux?

vivement énergiquement; **chandeliers** *candlesticks*; **argenterie** objets en argent; **ramené** *brought*; **méprise** erreur; **recula** *withdrew*; **retirer** partir; **s'éloignèrent** *moved away*; **s'évanouir** *to faint*; **honnête** *honest*; **appartenez** *belong*; **âme** *soul*

Essential Instruction

1. Continue the recording of the scene among the bishop, Jean Valjean, and the **gendarmes.**
2. Have students identify parts of the reading that they do not understand. Collaborate as a class to respond to their questions.
3. Answer the **Pendant la lecture** questions in the margins.
4. Supplementary questions: What physical descriptions of Jean Valjean describe his emotional state throughout the scene? In what ways was the bishop dishonest? Can a lie be justifiable?
5. Discuss the question in **Post-lecture** as a class. Write the various opinions on the board. Have students copy them in their notebooks as a reference for future compositions.
6. Students answer the questions in **Le monde visuel** in small groups. Bring the groups together to discuss the topic as a class.
7. Play the scene from the musical ***Les Misérables*** and compare it to the passage. Have students do tasks 1–3 of **Activités d'expansion**.

Post-lecture  1.2

Pensez-vous que monseigneur Myriel change la vie de Jean Valjean par son acte de générosité? De quelle façon?

Le monde visuel  1.2, 3.1

On a assisté une hausse dramatique des illustrations des livres au 19ème siècle, dûe à l'arrivée de la lithographie et à l'impression offset. La popularité des livres et des histoires ont augmenté avec la sérialisation des magazines populaires et des ouvrages périodiques. La scène à la page 561 a été créée par un graveur sur bois anonyme. Avant 1860, les graveurs sur bois devaient couper le bois et peindre ou dessiner directement sur la surface taillée (*smooth*). Vous remarquez que plusieurs lignes parallèles se croisent à un angle afin de créér des tons contrastés. Qualifieriez-vous cette illustration du livre de classique, réaliste, ou impressionniste? Quels sont les deux personnages qui sont au point focal de l'image? Qu'est-ce que la porte ouverte pourrait symboliser pour Jean Valjean?

Activités d'expansion 1.3, 3.1, 3.2

Complétez les activités suivantes.

1. Écrivez un paragraphe dans lequel vous décrivez monseigneur Myriel et commentez la création de ce personnage par Victor Hugo. Servez-vous des détails de votre organigramme.
2. Lisez un résumé de la comédie musicale. Finalement, écrivez un paragraphe qui explique votre prédiction dans la question de Post-lecture et si vous aviez raison et de quelle manière.

 Search words: **les misérables résumé**

3. Transformé(e) par la générosité de monseigneur Myriel, vous voulez offrir un don à une fondation. Avec votre partenaire, recherchez des fondations francophones et faites votre choix. Faites une présentation à la classe dans laquelle vous:
   - expliquez le but de votre fondation
   - expliquez comment votre fondation aide les autres, peut-être avec un exemple
   - expliquez pourquoi le travail de cette fondation est important pour vous personnellement

 Search words: **fondation brigitte bardot, médecins sans frontières, fondation 30 millions d'amis, fondation abbé pierre, fondation pour l'enfance, fondation groupama, fondation greffe de vie, fondation claude pompidou, fondation d'auteuil, fondation nicolas hulot**

RESOURCES

 **Pre-test**

 ***Leçon* Quiz**

Answers

Post-lecture
Answers will vary.

Le monde visuel
Possible answer: Cette illustration est réaliste, car elle montre avec détails l'expression et l'interaction des personnages, l'évêque et Jean Valjean. La porte ouverte pourrait symboliser que Jean Valjean est libre de choisir de faire le bien ou le mal.

Activités d'expansion
All answers will vary.

Reference Desk

Before having students discuss **Le monde visuel**, briefly discuss the differences among **l'art classique**, **réaliste**, and **impressionniste**. Provide examples from each period to reinforce the distinctions among them.

Differentiated Learning

Accelerate
Ask students to write about a moment in their lives when an act of kindness touched them.

Decelerate
Offer students an opportunity to do well. Ask them to make flash cards of the irregular verbs. Give them an average-boosting quiz where they have to transform a verb in the **passé simple** to the **passé composé**.

Answers

All activities will vary.

Critical Thinking

Analysis

What impact does technology, like the Internet and social media sites, have on language globally?

Communication

Presentational: Cooperative Groups

Have students write a skit in which a career counselor interviews a young student about his/her future plans. The student offers some resistance to the counselor's suggestions before finally deciding on a path of study.

Projets finaux

A Connexions par Internet: Planification de carrière

1.2

Identifiez vos qualités

Pour choisir une profession, un métier, ou une spécialisation universitaire après le bac, il faut que vous déterminiez vos aspirations et vos ambitions. Mais votre personnalité et vos habitudes jouent aussi un rôle majeur dans votre décision. Passez le test ci-dessous. Il va indiquer l'environnement professionnel dont vous aurez besoin. Après avoir passé ce test, trouvé sur Internet, faites une liste de cinq professions ou métiers qui correspondent à vos aspirations.

1.	Au dernier moment	❑	ou	Ponctuel	❑
2.	Curieux	❑	ou	Ordonné	❑
3.	Aime l'improvisation	❑	ou	Suit les règles	❑
4.	Pas organisé	❑	ou	Organisé	❑
5.	Flexible	❑	ou	Structuré	❑
6.	Change de point de vue	❑	ou	Décisif	❑
7.	Aime découvre	❑	ou	Aime produire	❑
8.	Aime les changements	❑	ou	Résiste les changements	❑

Résultats:

Si vous avez sélectionné la plupart de vos réponses dans la liste de droite, vous préféreriez un environnement traditionnel, peut-être hiérarchique, où la production et les résultats sont importants et où vous serez apprécié pour votre diligence, formation, et expérience. Si vous avez sélectionné la plupart de vos réponses dans la liste de gauche, vous préféreriez travailler dans une compagnie qui suit un nouveau modèle, par exemple, une coopérative; ce genre de compagnie apprécierait votre esprit de camaraderie, votre désir d'évoluer et de proposer de nouvelles idées.

B Communautés en ligne

1.3, 3.2, 4.2

Aide aux devoirs/Interpretive and Presentational Communication

Créez une liste de cinq tâches (*tasks*) ou questions que vous avez sur le français (la grammaire, le vocabulaire, l'expression orale, le discours, etc.) ou la littérature francophone (les thèmes, comment écrire une composition, etc.). Faites semblant (*pretend*) d'être un(e) élève en France. Cherchez de l'aide sur Internet pour trouver des réponses. Qu'est-ce que vous avez appris? D'après vous, qui a le plus de soutien pour faire ses devoirs: les élèves français ou les élèves américains? Discutez en classe.

Search words: aide aux devoirs, sos devoirs, soutien scolaire

Essential Instruction

1. Students take the career preference test in **Activité A.**
2. Have students write a one-paragraph personal reaction to the test results, agreeing or disagreeing with the findings, and stating why.
3. For **Activité B**, students research the **Search words** in the computer lab to decide if French, (Canadian) or American students have more help online.
   Search words: **hippocampus, homework help**
4. Before making the video about **harcèlement** in **Activité C** students may want to see corresponding anti-bullying videos online to help them create their own.
5. In small groups, have students collaborate to do **Activité D.** One student acts as secretary to write the various answers.
6. Distribute copies of the graphic organizer, located in the **Copy Masters** supplement, for **Activité D.**

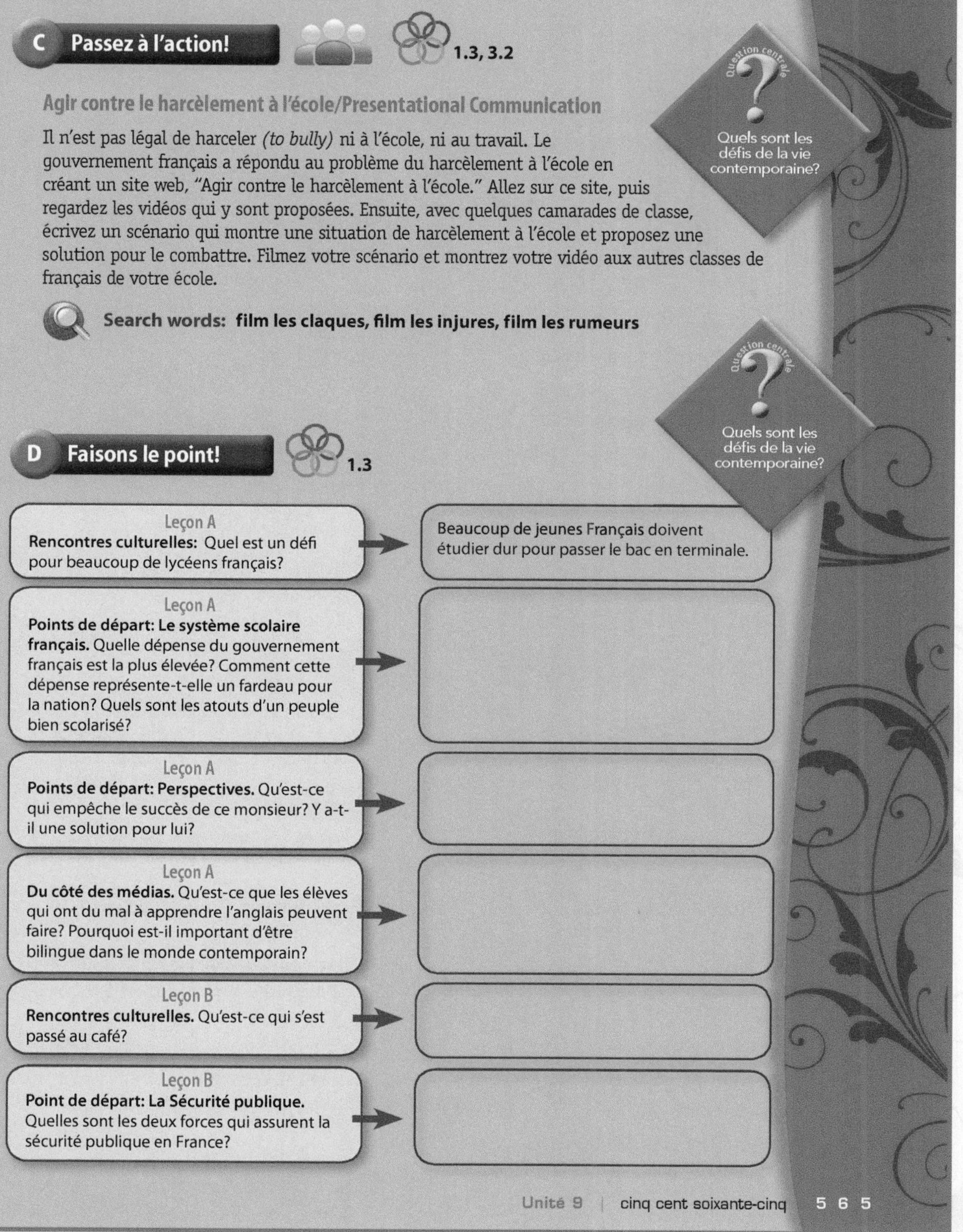

C Passez à l'action!

1.3, 3.2

Agir contre le harcèlement à l'école/Presentational Communication

Il n'est pas légal de harceler *(to bully)* ni à l'école, ni au travail. Le gouvernement français a répondu au problème du harcèlement à l'école en créant un site web, "Agir contre le harcèlement à l'école." Allez sur ce site, puis regardez les vidéos qui y sont proposées. Ensuite, avec quelques camarades de classe, écrivez un scénario qui montre une situation de harcèlement à l'école et proposez une solution pour le combattre. Filmez votre scénario et montrez votre vidéo aux autres classes de français de votre école.

Search words: film les claques, film les injures, film les rumeurs

D Faisons le point!

1.3

Leçon A **Rencontres culturelles:** Quel est un défi pour beaucoup de lycéens français?	Beaucoup de jeunes Français doivent étudier dur pour passer le bac en terminale.
Leçon A **Points de départ: Le système scolaire français.** Quelle dépense du gouvernement français est la plus élevée? Comment cette dépense représente-t-elle un fardeau pour la nation? Quels sont les atouts d'un peuple bien scolarisé?	
Leçon A **Points de départ: Perspectives.** Qu'est-ce qui empêche le succès de ce monsieur? Y a-t-il une solution pour lui?	
Leçon A **Du côté des médias.** Qu'est-ce que les élèves qui ont du mal à apprendre l'anglais peuvent faire? Pourquoi est-il important d'être bilingue dans le monde contemporain?	
Leçon B **Rencontres culturelles.** Qu'est-ce qui s'est passé au café?	
Leçon B **Point de départ: La Sécurité publique.** Quelles sont les deux forces qui assurent la sécurité publique en France?	

Answers

C *Answers will vary.*

D *Possible answers:*

Leçon A: Le budget de l'éducation nationale, qui représente 2.000€ par habitant. un peuple bien scolarisé donne du succès a l'enseignement; Il a du mal à trouver un travail parce qu'il n'a jamais passe le bac. Oui, il peut le repasser.; Ils peuvent faire des stages intensifs. L'anglais est une langue internationale.

Leçon B: Karim et Léo se sont fait voler leur ordinateur portable.; la gendarmerie et la police; *Students will reiterate their group answers.*

Leçon C: Quelqu'un peut utiliser des informations personnelles.; La culture sur place: Le/La Francophone avec qui vous avez parlé voulait parler de quel(s) défi(s)?; *Possible answer:* amis, goûts musicaux; *Possible answer:* On peut encourager la personne à voir que le bien est meilleur que le mal.; Projets finaux: Passez à l'action!: *Answers will vary.*

Reference Desk

Students discussed the **Question centrale** at the beginning of the unit. Consider having them work with a partner to refine their list of **défis de la vie contemporaine** discussed in **Unité 9**.

Special Needs Students

AD(H)D

This break is an excellent time for students with organizational problems to gather their information for the chapter. Using the chart as a guide, have students look through their notes on cultural information from the chapter.

At-Risk Students

Give students time to study in class. Make sure that they can ask their questions, no matter how basic, in a small study group where they feel comfortable asking for help.

RESOURCES

Listening Activity
Synthèse

Answers

A Script can be found in the front pages of the Annotated Teacher's Edition.

1. oui
2. oui
3. oui
4. non
5. oui
6. non
7. oui
8. non

B *Conversations will vary.*

Communication

Interpersonal: Paired practice

To practice the dialogue in **Activité B**, have students prepare both roles of the conversation. Place the students with a partner to practice. Set a timer and when time is called, tell the students to switch roles. When you call time a second time have the students switch partners and follow the same procedure to practice both parts.

Évaluation

emcl.com
LA *Synthèse*

A Évaluation de compréhension auditive

1.2

Interpretive Communication

Récit d'un vol

*Écoutez Marion décrire à un policier le vol auquel elle vient d'assister. Ensuite, dites **oui** ou **non** si elle a aidé avec les catégories ci-dessous.*

1. Description physique
2. Description des cheveux
3. Description d'âge
4. Description psychologique
5. Description de vêtements
6. Description de caractère
7. Description d'actions
8. Description de bijoux

B Évaluation orale

1.1, 3.2

Interpersonal Communication

Vous parlez avec un(e) ami(e). Dans votre conversation:

Demandez pourquoi votre ami(e) n'était pas aux cours d'histoire et d'anglais ce matin. Dites que vous avez pris beaucoup de notes, et que vous pouvez les lui passer.	Dites que vous avez séché les cours. Racontez ce qui s'est passé: Vous étiez dans le métro quand vous avez trébuché et votre tablette est tombée. Deux garçons l'ont prise.
Demandez comment étaient les deux garçons.	Décrivez les garçons: âge, taille, cheveux, yeux.
Demandez leur ethnie et ce qu'ils portaient.	Répondez avec une description.
Dites qu'il faut remplir une déclaration de vol.	Dites que vous êtes déjà allé(e) au commissariat de police. Dites que vous avez besoin de votre tablette pour le cours de maths.
Dites que vous pouvez lui prêter la vôtre dont vous n'avez pas besoin aujourd'hui.	Remerciez votre ami(e) et dites qu'il faut fixer un rendez-vous pour lui rendre la tablette.
Donnez l'heure et le lieu du rendez-vous.	Dites que vous verrez votre ami(e) plus tard.

Essential Instruction

1. Read through the sentences in **Activité A.** Play the recording.
2. Pair students to create the dialogue in **Activité B.** After they peer edit and practice, have them present it to the class or film it. Consider using the dialogue as an oral assessment.
3. Briefly discuss American culture in relation to the five different categories given in **Activité C.** Then ask students to write their answers.
4. Give students time in class to do **Activité D.** Students might want to write their response as a blog, letter, or an e-mail. Ask students to volunteer to read their response.
5. Have students use a graphic organizer of their choice to jot down ideas before doing **Activité E.**
6. For **Activité F,** students can use a storyboard to illustrate and make captions about how the Internet and technology impact their studies and their free time.

C Évaluation culturelle

 1.3, 2.1, 3.1, 3.2, 4.2, 5.1

Vous allez comparer les cultures francophones à votre culture. Vous aurez peut-être besoin de faire des recherches sur la culture américaine.

1. **Le système éducatif en France**
   Dites comment les Français veulent reformer le système éducatif en France. Puis, parlez des réformes que vous et vos amis désirez voir dans le système éducatif américain.
2. **Le bac**
   Est-ce que le bac marche bien pour les jeunes Français? Citez les statistiques. Est-ce que vous devez passer un examen à la fin du lycée? Donnez des arguments pour et contre.
3. **La sécurité publique**
   Dites de quoi s'occupent la police nationale et la police municipale en France. Puis, faites une liste d'agences qui s'occupent de la sécurité fédérale et au niveau de l'état, de la ville, et de la nation en Amérique.
4. **Les chiffres de la délinquance**
   Comparez les chiffres de la délinquance en France et aux États-Unis et formez des généralisations qui expliquent les différences.
5. **Internet et les réseaux sociaux**
   De quelles façons les ados français sont-ils branchés? Que pensez-vous des sites Internet français? Est-ce une bonne façon d'améliorer votre français? Comment?

D Évaluation écrite

 1.3

Imaginez que vous allez bientôt passer le bac. Parlez de vos sentiments et dites pourquoi vous les ressentez.

E Évaluation visuelle

 1.3

*Décrivez les cambrioleurs (*burglers*) et le crime. Répondez à ces questions: Où? Quand? Qui? Que?*

F Évaluation compréhensive

 1.3

Créez six illustrations cadrées qui montrent comment les jeunes se servent d'Internet et des produits numériques dans leur scolarisation ou dans leurs passe-temps. Si vous préférez, vous pouvez parler de votre expérience personnelle.

Answers

All activities will vary.

Expansion

Have students write a newspaper article about the robbery shown in **Activité C.** Encourage them to make up details to add interest to the article, for example, who was robbed, and where were they during the robbery?

Special Needs Students

Auditory Impairment

Pause the recording in **Activité A** frequently so that students with auditory difficulties can keep up, or administer the listening test separately from the students with no hearing issues.

Linguistically Challenged

Give students a prepared template for **Activité F** with three or four squares rather than six. Help them focus on the written aspect of the assignment before adding their drawings.

RESOURCES

Listening Pre-test D

***Unité* Test**

Game

Allez on montre!

Divide students into groups of four or five. Give one student, the flasher, a pile of cards with the English translation of vocabulary words written on them. The other students should each draw a grid with nine places on a sheet of plain white paper. The flasher reveals the first word, and the other students write its French translation in the first square and turn their paper face down. When everyone is done, the flasher says, "**Allez on montre!**" All students turn their papers face up, and the flasher checks the answers. Each student with a correct answer receives a point. When all nine squares have been filled in, the student with the most points wins.

Vocabulaire de l'Unité 9  1.2

à: à carreaux plaid *B*; **à part** aside from *A*; **à pois** polka dots *B*; **à rayures** striped *B*
accablé(e) overwhelmed *C*
africain(e) African *B*
s' **apercevoir (de)** to notice *B*
s' **approcher** to come closer *B*
l' **argot (m.)** slang *B*
arriver to happen *A*
asiatique Asian *B*
attristé(e) sad *A*
auparavant before *A*
le **bac (baccalauréat)** exam taken to obtain high school diploma *A*
la **bagarre** fight *A*
blanc: le blanc des yeux eye to eye *B*
bosser to work *[inform.] A*
bouclé(e) wavy (hair) *B*
bref in short *C*
le **buzz** buzz *C*
chauve bald *B*
un **chemisier** blouse *B*
un **chœur** choir *C*
choqué(e) shocked *C*
une **cinquantaine: d'une cinquantaine d'années** in one's fifties *B*
les **commérages (m.)** gossip *A*
le **commissariat** police station *B*
complètement completely *C*
costaud(e) stocky *B*
court(e) short (hair) *B*
craquer to lose it *C*
se **déchaîner** to get wild *C*
une **déclaration de vol** report of a theft *B*
découragé(e) discouraged *A*
les **défis (m.)** challenges *A*
délavé(e) washed out *C*
s' **effondrer** to collapse *A*; **s'effondrer de fatigue** to collapse from exhaustion *A*
encouragé(e) encouraged *A*
les **ennuis (m.)** trouble *A*
face à faced with *A*
la **façon** in the manner of *B*
se **faire: se faire arrêter** to get arrested *A*; **se faire bousculer** to get knocked into *A*
fier, fière proud *A*
filmer to film *C*
flirter to flirt *B*
frisé(e) curly (hair) *B*
frustré(e) frustrated *C*
le **gospel** gospel *C*
la **grêle** hail *A*
un(e) **groupie** fan *C*
honteux, honteuse ashamed *A*
incapable incapable *A*
interviewer to interview *C*
un **lâcheur, une lâcheuse** flake *[inform.] A*
une **liquette** shirt *C*
maigre skinny *B*
méditerranéen(ne) Mediterranean *B*
mi-long, mi-longue shoulder-length (hair) *B*
mince thin *B*
musclé(e) muscular *B*
n'importe: n'importe quel, quelle just any *C*; **n'importe qui** anyone *C*
paniqué(e) panicky *A*
par: par la suite consequently *C*
photogénique photogenic *C*
la **plupart de** most *C*
la **priorité** priority *A*
une **quarantaine: d'une quarantaine d'années** in one's forties *B*
raide straight (hair) *B*
une **réaction** reaction *C*
un **récit** account *A*
remplir to fill out *B*
se **rendre compte (de)** to realize *B*
ressentir to feel *A*
se **retrouver (sur)** to appear (on) *C*
rien nothing *B*
scandinave Scandinavian *B*
sécher to skip class *A*
se **sentir** to feel *A*
seul(e) alone, lonely *C*
un **show** show *C*
surexcité(e) overexcited *C*
surveiller to keep an eye on *B*
le **talent** talent *C*
un **tel, une telle** such a *C*
tétanisé(e) paralyzed *A*
la **tête** look *B*; **pas la tête à** not the type to *B*
tourmenter to torment *A*
tout(e): tout d'un coup all of a sudden *B*
trébucher to stumble *A*
une **trentaine: d'une trentaine d'années** in one's thirties *B*
un **type** guy *B*
l' **un(e)... l'autre** the one... the other *C*
vêtu(e) de dressed in *B*
une **vingtaine: d'une vingtaine d'années** in one's twenties *B*
vintage vintage *B*
visible visible *B*
voler to steal *B*
un **voleur** thief *B*

Possessive Pronouns... see p. 535

Learning Styles

Visual Learners

Students benefit from associating the vocabulary words in the context of the lessons and associating images with each word or term.

Auditory Learners

These students would benefit from hearing the recording of the words or saying them aloud.

Kinesthetic Learners

These students will tell you that they have to write words down to learn them.

Special Needs Students

Dyslexia

Students with dyslexia can be overwhelmed when they see the whole vocabulary list in one place. Help them divide the list into categories and identify the words they already know.

Unité

10 La culture des affaires

Culture

Products: Activity

Ask students to guess how much Americans spent on luxury items in each of the last five years. Has there been a change?

Citation

"Dans les affaires, l'esprit de décision va de pair avec le succès."

In business, decision-making goes hand in hand with success.

–Claire France, écrivain canadien

À savoir

Il y a seulement 150.000 Français qui travaillent dans le secteur "produits de luxe," mais ce secteur rapporte 35 milliards d'euros par an.

Essential Instruction

1. Ask students to name brands of French luxury products. What kind of products are they? Cosmetics? Clothing? Wine?
2. If French students were asked to name American luxury products, what might they mention?
3. The **Question centrale** suggests that the products and services of a country's economy are a window into its culture. Ask students to keep this in mind as they work their way through the chapter to see if that statement is true.
4. Explain that in **Unité 10**, students are going to study how the French and American economies are unique, and yet are interdependent in this era of globalization.
5. Ask students to read the **Contract de l'élève** to gain an overview of what they are going to learn.

Unité

10 La culture des affaires

Contrat de l'élève

Leçon A **I will be able to:**

- say where an item was made and express what I feared.
- discuss globalization and French luxury exports.

Leçon B **I will be able to:**

- say that I want to get away and ask how long someone has been in a certain place.
- discuss French trade competitiveness, French-U.S. trade, and manners in the French business environment.

Leçon C **I will be able to:**

- describe adaptability.
- discuss French business organization and the history of marketing in France.

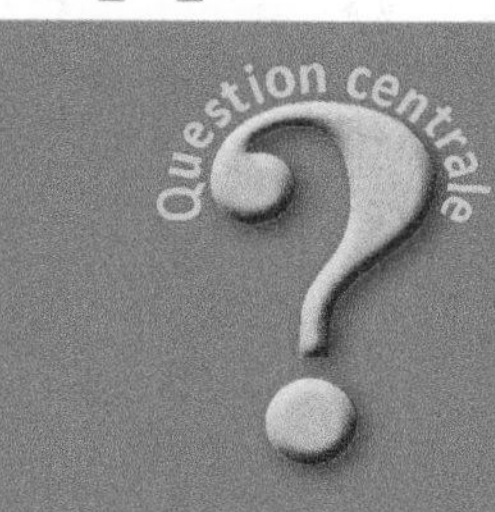

Qu'apprend-on de la culture d'un pays en étudiant son économie?

Quelle est la marque de ces bijoux?

Quel service est-ce que cette entreprise française offre?

Critical Thinking

Analysis

The title of **Unité 10** is **La culture des affaires** (*the culture of business*). Are the words culture and business incompatible, or is this an apt choice of wording?

Differentiated Learning

Accelerate

Have students write a short composition defending or disagreeing with the **Citation**, justifying their opinion with examples.

Decelerate

Have students go to a local department store and make a list of the French products that they find in the cosmetic and clothing departments.

Multiple Intelligences

Mathematical-Logical

Ask students to compare the statistics in **À savoir** with the corresponding values in the United States.

RESOURCES

 **e-visual 29, 30**

 **Workbook 1–4**

 **Flash Cards**

 **Listening Activities 1–2**

 **Drill & Practice Games**

Reference Desk

Remind students that **le champagne** is the beverage, and **la Champagne** is the province. Champagne is served in a glass called **une coupe**, whereas wine is served in **un verre à vin.**

Culture

Products: Information

The basic categories of perfume listed from the most to the least expensive are: perfume, **eau de parfum**, **eau de toilette**, **eau de cologne**, and body splash. The price increases as the concentration of essential fragrances and oils increases. As a rule of thumb, perfume contains 15–40% essential oils, **eau de parfum** 7–15%, **eau de toilette** 4–8%, **eau de cologne** 3–5%, and body splash the least. Several famous French perfume producers are **Lanvin**, **Dior**, and **Jean Patou**.

Leçon A

Vocabulaire actif

Les produits et où ils sont fabriqués

Où les produits ont-ils été fabriqués?

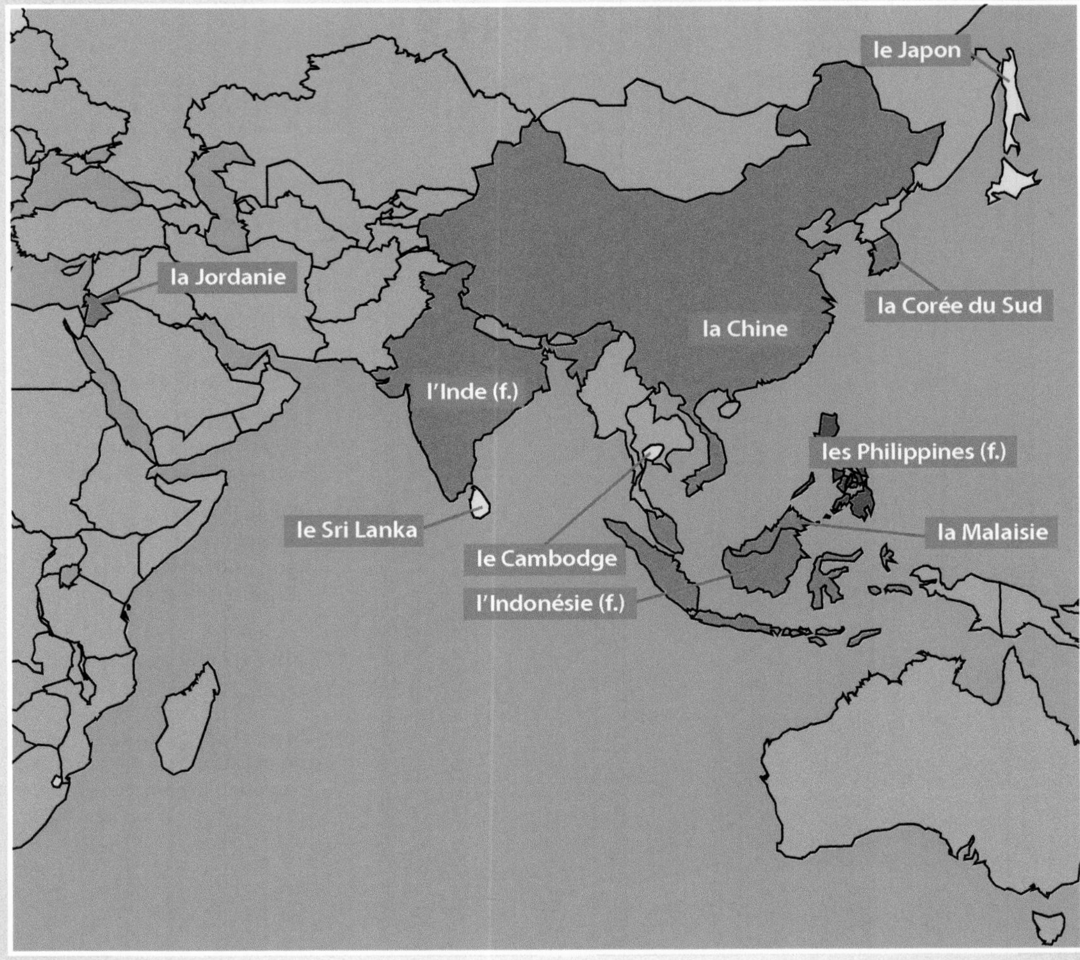

Un produit fabriqué....	
en	Chine, Indonésie, Inde, Jordanie, Corée du Sud, Malaisie
au	Cambodge, Canada, Mexique, Sri Lanka, Japon, Honduras
aux	Philippines, États-Unis

Essential Instruction

1. Put the countries listed under **un produit fabriqué** on the board in random order. Ask students how to say "in" for each country to see if they remember how to use **en**, **au**, and **aux**.
2. Have students listen to **Pour la conversation** twice and repeat the sentences the second time.
3. Have students copy the vocabulary from **Et si je voulais dire...?** into their notebooks.
4. Say the names of the **produits de luxe** and **les marques**. Have students repeat them.
5. It is important that students learn to pronounce the "t" in Moët and the "s" in Hermès as they are foreign names and therefore the silent last consonant rule does not apply.

Les grandes marques des produits de luxe

emcl.com
WB 2–4
LA 1–2
Games

Les produits de luxe	 **Les parfums:** pour femmes, pour hommes	**Les produits de beauté:** crème pour la peau, mascara, etc	**La joaillerie:** bracelets, colliers, bagues, etc
Les marques:	Chanel, Lancôme, Givenchy, Dior, Guerlain	Roc, Clarins, Caudalie, L'Oréal	Cartier, Dior
Les produits de luxe	 **Les montres**	**La mode:** la haute couture	**La maroquinerie:** bagages, sacs à main
Les marques:	Cartier, Dior, Hublot, Gucci	Dior, Cardin, Lacroix, Saint Laurent, Nina Ricci, Chanel, Jean-Paul Gaultier	Louis Vuitton, Lancel, Longchamp, Hermès
Les produits de luxe	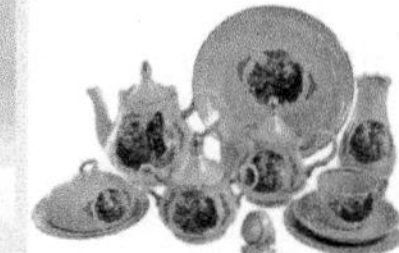 **La faïence:** vases, figurines, etc.	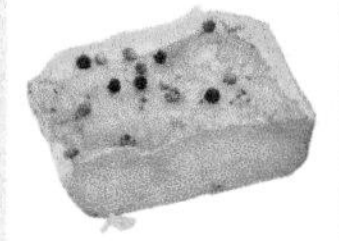 **Les produits alimentaires:** le pâté de foie gras	 **Le champagne**
Les marques:	Limoges, Sèvres	Montfort et Bizac	Moët et Chandon

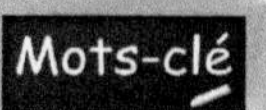

Mots-clé

Marque vient du normand *merc* (1119) apparenté à l'ancien norrois *merki* qui vient lui-même du germanique qui a donné "marcher," "marche". Le mot reste proche de son sens original de signe apposé sur un objet pour le rendre reconnaissable. C'est à partir de la moitié du XVIIème siècle qu'il s'applique à une pratique professionnelle. Cherchez ces expressions en ligne et expliquez ce qu'elles veulent dire:

C'est son image de marque.
Il a trouvé ses marques.

Pour la conversation   1.1, 1.2

How do I say where an item was made?

> **Il a été fabriqué en** Malaisie.
> *It was made in Malaysia.*

How do I express what I was afraid of?

> **C'est bien ce que je craignais.**
> *That's exactly what I was afraid of.*

Et si je voulais dire...? 

un bijou-fantaisie	*costume jewelry*
le caviar	*caviar*
une cravate en soie	*silk tie*
un joyau	*jewel*
un mouchoir brodé	*embroidered handkerchief*
de la cam, du toc *[inform.]*	*fake or imitation*

Reference Desk

Le foie gras (*duck* or *goose liver*) is served several ways: sautéed whole, as a smooth paste, or in a mousse. **Le pâté de foie gras** is a less expensive liver paste that contains liver as a base, but also other spices and ingredients may be added. **La foi** means "faith," **la foie** means "liver," **le foie gras** is the product. If you hear **une crise de foi(e)** out of context you would not know if it refers to a religious crisis or a liver flare up.

Critical Thinking

Analysis
Ask students to research the ban that was imposed on selling **foie gras**, notably in the state of California and the city of Chicago. Why? Do you agree or disagree?

Differentiated Learning

Accelerate
Ask students to research and explain in French the origins of the names Moët and Hermès.

Decelerate
Have students select labels of French luxury products and find corresponding American brands.

Multiple Intelligences

Visual-Spatial
Have students make facsimiles of the listed luxury product logos.

Musical-Rhythmic
Encourage students to search online and find music used to advertise these luxury items.

Answers

1

1. de voyager
2. son oncle et sa tante
3. à Paris
4. en Chine, au Japon, et aux Philippines
5. à Honduras et au Mexique
6. Louis Vuitton, Hublot, Givenchy, Cartier
7. serveuse

2

1. Cette stéréo a été fabriquée au Japon.
2. Ces sandales ont été fabriquées aux Philippines.
3. Cet ensemble a été fabriqué en Malaisie.
4. Cette voiture a été fabriquée en Corée du Sud.
5. Ce sac à main a été fabriqué en Jordanie.
6. Cette veste a été fabriquée au Sri Lanka.
7. Ce thé a été fabriqué en d'Indonésie.
8. Ce collier en or a été fabriqué en Inde.
9. Ce bracelet a été fabriqué au Cambodge.

Communication

Interpersonal: Paired Practice

Student A is in a large department store and would like to buy a gift for his/her mother. Student B plays the role of the salesperson offering suggestions for selecting French luxury items. Student A wants to see a large selection before making a purchase.

1 Céline fait le tour du monde.

1.2

Lisez le blogue de Céline.

Salut, tout le monde! Où suis-je? Dans la capitale de France!

Quand mon oncle et m'a tante m'ont proposé un voyage autour du monde, comment aurais-je pu résister? Nous sommes passé à Paris. Ma tante m'a emmenée à plusieurs boutiques et elle m'a acheté un sac à main Louis Vuitton, une montre Hublot, du parfum Givenchy, et un collier de perles Cartier. On part pour l'Asie demain. On va d'abord en Chine, puis au Japon, et finalement aux Philippines. Après ça on va à Honduras et au Mexique avant de rentrer à Montréal. J'ai l'impression d'être une princesse, mais bientôt ma vie réelle de serveuse et étudiante recommencera.

1. Qu'est-ce que Céline est en train de faire?
2. Qui l'accompagne?
3. Où est-elle maintenant?
4. Elle ira dans quels pays d'Asie?
5. Où ira-t-elle en Amérique du Sud?
6. Céline connaît quelles marques françaises après avoir fait du shopping avec sa tante?
7. Quel métier Céline fait-elle pendant qu'elle fait ses études?

2 Le lieu de fabrication

1.2

Indiquez le pays de fabrication de chaque produit.

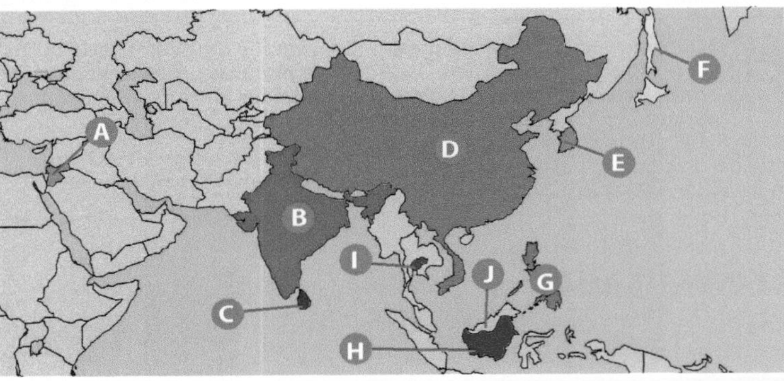

MODÈLE ce portable (**D.**)
Ce portable a été fabriqué en Chine.

1. cette stéréo (**F.**)
2. ces sandales (**G.**)
3. cet ensemble (**J.**)
4. cette voiture (**E.**)
5. ce sac à main (**A.**)
6. cette veste (**C.**)
7. ce thé (**H.**)
8. ce collier en or (**B.**)
9. ce bracelet (**I.**)

Essential Instruction

1. Students read **Activité 1** and answer the questions.
2. Have students do **Activité 2** orally and in writing, paying attention to the agreement of the past participle.
3. Students do **Activité 3** in partners. A brand name might be used twice. Dior makes cosmetics, clothing, and handbags, for example.
4. Play **Activité 4** stopping after each statement. If false, ask students to correct the statement to make it true.
5. Have students listen to **Activité 5** and write short answers. Put sample answers on the board reminding students that the answers will vary.
6. Allot time for students to prepare their answers for **Activité 6**. Have them circulate to ask classmates these questions. They should note the responses on a piece of paper. Debrief the class, making a summary of their preferences for questions 1–5.

3 Fabriqué en France

1.3

Dites à quelle marque vous associez chaque produit français de luxe. Choisissez une marque de la liste.

Louis Vuitton Clarins Moët et Chandon Hublot Roc
Saint Laurent Cartier Lancôme Limoges Montfort et Bizac

MODÈLE le maquillage
J'associe le maquillage à la marque Clarins.

1. la crème pour la peau
2. les montres
3. la haute couture
4. la maroquinerie
5. le champagne
6. la faïence
7. le parfum
8. le pâté de foie gras
9. la joaillerie

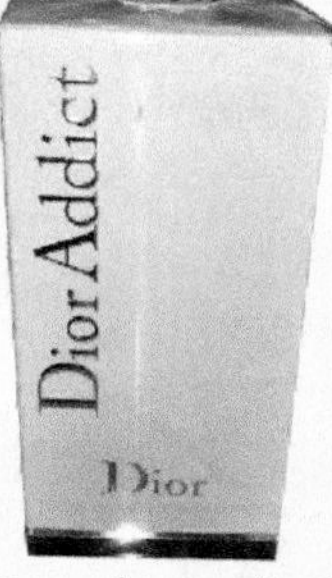

On associe ce parfum à Christian Dior.

Communiquez!

4 Fabriqué au Maroc

1.1, 1.2

Interpretive Communication

*Écrivez les numéros 1–8. Écoutez David et sa maman discuter des produits qu'ils achètent au Maroc. Ensuite, dites si les phrases que vous entendez sont vraies (**V**) ou fausses (**F**).*

Communiquez!

5 Les produits de luxe

Interpretive Communication

Écrivez les numéros 1–8 sur votre papier. Écoutez Rachida et Caroline discuter de l'industrie de luxe française. Ensuite, écrivez une réponse brève pour chaque question que vous entendez.

1.1, 1.2, 1.3

6 Questions personnelles

1.3

Répondez aux questions.

1. Quelle marque préfères-tu pour ces produits: montres, produits de beauté, maroquinerie, mode, produits électroniques?
2. Où voudrais-tu voyager en Asie?
3. Es-tu jamais allé(e) au Mexique? Si oui, où? Pour combien de temps?
4. Est-ce que tu mets du parfum avant de sortir le weekend? Si oui, quel parfum préfères-tu?
5. Où est-ce que ta montre a été fabriquée?

Answers

3

1. la crème pour la peau / Clarins, Roc
2. les montres / Cartier, Hublot
3. la haute couture / Louis Vuitton, Yves Saint-Laurent
4. la maroquinerie / Louis Vuitton
5. le champagne / Moët et Chandon
6. la faïence / Limoges
7. le parfum / Lancôme
8. le pâté de foie gras / Montfort et Bizac
9. la joaillerie / Cartier

4

Script can be found in the front pages of the Annotated Teacher's Edition.

1. V
2. V
3. F
4. V
5. F
6. V
7. V
8. V

5

Script can be found in the front pages of the Annotated Teacher's Edition.

1. l'industrie française du luxe
2. en faisant de recherche en ligne et en parlant à des personnes du secteur
3. un stage chez Guerlain
4. dans les parfums
5. des montres Cartier et des tee-shirts Chanel
6. en France
7. la maison Hermès
8. 40%

6 *Answers will vary.*

Differentiated Learning

Adapt

Students select **une marque de luxe** to research. Have them make a poster featuring a brief history, famous products, annual income, where their products are manufactured, and the location of international headquarters. They present their findings to the class. Consider displaying the posters in the classroom.

Accelerate/Decelerate

Consider having students work in mixed-level pairs to do **Activité 3** in the computer lab. Begin with partners reviewing the vocabulary words listed. Next, ask them to search each of the luxury brand names mentioned. Connecting a visual of the brand logo and packaging to the product reinforces meaning of the term.

Game

Une minute!

Provide each student in a group of five a blank sheet of paper. For one minute, ask each student to write as many vocabulary words from the chapter as he or she remembers. After one minute, call time and ask students to pass the papers to the right. The next student can correct any vocabulary words or write new ones. At the end of a time period, a representative from each group puts the words on the board. The winning group has the most words correct.

RESOURCES

 Dialogue Video

 Workbook 5

Answers

1. sa correspondante
2. de fabriqué
3. typiquement
4. parfums, produits de beauté, bijoux, produits alimentaires, mode, et maroquinerie
5. un foulard fabriqué en France

Reference Desk

1. Students may not know the meaning of these expressions: **l'embarras du choix** (*a multitude of choices*); **au-dessus** (*above*); **en dessous** (*below*). **Ci-dessus** and **ci-dessous** (*above* and *below*) refer to a written piece where things are cited above or below a certain sentence.
2. **Une écharpe** is often made of wool, is rectangular, and is used to protect from the cold. **Un foulard** is made of a lighter material and is square. **Un carré Hermès** is an expensive square, silk scarf in a classic or contemporary design.
3. **CPCH** (**Collier de perles, carré Hermès**) and **BCBG** (**bon chic, bon genre**) refer to a young, upper middle-class woman. A **NAP** (**Neuilly-Auteuil-Passy**) is someone who lives in some of the most expensive areas in Paris and has **le look.**

Connections

Music

"**Adieu foulard, adieu madras**" is a song from Martinique, believed to have been written in 1769, about a young woman who says goodbye to her "**doudou,**" the local word for sweetheart, as he parts for the sea.

Rencontres culturelles

emcl.com
WB 5

Un cadeau typiquement français

   1.1, 1.2, 5.1

Élodie fait du shopping avec son amie Coralie.

Coralie: Tu ne vas pas offrir ça à ta correspondante américaine! Tu as regardé, ce n'est même pas du "made in France." Il a été fabriqué en Malaisie.

Élodie: Tu as raison. Il faut que je lui trouve quelque chose de typiquement français!

Coralie: Tu as quand même le choix entre un parfum, des produits de beauté, un bijou....

Élodie: Tu peux ajouter aussi les produits alimentaires, la mode, et la maroquinerie, et on aura fait le tour!

Coralie: Finalement, tu as l'embarras du choix.

Élodie: C'est bien ce que je craignais... mais tu connais les prix de tous ces produits de luxe?

Coralie: Tu veux dire que tu crois que Chanel, Cartier, Dior, Gaultier, Vuitton, Hermès... c'est au-dessus de nos moyens?

Élodie: Je ne crois pas, j'en suis sûre! En tout cas, moi, je n'ai pas les moyens de lui acheter ça.

Coralie: Reste l'imagination: moins convenu, moins marqué, et plus original.

Élodie: Je crois que j'ai trouvé.... Viens, on y va!

Coralie: Où?

Élodie: Tu verras... pourquoi pas un joli foulard en soie fabriqué ici?

7 Un cadeau typiquement français

Complétez les phrases avec un mot ou une expression.

1. Élodie a du mal à trouver un cadeau "made in France" pour....
2. D'abord, elle considère quelque chose... Malaisie.
3. Elle prend la décision d'acheter quelque chose de... français.
4. Les produits français sont dans ces catégories: ....
5. Finalement, elle va envoyer... à sa correspondante américaine.

1.2, 1.3

Essential Instruction

1. Have students look at the photo of Élodie and Coralie. Where are they, and what might they be doing?
2. After viewing the video, ask general comprehension questions.
3. Play the recording with students following along in their books.
4. Give students time to answer **Activité 7**.
5. Ask various students to read and answer the questions.
6. For **Extension**, ask students to talk about the photo. How old are the people? Where are they? What are they doing? What might be in their shopping cart?
7. Have volunteers read each role. Encourage students to ask questions about vocabulary.
8. Students answer the **Extension** question as a class discussion.

Extension **La mondialisation à l'hypermarché**   1.2, 5.1

Un couple qui a pris la retraite cherche un produit qu'ils aiment à l'hypermarché.

Lui: Je ne trouve pas.
Elle: Mais il y en avait encore le mois dernier....
Lui: Mais tu vois bien il n'y a plus que des marques alimentaires que l'on ne connaît pas: ça vient d'où ça?
Elle: De Chine, d'Indonésie, de Malaisie....
Lui: Quand ils comprendront que ce n'est pas dix centimes qui feront la différence et que ce que l'on veut d'abord, c'est savoir d'où viennent les produits, surtout l'alimentaire.
Elle: Avec tout ce qu'on lit ou qu'on entend sur l'absence de contrôles, les produits frelatés reconditionnés, les conditions sanitaires pas toujours respectées, les mélanges douteux....
Lui: Ah! Elles sont là!
Elle: Comme d'habitude, ils les ont encore changées de place pour nous faire acheter autre chose.
Lui: J'en prends cinq boîtes d'un coup, comme ça on est sûr d'en avoir.
Elle: Ou moins on ne manquera pas de bonnes salades!
Lui: Y'en a marre de ces magasins où l'on passe plus de temps à chercher qu'à trouver!
Elle: Comme si on n'avait que ça à faire!

Extension De quoi est-ce que le couple de retraités se plaint? Pouvez-vous deviner ce qu'ils achètent?

1.2, 1.3

Answers

Extension

Ils se plaignent qu'il y a trop de variétés de produits de mauvaise qualité.

Reference Desk

Students might not know these expressions: **alimentaire** (*food products*); **produits frelatés** (products containing questionable ingredients); **une boîte** (*box* or *can* and *nightclub*); **un carton** (*cardboard box*). **Un récipient** is a general term for a container. **Y'en a marre** and **On en a ras le bol** mean that one is fed up.

Culture

Products: Information

A **hypermarché** is a superstore combining a supermarket and products usually found in a department store, hardware store, and pharmacy. The concept originated with The Carrefour Group, which is the second largest retailer in the world with three major markets in Europe, Latin America, and Asia. It has over 9,870 company-owned and franchised hypermarkets, supermarkets, cash and carry, and convenience stores.

Differentiated Learning

Accelerate

Find examples of **produits frelatés** which have appeared in French and American grocery stores in the past few years.

Decelerate

Luxury products for sale online are often **du toc.** Have students select a product such as a Dior bag, a Vuitton suitcase, or Chanel sunglasses and explain how to tell the difference between the authentic item and its imitation.

Search words: **how to detect the real (name of brand) from a fake**

Multiple Intelligences

Visual-Spatial

There are classic Dior bags named after famous people like Grace Kelly. There are also classic patterns of Hermès scarves. Encourage students to sketch a few to show in class.

RESOURCES

Workbook 6

Critical Thinking

Analysis

If a luxury item is marked **fabriqué en France** and it is actually manufactured in another country, is that a fraudulent representation? Can you find examples of luxury items where that is true?

Points de départ

emcl.com
WB 6

Question centrale

Qu'apprend-on de la culture d'un pays en étudiant son économie?

La France et la mondialisation 1.2, 3.1

La France a-t-elle peur de la mondialisation ou la France profite-t-elle de la mondialisation? La presse anglo-saxonne hésite toujours entre ces deux analyses. Si l'on se réfère aux* sondages*, on pourrait affirmer que les Français ont peur de la mondialisation: ils sont près des deux tiers (60%) à la considérer comme une menace* et seulement un tiers (30%) à la considérer comme une chance.

Ce qui fait peur dans la mondialisation, ce sont les déséquilibres*: dérégulation du commerce mondial; déséquilibres des échanges* commerciaux; délocalisation de l'industrie; crises de l'industrie financière spéculative qui menacent l'économie réelle; menaces agro-alimentaires avec les différentes épidémies*; menaces environnementales; menaces sur les cultures nationales.

Les compagnies françaises profitent de la mondialisation.

Mais si l'on regarde la réussite* économique, on peut dire que la France profite de la mondialisation; elle reste la cinquième puissance mondiale, et elle est le sixième pays exportateur du monde. L'économie française est le cinquième exportateur mondial de biens* (principalement des biens d'équipement), le quatrième pour les services, et le troisième pour les produits agricoles et agroalimentaires (premier producteur et exportateur agricole européen).

Search words: mondialisation france, globalisation France

Si l'on se réfère aux *If one refers to;* **sondages** *surveys;* **menace** *threat;* **déséquilibres** *items with inequalities;* **échanges** *trade;* **épidémies** *epidemics;* **réussite** *achievement, success;* **biens** *goods*

COMPARAISONS

Quels produits fabriqués à l'étranger est-ce que votre famille achète?

4.2

Produits

Louis Vuitton (1821–1892) a fondé une maison française de maroquinerie en 1854. Au XIXème siècle ses malles (*trunks*) étaient populaires pour les voyages transatlantiques en bateau. En 1998 **la marque Louis Vuitton** entre dans le prêt-à-porter: sacs à main, sandales, foulards de soie, etc. Les produits Louis Vuitton sont connus pour la toile (*fabric*) "Monogramme LV." Cherchez ce produit en ligne. 2.2

Essential Instruction

1. Ask students how the American economy is changing. Is manufacturing going to Asia? What effect does globalization have on their lives? Tell them the French feel these changes too.
2. Have students read **La France et la mondialisation.**
3. Divide the students into two teams assigning one a pro-globalization stance and the other opposing it. Have each team go online to research the **Search words** to prepare a for and against debate about the benefits and pitfalls of **la mondialisation.**
4. Have students read **l'Industrie du luxe** and answer the **Comparaisons** question.
5. Divide the class into six groups and randomly assign a task from **Activité 8.** Have students do a jigsaw presentation of all six tasks to share their research with the class.

L'Industrie du luxe  1.2, 2.1

Créée en 1847, la joaillerie Cartier fait des bijoux de luxe.

La France a 40% du marché mondial pour les produits de luxe. L'Oréal exporte les produits cosmétiques. LVMH est connu pour 60 marques prestigieuses. PPR est lié à* la mode et les bijoux, parmi autres produits. Ces compagnies contrôlent des marques comme Vuitton, Hennessy, Moët et Chandon, Dior, Donna Karan, Tag Heuer, Bulgari, Gucci, Yves Saint-Laurent, Bottega Veneta. Elles représentent aussi beaucoup d'euros, 60 milliards* pour ces trois majors. Elles se distinguent* aussi par des flagships spectaculaires sur les plus grandes avenues du monde qui sont devenues de véritables usines à rêve. Et des stars (Charlize Theron, Marion Cotillard, Jude Law) prêtent leur image pour promouvoir* ces grandes marques. Si les États-Unis restent le premier marché pour ces produits du luxe, la Chine arrive au quatrième rang* avec 13 milliards d'euros de chiffre d'affaire, 550 boutiques pour les grandes marques, et une croissance* de 20 à 30%.

 **Search words: dior parfum pub, dior homme sport jude law**

liés à *tied to;* **milliards** *billions;* **se distinguent** *stand out;* **promouvoir** *to promote;* **rang** *rank;* **croissance** *growth*

COMPARAISONS

Quelles sont les marques américaines qui sont exportées à l'étranger?

8 Activités culturelles  1.3, 2.2, 3.2

Faites les activités suivantes.

1. Faites une liste des peurs des Français attachées à la mondialisation.
2. Faites un graphique qui montre les pays qui représentent la cinquième puissance mondiale à la première puissance mondiale.
3. Indiquez les produits qui sont liés à ces marques: Hennessy, Donna Karan, Bulgari, Bottega Veneta.
4. Liez un produit de luxe à chacune de ces vedettes: Charlize Theron, Marion Cotillard, Jude Law, Sharon Stone. Regardez leurs clips en ligne. Expliquez le marketing de ces produits.
5. Trouvez cinq produits de luxe que vous voudriez acheter. Imprimez des photos de ces produits.
6. Faites des recherches pour trouver des produits de luxe dans votre état ou région. Écrivez une liste.

L'actrice Michelle Monaghan porte une robe Chanel.

Perspectives

L'écrivain québécois Marc Vachon a dit sur son blogue "Oser changer": "Sous l'effet de la mondialisation, dans la plupart des pays industrialisés, on note une augmentation du Produit intérieur brut (PIB) mais aussi une diminution du Bonheur intérieur brut (BIB)." (PIB = *GNP* en anglais.) Êtes-vous pour ou contre cet argument? Pourquoi?

Differentiated Learning

Accelerate
Ask students to write an essay answering the question in **Perspectives.**

Decelerate
Have students research Louis Vuitton, the history of the company, and the products, as suggested in the **Produits** activity.

Answers

1. la dérégulation du commerce mondial; les déséquilibres des échanges commerciaux; la délocalisation de l'industrie; les crises de l'industrie financière spéculative qui menacent l'économie réelle; les menaces agro-alimentaires avec les différentes épidémies; les menaces environnementales; les menaces sur les cultures nationales
2. *Graphs will vary.*
3. Hennessy: le cognac; Donna Karan: les vêtements; Bulgari: les parfums ; Bottega: la maroquinerie ; Veneta: la maroquinerie
4. *Possible answers:* Charlize Theron: Chanel; Marion Cotillard: Chanel; Jude Law: Dior; Sharon Stone: Dior
5. *Answers will vary.*
6. *Answers will vary.*

Perspectives
Answers will vary.

Communication

Interpersonal: Cooperative Groups

Instruct groups of students to create an original crossword puzzle in French with a separate answer key. Ask students to focus on the people, brand names, and products France produces as seen in this lesson. Check each group's puzzle for accuracy, and have students correct any errors. Then, have groups exchange puzzles and solve them.
Search words: templates for crossword puzzles

Critical Thinking

Analysis

One of the elements of globalization is to produce goods in countries where labor is less expensive so as to reduce cost. A negative side of this practice is the use of child labor in countries with reduced or no legal restrictions preventing abuse of children in factories. Is this justifiable for the bottom line? Debate.

Answers

9 *Answers will vary.*

Communication

Interpersonal: Cooperative Groups

Students study the kinds of stores at **La Défense.** Have them write a dialogue among three or four friends planning their shopping excursion. Ask students to mention where they want to shop, what they want to buy, and where they plan to have lunch.

Search Words: les quatre temps, la défense

Du côté des médias

Interpretive Communication 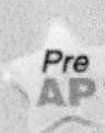  1.2

Regardez les logos des boutiques du centre commercial Les quatre temps, situé à La Défense, à Paris.

9 Les marques

 1.3,2.2

Faites les activités suivantes.

1. Faites une liste des marques françaises que vous connaissez.
2. Indiquez les domaines qu'elles couvrent (*cover*).
3. Tirez (*Draw*) des conclusions.

Essential Instruction

1. Students read **Du côté des médias** and do **Activité 9.** Make a master list of brands and their products that the groups have generated. Write them on the board in the different categories.
2. To do **Activité 10**, have student pairs visit the websites of the stores at **La Défense** to get gift ideas.
3. For **Activité 11**, if you have not done so already, organize a debate for and against **la mondialisation.** Students should find economic statistics on manufacturing and services in the United States ten years ago and today to use these numbers in their debate.
4. For **Activité 12**, have students identify the categories of American products and list at least three for each category. In addition, have them find out where these products' labels are produced in the world.

À vous la parole

10 Un cadeau américain

1.1, 5.2

Interpersonal Communication

Avec un partenaire, jouez les rôles d'un(e) élève américain(e) qui va passer l'été chez une famille française et son prof de français. L'élève voudrait offrir un cadeau typique des États-Unis à cette famille. Il/Elle propose des idées des produits fabriqués en Amérique et demande au prof si chacun sera une bonne idée pour une famille française. Le prof demande à l'élève ce qu'il sait de la famille française... où elle habite, les intérêts et les passe-temps de la famille. Ensemble, ils choisissent un bon cadeau fabriqué aux États-Unis pour la famille française.

11 Un débat sur la mondialisation

1.3, 5.1

Interpersonal Communication

Choisissez l'un de ces points de vue suivants: A. la mondialisation est bonne pour le consommateur ou l'économie; B. la mondialisation n'est pas bonne pour le consommateur ou l'économie. Révisez le vocabulaire du débat dans l'Unité 8, Leçon C. Finalement, trouvez quelqu'un qui a une opinion opposée à la vôtre et participez à un débat devant la classe.

12 Produits pour lesquels les États-Unis sont connus

1.3, 3.2

Interpretive/Presentational Communication

Recherchez les produits pour lesquels les États-Unis sont connus dans le monde. Préparez une table qui comprend les catégories, les types de produits, et les marques américaines, basée sur le modèle français à la page 573.

RESOURCES

Communicative Activities

Answers

All activities will vary.

Critical Thinking

Analysis

McDonald's is one of the largest restaurant chains in France. It has had a huge impact on the way the French eat. Have students visit the French McDonald's website. How is this company adapting to French tastes? In addition to the choice of cheese, what new products are offered that seem to blend the two cultures? Explain.

Reference Desk

Blended Instruction

Consider using blended instruction, a combination of in-class learning and computer-mediated instruction or learning opportunities. Ask students to complete activities on the computer, using their cell or smartphone, or other emerging electronic technology. This process will allow students to hone their tech skills and become more independent learners. Schedule routine Internet and e-book learning in class and in the lab.

Differentiated Learning

Expand

Have students visit **Les Quatre Temps** boutiques at **La Défense** and see if there have been any changes since this chart was published. What kinds of restaurants are there and what international cuisine is available? What other store names do they recognize which sell beauty products? Are they low or high-end products? Students will report their findings to the rest of the class.

Multiple Intelligences

Visual-Spatial

Encourage students to design their own department store. Have them choose from the brand names listed in **Du côté des médias** and identify the products associated with each one. Ask them to name their store and to describe the finished product to the class.

RESOURCES

 Pre-test

 *Leçon* Quiz

Answers

Script is available in the Audio Program Manual.

1. P
2. S
3. P
4. S

Reference Desk

1. As the students will see, there is a difference between standard and familiar French. If they are looking for an example in English of these two categories, tell students that if they were teaching foreigners English, they might be tempted to teach them "I've got to go." In reality the familiar form is "Ivgottago."
2. The consonant in the third person plural of –**re** verbs is followed by an **e**, therefore the consonant is pronounced.
3. The answer to a question starting **Ça fait longtemps que…?** is **Ça fait** + time **que…**

Communication

Presentational: Cooperative Groups

Ask students to make a list of common English expressions that change from standard to familiar pronunciation in daily conversation.

TPR

For **Activité D,** have students write **S** and **P** on two separate pieces of paper. Have them hold up the appropriate letter to indicate if the verb they hear is in the singular or plural.

Prononciation 1.1, 1.2

Liaisons in Standard French

- In the first- and second-person singular, liaison is avoided with **être** in standard French. In the third-person singular and plural, liaison is observed in standard French. More and more, French people are not making liaison with **euros** in standard French.

 **Style standard et familier**

Répétez les phrases, d'abord au style standard, puis au style familier.

Standard	Familier
1. Je suis‿en vacances.	Je suis‿en vacances.
2. Tu es_allé en‿Allemagne?	Tu es_allé en‿Allemagne?
3. On‿est‿en‿Angleterre.	On‿est‿en‿Angleterre.
4. Ils sont‿aux‿États‿-Unis.	Ils sont‿aux‿États‿-Unis.
5. Vingt‿euros?	Oui, ça coûte vingt euros.
6. Cent‿euros?	J'ai perdu cent euros.

 **Je réponds affirmativement.**

Écoutez les questions et répondez-y affirmativement en utilisant le français standard.

1. Où es-tu? (en vacances)
2. Où sont-ils? (aux États-Unis)
3. Ça coûte combien? (vingt euros)

Pronouncing –e After a Consonant

- The consonant at the end of some verbs is not pronounced, except in the plural. For example: **Elle part.** *but* **Elles partent.**

 **Transformez au pluriel!**

Vous allez entendre le verbe au singulier. Changez la phrase au pluriel.

1. Il sort à 18h00.	Ils sortent à 18h00.
2. Il perd les bagages.	Ils perdent les bagages.
3. Elle met du parfum.	Elles mettent du parfum.

 **C'est singulier ou pluriel?**

*Écoutez la phrase. Écrivez **S** si le pronom et le verbe sont au singulier, ou **P** s'ils sont au pluriel.*

Essential Instruction

1. Read Part A for the students. Have them note the difference in pronunciation between standard and familiar French.
2. Ask them to repeat the sentences after you in a group and individually.
3. Monitor students as they answer the questions in **Activité D** to assure they are making the correct liaisons.
4. Have students read to you the three sentences in the singular and the plural for **Activité C.**
5. Have students listen to **Les compagnies françaises.** Ask them to give you the corresponding English term for each type of business, and an example.
6. Have students listen and repeat **Pour la conversation.** Have them add the words to their vocabulary list.

Leçon B

Vocabulaire actif

emcl.com
WB 1–3
LA 1–2
Games

Les compagnies françaises

1.2

Les types de compagnies françaises

GUIDE ÉCONOME

une entreprise compagnie créé par des individus

une PME (Petite et Moyenne Entreprise) entreprise de 20 à 250 employés

une société compagnie créé par des groupes commerciaux

une SA (Société Anonyme) société avec des actionnaires

Une compagnie française

Danone est **une compagnie multinationale** française. C'est une Société Anonyme (SA).

C'est **un leader** dans **la production de** produits laitiers frais.

Son siège social est à Paris.

Il y a plusieurs **filiales** Danone aux États-Unis; leur siège social se trouve à White Plains dans l'état de New York.

Pour la conversation

1.1

How do I ask if someone's been here a long time?

› **Ça fait longtemps que** vous êtes en France?
How long have you been in France?

How do I say I wanted to get away?

› **Je voulais m'éloigner de** la capitale.
I wanted to get away from the capital.

Et si je voulais dire...?

un cadre	*company executive*
le comité directeur	*board of directors*
une firme	*firm*
un groupe	*concern*
un patron	*boss*
une succursale	*branch*

RESOURCES

e-visual 31

Workbook 1–3

Flash Cards

Listening Activities 1–2

Drill & Practice Games

Reference Desk

Some additional vocabulary students might not know:

1. **Le siège** is the legal headquarters of a company. **Le siège** means "a seat." It can also mean "siege," as in surrounding an enemy.
2. **Une filiale** is "a subsidiary" or "affiliate" of a larger organization. **Une succursale** is "a branch office" of a company or financial institution. **Les actionnaires** are "shareholders" who own **les actions** (*stock*). **Le conseil d'administration** is another term for "board of directors."

Differentiated Learning

Accelerate

Have students write a dialogue between two employees who live in Paris and are discussing their jobs. Have them use the expressions from **Pour la conversation.** Challenge students to include as many vocabulary words from **Et si je voulais dire...?** as possible. Present the scene to the class.

Decelerate

Have students make an organizational chart in French of an imaginary company, listing from the top to the bottom the executives who work there.

Special Needs Students

Dyslexia

Students may have to depend on their ear to learn when to make liaisons if they have trouble reading the phonetic markings in the lesson.

Social Anxiety

Choral responses give students with social anxiety a chance to practice speaking French in a safe way.

Answers

1

1. à Paris; à White Plains, NY
2. Danone
3. Elle a l'âge d'aller au lycée, entre 15 et 17 ans.
4. Elle va se spécialiser dans les affaires.
5. son amie Gabrielle
6. Elles feront les touristes.

compagnie; produits laitiers; yaourt; siège social; filiales; état

Reference Desk

Rendre visite à means "to visit (a person)." **Visiter** means "to visit (a place)." **Se spécialiser en** is "to major in (something)." **Le ménage** means "household." **Faire le ménage** is "to do the housework." **Déménager** (literally "to undo the house") means "to move."

Communication

Presentational: Paired Practice

Have students imagine a phone conversation between Catherine and Gabrielle in which they compare life in White Plains and in France. Ask them to make plans for Gabrielle's visit.

1 Je vis aux États-Unis!

Lisez le mail que Catherine écrit à sa copine, puis répondez aux questions.

À: Gabrielle
Cc:
Sujet: Devine où je suis!

Salut, Gabrielle!

Me voici à White Plains dans l'état de New York. On vient de déménager de Paris parce que mon père a un nouveau poste chez Danone… tu sais, la compagnie qui produit notamment des yaourts. C'est à White Plains où se trouve le siège américain des activités produits laitiers frais du groupe, appelé Dannon. Je vais à une vraie high school américaine. Après, je vais me spécialiser en affaires à New York. J'aime l'idée de vivre dans une autre culture. Il faut absolument que tu viennes me rendre visite! On fera les touristes à New York!

J'attends ta réponse,
Catherine

1. Où habitait Catherine, et où habite-t-elle maintenant?
2. Pour quelle compagnie son père travaille-t-il?
3. Quel âge a Catherine? Comment le savez-vous?
4. Qu'est-ce qu'elle va faire après être diplômée?
5. Qui est-ce qu'elle invite à lui rendre visite?
6. Quand Gabrielle lui rendra visite, qu'est-ce que les filles feront?

2 Danone

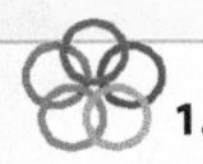

Complétez les phrases logiquement.

Danone est une… multinationale française. Cette société fabrique des… comme le…. Le … de Danone est à Paris. Danone a plusieurs… aux États-Unis, mais la compagnie est centralisée en Amérique dans l'… de New York à White Plains.

La compagnie Danone se trouve boulevard Haussmann à Paris.

Essential Instruction

1. Have students read **Activité 1**, then work in pairs to answer the questions.
2. Have students expand on question 6 of **Activité 1** by researching things to see and do in White Plains and nearby New York City.
3. Ask students to write a response to Catherine asking her more questions about her life in the United States.
4. As a class, complete **Activité 2**.
5. Have students define the terms in **Activité 3** before completing the exercise with the appropriate synonym.
6. Have students listen to **Activités 4** and **5** and respond using white boards.
7. Have students research online the companies in their area before doing **Activité 6**. Do these companies have international branches or manufacturing centers? Where?
8. Ask students to interview each other using **Activité 6** as a basis for conversation. Circulate to offer help where necessary.

3 Les synonymes

1.2

Des jeunes diplômés parlent de leurs premiers postes. Remplacez les mots en italique par des mots de vocabulaire de la liste.

entreprise SA production leader m'éloigner filiales

1. Benoît: Je travaille pour une *compagnie qui n'est pas très grande*. Nous sommes le *numéro un* des compagnies qui fabriquent les sacs de provisions.
2. Marie-Alix: Je cherchais un poste pour une compagnie qui a des *bureaux dans beaucoup de pays*. J'ai trouvé un poste chez Danone, le leader dans la *fabrication* de produits laitiers frais, à Paris.
3. Jean-Pierre: Je travaille pour une *grande compagnie* dans le secteur de l'informatique à Paris. Plus tard, j'aimerais *me mettre à une distance* de la capitale pour travailler aux États-Unis.

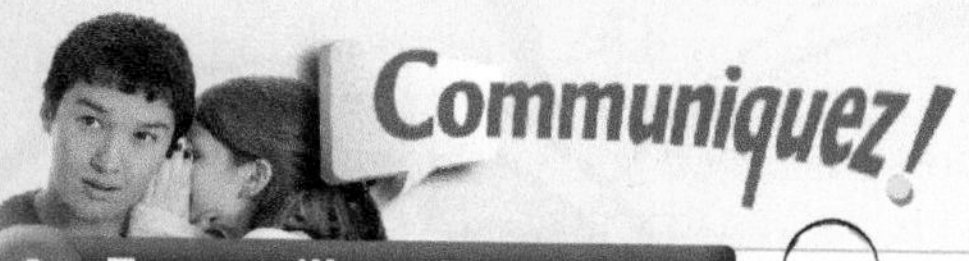

4 Tu travailles pour qui?

Interpretive Communication

Écrivez les numéros 1–6 sur votre papier. Écoutez les personnes décrire où elles travaillent. Ensuite, choisissez la lettre qui correspond au lieu de travail.

A. un siège social
B. une filiale
C. une PME
D. une grande multinationale

1.1, 1.2

Communiquez!

5 Je travaille chez GM.

Interpretive Communication

Écrivez les numéros 1–6 sur votre papier. Écoutez l'histoire et, ensuite, répondez aux questions que vous entendez.

1.1, 1.2

6 Questions personnelles

Répondez aux questions. 1.2, 1.3

1. Quelles sociétés y a-t-il dans ta région? Est-ce que tu aimerais y travailler? Pourquoi, ou pourquoi pas?
2. Quel est le siège social des grandes compagnies dans ta région?
3. As-tu déjà travaillé pour une compagnie? Si oui, c'était quelle sorte de compagnie—une PME, une société, ou une compagnie multinationale?
4. Ça fait longtemps que tu choisis des grandes marques pour tes vêtements?
5. Quand ta famille veut s'éloigner de votre ville, où allez-vous?

Je travaille pour l'entreprise Altran Technologies.

Answers

3
1. entreprise; leader
2. filiales; production
3. SA; m'éloigner

4
Script can be found in the front pages of the Annotated Teacher's Edition.
1. D
2. C
3. B
4. A
5. C
6. D

5
Script can be found in the front pages of the Annotated Teacher's Edition.
1. B
2. C
3. A
4. A
5. C
6. A

6 *Answers will vary.*

Reference Desk

White Plains, New York is the commercial center of Westchester County. It is a bedroom community of New York City because it is an easy 35 minutes by train into the city center. There are four malls with anchor stores such as Sears, Nordstrom, Neiman Marcus, and Bloomingdale's plus hundreds of smaller stores. Heineken and Dannon have their headquarters in White Plains.

Differentiated Learning

Accelerate

Have students visit **la version française** of the Dannon website and make a list of their products. In addition, have them report how the French company **Danone** is currently doing financially.
Search words: **yahoo finance**, **bloomberg**

Decelerate

Ask students to write a one-paragraph response to question 5 of **Activité 6.** Have them explain where and why they would like to move to a new location of their choice.

Multiple Intelligences

Visual-Spatial

Ask students to make a publicity poster for **Danone.** They may incorporate advertising wording from the website.

RESOURCES

 **Dialogue Video**

 **Workbook 4**

Answers

1. F: pour une compagnie multinationale
2. F: un cours de marketing
3. F: des produits laitiers
4. F: à Paris
5. V
6. V

Reference Desk

1. **Un auditeur libre** audits courses. One can either **tutoyer** or **vousvoyer** someone depending on the relationship.
2. **Suivre un cours** means "to take a course."
3. When the word **français** is capitalized it means a French person: **Le Français typique aime les fromages français.**

Culture

Perspectives: Information

Thunderbird School of Global Management, according to their website, "is the world's #1 ranked school of international business with more than 65 years of experience in developing leaders with the global mindset, business skills and social responsibility necessary to create real, sustainable value for their organizations, communities and the world." It is located in Glendale, Arizona.

Critical Thinking

Comparisons

Thunderbird is the top international business school located in the United States. Compare Thunderbird to **une grande école** such as **HEC** in France.

Rencontres culturelles

emcl.com
WB 4

Un Américain à Paris

   1.2

Léo et Justin font la connaissance d'un jeune homme d'affaires au café.

Dennis: C'est donc une interview pour votre cours de marketing à l'université?

Léo: Oui, c'est ça. Je dois interviewer quelqu'un qui travaille pour une compagnie multinationale. Mon copain est auditeur libre et suit le même cours que moi.... Ça fait longtemps que vous êtes en France?

Dennis: Tu peux me tutoyer... ça fait deux ans.

Léo: Bravo pour l'accent!

Dennis: Ce n'est pas trop difficile... travailler tous les jours en français avec des Français, ça aide....

Justin: Tu travailles pour quelle compagnie?

Dennis: Un groupe agroalimentaire qui est le leader mondial dans la production de produits laitiers frais.

Léo: Laisse-moi deviner. C'est Danone?

Dennis: Oui, c'est ça.

Justin: C'est où, le siège social?

Dennis: À Paris, dans le 9ème arrondissement. Mais, ce weekend je voulais m'éloigner de la capitale et trouver du soleil.

Justin: Quelles sont tes responsabilités?

Dennis: Je travaille pour le département de marketing. Plus précisément, sur des stratégies pour lancer nos produits dans des pays anglophones.

Justin: Tu peux parler un peu de ta formation?

Dennis: Après mon B.A., j'ai fait ma maîtrise à Thunderbird en Arizona où je me suis spécialisé en gestion et en français. L'université m'a trouvé un stage à Danone, et le hasard a fait le reste.

7 Un Américain à Paris

  1.2

*Indiquez si la phrase est vraie (**V**) ou fausse (**F**). Corrigez les phrases qui sont fausses.*

1. Il faut que Justin et Léo interviewent quelqu'un qui travaille pour une filiale américaine en France.
2. Justin et Léo suivent un cours de littérature à l'université.
3. Danone fabrique des produits chimiques.
4. Le siège social de Danone se trouve à Nice.
5. Dennis fait des stratégies pour lancer les produits de Danone dans des pays anglophones.
6. Il a fait ses études de gestion à Thunderbird, en Arizona.

Essential Instruction

1. Ask students to name top business schools in the United States. Explain that Thunderbird specializes in international business.
2. Play the video once for general comprehension. Ask students to explain the main storyline.
3. Ask students to write Dennis, Léo, and Justin on a piece of paper. Have them jot down details about each boy as they watch the video again.
4. Have students listen to the dialogue and compare what they wrote to the information in the reading.
5. Answer any questions students have about the dialogue before doing **Activité 7**.

Extension **L'émission de radio: "En France comme si vous y étiez"**   **1.1, 1.2**

Une journaliste interviewe des gens pour une émission de radio pour apprendre pourquoi ils ont choisi le français comme langue secondaire.

Historien italien: On ne peut pas faire de l'histoire si on ne connaît pas le travail de l'École des Annales: elle a changé l'approche de l'histoire. Ce qui n'est pas traduit en italien, je dois pouvoir le lire en français.

Prof allemande: Je suis spécialiste de Proust.... Même si il y a une excellente traduction en allemand... vous imaginez un *proustien* qui ne lirait pas le français!

Banquier britannique: Vous ne le savez peut-être pas, mais les français sont très forts dans la modélisation financière, leurs spécialistes sont très réputés et même si leurs cours sont en anglais, ils les donnent à Paris. Alors si vous voulez aussi profiter de la ville... et comment ne pas profiter de Paris!

Graphiste espagnole: Moi, je voulais être reçu à l'ENSAD, l'Ecole nationale des Arts décoratifs, parce que je voulais absolument travailler dans l'animation et vous savez que l'ENSAD est la meilleure porte d'entrée pour intégrer les grands studios d'animation... alors je suis passé par le français.

Extension Quelle raison pour étudier le français s'approche la plus de la vôtre?

1.3

Answers

Extension

Answers will vary.

Reference Desk

Marcel Proust (1871–1922) was a French novelist and critic. He is best known for his seven-volume novel ***À la Recherche du Temps Perdu*** (*Remembrance of Things Past*).

Communication

Interpersonal: Paired Practice

Ask one student to play the role of the journalist and the other an American being interviewed on French radio about why he/she has chosen to learn French. Students may give real or fantasy answers, but they must expand on their reasons why.

Differentiated Learning

Accelerate

Ask students to summarize in one sentence each why the Italian, German, and Spaniard in the dialogue have elected to learn French.

Decelerate

Have students write a short composition explaining why they have chosen to learn French.

RESOURCES

Workbook 5

Game

Circulez!

The purpose of the game is to learn the companies listed in **La France et la concurrence mondiale**, their functions, and products in a short amount of time. Each student assumes the name of a French company and defines it in one memorized sentence. Have students wear a name tag bearing the name of the company. At a "mocktail" party ask the students to circulate and introduce themselves with a prepared definition. "**Bonjour. Je m'appelle BNP. Je suis une des plus grandes banques de France.**" At the end of the mixer, call out the name of a company. The first person who defines the company correctly gets a point. Award a small prize to the overall winner.

Points de départ

emcl.com WB 5

Question centrale: Qu'apprend-on de la culture d'un pays en étudiant son économie?

La France et la concurrence mondiale

1.2, 3.1, 2.2

Le groupe EDF GDF offre l'électricité et le gaz en France et en Outre-Mer.

La France a placé, dans tous les secteurs, de grands groupes parmi les leaders mondiaux: banque et assurances (BNP, Axa), distribution (Carrefour), industrie pétrolière (Total), énergie (EDF et GDF Suez pour le gaz et l'électricité, Areva pour le nucléaire, Air Liquide pour le gaz industriel), industrie agroalimentaire (Danone), aéronautique (Airbus), industrie aérospatiale (Ariane), télécommunication (France Télécom et Vivendi), services informatiques (Cap Gemini), automobile (Renault-Nissan), matériel* électrique (Schneider électrique), industries pharmaceutiques (Sanofi-Avantis), constructions et travaux publics* (Vinci, Bouygues, Eiffage), services collectifs* (Veolia environnement), ciment* (Lafarge), pneumatiques (Michelin), transport aérien (Air France-KLM)... mais aussi optique (Essilor), et la publicité (Publicis et JC Decaux). Au total, quatorze leaders mondiaux, huit numéros deux, cinq dans les cinq premiers, et six autres dans les dix premiers.

Search words: insee commerce, insee économie

matériel *equipment;* **travaux publics** *public works projects;* **collectifs** *collective;* **ciment** *cement*

Produits

La France a lancé plusieurs **fusées** (*rockets*) sous le nom d'**Ariane.** La France fait partie de l'Agence spatiale européenne, ou l'ESA. On lance les fusées Ariane du centre spatial de Kourou en Guyane française.

COMPARAISONS

Les États-Unis sont classés à quel rang de la concurrence internationale?

4.2

Essential Instruction

1. Put the names on the board of the companies listed in parentheses. Ask students to identify the ones they know. Have them copy these names in their notebooks.
2. Have students read **Points de départ** and write a short description of each company next to the name.
3. Depending on the number of students in the class, assign each student the name of a major company, or all of them, to research. Ask students to add information gained from researching the **Search words**.
4. For **Le commerce entre la France et les États-Unis**, have students compare the list of French and American exports. How are they the same? How are they different? Ask if students are surprised at the number of luxury items exported by France and the lack of them by the United States.
5. Have students answer the two **Comparaisons** questions.

Le commerce entre la France et les États-Unis  1.2, 4.2

La France est la deuxième nation commerçante de l'Europe de l'Ouest, derrière l'Allemagne, qui est son partenaire privilégié*. Récemment, l'échange des biens* et services entre la France et les États-Unis a atteint* 67 milliards de dollars. La France est le huitième partenaire commercial des États-Unis. Vous trouverez ci-dessous les neufs premiers produits échangés* entre ces deux pays.

	Produits français vers les États-Unis		Produits américains vers la France
1	préparations médicales, dentaires*, et pharmaceutiques	1	moteurs pour avions civils
2	aviation civile	2	préparations médicales, dentaires, et pharmaceutiques
3	moteurs pour avions civils	3	aviation civile
4	collectibles (objets d'art, antiquités, timbres, etc.)	4	pièces aéronautiques pour avions civils
5	produits pétroliers	5	matériel médical
6	boissons alcoolisées autres que le vin	6	machines industrielles
7	vin	7	produits chimiques organiques
8	produits cosmétiques, produits d'entretien et d'hygiène	8	accessoires d'ordinateurs
9	pièces et outillage* automobiles	9	instruments de mesure et méthodes de test

Search words: **la diplomatie gouvernement france, insee commerce extérieur**

partenaire privilégié *primary trading partner;* **biens** *goods;* **a atteint** *attained;* **échangé** *exchanged;* **dentaire** *dental;* **outillage** *tools*

COMPARAISONS

Quel est le partenaire privilégié des États-Unis? Qu'est-ce que vous remarquez de cet exemple et de l'exemple de France-Allemagne?

 4.2

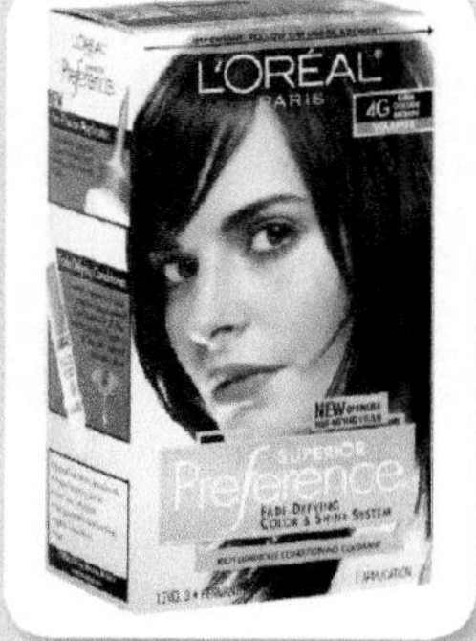

Les produits cosmétiques français l'Oréal sont distribués aux États-Unis depuis 1953.

Communication

Presentational: Paired Practice

Students engage in a debate in which one student argues that globalization is a negative because it is destroying language and culture as English becomes the lingua franca of the world. The other student argues the contrary.

Differentiated Learning

Expand

Arrange students into high and low-ability groups and give them the name of a French company. Have the groups imagine that they work for a public relations firm whose task it is to make an advertising pitch for their company. The students create a commercial or an ad to sell their product. Their sales pitch can be done live or filmed. Encourage students to find commercials online that they may want to incorporate into their presentation.

Special Needs Students

Dyslexia/Linguistically Challenged

Ask students to read **le commerce entre la France et les États-Unis** aloud to a partner. Ask them to summarize the information in the introduction in bullet points. Check their initial list to make sure they understand before continuing. Have them write in English the products listed.

Critical Thinking

Analysis

There is a French **dicton** (saying): "**L'heure, c'est l'heure. Après l'heure, c'est quelquefois l'heure. Avant l'heure n'est jamais l'heure.**" What does this mean, and how might it refer to a hostess preparing a dinner party?

Culture

Products: Information

L'Ecole française de la courtoisie is a service that offers cross-cultural training for foreigners working in France. It is a good source for a comparative study of customs and practices in France. **Search words: etiquette in france**, **l'école française de la courtoisie**

Expansion

Students interview an American businessman or woman. Ask them to explain to the American, point by point, the etiquette of business meetings and business dinners in France, and ask the American to comment on how these practices are the same or different in the United States. Have them report back to the class.

Bonnes manières

1.2, 4.1, 5.1

Réunion*, repas d'affaires, invitations—à chaque moment ses codes pour réussir un rapport avec une entreprise française.

Rendez-vous et réunions: Depuis le Moyen-Âge*, les Français ont la réputation de n'être jamais à l'heure à un rendez-vous. Pourtant les rendez-vous et réunions commencent en général à l'heure dite. L'internationalisation a mis de la rigueur* dans la gestion du temps. Un écart* de cinq minutes reste toutefois toléré. Les Français ne fixent que rarement l'heure de fin d'une réunion. Dans les premiers rendez-vous, le "vous" est de rigueur au premier contact; si le "tu" doit s'imposer, il le fera naturellement, par consensus. Généralement, c'est dans les moments de convivialité, hors* l'officialité qu'il s'imposera. Attention, les Français respectent peu les tours de parole et ont tendance à couper la parole: c'est le produit d'une culture du débat et de la polémique*.

Repas d'affaire: Ils ont beaucoup évolué. Plus courts (une heure maximum), et réduits* à entrée-plat ou plat-dessert. Pas ou peu de vin (on travaille, ou on conduit après) et beaucoup d'eau minérale. On pratique aussi les déjeuners de travail avec plateau-repas*. L'homme précède la femme pour entrer dans le restaurant et pour monter un escalier*. Le paiement doit se faire discrètement, en se déplaçant à la caisse.

Invitation à domicile: Il faut arriver après l'heure (dix minutes à un quart d'heure maximum) pour une invitation amicale*, à l'heure si c'est un dîner privé. Selon le degré d'officialité, fleurs pas encombrantes* pour Madame ou une bouteille de vin si c'est un dîner plus amical. Reste le casse-tête* des manières de table pour lesquelles il faut éviter le "bon appétit" en début de repas; trinquer* ou ne pas trinquer, cela dépend du degré d'officialité et de proximité. Pour l'ordre des couverts, commencer par ceux qui sont le plus à l'extérieur et progresser vers ceux placés le plus proche* de l'assiette; distinguer le verre à eau (toujours le plus grand) des verres à vin.

Search words: customs taboos in france, etiquette in france

Reunion *Meeting;* **Moyen-Âge** *Middle-Ages;* **rigueur** *strictness;* **écart** *delay;* **hors** *outside of;* **polémique** *argument;* **réduits** *reduced;* **plateau-repas** *TV dinner;* **escalier** *staircase;* **invitation amicable** *invitation to the home;* **encombrantes** *cumbersome;* **casse-tête** *puzzle;* **trinquer** *to toast;* **plus proche** *closest*

Mots-clé

Manière: féminin substantivé (1119) qui vient de l'adjectif *manier* qui signifie que l'on fait fonctionner à la main. Il est issu du latin *manuarus* lui-même dérivé de *manus* ("main"). C'est à partir de 1170 qu'il sera appliqué aux personnes avec le sens de "comportement considéré en société." Qu'est-ce que ces expressions veulent dire?

Ne fais pas de manières.
Il y a l'art et la manière.

Les repas d'affaire style cafétéria permettent de gagner du temps.

Essential Instruction

1. Explain to students that cultural practices differ from country to country and one of the benefits of studying French is becoming open and sensitive to different ways of acting.
2. Have students read and outline **Bonnes manières.**
3. After researching the **Search words**, ask students to add more information to their outline about what to do and not to do in business and social settings in France.
4. Ask students to use this information to do task 4 of **Activité 8.**
5. Give students a choice of the remaining tasks in **Activité 8.**
6. Have students examine the two graphics about French exports in order to complete **Activité 9.**

8 Activités culturelles

Faites les activités suivantes.

1. Recherchez une compagnie française et faites une présentation à la classe.
2. Montrez la présence des grands groupes leaders mondiaux français aux États-Unis.
3. Faites une liste des produits que les États-Unis importent de la France qu'ils n'y exportent pas, et vice-versa.
4. Faites la liste des choses à éviter dans les contacts avec les Français.
5. Écrivez un dialogue d'un repas d'affaire entre une femme d'affaires américaine et deux hommes d'affaires français.

Perspectives

"Auprès des politiciens, les finesses de l'étiquette, les subtilités de la diplomatie comptent moins que le succès."

—Robert Charbonneau, journaliste et écrivain québécois

Quel proverbe anglais exprime la même idée? Êtes-vous d'accord avec ce principe, ou pensez-vous que le moyen ou la méthode d'accomplir une chose est aussi important que le résultat?

Du côté des médias

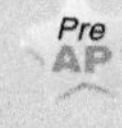

Interpretive Communication

Regardez les graphiques ci-dessous qui montrent les destinations des exportations françaises.

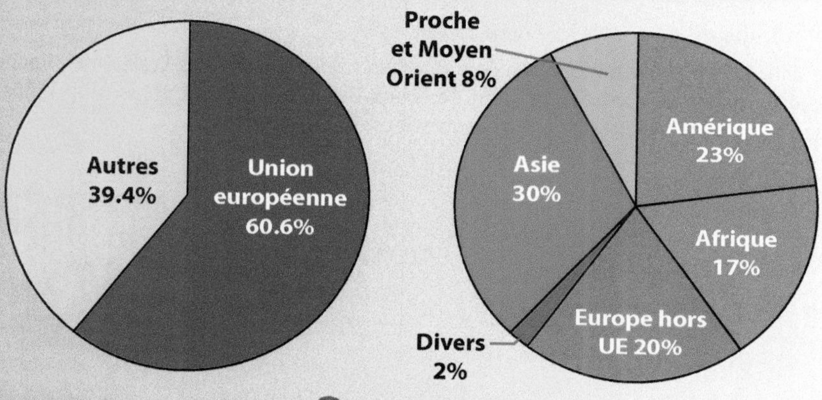

9 Exportations françaises

Faites les activités suivantes.

1. Dites à qui va le plus grand pourcentage de produits français à exporter.
2. Expliquez les généralisations que vous pouvez faire de ce tableau.
3. Faites un tableau semblable pour les domaines des exportations américaines.

Answers

1. *Presentations will vary.*
2. *Answers will vary.*
3. *Answers will vary.*
4. *Possible answers:* utiliser "tu" dans les premiers rendez-vous; passer devant une femme au déjeuner si on est un homme; payer devant tout le monde; arriver à une invitation à domicile en avance ou à l'heure; dire "bon appétit" n'importe quand.
5. *Dialogues will vary.*

Perspectives
Answers will vary.

9

1. à l'Union Européenne
2. *Possible answers*: l'Asie est la deuxième destination des exportations françaises, après l'U.E.; La France n'exporte pas beaucoup au Proche et Moyen-Orient; L'Amérique achète beaucoup de produits français.
3. *Graphs will vary.*

Communication

Presentational: Paired Practice

Students research etiquette for dining in a French home. Have them write a comic scene in which the American makes many **faux-pas** because of cultural misunderstandings. An example might be the American offering a large bouquet of chrysanthemums as a hostess gift when these flowers are only put on graves.
Search words: etiquette in France

Differentiated Learning

Accelerate
Have students answer the question for **Perspectives** then write a three-paragraph essay agreeing or disagreeing with the quotation.

Decelerate
Ask students to write a short composition discussing how arrival time is relative to the French depending on the situation. There are different standards for a French business meeting or dinner party. Ask them to comment if the same is true in the United States as well.

RESOURCES

Communicative Activities

Answers

All activities will vary.

Reference Desk

Blended Instruction

Consider using blended instruction, a combination of in-class learning and computer-mediated instruction or learning opportunities. Ask students to complete activities on the computer, using their cell or smartphone, or other emerging electronic technology. This process will allow students to hone their tech skills and become more independent learners. Schedule routine Internet and e-book learning in class and in the lab.

À vous la parole

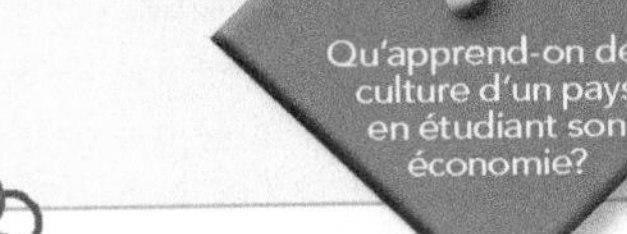

Communiquez!

10 Une compagnie multinationale américaine

1.3, 3.2

Presentational Communication

Recherchez une compagnie multinationale américaine, par exemple une compagnie technologique, sportive, aéronautique, ou alimentaire. Préparez un profil de cette compagnie dans lequel vous:

- identifiez le secteur
- dites de quel(s) produit(s) elle est le leader
- dites où se trouve son siège social
- dites où se trouve ses filiales
- donnez votre opinion des produits de cette compagnie

Communiquez!

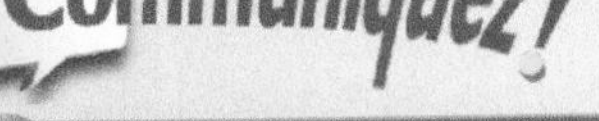

11 Le commerce entre le Canada et les États-Unis

1.3, 2.2, 3.2

Interpretive/Presentational Communication

Le Canada est le partenaire privilégié (*leading trade partner*) des États-Unis. Recherchez les dix principaux produits qui vont des États-Unis au Canada et vice-versa. Préparez un graphique pour montrer ce que vous avez appris.

Communiquez!

12 Bonnes manières en France

1.3, 2.2, 3.2

Presentational Communication

Imaginez que vous êtes en France et que votre compagnie américaine travaille avec une compagnie française. Hier soir un collègue français vous a invité à dîner chez lui. Écrivez un paragraphe dans votre journal qui décrit le dîner... l'heure de l'invitation, quand vous êtes arrivé(e) chez lui, ce que l'hôtesse vous a servi, et l'ordre des couverts dont vous vous êtes servi.

Essential Instruction

1. In class read through the instructions and expectations for **Stratégie communicative.**
2. For **Activité 10**, suggest that students select a company whose products they use and like.
3. To complete **Activité 11**, students can find pie chart makers online.
4. To personalize **Activité 12**, suggest that students ascribe names to the French family and a description of each person. Have them relate what the table looked like, the specific courses they ate, what was discussed, and what the students selected for a hostess gift.
5. To do the storyboard, brainstorm with students a product that they really like. It could be a sports car, a restaurant, designer jeans, or shoes. Once they find what they are passionate about, they will be ready to write an ad.
6. Using **Search words** about publicity, students get a feel for advertising styles, from straightforward sells to more surrealistic "surprise-at-the-end" ads.

Stratégie communicative

 Storyboard  1.3, 2.2, 3.2

Un scénario dessiné (*storyboard*) est composé d'images et de textes; il s'agit d'une sorte de brouillon (*draft*) qui permettra au filmage d'une publicité.

Suivez les étapes suivantes afin d'apprendre comment réaliser une pub. Ensuite, vous créerez votre propre scénario dessiné afin de vendre un produit américain sur le marché français. N'oubliez pas d'utiliser vos connaissances sur la culture française et ce qui plaît aux consommateurs en France.

1. Recherchez quelles sont les techniques de commercialisation telles que: *celebrity endorsement, avant-garde, facts and figures, weasel words, magic ingredients, diversion, transfer, plain folks, snob appeal, testimonial, bandwagon*. Choisissez-en une.
2. Regardez quelques pubs françaises en ligne et demandez-vous: Quelles techniques de commercialisation fonctionneraient pour les Français? En quoi les pubs françaises diffèrent-elles des pubs américaines? Qu'est-ce qui est important pour les Français?
3. Réalisez votre scénario dessiné en vous basant sur le template ci-dessous.

 **Search words: publicités (+ année), culture pub, pubs tv, best of publicités françaises**

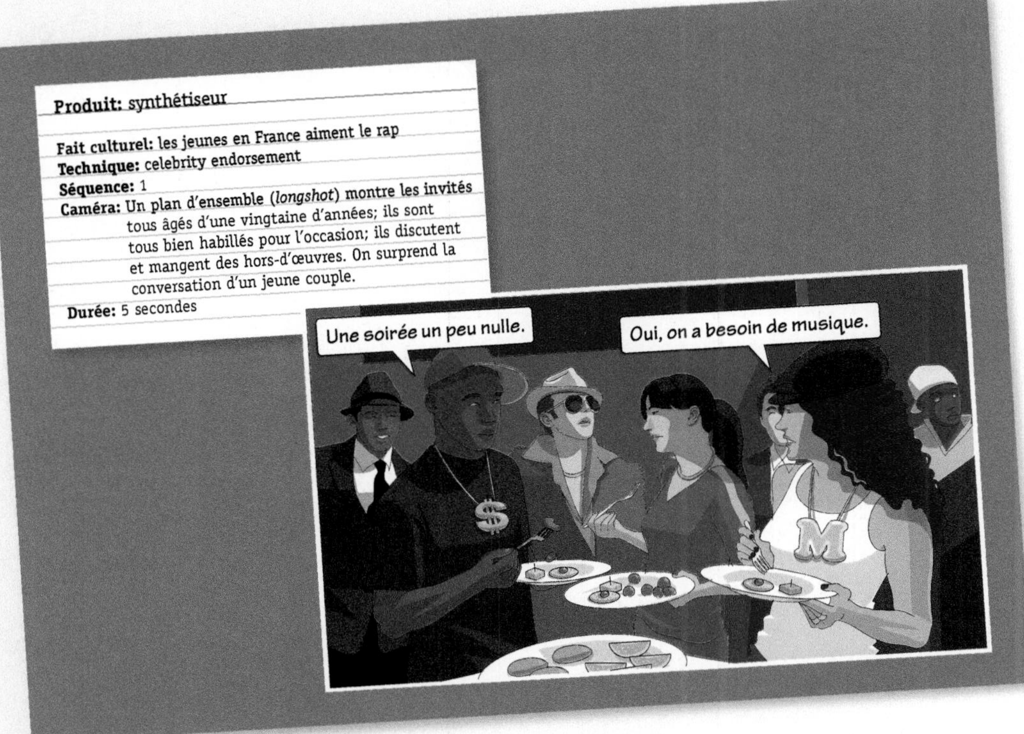

RESOURCES

 **Pre-test**

 ***Leçon* Quiz**

Reference Desk

Storyboards are essential tools in advertising. They provide the framework for creating an overview of television movies, cartoons, and advertisements as well. Have students check online for more ideas and tips on creating storyboards.
Search words: storyboards, what is a storyboard, how to make a storyboard

Differentiate Learning

Expand
Students can find online examples of promotions and discounts. In marketing their products they might want to include some **prix-chocs** and great sales.

Multiple Intelligences

Visual-Spatial
Ask students to illustrate the ideas of the group for their storyboards.

Musical-Rythmic
Have students be in charge of the music ideas to accompany the storyboards.

Connections

Humor

For a change of pace, have students watch **"Omar et Fred"** online as they do comedy sketches in French about the pitfalls of the customer service department. **Search words: le service après-vente**

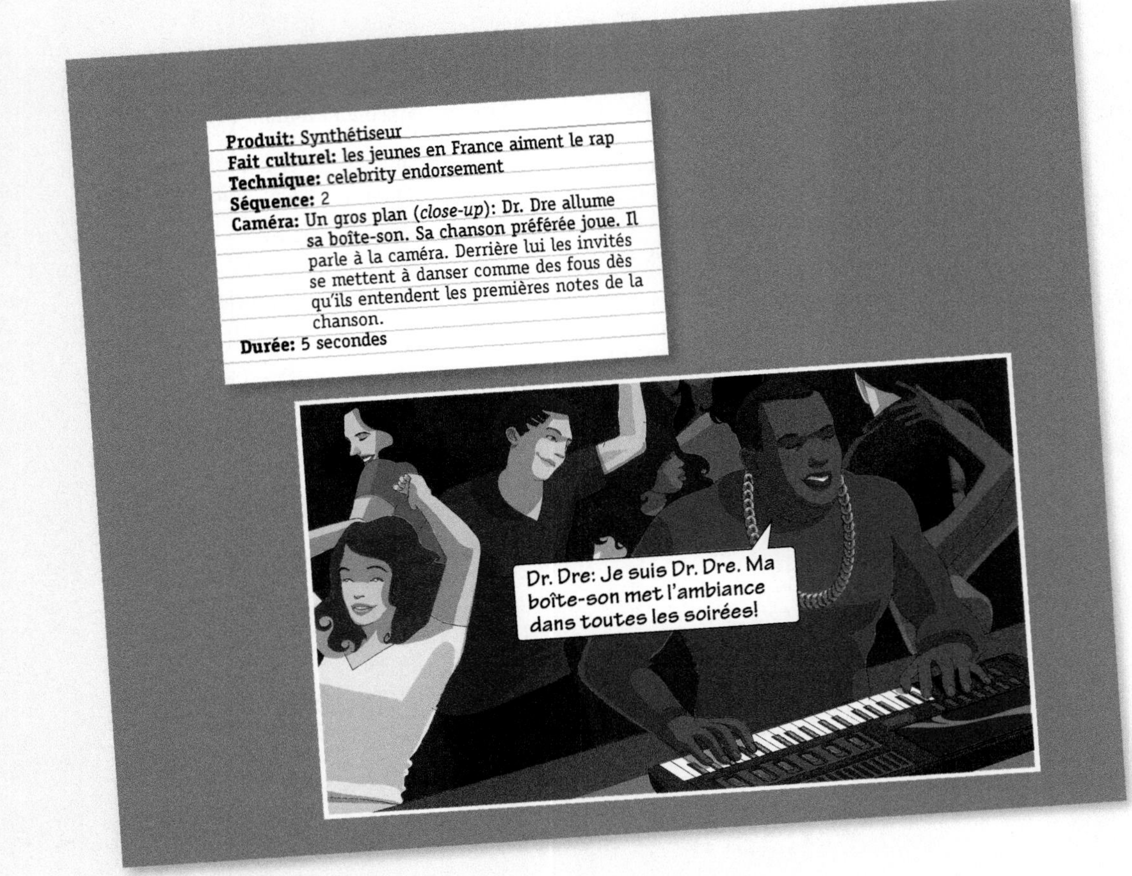

Essential Instruction

1. Have students submit their storyboard outline to you for suggestions and evaluation.
2. Students present their storyboards to the class as if they were in a "Mad Men" pitch session trying to sell their peers on the quality of the publicity.
3. For **Leçon C**, ask students to name in English the different departments of a major organization. Write these titles on the board from the top management on down.
4. Have students listen to **Les départements et les postes d'une compagnie** then copy the organizational chart in their notebooks.
5. Listen to **Et si je voulais dire...?** then ask students to add the vocabulary to their notebooks.
6. Add **département de technologie** to the chart.
7. Ask students to define the functions of each of the departments and the members of the staff.

Leçon C

Vocabulaire actif

emcl.com
WB 1–2
LA 1–2
Games

Les départements et les postes d'une compagnie

1.2

BIENVENUE À L'ENTREPRISE DELORS!

le, la PDG président(e) directeur/directrice général(e), le chef, la cheffe d'entreprise, le directeur financier, la directrice financière

le service du marketing

le, la responsable marketing

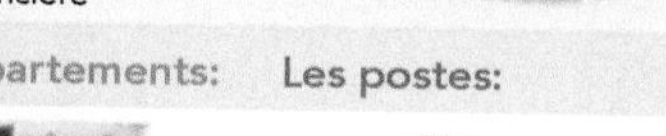

Nos départements: Les postes:

la gestion

le chef, la cheffe de groupe

le service des ventes

le vendeur, la vendeuse

la comptabilité

le, la comptable

le secrétariat

le, la secrétaire (administratif, -ive)

les ressources (f.) humaines

le, la DRH (directeur, directrice des ressources humaines)

le service après-vente (m.)

le chef, la cheffe de service

Pour la conversation

1.1

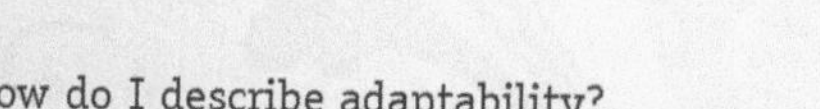

How do I describe adaptability?

> McDo met du fromage français dans leurs sandwichs **pour s'adapter à** notre goût.
>
> *McDonald's puts French cheese on their sandwiches to adapt to our taste.*

Et si je voulais dire...?

un(e) artisan(e)	*craftsman*
la conversion	*changeover*
la main d'œuvre	*manpower*
un ouvrier, une ouvrière	*blue-collar worker*
la restructuration	*restructuring*
la robotisation	*full automation*

RESOURCES

 e-visual 32

 Workbook 1–2

 Flash Cards

 Listening Activities 1–2

 Drill & Practice Games

Communication

Presentational: Cooperative Groups

Have students define what it takes to be a good secretary, salesperson, accountant, department head, etc. Have them write a job description for each. Upon completion have them peer edit each other's work. Ask students to make presentations to the class about each of the jobs they researched.

Search words: quelles sont les qualités pour être un(e) bon(ne)...

Differentiated Learning

Accelerate

Have students write a help wanted ad for their business to attract a competent accountant and sales person. Ask them to include a job description, hours, salary, and benefits.

Decelerate

Copy the photos that accompany each new vocabulary word in **Vocabulaire actif** and **Et si je voulais dire...?** and attach them to index cards. Work with students to create simplified definitions for each position then use the photos as cues to check learning. For example, manipulate the photos matching them to written definitions, or say the new word and have the students pick the corresponding photo.

Answers

1 *Drawings will vary.*

2

1. secrétaire
2. PDG
3. comptable
4. responsable marketing
5. vendeur
6. DRH

Reference Desk

Axa, **Crédit Agricole**, **l'Oréal**, **LVMH**, and **Alstrom** have been named the top five environmentally friendly companies emitting the least amount of CO_2 in the atmosphere. (**L'ONG Britannique** study)

Communication

Interpersonal: Paired Practice

Student A is **chef des ressources humaines.** Student B wants to get a job in a department of his/her choice. Imagine the interview between the two. Student A asks questions about Student B's background, interests, past job experience, and skills. Student B answers giving real or imagined details.

1 Nettoyez-Bio

La compagnie Nettoyez-Bio fabrique des produits pour nettoyer la maison sans polluer la terre. Faites un dessin de la compagnie décrite ci-dessous.

La compagnie Nettoyez-Bio se trouve devant une forêt qui est visible des fenêtres du secrétariat. Quand on entre la compagnie, Mlle Duclerc, la secrétaire vous accueille. À droite sont les bureaux—celui du PDG d'abord (M. Tissot), suivi de la comptable, Mme Garnier; du DRH, Mme Delavigne; et du responsable marketing, M. Dumont. Les employés sont derrière la secrétaire dans des box (*cubicles*). Le nom de la compagnie se trouve sur le mur à gauche.

2 Les employés

Donnez le nom de plusieurs employés dans une compagnie française.

1. La (**A.**) voit tout le monde qui entre et qui part.
2. Le (**B.**) est le responsable de la gestion de la compagnie.
3. La (**C.**) imprime un document financier.
4. La (**D.**) prépare une publicité.
5. Le (**E.**) va essayer de vendre le nouveau produit.
6. La (**F.**) interviewe un candidat.

Essential Instruction

1. Read **Activité 1** to the students as a dictation. Have students correct their work.
2. For **Activité 2**, ask students to identify the positions by reading the descriptions. For each position, ask for more details about their functions. For example, "What else does a receptionist do?"
3. Using the organization chart, students complete **Activité 3**.
4. Before assigning **Activité 4** ask students to describe each picture. Where might they be working? How long have they been working there? Give a physical description of each person. How old are they?

3 L'organisation de la compagnie

 1.2, 5.1

Complétez les phrases pour identifier les départements ou les personnes qu'on contacte dans les situations décrites.

1. Quand on téléphone à une compagnie, on parle souvent à un(e) employé(e) dans le....
2. Une personne qui veut acheter un produit contacte un... ou une....
3. Le PDG est responsable de la... de la compagnie.
4. Quand on accepte un poste dans une compagnie, on va aux... pour signer le contrat.
5. Pour comprendre les finances d'une compagnie, on contacte le comptable dans le département de....
6. Quand le PDG voudrait faire des publicités pour ses produits, il contacte le département de....

Communiquez!

4 Tu fais quoi?

  1.1, 1.2

Interpretive Communication

Écrivez les numéros 1–6 sur votre papier. Écoutez les descriptions. Puis, faites correspondre la description avec la bonne illustration.

A

B

C

D

E

F

Answers

1. service après-vente
2. vendeur, vendeuse
3. gestion/direction
4. ressources humaines
5. la comptabilité
6. marketing

Script can be found in the front pages of the Annotated Teacher's Edition.

1. B
2. A
3. D
4. F
5. E
6. C

Communication

Interpersonal: Paired Practice

Student A wants to make an appointment for a job interview with Student B who is head of human services. Have them role-play the scene.

Search words: **french conversation, making an appointment on the phone**

Differentiated Learning

Expand

Have students find a photo online of people in a business setting. Ask them to write a story with dialogue, using the photo as a point of departure, and integrating the business vocabulary of the lessons.

Search words: **google/images**, **business meeting**

Multiple Intelligences

Bodily-Kinesthetic

Ask students to act out the cues for **Activité 3** and have the rest of the class identify the department or person to contact.

Answers

Script can be found in the front pages of the Annotated Teacher's Edition.

1. F
2. V
3. F
4. V
5. F
6. F

6 *Answers will vary.*

Communication

Interpersonal: Paired Practice

Ask students to read **Mots-clés** about **franglais.** Have them search online for current English words that now are used in French such as **le zappeur**, **le buzz**, **le brushing**, etc. Are they correct translations of the English words? Have students also make a list of French words used daily in English such as **soupe du jour**, **au jus**, **nom de plume** etc.

5 Le travail en France

1.2

Interpretive Communication

*Écrivez les numéros 1–6 sur votre papier. Écoutez la conversation entre Marc et Henrike, une stagiaire allemande. Ensuite, indiquez si les phrases que vous entendez sont vraies (**V**) ou fausses (**F**).*

6 Questions personnelles

1.3, 5.1

Répondez aux questions.

1. Est-ce que tu as déjà travaillé pour une compagnie? Si oui, quel était ton poste?
2. As-tu jamais écrit à un PDG? Pour quelle raison?
3. Imagine que tu as fini tes études universitaires et tus cherches maintenant un poste. Qui est-ce que tu comptes contacter dans la compagnie où tu voudrais travailler? Pourquoi?
4. Qu'est-ce que tu ferais si tu travaillais pour le service du marketing?
5. Tu aimerais être vendeur ou vendeuse d'un produit que tu aimes? Si oui, duquel?

Essential Instruction

1. Have students listen to **Activité 5** and answer one comprehension question at a time. Stop the recording after each sentence and ask for the answer. Ask a volunteer to restate the original sentence.
2. Allow students to answer **Activité 6** honestly or with imagination since many have limited work experience.
3. Have students watch the video **Une compagnie multinationale américaine en France.** What do they remember about the conversation between Léo and Justin?
4. Students listen to the recording. In small groups have them list the companies mentioned, and explain how they have adapted to international markets.
5. In the same groups, have students do **Activité 7.** Upon completion, ask them to compare their lists with other groups.

Rencontres culturelles

emcl.com WB 3

Une compagnie multinationale américaine en France

Léo et Justin étudient ensemble. 1.1, 1.2

Léo: Génial ce que la prof de marketing nous a raconté....
Justin: Vous travailliez sur quoi?
Léo: Sur l'adaptation des compagnies multinationales aux besoins des marchés locaux.
Justin: Ah oui, je vois... contre l'idée reçue que mondialisation égale uniformisation.
Léo: Exactement! Elle nous a raconté comment 3M... tu connais 3M?
Justin: Oui, les rouleaux de Scotch™!
Léo: Oui, si tu veux.... Et aussi les Post-it™ et les éponges Scotch-Brite™, comme ça on aura fait le tour du supermarché! Donc, je disais que 3M avait eu l'idée géniale d'adapter des sandales avec de l'éponge en dessous pour qu'elles servent de serpillières aux Philippines... pas bête, non?
Justin: C'est comme les constructeurs automobiles qui sont obligés d'adapter leurs voitures pour les pays où l'on conduit à gauche....
Léo: Et puis McDo et Subway qui mettent du fromage français dans leurs sandwichs pour s'adapter à notre goût... et qui nous servent de la bière et du café *expresso*.
Justin: En Allemagne, ils proposent des hamburgers au porc, j'en ai goûté!
Léo: Et l'Oréal? C'est bien connu, l'Oréal fait du marketing ethnique avec des produits qui ciblent certaines couleurs de peaux. Sans parler de Kleenex™ qui nous réserve son papier toilette découpé en petits carrés.
Justin: Eh oui, Léo, le marché devient régional. Dis, tu es bilingue, diligent, et doué pour le marketing; tu comptes travailler pour une compagnie multinationale?
Léo: Je n'ai pas encore pris ma décision, mais cette possibilité m'intéresse.

Mots-clé Le **marketing** est un mot anglais et un mot franglais en France. Selon l'Académie française et quelques commissions, on devrait le remplacer avec "mercatique." Mais beaucoup de Français continuent à parler du "marketing."

Search words: délégation générale à la langue française

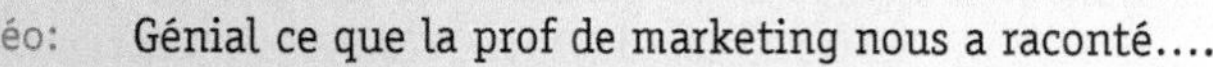

7 Une compagnie multinationale américaine en France

 1.3

Faites une liste des multinationales mentionnées dans le dialogue qui montrent la régionalisation dans la mondialisation.

RESOURCES

 **Dialogue Video**

 **Workbook 3**

Answers

7 3M; McDo; Subway; l'Oréal; Kleenex

Reference Desk

Here is some help with the vocabulary from the dialogue: **Génial!** by itself means "Great!" **L'idée géniale** means "a brilliant idea." The plural of **local** is **locaux. Cibler** is "to target." **Une serpillère** is a rough cotton cleaning cloth used for cleaning the floor. **Doué(e)** means "talented" or "gifted."

Culture

Perspectives: Information

There is a classic scene from the film ***Le Père Noël est une ordure*** where a young woman, Thérèse, gives her boyfriend Pierre a gift that she made. He thinks it is a **serpillère** because it is so ugly. She corrects him: It is a vest! This film can be downloaded to your computer, or you can search for it online.

Search words: **le père noël est une ordure, serpillère**

Differentiated Learning

Expand

Have students compare the menus of McDonald's in the United States with that of France, Germany, and India. Ask: Which items are different and which are the same? What modifications would be made to the menu in India? Why? Visit the Indian McDonald's website to confirm your assumptions.

Special Needs Students

Linguistically Challenged

Read **Une compagnie multinationale américaine en France** with the students. Ask them to highlight any cognates they see. Emphasize how much they already understand by identifying the words and expressions that they already know. Encourage them to listen to the conversation again and then read it out loud to help reinforce its meaning.

Answers

8

1. de l'adaptation des compagnies multinationales aux besoins des marchés
2. leur prof de marketing
3. les rouleaux de Scotch, les Post-it, les éponges Scotch-Brite
4. des sandales avec des éponges aux soles, qui servent de serpillères
5. Ils utilisent du fromage français dans leurs sandwichs, et servent des expressos et de la bière. Kleenex découpe son papier toilette en petits carrés.
6. travailler pour une compagnie multinationale

Extension

Il a du mal à s'adapter aux idées, projets, et réunions discontinus.

Reference Desk

1. **La voie** can refer to a physical path, train track, or lane on a highway. It can also refer to a theoretical path, as in a career path.
2. **D'ailleurs** means "by the way." **Ailleurs** means "elsewhere." There is a popular program on French TV called **"Nulle part ailleurs"** which means "No where else."
3. The word **foutu** is a very strong word. Emphasize that it should be used with caution.

8 Une compagnie multinationale américaine en France

1.2, 5.1

Répondez aux questions.

1. De quoi est-ce que Léo et Justin parlent?
2. Qui leur a appris que le marché devient régional?
3. Quels sont les trois produits fabriqués par 3M mentionnés?
4. Qu'est-ce que 3M a inventé pour le marché philippin?
5. Comment est-ce que McDo et Subway s'adaptent au marché français? Et Kleenex?
6. Léo s'intéresse à quelle possibilité?

Extension **Brad discute de son travail dans un bureau français.**

1.1, 1.2

Au bureau Raphaël et Brad prennent un café.

Raphaël: Alors Brad, pas trop difficile?
Brad: Non, c'est comme toi quand tu es venu travailler chez nous à San Diego, il faut s'adapter.
Raphaël: Je t'avais prévenu pourtant....
Brad: Mais la discontinuité! Impossible de rester sur une chose décidée; vous passez d'une chose à l'autre, revenez à la première, ça a changé entre temps, on ne sait pas pourquoi. Moi, j'aime faire une chose jusqu'au bout, puis l'autre et ainsi de suite.
Raphaël: Mais tout n'a pas besoin d'être dit; on comprend implicitement; chacun remplit les blancs... l'important c'est l'objectif, la manière, elle laisse la place à la créativité de chacun... chacun choisit sa voie pour y arriver.
Brad: C'est ça, c'est son affaire.
Raphaël: Notre foutu individualisme comme tu dis souvent!
Brad: C'est comme les réunions: on sait quand ça commence, mais on ne sait jamais quand ça finit... d'ailleurs ça ne finit pas.
Raphaël: Si! Ça finit!
Brad: Bon et bien, la suite au prochain café....

Extension Pourquoi Brad a-t-il des difficultés au bureau français? De quoi est-ce qu'il se plaint?

1.2

Essential Instruction

1. Do **Activité 8** as a class leading to a discussion of how companies adapt to international markets.
2. Have students make two columns with two headings: Brad and Raphaël. As students read the **Extension** conversation, have them note in the appropriate columns the cultural differences between them.
3. Ask students to read and take notes on **La structure de l'entreprise en France.** Have them use the **Search words**, plus add "intercultural management, France" to the list.
4. Use the **Extension** question to discuss the differences in approaches between the American and French business practices. Have students use their notes to enrich the discussion.
5. Write questions on the board that you would like them to know after reading **Le marketing en France**, or prepare a worksheet that they fill out as they read.

Points de départ

emcl.com WB 4

La structure de l'entreprise en France 1.2

Le PDG d'une société à structure hiérarchique se tient au centre des décisions.

Traditionnellement, la structure de l'entreprise française est hiérarchique, c'est-à-dire que le PDG, ou président-directeur général gère* la compagnie; c'est lui qui prend toutes les décisions importantes. Sous lui il y a des cadres supérieurs* et des cadres moyens* que le PDG dirige*. Un résultat de ce modèle est l'élitisme; l'entreprise embauche des diplômés des grandes écoles. Mais ce modèle, qui remonte à l'idée d'un gouvernement français centralisé depuis Napoléon, est en train de changer.

Un exemple de ce changement est la coopérative, qui, de l'autre côté, dépend des valeurs de partage*, d'humanisme, de transparence, et de participation. Les coopératives Scop redistribuent les profits aux employées et représentent environ 40.000 salariés.

Pour réussir dans le marché mondial, il faut changer le modèle traditionnel.

 **Search words: hec paris, les scop**

COMPARAISONS

Est-ce que vous connaissez une compagnie américaine? Comment est-elle structurée? 2.2

gère *manages;* **cadres supérieur** *senior executive;* **cadre moyen** *junior manager;* **dirage** *manages;* **partage** *sharing*

Le marketing en France  1.2

Les premières formes de marketing apparaissent* en France pendant le XVIIème et le XVIIIème siècles. La publicité est vraiment la "réclame*" après la guerre de 1870. "L'affichomanie" règne de 1850 à 1920 quand on voit les belles affiches artistiques comme celles de Toulouse-Lautrec qui réclament les cafés, les théâtres, et les cabarets de Paris. Entre les deux guerres arrive le "publicitaire" qui travaille dans une agence. Avant 1945, le problème le plus grave des entreprises est la capacité de production, pas la vente des produits pour lesquels les consommateurs ont déjà un appétit. L'invention de la radio pendant les années 1920 offre un autre champ pour la publicité; on répond avec le marketing de masse. "Les Trente Glorieuses" sont les années de 1950 à 1973 quand commencent les publicités télévisuelles. Les sondages d'opinion sont nouveaux en France pendant les 1950 et changent le marketing.

Avec les années 1960, un groupe de consommateurs importants viennent sur scène: les baby-boomers; c'est pendant cette époque que la publicité française se découvre parce que c'est une période de prospérité. Le marketing de nos jours se caractérise par l'émergence de nouveaux paradigmes tels que le marketing relationnel et électronique, même en ligne; les entreprises modernes doivent atteindre* la satisfaction de la clientèle.

 **Search words: musée de la publicité, l'univers de la publicité, publicité (+ 1920, 1930, etc.)**

apparaissent *appear;* **réclame** *advertisement;* **atteindre** *to meet*

RESOURCES

 **Workbook 4**

Communication

Presentational: Cooperative Groups

Ask students to guess what strategies are used to market to people their age. Extend this activity by having them create a survey to poll their classmates as to which marketing strategy works best to entice them personally to buy. Would it be advertising online, ads in popular magazines, product placement, or commercials on television? Ask them to share their findings with the class.
Search words: le marketing et les jeunes.

Critical Thinking

Analysis

Ask students: What do you think is the effect of advertising of tobacco and alcohol seen by young people? Does this influence the behavior of people your age?
Search words: social marketing to young people, l'alcool, la publicité et les jeunes

Differentiated Learning

Accelerate

Have students study an American company in their town and compare the structure to the French company described in the reading.

Decelerate

Ask students to find five funny French and American commercials (which are classroom appropriate) online. Have them show these to the class. Ask them to lead a discussion about French and American commercials.

Answers

 *Answers will vary.*

Perspectives
Answers will vary.

10
1. McDo (McDonald's); français (Orléans)
2. fromage au lait cru, camembert, emmental

Communication

Interpersonal: Cooperative Groups

Have students go online to find the definitions of the terms in "**Pub.**" Are there any corresponding slang terms in English for these categories?

Connections

Music

"**La femme image**" is a song which explores the life of a supermodel whose only purpose in life is to project the illusion of reality as dictated by whatever product she is representing.
Search words: la femme image, gilbert lafaille, tout m'étonne

La vache qui rit est un fromage français qui a changé son look à travers les années. Recherchez l'évolution de cette marque et regardez ses images changeantes.

Search words: l'univers de la publicité marques et personnages 2.2

L'argot des ados

"Pub" veut dire "publicité" en argot. Donnez des définitions pour "publiphile," "publipostage," et "publireportage" après avoir recherché ces mots en ligne. 4.1

La vache qui rit.

9 Activités culturelles 1.3, 3.2, 5.1, 5.2

Faites les activités suivantes.

1. Parlez à un(e) adulte qui travaille dans les affaires de la structure de sa compagnie. Ensuite, comparez la compagnie américaine à l'un des deux modèles français.
2. En travaillant avec un groupe, choisissez une décennie (de 1920 à 2010). Trouvez un exemple typique de la publicité de cette époque et présentez-la à la classe.
3. Comparez une publicité française à une publicité américaine de la même époque.

Perspectives

"Pour réussir sur le marché mondial, il faut changer le modèle traditionnel des affaires en France. Il vaut mieux que les entreprises françaises impliquent davantage les salariés et les cadres dans les processus de décision, favorisent l'initiative individuelle et la diversité, et aient une vision globale et une action locale." Ce point de vue, écrit par un jeune diplômé embauché par une compagnie traditionnelle, vous semble-t-il raisonnable? Justifiez votre avis et décrivez la sorte de compagnie pour laquelle vous voudriez travailler.

Du côté des médias

Pre AP

Lisez l'annonce ci-dessous.

10 Un fast-food américain s'adapte au marché français.

1. *Identifiez l'entreprise qui fait cette publicité et donnez son origine nationale.*
2. *Comparez le choix de fromages à ce fast-food en France et aux États-Unis.*

1.2, 2.2, 4.2

Essential Instruction

1. Arrange students randomly into two groups to do **Activité 9**. Have Group A do the first task. In addition, require them to research online articles on business that discuss the difference in French and American corporate structures. Which is more hierarchical?
2. Have Group B complete the second and third tasks. Ask them to find print illustrations of the American and French advertising of the decade they select.
3. Have Groups A and B do **Activité 10**.
4. For **Activité 11**, students choose their target category to investigate. Have them declare what they are going to do and why. Ask them to make a numbered chart (ten items) with the headings **Produit**, **Marque**, **Pays de fabrication**.
5. For **Activité 12**, have students analyze items in their category and answer the questions about them.
6. Have students do **Activité 13** to prepare for a whole-class discussion of **la mondialisation**.

La culture sur place

Mes expériences avec la mondialisation

Dans cette *Culture sur place*, vous allez rechercher les marques internationales dans votre vie. D'où viennent les produits que vous utilisez chaque jour? Quel est le lien entre ces produits et la culture?

11 Première Étape: Chercher et rechercher

1.3, 3.2

Choisissez une catégorie de la liste suivante. Vous allez rechercher d'où viennent ces produits dont vous vous servez régulièrement.

- les vêtements
- l'équipement sportif
- la nourriture
- les boissons
- les produits électroniques
- les produits cosmétiques, produits d'entretien et d'hygiène

Faites une liste des produits, donnez le pays de fabrication et des marques pour chacun. Préparez des pourcentages où c'est possible, par exemple, "Soixante pourcent de mes vêtements viennent d'Asie."

12 Deuxième Étape: Comparer

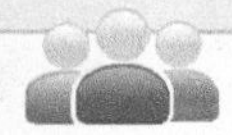

1.1, 2.2, 5.2

Partagez les informations de votre liste avec celles de quelques camarades de classe. Si plusieurs élèves ont choisi la même catégorie, combinez vos listes de marques et de pays de fabrication. Ensuite, discutez de vos découvertes avec les autres élèves en répondant à ces questions:

1. Est-ce que la plupart de ces produits (dans la catégorie que vous avez choisie) viennent de la même région ou du même pays?
2. Remarquez-vous d'autres motifs?
3. Quelle est votre hypothèse économique pour expliquer ces motifs et pourquoi un tel pays fabrique ceci ou cela?

13 Faire l'inventaire!

1.1, 2.2

Discutez ces questions en classe.

1. Après vos recherches, est-ce que vous pensez que vous vivez dans un marché mondial? Est-ce que votre point de vue a changé au cours de cette activité? Si oui, comment?
2. Est-ce que vous pensez qu'il y a un lien entre les produits et les cultures? Avez-vous trouvé, par exemple, un produit que vous pensez typiquement américain qui a été fabriqué à l'étranger?
3. Quelle est la fonction des frontières (*borders*) entre nations dans une époque de mondialisation? Trouvez-vous que les frontières entre les pays sont plus importantes, ou moins importantes, maintenant?
4. Selon vous, la mondialisation est-elle une menace ou un avantage?

Answers

All answers will vary.

Culture

Products: Information, Activity

JCDecaux Group is a multinational corporation that is the largest out-of-home advertising corporation in the world. Based in Neuilly-sur-Seine, Paris, it is known for its bus-stop advertising systems, billboards, and public bicycle rental systems in France and abroad. Have students find corresponding large American advertising companies.

Differentiated Learning

Accelerate

Have students write an essay explaining the impact **la mondialisation** has on their lives. Ask them to cite examples from the research they did in **La culture sur place**.

Decelerate

Have students inventory the cheeses in the dairy section of their grocery store. What kinds of cheeses are there, and where are they produced? Are they all pasteurized? Are they pasteurized in France?

Multiple Intelligences

Visual-Spatial

Ask students to investigate **La vache qui rit** in the **Produits** section and report to the class. Have them display pictures of the changing images of the product and share with the class.

Verbal-Linguistic

Have students make a commercial for **La vache qui rit**. Their commercial should include a jingle and of course a cow.

RESOURCES

Communicative Activities

Answers

All activities will vary.

Reference Desk

Blended Instruction

Consider using blended instruction, a combination of in-class learning and computer-mediated instruction or learning opportunities. Ask students to complete activities on the computer, using their cell or smartphone, or other emerging electronic technology. This process will allow students to hone their tech skills and become more independent learners. Schedule routine Internet and e-book learning in class and in the lab.

À vous la parole

Communiquez!

14 La publicité en France

1.3, 3.1, 3.2

Presentational Communication

Préparez une présentation visuelle qui montre le développement de la publicité depuis l'époque de Toulouse-Lautrec. Écrivez de petits textes en-dessous de chaque image qui montrent votre compréhension des changements dans le marketing jusqu'à l'époque moderne.

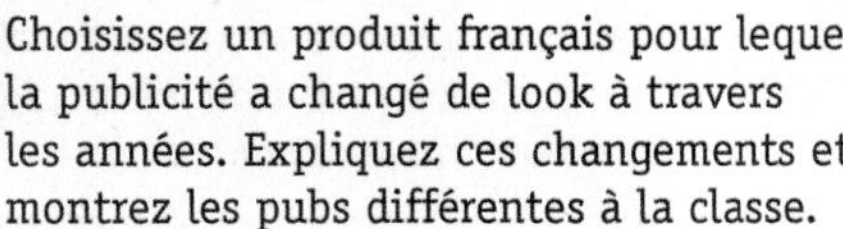

Communiquez!

15 Un produit au fil des années

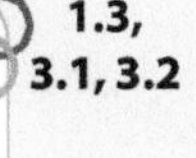

1.3, 3.1, 3.2

Presentational Communication

Choisissez un produit français pour lequel la publicité a changé de look à travers les années. Expliquez ces changements et montrez les pubs différentes à la classe.

Communiquez!

16 Ma pub pour le marché français

1.3

Presentational Communication

Faites une vidéo pour la pub pour laquelle vous avez fait le storyboard dans *Stratégie communicative.* Peut-être que vous aurez besoin d'aide de quelques camarades de classe. Montrez la vidéo à la classe.

Essential Instruction

1. For **Activité 14**, students use the **Search words** on p. 601. For more examples of contemporary ads, they can do more research online.
   Search words: **marie-claire, gq, ikea france**
2. To do **Activité 15**, students might consider: **Dubonnet**, a classic French liqueur; **Vittel**, **Vichy**, or **Evian** for water; or any of the luxury products listed on p. 573.
3. Encourage students who are assigned **Activité 16** to study the commercials for French products found online. Despite the fact that many commercials feature popular American songs, insist that they use French music.
4. Before listening to **Rencontre avec l'auteur**, ask students the **Pre-lecture** question. Have them list the ads and commercials they are most susceptible to.
5. After reading the **Rencontre avec l'auteur**, have students summarize the information to a partner.
6. Read through the **Stratégie de lecture** and ask students to create a chart like the one on the page.

Lecture thématique

14,99 €

Rencontre avec l'auteur   1.2

Frédéric Beigbeder (1965–) est un écrivain, un critique littéraire, un réalisateur et animateur de télévision français. Son roman *14,99 €,* intitulé, *99 francs* au début, est l'histoire d'Octave Parrango, un rédacteur publicitaire. Désenchanté par le marketing et conquis par la déception de la promesse d'une vie meilleure pour tous, il décide de se révolter contre son agence de pub en sabotant sa plus grande campagne. Quelles indications remarquez-vous qu'il va se rebeller dans cet extrait?

Pré-lecture  1.3

Comment êtes-vous influencé(e) par les publicités?

Stratégie de lecture  1.2

Tone

La tonalité, ou le ton d'un texte, est l'ensemble des procédés que l'auteur utilise pour provoquer des émotions particulières chez le lecteur, à travers les personnages, ou par le thème d'une œuvre littéraire. Dans un texte, on peut trouver différentes tonalités: familière, ironique, comique, sarcastique, sérieuse, sincère, ou cynique. Au fur et à mesure (*During*) de votre lecture, relevez au moins un exemple de la tonalité dans chaque paragraphe. Indiquez si cette tonalité est provoquée par les paroles du protagoniste, la réaction anticipée du lecteur, ou par le thème de la lecture. Un exemple a été fait pour vous.

Paragraphe	Provocation	Description du ton
1. "...eh oui, je pollue l'univers"	le protagoniste	dédaigneux, sarcastique
2.		
3.		

Outils de lecture  1.2

Addressing one's Audience in Fiction

De nos jours, il est rare qu'un écrivain s'adresse directement à ses lecteurs dans son œuvre de fiction. Mais, Beigbeder utilise le pronom "vous." À votre avis, quel genre de relation essaie-t-il de créér avec ses lecteurs? Quel est l'effet de cette intimité (*intimacy*)? Êtes-vous davantage attiré par l'histoire, ou vous sentez-vous plus distant? Pourquoi?

RESOURCES

 **Pre-test**

 ***Leçon* Quiz**

Answers

Rencontre avec l'auteur
Il se présente comme quelqu'un qui "pollue l'univers".

Pré-lecture
Answers will vary.

Stratégie de lecture
Possible answers:

2. "Je vous drogue à la nouveauté."; le protagoniste; agressive, cynique (la drogue tue)
3. "Votre souffrance dope le commerce."; le lecteur; sérieuse (le lecteur est en danger)
4. "Je passe ma vie à vous mentir."; le protagoniste; sincère, confessionnelle
5. "Vous ne m'échapperez pas." le protagoniste; menaçante

Outils de lecture
Possible answers:
Il essaie de confronter le lecteur par une approche directe. On se sent plus concerné, il est difficile d'objectiver une telle approche.

Reference Desk

Les émotions particulières can mean "particular emotions" or in the context of **Stratégie de lecture**, it means "personal emotions." **Lire**, **le lecteur**, **la lectrice**, **la lecture** are words of the same family. Synonyms for **de nos jours** are **aujourd'hui** and **actuellement**.

Differentiated Learning

Expand

Consider inviting one of the English teachers or the literacy coach from your school to talk with the students about tone. Ask him or her to highlight examples of tone from texts that the students have read in English class in order to create a stronger link between what they have already read and the excerpt from ***14,99€.***

Special Needs Students

Dyslexia, AD(H)D, Linguistically Challenged

To help students with reading difficulties, attention problems, and linguistic difficulties, focus on general comprehension as the goal. Prepare a worksheet for them with translations of difficult vocabulary that they can use as they do their readings.

Connections

Entertainment

In **Outil de lecture** it is pointed out that the speaker in ***14,99€*** speaks directly to the readers. Can students think of any piece of literature or a television show where this technique is used? ("Modern Family")

Answers

Pendant la lecture

1. publicitaire
2. les voitures
3. les gens malheureux qui veulent toujours plus
4. qu'il est toujours insatisfait
5. Oui, il gagne beaucoup d'argent et a toujours de belles voitures neuves.

Reference Desk

1. **"Connaissez-vous beaucoup de mecs qui gagnent 13K euros à mon âge?"** is a reference to a monthly income. In France, no one refers to an income on an annual basis. Ask students to calculate the protagonist's annual income in dollars. ($200K)
2. **"Je dépense donc je suis"** is a take off on Descartes' famous saying "**Je pense donc je suis**" or in latin, **"Cogito ergo sum." Assouvir** means "to satisify a hunger or thirst." It could also be used to satisfy intangible needs: **Assouvir vos désirs. Rabâcher** means "to rehearse." It also means to "hammer away at" or "to drill information repeatedly."
3. **Un creux** can mean "a hollow" as in a tree, or "an opening" in your schedule. **J'ai un creux le lundi à midi. Avoir un (petit) creux** means "to be a little hungry" as in your stomach is a little hollow.

Je me prénomme Octave et m'habille chez APC. Je suis publicitaire: eh oui, je pollue l'univers. Je suis le type (...) qui vous fait rêver de ces choses que vous n'aurez jamais. Ciel* toujours bleu, nanas* jamais moches, un bonheur parfait, retouché sur PhotoShop. Images léchées*, musiques dans le vent. Quand, à force d'économies, vous réussirez à vous payer la bagnole* de vos rêves, celle que j'ai shootée dans ma dernière campagne, je l'aurai déjà démodée*. J'ai trois vogues d'avance, et m'arrange toujours pour que vous soyez frustré. Le Glamour, c'est le pays où l'on n'arrive jamais.

> **Pendant la lecture**
> 1. Quelle est la profession du narrateur?

> **Pendant la lecture**
> 2. Il parle de quel produit?

Je vous drogue à la nouveauté*, et l'avantage avec la nouveauté, c'est qu'elle ne reste jamais neuve*. Il y a toujours une nouvelle nouveauté pour faire vieillir* la précédente. Vous faire baver*, tel est mon sacerdoce*. Dans ma profession, personne ne souhaite votre bonheur, parce que les gens heureux ne consomment* pas.

> **Pendant la lecture**
> 3.Quels consommateurs le narrateur apprécie-t-il?

Votre souffrance* dope* le commerce. Dans notre jargon, on l'a baptisée "la déception post-achat". Il vous faut d'urgence un produit, mais dès que vous le possédez, il vous en faut un autre. L'hédonisme n'est pas un humanisme: c'est du cash-flow. Sa devise? "Je dépense, donc je suis." Mais pour créer des besoins, il faut attiser* la jalousie*, la douleur*, l'inassouvissement*: telles sont mes munitions*. Et ma cible, c'est vous.

> **Pendant la lecture**
> 4. Que sait le narrateur du consommateur?

Je passe ma vie à vous mentir et on me récompense grassement*. Je gagne 13.000 euros (sans compter les notes de frais, la bagnole de fonction, les stock-options et le golden parachute). L'euro a été inventé pour rendre les salaires des riches six fois moins indécents. Connaissez-vous beaucoup de mecs qui gagnent 13K euros à mon âge? Je vous manipule et on me file la nouvelle Mercedes SLK (avec son toit qui rentre automatiquement dans le coffre) ou la BMW 78 ou la Porsche Boxter ou la Mazda MX5. (Personnellement, j'ai un faible pour le roadster BMW 78 qui allie esthétisme aérodynamique de la carrosserie* et puissance* grâce à* son 6 cylindres en ligne qui développe 321 chevaux, lui permettant de passer de 0 à 100 kilomètres/heure en 5,4 secondes.

> **Pendant la lecture**
> 5. Est-ce que le narrateur vit bien? Quelle en est la preuve?

J'interromps* vos films (...) à la télé pour imposer mes logos et on me paye des vacances à Saint-Barth ou Lamu ou Phuket ou Lascabanes (Quercy). Je rabâche* mes slogans dans vos magazines favoris et on m'offre un mas provençal*, ou un château périgourdin*, ou une villa corse*, ou une ferme ardéchoise*, ou un palais marocain, ou un

Ciel *Sky;* **nanas** filles; **léchées** *overpolished;* **bagnole** voiture; **démodée** pas à la mode; **nouveauté** nouveaux produits; **neuve** toute nouvelle; **vieillir** *to age;* **baver** *to drool;* **sacerdoce** *calling, vocation;* **consomment** *consume;* **souffrance** *suffering;* **dope** *dopes (like a drug);* **attiser** *to stir up;* **jalousie** *jealousy;* **douleur** *pain;* **inassouvissement** *built-up hunger;* **munitions** *ammunition;* **cible** *target;* **grassement** énormément; **carrosserie** *car body;* **puissance** *power;* **grâce à** *thanks to;* **interromps** *interrupt;* **rabâche** *rehearse;* **mas provençal** maison traditionnelle de Provence; **périgourdin** *from, of Périgord region;* **corse** *from, of Corsica;* **ardéchoise** *from, of Ardèche region*

Essential Instruction

1. Make a copy of the reading for students so that they can write on it noting vocabulary and questions they might have.
2. Play the recording once and ask students what they think the reading is about.
3. Replay the recording stopping at each paragraph to discuss the central idea. Have students answer the **Pendant la lecture** questions as you go along.
4. Ask students to find the places the author refers to on the world map.
5. Put students in small groups to complete the **Stratégie de lecture** grid, p. 605, which forms the basis for a class discussion. In addition, have them discuss **Outils de lecture.**

catamaran antillais, ou un yacht tropézien*. Je Suis Partout. Vous ne m'échapperez* pas. Où que* vous posiez vos yeux, trône ma publicité. Je vous interdis* de vous ennuyer. Je vous empêche de penser. Le terrorisme de la nouveauté me sert à vendre du vide. Demandez à n'importe quel surfeur: pour tenir à la surface, il est indispensable d'avoir un creux* au-dessous. Surfer, c'est glisser sur un trou béant* (les adeptes d'Internet le savent aussi bien que les champions de Lacanau). Je décrète* ce qui est Vrai, ce qui est Beau, ce qui est Bien. Je caste les mannequins (...) À force de les placarder*, vous les baptisez top-models; mes jeunes filles traumatiseront toute femme qui a plus de 14 ans. Vous idolâtrez mes choix. (...) Plus je joue avec votre subconscient, plus vous m'obéissez. Si je vante un yaourt sur les murs de votre ville, je vous garantis que vous allez l'acheter. Vous croyez que vous avez votre libre arbitre*, mais un jour ou l'autre, vous allez reconnaître mon produit dans le rayonnage* d'un supermarché, et vous l'achèterez comme ça juste pour goûter, croyez-moi, je connais mon boulot.

Pendant la lecture

6. Avec quoi le narrateur joue-t-il?

tropézien de Saint-Tropez; **échapper** *to escape;* **Où que** *Wherever;* **interdis** *forbid;* **creux** *hollow;* **béant** *gaping;* **décrète** *decree;* **placarder** *to affix posters;* **le libre arbitre** *free will;* **rayonnage** *shelving*

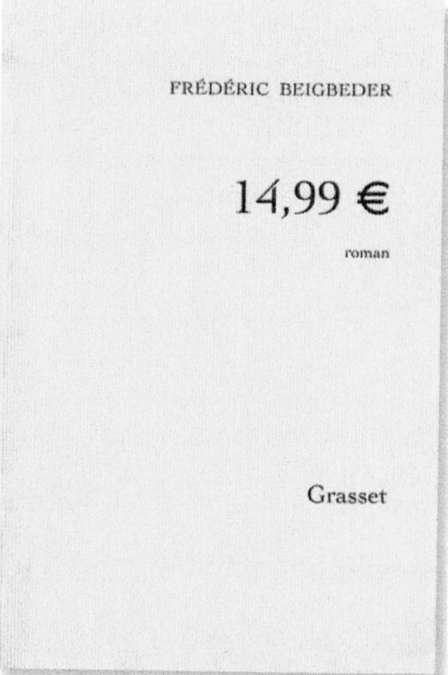

Answers

Pendant la lecture

6. avec le subconscient des consommateurs

Reference Desk

Frédéric Beigbeder, born September 21, 1965 outside of Paris, is a prolific French writer, filmmaker, and literary critic. He won the **Prix Interallié** in 2003 for his novel *Windows on the World* and the **Prix Renaudot** in 2009 for his book ***Un roman français***.

Differentiated Learning

Accelerate

Consider letting your high-ability students read at their own pace and answer the **Pendant la lecture** questions on their own. Encourage them to learn more about Frédéric Beigbeder online.

Decelerate

This is a formidable reading for low-ability learners. They will benefit from paragraph by paragraph explanations.

Multiple Intelligences

Visual-Spatial

Students may enjoy making a collage of the products the author mentions in the readings.

Answers

Post-lecture
Il veut dénoncer le côté inhumain de son travail.

Le monde visuel
Possible answer: Les cheveux de la femme se confondent avec le ciel, lui suggérant un pouvoir surnaturel.

1. *Paragraphs will vary.*
2. *Answers will vary.*
3. *Answers will vary.*
4. *Possible answer:* Je suis le type (...) qui vous fait rêver; J'ai trois vogues d'avance; Vous faire baver*, tel est mon sacerdoce.; on me récompense grassement; Connaissez-vous beaucoup de mecs qui gagnent 13K euros à mon âge?; Vous ne m'échapperez* pas.; Je décrète* ce qui est Vrai, ce qui est Beau, ce qui est Bien.; Vous idolâtrez mes choix.; Plus je joue avec votre subconscient, plus vous m'obéissez.; je vous garantis que vous allez l'acheter; croyez-moi, je connais mon boulot
5. *Answers will vary.*

Critical Thinking

Discussion
Ask students to keep a log for three days about the advertising that they are exposed to. Have them discuss if advertisers are manipulating them psychologically and emotionally. The last time they purchased an "impulse buy," what motivated them? Was it the advertising, special discounted offers, or other factors that won them over?

Post-lecture  1.2

Pourquoi est-ce que le narrateur avoue (*confesses*) le mauvais côté de son travail?

Le monde visuel  1.2, 3.1

Publicité pour Longchamp, 2006. © LEBON/GAMMA.

La publicité a depuis toujours eu une relation privilégiée avec l'art et la photographie. Il arrive que certaines publicités trouvent une place à part entière au sein d'une culture déterminée, et peuvent même en traverser ses frontières; l'un des meilleurs exemples étant les posters de Toulouse-Lautrec. Il arrive que les mêmes techniques de composition propres à la peinture ou à d'autres formes artistiques s'appliquent aussi à la publicité. Pour cette publicité, le photographe a placé le produit sous la meilleure lumière possible puisqu'il est le centre d'attention et ses couleurs ressortent sur le fond neutre. Qu'est-ce que cette photo-publicité a d'artistique?

17 Activités d'expansion  1.3, 5.2

Faites les activités suivantes.

1. Écrivez un paragraphe qui décrit les exemples de tonalité dans la sélection, en vous servant des informations dans votre grille.
2. Discutez pourquoi le protagoniste implique le lecteur/la lectrice dans son histoire. Partagez vos théories avec la classe.
3. Écrivez une lettre au protagoniste dans laquelle vous donnez votre point de vue du consommateur contemporain.
4. Faites une liste de mots et d'expressions qui montrent l'orgueil du narrateur.
5. Faites une publicité pour la radio, la télévision, ou les médias en ligne pour l'un des produits mentionnés dans l'extrait que vous venez de lire.

Essential Instruction

1. Read **Le monde visual** with the students. Ask them to bring in examples of photos used in advertisements that are very esthetic and artistic.
2. Read through the **Activités d'expansion**. Allow students to choose one of them.
3. Review the instructions in **Projets finaux**. Allow students to work with a partner on their chosen project.
4. Create a rubric that outlines your expectations and point values for each section.
5. Have students peer-edit their work before submitting the finished product.

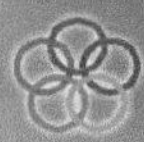

T'es branché?

Projets finaux

A Connexions par Internet: Les affaires

1.3, 3.2

Interpersonal Communication

Vous n'avez pas encore pris la décision de quelle sera votre spécialisation à l'université. Imaginez que vous vous intéressez à une profession dans laquelle vous pouvez travailler dans les affaires et communiquer en français. Recherchez une école d'affaires comme Thunderbird dans l'Arizona qui prépare ses étudiants pour une carrière en affaires et une deuxième langue. Discutez ce que vous avez appris avec des camarades de classe... le prix, les spécialisations, les cours, la formation en France, les stages, etc.

B Communautés en ligne

1.3, 3.2

Une nouvelle idée pour le monde/Presentational Communication

TEDx est une organisation qui facilite des conférences globales où on peut présenter des idées et des inventions. Recherchez le site ci-dessous et décrivez deux ou trois de ces idées/inventions qui vous intéressent. Choisissez celle que vous préférez et présentez-la à la classe. Ou bien, présentez une idée/invention originale.

Search words: tedx paris

C Passez à l'action!

1.3, 2.2, 3.2, 5.2

Le marché français dans notre région/Interpretive/Presentational Communication

Quels sont les liens de votre région avec la France? Recherchez les compagnies françaises dans votre région et les filiales des compagnies américaines en France de votre région. Partagez le travail; vous aurez besoin de camarades de classe qui pourront:

- Téléphoner à la Chamber of Commerce et à la Trade Commission de votre état.
- Contacter le consulat français avec un mail ou une lettre.
- Interviewer des employés des compagnies américaines qui ont une présence en France.
- Ècrire un sommaire de ce que vous avez appris.
- Préparer des graphiques.
- Choisir de la musique pour la présentation.
- Partagez ce que vous avez appris avec un sketch (*skit*), une présentation PowerPoint™, ou un autre produit créateur.

Search words: chamber of commerce, trade commission (+ nom de l'état), consulat français

Answers

All activities will vary.

Communication

Interpersonal: Cooperative Groups

Arrange the class into groups of equally high and low-ability students, and ask them to choose an activity. Have the lower-ability students do the research, and the higher-ability students prepare a response to questions with specific examples. Ask them to share their ideas with other groups.

Differentiated Learning

Accelerate

Encourage students to incorporate **La question centrale** into their **Projets finaux.**

Decelerate

Help students select a project, and give them help strategizing how they are going to do the work. Encourage them to see you when they have a problem.

Special Needs Students

AD(H)D

Divide the **Projets finaux** into manageable tasks to be completed on specific dates, for example, choosing a topic, devising a list of vocabulary and structures to use, conducting research if needed, completing the rough draft, editing, finalizing the presentation, and practicing.

At-Risk Students

The **Projets finaux** is an excellent opportunity for students to select a topic that interests them.

Answers

D *Answers will vary.*

Communication

Interpersonal: Cooperative Groups

Arrange students in high and low-ability groups to do a review of **Unité 10** using the **Activité D** graphic organizer.

D Faisons le point!

1.3

Remplissez les organigrammes pour montrer ce que vous avez appris dans cette unité.

Je comprends	Je ne comprends pas encore	Mes connexions

What did I do well to learn and use the content of this unit?	How can I apply what I have learned this year?
How can I effectively communicate to others what I have learned?	What was the most important concept I learned in this unit?

La compagnie AirFrance à Paris.

La chaîne d'hotels ibis fait partie du groupe français Accor.

Essential Instruction

1. For **Activité D**, distribute copies of the graphic organizer in the **Copy Masters** supplement.
2. Ask students to respond to **Activité A** by writing each response on a whiteboard for you to check.
3. Instruct partners to write a draft for **Activité B** and have them exchange scripts with other pairs for peer-review.
4. Encourage them to ask for any help on pronunciation before practicing and presenting to the class.

Évaluation 

A Évaluation de compréhension auditive

1.1, 1.2

Interpretive Communication
Le travail et l'économie

Écrivez les numéros 1–8 sur votre papier. Écoutez une femme et un homme discuter des métiers des membres de leur famille. Ensuite, écrivez une réponse brève à la question que vous entendez.

B Évaluation orale

1.1

Interpersonal Communication

Avec un partenaire, jouez les rôles d'un(e) étudiant(e) américain(e) qui fait un séjour en France et son ami(e) français(e) qui va l'aider à faire du shopping pour sa mère, son père, et sa sœur. Les parents de l'Américain(e) ont envoyé $350 pour que leur fils ou fille puisse leur acheter des produits de luxe.

Demandez si votre ami(e) américain(e) doit faire du shopping pour toute sa famille.	→ Dites que oui et qu'ils veulent des souvenirs typiquement français.
Demandez si ça fait longtemps que votre ami(e) cherche des cadeaux.	→ Dites que vous avez regardé, mais il semble que tous les bons produits sont fabriqués ailleurs.
Demandez combien votre ami(e) peut dépenser.	→ Dites que vos parents vous ont envoyé $350.
Dites à votre ami(e) de considérer les produits du luxe qui sont fabriqués en France. Demandez si sa sœur aime se maquiller.	→ Dites que oui.
Dites que vous pouvez aller ensemble au grand magasin et acheter des produits de beauté pour elle de la marque Clarins que votre cousine aime beaucoup.	→ Dites que vous êtes d'accord, mais que vous avez besoin de quelque chose pour vos parents aussi.
Dites que votre ami peut leur envoyer du parfum français de Chanel ou de Givenchy.	→ Dites si vous aimez cette idée ou vous avez une meilleure idée.

RESOURCES

Listening Activity
Synthèse

Answers

Script can be found in the front pages of the Annotated Teacher's Edition.

1. chez LVMH.
2. Elle est assistante de la DRH.
3. Oui, car elle aura des avantages pour acheter des produits de marque moins chers.
4. Il voulait s'éloigner de la France.
5. pour Apple
6. Parce qu'il est marié maintenant.
7. dans une PME.
8. Non, en Chine et en Tunisie.

B *Answers will vary.*

Reference Desk

Any of the **Évaluation** activities can be used as an assessment tool. Include additional visual prompts, similar to those in **Activité E**, which are particularly helpful for students with difficulty processing language.

Special Needs Students

AD(H)D/Dyslexia
Take this time to help students with attention difficulties and reading challenges to organize their materials and their time. Work with them to set up a study schedule so that they can get their unit review done in a structured manner.

Auditory Impairment
Use the practice listening test as an opportunity to assess what modifications you can do to help them hear well. Ask them if they would prefer taking the test in a different environment or if they need extra time to process the information in the questions.

At-Risk Students
At this point, some of your students are in danger of failing the class. Express your concern and see if you can help them in any way prepare for the unit test.

Answers

All activities will vary.

Reference Desk

1. **Activités E** and **F** require students to synthesize vocabulary and cultural information, specifically in the domain of business and marketing. Encourage them to review their notes and exercises before they complete these activities.
2. There are many websites that will help students review structure and vocabulary. The website Quizlet allows students and teachers to create review exercises tailored to specific lessons and then to share them with others. The site creates several different online games. This activity will appeal to your techie students.

C Évaluation culturelle

1.3, 2.1, 2.2, 3.1, 3.2, 4.2, 5.1

Vous allez comparer les cultures francophones à votre culture aux États-Unis. Vous aurez peut-être besoin de faire des recherches sur la culture américaine.

1. **La France et la mondialisation**
   Quelles sont les attitudes des Français envers la mondialisation? Faites un sondage de dix adultes américains pour pouvoir comparer les attitudes des deux pays.
2. **L'Industrie du luxe**
   Quel est le pourcentage du marché français pour les produits de luxe? Imaginez qu'on vous donne un coupon pour des produits de luxe qui vaut 4.000 euros. Quels produits de luxe achèteriez-vous? (Cherchez les prix en ligne.) Pouvez-vous trouver des produits similaires en Amérique? Si oui, quelles sont les marques?
3. **La France et la concurrence mondiale**
   Imaginez que vous allez travailler en France et que vous devez prendre beaucoup de décisions quand vous vous installez dans votre appartement. Faites une liste des compagnies dont vous allez vous servir pour ces services: bancaires, pétroliers, informatiques; vous devez aussi acheter une voiture. Faites une liste semblable pour les services dont vous vous servez aux États-Unis pour ces mêmes catégories.
4. **Le commerce entre la France et les États-Unis**
   En regardant la liste de produits que les deux pays échangent, faites une sommaire des secteurs qui sont forts en France et aux États-Unis. Expliquez les similarités et les différences marquantes.
5. **La structure des entreprises**
   Choisissez une compagnie américaine et dites si elle ressemble plutôt au modèle hiérarchique français ou à la coopérative française. Il est possible que la compagnie américaine ne suive ni le modèle hiérarchique ni le modèle coopérative. Dans ce cas, décrivez ce modèle américain.
6. **Les bonnes manières**
   Faites une liste de tabous (*taboos*) à éviter quand vous allez à une réunion, partagez un repas d'affaires, et allez chez un collègue en France. Faites une liste de tabous pour ces mêmes scénarios aux États-Unis.

D Évaluation écrite

1.3

Écrivez un paragraphe qui décrit comment une compagnie américaine s'adapte à la culture d'un pays francophone pour vendre ses produits. Pensez à un produit réel et faites des recherches en ligne pour regarder le site web de la compagnie ou ses publicités dans ce pays.

Essential Instruction

1. For **Activité C**, have students select three of the six activities to do in depth. They are responsible for outlining the information needed to complete the other three tasks.
2. Insist that the students spend at least ten minutes making an outline for **Activité D.** Have them write the composition in class to assure that it is their original work and so that you are on hand to help.
3. Ask students to examine the picture in **Activité E** and write a short story about Méline. Encourage them to use rich descriptions to make the story more interesting.
4. Using a storyboard graphic, have students complete **Activité F.**

E Évaluation visuelle

 1.1

Méline, une chanteuse de musique pop, fait du shopping à sa boutique préférée. Dites ce qu'elle achète et de quelle marque.

F Évaluation compréhensive

 1.3, 3.2

Créez une publicité pour un produit de luxe français qu'on va lancer (launch) *sur le marché américain. D'abord il faut que vous trouviez une stratégie (par exemple,* bandwagon, glittering generalities, celebrity endorsement) *et choisissez un groupe de consommateurs. Finalement, faites un storyboard avec quatre à six séquences.*

Answers

All activities will vary.

Reference Desk

For examples of the marketing strategies discussed in the unit, consider searching for images online of ads for French luxury items. Use these images to reinforce the differences among the strategies and to help students decide how they wish to proceed with **Activité F.**

Special Needs Students

Linguistically Challenged

Help students with language difficulties complete **Activités E** and **F.** Make sure that they know how to make an outline of their ideas before attempting to write.

Multiple Intelligences

Visual-Spatial

Consider having students create several images similar to **Activité E.** Use these for whole-class or partner practice.

RESOURCES

 Listening Pre-test D

 *Unité* Test

Game

Le pendu

Play Hangman to review unit vocabulary. The object is to spell words before the figure of a hanged man takes shape. A student at the board writes a set of broken lines corresponding to the number of letters of a word he or she chooses from the unit's vocabulary. One at a time students try to guess the word by calling out letters. The student at the board writes a letter on the appropriate line if a correct call is made. For each wrong call, he or she draws elsewhere on the board a line that would become part of a hanged man. Drawing begins with a line-by-line sketch of a gallows. The number of lines needed to form the whole image should be predetermined.

Vocabulaire de l'Unité 10  1.2

un(e) **actionnaire** stockholder *B*
l' **adaptation (f.)** adaptation *C*
adapter to adapt, to adjust *C*
s' **adapter (à)** to adapt (to) *C*
administratif, administrative administrative *C*
agroalimentaire food-processing *B*
ajouter to add *A*
anglophone English-speaking *B*
un **arrondissement** district, quarter *B*
un **auditeur, une auditrice libre** auditor of a class *B*
un **B.A.** Bachelor of Arts degree *B*
la **bière** beer *C*
bilingue bilingual *C*
c'est: c'est bien it's/that's exactly *A*
le **Cambodge** Cambodia *A*
le **champagne** champagne *A*
un **chef, une cheffe: chef, cheffe d'entreprise** president *C*
la **Chine** China *A*
cibler to target *C*
la **comptabilité** accounting *C*
le, la **comptable** accountant *C*
un **constructeur, une constructrice automobile** car manufacturer *C*
convenu(e) conventional *A*
la **Corée du Sud** South Korea *A*
un(e) **correspondant(e)** pen pal *A*
la **crème** cream, lotion *A*
découpé(e) (en) cut up (in) *C*
le **directeur, la directrice: directeur, directrice des ressources humaines (DRH)** director of human resources *C*; **directeur financier, directrice financière** C.F.O. *C*
doué(e) talented *C*
égal(e) equal *C*
s' **éloigner (de)** to get away (from)
l' **embarras (m.): avoir l'embarras du choix** to have too many choices *A*
une **éponge** sponge *C*
ethnique ethnic, multicultural *C*
fabriqué(e) (au, aux, en) made (in) *A*
la **faïence** earthenware *A*
faire: faire le tour explore all the possibilities *A*
une **figurine** figurine *A*
une **filiale** branch, subsidiary *B*
le **hasard** fate, luck *B*
la **haute couture** high fashion *A*
le **Honduras** Honduras *A*
l' **imagination (f.)** imagination *A*
l' **Inde (f.)** India *A*
un **individu** individual *B*
l' **Indonésie (f.)** Indonesia *A*
une **interview** interview *B*
le **Japon** Japan *A*
la **joaillerie** fine jewelry *A*
la **Jordanie** Jordan *A*
lancer to launch *B*
un **leader** leader *B*; **leader mondial** world leader *B*
local(e) local *C*
le **luxe** luxury *A*
une **maîtrise** Master's degree *B*
la **Malaisie** Malaysia *A*
le **marketing** marketing *B*
la **maroquinerie** leather goods *A*
une **marque** brand *A*
marqué(e) brand name *A*
le **Mexique** Mexico *A*
la **mondialisation** globalization *C*
multinational(e) multinational *B*
le **papier: papier toilette** toilet paper *C*
la **peau** skin *C*
les **Philippines (f.)** Philippines *A*
prendre: prendre une décision to make a decision *C*
un(e) **président(e): président directeur général (PDG)** CEO *C*
la **production** production *B*
un **produit: produit alimentaire** food product *A*; **produit laitier** dairy product *B*
proposer to offer *C*
régional(e) regional *C*
réserver (pour quelqu'un) to make especially (for someone) *C*
une **responsabilité** responsibility *B*
le, la **responsable** director, manager *C*
les **ressources (f.) humaines** human resources *C*
le **reste** rest *B*
un **rouleau** roll *C*
sans: sans parler de not to mention *C*
le **secrétaire (administratif), la secrétaire (administrative)** secretary *C*
le **secrétariat** reception area *C*
une **serpillière** mop *C*
le **service** department *C*; **service après-vente** post-sale support *C*
un **siège: siège social** headquarters *B*
une **société: Société Anonyme (SA)** public (incorporated) company *B*
le **Sri Lanka** Sri Lanka *A*
des **stratégies (f.)** strategies *B*
tutoyer to use the informal "**tu**" to address someone *B*
typiquement typical of *A*
l' **uniformisation (f.)** standardisation *C*
un **vase** vase *A*
les **ventes (f.)** sales *C*

Essential Instruction

1. Make copies of pp. 614–616 so that students can write notes and ideas on them.
2. Have students skim the questions before reading **Activité I**.
3. Ask them to do the same for **Activité II**. Correct both exercises immediately.
4. Assign **Activité III** to be done in class. Circulate to help with on-the-spot questions they have about their writing.

Unité 10 Bilan cumulatif 

I. Interpretive Communication: Print Text  1.2, 2.1

Lisez cet article sur le patrimoine français, puis répondez à la question.

C'est complètement fou à quel point les Français protègent leur patrimoine. Le gouvernement encourage les français à consommer français, à produire voitures françaises. Il se vante des produits de luxe français tels que la maroquinerie, le parfumerie, le vin, la champagne, et le foie gras. N'oubliez pas la langue! Le gouvernement est contre les mots anglais et invente des mots français pour les remplacer. Le gouvernement exige aussi que les radios françaises passe un minimum de chansons françaises pour préserver la langue et la culture française. De cette façon on ne fait pas partie de la globalisation.

1. D'après le texte que signifie le mot "patrimoine"?
   A. C'est une société matérialiste qui ne consomme que des produits chics et exclusifs.
   B. C'est l'ensemble des produits de luxe d'un pays.
   C. C'est ce qui constitue l'héritage culturel et linguistique d'un pays.
   D. C'est une philosophie née en France.

II. Interpretive Communication: Audio Text  1.1, 1.2

Écoutez le dialogue entre Taylor et son meilleur ami, puis répondez aux questions.

1. Qu'est-ce que cet étudiant américain désire?
   A. Améliorer son français et sa compréhension de la culture française.
   B. Étudier à l'université en France.
   C. Louer un appartement à Paris.
   D. Se marier avec une Française.
2. Quelle est la solution?
   A. Voyager en France avec sa prof de français.
   B. Voyager en France avec son ami.
   C. Trouver un stage dans une compagnie américaine en France.
   D. Faire le touriste.
3. Comment l'ami de Taylor prend-il la nouvelle?
   A. Il est content. Il rêve de faire la même chose.
   B. Il est fâché. Il ne comprend pas la décision que son ami a prise.
   C. Il décide de partir avec lui.
   D. Il se sent attristé de voir partir son ami.

III. Interpersonal Writing: E-mail Reply  1.3, 5.2

Vous allez écrire une réponse à un mail d'un homme d'affaires américain qui s'intéresse à importer des produits de luxe français. Il faut que vous répondiez à des questions sur votre gamme (line) *de produits et aborder les questions de prix et de croissance* (growth)*. Vous vous intéressez à entrer dans le marché américain. Vous voudriez faire la connaissance de l'Américain et propose une date de rendez-vous à Boston. Écrivez formellement et n'oubliez pas d'écrire une salutation au début et une formule de politesse* (closing) *à la fin de votre message.*

RESOURCES

 **Listening Units 9–10**

Answers

1. C

1. A
2. C
3. D

Paragraphs will vary.

Reference Desk

1. The **Bilan cumulative** is based on the French Language and Culture AP exam prepared by the College Board. It assesses students' proficiencies in the Interpersonal, Interpretive, and Presentational modes of communication. Students are also asked to demonstrate their understanding of the products, practices, and perspectives of the target cultures.
2. The Print Text section consists of a variety of authentic print materials such as articles and correspondence. A multiple-choice question follows the text.
3. The Audio Text is a professional recording, usually a dialogue. Encourage students to preview and skim the questions before listening. They should then answer the multiple-choice questions.
4. The E-mail reply is a free response test section. Students develop their interpersonal writing skills.

Differentiated Learning

Accelerate

Allow students to write at their own pace. They may peer edit their work upon completion.

Decelerate

Suggest that students first read the questions then have them cover the reading with a blank piece of paper and uncover the text sentence by sentence. This process helps them focus on the reading a little at a time and not be overwhelmed by the length.

Special Needs Students

Dyslexia/At-Risk Students

Consider modifying your assessment of spelling to ease the pressure students may experience.

Game

Le Jéopardy

Make a Jeopardy board with the headings: **Vocabulaire**, **Expressions**, **Entreprise**, **Publicité**, etc. Have students play the game in teams making questions from the cues you give them. Find Jeopardy game templates online.

Search words: **free flash jeopardy review generator**

Answers

Conversations will vary.

Reference Desk

In the Speaking section of the assessment, students are asked to participate in a conversation or make a cultural comparison using their presentational speaking skills.

De: Thomas Hamilton
Objet: Importation de produits de luxe aux USA

Monsieur,

Je suis à la recherche d'un exportateur français qui veut à son tour devenir partenaire dans la promotion de produits de luxe aux États-Unis. Nous sommes bien placés pour promouvoir les grandes marques en vogue puisque notre boutique et centre de distribution se sont situés dans la banlieue proche de Boston, entourés par un grand nombre de sociétés dans les domaines de technologie, d'assurances, et d'hôtellerie, aussi bien que les associations universitaires. Nos clients veulent à leur tour offrir des cadeaux promotionnels lors des conférences, des évènements, et des réunions. Nous nous intéressons à présenter plusieurs grandes marques sous un seul toit chez nous. Les parfums, les produits de beauté, les montres, les foulards et d'autres accessoires, les vêtements femme, et les fournitures bureau haut de gamme nous conviennent. Le marché est fort, et le secteur rapporte plusieurs milliards de dollars. Nous gardons l'espoir de pouvoir élargir notre territoire bientôt et répondre aux besoins de clients d'un grand nombre de villes américaines.

Pour toutes précisions complémentaires, je vous remercie de me contacter par messagerie électronique.

Veuillez agréer, Monsieur, mes sincères salutations.

Thomas Hamilton, propriétaire
Hamilton Highline Gifts
3400 Longwood Way
Burlington, Massachusetts
USA

IV. Interpersonal Speaking: Conversation

1.1

Vous allez avoir une conversation avec un agent de police au commissariat. Vous êtes touriste en France, et on vous a volé quelque chose d'important. Suivez les indications ci-dessous.

L'agent: Je peux vous aider, Monsieur?
Vous: **Dites ce qu'on vous a volé.**
L'agent: Et où ce vol a-t-il eu lieu?
Vous: **Dites qu'on vous a volé dans le métro en route vers la station Châtelet.**
L'agent: Et vous avez vu le voleur?
Vous: **Dites que oui, et décrivez le voleur: sa taille, son âge, la couleur de ses cheveux, son origine ethnique, ses vêtements.**
L'agent: (Il vous montre une photo.) C'est lui?
Vous: **Dites que vous êtes sûr que c'est lui, mais qu'il a les cheveux plus courts maintenant.**
L'agent: On l'a presque arrêté la semaine dernière. Ses vols sont toujours dans le métro. Comment est-ce qu'on peut vous contacter?
Vous: **Donnez-lui votre numéro de portable.**
L'agent: Auriez-vous le temps de remplir cette déclaration de vol?
Vous: **Dites que vous le remplirez à l'hôtel et que vous reviendrez demain matin.**
L'agent: Merci d'être venu. Je vous reverrai demain, alors.
Vous: **Remerciez l'agent et dites que vous le reverrez demain.**

Essential Instruction

1. Give students time to prepare their oral responses. If possible, allow them to record their work so that they can do it many times until they are pleased with it.
2. Students who have anxiety issues will benefit from not performing in front of the class.

Grammar Summary

The Grammar Summary is in alphabetical order.

Adjectives

Agreement of Regular Adjectives

Masculine	Masculine Plural	Feminine	Feminine Plural
	+ s	**masculine adjective + e**	**masculine adjective + es**
grand	grands	grande	grandes

Exceptions

Masculine	Masculine Plural	Feminine	Feminine Plural
Adjectives ending in **e** bête	**+ s** bêtes	no change bête	**+ s** bêtes
Adjectives ending in **n, l** bon intellectuel	**+ s** bons intellectuels	**double consonant + e** bonne intellectuelle	**double consonant + es** bonnes intellectuelles
Adjectives ending in **s** gros	no change gros	**double consonant + e** grosse	**double consonant + es** grosses
Adjectives ending in **eux** généreux	no change généreux	**-euse** généreuse	**-euses** généreuses

Irregular Adjectives

Masculine	Masculine Before a Vowel	Masculine Plural	Feminine	Feminine Plural
beau	bel	beaux	belle	**+ s**
nouveau	nouvel	nouveaux	nouvelle	
vieux	vieil	vieux	vieille	
frais		} **+ s**	fraîche	
cher			chère	
blanc			blanche	
long			longue	

Invariable Adjectives

Some adjectives do not change in the feminine or the plural form.

orange	marron	super	sympa	bon marché

Position of Adjectives

Article + Noun	+ Adjective
des stylos **bleus**	

Exceptions
beau, joli, nouveau, vieux, bon, mauvais, grand, petit, gros *(BAGS: beauty, age, goodness, size)*

Article + Adjective	+ Noun
une **belle** voiture	

Comparative of Adjectives

plus	(*more*)	**+ adj**	**+ que**	(*than*)
moins	(*less*)	**+ adj**	**+ que**	(*than*)
aussi	(*as*)	**+ adj**	**+ que**	(*as*)

Superlative of Adjectives

For regular adjectives placed after the noun

le/la/les + noun + **le/la/les** + **plus** + adjective

For adjectives placed before the noun

le/la/les + **plus** + adjective + noun

Exception: bon = le/la/les **meilleur**(e)(s)

Interrogative Adjective *quel*

Masculine	Masculine Plural	Feminine	Feminine Plural
quel	quels	quelle	quelles

Adjective *tout*

Masculine	Masculine Plural	Feminine	Feminine Plural
tout	tous	toute	toutes

Demonstrative Adjective

Singular			Plural
Masculine before a Consonant Sound **ce** colis	**Masculine before a Vowel Sound** **cet** aérogramme	**Feminine** **cette** lettre	**ces** livres

Indefinite Adjectives

aucun(e)... ne(n')	*not one, no*
autre	*other*
certain(e)	*certain*
chaque	*each, every*
même	*same*
plusieurs	*several*
quelque	*some*
tout/tous/toute(s)	*all, every*

Possessive Adjectives

Masculine	Feminine	Plural
mon	ma	mes
ton	ta	tes
son	sa	ses
notre	notre	nos
votre	votre	vos
leur	leur	leurs

Adverbs

assez	peut-être
beaucoup	souvent
bien	surtout
déjà	toujours
enfin	trop
mal	un peu
même	vite
peu	

Expressions of Quantity

assez de	une boîte de	une bouteille de
beaucoup de	un paquet de	un pot de
peu de	un morceau de	une tranche de
un peu de	un gramme de	un kilo de
trop de	un litre de	

Formation of Long Adverbs

Long adverbs are formed by adding **-ment** to the feminine form of an adjective.

Feminine Form of Adjective	+ ment
heureuse	heureusement
généreuse	généreusement

Position of Adverbs

Short Adverbs Qualifying Verbs

present tense	*passé composé*
J'aime **beaucoup** les animaux.	Tu as **trop** mangé.

Long Adverbs Qualifying Sentences

Modyfying Verbs	Modyfying Entire Sentence
Tu dessines **parfaitement**.	Nous avons fini, **heureusement**. **Heureusement**, nous avons fini.

Adverbial Expressions of Time

Tu vas à la teuf **demain soir**? **Ce matin**, le prof a apporté des gâteaux.

Comparative of Adverbs

plus	(*more*)	**+ adverb**	**+ que**	(*than*)
moins	(*less*)	**+ adverb**	**+ que**	(*than*)
aussi	(*as*)	**+ adverb**	**+ que**	(*as*)

Some adverbs have an irregular form:

Adverb	Comparative
bien (*well*)	**mieux** (*better*)
beaucoup (*a lot, much*)	**plus** (*more*)
peu (*little*)	**moins** (*less*)
mal (*badly*)	**pire, plus mal** (*worse*)

Superlative of Adverbs

For regular adjectives placed after the noun

le + **plus** + adverb

To form the superlative of **bien**, **beaucoup** and **peu**, put **le** before these adverbs' irregular comparative forms.

Adverb	Comparative	Superlative
bien *(well)*	**mieux** *(better)*	**le mieux** *(the best)*
beaucoup *(a lot, much)*	**plus** *(more)*	**le plus** *(the most)*
peu *(little)*	**moins** *(less)*	**le moins** *(the least)*
mal *(badly)*	**pire, plus mal** *(worse)*	**le pire, le plus mal** *(the worst)*

Articles

Indefinite Articles

<table>
<tr><th colspan="2">Singular</th><th>Plural</th></tr>
<tr><th>Masculine</th><th>Feminine</th><td rowspan="2">des</td></tr>
<tr><td>un</td><td>une</td></tr>
</table>

Definite Articles

<table>
<tr><th colspan="3">Singular</th><th>Plural</th></tr>
<tr><th colspan="2">Before a Consonant Sound</th><th rowspan="2">Before a Vowel Sound</th><td rowspan="3">les</td></tr>
<tr><th>Masculine</th><th>Feminine</th></tr>
<tr><td>le</td><td>la</td><td>l'</td></tr>
</table>

À + Definite Articles

<table>
<tr><th colspan="3">Singular</th><th>Plural</th></tr>
<tr><th colspan="2">Before a Consonant Sound</th><th rowspan="2">Before a Vowel Sound</th><td rowspan="3">aux</td></tr>
<tr><th>Masculine</th><th>Feminine</th></tr>
<tr><td>au</td><td>à la</td><td>à l'</td></tr>
</table>

De + Definite Articles

<table>
<tr><th colspan="3">Singular</th><th>Plural</th></tr>
<tr><th colspan="2">Before a Consonant Sound</th><th rowspan="2">Before a Vowel Sound</th><td rowspan="3">des</td></tr>
<tr><th>Masculine</th><th>Feminine</th></tr>
<tr><td>du</td><td>de la</td><td>de l'</td></tr>
<tr><th colspan="4">In the negative</th></tr>
<tr><td colspan="4">de</td></tr>
</table>

Partitive Articles

<table>
<tr><th colspan="2">Before a Consonant Sound</th><th>Before a Vowel Sound</th><th>In the Negative</th></tr>
<tr><th>Masculine</th><th>Feminine</th><td rowspan="2">de l'eau minérale</td><td rowspan="2">pas de coca
pas de viande
pas d'eau minérale</td></tr>
<tr><td>du coca</td><td>de la viande</td></tr>
</table>

C'est vs. il/elle est

c'est	vs.	ce n'est pas
C'est un ballon de foot.		Ce n'est pas un gâteau.
c'est	**vs.**	**il/elle est**
C'est un garçon. C'est une fille.		Il s'appelle Karim. Elle s'appelle Amélie.
ce sont	**vs.**	**ils/elles sont**
Ce sont des étudiants. Ce sont des étudiantes.		Ils sont sportifs. Elles sont sympa.

Negation

ne (n')… pas	Il **ne** joue **pas**. Il **n'**a **pas** joué.
ne (n')… plus	Elle **n'**aime **plus** les frites.
ne (n')… jamais	Nous **ne** dansons **jamais**.
ne (n')… personne	Vous **n'**invitez **personne**?
ne (n')…que	Ils **ne** mangent **que** des pâtes.
ne (n')… rien	Ma grand-mère **ne** comprend **rien**.
ne … ni … ni	On **ne** joue **ni** au foot **ni** au tennis.

Nouns

Irregular Plural Nouns

	Singular	Plural
no change	un bus	des bus
-al → **aux**	un cheval	des chev**aux**
-eu → **eux**	un jeu	des jeu**x**
-eau → **eaux**	un bateau	des bat**eaux**

Numbers

Cardinal Numbers	Ordinal Numbers
un	premier, premiēre
deux	deuxième
trois	troisième
quatre	quatrième
cinq	cinquième
six	sixième
sept	septième
huit	huitième
neuf	neuvième
dix, etc.	dixième, etc.

Prepositions

Prepositions before Cities, Countries, Continents

City (no article)	Masculine (le Japon)	Feminine (la France)	Plural (les États-Unis)
à	au	en	aux

Pronouns

Subject Pronouns

Singular	Plural
je	nous
tu	vous
il/elle/on	ils/elles

Direct Object Pronouns

Singular	Plural
me	nous
te	vous
le, la, l'	les

Indirect Object Pronouns

Singular	Plural
me	nous
te	vous
lui	leur

The Pronoun *en*

***en* replaces…**	
de + Noun	Tu manges du pain? Oui, j'en mange. Prenez de la viande! Prenez-en!
de + Noun after Expression of Quantity	Vous voulez un peu de café? Oui, j'en veux un peu. Il a apporté trois assiettes? Oui, il en a apporté trois.

The Pronoun *y*

y replaces...	
preposition + place	Ma grand-mère habite en Arizona. Ma grand-mère **y** habite.
certain verbs such as **penser à, réfléchir à** + thing	Je pense toujours aux falaises de Normandie. J'**y** pense toujours.

Order of Double Object Pronouns

Subject	+	**me** **te** **nous** **vous** **se**	+	**la** **les**	+	**lui** **leur**	+	**y**	+	**en**	+	Verb

In affirmative command, the order of pronouns is:

Verb	+	**le** **la** **l'** **les**	+	**lui** **leur**	+	**me** **toi** **nous** **vous**	+	**y**	+	**en**

Stress Pronouns

Singular	Plural
moi	nous
toi	vous
lui, elle	eux, elles

Possessive Pronouns

	Singular		Plural	
	Masculine	Feminine	Masculine	Feminine
mine	**le mien**	**la mienne**	**les miens**	**les miennes**
yours	**le tien**	**la tienne**	**les tiens**	**les tiennes**
his, hers, its, one's	**le sien**	**la sienne**	**les siens**	**les siennes**
ours	**le nôtre**	**la nôtre**	**les nôtres**	
yours	**le vôtre**	**la vôtre**	**les vôtres**	
theirs	**le leur**	**la leur**	**les leurs**	

Interrogative Pronouns

	Subject	Direct Object	Object of Preposition
People	qui qui est-ce qui	qui qui est-ce que	qui
Things	qu'est-ce qui	que qu' estj-ce-que	quoi

Interrogative Pronoun *lequel*

Masculine	Masculine Plural	Feminine	Feminine Plural
lequel	lesquels	laquelle	lesquelles

Relative Pronouns *qui* and *que*

	Subject	Object
People	qui l'homme qui parle	que le pull que je porte
Things	qui la prof qui est française	que le garçon que je connais

Relative Pronoun *dont*

dont = **de** + noun

Relative Pronouns *ce qui* and *ce que*

	Subject	Object
Things	**ce qui** J'aime **ce qui** est beau.	**ce que** Tu comprends **ce que** tu lis?

Demonstrative Pronouns

	Singular	Plural
Masculine	celui	ceux
Feminine	celle	celles

Indefinite Pronouns

aucun(e)... ne(n')	not one
un(e) autre	another
la plupart	most
plusieurs	several
quelqu'un	someone, somebody
quelque chose	something
tous les deux	both

Questions

Forming Questions

using **n'est-ce-pas**	Il fait chaud, **n'est-ce pas**? Ils regardent un DVD, **n'est-ce pas**?
using **est-ce que**	**Est-ce qu'**il fait chaud? **Est-ce qu'**ils regardent un DVD?
using **inversion:** Verb-Subject	**Fait-il** chaud? **Regardent-ils** un DVD?

Telling Time

Il est une **heure** Il est midi. Il est minuit.	...et quart.	...et demie.	...moins le quart.

Verbs

Regular Verbs—Present Tense

	-er **aimer**		
j'	aim**e**	nous	aim**ons**
tu	aim**es**	vous	aim**ez**
il/elle/on	aim**e**	ils/elles	aim**ent**

-ir finir			
je	fin**is**	nous	fin**issons**
tu	fin**is**	vous	fin**issez**
il/elle/on	fin**it**	ils/elles	fin**issent**

-re vendre			
je	vend**s**	nous	vend**ons**
tu	vend**s**	vous	vend**ez**
il/elle/on	vend	ils/elles	vend**ent**

Irregular Verbs—Present Tense

acheter			
j'	ach**è**te	nous	achetons
tu	ach**è**tes	vous	achetez
il/elle/on	ach**è**te	ils/elles	ach**è**tent

aller			
je	vais	nous	allons
tu	vas	vous	allez
il/elle/on	va	ils/elles	vont

avoir (avoir besoin de/avoir chaud/avoir faim/avoir froid/avoir soif)			
j'	ai	nous	avons
tu	as	vous	avez
il/elle/on	a	ils/elles	ont

boire			
je	bois	nous	buvons
tu	bois	vous	buvez
il/elle/on	boit	ils/elles	boivent

conduire			
je	conduis	nous	conduisons
tu	conduis	vous	conduisez
il/elle/on	conduit	ils/elles	conduisent

connaître			
je	connais	nous	connaissons
tu	connais	vous	connaissez
il/elle/on	connaît	ils/elles	connaissent

courir	
je cours	nous courons
tu cours	vous courez
il/elle/on court	ils/elles courent

croire	
je crois	nous croyons
tu crois	vous croyez
il/elle/on croit	ils/elles croient

devoir			
je	dois	nous	devons
tu	dois	vous	devez
il/elle/on	doit	ils/elles	doivent

dire	
je dis	nous disons
tu dis	vous dites
il/elle/on dit	ils/elles disent

dormir			
je	dors	nous	dormons
tu	dors	vous	dormez
il/elle/on	dort	ils/elles	dorment

écrire			
j'	écris	nous	écrivons
tu	écris	vous	écrivez
il/elle/on	écrit	ils/elles	écrivent

Irregular Verbs—Present Tense *continued*

être			
je	suis	nous	sommes
tu	es	vous	êtes
il/elle/on	est	ils/elles	sont

faire			
je	fais	nous	faisons
tu	fais	vous	faites
il/elle/on	fait	ils/elles	font

falloir
il faut

lire			
je	lis	nous	lisons
tu	lis	vous	lisez
il/elle/on	lis	ils/elles	lisent

mettre			
je	mets	nous	mettons
tu	mets	vous	mettez
il/elle/on	met	ils/elles	mettent

offrir			
j'	offre	nous	offrons
tu	offres	vous	offrez
il/elle/on	offre	ils/elles	offrent

ouvrir			
j'	ouvre	nous	ouvrons
tu	ouvres	vous	ouvrez
il/elle/on	ouvre	ils/elles	ouvrent

partir			
je	pars	nous	partons
tu	pars	vous	partez
il/elle/on	part	ils/elles	partent

plaire	
je plais	nous plaisons
tu plais	vous plaisez
il/elle/on plaît	ils/elles plaisent

pouvoir			
je	peux	nous	pouvons
tu	peux	vous	pouvez
il/elle/on	peut	ils/elles	peuvent

préférer			
je	préf**è**re	nous	préférons
tu	préf**è**res	vous	préférez
il/elle/on	préf**è**re	ils/elles	préf**è**rent

prendre			
je	prends	nous	prenons
tu	prends	vous	prenez
il/elle/on	prend	ils/elles	prennent

recevoir			
je	reçois	nous	recevons
tu	reçois	vous	recevez
il/elle/on	reçoit	ils/elles	reçoivent

savoir			
je	sais	nous	savons
tu	sais	vous	savez
il/elle/on	sait	ils/elles	savent

Irregular Verbs—Present Tense *continued*

sortir			
je	sors	nous	sortons
tu	sors	vous	sortez
il/elle/on	sort	ils/elles	sortent

vivre			
je	vis	nous	vivons
tu	vis	vous	vivez
il/elle/on	vit	ils/elles	vivent

suivre			
je	suis	nous	suivons
tu	suis	vous	suivez
il/elle/on	suit	ils/elles	suivent

voir			
je	vois	nous	voyons
tu	vois	vous	voyez
il/elle/on	voit	ils/elles	voient

venir			
je	viens	nous	venons
tu	viens	vous	venez
il/elle/on	vient	ils/elles	viennent

vouloir			
je	veux	nous	voulons
tu	veux	vous	voulez
il/elle/on	veut	ils/elles	veulent

Regular Imperatives

-er chanter	-ir choisir	-re pendre
Chante! Chantons! Chantez!	Choisis! Choisissons! Choisissez!	Prends! Prenons! Prenez!

Reflexive Verbs—Present Tense

se préparer	
je **me** prépare	nous **nous** préparons
tu **te** prépares	vous **vous** préparez
il/elle/on **se** prépare	ils/elles **se** préparent

Imperative of Reflexive Verbs

s'asseoir
Assieds-toi! Asseyons-nous! Asseyez-vous!

Expressing the Near Future

aller + Infinitive
Nous allons dîner.

Passé composé with *avoir*

avoir + past participle

-er verbs → é	-ir verbs → i	-re verbs → u
Nous avons gagné.	Tu as fini.	On a attendu.

Irregular Past Participles		
avoir—**eu**	boire—**bu**	conduire—**conduit**
connaître—**connu**	courir—**couru**	croire—**cru**
devoir—**dû**	dire—**dit**	écrire—**écrit**
être—**été**	faire—**fait**	falloir—**fallu**
lire—**lu**	mettre—**mis**	offrir—**offert**
ouvrir—**ouvert**	pleuvoir—**plu**	pouvoir—**pu**
prendre—**pris**	recevoir—**reçu**	savoir—**su**
suivre—**suivi**	vivre—**vécu**	voir—**vu**
vouloir—**voulu**		

Passé composé with *être*

Some of the verbs that use **être** as the helping verb in the **passé composé** are:

Infinitive	Past Participle
aller	**allé**
arriver	**arrivé**
descendre	**descendu**
devenir	**devenu**
entrer	**entré**
monter	**monté**
partir	**parti**
rentrer	**rentré**
rester	**resté**
retourner	**retourné**
revenir	**revenu**
sortir	**sorti**
vendre	**vendu**
venir	**venu**

Passé composé of Reflexive Verbs

se préparer	
je **me** suis couché(e)	nous **nous** sommes couché(e)s
tu **t'**es couché(e)	vous **vous** êtes couché(e)s
il **s'**est couché	ils **se** sont couchés
elle **s'**est couchée	elles **se** sont couchées
on **s'**est couché	

Present Participle

Verb	Present Participle
aller	allant
attendre	attendant
faire	faisant
finir	finissant
partir	partant

Some verbs have irregular present participles.

Verb	Present Participle
avoir	ayant
être	étant
savoir	sachant

Imperfect Tense

aller	
j'all**ais**	nous all**ions**
tu all**ais**	vous all**iez**
il/ elle/on all**ait**	ils/ elles/ all**aient**

Pluperfect Tense

	finir	rentrer
je (j')	**avais fini**	**étais rentré(e)**
tu	**avais fini**	**étais rentré(e)**
il/elle	**avait fini**	**était rentré(e)**
nous	**avions fini**	**étions rentré(e)s**
vous	**aviez fini**	**étiez rentré(e)(s)**
ils/elles	**avaient fini**	**étaient rentré(e)s**

Future Tense

finir	
je fini**rai**	nous fini**rons**
tu fini**ras**	vous fini**rez**
il/ elle/on fini**ra**	ils/ elles fini**ront**

Conditional Tense

choisir	
je choisi**rais**	nous choisi**rions**
tu choisi**rais**	vous choisi**riez**
il/ elle/on choisi**rait**	ils/ elles choisi**raient**

Past Conditional Tense

	mettre	**rentrer**	**se lever**
je (j')	**aurais mis**	**serais allé(e)**	**me serais levé(e)**
tu	**aurais mis**	**serais allé(e)**	**te serais levé(e)**
il/elle	**aurait mis**	**serait allé(e)**	**se serait levé(e)**
nous	**aurions mis**	**serions allé(e)s**	**nous serions levé(e)s**
vous	**auriez mis**	**seriez allé(e)(s)**	**vous seriez levé(e)(s)**
ils/elles	**auraient mis**	**seraient allé(e)s**	**se seraient levé(e)s**

Irregular Stems of Verbs in Future and Conditional Tense

Infinitive—Irregular stem		
aller—**ir**	s'asseoir—**assiér**	avoir—**aur**
courir—**courr**	devoir—**devr**	envoyer—**enverr**
être—**ser**	faire—**fer**	falloir—**faudr**
pleuvoir—**pleuvr**	pouvoir—**pourr**	recevoir—**recevr**
savoir—**saur**	venir—**viendr**	voir—**verr**
vouloir—**voudr**		

Future Tense after *quand*

quand + future	future

Future or Conditional Tense with *si*

si	+	present	future
si	+	imperfect	conditional
si	+	pluperfect	past conditional

Subjunctive of Regular Verbs

	tenter	**finir**	**attendre**
que je (j')	tent**e**	finiss**e**	attend**e**
que tu	tent**es**	finiss**es**	attend**es**
qu'il/elle	tent**e**	finiss**e**	attend**e**
que nous	tent**ions**	finiss**ions**	attend**ions**
que vous	tent**iez**	finiss**iez**	attend**iez**
qu'ils/elles	tent**ent**	finiss**ent**	attend**ent**

Subjunctive of Irregular Verbs

	aller	avoir	boire	croire	devoir
que je (j')	aill**e**	ai**e**	boiv**e**	croi**e**	doiv**e**
que tu	aill**es**	ai**es**	boiv**es**	croi**es**	doiv**es**
qu'il/elle	aill**e**	ai**t**	boiv**e**	croi**e**	doiv**e**
que nous	all**ions**	**ayons**	**buvions**	**croyions**	**devions**
que vous	all**iez**	**ayez**	**buviez**	**croyiez**	**deviez**
qu'ils/elles	aill**ent**	ai**ent**	boiv**ent**	croi**ent**	doiv**ent**

	être	faire	pouvoir	prendre	recevoir
que je (j')	soi**e**	fass**e**	puiss**e**	prenn**e**	reçoiv**e**
que tu	soi**es**	fass**es**	puiss**es**	prenn**es**	reçoiv**es**
qu'il/elle	soi**t**	fass**e**	puiss**e**	prenn**e**	reçoiv**e**
que nous	**soyons**	fass**ions**	puiss**ions**	**prenions**	**recevions**
que vous	**soyez**	fass**iez**	puiss**iez**	**preniez**	**receviez**
qu'ils/elles	soi**ent**	fass**ent**	puiss**ent**	prenn**ent**	reçoiv**ent**

	savoir	venir	voir	vouloir
que je (j')	sach**e**	vienn**e**	voi**e**	veuill**e**
que tu	sach**es**	vienn**es**	voi**es**	veuill**es**
qu'il/elle	sach**e**	vienn**e**	voi**t**	veuill**e**
que nous	sach**ions**	**venions**	**voyions**	voul**ions**
que vous	sach**iez**	**veniez**	**voyiez**	voul**iez**
qu'ils/elles	sach**ent**	vienn**ent**	voi**ent**	veuill**ent**

The Subjunctive after Impersonal Expressions

il est bon que	*it is necessary that*
il est essentiel que	*it is essential that*
il faut que	*it is necessary that*
il est important que	*it is important that*
il est impossible que	*it is impossible that*
il est indispensable que	*it is indispensable that*
il est nécessaire que	*it is necessary that*
il est possible que	*it is possible that*
il est surprenant que	*it is surprising that*
il est utile que	*it is useful that*
il se pourrait que	*it is possible that*
il vaut mieux que	*it is better that*

Other Expressions Requiring the Use of the Subjunctive

Expressions of Wish, Will, or Desire	Expressions of Emotions	
aimer que *to like, to love*	**être content(e) que** *to be happy that*	**avoir peur que** *to be afraid that*
desirer que *to want*	**être heureux/heureuse que** *to be happy that*	**regretter que** *to regret that*
exiger que *to require*	**être triste que** *to be sad that*	**s'inquiéter que** *to be worried that*
préférer que *to prefer*	**être désolé(e) que** *to be sorry that*	**Ça me surprend que…** *It surprises me that…*
souhaiter que *to wish, to hope*	**être fâché(e) que** *to be angry that*	**Ça m'embête que…** *It bothers me that…*
vouloir que *to want*	**être étonné(e) que** *to be surprised that*	**C'est dommage que…** *It's too bad that…*

Expressions of Doubt or Uncertainty		
(ne pas) penser que *to not think that*	Je **ne** pense **pas** qu'il **soit** français. *I don't think that he is French.*	**Penses-tu que** nous **ayons** assez d'argent? *Do you think we have enough money?*
(ne pas) croire que *to not believe that*	Elle **ne** croit **pas** que vous **partiez**. *She doesn't believe that you are leaving.*	**Croyez-vous qu'**il **fasse** beau demain? *Do you believe it will be nice tomorrow?*
(ne pas) être sûr que *to not be sure that*	Je **ne** suis **pas** sûr que ce **soit** vrai. *I am not sure this is true.*	**Êtes-vous sûr que** ce **soient** des chats? *Are you sure these are cats?*
(ne pas) être vrai que *to not be true that*	**Ce n'est pas vrai que** Mel **comprenne**. *It is not true that Mel understands.*	**Est-il vrai que** tes cousins **partent**? *Is it true that your cousins are leaving?*
(ne pas) être évident que *to not be obvious that*	**Il n'est pas évident que** nous **restions**. *It is not obvious that we'll stay.*	**Est-il évident que** nous **soyons** jumeaux? *Is it obvious that we are twins?*

Subjunctive after *pour que*

pour que + subjunctive	Je nourris les chevaux **pour qu'**ils **soient** forts. *I feed the horses so they be strong.*

Verbs + Infinitives

aimer	aller	désirer
devoir	falloir	pouvoir
préférer	venir	vouloir
Nous préférons faire du ski.		

Verbs + *à* + Infinitives

aider	s'amuser	apprendre
commencer	continuer	s'engager
hésiter	s'intéresser	inviter
se préparer	réussir	

Verbs + *de* + Infinitives

accepter	arrêter	choisir
conseiller	décider	demander
se dépêcher	dire	essayer
finir	offrir	oublier
promettre	rêver	

Past Infinitive

après	+	**avoir** **être**	+	past participle

Vocabulaire

Vocabulary terms from Level 1 and Level 2 of *T'es branché?* are included but do not have a unit number. Vocabulary terms from Level 3 include the unit number in which the term is introduced.

Français-Anglais

A

à at; in; on; to; *à bicyclette* on a bicycle; *À bientôt.* See you soon.; *à bord* on board; *à carreaux* plaid 9; *à cause de* because of 2; *à côté (de)* beside, next to; *À demain.* See you tomorrow.; *à droite* on the right; *à gauche* on the left; *à la fois* at the same time; *à la page* in fashion 2; *à l'arrière-plan (m.)* in the background 7; *à la télé* on TV; *à l'heure* on time; *à l'horizon* on the horizon; *à mi-temps* half-time 8; *à mon avis* in my opinion; *à mon goût* for my taste 5; *à part* aside from 9; *à pied* on foot; *à plein temps* full-time 8; *à pois* polka dots 9; *à propos de* about 2; *à rayures* striped 9; *à roulettes* on wheels; *à sa place* in its place 2; *à table* at the (dinner) table 2; *à vélo* by bike

abandonner to abandon 4
absolument absolutely 1
abstrait(e) abstract
accablé(e) overwhelmed 9
accéder to access 8
un **accélérateur** accelerator
un **accent** accent
accepter to accept
un **accessoire** accessory
un **accident** accident
un **accompagnateur, une accompagnatrice** home health worker
accompagner to accompany
un **accord** agreement 1; *mettre d'accord* to get people to agree 1
accorder to grant 8
un **accra de morue** cod fritter
accrocher to hang 3
un **accueil** welcome; *un centre d'accueil* reception center, shelter
accueil home page 5
accueillir to welcome 2
un **achat** purchase
acheter to buy
acquis(e) acquired 8
un **acteur, une actrice** actor
une **action** action 5; *l'action (f.)* action; *l'Action de grâce (f.)* Thanksgiving; *un film d'action* action movie
un(e) **actionnaire** stockholder 10
une **activité** activity
une **adaptation** adaptation 10
adapter to adapt, to adjust 10
s' **adapter (à)** to adapt (to) 10
l' **addition (f.)** bill
adieu farewell 8; *faire ses adieux* to bid farewell 8
administratif, administrative administrative 10
un(e) **adolescent(e)** teenager
adorer to adore
une **adresse** address; *un jeu d'adresse* game of skill
adressé (à) addressed (to) 5
s' **adresser (à)** to address (someone) 2
l' **aérobic (m.)** aerobics
un **aérogramme** air letter 6
aéronautique: le secteur aéronautique aviation industry
un **aéroport** airport
des **affaires (f.)** belongings, things; *les affaires (f.)* business 5; *affaires de ménage* house cleaning items; *affaires de toilette* toiletries; *un centre d'affaires* business center 5
affectueusement affectionately, with warm regards
une **affiche** poster
affolé(e) distraught 1; *être affolé(e)* to panic 1
affranchir to stamp 6
l' **affranchissement (m.)** postage 6
africain(e) African 9
l' **Afrique (f.)** Africa
agacer to annoy; *Tu m'agaces!* You're getting on my nerves!
l' **âge (m.)** age; *Tu as quel âge?* How old are you?
un(e) **agent(e)** agent; *agent de police* police officer
agir to act
s' **agir (de): il s'agit de** it's about
un **agneau** lamb
agréable pleasant 5
l' **agriculture (f.)** agriculture
agroalimentaire food-processing 10; *le secteur agroalimentaire* food industry
ah oh
l' **aide (f.)** assistance
aider to help
un(e) **aïeul(e)** ancestor 3
aimer to like, to love
l' **air (m.)** air; *avoir l'air* to look; *avoir l'air de* to seem like 1; *en plein air* outdoors
ajouter to add 10
un **album** album; *album concept* concept album 7
l' **alcoolisme (m.)** alcoholism
algérien(ne) Algerian
alimentaire food 10; *un produit alimentaire* food product 10
l' **Allemagne (f.)** Germany
l' **allemand (m.)** German *[language]*
allemand(e) German
aller to go; *je m'en vais* I'm going 2; *Tu trouves que... me va bien?* Does this... look good on me?; *Vas-y!* Go for it!
une **alliance** wedding ring 1
allô hello *[on telephone]*
alors so, then
l' **Alsace (f.)** Alsace region
alsacien(ne) from, of Alsace region
l' **aluminium (m.)** aluminum; *en aluminium* made of aluminum
une **amande** almond
une **ambiance** ambiance; atmosphere; *chaude ambiance* exciting/fun night
américain(e) American
amérindien(ne) Amerindian
l' **Amérique (f.): Amérique du Nord** North America; *Amérique du Sud* South America
un(e) **ami(e)** friend
l' **amour (m.)** love
un **amoureux, une amoureuse (de)** lover (of)
amoureux, amoureuse in love 6; *être amoureux/ amoureuse (de)* to be in love (with) 6
amusant(e) funny
amuser to amuse
s' **amuser** to have fun
un **an** year; *le Jour de l'an* New Year's Day
un **ananas** pineapple; *ananas montagne* mountain pineapple

un(e) **ancêtre** ancestor 3
ancien(ne) old 3
une **anecdote** anecdote 8
l' **anglais (m.)** English *[language]*
anglais(e) English
l' **Angleterre (f.)** England
anglophone English-speaking 10
un **animal** animal; *les animaux en voie de disparition* endangered species
un **animateur, une animatrice** TV host
animé(e): un dessin animé cartoon
une **année** year; *d'une cinquantaine d'années* in one's fifties 9; *d'une quarantaine d'années* in one's forties 9; *d'une trentaine d'années* in one's thirties 9; *d'une vingtaine d'années* in one's twenties 9; *en première année* in the first year
annexer to annex
un **anniversaire** birthday; *anniversaire de mariage* wedding anniversary
une **annonce** advertisement 8; *une petite annonce* want ad 8
annoncer to announce
un **anoli** anole
anonyme anonymous 10; *une Société Anonyme (SA)* public (incorporated) company 10
une **anthologie** anthology 6
les **Antilles (f.)** West Indies
un **anti-moustique** insect repellent
des **antirétroviraux (m.)** antiretroviral drugs
l' **antisémitisme (m.)** anti-Semitism
août August
l' **apartheid (m.)** Apartheid
s' **apercevoir (de)** to notice 9
un **apéritif** drink and food offered before the meal 2
un **appareil** camera, device; machine 6
un **appartement** apartment
appeler to call
s' **appeler** to be called
une **appli (application)** app (application)
appliquer to apply 7
apporter to bring
apprécier to like 5
apprendre to learn; to teach
s' **approcher** to come closer 9
appuyer to push
après after
l' **après-midi (m.)** afternoon
l' **après-vente (m.): un service après-vente** post-sale support 10
un **aquaparc** water park 1
arabe Arab
l' **argent (m.)** money; silver; *argent liquide* cash 6; *en argent* made of silver
l' **argot (m.)** slang 9
un(e) **aristocrate** aristocrat 8
une **armoire** wardrobe
arrêter to stop; *se faire arrêter* to get arrested 9
s' **arrêter** to stop
une **arrière-grand-mère** great-grandmother 3
un **arrière-grand-père** great-grandfather 3
l' **arrière-pays (m.)** back country
un **arrière-plan** background 7; *à l'arrière-plan* in the background 7
une **arrivée** arrival
arriver to arrive; to happen 9; *arriver (à)* to be able to; *arriver à faire quelque chose* to bring oneself to do something 6
un **arrondissement** district, quarter 10
arroser to water
l' **art (m.)** art; *les arts plastiques (m.)* visual arts; *un objet d'art* art object
un **article** magazine, newspaper article
artifice: un feu d'artifice firework
un(e) **artiste** artist
un **ascenseur** elevator 5
asiatique Asian 9
l' **Asie (f.)** Asia
un **aspirateur** vacuum cleaner; *passer l'aspirateur* to vacuum
s' **asseoir** to sit down
assez rather 6; *assez (de)* enough (of)
une **assiette** plate
assis(e) sitting
un(e) **assistant(e)** assistant 8
assister (à) to attend 1
une **assurance** insurance 8; *assurance maladie* health insurance 8
un **atelier** studio 7
un(e) **athlète** athlete
l' **athlétisme (m.)** athletics 2
attachant(e) likeable
attendre to expect (baby); to wait (for)
s' **attendre (à)** to expect (something) 4
Attention! Be careful!, Watch out!
atterrir to land
attractions: un parc d'attractions amusement park
attristé(e) sad 9
au in (the), on (the); to (the); with; *au bord de la mer* at the seaside; *au bout de* at the end of; *au chocolat* with chocolate; *au contraire* on the contrary 8; *au cours de* during, in the course of 8; *au-dessus de* above; *au fait* by the way; *au fond de* at the end of; *au moins* at least; *au premier plan* in the foreground; *Au revoir.* Good-bye.; *au secours* help; *au sucre* with sugar; *être au courant* to be informed, to know
l' **aube (f.)** dawn 7
une **auberge de jeunesse** youth hostel
une **aubergine** eggplant
aucun(e) any, none, no one 4; *aucun de nous ne (+ verb)* none of us (+ verb) 4; *ne (n')... aucun(e)* no, none, not any, not one 4; *sans aucun doute* without a doubt 4
un **auditeur, une auditrice libre** auditor of a class 10
aujourd'hui today
auparavant before 9
auquel, auquelle to which 5
aussi also, too; as; *aussi (+ adverb) que* as... as
aussitôt que as soon as 1
l' **Australie (f.)** Australia
un **auteur** author 7
une **autobiographie** autobiography 6
une **auto (automobile)** car; *auto tamponneuse* bumper car; *un constructeur, une constructrice automobile* car manufacturer 10; *un(e) designer automobile* automotive designer
un **autobus** bus; *en autobus* by bus
un(e) **autochtone** native
l' **automne (m.)** autumn
un **autoportrait** auto-portrait
une **autorisation** permit 6
autour de around 2
autre other; *l'un(e)... l'autre* the one... the other 9
autrefois formerly, in the past
autrement otherwise
aux at (the), in (the), to (the)
avance: en avance early
avancer: pour t'avancer to help you 2
s' **avancer (vers)** to move (toward)
avant before
avec with
l' **avenir (m.)** future
une **aventure** adventure; *le tourisme d'aventure* adventure tourism; *un film d'aventures* adventure movie
une **avenue** avenue
un **aveu** confession 7

un **avion** plane; *en avion* by plane
un **avis** opinion; *à mon avis* in my opinion
un(e) **avocat(e)** lawyer; *un cabinet d'avocats* law firm 1
avoir to have; *avoir... an(s)* to be... year(s) old; *avoir beau [inform.]* to do (something) in vain 8; *avoir besoin de* to need; *avoir bonne mine* to look healthy; *avoir chaud* to be hot; *avoir confiance* to trust; *avoir de la chance* to be lucky; *avoir droit à* to be entitled to 8; *avoir envie de* to feel like, to want; *avoir faim* to be hungry; *avoir froid* to be cold; *avoir hâte de* to be eager; *avoir horreur de* to hate; *avoir la chance (de)* to have the opportunity (to) 2; *avoir l'air* to look; *avoir l'air de* to seem like 1; *avoir l'embarras du choix* to have too many choices 10; *avoir les moyens* to be able to afford, to have the means 8; *avoir lieu* to take place; *avoir l'impression (de)* to have the impression (of) 6; *avoir l'occasion (de)* to have the opportunity (to) 4; *avoir mal (à...)* to be hurt, to have a/an... ache; *avoir mal au cœur* to feel nauseous; *avoir mauvaise mine* to look sick; *avoir peur (de)* to be afraid (of); *avoir peur du vide* to be afraid of heights; *avoir quel âge* to be how old; *avoir raison* to be right; *avoir soif* to be thirsty; *avoir tort* to be wrong 8; *avoir un petit air du pays* to look like (something from) my country
avril April
azur: la côte d'Azur French Riviera

B

un **B.A.** Bachelor of Arts degree 10
un **bac (baccalauréat)** exam taken to obtain high school diploma 9
le **bacon** bacon
un **bagage** piece of luggage; *faire enregistrer les bagages* to check one's luggage; *un compartiment à bagages* luggage compartment
une **bagarre** fight 9
une **bague** ring; *bague de diamants* diamond ring; *bague de fiançailles* engagement ring 1
une **baguette** long thin loaf of bread
baigner to bathe
une **baignoire** bathtub
un **bain** bath; *bain à remous* whirlpool bath 5; *un peignoir de bain* bathrobe
baisser to decrease 2
une **balade** ride, walk
un **balisier** botanical canna
une **ballade** ballad 3
un **ballon (de foot)** (soccer) ball
banal(e) banal
une **banane** banana
un **banc** bench
bancaire: une carte bancaire debit card 6
une **bande** group of friends 1
une **bande-annonce** film trailer 5
une **bande dessinée (BD)** comic strip
une **banlieue** suburb
une **banque** bank
un **banquier, une banquière** banker 6
le **bas** bottom
le **basket (basketball)** basketball
un **bassin** fountain, pond, pool
un **bateau** boat; *en bateau* by boat
un **bâton de ski** ski pole 4
une **batterie** drum set
bavard(e) talkative
béarnaise(e): une sauce béarnaise Béarnaise sauce 5
beau, bel, belle beautiful, handsome; *avoir beau [inform.]* to do (something) in vain 8
beaucoup a lot, very much; *beaucoup de* a lot of
un **beau-frère** stepbrother
un **beau-père** stepfather
la **beauté** beauty
les **beaux-arts (m.)** fine arts 7
un **bébé** baby 1
béchamel: une sauce béchamel béchamel sauce 5
beige beige
belge Belgian
la **Belgique** Belgium
une **belle-mère** stepmother
une **belle-sœur** stepsister
ben well
le **bénévolat** volunteer work 4
le **Bénin** Benin
béninois(e) Beninese
berbère Berber
un **besoin** need 8
un **best-seller** best seller
bête unintelligent
le **beurre** butter
une **bicyclette** bicycle; *à bicyclette* on a bicycle
bien really, well; *bien entendu* of course 5; *bien sûr* of course; *c'est bien* it's/that's exactly 10; *ça tombe bien* that works out well 2; *en y réfléchissant bien* on second thought 4
bientôt soon; *à bientôt* see you soon
bienvenue welcome
une **bière** beer 10
un **bijou** piece of jewelry
bilingue bilingual 10
une **bille** marble 1; *jouer aux billes* to play marbles 1
un **billet** bill *[money]*; ticket
la **biochimie** biochemistry 6
une **biographie** biography 6
la **biologie** biology
biologique organic
blanc, blanche white; *le blanc des yeux* eye to eye 9; *une sauce blanche* white sauce 5
la **blanchisserie** laundry 5; *un service blanchisserie* laundry service 5
blasé(e) blasé 5
un **blason** team logo
bleu(e) blue
un **blogue** blog
un **blogueur, une blogeuse** blogger 2
blond(e) blond
un **blouson** jacket
le **bœuf** beef; *bœuf bourguignon* beef burgundy
boire to drink
le **bois** wood 2; *en bois* wooden 2
une **boisson** drink
une **boîte** box 6; nightclub; *boîte (de)* can (of); *boîte aux lettres* mailbox 6; *boîte cartonnée* cardboard box 6; *en boîte* at/to the club
un **bol** bowl
bon(ne) good; *Bon Appétit!* Enjoy your meal!; *bon courage* good luck; *bon marché* cheap; *Bonne route!* Have a good trip!; *Bon voyage!* Have a good trip!; *le bon vieux temps* the good old days
bon so
bonjour hello
un **bonnet** hat; *bonnet en laine* wool hat
le **bord** edge, side; *au bord de la mer* by the seaside; *bord de mer* seaside; *monter à bord* to board
une **borne-fontaine** water hydrant
une **borne libre-service** self-service kiosk

un **bosquet** grove
bosser ***[inform.]*** to work 9
des **bottes (f.)** boots
la **bouche** mouth; *une bouche du métro* subway entrance
un **boucher, une bouchère** butcher
une **boucherie** butcher shop
bouclé(e) wavy (hair) 9
une **boucle d'oreille** earring
bouger to move
un **boulanger, une boulangère** baker
une **boulangerie** bakery
une **boule de neige** snowball 2
un **boulot** ***[inform.]*** job 8
un **bouquin** ***[inform.]*** book 6
la **Bourgogne** Burgundy 5
bourguignon(ne) from, of Burgundy 5
bousculer to shove 9; *se faire bousculer* to get knocked into 9
le **bout** end; *au bout de* at the end of
une **bouteille (de)** bottle (of)
une **boutique** shop
un **bracelet** bracelet
le **bras** arm
une **brasserie** café-restaurant
bref in short 9
la **Bretagne** Brittany region
breton(ne) from, of Brittany region
le **bricolage** do-it-yourself (DIY) projects 3
bricoler to do DIY projects 3
une **brochette** skewer
bronzer to tan
une **brosse: brosse à cheveux** hairbrush; *brosse à dents* toothbrush
se **brosser: se brosser les cheveux** to brush one's hair; *se brosser les dents* to brush one's teeth
le **brouillard** mist 7
brouillé(e): des œufs (m.) brouillés scrambled eggs
brun(e) brown, dark (hair)
brut(e): le Produit National Brut (PNB) GNP (Gross National Product) 2
une **bûche de Noël** yule log 2
un **buffet** buffet
un **bulletin météo(rologique)** weather forecast
un **bureau** desk, office; *bureau de change* foreign exchange counter 6; *bureau de tabac* news store that sells tobacco, stamps, lottery tickets; *bureau du proviseur* principal's office
le **Burkina Faso** Burkina Faso
burkinabè from, of Burkina Faso
un **bus** city bus; *en bus* by city bus
un **but** goal
un **buzz** buzz 9

C

c'est it is, that is, this is; *c'est bien* it's/that's exactly 10; *C'est ça.* That's right.; *c'est comme ça que...* that's how... 1; *C'est décidé.* It's settled.; *c'est dommage que...* it's too bad that... 5; *c'est pareil* it's the same; *C'est parti!* Here we go!; *c'est pour ça que* this/that is why; *c'est promis* it's a promise 6; *c'est sûr* that's for sure
ça it, this; that; *Ça fait combien?* How much is it?; *ça fait longtemps que* it's been a long time since; *ça m'est égal* it's all the same to me; *ça ne se fait pas* you shouldn't do that; *ça promet* it sounds promising 5; *ça tombe bien* that works out well 2; *Ça va?* How are things going?; *ça va se savoir* it will be revealed (known); *ça vaut* it's worth; *c'est pour ça que* that/this is why; *c'est comme ça que...* that's how... 1; *comme ça* like this, thus; *Rien que ça?* Is that all?
une **cabine d'essayage** dressing room
un **cabinet** office; *cabinet d'avocats* law firm 1; *cabinet dentaire* dentist's office; *cabinet du médecin* doctor's office
câblé(e): une chaîne câblée cable channel 5
le **cache-cache: jouer à cache-cache** to play hide-and-seek 1
cacher to conceal, to hide 7
se **cacher** to hide 7
un **cadeau** gift
un **cadre** setting
un **café** café; coffee; *café au lait* coffee with milk
un **cahier** notebook
un **caissier, une caissière** bank teller 6
un **calendrier** calendar
se **calmer** to calm oneself down
un(e) **camarade de classe** classmate
le **Cambodge** Cambodia 10
le **camembert** camembert cheese
une **caméra** camera
le **Cameroun** Cameroon
camerounais(e) Cameroonian
un **camion** truck
la **campagne** country(side)
le **camping** camping; *faire du camping* to go camping; *un terrain de camping* campground
le **Canada** Canada
canadien(ne) Canadian
la **canalisation** pipe(line)
un **canapé** sofa
un **canard** duck; *un magret de canard* duck breast 2
un **candidat** candidate 2
une **candidature** application 8; *une lettre de candidature* application letter 8
une **canne à pêche** fishing pole
un **canoë** canoe; *en canoë* by canoe; *faire du canoë* to go canoeing
une **cantine** school cafeteria
une **capitale** capital
un **capot** hood *[car]*
le **caramel** caramel; *une crème caramel* caramel custard
une **caravane** camper
une **caricature** caricature 7
un **carnaval** carnival
une **carotte** carrot
un **carré** square; *en carrés* in squares
carré(e) square 2
un **carreau: à carreaux** plaid 9
une **carte** card; map; menu; *carte bancaire* debit card 6; *carte cadeau* gift card; *carte de crédit* credit card; *carte d'embarquement* boarding pass; *carte postale* postcard; *carte SIM* SIM card
cartonné(e) (made out of) cardboard 6; *une boîte cartonnée* cardboard box 6
un **cas** case; *en tout cas* in any case
une **cascade** waterfall
une **casquette** cap
se **casser** to break 4; *se casser le poignet* to break one's wrist 4
une **casserole** saucepan
le **casting** casting 5
un **catalogue** catalog 6
une **catastrophe** catastrophe 5
une **cathédrale** cathedral
une **cause** cause; *à cause de* because of 2
causer to cause
une **caverne** cave
un **CD** CD
ce it; this; *ce, cet, cette, ces* that, these, this, those; *ce que* what; *ce qui* what; *ce mot-là* this (very) word
un **cédérom** CD
une **ceinture** belt; *ceinture de sécurité* seatbelt
cela it 3; that, this

célèbre famous
celui, celle that/this one, the one 6
cent (one) hundred
un **centre** center; *centre commercial* mall, shopping center; *centre d'accueil* reception center, shelter; *centre d'affaires* business center 5; *centre de remise en forme* fitness center 5
cependant however 8
des **céréales (f.)** cereal
un **cercle** circle, group 3
une **cerise** cherry
certain(e) certain, sure 5; *être certain que* to be certain that 5
un **certificat** certificate 6
ceux the ones, these, those 6
chacun(e) each (one) 5
une **chaîne** channel; *chaîne cablée* cable channel 5
une **chaise** chair
une **chaise-longue** chaise lounge
une **chambre** bedroom; hotel room; *un service de chambre* room service 5
un **champ** field; field of vision
le **champagne** champagne 10
champêtre rural, rustic 7; *une fête champêtre* garden party 7
un **champignon** mushroom
un **championnat** championship 2
la **chance: avoir de la chance** to be lucky; *avoir la chance (de)* to have the opportunity (to) 2; *tenter sa chance* to try one's luck 3
un **change** exchange 6; *un bureau de change* foreign exchange counter 6
changer to change
une **chanson** song; *chanson réaliste* chanson réaliste 7
un **chansonnier, une chansonnière** cabaret artist/singer
chanter to sing
un **chanteur, une chanteuse** singer
un **chapeau** hat
une **chapelle** chapel
chaque each
un **char** float
une **charcuterie** delicatessen
un **charcutier, une charcutière** deli owner
chargé(e): être chargé(e) (de) to be in charge (of)
charmant(e) charming
le **charme** charm
un **chat** cat
un **château** castle
chaud(e) hot; *chaude ambiance* exciting/fun night; *avoir chaud* to be hot; *il fait chaud* it's hot; *un chocolat chaud* hot chocolate
chauffer to heat (up) 2
une **chaussette** sock
une **chaussure** shoe; *chaussure de ski* ski boot 4
chauve bald 9
une **chauve-souris** bat
chef sir
un **chef, une cheffe** manager 8; *chef, cheffe d'entreprise* president 10; *chef d'orchestre* conductor 5; *chef du personnel* personnel manager 8
un **chef-d'œuvre** masterpiece
un **chemin** path, way
une **chemise** shirt
un **chemisier** blouse 9
un **chèque** check 6; *chèque de voyage* traveler's check 6
un **chéquier** checkbook 6
cher, chère dear; expensive
chercher to look for
un **chercheur, une chercheuse** researcher
chéri(e) honey
un **cheval** horse; *faire du cheval* to go horseback riding
les **cheveux (m.)** hair; *une brosse à cheveux* hairbrush; *se brosser les cheveux* to brush one's hair
la **cheville** ankle 4; *se fouler la cheville* to sprain an ankle 4
une **chèvre** goat
le **chevreuil** venison 2; *une côte de chevreuil* venison chop 2
chez at/to the house (home) of; *chez le kiné* at/to the physical therapy office 8; *chez moi* at/to my house
chic chic
un **chien** dog
un **chiffre** figure, number 8
la **chimie** chemistry
chimique chemical
la **Chine** China 10
un **chinois** conical strainer 2
le **chocolat** chocolate; *au chocolat* with chocolate; *un chocolat chaud* hot chocolate; *une mousse au chocolat* chocolate mousse
un **chœur** choir 9
choisir to choose; to decide
un **choix** choice; *avoir l'embarras du choix* to have too many choices 10
le **chômage** unemployment
choqué(e) shocked 9
une **chose** thing; *Tu en sais des choses.* You sure know a lot about it.
la **choucroute** sauerkraut; *choucroute garnie* sauerkraut with potatoes, sausages, smoked pork
chouette great
chut shh
une **chute** fall 8; *une chute d'eau* waterfall
cibler to target 10
un **ciné (cinéma)** movie theatre; *le cinéma* movies
un **ciné-club** film club 1
cinq five
une **cinquantaine** about fifty 9; *d'une cinquantaine d'années* in one's fifties 9
cinquante fifty
cinquième fifth
circuler to drive, to get around
cirer to polish 3
une **citation** quote 8
une **cité universitaire** university dormitory
un **citoyen, une citoyenne** citizen 8
un **citron** lemon; *un thé au citron* tea with lemon
civil(e) civil 6; *le génie civil* civil engineering 6
clair(e) clear
une **clarinette** clarinet
une **classe** class; *classe de neige* ski class 4
un **classique** classic 5
classique classical; *la musique classique* classical music
un **clavier** keyboard
une **clé** (ignition) key; *clé USB* USB key
un **clergé** clergy 8
un(e) **client(e)** guest 5
un **clignotant** blinker
la **climatisation** air conditioning
un **clip** video clip
cliquer to click
un **clou** nail 3; *enfoncer un clou* to hammer a nail 3
un **club** club 2
un **coca** cola
un **cochon** pig
le **cœur** heart; *avoir mal au cœur* to feel nauseous
un **coffre-fort** safe 5
un **coiffeur, une coiffeuse** hair stylist
une **coiffure** hairstyle; *un salon de coiffure* hair salon
le **coin** corner; *du coin* on the corner
un **colibri** hummingbird
un **colis** package 6

collé(e) glued, stuck
une **collection** collection
collectionner to collect 1
la **collectivité** community, society 8
un **collier** necklace; *collier de/en perles* pearl necklace
une **colline** hill
la **colonisation** colonization
combattre to fight
combien how much; *Ça fait combien?* How much is it?; *C'est combien le kilo?* How much per kilo?; *depuis combien de temps* how long; *Il coûte combien?* How much does it cost?
une **comédie** comedy; *comédie romantique* romantic comedy
un **comité** group 2; *en petit comité* with a few friends 2
commander to order
comme for; like; since; *comme ça* like this, thus; *comme ci, comme ça* so-so; *c'est comme ça que...* that's how... 1
commencer to begin; *pour commencer* for starters
comment how, what; *Comment allez-vous? [form.]* How are you?; *Comment est...?* What is... like?
des **commérages (m.)** gossip 9
un(e) **commerçant(e)** business, shopping; *un(e) petit(e) commerçant(e)* shopkeeper
un **commissariat** police station 9
une **compagnie** company 8
un **compartiment à bagages** baggage compartment
une **compétence** skill 5
complémentaire supplementary 8
complètement completely 9
un **complexe** center; *complexe sportif* sports center 1
la **complicité** connection 1
compliqué(e) complicated
composé(e) (de) made up (of) 5
un **compositeur, une compositrice** composer, songwriter
une **composition** composition
composter to validate (a ticket)
un **composteur** ticket-stamping machine
comprendre to include 5; to understand
compris(e) included
la **comptabilité** accounting 10
un(e) **comptable** accountant 10
un **compte** account 6; *se rendre compte (de)* to realize 9
compter to plan to do something
un **comptoir** (ticket) counter
un **concept** concept 7; *un album concept* concept album 7
un **concepteur de web** web designer
un **concert** concert; *concert R'n'B* R&B concert
un(e) **concierge** concierge 5
un **concombre** cucumber
condamné(e) condemned 8; *être condamné(e)* to be condemned 8
un **conducteur, une conductrice** driver
conduire to drive; *un permis (de conduire)* driver's license 8
le **confort** comfort 5
la **confiance: avoir confiance** to trust
la **confiture** jam
congolais(e) Congolese 6
conique cone-shaped 2
les **connaissances (f.)** knowledge 8
connaître to be familiar with (person, place, thing), to meet; to know; *faire connaître (à)* to introduce to someone
se **connaître** to know each other
une **connexion** connection 5; *connexion Wifi* wireless internet connection 5
un **conquérant** conqueror
conseiller to advise; to recommend 3
une **conserverie** canning company 3
consommer to consume
un **constructeur, une constructrice automobile** car manufacturer 10
un **consulat** consulate 4
un(e) **consultant(e)** consultant
une **consultation** consultation
consulter to consult 5
le **contact: garder le contact** to keep in touch 3
un **conte** tale; *conte de fées* fairy tale 3
contemporain(e) contemporary
content(e) happy; *être content(e) (de)* to be happy (about) 6
un **continent** continent
continuer to continue
le **contraire** opposite 8; *au contraire* on the contrary 8
un **contrat** contract 8
contre against, versus; *par contre* however, on the other hand 8
un **contrebandier, une contrebandière** smuggler
un **contrôle** test; *contrôle de sécurité* security checkpoint
un **contrôleur, une contrôleuse** ticket collector
convenir (à) to please; to suit; *si cela vous convient* if you'd like
convenu(e) conventional 10
une **conversation** conversation
convoqué(e) (à) called (in) 8; *être convoqué(e) (à)* to be called (in) 8
un **copain, une copine** (boy/girl) friend
un **coq** rooster; *le coq au vin* chicken cooked in wine
un **coquelicot** poppy 7
un **coquillage** seashell 1
une **coquille St-Jacques** scallop
un **corbeau** crow 7
une **corde** rope 1; *sauter à la corde* to jump rope 1
la **Corée du Sud** South Korea 10
une **corniche** cliff road
le **corps** body
correctement correctly 4
un(e) **correspondant(e)** pen pal 10
une **corvée** chore
costaud(e) stocky 9
un **costume** costume
une **côte** chop 2; coast; *côte de chevreuil* venison chop 2; *la côte d'Azur* French Riviera; *la Côte-d'Ivoire* Ivory Coast
un **côté** side; *à côté (de)* beside, next to; *de votre côté* as for you 2
le **coton** cotton; *en coton* made of cotton
le **cou** neck
couché(e) in bed
se **coucher** to go to bed
une **couleur** color; *De quelle(s) couleur(s)?* In what color(s)?
un **couloir** hallway
un **coup: coup de main** (helping) hand 2; *faire le coup (à quelqu'un)* to play a trick (on someone) 4; *jeter un coup d'œil (à)* to glance (at) 5; *tout d'un coup* all of a sudden 9
coupable guilty 6
couper to cut
un **couple** couple
le **courage: bon courage** good luck
courant: être au courant to be informed, to know
une **courgette** zucchini
courir to run 1
un **courrier** mail
un **cours** class, course; *cours particulier* private class 1; *au cours de* during, in the course of 8
court(e) short (hair) 9
le **couscous** couscous

un(e) **cousin(e)** cousin; *cousin(e) germain(e)* first cousin 3

un **coussin** pillow

un **couteau** knife; *couteau suisse* Swiss army knife

coûter to cost

la **couture** fashion design 10; *la haute couture* high fashion 10

une **couturière** dress-maker

le **couvert** table setting; *mettre le couvert* to set the table

un **crabe** crab

craindre to fear; *Je crains que non.* I'm afraid not. 2

craquer to lose it 9

un **crayon** pencil

le **crédit: une carte de crédit** credit card

créer to create

une **crème** cream, lotion 10; *crème caramel* caramel custard; *crème solaire* sunscreen

une **crémerie** dairy store

le **créole** Creole *[language]*

créole Creole

une **crêpe** crêpe; *un stand de crêpes* crêpe stand

une **crêperie** crêpe restaurant

une **crevette** shrimp

un **cri** cry; *pousser un cri* to scream

une **crise** crisis 3; *la grande crise* Great Depression 3

un(e) **critique** critic 5; *une critique* review 5

croire to believe, to think

un **croissant** croissant

un **croque-monsieur** grilled ham and cheese sandwich

des **crudités (f.)** raw vegetables

cubique cubical 2

cueillir to pick 7

une **cuiller** spoon

une **cuillère-mesure** measuring spoon 2

le **cuir** leather; *en cuir* made of leather

cuire to cook 2

la **cuisine** cooking; kitchen

un **cuisinier, une cuisinière** chef, cook

une **cuisinière** stove

culturel, culturelle cultural

une **cure** spa treatment

un **CV** CV (Curriculum vitae) 8

cylindrique cylindrical 2

D

d'abord first of all

d'accord OK

d'habitude usually

d'ailleurs moreover 8

une **dame** lady

danois(e) from, of Denmark

dans in

un **danseur, une danseuse** dancer

une **date** date

davantage more

de any, some; by, made of; from, of; *de diamants* made of diamonds; *de lin* made of linen; *de neuf* new; *de perles* made of pearls; *de plus en plus* more and more 7; *de toute façon* in any case 4; *De quelle(s) couleur(s)?* In what color(s)?

débarasser la table to clear the table

un **débat** debate 8

un **déboulé** ***[Mart.]*** parade

debout standing

se **débrouiller** to get by 6; to take care of things 8

un **début** beginning

une **décapotable** convertible

décembre December

se **déchaîner** to get wild 9

décider to decide; *C'est décidé.* It's settled.

se **décider** to make up one's mind 6

une **décision** decision 10; *prendre une décision* to make a decision 10

une **déclaration** declaration, statement 9; *déclaration de vol* report of a theft 9

décoller to take off *[airplane]*

décontracté(e) relaxed

découpé(e) (en) cut up (in) 10

découragé(e) discouraged 9

une **découverte** discovery

découvrir to discover; *faire découvrir (à)* to introduce to someone

décrire to describe

un **défi** challenge 9

un **défilé** parade

un **degré** degree

se **déguiser** to disguise oneself, to dress up

déjà already

le **déjeuner** lunch

déjouer un tour to undo a spell 3

délavé(e) washed out 9

délicieux, délicieuse delicious

demain tomorrow; *À demain.* See you tomorrow.

demander to ask (for); *demander le chemin* to ask for directions; *demander un service* to ask for a favor

démarrer to start

un **déménagement** move (house)

déménager to move 1

demeurer to live 7

demi(e) half; *et demie* half past

un **demi-frère** half-brother

une **demi-sœur** half-sister

une **démocratie** democracy 2

une **demoiselle d'honneur** bridesmaid 1

une **dénomination** denomination 5

une **dent** tooth; *une brosse à dents* toothbrush; *se brosser les dents* to brush one's teeth

dentaire: un cabinet dentaire dentist's office

le **dentifrice** toothpaste

un(e) **dentiste** dentist

un **départ** departure; *des préparatifs (m.) de départ* travel preparations 4

un **département** department

se **dépêcher (de)** to hurry

dépendre (de) to depend (on) 2

se **déplacer** to get around

déposer to deposit 6

depuis for; since; *depuis combien de temps* how long; *Depuis le temps!* At last!; *depuis quand* since when

un **député** deputy 8

déranger to bother 2

dernier, dernière last; *le dernier, la dernière* the latest 6

derrière behind

des any; from (the), of (the); some

désagréable unpleasant

descendre to get off, to go down

une **descente** descent

une **description** description 5

se **déshabiller** to get undressed

un(e) **designer automobile** automotive designer

désirer to want

désolé(e) sorry

le **désordre** disorder

dès que as soon as

un **dessert** dessert

un **dessin** drawing; *dessin animé* cartoon

dessiner to draw

dessus on, over (it); *au-dessus de* above

le **destin** destiny

une **destination** destination

un **détail** detail

se **détendre** to relax

détester to detest 1

détruit(e) destroyed

deux two

deuxième second

deuxièmement secondly 8

devant in front of
un **développement** development; *développement durable* sustainable development; *le secteur de développement durable* sustainable development industry
devenir to become
deviner to guess
une **devise** motto
devoir to have to; to owe 7
un **devoir** assignment; *les devoirs (m.)* homework
un **diabolo menthe** lemon-lime soda with mint syrup
un **dialogue** dialogue 5
un **diamont** diamond; *une bague de diamants* diamond ring
un **dictature** dictatorship 2
un **dictionnaire** dictionary
un **dieu: mon Dieu** my god 5
différemment differently 4
différent(e) different
difficile difficult
une **difficulté** difficulty 8
dijonnais(e) from, of Dijon 5
diligent(e) diligent
dimanche Sunday
une **dimension** dimension 6
la **dinde** turkey 2; *dinde aux marrons* turkey with chestnuts 2
un **dindon** turkey
dîner to have dinner
le **dîner** dinner
le **dioxyde de carbone** carbon dioxide
la **diplomatie** diplomacy; *user de diplomatie* to use diplomacy
dire to say, to tell; *joliment dit* nicely said; *(noun) te dit?* How do you feel about (noun)? 4; *vouloir dire* to mean
se **dire** to say to oneself
direct(e): en direct de live from
un **directeur, une directrice** director 5; *directeur, directrice des ressources humaines (DRH)* director of human resources 10; *directeur financier, directrice financière* C.F.O. 10; *un président directeur général (PDG)* C.E.O. 10
une **direction** direction
dis say; *dis donc* well
une **discographie** discography
une **discothèque** nightclub 1
un **discours** speech 8; *faire un discours* to make a speech 8
une **discussion** discussion
discuter (de) to discuss
disparaître to disappear
disponible free
disposé(e) laid out
disputer: se faire disputer (par) to get in trouble (with) 3
se **disputer** to argue
dissimuler to hide
une **distance** distance
un **distributeur (automatique)** ATM 6
le **divertissement** entertainment; *l'industrie (f.) du divertissement* entertainment industry
divorcé(e) divorced
dix ten
dix-huit eighteen
dixième tenth
dix-neuf nineteen
dix-sept seventeen
un **documentaire** documentary
le **doigt** finger; *doigt de pied* toe
un **domaine** field, sector; property 4; *domaine de la santé* health sector; *domaine des sciences et techniques* science and technology sector
dommage pity, shame 5; *c'est dommage que...* it's too bad that... 5
un **don: faire un don (de)** to give
donc so, therefore; *dis donc* well
donner to give; *donner lieu à* to give rise to 7
dont about which/whom, of which/whom 6; whose
dormir to sleep
un **dortoir** dormitory
le **dos** back
le **doublage** dubbing 5
doublé(e) dubbed 5
une **douceur** gentleness; *douceur de vivre* relaxed style of life
une **douche** shower
doué(e) talented 10
un **doute** doubt 4; *sans aucun doute* without a doubt 4
douter to doubt 5
douze twelve
dramatique dramatic 2
un(e) **dramaturge** playwright 7
un **drame** drama
un **drap** sheet
un **drapeau** flag
la **drogue** drugs
un **droit** right 2; *le droit* law 6; *les droits de l'homme* human rights 2; *avoir droit à* to be entititled to 8
la **droite: à droite** to the right; *à droite de* to (on) the right of; *tout droit* straight ahead
drôle funny
du about (the); any; from (the); of (the); on (the); some; *du coin* on the corner
dur(e) difficult
durable: le développement durable sustainable development; *le secteur de développement durable* sustainable development industry
une **durée** duration, length 5
duquel, duquelle from which 5
un **DVD** DVD
dynamique dynamic

E

l' **eau (f.)** water; *eau minérale* mineral water; *une chute d'eau* waterfall; *une grande eau* fountain; *une masse d'eau* body of water; *une source d'eau* spring
une **écharpe** scarf
un **éclair** eclair
une **école** school
une **économie** economy 2
économique economic; *la gestion économique d'entreprise* economic business management 6
économiser to save (up)
l' **écoute (f.): en écoute libre** listening trial
écouter to listen (to); *écouter de la musique* to listen to music; *écouter mon lecteur MP3* to listen to my MP3 player; *écoute...* look... 2
un **écran** monitor, screen
écrire to write
un **écrivain** writer
une **éducation** education; *éducation physique et sportive (EPS)* gym class
un **effet** effect; *l'effet de serre* greenhouse effect
efficacement efficiently
s' **effondrer** to collapse 9; *s'effondrer de fatigue* to collapse from exhaustion 9
égal(e) equal 10; *ça m'est égal* it's all the same to me
une **église** church
égoïste selfish
eh bien well
une **élastique: faire du saut à l'élastique** to bungee jump 4

une **élection** election 2; *élection présidentielle* presidential elections 2
électrique electric
électronique electronic 5
l' **électro pop (m.)** Electro pop music
un(e) **élève** student
éliminer to eliminate
elle her; it; she
elles them (f.); they (f.)
éloigné(e) distant 3
s' **éloigner (de)** to distance oneself (from) 7; to get away (from) 10
l' **embarquement (m.)** boarding; *une carte d'embarquement* boarding pass; *une porte d'embarquement* boarding gate
l' **embarras (m.): avoir l'embarras du choix** to have too many choices 10
embaucher to hire 8
embêter to annoy 2
embrasser to kiss
une **émission** television program; TV show; *émission de musique* music show; *émission de télé-réalité* reality TV show
emmener to bring (person)
une **émotion** emotion 5
s' **empêcher (de)** to refrain (from) 2; *ne pas pouvoir s'empêcher (de)* cannot help (but) 2
un **emploi** job
un(e) **employé(e)** employee 3
emporter to take (away) 4
emprunter to borrow
emprisonner to imprison 2
en any, about it/them, from it/them, of it/them, some; at; by; in; made of; of *[pronoun]*; on; upon, while 4; *en aluminium, plastique* made of aluminum, plastic; *en argent* made of silver; *en autobus* by bus; *en avance* early; *en avion* by plane; *en bateau* by boat; *en bois* wooden 2; *en boîte* at/to the club; *en bus* by city bus; *en canoë* by canoe; *en ce moment* at the moment 6; *en coton* made of cotton; *en cuir* made of leather; *en direct de* live from; *en écoute libre* listening trial; *en face de* across from; *en famille* with family; *en forme de poire* pear-shaped 2; *en gros plan* in a close-up 7; *en guerre* at war 2; *en haut* at the top; *en laine* made of wool; *en ligne* online; *en métal* made of metal 2; *en métro* by subway; *en or* made of gold; *en ordre* in order; *en panne* broken down; *en perles* made of pearls; *en petit comité* with a few friends 2; *en pirogue* by pirogue; *en plein air* outdoors; *en plus* in addition to; *en première année* in the first year; *en R.E.R.* by R.E.R.; *en retard* late; *en route* on the way; *en scooter* by scooter; *en skiant* while skiing 4; *en soie* made of silk; *en solde* on sale; *en taxi* by taxi; *en tournée* on tour 7; *en tout cas* in any case; *en train* by train; *en velours* made of velvet; *en ville* downtown; *en voiture* by car; *en voiture électrique* by electric car; *en voiture hybride* by hybrid car; *en un sens* in a way; *en y réfléchissant bien* on second thought 4; *en y regardant de plus près* on a closer look 4; *je m'en vais* I'm going 2; *Tu en sais des choses.* You sure know a lot about it.
encaisser to cash 6
enchanté(e) delighted
encore more; still
encouragé(e) encouraged 9
encourager to encourage 2
un **endettement** debt 2
un **endroit** place
l' **énergie (f.)** energy; *énergie nucléaire* nuclear energy; *énergie solaire* solar energy
énergique energetic
l' **enfance (f.)** childhood 1
un **enfant** child; *garder un enfant* to babysit 3
enfantin(e) childish 1
enfin come on; finally; well
enfoncer un clou to hammer a nail 3
un **engagement** engagement
s' **engager** to be committed to, to commit to
l' **engrais (m.)** fertilizer
des **ennuis (m.)** trouble 9
s' **ennuyer** to get bored 4
une **enquête** survey
enregistrer: faire enregistrer les bagages to check one's luggage
enseigner to teach
ensemble together
un **ensemble** outfit
ensuite next
entendre to hear; *bien entendu* of course 5
s' **entendre** to get along
enthousiaste enthusiastic
entièrement completely, entirely 8
s' **entraîner** to practice (sports) 2
entre between
une **entrée** appetizer
une **entreprise** business, company 1; *la gestion économique d'entreprise* economic business management 6; *un chef, une cheffe d'entreprise* president 10; *une petite et moyenne entreprise (PME)* small business 1
entrer to come in, to enter; *entrer à l'université* to go to college
un **entretien** interview 8
envahi(e) invaded 2
une **enveloppe** envelope
l' **environnement (m.)** environment
l' **envoi (m.)** send button
un **envoûtement** spell
envoyer to send; *envoyer des textos* to send text messages
une **éolienne** wind turbine
l' **épaule (f.)** shoulder
épicé(e) spicy
une **épicerie** grocery store
un **épicier, une épicière** grocery store owner
une **éponge** sponge 10
une **époque** era, period
éprouver to feel 5
l' **EPS (f.)** gym class
équestre: faire une randonnée équestre to go on a trail ride 4
une **équipe** team
équipé(e) equipped 5
un **érable** maple tree; *le sirop d'érable* maple syrup
un **e-reader** e-reader
l' **escalade (f.): faire de l'escalade** to rock climb 4
un **escargot** snail
un **espace** area
l' **Espagne (f.)** Spain
l' **espagnol (m.)** Spanish *[language]*
espagnol(e) Spanish
espérer to hope
un **essai** essay
essayer to try (on)
l' **essence (f.)** gasoline
essentiel, essentielle essential 4
un **essuie-glace** windshield wiper
l' **est (m.)** east
est-ce que *[phrase introducing a question]*
l' **estomac (m.)** stomach
et and; *et demie* half past; *et quart* quarter past
un **étage** floor, story; *le premier étage* the second floor
un **étang** pond

un **état** state 8
les **États-Unis (m.)** United States
l' **été (m.)** summer
ethnique ethnic, multicultural 10
une **étoile** star 5
étonné(e) surprised 5; *être étonné que* to be surprised that 5
étonner to surprise
être to be; *être à* to belong to 8; *être affolé(e)* to panic 1; *être amoureux/ amoureuse (de)* to be in love (with) 6; *être au courant* to be informed, to know; *être certain que* to be certain that 5; *être chargé(e) (de)* to be in charge (of); *être condamné(e)* to be condemned 8; *être content(e) (de)* to be happy (about) 6; *être convoqué(e) (à)* to be called (in) 8; *être d'accord* to agree; *être de retour* to be back; *être d'origine (+ adjective)* to come from (+ country) 3; *être en (bonne, mauvaise) forme* to be in (good, bad) shape; *être en train de (+ infinitive)* to be (busy) doing something; *être étonné que* to be surprised that 5; *être évident que* to be obvious that 5; *être fâché(e)* to be angry 1; *être libre* to be free; *être obligé(e) (de)* to be obligated (to) 8; *être occupé* to be busy; *être perso [inform.]* to be egotistical 8; *être situé(e)* to be located; *être sur place* to be there; *être vert* to be environmentally friendly; *ce n'est pas la peine* it's not worth it 1; *je ne suis pas trop d'humeur pour* I'm not in the mood for 5; *Il était une fois....* Once upon a time (there was).... 3; *Nous sommes le (+ date).* It's the (+ date).
étroit(e) narrow 2
des **études (f.)** studies
un(e) **étudiant(e)** student
étudier to study
euh um
un **euro** euro
l' **Europe (f.)** Europe
eux them
évidemment obviously
évident(e) obvious 5; *être évident que* to be obvious that 5
un **évier** sink
éviter to avoid
exactement exactly
exagérer to exaggerate
une **excursion** trip; *faire une excursion* to take a trip
exiger to require 5
exister to exist
une **expérience** experience
expliqué(e) explained
expliquer to explain
un **exposé** presentation
une **exposition** exhibit
l' **expressionnisme (m.)** expressionism 7
expressionniste expressionist 7
extraordinaire extraordinary

F

une **fable** fable 3
fabriqué(e) (au, aux, en) made (in) 10
fabuleux, fabuleuse fabulous
une **fac (faculté)** college
face: face à faced with 9; *en face de* across from
fâché(e) angry 1; *être fâché(e)* to be angry 1
facile easy
une **façon** way 4; *la façon* in the manner of 9; *de toute façon* in any case 4
un **facteur, une factrice** mailman, mailwoman 6
une **facture** bill 8
la **faïence** earthenware 10
la **faim** hunger; *avoir faim* to be hungry
faire to do, to make; *faire connaître (à)* to introduce to someone; *faire découvrir (à)* to introduce to someone; *faire de la gym (gymnastique)* to do gymnastics; *faire de la luge* to go sledding 4; *faire de la planche à voile* to wind surf 4; *faire de la plongée sous-marine* to go scuba diving; *faire de la raquette à neige* to go snowshoeing 4; *faire de la voile* to go sailing; *faire de l'escalade* to rock climb 4; *faire des sauts à ski* to go off ski jumps 4; *faire du camping* to go camping; *faire du canoë* to go canoeing; *faire du cheval* to go horseback riding; *faire du footing* to go running; *faire du kayak* to go kayaking; *faire du parachutisme ascensionnel* to go parasailing; *faire du patinage (artistique)* to (figure) skate; *faire du roller* to in-line skate; *faire du saut à l'élastique* to bungee jump 4; *faire du scooter des mers* to jet ski; *faire du shopping* to go shopping; *faire du ski (alpin)* to (downhill) ski; *faire du ski de fond* to cross-country ski 4; *faire du ski joering* to skijor 4; *faire du ski nautique* to go water-skiing; *faire du snowboard* to snowboard 4; *faire du speed riding* to speed ride 4; *faire du sport* to play sports; *faire du taxi-ski* to take a ski-taxi ride 4; *faire du télémark* to telemark ski 4; *faire du vélo* to bike; *faire enregistrer les bagages* to check one's luggage; *faire grève* to go on strike 2; *faire griller* to barbecue; *faire la connaissance (de)* to meet; *faire la cuisine* to cook; *faire la lessive* to wash clothes; *faire la vaisselle* to wash the dishes; *faire le coup (à quelqu'un)* to play a trick (on someone) 4; *faire le ménage* to do housework; *faire le plein* to fill up the gas tank; *faire les courses* to go grocery shopping; *faire le tour* to explore all the possibilities 10; *faire le touriste* to be a tourist; *faire marcher* to make (something) work; *faire mes devoirs* to do my homework; *faire partie (de)* to belong (to); *faire sa valise* to pack 4; *faire sécher le linge* to dry clothes; *faire semblant (de)* to pretend (to) 1; *faire ses adieux* to bid farewell 8; *faire un don (de)* to give; *faire une excursion* to take a trip; *faire une intervention* to organize an intervention; *faire une liste* to make a list; *faire une nuit blanche* to stay up all night; *faire une promenade* to go for a walk; *faire une promesse* to make a promise; *faire une randonnée à pied* to hike; *faire une randonnée équestre* to go on a trail ride 4; *faire une visite guidée* to go on a guided tour; *faire un discours* to make a speech 8; *faire un séjour* to stay 4; *faire un stage* to intern 8; *faire un tour* to go on a ride; to go on a tour; *faire un tour de grande roue* to go on a Ferris wheel ride; *faire un tour de manège* to go on a carnival ride; *faire un tour de montagnes russes* to go on a roller coaster ride; *faire un voyage* to go on a trip; *arriver à faire quelque chose* to bring oneself to do something 6

se **faire: se faire arrêter** to get arrested 9; *se faire bousculer* to get knocked into 9; *se faire disputer (par)* to get in trouble (with) 3; *se faire muter* to get reassigned 1; *se faire soigner* to seek (medical) treatment 8; *se faire vacciner* to get a shot 4; *ça ne se fait pas* you shouldn't do that
le **faisan** pheasant 5
fait: au fait by the way; *Ça fait combien?* How much is it?; *il fait beau* it's beautiful out; *il fait chaud* it's hot; *il fait du soleil* it's sunny; *il fait du vent* it's windy; *il fait frais* it's cool; *il fait froid* it's cold; *il fait mauvais* the weather's bad; *on te fait* they (one) make(s) you 8; *Quel temps fait-il?* What's the weather like?; *tout à fait* completely
une **falaise** cliff
falloir to be necessary, to have to; *il faut* it is necessary, one has to/must, we/you have to/must
une **famille** family; *famille monoparentale* single-parent family 1; *famille nucléaire* nuclear family 1; *famille recomposée* blended family 1; *en famille* with family
la **fantaisie** fantasy
farci(e) stuffed
la **fatigue** fatigue 9; *s'effondrer de fatigue* to collapse from exhaustion 9
fatigué(e) tired
la **faune** fauna, wildlife
faut: il me faut I need
un **fauteuil** armchair
un **fax** fax 5
une **fée** fairy 3; *un conte de fées* fairy tale 3
une **femme** wife; woman; *femme d'affaires* businesswoman; *femme poète* poet 7; *femme politique* female politician
une **fenêtre** window
un **fer à repasser** (clothes) iron
une **ferme** farm
fermenté(e) fermented 5
fermer to close
un **fermier, une fermière** farmer
un **festival** festival 1
une **fête** holiday; party; *fête champêtre* garden party 7; *fête foraine* carnival; *fête nationale* national holiday
fêter to celebrate
un **feu: feu d'artifice** firework; *feu de joie* bonfire
une **feuille de papier** sheet of paper
un **feuilleton** TV soap opera
février February
les **fiançailles (f.)** engagement 1; *une bague de fiançailles* engagement ring 1
se **ficher: s'en ficher** to not care 1
un **fichier multimédia** multimedia file
fier, fière proud 9
la **fièvre** fever
une **figure** figure 7; *la figure* face
une **figurine** figurine 10
filer ***[inform.]*** to run
une **filiale** branch, subsidiary 10
une **fille** daughter; girl
un **film** film; *film d'action* action movie; *film d'aventures* adventure movie; *film d'horreur* horror movie; *film de science-fiction* science fiction movie; *film musical* musical; *film policier* detective movie; *tourner un film* to shoot a movie 5
filmer to film 9
un **fils** son
filtrer to filter 2
fin(e) fine
un **final** finale 5
finalement in the end 3
les **finances (f.)** finances 6
financier, financière financial 10; *un directeur financier, une directrice financière* C.F.O. 10
finir to finish
un **fitness** gym, health club
un(e) **fleuriste** florist
un **fleuve** river
flirter to flirt 9
la **flore** flora
une **flûte** flute
le **foie gras** goose liver pâté 2
une **fois** occasion, time; *à la fois* at the same time; *Il était une fois....* Once upon a time (there was).... 3
folklorique: la musique folklorique folk music
le **fond: au fond (de)** at the end (of); *faire du ski de fond* to cross-country ski 4; *le ski de fond* cross-country skiing 4
le **foot** soccer
un **footballeur, une footballeuse** soccer player
le **footing** running
une **force** strength
forestier, forestière with mushrooms
une **forêt** forest
un **forfait de ski** ski pass 4
un **forgeron** blacksmith
une **formation** education, training 8
une **forme** shape 2; *en forme de poire* pear-shaped 2; *être en (bonne, mauvaise) forme* to be in (good, bad) shape; *un centre de remise en forme* fitness center 5
formidable awesome
fort(e) strong
un **fou, une folle** crazy person
un **foulard** scarf
une **foule** crowd
se **fouler** to sprain 4; *se fouler la cheville* to sprain an ankle 4
un **four** oven
une **fourchette** fork
un **fourre-tout** carry-all
frais, fraîche cool; fresh; *il fait frais* it's cool
une **fraise** strawberry
le **français** French *[language]*
français(e) French
francanadien(ne) from, of French-speaking Canada
la **France** France
francophone French-speaking
la **Francophonie** French-speaking world 3
un **frein** brake
fréquenter to frequent, to hang out
un **frère** brother
un **frigo** refrigerator
frisé(e) curly (hair) 9
des **frissons (m.)** chills; shakes
frit(e) deep-fried
des **frites (f.)** French fries
froid(e) cold; *avoir froid* to be cold; *il fait froid* it's cold
le **fromage** cheese
un **fruit** fruit; *les fruits de mer (m.)* seafood; *une tarte aux fruits* fruit tart
frustré(e) frustrated 9
fumé(e) smoked 2; *le saumon fumé* smoked salmon 2
le **funk** funk music
un **fuseau de ski** ski pants 4
futur(e) future 6

G

le **Gabon** Gabon
gabonais(e) Gabonese
gagner to win; *gagner du temps* to save time

une **galerie** gallery; *galerie des miroirs déformants* fun house
une **galette** buckwheat crêpe
un **gant** glove 4; *gant de toilette* washcloth
un **garage** auto shop
garanti(e) guaranteed
garantir to guarantee 5
un **garcon** boy; *garçon d'honneur* best man 1
garder to keep, to take care of 3; *garder le contact* to keep in touch 3; *garder un enfant* to babysit 3
une **gare** train station
garni(e): la choucroute garnie sauerkraut with potatoes, sausages, smoked pork
la **Gascogne** Gascony region
gascon(ne) from, of Gascony region
la **gastronomie** gastronomy 5
un **gâteau** cake
gauche: à gauche on the left; *à gauche de* on/to the left of
géant(e) giant
généalogique genealogical 3; *des recherches (f.) généalogiques* genealogical research 3
général(e) general 8; *un président directeur général (PDG)* CEO 10
une **génération** generation 3
généreux, généreuse generous
génial(e) fantastic, great, terrific
le **génie** engineering 6; *génie civil* civil engineering 6
le **génocide** genocide
le **genou** knee
un **genre** type
des **gens (m.)** people
gentil, gentille nice
germain(e): un(e) cousin(e) germain(e) first cousin 3
la **gestion** management 6; *gestion économique d'entreprise* economic business management 6
une **glace** ice cream; mirror; *glace à la vanille* vanilla ice cream; *glace au chocolat* chocolate ice cream
une **glacière** cooler
la **gorge** throat
un **gorille** gorilla; *gorille des montagnes* mountain gorilla
le **gospel** gospel 9
gourmand(e) fond of food
un **goût** taste 5; *à mon goût* for my taste 5
goûter to taste
le **goûter** snack
gouverné(e) ruled 8
un **gouvernement** government
des **graffiti (m.)** graffiti 3
un **gramme (de)** a gram (of)
grand(e) big, large, tall; *la grande crise* Great Depression 3; *la grande roue* Ferris wheel; *faire un tour de grande roue* to go on a Ferris wheel ride; *une grande eau* fountain
grandir to grow; to grow up 3
une **grand-mère** grandmother
un **grand-oncle** great uncle 3
un **grand-père** grandfather
les **grands-parents (m.)** grandparents
une **grand-tante** great aunt 3
une **grange** barn
graphique graphic 6
un(e) **graphiste** graphic designer
gras greasy, oily 2; *le foie gras* goose liver pâté 2
gratuit(e) free
grave serious
gravé(e) engraved
la **grêle** hail 9
une **grève** strike 2; *faire grève* to go on strike 2
grillé(e) grilled; *le pain grillé* toast
griller to grill; *faire griller* to barbecue
la **grippe** flu
gris(e) grey
une **grive** thrush
gros, grosse big, fat, large; *en gros plan* in a close-up 7
grossir to gain weight
un **groupe** group
un(e) **groupie** fan 9
la **Guadeloupe** Guadeloupe
une **guerre** war; *en guerre* at war 2
guéri(e) healed 8
un **guichet** ticket booth
un **guide** guide; guidebook; *guide touristique* tourist guide; *le guide Michelin* Michelin guidebook
guidé(e) guided; *une visite guidée* guided tour; *faire une visite guidée* to go on a guided tour
guillotiner to decapitate 8
une **guitare** guitar
la **Guyane (française)** French Guyana
la **gym (gymnastique)** gymnastics; *faire de la gym (gymnastique)* to do gymnastics

H

s' **habiller** to get dressed
un(e) **habitant(e)** inhabitant, resident
habiter to live
haïtien(ne) Haitian
un **hall** lobby 5
un **hamac** hammock
un **hamburger** hamburger
un **hameau** hamlet
hanté(e): une maison hantée haunted house
des **haricots verts (m.)** green beans
le **hasard** fate, luck 10
la **hâte: avoir hâte de** to be eager
une **hausse** increase 2
le **haut** top
haut(e) high; *en haut* at the top
la **haute couture** high fashion 10
une **herbe** herb 2
un **héros, une héroïne** hero, heroine
hésiter to hesitate
l' **heure (f.)** hour, o'clock, time; *à l'heure* on time; *Quelle heure est-il?* What time is it?
heureusement fortunately
heureux, heureuse happy; *Très heureux/heureuse.* Pleased to meet you. 3
un **hibiscus** hibiscus
hier yesterday
le **hip-hop** hip-hop
une **histoire** story 3; *l'histoire (f.)* history
un **hit** ***[inform.]*** hit 2
l' **hiver (m.)** winter
un **HLM** subsidized housing 3
hollandais(e): une sauce hollandaise hollandaise sauce 5
un **homme** man; *homme d'affaires* businessman; *homme de ménage* janitor 5; *homme politique* male politician; *les droits (m.) de l'homme* human rights 2
le **Honduras** Honduras 10
l' **honneur (m.)** honor 1; *une demoiselle d'honneur* bridesmaid 1; *un garçon d'honneur* best man 1
honteux, honteuse ashamed 9
un **hôpital** hospital 8
l' **horizon (m.)** horizon; *à l'horizon* on the horizon
l' **horreur (f.)** horror; *avoir horreur de* to detest, to hate; *un film d'horreur* horror movie
horrible awful, horrible
un **hors-d'œuvre** appetizer 2
un **hors-piste** off-piste skiing 4
l' **hospitalité (f.)** hospitality
un **hôtel** hotel; *hôtel de ville* city hall
une **hôtesse de l'air** female flight attendant

l' **huile (f.)** oil *[car]*
huit eight
huitième eighth
une **huître** oyster 2
humain(e) human 10; *les ressources (f.) humaines* human resources 10; *un directeur, une directrice des ressources humaines (DRH)* director of human resources 10
humanitaire humanitarian
une **humeur** humor, mood 5; *je ne suis pas trop d'humeur pour* I'm not in the mood for 5
humide humid 4
hybride hybrid

I

ici here
une **icône** icon
l' **idéalisme (m.)** idealism 2
une **idée** idea; *Bonne idée!* Good idea!
une **identité** identity 4; *une pièce d'identité* piece of identification 4
il he; it; *il se pourrait que* it's possible that 4; *il vaut mieux que* it's better that 4; *il y a* there are/is; *il y a (+ time)* (time) ago
une **île** island 4
illustrer to illustrate 8
ils they (m.)
une **image** image, picture
l' **imaginaire (m.)** fantasy 6
une **imagination** imagination 10
imaginer to imagine
immense immense 7
un **immeuble** apartment building
l' **important (neutr.)** what's important
important(e) important 4
impossible impossible
imprécis(e) vague 5
imprenable unobstructed 5
une **impression** impression 5; *avoir l'impression (de)* to have the impression (of) 6
l' **impressionnisme (m.)** Impressionism 7
un(e) **impressionniste** Impressionist 7
impressionniste Impressionist
une **imprimante** printer
imprimer to print
improviser to improvise 2
incapable incapable 9
incroyable incredible
l' **Inde (f.)** India 10
les **indigènes (m.)** native people
indiquer to indicate, to point out/to
indispensable indispensable 4
un **individu** individual 10
individuel, individuelle individual 3; *une maison individuelle* single-family house 3
l' **Indonésie (f.)** Indonesia 10
une **industrie** industry; *industrie du divertissement* entertainment industry
un **infirmier, une infirmière** nurse
une **inflation** inflation 2; *un taux d'inflation* inflation rate 2
influencer to influence 8
l' **infographie (f.)** computer graphics 6
les **informations (infos) (f.)** news
l' **informatique (f.)** computer science; information technology; *le secteur de l'informatique* information technology industry
informer to inform
un **ingénieur** engineer
l' **initiative (f.): un syndicat d'initiative** tourist information office
inquiet, inquiète worried
s' **inquiéter** to worry 1
une **inquiétude** worry
s' **inscrire** to register; *s'inscrire en letters* to declare a major in Humanities
un **insecte** insect
insister (sur) to insist (on)
installer to install
s' **installer** to get settled
un **instant** moment; *pour l'instant* for the moment
un **instituteur, une institutrice** elementary school teacher
un **instrument** musical instrument
s' **intégrer (à)** to integrate (into) 6
intelligent(e) intelligent
intense intense 5
intéressant(e) interesting
intéressé(e) interested 1
intéresser to interest
s' **intéresser (à)** to be interested (in)
une **interface** interface
l' **intérieur (m.)** inside
international(e) international
(l') **Internet (m.)** Internet
un **interprète** performer 7
une **intervention: faire une intervention** to organize an intervention
une **interview** interview 10
interviewer to interview 9
intimiste intimate 7
introduire to introduce 8
l' **inutile (m.)** what is useless
une **invention** invention 7
une **invitation** invitation 2
un(e) **invité(e)** guest
inviter to invite
l' **Italie (f.)** Italy
italien(ne) Italian
un **itinéraire** itinerary
ivoirien(ne) from, of the Ivory Coast

J

la **jambe** leg
le **jambon** ham; *jambon persillé* ham and pork dish made with chopped parsley 5
janvier January
le **Japon** Japan 10
japonais(e) Japonese
la **joaillerie** fine jewelry 10
un **jardin** garden, park
le **jasmin** jasmine
jaune yellow
le **jazz** jazz music
je/j' I
un **jean** jeans
jeter to throw 5; *jeter un coup d'œil (à)* to glance (at) 5; *N'en jette plus! [inform.]* Enough! Stop it! 8
un **jet ski** jet ski
un **jeu: jeu d'adresse** game of skill; *jeu télévisé* (TV) game show; *jeu vidéo* video game; *les Jeux Olympiques (m.)* Olympic Games
jeudi Thursday
jeune young
un(e) **jeune** young man/woman
la **jeunesse** youth 2
joering: faire du ski joering to skijor 4
joindre to attach
joli(e) pretty
joliment dit nicely said
la **Jordanie** Jordan 10
jouer to play; *jouer à cache-cache* to play hide-and-seek 1; *jouer à la marelle* to play hopscotch 1; *jouer à la poupée* to play with dolls 1; *jouer au basket (basketball)* to play basketball; *jouer au foot (football)* to play soccer; *jouer au hockey sur glace* to play ice hockey; *jouer aux billes* to play marbles 1; *jouer aux jeux*

vidéo to play video games; *jouer aux petites voitures* to play with toy cars 1; *jouer de (+ instrument)* to play (instrument); *jouer un rôle* to play a role; *jouer un tour* to place a spell on 3

un **jour** day; one day, someday; *le Jour de l'an* New Year's Day

un **journal** newspaper

une **journée** day

juillet July

juin June

jumeau, jumelle twin; *un lit jumeau* twin-sized bed

des **jumelles (f.)** binoculars

junior junior 8

une **jupe** skirt

un **jus** juice; *jus d'orange* orange juice; *jus de pamplemousse* grapefruit juice; *jus de pomme* apple juice

jusqu'à until

juste fair; just 3; only

justement fittingly 3

K

un **kayak: faire du kayak** to go kayaking

le **ketchup** ketchup

kiffer *[inform.]* to like

un **kilo (de)** kilogram (of)

un **kilomètre** kilometer

un(e) **kiné (kinésithérapeute)** physical therapist 8; *chez le kiné* at/to the physical therapy office 8

un **kiosque** stand; *kiosque à journaux* newsstand

un **klaxon** horn

L

là there

là-bas over there

un **labo (laboratoire)** science lab; *laboratoire de recherches* research laboratory 1

un **lac** lake

un **lâcheur, une lâcheuse *[inform.]*** flake 9

laid(e) ugly

la **laine** wool; *en laine* made of wool; *un bonnet en laine* wool hat

laisser to leave, to let; *Laisse-moi finir!* Let me finish!

le **lait** milk

un **lambi** lambis

une **lampe** lamp; *lampe de poche* flashlight

lancer to launch 10

une **langouste** spiny lobster

une **langue** language

un **lapin** rabbit

large wide 2

une **largeur** width; *régler la largeur du champ* to adjust the zoom

latier, latière dairy 10; *un produit laitier* dairy product 10

laver: une machine à laver washing machine

se **laver** to wash (oneself)

un **lave-vaisselle** dishwasher

le, la, l' it *[object pronoun]*; the

un **leader** leader 10; *leader mondial* world leader 10

un **lecteur: lecteur de DVD** DVD player; *lecteur de MP3* MP3 player

la **lecture** reading

une **légende** legend

un **légume** vegetable

le **lendemain** next day

les the; them

la **lessive: faire la lessive** to wash clothes

une **lettre** letter; *lettre de candidature* application letter 8; *lettre de motivation* cover letter 8; *une boîte aux lettres* mailbox 6

les **lettres (f.)** Humanities; *s'inscrire en lettres* to declare a major in Humanities

le, la **leur** theirs 9

leur their; to them

leurs their

lèver: Lève la tête! Look up!

se **lever** to get up

la **lèvre:** *un rouge à lèvres* lipstick

une **librairie** bookstore

libre free; *en écoute libre* listening trial; *un auditeur, une auditrice libre* auditor of a class 10; *une borne libre-service* self-service kiosk

une **licorne** unicorn

un **lien** link

un **lieu** place 5; *avoir lieu* to take place; *donner lieu à* to give rise to 7

une **ligne** line 7; *la ligne* figure; *en ligne* online

une **limonade** lemon-lime soda

le **lin** linen; *de lin* made of linen; *un mouchoir de lin* linen handkerchief

le **linge: faire sécher le linge** to dry clothes

une **liquette** shirt 9

une **liquide** liquid 6; *l'argent (m.) liquide* cash 6

lire to read

une **liste** list; *faire une liste* to make a list

un **lit** bed; *lit jumeau* twin-sized bed; *lits superposés* bunk beds

un **litre (de)** liter (of)

un **livre** book; *livre de poche* paperback 6

une **livre** pound

un **lobby** lobby 5

local(e) local 10

un(e) **locataire** tenant 3

un **lockscreen** lock screen

un **logement** housing 3

un **logiciel** software

loin (de) far (from)

long, longue long; *un long métrage* feature film 5

le **long de** alongside

longtemps: ça fait longtemps que it's been a long time since

une **longueur** length 2

un **look** look 2; *look tradi* traditional look 2

lorsque when 1

louer to rent

la **luge: faire de la luge** to go sledding 4

lui to her/him

une **lumière** light

un **lump** lumpfish 2; *des œufs (m.) de lump* lumpfish roe 2

lundi Monday

des **lunettes (f.)** glasses; *lunettes de soleil* sunglasses

lutter to fight

le **luxe** luxury 10

le **Luxembourg** Luxembourg

luxembourgeois(e) from, of Luxembourg

le **Lyonnais** Lyon region

lyonnais(e) from, of Lyon

le **lyrisme** lyricism 7

M

un **machin** thing 2

une **machine** machine; *machine à laver* washing machine

madame (Mme) Ma'am, Mrs., Ms.

mademoiselle (Mlle) Miss, Ms.

un **magasin** store

un **magazine** magazine

maghrébin(e) from, of the Maghreb

un(e) **magicien(ne)** magician 3

magique magical

un **magret de canard** duck breast 2

mai May

maigre skinny 9

maigrir to lose weight

un **maillot** jersey; *maillot de bain* bathing suit

la	**main** hand; *la main dans la main* hand in hand; *un coup de main* (helping) hand 2
	maintenant now
	maints many 5
le	**maire, madame le maire** mayor
	mais but
une	**maison** home, house; *maison de rêve* dream house; *maison hantée* haunted house; *maison individuelle* single-family house 3; *maison mitoyenne* row house 3
un	**maître, une maîtresse** master, mistress 3
une	**maîtrise** Master's degree 10
	mal badly; *avoir mal (à...)* to be hurt, to have a/an... ache; *Ça va mal.* Things are going badly.; *le plus mal* the worst; *plus mal* worse
un(e)	**malade** sick person
	malade sick
une	**maladie** illness; *une assurance maladie* health insurance 8
la	**Malaisie** Malaysia 10
le	**Mali** Mali
	malien(ne) Malian
	Mamy grandma
la	**Manche** English Channel
une	**mandarine** mandarin orange 2
un	**manège: faire un tour de manège** to go on a carnival ride
un	**manga** manga 6
	manger to eat
une	**mangouste** mongoose
une	**mangrove** mangrove
une	**manière** way 3
une	**manif (manifestation)** street demonstration
un	**mannequin** model
	manquer to lack
un	**manteau** coat
le	**maquillage** make-up
se	**maquiller** to put on make-up
un(e)	**marchand(e)** merchant
un	**marché** outdoor market; *le marché* market *[financial]*; *marché aux puces* flea market
	marcher to walk; to work; *faire marcher* to make (something) work
	mardi Tuesday
une	**marée** tide; *marée noire* oil slick
la	**marelle: jouer à la marelle** to play hopscotch 1
un	**mari** husband
un	**mariage** wedding; *un anniversaire de mariage* wedding anniversary
un	**marié** groom
une	**mariée** bride; *une robe de mariée* wedding dress
se	**marier** to get married
	marin(e): une tortue marine sea turtle
	marinier, marinière: une sauce marinière white wine sauce 5
le	**marketing** marketing 10
la	**maroquinerie** leather goods 10
une	**marque** brand 10
	marqué(e) brand name 10
	marquer to score
une	**marraine** godmother 1
un	**marron** chestnut 2; *la dinde aux marrons* turkey with chestnuts 2
	marron brown
	mars March
un	**marteau** hammer 3
	martiniquais(e) from, of Martinique
la	**Martinique** Martinique
un	**mas** ***[Mart.]*** mask
le	**mascara** mascara
un	**masque** mask; *masque de ski* ski goggles 4
une	**masse d'eau** body of water
un	**massif** mountain range
un	**match** game
un	**matelas pneumatique** inflatable water mattress
les	**maths (f.)** math
une	**matière** class subject
le	**matin** morning
la	**matinée** morning
	mauvais(e) bad; *il fait mauvais* the weather is bad
la	**mayonnaise** mayo
	me (m') me; to me
un(e)	**mécanicien(ne)** mechanic
la	**mécanique** mechanics 3
	méchant(e) mean
une	**médaille** medal 2
un	**médecin** doctor; *un cabinet de médecin* doctor's office
la	**médecine** medicine 6
les	**médias (m.)** media 2
une	**médiathèque** media center
	médical(e) medical 8
	médicalisé(e) medicalized 8
	méditerranéen(ne) Mediterranean 9
se	**méfier (de)** to be wary (of) 3
les	**meilleurs (m.)** the best
la	**mélancolie** melancholy 7
	mélanger to mix 2
une	**mélodie** melody 7
un	**melon** melon
	même even; same; *même que [inform.]* that 3; *quand même* after all, regardless 2
le	**ménage** household, housework; *des affaires (f.) de ménage* house cleaning items; *faire le ménage* to do housework; *un homme de ménage* janitor 5
la	**menthe** mint; *un diabolo menthe* lemon-lime soda with mint syrup
	mentir to lie 7
un	**menu fixe** fixed menu
une	**mer** sea; *mer des Caraïbes* Caribbean Sea; *mer Méditerranée* Mediterranean Sea; *mer du Nord* North Sea; *au bord de la mer* by the seaside; *le bord de mer* seaside; *les fruits de mer (m.)* seafood
	merci thank you
	mercredi Wednesday
une	**mère** mother
	merveilleux, merveilleuse marvelous
	mesdemoiselles (f.) plural of "**mademoiselle**"
un	**message** message
une	**messagerie** messaging
	mesurer to measure 2
	mesureur: un verre mesureur measuring cup 2
un	**métal** metal 2; *en métal* made of metal 2
la	**météo** weather; weather forecast; *un bulletin météo(rologique)* weather forecast
une	**méthode** method 7
un	**métier** job
un	**métrage: long métrage** feature film 5
le	**métro** subway; *en métro* by subway
un	**metteur en scène** director
	mettre to put (on), to set; *mettre d'accord* to get people to agree 1; *mettre en pratique* to put into practice 8; *mettre en valeur* to accentuate; *mettre le couvert* to set the table
se	**mettre: se mettre en mode photo** to go into photo mode; *mets-toi devant l'écran* place yourself in front of the TV
un	**meuble** piece of furniture
	meunier, meunière rolled in flour and sautéed
le	**Mexique** Mexico 10
un	**micro-onde** microwave
	midi noon
le	**mien, la mienne** mine 9

mieux better; *mieux que* better than; *il vaut mieux que* it's better that 4; *le mieux* the best; *se porter mieux* to feel/do better
mille thousand
un **millefeuille** layered custard pastry
un **million** million
mi-long, mi-longue shoulder-length (hair) 9
mince thin 9
mince darn, shoot
une **mine** appearance, expression
minuit midnight
une **minute** minute
un **miroir** mirror; *une galerie des miroirs déformants* fun house
une **mission** mission
la **mi-temps: à mi-temps** half-time 8
mitoyen(ne) adjoining 3; *une maison mitoyenne* row house 3
un **mixer** blender 2
une **MJC** community center 1
moche ugly
la **mode** fashion 2
un **mode: se mettre en mode photo** to go into photo mode
moderne modern
moderniser to modernize
moi me
moins less; *moins le quart* quarter to; *moins (+ adverb) + que* less... than; *au moins* at least; *le moins* the least
un **mois** month
un **moment** moment; *en ce moment* at the moment 6
mon, ma, mes my; *mon Dieu* my god 5
le **monde** everyone, world; *tout le monde* everybody
mondial(e) world 10; *un leader mondial* world leader 10
la **mondialisation** globalization 10
monégasque from, of Monaco 5
un **moniteur, une monitrice** instructor 4; *un moniteur* monitor
la **monnaie** cash 6
monoparental(e): une famille monoparentale single-parent family 1
un **monospace** minivan
monsieur (M.) Mr., sir
une **montagne** mountain; *un ananas montagne* mountain pineapple; *faire un tour de montagnes russes* to go on a roller coaster ride
monter to get in/on, to go up; *monter à bord* to board
une **montre** watch
montrer to show
un **monument** monument
se **moquer (de)** to make fun (of)
la **moquette** carpeting 3
une **morale** moral 7
un **morceau (de)** piece (of)
la **mort** death 5; *une trompette de la mort* trumpet of the dead mushroom 5
mort(e) dead
une **morue** cod; *un accra de morue* cod fritter
une **mosquée** mosque
un **mot** word; *ce mot-là* this (very) word
la **motivation** motivation 8; *une lettre de motivation* cover letter 8
un **mouchoir** handkerchief; *mouchoir de lin* linen handkerchief
mourir to die 8
une **mousse au chocolat** chocolate mousse
la **moutarde** mustard
un **mouton** sheep
un **mouvement** movement
un **moyen** means; *moyen de transport* means of transportation; *avoir les moyens* to be able to afford, to have the means 8
moyen(ne) medium; *une petite et moyenne entreprise (PME)* small business 1
multinational(e) multinational 10
un **multiplexe** multiplex cinema 5
la **multiplication** multiplication 8; *une table de multiplication* multiplication table 8
un **mur** wall 3
mûr(e) ripe
musclé(e) muscular 9
un **musée** museum
musical(e) musical; *un film musical* musical
un **music-hall** music hall
la **musique** music; *musique alternative* alternative music; *musique classique* classical music; *musique folklorique* folk music; *musique pop* pop music; *une émission de musique* music show
muter to transfer 1; *se faire muter* to get reassigned 1
un **mystère** mystery 6

N

n'est-ce pas isn't that so
n'importe: n'importe quel, quelle just any 9; *n'importe qui* anyone 9
nager to swim
un **nanar** flop 5
les **nanotechnologies (f.)** nanotechnology 1
une **nappe** tablecloth
une **nation** nation 2
national(e) national; *le Produit National Brut (PNB)* GNP (Gross National Product) 2; *une fête nationale* national holiday
la **nature** nature; *nature morte* still life
naviguer to browse
un **nay** ney *[instrument]*
ne: ne (n')... aucun(e) no, none, not any, not one 4; *ne (n')... jamais* never; *ne (n')... ni... ni* neither... nor 4; *ne (n')... pas* not; *ne (n')... pas encore* not yet; *ne (n')... personne* nobody, no one, not anyone; *ne (n')... plus* no longer, not anymore; *ne (n')... que* only 4; *ne (n')... rien* nothing; *N'en jette plus! [inform.]* Enough! Stop it! 8
néanmoins nevertheless 8
nécessaire necessary
la **neige** snow 2; *faire de la raquette à neige* to go snowshoeing 4; *une boule de neige* snowball 2; *une classe de neige* ski class 4
neiger to snow; *il neige* it's snowing
le **néo-classicisme** neoclassicism 7
néoclassique neo-classic 7
le **néo-impressionnisme** Neo-impressionism 7
nettoyer to clean
neuf nine
neuf, neuve new; *de neuf* new; *Quoi de neuf?* What's new?
neuvième ninth
le **nez** nose
ni neither, nor 4; *ne (n')... ni... ni* neither... nor 4
niçois(e): une salade niçoise tuna salad
un **niveau** level
les **noces (f.): un voyage de noces** honeymoon 1
Noël Christmas; *le réveillon de Noël* Christmas Eve celebration 2; *une bûche de Noël* yule log 2; *un sapin de Noël* Christmas tree 2
noir(e) black
un **nom** name
un **nombre** number
non no; *non plus* neither; *Je crains que non.* I'm afraid not. 2

le **nord** north; *l'Amérique du Nord (f.)* North America
normand(e) from, of Normandy region
la **Normandie** Normandy region
une **note** grade
le, la **nôtre** ours 9
notre, nos our
nourrir to feed
la **nourriture** food
nous to us; us; we; *aucun de nous ne (+ verb)* none of us (+ verb) 4
nouveau new; *nouvel, nouvelle* new
le **Nouveau-Brunswick** New Brunswick
une **nouveauté** new release 5
une **nouvelle** short story 6
novembre November
nucléaire nuclear; *une famille nucléaire* nuclear family 1
la **nuit** night; *faire une nuit blanche* to stay up all night
nul, nulle bad
un **numéro** number; *numéro de téléphone* phone number
le **Nutella** spread made of hazelnut and chocolate

O

un **objet** object; *objet d'art* art object
obligatoire mandatory
obligé(e) (de) obligated (to) 8; *être obligé(e) (de)* to be obligated (to) 8
observer to observe
obtenir to obtain 4
une **occasion** chance, occasion 4; *avoir l'occasion (de)* to have the opportunity (to) 4
occupé(e) busy; *être occupé(e)* to be busy
occuper to occupy
s' **occuper (de)** to take care (of)
un **océan** ocean; *océan Atlantique* Atlantic Ocean; *océan Indien* Indian Ocean; *océan Pacifique* Pacific Ocean
octobre October
l' **œil (m.)** eye; *jeter un coup d'œil (à)* to glance (at) 5
un **œuf** egg; *œufs brouillés* scrambled eggs; *œufs de lump (m.)* lumpfish roe 2; *œufs sur le plat* eggs sunny side up
une **œuvre** work; *un hors-d'œuvre* appetizer 2
un **office** office 4; *office de tourisme* tourist office 4
officiel, officielle official
offrir to give, to offer
oh oh; *oh là là* oh dear, oh no, wow
un **oignon** onion
un **oiseau** bird
une **olive** olive
une **omelette** omelette
on one, they, we; *on te fait* they (one) make(s) you 8
un **oncle** uncle
une **ONG (organisation non gouvernementale)** NGO (non-governmental organization)
onze eleven
l' **or (m.)** gold; *en or* made of gold
une **orange** orange
orange orange
une **orangerie** orangery
un **orchestre** orchestra 5; *un chef d'orchestre* conductor 5
une **orchidée** orchid; *orchidée suspendue* tropical orchid
un **ordre** order; *en ordre* in order
un **ordinateur** computer; *ordinateur portable* laptop computer
l' **oreille (f.)** ear; *une boucle d'oreille* earring
organisé(e) organized 4
original(e) original 5; *une version originale (V.O.)* original version 5
une **origine** origin 3; *être d'origine (+ adjective)* to come from (+ country) 3
ou or
où when; where
oublier to forget
un **oud** oud *[instrument]*
l' **ouest (m.)** west
oui yes
ouille ouch
un **ours** bear; *ours polaire* polar bear
une **ouverture** opening 8
ouvrir to open

P

une **page: à la page** in fashion 2
le **pain** bread; *pain grillé* toast; *pain perdu* French toast
la **paix** peace 2
pâle pale 7
une **pamplemousse** grapefruit; *un jus de pamplemousse* grapefruit juice
un **panda** panda; *panda géant* giant panda
paniqué(e) panicky 9
une **panne: en panne** broken down
un **panneau** panel
un **pantalon** pants
le **papier** paper; *papier peint* wallpaper 3; *papier toilette* toilet paper 10; *une feuille de papier* sheet of paper
un **papillon** butterfly
Papy grandpa
un **paquet** package; *paquet (de)* packet (of)
par through, via; with; *par contre* however, on the other hand 8; *par la suite* consequently 9
le **parachutisme ascensionnel: faire du parachutisme ascensionnel** to go parasailing
paraître to appear, to seem 5
un **parasol** (beach) umbrella
un **parc** park; *parc d'attractions* amusement park
parce que because
pardi of course *[regional]*
pardon pardon me
un **pare-brise** windshield
pareil, pareille the same; *c'est pareil* it's the same
les **parents (m.)** parents
paresseux, paresseuse lazy
parfait(e) perfect 5
parfaitement perfectly
parfois sometimes
un **parfum** perfume, scent
parisien(ne) from, of Paris
parlementaire parliamentary
parler to speak, to talk; *parler de* to be about 6; *sans parler de* not to mention 10
se **parler** to talk to each other/one another
parles: tu parles yeah right
des **paroles (f.)** lyrics
le **parquet** hardwood flooring 3
part: à part aside from 9
partager to share 5
un **parti** party 2; *parti politique* political party 2; *le parti politique socialiste* socialist political party 2
particulier, particulière personal 1; *un cours particulier* private class 1
une **partie** part 7; *faire partie (de)* to belong (to)
partir to leave; *partir en voyage* to take a journey 8; *C'est parti!* Here we go!
partout everywhere
pas not; *pas du tout* not at all; *pas la tête à* not the type to 9; *pas mal* not bad; *pas très bien* not very well; *ne (n')... pas* not

un **passager, une passagère** passenger
un(e) **passant(e)** passer-by 3
le **passé** past 4
un **passeport** passport 4
passer to go through; to move over (something), to pass; to play 2; to spend (time); *passer à la radio* to play on the radio 2; *passer de... à* to move from... to 7; *passer l'aspirateur* to vacuum; *on passe... ...* is playing (at the movies) 2
se **passer** to happen 8
un **passe-temps** pastime
une **passion** passion
passionnant(e) fascinating
passionné(e) (de) passionate (about)
passionnément passionately 2
une **passoire** colander 2
une **pastèque** watermelon
le **pâté** pâté
des **pâtes (f.)** pasta
le **patinage (artistique)** (figure) skating
une **pâtisserie** bakery, pastry shop
une **pause** pause 5
pauvre poor
la **pauvreté** poverty
payer to pay
un **payeur, une payeuse** someone who pays
un **pays** country
un **paysage** landscape
la **peau** skin 10
une **pêche** peach; *la pêche* fishing; *une canne à pêche* fishing pole
pêcher to fish
un **pêcheur, une pêcheuse** fisherman, fisherwoman 3
un **peigne** comb
se **peigner** to comb one's hair
un **peignoir de bain** bathrobe
peindre to paint 3
une **peine: ce n'est pas la peine** it's not worth it 1
peint(e): le papier peint wallpaper 3
un(e) **peintre** painter
une **peinture** painting; *la peinture* painting 7
une **pelouse** lawn
pendant during; for; *pendant que* while 3; *pendant que tu y es* while you're at it
une **pendule** clock
penser to think
perdre to lose
perdu(e) lost; *le pain perdu* French toast
un **père** father
une **perle** pearl; *un collier de/en perles* pearl necklace
un **permis (de conduire)** driver's license 8
une **perruque** wig 8
persillé(e): le jambon persillé ham and porc dish made with chopped parsley 5
perso *[inform.]* egotistical 8; *être perso [inform.]* to be egotistical 8
une **personnalité** celebrity
une **personne** person; *ne (n')... personne* no one, nobody, not anyone
un **personnel** personnel, staff 8; *un chef du personnel* personnel manager 8
personnel, personnelle personal 2
personnellement personally 5
une **perspective** perspective
persuadé(e) convinced 4; persuaded
peser to weigh 6
petit, petite little, short, small; *en petit comité* with a few friends 2; *jouer aux petites voitures* to play with toy cars 1; *une petite annonce* want ad 8; *une petite voiture* toy car 1
un(e) **petit(e) commerçant(e)** shopkeeper
le **petit déjeuner** breakfast
une **petite et moyenne entreprise (PME)** small business 1
des **petits pois (m.)** peas
le **pétrole** petroleum
(un) **peu** (a) little; *un peu de* a little of
un **peuple** people 8
la **peur: avoir peur (de)** to be afraid (of); *avoir peur du vide* to be afraid of heights
peut-être maybe
une **pharmacie** drugstore
les **Philippines (f.)** Philippines 10
une **photo** photo; *prendre (quelque chose) en photo* to take a picture (of something); *re-photo* another photo
photogénique photogenic 9
la **physique** physics
un(e) **pianiste** pianist
un **piano** piano
une **pièce** play; room; *pièce (de monnaie)* coin 6; *pièce d'identité* piece of identification 4; *pièce de théâtre* play 6
le **pied** foot; *à pied* on foot; *faire une randonnée à pied* to hike
un(e) **pilote** pilot
un **pinceau** paintbrush 7
piqueniquer to picnic
un **piranha** piranha
un **pirate** pirate
pire worse; *le pire* the worst
une **pirogue** pirogue; *en pirogue* by pirogue
une **piscine** swimming pool
une **pizza** pizza
un **placard** closet
une **place** place 2; square; *à sa place* in its place 2; *sur place* on the premises 4
une **plage** beach; *une serviette de plage* beach towel
se **plaindre** to complain
une **plaine** plain
une **plainte** complaint 7
plaire (à) to please 7
un **plaisir** pleasure
un **plan** city map; shot 7; *en gros plan* in a close-up 7; *le premier plan* foreground; *au premier plan* in the foreground
la **planche à voile: faire de la planche à voile** to wind surf 4
une **planète** planet
planifier to plan 4
une **plante** plant
la **plastique** plastic; *en plastique* made of plastic
un **plat** dish; *plat principal* main dish; *des œufs (m.) sur le plat* eggs sunny side up
plat(e) flat, lifeless 5
un **plateau** platter
plein(e) full; *plein (de)* a lot (of) 8; *à plein temps* full-time 8; *en plein air* outdoors; *faire le plein* to fill up the gas tank
pleurer to cry
pleuvoir to rain; *il pleut* it's raining
la **plongée sous-marine: faire de la plongée sous-marine** to go scuba diving
plonger to dive
la **plupart de** most 9
plus more; *plus mal* worse; *plus (+ adverb) + que* more... than; *plus de (+ noun)* more; *de plus en plus* more and more 7; *en plus* in addition to; *en y regardant de plus près* on a closer look 4; *le/la/les plus (+adjectif)* the most (+ adjective); *le plus* the most; *le plus mal* the worst; *ne (n')... plus* no longer, not anymore; *non plus* neither

plusieurs several
plutôt instead; quite 5; rather
un **pneu** tire
pneumatique: un matelas pneumatique inflatable water mattress
une **poche** pocket; *une lampe de poche* flashlight; *un livre de poche* paperback 6
une **poêle** frying pan
un **poème** poem
la **poésie** poetry 6
un **poète, une femme poète** poet 7
poétique poetic 7
le **poignet** wrist 4; *se casser le poignet* to break one's wrist 4
un **point de vue** viewpoint
une **poire** pear; *en forme de poire* pear-shaped 2
un **pois** polka dot 9; *à pois* polka dots 9
un **poisson (rouge)** (gold)fish
la **poitrine** chest
le **poivre** pepper
un **poivron** bell pepper
policier, policière detective; *un film policier* detective movie
la **politique** politics 2
politique political; *le parti politique socialiste* socialist political party 2; *les sciences (f.) politiques (sciences po)* political science 6; *une femme politique* female politician; *un homme politique* male politician; *un parti politique* political party 2
polluant polluting
pollué(e) polluted
polluer to pollute
un **pollueur, une pollueuse** polluter
la **pollution** pollution
une **pomme** apple; *un jus de pomme* apple juice; *une tarte aux pommes* apple pie
un **pont** bridge
pop: la musique pop pop music
populaire popular 7
le **porc** pork
un **port** port; *port micro-USB* USB port
un **portable** cell phone
portable: une téléphone portable cell phone
une **porte** door; *porte d'embarquement* boarding gate
un **portefeuille** wallet
porter to wear
se **porter: se porter mieux** to feel/do better
un **portrait** portrait
posé(e) set down 2
poser to put down 2; to put up 3
une **position** position 7; *prendre position (sur)* to take a position (on) 7
le **positionnement** positioning 6
une **possibilité** possibility
possible possible
postal(e): une carte postale postcard
un **poste** job position 1
une **poste** post office
un **postier, une postière** postal worker 6
un **pot (de)** a jar (of)
un **potage** soup
une **poubelle** garbage can
une **poule** hen
le **poulet** chicken
une **poupée** doll 1; *jouer à la poupée* to play with dolls 1
pour for; *pour commencer* for starters; *pour que* so that 7; *pour t'avancer* to help you 2; *c'est pour ça que* that/this is why
pourquoi why
pousser un cri to scream
pouvoir to be able (to); *ne pas pouvoir s'empêcher (de)* cannot help (but) 2
se **pouvoir: il se pourrait que** it's possible that 4
un **pouvoir** power
une **pratique** practice 8; *mettre en pratique* to put into practice 8
pratique practical 5
précisément precisely
des **précisions (f.)** specific information 5
préféré(e) favorite
préférer to prefer
premier, première first; *au premier plan* in the foreground; *en première année* in the first year; *le premier plan* foreground; *les premiers secours (m.)* first-aid; *une trousse de premiers secours* first-aid kit
une **première** première (of movie) 6
premièrement firstly 8
prendre to have (food or drink), to take; *prendre des vacances* to take a vacation; *prendre (quelque chose) en photo* to take a picture (of something); *prendre position (sur)* to take a position (on) 7; *prendre une décision* to make a decision 10
un **prénom** first name
des **préparatifs (m.)** preparations 4; *préparatifs de départ* travel preparations 4
préparer to make; to prepare
se **préparer** to get (oneself) ready
une **préposition** preposition
près de near; *en y regardant de plus près* on a closer look 4
le **présent** present 8
un **présentateur, une présentatrice** news anchor
présenter (à) to introduce (to someone)
un(e) **président(e)** president 10; *président directeur général (PDG)* CEO 10
présidentiel, présidentielle presidential 2; *les élections (f.) présidentielles* presidential elections 2
presque almost; nearly
des **prestations (f.)** amenities 5
prêt(e) ready
le **prêt-à-porter** ready-to-wear 2
prêter to lend
les **prévisions (f.)** forecast
prévu(e) planned 2
une **princesse** princess 1
principal(e) main; *un plat principal* main dish
le **printemps** spring
un **priorité** priority 9
un **prisonnier, une prisonnière** prisoner 2
privé(e) private 8
un **problème** problem
prochain(e) next
une **production** production 10
un **produit** product 2; *produit alimentaire* food product 10; *produit laitier* dairy product 10; *le Produit National Brut (PNB)* GNP (Gross National Product) 2
un(e) **prof** teacher
une **profession** profession; *Quelle est votre profession?* What is your profession?
un **professionnel, une professionnelle** professional
un **profil** profile
profiter to take advantage of; *profiter de* to benefit from
un **programme** plan
le **progrès** progress
un **projet** project
projeter to plan
prolongé(e) extended
une **promenade** walk
se **promener** to go for a walk

une **promesse: faire une promesse** to make a promise
promettre to promise; *ça promet* it sounds promising 5
promis(e) promised 6; *c'est promis* it's a promise 6
une **promo** sale
un **propos: à propos de** about 2
proposer to offer 10; to suggest
propre clean 3
protéger to protect
provençal(e) from, of Provence
la **Provence** Provence
une **province** province
un **proviseur** principal
des **provisions (f.)** supplies
prudemment carefully
la **psychologie** psychology 6
puisque since 2
puissant(e) powerful
puis then
un **puits** well
un **pull** sweater
un **pyjama** pyjamas

Q

qu'est-ce que what; *Qu'est-ce qu'elle a?* What's wrong with her?; *Qu'est-ce que tu aimes faire?* What do you like to do?; *Qu'est-ce que tu fais?* What are you doing?
qu'est-ce qui what
un **quai** platform
une **qualité** quality 8
quand when; *quand même* after all, regardless 2; *depuis quand* since when
une **quarantaine** about forty 9; *d'une quarantaine d'années* in one's forties 9
quarante forty
un **quart** quarter; *et quart* quarter past; *moins le quart* quarter to
un **quartier** area, district
quatorze fourteen
quatre four
quatre-vingt-dix ninety
quatre-vingts eighty
quatrième fourth
que as, than; that; which; whom 2; *aussitôt que* as soon as 1; *dès que* as soon as; *même que [inform.]* that 3; *ne(n')... que* only 4; *pendant que* while 3; *pour que* so that 7
le **Québec** Quebec
québécois(e) from, of Quebec
quel, quelle what, which; *n'importe quel, quelle* just any 9
quelque a few, some 5
quelque chose something; *arriver à faire quelque chose* to bring oneself to do something 6
quelqu'un somebody, someone
une **question** question
qui that, who; which; *ce qui* what; *n'importe qui* anyone 9
une **quiche** quiche
quinze fifteen
quitter to leave
se **quitter** to leave one another 1
quoi what; you know what I mean; *Quoi de neuf?* What's new?
quotidien(ne) daily

R

le **racisme** racism
racler to scrape, to scrub 2
raconter to tell
la **radiation** radiation
une **radio** radio; *passer à la radio* to play on the radio 2
le **raï** Rai music
raide straight (hair) 9
un **raisin** grape
la **raison: avoir raison** to be right
ramasser to pick up 1
un **ramier** woodpigeon
une **randonnée** hike; *faire une randonnée à pied* to hike; *faire une randonnée équestre* to go on a trail ride 4
ranger to arrange, to pick up
le **rap** rap music
rapide fast
rapidement quickly 3
se **rappeler** to remember
un **rapport** relationship 2
rapporter to bring in 10
la **raquette à neige: faire de la raquette à neige** to go snowshoeing 4
se **raser** to shave
un **rasoir** razor
se **rassurer** to reassure (oneself); *rassure-toi* don't worry
la **ratatouille** ratatouille
raté(e) failed
rater to mess up 2
un **raton laveur** raccoon
une **rayure** stripe 9; *à rayures* striped 9
une **réaction** reaction 9
un **réalisateur, une réalisatrice** movie director 5
réalisé(e) (par) directed (by) 2
réaliser to direct (movie) 6; to realize
le **réalisme** realism 7
réaliste realistic; *une chanson réaliste* chanson réaliste 7
la **réalité** reality 6
une **réception** reception 1; *la réception* reception desk
un(e) **réceptionniste** hotel clerk
une **recette** recipe
recevoir to get, to host, to receive
un **réchaud** portable stove
réchauffer to heat up
la **recherche** research 1; *des recherches* research 3; *des recherches généalogiques* genealogical research 3; *un laboratoire de recherches* research laboratory 1
rechercher to look for/into 7
un **récit** account 9
une **récompense** award 2
recomposé(e): une famille recomposée blended family 1
reconnaître to recognize
se **reconnaître** to see oneself as 7
rectangulaire rectangular 2
un **recueil** collection 6
récupérer to recapture 2
recycler to recycle
une **rédaction** composition
rédiger to write 8
réduire to reduce 2
une **rééducation** physical therapy 8
réfléchir (à) to consider, to think over; *en y réfléchissant bien* on second thought 4
un **reflet** reflection 7
une **réflexion** thought
un **regard** look
regarder to watch; *en y regardant de plus près* on a closer look 4
se **regarder** to look at oneself
le **reggae** reggae music
un **régime** regime 8
une **région** region
régional(e) regional 10
un **réglage** adjustment
régler to adjust; to pay; *régler la largeur du champ* to adjust the zoom
un **regret** regret 1
regretter to be sorry 5
une **reine** queen
une **religieuse** cream puff pastry
remarquable remarkable
remarque look, well
remarquer to notice
rembourser to reimburse
un **remède** remedy, solution
remercie: je vous remercie (de) ***[form.]*** thank you (for)

remettre to put back
se **remettre (à)** to start something again; *on s'y remet* let's get back to it
une **remise: un centre de remise en forme** fitness center 5
un **remous: un bain à remous** whirlpool bath 5
remplacer to replace
remplir to fill out 9; to fill up
remuer to stir, to toss 2
un **renard** fox 7
se **rencontrer** to meet (someone)
un **rendez-vous** meeting
rendre to give back, to return; to turn in; *rendre un service (à quelqu'un)* to do (someone) a favor; *rendre visite à (+ person)* to visit (person)
se **rendre (à)** to go, to show up; *se rendre compte (de)* to realize 9
se **renseigner** to get information 4
la **rentrée** back to school/work after vacation
rentrer to come back, to come home, to return
réparer to repair
un **repas** meal
repasser to iron; *un fer à repasser* (clothes) iron
repeindre to repaint 3
re-photo another photo
répondre to respond 8
un **reportage** news report; *reportage sportif* sports coverage
se **reposer** to rest
un(e) **représentant(e)** representative
une **république** republic 8; *la République d'Haïti (Haïti)* Republic of Haiti
le **R.E.R.** express train from Paris to suburbs; *en R.E.R.* by R.E.R.
une **reservation** reservation
réserver to make a reservation; *réserver (pour quelqu'un)* to make especially (for someone) 10
une **résidence** residence 3; *une résidence secondaire* second home 3
une **résolution** resolution
respiratoire respiratory
respirer to breathe
une **responsabilité** responsibility 10
un(e) **responsable** director, manager 10
responsable responsible
ressembler (à) to resemble
ressentir to feel 9
une **ressource** resource 10; *ressources humaines* human resources 10; *un directeur,une directrice des ressources humaines (DRH)* director of human resources 10
un **restaurant** restaurant; *tenir un restaurant* to own a restaurant 3
le **reste** rest 10
rester to be left; to remain, to stay
un **resto-U (restaurant universitaire)** university cafeteria
retirer to withdraw 6
un **retour** return; *être de retour* to be back
retourner to return
se **retrouver** to meet; *se retrouver (sur)* to appear (on) 9
un **rétroviseur** rear-view mirror
la **Réunion** Reunion 4
se **réunir** to meet
réussir (à) to pass (a test), to succeed
un **rêve** dream; *une maison de rêve* dream house
se **réveiller** to wake up
le **réveillon de Noël** Christmas Eve celebration 2
réveillonner to celebrate Christmas/New Year's Eve 2
revenir to come back; to return
des **revenus (m.)** income 2
rêver to dream
revoir to see again
une **révolution** revolution
le **rez-de-chaussée** ground floor
un **rhume** cold
une **riad** riad
riche rich, wealthy
rien nothing 9; *Rien que ça?* Is that all?; *ne (n')... rien* nothing
rigoler to laugh
rire to laugh
une **rive** river bank
une **rivière** river
une **robe** dress; *robe de mariée* wedding dress
le **rock** rock (music)
le **rococo** rococo style 7
rococo rococo 7
un **roi** king
un **rôle** role
le **roller** in-line skating
un(e) **Romain(e)** Roman 5
un **roman** novel
un **romancier, une romancière** novelist 7
romantique Romantic 7
le **romantisme** Romanticism 7
rond(e) round 2
une **rondelle** circular piece of food; *en rondelles* in circles
rose pink
une **roue: la grande roue** Ferris wheel; *faire un tour de grande roue* to go on a Ferris wheel ride
rouge red
un **rouge à lèvres** lipstick
un **rouget** goatfish
rougir to blush
un **rouleau** roll 10
une **roulette** wheel; *à roulettes* on wheels; *une valise à roulettes* suitcase with wheels
une **route** highway, road, route; *Bonne route!* Have a good trip!; *en route* on the way
une **routine** routine
roux, rousse red (hair)
une **rue** street
rusé(e) cunning 3
le **Rwanda** Rwanda

S

s'il vous plaît please
le **sable** sand 1
un **sac** bag; *sac à dos* backpack; *sac à main* purse; *sac de couchage* sleeping bag
la **Saint-Jean** national Quebec holiday
la **Saint-Valentin** Valentine's day
une **saison** season
une **salade** lettuce; salad; *salade niçoise* tuna salad
un **salaire** salary 8
sale dirty 3
salé(e) salty, savory
une **salle** room; *salle de classe* classroom; *salle à manger* dining room; *salle de bains* bathroom; *salle d'informatique* computer lab
un **salon** living room; *salon de coiffure* hair salon
la **salsa** salsa music 7
salut good-bye, hi
samedi Saturday
une **sanction** punishment
des **sandales (f.)** sandals
un **sandwich** sandwich; *sandwich au fromage* cheese sandwich; *sandwich au jambon* ham sandwich
sanitaire health, sanitary
sans without 4; *sans aucun doute* without a doubt 4; *sans parler de* not to mention 10
un **sans-abri** homeless person
la **santé** health; *le domaine de la santé* health sector
un **sapin** fir tree 2; *sapin de Noël*

Christmas tree 2
une **satire** satire 7
une **sauce** sauce 2; *sauce béarnaise* Béarnaise sauce 5; *sauce béchamel* béchamel sauce 5; *sauce blanche* white sauce 5; *sauce hollandaise* hollandaise sauce 5; *sauce marinière* white wine sauce 5
une **saucisse** sausage
le **saucisson** salami
sauf except
le **saumon** salmon; *saumon fumé* smoked salmon 2; *une terrine de saumon* salmon loaf
un **saut: faire des sauts à ski** to go off ski jumps 4; *faire du saut à l'élastique* to bungee jump 4; *un tremplin de saut à ski* ski jump 4
sauter to jump 1; *sauter à la corde* to jump rope 1
sauvage wild
sauvegarder to protect; to save
savoir to figure out, to know how; to know; *Tu en sais des choses.* You sure know a lot about it.
se **savoir** to be known; *ça va se savoir* it will be revealed (known)
un **savon** soap
un **saxophone** saxophone
scandinave Scandinavian 9
une **scène** scene; *sur scène* on-stage 7
les **sciences (f.)** science; *sciences politiques (sciences po)* political science 6 ; *le domaine des sciences et techniques* science and technology sector
la **science-fiction** science fiction; *un film de science-fiction* science fiction movie
schuss: tout schuss full throttle 4
un **scooter** scooter; *en scooter* by scooter; *faire du scooter des mers* to jet ski
scotché(e) (à) glued (to)
une **sculpture** sculpture
une **séance** film showing; session 8
un **sèche-cheveux** hairdryer
un **sèche-linge** clothes dryer
sécher to dry; to skip (class) 9; *faire sécher le linge* to dry clothes
secondaire secondary 3; *une résidence secondaire* second home 3
un **secours: au secours** help
un **secret** secret
un **secrétaire (administratif), une secrétaire (administrative)** secretary 10
le **secrétariat** reception area 10
un **secteur** industry; *secteur aéronautique* aviation industry; *secteur agroalimentaire* food industry; *secteur de développement durable* sustainable development industry; *secteur de l'informatique* information technology industry
la **sécurité** security; *sécurité sociale (sécu)* French national health and pension insurance 8; *une ceinture de sécurité* seatbelt; *un contrôle de sécurité* security checkpoint
séduire to seduce 7
seize sixteen
un **séjour** living room; stay; *faire un séjour* to stay 4
le **sel** salt
selon according to
une **semaine** week
semblant(e): faire semblant (de) to pretend (to) 1
sembler to seem
le **Sénégal** Senegal
sénégalais(e) Senegalese
un **sens** sense, way; *en un sens* in a way
une **sensation** feeling, sensation
un **sentier** path
sentir to smell; *Ça sent quoi?* What does it smell like?
se **sentir** to feel 9
sept seven
septembre September
septième seventh
une **série** series; *toute une série (de)* whole series (of)
le **sérieux** seriousness
sérieux, sérieuse serious
un **serpent** snake
une **serpillière** mop 10
un **serveur, une serveuse** server
servi(e) served 5
un **service** department 10; favor; service 5; *service après-vente* post-sale support 10; *service blanchisserie* laundry service 5; *service de chambre* room service 5; *demander un service* to ask for a favor; *rendre un service (à quelqu'un)* to do (someone) a favor
une **serviette** napkin; towel; *serviette de plage* beach towel
servir to serve; *servir (à)* to be used (for) 2
se **servir (de)** to use
seul(e) alone, lonely 9
seulement only 4
un **shampooing** shampoo
le **shopping** shopping
un **short** shorts
un **show** show 9
si how about, if only, what if; if; so 2; yes *[on the contrary]*; *si cela vous convient* if you'd like
le **SIDA** AIDS
un **siège** seat; *siège social* headquarters 10
le **sien, la sienne** his, hers, one's 9
signaler to signal
signer to sign 6
SIM: une carte SIM SIM card
simple simple
simplement simply; *tout simplement* simply
le **sirop** syrup; *sirop d'érable* maple syrup
un **sitcom** sitcom
un **site** site; *site web* website
une **situation** situation
situé(e) located
six six
sixième sixth
un **skatepark** skateboard park 1
un **ski** ski 4; *le ski (alpin)* (downhilll) skiing; *le ski de fond* cross-country skiing 4; *faire des sauts à ski* to go off ski jumps 4; *faire du ski de fond* to cross-country ski 4; *faire du ski joering* to skijor 4; *faire du ski nautique* to go water-skiing; *un bâton de ski* ski pole 4; *une chaussure de ski* ski boot 4; *une station de ski* ski resort 4; *un forfait de ski* ski pass 4; *un fuseau de ski* ski pants 4; *un masque de ski* ski goggles 4; *un tremplin de saut à ski* ski jump 4
skier to ski 4; *en skiant* while skiing 4
un **skype** skype call
skyper to skype
un **smartphone** smartphone
un **smoking** tuxedo
un **SMS** text message
le **snowboard** snowboarding 4; *faire du snowboard* to snowboard 4
le **speed riding: faire du speed riding** to speed ride 4
social(e) social 8; *la sécurité sociale (sécu)* French national health and pension insurance 8; *un siège social* headquarters 10
socialiste socialist 2; *le parti politique socialiste* socialist

political party 2
une **société** company; *Société Anonyme (SA)* public (incorporated) company 10
une **sœur** sister
la **soie** silk; *en soie* made of silk
la **soif: avoir soif** to be thirsty
soigner to treat 8; *se faire soigner* to seek (medical) treatment 8
des **soins (m.)** care, treatment 8
le **soir** evening; *tous les soirs* every night
une **soirée** evening; evening out 1
soixante sixty
soixante-dix seventy
solaire solar; *la crème solaire* sunscreen; *l'énergie (f.) solaire* solar energy; *un panneau solaire* solar panel
solde: en solde on sale
le **soleil** sun; *des lunettes (f.) de soleil* sunglasses; *il fait du soleil* it's sunny
la **solidarité** solidarity
une **solution** solution
sombre dark
un **sommet** peak 4
son, sa, ses her, his, one's, its
un **sonnet** sonnet 7
un **sorcier** wizard 7
une **sorte** kind, sort
une **sortie** exit; release 5
sortir to come out; to go out; to take out
se **sortir: s'en sortir** to overcome
un **souci** worry 2
souffrir to suffer 2
souhaiter to hope, to wish 5
la **soupe** soup
un **soupir** sigh 7
une **source d'eau** spring
sourire to smile 1
un **sourire** smile 1
une **souris** mouse
sous under
sous-titré(e) subtitled 5
un **sous-titre** subtitle 5
soutenir to support
se **souvenir (de)** to remember
un **souvenir** memory
souvent often
soviétique Soviet 5
une **spatule** spatula 2
se **spécialiser (en)** to major (in)
une **spécialité** specialty; *spécialité du jour* daily special
une **spectacle** show
sphérique spherical 2
splendide gorgeous
un **sport** sport; *une voiture de sport* sports car
sportif, sportive athletic; *un complexe sportif* sports center 1; *un reportage sportif* sports coverage
un **spot publicitaire** commercial
le **Sri Lanka** Sri Lanka 10
un **stade** stadium
un **stage** internship 8; *faire un stage* to intern 8
un(e) **stagiaire** intern 8
un **stand de crêpes** crêpe stand
une **station** station; *station de ski* ski resort 4
une **station-service** gas station
une **statue** statue
un **steak-frites** steak with fries
le **step** step aerobics
une **stéréo** stereo
stéréotypé(e) stereotypical 5
un **steward** male flight attendant
une **stratégie** strategy 10
strict(e) strict
un **studio** studio apartment 3
un **style** style 5
un **stylo** pen
le **succès** success 7
le **sucre** sugar; *au sucre* with sugar
sucré(e) sweet
le **sud** south; *l'Amérique du Sud (f.)* South America; *la Corée du Sud* South Korea 10
suffire to be enough 3
la **Suisse** Switzerland
suisse Swiss; *un couteau suisse* Swiss army knife
la **suite** (the) rest 3; *par la suite* consequently 9; *tout de suite* right away
suivant(e) following 5
suivre to follow, to take (a class)
un **sujet** subject
super awesome; really, very
superbe excellent
un **super-héros** superhero 1
un **supermarché** supermarket
superposé(e): des lits (m.) superposés bunk beds
un **supplément** additional cost
sur about; of; on; *sur place* on the premises 4; *sur scène* on-stage 7; *être sur place* to be there
sûr(e) sure; *bien sûr* of course; *c'est sûr* that's for sure
surexcité(e) overexcited 9
surfer to surf; *surfer sur Internet* to surf the Web
surprenant(e) surprising 4
surprend: ça ne me surprend pas it doesn't surprise me
surpris(e) surprised
une **surprise** surprise
le **surréalisme** surrealism 7
surtout especially; mostly
surveiller to keep an eye on 9
survivre to survive
le **swing** swing music 7
sympa nice
synchroniser to synchronize
un **syndicat d'initiative** tourist information office
un **synopsis** movie synopsis 5
un **synthé(tiseur)** synthesizer
un **système** system 8

T

t'appelles: Tu t'appelles comment? What's your name?
le **tabac: un bureau de tabac** news store that sells tobacco, stamps, lottery tickets
une **table** table; *table de multiplication* multiplication table 8; *à table* at the (dinner) table 2; *débarrasser la table* to clear the table
un **tableau** chalkboard; painting; *tableau des arrivées et des départs* arrival and departure timetable
une **tablette** tablet
une **tache** spot
un **taf** work
tahitien(ne) Tahitian
une **taille** size; *de taille moyenne* of average height; *Quelle taille faites-vous?* What size are you?
un **taille-crayon** pencil sharpener
un **tailleur** tailor
un **talent** talent 9
un **tambour** drum
tamponneuse: une auto tamponneuse bumper car
tant pis too bad
une **tante** aunt
taper to type
un **tapis** rug
tard late
une **tarte** pie; *tarte aux fruits* fruit tart; *tarte aux pommes* apple pie
une **tartine** bread with butter, jam
une **tasse** cup
un **taxi** taxi; *en taxi* by taxi
un **taxi-ski: faire du taxi-ski** to take a ski-taxi ride 4
un **taux** rate 2; *taux d'inflation* inflation rate 2

te (t') to you, you
un(e) **technicien(ne) de centrale solaire** solar plant technician
la **technique** technology; *le domaine des sciences et techniques* science and technology sector
la **techno** techno music
un **tee-shirt** T-shirt
un **tel, une telle** such a 9
une **télé (télévision)** television, TV; *télé câblée* cable TV; *à la télé* on TV
télécharger to download
une **télécommande** TV remote control
le **télémark: faire du télémark** to telemark ski 4
un **téléphone portable** cell phone
téléphoner to phone (someone), to make a call
la **téléréalité** reality TV; *une émission de télé-réalité* reality TV show
un **télésiège** ski lift 4
télévisé(e) televised; *un jeu télévisé* (TV) game show
tellement so much
la **température** temperature
le **temps** time; weather; *à plein temps* full-time 8; *depuis combien de temps* how long; *Depuis le temps!* At last!; *gagner du temps* to save time; *le bon vieux temps* the good old days; *Quel temps fait-il?* What's the weather like?; How's the weather?; *tout le temps* all the time
la **tendresse** tenderness 6
tenir: tenir un restaurant to own a restaurant 3
des **tennis (m.)** sneakers
une **tente** tent
tenter to tempt; *tenter sa chance* to try one's luck 3
un **terrain de camping** campground
une **terrasse** terrace
la **terre** land
une **terrine de saumon** salmon loaf
un **territoire** territory 2
le **terrorisme** terrorism
un **testeur de jeux vidéo** video game tester
tétanisé(e) paralyzed 9
une **tête** head; look 9; *Lève la tête!* Look up!; *pas la tête à* not the type to 9
une **teuf** party
un **texte** text 7
un **texto** text message
un **thé** tea; *thé au citron* tea with lemon
un **théâtre** theatre; *une pièce de théâtre* play 6
un **thème** theme 7; topic
thermal(e) hydrotherapeutic
le **thon** tuna
un **thriller** thriller
un **ticket** ticket
le **tien, la tienne** yours 9
tiens here; hey
un **tigre** tiger; *tigre de Sumatra* Sumatran tiger
un **timbre** stamp 1
timide shy
un **tissu** fabric
un **titre** title 6
un **toast** canapé 2
le **Togo** Togo
togolais(e) Togolese
toi you
une **toile** canvas 7
les **toilettes (f.)** toilet; *des affaires (f.) de toilette* toiletries; *le papier toilette* toilet paper 10; *un gant de toilette* washcloth
un **toit** roof
la **tolérance** tolerance
une **tomate** tomato
tomber to fall 8; *tomber en panne* to break down; *tomber sur* to discover accidentally 5; *ça tombe bien* that works out well 2
un **ton** tone 5
ton, ta your; *tes* your
une **tondeuse** lawn mower
tondre to mow
top awesome; *C'est le top!* That's awesome!
un **tort** wrongdoing 8; *avoir tort* to be wrong 8
une **tortue** turtle; *tortue marine* sea turtle
tôt early
total(e): Total vintage! It has a totally vintage look!; *la totale* the whole deal
une **touche** key *[on keyboard]*
toucher to touch
toujours always; still
un **tour** tour; *déjouer un tour* to undo a spell 3; *faire le tour* explore all the possibilities 10; *faire un tour* to go on a ride; to go on a tour; *faire un tour de grande roue* to go on a Ferris wheel ride; *faire un tour de manège* to go on a carnival ride; *faire un tour de montagnes russes* to go on a roller coaster ride; *jouer un tour* to place a spell on 3
une **tour** tower
la **Touraine** Touraine region
tourangeau, tourangelle from, of Touraine region
le **tourisme** tourism 4; *tourisme d'aventure* adventure tourism; *un office de tourisme* tourist office 4
un(e) **touriste** tourist; *faire le touriste* to be a tourist
touristique touristy 3
tourmenter to torment 9
tourné(e) filmed 2
une **tournée** tour 7; *en tournée* on tour 7
tourner to turn; *tourner (un film)* to shoot (a movie) 5
un **tournevis** screwdriver 3
la **Toussaint** All Saints Day
tout(e) all; every; everything 3; *tous les soirs* every night; *tout à fait* completely; *Tout ça!* All that!; *tout de suite* right away; *tout d'un coup* all of a sudden 9; *tout le monde* everybody; *tout le temps* all the time; *tout schuss* full throttle 4; *tout simplement* simply; *toute une série (de)* whole series (of); *de toute façon* in any case 4; *en tout cas* in any case; *tu n'y es pas du tout* you don't get it 4
une **trace** ***[Mart.]*** path
tradi(e) traditional 2; *un look tradi* traditional look 2
traditionnel, traditionnelle traditional
un **train** train; *en train* by train
traîner to dawdle
traire to milk
un **traitement** treatment 8
une **tranche (de)** a slice (of)
tranquille calm, quiet 2
un **transport** transportation; *un moyen de transport* means of transportation
travailler to work
traverser to cross
trébucher to stumble 9
treize thirteen
un **tremblement de terre** earthquake
un **tremplin de saut à ski** ski jump 4
trente thirty
une **trentaine** about thirty 9; *d'une trentaine d'années* in one's thirties 9
très very; *Très heureux/heureuse.* Pleased to meet you. 3
un **trésor** treasure

	triste sad
	trois three
	troisième third
un	**trombone** trombone
une	**trompette** trumpet; *trompette de la mort* trumpet of the dead mushroom 5
un	**trône** throne 8
	trop too; *trop de* too much of
une	**trousse** pencil case; *trousse de premiers secours* first-aid kit
	trouver to find
se	**trouver** to be located
un	**truc** thing
	tu you; *tu n'y es pas du tout* you don't get it 4
	tuer to kill 2
la	**Tunisie** Tunisia
	tunisien(ne) Tunisian
	tutoyer to use the informal "**tu**" to address someone 10
un	**type** type 1
	typiquement typical of 10

U

	un a, an; one
	une a, an, one
l'	**un(e)... l'autre** the one... the other 9
une	**uniformisation** standardisation 10
l'	**Union européenne (f.)** European Union
l'	**univers (m.)** universe
	universel, universelle universal 2
	universitaire university; *une cité universitaire* university dormitory
une	**université** university; *entrer à l'université* to go to college
un	**USB: un port micro-USB** USB port
	user de diplomatie to use diplomacy
une	**usine** factory
un	**ustensile** utensil 2
	usurper to usurp 2
	utile useful 4

V

des	**vacances (f.)** vacation; *prendre des vacances* to take a vacation
un	**vacancier, une vacancière** vacationer
	vacciner (contre) to vaccinate (against) 4; *se faire vacciner* to get a shot 4
une	**vache** cow
la	**vaisselle: faire la vaisselle** to wash the dishes
une	**valeur** worth 2
une	**valise** suitcase; *valise à roulettes* suitcase with wheels; *faire sa valise* to pack 4
une	**vallée** valley
	valoir to be valued as/at 7; to be worth 4; *il vaut mieux que* it's better that 4
une	**variation** variation 7
	vas: Tu vas bien? Are things going well?
un	**vase** vase 10
le	**veau** veal 5
une	**vedette** star 5
un	**vélo** bike; *à vélo* by bike
le	**velours** velvet; *en velours* made of velvet
un	**vendeur, une vendeuse** salesperson
	vendre to sell
	vendredi Friday
	venir to come; *venir de (+ infinitive)* to have just
le	**vent** wind; *il fait du vent* it's windy
les	**ventes (f.)** sales 10
le	**ventre** stomach
	vérifier to check
un	**verre** glass; *verre mesureur* measuring cup 2
	vers around; towards
	verser to pour 2
une	**version** version; *version originale (V.O.)* original version 5
	vert(e) green
une	**veste** jacket
des	**vêtements (m.)** clothes
un(e)	**vétérinaire** veterinarian
	vêtu(e) de dressed in 9
	veux: je veux bien I'd like that
la	**viande** meat 5
le	**vide: avoir peur du vide** to be afraid of heights
une	**vie** life
la	**vieillesse** old age 7
le	**Vietnam** Vietnam 4
	vieux, vieil, vieille old; *le bon vieux temps* the good old days
	vif, vive vivid
une	**villa** villa 3
un	**village** village
une	**ville** city; *en ville* downtown
la	**vinaigrette** vinaigrette salad dressing
	vingt twenty
une	**vingtaine** about twenty 9; *d'une vingtaine d'années* in one's twenties 9
	vintage vintage 9
la	**violence** violence
	violet, violette purple
un	**violon** violin
un	**violoncelle** cello
une	**vis** screw 3
un	**visa** visa 4
	visible visible 9
une	**visite** visit; *une visite guidée* guided tour; *faire une visite guidée* to go on a guided tour; *rendre visite à (+ person)* to visit (person)
	visiter to visit
	vite fast, quickly
	vivre to live; *une douceur de vivre* relaxed style of life
	voici here, here is
une	**voie** path; train track; *les animaux en voie de disparition* endangered species
	voilà here are/is
une	**voile: faire de la planche à voile** to wind surf 4; *faire de la voile* to go sailing
un	**voilier** sailboat
	voir to see
se	**voir** to see each other/one another
une	**voiture** car; *voiture de sport* sports car; *voiture électrique* electric car; *voiture hybride* hybrid car; *en voiture* by car; *jouer aux petites voitures* to play with toy cars 1; *une petite voiture* toy car 1
un	**vol** flight; theft 9; *une déclaration de vol* report of a theft 9
un	**volant** steering wheel
un	**volcan** volcano 4
	voler to steal 9
un	**voleur** thief 9
	volontiers gladly
	volumineux, volumineuse voluminous 7
	voter to vote 2
le, la	**vôtre** yours 9
	votre, vos your; *de votre côté* as for you 2
	vouloir to want; *vouloir dire* to mean
	vous to you; you
un	**voyage** trip; *voyage de noces* honeymoon 1; *faire un voyage* to go on a trip; *partir en voyage* to take a journey 8; *un chèque de voyage* traveler's check 6
	voyager to travel
un	**voyageur, une voyageuse** traveller

un(e) **voyant(e)** fortune teller
vrai(e) real 5; true
vraiment really
une **vue** view; *Quelle belle vue!* What a beautiful view!; *un point de vue* viewpoint

W

un **wagon-restaurant** dining car
wahou wow 8
les **W.C. (m.)** toilet
le **web: un concepteur de web** web designer
le **weekend** weekend
le **Wi-Fi** wireless internet 5; *une connexion Wi-Fi* wireless internet connection 5
la **world** world music

Y

y there *[pronoun]*; it *[pronoun]*
un **yaourt** yogurt
les **yeux (m.)** eyes; *le blanc des yeux* eye to eye 9
le **yoga** yoga

Z

zéro zero

Vocabulary

Vocabulary terms from Level 1 and Level 2 of *T'es branché?* are included but do not have a unit number. Vocabulary terms from Level 3 include the unit number in which the term is introduced.

English-French

A

a un; une; *a few* quelque 5; *(a) little* (un) peu; *a little of* un peu de; *a lot* beaucoup; *a lot (of)* plein (de) 8; *a lot of* beaucoup de; *You sure know a lot about it.* Tu en sais des choses.

to **abandon** abandonner 4
to be **able** arriver (à); pouvoir; *to be able to afford* avoir les moyens 8; *cannot help (but)* ne pas pouvoir s'empêcher (de) 2
about à propos de 2; sur; *about (the)* du; *about fifty* une cinquantaine 9; *about forty* une quarantaine 9; *about it/them* en; *about thirty* une trentaine 9; *about twenty* une vingtaine 9; *about which/whom* dont 6; *it's about* il s'agit de; *to be about* parler de 6
above au-dessus de
absolutely absolument 1
abstract abstrait(e)
accelerator un accélérateur
accent un accent
to **accentuate** mettre en valeur
to **accept** accepter
to **access** accéder 8
accessory un accessoire
accident un accident
accidentally: to discover accidentally tomber sur 5
to **accompany** accompagner
according to selon
account un compte 6; un récit 9
accountant un(e) comptable 10
accounting la comptabilité 10
ache: to have a/an... ache avoir mal (à)...
acquired acquis(e) 8
across from en face de
to **act** agir
action l'action (f.); une action 5; *action movie* un film d'action
activity une activité
actor un acteur, une actrice
to **adapt** adapter 10; *to adapt (to)* s'adapter (à) 10
adaptation une adaptation 10
to **add** ajouter 10
addition: in addition to en plus
additional cost un supplément
to **address (someone)** s'adresser (à) 2; *to use the informal "tu" to address someone* tutoyer 10
address une adresse
addressed (to) adressé (à) 5
adjoining mitoyen(ne) 3
to **adjust** adapter 10; régler; *to adjust the zoom* régler la largeur du champ
adjustment un réglage
administrative administratif, administrative 10
to **adore** adorer
adventure une aventure; *adventure movie* un film d'aventure; *adventure tourism* le tourisme d'aventure
advertisement une annonce 8; *want ad* une petite annonce 8
to **advise** conseiller
aerobics l'aérobic (m.); *step aerobics* le step
affectionately affectueusement
to **afford: to be able to afford** avoir les moyens 8
to be **afraid (of)** avoir peur (de); *to be afraid of heights* avoir peur du vide; *I'm afraid not.* Je crains que non. 2
Africa l'Afrique (f.)
African africain(e) 9
after après; *after all* quand meme 2
afternoon l'après-midi (m.)
again: to see again revoir; *to start something again* se remettre (à)
against contre
age l'âge (m.); *old age* la vieillesse 7
agent un(e) agent(e)
ago: (time) ago il y a (+ time)
to **agree** être d'accord; *to get people to agree* mettre d'accord 1
agreement un accord 1
agriculture l'agriculture (f.)
AIDS le SIDA
air l'air (m.); *air conditioning* la climatisation; *air letter* un aérogramme 6
airplane un avion
airport un aéroport
album un album; *concept album* un album concept 7
alcoholism l'alcoolisme (m.)
Algerian algérien(ne)
all tout(e), tous, toutes; *all of a sudden* tout d'un coup 9; *All that!* Tout ça!; *all the time* tout le temps; *after all* quand meme 2; *Is that all?* Rien que ça?; *to explore all the possibilities* faire le tour 10; *to stay up all night* faire une nuit blanche
almond une amande
almost presque
alone seul(e) 9
along: to get along s'entendre
alongside le long de
already déjà
Alsace region l'Alsace (f.); *from, of Alsace region* alsacien(ne)
also aussi
aluminum l'aluminium (m.); *made of aluminum* en aluminium
always toujours
ambiance une ambiance
amenities des prestations (f.) 5
America: North America l'Amérique du Nord (f.); *South America* l'Amérique du Sud (f.)
American américain(e)
Amerindian amérindien(ne)
to **amuse** amuser
amusement park un parc d'attractions
ancestor un(e) aïeul(e) 3; un(e) ancêtre 3
anchor: news anchor un présentateur, une présentatrice
and et
anecdote une anecdote 8
angry fâché(e) 1; *to be angry* être fâché(e) 1
animal un animal
ankle la cheville 4; *to sprain an ankle* se fouler la cheville 4
to **annex** annexer
anniversary: wedding anniversary un anniversaire de mariage
to **announce** annoncer
to **annoy** agacer; embêter 2

anole un anoli
anonymous anonyme 10
another: another photo re-photo; *to leave one another* se quitter 1
anthology une anthologie 6
antiretroviral drugs les antirétroviraux (m.)
anti-Semitism l'antisémitisme (m.)
any aucun(e) 4; d', de; des, du, en; *in any case* de toute façon 4; en tout cas; *just any* n'importe quel, quelle 9; *not any* ne (n')... aucun(e) 4
anyone n'importe qui 9
Apartheid l'apartheid (m.)
apartment un appartement; *apartment building* un immeuble; *studio apartment* un studio 3
app (application) une appli (application)
to **appear** paraître 5; *to appear (on)* se retrouver (sur) 9
appearance une mine
appetizer une entrée; un hors-d'œuvre 2
apple une pomme; *apple juice* un jus de pomme; *apple pie* une tarte aux pommes
application une candidature 8; *application letter* une lettre de candidature 8
to **apply** appliquer 7
April avril
Arab arabe
area un espace; un quartier; *reception area* le secrétariat 10
to **argue** se disputer
aristocrat un(e) aristocrate 8
arm le bras
armchair un fauteuil
around autour de 2; vers; *to get around* se déplacer
to **arrange** ranger
arrested: to get arrested se faire arrêter 9
arrival une arrivée; *arrival and departure timetable* un tableau des arrivées et départs
to **arrive** arriver
art l'art (m.); *art object* un objet d'art; *Bachelor of Arts degree* un B.A. 10; *fine arts* les beaux-arts (m.) 7
article: magazine article un article; *newspaper article* un article
artist un(e) artiste

as aussi, que; *as... as* aussi (+ adverb) que; *as for you* de votre côté 2; *as soon as* aussitôt que 1; dès que
ashamed honteux, honteuse 9
Asia l'Asie (f.)
Asian asiatique 9
aside from à part 9
to **ask (for)** demander; *to ask for a favor* demander un service; *to ask for directions* demander le chemin
assignment un devoir
assistance l'aide (f.)
assistant un(e) assistant(e) 8
at à; en; *at (the)* au, aux; *At last!* Depuis le temps!; *at least* au moins; *at my house* chez moi; *at the end of* au bout de; au fond de; *at the house (home) of* chez; *at the moment* en ce moment 6; *at the same time* à la fois; *at the seaside* au bord de la mer; *at the (dinner) table* à table 2; *at the top* en haut; *at/to the club* en boîte; *at/to the physical therapy office* chez le kiné 8; *at war* en guerre 2
athlete un(e) athlète
athletic sportif, sportive
athletics l'athlétisme (m.) 2
ATM un distributeur (automatique) 6
atmosphere une ambiance
to **attach** joindre
to **attend** assister (à) 1
auditor of a class un auditeur, une auditrice libre 10
August août
aunt une tante; *great aunt* une grand-tante 3
Australia l'Australie (f.)
author un auteur 7
autobiography une autobiographie 6
automotive designer un(e) designer automobile
auto-portrait un autoportrait
auto shop un garage
autumn l'automne (m.)
avenue une avenue
aviation: aviation industry le secteur aéronautique
to **avoid** éviter
award une récompense 2
away: right away tout de suite; *to get away (from)* s'éloigner (de) 10
awesome formidable; super; top; *That's awesome!* C'est le top!

awful horrible

B

baby un bébé 1
to **babysit** garder un enfant 3
Bachelor of Arts degree un B.A. 10
back le dos; *back country* l'arrière-pays (m.); *back to school/work after vacation* la rentrée; *let's get back to it* on s'y remet; *to be back* être de retour; *to give back* rendre; *to put back* remettre
background un arrière-plan 7; *in the background* à l'arrière-plan 7
backpack un sac à dos
bacon le bacon
bad mal; mauvais; nul, nulle; *it's too bad that...* c'est dommage que... 5; *the weather is bad* il fait mauvais
badly mal; *Things are going badly.* Ça va mal.
bag un sac; *sleeping bag* un sac de couchage
baker un boulanger, une boulangère
bakery une boulangerie, une pâtisserie
bald chauve 9
ballad une ballade 3
banal banal(e)
banana une banane
bank une banque; *bank teller* un caissier, une caissière 6; *river bank* une rive
banker un banquier, une banquière 6
to **barbecue** faire griller
barn une grange
basketball le basket (basketball)
bat une chauve-souris
bath un bain; *whirlpool bath* un bain à remous 5
to **bathe** baigner
bathing suit un maillot de bain
bathrobe un peignoir de bain
bathroom une salle de bains
bathtub une baignoire
to **be** être; *to be able (to)* pouvoir; arriver (à); *to be about* parler de 6; *to be afraid (of)* avoir peur (de); *to be afraid of heights* avoir peur du vide; *to be angry* être fâché(e) 1; *to be a tourist* faire le touriste; *to be back* être de retour; *to be busy* être occupé(e); *to be*

(busy) doing something être en train de (+ infinitive); *to be called* s'appeler; *to be called (in)* être convoqué(e) (à) 8; *to be certain that* être certain que 5; *to be cold* avoir froid; *to be committed to* s'engager; *to be condemned* être condamné(e) 8; *to be eager* avoir hâte de; *to be egotistical* être perso *[inform.]* 8; *to be enough* suffire 3; *to be entitled to* avoir droit à 8; *to be environmentally friendly* être vert; *to be familiar with (person, place, thing)* connaître; *to be free* être libre; *to be happy (about)* être content(e) (de) 6; *to be hot* avoir chaud; *to be how old* avoir quel âge; *to be hungry* avoir faim; *to be hurt* avoir mal (à...); *to be in charge (of)* être chargé(e) (de); *to be informed* être au courant; *to be in love (with)* être amoureux/amoureuse (de) 6; *to be in (good, bad) shape* être en (bonne, mauvaise) forme; *to be interested (in)* s'intéresser (à); *to be left* rester; *to be located* être situé(e), se trouver; *to be lucky* avoir de la chance; *to be necessary* falloir; *to be obligated (to)* être obligé(e) (de) 8; *to be obvious that* être évident que 5; *to be right* avoir raison; *to be sorry* regretter 5; *to be surprised that* être étonné que 5; *to be there* être sur place; *to be thirsty* avoir soif; *to be used (for)* servir (à) 2; *to be valued as/at* valoir 7; *to be wary (of)* se méfier (de) 3; *to be worth* valoir 4; *to be wrong* avoir tort 8; *to be... year(s) old* avoir... an(s); *I'm not in the mood for* je ne suis pas trop d'humeur pour 5

beach une plage; *beach towel* une serviette de plage

bear un ours; *polar bear* un ours polaire

Béarnaise sauce une sauce béarnaise 5

beautiful beau, bel, belle; *It's beautiful out.* Il fait beau.

beauty la beauté

because parce que; *because of* à cause de 2

béchamel sauce une sauce béchamel 5

to **become** devenir

bed un lit; *bunk beds* des lits superposés; *in bed* couché(e); *to go to bed* se coucher; *twin-sized bed* un lit jumeau

bedroom une chambre

beef le bœuf; *beef burgundy* le bœuf bourguignon

beer une bière 10

before auparavant 9; avant; *drink and food offered before the meal* un apéritif 2

to **begin** commencer

beginning un début

behind derrière

beige beige

Belgian belge

Belgium la Belgique

to **believe** croire

to **belong (to)** être à 8; faire partie (de)

belongings des affaires (f.)

belt une ceinture

bench un banc

to **benefit from** profiter de

Benin le Bénin

Beninese béninois(e)

Berber berbère

beside à côté de

best: best man un garçon d'honneur 1; *the best* les meilleurs (m.); le mieux

best seller un best-seller

better mieux; *better than* mieux que; *it's better that* il vaut mieux que 4; *to do/feel better* se porter mieux

between entre

bicycle une bicyclette; *on a bicycle* à bicyclette

to **bid farewell** faire ses adieux (m.) 8

big grand(e); gros, grosse

to **bike** faire du vélo; *by bike* à vélo

bike un vélo

bilingual bilingue 10

bill l'addition (f.); une facture 8; *bill [money]* un billet

binoculars des jumelles (f.)

biochemistry la biochimie 6

biography une biographie 6

biology la biologie

bird un oiseau

birthday un anniversaire

black noir(e)

blacksmith un forgeron

blasé blasé(e) 5

blended: blended family une famille recomposée 1

blender un mixer 2

blinker un clignotant

blog un blogue

blogger un blogueur, une blogeuse 2

blond blond(e)

blouse un chemisier 9

blue bleu(e)

to **blush** rougir

to **board** monter à bord

boarding l'embarquement (m.); *boarding gate* une porte d'embarquement; *boarding pass* une carte d'embarquement

boat un bateau; *by boat* en bateau

body le corps; *body of water* une masse d'eau

bonfire un feu de joie

book un bouquin *[inform.]* 6; un livre

bookstore une librairie

boot une botte; *ski boot* une chaussure de ski 4

bored: to get bored s'ennuyer 4

to **borrow** emprunter

botanical canna un balisier

to **bother** déranger 2

bottle (of) une bouteille (de)

bottom le bas

bowl un bol

box une boîte 6; *cardboard box* une boîte cartonnée 6

boy un garçon

bracelet un bracelet

brake un frein

branch une filiale 10

brand une marque 10; *brand name* marqué(e) 10

bread le pain; *long thin loaf of bread* une baguette; *bread with butter, jam* une tartine

to **break** se casser 4; *to break down* tomber en panne; *to break one's wrist* se casser le poignet 4

breakfast le petit déjeuner

breast: duck breast un magret de canard 2

to **breathe** respirer

bride une mariée

bridesmaid une demoiselle d'honneur 1

bridge un pont

to **bring** apporter; *to bring (person* emmener; *to bring in* rapporter 10; *to bring oneself to do something* arriver à faire quelque chose 6

Brittany region la Bretagne; *from, of Brittany region* breton(ne)

broken down en panne
brother un frère; *half-brother* un demi-frère; *stepbrother* un beau-frère
brown marron; *brown (hair)* brun(e)
to **browse** naviguer
to **brush: to brush one's hair** se brosser les cheveux; *to brush one's teeth* se brosser les dents
buckwheat crêpe une galette
buffet un buffet
building: apartment building un immeuble
bumper car une auto tamponneuse
to **bungee jump** faire du saut à l'élastique 4
bunk beds des lits (m.) superposés
Burgundy la Bourgogne 5; *from, of Burgundy* bourguignon(ne) 5
Burkina Faso le Burkina Faso; *from, of Burkina Faso* burkinabè
bus un autobus; *by bus* en autobus
business les affaires (f.) 5; une entreprise 1; *business center* un centre d'affaires 5; *economic business management* la gestion économique d'entreprise 6; *small business* une petite et moyenne entreprise (PME) 1
business commerçant(e)
businessman un homme d'affaires
businesswoman une femme d'affaires
busy occupé(e)
to be **busy** être occupé(e); *to be (busy) doing something* être en train de (+ infinitive)
but mais
butcher un boucher, une bouchère; *butcher shop* une boucherie
butter le beurre
butterfly un papillon
button: send button l'envoi (m.)
to **buy** acheter
buzz un buzz 9
by à; de; en; *by bike* à vélo; *by boat* en bateau; *by bus* en autobus; *by canoe* en canoë; *by car* en voiture; *by city bus* en bus; *by electric car* en voiture électrique; *by hybrid car* en voiture hybride; *by pirogue* en pirogue; *by plane* en avion; *by R.E.R.* en R.E.R.; *by scooter* en scooter; *by subway* en métro; *by taxi* en taxi; *by the way* au fait; *by train* en train; *to get by* se débrouiller 6

C

cabaret artist/singer un chansonnier, une chansonnière
cable channel une chaîne câblée 5
café un café
café-restaurant une brasserie
cafeteria: school cafeteria une cantine; *university cafeteria* un resto-U (restaurant universitaire)
cake un gâteau
calendar un calendrier
to **call** appeler
to be **called** s'appeler; *to be called (in)* être convoqué(e) (à) 8
called: called (in) convoqué(e) (à) 8
to **calm oneself down** se calmer
calm tranquille 2
Cambodia le Cambodge 10
camembert cheese le camembert
camera un appareil, une caméra
Cameroon le Cameroun
Cameroonian camerounais(e)
camper une caravane
campground un terrain de camping
camping le camping; *to go camping* faire du camping
can (of) une boîte (de); *garbage can* une poubelle
Canada le Canada
Canadian canadien(ne)
canapé un toast 2
candidate un candidat 2
canning company une conserverie 3
canoe un canoë; *by canoe* en canoë; *to go canoeing* faire du canoë
canvas une toile 7
cap une casquette
capital une capitale
car une auto (automobile); une voiture; *car manufacturer* un constructeur, une constructrice automobile 10; *bumper car* une auto tamponneuse; *by car* en voiture; *dining car* un wagon-restaurant; *electric car* une voiture électrique; *hybrid car* une voiture hybride; *sports car* une voiture de sport; *toy car* une petite voiture 1; *to play with toy cars* jouer aux petites voitures 1
caramel le caramel; *caramel custard* une crème caramel
carbon dioxyde le dioxyde de carbone
card une carte; *credit card* une carte de crédit; *debit card* une carte bancaire 6; *SIM card* une carte SIM
cardboard: (made out of) cardboard cartonné(e) 6; *cardboard box* une boîte cartonnée 6
to **care: to not care** s'en ficher 1;
care des soins (m.) 8; *to take care of* garder 3; s'occuper (de); *to take care of things* se débrouiller 8
careful: Be careful! Attention!
carefully prudemment
caricature une caricature 7
carnival un carnaval; une fête foraine; *to go on a carnival ride* faire un tour de manège
carpeting la moquette 3
carrot une carotte
carry-all un fourre-tout
cartoon un dessin animé
case un cas; *in any case* de toute façon 4; en tout cas
to **cash** encaisser 6
cash l'argent (m.) liquid, la monnaie 6
casting le casting 5
castle un château
cat un chat
catalog un catalogue 6
catastrophe une catastrophe 5
cathedral une cathédrale
to **cause** causer
cause une cause
cave une caverne
CD un CD; un cédérom
to **celebrate** fêter; *to celebrate Christmas/New Year's Eve* réveillonner 2
celebration: Christmas Eve celebration le réveillon de Noël 2
celebrity une personnalité
cello un violoncelle
cell phone un portable; une téléphone portable
center un centre; un complexe; *business center* un centre d'affaires 5; *community center* une MJC 1; *fitness center* un centre de remise en forme 5; *reception center* un centre

d'accueil; *shopping center* un centre commercial; *sports center* un complexe sportif 1
C.E.O. un président directeur général (PDG) 10
cereal des céréales (f.)
certain certain(e) 5; *to be certain that* être certain que 5
certificate un certificat 6
C.F.O. un directeur financier, une directrice financière 10
chair une chaise
chaise lounge une chaise-longue
chalkboard un tableau
challenge un défi 9
champagne le champagne 10
championship un championnat 2
chance une occasion 4
to **change** changer
channel une chaîne; *cable channel* une chaîne câblée 5
chanson réaliste une chanson réaliste 7
chapel une chapelle
charge: to be in charge (of) être chargé(e) (de)
charm le charme
charming charmant(e)
cheap bon marché(e)
to **check** vérifier; *to check one's/ luggage* faire enregistrer les bagages
check un chèque 6; *traveler's check* un chèque de voyage 6
checkbook un chéquier 6
checkpoint: security checkpoint un contrôle de sécurité
cheese le fromage; *camembert cheese* le camembert; *cheese sandwich* un sandwich au fromage
chef un cuisinier, une cuisinière
chemical chimique
chemistry la chimie
cherry une cerise
chest la poitrine
chestnut un marron 2; *turkey with chestnuts* la dinde aux marrons 2
chic chic
chicken le poulet; *chicken cooked in wine* le coq au vin
child un enfant
childhood l'enfance (f.) 1
childish enfantin(e) 1
chills des frissons (m.)
China la Chine 10
chocolate le chocolat; *chocolate mousse* une mousse au chocolat; *hot chocolate* un chocolat chaud; *spread made of hazelnut and chocolate* le Nutella; *with chocolate* au chocolat
choice un choix; *to have too many choices* avoir l'embarras du choix 10
choir un chœur 9
to **choose** choisir
chop une côte 2; *venison chop* une côte de chevreuil 2
chopped: ham and pork dish made with chopped parsley le jambon persillé 5
chore une corvée
Christmas Noël; *Christmas Eve celebration* le réveillon de Noël 2; *Christmas tree* un sapin de Noël 2; *to celebrate Christmas/New Year's Eve* réveillonner 2
church une église
cinema: multiplex cinema un multiplexe 5
circle un cercle 3
circular: circular piece of food or object une rondelle
citizen un(e) citoyen(ne), 8
city une ville; *city bus* un bus; *by city bus* en bus; *city hall* un hôtel de ville
civil civil(e) 6; *civil engineering* le génie civil 6
clarinet une clarinette
class une classe; un cours; *class subject* la matière; *auditor of a class* un auditeur, une auditrice libre 10; *gym class* l'éducation physique et sportive (EPS) (f.); *private class* un cours particulier 1; *ski class* une classe de neige 4
classic un classique 5
classical classique; *classical music* la musique classique
classmate un(e) camarade de classe
classroom la salle de classe
to **clean** nettoyer
clean propre 3
to **clear: to clear the table** débarasser la table
clear clair(e)
clergy un clergé 8
to **click** cliquer
cliff une falaise; *cliff road* une corniche
to **climb: to rock climb** faire de l'escalade 4
clip: video clip un clip
clock une pendule
to **close** fermer
closer: on a closer look en y regardant de plus près 4; *to come closer* s'approcher 9
closet un placard
close-up: in a close-up en gros plan 7
clothes des vêtements (m.); *clothes dryer* un sèche-linge; *to dry clothes* faire sécher le linge; *to wash clothes* faire la lessive
club un club 2; *at/to the club* en boîte; *film club* un ciné-club 1
coast une côte
coat un manteau
cod une morue; *cod fritter* un accra de morue
coffee un café; *coffee with milk* un café au lait
coin une pièce (de monnaie) 6
cola un coca
colander une passoire 2
cold un rhume
cold froid; *it's cold* il fait froid; *to be cold* avoir froid
to **collapse** s'effondrer 9; *to collapse from exhaustion* s'effondrer de fatigue 9
to **collect** collectionner 1
collection une collection; un recueil 6
college une fac (faculté); *to go to **college*** entrer à l'université
colonization la colonisation
color une couleur; *In what colors?* De quelle(s) couleur(s)?
to **comb one's hair** se peigner
comb un peigne
to **come** venir; *to come back* rentrer; revenir; *to come closer* s'approcher 9; *to come from (+ country)* être d'origine (+ adjective) 3; *to come home* rentrer; *to come in* entrer; *to come out* sortir; *come on* enfin
comedy une comédie; *romantic comedy* une comédie romantique
comfort le confort 5
comic strip une bande dessinée (BD)
commercial un spot publicitaire
to **commit** to s'engager
to be **committed** to s'engager
community la collectivité 8; *community center* une MJC 1
company une compagnie 8; une entreprise 1; une

société; *canning company* une conserverie 3; *public (incorporated) company* une Société Anonyme (SA) 10
compartment: baggage compartment un compartiment à bagages
to **complain** se plaindre
complaint une plainte 7
completely complètement 9; entièrement 8; tout à fait
complex un complexe
complicated compliqué(e)
composer un compositeur, une compositrice
composition une composition; une rédaction
computer un ordinateur; *computer graphics* l'infographie (f.) 6; *computer lab* la salle d'informatique; *computer science* l'informatique (f.); *laptop computer* un ordinateur portable
to **conceal** cacher 7
concept un concept 7; *concept album* un album concept 7
concert un concert
concierge un(e) concierge 5
condemned condamné(e) 8; *to be condemned* être condamné(e) 8
conductor un chef d'orchestre 5
cone-shaped conique 2
confession un aveu 7
Congolese congolais(e) 6
conical strainer un chinois 2
connection la complicité 1; une connexion 5; *wireless internet connection* une connexion Wifi 5
conqueror un conquérant
consequently par la suite 9
to **consider** réfléchir (à)
consulate un consulat 4
to **consult** consulter 5
consultant un(e) consultant(e)
consultation une consultation
to **consume** consommer
contemporary contemporain(e)
continent un continent
to **continue** continuer
contract un contrat 8
contrary: on the contrary au contraire 8
conventional convenu(e) 10
conversation une conversation
convertible une décapotable
convinced persuadé(e) 4
to **cook** cuire 2; faire la cuisine
cooking la cuisine
cool frais, fraîche; *it's cool* il fait frais
cooler une glacière
corner le coin; *on the corner* du coin
correctly correctement 4
to **cost** coûter
cost: additional cost un supplément
costume un costume
cotton le coton; *made of cotton* en coton
counter: foreign exchange counter un bureau de change 6
to **count** on compter
counter (ticket) un comptoir
country un pays; *country(side)* la campagne; *back country* l'arrière-pays (m.)
couple un couple
course un cours
course: in the course of au cours de 8; *of course* bien entendu 5; bien sûr
couscous le couscous
cousin un(e) cousin(e); *first cousin* un(e) cousin(e) germain(e) 3
coverage: sports coverage reportage sportif
cover letter une lettre de motivation 8
cow une vache
crab un crabe
crazy person un fou, une folle
cream une crème 10; *cream puff pastry* une religieuse
to **create** créer
credit card une carte de crédit
Creole *[language]* le créole
Creole créole
crêpe une crêpe; *buckwheat crêpe* une galette; *crêpe restaurant* une crêperie; *crêpe stand* un stand de crêpes
crisis une crise 3
critic un(e) critique 5
croissant un croissant
to **cross** traverser
cross-country skiing le ski de fond 4; *to cross-country ski* faire du ski de fond 4
crow un corbeau 7
crowd une foule
to **cry** pleurer
cry un cri
cubical cubique 2
cucumber un concombre
cultural culturel, culturelle
cunning rusé(e) 3
cup une tasse; *measuring cup* un verre mesureur 2
curly (hair) frisé(e) 9
custard: caramel custard une crème caramel
to **cut** couper
cut up (in) découpé(e) (en) 10
CV (Curriculum vitae) un CV 8
cylindrical cylindrique 2

D

daily quotidien(ne); *daily special* une spécialité du jour
dairy store une crémerie
dancer un danseur, une danseuse
dark sombre; *dark (hair)* brun(e)
darn mince
date une date
daughter une fille
to **dawdle** traîner
dawn l'aube (f.) 7
dairy latier, latière 10; *dairy product* un produit laitier 10
day un jour; une journée; *New Year's Day* le Jour de l'an; *next day* le lendemain; *one day, someday* un jour; *the good old days* le bon vieux temps; *Valentine's day* la Saint-Valentin
dead mort(e); *trumpet of the dead mushroom* une trompette de la mort 5
dear cher, chère
death la mort 5
debate un débat 8
debit card une carte bancaire 6
debt un endettement 2
to **decapitate** guillotiner 8
December décembre
to **decide** choisir; décider
decision une décision 10; *to make a decision* prendre une décision 10
declaration une déclaration 9
to **declare a major in Humanities** s'inscrire en letters
to **decrease** baisser 2
deep-fried frit(e)
degree un degré; *Bachelor of Arts degree* un B.A. 10; *Master's degree* une maîtrise 10
delicatessen une charcuterie
delicious délicieux, délicieuse
delighted enchanté(e)
deli owner un charcutier, une charcutière
democracy une démocratie 2
demonstration: street demonstration une manif (manifestation)

Denmark: from, of Denmark danois(e)
denomination une dénomination 5
dentist un(e) dentiste; *dentist's office* un cabinet dentaire
department un department; un service 10
departure un départ
to **depend (on)** dépendre (de) 2
to **deposit** déposer 6
depression: Great Depression la grande crise 3
deputy un député 8
descent une descente
to **describe** décrire
description une description 5
design: fashion design la couture 10
designer; *automotive designer* un(e) designer automobile; *web designer* un concepteur de web
desk un bureau; *reception desk* la réception
dessert un dessert
destination une destination
destiny le destin
destroyed détruit(e)
detail un détail
detective policier, policière; *detective movie* un film policier
to **detest** avoir horreur de; détester 1
development un développement; *sustainable development* le développement durable; *sustainable development industry* le secteur de développement durable
device un appareil
dialogue une dialogue 5
diamond un diamont; *diamond ring* une bague de diamants
dictatorship une dictature 2
dictionary un dictionnaire
to **die** mourir 8
different différent(e)
differently différemment 4
difficult difficile; dur(e)
difficulty une difficulté 8
Dijon: from, of Dijon dijonnais(e) 5
diligent diligent(e)
dimension une dimension 6
dining: dining car un wagon-restaurant; *dining room* la salle à manger
to have **dinner** dîner
dinner le dîner
diploma: exam taken to obtain high school diploma un bac (baccalauréat) 9
diplomacy la diplomatie; *to use diplomacy* user de diplomatie
to **direct (movie)** réaliser 6
directed (by) réalisé(e) (par) 2
direction une direction
director un directeur, une directrice 5; un metteur en scène; un(e) responsable 10; *director of human resources* un directeur, une directrice des ressources humaines (DRH) 10; *movie director* un réalisateur, une réalisatrice 5
dirty sale 3
to **disappear** disparaître
discography une discographie
discouraged découragé(e) 9
to **discover** découvrir; *to discover accidentally* tomber sur 5
discovery une découverte
to **discuss** discuter (de)
discussion une discussion
to **disguise oneself** se déguiser
dish un plat; *ham and pork dish made with chopped parsley* le jambon persillé 5; *main dish* un plat principal; *to wash the dishes* faire la vaisselle
dishwasher un lave-vaisselle
disorder le désordre
to **distance: to distance oneself (from)** s'éloigner (de) 7
distance une distance
distant éloigné(e) 3
distraught affolé(e) 1
district un arrondissement 10; un quartier
to **dive** plonger
divorced divorcé(e)(s)
to **do** faire; *to do (someone) a favor* rendre un service (à quelqu'un); *to do DIY projects* bricoler 3; *to do (something) in vain* avoir beau *[inform.]* 8; *to do gymnastics* faire de la gym (gymnastique); *to do housework* faire le ménage; *to do my homework* faire mes devoirs; *to bring oneself to do something* arriver à faire quelque chose 6; *you shouldn't do that* ça ne se fait pas
doctor un médecin; *doctor's office* un cabinet de médecin
documentary un documentaire
dog un chien
do-it-yourself (DIY) projects le bricolage 3; *to do DIY projects* bricoler 3
doll une poupée 1; *to play with dolls* jouer à la poupée 1
don't worry rassure-toi
door une porte
dormitory un dortoir; *university dormitory* une cité universitaire
dot: polka dot un pois 9; *polka dots* à pois 9
doubt un doute 4; *without a* ***doubt*** sans aucun doute 4
down: broken down en panne; *set down* posé(e) 2; *to break down* tomber en panne; *to put down* poser 2
to **download** télécharger
downtown en ville
drama un drame
to **draw** dessiner
drawing un dessin
to **dream** rêver
dream un rêve; *dream house* une maison de rêve
dress une robe; *wedding dress* une robe de mariée
dressed: dressed in vêtu(e) de 9; *to get dressed* s'habiller
dressing room une cabine d'essayage
dress-maker une couturière
to **dress up** se déguiser
to **drink** boire
drink une boisson; *drink and food offered before the meal* un apéritif 2
to **drive** circuler; conduire
driver un conducteur, une conductrice; *driver's license* un permis (de conduire) 8
drugs la drogue
drugstore une pharmacie
drum un tambour; *drum set* une batterie
to **dry** sécher; *to dry clothes* faire sécher le linge
dryer: clothes dryer un sèche-linge
dubbed doublé(e) 5
dubbing le doublage 5
duck un canard; *duck breast* un magret de canard 2
duration une durée 5
during au cours de 8; pendant
DVD un DVD; *DVD player* un lecteur de DVD
dynamic dynamique

E

each chaque; *each (one)* chacun(e) 5
to be **eager** avoir hâte de

ear l'oreille (f.)
early en avance; tôt
earring une boucle d'oreille
earthenware la faïence 10
earthquake un tremblement de terre
east l'est (m.)
easy facile
to **eat** manger
eclair un éclair
economic économique; *economic business management* la gestion économique d'entreprise 6
economy une économie 2
edge le bord
education une education; une formation 8
effect un effet; *greenhouse effect* l'effet de serre
efficiently efficacement
egg un œuf; *scrambled eggs* des œufs brouillés; *eggs sunny side up* des œufs sur le plat
eggplant une aubergine
egotistical perso *[inform.]* 8; *to be egotistical* être perso *[inform.]* 8
eight huit
eighteen dix-huit
eighth huitième
eighty quatre-vingts
election une élection 2; *presidential election* une élection présidentielle 2
electric électrique
electronic électronique 5
Electro pop music l'électro pop (m.)
elementary school teacher un instituteur, une institutrice
elevator un ascenseur 5
eleven onze
to **eliminate** éliminer
emotion une émotion 5
employee un(e) employé(e) 3
to **encourage** encourager 2
encouraged encouragé(e) 9
end le bout; *at the end (of)* au bout (de); au fond (de); *in the end* finalement 3
endangered species les animaux (m.) en voie de disparition
energetic énergique
energy l'énergie (f.); *nuclear energy* l'énergie nucléaire; *solar energy* l'énergie solaire
engagement les fiançailles (f.) 1; un engagement; *engagement ring* une bague de fiançailles 1
engineer un ingénieur
engineering le genie 6; *civil engineering* le génie civil 6
England l'Angleterre (f.)
English ***[language]*** l'anglais (m.)
English anglais(e) *English Channel* la Manche
English-speaking anglophone 10
engraved gravé(e)
enjoy: Enjoy your meal! Bon Appétit!
enough (of) assez (de); *Enough! Stop it!* N'en jette plus! *[inform.]* 8; *to be enough* suffire 3
to **enter** entrer
entertainment le divertissement; *entertainment industry* l'industrie (f.) du divertissement
enthusiastic enthousiaste
entirely entièrement 8
entitled: to be entitled to avoir droit à 8
envelope une enveloppe
environment l'environnement (m.)
equal égal(e) 10
equipped équipé(e) 5
era une époque
e-reader un e-reader
especially surtout; *to make especially (for someone)* réserver (pour quelqu'un) 10
essay un essai
essential essentiel, essentielle 4
ethnic ethnique 10
euro un euro
Europe l'Europe (f.)
European Union l'Union (f.) européenne
eve: Christmas Eve celebration le réveillon de Noël 2; *to celebrate Christmas/New Year's Eve* réveillonner 2
even même
evening le soir; une soirée; *evening out* une soirée 1
every tout(e); *every night* tous les soirs
everybody tout le monde
everyone le monde
everything tout(e) 3
everywhere partout
exactly exactement; *it's/that's exactly* c'est bien 10
to **exaggerate** exagérer
exam taken to obtain high school diploma un bac (baccalauréat) 9
excellent superbe
except sauf
exchange un change 6; *foreign exchange counter* un bureau de change 6
exhaustion: to collapse from exhaustion s'effondrer de fatigue 9
exhibit une exposition
exciting/fun night chaude ambiance
to **exist** exister
exit une sortie
to **expect: expect (baby)** attendre; *to expect (something)* s'attendre (à) 4
expensive cher, chère
experience une expérience
to **explain** expliquer
explained expliqué(e)
to **explore all the possibilities** faire le tour 10
expression une mine
expressionism l'expressionnisme (m.) 7
expressionist expressionniste 7
express train from Paris to suburbs le R.E.R.
extended prolongé(e)
extraordinary extraordinaire
eye l'œil (m.); *eyes* les yeux (m.) *eye to eye* le blanc des yeux 9; *to keep an eye on* surveiller 9

F

fable une fable 3
fabric un tissu
fabulous fabuleux, fabuleuse
face la figure
faced with face à 9
factory une usine
failed raté(e)
fair juste
fairy une fée 3; *fairy tale* un conte de fées 3
to **fall** tomber 8
fall une chute 8
to be **familiar with (person, place, thing)** connaître
family une famille; *blended family* une famille recomposée 1; *nuclear family* une famille nucléaire 1; *single-parent family* une famille monoparentale 1; *with family* en famille
famous célèbre
fan un(e) groupie 9
fantastic génial(e)
fantasy la fantaisie; l'imaginaire (m.) 6

far (from) loin (de)
farewell adieu 8; *to bid farewell* faire ses adieux (m.) 8
farm une ferme
farmer un fermier, une fermière
fascinating passionnant(e)
fashion la mode 2; *fashion design* la couture 10; *high fashion* la haute couture 10; *in fashion* à la page 2
fast rapide; vite
fat gros, grosse
fate le hasard 10
father un père; *stepfather* un beau-père
fatigue la fatigue 9
fauna la faune
favor un service; *to ask for a favor* demander un service; *to do (someone) a favor* rendre un service (à quelqu'un)
favorite préféré(e)
fax un fax 5
to **fear** craindre
feature film un long métrage 5
February février
to **feed** nourrir
to **feel** éprouver 5; ressentir 9; se sentir 9; *to feel/do better* se porter mieux; *to feel like* avoir envie de; *to feel nauseous* avoir mal au cœur; *How do you feel about (noun)?* (noun) te dit? 4
feeling une sensation
female politician une femme politique
fermented fermenté(e) 5
Ferris wheel la grande roue; *to go on a Ferris wheel ride* faire un tour de grande roue
fertilizer l'engrais (m.)
festival un festival 1
fever la fièvre
few: a few quelque 5; *with a few friends* en petit comité 2
field un champ; un domaine; *field of vision* un champ
fifteen quinze
fifth cinquième
fifty cinquante; *about fifty* une cinquantaine 9; *in one's fifties* d'une cinquantaine d'années 9
to **fight** combattre; lutter
fight une bagarre 9
figure la ligne; un chiffre 8; une figure 7
to **figure out** savoir
to **fill: to fill out** remplir 9; *to fill up* remplir; *to fill up the gas tank* faire le plein
to **film** filmer 9
film un film; *film club* un ciné-club 1; *film showing* une séance; *film trailer* une bande-annonce 5; *feature film* un long métrage 5
filmed tourné(e) 2
to **filter** filtrer 2
finale un final 5
finally enfin
finances les finances (f.) 6
financial financier, financière 10
to **find** trouver
fine fin(e); *fine arts* les beaux-arts (m.) 7; *fine jewelry* la joaillerie 10
to **finish** finir
finger le doigt
firework un feu d'artifice
firm: law firm un cabinet d'avocats 1
first premier, première; *first cousin* un(e) cousin(e) germain(e) 3; *first name* un prénom; *first of all* d'abord; *in the first year* en première année
first-aid les premiers secours (m.); *first-aid kit* une trousse de premiers secours
firstly premièrement 8
fir tree un sapin 2
to **fish** pêcher
fish un poisson; *goldfish* un poisson rouge
fisherman, fisherwoman un pêcheur, une pêcheuse 3
fishing la pêche; *fishing pole* une canne à pêche
fitness center un centre de remise en forme 5
fittingly justement 3
five cinq
fixed menu un menu fixe
flag un drapeau
flake un lâcheur, une lâcheuse *[inform.]* 9
flashlight une lampe de poche
flat plat(e) 5
flight un vol; *female flight attendant* une hôtesse de l'air; *male flight attendant* un steward
to **flirt** flirter 9
float un char
floor un étage; *the ground floor* le rez-de-chaussée; *the second floor* le premier étage
flooring: hardwood flooring le parquet 3
flop un nanar 5
flora la flore
florist un(e) fleuriste
flour: rolled in flour and sautéed meunier; meunière
flu la grippe
flute une flûte
folk music la musique folklorique
to **follow** suivre
following suivant(e) 5
fond of food gourmand(e)
food la nourriture; *food industry* le secteur agroalimentaire; *food product* un produit alimentaire 10; *drink and food offered before the meal* un apéritif 2
food-processing agroalimentaire 10
foot le pied; *on foot* à pied
for comme; depuis; pendant; pour; *for my taste* à mon goût 5; *for starters* pour commencer; *as for you* de votre côté 2
forecast les prévisions (f.); *weather forecast* la météo; un bulletin météo(rologique)
foreground le premier plan; *in the foreground* au premier plan
foreign exchange counter un bureau de change 6
forest une forêt
to **forget** oublier
fork une fourchette
formerly autrefois
fortunately heureusement
fortune teller un(e) voyant(e)
forty quarante; *about forty* une quarantaine 9; *in one's forties* d'une quarantaine d'années 9
fountain un bassin, une grande eau
four quatre
fourteen quatorze
fourth quatrième
fox un renard 7
France la France
free disponible; gratuit(e); libre; *to be free* être libre
French *[language]* le français; *French Guyana* la Guyane (française)
French français(e); *French fries* des frites (f.); *French national health and pension insurance* la sécurité sociale (sécu) 8; *French Riviera* la côte d'Azur; *French toast* le pain perdu
French-speaking francophone; *French-speaking world* la Francophonie 3; *from, of French-speaking Canada* francanadien(ne)

to **frequent** fréquenter
fresh frais, fraîche
Friday vendredi
friend un(e) ami(e); *(boy/girl) friend* un copain, une copine; *group of friends* une bande 1; *with a few friends* en petit comité 2
friendly: to be environmentally friendly être vert
fritter: cod fritter un accra de morue
from d', de; *from (the)* des, du; en *[pronoun]*; *from it/them* en; *from which* duquel, duquelle 5; *aside from* à part 9; *live from* en direct de; *to come from (+ country)* être d'origine (+ adjective) 3
front: in front of devant
fruit un fruit; *fruit tart* une tarte aux fruits
frustrated frustré(e) 9
frying pan une poêle
full plein(e); *full throttle* tout schuss 4
full-time à plein temps 8
fun: fun house une galerie des miroirs déformants; *to have fun* s'amuser; *to make fun (of)* se moquer (de)
to **function** marcher
funk music le funk
funny amusant(e); drôle
furniture: piece of furniture un meuble
future l'avenir (m.)
future futur(e) 6

G

Gabon le Gabon
Gabonese gabonais(e)
to **gain weight** grossir
gallery une galerie
game un match; *game of skill* un jeu d'adresse; *(TV) game show* un jeu télévisé
garbage can une poubelle
garden un jardin; *garden party* une fête champêtre 7
gas: gas station une station-service; *to fill up the gas tank* faire le plein
Gascony region la Gascogne; *from, of Gascony region* gascon(ne)
gasoline l'essence (f.)
gastronomy la gastronomie 5
gate: boarding gate une porte d'embarquement
genealogical généalogique 3; *genealogical research* des recherches (f.) généalogiques 3
general général(e) 8
generation une génération 3
generous généreux, généreuse
genocide le génocide
gentleness une douceur
German *[language]* l'allemand (m.)
German allemand(e)
Germany l'Allemagne (f.)
to **get** recevoir; *to get along* s'entendre; *to get around* circuler; se déplacer; *to get arrested* se faire arrêter 9; *to get a shot* se faire vacciner 4; *to get away (from)* s'éloigner (de) 10; *to get bored* s'ennuyer 4; *to get by* se débrouiller 6; *to get dressed* s'habiller; *to get information* se renseigner 4; *to get in/on* monter; *to get in trouble (with)* se faire disputer (par) 3; *to get knocked into* se faire bousculer 9; *to get married* se marier; *to get off* descendre; *to get people to agree* mettre d'accord 1; *to get (oneself) ready* se préparer; *to get reassigned* se faire muter 1; *to get settled* s'installer; *to get undressed* se déshabiller; *to get up* se lever; *to get wild* se déchaîner 9; *let's get back to it* on s'y remet; *you don't get it* tu n'y es pas du tout 4
giant géant(e)
gift un cadeau; *gift card* une carte cadeau
girl une fille
to **give** donner; faire un don (de); offrir; *to give back* rendre; *to give rise to* donner lieu à 7
gladly volontiers
to **glance (at)** jeter un coup d'œil (à) 5
glass un verre
glasses des lunettes (f.)
globalization la mondialisation 10
glove un gant 4
glued collé(e); *glued to* scotché(e) à
GNP (Gross National Product) le Produit National Brut (PNB) 2
to **go** aller; se rendre (à); *to go camping* faire du camping; *to go canoeing* faire du canoë; *to go down* descendre; *to go for a walk* faire une promenade; se promener; *to go grocery shopping* faire les courses; *to go horseback riding* faire du cheval; *to go into photo mode* se mettre en mode photo; *to go kayaking* faire du kayak; *to go off ski jumps* faire des sauts à ski 4; *to go on a carnival ride* faire un tour de manège; *to go on a Ferris wheel ride* faire un tour de grande roue; *to go on a guided tour* faire une visite guidée; *to go on a ride* faire un tour; *to go on a roller coaster ride* faire un tour de montagnes russes; *to go on a tour* faire un tour; *to go on a trail ride* faire une randonnée équestre 4; *to go on a trip* faire un voyage; *to go on strike* faire grève 2; *to go out* sortir; *to go parasailing* faire du parachutisme ascensionnel; *to go running* faire du footing; *to go sailing* faire de la voile; *to go scuba diving* faire de la plongée sous-marine; *to go shopping* faire du shopping; *to go sledding* faire de la luge 4; *to go snowshoeing* faire de la raquette à neige 4; *to go through* passer; *to go to bed* se coucher; *to go to college* entrer à l'université; *to go up* monter; *to go water-skiing* faire du ski nautique; *Go for it!* Vas-y!; *Here we go!* C'est parti!; *I'm going* je m'en vais 2
goal un but
goat une chèvre
goatfish un rouget
god: my god mon Dieu 5
godmother une marraine 1
goggles: ski goggles un masque de ski 4
gold l'or (m.); *made of gold* en or
good bon(ne); *good-bye* au revoir, salut; *Good idea!* Bonne idée!; *good luck* bon courage; *the good old days* le bon vieux temps; *Have a good trip!* Bonne route!; Bon voyage!
goods: leather goods la maroquinerie 10
goose liver pâté le foie gras 2
gorgeous splendide
gorilla un gorille; *mountain gorilla* un gorille des montagnes
gospel le gospel 9

gossip des commérages (m.) 9
government un gouvernement
grade une note
graffiti des graffiti (m.) 3
gram (of) un gramme (de)
to **grant** accorder 8
grandfather un grand-père
grandma Mamy
grandmother une grand-mère
grandpa Papy
grandparents les grands-parents (m.)
grape un raisin
grapefruit un pamplemousse; *grapefruit juice* un jus de pamplemousse
graphic: computer graphics l'infographie (f.) 6
graphic graphique 6; *graphic designer* un(e) graphiste
greasy gras 2
great chouette; génial(e); *great aunt* une grand-tante 3; *Great Depression* la grande crise 3; *great uncle* un grand-oncle 3
great-grandfather un arrière-grand-père 3
great-grandmother une arrière-grand-mère 3
green vert(e); *green beans* des haricots verts (m.)
grey gris(e)
to **grill** griller
grilled grillé(e)
grocery store une épicerie; *grocery store owner* un épicier, une épicière
groom un marié
ground floor le rez-de-chaussée
group un cercle 3; un comité 2; un groupe; *group of friends* une bande 1
grove un bosquet
to **grow** grandir; *to grow up* grandir 3
Guadeloupe la Guadeloupe
to **guarantee** garantir 5
guaranteed garanti(e)
to **guess** deviner
guest un(e) client(e) 5; un(e) invité(e)
guide un guide
guidebook un guide; *Michelin guidebook* le guide Michelin
guided guidé(e); *guided tour* une visite guidée; *to go on a guided tour* faire une visite guidée
guilty coupable 6
guitar une guitare
gym un fitness; *gym class* l'éducation physique et sportive (l'EPS) (f.)
gymnastics la gym (gymnastique)

H

hail la grêle 9
hair les cheveux (m.); *hair salon* un salon de coiffure; *hair stylist* un coiffeur, une coiffeuse; *to brush one's hair* se brosser les cheveux; *hairbrush* une brosse à cheveux; *hairstyle* une coiffure
hairdryer un sèche-cheveux
Haitian haïtien(ne)
half demi(e); *half past* et demi(e)
half-brother un demi-frère
half-sister une demi-sœur
half-time à mi-temps 8
hallway un couloir
ham le jambon; *ham and pork dish made with chopped parsley* le jambon persillé 5; *ham sandwich* un sandwich au jambon
hamburger un hamburger
hamlet un hameau
to **hammer a nail** enfoncer un clou 3
hammer un marteau 3
hammock un hamac
hand la main; *(helping) hand* un coup de main 2; *hand in hand* la main dans la main; *on the other hand* par contre 8
handkerchief un mouchoir; *linen handkerchief* un mouchoir de lin
handsome beau, bel, belle
to **hang** accrocher 3; *to hang out* fréquenter
to **happen** arriver 9; se passer 8
happy content(e), heureux, heureuse; *to be happy (about)* être content(e) (de) 6
hardwood flooring le parquet 3
hat un bonnet; un chapeau; *wool hat* un bonnet en laine
to **hate** avoir horreur de
haunted house une maison hantée
to **have** avoir; *(food or drink)* prendre; *to have a/an... ache* avoir mal (à...); *to have dinner* dîner; *to have fun* s'amuser; *to have just* venir de (+ infinitive); *to have the impression (of)* avoir l'impression (de) 6; *to have the means* avoir les moyens 8; *to have the opportunity (to)* avoir la chance (de) 2; avoir l'occasion (de) 4; *to have to* devoir; falloir; *to have too many choices* avoir l'embarras du choix 10; *Have a good trip!* Bonne route!; Bon voyage!;
hazelnut: spread made of hazelnut and chocolate le Nutella
he il
head la tête
headquarters un siège social 10
healed guéri(e) 8
health la santé; *health club* un fitness; *health sector* le domaine de la santé; *French national health and pension insurance* la sécurité sociale (sécu) 8; *health insurance* une assurance maladie 8
health sanitaire;
to **hear** entendre
heart le cœur
to **heat (up)** chauffer 2; réchauffer
heights: to be afraid of heights avoir peur du vide
hello bonjour; *[on the telephone]* allô
to **help** aider; *to help you* pour t'avancer 2; *cannot help (but)* ne pas pouvoir s'empêcher (de) 2
help au secours
hen une poule
her elle; sa, ses, son
herb une herbe 2
here ici; tiens; voici; *here are/is* voilà; *here is* voici; *Here we go!* C'est parti!
hero, heroine un héros, une héroïne
hers le, la sien(ne) 9
to **hesitate** hésiter
hey tiens
hi salut
hibiscus un hibiscus
to **hide** cacher, se cacher 7; dissimuler
hide-and-seek: to play hide-and-seek jouer à cache-cache 1
high haut(e); *high fashion* la haute couture 10
high school un lycée; *exam taken to obtain high school diploma* un bac (baccalauréat) 9
highway une route
to **hike** faire une randonnée à pied
hike une randonnée
hill une colline
hip-hop le hip-hop
to **hire** embaucher 8

his le, la sien(ne), 9; sa, ses, son
history l'histoire (f.)
hit un hit *[inform.]* 2
holiday une fête; *national holiday* une fête nationale; *national Quebec holiday* la Saint-Jean
hollandaise sauce une sauce hollandaise 5
home une maison; *home health worker* un accompagnateur, une accompagnatrice; *home page* accueil 5; *second home* une résidence secondaire 3
homeless person un sans-abri
homework les devoirs (m.)
honey chéri(e)3
honeymoon un voyage de noces 1
honor l'honneur (m.) 1
Honduras le Honduras 10
hood ***[car]*** un capot
to **hope** espérer; souhaiter 5
hopscotch: to play hopscotch jouer à la marelle 1
horizon l'horizon (m.); *on the horizon* à l'horizon
horn un klaxon
horrible horrible
horror l'horreur (f.); *horror movie* un film d'horreur
horse un cheval
horseback: to go horseback riding faire du cheval
hospital un hôpital 8
hospitality l'hospitalité (f.)
to **host** recevoir
host: TV host un animateur, une animatrice
hot chaud(e); *hot chocolate* un chocolat chaud; *to be hot* avoir chaud; *it's hot* il fait chaud
hotel un hôtel; *hotel clerk* un(e) réceptionniste; *hotel room* une chambre
hour une heure
house une maison; *house cleaning items* des affaires (f.) de ménage; *dream house* une maison de rêve; *fun house* une galerie des miroirs déformants; *haunted house* une maison hantée; *row house* une maison mitoyenne 3; *single-family house* une maison individuelle 3
household le ménage
housework le ménage; *to do housework* faire le ménage
housing un logement 3; *subsidized housing* un HLM 3
how comment; *how about* si; *How are things going?* Ça va?; *How are you?* Comment allez-vous? *[form.]*; *How do you feel about (noun)?* (noun) te dit? 4; *how long* depuis combien de temps; *how much* combien; *How much is it?* Ça fait combien?; *How much per kilo?* C'est combien le kilo?; *How old are you?* Tu as quel âge?; *How's the weather?* Quel temps fait-il?; *that's how...* c'est comme ça que... 1
however cependant, par contre 8
human humain(e) 10; *human resources* les ressources (f.) humaines 10; *human rights* les droits (m.) de l'homme 2; *director of human resources* un directeur, une directrice des ressources humaines (DRH) 10
humanitarian humanitaire
Humanities les lettres (f.); *to declare a major in Humanities* s'inscrire en lettres
humid humide 4
hummingbird un colibri
humor une humeur 5
hundred: (one) hundred cent
hunger la faim
to be **hungry** avoir faim
to **hurry** se dépêcher (de)
to be **hurt** avoir mal (à...)
husband un mari
hybrid hybride
hydrant: water hydrant une borne-fontaine
hydrotherapeutic thermal(e)

I

I j'/je
ice cream une glace; *chocolate ice cream* une glace au chocolat; *vanilla ice cream* une glace à la vanille
ice-skating (figure skating) le patinage (artistique)
icon une icône
idea une idée
idealism l'idéalisme (m.) 2
identity une identité 4
identification: piece of identification une pièce d'identité 4
if si; *if only* si; *if you'd like* si cela vous convient
illness une maladie
to **illustrate** illustrer 8
image une image
to **imagine** imaginer
imagination une imagination 10
immense immense 7
important important(e) 4; *what's important* l'important (neutr.)
impossible impossible
impression une impression 5; *to/have the impression (of)* avoir l'impression (de) 6
Impressionism l'impressionnisme (m.) 7
Impressionist un(e) impressionniste 7
Impressionist impressionniste
to **imprison** emprisonner 2
to **improvise** improviser 2
in à; dans, en; *in a close-up* en gros plan 7; *in addition to* en plus; *in any case* de toute façon 4; en tout cas; *in a way* en un sens; *in circles* en rondelles; *in fashion* à la page 2; *in front of* devant; *in its place* à sa place 2; *in love* amoureux, amoureuse 6; *in my opinion* à mon avis; *in one's fifties* d'une cinquantaine d'années 9; *in one's forties* d'une quarantaine d'années 9; *in one's thirties* d'une trentaine d'années 9; *in one's twenties* d'une vingtaine d'années 9; *in order* en ordre; *in short* bref 9; *in the* au, aux; *in the background* à l'arrière-plan 7; *in the course of* au cours de 8; *in the end* finalement 3; *in the first year* en première année; *in the foreground* au premier plan; *in the manner of* la façon 9; *in the past* autrefois; *in the spring* au printemps; *In what colors?* De quelle(s) couleur(s)?; *in winter* en hiver
incapable incapable 9
to **include** comprendre 5
included compris(e)
income des revenus (m.) 2
increase une hausse 2
incredible incroyable
India l'Inde (f.) 10
to **indicate** indiquer
indispensable indispensable 4
individual un individu 10
individual individuel, individuelle 3
Indonesia l'Indonésie (f.) 10

industry une industrie; un secteur; *aviation industry* le secteur aéronautique; *entertainment industry* l'industrie du divertissement; *food industry* le secteur agroalimentaire; *information technology industry* le secteur de l'informatique; *sustainable development industry* le secteur de développement durable
inflatable water mattress un matelas pneumatique
inflation une inflation 2; *inflation rate* un taux d'inflation 2
to **influence** influencer 8
to **inform** informer
informal: to use the informal "*tu*" to address someone tutoyer 10
information: information technology l'informatique (f.); *information technology industry* le secteur de l'informatique; *specific information* des précisions (f.) 5; *to get information* se renseigner 4
to be **informed** être au courant
inhabitant un(e) habitant(e)
in-line skating le roller
insect un insecte; *insect repellent* un anti-moustique
inside l'intérieur (m.)
to **insist (on)** insister (sur)
to **install** installer
instructor un moniteur, une monitrice 4
insurance une assurance 8; *French national health and pension insurance* la sécurité sociale (sécu) 8; *health insurance* une assurance maladie 8
instrument: musical instrument un instrument
to **integrate (into)** s'intégrer (à) 6
intelligent intelligent(e)
intense intense 5
to **interest** intéresser
to be **interested (in)** s'intéresser (à)
interested intéressé(e) 1
interesting intéressant(e)
interface une interface
international international(e)
Internet l'Internet (m.); *wireless Internet connection* une connexion Wifi 5
to **intern** faire un stage 8
intern un(e) stagiaire 8
internship un stage 8
intervention: to organize an intervention faire une intervention
to **interview** interviewer 9
interview un entretien 8; une interview 10
intimate intimiste 7
to **introduce** introduire 8; *to introduce (to someone)* présenter (à); *to introduce to someone* faire connaître (à), faire découvrir (à)
invaded envahi(e) 2
invention une invention 7
invitation une invitation 2
to **invite** inviter
to **iron** repasser
iron *[clothes]* un fer à repasser
is: isn't that so n'est-ce pas
island une île 4
it ça, ce; cela 3; elle, il; l', la, le *[object pronoun]*; y *[pronoun]*; *it doesn't surprise me* ça ne me surprend pas; *It has a totally vintage look!* Total vintage!; *it is* c'est; *it is necessary* il faut; *it/that means* ça veut dire; *it will be revealed (known)* ça va se savoir; *it's all the same to me* ça m'est égal; *it's a promise* c'est promis 6; *It's beautiful out.* Il fait beau.; *it's been a long time since* ça fait longtemps que; *it's better that* il vaut mieux que 4; *it's cold* il fait froid; *it's cool* il fait frais; *it's hot* il fait chaud; *it's not worth it* ce n'est pas la peine 1; *it sounds promising* ça promet 5; *it's possible that* il se pourrait que 4; *it's raining* il pleut; *It's settled.* C'est décidé.; *it's snowing* il neige; *it's sunny* il fait du soleil; *it's/that's exactly* c'est bien 10; *It's the (+ date).* Nous sommes le (+ date).; *it's the same* c'est pareil; *it's too bad that...* c'est dommage que... 5; *it's windy* il fait du vent; *You sure know a lot about it.* Tu en sais des choses.
its sa, ses, son
Italian italien(ne)
Italy l'Italie (f.)
items: house cleaning items des affaires (f.) de ménage
itinerary un itinéraire
Ivory Coast la Côte-d'Ivoire; *from, of the Ivory Coast* ivorien(ne)

J

jacket un blouson; une veste
jam la confiture
janitor un homme de ménage 5
January janvier
Japan le Japon 10
Japonese japonais(e)
jar (of) un pot (de)
jasmine le jasmin
jazz music le jazz
jeans un jean
jersey un maillot
to **jet ski** faire du scooter des mers
jet ski un jet ski
jewelry: fine jewelry la joaillerie 10; *piece of jewelry* un bijou
job un boulot *[inform.]* 8; un emploi; un métier; *job position* un poste 1
Jordan la Jordanie 10
journey: to take a journey partir en voyage 8
juice un jus; *apple juice* un jus de pomme; *grapefruit juice* un jus de pamplemousse; *orange juice* jus d'orange
July juillet
to **jump** sauter 1; *to jump rope* sauter à la corde 1; *to bungee jump* faire du saut à l'élastique 4
jump: ski jump un tremplin de saut à ski 4; *to go off ski jumps* faire des sauts à ski 4
June juin
junior junior 8
just juste 3; *just any* n'importe quel, quelle 9; *to have just* venir de (+ infinitive)

K

kayaking: to go kayaking faire du kayak
to **keep** garder 3; *to keep an eye on* surveiller 9; *to keep in touch* garder le contact 3
ketchup le ketchup
key *[ignition]* une clé; *[on keyboard]* une touche
keyboard un clavier
to **kill** tuer 2
kilogram (of) un kilo (de)
kilometer un kilomètre
kind une sorte
king un roi
kiosk: self-service kiosk une borne libre-service
to **kiss** embrasser
kit: first-aid kit une trousse de premiers secours

kitchen la cuisine
knee le genou
knife un couteau; *Swiss army knife* un couteau suisse
knocked: to get knocked into se faire bousculer 9
to **know** connaître; être au courant; savoir; *to know how* savoir; *to know each other* se connaître; *You sure know a lot about it.* Tu en sais des choses.
knowledge les connaissances (f.) 8
to be **known** se savoir
Korea: South Korea la Corée du Sud 10

L

laboratory: computer lab une salle d'informatique; *research laboratory* un laboratoire de recherches 1; *science lab* un labo (laboratoire)
to **lack** manquer
lady une dame
laid out disposé(e)
lake un lac
lamb un agneau
lambis un lambi
lamp une lampe
to **land** atterrir
land la terre
landscape un paysage
language une langue
large grand(e); gros, grosse
last dernier, dernière; *At last!* Depuis le temps!
late en retard; tard
latest: the latest le dernier, la dernière 6
to **laugh** rigoler; rire
to **launch** lancer 10
laundry la blanchisserie 5; *laundry service* un service blanchisserie 5
law le droit 6; *law firm* un cabinet d'avocats 1
lawn une pelouse; *lawn mower* une tondeuse
lawyer un(e) avocat(e)
lazy paresseux, paresseuse
leader un leader 10; *world leader* un leader mondial 10
to **learn** apprendre
least: at least au moins; *the least* le moins
leather le cuir; *leather goods* la maroquinerie 10; *made of leather* en cuir
to **leave** laisser; partir; quitter; *to leave one another* se quitter 1

left: on the left à gauche; *on/to the left of* à gauche de; *to be left* rester
leg la jambe
legend une légende
lemon un citron; *tea with lemon* un thé au citron
lemon-lime soda with mint syrup un diabolo menthe
to **lend** prêter
length une durée 5; une longueur 2
less moins; *less... than* moins (+ adverb) + que
to **let** laisser; *Let me finish!* Laisse-moi finir!
letter une lettre; *air letter* un aérogramme 6; *application letter* une lettre de candidature 8; *cover letter* une lettre de motivation 8
lettuce une salade
level un niveau
license: driver's license un permis (de conduire) 8
to **lie** mentir 7
life une vie; *relaxed style of life* une douceur de vivre
lifeless plat(e) 5
lift: ski lift un télésiège 4
light une lumière
to **like** aimer; apprécier 5; kiffer *[inform.]*; *if you'd like* si cela vous convient; *like this* comme ça
like: to seem like avoir l'air de 1
likeable attachant(e)
line une ligne 7
linen le lin; *linen handkerchief* un mouchoir de lin; *made of linen* de lin
link un lien
lip la lèvre
lipstick un rouge à lèvres
liquid une liquide 6
list une liste; *to make a list* faire une liste
to **listen (to)** écouter; *to listen to music* écouter de la musique; *to listen to my MP3 player* écouter mon lecteur MP3
listening trial en écoute libre
liter (of) un litre (de)
little petit(e); *(a) little* (un) peu; *a little of* un peu de
to **live** demeurer 7; habiter; vivre
live from en direct de
liver: goose liver pâté le foie gras 2
living room un salon, un séjour

loaf: salmon loaf une terrine de saumon
lobby un hall, un lobby 5
lobster: spiny lobster une langouste
local local(e) 10
located situé(e); *to be located* être situé(e); se trouver
lock screen un lockscreen
log: yule log une bûche de Noël 2
logo: team logo un blason
lonely seul(e) 9
long long, longue; *how long* depuis combien de temps; *it's been a long time since* ça fait longtemps que
to **look** avoir l'air; *to look at oneself* se regarder; *to look for* chercher; *to look for/into* rechercher 7; *to look healthy* avoir bonne mine; *to look like (something from) my country* avoir un petit air du pays; *to look sick* avoir mauvaise mine; *Does this... look good on me?* Tu trouves que... me va bien?; *Look up!* Lève la tête!
look un look 2; une tête 9; *on a closer look* en y regardant de plus près 4; *traditional look* un look tradi 2
look remarque; un regard; *look...* écoute... 2
to **lose** perdre; *to lose it* craquer 9; *to lose weight* maigrir
lost perdu(e)
lot: a lot beaucoup; *a lot (of)* plein (de) 8; *a lot of* beaucoup de
lotion une crème 1
to **love** aimer
love l'amour (m.); *in love* amoureux, amoureuse 6; *to be in love (with)* être amoureux/amoureuse (de) 6
lover (of) un amoureux, une amoureuse (de)
luck le hasard 10; *good luck* bon courage; *to try one's luck* tenter sa chance 3
to be **lucky** avoir de la chance
luggage: piece of luggage un bagage; *luggage compartment* un compartiment à bagages; *to check one's luggage* faire enregistrer les bagages
lumpfish un lump 2; *lumpfish roe* des œufs (m.) de lump 2
lunch le déjeuner

Luxembourg le Luxembourg; *from, of Luxembourg* luxembourgeois(e)
luxury le luxe 10
Lyon region le Lyonnais; *from, of Lyon* lyonnais(e)
lyricism le lyrisme 7
lyrics des paroles (f.)

M

Ma'am madame (Mme)
machine un appareil 6; *washing machine* une machine à laver
made: made (in) fabriqué(e) (au, aux, en) 10; *made of* de, en; *made of aluminum* en aluminium; *made of cotton* en coton; *made of diamonds* de diamants; *made of gold* en or; *made of leather* en cuir; *made of linen* de lin; *made of metal* en métal 2; *made of pearls* de/en perles; *made of plastic* en plastique; *made of silk* en soie; *made of silver* en argent; *made of velvet* en velours; *made of wool* en laine; *made up (of)* composé(e) (de) 5
magazine un magazine; *magazine article* un article
Maghreb: from, of the Maghreb maghrébin(e)
magical magique
magician un(e) magicien(ne) 3
mail un courrier
mailbox une boîte aux lettres 6
mailman, mailwoman un facteur, une factrice 6
main principal(e); *main dish* un plat principal
to **major (in)** se spécialiser (en)
to **make** faire; préparer; *to make a call* téléphoner; *to make a decision* prendre une décision 10; *to make a list* faire une liste; *to make a promise* faire une promesse; *to make a reservation* réserver; *to make a speech* faire un discours 8; *to make especially (for someone)* réserver (pour quelqu'un) 10; *to make fun (of)* se moquer (de); *to make up one's mind* se décider 6; *to make (something) work* faire marcher; *they (one) make(s) you* on te fait 8
make-up le maquillage; *to put on make-up* se maquiller
Malaysia la Malaisie 10
male politician un homme politique
Mali le Mali
Malian malien(ne)
mall un centre commercial
man un homme; *best man* un garçon d'honneur 1
management la gestion 6; *economic business management* la gestion économique d'entreprise 6
manager un chef, une cheffe 8; un(e) responsible 10; *personnel manager* un chef du personnel 8
mandarin orange une mandarine 2
mandatory obligatoire
manga un manga 6
mangrove une mangrove
manner: in the manner of la façon 9
manufacturer: car manufacturer un constructeur, une constructrice automobile 10
many maints 5; *to have too many choices* avoir l'embarras du choix 10
map une carte; *city map* un plan
maple: maple tree un érable; *maple syrup* le sirop d'érable
marble une bille 1; *to play marbles* jouer aux billes 1
market ***[financial]*** le marché; *flea market* un marché aux puces; *outdoor market* un marché
marketing le marketing 10
married: to get married se marier
Martinique la Martinique; *from, of Martinique* martiniquais(e)
marvelous merveilleux, merveilleuse
mascara le mascara
mask un mas *[Mart.]*, un masque
master: master, mistress un maître, une maîtresse 3; *Master's degree* une maîtrise 10
masterpiece un chef-d'œuvre
math les maths (f.)
mattress: inflatable water mattress un matelas pneumatique
May mai
may: May I help you? Je peux vous aider?
maybe peut-être
mayo la mayonnaise
mayor le maire, madame le maire
me m', moi; me; *to me* me
meal un repas; *drink and food offered before the meal* un apéritif 2
to **mean** vouloir dire; *it/that means* ça veut dire
mean méchant(e)
means un moyen; *means of transportation* un moyen de transport; *to have the means* avoir les moyens 8
to **measure** mesurer 2
measuring: measuring cup un verre mesureur 2; *measuring spoon* une cuillère-mesure 2
meat la viande 5
mechanic un(e) mécanicien(ne)
mechanics la mécanique 3
medal une médaille 2
media les médias (m.) 2; *media center* une médiathèque
medical médical(e) 8
medicalized médicalisé(e) 8
medicine la médecine 6
Mediterranean méditerranéen(ne) 9
medium moyen(ne)
to **meet** connaître; faire la connaissance (de); se retrouver; se réunir; *to meet (someone)* se rencontrer; *Pleased to meet you.* Très heureux/heureuse. 3
meeting un rendez-vous
melancholy la mélancolie 7
melody une mélodie 7
melon un melon
memory un souvenir
to **mention: not to mention** sans parler de 10
menu une carte
merchant un(e) marchand(e)
message un message
messaging une messagerie
to **mess up** rater 2
metal un métal 2; *made of metal* en métal 2
method une méthode 7
Mexico le Mexique 10
microwave un micro-onde
midnight minuit
to **milk** traire
milk le lait
million un million
mind: to make up one's mind se décider 6
mine le, la mien(ne) 9
mineral water une eau minéral
minivan un monospace
mint la menthe; *lemon-lime soda with mint syrup* un diabolo menthe

minute une minute
mirror une glace; un miroir; *rear-view mirror* un rétroviseur
Miss mademoiselle (Mlle)
mission une mission
mist le brouillard 7
to **mix** mélanger 2
mode: to go into photo mode se mettre en mode photo
model un mannequin
modern moderne
to **modernize** moderniser
moment un instant; un moment; *at the moment* en ce moment 6; *for the moment* pour l'instant
Monaco: from, of Monaco monégasque 5
Monday lundi
money l'argent (m.)
mongoose une mangouste
monitor un écran; un moniteur
month un mois
monument un monument
mood une humeur 5; *I'm not in the mood for* je ne suis pas trop d'humeur pour 5
mop une serpillière 10
moral une morale 7
more davantage; encore; plus; plus de (+ noun); *more and more* de plus en plus 7; *more... than* plus (+ adverb) + que
moreover d'ailleurs 8
morning la matinée; le matin
most la plupart de 9; *the most* le plus; *the most (+ adjective)* le/la/les plus (+ adjectif)
mostly surtout
mother une mère; *stepmother* une belle-mère
motivation la motivation 8
motto une devise
mountain une montagne; *mountain pineapple* un ananas montagne; *mountain range* un massif
mouse une souris
mousse: chocolate mousse une mousse au chocolat
mouth la bouche
to **move** bouger; déménager 1; *to move from... to* passer de... à 7; *to move over (something)* passer; *to move (toward)* s'avancer (vers)
move (house) un déménagement
movement un mouvement
movie: movie director un réalisateur, une réalisatrice 5; *movies* le cinéma; *action movie* un film d'action; *adventure movie* un film d'aventure; *detective movie* un film policier; *horror movie* un film d'horreur; *movie theatre* un ciné (cinéma); *science fiction movie* un film de science-fiction; *to shoot a movie* tourner un film 5
to **mow** tondre
MP3 player un lecteur de MP3
Mr. monsieur (M.)
Mrs. madame (Mme)
Ms. madame (Mme), mademoiselle (Mlle)
much: so much tellement; *very much* beaucoup; *How much is it?* Ça fait combien?
multicultural ethnique 10
multimedia file un fichier multimédia
multinational multinational(e) 10
multiplex cinema un multiplexe 5
multiplication la multiplication 8; *multiplication table* une table de multiplication 8
muscular musclé(e) 9
museum un musée
mushroom un champignon; *trumpet of the dead mushroom* une trompette de la mort 5; *with mushrooms* forestier, forestière
music la musique; *music show* une émission de musique; *alternative music* la musique alternative; *classical music* la musique classique; *Electro pop music* l'électro pop (m.); *folk music* la musique folklorique; *funk music* le funk; *jazz music* le jazz; *pop music* la musique pop; *Rai music* le raï; *rap music* le rap; *reggae music* le reggae; *salsa music* la salsa 7; *swing music* le swing 7; *techno music* la techno
musical un film musical; *musical instrument* un instrument
music-hall un music-hall
mustard la moutarde
my ma, mes, mon; *my god* mon Dieu 5
mystery un mystère 6

N

nail un clou 3; *to hammer a nail* enfoncer un clou 3
name un nom; *brand name* marqué(e) 10; *first name* un prénom; *What's your name?* Tu t'appelles comment?
nanotechnology les nanotechnologies (f.) 1
napkin une serviette
narrow étroit(e) 2
nation une nation 2
national national(e); *national holiday* une fête nationale; *national Quebec holiday* la Saint-Jean; *French national health and pension insurance* la sécurité sociale (sécu) 8; *GNP (Gross National Product)* le Produit National Brut (PNB) 2
native un(e) autochtone; *native people* les indigènes (m.)
nature la nature
nauseous: to feel nauseous avoir mal au cœur
near près de
nearly presque
necessary nécessaire; *to be necessary* falloir
neck le cou
necklace un collier; *pearl necklace* un collier de/en perles
to **need** avoir besoin de; *I need* il me faut
need un besoin 8
neither ni 4; non plus; *neither... nor* ne (n')... ni... ni 4
neo-classic néoclassique 7
neoclassicism le néo-classicisme 7
Neo-impressionism le néo-impressionnisme 7
nerves: You're getting on my nerves! Tu m'agaces!
never ne (n')... jamais
nevertheless néanmoins 8
new de neuf, neuf, neuve; nouveau, nouvel; nouvelle; *New Brunswick* le Nouveau-Brunswick; *new release* une nouveauté 5; *New Year's Day* le Jour de l'an; *to celebrate Christmas/New Year's Eve* réveillonner 2; *What's new?* Quoi de neuf?
news les informations (infos) (f.); *news anchor* un présentateur, une présentatrice; *news report* un reportage; *news store that sells tobacco, stamps, lottery tickets* un bureau de tabac
newspaper un journal; *newspaper article* un article

newsstand un kiosque à journaux
next ensuite; prochain(e); *next day* le lendemain; *next to* à côté (de)
ney ***[instrument]*** un nay
NGO (non-governmental organization) une ONG (organisation non gouvernementale)
nice gentil, gentille; sympa
nicely said joliment dit
night la nuit; *every night* tous les soirs; *exciting/fun night* chaude ambiance; *to stay up all night* faire une nuit blanche
nightclub une boîte; une discothèque 1
nine neuf
nineteen dix-neuf
ninety quatre-vingt-dix
ninth neuvième
no ne (n')... aucun(e) 4; non; *no longer* ne (n')... plus; *no one* aucun(e) 4; ne (n')... personne
nobody ne (n')... personne
none aucun(e) 4; ne (n')... aucun(e) 4; *none of us (+ verb)* aucun de nous ne (+ verb) 4
noon midi
nor ni 4; *neither... nor* ne (n')... ni... ni 4
Normandy region la Normandie; *from, of Normandy region* normand(e)
north le nord; *North America* l'Amérique du Nord (f.)
nose le nez
not ne (n')... pas, pas; *not any* ne (n')... aucun(e) 4; *not anymore* ne (n')... plus; *not anyone* ne (n')... personne; *not at all* pas du tout; *not bad* pas mal; *not one* ne (n')... aucun(e) 4; *not the type to* pas la tête à 9; *not to mention* sans parler de 10; *not well* pas très bien; *not yet* ne (n')... pas encore; *I'm afraid not.* Je crains que non. 2
notebook un cahier
nothing ne (n')... rien; rien 9
to **notice** remarquer; s'apercevoir (de) 9
novel un roman
novelist un romancier, une romancière 7
November novembre
now maintenant
nuclear nucléaire; *nuclear family* une famille nucléaire 1
number un chiffre 8; un nombre, un numéro; *phone number* un numéro de téléphone
nurse un infirmier, une infirmière

O

obligated (to) obligé(e) (de) 8; *to be obligated (to)* être obligé(e) (de) 8
to **obtain** obtenir 4
obvious évident(e) 5; *to be obvious that* être évident que 5
occasion une occasion 4
o'clock l'heure (f.)
object un objet; *art object* un objet d'art
to **observe** observer
obviously évidemment
occasion une fois
to **occupy** occuper
ocean un océan; *Atlantic Ocean* l'océan Atlantique; *Indian Ocean* l'océan Indien; *Pacific Ocean* l'océan Pacifique
October octobre
of de/d'; en; sur; *of (the)* des; du; *of average height* de taille moyenne; *of course* bien entendu 5; bien sûr; pardi *[regional]*; *of it/them* en; *of which/whom* dont 6; *because of* à cause de 2
to **offer** offrir; proposer 10
office un bureau; un office 4; *at/to the physical therapy office* chez le kiné 8; *dentist's office* un cabinet dentaire; *doctor's office* un cabinet du médecin; *principal's office* le bureau du proviseur; *tourist information office* un syndicat d'initiative; *tourist office* un office de tourisme 4
official officiel, officielle
off-piste skiing un hors-piste 4
often souvent
oh ah, oh; *oh dear* oh là là; *oh no* oh là là
oil ***[car]*** l'huile (f.); *oil slick* une marée noire
oily gras 2
OK d'accord
old ancien(ne) 3; vieux, vieil, vieille; *old age* la vieillesse 7; *the good old days* le bon vieux temps
on à, en; dessus; sur; *on a bicycle* à bicyclette; *on a closer look* en y regardant de plus près 4; *on board* à bord; *on foot* à pied; *on sale* en solde; *on second thought* en y réfléchissant bien 4; *on the* au, du; *on the contrary* au contraire 8; *on the corner* du coin; *on the horizon* à l'horizon; *on the left* à gauche; *on the other hand* par contre 8; *on the premises* sur place 4; *on the right* à droite; *on the way* en route; *on time* à l'heure; *on tour* en tournée 7; *on TV* à la télé; *on wheels* à roulettes; *come on* enfin
Once upon a time (there was).... Il était une fois.... 3
one on; un; une; *one's* le, la sien(ne) 9; sa, ses, son; *no one* aucun(e) 4; *not one* ne (n')... aucun(e) 4; *that/this one* celui, celle 6; *the one* celui, celle 6; *the ones* ceux 6; *the one... the other* l'un(e)... l'autre 9
oneself: to distance oneself (from) s'éloigner (de) 7; *to say to oneself* se dire; *to see oneself as* se reconnaître 7
onion un oignon
online en ligne
only juste; ne (n')... que, seulement 4
on-stage sur scène 7
to **open** ouvrir
opening une ouverture 8
opinion un avis; *in my opinion* à mon avis
opportunity: to have the opportunity (to) avoir la chance (de) 2; avoir l'occasion (de) 4
opposite le contraire 8
or ou
orange une orange; *orange juice* un jus d'orange; *mandarin orange* une mandarine 2
orange orange
orangery une orangerie
orchestra un orchestre 5
orchid une orchidée; *tropical orchid* une orchidée suspendue
to **order** commander
order un ordre; *in order* en ordre
organic biologique
to **organize an intervention** faire une intervention
organized organisé(e) 4
origin une origine 3
original original(e) 5; *original version* une version originale (V.O.) 5

other autre; *on the other hand* par contre 8; *the one... the other* l'un(e)... l'autre 9
otherwise autrement
ouch ouille
oud *[instrument]* un oud
our nos, notre
ours le, la nôtre 9
out: evening out une soirée 1; *washed out* délavé(e) 9
outdoors en plein air
outfit un ensemble
oven un four
over (it) dessus; *over there* là-bas
to **overcome** s'en sortir
overexcited surexcité(e) 9
overwhelmed accablé(e) 9
to **owe** devoir 7
to **own a restaurant** tenir un restaurant 3
owner: grocery store owner un épicier, une épicière
oyster une huître 2

P

to **pack** faire sa valise 4
package un colis 6; un paquet
packet (of) un paquet (de)
page: home page accueil 5
to **paint** peindre 3
paintbrush un pinceau 7
painter un(e) peintre
painting la peinture 7; une peinture; un tableau
pal: pen pal un(e) correspondant(e) 10
pale pâle 7
pan: frying pan une poêle
panda un panda; *giant panda* un panda géant
panel un panneau
to **panic** être affolé(e) 1
panicky paniqué(e) 9
pants un pantalon; *ski pants* un fuseau de ski 4
paper le papier; *sheet of paper* une feuille de papier; *toilet paper* le papier toilette 10
paperback un livre de poche 6
parade un déboulé *[Mart.]*, un défilé
paralyzed tétanisé(e) 9
parasailing: to go parasailing faire du parachutisme ascensionnel
pardon me pardon
parents les parents (m.)
Paris: from, of Paris parisien(ne)
park un jardin; un parc; *amusement park* un parc d'attractions; *skateboard park* un skatepark 1; *water park* un aquaparc 1
parliamentary parlementaire
parsley: ham and pork dish made with chopped parsley le jambon persillé 5
part une partie 7
party une fête, une teuf; un parti 2; *garden party* une fête champêtre 7; *political party* un parti politique 2; *socialist political party* le parti politique socialiste 2
to **pass** passer; *to pass (a test)* réussir (à)
pass: boarding pass une carte d'embarquement; *ski pass* un forfait de ski 4
passenger un passager, une passagère
passer-by un(e) passant(e) 3
passion une passion
passionate (about) passionné(e (de)
passionately passionnément 2
passport un passeport 4
past le passé 4
pasta des pâtes (f.)
pastime un passe-temps
pastry: pastry shop une patisserie; *cream puff pastry* une religieuse; *layered custard pastry* un millefeuille
pâté le pâté; *goose liver pâté* le foie gras 2
path un chemin; un sentier; une trace *[Mart.]*; une voie
pause une pause 5
to **pay** payer; régler; *someone who pays* un payeur, une payeuse
peace la paix 2
peach une pêche
peak un sommet 4
pear une poire
pear-shaped en forme de poire 2
pearl une perle; *pearl necklace* un collier de/en perles
peas des petits-pois (m.)
pen un stylo; *pen pal* un(e) correspondant(e) 10
pencil un crayon; *pencil case* une trousse; *pencil sharpener* un taille-crayon
pension: French national health and pension insurance la sécurité sociale (sécu) 8
people des gens (m.); un peuple 8; *native people* les indigènes (m.); *to get people to agree* mettre d'accord 1
pepper le poivre; *bell pepper* un poivron
perfect parfait(e) 5
perfectly parfaitement
performer un interprète 7
perfume un parfum
period une époque
permit une autorisation 6
person une personne; *crazy person* un fou, une folle; *homeless person* un sans-abri
personal particulier, particulière 1; personnel, personnelle 2
personally personnellement 5
personnel un personnel 8; *personnel manager* un chef du personnel 8
perspective une perspective
persuaded persuadé(e)
petroleum le pétrole
pheasant le faisan 5
Philippines les Philippines (f.) 10
to **phone (someone)** téléphoner
phone: cell phone un téléphone portable
photo une photo; *another photo* re-photo; *to go into photo mode* se mettre en mode photo
photogenic photogénique 9
physical: physical therapist un(e) kiné (kinésithérapeute) 8; *physical therapy* une rééducation 8; *at/to the physical therapy* office chez le kiné 8
physics la physique
pianist un(e) pianiste
piano un piano
to **pick** cueillir 7; *to pick up* ramasser 1; ranger
to **picnic** piqueniquer
picture une image; *to take a picture (of something)* prendre (quelque chose) en photo
pie une tarte; *apple pie* une tarte aux pommes
piece (of) un morceau (de); *piece of furniture* un meuble; *piece of identification* une pièce d'identité 4; *piece of jewelry* un bijou; *piece of luggage* un bagage
pig un cochon
pillow un coussin
pilot un(e) pilote
pineapple un ananas; *mountain pineapple* un ananas montagne
pink rose
pipe(line) la canalisation
piranha un piranha

pirate un pirate
pirogue une pirogue; *by pirogue* en pirogue
pity dommage 5
pizza une pizza
to **place: to place a spell on** jouer un tour 3
place un endroit; un lieu 5; une place 2; *in its place* à sa place 2; *place yourself in front of the TV* mets-toi devant l'écran; *to take place* avoir lieu
plaid à carreaux 9
plain une plaine
to **plan** planifier 4; projeter; *to plan to do something* compter
plan un programme
plane un avion; *by plane* en avion
planet une planète
planned prévu(e) 2
plant une plante
plastic la plastique; *made of plastic* en plastique
plate une assiette
platform un quai
platter un plateau
to **play** jouer; passer 2; *to play (instrument)* jouer de (+ instrument); *to play a role* jouer un rôle; *to play a trick (on someone)* faire le coup (à quelqu'un) 4; *to play basketball* jouer au basket (basketball); *to play hide-and-seek* jouer à cache-cache 1; *to play hopscotch* jouer à la marelle 1; *to play ice hockey* jouer au hockey sur glace; *to play marbles* jouer aux billes 1; *to play on the radio* passer à la radio 2; *to play soccer* jouer au foot (football); *to play sports* faire du sport; *to play video games* jouer aux jeux video; *to play with dolls* jouer à la poupée 1; *to play with toy cars* jouer aux petites voitures 1; *... is playing (at the movies)* on passe... 2
play une pièce; une pièce de théâtre 6
pleasant agréable 5
to **please** convenir (à); plaire (à) 7
please s'il vous plaît
pleased: Pleased to meet you. Très heureux/heureuse. 3
pleasure un plaisir
pocket une poche
poem un poème
poet un poète, une femme poète 7
poetic poétique 7
poetry la poésie 6
to **point out/to** indiquer
pole: fishing pole une canne à pêche; *ski pole* un bâton de ski 4
police: police officer un agent de police; *police station* un commissariat 9
to **polish** cirer 3
political politique; *political party* un parti politique 2; *political science* les sciences (f.) politiques (sciences po) 6; *socialist political party* le parti politique socialiste 2
politician: female politician une femme politique; *male politician* un homme politique
politics la politique 2
polka dot un pois 9; *polka dots* à pois 9
to **pollute** polluer
polluted pollué(e)
polluter un pollueur, une pollueuse
polluting polluant
pollution la pollution
pond un bassin; un étang
pool un bassin
poor pauvre
pop music la musique pop
poppy un coquelicot 7
popular populaire 7
pork le porc; *ham and pork dish made with chopped parsley* le jambon persillé 5
port un port; *USB port* un port micro-USB
portable stove un réchaud
portrait un portrait
position une position 7; *job position* un poste 1; *to take a position (on)* prendre position (sur) 7
positioning le positionnement 6
possibility une possibilité; *to explore all the possibilities* faire le tour 10
possible possible; *it's possible that* il se pourrait que 4
postage l'affranchissement (m.) 6
postal worker un postier, une postière 6
postcard une carte postale
poster une affiche
post office une poste
post-sale support un service après-vente 10
potato une pomme de terre
pound une livre
to **pour** verser 2
poverty la pauvreté
power un pouvoir
powerful puissant(e)
practical pratique 5
to **practice (sports)** s'entraîner 2
practice une pratique 8; *to put into practice* mettre en pratique 8
precisely précisément
to **prefer** préférer
première (of movie) une première 6
premises: on the premises sur place 4
preparations des préparatifs (m.) 4; *travel preparations* des préparatifs (m.) de départ 4
to **prepare** préparer
preposition une préposition
present le présent 8
presentation un exposé
president un chef, une cheffe d'entreprise, un(e) president(e) 10
presidential présidentiel, présidentielle 2; *presidential election* une élection présidentielle 2
to **pretend (to)** faire semblant (de) 1
pretty joli(e)
princess une princesse 1
principal un proviseur
to **print** imprimer
printer une imprimante
priority un priorité 9
prisoner un prisonnier, une prisonnière 2
private privé(e) 8; *private class* un cours particulier 1
problem un problème
product un produit 2; *dairy product* un produit laitier 10; *food product* un produit alimentaire 10; *GNP (Gross National Product)* le Produit National Brut (PNB) 2
production une production 10
profession une profession
professional un professionnel, une professionnelle
profile un profil
program: television program une émission
progress le progrès
project un projet; *do-it-yourself (DIY) projects* le bricolage 3; *to do DIY projects* bricoler 3

to **promise** promettre
promise une promesse; *to make a promise* faire une promesse; *it's a promise* c'est promis 6
promised promis(e) 6
promising: it sounds promising ça promet 5
property un domaine 4
to **protect** protéger, sauvegarder
proud fier, fière 9
Provence la Provence; *from, of Provence* provençal(e)
Province une province
psychology la psychologie 6
public: public (incorporated) company une Société Anonyme (SA) 10
punishment une sanction
purchase un achat
purple violet, violette
purse un sac à main
to **push** appuyer
to **put (on)** mettre; *to put back* remettre; *to put down* poser 2; *to put into practice* mettre en pratique 8; *to put on make-up* se maquiller; *to put up* poser 3
pyjamas un pyjama

Q

quality une qualité 8
quarter un arrondissement 10; un quart; *quarter past* et quart; *quarter to* moins le quart
Quebec le Québec; *from, of Quebec* québécois(e)
queen une reine
question une question
quiche une quiche
quickly rapidement 3; vite
quiet tranquille 2
quite plutôt 5
quote une citation 8

R

rabbit un lapin
raccoon un raton laveur
racism le racisme
radiation la radiation
radio une radio; *to play on the radio* passer à la radio 2
Rai music le raï
to **rain** pleuvoir; *it's raining* il pleut
range: mountain range un massif
rap music le rap
ratatouille la ratatouille
rate un taux 2; *inflation rate* un taux d'inflation 2
rather assez 6; plutôt
raw vegetables des crudités (f.)
razor un rasoir
R&B concert un concert R'n'B
reaction une réaction 9
to **read** lire
reading la lecture
ready prêt(e); *to get (oneself) ready* se préparer
ready-to-wear le prêt-à-porter 2
real vrai(e) 5
realism le réalisme 7
réaliste: chanson réaliste une chanson réaliste 7
realistic réaliste
reality la réalité 6; *reality TV* la téléréalité; *reality TV show* une émission de télé-réalité
to **realize** réaliser; se rendre compte (de) 9
really bien; super; vraiment
rear-view mirror un rétroviseur
reassigned: to get reassigned se faire muter 1
to **reassure (oneself)** se rassurer
to **recapture** récupérer 2
to **receive** recevoir
reception une réception 1; *reception area* le secrétariat 10; *reception center* un centre d'accueil; *reception desk* la réception
recipe une recette
to **recognize** reconnaître
to **recommend** conseiller 3
rectangular rectangulaire 2
to **recycle** recycler
red rouge; *red (hair)* roux, rousse
to **reduce** réduire 2
reflection un reflet 7
to **refrain (from)** s'empêcher (de) 2
refrigerator un frigo
regardless quand même 2
regards: with warm regards affectueusement
reggae music le reggae
regime un régime 8
region une région
regional régional(e) 10
to **register** s'inscrire
regret un regret 1
to **reimburse** rembourser
relationship un rapport 2
to **relax** se détendre
relaxed décontracté(e); *relaxed style of life* une douceur de vivre
release une sortie 5; *new release* une nouveauté 5
to **remain** rester
remarkable remarquable
remedy un remède
to **remember** se rappeler, se souvenir (de)
to **rent** louer
to **repaint** repeindre 3
to **repair** réparer
repellent: insect repellent un anti-moustique
to **replace** remplacer
report: report of a theft une déclaration de vol 9; *news report* un reportage
representative un(e) représentant(e)
republic une république 8; *Republic of Haiti* la République d'Haïti (Haïti)
to **require** exiger 5
R.E.R.: by R.E.R. en R.E.R.
research des recherches 3 la recherche 1; *research laboratory* un laboratoire de recherches 1; *genealogical research* des recherches (f.) généalogiques 3
researcher un chercheur, une chercheuse
to **resemble** ressembler (à)
reservation une reservation; *to make a reservation* réserver
residence une résidence 3
resident un(e) habitant(e)
resolution une résolution
resort: ski resort une station de ski 4
resource une ressource 10; *human resources* les ressources humaines 10; *director of human resources* un directeur, une directrice des ressources humaines (DRH) 10
respiratory respiratoire
to **respond** répondre 8
responsibility une responsabilité 10
responsible responsable
to **rest** se reposer
rest le reste 10; *(the) rest* la suite 3
restaurant un restaurant; *to own a restaurant* tenir un restaurant 3
to **return** rendre; rentrer, retourner, revenir
return un retour
Reunion la Réunion 4
revealed: it will be revealed (known) ça va se savoir
review une critique 5
revolution une révolution

riad une riad
rich riche
to **ride: to speed ride** faire du speed riding 4
ride une balade; *to go on a carnival ride* faire un tour de manège; *to go on a Ferris wheel ride* faire un tour de grande roue; *to go on a ride* faire un tour; *to go on a trail ride* faire une randonnée équestre 4; *to take a ski-taxi ride* faire du taxi-ski 4
right un droit 2; *right away* tout de suite; *human rights* les droits (m.) de l'homme 2; *That's right.* C'est ça.; *to be right* avoir raison; *to the right* à droite; *to (on) the right of* à droite de; *yeah right* tu parles
ring une bague; *diamond ring* une bague de diamants; *engagement ring* une bague de fiançailles 1; *wedding ring* une alliance 1
ripe mûr(e)
rise: to give rise to donner lieu à 7
river un fleuve; une rivière; *river bank* une rive
riviera: French Riviera la côte d'Azur
road une route; *cliff road* une corniche
rock (music) le rock
to **rock climb** faire de l'escalade 4
rococo rococo 7
rococo style le rococo 7
roe: lumpfish roe des œufs (m.) de lump 2
role un rôle
roll un rouleau 10
rolled in flour and sautéed meunier, meunière
roller coaster: to go on a roller coaster ride faire un tour de montagnes russes
Roman un(e) Romain(e) 5
Romantic romantique 7
Romanticism le romantisme 7
roof un toit
room une pièce; une salle; *room service* un service de chambre 5; *bathroom* une salle de bains; *classroom* une salle de classe; *dining room* une salle à manger; *hotel room* une chambre; *living room* un salon
rooster un coq
rope une corde 1; *to jump rope* sauter à la corde 1
round rond(e) 2
route une route
rug un tapis
ruled gouverné(e) 8
to **run** courir 1; filer *[inform.]*
running le footing
rural champêtre 7
rustic champêtre 7
Rwanda le Rwanda

S

sad attristé(e) 9; triste
safe un coffre-fort 5
sailboat un voilier
sailing: to go sailing faire de la voile
saint: All Saints Day la Toussaint
salad une salade; *tuna salad* une salade niçoise
salami le saucisson
salary un salaire 8
sale une promo; *on sale* en solde
sales les ventes (f.) 10
salesperson un vendeur, une vendeuse
salmon le saumon; *salmon loaf* une terrine de saumon; *smoked salmon* le saumon fumé 2
salon: hair salon un salon de coiffure
salsa music la salsa 7
salt le sel
salty salé(e)
same même; *at the same time* à la fois; *it's all the same to me* ça m'est égal; *it's the same* c'est pareil; *the same* pareil, pareille
sand le sable 1
sandals des sandales (f.)
sandwich un sandwich; *cheese sandwich* un sandwich au fromage; *ham sandwich* un sandwich au jambon; *grilled ham and cheese sandwich* un croque-monsieur
sanitary sanitaire
satire une satire 7
Saturday samedi
sauce une sauce 2; *Béarnaise sauce* une sauce béarnaise 5; *béchamel sauce* une sauce béchamel 5; *hollandaise sauce* une sauce hollandaise 5; *white sauce* une sauce blanche 5; *white wine sauce* une sauce marinière 5
saucepan une casserole
sauerkraut la choucroute; *sauerkraut with potatoes, sausages, smoked pork* la choucroute garnie
sausage une saucisse
sautéed: rolled in flour and sautéed meunier, meunière
to **save** sauvegarder; *to save (up)* économiser; *to save time* gagner du temps
savory salé(e)
saxophone un saxophone
to **say** dire; *to say to oneself* se dire; *nicely said* joliment dit
scallop une coquille St-Jacques
Scandinavian scandinave 9
scarf une écharpe; un foulard
scene une scène
scent un parfum
school une école; *school cafeteria* une cantine
science la science; les sciences; *science and technology sector* le domaine des sciences et techniques; *science fiction* la science-fiction; *science fiction movie* un film de science-fiction; *science lab* un labo (laboratoire); *political science* les sciences politiques (sciences po) 6
scooter un scooter; *by scooter* en scooter
to **score** marquer
scrambled eggs des œufs (m.) brouillés
to **scrape** racler 2
to **scream** pousser un cri
screen un écran
screw une vis 3
screwdriver un tournevis 3
to **scrub** racler 2
scuba diving: to go scuba diving faire de la plongée sous-marine
sculpture une sculpture
sea une mer; *sea turtle* une tortue marine; *Caribbean Sea* la mer des Caraïbes; *Mediterranean Sea* la mer Méditerranée; *North Sea* la mer du Nord
seafood les fruits de mer (m.)
seashell un coquillage 1
seaside le bord de mer; *by the seaside* au bord de la mer
season une saison
seat un siège
seatbelt une ceinture de sécurité
second deuxième; *second home* une résidence secondaire 3; *on second thought* en y réfléchissant bien 4
secondary secondaire 3
secondly deuxièmement 8

secret un secret
secretary un secrétaire (administratif), une secrétaire (administrative) 10
sector un domaine; *health sector* le domaine de la santé; *science and technology sector* le domaine des sciences et techniques
security la sécurité; *security checkpoint* un contrôle de sécurité
to **seduce** séduire 7
to **see** voir; *to see again* revoir; *to see each other/one another* se voir; *to see oneself as* se reconnaître 7; *See you soon.* À bientôt.; *See you tomorrow.* À demain.
to **seek (medical) treatment** se faire soigner 8
to **seem** paraître 5; sembler; *to seem like* avoir l'air de 1
selfish égoïste
self-service kiosk une borne libre-service
to **sell** vendre
to **send** envoyer; *to send text messages* envoyer des textos (m.)
send button l'envoi (m.)
Senegal le Sénégal
Senegalese sénégalais(e)
sensation une sensation
sense un sens
September septembre
series une série; *whole series (of)* toute une série (de)
serious grave; sérieux, sérieuse
seriousness le sérieux
to **serve** servir
served servi(e) 5
server un serveur, une serveuse
service un service 5; *laundry service* un service blanchisserie 5; *post-sale support* un service après-vente 10; *room service* un service de chambre 5
session une séance 8
to **set** mettre; *to set the table* mettre le couvert; *to set oneself down* se mettre
set down posé(e) 2
setting un cadre
settled: It's settled C'est decidé; *to get settled* s'installer
seven sept
seventeen dix-sept
seventh septième
seventy soixante-dix
several plusieurs

shakes des frissons (m.)
shame dommage 5
shampoo un shampooing
shape une forme 2
to **shave** se raser
she elle
sheet un drap; *sheet of paper* une feuille de papier
sheep un mouton
shelter un centre d'accueil
shh chut
shirt une chemise; une liquette 9
shoe une chaussur
shocked choqué(e) 9
to **shoot (a movie)** tourner (un film) 5
shoot mince
shop une boutique; *butcher shop* une boucherie
shopkeeper un(e) petit(e) commerçant(e)
shopping commerçant(e); le shopping; *shopping center* un centre commercial
short petit(e); *short (hair)* court(e) 9; *short story* une nouvelle 6; *in short* bref 9
shorts un short
shot un plan 7; *to get a shot* se faire vacciner 4
shoulder l'épaule (f.)
shoulder-length (hair) mi-long, mi-longue 9
to **shove** bousculer 9
to **show** montrer; *to show up* se rendre (à)
show une spectacle; un show 9; *(TV) game show* un jeu télévisé; *music show* une émission de musique; *reality TV show* une émission de télé-réalité; *TV show* une émission
shower une douche
shrimp une crevette
shy timide
sick malade; *sick person* un(e) malade
side le bord; un côté
sigh un soupir 7
to **sign** signer 6
to **signal** signaler
silk la soie; *made of silk* en soie
silver l'argent (m.); *made of silver* en argent
SIM card une carte SIM
simple simple
simply simplement; tout simplement
since comme; depuis; puisque 2; *since when* depuis quand

to **sing** chanter
singer un chanteur, une chanteuse
single: single-parent family une famille monoparentale 1
sink un évier
sir chef; monsieur (M.)
sister une sœur; *half-sister* une demi-sœur; *stepsister* une belle-sœur
sitcom un sitcom
to **sit down** s'asseoir
site un site
sitting assis(e)
situation une situation
six six
sixteen seize
sixth sixième
sixty soixante
size une taille
to **skate: to (figure) skate** faire du patinage (artistique); *to in-line skate* faire du roller
skateboard park un skatepark 1
skating: (figure) skating le patinage artistique
skewer une brochette
to **ski** skier 4; *to (downhill) ski* faire du ski (alpin); *to cross-country ski* faire du ski de fond 4; *to telemark ski* faire du télémark 4
ski un ski 4
ski: ski boot une chaussure de ski 4; *ski class* une classe de neige 4; *ski goggles* un masque de ski 4; *ski jump* un tremplin de saut à ski 4; *ski lift* un télésiège 4; *ski pants* un fuseau de ski 4; *ski pass* un forfait de ski 4; *ski pole* un bâton de ski 4; *ski resort* une station de ski 4; *to go off ski jumps* faire des sauts à ski 4
skiing: skiing (downhill) le ski (alpin); *cross-country skiing* le ski de fond 4; *off-piste skiing* un hors-piste 4; *while skiing* en skiant 4
to **skijor** faire du ski joering 4
skill une compétence 5; *game of skill* un jeu d'adresse
skin la peau 10
skinny maigre 9
to **skip (class)** sécher 9
skirt une jupe
ski-taxi: to take a ski-taxi ride faire du taxi-ski 4
to **skype** skyper
skype call un skype
slang l'argot (m.) 9

sledding: to go sledding faire de la luge 4
to **sleep** dormir
slice (of) une tranche (de)
small petit(e); *small business* une petite et moyenne entreprise (PME) 1
smartphone un smartphone
to **smell** sentir; *What does it smell like?* Ça sent quoi?
to **smile** sourire 1
smile un sourire 1
smoked fumé(e) 2; *smoked salmon* le saumon fumé 2
smuggler un contrebandier, une contrebandière
snack le goûter
snail un escargot
snake un serpent
sneakers des tennis (m.)
snow la neige 2
snowball une boule de neige 2
to **snowboard** faire du snowboard 4
snowboarding le snowboard 4
snowing: it's snowing il neige
snowshoeing: to go snowshoeing faire de la raquette à neige 4
so alors; bon; donc; si 2; *so much* tellement; *so-so* comme ci, comme ça; *so that* pour que 7
soap un savon
soap opera: TV soap opera un feuilleton
soccer le foot; *soccer ball* un ballon de foot; *soccer player* un footballeur, une footballeuse
social social(e) 8
socialist socialiste 2; *socialist political party* le parti politique socialiste 2
society la collectivité 8
sock une chaussette
soda: lemon-lime soda une limonade; *lemon-lime soda with mint syrup* diabolo menthe
sofa un canapé
software un logiciel
solar solaire; *solar energy* l'énergie (f.) solaire; *solar panel* un panneau solaire
solidarity la solidarité
solution un remède; une solution
some d', de, des, du; en; quelque 5
somebody quelqu'un
someday un jour
someone quelqu'un; *to introduce to someone* faire connaître (à), faire découvrir (à); *to use the informal "tu" to address someone* tutoyer 10
something quelque chose; *to bring oneself to do something* arriver à faire quelque chose 6
sometimes parfois
son un fils
song une chanson
songwriter un compositeur, une compositrice
sonnet un sonnet 7
soon bientôt; *as soon as* aussitôt que 1; dès que
to be **sorry** regretter 5
sorry désolé(e)
sort une sorte
to **sound: it sounds promising** ça promet 5
soup la soupe; un potage
south le sud; *South America* l'Amérique du Sud (f.); *South Korea* la Corée du Sud 10
Soviet soviétique 5
Spain l'Espagne (f.)
Spanish ***[language]*** l'espagnol (m.)
Spanish espagnol(e)
spa treatment une cure
spatula une spatule 2
to **speak** parler
specialty une spécialité
species: endangered species les animaux (m.) en voie de disparition
specific information des précisions (f.) 5
speech un discours 8; *to make a speech* faire un discours 8
speed: to speed ride faire du speed riding 4
spell un envoûtement; *to place a spell on* jouer un tour 3; *to undo a spell* déjouer un tour 3
to **spend (time)** passer
spherical sphérique 2
spicy épicé(e)
spiny lobster une langouste
sponge une éponge 10
spoon une cuiller; *measuring spoon* une cuillère-mesure 2
sport un sport; *sports car* une voiture de sport; *sports center* un complexe sportif 1; *sports coverage* un reportage sportif
spot une tache
to **sprain** se fouler 4; *to sprain an ankle* se fouler la cheville 4
spread made of hazelnut and chocolate le Nutella
spring le printemps; une source d'eau; *in the spring* au printemps
square un carré; une place; *in squares* en carrés
square carré(e) 2
Sri Lanka le Sri Lanka 10
stadium un stade
staff un personnel 8
to **stamp** affranchir 6
stamp un timbre 1
stand un kiosque; *crêpe stand* un stand de crêpes
standardisation une uniformisation 10
standing debout
star une étoile, une vedette 5
to **start** démarrer; *to start something again* se remettre (à)
starters: for starters pour commencer
state un état 8
statement une déclaration 9
station une station; *gas station* une station-service; *police station* un commissariat 9
statue une statue
to **stay** faire un séjour 4; rester; *to stay up all night* faire une nuit blanche
stay un séjour
steak with fries un steak-frites
to **steal** voler 9
steering wheel un volant
step: step aerobics le step; *stepbrother* un beau-frère; *stepfather* un beau-père; *stepmother* une belle-mère; *stepsister* une belle-sœur
stereo une stéréo
stereotypical stéréotypé(e) 5
still encore; toujours; *still life* une nature morte
to **stir** remuer 2
stockholder un(e) actionnaire 10
stocky costaud(e) 9
stomach l'estomac (m.), le ventre
to **stop** arrêter; s'arrêter; *Enough! Stop it!* N'en jette plus! *[inform.]* 8
store un magasin; *dairy store* une crémerie; *grocery store* une épicerie
story une histoire 3; un étage; *short story* une nouvelle 6
stove une cuisinière; *portable stove* un réchaud
straight: straight (hair) raide 9; *straight ahead* tout droit
strainer: conical strainer un chinois 2
strategy une stratégie 10
strawberry une fraise
street une rue; *street demonstration* une manif (manifestation)

strength une force
strict strict(e)
strike une grève 2; *to go on strike* faire grève 2
stripe une rayure 9; *striped* à rayures 9
strong fort(e)
stuck collé(e)
student un(e) élève; un(e) étudiant(e)
studies des études (f.)
studio un atelier 7; *studio apartment* un studio 3
to **study** étudier
stuffed farci(e)
to **stumble** trébucher 9
style un style 5
stylist: hair stylist un coiffeur, une coiffeuse
subject un sujet
subsidiary une filiale 10
subsidized housing un HLM 3
subtitle un sous-titre 5
subtitled sous-titré(e) 5
suburb une banlieue
subway le metro; *subway entrance* une bouche du métro; *by subway* en métro
to **succeed** réussir (à)
success le succès 7
such a un tel, une telle 9
sudden: all of a sudden tout d'un coup 9
to **suffer** souffrir 2
sugar le sucre; *with sugar* au sucre
to **suggest** proposer
to **suit** convenir (à)
suitcase une valise; *suitcase with wheels* une valise à roulettes
summer l'été (m.)
Sunday dimanche
sunglasses des lunettes (f.) de soleil
sunny: eggs sunny side up des œufs (m.) sur le plat; *it's sunny* il fait du soleil
sunscreen la crème solaire
superhero un super-héros 1
supermarket un supermarché
supplementary complémentaire 8
supplies des provisions (f.)
to **support** soutenir
sure certain(e) 5; sûr(e); *that's for sure* c'est sûr
to **surf** surfer; *to surf the Web* surfer sur Internet; *to wind surf* faire de la planche à voile 4
to **surprise** étonner; *it doesn't surprise me* ça ne me surprend pas
surprise une surprise
surprised étonné(e) 5; surpris(e); *to be surprised that* être étonné que 5
surprising surprenant(e) 4
surrealism le surréalisme 7
survey une enquête
to **survive** survivre
sustainable: sustainable development le développement durable; *sustainable development industry* le secteur de développement durable
sweater un pull
sweet sucré(e)
to **swim** nager
swimming pool une piscine
swing music le swing 7
Swiss suisse; *Swiss army knife* un couteau suisse
Switzerland la Suisse
to **synchronize** synchroniser
synopsis: movie synopsis un synopsis 5
synthesizer un synthé(tiseur)
syrup le sirop; *maple syrup* le sirop d'érable
system un système 8

T

table une table; *table setting* le couvert; *at the (dinner) table* à table 2; *multiplication table* une table de multiplication 8; *to clear the table* débarrasser la table
tablecloth une nappe
Tahitian tahitien(ne)
tailor un tailleur
to **take** prendre; *to take (a class)* suivre; *to take (away)* emporter 4; *to take advantage of* profiter; *to take a journey* partir en voyage 8; *to take a picture (of something)* prendre (quelque chose) en photo; *to take a position (on)* prendre position (sur) 7; *to take a ski-taxi ride* faire du taxi-ski 4; *to take a trip* faire une excursion; *to take a vacation* prendre des vacances; *to take care (of)* s'occuper (de); *to take care of* garder 3; *to take care of things* se débrouiller 8; *to take off [airplane]* décoller; *to take out* sortir; *to take place* avoir lieu
tale un conte; *fairy tale* un conte de fées 3
talent un talent 9
talented doué(e) 10
to **talk** parler; *to talk to each other/one another* se parler
talkative bavard(e)
tall grand(e)
to **tan** bronzer
to **target** cibler 10
tart: fruit tart une tarte aux fruits
to **taste** goûter
taste un gout 5; *for my taste* à mon goût 5
taxi un taxi; *by taxi* en taxi
tea un thé; *tea with lemon* un thé au citron
to **teach** apprendre; enseigner
teacher un(e) prof; *elementary school teacher* un instituteur, une institutrice
team une équipe; *team logo* un blason
technician un(e) technicien(ne); *solar plant technician* un(e) technicien(ne) de centrale solaire
technology la technique; *science and technology sector* le domaine des sciences et techniques
techno music la techno
teenager un(e) adolescent(e)
teeth: to brush one's teeth se brosser les dents
telemark: to telemark ski faire du télémark 4
televised télévisé(e)
television une télé (télévision); *television program* une émission
to **tell** dire; raconter
teller: bank teller un caissier, une caissière 6
temperature la température
to **tempt** tenter
ten dix
tenant un(e) locataire 3
tenderness la tendresse 6
tent une tente
tenth dixième
terrace une terrasse
terrific génial(e)
territory un territoire 2
terrorism le terrorisme
test un contrôle
text un texte 7; *text message* un SMS; un texto
than que
Thanksgiving l'Action de grâce (f.)
thank you merci; *thank you (for)* je vous remercie (de) *[form.]*

that ça; ce, cet, cette, ces; cela; même que *[inform.]* 3; que; qui; *that is* c'est; *that's for sure* c'est sûr; *that's how...* c'est comme ça que... 1; *That's right.* C'est ça.; *that/this one* celui, celle 6; *that works out well* ça tombe bien 2; *Is that all?* Rien que ça?; *so that* pour que 7; *you shouldn't do that* ça ne se fait pas
the le, la, l'; les; *the most (+ adjectif)* le/la/les plus (+ adjective); *the one* celui, celle 6; *the ones* ceux 6
theatre un théâtre
theft un vol 9; *report of a theft* une déclaration de vol 9
thief un voleur 9
their leur, leurs
theirs le, la; leur 9
them elles; eux; les; *to them* leur
theme un thème 7
then alors, puis
therapist: physical therapist un(e) kiné (kinésithérapeute) 8
therapy: at/to the physical therapy office chez le kiné 8; *physical therapy* une rééducation 8
there là; y *[pronoun]*; *Are we going (there)?* On y va?; *over there* là-bas; *to be there* être sur place
therefore donc
these ce, cet, cette, ces; ceux 6
they on; *they (f.)* elles; *they (m.)* ils; *they (one) make(s) you* on te fait 8
thin mince 9
thing une chose; un machin 2; un truc; *things* des affaires (f.); *to take care of things* se débrouiller 8
to **think** croire; penser; *to think over* réfléchir (à)
third troisième
to be **thirsty** avoir soif
thirteen treize
thirty trente; *about thirty* une trentaine 9; *in one's thirties* d'une trentaine d'années 9
this ce, cet, cette, ces; cela; *this is* c'est; *that/this is why* c'est pour ça que; *this (very) word* ce mot-là; *like this* comme ça
those ce, cet, cette, ces; ceux 6
thought une réflexion; *on second thought* en y réfléchissant bien 4
thousand mille
three trois
thriller un thriller
throat la gorge
throne un trône 8
throttle: full throttle tout schuss 4
through par
to **throw** jeter 5
thrush une grive
Thursday jeudi
thus comme ça
ticket un billet; un ticket; *ticket booth* un guichet; *ticket collector* un contrôleur, une contrôleuse
ticket-stamping machine un composteur
tide une marée
tiger un tigre; *Sumatran tiger* un tigre de Sumatra
time l'heure (f.); le temps; une fois; *all the time* tout le temps; *at the same time* à la fois; *it's been a long time since* ça fait longtemps que; *on time* à l'heure; *to save time* gagner du temps; *What time is it?* Quelle heure est-il?
tire un pneu
tired fatigué(e)
title un titre 6
to à; *to him* lui; *to her* lui; *to me* moi; *to my house* chez moi; *to the* au; aux; *to which* auquel, auquelle 5; *to you* te; vous; *eye to eye* le blanc des yeux 9
toast le pain grillé; *French toast* le pain perdu
tobacco: news store that sells tobacco, stamps, lottery tickets un bureau de tabac
today aujourd'hui
toe le doigt de pied
together ensemble
Togo le Togo
Togolese togolais(e)
toilet les toilettes (f.), les W.C. (m.); *toilet paper* le papier toilette 10
toiletries des affaires (f.) de toilette
tolerance la tolérance
tomato une tomate
tomorrow demain; *See you tomorrow.* À demain.
tone un ton 5
too aussi; trop; *too bad* tant pis; *too much of* trop de; *it's too bad that...* c'est dommage que... 5; *to have too many choices* avoir l'embarras du choix 10
tooth une dent
toothbrush une brosse à dents
toothpaste le dentifrice
top le haut; *at the top* en haut
topic un thème
to **torment** tourmenter 9
to **toss** remuer 2
to **touch** toucher
touch: to keep in touch garder le contact 3
tour une tournée 7; un tour; *guided tour* une visite guidée; *on tour* en tournée 7; *to go on a guided tour* faire une visite guidée; *to go on a tour* faire un tour
Touraine region la Touraine; *from, of Touraine region* tourangeau, tourangelle
tourism le tourisme 4; *adventure tourism* le tourisme d'aventure
tourist un(e) touriste; *tourist guide* un guide touristique; *tourist information office* un syndicat d'initiative; *tourist office* un office de tourisme 4; *to be a tourist* faire le touriste
touristy touristique 3
towards vers
towel une serviette; *beach towel* une serviette de plage
tower une tour
toy: toy car une petite voiture 1; *to play with toy cars* jouer aux petites voitures 1
traditional tradi(e) 2; traditionnel, traditionnelle; *traditional look* un look tradi 2
trail: to go on a trail ride faire une randonnée équestre 4
trailer: film trailer une bande-annonce 5
train un train; *train station* une gare; *train track* une voie; *by train* en train; *express train from Paris to suburbs* le R.E.R.
training une formation 8
to **transfer** muter 1
transportation un transport; *means of transportation* un moyen de transport
to **travel** voyager
travel preparations des préparatifs (m.) de départ 4
traveler's check un chèque de voyage 6
traveller un voyageur, une voyageuse

tray un plateau
treasure un trésor
to treat soigner 8
treatment des soins (m.) 8; un traitement 8; *to seek (medical) treatment* se faire soigner 8
tree: Christmas tree un sapin de Noël 2; *fir tree* un sapin 2; *maple tree* un érable
trial: listening trial en écoute libre
trick un coup 4; *to play a trick (on someone)* faire le coup (à quelqu'un) 4
trip une excursion; un voyage; *Have a good trip!* Bonne route!; *to go on a trip* faire un voyage; *to take a trip* faire une excursion
trombone un trombone
trouble des ennuis (m.) 9; *to get in trouble (with)* se faire disputer (par) 3
truck un camion
true vrai(e)
trumpet une trompette; *trumpet of the dead mushroom* une trompette de la mort 5
to trust avoir confiance
to try: to try (on) essayer; *to try one's luck* tenter sa chance 3
T-shirt un tee-shirt
Tuesday mardi
tuna le thon; *tuna salad* une salade niçoise
Tunisia la Tunisie
Tunisian tunisien(ne)
turkey la dinde 2; un dindon; *turkey with chestnuts* la dinde aux marrons 2
to turn tourner; *to turn in* rendre
turtle une tortue; *sea turtle* une tortue marine
tuxedo un smoking
TV une télé (télévision); *TV host* un animateur, une animatrice; *TV remote control* une télécommande; *TV show* une émission; *TV soap opera* un feuilleton; *cable TV* une télé câblée; *on TV* à la télé; *reality TV* la téléréalité; *reality TV show* une émission de télé-réalité
twelve douze
twenty vingt; *about twenty* une vingtaine 9; *in one's twenties* d'une vingtaine d'années 9
twin jumeau, jumelle; *twin-sized bed* un lit jumeau
two deux
to type taper
type un genre; un type 1; *not the type to* pas la tête à 9
typical of typiquement 10

U

ugly laid(e); moche
um euh
umbrella (beach) un parasol
uncle un oncle; *great uncle* un grand-oncle 3
under sous
to understand comprendre
to undo a spell déjouer un tour 3
undressed: to get undressed se déshabiller
unemployment le chômage
unicorn une licorne
unintelligent bête
United States les États-Unis (m.)
universal universel, universelle 2
universe l'univers (m.)
university une université; *university cafeteria* un resto-U (restaurant universitaire); *university dormitory* une cité universitaire
university universitaire
unobstructed imprenable 5
unpleasant désagréable
until jusqu'à
up: cut up (in) découpé(e) (en) 10; *Look up!* Lève la tête!; *to get up* se lever; *to grow up* grandir 3; *to make up one's mind* se décider 6; *to pick up* ramasser 1; *to put up* poser 3; *to wake up* se réveiller
upon en 4; *Once upon a time (there was)....* Il était une fois.... 3
us nous; *none of us (+ verb)* aucunde nous ne (+ verb) 4; *to us* nous
USB: USB key une clé USB; *USB port* un port micro-USB
to use se servir (de); *to use diplomacy* user de diplomatie; *to use the informal "***tu***" to address someone* tutoyer 10
used: to be used (for) servir (à) 2
useful utile 4
useless: what is useless l'inutile (m.)
usually d'habitude
to usurp usurper 2
utensil un ustensile 2

V

vacation des vacances (f.); *back to school/work after vacation* la rentrée; *to take a vacation* prendre des vacances
vacationer un vacancier, une vacancière
to vaccinate (against) vaccine (contre) 4
to vacuum passer l'aspirateur
vacuum cleaner un aspirateur
vague imprécis(e) 5
vain: to do (something) in vain avoir beau *[inform.]* 8
Valentine's day la Saint-Valentin
to validate (a ticket) composter
valley une vallée
valued: to be valued as/at valoir 7
variation une variation 7
vase un vase 10
veal le veau 5
vegetable un légume; *raw vegetables* des crudités (f.)
velvet le velours; *made of velvet* en velours
venison le chevreuil 2; *venison chop* une côte de chevreuil 2
version une version; *original version* une version originale (V.O.) 5
versus contre
very super; très
veterinarian un(e) vétérinaire
via par
video: video clip un clip; *video games* les jeux vidéo (m.); *video game tester* un testeur de jeux vidéo
Vietnam le Vietnam 4
view une vue; *What a beautiful view!* Quelle belle vue!
viewpoint un point de vue
villa une villa 3
village un village
vinaigrette salad dressing la vinaigrette
vintage vintage 9
violence la violence
violin un violon
visa un visa 4
visible visible 9
to visit visiter; *to visit (person)* rendre visite à (+ person)
visual arts les arts plastiques (m.)
vivid vif, vive
volcano un volcan 4
voluminous volumineux, volumineuse 7

to **volunteer work** le bénévolat 4
to **vote** voter 2

W

to **wait (for)** attendre
to **wake up** se réveiller
to **walk** marcher
walk une balade; une promenade; *to go for a walk* se promener
wall un mur 3
wallet un portefeuille
wallpaper le papier peint 3
to **want** avoir envie de; désirer; vouloir
want ad une petite annonce 8
war une guerre; *at war* en guerre 2
wardrobe une armoire
wary: to be wary (of) se méfier (de) 3
to **wash: to wash (oneself)** se laver; *to wash clothes* faire la lessive; *to wash the dishes* faire la vaisselle
washcloth un gant de toilette
washed out délavé(e) 9
washing machine une machine à laver
to **watch** regarder; *Watch out!* Attention!
watch une montre
to **water** arroser
water l'eau (f.); *water hydrant* une borne-fontaine; *water park* un aquaparc 1; *body of water* une masse d'eau
waterfall une cascade; une chute d'eau
watermelon une pastèque
water-skiing: to go water-skiing faire du ski nautique
wavy (hair) bouclé(e) 9
way un chemin; une façon 4; une manière 3; un sens; *by the way* au fait; *in a way* en un sens; *on the way* en route
we on; nous
wealthy riche
to **wear** porter
weather la météo; le temps; *weather forecast* la météo; un bulletin météo(rologique); *the weather's bad* il fait mauvais
web designer un concepteur de web
website un site web
wedding un mariage; *wedding anniversary* un anniversaire de mariage; *wedding dress* une robe de mariée; *wedding ring* une alliance 1
Wednesday mercredi
week une semaine
weekend le weekend
to **weigh** peser 6
to **welcome** accueillir 2
welcome un accueil
welcome bienvenue
well un puits
well ben; bien, eh bien; dis donc; enfin; remarque; *Are things going well?* Tu vas bien?; *that works out well* ça tombe bien 2
west l'ouest (m.); *West Indies* les Antilles (f.)
what ce que; ce qui; comment; quel, quelle; qu'est-ce que; qu'est-ce qui; quoi; *What a beautiful view!* Quelle belle vue!; *What are you doing?* Qu'est-ce que tu fais?; *What do you like to do?* Qu'est-ce que tu aimes faire?; *What does it smell like?* Ça sent quoi?; *what if* si; *what is useless* l'inutile (m.); *What is your profession?* Quelle est votre profession?; *What size are you?* Quelle taille faites-vous?; *What's the weather like?* Quel temps fait-il?; *what's important* l'important (neutr.); *What's new?* Quoi de neuf?; *What's wrong with her?* Qu'est-ce qu'elle a?; *What's your name?* Tu t'appelles comment?; *you know what I mean* quoi
wheel une roulette; *Ferris wheel* la grande roue; *on wheels* à roulettes; *steering wheel* un volant; *suitcase with wheels* une valise à roulettes; *to go on a Ferris wheel ride* faire un tour de grande roue
when lorsque 1; où; quand; *since when* depuis quand
where où
which que; quel, quelle; qui; *about which/whom* dont 6; *from which* duquel, duquelle 5; *of which/whom* dont 6; *to which* auquel, auquelle 5
while en 4; pendant que 3; *while skiing* en skiant 4; *while you're at it* pendant que tu y es
whirlpool bath un bain à remous 5
white blanc, blanche; *white sauce* une sauce blanche 5; *white wine sauce* une sauce marinière 5
who qui
whole: whole series (of) toute une série (de); *the whole deal* la totale
whom que 2
whose dont
why pourquoi
wide large 2
width une largeur
wife une femme
wig une perruque 8
wild sauvage; *to get wild* se déchaîner 9
wildlife la faune
to **win** gagner
to **wind surf** faire de la planche à voile 4
wind turbine une éolienne
window une fenêtre
windshield un pare-brise; *windshield wiper* un essuie-glace
windy: it's windy il fait du vent
wine: chicken cooked in wine le coq au vin; *white wine sauce* une sauce marinière 5
winter l'hiver (m.)
wireless internet le Wi-Fi 5; *wireless internet connection* une connexion Wifi 5
to **wish** souhaiter 5
with au; avec; par; *with a few friends* en petit comité 2; *with chocolate* au chocolat; *with family* en famille; *with mushrooms* forestier, forestière; *with sugar* au sucre; *with warm regards* affectueusement
to **withdraw** retirer 6
without sans 4; *without a doubt* sans aucun doute 4
wizard un sorcier 7
woman une femme
wood le bois 2
wooden en bois 2
woodpigeon un ramier
wool la laine; *wool hat* un bonnet en laine; *made of wool* en laine
word un mot; *this (very) word* ce mot-là
to **work** bosser *[inform.]* 9; marcher; travailler; *that works out well* ça tombe bien 2
work une œuvre; un taf; *volunteer work* le bénévolat 4
worker: postal worker un postier, une postière 6
world le monde; *world music* la world; *French-speaking world* la Francophonie 3

world mondial(e) 10; *world leader* un leader mondial 10
worried inquiet, inquiète
to **worry** s'inquiéter 1
worry une inquiétude; un souci 2; *don't worry* rassure-toi
worse pire, plus mal
worst: the worst le pire, le plus mal
to be **worth** valoir 4; *it's not worth it* ce n'est pas la peine 1
worth une valeur 2
wow oh là là; wahou 8
wrist le poignet 4; *to break one's wrist* se casser le poignet 4
to **write** écrire; rédiger 8
writer un écrivain
to be **wrong** avoir tort 8
wrongdoing un tort 8

Y

yeah right tu parles
year un an, une année; *New Year's Day* le Jour de l'an; *in the first year* en première année; *to celebrate Christmas/New Year's Eve* réveillonner 2
yellow jaune
yes oui; *yes [on the contrary]* si
yesterday hier
yoga le yoga
yogurt le yaourt
you te/t', toi, tu, vous; *as for you* de votre côté 2; *to help you* pour t'avancer 2; *you don't get it* tu n'y es pas du tout 4
young jeune
young man/woman un(e) jeune
your ton, ta; tes, votre, vos
yours le, la tien(ne), le, la vôtre 9
youth la jeunesse 2; *youth hostel* une auberge de jeunesse
yule log une bûche de Noël 2

Z

zero zéro
zoom: to adjust the zoom régler la largeur du champ
zucchini une courgette

Grammar Index

Credits

Abbreviations: top (t), bottom (b), right (r), center (c), left (l)

Photo Credits

Cover: iStockphoto/Famous pavilion by the pool in Jardin Menara, Marrakesh, (Morocco). © Magdalena Jankowska
@laurent/iStockphoto: ix (b); 573 (*maroquinerie*)
4x6/iStockphoto: 524 (raides)
4FR – Photography(Nils Kahle)/iStockphoto: 176
Ababsolutum/iStockphoto: 109
Arcurs, Yuri/Fotolia.com: 524 (chauve)
Adaszku/iStockphoto: 418 (t)
Admedia/SIPA Press: 101
AF Studio/iStockphoto: 325 (*gestion*)
AGfoto/iStockphoto: 084 (b)
Albrektsen, Peter/iStockphoto: 107 (#1)
Alejandro Photography/iStockphoto: 402
AlexMax/iStockphoto: 411 (Modèle (b))
Alija/iStockphoto: 111 (t); 378
Alix William/SIPA Press: 367
Alliance Française Minneapolis/St-Paul: 147
Alpamayo Software, Inc./iStockphoto: 520 (#C)
Ames, Christopher/iStockphoto: 569 (tr)
Anastasia_art/Fotolia.com: 420 (t)
Anderson, Leslie: vi (tl); vii (bl); ix (t); 019; 023 (*collectionner des coquillages*); 019; 025 (*Modèle*); 042 (#3, #7); 048 (*demoiselle d'honneur; baguede fiançailles; gâteau de mariage*); 054; 094 (wooden spoon, strainer); 095 (*Modèle*, #6); 096 (Activity 3: *Modèle*, #1, #2, #6; Activity 4: *Modèle*); 103 (*Modèle*, strainer, #7, #11); 107 (#2, #5); 140 (mother); 176 (*une maison mitoyenne*); 177 (*enfoncer un clou, propre*); 290; 304 (b); 324 (*banquière*); 324 (*un chéquier*); 327; 362 (#7 l, #7 r); 384; 386; 396 (br); 405; 411 (#5, #6, #7); 425 (l); 443 (b); 457 (#5); 477; 514 (b); 573 (*parfums, produits de beauté,champagne*); 575(t); 576(b); 589; 607
Andrea Zanchi Photography/iStockphoto: 506
Andresr/Fotolia.com:545 (b)
Andrew Lever Photography/iStockphoto: 140 (*le cousin germain*)
Andrey/iStockphoto: 372 (r)
Andronov, Leonid/Fotolia.com: 466
Anna k./Fotolia.com: 107 (#3)
Antonino, Matthew/iStockphoto: 097 (t)
Apesteguy/SIPA Press: 257 (b); 273 (b)
Araraadt/Fotolia.com: 076 (*huîtres*)
Archideaphoto/iStockphoto: 177 (living room)
Arcurs, Yuri/Fotolia.com: 303; 595 (*gestion, chef de groupe*)
Arnau, Xavier/iStockphoto: 063 (b) 118
Arsenik Studios Inc./iStockphoto: 276; 288 (t)
Art12321/iStockphoto: 325 (*infographie*)
Asenova, Eli/iStockphoto: 096 (Activity 4: #6)
Ashukian, Susan/iStockphoto: 025 (#2)
Atahac/Fotolia.com: 167 (b)
Auremar/Fotolia.com: vi (mailbox)
Auruskevicius, Marijus/iStockphoto: 103 (#3)
Avatar/iStockphoto: 278 (# GA); 457 (#4)
B/iStockphoto: 177 (*installer la moquette, sale*)
Baker, Matt/iStockphoto: 095 (#3)
Baltel/SIPA Press: 192; 323 (b)
Barbacetto, Guy/Fotolia.com: x (bl)
Bareta, Valery/Fotolia.com: 273 (t)
Beboy/Fotolia.com: 570
Becchetti, Simone/iStockphoto: 318; 488 (#1)
Becker, Brooke Elizabeth/iStockphoto: 096 (Activity 4: #4)
Bedo/iStockphoto: 268 (*chaînes cablées*)
Benamalice/Fotolia.com: 042 (#1)
Benaroch/SIPA Press: 605
Berg, Sanne/iStockphoto: 467
Bergquist, Sonee: 117
Beyond Images/iStockphoto: 531 (b)
Biafore, Joe/iStockphoto: 283 (#11)
Bianchini, Fabio/iStockphoto: 103 (#9)
Biffspandex.com/iStockphoto: 595 (*ressources humaines*)
Bikeriderlondon/Shutterstock.com: 048 (t)
Bing/iStockphoto: 148 (r)
Blackwaterimages/iStockphoto: 543 (*accablée*)
Blue Cutler/iStockphoto: 545 (#3)
Blue Moon/Fotolia.com: 388 (b); 420 (b)
Bokach, Natallia/iStockphoto: 411 (#8)
Bonnie J Graphic Design/iStockphoto: 009
Borghi, Pierre/Fotolia.com: 137 (b)
Box photography/iStockphoto: 362 (#4 b)
Boumen&Japet/iStockphoto: 411 (#2)
Bowdenimages/iStockphoto: 548
Braun, Svetlana/iStockphoto: 545 (#5)
Brave-carp/iStockphoto: 232 (t)
Brian Scantlebury Photos/iStockphoto: 345
Brittak/iStockphoto: 031
Brkovic, Ugurhan Betin/iStockphoto: 268 (*une connexion wifi*)
Brown, Ken/iStockphoto: 381 (*salle expressionniste*); 406 (t); 415 (*un poète*)
Brundin, Gustaf/iStockphoto: 094 (frying pan)
Bryson, Jani/iStockphoto: 111 (b)
Bryukhanova, Anna/iStockphoto: 610 (t)
Bst2012/Fotolia.com: v (bc)
Buzbuzzer/iStockphoto: v (bl); x (tl); 148 (l)
C-Foto.dk/iStockphoto: 520 (#E)
Çaglav, Hakan/iStockphoto: 004 (*aquaparc*)
Caimacanul/iStockphoto: 573 (montres)
Candy Box Images/iStockphoto: 130 (r); 590
Captura/iStockphoto: 073 (tl); 301
Capture the Moment
Cat London Photography/iStockphoto: 546 (t)
Photography, LLC/iStockphoto: 525 (*à carreaux*)
Carillet, Joel/iStockphoto: 452
Casacci, Robert/Fotolia.com: 032 (b)
Casey, Cheryl/Fotolia.com: 048 (*voyage de noces*)
Caucino, Roberto/iStockphoto: 232 (b)
Chagin-art/iStockphoto: 209
Chantal S./Fotolia.com: 076 (*magret de canard*); 143 (Etienne, Marguerite); 169
Charleton, Brett/iStockphoto: v (br)
Cherokeedxb/iStockphoto: 278 (# B)
Chevalier, Denise: x (br); 211 (r)
Chezvik/Fotolia.com: 573 (*faïence*)
Chic Type/iStockphoto: 362 (#5 l)
Chris32m/Fotolia.com: 097 (b)
Chris Bernard Photography/iStockphoto: 525 (*à rayures*)
Chris Gramly Photography/iStockphoto: viii (b)
Clearandtransparent/iStockphoto: 075 (t); 84 (t)
Clicknique/=iStockphoto: 543 (*surexcitée*)
Closs, Sébastien/Fotolia.com: 272 (b)
Collet, Guillaume/SIPA Press: 298 (t)
Cordier, Jean-Jacques/Fotolia.com: 288 (b)
Côte, Sébastien/iStockphoto: x (tr)
Cowan, Paul/iStockphoto: 281 (*le veau*)
Cr-Management GmbH & Co. KG/iStockphoto: 525 (*faible*)
Creativeye99/iStockphoto: 283 (#6, #8, #9)
Creative Shot/iStockphoto: 457 (*Modèle* l)
Cristalconcept/Fotolia.com: vii (cr)
Cudic, Damir/iStockphoto: 137 (tl); 253; 403
Cvetanovski/Fotolia.com: 042 (*Modèle*)
Dag, Durrich/iStockphoto: 457 (tl)
Dagphoto/iStockphoto: 206 (#8)
Damjanac, Svetlana/iStockphoto: iii (tl); 595 (*service des ventes*)
De Bruyne, Hendrik/iStockphoto: 185
Dean Mitchell Photography/iStockphoto: 270; 448
Deejpilot/iStockphoto: 266
Denis, Christophe/Fotolia.com: 001 (tr); 053 (t)
Deniztuyel/iStockphoto: 411 (#3)
De Sazo, Serge/Gamma-Rapho/Getty Images: 498
Desscouleurs, Marco/Fotolia.com: 176 (*une maison individuelle*)
Deva/iStockphoto: 575(b)
Devanne, Philippe/Fotolia.com: 287 (t); 457 (#1)
DeWeese-Frank, Michael/iStockphoto: 096 (Activity 4: #5)
Dexter_s/iStockphoto: 080 (r)
Diederich, Diane/iStockphoto.com: 077 (*Il les emmène...*)
Dietl, Jeanette/Fotolia.com: iv (br)
Diez-artwork/Fotolia.com: 307 (b)
Digihelion photostudio/iStockphoto: iv (cl)
Digital planet design/iStockphoto: 155; 441 (b)
Digital Skillet/iStockphoto: 130 (l)
Dixon, Matthew/iStockphoto: 344
Dolgikh, George/iStockphoto: 500
Doug Berry Images/iStockphoto: 224 (*un moniteur/une monitrice*)
Draghici, Alexandra/iStockphoto: 103 (#8)
DRB Images/iStockphoto: 004 (*détester; être fâché(e); s'affoler; réfléchir*); 525 (*maigre*); 543 (Abdoul)
Drillon, Jean-Claude/Fotolia.com: 048 (*alliances*); 055
Drivepix/Fotolia.com: 507 (b); 514 (t)
Duncan1890/iStockphoto: 381 (*salle néo-classique*); 441 (tl)
Duris, Guillaume/Fotolia.com: vi (man at ATM)
Dutourdumonde/Fotolia.com: 450 (b)
DWP/Fotolia.com: 004 (*discothèque*)
EasyBuy4u/iStockphoto: xi (tr)
Eclypse78/Fotolia.com: 143 (Pierre)
Edstock/iStockphoto: 265 (tl); 306; 379 (t); 404; 406 (b); 483; 540; 579 (b)
Edward Shaw Photography/iStockphoto: 201 (b)
Elenathewise/iStockphoto: 457 (tr)

Éléonore H/Fotolia.com: 025 (#3)
Elnur/iStockphoto: 206 (#2)
EMC Publishing, LLC: ix (c); 023 (*jouer aux billes*); 094 (kitchen); 095 (#5); 096 (Activity 4: #2); 103 (#5); 140 (*l'arrière-grand-mère; le grand-oncle; la grand-tante;* grandpa; grandma); 206 (#1); 234; 281 (*marinière*); 283 (#7); 325 (*droit*); 325 (*médecine*); 325 (*langues*); 362 (#1 l, #1 r, #2 r, #5 r); 447; 457 (#8); 488 (#3); 595 (*secrétariat, service après-vente, DRH, chef de service*);
Emergent Designs/iStockphoto: 350
Emilie/Fotolia.com: 213
Eric Foltz Photography/iStockphoto: 206 (#5)
Eric's Photo Lab/iStockphoto: 525 (*à pois*)
Estionx/Fotolia.com: 355 (#1 t)
Ewg3D/iStockphoto: 107 (*Modèle*)
Eyecrave LLC/iStockphoto: 524 (frisés)
Eye Design Photo Team/iStockphoto: 518
Felker, Inna, Inc./iStockphoto: 037 (t)
Ffolas/iStockphoto: 457 (#2)
FiremanYU/iStockphoto: 158 (bl)
Floortjee/iStockphoto: 389 (l)
FOOD-pictures/Fotolia.com: 076 (*dinde aux marrons*)
Foreman, Richard/iStockphoto: 595 (*secrétaire*)
Forestpath/Fotolia.com: 023 (*famille nucléaire*)
Fotoclick/iStockphoto: 017 (#5)
Fotostorm/iStockphoto: 158 (br)
Franklin, David/iStockphoto: 411 (Modèle (t)); 457 (#3)
Frischhut, Thomas/Tellus Vision Production AB, Lund, Sweden: 008; 028; 051; 081; 98; 112; 145 (t); 165; 181; 208; 228; 236; 246; 271; 285; 302; 328; 343; 357; 464; 481; 511 (tl, cl); 519; 529; 547; 576(t); 586; 599
Fromer, Jill/iStockphoto: 095 (#2)
Fstop123/iStockphoto: 510 (#3)
Ftwitty/iStockphoto: 269 (le concierge)
Gajik, Miodrag/iStockphoto: 166
Galushko, Sergey/iStockphoto: 096 (Activity 4: #1)
Garbet, Peter/iStockphoto: 583 (*Venise Verte*)
Gary/Fotolia.com: 202
Gaspr13/iStockphoto: 206 (#9)
Gavran333/iStockphoto: 103 (*Modèle*, colander)
Gbh007/iStockphoto: 023 (*courir*)
Gblue.com/iStockphoto: 573 (*joaillerie*)
Geoff/Fotolia.com: 191 (l)
Georgeclerk/iStockphoto: 227
GeorgiosArt/iStockphoto: 492
Gezzeg/Fotolia.com: 356
Giacobbe, Marzia/Fotolia.com: 281 (*béchamel*)
Gillow, Mark/iStockphoto: 283 (*Modèle*)
Gina191/Fotolia.com: 176 (*une villa*)
Gold, Marina/iStockphoto: 458
Goldberg, Beryl: 001 (tl)
GoodOlga/iStockphoto: 206 (#4)
Goodluz/Fotolia.com: 309
Graffizone/iStockphoto: 602 (t)
Grafissimo/iStockphoto: 415 (satire)
Gremlin/iStockphoto: 517 (t)
Green Machine/iStockphoto: 488 (Modèle l)
Greig, Johnny/iStockphoto: 524 (mi-longs)
Gruau, J./Fotolia.com: 183
Guilane-Nachez,Erica/Fotolia.com: vii (tr)
Guillaumecd/Fotolia.com: 201 (tr)
Gvozdikov, Anton/Fotolia.com: 215
Hadyniak, Bartosz/iStockphoto: 468 (t)
Hakusan/iStockphoto: 520 (#F)
Hancu, Adrian/iStockphoto: 278 (# F)
Hayes Photos/iStockphoto: 463 (b)
Helenedevun/Fotolia.com: 184 (b)
Herreid, Allison/iStockphoto: 095 (#7)
HLPhoto/Fotolia.com: 281 (*le bœuf*)
HooRoo Graphics/iStockphoto: 524 (*longs*)
Hoppe, Sven/iStockphoto: 441 (tr)
Horstklinker/iStockphoto: 381 (*salle rococo*); 442
Hosteller, Loresta/iStockphoto: 077 (*Les Lombard...*)
Hrabar, Vitaliy/iStockphoto.com: 077 (*Mme Lombard...*)
Hronos7/iStockphoto: 238
HultonArchive/iStockphoto: 425 (r)
laartist/iStockphoto: 286
Ildi_Papp/iStockphoto: 281 (*hollandaise*)
Illini, Davide/iStockphoto: 281 (*béarnaise*)
Ilustrez-vous/Fotolia.com: 076 (*foie gras*); 573 (*produits alimentaires*)
Images by Barbara/iStockphoto: 143 (Jean-Luc)
Iofoto/iStockphoto: 143 (Rose)
lostinbids/iStockphoto.com: 289; 484 (t)
Iropa/iStockphoto: 362 (#3 l)
Izusek/iStockphoto: 543 (*frustrée*)
JackF/iStockphoto: 206 (#6)
Jag_cz/Fotolia.com: 415 (*fable*)
Jamie Carroll, LLC/iStockphoto: 566
Jani Bryson Studios, Inc./iStockphoto: 036
Jansen, Silvia/iStockphoto: 164
Jasmina/iStockphoto: 520 (#B)
JavierGil1000/iStockphoto: 396 (bl)
Jcarillet/iStockphoto: 167 (t)
Jeka/Shutterstock.com: 476
Jhorrocks/iStockphoto: 543 (*surprise*); 546 (b)
Jim Vallee Photography/iStockphoto: 143 (b)
JJAVA/Fotolia.com: 115 (b)
Jlmatt/iStockphoto: 557
Jmorse2000/iStockphoto: 145 (b)
Joshua Hodge Photography/iStockphoto: 510 (#4)
JPC-PROD/Fotolia.com: 550
Juanmonino/iStockphoto: 528
Justin Ward Photography/iStockphoto: 438; 517 (b)
Kablonk Micro/Fotolia.com: 023 (*jouer à la marelle*)
Kali Nine LLC/iStockphoto: 023 (*jouer à cache-cache; sauter à la corde*); 119; 342 (t)
Karandaev, Evgeny/iStockphoto: 094 (measuring glass); 103 (#4r)
Kaspi - Kilikpela's Aperture Studio Photography Inc./iStockphoto: iv (tl); viii (cr)
Kativ/iStockphoto: 429
Keating, Courtney/iStockphoto: 082; 595 (comptabilité, comptable)
Keres, Jasminka/Fotolia.com: 231
Kgtoh/iStockphoto: 268 (*un service de chambre*); 278 (# H)
Kirilart/iStockphoto: 381 (*salle romantique*)
Kishan, Sergey/iStockphoto: 365 (b)
Klubovy/iStockphoto: 190
Knape/iStockphoto: 023 (*jouer à la poupée*)
Knight, Michael/iStockphoto: 095 (#4)
Kohlhuber, Robert/iStockphoto: 305 (t)
Kollidas, Georgios/Fotolia.com: 449; 513
Kontrast-fotodesign/iStockphoto: 153
Kozachenko, Andrey/iStockphoto: 103 (#10)
Kravchenko, Andriy/iStockphoto: 095 (#1)
Kun, Emilia/iStockphoto: 103 (#6)
Kupicoo/iStockphoto: 545 (#1); 585
Kurhan/Fotolia.com: 034
Kyogoyugo/iStockphoto: 283 (#2)
Kzenon/iStockphoto: 100
Laflor Photography/iStockphoto: 023 (*faire des châteaux de sable*); 279 (tr); 545 (*Modèle*)
Lakov Kalinin/iStockphoto: 025 (#1)
Larionova, Anna/iStockphoto: 096 (3:#3)
Laughingmango/iStockphoto: 268 (*un centre de remise en forme*)
Launois, Thomas/Fotolia.com: 044
Lauri/iStockphoto: 017 (#3)
L. Bouvier/Fotolia.com: 247 (b)
LEBON/GAMMA. *Publicité pour Longchamp*. 2006: 608
Leezsnow/iStockphoto: 450 (t)
Lempérière, Francis/Fotolia.com: 025 (#5)
Leontura/iStockphoto: 329
Lido/Sipa Press: 122; 313; 433
Life on White/iStockphoto: 538 (b)
Light Touch/iStockphoto: 571 (b); 588
Lindquist, Mary: 321 (tl); 321 (b); 322; 358 (t); 377 (tl, tr)
Ling Jonathan/iStockphoto: 292 (r)
Lisa Howard Photography/iStockphoto: 207
LLC Photography/Fotolia.com: 023 (*jouer aux petites voitures*)
LM/iStockphoto: 362 (#2 l)
Lobanov, Dmitry/Fotolia.com: 074
Loonger/iStockphoto: 394
Losevsky, Pavel/Fotolia.com: 324 (*banque*)
Loskutnikov, Maxim/Fotolia.com: 176 (*une ancienne ferme*)
LuminaStock/iStockphoto: 524 (courts)
Luncentius/iStockphoto: 424
Lye, Johnny/iStockphoto: 107 (#6)
M&H Sheppard/iStockphoto: iii (tr)
Maceo/Fotolia.com: 076 (*côtes de chevreuil*); 281 (*le chevreuil*)
Machine Headz/iStockphoto: 545 (#2)
Makenoodle,/iStockphoto: 569 (tl)
Mammut Vision/Fotolia.com: 004 (*ciné-club*)
Mangostock/iStockphoto: 524 (tr)
Manley, Andrew/iStockphoto: 284; 549
Marcus Clackson Photography/iStockphoto: 600
Margouillat photo/Fotolia.com: 076 (*saumon fumé*)
Mariait/iStockphoto: 216
Marin, Tomas/iStockphoto: 457 (Modèle r)
Markovka/Shutterstock.com: 096 (3: #5)
Marta P./Fotolia.com: 099
Mayer, Marco/iStockphoto: 073 (tr); 283 (#10)
Maxphotography/iStockphoto: 201 (tl)
McComber, Nicolas/iStockphoto: 407; 510 (*Modèle*)
McKinnon, Peter/iStockphoto: 278 (# E); 337 (l)
Mediaphotos/iStockphoto: 490
MellyB/iStockphoto: 179
Meryll/Fotolia.com: 324 (*On retire de l'argent...*)
Messina, Sandro/iStockphoto: 073 (b); 573 (*mode*)
Mgay photo/iStockphoto: 324 (*chèques de voyage*)
Michaeljung/Fotolia.com: 143 (Thibault); 485; 525 (*gros*); 598
Michael C/iStockphoto: 396 (t)
Micromonkey/Fotolia.com: 083
Mika/iStockphoto: 195
Mimon/Fotolia.com: vii (tl); viii (br)

MIP Studios/iStockphoto: 281 (*le faisan*)
Mirabelle Pictures/Fotolia.com: 080 (l)
Mizioznikov, Felix/Shutterstock .com: 048 (*garcon d'honneur*)
MKucova/iStockphoto: 076 (*boules de neige*)
Mlenny Photography/iStockphoto: 479; 611 (r)
Mmac72/iStockphoto: 507 (t); 531 (t)
Mnich, Marek/iStockphoto: 094 (spatula)
Monat, Antoine/Fotolia.com: 404 (t)
Monkey Business/Fotolia.com: 004 (*soirée*); 220 (b); 592
Monkey Business Images/iStockphoto: 224 (br); 245 (r); 524 (tl); 581
Monu, Nicholas/iStockphoto: 520 (#D)
Moramora/Fotolia.com: 191 (r)
Moran, Ellen/iStockphoto: 120
Morane/Fotolia.com: 224 (ski resort)
Mordolff, Dmitry/iStockphoto: 380 (b)
Morley, Mike/iStockphoto: 292 (l)
M.studio/Fotolia.com: 229
Mrundbaken/iStockphoto: 023 (*faire semblant d'être une princesse*)
Mukherjee, Peter/iStockphoto: 114
Muralinath/iStockphoto: 488 (#2)
NadyaPhoto/iStockphoto: 140 (*la cousine germaine*)
Natali_ua/Fotolia.com: 177 (*poser le papier peint*)
Nazdravie/iStockphoto: 268 (*une clé électronique*); 278 (# A)
Nelis/iStockphoto: 177 (*un tournevis/une vis*)
Nico75/Fotolia.com: 297
Nikonaft/iStockphoto: 578
Nivière/Villard/Dupuy/Florent/SIPA Press: 305 (b)
Nolimitpictures/iStockphoto: 411 (#1); 520 (#A)
Nyul/Fotolia.com: 143 (Maude)
Nyul/iStockphoto: 595 (*service du marketing, responsable marketing*)
Olivier.P/Fotolia.com: 332
Olson, Tyler/Fotolia.com: 017 (*Modèle*)
OMG Images/iStockphoto: 418 (b); 554
Onebluelight/iStockphoto: 023 (*collectionner des timbres*); 077 (*M. Lombard…*)
OnFilm/Istockhoto: 381 (*salle impressionniste*)
Ostill/iStockphoto: 003 (b); 032 (t)
Ozmen, Merih Una/iStockphoto: 103 (#4 l)
Pagadesign/iStockphoto: 325 (*sciences politiques*)
Pafe/iStockphoto: 172
Palut, Jacques/Fotolia.com: 281 (*le lapin*)
Panosian, Greg S./iStockphoto: 443 (t)
PAO joke/Fotolia.com: 176 (*une résidence secondaire*)
Paray, Jacques/Ville de Saint-Germain-en-Laye: 037 (b)
Pashin Georgiy/iStockphoto: 042 (#6)
Paylessimages/Fotolia.com: 535
Pelikh, Anastasia/iStockphoto: 512
Penney, Daniel/SenegalVenture Missionaries: 139 (b); 184; 248 (t)
Perry, Shelly/iStockphoto: 509 (tr)
PeskyMonkey/iStockphoto: 366 (r)
Peterchen/Fotolia.com: 143 (Hugo)
Phillips, Alan/iStockphoto: xi (bl)
Photobac/iStockphoto: 324 (*de la monnaie*)
Photocrew/Fotolia.com: 281 (*le jambon*)
Photodjo/iStockphoto: 365 (t)
Photographer Sanne Berg/iStockphoto: 411 (#4)
Photoiron/Fotolia.com: 457 (#6)
Photo Note Cards/025 (#4)
Photos by Vicky Leon/iStockphoto: 456
Photovideostock/iStockphoto: xi (br); 265 (b)
Piccillo Photography/iStockphoto: 525 (*mince*)
Pieraccini, Massimiliano/iStockphoto: 137 (tr)
Pixarno/Fotolia.com: 35
P.M. Augustavo Photography/iStockphoto: 355 (#4); 505 (tl); 511 (b)
PMG/SIPA Press: 352
Prandina, Marco/iStockphoto: 381 (*salle réaliste*)
Prève, Béatrice/Fotolia.com: 224 (*un télésiège*)
Pressmaster/Fotolia.com: 601
Private/iStockphoto: 545 (#4)
Prudek, Daniel/Fotolia.com: 212, 203 (b)
Pwillitts/Fotolia.com: 042 (#4)
Qingwa LLC/iStockphoto: 421 (t)
Randy Plett Photographs/iStockphoto: 143 (Cécile)
Raoulgalop/Fotolia.com: 532
Rapid Eye Media/iStockphoto: 017 (#4); 577
Raths, Alexander/iStockphoto: 143 (Philippe); 543 (*choquée*)
RayCan/Fotolia.com: iv (bl)
Razvan/iStockphoto: 569 (b)
Revel Pix LLC/iStockphoto: 198
Rich Legg | Legacy One Photography/iStockphoto: 510 (#2); 510 (#1); 525 (*costaud*)
Richard/iStockphoto: 146 (t)
Richter, Dirk/iStockphoto: 283 (#4)
Ridofranz/iStockphoto: 220 (t)
RKH Pictures/iStockphoto: 029
Robynmac/iStockphoto: 283 (#1)
Robyvannucci/iStockphoto: 457 (7)
Rodriguez, Andres/Fotolia.com: 595 (*vendeur*)
Rogers, Chris/iStockphoto: 430
Roland, Yves/Fotolia.com: 076 (t)
Rook76/Fotolia.com: 355 (#1 b)
Rosenberg, Anthony/iStockphoto: 094 (pan)
Roudlove, Hazel/Fotolia.com: 042 (#5)
Ruf, Vincent/iStockphoto: 203 (c); 230 (t)
Runnerphoto/Fotolia.com: 003 (t); 053 (b)
Ruslan, Omega/iStockphoto: 224 (*une piste*); 488 (#4)
Ryan Kelly Photography/iStockphoto: 017 (#2)
Ryo_stockPhoto/iStockphoto: 362 (*Modèle* r)
Ryzhkov/iStockphoto: 281 (*blanche*)
Santa Maria Design Group/iStockphoto: 525 (*fort*)
Santrac, Zeljko/iStockphoto.com: 077 (*Chloé…*)
Sarjeant, Iain/iStockphoto: 298 (b)
Sasar/iStockphoto: 324 (*un billet, une pièce*)
Sassyphotos/Fotolia.com: 488 (#5)
S. Bossert/iStockphoto: 265 (tr)
Scanrail/iStockphoto: 488 (*Modèle* r)
Scorpion66/iStockphoto: 140 (*l'arrière-grand-père*)
Screve, Thomas/Fotolia.com: 267 (t); 287 (b)
Sebastien Cote Photographe/iStockphoto: 222
Secondcorner/Fotolia.com: 415 (*recueil, sonnet*)
Seeden, Lynn/iStockphoto: 096 (Activity 4: #3)
See Hear Media, Inc./iStockphoto: 268 (*un centre d'affaires*)
Seraficus/iStockphoto: 268 (*un service blanchisserie*)
Sergio37_120/Fotolia.com: 076 (*mandarines*)
Severija/iStockphoto: 177 (*peindre les murs*)
Shapecharge Photography/iStockphoto: 140 (father)
Sharon Dominick Photography/iStockphoto: 465
Shaun Lowe Photographic/iStockphoto: 158
ShkYo30/Fotolia.com: viii (cl); 533 (l)
Shot Studio/Fotolia.com: vi (br); 005
Shu, Kristina/iStockphoto: 103 (#1)
Silvrshootr/iStockphoto: 206 (#7)
Simply Creative Photography/iStockphoto: 042 (#2)
Simson, David/images by 'David SimsonB-6940 SEPTON (dasphoto@hotmail.com): 002; 004 (*festival; skatepark; MJC; complexe sportif*); 010; 011; 017 (#1; #6); 023 (*famille monoparentale*); 027; 052; 059; 061; 063 (t); 358 (b); 359
Sinitar Photo/iStockphoto: 463 (t)
Sirichoo, Tupporn/iStockphoto: 103 (#2)
Skampixel/Fotolia.com: 505 (tr)
Skynesher/iStockphoto: 474; 482
SLDigi/Fotolia.com: 023 (*faire semblant d'être un superhéro*)
Smith, Maxfield/iStockphoto: 279 (tl)
Sol Stock/iStockphoto: vii (singer)
Solivo/Fotolia.com: 380 (tl)
SoopySue/iStockphoto: 330
Southmind/Fotolia.com: 075 (b)
Spaxiax/iStockphoto: 538 (t)
Spiderbox Photography Inc./iStockphoto: 595 (*PDG*)
Sportstock/iStockphoto: 248 (b)
Springfield Gallery/Fotolia.com: iv (tr)
Stay Media Productions/iStockphoto: 325 (*chimie-biochimie*); 325 (*gestion*)
Stelian/Fotolia.com: 415 (fox)
Stefcervos/Fotolia.com: v (tr); 247 (t)
Steve Debenport Imagery/iStockphoto: 158 (t); 278 (# D); 421 (b)
Stiop, Alexey/iStockphoto: 103 (#12)
Stock_IMG/iStockphoto: 362 (#4 t)
StockLib/iStockphoto: 079
Stocksnapper/iStockphoto: 362 (*Modèle* l); 560
Stokkete/iStockphoto: 372 (l)
Stuart Rayner Photographer Limited/iStockphoto: 521
Studiocasper/iStockphoto: 268 (*la climatisation*)
Suchan/iStockphoto: 533 (r)
Supermimicry/iStockphoto: 283 (#3)
Szasz-Fabian, Erika/Fotolia.com: 004 (*cours particulier*)
Take A Pix Media/iStockphoto: 245 (r)
Tangopaso: 584
Techno/iStockphoto: 206 (#3); 224 (*un tremplin de sauts à ski*)
Terex/iStockphoto: 268 (*un bain à remous*)
Theasis/iStockphoto: 173
TheBiggles/iStockphoto: 583 (b)
Thinair28/iStockphoto: 334
Thomas_EyeDesign/iStockphoto: 143 (*Étienne*)
Thornberg, Lisa/iStockphoto: 077 (*Les Lombard mettent…*)
Tiler84/iStockphoto: 362 (#3 r)
Tilio & Paolo/Fotolia.com: 468 (b)
Toker, Ilyas/iStockphoto: 268 (*un coffre-fort*)
Tom Fullum Photography/iStockphoto: 143 (*Marguerite*)
Tomos3/iStockphoto: 268 (*l'ascenseur*)
Toutenphoton/Fotolia.com: 138; 182
Track5/iStockphoto: 197; 505 (b); 537 (b)
Traveler1116/iStockphoto: 415 (*une romancière*); 450 (c)
Tree4Two/iStockphoto: 379 (b); 423; 484 (b); 583 (*Norauto*)
Trojanowski, Tomasz/Fotolia.com: 001 (b)
Tropicalpix/iStockphoto.com: 210
Tsokur/iStockphoto: 524 (bouclés)
Tsidvintsev, Andrey/iStockphoto: 587
Tsvetkov, Todor/iStockphoto: 543 (*seule*)
Tupungato/iStockphoto: 321 (tr); 323 (t); 583 (*BNP*); 610 (b)

Tupungato/iStockphoto: 321 (tr); 323 (t); 583 (*BNP*); 610 (b)
Ulga/iStockphoto: 283 (#5)
Unclesam/Fotolia.com: 096 (Activity 3: #4); 129
Vankad/Fotolia.com: 143 (Sylvie)
Vasiliki/iStockphoto: 177 (*accrocher des tableaux*)
Venturini-Autieri, Marco/iStockphoto: vi (bl)
VichoT/iStockphoto: 251
Vikram Raghuvanshi Photography/iStockphoto: 509 (tl)
Vidady/Fotolia.com: 094 (colander)
Videographer/iStockphoto: 410
Villard/Niviere/SIPA Press: 267 (b); 274
Villesèche, Florian/Fotolia.com: 139 (t); 168
Volschenkh/iStockphoto: 324(*le bureau de change*)
Wacquier, Alain/Fotolia.com: 076 (*bûche*)
Wdstock/iStockphoto: 571 (t); 579 (t)
Webb, Diane/iStockphoto: 115 (t)
Weibell, Trista/iStockphoto: 269 (*Le réceptionniste…*)
Whitemay/iStockphoto: 145 (c)
Wicki58/iStockphoto: 177 (*cirer le parquet*)
Wiedemann, Ken/iStockphoto: 230 (b)
Windu/Fotolia.com: 362 (#6 t)
Winhorse/iStockphoto: 583 (*Air France*)
Wilson, Mathhias/iStockphoto: 342 (b)
Witthaya/Fotolia.com: 107 (#4)
Woodcock, Carolyn/iStockphoto: 094 (measuring spoons)
Yakovenko, Pavel/iStockphoto: 537 (t)
Yemelyanov, Maksym/Fotolia.com: 325 (*genie-civil*)
Yeulet, Catherine/iStockphoto: 113
YinYang/iStockphoto: vi (cl); 278 (# c); 324 (*caissière*); 337 (r); 366 (l)
Yuhirao/iStockphoto: 023 (*famille recomposée*)
Yula-designs/iStockphoto: 291; 295
Yulkapopkova/iStockphoto: 224 (bl)
Yvann K/Fotolia.com: 272 (t)
Zarubina, Elena/Fotolia.com: 149
Zbruch/iStockphoto: 325 (*lettres*)
Zerbor/iStockphoto: 488 (#5)
Zhan, Tian/iStockphoto: 377 (b)
Zilli/iStockphoto: 525 (women portrait)
Zirkel, Kenneth C./iStockphoto: 094 (blender)
Ziutograf/iStockphoto: xi (tl)
ZU_09/iStockphoto: 415 (*un dramaturge*)

Reading Credits

Guitry, Sacha, "Deux couverts," Librairie Théâtrale, 1914. (comedy): 123–127
Prevert, Jacques, "Familiale," in *Paroles*, @Editions GALLIMARD. (poetry): 434
Raynaud, Fernand, "Les croissants." (comedy): 314
Satrapi, Marjane, *Persepolis* (comics), *Tome 3*, Coll. Ciboulettes, 2002: 368–369

Art Credits

Akg-images. Walter Limot. History. World War II.-A French sentry on a railway track.-Photo (multiple exposure), 1939. Handwritten descr.: "Avant la defaite". 1939
Anonymous. Hugo, Victor; French poet; 1802–1885. Works: Les Misérables (Novel, 1862); "Jean Valjean - épisode des chande-liers". Wood engraving, anon. From: V. Hugo, Les Misérables, 5 volumes, Paris (Eugène Hugues) 1879–1882. Photo: akg-images: 561
Cailleux, Christian. *Le restaurant*. 2011: 315 (b)
Chéri Samba. *Le Nid dans le nid*, 1996. Acrylic on canvas, sequins and glued mixed medium 53 x 79 inches 135 x 203 cm. Courtesy CAAC - The Pigozzi Collection, Geneva© Chéri Samba: 389 (br)
Cousin le Jeune, Jean (1522–1594). *Portrait de Joachim du Bellay*/Bibliothèque Nationale de Paris: 255
Delorme, Cécile. *Retour du marché*.2005: 193
Édouard, Albert/Rmn. CNAC/MNAM/Dist. Réunion des Musées Nationaux/Art Resource, NY: *Immeuble, rue Croulebarbe*, Paris: 067
The Bridgeman Art Library International: *Portrait of Marcel Renoux aged about 13 or 14* (oil on canvas) by Renoux, Jules Ernest (1863–1932) Private Collection/Giraudon: 128; Ulysse découvre Astyanax caché dans le tombeau d'Hector, c. 1654–1656. Sébastien Bourdon. Collection privée./Photo © Agnew's, London, UK: 257; *They Have Just Plucked Someone*, caricature from series *Les beaux ours de la vie*, by Honore Daumier, 1846, 1808–1879/ De Agostini Picture Library: 315 (t); The Loing Canal, 1892 (oil on canvas), Sisley, Alfred (1839–99)/Musée d'Orsay, Paris, France/Giraudon: 383; *Sunday Afternoon on the Island of La Grande Jatte*, 1884–86 (oil on canvas), Seurat, Georges Pierre (1859–91)/The Art Institute of Chicago, IL, USA: 385 (t); *Cafe Terrace, Place du Forum, Arles, 1888* (oil on canvas), Gogh, Vincent van (1853–90)/Rijksmuseum Kroller Muller, Otterlo, Netherlands: 385 (b); *Mother and child* (pastel on paper), Cassatt, Mary Stevenson (1844–1926)/ Private Collection/Giraudon: 387 (t); *Impression: Sunrise*, 1872 (oil on canvas), Monet, Claude (1840–1926)/Musée Marmottan Monet, Paris, France/Giraudon: 387 (b); *The Pine Tree at St. Tropez*, 1909 (oil on canvas), Signac, Paul (1863–1935)/Pushkin Museum, Moscow, Russia: 388 (t); *Opening of the Estates General at Versailles on 5th May 1789*, 1839 (oil on canvas), Couder, Louis Charles Auguste (1790–1873)/Chateau de Versailles, France/Giraudon: 444 (t); *Farewell to Louis XVI by his Family in the Temple*, 20th January 1793, Hauer, Jean-Jacques (1751–1829)/Musee de la Ville de Paris, Musee Carnavalet, Paris, France/Giraudon: 444 (bl); 'I Die Innocent, I Pardon My Enemies', plate from 'The Story of France', by Mary MacGregor, 1920 (coloured lithograph), Rainey, William (1852–1936) (after)/Private Collection/The Stapleton Collection: 444 (bl)
Samba, Chéri. *Le Nid dans le nid*, 1996. CAAC (Contemporary African Art Collection by Jean Pigozzi): 389

Realia Credits

4Temps&CNIT: 580
Académie Goncourt: 427
ancestry.fr: 146 (b)
CLD de l'Île d'Orléans: 150, 151
Connaissance des Arts : Auteur : Virginie Huet, Source : www.connaissancedesarts.com, ©SFPA – Connaissance des Arts 2013: 391
Crédit Mutuel: 332
L'Atelier des chefs: 289 (www.atelierdeschefs.fr/fr/live; This site offers information on French cuisine and cooking classes)
La Poste: 360
Le Cordon Bleu, Paris: 101
Les enfoirés: 408
Festival de Cannes: 307
francebillet.com: 551
France Volontaires: 249
Guide des stations Savoie/Mont-Blanc (www.savoie-mont-blanc.com): 231
Hugues CHAN-NG-YOK, www.liledelareunion.com: 213
James Noël: 424
Judo Club de Sorgues: 116
McDonald d'Orléans: 602
metrofrance.com: Courrier du cœur: 012
Mairie d'Évry: 495
Ministère de la Culture et de la Sauvegarde du Patrimoine de Tunisie: 170
Ministère de l'Éducation Nationale@eduscol.education.fr — MEN — droits réservés: 515
Ministère de l'Intérieur et de la Sécurité Publique/Commissariat de Voie Publique, Paris: 539
Monaco Monte-Carlo: 275
Opodo.fr: 185
Poésie en liberté (www.poesie-en-liberte.com): 426
Quizbiz.com: 470
SNE: 347
St Paul de Vence.com. Crédit photographique: Jacques Gomot—Office de Tourisme de Saint-Paul de Vence (tl, br): 033
Théâtre du Chatelet/T. Chaine: 392

We have attempted to locate owners of copyright materials used in this book. If an error or omission has occurred, EMC Publishing, LLC will acknowledge the contribution in subsequent printings.

Appendix

Phonetic Alphabet

L'alphabet phonétique pour le français

In its *Prononciation* sections, *T'es branché?* uses the standard phonetic symbols of the International Phonetic Alphabet (IPA). This system was created by the International Phonetic Association as a way to represent the different sounds of spoken languages. The comprehensive list below contains the symbols most commonly used for the French language.

Voyelles

[a] ami, mamy
[ɑ] pâtes, bas
[e] été, nager
[ɛ] étais, belle
[ə] le, demain
[œ] œuf, sœur
[ø] peu, bleu, œufs
[i] dix, gris
[o] dos, chaud
[ɔ] bol, bottes
[u] nous, douze
[y] pur, sucre, bûcher

Voyelles nasales

[ɑ̃] banque, chambre, enchanté
[ɛ̃] cinq, impatient
[ɔ̃] bonbons, long
[œ̃] un, lundi, parfum

Consonnes

[b] bien, bonbon
[k] café, ski, quinze
[ʃ] chaud, chien, short
[d] douze, dents
[f] neuf, pharmacie
[g] gris, gant
[ʒ] jaune, géant, aubergine
[ɲ] agneau, mignon, peigner
[l] lampe, mille
[m] mille, mère
[n] nage, noir
[ŋ] le smoking
[p] père, pêche
[R] rare, père
[s] cela, français, poisson, attention, soixante
[t] tarte, théâtre
[v] violet, avion, wagon
[z] visage, zèbre

Semi-consonnes

[j] adieu, œil, fille, yaourt
[ɥ] nuit, fruit, huit
[w] oui, boire, ouest

Functions in Level 1 Textbook

Unité 1

Leçon A:

- Je l'ai rencontré… *(au ciné-club)*.
- Tu ferais bien de… *(l'inviter à la maison)*.
- Ce n'est pas la peine de t'inquiéter.
- Tu as l'air de… *(bien l'aimer)*.

Leçon B:

- J'ai découvert… *(la vie des supermarchés ici)*.
- C'est comme ça que… *(l'on est arrivé à Nice)*.
- Tu proposes… *(quoi)*?

Leçon C:

- Je m'en fiche.
- J'aimerais bien travailler… *(dans un laboratoire de recherches)*.

Unité 2

Leçon A:

- Je ne te dérange pas?
- Vous aimeriez… *(la soirée du réveillon avec nous)*?
- Pourquoi pas? On n'a rien de prévu.
- Ça tombe bien.

Leçon B:

- Tu pourrais me donner un coup de main?
- Avec plaisir.
- Je crains que non.
- Ça dépend.
- Tu peux me passer… *(la passoire)*?

Leçon C:

- Je ne peux pas m'empêcher de… *(penser aux gens qui souffrent dans le monde)*.
- *(Élodie)*… a raison.
- *(Et à votre table,)*… vous parlez de quoi?

Unité 3

Leçon A:

- Mes aïeux sont arrivés de… *(Bretagne et)* se sont installés… *(au Québec)*.

Leçon B:

- Il était une fois… *(un petit garçon, Fahim)*.

Leçon C:

- Très heureux/heureuse.
- J'ai grandi dans… *(un HLM qui n'était pas très propre)*.
- On dirait que… *(cela a été fait par un professionnel)*!

Unité 4

Leçon A:

- *(Chamonix)*... te dit?
- Sans aucun doute.
- Je suis persuadé(e).
- Je vois les choses un peu différemment.

Leçon B:

- Il faut que je... *(revienne en skiant correctement)*.
- Tu auras l'occasion d'... *(apprendre)*.
- *(Ça,)*... je m'y attendais!

Leçon C:

- Vous ferez ce que vous voulez, moi c'est... *(balade sur le domaine)*.
- Il est important que... *(tu ne te foules pas la cheville ou que tu ne te casses pas le poignet)*!

Unité 5

Leçon A:

- Je voudrais que vous me donniez quelques précisions sur... *(les prestations de l'hôtel)*.

Leçon B:

- Puis-je savoir quelles sont les spécialités?
- Il est servi avec... *(de la moutarde)*?

Leçon C:

- Je ne suis pas trop d'humeur pour... *(une comédie dramatique)*.
- Il paraît que c'est... *(très drôle)*.
- Quelles sont... *(tes)* impressions... *(du film)*?
- Je ne partage pas... *(ton)* avis.

Unité 6

Leçon A:

- Je voudrais ouvrir un compte et obtenir... *(une carte bancaire)*.
- C'est promis!

Leçon B:

- Ça parle de quoi?
- Je n'arriverai jamais à me décider!

Leçon C:

- Il me faut une assez grande boîte....
- Quels sont ceux que tu veux envoyer?
- Ceux que j'ai achetés l'autre jour à la librairie.

Unité 7

Leçon A:

- *Les coquelicots* a été peint en... *(1873)*.
- Avec ce tableau,... *(Renoir)* recherche de plus en plus... *(les effets de lignes)*.
- Avec cette méthode,... *(Seurat)* s'éloignait des... *(impressionnistes)*.
- *(L'artiste a utilisé le jaune)*... pâle.

Leçon B:

- Il passe de... *(la caricature)* à... *(la chanson engagée)*.
- Ses chansons... *(du temps qui passe et des amours tristes)* lui ont valu d'immenses succès.
- *(Brel)*... c'est le goût pour... *(la musique populaire)*.
- *(Elle)*... a séduit plusieurs générations qui se sont reconnues dans... *(le lyrisme intimiste de ses textes)*.

Leçon C:

- *(Ses* Amours*)*... donnent lieu à des variations sur les thèmes de... *(la plainte, du soupir, de l'aveu, et de la mélancolie)*.
- C'est une œuvre... *(politique)* qui prend position sur... *(la guerre)*.
- *(La poésie)*... est la partie la plus volumineuse de l'œuvre de... *(Victor Hugo)*.
- C'est à... *(Apollinaire)* qui l'on doit l'invention du... *(mot "surréalisme")*.
- C'est une figure de la culture... *(populaire)*.

Unité 8

Leçon A:

- Il était obligé de... *(faire venir les députés)*....
- On te fait... (étudier tout ça)?

Leçon B:

- Il y a plein de... *(modelés)*.
- J'ai beau... *(chercher des modèles pour la lettre de motivation)*....

Leçon C:

- *(Mamy)*... a droit à... *(une voiture médicalisée)*....
- *(Elle)*... a les moyens de... *(payer un taxi normal)*.
- On peut en discuter davantage plus tard.

Unité 9

Leçon A:

- Tu ne semblais pas... *(très bien)*.
- J'étais incapable de... *(décider quelle était la priorité)*....

Leçon B:

- Tu ne t'es aperçu de rien?
- Je me suis rendu compte que... *(mon ordinateur n'était plus là)*.

Leçon C:

- Vous avez eu l'idée de... *(mettre votre vidéo sur YouTube tout de suite)*?
- Je ne m'y attendais pas....

Unité 10

Leçon A:

- Il a été fabriqué en... *(Malaisie)*.
- C'est bien ce que je craignais.

Leçon B:

- Ça fait longtemps que... *(vous êtes en France)*?
- Je voulais m'éloigner de... *(la capitale)*.

Leçon C:

- *(McDo met du fromage français dans leurs sandwichs)*... pour s'adapter à... *(notre goût)*.

Additional Sources of Information

Below you will find search words to help you and your students to find Internet sites for a multitude of activities to enrich your classroom instruction.

Amusement Parks:
- fétes des loges
- fétes foraines europe
- parc d'astérix

Francophone News:
- allafrica
- france amérique
- jeune afrique
- l'actualité
- l'humanité
- le devoir
- le figaro
- le monde.fr
- libération
- tv5

Francophonie:
- franc parler
- francofil.net
- organisation internationale de la francophonie

French Cheeses:
- ermitage fromage
- petit lexique du chabichou et des fromages de chèvre

Governmental Sites:
- ambassade de france
- campus france
- campus france resource center
- french embassy washington dc
- ministere de l'education nationale
- union europeenne

Grammar:
- conjuguemos french
- french.about.com

International NGOs:
- ATD quart monde
- croix rouge
- medecin sans frontières

Miscellaneous:
- ABU france
- canal plus
- centre belge de la bande dessinée
- fuaj
- phosphore france

Online Activities:
- corporate classroom connect
- fsl activities with m. renaud

Paris:
- aéroports de paris
- arrondissements paris.fr
- centre pompidou
- la sorbonne
- louvre
- montmartre
- musée d'orsay
- paris office du tourisme
- ratp paris
- université vincennes
- versailles site officiel

Pedagogical Sites and Testing:
- ap central french
- carla mn
- center for applied linguistics language testing
- le cndp
- linguafolio
- planète enseignante

Radio Stations:
- europe1
- radio canada
- radio france internationale
- rci martinique
- tf1 en direct

Teacher Associations:
- aatf
- actfl
- alliance française
- alliance française usa
- center for applied linguistics

Technology
- cnes
- cnrs
- france télécom
- insee
- peugeot-citroen
- renault site officiel
- sncf

Tourist Offices:
- bordeaux tourisme
- écotourisme antilles
- écotourisme guadeloupe
- grenoble tourisme
- guyane francaise tourisme
- montréal tourisme
- nice tourisme
- normandie tourisme
- office du tourisme alsace
- office du tourisme antilles françaises
- office du tourisme bretagne
- office du tourisme cameroun
- office du tourisme lyon
- office du tourisme maroc
- office du tourisme marseille
- office du tourisme quebec
- office du tourisme strasbourg
- office national de tourisme algérien
- office national de tourisme tunisien
- parc national guadeloupe
- provence tourisme
- rouen tourisme
- sénégal tourisme
- site officiel office du tourisme belgique
- site officiel office du tourisme côte d'azur
- tourisme bretagne
- tourisme bruxelles
- tourisme côte d'ivoire
- tourisme d'aventure france
- tourisme d'aventure guyane
- tourisme d'aventure et écotourisme
- tourisme gascogne
- tourisme guadeloupe
- tourisme kabylie
- tourisme loire
- tourisme luxembourg
- tourisme martinique

Culture Index

Poetry

Places

Sports / Games

Technology

French Survey Respondents

In 2009, we conducted a survey of French teachers to find out what they wanted in a new French textbook series. We would like to thank the following teachers for their participation, which helped us design *T'es branché?*

Alabama: Judy Byram, Melissa Copeland, Chris Eubanks, Shelley Fordice, Julie Norvelle Fantoni, Cheryl Hall, Cindy Lepore, Stephanie McGee, Maxanna Nichols-Lefebvre, Sara C. Runner, Susanne Rives, Candance Thomason; **Alaska:** Virginia G. Boyd, Claudia Markham, Kathleen Walgren; **Arizona:** Catherine Burke, Linda Dunbar, Ruth Eiseman, Sarah Fowler, Jarred Gainey, Margaret Hanna, Ann-Marie Hyland, Hope Loveland, Randall Nissly, Jennifer Patrick, Leigh Thomas, Diane Waters; **Arkansas:** Chris Becnel, Nola Harrison, Carey Lagarrigue, Gray Langston, Jan Nixon, Kim Scarbrough; **California:** Maria Adame, Sally K. Adams, Joan Adometto Taylor, Judy Avila, Silvia Battigalli, Anne Bazile, Nathalie Bellitti, Mary Anne Berry, Justin Brooks, Ariene Borutzki, Leah Boselli, Kathy Calvin,Corinne Carlson, Samantha Carr, Karina Chin, Rachel Cornec, Sandy Dana-Kildow, Sebastian P. DeClerck, James DeKay, Susan DeLateur, Michael Delbar, Karen Donner, Mary Dowden, Yvonne Duong, Lynda Fine, Lorraine Fong, Joan Fox, Shelley Friedman, Natalie Freitas, Edwige Gamache, Andrea Gannon, Patricia Grogan, Rhonda Habsersham, Janet Hedeline, Lynn Heyman-Hogue, Sharon Hendrickson, Mira Jamadi, Eva Johnson, Shana Kamper, Karen Kessinger, Michelle Klein, Patti Kussman, Brigitte Kyle, Jessica Lawrence, Denise LeBiavant, Valerie Lent, Cecile Lunetta, Azita Mahmoudi, Michelle Marriott, Sheila McCumber, Sadie Medina, Lise Melin, Deborah Mogel, Micheline Moreau, Starlight Murray, Mariela Neira, Sara Niles, Todd Oesterman, Yvonne Oliver, Brenda Parrish, Carolyn Quinby, Karen Ransom, Dee Robbins, Jetta Rodal, Linda Rosenberg, Rachel Safier, Melisa Salvato, Allison Sass, Robert Schaffer, Claudine Senac-Urtecho, Bertha Sevilla, Francine W. Shivers, Michelle Shockey, Audrey Smith, Patty Stephenson, Judy Stout, Isabelle Teraoka, Tatjana Trout, Beth Tudor, Judith Uriarte, Mary Van de BovenKamp, Geraldine Van Roie Stoddard, Christine Veilleux, Verna Verspieren, Barbara Vinolus, Elizabeth Vitanza, , Agnieszka Waclawek, Catherine Welter, Judy Werner, Jacki Williams-Jones, Francois Wolman; **Colorado:** Jane Backer, Laura Battisti, Leslie Casanova, Debbie Cody, Anne Damanti, Lisa Davis, Ellen Grimsdale, Paul Kirschling, Elaine Kurbegov, Marlene Ladouceur, Patty Ross-Baldwin, Florence Schranz, Ann Snow, Austin Wallace, Linda Zimmerman; **Connecticut:** Magdalena Alvarado, Garry Apgar, Ann Barton, Lisa Ahlstrom-Nasy, Martine Berliet, Maria Cahill, Constance Carrington, Nathalie Casey, Carol Coderre-Marx, Rossana Crudele, Aline Dennison, Justin Ehrenberg, Abdoulaye Fall, Mark Foster, Myriam Franquesa, Paula Greenfield, Diane Holskin, Susan Hudson, Ruth Jones, Nancy Katsaros, Angela Kelleher, Thomas Kelly, Corrine Khawaja, Bruno Koffi, Barbara H. Lathrop, Kathy Martin-Ocain, Susan Mason, Gail McKenna, Nancy Moran, Mary E. Perlot, Nicandra Perusi, Barbara C. Polley, Dorothy Raviele, Claudine Rose, Jane See, Ed Smith, Jennifer Sturges, Renee M. Sylvestre, Ann Trinkaus, Magioula Tsilibocos, Patricia Villella, Heather Way, Emily Wentworth, Marianna Wikarska, Sandra P. Wilson, Linda Zabor; **Delaware:** Megan Cover, Roch Luberti, Mary Ann Ryan, Pamela Scholla, Joyce Strojny; **Florida:** Shirley R. Bayard, Sandra Bierkan, Christelle Carter, Sansan Dah, Valerie Eastman, Valerie Gentilini, Gianina Ireland, Susan Laffitte, Herve le Guilloux, Laura Hollands, H. Leonard, Sheila Mansier, Barbara M. Murray, Mary B. Noblin, Susan Olevia-Wagner, Sherry Parker, Erin Pendergast, Doriane Rencker, Simone Schoeni, Sorela Schultz, Teresa Suarez, Mary C. Sweet, Brenda Velez, Kathryn Anne Vensel, Barbara Woolley, Paula Yaniglos; **Georgia:** Patricia Bailey, Valerie Bathurst, Denise Bedell, Christy Belbey, Claire Bell, Kristen Bintlift, David Bobkowski, Nan Brightwell, Sally Brock, Agnes Browning, Angela Burgess, Brita Buhrman, Cecilia Burns, Karen Canady, Fejokwuc Comfort, Liana Cox, Caryn Craft, Michele Diament, Michael Dockery, Gabrielle Durden-Coffee, Gail Ehrhart, Catherine Francisse, Reesa Frezier, Judy Fritz, Tracey Glass Fuchs, Rhonda Habersham, Shanda D. Hester, Nessa Hoppe, Valerie Hughey, Elizabeth John, Jeanne S. Jones, Mary Lane Jukes, Edna-May King, Susan Logan, Phyllis Loiacono, Patricia A. B. Macmillan, Rachel G. Martellus, Irene Marxsen, Alanna McEachin, Lesya McGee, Katy McManus, Eugenia McMillan, Jennifer Miller, Amie Muir, Nancy Nichols, Laure-Anne Pennelli, Kathleen A. Porto, Christohe Powers, Benjamin Riekhof, Tracy Rucker, Sharon Shirah, Marianne Simeneta, Katie Sisterhen, Travis Spell, Carol Stevens, Kenneth Swanson, Cynthia Toups, Lauren Watson, Kristin Webb, Jeanette Webster-Whyte, Marylou Wiesendanger, Debra Welch, Valerie White, Elizabeth Williams, Jennifer Willis, Thelma Wise; **Hawaii:** Erin C. Cleveland, Kathie Dinges, Dayna Fukunaga, Catherine Pettit, Norma Young; **Idaho:** Gabrielle Applequist, Sharon Bartlow, Jerre Coleman, Claudia Creek, Sally Husted, Aliene Shearer, Dana L. Stockman; **Illinois:** Jason Anderson, Martha Behlow, Caryn Boltz, Jo Anne A. Bratkovich, Liette Brisebois, Tracy Cowper, Angelique Dorchies, Cynthia Driesner, Sharon Eichensehr, Carolyn Fitzgerald, Julie Frost, Michelle Garesche, Barb Goldberg, Sandra Grandolfo, Francis Greaux, Sue Harsa, Ann K. Hartman, Melanie Hillegass, Andrea K. Isabelli, Kathleen Iverson, Jura Jancys, Eric Laird, Lynette Lang, Toni Lowery, Melissa Lo, Joyce Marconcini, Suzanne McKeigue, Michelle Morelli, Maryann Pliss, Sara Kahle Ruiz, Janet Rzeszutko, Michele Salkauskas, Heather Song, Laura Sperling, Roz Sunquist, William Swiderski, Jeanne Trengove, Judy Weiss; **Indiana:** Michele Balma, Elizabeth Breidinger, Alisha Burcham, Heather Carey, Gwen Craig, Susie Deneen, Philip D. Didier, Kristy Donley, Rebecca Elkins, Melanie Enkoff, Pamela Forth, Diane Furtwangler, Jessica Geisinger, Sara Harrison, Cheryl Herman, Jill Hildgemeier, Kathy Jaroszewski, Ellen Landers, Martha Layton, Lisa Liberge, Bryan Macke, Vicki Mannweiler, Paula Morton, Debora Olejniczek, Andrea S. Pieh, Regina Portman, Adrienne Qualls, Carol Shumate, Beth Strodel, Kimberly Summers, Susan Van Fleit, Safia Virgil, Janice Vote, Lisa Walborn, Jill Wiley, Kay A. Wood; **Iowa:** Michele Marie Arman, Laura Catron, Jae Dwyer, Vicki Gallagher, Christine K. Gilbertson, Janet Johnson, Deb Paulsen, Melanie Sartori, Erin Schafer, Christina Snyder-Scott; **Kansas:** Melanie Adams, Christina Beard, Rebecca Bock, Sandra Chastan, Linda S. Clark, Jan Denning, Lisa DeVore, Clara A. George, April S. Gomez, Nora Kelting, Susan Lehr, Karen Pearson, Leslie Ransdall, Alyssa Rydant, Christa L. Ruhlen, Vicki Swetz; **Kentucky:** Elizabeth W. Cooke, Jocelyne Cross, Scottye Eakin, Jennifer Kirby, Elizabeth B. Rambo, Susan Robbins; **Louisiana:** Marilyn J. Ashton, Theresa Barr, Yannick Brignac, Mimi Brooks, Pam Broussard, Valerie Burton, Isabelle Callens-Shirazi, Marie Cipolla, Vicki K. Clem, Charles Darby, Marguerite Dietrich, Brother Derek W. Foster, William Gautreaux, Cosima Hasenstein, Mary C. Herget, Linda Lafont, Norma Michaud, Marie-France Price, Martine Smith, Rebeccah Smith, Stephanie Viator; **Maine:** Kristen Andrews, Andrea AskenDunn, Seth Briggs, Linda Butt, Lisa Charlier, Leslie Harlin, Irene Marchenay, Margaret Nulle, Anne E. Smith; **Maryland:** Amanda Arnoult, Larissa Arist, Monique Briend-Walker, Denise W. Diegel, Elizabeth Foyle, Elizabeth Gray, Nancy Claire Gritzinger, Kenneth Haines, Kathleen Kirk-Leason, Marie-Pierre Manrique, Phyllis McCauley, Paul Newhouse, Keila Oropeza, Angela Porcella, Lexi Sargent, Emilie Shipman, Robert A. Silkworth, Debora Speier, Jeanne Touzeau, Richard Tuckerman, Laurie Whitley, Teresa Wilson, Yimei Wu; **Massachusetts:** Marie Dunell, Justin Evans, Rina Farber-Mazor, Christine Geueke, Christopher Johnson, Janice Joyce, Norma Kozaka, Deborah Leavitt, Michelle Lewison, Susanne Markus, Robert F. Peolquin, Yiota Simoglou; **Michigan:** Dick Ahlers, Faye M. Amo, Amy Begnene, Michelle Burley, Nancy Busard, Crystal Cannon, Amy Clement, Susan Clugston, Laura Davis, Kelley DeGraaf, Veronica Dewey, Mary Drouillard, Sheryl Foster, Kim Frisinger, Eileen Gifford, Christine Haack, Cindy Hern, Valerie Jablonski, Jennifer M. Kay, Michelle Kuehnlein, Marti Larson, Jeanine LeMieux, Sheryl Moll, Diana Morgenstern, Theresa Nilsen, Victoria Potter, Kathy Refice, Pam Romanelli, Kim Rouvelin, Melissa Saeed, Sister Rose Sam, Melissa Samluk, Barbara St. Louis, Patrick Teahan, Dana Tipurita, Raghida West; **Minnesota:** Susan Brown, Jen Bouchard, Michele Campbell, Kari Christensen, Joyce Cogdell-Travis, Coleen Colton, K. Droske, Jessica Gillespie, Camilla J. Glattly, Laurie Hennen, Phyllis Hicks, Sara Holcombe, Margaret Laboe, Amy Lemme, Elizabeth Manning, Elizabeth Marin, Mary Lynn Montgomery, Susan Palmer, Kris Rydland, Sue

Sebghati, Twyla Sha, Kathleen Stoddart, Christina Sturm, Kyle Sweeney, Scott Swedin,; **Mississippi:** Bridget Carmody, Susan Callon, Debbie Gorney, Brigitte Herbert, Jessica Powell, Janis Risley, Jacquelyn Sergi, Jacqueline Wilson; **Missouri:** Vicki Barmann, Julie Begnaud, Fran Burnet, April Burton, Lauren Coleman, Teresa Connolly, Anne-Marie Coreggia, Linda Crane, Judith Crenshaw, Lynne Evans, Karen Gibson, Kathryn L. Hedrick, Annie Hilmes, Nita Jackson, Andrea Junkans, Richard Keefe, Jenifer Kidwell, Nicole King, Chad Lower, Catherine Marquart, Sandy Mason, Kimberlee Moyer, Myriam Palmer, Sarah Rausch, Sarah Scoggins, Laura Snead, Amy Sternke, Mike Summers, Jennifer Tadsen, Lori Turnage, Della Thompson, Julie West, Krista White; **Nebraska:** Jeanne Cronin, Kathy Hardenbergh, Pamela Kooiker; **Nevada:** Richard Bangert, Jonathan Reynolds, Leslie Righetti, Ginnae Stamanis; **New Hampshire:** Leslie Anton, Evelyn Christoph, Elaine Jubinville, David Page, Jayne Wing; **New Jersey:** Gerard Amsellem, Lauren Arcusi, Debbie Barca, Angela Barone, Bonnie Baumert, Karen Beetham, Helene Blanton, Joan Bonnell, G. Cahayla, Eileen Campanella, Geraldine G. Castaldo, Alda Cornec, Claire D'Angelo, Kerrie Decker, Claudy Delne, Phyllis Dimick, Meredith Donato, Maria Kostis Economals, Laurence Farhat, Brigitte Fischer, Diana Flynn, Cynthia Foxworth, Martine Gabler, Kinga Galica, Linda Geldmacher, Sylvia Guensch, Marie-Marthelle Guervil, Jenn Haff, Suzanne Hennessey, Carol Hill, Maryanne Kain, Rebecca Kazimir, Raana Khan, Maria Kostis, Karen Kozlowski, Barbara A. Lehman, Karen Lester, Joan Lipkowitz, Jeanine Losito, Marianne Ly, Sonia Magalhaes, Carol McKay, Carol Milich, Daniel Moraske, Valerie Morris, Nancy Mousavi, Cristin O'Connor, Ellen O'Meara, Ellen Reiss, Jane Roxbury, Kimberlee J. Safranek, Fritzner Salomon, Paula Schaffer, Susan Shourds, Diana Shults, Lise Simard, Debra Soriano, Joelle Stark, Laura Thomas, Margaret Tisa, Stephanie Walczak, Marguerite Wall, Tammy Wubbenhorst, Marlene Yoskowitz, Susan Roque Zeitz; **New Mexico:** John Coleman, Louise Gentile, Suzanne Holman; **New York:** Elsie Augustave, Jeff Brown, Nancy Burns, Susan Chatoui, Tom Davian, Paula DeFlippo, Ousmane Diouf, Mary Ellen Donovan, Elizabeth A. Ernenwein, Alba Gallegos, Andrea Grady, Marie Guagliardo-Day, Lisa Judd, Laurine Haefner, Rose Marie Hawver, Lizette Liebold, Louise J. Lindemann, Patricia Long, Matthew Nani, Monique Navalet, Denise Nichols, Debbie Pelletiere, Giovanni Ruggiero, Ellen Scheiderer, Catherine Scher, Kathryn Siegel, Alla Shustorovich, Jo Ann Thomasson, Jerry Treadwell, Laura Veralli, Lindsay Wahler, Wendy Winters, Lauren Wood-Radcliffe; **North Carolina:** Debra Ashe, Abeer Awad, Erin Bockoras, Maria G. Bonito, Stephanie Casstevens, Elizabeth Conine, Carolyn L. Cooper, Mary Turner Dalton, Ann Herminjard Davis, Richard Dubois, Teresa Engebretsen, Erin Feltman, Shannon Ferguson, Evelyn Marie Freeman, Jill Friesen, Angela Hagler, Angela Harris, Stephanie Hellert, Ana Hummel, James T. Hunter, Dawn Jones, Kim Lemons, Alicia Lewis, Sylvie Little, Kathryn C. Marker, Deborah P. Marks, Victoria Matisko, Sue Mead, Roland Menestres, Laraleigh Moffitt, Symphorien Momet, Wanda Moore, Wendy Mumy, Kristen Noland, Annie P.G. Norris, Hannah Pao, Alix Pavlic Phillips, Leslie Pyler, Kathleen Rhodes, Cynthia Richards, Julia Royall, Diane Smith, James Sonier, Ashlee Bree Stillings, Dyana Walker Talford, Alain Tourrret, Sarah Walden, Ines Weikel, Sharon Williams, Kim Young; **North Dakota:** Patricia Jessen, Melissa R. Klajda, Valerie Kling, Lynee Meier; **Ohio:** Brandon Arnold, Maria Baker, Madith Barton, Shelbrey Blanc, Patricia Boon, Marguerite Bourgeois, Audra Buckley, Rebekah Clark, Nancy Compton, Parthena Draggett, Lisa Devlin, Carol J. Drescher, Kim Easley, Susan M. Eynon, Rachel Fawcett, Erin Gavula, Marianne Gooding, Suzanne Gyurgyik, Vinka Hartman, Suzanne Heacock, Jeanette Marie Hecker, Tina Hodge, Etchri Kekessi, Kelli Izzo, Patricia Jawyn, Madeline LaJeunesse, Tracy Loar, Cynthia Mathias, Judith Mielbrecht, Linda Morell, JoAnn O'Connor, Gretchen Petrie, Juliana Porter, Davara Potel, Ann Marie Radefeld, Ann Ryan, Robert J. Roesbery, Jeff Royer, D. Saunders, Ellen Schaf, Patricia Schorr, Lynne Sebring, Lynette A. Seith, Cheryl Shank, Jacqueline Shrake, Kathryn M. Siegel, Adrienne Six, Bonnie Thompson, Mary Russell Townsend, Milton Alan Turner, Susan Vrooman, Stephanie Waugh, Melinda White, Barbara Yedidsion, Kimberly Young, Nicole Zistler; **Oklahoma:** Patricia Box, Joan King, Janet Gorton, Carol Little, Melinda Minshall, Julie Nesser, Jennifer Taylor, Micki Taylor, Wendy Toscani; **Oregon:** Penny Bazanele, Angela Barley, Eloise S. Bates, Terry Benge, David Burke, Rhonda Case, Mike Curtis, Brenda Eichten, Annette Hallaux, Gina Johnson, Marc McAvoy, Laurelin Muir, Sandra Rands, Jean Redrejo, Anick Southwood, Lexie Tombleson, Kathleen Williams, Erica Zimmerman; **Pennsylvania:** Denis N. Asselin, Colette Ballew, Pamela Barentine, Brenda Barndt, Betty Benton, Linda Bistline, Linda Blum, Colleen Bognet, Mary Bollinger, Kathleen H. Brown, Carolyn Busque, Gloria Carfagno, Gregory W. Coleman, Cindy Comstock, Bruce A. Cope, Virginia Cosgrove, Elaine Danford, Linda Donahue, Sandra Dubnansky, Michelle Emery, Jill Fersch, Karen Fickes, Lydia Fichtman, Linda E. Fosselman, Paula Foster, Linda Girard, Jessica Grey, Andrew D. Grim, Dorothea Hackett, Scott Holland, Maureen Klingaman, Andrea Kupprion, Tricia Larson, Annette Lee, Susan Lobb, Cecile McKernan, Nancy McKnight, Ann Menichelli, Linda Mercier, Amy Montgomery, Laura Nagle, Laurie Neilson, Courtney Nelson, Jill Nickerson, Claudine Nicolay, Hallie Olson, Conni Petrie, Andrew Reaman, Joanne Robb, Regina Rooney, Anita Sapalidis, Jennifer Sharp, Susan Shelley, Susan E. Shuman, Kathy Simonovich, R. Sklar, Jan Hostler Stewart, Kyrston Strauch, Deborah A. Swann, Kathleen Tatala, Alan M. Tomaszewski, Jill Trate, Amy Varacalli, Maureen L. Verwey, Nicole Wagner, Vanessa Weinlein, Ellen R. Wiberley, Katie Wilhelm, Diane Yanez, Barbara Zaun; **Rhode Island:** Sarah Brady, Kathleen DePasquale, Coleen Griffith, Sandra Tessier; **South Carolina:** Cathy Bouabre, Susannah Elliot, Jill Hnat, Kristina Holst, Sara Johnson, Justin T. Jones, Marisa Keenan, Lilly Mikol, Michele Mouyeos, Jennifer Teague; **South Dakota:** Jane Perman; **Tennessee:** Marsha Barrom, Marcia Bowen, Elizabeth Buchignani, Edith Jane Cain, Melanie L. Calhoun, Dustin Denzin, Marina Fernandez, Maureen Garrett, Janet Kaller Geerlings, Larry Justis, Ashley Lawrence, Laura Leonard, Alexis Mattingly, Katie Paduch-Ledford, Jacob Truax, Robin Lynn Woo; **Texas:** Ann Abercrombie, Andrea Adams, Veronica Angel, Cheryl Babb, Joanna Gipson Bacon, Rose E. Balboa, Dawn M. Baraett, Maria Barraza, Penny Beauchamp, Allison Bennett, Claire Breaux, Kathleen Carsey, Jose H. Castro, Richard J. Catania, Ann Clogan, Jacqueline Costanza, Randi Costenbader, Leslie Cushman, Lan Doan, Florence Dossett, Susan Dworaczyk, Francisca Florent, Allison Foster, Karlyn Fuquay, Erin Gallagher, M. Carla Geiger, Cathy Gelzleichter, Everett Gillette, Stacey Griffin, Rita A. Guidry, Julie Hanson, Phill Hemmings, Esther Hendrick, Jenifer Herndon, Melissa Hezlep, Bruce Hoang, Kitty Hutchcroft, Diana Jacob, Jeanne Johnson, Anne Jones, Penny Korenek, Aaron Levine, Cecilee C. Lindsey, Leigh Marshall, Joel Mayer, Cindy McBrayer, Denise McCage, Rita Mendoza, Diane Meyrat, Patricia Mills, Adam Morton, Deborah Murphy, Mark Myers, Cathy Nacol, Mary Nichols, Rhonda Palmer, Terry Pierce, Elizabeth Porter, Micaela Pitre, Natalya Belova Ramirez, Beverly Randall, Celeste Renza-Guren, Heather Richardson, Jill A. Rock, Serge Schragin, Rachel Schulz, Tara Smith, Maribel Squibb, Karen Stephens, Dore Sulistyo, Gail Sutcliffe, Roger Thomas, J. M. Turner, Kristen Villalvazo, Alicia Villarreal, R. D. Wade, Elizabeth Walker, Brandon Walters, Sharon Wendzel, Mary Westlake, Kristin Wright, Pamela Young, Amina Ztot; **Utah:** Christina Brown, Art Burnah, Alisan Mills, Dave Miller, Lorraine Peterson; **Vermont:** Diane Ingham, Norman W. McLure, Kendrda Paupst; **Virginia:** Amanda Amos, Kandie Bradshaw, Susan Broaddus, Kay Choi, Anna Collins, Susan Courtney, Cynthia Dahl, Genevieve Delfosse, Kathy Flinn, LaVerne E. Flowers, Monica Johnston, Rinata Lewis, Sue McCloud, Lynn McCrady, Michelle M. Morningstar, Elizabeth Schollaert, Craig F. Seal, Ghislaine Tulou, Cynthia van de Kamp, Dawn Whitehurst; **Washington:** Catherine Blair, Olivia Caulhez, Roslyn Cooper, Svetlana Cuello, Daniel Dole, Ann Elliot, Jeanne Federovitch, Greg Isham, Jenny Hallenbeck, Tina Irish, Gregg Kasner, Josette Martin, Merissa McGregor, Molly McKinnon, Sarah McMenamin, Kara Miller, Heidi Monrad, Meghan Morahan, JoAnne Peterson, Kathleen Pointec, Esther Reiquam, Robert Slabodnik, Kaisa Swenddal-White, Deana Wiatr; **West Virginia:** Rita Denton; **Wisconsin:** Ramona Armour, Margaret Bussone, Linda Christen, Guy Dayen, Natalia DeLaat, Maura Devanie, Jana Gasiorkiewicz, Kathy A. Hawkins, Susanne Krasovich, Mary A. Martin, Jennifer Muchka, Julie Nji, Angela Olson, Jamie Pittmann, Vicky Thompson, Deborah Waither, Michelle Webster, Sally Weems, Brian Wopat